TAXATION OF INTERNATIONAL TRANSACTIONS

MATERIALS, TEXT AND PROBLEMS

Fourth Edition

■ ■ ■

By

Charles H. Gustafson

Professor of Law
Georgetown University Law Center

Robert J. Peroni

Fondren Foundation Centennial Chair for Faculty Excellence
The University of Texas School of Law

Richard Crawford Pugh

Distinguished Professor of Law Emeritus
University of San Diego School of Law

AMERICAN CASEBOOK SERIES®

WEST®
A Thomson Reuters business

Mat #40901801

610 Opperman Drive
St. Paul, MN 55123
1–800–313–9378

Printed in the United States of America

ISBN: 978–0–314–91171–1

DEDICATION

We dedicate this book to the thousands of students with whom we have worked and who have helped us to gain insights about tax law and tax law pedagogy.

Professor Gustafson also dedicates this book to his loving and supportive wife, Kate Gustafson.

Professor Peroni also dedicates this book to his loving and supportive parents, the late Emil Peroni and Betty Peroni.

Professor Pugh also dedicates this book to his loving and supportive wife, Nan Pugh.

PREFACE

The observation that law is being globalized has become something of a cliché. Like many clichés, the observation is true. Practitioners throughout the United States and in other countries are discovering that their work compels them to address problems with international dimensions.

The effects of an increasingly global marketplace, coupled with the mobility of people and ideas, have affected tax practitioners as well. In the United States the taxation of international transactions was once the province of a relatively limited number of specialized practitioners located primarily in a number of major cities. But the rapid growth of trade and investment arrangements that cross national boundaries has changed the picture materially. Attorneys, accountants, consultants and executives who may never have contemplated a career involving international trade and investment are finding themselves involved in business planning decisions that require analysis of many international factors.

This book is designed to serve as an initial step in the process of confronting one aspect of modern international trade and investment realities—the determination and administration of U.S. income tax liabilities resulting from international transactions. This area of the income tax law is particularly complex. There are a number of factors contributing to its complexity. The general complexity of the U.S. tax law is obviously a basic ingredient, as is the complexity of the foreign tax systems that may affect the analysis of any problem. Moreover, international trade and investment transactions are themselves often very complicated, and the complications are compounded by the sometimes conflicting demands of two or more national tax regimes. Technological changes, such as the evolution of electronic commerce, impose new strains on existing rules and procedures.

Another source of challenge is the seemingly constant change in the law. U.S. income tax law affecting international transactions has been subject to almost continuous change and adjustment over the past 50 years. In a familiar pattern, many of these changes have given rise to development of tax-avoidance techniques that in turn have attracted further legislative action intended to protect national revenues. One challenging element of the frequency of change that confronts this edition is the possibility that individual and corporate income tax rates will be changing just when the book is being published. Throughout the book, we have used a 35–percent tax rate as examples for both individual and corporate taxpayers. As we go to press, there is a debate about possible actions by Congress at the end of 2010 that may result in changes in those rates.

This volume is designed primarily for use in law schools, business schools and schools of management. As an introductory course book, it necessarily leaves some stones unturned and is not intended to be the basis for advice to clients. It does, however, provide students with an opportunity to explore in considerable detail the basic topography of tax considerations that confronts foreign individuals and entities that would participate in the U.S. economy and U.S. individuals and entities that seek to generate income abroad. As such, it will be useful to those who contemplate at least the possibility of further work in the field as well as those who may need or wish to be able to recognize when an international tax specialist should be consulted.

The textual discussion, cases, rulings and other materials in the volume are accompanied by problems designed to demonstrate the operation of the applicable provisions and to provide focus for an examination of the policy considerations that relate to them. Some of the problems are designed to demonstrate specific points. Others provide an opportunity to apply relevant provisions in the context of a tax planning exercise. Many of the problems include references to other countries. Such references are used to facilitate discussion. However, the problems do not actually reflect the laws of any country other than the United States. In a number of instances, the problems require the analysis of the impact of treaty provisions that might be in effect. Such references do not, unless otherwise indicated, represent treaties that are actually in force between the United States and the country or countries identified in the problem.

We fully recognize that there are more materials in the course book than can be addressed in most course or seminar offerings. The book has been prepared with the expectation that professors will choose among topics that are to be addressed in a particular course or seminar offering, and we have sought to facilitate the selection process by using a paragraph numbering system.

Chapter 1 serves as an introduction to the conceptual and administrative considerations that inhere in the establishment of a structure for taxing the income deriving from international transactions. It introduces the principal policy considerations relevant to any evaluation of international taxing provisions. It reflects the influence of international law considerations, including particularly jurisdictional limitations, on the formulation of international tax policy and introduces tax treaties as a source of income tax law to which students may not previously have been exposed.

Chapter 2 reflects the process by which specific items of income and expense are attributed to geographical areas (usually countries) for various tax reasons by examining the so-called "source rules." These source rules are invoked for different purposes throughout the book.

Chapters 3 and 4 deal with "inbound transactions" (the taxation of income realized from investments and activities in the United States by foreign individuals and entities). The effect of tax treaties on inbound transactions is reflected throughout these chapters.

Most of the remainder of the book concerns the U.S. income tax treatment of "outbound transactions" (the taxation of income realized from investments and activities abroad by U.S. individuals and entities). Chapters 5 and 7 deal with aspects of the foreign tax credit and the limitations thereon. Chapter 5 also considers alternative approaches to mitigating international double taxation for U.S persons, including the foreign earned income exclusion and the impact of tax treaties. Chapter 6 deals with various provisions intended to limit the ability of U.S. investors to avoid or defer U.S. taxes on foreign investment and business activities by using foreign corporations. Chapter 9 deals with issues arising from the use of foreign currencies.

The materials on transfer pricing set forth in Chapter 8 and the materials in Chapter 10 dealing with international tax-free exchanges apply to both inbound and outbound transactions.

Chapter 11 (international sale of goods), Chapter 12 (exploitation of intangible property rights abroad) and Chapter 13 (direct investment abroad) are intended for use in particular by professors who may wish to give an international tax planning emphasis to the treatment of outbound transactions.

Chapter 14 deals with two areas, the anti-international boycott rules and the Foreign Corrupt Practices Act, in which essentially political objectives have been advanced through the use of tax law provisions.

The materials covered in this volume generally reflect developments through November 1, 2010.

We have adopted a number of editing practices for this volume. Most footnotes are omitted from judicial opinions. Those that appear bear their original numbers in the opinions. Deletions of portions of judicial opinions, revenue rulings and other materials are indicated by ellipses.

This volume reflects a revised examination of the issues involved in the taxation of international transactions and introduces some new material not covered in the prior editions of the book. It is by necessity the product of our collective years in the classroom teaching international taxation and our various professional experiences. We are interested in your reflections about it. We have very much appreciated the comments and suggestions by professors and students who have used the earlier editions, including particularly Alice Abreu, Peter Blessing, Karen Brown, Glenn Coven, Joe Dodge, Cliff Fleming, Deborah Geier, Tracy Kaye, Michael Kirsch, Dan Lathrope, Julie Roin, Adam Rosenzweig, Stephen Shay, Bill Sherman, Jeff Strnad, Steve Wrappe and Eric Zolt. We welcome comments and suggestions with respect to this edition.

You may reach us at:

gustafso@law.georgetown.edu

rperoni@law.utexas.edu

rpugh@sandiego.edu

We also wish to express our appreciation to the Georgetown University Law Center, the University of San Diego School of Law and the University of Texas School of Law for their support of this project.

The book, although a new work, has a rich ancestry which we wish to acknowledge. It derives from a volume entitled *Taxation of International Transactions* by Charles H. Gustafson and Richard C. Pugh and published by

CCH, Inc. That volume in turn was a revised and expanded version of *Taxation of Transnational Transactions* by the late Robert Hellawell, of Columbia University, and Richard C. Pugh, which was also published by CCH, Inc.

CHARLES H. GUSTAFSON
ROBERT J. PERONI
RICHARD CRAWFORD PUGH

SUMMARY OF CONTENTS

Table of Contents

Page

TABLE OF INTERNAL REVENUE CODE SECTIONS

UNITED STATES

UNITED STATES CODE ANNOTATED

26 U.S.C.A.—Internal Revenue Code

Sec.	This Work Par.
1	1020
1	1145
1	1195
1	1285
1	4160
1	4175
1	5000
1	5330
1	5370
1(c)	6365
1(h)(1)(C)	10,088
1(h)(11)	10,135
1(h)(11)	1020
1(h)(11)	5265
1(h)(11)	6015
1(h)(11)	6240
1(h)(11)	6245
1(h)(11)	6300
1(h)(11)	6305
1(h)(11)	6315
1(h)(11)	6365
1(h)(11)(C)(iii)	6300
1(h)(11)(C)(iii)	6305
1(h)(11)(C)(iii)	6315
1(h)(11)(C)(iv)	5265
5(b)(1)	11,185
11	1020
11	1145
11	5000
11	6165
16(a)	10,088
27	5005
55	4200
59(a)	7150
59(a)(3)	7050
61	1020
61	2225
61	9040
63	5130
71	2195
71(c)	4050
78	13,070
78	5135

UNITED STATES CODE ANNOTATED

26 U.S.C.A.—Internal Revenue Code

Sec.	This Work Par.
78	5150
78	6020
78	6065
78	7115
78	7130
103	4027
103	9080
106	12,090
108	9080
114 (former)	11,230
114(a) (former)	11,230
114(b)	11,230
114(c)(1) (former)	11,230
114(c)(2) (former)	11,230
114(d) (former)	11,230
114(d) (former)	7040
114(e) (former)	11,230
119	5350
162	10,090
162	3005
162	5050
162	5370
162	9020
162	9065
162	9075
162(a)(2)	1185
162(a)(2)	2130
162(a)(2)	5355
162(a)(2)	9065
162(c)	14,095
162(c)	5150
163(f)(2)(B)	4040
163(j)	10,088
163(j)	4270
163(j)	4280
163(j)(1)	4270
163(j)(1)(A)	4270
163(j)(2)(A)	4270
163(j)(2)(B)	4270
163(j)(2)(B)(iii)	4270
163(j)(2)(C)	4270
163(j)(3)(A)	4270
163(j)(3)(B)	4270
163(j)(4)	4270
163(j)(5)(B)	4270
163(j)(6)(D)	4270
163(j)(6)(D)(ii)(I)	4270

UNITED STATES CODE ANNOTATED

26 U.S.C.A.—Internal Revenue Code

UNITED STATES CODE ANNOTATED
26 U.S.C.A.—Internal Revenue Code

Sec.	This Work Par.
334(b)(1)	10,140
334(b)(1)	10,145
336	10,010
337	10,010
337(a)	10,010
337(a)	10,100
337(b)	10,100
338(a)	5253
338(a)	5315
351	10,000
351	10,005
351	10,023
351	10,025
351	10,030
351	10,035
351	10,080
351	10,090
351	10,130
351	10,150
351	12,000
351	12,040
351	12,080
351	12,130
351	12,135
351	12,140
351	12,155
351	12,195
351	12,200
351	13,075
351	4225
351	7075
351	9050
351(a)	12,080
354	10,015
354	10,025
354	10,035
354	10,080
354	10,085
354	10,130
354(a)	10,035
355	10,015
355	10,020
355	10,025
355	10,035
355	10,110
355	10,130
355	10,160
355	10,170
355	10,180
355(a)	10,110
355(a)(1)(D)	10,020
355(b)(2)	10,020
355(d)	10,020
355(e)	10,020
355(f)	10,020
355(g)	10,020
356	10,015
356	10,025
356	10,035
356	10,080
356	10,110
356	10,130

UNITED STATES CODE ANNOTATED
26 U.S.C.A.—Internal Revenue Code

Sec.	This Work Par.
357	10,015
358	10,015
358	10,023
358	10,030
361	10,015
361	10,025
361	10,035
361	10,070
361	10,080
361	10,090
361	10,130
361	12,000
361	12,130
361	12,200
362	10,023
362	10,030
362(a)	10,000
362(a)	10,023
362(a)	10,030
362(b)	10,015
362(e)	10,023
362(e)(1)	10,023
362(e)(2)	10,023
362(e)(2)(A)(i)	10,023
362(e)(2)(A)(ii)	10,023
362(e)(2)(B)	10,023
362(e)(2)(C)	10,023
367	10,000
367	10,005
367	10,010
367	10,015
367	10,025
367	10,030
367	10,088
367	10,110
367	12,130
367	12,131
367	6060
367(a)	10,000
367(a)	10,005
367(a)	10,015
367(a)	10,025
367(a)	10,030
367(a)	10,035
367(a)	10,040
367(a)	10,045
367(a)	10,070
367(a)	10,080
367(a)	10,088
367(a)	10,090
367(a)	10,095
367(a)	10,115
367(a)	10,120
367(a)	10,130
367(a)	12,130
367(a)(1)	10,015
367(a)(1)	10,030
367(a)(1)	10,035
367(a)(1)	10,040
367(a)(1)	10,070
367(a)(1)	10,080
367(a)(1)	10,085

UNITED STATES CODE ANNOTATED

26 U.S.C.A.—Internal Revenue Code

UNITED STATES CODE ANNOTATED

26 U.S.C.A.—Internal Revenue Code

Sec.	This Work Par.
482	12,275
482	12,285
482	12,295
482	12,300
482	12,305
482	13,015
482	13,075
482	1125
482	4025
482	6025
482	8000
482	8005
482	8010
482	8015
482	8020
482	8025
482	8035
482	8040
482	8045
482	8050
482	8070
482	8075
482	8077
482	8080
482	8085
482	8100
482	8120
482	8125
482	8140
482	8145
482	8150
482	8155
482	8160
482	8170
482	8175
482	8185
483	12,110
483	12,195
483	8050
483(d)(4)	12,110
531—537	6000
531	6280
531—537	6365
531	6365
532(a)	6365
532(b)(4)	6365
533(a)	6365
533(b)	6365
535	6365
535(b)(10)	6365
535(d)(1)	6365
535(d)(2)	6365
541—547	6000
541	6000
551—558	6025
551—558	6000
553	6000
553(a)(5)	6125
611	5050
613	5050
684	10,125
701	6180

UNITED STATES CODE ANNOTATED

26 U.S.C.A.—Internal Revenue Code

Sec.	This Work Par.
702	6180
702(a)(7)	6180
702(b)	6180
704(b)	5300
707(b)(1)	4040
707(b)(1)	4102
707(b)(1)	4270
721	7075
721(c)	10,125
721(c)	12,131
721(d)	10,090
721(d)	12,131
761	13,150
806	10,088
842(b)	3188
861	11,080
861—865	2000
861	2000
861	5253
861	5255
861	6090
861(a)(1)	1285
861(a)(1)	2005
861 (a)(1)	5253
861(a)(1)(B)	2005
861(a)(1)(B)(i)	2005
861(a)(1) (c)	5253
861(a)(2)	2010
861(a)(2)(A)	4045
861(a)(2)(B)	2010
861(a)(2)(B)	3230
861(a)(2)(B)	4045
861(a)(2)(D)	11,225
861(a)(3)	11,070
861(a)(3)	2025
861(a)(3)	2035
861(a)(3)	3010
861(a)(3)	3190
861(a)(3)	5345
861(a)(4)	10,090
861(a)(4)	12,040
861(a)(4)	12,090
861(a)(4)	12,115
861(a)(4)	12,125
861(a)(4)	2015
861(a)(4)	2175
861(a)(4)	4152
861(a)(5)	2155
861(a)(5)	4205
861(a)(6)	10,030
861(a)(6)	11,070
861(a)(6)	12,090
861(a)(6)	2115
861(a)(6)	2175
861(a)(9)	2211
861(b)	2225
862	2000
862	6090
862(a)(1)	2005
862(a)(2)	2010
862(a)(3)	11,070
862(a)(3)	2025

UNITED STATES CODE ANNOTATED
26 U.S.C.A.—Internal Revenue Code

Sec.	This Work Par.
862(a)(3)	5345
862(a)(4)	10,090
862(a)(4)	12,040
862(a)(4)	12,115
862(a)(4)	12,125
862(a)(4)	12,130
862(a)(4)	12,131
862(a)(4)	12,195
862(a)(4)	13,075
862(a)(4)	2015
862(a)(5)	13,075
862(a)(5)	2105
862(a)(6)	10,000
862(a)(6)	11,070
862(a)(6)	11,080
862(a)(6)	2115
862(a)(6)	2175
862(a)(9)	2211
863	2000
863	2160
863(b)	11,005
863(b)	11,240
863(b)(2)	11,065
863(b)(2)	11,135
863(b)(2)	13,070
863(b)(2)	2160
863(c)	2180
863(d)	2180
863(e)	2180
864	2000
864	5253
864(b)	1145
864(b)	3005
864(b)	3010
864(b)	3030
864(b)	3110
864(b)	3190
864(b)	4160
864(b)(1)	1145
864(b)(1)	3010
864(b)(2)	1145
864(b)(2)(A)	3015
864(b)(2)(B)	3015
864(b)(2)(B)(ii)	3015
864(b)(2)(C)	3015
864(c)	1145
864(c)	3110
864(c)(2)	11,070
864(c)(2)	1145
864(c)(2)	3100
864(c)(2)	3185
864(c)(2)	6075
864(c)(2)(B)	3100
864(c)(3)	11,070
864(c)(3)	1145
864(c)(3)	3100
864(c)(3)	3120
864(c)(3)	4115
864(c)(4)	11,070
864(c)(4)	1145
864(c)(4)	3120
864(c)(4)	3130

UNITED STATES CODE ANNOTATED
26 U.S.C.A.—Internal Revenue Code

Sec.	This Work Par.
864(c)(4)	3135
864(c)(4)(A)	3120
864(c)(4)(B)(i)	3120
864(c)(4)(B)(ii)	3120
864(c)(4)(B)(iii)	11,080
864(c)(4)(B)(iii)	3120
864(c)(5)	1145
864(c)(5)	2150
864(c)(5)	3045
864(c)(5)(A)	3045
864(c)(5)(A)	3120
864(c)(6)	3115
864(c)(7)	10,105
864(c)(7)	3115
864(d)	6195
864(d)(1)	11,235
864(d)(1)	6090
864(d)(1)	7010
864(d)(2)	6090
864(d)(3)	6090
864(d)(4)	6090
864(d)(5)(A)	6090
864(d)(5)(A)(i)	11,235
864(d)(6)	11,235
864(d)(6)	6090
864(d)(6)	7010
864(d)(7)	11,235
864(d)(7)	6090
864(e)(1)	2230
864(e)(2)	2230
864(e)(2)	3140
864(e)(5)	5253
864(e)(7)(B)	2230
864(e)(7)(C)	7145
864(e)(7)(F)	2230
864(f)	2230
864(f)	7145
864(f)(4)(C)	2230
864(f)(5)(C)	2230
864(f)(6)	2230
864(g)	2240
865	1150
865	2000
865	2110
865	2115
865	2130
865	2175
865(a)	10,090
865(a)	12,090
865(a)	12,115
865(a)	13,075
865(a)	2110
865(a)	2130
865(a)	2165
865(a)	4110
865(a)(1)	12,115
865(b)	10,000
865(b)	10,030
865(b)	11,005
865(b)	11,065
865(b)	11,070
865(b)	11,240

UNITED STATES CODE ANNOTATED
26 U.S.C.A.—Internal Revenue Code

UNITED STATES CODE ANNOTATED
26 U.S.C.A.—Internal Revenue Code

UNITED STATES CODE ANNOTATED

26 U.S.C.A.—Internal Revenue Code

UNITED STATES CODE ANNOTATED

26 U.S.C.A.—Internal Revenue Code

UNITED STATES CODE ANNOTATED

26 U.S.C.A.—Internal Revenue Code

Sec.	This Work Par.
901	13,155
901	14,070
901	14,085
901	14,090
901	3135
901	5005
901	5010
901	5015
901	5060
901	5070
901	5075
901	5095
901	5120
901	5150
901	5180
901	5215
901	5300
901	6000
901	7005
901	7010
901—908	7150
901(a)	5015
901(a)	5133
901(a)—(c)	5010
901(b)	5015
901(b)(4)	5010
901(c)	5010
901(d)(1)	11,005
901(d)(1)(B)	7030
901(e)	13,015
901(e)	5050
901(f)	5050
901(f)	5275
901(i)	5110
901(i)	5120
901(j)	5125
901(j)	5275
901(j)	6025
901(j)(3)	5125
901(j)(3)	5275
901(j)(5)	5125
901(k)	5315
901(*l*)	5315
901(m)	5253
901(m)	5315
902	10,175
902	11,225
902	13,070
902	13,075
902	13,135
902	13,150
902	14,070
902	14,085
902	1160
902	3135
902	5000
902	5005
902	5010
902	5135
902	5145
902	5150
902	5160

UNITED STATES CODE ANNOTATED

26 U.S.C.A.—Internal Revenue Code

Sec.	This Work Par.
902	5170
902	5175
902	5180
902	5190
902	5200
902	5205
902	5215
902	5245
902	5250
902	6000
902	6065
902	6200
902	6240
902	6255
902	6300
902	7000
902	7005
902	7010
902	7030
902	7042
902	7085
902	7130
902	7160
902	9000
902	9120
902(a)	5135
902(a)	5150
902(a)	5175
902(a)	5200
902(a)	6065
902(a)(1)	5190
902(b)	6065
902(b)(2)	5145
902(b)(2)	6065
902(b)(2)(B)	5145
902(b)(2)(B)	6065
902(b)(2)(B)(iii)	5145
902(b)(2)(B)(iii)	6065
902(c)(1)	5150
902(c)(2)	5150
902(c)(2)(A)	5150
902(c)(3)	5150
902(c)(3)(A)	5150
902(c)(4)(A)	5150
902(c)(6)(A)	5150
902(c)(7)	5135
903	12,015
903	5010
903	5015
903	5075
903	5095
903	5150
903	7005
903	7010
903(d)(3)	12,125
904	10,025
904	10,090
904	11,005
904	11,240
904	12,015
904	12,175
904	13,005

UNITED STATES CODE ANNOTATED

26 U.S.C.A.—Internal Revenue Code

Sec.	This Work Par.
904	13,020
904	13,070
904	13,075
904	13,120
904	14,070
904	14,075
904	14,090
904	2130
904	5000
904	5005
904	5010
904	5015
904	5110
904	5215
904	5225
904	5230
904	5245
904	5250
904	5265
904	5270
904	5275
904	6240
904	7010
904	7042
904	7055
904	7060
904	7070
904	7080
904	7140
904	7160
904	7175
904	8150
904(a)	11,005
904(a)	12,130
904(a)	1160
904(a)	5220
904(a)	5230
904(a)	7000
904(a)	7005
904(b)	5265
904(b)(2)(A)	5265
904(b)(2)(B)	5265
904(c)	10,175
904(c)	12,005
904(c)	13,070
904(c)	5225
904(c)	5250
904(c)	7070
904(d)	12,125
904(d)	12,195
904(d)	13,005
904(d)	13,070
904(d)	1160
904(d)	5220
904(d)	5240
904(d)	5245
904(d)	5250
904(d)	5270
904(d)	6255
904(d)	7030
904(d)	7170
904(d)(1)	11,135

UNITED STATES CODE ANNOTATED

26 U.S.C.A.—Internal Revenue Code

Sec.	This Work Par.
904(d)(1)	11,180
904(d)(1)	11,225
904(d)(1)	13,070
904(d)(1)	5220
904(d)(1)	5245
904(d)(1)	5250
904(d)(1)	5285
904(d)(1)	7000
904(d)(1)	7005
904(d)(1)	7150
904(d)(1)	7165
904 (d)(1)	7045
904(d)(1)(A)	11,005
904(d)(1)(A)	12,015
904(d)(1)(A)	12,125
904(d)(1)(A)	12,190
904(d)(1)(A)	13,075
904(d)(1)(A)	5245
904(d)(1)(A)	5250
904(d)(1)(A)	7005
904(d)(1)(A)	7010
904(d)(1)(A)	7170
904(d)(1)(B)	11,005
904(d)(1)(B)	11,015
904(d)(1)(B)	11,235
904(d)(1)(B)	12,005
904(d)(1)(B)	12,015
904(d)(1)(B)	12,125
904(d)(1)(B)	12,190
904(d)(1)(B)	13,070
904(d)(1)(B)	13,120
904(d)(1)(B)	13,140
904(d)(1)(B)	13,145
904(d)(1)(B)	5220
904(d)(1)(B)	5245
904(d)(1)(B)	5250
904(d)(1)(B)	6255
904(d)(1)(B)	7005
904 (d)(1)(B)	7015
904(d)(1)(B)	7025
904(d)(1)(B)	7045
904(d)(1)(B)	7175
904(d)(1)(C)	5245
904(d)(1)(C)	7020
904(d)(1)(D)	5245
904 (d)(1)(D)	7025
904(d)(1)(E)	5245
904(d)(1)(E)	6255
904(d)(1)(E)	7030
904(d)(1)(E) (former)	13,135
904(d)(1)(E) (former)	7085
904(d)(1)(F) (former)	7040
904(d)(1)(G) (former)	11,180
904(d)(1)(G) (former)	7040
904(d)(1)(H) (former)	11,180
904(d)(1)(H) (former)	7040
904(d)(1)(I)	5245
904(d)(1)(I)	6255
904(d)(1)(I)	7045
904(d)(1)(I) (former)	5245
904(d)(1)(I) (former)	7005
904(d)(1)(I) (former)	7165

UNITED STATES CODE ANNOTATED
26 U.S.C.A.—Internal Revenue Code

UNITED STATES CODE ANNOTATED

26 U.S.C.A.—Internal Revenue Code

UNITED STATES CODE ANNOTATED

26 U.S.C.A.—Internal Revenue Code

UNITED STATES CODE ANNOTATED

26 U.S.C.A.—Internal Revenue Code

Sec.	This Work Par.
921—927	11,160
921 (former)	2120
921(a) (former)	11,160
921(a) (former)	11,175
921—927	11,230
922	2120
922(a)	11,165
922(a)(1)(D)(i)—(ii) (former)	11,165
922(a)(1)(D)(iii) (former)	11,165
922(a)(1)(E) (former)	11,165
922(a)(2) (former)	11,165
923(a)(2) (former)	11,175
923(a)(3) (former)	11,175
923(b) (former)	11,170
924(b)(1) (former)	11,170
924(b)(1)(A)	11,170
924(b)(1)(B) (former)	11,170
924(c) (former)	11,170
924(d) (former)	11,170
924(e)	11,170
925(a) (former)	11,170
925(a) (former)	11,175
927(a)(2)(B) (former)	11,175
927(e)(3) (former)	11,165
927(e)(3) (former)	11,170
931—936	5000
936	5000
936	5210
936(h)(3)(B)	10,090
936(h)(3)(B)	12,000
936(h)(3)(B)	12,130
936(h)(3)(B)	13,075
936(h)(3)(B)	6275
936(h)(3)(B)	8135
936(h)(3)(B)(i)	12,140
941(a)(1) (former)	11,230
941(a)(5)(A) (former)	11,230
941(a)(5)(B) (former)	11,230
941(b)(1) (former)	11,230
941(c)(1)(B) (former)	11,230
941—943	11,230
942	11,230
942(a)(1)	11,230
942(a)(3) (former)	11,230
942(b)(1) (former)	11,230
942(c)(1) (former)	11,230
942(c)(2) (former)	11,230
942(c)(3)	11,230
943(a)(1)(A) (former)	11,230
943(a)(1)(B) (former)	11,230
943(a)(1)(C) (former)	11,230
943(a)(2)	11,230
943(a)(3) (former)	11,230
943(a)(4)	11,230
943(b)(1)(B) (former)	11,230
943(b)(3) (former)	11,230
943(e)(1) (former)	11,230
943(e)(2)	11,230
951	11,135
951—964	6000
951	6015
951	6020

UNITED STATES CODE ANNOTATED

26 U.S.C.A.—Internal Revenue Code

Sec.	This Work Par.
951	6025
951	6065
951	6180
951	6240
951	6245
951	6250
951(a)	6015
951(a)	6020
951(a)	6065
951(a)	6080
951(a)	6085
951(a)	6180
951(a)	6240
951(a)	6365
951(a)(1)	6015
951(a)(1)	6020
951(a)(1)	6065
951(a)(1)	6255
951(a)(1)	7042
951(a)(1)(A)	6020
951(a)(1)(A)	6065
951(a)(1)(A)	6080
951(a)(1)(A)	6085
951(a)(1)(A)	6195
951(a)(1)(A)	6245
951(a)(1)(A)	6330
951(a)(1)(A)	7095
951(a)(1)(A)	7115
951(a)(1)(A)	7135
951(a)(1)(A)	7160
951(a)(1)(A)	7170
951(a)(1)(A)	9000
951(a)(1)(A)	9025
951(a)(1)(A)	9110
951(a)(1)(A)	9120
951(a)(1)(A)(i)	6015
951(a)(1)(A)(i)	6065
951(a)(1)(A)(i)	6105
951(a)(1)(A)(i)	6240
951(a)(1)(A)(ii)	6015
951(a)(1)(A)(iii)	6015
951(a)(1)(B)	13,120
951(a)(1)(B)	6015
951(a)(1)(B)	6020
951(a)(1)(B)	6200
951(a)(1)(B)	6235
951(a)(1)(B)	6240
951(a)(1)(B)	7095
951(a)(1)(B)	7115
951(a)(1)(B)	7130
951(a)(1)(B)	7135
951(a)(1)(B)	7160
951(a)(1)(B)	7170
951(a)(1)(B)	9025
951(a)(1)(B)	9120
951(a)(1)(C) (former)	6015
951(a)(1)(i)	6065
951(a)(2)	6015
951(a)(2)(A)	6065
951(a)(2)(B)	6065
951(b)	14,080
951(b)	5135

UNITED STATES CODE ANNOTATED

26 U.S.C.A.—Internal Revenue Code

UNITED STATES CODE ANNOTATED

26 U.S.C.A.—Internal Revenue Code

UNITED STATES CODE ANNOTATED

26 U.S.C.A.—Internal Revenue Code

UNITED STATES CODE ANNOTATED
26 U.S.C.A.—Internal Revenue Code

UNITED STATES CODE ANNOTATED
26 U.S.C.A.—Internal Revenue Code

UNITED STATES CODE ANNOTATED
26 U.S.C.A.—Internal Revenue Code

UNITED STATES CODE ANNOTATED

26 U.S.C.A.—Internal Revenue Code

Sec.	This Work Par.
999(b)(2)	14,060
999(b)(2)(A)	14,075
999(b)(3)	14,015
999(b)(3)	14,020
999(b)(3)	14,045
999(b)(3)(A)(ii)	14,025
999(b)(4)	14,015
999(b)(4)	14,040
999(b)(4)(A)	14,080
999(b)(4)(B)	14,080
999(c)	14,005
999(c)	14,065
999(c)(1)	11,230
999(c)(1)	14,010
999(c)(1)	14,070
999(c)(2)	14,085
999(c)(2)	14,090
999(e)	14,045
999(e)	14,055
999(e)(1)	14,010
999(e)(2)	14,010
999(f)	14,080
1001	10,088
1001	9000
1014	6245
1014	6315
1031	9045
1032	10,015
1058	6120
1058(b)	6120
1059A	8120
1202	1020
1202(c)	1020
1211	10,095
1211	1020
1211(a)	5310
1212	1020
1221(a)(1)	10,030
1221(a)(1)	10,045
1221(a)(1)	12,025
1221(a)(1)	6090
1221(a)(1)	6100
1221(a)(2)	6100
1221(a)(3)	10,045
1221(a)(3)(A)	12,045
1221(a)(8)	6100
1221(b)(3)	12,045
1222	12,050
1222	12,060
1222	12,075
1222	12,125
1222	12,160
1222	2175
1222(3)	12,050
1231	12,005
1231	12,015
1231	12,025
1231	12,030
1231	12,035
1231	12,040
1231	12,045
1231	12,050

UNITED STATES CODE ANNOTATED

26 U.S.C.A.—Internal Revenue Code

Sec.	This Work Par.
1231	12,060
1231	12,130
1231	13,075
1231(a)(3)(A)(ii)(II)	12,050
1231(b)	12,025
1231(b)(1)	12,050
1231(b)(1)(A)	12,025
1231(b)(1)(B)	12,025
1231(b)(1)(C)	12,045
1235	12,025
1235	12,050
1235	12,060
1235	2175
1235(a)	12,110
1245	13,075
1246 (former)	6000
1247 (former)	6000
1248	10,000
1248	10,010
1248	10,080
1248	10,088
1248	10,130
1248	10,135
1248	10,150
1248	10,155
1248	10,170
1248	10,175
1248	13,120
1248	6000
1248	6065
1248	6240
1248	6245
1248	9025
1248	9110
1248	9120
1248(a)	10,110
1248(a)	10,135
1248(a)	6015
1248(a)	6085
1248(a)	6245
1248(a)	7130
1248(a)	7135
1248(a)	7170
1248(a)(2)	10,130
1248(a)(2)	10,150
1248(b)	6245
1248(b)	6250
1248(c)(2)	10,150
1248(d)(1)	6245
1248(d)(4)	6245
1248(d)(6)	6245
1248(h)	6245
1249	12,095
1249	12,100
1249	12,125
1249	12,130
1249	12,195
1249	13,075
1249	13,120
1249	6000
1249	6260
1249(b)	12,095

UNITED STATES CODE ANNOTATED
26 U.S.C.A.—Internal Revenue Code

UNITED STATES CODE ANNOTATED
26 U.S.C.A.—Internal Revenue Code

UNITED STATES CODE ANNOTATED
26 U.S.C.A.—Internal Revenue Code

UNITED STATES CODE ANNOTATED
26 U.S.C.A.—Internal Revenue Code

UNITED STATES CODE ANNOTATED
26 U.S.C.A.—Internal Revenue Code

Table of I.R.S. Notices

IRS NOTICES

Table of I.R.S. Revenue Procedures

REVENUE PROCEDURES

Rev.Proc.	This Work Par.
68–23	10,025
69–19	12,150
93–22A	1235
99–32	8005
2007–13	8077

TABLE OF I.R.S. REVENUE RULINGS

REVENUE RULINGS

Rev.Rul.	This Work Par.
54–409	12,090
55–296	**5030**
58–353	12,050
60–55	**2030**
60–226	12,090
64–56	12,025
64–56	12,035
64–56	12,040
64–56	12,050
64–56	12,075
64–56	12,080
64–56	12,140
64–56	**12,145**
64–56	12,150
64–56	12,155
64–184	3010
68–443	**2020**
68–522	5035
69–108	**2200**
69–156	12,155
69–479	3010
69–482	12,060
69–482	12,080
70–424	**3040**
70–426	**13,130**
70–426	13,135
70–543	4165
71–141	5135
71–564	12,080
71–564	12,150
72–87	4125
72–330	5390
72–423	5345
73–522	**3090**
73–522	4020
74–7	**9070**
74–108	**2085**
74–459	5180
74–555	2065
74–555	2170
75–7	11,105
75–7	**11,120**
75–253	**3125**
76–215	5045
76–322	3165
76–435	3220

REVENUE RULINGS

Rev.Rul.	This Work Par.
77–167	5345
78–63	5045
78–83	**8030**
78–234	**5100**
79–74	5140
79–152	1270
79–388	2100
80–17	1185
80–362	**4145**
81–112	1225
83–177	2095
84–17	**3205**
84–78	**2170**
84–125	5133
84–152	**4080**
84–153	4085
84–160	**4230**
85–3	5135
85–193	4125
86–154	**3105**
87–38	2050
87–39	**5085**
87–64	3135
87–71	**8095**
88–8	13,030
89–72	6180
90–31	6245
90–79	**9090**
90–79	9095
90–80	**3215**
90–112	**6230**
91–7	3095
91–32	3070
91–32	3220
91–58	5365
91–58	5390
95–56	4095
97–48	**11,120**
97–48	11,125
2003–8	5090
2004–3	3190
2004–75	4020
2004–76	13,035
2005–3	5125
2005–3	5365
2009–14	2211

TABLE OF CASES

The principal cases are in bold type. Cases cited or discussed in the text are in roman type. References are to paragraphs. Cases cited in principal cases and within other quoted materials are not included.

TAXATION OF INTERNATIONAL TRANSACTIONS

MATERIALS, TEXT AND PROBLEMS

Fourth Edition

CHAPTER 1

INTRODUCTION AND OVERVIEW

■ ■ ■

A. BACKGROUND

[¶ 1000]

1. SCOPE OF THE INQUIRY

The materials in this book deal with the ways in which the U.S. income tax system applies to transactions that in some respect involve one or more other countries. Accordingly, they concern the taxation of the income of foreign entities and individuals doing business or investing in the United States and the taxation of income earned by U.S. entities and individuals from exporting, licensing, rendering services, engaging in other business activities or investing outside the United States.

[¶ 1005]

2. TYPES AND EVOLUTION OF INTERNATIONAL BUSINESS TRANSACTIONS

While there is an almost infinite array of pathways to the establishment of international business arrangements, there are also a number of recurring themes. Many U.S. corporations have become involved in foreign countries through a gradual process. The process often begins with the initiation of exports to foreign markets. Export sales, which may have begun in a modest way using foreign agents or distributors, are often followed by the establishment of foreign sales operations and facilities. The next step might involve the licensing of foreign patents or knowhow to independent licensees abroad in exchange for royalties as a means of obtaining an additional return on research and development expenditures in the United States. At some later point the corporation may need to expand its production capabilities. Now more familiar with the potential advantages and disadvantages of foreign operations, the corporation's executives may start to consider direct investment opportunities abroad as realistic alternatives to additional investment within the United States.

Sometimes, of course, the process is accelerated. U.S. corporations may acquire foreign businesses or establish joint ventures with foreign interests. Sometimes business executives may feel that there is no practical choice. In many instances, the decision to invest abroad results from the attempt to defend foreign market positions, developed perhaps through exports or licensing, against stiff foreign competition. Some foreign investment derives from the imposition of legal requirements by foreign governments that effectively compel local investment as a precondition to participating in the market of the foreign country. These phases or stages of penetration of foreign markets may occur simultaneously in different countries and even within a single country.

When foreign businesses elect to enter the United States, a similar process of fashioning appropriate arrangements is involved. Again, the process may involve a phased economic penetration of the U.S. market through exports, licensing and eventually direct investment or an immediate plunge through acquisition of a U.S. business or establishment of a joint venture with a U.S. partner.

Whether the process involves trade or investment by U.S. persons abroad or by foreign persons in the United States and whether the process is gradual or swift, it continues unabated. Among its consequences is that many professionals who might never have expected a career in international practice are confronting the legal, financial and tax aspects of the expanded international activity of their clients.

During the past few decades, the nature of business activity in the United States and around the world has been changing. Services as a percentage of the overall economy have been growing, including many types of highly mobile services activities, such as financial services. Electronic commerce has fast become an increasingly important component of the global economy. Moreover, even traditional businesses, such as manufacturers, have been making ever greater use of the Internet and electronic media. In addition, for decades a significant and growing portion of business activity has been conducted through the use of media, such as telephone, radio, television and facsimile, rather than through the physical presence of an office or plant or an agent of the business in the country in which the customer or client is located. The rapid evolution of the Internet has accelerated this trend. All of these changes place great pressure on the existing rules of international taxation, many of which were developed in an era when physical manufacturing and traditional sales activities dominated the U.S. and world economies.

[¶ 1010]

3. INTERNATIONAL ECONOMIC INTEGRATION OF MULTINATIONAL ENTERPRISES

It is a cliché to observe that nations are increasingly interdependent in economic and political terms. The degree of economic integration of multinational enterprises makes it very difficult in many instances to identify distinct categories of taxpayers. Large multinational corporate organizations often include many separate entities incorporated and operating in many different nations. The net result has been characterized as a "global assembly line" in which the eventual profits accruing to the organization are attributable to investments and activities in at least several countries.

Moreover, ownership of the multinational corporation (a term usually referring to an integrated system of entities) is often shared among investors in many different countries. It is not always obvious, therefore, how to identify who and what are to be treated as domestic and as foreign for tax purposes.

The literature of economics, business, finance and even diplomacy and political science is well stocked with often conflicting analyses of the value and risks created by the operation of large multinational corporations. The focus here is necessarily restricted to the methods by which their income is and should be taxed.

[¶ 1015]

4. MAGNITUDE OF INTERNATIONAL TRANSACTIONS

The following data relating to changes in the flow of investment into and out of the United States and in other international transactions suggest the growing importance of international trade and investment in the overall economy of the United States. They also suggest that some of the factual assumptions that have contributed to the structuring of U.S. income tax policies should be reviewed. Many of the key U.S. international tax provisions were enacted many years ago, when the flow of U.S. investment abroad greatly exceeded the flow of foreign investment into the United States. Today, the United States is a net importer of investment capital and cross-border investment represents a much greater proportion of the overall economy of the United States.

U.S. International Transactions by Type of Transaction, Selected Years, 1990–2008

[In millions of dollars (706,975 represents $706,975,000,000)]

Type of transaction	1990	1995	2000	2005	2006	2007	2008
Exports of goods and services and income receipts	**706,975**	**1,004,631**	**1,421,515**	**1,816,723**	**2,133,905**	**2,462,099**	**2,591,233**
Exports of goods and services	535,233	794,387	1,070,597	1,281,460	1,451,684	1,643,168	1,826,596
Goods, balance of payments basis	387,401	575,204	771,994	892,337	1,015,812	1,138,384	1,276,994
Services	147,832	219,183	298,603	389,122	435,873	504,784	549,602
Transfers under U.S. military agency sales contracts	9,932	14,643	13,790	19,539	23,913	25,436	22,571
Travel	43,007	63,395	82,400	81,799	85,789	97,050	110,090
Passenger fares	15,298	18,909	20,687	20,970	22,036	25,636	31,623
Other transportation	22,042	26,081	29,803	41,281	46,225	51,550	58,945
Royalties and license fees	16,634	30,289	43,233	64,395	70,727	83,824	91,599
Other private services	40,251	65,048	107,904	160,051	186,028	220,077	233,529
U.S. government miscellaneous services	668	818	786	1,087	1,155	1,212	1,245
Income receipts	171,742	210,244	350,918	535,263	682,221	818,931	764,637
Income receipts on U.S.-owned assets abroad	170,570	208,065	348,083	532,373	679,338	815,960	761,593
Direct investment receipts	65,973	95,260	151,839	294,538	324,816	363,247	370,747
Other private receipts	94,072	108,092	192,398	235,120	352,122	450,480	385,940
U.S. government receipts	10,525	4,713	3,846	2,715	2,400	2,233	4,906
Compensation of employees	1,172	2,179	2,835	2,890	2,883	2,971	3,044
Imports of goods and services and income payments	**–759,290**	**–1,080,124**	**–1,780,296**	**–2,459,633**	**–2,846,179**	**–3,072,675**	**–3,168,938**
Imports of goods and services	–616,097	–890,771	–1,450,432	–1,996,728	–2,212,043	–2,344,590	–2,522,532
Goods, balance of payments basis	–498,438	–749,374	–1,226,684	–1,683,188	–1,863,072	–1,969,375	–2,117,245
Services	–117,659	–141,397	–223,748	–313,540	–348,972	–375,215	–405,287
Direct defense expenditures	–17,531	–10,043	–13,473	–30,075	–31,032	–32,820	–36,452
Travel	–37,349	–44,916	–64,705	–68,970	–72,104	–76,354	–79,743
Passenger fares	–10,531	–14,663	–24,274	–26,149	–27,501	–28,437	–32,597
Other transportation	–24,966	–27,034	–41,425	–61,937	–65,318	–67,100	–72,143
Royalties and license fees	–3,135	–6,919	–16,468	–24,612	–23,518	–24,656	–26,616
Other private services	–22,229	–35,199	–60,520	–97,818	–125,478	–141,664	–153,267
U.S. government miscellaneous services	–1,919	–2,623	–2,883	–3,979	–4,021	–4,184	–4,469
Income payments	–143,192	–189,353	–329,864	–462,905	–634,136	–728,085	–646,406
Income payments on foreign-owned assets in the U.S.	–139,728	–183,090	–322,345	–453,615	–624,646	–718,019	–636,043
Direct investment payments	–3,450	–30,318	–56,910	–121,333	–150,770	–126,532	–120,862
Other private payments	–95,508	–97,149	–180,918	–228,408	–338,897	–427,159	–349,871
U.S. government payments	–40,770	–55,623	–84,517	–103,874	–134,979	–164,328	–165,310
Compensation of employees	–3,464	–6,263	–7,519	–9,290	–9,490	–10,066	–10,364
Unilateral current transfers, net	**–26,654**	**–38,074**	**–58,645**	**–105,772**	**–91,273**	**–115,996**	**–128,363**
U.S. government grants	–10,359	–11,190	–16,714	–33,647	–27,733	–34,437	–36,003
U.S. government pensions and other transfers	–3,224	–3,451	–4,705	–6,303	–6,508	–7,323	–8,390
Private remittances and other transfers	–13,070	–23,433	–37,226	–65,822	–57,032	–74,236	–83,970
Capital account transactions, net	–6,579	–927	–1,010	11,344	–3,906	–1,895	953

Type of transaction	1990	1995	2000	2005	2006	2007	2008
U.S. assets abroad, net (increase/financial outflow (–))	**–81,234**	**–352,264**	**–560,523**	**–546,631**	**–1,285,729**	**–1,472,126**	**–106**
U.S. official reserve assets, net	–2,158	–9,742	–290	14,096	2,374	–122	–4,848
Special drawing rights	–192	–808	–722	4,511	–223	–154	–106
Reserve position in the International Monetary Fund	731	–2,466	2,308	10,200	3,331	1,021	–3,473
Foreign currencies	–2,697	–6,468	–1,876	–615	–734	–989	–1,269
U.S. government assets, other than official reserve assets	2,317	–984	–941	5,539	5,346	–22,273	–529,615
U.S. credits and other long-term assets	–8,410	–4,859	–5,182	–2,255	–2,992	–2,475	–2,202
Repayments on U.S. credits and other long-term assets	10,856	4,125	4,265	5,603	8,329	4,104	2,354
U.S. foreign currency holdings and U.S. short-term assets, net	–130	–250	–24	2,191	9	–23,902	–529,766
U.S. private assets, net	–81,393	–341,538	–559,292	–566,266	–1,293,449	–1,449,731	534,357
Direct investment	–37,183	–98,750	–159,212	–36,235	–244,922	–398,597	–332,012
Foreign securities	–28,765	–122,394	–127,908	–251,199	–365,129	–366,524	60,761
U.S. claims on unaffiliated foreigners reported by U.S. nonbanking concerns	–27,824	–45,286	–138,790	–71,207	–181,299	–40,517	372,229
U.S. claims reported by U.S. banks	12,379	–75,108	–133,382	–207,625	–502,099	–644,093	433,379
Foreign-owned assets in the United States, net (increase/financial inflow(+))	**139,357**	**435,102**	**1,038,224**	**1,247,347**	**2,065,169**	**2,129,460**	**534,071**
Foreign official assets in the U.S., net	33,910	109,880	42,758	259,268	487,939	480,949	487,021
U.S. government securities	30,243	72,712	35,710	213,334	428,401	269,897	543,498
Other U.S. government liabilities	1,868	–105	–1,825	–421	2,816	5,342	8,626
U.S. liabilities reported by U.S. banks	3,385	34,008	5,746	26,260	22,365	109,019	–153,443
Other foreign official assets	–1,586	3,265	3,127	20,095	34,357	96,691	88,340
Other foreign assets in the U.S., net	105,447	325,222	995,466	988,079	1,577,230	1,648,511	47,050
Direct investments in U.S.	48,494	57,776	321,274	112,638	243,151	275,758	319,737
U.S. Treasury securities	–2,534	91,544	–69,983	132,300	–58,229	66,807	196,619
U.S. securities other than U.S. Treasury securities	1,592	77,249	459,889	450,386	683,245	605,652	–126,737
U.S. currency flows	16,586	8,840	–3,357	8,447	2,227	–10,675	29,187
U.S. liabilities to unaffiliated foreigners reported by U.S. nonbanking concerns	45,133	59,637	170,672	69,572	244,793	201,681	–45,167
U.S. liabilities reported by U.S. banks	–3,824	30,176	116,971	214,736	462,043	509,288	–326,589
Financial derivatives, net	**(NA)**	**(NA)**	**(NA)**	**(NA)**	**29,710**	**6,222**	**–28,905**
Statistical discrepancy	*27,425*	*31,656*	*–59,265*	*36,623*	*–1,698*	*64,912*	*200,055*
Balance on goods	–111,037	–174,170	–454,690	–790,851	–847,260	–830,992	–840,252
Balance on services	30,173	77,786	74,855	75,582	86,901	129,569	144,316
Balance on income	28,550	20,891	21,054	72,358	48,085	90,845	118,231
Balance on current account	–78,968	–113,567	–417,426	–748,683	–803,547	–726,573	–706,068

NA: Data not available for year indicated.
Source: U.S. Bureau of Economic Analysis, Survey of Current Business, July 2009. Also see <http://www.bea.gov/scb/index.htm>.

[¶ 1020]

5. REVIEW OF SOME BASIC PROPOSITIONS OF U.S. INCOME TAX LAW

It is useful at the start of a study of international taxation to reflect on some basic and familiar principles of U.S. income tax law. While

Section 61 of the Internal Revenue Code commands that "gross income means all income from whatever source derived," there is a broad array of exemptions and exclusions that must be considered along with deductions to determine the amount (called "taxable income") finally subject to the applicable tax rates. The product of that process, the tentative tax liability, is then reduced by any applicable tax credits to arrive at the net tax due to the U.S. government or refund owed to the taxpayer.

The rules for taxing the return to labor and the return to capital have evolved in many respects as two general systems. Each system applies some common doctrines, such as the rule requiring an event of realization, under which income or loss is considered to arise from transactions and other income- or expense-generating events rather than from periodic evaluations of the taxpayer's wealth or actual measurement of the taxpayer's consumption expenditures. Each system is also marked by its own series of exceptions and specific applications.

Although tax rates have been reduced in recent decades, a progressive rate structure for individuals has been a consistent element of the U.S. income tax system. The individual tax rate schedule as recently as 1980 reflected many tax rate levels increasing to a maximum of 70 percent. Before tax legislation enacted in 2001 and 2003, the individual rate schedule reflected in Section 1, had just five rates: 15 percent, 28 percent, 31 percent, 36 percent and 39.6 percent. The 2001 and 2003 legislation added a new 10–percent rate bracket and phased in reductions to the tax rates above 15 percent, including a reduction in the top marginal rate to 35 percent.[1] Thus, under current law, in effect through only 2010, unless extended in subsequent legislation, the individual rate schedule has six rates: 10 percent, 15 percent, 25 percent, 28 percent, 33 percent and 35 percent.[2] If Congress does not act to extend the 2001 and 2003 tax cuts, the individual tax rate structure will revert to its pre-2001 form in 2011.

In 1986, Congress eliminated the preferential rates of tax on long-term capital gains. However, in 1990, Congress took what has proved to be the first step in restoring preferential treatment. It provided for a maximum rate of 28 percent for individuals but no preference for corporations. In 1993, Congress retained the maximum 28–percent rate on long-term capital gains for individuals and added a new, targeted preference for certain capital gains in Section 1202. Section 1202 allows noncorporate investors to exclude from gross income up to 50 percent of the gain they realize on the disposition of certain "qualified small business stock" held for more than five years.[3] As a result of legislation enacted in 1997, 1998

1. This top marginal rate decrease, together with the other individual rate cuts enacted in 2001 and 2003, are scheduled to expire after 2010, unless extended in subsequent legislation.

2. Because of the phaseout of personal exemptions and the reductions in itemized deductions applicable to relatively high-income taxpayers, the top *effective* marginal tax rate for individuals, however, can exceed 35 percent. Legislation enacted in 2001 provided a five-year phased in repeal of these provisions, starting in 2006. However, the repeal of these provisions also is scheduled to expire after 2010, unless extended in subsequent legislation.

3. Qualified small business stock is stock (issued after August 10, 1993) of a domestic C corporation (with certain exceptions) that uses at least 80 percent by value of its assets in the active conduct of one or more qualified businesses. § 1202(c).

and 2003, the preferential top rate for an individual taxpayer's gains from the sale of capital assets (other than collectibles, the taxable portion of the gain from the sale of qualified small business stock or certain depreciation recapture on depreciable real property) held for more than one year was first reduced to 20 percent and then to 15 percent.[4]

Moreover, apart from the capital gain rate preferences for individual taxpayers, the distinction between the treatment of transactions producing capital gain or loss and transactions producing ordinary income or loss retains importance because of the special limitations on the deduction of capital losses. Under Section 1211, in the case of corporations, capital losses may be deducted only against capital gains and, in the case of individuals, may be deducted only against capital gains and a limited amount of ordinary income. (Under Section 1212, any excess of capital losses over capital gains that cannot be currently deducted may be carried forward indefinitely (until death) by individual taxpayers and carried back three years and carried forward five years by corporate taxpayers.) Further, distinctions between trade or business activities and investment transactions often bear other important tax consequences.

The application of a system of double taxation for corporate earnings in most situations has long been a central element of the U.S. taxing structure. Historically, the top rate of corporate income tax has been near 50 percent. The 1986 Act, however, reduced the top nominal marginal corporate rate under Section 11 to 34 percent. The 1993 Act increased the top nominal marginal corporate rate to 35 percent on taxable income in excess of $10 million.[5] The shareholder is also generally taxed when corporate earnings and profits are distributed or the shareholder sells the corporation's stock.[6] If the shareholder sells the corporation's stock or the corporate distribution takes the form of a liquidation or a redemption that meaningfully reduces the shareholder's percentage interest in the corporation (rather than an ordinary dividend distribution which does not), the

4. For gain from the sale of capital assets that are "collectibles" and that are held for more than one year and for the taxable portion of gain from the sale of qualified small business stock, the top rate remains 28 percent. For certain depreciation recapture gain on depreciable real property held for more than one year, the top rate is now 25 percent. For individual taxpayers whose ordinary income is taxed in the 15 percent or lower rate brackets in Section 1, the 1997 legislation added a preferential rate of ten percent for gain from the sale of capital assets (other than collectibles, the taxable portion of the gain from the sale of qualified small business stock or certain depreciation recapture gain on depreciable real property) held more than one year. The 2003 legislation further reduced the preferential rate for such low-bracket taxpayers' long-term capital gains to five percent for tax years starting before 2008 and 0 percent for tax years starting in 2008. The reductions in the capital gain tax rates enacted in 2003 are scheduled to expire for tax years starting after 2010, unless extended in subsequent legislation.

5. Because of the phaseout of the rates below 34 percent and 35 percent for certain high-income corporations, the top *effective* marginal tax rate for corporations, however, can reach as high as 39 percent.

6. However, a corporate shareholder may qualify for a 70–, 80– or 100–percent dividends-received deduction with respect to ordinary dividend distributions from a U.S. corporation. See § 243. A more limited dividends-received deduction may be available for dividends from ten-percent owned foreign corporations, but only with respect to the U.S.-source portion of the dividends. See § 245.

shareholder is taxed only on the gain from the sale or exchange of the corporation's stock (i.e., amount realized on the sale minus the shareholder's basis in the stock) and, in the case of an individual shareholder, such gain may be taxed at the preferential capital gains rates. If the distribution is treated as dividend income under the corporate tax provisions of the Code, such dividend income is characterized as ordinary income. Under the 2003 legislation, however, such dividend income will be taxed to an individual shareholder at the preferential capital gains rates (currently at a top rate of 15 percent) if it meets the definition of "qualified dividend income."[7] If Congress does not act to extend this special tax treatment of individuals' qualified dividend income, such income will again be taxed at ordinary income tax rates in 2011.

While each corporation is a separate taxpayer, there are situations in which the separateness is disregarded. U.S corporations under 80-percent common control can, for example, file consolidated returns. Moreover, the double taxation of business operations can be avoided in some cases by using S corporations, partnerships or limited liability companies that elect to be treated as partnerships for U.S. tax purposes (the earnings of which generally bear tax only at the shareholder, partner or member level).

The notion of tax-free exchanges of property in various transactions in which realization of gain or loss does not compel its recognition is another important element of U.S. income tax jurisprudence. The tax-free exchange provisions (sometimes called "nonrecognition provisions") in particular play an important role in the setting up of corporations and in acquisitions and restructurings involving one or more corporations.

As discussed in Chapter 11, the American Jobs Creation Act of 2004 (hereinafter "2004 JOBS Act") added Section 199 to the Code, which allows both individual and corporate taxpayers a special deduction against income from production activities in the United States. This deduction currently is equal to nine percent of the taxpayer's so-called qualified production activities income, i.e., the excess of the taxpayer's domestic production gross receipts over the sum of its cost of goods sold that are allocable to such receipts and the other expenses, losses or deductions that are properly allocable to such receipts. In essence, this deduction reduces the effective rate of tax on a taxpayer's qualified production activities income. The purpose of this deduction is to encourage taxpayers to conduct their manufacturing activities in the United States, rather than abroad, regardless of whether their products are sold for export or within the United States.

---

7. See § 1(h)(11). Such qualified dividend income, however, retains its basic character as ordinary income and is not treated as capital gain income for other purposes in the Code, e.g., the capital loss limitation in Section 1211. In addition, unlike proceeds from the sale or exchange of stock (including stock redemptions meeting certain requirements in the Code), qualified dividend income may not be reduced by a shareholder's basis in the stock. As mentioned in the text above, the reductions in the rate of tax on qualified dividend income in Section 1(h)(11) will expire for tax years starting after 2010, unless they are extended in subsequent legislation.

It is important to mention that U.S. courts have developed several common law doctrines, including the economic-substance doctrine and the closely related business-purpose, substance-over-form, sham-transaction, and step-transaction doctrines, which may come into play when a taxpayer attempts to manipulate the form of a transaction and thereby obscure its substance to achieve a tax-avoidance purpose. The U.S. Treasury Department and Internal Revenue Service (hereinafter "IRS") have similarly adopted various regulations and rulings containing so-called anti-abuse rules to combat tax-avoidance plans that conflict with the policies underlying the Code provision at issue. Moreover, in 2010, Congress codified the economic-substance doctrine in new Section 7701(*o*) and imposed a new strict liability penalty on tax underpayments attributable to transactions lacking economic substance under this statutory provision.

Finally, it should be emphasized that U.S. tax rules determine a taxpayer's U.S. tax liability from international transactions. The fact that a transaction takes place wholly or partially within a foreign country does not mean that foreign tax law will govern the determination of the taxpayer's U.S. tax liability. However, foreign law will often be considered in the application of U.S. tax provisions.

[¶ 1025]

B. BASIC QUESTIONS: DESIGNING A SYSTEM FOR TAXING INTERNATIONAL TRANSACTIONS

It may be somewhat daunting, after starting to master the techniques and applications of the U.S. tax system, to reflect critically upon the basic assumptions of the ways in which that system taxes complicated international transactions. To provide an opportunity for reflection not affected by the tax regime that is already in place, try your hand at the following exercise.

[¶ 1030]

1. ASSIGNMENT: THE INDUSTRIA PROJECT

Industria is a country very much like the United States. It has an income tax system that contains the basic elements of the U.S. income tax system referred to in the previous section. The Government of Industria is not sure, however, how its taxing mechanisms should be applied to international transactions. It has hired a group of experts, including you, to design an appropriate system and has agreed to pay a handsome fee for the effort. This may be your last chance to undertake a pure reflection on the appropriate taxation of international transactions without the implicit assumptions arising from the current U.S. approach to the matter. How should Industria's system for taxing income and loss from international transactions be structured?

[¶ 1035]

2. CATEGORIES OF INTERNATIONAL TRANSACTIONS

A good first step would be to identify the nature and scope of transactions that must be considered in the analysis. Since Industria uses basic U.S. income tax concepts, income tax consequences are usually triggered by transactions in which taxpayers realize income, gain or loss or make expenditures. For purposes of the Industria Project, the types of transactions that might usefully be considered readily divide into two basic categories: the taxation of income earned in Industria by "outsiders" and the taxation of income earned outside of Industria by Industrians.

In fact, this basic demarcation is widely used in international tax parlance. The first category is often referred to as "inbound transactions" because foreign entities or individuals are coming into the economy of the host country in one way or another. The second category is often referred to as "outbound transactions" because domestic entities or individuals are venturing abroad in income-seeking enterprises.

The specific nature of both inbound and outbound transactions will depend on the economic factors being exploited. The two obvious alternatives are labor and capital, but the specific ways in which the factors of economic production can be exploited are almost infinite.

[¶ 1040]

3. TAXATION OF INTERNATIONAL LABOR

The Industria Project will require a definition of insiders and outsiders. That is, however, only the start of the analysis. The extent, if any, of the Industrian income tax burden appropriately imposed on foreign labor in Industria will depend on the application of sometimes complex and sometimes inconsistent considerations of income tax policy. Does Industria wish to encourage domestic use of foreign labor? Is it fair to tax an outsider who may not enjoy all of the political, social and economic advantages of an Industrian?

If an Industrian lives and works abroad, should there be any Industrian tax? The answer to this question depends in substantial measure on the political and economic rationale for the income tax system. An Industrian living overseas may have less political allegiance and may be using fewer governmental resources than an Industrian living at home (although protections afforded by the Industrian defense, diplomatic and consular establishments may be very important to the former). His or her expenses may be higher or lower. There may be income taxes and other taxes to be paid in the other country.

[¶ 1045]

4. TAXATION OF INTERNATIONAL INVESTMENT

Income from the exploitation of capital is usually defined by the nature of the capital. Loans produce interest. Stocks produce dividends. Technology produces royalties. Land produces rents. All forms of property may produce gain or loss upon disposition.

Whether the focus is on the foreign capitalist who earns income from Industria or the Industrian capitalist who earns income abroad, the same basic questions must be answered. The analysis might usefully be divided into two parts. One is to determine the "correct" way to apply Industrian tax principles to the transactions in question. The second is to determine whether to vary the application of those principles either to encourage or discourage the particular type of transaction.

[¶ 1050]

5. TAXATION OF INTERNATIONAL TRADE

Profits can, of course, arise from transactions in which there has been no meaningful investment in the place where the profit accrues. When foreign entities import into Industria products that have been produced elsewhere, should there be an Industrian income tax? Should income earned by Industrians who export be taxed by Industria in the same way as other income?

[¶ 1055]

6. SOME SPECIFIC QUESTIONS

In connection with the Industria Project, the government has asked you to respond to some specific questions:

—If a distinction between "outsiders" and Industrians is to be made, definitional standards must be applied. What criteria should be used?

—Should a corporation be treated as foreign or domestic according to its place of incorporation, its place of operation or the location of its management or its shareholders?

—Is it appropriate to respect the separateness of corporate entities for income tax purposes when they are owned or controlled by the same interests?

—Should current tax be imposed on income of an Industrian earned abroad either directly or through a foreign corporation?

—Should there be a difference in the approach to taxing the returns to labor and capital?

—Should a distinction be drawn between the treatment of trade or business income and passive investment income?

—Should consideration be given to the *foreign* tax burdens of either Industrian or "outside" taxpayers?

—Are there any administrative difficulties that would require modification of otherwise sound taxing principles?

—Should the Industrian rules for taxing various international transactions be designed to favor, discourage or treat neutrally such transactions?

—Are there any issues that should be raised with other governments in the establishment or implementation of Industria's international taxing regime?

[¶ 1060]

7. POSSIBLE LINES OF ANALYSIS

These are not new questions. The U.S. Congress began to address them as soon as the constitutionally valid income tax was established in 1913. The materials in this book will reflect that different answers have been provided at different times. A group of international tax experts was commissioned by the League of Nations in 1922 to consider the problem of double taxation of international transactions. Their study took place just about the time that initial approaches of the U.S. income tax system to the treatment of international transactions were being formulated. In developing recommendations for the Industria Project, it might be useful to consider some of the observations contained in the following excerpt from the Report on Double Taxation to the Financial Committee of the League of Nations by the Panel of Experts (Prof. Bruins, Commercial University, Rotterdam; Prof. Senator Einaudi, Turin University; Prof. Seligman, Columbia University, New York; Sir Josiah Stamp, K.B.E., London University) 18–20 (1923):

> The older theory of taxation was the exchange theory, which was related directly to the philosophical basis of society in the "social contract," according to which the reason and measure of taxation are in accordance with the principles of an exchange as between the government and the individual. This took two forms: the cost theory and the benefit theory. The cost theory was that taxes ought to be paid in accordance with the cost of the service performed by the Government. The benefit theory was that taxes ought to be paid in accordance with the particular benefits conferred upon the individual. Neither the cost nor the benefit theory was able to avoid or to solve the problem of international double taxation. For the services con-

ferred by a given government affect not only the person of the taxpayer resident within that government's area (his personal safety, health and welfare) but also the property that he possesses within the limits of that area (not, of course, the property outside it), the services by which that property benefits being its physical defence from spoliation, its protection from various kinds of physical deterioration and the maintenance of a system of legal rights surrounding it. Where the property was in one State and the person in another State, the complications were obvious. There was, moreover, no satisfactory method of apportioning either the cost or the benefit.

There is, however, no need to enter into the details of these methods, as the entire exchange theory has been supplanted in modern times by the faculty theory or theory of ability to pay. This theory is more comprehensive than the preceding theory, because it includes what there is of value in the benefit theory. So far as the benefits connected with the acquisition of wealth increase individual faculty, they constitute an element not to be neglected. The same is true of the benefits connected with the consumption side of faculty, where there is room even for consideration of the cost to the government in providing a proper environment which renders the consumption of wealth possible or agreeable. The faculty theory is the more comprehensive theory.

The objection may be made that faculty does not attach to things, and that many taxes are imposed upon things or objects. This is true of the so-called real or impersonal taxes as opposed to personal taxes. This distinction, however, must not prevent the recognition of the fact that all taxes are ultimately paid by persons. So-called real or impersonal taxes—taxes *in rem*, as the English-speaking countries term them—which are often chosen for reasons of administrative convenience, are ultimately defrayed by persons and, through the process of economic adjustment, ultimately affect the economic situation of the individual.

When we deal with the question of personality, we are confronted by the original idea of personal political allegiance or nationality. It is first of all necessary to consider briefly the issues that arise upon *political allegiance*. A citizen of a country living abroad is frequently held responsible to his own country, though he may have no other ties than that of citizenship there. His is a political fealty which may involve political duties and may also confer political rights. It may well be that the political rights are such as to imply a political obligation or duty to pay taxes.

In modern times, however, the force of political allegiance has been considerably weakened. The political ties of a nonresident to the mother-country may often be merely nominal. His life may be spent abroad, and his real interests may be indissolubly bound up with his new home, while his loyalty to the old country may have almost completely disappeared. In many cases, indeed, the new home will also become the place of a new political allegiance. But it is well known that in some countries the political bond cannot be dissolved even by permanent emigration; while it frequently happens that the immigrant has no desire to ally himself politically with what is socially and commercially his real home. In the modern age of the international migration of persons as well as of capital, political allegiance no longer forms an adequate test of individual fiscal obligation. It is fast breaking down in practice, and it is clearly insufficient in theory.

A second possible principle which may be followed is that of mere temporary *residence*; everyone who happens to be in the town or State may be taxable there. This, however, is also inadequate. If a traveller chances to spend a week in a town when the tax collector comes around, there is no good reason why he should be assessed on his entire wealth by this particular town; the relations between him and the government are too slight. Moreover, as he goes from place to place, he may be taxable in each place or in none. Temporary residence is plainly inadmissible as a test.

A third possible principle is that of *domicile* or *permanent residence*. This is a more defensible basis, and has many arguments in its favour. It is obviously getting further away from the idea of mere political allegiance and closer to that of economic obligation. Those who are permanently or habitually resident in a place ought undoubtedly to contribute to its expenses. But the principle is not completely satisfactory. For, in the first place, a large part of the property in the town may be owned by outsiders: if the government were to depend only on the permanent residents, it might have an insufficient revenue even for the mere protection of property. In the second place, most of the revenues of the resident population may be derived from outside sources, as from business conducted in other States: in this case, the home government would be gaining at the expense of its neighbour. Thirdly, property-owners like the absentee landlords of Ireland or the stockholders of railways in the western States of America cannot be declared devoid of all obligations to the place whence their profits are derived. Domicile, it is obvious, cannot be the exclusive consideration.

A fourth possible principle is that of the *location* of the wealth. This again is undoubtedly to a certain extent legitimate. For a man who owns property has always been considered to have such a close relation with the government of the town or country where his property is situated as to be under a clear obligation to support it.

While the principle of location or *situs* seemed to be adequate as long as we were dealing with the older taxes on property owned by the living or passing on death, the term became inadequate under the more modern systems of the taxation of income or earnings. It has become customary, therefore, to speak of the principle of location in the case of property, and the principle of origin in the case of income. Further consideration makes us realise that these two principles are not exactly coterminous; because, even though the income may be earned in a certain place, after it has been earned it becomes property, and is therefore susceptible of a different *situs*. Tangible, corporeal property is more difficult of movement, and in some cases, where it consists of immovables, cannot be moved at all; but certain forms of incorporeal property can be easily moved. The legal writers and the courts attempt to surmount certain of the resulting difficulty by distinguishing between the *actual* and the *constructive* location of property. We thus have the possibility of income originating in country A by trading within that country or physically arising from crops, property, etc. in that country, being actually found, so far as it consists, for instance, of securities, in a strong box in country B; so that in one sense the property, or the right to it, may be said to exist in country B. It may, however, well be that the whole apparatus producing the income that is non-physical, namely; the brains and control and direction, without which the physical adjuncts would be sterile and ineffective, are in country C; and therefore it may be said in another sense that the origin of the income is where the intellectual element among the assets is to be found. Finally, it may be said that the location of the property is country D, where the owner of the property has his residence. There is thus a possible difference between the theory of origin and the theory of location, if one examines the legal view of the matter.

Apart from these considerations, however, and chiefly for reasons which are just the reverse of those mentioned in the preceding case, the location or origin of the wealth cannot be the only test. Permanent residents owe some duty to the place where they live, even if the property is situated or their income derived elsewhere.

Practically, therefore, apart from the question of nationality, which still plays a minor role, the choice lies between the principle of domicile and that of location or origin. Taking the field of taxation as a whole, the reason why tax authorities waver between these two principles is that each may be considered as a part of the still broader principle of economic interest or *economic allegiance*, as against the original doctrine of political allegiance. A part of the total sum paid according to the ability of a person ought to reach the competing authorities according to the economic interest under each authority. The ideal solution is that the individual's whole faculty should be taxed, but that it should be taxed only once, and that the liability should be divided among the tax districts according to his relative interests in each. The individual has certain economic interests in the place of his permanent residence or domicile, as well as in the place or places where his property is situated or from which his income is derived. If he makes money in one place he generally spends it in another.

* * *

The starting-point of the modern theory must therefore be the doctrine of economic allegiance. In the most complex communities, with more fully developed taxation expedients, this doctrine is given quantitative expression by reference to terms of economic faculty or ability of the individual to pay. That is to say, the taxes, though measured by things, eventually fall upon persons and ought to fall upon them in the aggregate according to the total resources of the individuals, leading to progressively larger sums being paid by the people who are richer. The point is that when the money has left the pocket of the individual, its destination is not a single one but is due to all those governments to whom the individual owes economic allegiance. How, then, should the sum that he finally pays reach these several governments which render him service? The problem consists in ascertaining where the true economic interests of the individual are found. It is only after an analysis of the constituent elements of this economic allegiance that we shall be able to determine where a person ought to be taxed or how the division ought to be made as between the various sovereignties that impose the tax.

[¶ 1065]

NOTE

The above observations were published in 1923. How well have they withstood the test of time? How would a panel of experts appointed today by the United Nations deal with the same issues of international taxation in the light of our modern global economy?

C. REACH OF U.S. TAX JURISDICTION: THE ROLE OF INTERNATIONAL LAW

[¶ 1070]

1. JURISDICTION TO TAX

The jurisdictional power of a nation to tax the income from international transactions is well established in the principles of customary international law. But these principles contain broadly recognized limitations on the power to exercise such jurisdiction. Under these principles, the exercise of jurisdiction to tax may be based on one or more different factors. These factors include:

—Nationality.

—Domicile or residence.

—Presence or doing business within the country.

—Location within the country of property or transactions from which income is derived.

See generally Restatement (Third) of the Foreign Relations Law of the United States §§ 411, 412 (A.L.I. 1986). The exercise by a nation of taxing jurisdiction not appropriately founded on one or more of these factors would constitute a violation of customary international law. A brief reflection on the alternative jurisdictional bases for the exercise of taxing authority, however, will make it clear that the permissible power of a nation to tax will often reach beyond its own borders.

The exercise of extraterritorial taxing jurisdiction (the taxation of individuals and entities outside of the boundaries of the nation) necessarily implies a risk that income produced by a taxpayer from international transactions will be subjected to the demands of the tax laws of two or more nations even though each nation is acting within the prescriptions of international law. As discussed throughout this book, the U.S. approach to taxing international transactions reflects both an aggressive assertion of the jurisdictional power to tax and a concern about the possibility that multiple national income tax burdens will accrue to the same taxpayer on the same item of income. Specifically, the United States and many other countries use some form of a worldwide or extraterritorial system for taxing international income. Under such a system, a domestic taxpayer's worldwide income, regardless of source, is subject to taxation by the country of residence (i.e., the United States in the case of a U.S. citizen, resident alien or corporation). However, in order to mitigate international double taxation, the country of residence grants the domestic taxpayer a dollar-for-dollar credit for foreign income taxes paid by the domestic taxpayer on foreign-source income. Moreover, the United States and other countries that have extraterritorial systems typically have limited exemptions from tax for certain favored types of foreign-source income. For example, the United States exempts a U.S. citizen or resident alien who meets certain tests from tax on a specified amount of compensation income from foreign sources. See § 911, which is discussed in detail in Chapter 5.

A growing number of countries, including Australia, Canada, Japan, the United Kingdom and a number of the European countries, use some version of an exemption or territorial source system for taxing international income. Under such a system, many types (but typically not all) of a domestic taxpayer's income from foreign sources are exempt from tax in the country of residence. For example, in the Netherlands and some other countries with territorial systems, both foreign-source income earned directly by a domestic taxpayer as well as foreign-source dividends from a foreign subsidiary of a Dutch corporation are exempt from tax in the country of residence. Most countries with territorial systems do exercise residence-based taxing jurisdiction over certain types of foreign-source income, such as passive income or income earned in certain low-tax or no-tax foreign jurisdictions, i.e., such income is taxable in the country of residence notwithstanding the general territorial approach to taxing international transactions in such countries.

Various commentators in the United States have argued that the United States should move its international tax rules in the direction of an exemption or territorial system. As discussed below, they argue that such a move is necessary to foster the competitiveness of U.S. multinational corporations in the global economy. Yet, in recent years, many U.S. multinational corporations have resisted these efforts and instead lobbied for "reforms" of the current hybrid U.S. international tax system, undoubtedly because they have discovered that a coherent and nonelective exemption system might well increase the effective rate of U.S. tax on foreign-source income over the somewhat incoherent and elective rules of existing law, at least for some industries. The 2004 JOBS Act is a product of those lobbying efforts. Through a variety of changes favoring U.S. multinational businesses (which will discussed in detail throughout this book), the JOBS Act reduced the effective rate of U.S. tax on many types of foreign-source income and arguably moved the U.S. international tax system further away from an extraterritorial, worldwide approach and markedly in the direction of an elective, incoherent and poorly designed exemption or territorial system. In any event, a properly designed and comprehensive worldwide system for taxing international income might well raise more revenue than either our existing incoherent U.S. international tax rules or a coherent and properly designed exemption or territorial system.

[¶ 1075]

2. ROLE OF TAX TREATIES

International law is relevant to the income taxation of international transactions for another important reason. In addition to all of the usual sources of U.S. income tax law, income tax treaties play an important role in the income tax structure applicable to international transactions. As of November 1, 2010, there were in force bilateral treaties between the United States and over 57 countries. Many more treaties are in various stages of negotiation. The analysis of the tax consequences of international transactions must include the impact of any applicable treaties. The last portion of this Chapter (¶¶ 1235 et seq.) provides an introduction to the way in which tax treaties apply.

[¶ 1080]

3. INTERNATIONAL ENFORCEMENT PROBLEMS

As an example of comity in international relations, nations are often permitted to file civil actions in the courts of friendly countries. However, long-standing international practice has denied the application of comity in the case of attempts to litigate to enforce the tax laws of another country. (This practice is sometimes called the "revenue rule.") The United States does not sue for U.S. taxes due in the courts of other countries even though taxpayers may be found there; and other nations do not sue in the United States to enforce their tax laws. See Restatement (Third) of the Foreign Relations Law of the United States § 483 (A.L.I. 1986).

The absence of access to foreign judicial fora for enforcement has an important bearing on the evolution of tax law and practice with respect to international transactions. If foreign courts are unavailable, how can tax liabilities be enforced against absent foreign persons? As will be discussed in Chapter 4, most countries (including the United States) rely on withholding taxes as an essential tool in collecting taxes on certain domestic-source income from foreign persons not present within the taxing country. In effect, by reason of the withholding provisions, the payor of the domestic-source income to the foreign person must collect the tax and pay it over to the domestic tax authority for the account of the foreign person or be liable itself to the source country for the tax.

D. SOME BASIC CONCEPTUAL AND POLICY ISSUES

[¶ 1085]

1. INTRODUCTION

While the League of Nations experts worked in a simpler time, their observations provide a worthwhile introduction to issues that are still being debated. It may also be useful before launching into the detailed examination of the U.S. approach to the taxation of international transactions to consider some other basic issues and concepts that appear as recurring themes throughout the book. Many of the economic arguments that relate to the establishment of an appropriate taxing policy are complex. Moreover, there is no consensus among economists or other tax policy analysts about many important issues. The following materials, therefore, can only suggest the breadth and complexity of the underlying questions.

[¶ 1090]

2. STANDARDS OF INTERNATIONAL TAX NEUTRALITY

While there has long been disagreement between economists about the extent to which U.S. tax policy affects the level of investment by U.S. corporations abroad, it would appear both a priori and on the basis of empirical data that significant tax savings do influence at the margin where new investments are made. For example, many U.S. corporations have made substantial investments in manufacturing facilities in countries where special tax incentives, including tax holidays for a period of years, have been available.

There has been an ongoing debate for many years focused on whether U.S. tax policy should encourage or discourage foreign investment or treat it "neutrally." The debate has been complicated by a lack of agreement on what it means to treat income from foreign investment "neutrally." There are now at least four competing approaches to international tax neutrality, which are commonly labelled as capital-export neutrality, capital-import neutrality, national neutrality and capital-ownership neutrality. See, e.g., Staff of Joint Comm. on Tax'n, 102d Cong., 1st Sess., Factors Affecting the International Competitiveness of the United States, at 232–48 (1991); Staff of Joint Comm. on Tax'n, 110th Cong., 2d Sess., Economic Efficiency and Structural Analyses of Alternative U.S. Tax Policies for Foreign Direct Investment, at 12, 13 n.37 (2008). As you will see throughout this book, the U.S. international tax rules have elements that reflect all four neutrality approaches.

Capital-export neutrality is achieved when the U.S. investor pays the same total amount of U.S. and foreign tax on foreign-source income before tax as the total U.S. tax it pays on U.S.-source income before tax. Stated differently, under capital-export neutrality, the U.S. investor pays the same total (U.S. and foreign) tax on all income, regardless of where the income is earned. Thus, the decision to invest in the United States or abroad is not affected by U.S. or foreign tax consequences; the investment is made wherever pre-tax returns are greatest. The foreign tax credit approach to mitigating double taxation is compatible with capital-export neutrality, but pure capital-export neutrality would call for the refunding of any credit for foreign tax to the extent that it exceeds the U.S. tax that would otherwise apply. Assuming the existence of perfect competition, capital-export neutrality will result in the most efficient international allocation of capital.[8] Professor Peggy Musgrave first developed this effi-

8. In a report issued near the end of the Clinton Administration, the U.S. Treasury Department concluded: "A basic economic analysis indicates that capital export neutrality is probably the best policy for promoting economic efficiency in a tax system that includes taxes on income of capital." U.S. Treas. Dep't, The Deferral of Income Earned Through U.S. Controlled Foreign

ciency benchmark and the U.S. Treasury Department has generally favored this neutrality standard, although that was not the approach followed by the Administration of President George W. Bush.

Capital-import neutrality focuses on the country in which the investment is made. All firms operating in the same industry in a particular country, whether owned by local or foreign interests, are taxed at the same level. The exemption or territorial approach to eliminating double taxation is compatible with capital-import neutrality. Only the country in which the investment is made imposes tax; the country of the investor's residence exempts foreign-source income. Capital-import neutrality is sometimes called "competitive neutrality" because all competing firms in the same market are subject to the same tax burden and this form of neutrality encourages the most efficient use of resources within a given capital-importing country. Multinational business enterprises have advocated this neutrality standard and used it to argue that the U.S. tax system should be changed to exempt all foreign-source income from tax to increase the competitiveness of U.S. enterprises operating abroad. In recent years, the Treasury Department of the Administration of George W. Bush and many Republican and conservative Democratic members of Congress have increasingly favored this neutrality standard. It is fair to say that the 2004 JOBS Act moved the U.S. international tax system markedly in the direction of capital-import neutrality.

National neutrality is designed to ensure that total returns on capital (which are shared between the U.S. persons making the investment abroad and the U.S. Treasury) are the same whether the investment is made in the United States or abroad. The same amount of current tax should be payable to the U.S. Treasury whether the earnings are from U.S. investment or from foreign investment. Under this approach, foreign income taxes should be deductible (rather than creditable) because net foreign-source income after payment of foreign taxes should be equal to net U.S.-source income before payment of U.S. tax. Thus, this approach favors domestic investment over foreign investment. Under national neutrality, U.S. national revenues are increased at the cost of reducing world income since it does not encourage the most efficient allocation of resources internationally. Labor unions have been the leading advocates of this neutrality standard because they believe that this approach discourages U.S. corporations from moving their operations abroad and thus maximizes domestic employment.

Corporations: A Policy Study 53 (Dec. 2000). Similarly, the Joint Committee Staff earlier concluded: "Economic analysis can demonstrate that for any capital import-neutral tax policy there is almost always a superior revenue-neutral capital export-neutral policy." Staff of Joint Comm. on Tax'n, 102d Cong., 1st Sess., Factors Affecting the International Competitiveness of the United States, at 5 (1991). By contrast, a more recent report by the Joint Committee Staff was more equivocal and stated that "[t]he literature on the theory of international taxation provides no clear direction" on the issue of whether a worldwide system of taxation based on capital-export neutrality is more economically efficient than an exemption system based on capital–import neutrality. Staff of Joint Comm. on Tax'n, 106th Cong., 1st Sess., Overview of Present–Law Rules and Economic Issues in International Taxation, at § IV.D (1999).

Capital-ownership neutrality is a relatively recent efficiency benchmark, first developed by Professors Mihir Desai and James Hines, Jr., which requires that the international tax rules of a country not distort ownership patterns of assets. See, e.g., Desai & Hines, Jr., "Evaluating International Tax Reform," 56 Nat'l Tax J. 487 (2003). In theory, capital-ownership neutrality is met by conformity among countries' international tax rules, whether that conformity is met by all countries adopting worldwide systems with a foreign credit mechanism for mitigating international double taxation or by all countries adopting exemption or territorial systems. However, as a practical matter, in a world in which a growing number of countries have moved to adopt exemption systems, capital-ownership neutrality would require the United States to abandon its worldwide system and adopt an exemption system. Moreover, many capital-ownership neutrality proponents, like capital-import neutrality proponents, argue that competitiveness concerns dictate that the United States move to an exemption system for taxing foreign-source income.

[¶ 1095]

3. INTERNATIONAL DOUBLE TAXATION

A central focus of international taxation (and, therefore, a central focus of this book) is international double taxation. International double taxation exists in its purest form when a single item of income is subject to income tax by more than one country. The phenomenon occurs constantly in international business operations because nation-states impose their taxes on a variety of jurisdictional bases under international law, and these bases often overlap. Here it will suffice to suggest a simple example. Assume a given item of income may be taxed by Country A because it is received by a corporation organized under the laws of Country A, which taxes domestic corporations on their worldwide income. Country B may seek to tax the same item of income because it is earned or arises in (or—to use the international tax jargon—has its "source" in) the territory of Country B. This might occur, for example, because a domestic corporation of Country A has a branch office engaged in business operations in Country B.

Some of the basic mechanisms of international taxation have as their principal purpose the elimination or mitigation of international double taxation. Four principal mechanisms have been used to deal with the double taxation problem.

First, Country A can elect to use an "exemption" or "territorial" system of taxation and exempt income earned abroad from its tax. Under this approach, there is no double taxation because only Country B imposes tax on the income earned in Country B. In effect, Country A relinquishes any taxing jurisdiction over the income earned outside its borders. If the

Country B tax rates are lower than the Country A rates, then Country A individuals and corporations will have an incentive to reduce their tax burden by moving business operations and investments to Country B. This approach to mitigating international double taxation reflects application of the capital-import neutrality and capital-ownership neutrality principles discussed above. Its proponents maintain that an exemption or territorial system for taxing international income would enhance the competitiveness of Country A residents when they engage in business or investment activities in foreign countries.

Second, Country A could follow the capital-export neutrality principle discussed above and grant a dollar-for-dollar credit against the tax it would otherwise impose for each dollar of Country B tax that has been paid on income earned there. Under this foreign tax credit approach, if the Country B tax is less than the Country A tax, the effective overall tax burden after the foreign tax credit is equal to the Country A tax, and Country A individuals and corporations will have the same total tax burden regardless of whether they locate their business operations and investments in Country A or Country B. If the Country B tax is the higher tax, there are two possibilities. Either the total tax burden equals the rate of the Country B tax or Country A refunds to the Country A individual or corporation the excess of the Country B tax over the Country A tax. (The latter possibility is more theoretical than real; for obvious reasons, it has not been adopted in practice, although it would be consistent with capital-export neutrality.)

Third, Country A may treat the Country B tax as a deduction (as income taxes paid to states within the United States are) in calculating the net income subject to the Country A tax. As illustrated in the chart below, the deduction method, unlike the exemption or tax credit method, mitigates, but does not eliminate, double taxation. Therefore, the deduction method may serve to discourage international investment by Country A individuals and corporations. This approach to mitigating international double taxation reflects application of the national neutrality principle discussed above.

The chart below illustrates the consequences of full double taxation by Countries A and B, and the exemption, foreign tax credit and deduction approaches to eliminating or mitigating international double taxation. The assumptions are that a Country A corporation has a branch in Country B earning income from sources in Country B. The taxable income ("TI") of the branch is $100, which, absent any mechanism to prevent or reduce double taxation, would be subject to a 30–percent Country B income tax and to a 35–percent Country A tax. (The numbers in parentheses indicate the results if the Country B tax is 40 percent, none of which is refunded by Country A.)

MECHANISMS FOR ELIMINATING OR REDUCING INTERNATIONAL DOUBLE TAXATION

			Double Tax	*Exemption*	*Credit*		*Deduction*
(1)	B Branch TI	=	100	100	100		100
(2)	B Tax [30% of (1)]	=	30	30	30(40)	Less B Tax	30
(3)	TI to A Corp.	=	100	0	100		70
(4)	Tentative A Tax [35% of (1)]	=	35	0	35		
(5)	Less tax credit	=	0		30(40)		
(6)	Final A Tax	=	35	0	5(0)	[35% of (3)]	24.5
(7)	Total A and B Tax	=	65	30	35(40)		54.5

The three foregoing mechanisms—the exemption, the foreign tax credit and the deduction—are *unilateral* devices for mitigating double taxation because they are formulated by Country A, the country of residence, without reaching agreement with Country B or any other country. There is a fourth mechanism—the income tax treaty—that is a *bilateral* device for mitigating double taxation. This approach involves Country A, the country of residence, reaching agreement with Country B, the country of source, regarding the allocation of taxing jurisdiction over income realized by residents of one country from sources within the other country. A tax treaty can be entered into by Country A and Country B that will preclude one state from exercising the taxing jurisdiction it could otherwise exercise under international law. Alternatively, a treaty may permit both countries to tax the income, but limit the amount of the tax that the source country will be permitted to impose. The latter mechanism in effect divides the tax revenues between Country A and Country B.

The premise of mechanisms to eliminate or mitigate double taxation, and of the hundreds of bilateral tax treaties in force throughout the world that are directed toward that end, is that the source country in which the income arises or is earned has initial and primary jurisdiction to tax such income. This basic principle of international taxation reflects the reality that the source country normally has the power to impose its tax on income arising in its territory before that income leaves the country.

[¶ 1100]

4. DEFERRAL PRINCIPLE

Other basic principles of U.S. taxation of the income from international transactions can be evaluated against the four approaches to tax neutrality discussed at ¶ 1090. One illustration of such evaluation may be offered here. The issue relates to what has come to be called the principle of tax deferral, and it is basic and important enough to warrant an early introduction in any discussion of the U.S. taxation of income from international transactions.

The term "deferral," as used in connection with debate over the issue raised here, bears a somewhat pejorative coloration because it implies, as many tax policy analysts would argue, that some special concession is being conferred. For that reason, some commentators refer to this element of the international tax rules as the "deferral privilege." In another sense, deferral may be regarded simply as a reference to the consequences of treating the foreign subsidiary as a separate legal person (and separate taxpayer). This is the approach adopted in the United States and in most foreign countries except in extraordinary circumstances. In any event, "deferral" is a convenient, shorthand way to refer to the phenomenon described below, and the term has become part of the "coin" of the international tax law realm.

When a U.S. corporation establishes a branch in a foreign Country X, the branch has no separate legal identity; no form of business organization under the laws of Country X is involved. The branch is simply an extension of the legal personality of the U.S. corporation and, accordingly, the income or loss of the branch is included in the income or loss of the U.S. corporation. If the branch has income from outside the United States, that foreign-source income is taxed in the United States as part of the U.S. corporation's income because, as will be discussed below, the United States generally taxes the worldwide income of a U.S. corporation. The branch's foreign-source income may also be subject to tax in Country X, in which case double taxation is eliminated or reduced by the foreign tax credit accorded by the United States with respect to the Country X tax. (Alternatively, if Country X and the United States have entered into an income tax treaty, the branch's income may be exempt from Country X tax under the terms of the treaty.)

By contrast, if the U.S. corporation conducts its business in Country X through a subsidiary corporation organized under the laws of Country X, the income of the Country X corporation from sources outside the United States is not generally subject to U.S. tax. The separate legal personality of the Country X corporation is respected for U.S. tax purposes, and no U.S. tax can normally be imposed unless and until the foreign earnings of the Country X corporation are distributed as a dividend or otherwise to the U.S. parent corporation. In international tax parlance, the U.S. tax is "deferred" unless and until the foreign earnings of the Country X corporation are distributed to the U.S. parent corporation (or the U.S. parent corporation sells the stock in the Country X corporation).[9]

Note that as a result of the deferral principle, there is a fundamental difference between the U.S. taxation of the foreign branch of the U.S.

---

9. If the period of deferral is long enough, the deferral has substantially the same effect as exempting the foreign income from tax.

corporation and the U.S. taxation of the wholly owned foreign subsidiary of the U.S. corporation. Those opposed to this difference argue that capital-export neutrality calls for the elimination of deferral and the taxing of the foreign subsidiary in the same manner as the foreign branch.

Those supporting deferral have invoked capital-import neutrality and, more recently, capital-ownership neutrality. They argue that the U.S. corporation would be placed at a serious competitive disadvantage if, for example, it were subjected to full U.S. tax on the undistributed earnings of a Country M manufacturing subsidiary which are exempt from Country M tax under a tax holiday regime aimed at attracting foreign investment to Country M. The disadvantage results because the U.S. tax on the undistributed earnings of the Country M subsidiary would cancel the benefit of the Country M tax exemption. By contrast, other Country M manufacturing subsidiaries owned, for example, by a corporation organized in a foreign country that follows the deferral principle, Country Z, would enjoy the full benefit of the exemption from Country M tax since no taxes would be imposed in Country Z unless and until the earnings were remitted by the Country M subsidiary to its Country Z parent corporation.

Congress has thus far declined to enact proposals to eliminate deferral entirely with respect to all foreign corporations owned by U.S. shareholders. However, significant exceptions to deferral have been adopted in certain situations, particularly involving the use of U.S.-owned foreign corporations in tax haven countries, with respect to which Congress has been persuaded that the potential for abuse is high. The two most important of these anti-deferral regimes are the controlled foreign corporation ("CFC") provisions in Subpart F of the Code (i.e., Sections 951 through 965) and the passive foreign investment company ("PFIC") provisions in Sections 1291 through 1298. When Congress determines that anti-abuse measures are necessary in response to an instance of deferral, it typically chooses between three conceptual ways of dealing with the issue: immediate taxation of the U.S. shareholder's share of the foreign corporation's foreign earnings on which U.S. tax would otherwise be deferred, imposition of an interest charge on the deferred tax or immediate taxation of the increase in the fair market value of the U.S. shareholder's stock from the beginning to end of the tax year (a "mark-to-market" approach).

[¶ 1105]

5. DOMESTIC EFFECTS OF FOREIGN INVESTMENT

One of the most widely debated and important issues underlying the establishment of appropriate international tax policy is whether foreign investment by domestic investors results in lost jobs for the domestic labor force that would have been employed if the new investment had been made at home. The effect of foreign investment on the U.S. economy is a difficult matter to predict and, as you would expect, a matter on which there is much disagreement. In large part it turns on the question of whether foreign investment lessens investment made in the United States—that is, whether foreign investment is made as a substitute for U.S. investment or as an addition to it. This, too, is a difficult question to answer, as the following excerpt (Staff of Joint Comm. on Tax'n, 102d Cong., 1st Sess., Factors Affecting the International Competitiveness of the United States, at 234–36 (1991)) demonstrates:

The distribution of income between capital and labor

The location of investment has important implications for the distribution of income. In general, increased capital formation increases the productivity of labor. With more output per worker, labor income (including wages and other forms of compensation) increases. Any reallocation of investment from the United States to foreign localities, for whatever reason, will reduce the productivity of U.S. workers and therefore their compensation. The remaining smaller pool of capital in the United States will receive a higher rate of return as investors drop the least profitable investment projects.

It is important to note that despite the decline in wages resulting from the reallocation of capital, an increase in overall income may nonetheless occur. A situation of unrestricted capital flows is considered optimal because it maximizes total income. If total national income increases due to the freedom of capital flows and an outflow of capital reduces domestic wages, then the increase in capital income necessarily exceeds the decline in wages.

Similarly, any increase in inbound investment into the United States increases the productivity of U.S. workers and their income. Increased investment by foreign persons in the United States also reduces the return on capital in the United States. If capital inflows are the result of free-market policies, they increase national welfare. However, as in the case of outbound investment, not all sectors of the economy will necessarily be better off.

The effect of outbound investment on domestic investment

A critical factor in determining the effects of international capital flows on the distribution of income is whether domestic saving increases in response to the availability of outbound investment opportunities. If outbound investment does not reduce domestic investment, then outbound investment will not reduce labor income (although by increasing returns on capital it may reduce labor's share of income). However, if outbound investment results in a reduction of the U.S. capital stock, labor income will also decline. The importance of one's assumption about the effect of outbound investment on domestic savings can hardly be overemphasized. Many conclusions and policy prescriptions derived from the theory of international taxation depend on this assumption. Unfortunately, little empirical research has been undertaken to determine the direct effect of investment overseas by U.S. investors on U.S. savings and on investment in the United States.

One way that outbound investment can affect domestic investment is illustrated by the case of a "runaway plant." The term "runaway plant" usually refers to the relocation to a foreign country of a U.S. production facility owned by U.S. persons. Even if this phenomenon is observed, it does not necessarily lead to the conclusion that U.S. investors collectively reduce investment in the United States by the amount of the outbound investment or by any other amount. Facilities which had been located in the United States may have been substantially funded by domestic debt and now could be funded by foreign debt. If this were the case, outbound investment may make available domestic debt capital for other investments in the United States. Similarly, unemployed workers and other resources made available as a result of the plant relocation may provide new investment opportunities for other domestic investors. Therefore, if a U.S. plant does relocate, it is uncertain how much (or, strictly speaking, whether) U.S. investment has declined by virtue of that fact. If lower rate financing and inexpensive labor become available as a result of outbound investment, runaway plants conceivably might not reduce U.S. domestic investment. However, it is unclear to what extent these newly available resources might increase domestic investment.

[¶ 1110]

6. TAX FAIRNESS: HORIZONTAL AND VERTICAL EQUITY

Fairness or equity is an important attribute of a soundly designed tax system. Two measures of equity are generally used by tax policy analysts in evaluating income tax provisions—horizontal equity and vertical equity. Horizontal equity requires that persons with equal economic incomes bear an equal tax burden (i.e., persons who are similarly situated should bear similar tax burdens). Vertical equity focuses on the distribution of the tax burden among persons with different levels of economic income and requires that persons with different economic incomes bear an "appropriately" different tax burden. To apply vertical equity, one must decide what is an appropriate distribution of the tax burden—proportional (i.e., flat rate), regressive or progressive. The standard measure in the federal income tax system has been a progressive distribution of the income tax burden, although the degree of progressivity in the tax system has varied over the years.

The capital-export neutrality standard may be viewed as consistent with horizontal equity because under that standard those persons with the same economic incomes bear the same total (U.S. and foreign) tax burden regardless of where they make their investments (at home or abroad). Thus, international tax provisions that promote capital-export neutrality, such as the basic foreign tax credit provisions, can be viewed as consistent with horizontal equity. On the other hand, the capital-import neutrality standard may be viewed as inconsistent with horizontal equity because it allows differences in tax burden based on the source of the income. Accordingly, the territorial or exemption system for mitigating double taxation, which implements the capital-import neutrality standard, is generally viewed as violating horizontal equity because it exempts one category of income (i.e., foreign-source income) from taxation by the country of residence.

Capital-export neutrality also may be viewed as consistent with vertical equity, particularly if one decides that a progressive distribution of the tax burden is the appropriate one. As stated in a 1977 Treasury Report: "[T]he income redistribution objective manifested by the use of progressive income taxes implies that a country should impose taxes on the entire income of residents." U.S. Treas. Dep't, Blueprints for Basic Tax Reform 99 (Jan. 1977). Thus, a residence-based tax system (which taxes a U.S. person's worldwide income combined with allowing a foreign tax credit for foreign taxes paid on foreign-source income) is consistent with vertical equity because a taxpayer will pay total (U.S. and foreign) taxes based on the taxpayer's level of worldwide income.

The traditional tax equity analysis, already complex and controverted, is obviously more difficult to apply to the taxation of foreign persons because only a small part of their total worldwide income may be taxed in a particular source country. To whom should such foreign taxpayers be compared in measuring horizontal equity? Should the foreign taxpayer's income from outside the source country be considered in applying principles of vertical equity? As a practical matter, how would the source country be able to take such income into account, if it wanted to do so?

[¶ 1115]

7. COMPLEXITY

Complexity has become a key issue in international taxation, as it has in other areas of taxation. Complex tax provisions undermine voluntary compliance and make administration of the tax system by the IRS more difficult. They impose significant administrative costs on the IRS and significant compliance costs on U.S. taxpayers. Complex tax provisions also place a premium on tax planning, which results in another tax-related cost for taxpayers. Those taxpayer compliance and tax planning costs, in turn, may result in increased prices for the goods and services offered by U.S. taxpayers in the global marketplace, thus undermining the competitiveness of U.S. taxpayers in international trade. See, e.g., U.S. Treas.

Dep't, International Tax Reform: An Interim Report 1 (Jan. 1993). Therefore, simplification of the international tax provisions should be a serious goal of tax policy analysts.

By any measure, the U.S. international tax rules are among the most complicated provisions in the entire Internal Revenue Code. There are several sources of this complexity. First, as in other areas of the tax law, there are a number of international tax provisions that are designed to serve some economic or political policy objective apart from raising revenue. As discussed below, these types of tax provisions, which represent subsidies or penalties administered through the tax system, add complexity to the tax system.

Second, the U.S. rules for taxing international transactions often represent compromises among the competing policy approaches. Some provisions are based on the capital-export neutrality standard, some are based on capital-import neutrality and others are based on national neutrality. Thus, the provisions do not work in a coordinated fashion to achieve a common policy goal but instead seek to implement conflicting policy objectives, resulting in a sometimes incoherent set of rules governing even a single transaction.

Third, the underlying transactions in the international area are often very complicated. Thus, any tax rules designed to apply to such transactions are likely to be complicated in both content and operation.

Finally, concerns about the complexity of income tax provisions may conflict with other tax policy concerns. For example, a tax proposal that attempts to improve the measurement of economic income subject to tax, and thereby improve the fairness and efficiency of the tax system, may increase the complexity of the tax system (sometimes significantly so). Yet, a sound tax policy analysis may well conclude that the proposal should be adopted because the equity and efficiency benefits advanced by the proposal outweigh the complexity concerns. Thus, some of the most complicated U.S. international tax rules were adopted because they were thought by Congress to improve significantly the fairness and efficiency of the tax system, notwithstanding their complexity.

As you study the various international tax provisions discussed in this book, you should think about at least two questions relating to the issue of complexity. First, do the tax policy benefits achieved by a complex tax provision outweigh whatever administrative and compliance costs that the provision imposes on the IRS and taxpayers? Second, can the same policy objectives be accomplished with a less complex provision?

[¶ 1120]

8. USE OF TAX LAW TO ACHIEVE NONTAX OBJECTIVES

The Code has often been used to advance governmental objectives that do not necessarily derive from tax policy considerations. Tax provisions that advance such objectives are sometimes called "tax expenditure" provisions and tax expenditure theorists maintain that such provisions should be evaluated as indirect subsidies or government programs implemented through the tax system. Some derive from economic considerations, such as credits for research and development and for certain other forms of investment. Others reflect social concerns, such as the deduction for charitable contributions.

Many tax policy analysts argue that the tax laws should not be used to advance such objectives because tax expenditure provisions increase the complexity of the income tax system and place implementation of the nontax economic or social policy objectives in the hands of an agency (the IRS) without the necessary expertise to effectively perform such implementation. By contrast, others argue that the tax laws should be used to advance such objectives because tax expenditure provisions provide an inexpensive (in terms of costs of implementation) way to direct funds in desired directions.

The same questions arise in the taxation of international activities. Opportunities arise for advancing economic, political and social objectives that do not derive from tax policy concerns. The cost of pursuing these objectives is usually measurable in tax revenues lost and increased complexity. The benefits, as always, are very difficult to measure accurately.

Not all attempts to induce behavior through taxing mechanisms lose revenues. In several instances the Congress has effectively denied tax benefits under the generally applicable international rules for certain taxpayers to advance international political objectives. These provisions are sometimes called "tax penalty" or "negative tax expenditure" provisions. For example, as discussed in Chapter 14, the Code contains tax penalties for cooperation with the Arab boycott of Israel. Also, foreign tax credits are denied as a sanction against unacceptable political conduct by foreign nations, such as supporting international terrorism, as discussed at ¶ 5125. Is it appropriate to use the tax system to achieve such international political objectives? How effective are these provisions in achieving their non-revenue raising objectives?

[¶ 1125]

9. TRANSFER PRICING AND OTHER SPECIAL ADMINISTRATIVE PROBLEMS

Whenever a transaction involves related parties located in two countries with differing tax rates, there may be an economic inducement for the parties to fix an artificial price to be paid by the party receiving a benefit. The objective of adopting an artificial price may be to shift income from the high-tax country to the low-tax country. The U.S. tax system, like most others, vests the revenue collection agency (the IRS) with authority to adjust the price between the related parties as necessary to reflect their incomes clearly. See § 482. This is accomplished by adjusting the price so that it is equal to the price that might have been fixed for a comparable transaction by independent persons dealing at arm's length. The difficult issue of evaluating (and, when necessary, adjusting) the price on transactions between related parties against an arm's length standard has come to be widely identified as the "transfer pricing" issue. It is an important feature of both national tax systems and international tax treaties, and is the focus of Chapter 8.

As will be discussed throughout this book, there are many other provisions in the Code that are explicable primarily by way of reference to administrative realities. There are special problems that arise in the context of international transactions. The IRS has been armed with extraordinary powers to collect information and taxes. When income derives from international transactions, however, the taxpayer or the proceeds of the transaction may be outside of the United States. The IRS's special powers are generally limited by national borders. To what extent is it justifiable to define income tax liabilities to reflect these administrative realities?

[¶ 1130]

10. REACTIONS BY FOREIGN GOVERNMENTS TO U.S. INTERNATIONAL TAX RULES

The application of a nation's tax policies to international transactions necessarily involves some considerations not necessarily present when other areas of tax law are being formulated. There is in particular the virtual certainty that at least one other country will always have a direct interest in the way that a nation's tax rules apply to an international transaction. U.S. tax policymakers must, therefore, consider the effect of U.S. policies on other countries and the possibility that other countries will be moved to modify their own laws in response to actions of the United States. In some instances, representatives of governments have been able to negotiate at least some aspects of the way in which their taxing mechanisms will operate to coordinate their respective requirements. In other instances, no intergovernmental cooperation has occurred and the taxpayer caught by the conflicting demands of multiple taxing systems is left to traditional forms of legal self-defense.

[¶ 1133]

11. THE PROBLEM OF CROSS-BORDER TAX ARBITRAGE

A particular international transaction or investment will frequently involve the interaction of two or more national tax systems and perhaps one or more international double tax treaties. Occasionally, separate tax systems implicated in an international transaction may accord inconsistent treatment to the transaction or the business entity involved. These differences in treatment can generate multiple tax benefits or burdens arising from the same transaction, and the parties may be able to structure the transaction to produce tax benefits under both systems. Distinct tax systems may characterize the transaction differently or may apply inconsistent source rules to the transaction. An illustration would be an international transfer of intangible property, such as a patent or copyright, which may be characterized by one tax system as a sale and by the other as a license, and the result may be that a different source rule may be applied in each country. Even if the transaction is characterized consistently by the two systems, inconsistent source or taxation rules may be applicable.

Inconsistencies in the treatment of a transaction can also arise in a variety of other contexts. For example, if a foreign law firm renders services outside the United States for a U.S. client, the resulting fee would be treated as foreign-source income under the U.S. source rules but may be treated as U.S.-source income under a foreign tax system which sources the income at the location of the client. The result of the inconsistent source rules may be that the fee is exempt from tax in both countries (sometimes referred to as the phenomenon of "double nontaxation"). In addition, inconsistent rules relating to characterization of entities can result in a royalty payment being deductible in one country because the entity is treated as a corporation in that country entitled to deduct the payment without a corresponding inclusion of royalty income in the other country because, under the law of the latter, the payor is treated as a branch that has simply made a payment to the entity of which it is a part, both being considered parts of a single legal entity. (Such an entity is commonly referred to as a "hybrid entity.") Inconsistent residence rules may result in double taxation of income if the recipient of the income involved is found to be a resident of each of two countries with the result that it is taxable in both or if the recipient is not held to be a resident of either of the countries concerned, the income may be exempt from tax altogether. Thus, when inconsistent rules relating to such matters as determining the source of income, entity characterization and residence are applied in the countries concerned, there may be not only the possibility of international double taxation but also the possibility of obtaining a tax benefit in both countries. Exploiting inconsistencies between such rules in order to obtain a tax benefit is often referred to as international or cross-border tax arbitrage.

The question presented is how the United States and the foreign country should deal with such cross-border arbitrage issues. In some cases, specific anti-abuse rules are formulated in a statutory provision (such as the dual consolidated loss rules of Section 1503(d), discussed at ¶ 13,065) or in a regulation provision. In other cases, the IRS attempts to use judicial doctrines, such as economic substance, substance over form or sham transaction, to strike down specific international transactions that it views as abusive (often falling under the rubric "tax shelter"). The government's success in using these doctrines in recent litigation in the international tax arena is decidedly mixed. Although the government has been successful in persuading courts to use these doctrines to disallow the tax benefits in some cross-border transactions, in other cases U.S. court of appeals judges have been quite reluctant to apply these doctrines to invalidate transactions that comply with the letter of the Code and regulations.[10] It remains to be seen whether the government will have greater success in applying the codified version of the economic-substance doctrine in new Section 7701(*o*) to attack these types of transactions.

Yet another approach in the case of certain cross-border arbitrage transactions that fall within the "tax shelter" category is to require disclosure by taxpayers and their "material advisors" with respect to "reportable transactions." See §§ 6011 and 6111; Reg. § 1.6011–4. These are certain transactions identified in regulations issued by the Treasury and the IRS as being of a type having a potential for tax avoidance or evasion. See § 6707A(c)(1). Material advisors also are required to maintain lists identifying each person with respect to whom they acted as a material advisor for a reportable transaction. See § 6112. Part and parcel of these disclosure and list maintenance regimes is the imposition of hefty monetary penalties if the disclosure and list maintenance requirements are not followed. See §§ 6707A and 6708. Note that tax attorneys and accountants who advise taxpayers with respect to "reportable transactions" may be "material advisors" subject to these requirements.

Finally, under an important financial accounting standards interpretation issued in 2006, generally accepted accounting principles now re-

---

10. Compare ACM Partnership v. Commissioner, 157 F.3d 231 (3d Cir. 1998), cert. denied, 526 U.S. 1017 (1999) (losses arising in a cross-border tax shelter transaction involving the contingent installment sale provisions disallowed because transaction lacked economic substance), with Compaq Computer Corp. v. Commissioner, 277 F.3d 778 (5th Cir. 2001) (appellate court upheld the validity of a tax-avoidance transaction involving the foreign tax credit), excerpted at ¶ 5310; and IES Industries, Inc. v. United States, 253 F.3d 350 (8th Cir. 2001) (upholding the validity of a transaction very similar to the one in the *Compaq* case).

quire corporations that prepare financial statements to identify and quantify uncertain tax positions. See Financial Accounting Standards Board, Interpretation No. 48, Accounting for Uncertainty in Income Taxes (June 2006) (often called "FIN 48"). This means that the corporation must identify and quantify for financial accounting purposes an uncertain tax position concerning a specific federal tax return for which the corporation is required to maintain a reserve amount under FIN 48. The Treasury and the IRS have announced that they are developing a proposal to require certain corporations that have both uncertain tax positions and assets of $10,000,000 or more to file a proposed Schedule UTP disclosing such uncertain tax positions if such corporations or a related party issued audited financial statements. See IRS Announcement 2010–9, 2010–1 C.B. 408; IRS Announcement 2010–17, 2010–1 C.B. 515; IRS Announcement 2010–30, 2010–1 C.B. 668. In addition, the Treasury and IRS have issued proposed regulations that would require corporate taxpayers to file a Schedule UTP in accordance with the forms, instructions and other guidance provided by the IRS. REG–119046–10, 2010–2 C.B. 415. These financial accounting and tax reporting requirements can apply to uncertain tax positions involving the international tax rules, including issues arising in cross-border arbitrage transactions.

These cross-border arbitrage issues and how the United States and other countries should deal with them are discussed throughout this book in the specific contexts in which they arise.

[¶ 1135]

12. REVENUE NEEDS OF U.S. GOVERNMENT

No full consideration of income tax policy can ignore the political realities attending the U.S. government's budgetary needs and concerns. While the historic U.S. budget deficits of the 1980s and 1990s had abated and a federal budget surplus temporarily emerged in the late 1990s, the combination of an economic downturn in the United States during the period from 2000 through 2003, the large tax cuts proposed by the Bush Administration and enacted into law by Congress in 2001 through 2004, the costly wars in Iraq and Afghanistan, the financial crisis and serious recession in 2008 and 2009 and the costly economic stimulus program enacted in 2009 have produced very large deficits once again. Thus, the U.S. government's need for tax revenue retains a prominent position on the political agenda. Accordingly, as with other portions of the Code, international tax proposals that effectively reduce U.S. tax collections, even when supported by sound economic analysis and income tax theory, must also confront this difficult political hurdle. In some respects the political problem is no different than for proposals that affect domestic investment; but far fewer constituents are directly involved in international than domestic transactions. Further, in the case of proposals that reduce U.S. taxes on foreign persons, the direct beneficiaries of the proposals (foreign persons) cannot vote. In fact, because foreign persons cannot vote, they are a tempting target for tax *increase* proposals by U.S. political leaders who need tax revenue but do not want to alienate their voting constituents.

E. SOME BASIC PRINCIPLES OF U.S. INTERNATIONAL TAXATION

[¶ 1140]

1. FOREIGN PERSONS

Foreign persons (principally nonresident aliens and foreign corporations) are subject to two different U.S. taxing regimes. One regime applies to income that is connected with the conduct of a trade or business in the United States. The other regime applies to certain specified types of nonbusiness income from U.S. sources. The rules for determining the source of a taxpayer's income and deductions are explored in Chapter 2.

[¶ 1145]

a. Trade or Business Income

If a foreign person conducts a trade or business in the United States, the *net income* effectively connected with the U.S. business activity will be taxed at the usual U.S. rates. §§ 871(b) and 882. At present, as a result of tax cuts enacted in 2001 and 2003, the top nominal marginal rate paid by individual taxpayers is 35 percent, although most long-term capital gains may be taxed at a lower maximum rate of 15 percent. § 1. (As noted earlier, if Congress does not act to extend the 2001 and 2003 tax rate cuts, the top nominal marginal rate on individual taxpayers will revert back to 39.6 percent and the top preferential tax rate for most long-term capital gains will revert back to 20 percent in 2011.) The top nominal marginal tax rate paid by the most profitable corporations is 35 percent. § 11. There is no preferential tax rate for a corporate taxpayer's long-term capital gains under current law.

The determination of whether a foreign person is engaged in the conduct of a trade or business in the United States generally involves a facts-and-circumstances analysis. Under the case law and the IRS rulings, a U.S. trade or business will generally be found to exist if a foreign person's business activity in the United States is regular, continuous and considerable. A mere isolated or sporadic act will not generally constitute a U.S. trade or business. The Code does provide, however, that *any* performance of services in the United States generally will be treated as a U.S. trade or business. § 864(b). This rule is subject to a de minimis exception for a nonresident alien individual who is working for a foreign employer, earns no more than $3,000 of compensation for his or her U.S.

work and is present in the United States for no more than 90 days during the year. § 864(b)(1). The Code also contains safe harbors for certain trading activities in stock, securities and commodities under which such trading activities will not constitute a U.S. trade or business. § 864(b)(2).

The trade or business regime for taxing a foreign person's U.S. trade or business income applies to income that is "effectively connected" with the conduct of the U.S. trade or business, as determined in Section 864(c). The income taxable under this regime includes certain U.S.-source investment-type income (such as interest, dividends, rents and royalties) and capital gains, but only if such income and gains are treated as effectively connected income under the tests in Section 864(c)(2) (which focus on the factual connection of the income or gains to the U.S. trade or business). It also includes other types of U.S.-source income of the foreign person (such as income from the sale of inventory) regardless of whether such income has an actual factual connection to the foreign person's U.S. trade or business. § 864(c)(3). Although foreign-source income of a foreign person is usually not subject to U.S. tax, several specified types of a foreign person's foreign-source income that are attributable to a U.S. office or fixed place of business may be subject to U.S. tax under this trade or business regime. § 864(c)(4) and (5).

This regime taxes the foreign person's *net* income derived from the U.S. trade or business (effectively connected gross income minus allowable deductions attributable to the U.S. trade or business). The rules for allocating and apportioning deductions (discussed in Chapters 2 and 3) are used to determine which of the foreign person's potential deductions are attributable to the U.S. trade or business income. Certain credits may also be available for activities attributable to the U.S. trade or business.

In the case of a foreign corporation that conducts a U.S. trade or business through an unincorporated branch, an additional 30–percent tax (called the "branch profits tax") will generally apply when a foreign corporation's U.S. trade or business earnings are not reinvested in the U.S. branch. § 884. The branch profits tax is intended to achieve rough parity between foreign corporations conducting a U.S. business through a U.S. subsidiary and those conducting a U.S. business through a U.S. branch.

A foreign person's U.S. trade or business income generally is not subject to withholding of tax at the source. However, a foreign person's trade or business income from personal services is subject to withholding. §§ 1441(c)(1) and 1442(a). Moreover, a foreign person's share of partnership taxable income that is effectively connected with a U.S. trade or business is subject to withholding. § 1446.

The ways in which the U.S. taxes on a foreign person's U.S. trade or business income are determined and administered are explored in Chapter 3.

[¶ 1150]

b. Other U.S.–Source Income

If a foreign person receives U.S.–source income in respect of investments not effectively connected with the conduct of a trade or business within the United States (such as dividends, interest, rents or royalties), the *gross amount* of the payment generally will be subject to a tax of 30 percent. §§ 871(a) and 881(a). This U.S. tax on a foreign person's nonbusiness income from U.S. sources is collected and enforced through withholding provisions, which require the payor of the income to withhold the 30–percent tax from the income and pay it over to the U.S. Treasury for the account of the foreign person. §§ 1441 and 1442.

Not all U.S.-source investment income of a foreign person is subject to U.S. tax, however. For various policy reasons, U.S.-source interest on certain forms of indebtedness (e.g., interest from deposits in U.S. banks and interest on certain debt obligations that qualifies as so-called "portfolio interest") is exempt from tax. §§ 871(h), (i) and 881(c), (d). In addition, an exemption is provided for certain income of a foreign government or an international organization (such as the United Nations or the World Bank) from investments in U.S. securities. § 892.

In addition, a foreign person is generally not subject to U.S. tax on gains from the sale of property that are not effectively connected with a U.S. trade or business, even if they derive from investment in the United States. Thus, for example, a foreign person generally does not pay U.S. tax on gains from the sale of investment stock or securities in a U.S. corporation. There are, however, two principal exceptions to this rule. First, a foreign person pays U.S. tax at usual rates on gain from the sale of U.S. real property and from the sale of stock in a U.S. corporation a significant portion of the assets of which consist of U.S. real property. § 897. This tax on gain from the sale of "U.S. real property interests" is partly collected and enforced through a withholding provision, which may require the purchaser of U.S. real property or the stock in such a U.S. corporation to withhold ten percent of the price paid for the real property or stock. § 1445. Second, a foreign person is subject to a 30–percent tax on certain U.S.-source gains from the sale of intangible property (such as patents, copyrights, goodwill, trademarks and other like property) to the extent the gains are attributable to payments that are contingent on the productivity, use or disposition of the property sold. §§ 871(a)(1)(D) and 881(a)(4).[11] This tax is also collected through withholding. §§ 1441 and 1442.

11. A nonresident alien individual is also theoretically subject to a 30–percent tax on his or her U.S.-source capital gains (in excess of any U.S.-source capital losses) derived in a year during which he or she is physically present in the United States for periods totaling at least 183 days. § 871(a)(2). This latter exception rarely applies, however, because, as discussed in the next section of this Chapter, an alien who is physically present in the United States for 183 days or

The ways in which the U.S. taxes on a foreign person's nonbusiness income from U.S. sources are determined and administered are explored in Chapter 4.

2. U.S. PERSONS

[¶ 1155]

a. Taxation of Worldwide Income

The basic rule of the U.S. income tax system is that U.S. citizens, resident aliens and corporations are subject to tax on worldwide income regardless of the country from which the income derives, the country in which payment is made or the currency in which the income is received. Foreign currency is, however, treated as a noncash form of income that must be converted into U.S. dollar values. The timing and implementation of the translation of foreign currency into dollars are addressed in Chapter 9.

[¶ 1160]

b. Relief From Double Taxation

U.S. taxation of the worldwide income of U.S. citizens, resident aliens and corporations obviously opens the door to double taxation because foreign income is likely to have been taxed in the country where it was earned. The foreign tax credit provisions (the complexity of which is reflected by the materials in Chapters 5 and 7) effectively mitigate or eliminate multiple taxation by allowing a U.S. taxpayer a dollar-for-dollar credit, against U.S. income taxes otherwise payable, for foreign income taxes paid on foreign income.

In addition, a U.S. corporation conducting business operations abroad through a ten-percent-or-more-owned foreign corporation is allowed a credit (called the "indirect" or "deemed paid" credit) for a portion of the foreign corporate income taxes paid by the foreign corporation. The credit is available at the time when the U.S. parent corporation receives dividend distributions from the foreign corporation. § 902. The purpose of this provision is to achieve rough parity, for foreign tax credit purposes, between U.S. corporations operating abroad through foreign branches and those operating abroad through foreign corporations.

To ensure that the foreign tax credit is not used to offset U.S. taxes on U.S.-source income, Section 904(a) limits the allowable foreign tax credit to the taxpayer's U.S. tax liability (before credit) on its foreign-source taxable income. Moreover, to prevent a taxpayer from crediting

more during a year is usually treated as a resident alien for tax purposes and subject to U.S. tax on worldwide income. Moreover, under Section 865, capital gains realized on the sale of personal property by a nonresident alien are frequently treated as foreign-source income and, thus, seldom subject to U.S. tax.

foreign taxes on one type of (usually high-taxed) foreign income against U.S. taxes on other types of (usually low-taxed) foreign income, Section 904(d) contains complex limitations on the foreign tax credit based on specified types of foreign-source income. Thus, the source rules (and the rules for allocating and apportioning deductions), discussed in Chapter 2, are important to U.S. taxpayers in applying the foreign tax credit limitations. A key international tax planning objective of U.S. taxpayers is to enlarge the amount of taxable income that is treated as arising from foreign sources and subject to little or no foreign tax and thereby increase the amount of foreign tax credits allowed under these limitations.

An alternative device for mitigating international double taxation—exemption from tax of foreign-source income—is used in a few situations under the Code. Thus, for example, as indicated above, U.S. citizens and resident aliens living and working abroad may exclude from gross income up to a specified dollar amount of foreign compensation income ($80,000 for 2002 and thereafter, but adjusted for inflation for calendar years after 2005; the inflation-adjusted amount for 2011 is $92,900) and exclude or deduct certain housing costs, subject to a limitation, if they meet the eligibility requirements. See § 911, discussed in Chapter 5.

[¶ 1165]

c. Deferral of U.S. Tax on Foreign Income of Foreign Corporations

As discussed earlier in this Chapter, one of the basic principles of U.S. international taxation is that a U.S. person who conducts operations abroad through a separately incorporated foreign corporation generally pays no U.S. tax on the foreign corporation's foreign-source earnings until those earnings are repatriated to the United States through a dividend or otherwise (the "deferral" principle). By contrast, a U.S. person who conducts operations abroad through an unincorporated branch must pay current U.S. tax on its worldwide earnings (including the foreign-source earnings of the branch). However, to prevent abuse of this deferral principle, Congress has enacted a number of exceptions to the deferral rule that are principally directed at certain types of readily movable or low-taxed foreign income. The 2004 JOBS Act reduced the number of these exceptions from six to three: the controlled foreign corporation provisions of Subpart F (the most important of these anti-deferral regimes), the passive foreign investment company rules and the accumulated earnings tax. As a practical matter, however, the accumulated earnings tax regime rarely applies to a foreign corporation. The most significant of these exceptions (i.e., the controlled foreign corporation provisions and the passive foreign investment company provisions) generally require a U.S. shareholder of the foreign corporation either to include in income currently as a constructive dividend all or some defined part of the foreign corporation's foreign-source earnings or to pay an interest charge on the deferred U.S. tax on the foreign corporation's earnings. These highly complex anti-deferral regimes are explored in Chapter 6.

F. WHO IS TAXED ON WORLDWIDE INCOME?

1. INDIVIDUALS

[¶ 1170]

a. Citizens

The United States taxes the worldwide income of U.S. citizens, regardless of where they reside or are domiciled. This approach differs markedly from almost all other countries that do not tax unrepatriated foreign earnings of citizens residing or domiciled abroad. Nevertheless, the Supreme Court in 1924 sustained the broad reach of the U.S. tax law as a permissible exercise of taxing jurisdiction under the principles of customary international law based on nationality.

[¶ 1175]

COOK v. TAIT

Supreme Court of the United States, 1924.
265 U.S. 47.

JUSTICE MCKENNA delivered the opinion of the Court.

* * *

Plaintiff is a native citizen of the United States, and was such when he took up his residence and became domiciled in the City of Mexico. A demand was made upon him by defendant in error, designated defendant, to make a return of his income for the purpose of taxation under the Revenue Laws of the United States. Plaintiff complied with the demand, but under protest, the income having been derived from property situated in the City of Mexico. A tax was assessed against him in the sum of $1,193.38, the first installment of which he paid, and for it, as we have said, this action was brought.

The question in the case, and which was presented by the demurrer to the declaration is, as expressed by plaintiff, whether Congress has power to impose a tax upon income received by a native citizen of the United States who, at the time the income was received, was permanently resident and domiciled in the City of Mexico, the income being from real and personal property located in Mexico.

Plaintiff assigns against the power, not only his rights under the Constitution of the United States, but under international law, and in support of the assignments cites many cases. It will be observed that the foundation of the assignments is the fact that the citizen receiving the income, and the property of which it is the product, are outside of the territorial limits of the United States. These two facts, the contention is, exclude the existence of the power to tax. Or to put the contention another way, as to the existence of the power and its exercise, the person receiving the income, and the property from which he receives it, must both be within the territorial limits of the United States to be within the taxing power of the United States. The contention is not justified, and that it is not justified is the necessary deduction of recent cases. In *United States v. Bennett*, 232 U.S. 299, the power of the United States to tax a foreign built yacht owned and used during the taxing period outside of the United States by a citizen domiciled in the United States was sustained. The tax passed on was imposed by a tariff act, but necessarily the power does not depend upon the form by which it is exerted.

It will be observed that the case contained only one of the conditions of the present case, the *property* taxed was outside of the United States. In *United States v. Goelet*, 232 U.S. 293, the yacht taxed was outside of the United States but owned by a citizen of the United States who was "permanently resident and domiciled in a foreign country." It was decided that the yacht was not subject to the tax—but this as a matter of construction. Pains were taken to say that the question of power was determined "wholly irrespective" of the owner's "permanent domicile in a foreign country." And the Court put out of view the situs of the yacht. That the Court had no doubt of the power to tax was illustrated by reference to the income tax laws of prior years and their express extension to those domiciled abroad. The illustration has pertinence to the case at bar, for the case at bar is concerned with an income tax, and the power to impose it.

We may make further exposition of the national power as the case depends upon it. It was illustrated at once in *United States v. Bennett* by a contrast with the power of a State. It was pointed out that there were limitations upon the latter that were not on the national power. The taxing power of a State, it was decided, encountered at its borders the taxing power of other States and was limited by them. There was no such limitation, it was pointed out, upon the national power; and the limitation upon the States affords, it was said, no ground for constructing a barrier around the United States "shutting that government off from the exertion of powers which inherently belong to it by virtue of its sovereignty."

The contention was rejected that a citizen's property without the limits of the United States derives no benefit from the United States. The contention, it was said, came from the confusion of thought in "mistaking the scope and extent of the sovereign power of the United States as a nation and its relations to its citizens and their relations to it." And that power in its scope and extent, it was decided, is based on the presumption that government by its very nature benefits the citizen and his property wherever found, and that opposition to it holds on to citizenship while it "belittles and destroys its advantages and blessings by denying the possession by government of an essential power required to make citizenship completely beneficial." In other words, the principle was declared that the government, by its very nature, benefits the citizen and his property wherever found and, therefore, has the power to make the benefit complete. Or, to express it another way, the basis of the power to tax was not and cannot be made dependent upon the situs of the property in all cases, it being in or out of the United States, and was not and cannot be made dependent upon the domicile of the citizen, that being in or out of the United States, but upon his relation as citizen to the United States and the relation of the latter to him as citizen. The consequence of the relations is that the native citizen who is taxed may have domicile, and the property from which his income is derived may have situs, in a foreign country and the tax be legal—the government having power to impose the tax.

* * *

[¶ 1180]

NOTES

1. The Court discusses the relationship between the imposition of tax burdens by government and the benefits of government to the taxpayer. Compare the 1923 analysis of the League of Nations experts set forth at ¶ 1060. Does the benefit/burden analysis provide a rationale for determining the appropriate reach of extraterritorial taxing jurisdiction? Does such an analysis lead inexorably to the taxation of worldwide income for U.S. citizens because they enjoy the benefits of citizenship even while residing abroad? Does the same rationale apply for aliens who reside in the United States?

2. As discussed in Chapter 5, in order to mitigate international double taxation, the United States allows U.S. individual and corporate taxpayers a dollar-for-dollar credit against their U.S. income tax for foreign income taxes paid on foreign-source income. Moreover, the Internal Revenue Code contains a number of exceptions to the extraterritorial reach of the U.S. taxing system. For example, as mentioned earlier in this Chapter, a U.S. citizen or resident alien who meets certain tests can elect to exclude from gross income up to a specified amount of compensation income from foreign sources ($92,900, for 2011, as adjusted for inflation) and exclude or deduct certain housing costs over a base amount. See § 911. Does the Court's opinion require that Congress enact such provisions to mitigate international double taxation?

[¶ 1185]

b. Resident Aliens

Individuals who are classified as resident aliens under the Code are also taxed on their worldwide income. In general, they are subject to the same U.S. tax treatment as U.S. citizens.

Pre-Section 7701(b) law. The definition of a "resident alien" for U.S. income tax purposes, however, is not congruent with the definition under immigration laws. Historically, a rather subjective definition was applied for tax purposes. The effect was that aliens classified as nonresidents under the immigration laws were sometimes characterized as U.S. residents for income tax purposes because the focus of their economic and other interests was located in the United States. See, e.g., Park v. Commissioner, 79 T.C. 252 (1982), aff'd without published opinion, 755 F.2d 181 (D.C.Cir.1985), in which a taxpayer who had held temporary visas over many years and who was domiciled in Korea was held to be a resident alien for tax purposes. The Tax Court cited the "taxpayer's deep and continuing involvement in business, social and political affairs" of Washington, D.C. This "involvement" included widespread lobbying activities on Capitol Hill and a listing in the Washington Social Directory.

Current law: "green card" and "substantial presence" tests. This somewhat subjective approach was criticized because of concerns centered on predictability and consistency. As a result, in 1984, a new statutory definition was adopted as Section 7701(b) of the Code. A resident alien is now defined to be an individual who is a permanent resident of the United States under the immigration laws (the so-called green card test) or any alien who meets the "substantial presence test."

The substantial presence test is a relatively simple formula intended to identify aliens who spend substantial periods of time within the United States. The test will be met if the alien was present within the United States during the tax year on at least 31 days and was present within the United States for 183 days during the tax year and the two preceding years, as determined under the following formula:

Current year	one day is one day
First preceding year	one day is 1/3 of a day
Second preceding year	one day is 1/6 of a day

Except for regular commuters from Canada and Mexico, individuals temporarily present in the United States as regular members of a crew of a foreign vessel engaged in international transportation, certain travelers in transit between two points outside the United States and present for less than 24 hours and certain other individuals described in Section 7701(b)(5) (discussed below), an individual is present on any day in which he or she was physically present in the United States at any time during the day. Partial days count as full days. § 7701(b)(7).

The application of the test can be shown with a simple example. Suppose that Sven, a nonresident alien under the immigration law, is present within the United States on 120 days for each of three consecutive years. He will be considered present for purposes of the test for 180 days (120 days for the current year plus 40 days for last year plus 20 days for the prior year). Accordingly, Sven will not be characterized as a resident alien for tax purposes. However, should Sven be present within the United States for 125 days during the current year he would be characterized as a resident alien (the formula now yields 185 days) for the current year despite the fact that his immigration status has not changed. He would also meet the substantial presence test if he were present in the United States for 122 days in each of the three years.

Certain days of presence excluded for purposes of substantial presence test. Section 7701(b)(5) provides that time spent in the United States by certain persons (including diplomats or full-time employees of certain international organizations, such as the United Nations, the International Monetary Fund and the World Bank, and their families, teachers, trainees and students and professional athletes temporarily in the United States to perform at a charitable sports events) will not be counted for purposes of the substantial presence test. The statute and regulations refer to such persons as "exempt individuals." Moreover, the substantial presence test does not count days of presence of an individual who is physically unable to leave the United States because of a medical condition that arose while the individual was present in the United States. § 7701(b)(3)(D)(ii).

"Closer connection" exception to substantial presence test. If an alien is actually present during fewer than 183 days during the current year and is able to show that he or she has a "tax home" in another country to which a "closer connection" exists, that alien will not be treated as a resident regardless of the results of applying the substantial presence test. § 7701(b)(3)(B). A "tax home" is the place determined to be home for purposes of applying the "away-from-home" test for the deductibility of traveling expenses under Section 162(a)(2).

The regulations provide that a taxpayer will have a "closer connection" to a foreign country if the individual "has maintained more significant contacts" with the foreign country than with the United States. Reg. § 301.7701(b)–2(d)(1). The relevant factors to be weighed in the comparison include the location of the:

—Taxpayer's permanent home.

—Taxpayer's family.

—Taxpayer's personal belongings.

—Social, political, cultural or religious organizations with which the taxpayer has a current relationship.

—Place of the taxpayer's routine personal banking activities.

—Place where the taxpayer's business activities are conducted.

—Jurisdiction issuing the taxpayer's driver's license.

—Jurisdiction in which the taxpayer votes.

—Place designated by the taxpayer as his or her residence on official forms and documents.

This closer connection exception does not apply, however, to an alien who has an application pending for a green card or who has taken other steps to apply for status as a lawful permanent U.S. resident. § 7701(b)(3)(C).

First-year election. A third way for an alien to be treated as resident of the United States under Section 7701(b) is the so-called first-year election, a provision that is simple in concept but amazingly complicated in its operation and requirements. § 7701(b)(1)(A)(iii) and (b)(4). An alien may make this election if the following five requirements are met:

(1) The alien individual is not a resident of the United States under either the green card test or the substantial presence test for the election year (if the alien is a U.S. resident under either of those tests, the alien has no election and must be treated as a U.S. resident for federal tax purposes), § 7701(b)(4)(A)(i);

(2) The alien individual was not a resident of the United States under the green card test, the substantial presence test or the first-year election provision for the calendar year immediately before the election year, § 7701(b)(4)(A)(ii);

(3) The alien individual is a resident of the United States under the substantial presence test for the calendar year immediately after the election year (the consequence of this requirement is that an alien individual typically will not know whether he or she qualifies for the election provision until after filing the original return for the election year; thus, this election is often made by a qualifying alien individual filing an amended return for the election year), § 7701(b)(4)(A)(iii);

(4) The alien individual is present in the United States for a period of at least 31 consecutive days in the election year, § 7701(b)(4)(A)(iv)(I); and

(5) The alien individual is present in the United States for at least 75 percent of the number of days in the "testing period." The testing period starts with the first day of the 31–day period referred to in (4) above and ends with the last day of the election year. For purposes of this requirement, the statute treats an individual as present in the United States for up to five days during the testing period even though the individual is actually absent from the United States during those days. § 7701(b)(4)(A)(iv)(II).

In applying these requirements, an alien individual's days of presence as an "exempt individual" within the meaning of Section 7701(b)(5) (e.g., as a foreign government-related individual, teacher, trainee or student) do not count as days of U.S. presence. § 7701(b)(4)(D) and (b)(3)(D)(i).

Other rules. There are also some rather complex rules in Section 7701(b)(2) and (b)(4)(C) for determining when characterization as a resident alien begins and ends. However, the net effect of Section 7701(b) has been to add some substantial predictability to the important question of whether an alien is going to be taxed in the United States on worldwide income.

Consequences of resident alien classification. Classification as a resident alien of the United States may not necessarily bring solely bad tax news. While resident aliens are generally entitled to the various deductions available under the Code, deductions for nonresident aliens are usually limited to those deriving from U.S. business activities. The timing of initial residence, therefore, can be a crucial question. For example, Rev. Rul. 80–17, 1980–1 C.B. 45, dealt with a citizen of a foreign country who left that country under a limited visa to become a U.S. resident. The taxpayer left behind assets in a business and some corporate stock. The policy of the foreign government was to prevent those citizens leaving on such a visa from receiving or enjoying property left within the country. When the taxpayer did not return upon the expiration of the U.S. visa, the taxpayer's foreign properties were confiscated. The IRS ruled that the taxpayer's ownership rights had effectively terminated upon departure from the foreign country, which occurred before the taxpayer became a resident of the United States. The foreign losses by reason of the confiscation, therefore, were not deductible for U.S. tax purposes.

[¶ 1190]

PROBLEMS

1. Compare the so-called "objective" tests for determining U.S. residence in Section 7701(b) and the myriad of exceptions and special rules used in applying such tests with the facts-and-circumstances approach used under prior law (which looked to the center of the alien's economic activities). Has the law really changed all that much and, if so, in which direction?

2. Assume that your client, Wolfgang, an unmarried German citizen, is present in the United States in connection with his work as an export sales employee of a German corporation for the following number of days during the calendar years at issue: year 1 (138 days), year 2 (150 days) and year 3 (120 days). He comes to the United States on temporary business visas.

When in the United States, Wolfgang operates out of a small office in Boston leased by his employer. He owns a townhouse in Boston, where he keeps a car registered in Massachusetts and personal belongings such as furniture and clothes. He is a member of a country club outside Boston. He was born and raised in Munich, Germany and owns an apartment there, where he keeps a car (which is registered in Germany) and personal belongings (such as furniture, an art collection and clothing). He is a member of a golf club in Germany. All of his family members live in Germany. The principal office of his employer, where he is headquartered, is located in Munich, Germany. He has an international driver's license. He is taxed as a

German resident in Germany and on all official documents identifies himself as a German resident. He votes in Germany.

Wolfgang does not hold a green card, which would confer on him status as a lawful permanent resident in the United States, and he has not elected to be treated as a U.S. resident. (For purposes of this Problem, ignore the effect of the United States–Germany Tax Treaty on your analysis.) Will Wolfgang be treated as a U.S. resident for year 3 under Section 7701(b)? What advice would you give him to minimize the likelihood that he will be treated as a U.S. resident in year 4?

3. Mary, a citizen of Brazil, has never been present in the United States before year 1. On the afternoon of February 9 of year 1, she arrives in the United States to attend a business convention and returns to Brazil on the afternoon of February 14 of year 1. On the afternoon of March 19 of year 1, she comes to the United States for a ten-day vacation (i.e., she has a roundtrip airline ticket with a March 28 return date). During that vacation, on the evening of March 23 of year 1, she collapses at a restaurant and is rushed to a local hospital. Mary is diagnosed as having a rare virus that requires immediate medical attention and hospitalization. She is released from the hospital on the afternoon of April 10 of year 1, and she flies home to Brazil on the evening of April 12 of year 1. On the morning of June 5 of year 1, Mary moves to the United States to live and work, and Mary remains in the United States until the morning of November 10 of year 1, when she returns to Brazil. In the early morning of December 12 of year 1, Mary flies from Brazil to Paris, France for a business meeting. Her flight connects through the airport in Atlanta, Georgia, and she has a four-hour layover in Atlanta. During that layover, she takes a cab from the airport to an Atlanta suburb to visit some friends, and then returns to the airport to pick up the connecting flight. On December 27 of year 1, Mary comes to Palm Springs, California for a New Year's celebration. She returns to Brazil on the morning of January 3 of year 2, and does not return to the United States at any time during the remainder of year 2.

Mary is not a lawful permanent resident of the United States and she has not elected to be treated as a U.S. resident. Will Mary be treated as a U.S. resident under Section 7701(b) for year 1 or year 2? If so, when does Mary's U.S. residency begin and when does it end?

4. Under what circumstances would an alien individual want to make the first-year election to be a U.S. resident for U.S. tax purposes in Section 7701(b)(4)?

5. Suppose that a foreign citizen and resident is considering immigration into the United States and owns both appreciated assets (value greater than basis) and depreciated assets (value less than basis) that she is thinking of selling. What practical tax planning steps should be suggested?

[¶ 1195]

c. Certain Former U.S. Citizens and Long–Term Permanent Residents—Special Rules for a Special Taxpayer Class

The taxation of worldwide income that confronts U.S. citizens may entice some to renounce their citizenship and become nonresident aliens.[12] Such a shift to the other side of the main individual taxpayer dividing line would, for example, ordinarily eliminate U.S. taxes on most capital gains from U.S. sources not connected with a U.S. trade or business or not deriving from the disposition of U.S. real property interests.

Section 877, enacted in 1966, was designed to defend against such a possibility. Section 877 effectively taxed a nonresident on all income from U.S. sources and on gains realized with respect to stock and securities in U.S. corporations and certain other property during the ten years following loss of citizenship. Moreover, if Section 877 applied, the taxpayer was taxed at the graduated tax rates in Section 1 applicable to U.S. citizens and resident aliens rather than the rates applicable to nonresident alien individuals in Section 871. § 877(b). Under the original version of the provision, Section 877 applied to such a former U.S. citizen unless he or she could show that the loss of citizenship "did not have for one of its principal purposes the avoidance of taxes." Former § 877(a). Is this extension of U.S. taxing jurisdiction consistent with the principles of international law discussed earlier in this Chapter?

Various versions of Section 877 (pre–2008 law). As noted above, the application of the original version of Section 877 required a facts-and-circumstances analysis of a taxpayer's purpose for expatriation before taxation under Section 877 was triggered. Congress was concerned that the original version of Section 877 was difficult for the IRS to administer and that expatriates were too easily able to avoid its application by arguing that their intent for expatriation was not tax avoidance. Accordingly, in 1996, Congress added former Section 877(a)(2) to the Code in an attempt to enhance the effectiveness of Section 877 in preventing former U.S. citizens from avoiding their fair share of U.S. taxes. Former Section 877(a)(2) provided that an individual was conclusively presumed to have a principal purpose of tax avoidance for the loss of U.S. citizenship if (i) the individual's average annual net income tax for the five tax years before the date of loss of U.S. citizenship was more than $100,000 *or* (ii) the individual's net worth on such date was at least $500,000. (The $100,000 and $500,000 thresholds were increased by an inflation adjustment for years after 1996.)

12. Reg. § 1.1–1(c) provides that every person born or naturalized in the United States and subject to its jurisdiction is a U.S. citizen. Reg. § 1.1–1(c) also provides that the Immigration and Nationality Act, 8 U.S.C.A. §§ 1401 et seq., governs the determination of when U.S. citizenship is acquired and lost for federal tax purposes. However, as discussed in the text above, Section 877A(g)(4), enacted in 2008, contains statutory rules for determining when an individual will be treated as relinquishing his or her U.S. citizenship for federal tax purposes.

This presumption did not apply, however, in the case of certain individuals described in former Section 877(c) who, within one year of the loss of U.S. citizenship, submitted a ruling request for the IRS's determination as to whether tax avoidance was one of the principal purposes for such loss. Individuals who may have qualified for this exception to the presumption included an individual who became a citizen of the United States and another country at birth and continued to be a citizen of the other country after the loss of U.S. citizenship, or an individual who, within a reasonable period after the loss of U.S. citizenship, became a citizen of the country in which the individual was born, the country in which the individual's spouse was born or the country in which either of the individual's parents was born. Former § 877(c)(2)(A). Other individuals who may have qualified for the exception were an individual who was present in the United States for 30 days or less during each of the ten years before the loss of U.S. citizenship, an individual whose loss of U.S. citizenship occurred before he or she attained the age of 18½ and any other individual excepted from the presumption by regulation. Former § 877(c)(2)(B) through (D).

Pursuant to a congressional mandate made in the 1996 legislation, the Treasury Department conducted and issued a study of the effectiveness of the expatriation tax rules in Section 877. See U.S. Treas. Dep't, Income Tax Compliance by U.S. Citizens and U.S. Lawful Permanent Residents Residing Outside the United States and Related Issues (May 1998). In addition, the Staff of the Joint Committee on Taxation, working with the Government Accounting Office, also conducted a study of the revised Section 877 rules and the various federal governmental agencies' procedures for enforcing those rules and concluded "that there is little or no enforcement of the special tax and immigration rules applicable to tax-motivated citizenship relinquishment and residency termination." Staff of Joint Comm. on Tax'n, 108th Cong., 1st Sess., Review of the Present–Law Tax and Immigration Treatment of Relinquishment of Citizenship and Termination of Long–Term Residency, at 5 (2003). These studies played a significant part in encouraging Congress to revisit the Section 877 rules as part of its consideration of legislation that was enacted into law as part of the 2004 JOBS Act.

The 2004 JOBS Act replaced the prior law rules of Section 877 (which combined objective standards for determining tax avoidance with a subjective standard for taxpayers who failed to meet the objective standard thresholds) with revised objective standards. Thus, under the revised version of Section 877, the subjective, facts-and-circumstances approach to determining tax-avoidance motive under the prior versions of Section 877 no longer applied, and the prior case law under Section 877 was of relevance only to taxpayers who relinquished U.S. citizenship (or terminated long-term resident alien status) before the effective date of the JOBS Act changes. Under the revised objective standards in Section 877(a)(2), the alternative tax regime in Section 877 applied to any individual who lost U.S. citizenship within the 10–year period immediately before the close of the tax year, if—

(1) the individual's average annual net income tax for the period of five tax years ending before the date of loss of U.S. citizenship was greater than $124,000 (subject to a cost-of-living adjustment for calendar years after 2004);

(2) the individual's net worth as of such date was at least $2,000,000; or

(3) the individual failed to certify under penalties of perjury that he or she met the requirements of the income tax title for the five preceding tax years or failed to submit such evidence of compliance as the Treasury Department may require.

The 2004 JOBS Act revised and narrowed the exceptions in Section 877(c) to provide only two basic exceptions. If either exception applied, an individual was not subject to the alternative tax regime in Section 877 by reason of either the average annual net income tax standard or the $2,000,000 net worth standard in Section 877(a)(2)(A) and (B). § 877(c)(1).

The first of these exceptions, in revised Section 877(c)(2), applied to an individual who (1) became at birth a U.S. citizen and a citizen of another country and continued citizenship in the other country, and (2) had no substantial contacts with the United States. To be treated as having had no substantial contacts in the United States, an individual must never have been a U.S. resident (within the meaning of Section 7701(b)), must never have held a U.S. passport and must not have been present in the United States for more than 30 days during any one of the ten calendar years before the individual's loss of U.S. citizenship.

The second exception, in revised Section 877(c)(3), applied to an individual who met four requirements:

(1) the individual became a U.S. citizen at birth;

(2) neither of the individual's parents was a U.S. citizen at the time of the individual's birth;

(3) the individual's loss of U.S. citizenship occurred before the individual reaches age 18½; and

(4) the individual was not present in the United States for more than 30 days during any one of the ten calendar years before the individual's loss of U.S. citizenship.

The JOBS Act also eliminated the ruling request process for seeking exemption from Section 877 treatment that had been enacted in 1996.

Application of Section 877 to long-term residents. The 1996 legislation had extended the reach of Section 877 to encompass certain "long-term residents" of the United States who terminate U.S. residence or who commence to be treated as residents of another country pursuant to a U.S. tax treaty and who do not waive treaty benefits. § 877(e)(1). Under the JOBS Act version of 877, the provision applied to such long-term residents if they met one of the objective triggers for the application of Section 877 in revised Section 877(a)(2). A long-term resident for this purpose was an individual who was a lawful permanent resident of the United States for at least eight of the 15 years before termination of U.S. residence. § 877(e)(2). Section 877 applied to such long-term residents for ten tax years after the termination of U.S. residence.

Special source rules for Section 877 purposes. Section 877(d)(1) contained special source rules that treated an expatriate's gains from the sale of certain property as income derived from U.S. sources. These special source rules overrode the usual source-of-income rules discussed in Chapter 2, but applied only for purposes of Section 877. For example, under one of these special source rules, gain from the sale or exchange of real or personal property (other than stock or debt obligations) located in the United States was treated as U.S.-source income. § 877(d)(1)(A). Another special source rule treated as U.S.-source income gain from the sale of stock in U.S. corporations or debt obligations of U.S. persons, the United States, a State or political subdivision of the United States or the District of Columbia. § 877(d)(1)(B).

Constitutionality of Section 877. In Di Portanova v. United States, 690 F.2d 169, 179–80 (Ct.Cl.1982), the taxpayer argued that the application of Section 877 to him was unconstitutional on the grounds that it represented an invalid exercise of personal jurisdiction and that it was a denial of due process. The court rejected both arguments and offered some interesting observations about the breadth of the authority that Congress may exercise in the creation and development of the income tax system (including the structure of the tax system as it applies to aliens):

> [First, the plaintiff] argues that the provision is an invalid exercise of personal jurisdiction over him. We have held, however, that section 877(a) is a source-based tax.
>
> The plaintiff recognizes that the United States may tax United States source income at any rate. He contends, however, that Congress cannot base the rate of tax upon the identity of the taxpayer, i.e., expatriates rather than nonresident citizens, and that when it attempts to do that, it is exercising personal jurisdiction over a nonresident alien.
>
> The plaintiff has not shown why this claim of discriminatory treatment * * * converts the tax into one based on personal jurisdiction. If the plaintiff contends that Congress may never tax nonresident aliens on the basis of personal characteristics, he brings into question the distinctions between citizens and aliens and between residents and nonresidents, both personal characteristics from which the plaintiff seeks to benefit. It would be possible for Congress to tax

nonresident aliens on their United States income at the same rates it taxes citizens and residents, but it has not done so.

Congress constitutionally may treat nonresident aliens as a special class and subject that class to different tax rates. In *Barclay & Co. v. Edwards*, 267 U.S. 442, 449–50 * * * (1924), the Court held that foreign corporations "constituted a class all by themselves and could be properly so treated by Congress.... The power of Congress in levying taxes is very wide, and where a classification is made of taxpayers that is reasonable, and not merely arbitrary and capricious, the Fifth Amendment can not apply."

The plaintiff has not shown why Congress may not also draw reasonable distinctions between various classes of nonresident aliens. Section 877 taxes expatriates only on their United States source income. It is therefore a source-based tax. The plaintiff's complaints about distinctions drawn between expatriates and aliens who were never citizens of this country are judged by the traditional due process and equal protection standards and are dealt with below.

[Second, the] plaintiff argues that section 877(a) denies him due process because "the means are unnecessary [and] inappropriate to the proposed end, are unreasonably harsh or oppressive, when viewed in the light of the expected benefit, ... [and] the guarantee of due process is infringed." * * *

Congress has wide discretion in deciding whom to tax and how much. * * * This court has said the test is one of minimum rationality. * * * There is a strong policy against invalidating tax statutes, and any rational basis for a taxing statute will justify it. * * *

The plaintiff contends section 877 is ill-suited to preventing tax avoidance because it does not cover all instances. Such arguments, however, are better addressed to Congress. Section 877 was not designed to prevent all tax avoidance. It "was enacted to forestall tax-motivated expatriation." *Kronenberg v. Commissioner*, 64 T.C. 428, 434 (1975) * * *.

The possibility that Congress might draft a better or a more comprehensive statute is not a reason for invalidating the present one. Congress certainly had a reasonable basis for concluding that United States citizens who expatriate themselves with a principal purpose of avoiding taxes should not be given the favorable tax treatment that nonresident aliens generally receive.

Mark-to-market regime in Section 877A of current law (enacted in 2008). Section 877A, enacted in 2008, imposes a new mark-to-market taxing regime on certain U.S. citizens who relinquish their U.S. citizenship and certain long-term U.S. resident aliens who terminate their U.S. residency. Under this regime, the former U.S. citizen or U.S. resident alien is subject to income tax on the net unrealized gain in their property as if the property had been sold for its fair market value on the day before the expatriation or termination of U.S. residency. Gains from this deemed sale are taken into account at that time without regard to other provisions in the Code (i.e., exclusion and nonrecognition provisions are generally ignored with respect to gains), but losses from the deemed sale generally are taken into account only to the extent otherwise provided by other provisions of the Code (i.e., loss disallowance and nonrecognition provisions generally prevent losses on the deemed sale from being taken into account). Any net gain (i.e., total gains from the deemed sale transaction that are taken into account in excess of the total losses from the deemed sale transaction that are taken into account) on this deemed sale is recognized and taxable to the extent it exceeds an exemption amount of $600,000 (the exemption amount is indexed for inflation for years after 2008; e.g., $636,000 is the exemption amount for 2011). Stated differently, only the net gain, if any, in excess of the exemption amount is subject to U.S. income tax under this regime. Any gains or losses later realized by the former U.S. citizen or U.S. resident alien are to be reduced by the gains and losses taken into account under this mark-to-market regime, without regard to the exemption amount. § 877A(a). This mark-to-market regime applies to most types of property interests held by the individual on the date of relinquishment of U.S. citizenship or termination of U.S. residency, except with respect to certain items such as deferred compensation items, interests in nongrantor trusts and certain specified tax deferred accounts that are subject to their own special rules under this provision. § 877A(c)-(f).

This mark-to-market regime applies to any U.S. citizen who relinquishes citizenship and any long-term U.S. resident alien who terminates residency, if such individual either (1) has an average annual net *income tax liability* for the five prior years ending before the date of the loss of U.S. citizenship or termination of long-term U.S. residency that exceeds $124,000 (this amount is to adjusted for inflation for years after 2008; the amount for 2011 is $147,000); (2) has a net worth of at least $2,000,000 on the date of the loss of U.S. citizenship or termination of long-term U.S. residency; *or* (3) fails to certify under penalties of perjury that he or she has complied with all U.S. federal income tax obligations for the prior five years or fails to submit such evidence of compliance as the IRS may require. This mark-to-market regime, instead of Section 877 of prior law, applies to any U.S. citizen or long-term U.S. resident alien who meets one of the tests discussed above and does not meet either of the exceptions discussed below and whose act of relinquishment of U.S. citizenship or act of termination of U.S. residency occurs on or after the enactment of the 2008 legislation (i.e., June 17, 2008). The definition of "long-term resident" for purposes of this mark-to-market regime is the same as it was under Section 877(e)(2) of prior law (discussed above). § 877A(g)(5).

Certain individuals, however, will not be subject to this mark-to-market regime, notwithstanding that they meet the objective benchmarks described above, provided that they qualify for one of the two exceptions provided in the statute. The first exception exempts from this mark-to-market regime an individual who both (1) became at birth a U.S. citizen and a citizen of another country, and continues to be a citizen of, and is taxed as a resident of, such other country, and (2) has been a resident of the United States (within the meaning of the substantial presence test in Section 7701(b)(1)(A)(ii)) for not more than ten taxable years during the 15–taxable year period ending with the taxable year during which the act of expatriation occurs. The second exception exempts from this mark-to-market regime an individual who (1) relinquishes U.S. citizenship before the individual attains age 18½, and (2) has been a resident of the United States (within the meaning of the substantial presence test in Section 7701(b)(1)(A)(ii)) for not more than ten taxable years before the date of relinquishment. § 877A(g)(1)(B).

An individual may elect to defer payment of the tax imposed on the deemed sale of property under this mark-to-market regime on a property-by-property basis. Under the election, the deferred tax is due and payable when the return is due for the taxable year in which the individual actually disposes of the property. The election is irrevocable and interest is imposed for the period that the tax is deferred at the rate normally applicable to individual income tax underpayments. In addition, in order to elect to defer the tax, the individual must furnish a bond to the Treasury conditioned upon payment of the deferred tax due. § 877A(b).

Is this imposition of an income tax on the net unrealized gain of certain individuals constitutionally valid under the Sixteenth Amendment to the U.S. Constitution? Is this mark-to-market taxing regime consistent with the principles of international law discussed earlier in this Chapter?

Determining when an individual will be treated as relinquishing U.S. citizenship. Under the 2008 legislation, an individual is treated as relinquishing U.S. citizenship on the earliest of the following four dates:

(1) the date the individual renounces his or her U.S. nationality before a U.S. diplomatic or consular officer pursuant to a specified provision of the Immigration and Nationality Act (but only if the renunciation is subsequently approved by the issuance to the individual of a loss of nationality by the U.S. State Department);

(2) the date the individual furnishes to the U.S. State Department a signed statement of voluntary relinquishment of U.S. nationality confirming the performance of an act of expatriation specified in a particular provision of the Immigration and Nationality Act (but only if the voluntary relinquishment is subsequently approved by the issuance to the individual of a loss of nationality by the U.S. State Department);

(3) the date the U.S. State Department issues to the individual a certificate of loss of nationality; or

(4) the date a U.S. court cancels a naturalized citizen's certificate of naturalization.

§ 877A(g)(4).

Information reporting requirements in Section 6039G. The 1996 legislation added Section 6039G to the Code, which requires an individual who loses U.S. citizenship (or a long-term permanent resident who terminates U.S. residence) to provide a statement containing certain specified information. The 2004 JOBS Act and the 2008 legislation revised the information reporting requirements in Section 6039G. Under the revised provision, an individual to whom Section 877(b) or Section 877A applies for any tax year must provide a statement that includes (1) the taxpayer's taxpayer identification number, (2) the mailing address of the individual's principal foreign residence, (3) the foreign country in which the individual is residing, (4) the foreign country of which the individual is a citizen, (5) a detailed description of the individual's income, assets and liabilities, (6) the number of days that the individual was physically present in the United States during the tax year; and (7) any other information that the Treasury may require. If an individual fails to file this statement by the due date, the individual is subject to a penalty of $10,000, unless the individual can show that the failure is due to reasonable cause. § 6039G(c).

[¶ 1200]

PROBLEM

Hacker is a U.S. citizen who has lived in California all his life. During the past five years, he started and developed a computer company. His original investment was $100,000. His stock is now worth $100 million. He wishes to sell his company but prefers to avoid U.S. taxation. He is prepared to renounce his U.S citizenship and become a citizen and resident of Monaco, a foreign country where he will have no income taxes. Advise him with respect to the U.S. tax consequences of such an action. Is there a way to assure that his tax objective could be achieved?

[¶ 1205]

2. U.S. CORPORATIONS

Domestic corporations, referred to in this book as "U.S. corporations," are defined by Section 7701(a)(4) to be corporations organized under the laws of the United States, any state or the District of Columbia. (Any corporation not organized under the laws of the United States, any state or the District of Columbia is a "foreign corporation" under current law, regardless of the location of its head office or place of management. See § 7701(a)(5).) Like U.S. citizens and resident aliens, U.S. corporations are subject to U.S. taxation on worldwide income. The jurisdictional basis is again the nationality principle.

The application of that principle in this context can bring results that may seem surprising. Suppose that a group of individuals who are citizens and residents of Mexico owns a corporation that has property and operates only in Germany, employs only German nationals and sells products only in Germany. If the incorporation papers were filed in Delaware, the corporation would be a U.S. corporation subject to U.S. taxation on its worldwide income.

By contrast, suppose that a corporation whose stock will be publicly traded on the New York Stock Exchange and owned by investors from many countries, including a significant percentage by U.S. persons, is organized under Bermuda law. The corporation's head office and place of management are located in the United States and, although it conducts business throughout the world, it earns a majority of its income in the United States. Under current law, this corporation is a foreign corporation and subject to only the limited U.S. taxing jurisdiction applicable to foreign persons, despite its close economic connection to the United States.

It should be noted that a significant number of other countries use a different test for determining the residence of corporations. In those countries, a corporation is treated as resident of the country in which its head office or primary place of management and control is located. Recognizing that the current approach under U.S. tax law for determining corporate residence is artificial and subject to tax abuse, the Staff of the Joint Committee on Taxation proposed a statutory change under which the residence of a publicly traded foreign-incorporated entity would be based on the location of its primary place of management and control. See Staff of Joint Comm. on Tax'n, 109th Cong., 1st Sess., Options to Improve Tax Compliance and Reform Tax Expenditures, at 179–80 (2005). This proposal is discussed in more detail at ¶ 6060.

[¶ 1210]

3. PARTNERSHIPS

Partnerships are not taxpayers under U.S. tax law. The income tax consequences of operating in a partnership form are attributed to the respective partners under the terms of the partnership agreement and the provisions of Subchapter K of the Code. The consequences of using a partnership in international transactions accordingly will be attributed to the respective partners, and the ways in which the international tax rules apply will depend on whether the partner is a U.S. or foreign person. Moreover, limited liability companies (whether organized under U.S. or foreign law) may often elect to be treated as partnerships for U.S. tax purposes.

[¶ 1215]

a. U.S. Partnerships

The difference between the U.S. tax consequences for a foreign investor using a U.S. partnership (or a U.S. limited liability company classified as a partnership for U.S. tax purposes) and one using a U.S. corporation is substantial. For example, if a business organization, 50 percent of the equity of which is owned by a U.S. citizen and 50 percent by a nonresident alien, is created under U.S. law and is characterized as a U.S. corporation, it will be subject to U.S. taxation on its worldwide income. On the other hand, if the organization is characterized as a partnership, the partnership's income taxable to the U.S. partner will include that partner's share of the partnership's worldwide income, whereas the partnership income taxable to the foreign partner will include only that partner's share of the partnership's income from U.S. sources or income that is effectively connected with the partnership's U.S. business.

[¶ 1220]

b. Foreign Partnerships

The characterization of foreign business entities will also have an important impact on U.S. taxes for U.S. participants. A U.S. shareholder of a foreign corporation will normally be taxed only when profits are repatriated in the form of corporate distributions or on gain from the sale of the corporation's stock. A U.S. partner in a foreign partnership (or a U.S. member of a foreign limited liability company that is treated as a partnership for U.S. tax purposes), however, will be taxed immediately on its share of the entity's income. The question of whether a foreign entity is an "association" taxable under the Code as a corporation or a partnership that is not a taxpayer under the Code is one of U.S. law regardless of the characterization of the entity under the law of the country where it is organized. In some instances, an entity that is characterized as a company under the laws of the country where it is organized (such as a civil law limited liability company) may nevertheless be characterized as a partnership, and therefore not a taxpayer, for U.S. tax purposes. As discussed in the next section, under the entity classification system contained in the current regulations under Section 7701, many types of foreign business entities may elect classification as a partnership or corporation for U.S. tax purposes.

To illustrate the significance of the characterization issue, consider the following situation:

The president of Universal Chemical Corp., a U.S. corporation, is intrigued with the prospects for investment in the Russian Federation. The president has visited Russia three times to discuss the outlines of a joint venture to produce and market chemicals in Eastern Europe. The president has signed a "memorandum of understanding" with representatives of a Russian enterprise calling for the establishment of a "joint venture vehicle in the Russian Federation that will be owned equally by a Russian enterprise and by Universal." Under applicable Russian Federation laws, there will be no income taxes for five years. By contrast, under applicable U.S. laws, there will be substantial profits potentially subject to U.S. taxes. However, all profits of the venture are to be reinvested during that period. Does it matter whether the joint venture vehicle is characterized as a corporation or a partnership for U.S. tax purposes so long as there are no taxes imposed by the Russian Federation?

[¶ 1223]

4. BUSINESS ENTITY CLASSIFICATION FOR U.S. TAX PURPOSES

As mentioned above, under current U.S. tax law, the classification of business entities, both U.S. and foreign, is made under a system that in many instances permits a taxpayer to elect whether to have a business entity treated as a separate corporation or a fiscally transparent entity (i.e., treated, for U.S. tax purposes, as a partnership or disregarded as an entity separate from its owner). The largely elective nature of this determination under the current regulations has caused this classification system to be called the "check-the-box" entity classification rules. See Reg. §§ 301.7701–2, –3.

It should be emphasized, however, that not all business entities may elect their classification for U.S. tax purposes. Certain entities are treated as "per se" corporations for U.S. tax purposes. The types of entities that are treated under the regulations as per se corporations include entities incorporated under state law incorporation statutes and certain foreign entities listed in the regulations. See Reg. § 301.7701–2(b). This list of foreign entities treated as per se corporations includes a French Société Anonyme, a German Akteingesellschaft, a Hong Kong Public Limited Company and a United Kingdom Public Limited Company, as well as numerous others. Reg. § 301.7701–2(b)(8)(i). The Treasury and the IRS add foreign entities to this list from time to time.

Business entities not treated as per se corporations under the regulations are called "eligible entities" and may elect their classification for tax purposes. If the entity has two or more members, it can elect to be classified for U.S. tax purposes as either an association taxable as a corporation or a partnership. If the entity has only a single owner, it can elect to be classified as an association taxable as a corporation or to be disregarded as an entity separate from its owner. Reg. § 301.7701–3(a). In tax parlance, the latter has come to be known by the oxymoronic phrase, "disregarded entity."

If no election is made, default rules in the regulations apply. Under those default rules, if no entity classification election is made, a U.S. eligible entity is treated as a partnership if it has two or more members or is disregarded as entity separate from its owner if it has a single owner. If the entity is a foreign eligible entity and no election is made, the foreign entity is (1) treated as a partnership if it has two or more members and at least one member does not have limited liability, (2) treated as an association taxable as a corporation if all members have limited liability or (3) disregarded as an entity separate from its owner if it has a single owner that does not have limited liability. Reg. § 301.7701–3(b).

This description of the entity classification rules is meant to provide only a brief introduction to them. These rules are covered in detail at ¶¶ 13,035 et seq.

[¶ 1225]

5. TRUSTS AND ESTATES

Trusts and estates can be income taxpayers. U.S. trusts and estates are subject to U.S. taxation on their worldwide income. Foreign trusts and estates are taxable under the rules that apply generally for foreign persons.

Section 7701(a)(30)(E) contains a two-part test for determining whether a trust is a U.S. or foreign trust. If both parts of the test are met, the trust is a U.S. trust. If either part of the test is not met, the trust is a foreign trust. § 7701(a)(31)(B). Under the first part of the test, a U.S. court must exercise primary supervision over administration of the trust. Under the second part of the test, one or more U.S. fiduciaries must have the authority to control all substantial decisions of the trust.

Section 7701(a)(31)(A) defines a foreign estate as one that is not subject to taxation on its worldwide income. Under this rather circular definition, an estate is a foreign estate if it is taxable by the United States in a manner similar to a nonresident alien individual. Any other estate is treated as a U.S. estate. § 7701(a)(30)(D). Under the revenue rulings and cases, the IRS and the courts have considered various factors to determine whether U.S. taxation of an estate is comparable to that of a nonresident alien individual. These factors include the location of the estate assets, the country under whose laws the estate is administered and the nationality and residence of the executor, the decedent and the beneficiaries. See, e.g., Rev. Rul. 81–112, 1981–1 C.B. 598.

[¶ 1230]

PROBLEM

U.S. Cleanliness, Inc. ("Usclean") is a large publicly held Delaware corporation, which is traded on the New York Stock Exchange and which owns and operates laundries throughout the United States. Campania Cleanliness, Ltd. ("Camclean") is a wholly owned subsidiary of Usclean, organized under the laws of Campania and engaged in owning and operating dry cleaning establishments throughout Campania, in several countries of Latin America and, in a small way, in the United States. Camclean has income from the following sources:

1. Interest on a loan made to a New York corporation engaged in business solely in the United States (this interest is unrelated to the business referred to in paragraph 9 below).

2. Royalties from an independent licensee in the United States that has a nonexclusive license under a U.S. patent owned by Camclean (unrelated to the business referred to in paragraph 9 below).

3. Dividends on 1,000 shares of General Motors stock owned by Camclean as a portfolio investment (unrelated to the business referred to in paragraph 9 below).

4. Capital gain on the sale of the 1,000 shares of General Motors stock referred to in paragraph 3 above and unrelated to the business referred to in paragraph 9 below.

5. Capital gain from the sale of a U.S. patent owned by Camclean for annual payments for ten years equal to five percent of the annual net sales of the patented product.

6. Conduct of the dry cleaning business in Campania.

7. Conduct of the dry cleaning business in several Latin American countries.

8. Dividends from a U.S. subsidiary that is engaged in the business of selling dry cleaning solvents in the United States.

9. Conduct of the dry cleaning business in the United States through an unincorporated branch.

Which of the above items of income could be taxed by the United States under international law? In each case, what would be the basis under international law for the exercise of jurisdiction to tax? Which of the items should be taxable in the United States? Which items should be taxed at the 30–percent flat rate on gross income? Which should be taxed at the regular corporate rate on net income? The source-of-income rules actually used by the United States are discussed in Chapter 2. For this problem assume that the sources of the income items are as follows:

Items 1, 2, 3, 5, 8 and 9: United States;

Items 4 and 6: Campania;

Item 7: Latin America.

G. THE ROLE OF INCOME TAX TREATIES IN INTERNATIONAL TAXATION

[¶ 1235]

1. INTRODUCTION

Section 894(a)(1) states that the provisions of the Code "shall be applied to any taxpayer with due regard to any treaty obligation of the United States which applies to such taxpayer." This brief formulation introduces another important element in the analysis of the income tax consequences of international transactions. No analysis of an international tax issue will be complete until the possible application of treaty provisions has been thoroughly considered.

The United States has entered into bilateral income tax treaties with 57 countries. As of November 1, 2010, there were in force income tax treaties between the United States and the following countries:

Australia	Iceland	Philippines
Austria	India	Poland
Bangladesh	Indonesia	Portugal
Barbados	Ireland	Romania
Belgium	Israel	Russian Federation
Bermuda	Italy	Slovak Republic
Bulgaria	Jamaica	Slovenia
Canada	Japan	South Africa
China	Kazakhstan	Spain
Cyprus	Korea (South)	Sri Lanka
Czech Republic	Latvia	Sweden
Denmark	Lithuania	Switzerland
Egypt	Luxembourg	Thailand
Estonia	Mexico	Trinidad and Tobago
Finland	Morocco	Tunisia
France	Netherlands	Turkey
Germany	New Zealand	Ukraine
Greece	Norway	United Kingdom
Hungary	Pakistan	Venezuela

Further, the treaty with the former Union of Soviet Socialist Republics remains in effect for the following nine countries that are members of the Commonwealth of Independent States (see Rev. Proc. 93–22A, 1993–2 C.B. 343):

Armenia	Georgia	Tajikistan
Azerbaijan	Kyrgyz Republic	Turkmenistan
Belarus	Moldova	Uzbekistan

This is not a static list. Some existing treaties are being renegotiated. Many other potential treaties are in various stages of negotiation. Some new treaties may come into force as this book is being published. Information regarding the status of treaty negotiations and renegotiations is usually made available by the Treasury Department.

Each of the treaties listed above basically deals with the same matters. Many of the treaties contain common provisions addressing the same issue. It is important to note, however, that the similar purpose and structure of the various treaties does not reflect congruity of substance. Almost every treaty is different in at least some respects. While interpretations of language used in one treaty may be useful in interpreting the same language of another, it is essential to focus on the terms of the specific treaty that may apply to a particular situation.

There are, in addition to the income tax treaties listed above, other international agreements in force between the United States and foreign countries that have an impact, directly or indirectly, on issues of tax law and administration. There are, for example, special agreements called "Tax Information Exchange Agreements," which provide for the exchange of information between governments. Certain treaties dealing with trade and investment relationships, such as Bilateral Investment Treaties and Treaties of Friendship, Commerce and Navigation, contain provisions that may apply in the context of particular tax issues. Mutual Legal Assistance Treaties (sometimes referred to as "MLATs") provide for assistance in criminal matters, including tax crimes. Despite the possible relevance of such agreements, the discussion in this book is limited to the impact of bilateral income tax treaties on the taxation of international transactions.

[¶ 1240]

2. PURPOSES OF TREATIES

The tax treaties generally advance a series of objectives, usually on a reciprocal basis. Their fundamental rationale is to prevent taxes from interfering with the free flow of international trade and investment. Their basic thrust is the avoidance of double taxation of income from international transactions by limiting the jurisdiction that each treaty country may exercise to tax income from domestic sources realized by residents of the other country. Most provide clarification in certain respects of areas in which the application of the tax laws of the treaty partners may be ambiguous or unpredictable. Most treaties also provide for cooperation between the taxing agencies of the respective countries in matters of tax administration.

[¶ 1245]

3. MODEL TREATIES

From time to time the Treasury Department will publish its Model Treaty. In general, the Model Treaty reflects the current position of U.S.

representatives in negotiating treaty arrangements with other countries. It does not, therefore, necessarily reflect the specific provisions of any treaty actually in force. The most recent Model Treaty published is the 2006 Model Treaty (set forth as Appendix A and hereinafter referred to as the "U.S. Model Treaty"). The Treasury Department has also published a Technical Explanation to that 2006 Model Treaty (set forth as Appendix B).

The U.S. Model Treaty is not the only prototype that has been devised and used. The Organization for Economic Cooperation and Development (OECD) (whose members include virtually all of the major industrialized countries) has published a series of model treaties for the elimination of double taxation, together with particularly useful commentaries on the model treaty provisions. Although U.S. representatives have, from time to time, expressed disagreement with some of the articles in the OECD model treaties, the OECD models have greatly influenced tax treaty policy on the part of the United States and other developed countries.

In addition, the United Nations in 1980 published a model treaty for use between developed and developing countries. The United Nations model has been less influential on U.S. treaty policy than have the OECD models.

[¶ 1250]

4. U.S. TREATY–MAKING PROCESS

Under the U.S. Constitution, the U.S. Executive Branch has the exclusive province to negotiate all treaties (including tax treaties) as part of its authority to conduct U.S. foreign relations. Although the State Department has the primary jurisdiction over foreign relations within the Executive Branch, it is the Treasury Department, acting through its Assistant Secretary for Tax Policy and its International Tax Counsel, that actually negotiates tax treaties with the appropriate authorities of the foreign country. If agreement on the treaty is reached with the foreign country, the President signs the treaty on behalf of the United States and sends it to the U.S. Senate for its advice and consent. (Note that, under the Constitution, the U.S. House of Representatives has no formal role in the approval of treaties.) The Senate then refers the treaty to its Foreign Relations Committee (not the Finance Committee), which holds hearings on the matter. If the Senate Foreign Relations Committee approves the treaty, it sends the treaty to the full Senate for its consideration. (The Senate has, on occasion, rejected a tax treaty or approved a treaty with reservation as to a particular provision.) Once the Senate approves the treaty by a two-thirds vote of its members, the treaty actually becomes effective only if and when the U.S. Executive Branch exchanges instruments of ratification with the foreign treaty country. See Federal Income

Tax Project—International Aspects of United States Income Taxation II—Proposals on United States Income Tax Treaties 15–22 (A.L.I. 1992).

[¶ 1255]

5. ALLOCATION OF TAXING JURISDICTION OVER INCOME ITEMS

As mentioned above, the basic purpose of U.S. tax treaties is to mitigate international double taxation by providing for the reciprocal reduction of taxes based on the exercise of source taxing jurisdiction by the United States and its foreign treaty partner with respect to certain income items specified in the treaty. Through the treaty, the country of source relinquishes to (or shares with) the country of residence taxing jurisdiction over the specified items of income. In other words, a treaty generally reduces or eliminates U.S. taxes on certain items of U.S.-source income earned by residents of the foreign treaty country and reduces or eliminates taxes imposed by the foreign treaty country on certain items of income earned by U.S. residents from sources in that country. In addition, a treaty will allocate taxing jurisdiction over certain other types of income (for example, most types of capital gains on the sale of personal property) exclusively to the recipient's country of residence.

Business income (other than personal service income). Treaties typically provide that "business profits" from a business are exempt from tax in the country of source unless the profits are attributable to a permanent establishment in the source country. A permanent establishment is typically defined to include a fixed place of business, such as a place of management, a branch, an office, a factory, a workshop and a mine, an oil or gas well, a quarry or any other place of extracting natural resources. A foreign person also may be treated as having a permanent establishment by reason of the activities of a dependent agent, such as an employee, who acts on behalf of the foreign person and has and habitually exercises in the source country an authority to conclude contracts that are binding on the foreign person. Thus, under a U.S. treaty, a resident of the foreign treaty partner generally will be exempt from U.S. tax on business profits derived from a business in the United States provided that the business is not carried on through a permanent establishment. This treaty exemption typically applies to a foreign person's income from sales operations in the United States conducted with no U.S. office, branch or other fixed place of business and no use of dependent agents located in the United States to conclude sales contracts.

Personal service income. Tax treaties often provide an exemption from tax in the source country for income from personal services performed in an independent capacity (e.g., as a lawyer, engineer or accountant) provided that such income is not attributable to a permanent establishment or a fixed base (the personal service income counterpart to the permanent establishment concept). Tax treaties also often provide an exemption for an employee's personal service income provided that the employee is present in the country for not more than a specified number of days (e.g., 183 days) during the year and the compensation is paid by a nonresident employer that does not have a permanent establishment or fixed base (sometimes referred to as the "commercial traveler's exemption"). Thus, under a U.S. treaty, a resident of the foreign treaty partner who is performing services in the United States as an independent contractor typically will be exempt from U.S. tax on the personal service income provided that the income is not attributable to a permanent establishment or a fixed base in the United States. Also, a resident of the foreign treaty country who is performing services as an employee in the United States will be exempt from U.S. tax provided that the employee works for a foreign employer, the compensation is not borne as a deductible expense by a permanent establishment or fixed base that the employer has in the United States and the employee is not present in the United States for more than 183 days during the year. Moreover, U.S. tax treaties often contain other special provisions relating to the taxation of the personal service income of artists and athletes, professors and students and for income earned from services performed on behalf of the government of the treaty partner.

Nonbusiness income. Tax treaties typically reduce or eliminate the withholding tax on at least some items of investment-type income such as interest, dividends, rents and royalties not attributable to a business conducted through a permanent establishment. Thus, a U.S. treaty typically reduces or eliminates the 30–percent withholding tax on U.S.-source, nonbusiness income (such as interest, dividends or royalties) derived by residents of the foreign treaty partner.

Capital gains. Tax treaties typically provide that capital gains may be taxed only by the country of residence, with two important exceptions. First, tax treaties typically confirm that gains from the sale of personal property attributable to a permanent establishment or fixed base may be taxed by the country in which the permanent establishment or fixed base is located. Second, treaties typically confirm that gains from the alienation of real property or stock in a corporation at least one-half of the assets of which consist of real property may be taxed by the country in which the real property is located. Thus, treaties permit the United States to impose U.S. tax under Section 897 on gain from the sale of U.S. real property or stock in a U.S. corporation at least one-half of the assets of which consists of U.S. real property.

Other income. Finally, modern U.S. tax treaties typically allocate exclusive taxing jurisdiction to the treaty country of residence over items of income, wherever arising, that are not covered by other articles in the treaty. See, e.g., U.S. Model Treaty, Art. 21.

[¶ 1260]

6. RELIEF FROM DOUBLE TAXATION

To mitigate or eliminate international double taxation, U.S. tax treaties typically contain a commitment by the United States to allow its residents and citizens a foreign tax credit, in accordance with the provisions of U.S. law, for taxes paid to the foreign treaty country. See, e.g., U.S. Model Treaty, Art. 23(2). This credit under the treaty is subject to the various limitations on the foreign tax credit of U.S. law. The treaties also typically contain a reciprocal commitment by the foreign treaty country either to allow its residents and citizens a credit for taxes paid to the United States on income derived from sources within the United States or to exempt its residents and citizens from tax on such income.

7. SCOPE OF TREATY BENEFITS

[¶ 1265]

a. Taxes Covered

A U.S. tax treaty typically specifies the taxes of the foreign treaty partner to which the treaty applies. The treaty also typically provides that it applies only to federal income taxes and to certain other federal taxes in the United States and to "identical or substantially similar taxes" of the foreign treaty partner or the United States that may be enacted after the treaty is signed. See, e.g., U.S. Model Treaty, Art. 2(4).

By contrast, the OECD Models apply to taxes "imposed on behalf of a Contracting State or of its political subdivisions or local authorities." No U.S. treaty currently in force contains a provision affecting state and local taxes in the United States. The treaty signed in 1975 between the United States and the United Kingdom would have applied to "taxes on income imposed by political subdivisions or local authorities." After extensive hearings the Senate approved the treaty but with a reservation as to that provision. Unhappiness on the part of a number of foreign governments with respect to the application of unitary, or formulary, income tax methods by certain states of the United States led to efforts to thwart the practice through provisions in tax treaties. The vigorous opposition by state authorities, however, overcame those efforts.

[¶ 1270]

b. Beneficiaries of Treaty Provisions

The treaty benefits of clarification and tax reduction are generally made available to "residents" of the parties to the treaty. The treaty typically defines a "resident" as a person who, under the laws of that country, is liable to tax therein by reason of "domicile, residence, citizenship, place of management, place of incorporation, or any other criterion of a similar nature." The treaty then typically contains so-called "tie-breaker" rules, which specify how residence is to be determined if a taxpayer is regarded as a resident of both countries under their respective laws and the general tests in the treaty. E.g., U.S. Model Treaty, Art. 4(3).

Under the saving clause, treaty benefits are not generally accorded by a contracting state to its own citizens and residents. For example, the U.S. Model Treaty provides that (except as provided in Article 1(5)), the treaty "shall not affect the taxation by a Contracting State of its residents * * * and its citizens." U.S. Model Treaty, Art. 1(4). Thus, a U.S. tax treaty generally does not reduce U.S. taxes on the income of U.S. citizens, resident aliens and corporations (with certain exceptions discussed at ¶ 5380); its principal importance to such U.S. taxpayers is that it reduces the taxes imposed by the foreign treaty country on income they derive in that country.

The treaty also typically provides that a Contracting State may tax a former citizen or former long-term resident for the period of ten years after the loss of such status "in accordance with the laws of that Contracting State." U.S. Model Treaty, Art. 1(4). The application of Section 877 (see ¶ 1195) was not negated, therefore, by renouncing U.S. citizenship or ending long-term U.S. residence in favor of citizenship or residence in a treaty country.

The IRS has ruled that Section 877 of prior law would apply even if a treaty did not specifically reserve the right to tax former citizens in such situations. Rev. Rul. 79–152, 1979–1 C.B. 237. However, the application of Section 877 to a taxpayer who had renounced U.S. citizenship and established a residence in Canada was rejected under the terms of the 1942 former United States–Canada Tax Treaty. The court concluded that Congress had not intended to overrule existing treaty obligations when it enacted Section 877. See Crow v. Commissioner, 85 T.C. 376 (1985).

[¶ 1275]

c. "Treaty Shopping" Problem

Under the terms of most U.S. treaties that have come into force, a corporation organized under the laws of its treaty partner is entitled to the reduction of U.S. taxes on various types of U.S.-source income and the other benefits in the treaty. The relative ease of corporate organization and operation has led foreign investors residing in a country that has no tax treaty with the United States (or has a less favorable treaty with the United States) to establish a corporation in a country that has a favorable treaty with the United States. In some cases, the treaty country in which the corporation is established is itself a tax haven so that the corporation will be subject to little or no tax in that country. Moreover, the corporation often has little or no economic presence in the treaty country; the principal purpose for forming the corporation in the treaty country is to take advantage of the country's tax treaty with the United States. Thus, unless some method to successfully attack this device can be found, foreign investors will be able to obtain U.S. treaty benefits in their treaty country of choice merely by setting up a corporation in that country. Selecting a country with a favorable treaty through which an investment or transaction in the United States can be channelled has come to be known as "treaty shopping."

The United States takes this treaty shopping problem very seriously and uses a number of approaches to deal with it. First, in certain cases, the IRS has succeeded in arguing that the corporation established in the treaty country did not in substance "receive" the U.S.-source income as to which it was claiming treaty benefits but was a mere "conduit" for receipt of the income by its shareholders, the foreign investors resident in some other country. A leading case in this area is the Tax Court's decision in *Aiken Industries, Inc. v. Commissioner*, at ¶ 4070.

Second, in certain cases the United States has included anti-treaty shopping rules in the Code that apply to a particular provision. For example, the branch profits tax provisions, discussed at ¶ 3230, contain their own anti-treaty shopping provisions in Section 884(e).

Third, the Treasury Department and the IRS have issued so-called anti-conduit regulations under the authority of Section 7701(*l*) of the Code. These regulations, which are discussed at ¶ 4095, give the IRS broad authority to recharacterize certain conduit-financing arrangements in accordance with their economic substance. After recharacterization of the arrangement under these regulations, the ultimate owner of the U.S.-source income may not be the interposed corporation formed in the treaty country for treaty shopping purposes.

Finally, and most important of all, the U.S. Treasury Department in its treaty negotiations now insists on the inclusion of "limitation-of-benefits" provisions in its tax treaties, and all treaties concluded by the United States since 1981 contain some form of such provisions. These limitation-of-benefits provisions vary from treaty to treaty, of course, but they typically provide that certain treaty benefits are not available to a corporation formed in the treaty country if more than a specified percentage (e.g., 50 percent) of its stock is held by residents of countries other than the United States or the foreign treaty country. See ¶ 4090.

[¶ 1280]

d. Nondiscrimination Provision

Because the fundamental rationale of income tax treaties is to prevent taxes from interfering with the free flow of international trade and investment, a U.S. tax treaty typically contains a nondiscrimination provision under which the United States and its treaty partner both agree that in the exercise of source-based tax jurisdiction each country will not tax nationals of the other country more heavily than its own nationals in the same circumstances. See Federal Income Tax Project—International Aspects of United States Income Taxation II—Proposals on United States Income Tax Treaties 253 (A.L.I. 1992). Specifically, such a provision typically provides that nationals of the treaty country shall not be subjected to taxation in the other country (or any requirement connected with such taxation) that is more burdensome than the taxation (and connected requirements) to which nationals of that other country in the same circumstances are subjected. E.g., U.S. Model Treaty, Art. 24. For example, this provision prevents the United States from taxing nationals of its foreign treaty partner who are U.S. resident aliens more heavily than U.S. citizens in the same circumstances.

Moreover, this nondiscrimination provision also typically provides that a permanent establishment which an enterprise of a treaty country has in the other source country shall not be less favorably taxed by the source country than enterprises of the source country carrying on the same activities. For example, the United States cannot tax the U.S. branch of a treaty partner corporation that is carrying on a business through a U.S. permanent establishment more heavily than it taxes a U.S. corporation carrying on the same business in the United States.

Further, the nondiscrimination provision typically provides that interest, royalties and other disbursements paid by a resident of the source treaty country to a resident of the other treaty country shall, for purposes of determining the payor's taxable profits, be deductible under the same conditions as if they had been paid to a resident of the source country. For example, the United States cannot deny a deduction for interest or royalties paid to a resident of its treaty partner if it allows a deduction for interest or royalties paid to a U.S. resident under the same conditions.

Finally, the nondiscrimination provision typically provides that an enterprise of the source treaty country, the capital of which is wholly or partly owned or controlled by residents of the other treaty country, shall not be subjected to taxation (or any requirement connected with such taxation) in the source country that is more burdensome than the taxation (and connected requirements) to which other similar source country enterprises are subjected. For example, the United States cannot tax a U.S. corporation wholly owned by residents of its treaty partner more heavily than similarly situated U.S. corporations wholly owned by U.S. persons.

[¶ 1285]

PROBLEMS

1. Review the facts involving your client, Wolfgang, the German citizen in Problem 1 at ¶ 1190. If Wolfgang is treated as a U.S. resident for year 3

under Section 7701(b) and is also treated as a resident of Germany for German tax purposes, is any relief available under the United States–Germany income tax treaty, assuming that it contains a provision identical to Article 4 of the U.S. Model Treaty in Appendix A? Applying Article 4 of that treaty, is Wolfgang a resident of the United States or Germany under the treaty?

2. Arlene, another German citizen and resident, is not a U.S. resident under any of the tests in Section 7701(b). During the current year, she earns $10,000 of interest income from a loan she made to a U.S. resident individual debtor (which would be treated as U.S.-source income under Section 861(a)(1) and would be subject to a 30–percent gross basis tax under Section 871(a)(1)(A)). She also earns $10,000 of U.S.-source compensation income for services rendered on a management consulting job that she undertakes for a U.S. client (which would be treated as U.S.-source income under Section 861(a)(3) and, by reason of Section 871(b), would be subject to tax at the usual rates in Section 1). Assume that Arlene is an independent contractor and does not have an office or other fixed place of business in the United States, and that Germany has entered into an income tax treaty with the United States that is identical to the U.S. Model Treaty in Appendix A. How would Arlene's U.S. tax treatment be changed by the relevant provisions in Articles 11(1), 5 and 7 of the treaty?

[¶ 1290]

8. ADMINISTRATIVE COOPERATION

An essential purpose of the tax treaties is to increase the cooperation of the tax authorities of the two countries in the administration of their respective tax laws. This cooperation takes many forms. The treaties typically authorize the United States and its treaty partner to exchange information filed by, and relating to the activities of, taxpayers engaged in international transactions. This exchange of information provides an important tool for facilitating international audits and combatting tax avoidance and evasion. Section 6103(k)(4) specifically authorizes the IRS to share taxpayer information with treaty partners of the United States.

Administrative cooperation can also provide benefits to taxpayers. U.S. tax treaties typically contain a provision that authorizes both countries to challenge transfer prices between "associated enterprises" but counsels both to have regard for the laws of the other country. The treaties also typically provide for the "competent authorities" of the two countries to endeavor to apply their laws in such a way as to avoid taxation that is contrary to the provisions of the treaty, including double taxation of the same income. This provision typically gives the competent authorities broad authority to consult and resolve double taxation issues whether or not they are specifically covered by the treaty. This provision is invoked frequently in situations where tax officials of the two countries are contending for inconsistent transfer pricing adjustments based on transactions between related entities. See generally Chapter 8.

The competent authority mechanism under U.S. tax treaties provides an administrative procedural device to mitigate double taxation, but does not give the taxpayer a judicially enforceable remedy. Moreover, the competent authorities' decision with respect to one taxpayer is not precedential authority with respect to any other taxpayer under the same or any other treaty. As stated by the Tax Court in Filler v. Commissioner, 74 T.C. 406, 408–09 (1980), at ¶ 5385, with respect to a prior version of the United States–France Tax Treaty:

> * * * Article 25, which is entitled "Mutual Agreement Procedure," * * * provides for an international administrative procedure in which the "competent authority" of one country confers with the "competent authority" of the other with a view to resolving difficulties in the application of the convention. The two competent authorities may reach an agreement in respect of the imposition of taxes in a specific case that can supersede the application of the national law of either country. The procedure is entirely administrative, not judicial, and paragraph (1) of article 25 contemplates that the taxpayer may invoke it by "present[ing] his case to the competent authority of the Contracting State of which he is a resident." In this case, petitioner is a resident of France; accordingly, if he were to proceed under article 25, it is incumbent upon him to present the matter to the competent authority of France.[4] Certainly, this Court is not empowered to initiate any competent authority proceedings or to represent the United States in any negotiations with the competent authority of France.
>
> If petitioner wishes to proceed under article 25, he must invoke competent authority proceedings in an appropriate manner,[5] not by attempting to present his case on the merits to this Court. We have jurisdiction only to decide whether the deficiency determined by the Commissioner is correct under the laws of the United States, as such laws may be affected by substantive provisions of the convention. And, as we have already pointed out, there is no dispute as to the correctness of the deficiency under our Internal Revenue Code. There remains only the question whether any substantive provisions of the convention require a different result.

There has been increasing discussion, particularly among European governments, about the use of arbitration and other alternative dispute

4. We express no opinion as to whether, in addition to the procedure specified in art. 25, petitioner might be permitted to invoke competent authority proceedings by presenting his case to the competent authority of the United States. * * *

5. Petitioner contends that he has already unsuccessfully sought relief from the French authorities. However, we have no indication that he has attempted to invoke the "competent authority" procedure as opposed to merely seeking relief from the French officials in administering their own law. Those officials apparently relied upon art. 15 of the convention in denying relief to petitioner, and we think they did so erroneously * * *. But there is nothing before us to show that "competent authority" proceedings were involved. In any event, this Court is not a proper forum in which to engage in or review any such proceedings.

resolution procedures for resolving differences under the mutual agreement provisions. A growing number of U.S. tax treaties also contemplate the possible use of arbitration. See, e.g., United States–Mexico Treaty (Art. 26). Moreover, as discussed at ¶ 8195, some U.S. tax treaties recently have included provisions obligating the treaty partners to submit to binding arbitration in certain instances. See, e.g., United States–Canada Treaty (Art. 21(6) and (7)); United States–Germany Treaty (Art. 25(5) and (6)).

[¶ 1295]

9. RELATIONSHIP BETWEEN TREATIES AND THE CODE

Often the terms of a U.S. tax treaty modify the tax results that one would otherwise obtain under the Code.[13] Section 7852(d)(1), however, provides that "[f]or purposes of determining the relationship between a provision of a treaty and any law of the United States affecting revenue, neither the treaty nor the law shall have preferential status by reason of its being a treaty or law." This rather enigmatic formulation is another (albeit convoluted) way of stating a basic principle of U.S. jurisprudence with respect to the posture of treaties: under the U.S. Constitution (art. VI, cl. 2), U.S. treaties and federal statutes have equal status as the supreme law of the land and, thus, whenever there is a conflict between the two, the later in time prevails. See Restatement (Third) of the Foreign Relations Law of the United States § 115 (A.L.I. 1986).

The obvious application of this principle occurs normally when a new tax treaty is concluded that reduces U.S. tax burdens for foreign persons in the ways described in this Chapter. Because the treaty is later in time, the courts in the United States will apply the treaty and the U.S. tax burdens of a resident of the foreign treaty partner will be lowered.

The converse of the rule above is also true. If a U.S. statute is enacted that is inconsistent with an existing treaty provision, the statute, being later in time, will prevail and the benefits of the treaty will not be available. A U.S. court will apply this principle even though the result is to place the United States in violation of the treaty and, therefore, in violation of international law. This practice differs from that of many countries where a treaty is considered to be a higher source of law than a statute. It should be noted, however, that as a rule of interpretation, U.S.

13. If a taxpayer takes the position that any U.S. tax treaty overrules or modifies any Code provision with respect to the taxpayer's U.S. tax liability, Section 6114 generally requires the taxpayer to disclose the position in a statement attached to the tax return (or an IRS form designed for this purpose, if no return is required). Failure to make the required disclosure may subject the taxpayer to a penalty of $1,000 ($10,000 for corporate taxpayers) for each such failure. § 6712. The purposes of this disclosure requirement are (1) to bring to the attention of Congress and the IRS conflicts between U.S. tax treaties and Code provisions, and (2) to assist the IRS in administering the tax system by bringing untested or questionable treaty positions to its prompt attention. Note that Reg. § 301.6114–1(c) waives this disclosure requirement with respect to certain treaty return positions.

courts generally strive to construe U.S. treaties and federal statutes so as not to conflict with each other. Restatement (Third) of the Foreign Relations Law of the United States § 114 (A.L.I. 1986).

Congress has enacted legislation in conflict with treaty obligations on a number of occasions. The frequency of such actions in the 1980s produced a new term—the "treaty override." Perhaps the most notable exercise of the treaty override authority occurred with the passage of Section 897 as part of the Foreign Investment in Real Property Tax Act in 1980 (see ¶¶ 4185 et seq.). Many U.S. treaties at the time provided that the source country would impose no taxes on certain capital gains. As discussed in Chapter 4, Section 897 results in a tax not only on gains realized on sales of real estate itself but also on gains realized from the sale of stock in U.S. corporations a significant portion of the assets of which consist of U.S. real estate.

The enthusiasm of treaty partners for such intentional violations of treaty obligations is understandably restrained. In the case of Section 897, Congress provided that its provisions would not apply for a four-year period in respect of a taxpayer entitled to the benefit of a treaty with inconsistent provisions. It was anticipated that the Treasury Department would use the four years to renegotiate the treaties under which modification was necessary to be consistent with Section 897.

In many instances, it is clear that new legislation is not intended to modify or interfere with treaty commitments. Congress either makes it clear in the text of the particular tax act or its legislative history that no override was intended or the nature of the tax provision is such that no conflict with existing treaty commitments is likely to be found (i.e., the new tax provision is likely to be interpreted as harmonious with existing treaty commitments). A particularly difficult problem arises, however, in massive consolidations of the tax laws such as those which occurred in the adoption of the Internal Revenue Code of 1954 and the Tax Reform Act of 1986. The 1954 Code contained a provision stating that it was not intended to replace existing treaty arrangements. No such provision was included in the Tax Reform Act of 1986. Did the 1986 Act effectively nullify all inconsistent provisions of existing treaties?

This question generated some concern among U.S. treaty partners and considerable debate in Washington. The result of this debate was the enactment of the current version of Section 7852(d)(1), as part of technical corrections legislation enacted in 1988, which is intended to codify the later-in-time rule of treaty interpretation. The 1988 legislation also identified a number of changes enacted in the 1986 Act that were *not* intended to override existing treaty obligations and a few such changes that *were* intended to override existing treaty obligations under the later-in-time rule. With respect to 1986 Act changes other than those identified as being in conflict with existing treaties, the 1988 legislative history indicated generally that "Congress intended harmonious construction of the [1986]

Act and U.S. income tax treaties to the extent possible,'' and identified several other 1986 Act changes that Congress viewed as consistent with existing treaties despite arguments to the contrary. S. Rep. No. 445, 100th Cong., 2d Sess. 320–21 (1988). The 1988 legislative history finally concludes that if other conflicts between the 1986 Act and existing treaties are found to exist, the later-in-time rule in Section 7852(d)(1) applies in determining which provision controls. Id. at 321. Is this a clear and appropriate resolution of the treaty override question with respect to the 1986 Act?

CHAPTER 2

SOURCE RULES FOR INCOME AND DEDUCTIONS

■ ■ ■

[¶ 2000]

A. INTRODUCTION: THE RELEVANCE OF SOURCE RULES

The answer to many questions about the income taxation of international transactions depends upon an identification of the country in which the income is properly deemed to have been generated. Put in the language of tax policy and practice, the task is to determine the *source* of the income concerned. Almost every country, therefore, has adopted rules for determining the source of income. Although the source rules of different countries are not congruent, many reflect approaches similar to those used in the United States.

The focus of this Chapter is, of course, upon the source rules applied by the United States. They are in many instances somewhat complex and confusing. The U.S. source rules in general derive from an attempt to identify the geographic locus of the economic activity or financial arrangements that generated the income. The question is always whether income and related deductions and credits derive from inside or outside the United States. According to Section 7701(a)(9) the " 'United States' when used in a geographical sense includes only the States and the District of Columbia." As you reflect on the specific source rules developed and applied in the United States, consider whether they identify the proper conceptual source of income or deductions and whether there might be other criteria that, if applied, would produce a different and more appropriate result.

Source rules apply in a number of quite different contexts. One important application of the source rules is the determination of U.S. income tax liability for foreign persons. The rules for determining the tax liability of foreign persons are explored in Chapters 3 and 4. It is sufficient for now to observe that, except in rare circumstances, a foreign person who has no U.S.-source income will have no U.S. income tax liability.

The source of income is also essential to the calculation of the foreign tax credit, discussed in Chapters 5 and 7. Because the foreign tax credit is intended to limit or mitigate double taxation of foreign-source income, the credit is generally accorded only with respect to foreign taxes on foreign-source income and is primarily applicable to U.S. persons. Moreover, the application of certain important limitations on the foreign tax credit depends on the amount of foreign tax on various categories of foreign-source income.

Additional applications of the source rules affect a number of other issues addressed in this book. The materials in this Chapter deal solely with the determination of source. The consequences of that determination will depend on the purpose for which the determination is being made. While the same source rules will generally apply regardless of the purposes for which they are being invoked, some special source rules apply in determining limitations on the foreign tax credit.

Because the source rules depend upon the nature of the income whose source is in question, the starting point in the analysis will be the correct classification of the item of income whose source is being determined. As some of the ensuing materials indicate, there are many transactions in which the appropriate characterization of an item of income is not readily apparent.

Most of the source rules are specified in Sections 861 through 865 of the Code. Section 861 identifies categories of U.S.-source income. Section 862 identifies categories of foreign-source income. Section 863 deals with categories of income that are partially U.S.- and partially foreign-source. Section 864 defines a number of relevant terms and prescribes rules for allocating certain expenses to U.S.- and foreign-source income. Section 865 establishes elaborate rules for determining the source of income derived from the sale of various types of personal property. Where source rules have not been prescribed in the Code, they have been developed by regulation and other administrative guidance and by judicial interpretation purporting to reflect the principles of the statutory prescriptions. Source rules also appear occasionally in tax treaties. The source rules, however established, do not depend upon the place of the payment or receipt of income.

Because it is necessary to determine net income from U.S. and foreign sources in a number of instances, special source rules have been developed for allocating deductions (and sometimes credits) to the appropriate source category. The materials in this Chapter also address these provisions.

[¶ 2005]

B. INTEREST

Section 861(a)(1) demonstrates the manner in which Congress has sought to identify the geographic place from which income is derived. The source of interest depends generally on the residence of the debtor who pays the interest. Accordingly, interest payments from U.S. residents and U.S. corporations are generally characterized as U.S.-source income. Interest paid by foreign corporations and nonresidents, including U.S. citizens residing abroad, will generally be characterized as foreign-source income. § 862(a)(1). The residence of the debtor is determined at the time of an interest payment. Reg. § 1.861–2(a)(2)(i).

There have been several exceptions to the usual source rules for interest. Interest on deposits paid by foreign branches of commercial banking business and savings institutions is treated as foreign-source income even though the payer is a U.S. corporation. § 861(a)(1)(B)(i). For many years interest paid by certain U.S. corporations in other circumstances was deemed to constitute foreign-source income, at least in part. If at least 80 percent of the debtor's gross income (over the three years prior to the year in which the interest was paid) had derived from foreign-source income attributable to the active conduct of a foreign trade or business, all of the interest paid was treated as foreign-source. If interest was paid by such a U.S. corporation to a related lender, only a portion of the interest was treated as foreign-source income. Concerned with the extent to which taxpayers were able to exploit this exception and seeking additional revenues, Congress enacted legislation in 2010 that terminated the source-rule exception. Some of the consequences of the source-rule exception were, however, grandfathered by the 2010 legislation. They are discussed at ¶ 4042.

While interest paid by foreign corporations is usually deemed to be from foreign sources, Section 884(f)(1) provides that interest paid by the U.S. trade or business of a foreign corporation will be treated "as if it were paid by a domestic corporation."

For purposes of this source rule, U.S. "residents" include domestic and foreign partnerships engaged in a trade or business in the United States. Reg. § 1.861–2(a)(2). However, if the foreign partnership is "predominantly engaged in the active conduct of a trade or business outside of the United States," interest payments will be treated as U.S.-source income only to the extent that they are paid by a U.S. trade or business of the partnership and are allocable to income effectively connected (or treated as effectively connected) with such a U.S. trade or business. § 861(a)(1)(B).

[¶ 2010]

C. DIVIDENDS

Dividends from U.S. corporations are generally treated as U.S.-source income. § 861(a)(2). Dividends from foreign corporations are generally treated as foreign-source income. § 862(a)(2).

Dividends from a foreign corporation will, however, be treated at least in part as U.S.-source income if 25 percent or more of the corporation's gross income from all sources for a base period was effectively connected with the conduct of a U.S. trade or business. In that event, the amount of dividends deemed to be from U.S. sources will be a percentage determined by the ratio between the gross income effectively connected with the U.S. trade or business and the total gross income of the corporation. § 861(a)(2)(B). The base period is the three tax years ending with the tax year preceding the declaration of the dividend. Note that the exception will apply even if the U.S. trade or business does not itself produce a profit.

[¶ 2015]

D. RENTALS AND ROYALTIES

The source of rental and royalty income is determined by the place where the property is located or used. §§ 861(a)(4) and 862(a)(4). Accordingly, the source of rental income for tangible property will depend on the place where the property is physically located. The source of royalty income for intangible properties, such as patents, copyrights, trade secrets, trademarks and goodwill, depends on where the rights are used, which is generally the country in which the intangible property derives its legal protection. The following Ruling applies this principle when trademarked products are sold in the United States for resale and use abroad.

[¶ 2020]

REVENUE RULING 68–443

1968–2 C.B. 304.

Advice has been requested whether the place of initial sale of a product that bears a trademark is the controlling factor in the determination of the source of the royalties paid for the use of the trademark under the circumstances described.

X, a resident foreign corporation, owns a trademark for certain products in many foreign countries. *X* corporation entered into a license agreement with *Y*, a domestic corporation, pursuant to which *Y* was given the right to place the foreign trademark owned by *X* on *Y*'s products and sell the trademarked products. The United States trademark for these products is owned by *Z*, an unrelated party. The license agreement between *X* and *Y* is a conventional trademark license agreement for a limited period of time and includes customary provisions to identify and protect the licensor's proprietorship of this mark. Under the terms of the license, *Y* corporation pays *X* corporation a royalty measured by a percentage of the initial sales price of the trademarked products.

Y manufactures the trademarked products in the United States and sells them to foreign buyers in the United States for resale and consumption in foreign countries; all rights, title, and interest of *Y* in the products pass to the foreign buyers within the United States. Thus, the initial sale of the trademarked products is regarded as having taken place in the United States.

The specific question presented is whether, by reason of the initial sale of the products to the foreign buyers in the United States, *Y* corporation has "used" the foreign trademark in the United States and the royalties paid by *Y* to *X* are income from sources within the United States.

Section 861(a)(4) * * * states, in part, that royalties for the use of or for the privilege of using in the United States trademarks and other like property shall be treated as income from sources within the United States.

Section 862(a)(4) * * * states, in part, that royalties for the use of or for the privilege of using without the United States trademarks and other like properties shall be treated as income from sources without the United States.

The gist of a trademark is its association in the public mind with the product, it being the identifying mark of the trade. * * *

The function of a trademark is to designate the goods as the product of a particular trader and to protect his goodwill against the sale of another's product as his. * * *

In the instant case the character of *X* corporation's income is royalty income measured by a percentage of the sales of the foreign trademarked products. The initial sale of the trademarked products to foreign shippers is a means of placing the products in the avenues of commerce with a view towards their ultimate consumption outside the United States. Although the amount of the royalty income is measured by the sales of the trademarked products, the place of sale does not necessarily determine the source of such royalty income.

Since *Z* owns the United States trademark to these products, the products manufactured by *Y* and identified by the trademark under the license from *X* cannot be sold in the United States for consumption in the United States. Moreover, the foreign countries do not protect the foreign trademarks in the United States. It is concluded, therefore, that the royalties paid by *Y* to *X* are paid for the use of the trademarks in the foreign countries and that the place of initial sale of the trademarked products is not the controlling factor in the determination of the source of income.

Accordingly, in the instant case, where products are ultimately used in the foreign country where their trademark is protected, a royalty, received by *X* for the use of the foreign trademark, is income from sources outside the United States despite the fact that the initial sale of the trademarked articles took place in the United States.

[¶ 2021]

NOTE

Application of the rule for determining the source of royalty income in practice can be a very challenging task. Arrangements for the exploitation of intellectual property interests often involve rights protected by the laws of the United States and perhaps several other countries, thereby requiring an allocation between U.S.- and foreign-source income.

E. COMPENSATION FOR PERSONAL SERVICES

[¶ 2025]

1. GENERAL RULE

The source of income from the performance of personal services is the place where the services are performed. §§ 861(a)(3) and 862(a)(3). The application of this rather simple principle can, however, be attended by substantial complexity. The first question is whether the income is in fact compensation for the performance of services.

[¶ 2030]

REVENUE RULING 60–55

1960–1 C.B. 270.

Advice has been requested whether commissions received by a corporation, organized and operating in a foreign country, from a domestic corporation constitute income from sources without the United States within the meaning of section 862 * * *.

The taxpayer corporation, organized under the laws of a foreign country, is engaged in the purchase in the United States and sale in foreign countries of various types of machinery manufactured by a domestic company of the United States.

The foreign corporation maintains its sales and servicing personnel permanently outside the United States. Such sales personnel travel throughout other foreign countries taking orders for and promoting the sale of the items manufactured by the domestic corporation.

In some instances, for various reasons, foreign customers order merchandise directly from the domestic corporation and require shipment directly to themselves, thus depriving the taxpayer of the sale. In such instances, the domestic corporation has obligated itself, by contract, to pay a commission to the foreign corporation in recognition of the fact that the sale would not have been made except for the promotional work done by the latter in foreign countries.

> Section 862 * * * provides [that foreign-source income includes] * * * compensation for labor or personal services performed without the United States.

In *British Timken Limited v. Commissioner*, 12 T.C. 880, acquiescence, C.B. 1949–2, 1, a foreign corporation entered into an agreement with an American associate for the latter to supply the foreign customers of the former with a product previously sold through the foreign corporation. Under such agreement, the American firm paid the foreign corporation a commission on such sales. The court, in determining that such commissions constituted income from sources without the United States, stated as follows:

> * * * we do not regard the fact that the situs of the sales was within the United States as determinative of the source of petitioner's income. * * * It is the situs of the activity or property which constitutes the source of the compensation paid and not the situs of the sales by which it is measured that is of critical importance. * * *

It has been repeatedly held that the place where the services are performed, and not where the compensation is paid, controls in determining the source of income derived from the performance of labor or personal services. * * *

The facts of the instant case appear to bring it within the rationale of * * * *British Timken Limited* * * *, inasmuch as the commissions were paid to the taxpayer by the domestic corporation in recognition of the fact that the sales would not have been made except through the services of the taxpayer. Such services consisted of promotion of the products of the domestic corporation by the taxpayer exclusively in foreign countries.

Accordingly, it is held that commissions received by a corporation operating exclusively in a foreign country from a domestic corporation for securing purchase orders from foreign customers constitute income from sources without the United States within the meaning of section 862 * * * to the extent that they constitute a reasonable allowance for services actually rendered.

[¶ 2035]

2. DE MINIMIS EXCEPTIONS

There is a limited exception to the application of the compensation source rule for certain individuals who work very briefly in the United States. Section 861(a)(3) provides that compensation earned by nonresident aliens will not be considered to be from U.S. sources if the taxpayer is present in the United States for a period or periods not exceeding 90 days during a tax year, if the compensation does not exceed $3,000 and if the work is performed on behalf of a foreign individual or entity not engaged in a U.S. trade or business or the foreign office or branch of a U.S. person or entity. If the compensation for services performed in the United States exceeds $3,000, however, the entire amount is treated as U.S.-source income. Further, compensation paid to a nonresident alien while serving temporarily in the United States as a regular member of the crew of a foreign vessel engaged in transportation between the United States and a foreign country or U.S. possession will be treated as foreign-source income. Because such foreign-source income is not subject to U.S. taxation, these source rules provide an effective exemption. See also ¶ 3010.

[¶ 2040]

3. ALLOCATION OF COMPENSATION INCOME

If services are performed partly within and partly without the United States, compensation will be apportioned between U.S. and foreign sources. The regulations provide that the method of apportionment "is determined on the basis that most correctly reflects the proper source of income under the facts and circumstances of the particular case." Reg. § 1.861–4(b)(1)(i). In many instances, the apportionment will reflect the number of days worked within and without the United States. But even this rather obvious approach can be accompanied by complexities of implementation.

[¶ 2045]

STEMKOWSKI v. COMMISSIONER

United States Court of Appeals, Second Circuit, 1982.
690 F.2d 40.

OAKES, CIRCUIT JUDGE:

* * *

FACTS

Taxpayer was traded prior to the beginning of taxable year 1971 to the New York Rangers, who play their home games at Madison Square Garden in New York City. He had previously signed a two-year NHL

Standard Player's Contract with the Detroit Red Wings, and this contract was assigned to and assumed by the Rangers. The contract provided for compensation of $31,500 in the 1970–71 season and $35,000 in the 1971–72 season plus various NHL bonuses, including a $1500 bonus for each round won in the play-offs. The player agreed to give his services in all "league championship" (i.e., regular season), exhibition, and play-off games, to report in good physical condition to the club training camp at the time and place fixed by the club, to keep himself in good physical condition at all times during the season, and to participate in any and all promotional activities of the club and the league that in the opinion of the club promoted the welfare of the club or professional hockey.

In addition to their rights under this contract, NHL players in 1971 were entitled under the NHL's Owner–Player Council Minutes and Agreements to receive $25 per exhibition game plus $25 per week of training camp unless they had played fifty or more games in the previous season, in which case they received $600 in lieu of payments for exhibition games and training camp allowances other than transportation, food, and lodging. The players were also provided with medical and disability coverage, per diem expenses while traveling during the regular season, and various other benefits.

An NHL player's year is divided into four periods: (1) training camp, including exhibition games, beginning in September and lasting approximately thirty days; (2) the "league championship" or regular season of games beginning in October and lasting until April of the following year; (3) the play-off competition, which ends in May; and (4) the off-season, which runs from the end of the regular season for clubs that do not make the play-offs, or from a club's last play-off game, to the first day of training camp. Stemkowski lived in Canada during all of the off-season and most of the training camp period and played in Canada fifteen days out of 179 during the regular season and five out of twenty-eight days during the play-offs. When he was not living in Canada or traveling to games elsewhere, he lived in Long Beach, New York, near New York City, where he shared a rented house with other professional hockey players. * * *

The less time Stemkowski was in the United States during the period covered by his contract, the less United States tax he owes. Thus, Stemkowski could reduce his tax liability either by showing that he was in Canada for a longer period during the time covered by the contract or, as is at issue here, that the contract covered a time during which he was in Canada. The Tax Court held that the total number of days for which Stemkowski was compensated under his contract was not 234 (all but the off-season) as he had claimed on his tax return, or 365 as he had claimed before the Tax Court, but only 179, the number of days in the regular season. The Tax Court held that Stemkowski could not use days spent in

Canada during training camp, the play-offs, or the off-season in calculating his foreign-source exclusion from income. * * *

DISCUSSION

* * *

The first issue is the Tax Court's determination of the portion of Stemkowski's compensation under the NHL Standard Player's Contract that was drawn from United States sources. As a nonresident alien, Stemkowski was taxable on income connected with the conduct of a trade or business, including the performance of personal services, within the United States. I.R.C. §§ 871(b), 864(b). Where services are performed partly within and partly outside the United States, but compensation is not separately allocated, [Reg. §] 1.861–4(b)(1975) allocates income to United States sources on a "time basis":

> [T]he amount to be included in gross income will be that amount which bears the same relation to the total compensation as the number of days of performance of the labor or services within the United States bears to the total number of days of performance of labor or services for which the payment is made.

This regulation applies to Stemkowski because the NHL Standard Player's Contract does not distinguish between payments for services performed within and outside the United States.

The parties disagree on what components of a hockey player's year are covered by the basic compensation in the NHL Standard Player's Contract, and therefore on how to compute the time-basis ratio. The taxpayer contends here as he did before the Tax Court that the contract salary compensates him for training camp, play-off, and even off-season services. The Commissioner argues and the Tax Court held that the contract salary covers only the regular season, and therefore that contract salary should be allocated to United States income in the same proportion that the number of days played in the United States during the regular season (164) bears to the total number of days in the regular season (179). We agree with the Commissioner and the Tax Court that the contract does not cover off-season services, but we hold that the Tax Court's finding that the contract does not compensate for training camp and the play-offs as well as the regular season is clearly erroneous. * * *

The Tax Court's holding was premised on provisions in the NHL contract and other players' agreements, and on the testimony of league and club officials. The first paragraph of the NHL Standard Player's Contract provides that if a player is "not in the employ of the Club for the whole period of the Club's games in the National Hockey League Championship Schedule," i.e., for the entire regular season, then he receives only part of his salary, in the same ratio to his total salary as the "ratio of the number of days of actual employment to the number of days of the League Championship Schedule of games." Paragraph 15 provides that if a player is suspended, he will not receive that portion of his salary equal to the ratio of "the number of days (of) suspension" to the "total number of days of the League Championship Schedule of games." The Tax Court concluded from these two paragraphs, and from the NHL's further agreements to pay players separate bonuses for participating in the play-offs and flat fees plus travel, room, and board for participating in training camp and pre-season exhibition games, that the basic contract salary did not cover play-off or training camp services.

We cannot uphold that finding, as we believe it clearly erroneous. The formulas for docking salary given in the contract's first and fifteenth paragraphs are not persuasive evidence that the salary compensates only for the regular season. These formulas may well use the number of days in the regular season in their denominators for administrative convenience (e.g., because the number of days to be spent in the play-offs cannot be known in advance) or to maximize the salary penalty per day lost. As to the testimony relied upon by the Tax Court, to a certain extent the owners and league officials have an interest in having the contract cover the shortest possible time span so as to maximize loss to suspended or striking players. Furthermore, two of the league and club officials, Leader and McFarland, testified that at least training camp time was included in the contract. The contract's plain language, moreover, requires in Paragraph 2(a) that a player "report to the Club training camp ... in good physical condition," and a player who fails to report to training camp and participate in exhibition games is subject under Paragraph 3 to a $500 fine, deductible from his basic salary. True, experienced players were paid $600 plus room and board for training camp under the Owner–Player Council minutes and Agreements, but we read those Agreements as providing that amount merely to cover the additional expenses of being away from home at training camp.

Paragraph 2 of the contract also plainly requires a player's participation in play-off games in exchange for basic contract salary. While it is true that bonuses are provided for play-off games won, these are simply added incentives, above and beyond salary, to get into and win the play-offs. In this respect, they are just like other incentive bonuses the contract provides to influence conduct during even the regular season, e.g., bonuses for the club's finishing in third place or better ($2500 in this case), or for the number of goals a player scores per season above certain minimums (at least $100 per goal over 20). Furthermore, players are required to participate in all play-off games for which they are eligible. Players may be terminated for failure to participate in the play-offs, but players receive nothing for the play-off games that they lose. Thus, we hold that the basic contract salary covered both play-off and training camp services.

We agree, however, that the off-season is not covered by the contract. During the off-season, the contract imposes no specific obligations on a player. Stemkowski argues that the obligation to appear at training camp "in good condition" makes off-season conditioning a contractual obligation. Fitness is not a service performed in fulfillment of the contract but a condition of employment. There was no evidence that Stemkowski was required to follow any mandatory conditioning program or was under any club supervision during the off-season. He was required to observe, if anything, only general obligations, applicable as well throughout the year, to conduct himself with loyalty to the club and the league and to participate only in approved promotional activities.

* * *

[¶ 2050]

NOTES

1. Stemkowski's working year was divided into the following parts for purposes of the prescribed allocation:

	Total Days	*Days in United States*
Training camp in Canada	27	0
Regular season	179	164
Playoffs	28	23
	234	187

He spent 131 off-season days outside of the United States.

2. In Favell, Jr. v. United States, 16 Cl.Ct. 700 (1989), nonresident alien professional hockey players were also required to effect an allocation on the basis of training camp, the regular season and post-season play-offs even though the league contracts required players to report for training in good physical condition. The court held that time devoted to off-season conditioning would not count because no compensable services were performed during the off-season period:

> It is not surprising, perhaps even to be expected, that hockey players are supposed to maintain a level of physical ability, under the Standard Player's Contracts at issue, in order to ably perform as professionals in their field. The court notes that professional athletes, like members of all professions, are expected to maintain a minimum level of ability to perform, or else risk losing their positions. In common parlance, maintaining an ability to properly perform a professional obligation is not generally compensated separately, but is assumed a condition for retaining employment. The words of the contracts at issue here do not suggest otherwise. For example, a college professor must be aware of all new developments in his or her field of expertise. A lawyer is required to keep abreast of new developments in the law, and a doctor must keep advised of rapidly changing technology and pharmacology to maintain the requi-

> site level of competence necessary to practice medicine. In the case of the professional hockey player plaintiffs, they are being required by their profession and the contracts they signed to maintain the required level of skill and physical fitness to play hockey, or else they risk demotion, suspension, or loss of employment. Such a requirement is a condition of the professional's continued employment and seemingly not unusual for professionals in various disciplines which require continuous competence.

16 Cl.Ct. at 724–25.

3. The IRS reconsidered its position and adopted the *Stemkowski* approach in Rev. Rul. 87–38, 1987–1 C.B. 176. It agreed, however, that per diem allowances received during the period at the training camp in Canada would constitute foreign-source income. The source of other per diem amounts paid for participating in specific games would be determined by the location of the games.

4. Regulations issued in 2005 emphasize that the allocation of employee compensation for individual taxpayers "is determined on a time basis" unless the taxpayer can persuade the IRS that an "alternative basis more properly determines the source of the compensation." Reg. § 1.861–4(b)(2)(ii)(A) and (C). An amount of compensation for labor or personal services performed in the United States determined on a time basis "is the amount that bears the same relation to the individual's total compensation as the number of days of performance of the labor or personal services of the individual within the United States bears to his or her total number of days of performance of labor or personal services." Further, the regulations establish a presumption that the relevant time period for allocation purposes is the calendar year. Reg. § 1.861–4(b)(2)(ii)(E). Regulations proposed in 2007 provide that in certain situations the allocation of source will be effected on an "event basis." Examples includes situations involving professional athletes and musicians who contract to perform in the United States and other countries. Prop. Reg. § 1.861–4(b)(2)(ii)(G).

Special source rules are prescribed for certain fringe benefits. Housing fringe benefits, education fringe benefits and local transportation fringe benefits will be sourced at the individual's principal place of work. Tax reimbursement fringe benefits will be sourced at the location of the jurisdiction imposing the tax. Hazardous or hardship duty pay fringe benefits will be sourced at the location of the hazardous or hardship duty zone. Moving expense reimbursement fringe benefits will be sourced at the employee's new principal place of work. Reg. § 1.861–4(b)(2)(ii)(D).

The regulations continue to provide that the source allocation of compensation income for entities and independent contractors "is determined on the basis that most correctly reflects the proper source of the income under the facts and circumstances of the particular case." Reg. § 1.861–4(b)(1) and (b)(2)(i).

[¶ 2055]

4. COMPENSATION OR ROYALTY INCOME?

Even when the source rules are clear, questions may arise regarding the appropriate characterization of the item of income with respect to which source is in question. For example, in a number of cases it has been necessary to distinguish compensation income from royalties.

[¶ 2060]

BOULEZ v. COMMISSIONER

United States Tax Court, 1984.
83 T.C. 584, aff'd, 810 F.2d 209 (D.C.Cir.1987).

[Pierre Boulez, a citizen of France, is a world-renowned music director and orchestra conductor. Mr. Boulez concluded a contract with CBS Records under which recordings would be made by the New York Philharmonic Orchestra and several other orchestras under his direction. The contract provided that "royalties" would be paid to Boulez based upon a percentage of the proceeds derived by CBS Records from the sale of the records with percentages varying depending upon a number of factors. Under the contract CBS Records retained the property rights to the master recordings, matrices and phonograph records produced under the agreement.

During the tax years in question, Boulez was a resident of Germany so that the United States–Germany Tax Treaty was applicable to him. Under the terms of the treaty, royalties were exempt from U.S. tax, but compensation income from U.S. sources was taxable in the United States. The recordings were made in the United States, and the IRS took the position that the payments, although characterized as "royalties" in the contract, were in substance compensation payments measured by record sales.]

KÖRNER, JUDGE: * * *.

* * *

1. THE FACTUAL QUESTION

By the contract entered into between petitioner and CBS Records in 1969, as amended, did the parties agree that petitioner was licensing or conveying to CBS Records a property interest in the recordings which he was retained to make, and in return for which he was to receive "royalties?" Petitioner claims that this is the case, and he bears the burden of proof to establish it. * * *

The contract between the parties is by no means clear. On the one hand, the contract consistently refers to the compensation which petitioner is to be entitled to receive as "royalties," and such payments are tied directly to the proceeds which CBS Records was to receive from sales of recordings which petitioner was to make. Both these factors suggest that the parties had a royalty arrangement, rather than a compensation arrangement, in mind in entering into the contract. We bear in mind, however, that the labels which the parties affix to a transaction are not necessarily determinative of their true nature, * * * and the fact that a party's remuneration under the contract is based on a percentage of future sales of the product created does not prove that a licensing or sale of property was intended, rather than compensation for services. *Karrer v. United States*, * * * 152 F.Supp. 66 ([Ct.Cl.] 1957).

On the other hand, the contract between petitioner and CBS Records is replete with language indicating that what was intended here was a contract for personal services. Thus, paragraph 1 * * * clearly states that CBS Records was engaging petitioner "to render your services exclusively for us as a producer and/or performer * * *. It is understood and agreed that such engagement by us shall include your services as a producer and/or performer." Paragraph 3 of the contract then requires petitioner to "perform" in the making of a certain number of recordings in each year. Most importantly, in the context of the present question, paragraph 4 of the contract * * * makes it clear that CBS considered petitioner's services to be the essence of the contract: petitioner agreed not to perform for others with respect to similar recordings during the term of the contract, and for a period of five years thereafter, and he was required to "acknowledge that your services are unique and extraordinary and that we shall be entitled to equitable relief to enforce the provision of this paragraph 4."

Under paragraph 5 of the contract * * *, it was agreed that the recordings, once made, should be entirely the property of CBS Records, "free from any claims whatsoever by you or any person deriving any rights or interests from you." Significantly, nowhere in the contract is there any language of conveyance of any alleged property right in the recordings by petitioner to CBS Records, nor any language indicating a licensing of any such purported right, other than the designation of petitioner's remuneration as being "royalties." The word "copyright" itself is never mentioned. Finally, under paragraph 13 of the contract, CBS Records was entitled to suspend or terminate its payments to petitioner "if, by reason of illness, injury, accident or refusal to work, you fail to perform for us in accordance with the provisions of this agreement."

Considered as a whole, therefore, and acknowledging that the contract is not perfectly clear on this point, we conclude that the weight of the evidence is that the parties intended a contract for personal services, rather than one involving the sale or licensing of any property rights which petitioner might have in the recordings which were to be made in the future.

2. THE LEGAL QUESTION

Before a person can derive income from royalties, it is fundamental that he must have an ownership interest in the property whose licensing or sale gives rise to the income. Thus, in *Patterson v. Texas Co.*, 131 F.2d 998, 1001 (5th Cir. 1942), the Court of Appeals adopted the definition of a "royalty" as "a share of the product or profit reserved by the owner for permitting another to use the property." Likewise, in *Hopag S.A. Holding De Participation, etc. v. Commissioner*, 14 T.C. 38 (1950), this Court held that in order for a payment to constitute a "royalty," the payee must have an ownership interest in the property whose use generates the payment * * *.

In its definition of royalties, the treaty embodies the same fundamental concept of ownership. Thus, in article VIII(3)(a) "royalties" are defined to mean "amounts paid as consideration for the use of, or *the right to use*, copyrights, artistic or scientific works * * * *or other like property or rights,*" and article VIII(3)(b) also states that the term "royalties" "shall include gains derived from the alienation of *any right for property* giving rise to such royalties." (Emphasis supplied.)

It is clear, then, that the existence of a property right in the payee is fundamental for the purpose of determining whether royalty income exists, and this is equally true under our domestic law as well as under the treaty.

Did the petitioner have any property rights in the recordings which he made for CBS Records, which he could either license or sell and which would give rise to royalty income here? We think not.

As noted in our findings, the basic contract between petitioner and CBS Records was executed in 1969. At that time, petitioner had no copyrightable property interest in the recordings which he made for CBS Records under the Copyright Act of 1909, as amended, * * * and petitioner concedes that this was so. * * *

Petitioner contends, however, that the Copyright Act of 1909 was amended by the Sound Recording Amendment of 1971 * * * and by virtue of this amendment, petitioner then acquired copyrightable property interests in the recordings which he thereafter made for CBS Records.

We think that petitioner is correct, in that the Sound Recording Amendment of 1971, *supra*, did amend the Copyright Act of 1909 so as to create, for the first time, copyrightable property interests in a musical director or performer such as petitioner who was making sound recordings of musical works, a property right which had not existed theretofore. * * * In discussing the changes made by the Sound Recording Amendment of 1971, and the new property rights therein created in both record producers such as CBS Records and performers such as petitioner, the legislative history contains the following significant statement: "As in the case of motion pictures, the bill does not fix the authorship, or the resulting ownership, of sound recordings, but leaves these matters to the employment relationship and bargaining among the interests involved." H. Rept. 92–487 (1971) * * *.

In spite of this change in the law in 1971, however, petitioner's contractual relationship with CBS Records went on as before. Neither the amendment to that contract of 1971, nor the further amendment in 1974, made any reference to the change of the copyright laws, nor modified the basic contract in any respect which would be pertinent to the instant question. We conclude, therefore, that the parties saw no need to modify their contract because they understood that even after the Sound Recording Amendment of 1971, petitioner still had no licensable or transferable property rights in the recordings which he made for CBS Records, and we think this was correct.

The Copyright Act of 1909, even after its amendment by the Sound Recording Amendment of 1971, describes the person having a copyrightable interest in property as the "author or proprietor," (17 U.S.C. sec. 9), and further provides that "the word 'author' shall include an employer in the case of works made for hire." 17 U.S.C. sec. 26. The above is a statutory enactment of the long-recognized rule that where a person is employed for the specific purpose of creating a work, including a copyrightable item, the fruits of his labor, carried out in accordance with the employment, are the property of his employer. The rule creates a rebuttable presumption to this effect, which can be overcome by express contractual provisions between the employee and the employer, reserving to the former the copyrightable interest * * *.

Here, the petitioner, a musical conductor of world-wide reputation, was employed to make recordings for CBS Records, and in doing so, was to exercise his peculiar and unique skills in accordance with his experience, talent, and best judgment. In these circumstances, we do not think that petitioner was an "employee" in the common law sense, but rather was an independent contractor, with the same relationship to CBS Records as a lawyer, an engineer, or an architect would have to his client, or a doctor to his patient * * *. This, however, provides no grounds for distinction, since the "works for hire" rule applies to independent contractors just as it does to conventional employees. * * *

In the instant case, the application of the "works for hire" rule means that petitioner had no copyrightable property interest in the recordings which he created for CBS Records, even after 1971. Petitioner was engaged for the specific purpose of making the recordings in question; his contract with CBS Records reserved no property rights in the recordings to him, and indeed made it specific that all such rights, whatever they were, were to reside in CBS Records. Under these circumstances, we do not think that petitioner has overcome the statutory presumption of the "works for hire" rule, nor that he has shown that he had any property interest in the recordings, either before 1971 or thereafter, which he could either license or sell to CBS Records so as to produce royalty income within the meaning of the treaty. This conclusion, in turn, reinforces our belief, which we have found as a fact, that the contract between petitioner and CBS was one for the performance of personal services.

* * *

[¶ 2065]

NOTES

1. In Ingram v. Bowers, 57 F.2d 65 (2d Cir.1932), Judge Learned Hand concluded that Enrico Caruso, the famous Italian tenor, had received compensation income as a result of recording for Victor Records even though the contract provided for the payment of "royalties." Caruso had sung (and recorded) in the United States. The records were sold within the United States and abroad. Caruso, a nonresident alien, contended that the foreign-source "royalties" deriving from foreign record sales were not subject to U.S. tax. However, Caruso had no property interest in the recordings or the copyrights. Accordingly, the "royalties" were simply a form of compensation income all of which was treated as U.S.-source income taxable in the United States.

2. In Karrer v. United States, 152 F.Supp. 66 (Ct.Cl.1957), the taxpayer was a nonresident alien who was employed as a scientist by a foreign corporation to perform research services in Switzerland. Under the terms of the employment agreement, the taxpayer received a percentage of the proceeds of the sale within the United States of synthetic vitamins produced with his inventions. The court held that payments to the taxpayer constituted foreign-source compensation income even though they were measured by proceeds of sales in the United States "because the employee's right to such payments derives from his services to his employer and not from any rights in inventions owned by the employee." 152 F.Supp. at 72.

3. In Rev. Rul. 74–555, 1974–2 C.B. 202, the nonresident alien taxpayer was an author who had entered into a contract with a U.S. corporation granting the corporation the first U.S. serial rights in his output of both long and short stories as well as the right to publish all of his new books. All of the works would be written outside of the United States. The IRS ruled that payments under the contract were to be taxed as royalties and not as compensation income. The Ruling noted that the contract did not commit the taxpayer to write anything and was, therefore, "neither a contract of employment nor a contract for the rendition of personal services." The rights constituted "licenses for the use of or for the privilege of using copyrights in the United States." As such, the payments were U.S.-source income subject to U.S. tax.

4. Jack Kramer, a legendary tennis player, agreed to allow a sporting goods company to produce a "signature line" of tennis racquets. He agreed to use his best efforts to promote the products and was paid 2.5 percent of the

net income derived therefrom. The Tax Court held that 70 percent of the income was properly characterized as a royalty for the right to use Kramer's name. The remaining 30 percent was characterized as compensation for the personal services he rendered to the company. The compensation income was taxed at a lesser maximum rate than the royalty income. Kramer v. Commissioner, 80 T.C. 768 (1983). A similar issue may arise in circumstances in which an athlete, such as a professional golfer, agrees to compete while wearing the logo of a sponsoring company. Should the source of such income be regarded as compensation or as a royalty for using the athlete's image and reputation?

[¶ 2070]

5. PAYMENT TO INDUCE EXECUTION OF EMPLOYMENT CONTRACT

Suppose that a taxpayer receives a lump-sum payment upon signing an employment contract that calls for the performance of services both within and without the United States. Is the payment solely attributable to the act of signing the contract or is it a portion of the compensation payable under the contract? In Linseman v. Commissioner, 82 T.C. 514 (1984), the taxpayer was yet another nonresident alien hockey player. He received a "signing bonus" for executing a contract with a professional hockey team in the United States. The Tax Court held that the signing bonus should be allocated between U.S. and foreign sources on the basis of the number of games contemplated to be played during the season within and without the United States. It explained its decision:

> [I]rrespective of any theoretical considerations as to the nature of a sign-on bonus [which the IRS argued was payment for a covenant not to compete], the primary purpose for such a bonus is to induce the player to sign a contract to play with the bonus-paying club. * * * Whatever the specifics of the sign-on agreement, the fact remains that the underlying purpose of such an agreement is to induce the player to perform the affirmative act of playing. It is that act which puts flesh on the bones of the sign-on agreement.

82 T.C. at 521–522.

[¶ 2075]

6. WHERE DOES ONE NOT COMPETE?

Payments received in return for a covenant not to compete are generally treated as compensation income. The following materials address the interesting question: If one agrees to do and does nothing, where does one do (or not do) it?

[¶ 2080]

KORFUND COMPANY, INC. v. COMMISSIONER

United States Tax Court, 1943.
1 T.C. 1180.

[This case required the determination of the source of payments from a U.S. corporation to a German corporation ("Zorn") and a nonresident German citizen ("Stoessel") under contracts in which, among other things, they had agreed not to compete in the United States and Canada.]

* * *

DISNEY, JUDGE: * * *.

* * *

The sole point of difference between the parties as to this income is whether it was earned from sources within the United States * * * and that, as already indicated, turns upon the source of the income derived from agreements not to compete with petitioner in the United States and Canada or give advice for the organization of, or to, a competitor.

The petitioner's contention is based upon the theory that the income was paid for agreements to refrain from doing specific things—negative acts. No defaults occurred and during the period of compliance the promisors were residents of Germany. Petitioner's contention is that negative performance is based upon a continuous exercise of will, which has its source at the place of location of the individual, and that, as the mental exertion involved herein occurred in Germany, the source of the income was in that country, not in the United States where the promise was given. The respondent's view of the question is, in short, that, as the place of performance would be in the United States if Zorn and Stoessel had violated their contractual obligations, abstinence of performance occurs in the same place. * * *

* * *

In *Sabatini v. Commissioner*, 98 Fed.(2d) 753, the taxpayer was an author and a subject of Great Britain. He was not in the United States before, nor during, the taxable years. By contract executed outside the United States he gave to a publisher in this country, among other rights, the right to publish certain books, as to some of which copyrights were not obtainable. As to these the taxpayer, by the contract above mentioned, agreed not to authorize any other publisher to publish the books in the United States so long as the *publisher* left in print its editions of the books. The taxpayer was to receive under the contracts amounts determinable from the number of volumes sold. * * * [The court held] that the income paid based upon the sale of these books was derived by the taxpayer from sources within the United States * * *.

* * *

We think the question here is governed by the principles laid down in the *Sabatini* * * * [and other] cases. Zorn had a right to compete with petitioner in the United States and Canada and for that purpose to form a competitive company or to assist others in forming one. Likewise, Stoessel had a right to serve other corporations or individuals in the United States engaged in a business similar to petitioner's as a consultant and to furnish them information of value to their business. They were willing to and did give up these rights in this country for a limited time for a consideration payable in the United States, just as did Sabatini in "foregoing his right to authorize others for a time to publish the works here." The Circuit Court in that case calls the exclusive right to publish an interest in property in the United States; so here, in our opinion, the rights of Stoessel and Zorn to do business in this country, in competition with the petitioner, were interests in property in this country. They might have received amounts here for services or information, but were willing to forego that right and possibility for a limited period for a consideration. What they received was in lieu of what they might have received. The situs of the right was in the United States, not elsewhere, and the income that flowed from the privileges was necessarily earned and produced here. Petitioner is merely using it, so to speak, for a specified time, subject to periodical payments to the owners of the rights. Upon the termination of the contracts the rights reverted to Zorn and Stoessel, and they were then free to exercise them independent of the agreements entered into with petitioner. These rights were property of value and the income in question was derived from the use thereof in the United States.

* * *

We find and hold that the source of all of the income in question was in the United States and is subject to withholding tax in the taxable year. * * *

[¶ 2085]

REVENUE RULING 74–108

1974–1 C.B. 248.

Advice has been requested whether a sign on fee, paid to a nonresident alien individual by a domestic corporation pursuant to a "sign on agreement" (agreement), is income from sources within the United States subject to income tax withholding under section 1441(a) * * *.

The taxpayer, a domestic corporation, operates a professional soccer club in the United States. The club is a member of a professional league affiliated with the governing body of world-wide professional soccer. The taxpayer entered into an agreement with a nonresident alien individual during the current taxable year. In order to induce the nonresident alien individual to sign the agreement, the taxpayer paid him a sign on fee. The agreement was executed by the taxpayer and the nonresident alien individual outside the United States.

The sign on fee is paid to induce the player to sign and become bound by the provisions of the agreement. The agreement does not require the player actually to play for the club; it is merely a preliminary agreement that is separate and distinct from a "uniform player" contract which binds a player to play soccer for a salary. When a player enters into an agreement, the taxpayer places him on its reserve list thereby protecting such player from recruiting efforts of any other club and preventing him from negotiating to play or playing for any other professional soccer club. No part of the sign on fee is attributable to future services, but the team anticipates the agreement and fee will induce the player to sign and become bound by the uniform player contract if the club wishes to use his services and a separate employment contract is negotiated for this purpose.

The professional soccer league with which the taxpayer's team is affiliated includes eleven members. Seven of the member teams, including the taxpayer, are located within the United States and the remaining four are located without the United States. The taxpayer's team schedule provides for some of its soccer games to be played in the United States and the remainder to be played in foreign countries.

* * *

Rev. Rul. 58–145, 1958–1 C.B. 360, provides that bonuses, which are not predicated on continuing employment, made to new baseball players solely for signing their first contracts, do not represent remuneration for services performed. Such bonuses are taxable to the baseball player as ordinary income in the taxable year received. Accordingly, in the instant case the sign on fee, which is similar to a bonus, paid to the nonresident alien individual is not compensation for labor or personal services for purposes of the source of income rules in section 861(a)(3) or section 862(a)(3) * * *.

The sign on fee, or bonus, was paid to insure that if the nonresident alien individual did play professional soccer, he would provide his services for the taxpayer only and to no other professional soccer club. * * * The bonus was paid as compensation for the promises made by the nonresident alien individual in the sign on agreement which in essence amounted to a covenant not to compete.

Compensation received for a promise not to compete is taxable as ordinary income and does not constitute income from the sale of property either real or personal. * * * Such compensation is fixed or determinable annual or periodical income and its source is the place where the promisor forfeited his right to act. *Korfund Co.*, 1 T.C. 1180 (1943). Therefore, amounts paid to a nonresident alien for his promise not to compete in the United States are subject to withholding under section 1441(a) * * *.

In the instant case the sign on fee is paid for the nonresident alien individual's promise not to compete both within and without the United States. Therefore, the sign on fee is attributable to sources both within and without the United States and the income must be apportioned appropriately. See section 863(b) * * * pertaining to the reporting of income partly from within and partly from without the United States.

Accordingly, a portion of the sign on fee in the instant case is income from sources within the United States and is subject to withholding under the provisions of section 1441(a) * * *. The basis upon which the sign on fee is allocated as income from sources within and sources without the United States must be reasonable and based on the facts and circumstances in each case. For example, in some cases it may be reasonable to make the allocation on the basis of the relative value of the taxpayer's services within and without the United States, or on the basis of the portion of the year during which soccer is played within and without the United States. Where a reasonable basis for allocation does not exist, the entire sign on fee is income from sources within the United States and is subject to section 1441(a).

[¶ 2090]

NOTES

1. Compare the analysis in the Ruling to the court's decision in *Linseman*, at ¶ 2070.

2. The withholding requirements of Sections 1441 et seq. are explored at ¶ 4120. In general payors of certain types of U.S.-source income are required thereby to withhold 30 percent of such income when paid to foreign persons. The amount withheld is then paid to the IRS on behalf of the payee, who is the taxpayer.

[¶ 2095]

7. PAYMENTS IN LIEU OF COMPENSATION

Suppose that a foreign person is entitled to compensation for services performed abroad on behalf of a U.S. corporation. It is clear that the compensation income is foreign-source income despite the nationality of the payor. What if the U.S. corporation breaches the contract and is required by a U.S. court to pay damages to the foreign person? If the payment is treated under the interest source rules, which focus on the identity and residence of the debtor, the payments would probably be characterized as from U.S. sources. The IRS has ruled, however, that such damage payments will be regarded as foreign-source income because the services would have been performed abroad and the payments effectively substituted for foreign-source compensation income. Rev. Rul. 83–177, 1983–2 C.B. 112.

[¶ 2100]

8. MIXED CHARACTERIZATION

In some situations, receipts of income will consist of several forms requiring the application of different source rules and producing different results. For example, suppose that a nonresident alien performs services abroad for a U.S. corporation. When the corporation fails to pay the compensation owed, a suit is filed in a U.S. court. The nonresident alien collects compensation with interest. The damages will be treated as foreign-source compensation income; the interest will probably be U.S.-source income.

In Rev. Rul. 79–388, 1979–2 C.B. 270, the taxpayer was a nonresident alien who had been employed by a U.S. corporation. During his years with the corporation, the taxpayer had worked both for a foreign branch and in the United States. The IRS ruled that payments from the corporation's pension plan were foreign-source income to the extent the payments were attributable to corporate contributions during the period that the taxpayer had worked overseas. However, the portion of the payments attributable to corporate contributions while the taxpayer worked in the United States or to profits of the U.S. pension trust constituted U.S.-source income.

[¶ 2105]

F. SALE OF REAL PROPERTY

Gain from the sale of real property is, unsurprisingly, sourced at the place where the property is located. Accordingly, the sale of land, buildings and other real property located in the United States will generate U.S.-source income. § 861(a)(5). Gain realized from the disposition of land and buildings located elsewhere will be treated as foreign-source income. § 862(a)(5).

G. SALE OF PERSONAL PROPERTY

[¶ 2110]

1. PURCHASE AND SALE OF PERSONAL PROPERTY

Section 865 prescribes the rules for determining the source of gain or loss from the sale of personal property. Section 865 sets forth an apparent rule of general application based upon the residence of the seller, and a special definition of "residence" for situations in which the section applies. § 865(a) and (g). However, source determinations will often depend upon the application of a series of exceptions which reflect a number of variables, including particularly whether the property is inventory and whether the property has been used in connection with a U.S. trade or business.

[¶ 2115]

a. Inventory Property

The source of income realized from the purchase and sale of inventory property will generally be determined by the situs of the property at the time of the transfer of title. §§ 861(a)(6), 862(a)(6) and 865(b). This so-called "passage-of-title" test had generally been applied to all sales of personal property prior to the adoption of Section 865 in 1986.

The place and time of sale are the place where and the time when the rights, title and interest of the seller in the property are transferred to the buyer. This rule derives from the law of sales and generally allows the parties to arrange title passage wherever they choose. Tax motives for the choice are generally not grounds for challenge. Such a result may be wholly justifiable for purposes of commercial and financial law. However, the rule opens the door to manipulation of the source rules and, therefore, tax consequences. Is this consistent with the general objectives of tax policy?

Reg. § 1.861–7(c) qualifies the passage-of-title rule by providing that, when the sales transaction is arranged in a particular manner for the primary purpose of tax avoidance, "all factors of the transaction, such as negotiations, the execution of the agreement, the location of the property, and the place of payment, will be considered, and the sale will be treated as having been consummated at the place where the substance of the sale occurred." While courts recognize the qualification, they tend to find reasons for not applying it, as in the case below.

[¶ 2120]

A.P. GREEN EXPORT CO. v. UNITED STATES

United States Court of Claims, 1960.
284 F.2d 383.

[The issue was whether a U.S. corporation qualified under the 1939 Code as a Western Hemisphere trade corporation and, therefore, was entitled to a substantial tax rate reduction accorded to such corporations. The requirements included doing all business in the Western Hemisphere, deriving 90 percent or more of gross income from the active conduct of a trade or business and deriving 95 percent or more of gross income from sources outside the United States. See former §§ 921 and 922. The latter requirement provided the issue in this case. The Western Hemisphere trade corporation provisions have since been repealed.]

JONES, CHIEF JUDGE:

* * *

Plaintiff is a wholly owned subsidiary of the A.P. Green Fire Brick Company, Inc., and was formed for the specific purpose of operating as a

Western Hemisphere trade corporation. Its sole business consisted of buying fire brick and other refractory products from the parent company and selling them either to A.P. Green Fire Brick Company, Ltd., a fully owned Canadian subsidiary of the parent company, or to various unaffiliated customers in Central or South America. The plaintiff maintained no sales force or business establishment outside the United States. As orders or inquiries came in, plaintiff would respond with an offer describing the goods specifically. The goods were priced c.i.f. port of entry or occasionally f.o.b. factory, Mexico, Missouri, with all delivery costs figured in the price quotations. Plaintiff carefully noted in each offer:

> "This quotation shall be binding upon A.P. Green Export Company upon acceptance by you and the placing of that acceptance in the mails.
>
> "Title to these goods and responsibility for their shipment and safe carriage shall be in A.P. Green Export Company until their delivery to the customer at destination."

In due course these offers were accepted and returned by mail. Shipment was by public carrier on rail and water often under a straight bill of lading with the buyer named as consignee. In most cases freight charges were prepaid by the plaintiff. Insurance was purchased by the plaintiff for his benefit but the policy was negotiable and covered the goods 15 to 30 days beyond their arrival at the final port. Documents were surrendered against acceptance after delivery; payment was by 30–day sight drafts. Frequently, these drafts were discounted by plaintiff's bank before their acceptance, always with full recourse to the plaintiff. Standard commercial practices were followed throughout.

* * *

The title-passage test as determinative of where a sale has occurred, and * * * where plaintiff's income was derived, is open to serious criticism, for it causes the incidence of the United States tax to depend upon the vagaries of the law of sales. The time and place of passage of title to ascertained goods is subject to the consensual arrangements of the parties. Williston on Sales, sec. 259, 2d ed. * * * This all-important consent is most frequently expressed by the parties, but if not it is determined at the time of controversy by a number of presumptions set up by the law of sales. These fairly complex rules regarding passage of title are extremely important in determining such questions as the risk of loss of goods in transit, or the rights of successive creditors, but have little or no bearing on the question of where income is earned and how it should be apportioned among the various countries in which business is conducted. * * * The title-passage test has been further criticized as imposing inequitable tax burdens on taxpayers engaged in substantially similar transactions, such as upon exporters, some of whose customers require that property in the goods passes in the United States. * * *

Whatever its weaknesses, however, the title-passage test as determinative of place of sale and source of income has been overwhelmingly adopted by the courts in recent decisions. * * * We believe no other suitable test providing an adequate degree of certainty for the taxpayer has been proposed. The use of vague "contacts" or "substance of the transaction" criteria would make it more difficult for corporations engaged in Western Hemisphere trade to plan their operations so as to receive the deductions granted them only if they derive their income from sources outside the United States. Tests based upon the destination of the property sold or on the locus of the selling activity are equally vulnerable to the charge of unfair discrimination. See United States v. Balanovski, 236 F.2d 298 * * *.

If then the passage of title does control the place of sale and the source of income, logic demands that we specify the place where title to the goods passed. It is a black letter rule of the law of sales that title to specific goods passes from the seller to the buyer in any manner and on any condition explicitly agreed on by the parties. * * * Examination of the sales contracts before us shows that the parties expressed their intentions as follows:

> "Title to these goods and the responsibility for their shipment and safe carriage shall be in the A.P. Green Export Company until their delivery to the customer at destination."

Such a clear statement, undoubtedly binding upon the parties in an ordinary sales or contract dispute, would seem to end our inquiry into the intention of the parties. But the Government urges that the terms of shipment raise presumptions that the parties intended to pass title in the United States contrary to their stated intentions, and that we must acknowledge the effect of these presumptions. We find no merit in this contention. It is true that in some instances the shipping terms, particularly the c.i.f. (cost, insurance, and freight) transactions, indicate presumptively that title passed at the place of shipment. * * * But the authorities are agreed that these presumptions are useful in ascertaining intention only if no *express* intention of the parties appears. * * * The Government does not suggest the expressions in the contract were fraudulent. It does maintain that we must disregard the *stated* intentions of the parties in determining where title passed because the ultimate motive for these statements was the plaintiff's desire to avoid a tax.

We believe the Government has erred in failing to distinguish two separate legal consequences flowing from the same act of expression by the parties, the consequences being the passage of title and the avoidance of a tax. Title passes in a sales transaction as a result of the mutual arrangement of the buyer and the seller, whatever the reason or motivation for the consent. It would be an unjustified distortion of this law for us to disregard the parties' stated intention to pass title outside the United States because they were principally motivated by a desire to avoid a tax.

This is *not* to say that under the tax law, in an atmosphere of tax avoidance, we may not find that the passage of title no longer governs the place of sale and the source of income. The next section of our opinion covers this problem. It is perfectly clear, however, that the parties intended to pass title to the goods outside the United States; this being determinative, we find that title to the goods did pass outside the United States.

* * * We now come to the problem of tax avoidance to which we have just referred. The Government urges that we examine the transactions here in the penetrating light of Gregory v. Helvering, 293 U.S. 465, * * * for it claims that plaintiff's principal purpose in organizing and operating the export corporation was tax avoidance.

Organizing a Western Hemisphere trade corporation does not constitute tax avoidance and the Commissioner * * * has so ruled * * *. Neither the motives, occasion for, nor the time of the *organization* of the plaintiff corporation affects its eligibility for tax relief. The Code provisions themselves have created this new business norm, a norm motivated entirely by a tax result.

The questions concerning the methods of operating the export corporation are not so easily answered. The facts show that the plaintiff delayed the passage of title with at least one eye on the Revenue Code. * * * May we, therefore, depart from the title-passage test in determining the place of sale and source of plaintiff's income? The defendant says we must and submits in support a ruling by the Commissioner which states:

> "Where the sales transaction is arranged for the primary purpose of tax avoidance, the foregoing rules (passage of title test) will not be applied. In such case, all factors of the transaction such as negotiations, execution of the agreement, location of the property and place of payment will be considered, and the sale will be treated as having been consummated at the place where the substance of the sale occurred." [G.C.M. 25131, 1947–2 Cum.Bull. 85.]

The defendant also relies on United States v. Balanovski * * *. At first glance the Balanovski case seems to give little support to the defendant's position. There, the facts showed that goods were purchased in the United States and sold to the Argentine Government. In determining the source of income of the Argentine broker, Balanovski, the district court applied a "substance of the transaction" test and determined that Balanovski had not earned income in the United States. The Court of Appeals for the Second Circuit reversed the district court on the exact point of where the sales had taken place. It rejected the "substance of the transaction" test and rested its decision on the traditional ground of looking to the point of passage of title.

But the final passage of Judge Clark's opinion in Balanovski, supra, is notable:

> "Of course this test [title-passage] may present problems, as where passage of title is formally delayed to avoid taxes. Hence it is not necessary, nor is it desirable, to require rigid adherence to this test under all circumstances."

The Government concludes from this that in instances where passage of title is formally delayed to avoid taxes the court would feel free to look beyond the question of where title passed. Furthermore, it is suggested that the court tacitly accepted a "substance of the transaction" criterion as only by examining the indicia of substance would it be possible to decide whether passage of title was delayed merely to avoid taxes.

Along with this we must consider the statement of Judge Learned Hand in the Gregory case that "a transaction, otherwise within an exception of the tax law, does not lose its immunity, because it is actuated by a desire to avoid, or, if one choose, to evade, taxation. Any one may so arrange his affairs that his taxes shall be as low as possible; he is not bound to choose that pattern which will best pay the Treasury; there is not even a patriotic duty to increase one's taxes." 69 F.2d 809, at page 810 * * *. It is undeniable that this is a doctrine essential to industry and commerce in a society like our own in which as far as possible business is always shaped to the form best suited to keep down taxes. * * * The question always is whether the transaction under scrutiny is in fact what it appears to be in form. A corporate reorganization may be illusory; a contract of sale may be intended only to deceive others. In such cases the transaction as a whole is different from its appearance. It is the intent that controls, but the intent which counts is one which contradicts the apparent transaction, not the intent to escape taxation. * * *

Why the parties in the present case wished to make the sales as they did is one thing, but that is irrelevant under the Gregory case so long as the consummated agreements were no different than they purported to be, and provided the retention of title was not a sham but had a commercial purpose apart from the expected tax consequences. * * * Plaintiff's operations meet these tests. The facts show that the parties did intend title to pass outside the United States. There was no sham. Retaining title until delivery served a legitimate business purpose apart from the expected tax consequences. A moment's contemplation of the current headline disputes among countries all over the world underscores the prudence of exporters who retain title to goods until delivery. A sudden trade embargo, a seizure or a nationalization of an industry, a paralyzing nationwide strike—under these circumstances the exporter who retains title diverts his shipments with little difficulty to friendlier ports and markets. Of additional significance is the fact that retaining title permits the shipper to insure his goods in the United States. If loss occurs he can recover directly and in dollars with the obvious benefits of avoiding circuitous litigation and the fluctuations of foreign currency.

On the other hand, we recognize that plaintiff would have received certain other benefits by passing title to his goods in the United States. Plaintiff was faced with a choice of two legitimate courses of conduct, either of which would be commercially sound and justifiable. We are not prepared to say that in this situation plaintiff was bound to choose that course which would best pay the Treasury.

Our conclusion from all of the above is that the sales were made outside the United States. However, our conclusion would be no different if we followed the defendant's suggestion and went beyond the passage of title to the other elements "of substance" in the transactions. Orders were solicited outside the United States. In every case, the contract of sale was made outside the United States; the destinations of the goods and the competitive markets for the goods were outside the United States. In most cases, the place of payment was outside the United States.

* * *

[¶ 2125]

NOTE

Under the court's analysis, when might the IRS succeed in the application of a rule other than title passage? Can taxpayers always devise some adequately convincing business reason for passing title outside the United States? In United States v. Balanovski, 236 F.2d 298 (2d Cir.1956), cert. denied, 352 U.S. 968 (1957)(as evidenced from the discussion in the *Green Export* opinion), the court seemed to leave open the possibility of a different result by observing that the test "may present problems, as where passage of title is formally delayed to avoid taxes. Hence it is not necessary, nor is it desirable, to require rigid adherence to [the passage-of-title] test under all circumstances." 236 F.2d at 306.

There may thus be limits to the application of the passage-of-title test. Suppose, for example, that a foreign corporation were to buy from its U.S. producer-parent corporation and resell to a purchaser located in the United States while passing title outside of the United States. The foreign subsidiary argues that the resulting profit was not from U.S. sources and therefore not subject to U.S. tax. The IRS might then be in a very strong position to urge the application of the exception to the passage-of-title test and to argue that the passage of title abroad should be disregarded for tax purposes. This scheme may also fail because of the controlled foreign corporation provisions of the Code. See § 954(d), discussed in Chapter 6.

[¶ 2130]

b. Noninventory Personal Property Not Subject to a Special Rule

Section 865(a) effectively provides that the source of income derived from the sale of noninventory personal property will be determined by the residence of the seller unless a special rule applies to the property or the transaction. When there is no such special provision and Section 865(a) applies, gains realized by a U.S. resident are U.S.-source income; the source of such income realized by a foreign resident is foreign. The legal or financial characteristics of the sale will not affect the determination of source.

A "U.S. resident" for purposes of applying these source rules is defined as a U.S. citizen or a resident alien with no "tax home" in a foreign country, a nonresident alien with a "tax home" in the United States and U.S. corporations, trusts and estates. § 865(g). A "tax home" is a taxpayer's home for purposes of determining the deductibility of travel expenses under Section 162(a)(2). However, if an individual's "abode" is in the United States, the tax home will be deemed to be in the United States. § 911(d)(3). Moreover, a U.S. citizen or resident alien will not be treated as a foreign resident unless an income tax equal to at least ten percent of the gain derived from the sale is actually paid to a foreign country with respect to it. § 865(g)(2).

The provisions of Section 865 are generally directed to the treatment of gains from the sale of personal property. However, Section 865(j) directs the Treasury to prescribe regulations relating to the treatment of losses from sales of personal property. The basic approach of the regulations, sometimes referred to as the "reciprocal to gain principle," is to treat losses in the same source category that would have obtained if gain had been realized in the transaction. Reg. §§ 1.865–1 and–2. The Tax Court applied the residence-of-the-seller source rule to losses in International Multifoods Corp. v. Commissioner, 108 T.C. 579 (1997). As a result, the loss realized upon the sale of stock of a Brazilian corporation by a U.S. corporation was considered to be from U.S. sources for purposes of computing the U.S. corporation's foreign tax credit limitation under Section 904. The stock did not qualify as stock of an affiliate under Section 865(f).

[¶ 2135]

c. Depreciable or Amortizable Tangible Personal Property

Section 865(c) establishes a form of recapture rule by providing that gain realized from the sale of depreciable or amortizable tangible personal property will be treated as U.S.-source income to the extent that depreciation or amortization deductions were previously allocated against U.S.-source income. The special rule effectively denies foreign persons the opportunity to take such deductions against U.S. income and then avoid tax on the sale of the property. The rules for determining the taxable income of foreign persons are discussed in Chapters 3 and 4. If depreciation deductions offset foreign-source income, recapture gain is foreign-source. § 865(c)(1). If depreciation deductions were taken against both

U.S.- and foreign-source income, the recapture amount will generally be allocated proportionately. To the extent that gain exceeds the depreciation or amortization deductions recaptured under this provision, the source rules for inventory property will apply. § 865(c)(2).

The operation of this recapture rule can be demonstrated by a simple example. Suppose that a foreign person acquires for $100,000 machinery that is used in connection with a U.S. trade or business. Under provisions analyzed in Chapter 3, the foreign person may take depreciation deductions against the U.S.-source income generated from the operation of the business. Suppose that such deductions of $20,000 were taken against such U.S.-source income, thereby reducing the adjusted basis of the asset to $80,000, before the foreign person discontinued its U.S. operation and sold the asset to a foreign purchaser with title passing overseas. If the asset were later sold for $90,000, the gain of $10,000 would be treated as U.S.-source income under the recapture rule. If, instead, the asset were later sold for $110,000, $20,000 of the gain would be treated as U.S.-source income under the recapture provision. The remaining gain of $10,000 would be treated as foreign-source income under the title-passage test.

[¶ 2140]

d. Gain From Sale of Intangible Property

The source of gain realized from the sale of intangible property will generally be determined by the residence of the taxpayer if there is a fixed price. However, to the extent that payments are contingent on the productivity, use or disposition of the intangible property, the source of income will be determined by reference to the source rules for royalty income discussed at ¶ 2015 even if the transaction is characterized as a sale by the parties and the relevant documents. § 865(d)(1). Gain realized from the sale of goodwill will generally be deemed to be from sources in the country where the goodwill was generated. § 865(d)(3). To the extent that amortization deductions have been taken against U.S.- or foreign-source income in respect of intangible property other than goodwill, however, gain not exceeding the deductions taken will be treated as U.S.- or foreign-source income respectively. §§ 865(d)(4)(A) and 865(c)(1).

In many instances it will be difficult to distinguish goodwill from other intangible property. In International Multifoods Corp. v. Commissioner, 108 T.C. 25 (1997), the taxpayer, a U.S. corporation, sold its Asian and Pacific Mister Donut operations for $2,050,000. In determining the source of gain realized in the transaction, the court held that goodwill was not sold separately from the sale of franchise rights and trademarks. Accordingly, no portion of the gain could be sourced under the special rule for goodwill; because the taxpayer was a U.S. resident, all of the gain was determined to be U.S.-source income under Section 865(d)(1)(A). The court noted that intangible assets such as trademarks and franchises are "inextricably related" to goodwill and concluded that the special source rule for goodwill

> is applicable only where goodwill is separate from the other intangible assets that are specifically listed in section 865(d)(2). If the sourcing provision contained in section 865(d)(3) also extended to the goodwill element embodied in the other intangible assets enumerated in section 865(d)(2), the exception would swallow the rule. Such an interpretation would nullify the general rule that income from the sale of an intangible asset by a U.S. resident is to be sourced in the United States.

108 T.C. at 37–38. The portion of the sales price properly attributable to a covenant not to compete in the buyer's foreign territory was, however, treated as foreign-source income.

[¶ 2145]

e. Gain From Sale of Stock in Foreign Affiliated Corporation

Section 865(f) establishes a special source rule for the sale of stock by a U.S. corporation in a foreign "affiliate" corporation. If the sale occurs in the country in which the affiliate conducts an active trade or business and if more than 50 percent of its gross income during a base period derived from the active conduct of a trade or business in that country, gain will be treated as foreign-source income. The base period is the three tax years prior to the year of the sale. The foreign corporation will generally be treated as an "affiliate" if the U.S. corporation owns, directly or indirectly, at least 80 percent of the total voting power and value of its stock. §§ 865(i)(4) and 1504(a).

[¶ 2150]

f. Special Exception Where Sales Derive From Office or Fixed Place of Business Maintained by Resident in Another Country

Income from certain personal property sales by U.S. residents attributable to an office or fixed place of business maintained in a foreign country will be treated as foreign-source income if an income tax of at least ten percent is actually paid to a foreign country with respect to such income. § 865(e)(1). This special rule does not, however, modify the rules applicable to sales of inventory, depreciable property, intangible property treated under the royalty source rules, goodwill or stock of a foreign affiliate.

Income from certain sales of personal property by nonresidents which are attributable to an office or other fixed place of business in the United

States will be treated as U.S.-source income. Such treatment will apply to inventory unless it is sold "for use, disposition, or consumption outside the United States" and a foreign office or fixed place of business "materially participated" in the sale. § 865(e)(2).

The principles set forth in Section 864(c)(5), which are discussed at ¶ 3045, determine whether a taxpayer has an office or other fixed place of business and whether a sale is attributable thereto. § 865(e)(3).

[¶ 2155]

g. Gain From Sale of Stock Treated as U.S. Real Property Interest

Special taxing rules have been created to tax gain realized by foreign investors in U.S. real property and gains realized by foreign shareholders of U.S. corporations that are principally invested in U.S. real property. Under Section 897, a "United States real property interest" is defined to include both real property located in the United States and stock in such U.S. corporations. A special source rule was also adopted to implement the taxing provisions. Section 861(a)(5) provides that gains realized from the sale of U.S. real property interests are to be treated as U.S-source income. Section 897 is discussed at ¶¶ 4185 et seq.

[¶ 2160]

2. PRODUCTION AND SALE OF INVENTORY PROPERTY

While Section 863(b)(2) of the Code requires that gain from the production and sale of inventory property be allocated between U.S. and foreign sources where the production and the sale do not both occur either inside or outside the United States, the method of allocation is not statutorily prescribed. The appropriate method of allocation has been the subject of much discussion and debate because the allocation is likely to have a significant effect on the tax burden of manufacturers that export a portion of their product. For example, because of the way in which the limitations on the foreign tax credit are determined (see Chapters 5 and 7), it is usually in the interest of a U.S. exporter to maximize its foreign-source allocation of the income derived from the manufacture and export activity. Under specified circumstances, the regulations permit the taxpayer to use one of three methods to effect the allocation. Reg. § 1.863–3(b).

The objective of the regulations is to divide the total profits between the production function and the sales and distribution functions for purposes of appropriately determining the source of the income. "Production" for these purposes includes inventory that is "created, fabricated, manufactured, extracted, processed, cured or aged." Reg. § 1.863–

3(c)(1)(i)(A). The generally applicable method is to allocate half of the gross income from the sale to production activity and half to sales activity (sometimes called the "50–50 method"). Reg. § 1.863–3(b)(1). The portion allocated to production activity is divided between U.S. and foreign sources based on the comparative adjusted bases of production assets (tangible and intangible assets owned directly by the taxpayer that are used to produce the inventory concerned) located inside and outside the United States. Reg. § 1.863–3(c). Thus, if a product were wholly produced within the United States, half of the gross income realized upon its sale would be treated as U.S.-source income. The production assets formula used by the taxpayer may be challenged by the IRS when the taxpayer has sought to manipulate its application to reduce U.S. tax liability. Reg. § 1.863–3(c)(1)(iii).

The source of the portion of gross income allocated to the sales activity is normally determined by application of the passage-of-title test discussed at ¶ 2115. Reg. § 1.863–3(c)(2). If title on all export sales is passed outside the United States, the remaining half of the gross income will be foreign-source. The application of the passage-of-title test is subject to two qualifications. First, if the transaction is arranged in a particular manner for the primary purpose of tax avoidance, the substance of the transaction will determine source. See Reg. § 1.861–7(c). Second, if the property is wholly produced in the United States and is sold for use, consumption or disposition in the United States, the place of sale (and, therefore, the source of income) will be presumed to be the United States. Reg. § 1.863–3(c)(2).

In lieu of the 50–50 method, the taxpayer may elect to base the allocation upon an independent factory price ("IFP") that is "fairly established" by sales to unrelated parties. Reg. § 1.863–3(b)(2)(i). Such a price will be fairly established only if the taxpayer regularly sells part of its output to wholly independent distributors or other selling concerns in such a way as reasonably to reflect the income earned from production activity. If the taxpayer elects to use this method, the amount of the gross sales price equal to the IFP will be treated as attributable to production activity. The excess will be attributed to the sales activity. If the taxpayer elects to use this method, it must be used for sales of inventory items that are "substantially similar in physical characteristics and function, and are sold at a similar level of distribution." Reg. § 1.863–3(b)(2)(ii).

Under a third approach, the IRS may in some cases agree to the use of the taxpayer's usual books of account. Reg. § 1.863–3(b)(3).

Finally, it should be noted that taxpayers may elect to apply the allocation principles set forth in the regulations to determine the source of taxable, rather than gross, income from sales governed by Section 863. Reg. § 1.863–2(b).

The differences between the 50–50 and the IFP methods, which are explicitly authorized in the regulations, can be demonstrated in a simple example. Suppose that American Fabricator, a U.S. corporation, produces widgets at a cost of $40 per unit. The company sells widgets to foreign consumers for $100 per unit, with title passing outside of the United States. The company also sells the product to independent distributors at the factory for $80 per unit. The company realizes income of $60 per unit from its sales to foreign consumers. Under the 50–50 method, $30 is treated as U.S.-source manufacturing income and $30 is treated as foreign-source sales income. However, if the IFP method is used, $40 will be treated as U.S.-source manufacturing income (the IFP of $80 less the cost of $40) and only $20 will be treated as foreign-source sales income. In most instances, the corporation would prefer for U.S. income tax purposes to maximize its foreign-source income to maximize foreign tax credits. Accordingly, it would in this instance use the 50–50 method.

A different approach applies in respect of natural resources. In essence the gross receipts from the sale abroad of products derived "from the ownership or operation of any farm, mine, oil or gas well, other natural deposits, or timber within the United States" must be allocated on the basis of the fair market value of the product at the export terminal. The same approach is applied for such products derived in other countries and imported into the United States. Reg. § 1.863–1(b).

[¶ 2165]

3. SALE OF INTANGIBLE PROPERTY, ROYALTY OR COMPENSATION FOR SERVICES?

To the extent payments for the sale of intangible property rights are "contingent upon productivity, use, or disposition," any gain must be sourced according to the royalty rules. § 865(d)(1)(B). The rationale for this exception is that such payment terms more closely resemble those commonly used in licensing agreements. The special rule is also intended to defend against excessively facile opportunities for taxpayers to avoid U.S. tax by concluding arrangements that would invoke inappropriate source rules. If the purchase price is fixed, the gain is sourced under the general rule of Section 865(a) in the taxpayer's country of residence. § 865(d)(1)(A).

As indicated in earlier portions of this Chapter, in some transactions several different source rules might arguably apply. In the Ruling that follows, the IRS analyzes a transaction that might alternatively be characterized as a sale, as a royalty or as compensation for services. Note that the results of applying the possible source rules may differ dramatically under the alternative characterizations.

[¶ 2170]

REVENUE RULING 84–78

1984–1 C.B. 173.

ISSUE

Whether the amount that a domestic corporation receives from a foreign corporation for the right to broadcast a live boxing match taking place in the United States via closed circuit television only in the country in which the foreign corporation is incorporated is foreign source income under the circumstances described below.

FACTS

Situation 1. A domestic corporation, *Y*, obtained from the contestants in a prize fight, which will take place in the United States, the exclusive rights to broadcast the fight live and to record the broadcast for subsequent viewing. *Y* entered into a contract with *FX*, a foreign corporation incorporated in foreign country *FC*. The contract provides that for a stipulated lump-sum payment to be paid by *FX* to *Y*, *FX* will have the right to broadcast the prize fight via closed circuit television only to an audience in *FC*. The payment that *Y* receives from *FX* under the contract is to be refunded to *FX* if the fight is cancelled for any reason. The broadcast and the simultaneous recording of the broadcast will be protected under the copyright laws of Title 17 of the United States Code * * *. The broadcast right that *Y* transfers to *FX* is nonexclusive, and the duration of such right is only for the live showing of the fight. *FX*'s right to broadcast the prize fight does not include recording rights for subsequent viewing. The contract is negotiated, executed and the consideration is paid in the United States.

Situation 2. The facts are the same as in Situation 1, except that *Y* transfers to a foreign corporation, *FXB*, incorporated in foreign country *FCB*, a broadcasting right in the specified prize fight that is exclusive and exercisable only in *FCB*.

* * *

[The Ruling then summarized the source rules that were then in effect and arguably applicable to the transactions (income from the sale of personal property, royalty income or compensation income for the performance of services) and cited Rev. Rul. 74–555, summarized at ¶ 2065, Note 3.]

Rev. Rul. 54–409, 1954–2 C.B. 174, holds that a copyright is divisible into separate properties, and that if the owner of a copyright granted to another the exclusive right to exploit the copyrighted work in a particular medium throughout the life of the copyright, then the consideration received for the use of the copyright would be treated as proceeds from the sale of property * * *.

The source of the payment received by *Y* in exchange for the grant of the right to broadcast the prize fight as United States or foreign income is dependent upon whether the characterization of the income is compensation for labor or personal services, income derived from the sale of personal property, or royalties for the use of or for the privilege of using a copyright or other like property, or some other type of income.

Situation 1. The contract entered into between *Y* and *FX* does not give *FX* any control over when or where the prize fight will take place or how the arrangements for the fight will be made, nor does it confer any legal rights over the contestants in the fight; it merely gives *FX* the right to broadcast the fight if it occurs. Further, the activities of *Y* are not exclusively performed for the benefit of *FX*, such that *FX* would own the product of *Y*'s labor. *See Ingram v. Bowers*, 57 F.2d 65 (2d Cir.1932) * * * . Accordingly, the payment received by *Y* is not compensation for labor or personal services.

The broadcasting right that *Y* transfers to *FX* is not exclusive, and the duration of such right is not for the remaining life of *Y*'s copyright, but is only for the live broadcast of the specified prize fight. *FX* cannot exploit the broadcast for the life of the copyright since it has no recording rights. The payment that *Y* receives from *FX* for such right, therefore, is not income derived from the sale of personal property. Rev. Ruls. 54–509 and 60–226. The payment that *Y* receives from *FX* for such right is for the use of, or for the privilege of using, a copyright without the United States.

Situation 2. Although the broadcasting right that *Y* transfers to *FXB* is exclusive, the duration of such right is not for the remaining life of *Y*'s copyright, but is limited only to the live broadcast of the specified prize fight. Because the broadcasting right that *Y* transfers is for less than the remaining life of *Y*'s copyright, the payment that *Y* receives from *FXB* for such right is not income derived from the sale of personal property, even though the right is for the exclusive use of *FXB*. *See* * * * *Pickren v. United States*, 249 F.Supp. 560 (M.D.Fla.1965), *aff'd*, 378 F.2d 595 (5th Cir.1967), in which the court held that the grant of exclusive rights in secret formulas and trade names for less than the remaining lives of such properties did not constitute a sale. The payment that *Y* receives from *FXB* for the broadcasting right is for the use of, or for the privilege of using, a copyright without the United States. * * *

HOLDINGS

Situation 1. The payment that *Y* receives from *FX* is foreign source income under section 862(a)(4).

Situation 2. The payment that *Y* receives from *FXB* is foreign source income under section 862(a)(4).

[¶ 2175]

4. CHALLENGES OF NEW TECHNOLOGIES

New technology and new transactions often raise difficult issues of tax policy and administration in part because existing rules were developed to deal with other situations. The dramatic expansion in electronic commerce facilitated by the use of the Internet and other new technology is subjecting existing tax principles to new pressures. One area of concern is the application of source rules to electronic commerce transactions. Suppose, for example, that a corporation delivers electronically software or a digital product to a customer on the Internet. The customer can download the product and use it commercially. Depending upon the nature of the transaction and the property interests involved, the income to the corporation might appropriately be characterized as a royalty for the use of technology, profit from the sale of a product or a payment for services that it has rendered.

A complex set of regulations provides guidance with respect to computer program transactions. Reg. § 1.861–18. A computer program is defined to be "a set of statements or instructions to be used directly or indirectly in a computer in order to bring about a certain result." The term includes "any media, user manuals, documentation, data base or similar item if * * * [they are] incidental to the operation of the computer program." Reg. § 1.861–18(a)(3). Transactions involving computer programs will generally be classified as the transfer of a "copyright right" in a computer program, the transfer of a copy of the computer program, the provision of services for the development or modification of the computer program or the provision of knowhow relating to computer programing techniques. Reg. § 1.861–18(b)(1).

Computer programs are generally protected by copyright law. Consequently, the rules for characterizing computer program transactions are guided by copyright principles found in both U.S. and foreign copyright laws. T.D. 8785, 1998–2 C.B. 494, 495. Copyright law generally protects computer programs and distinguishes between transactions in a copyright and in the subject of a copyright. Under U.S. copyright law, exclusive rights, such as the right to reproduce copies of the copyrighted works, are granted to the owner of a computer program copyright. In contrast, the purchaser of a copy of a computer program generally possesses only the right to sell or use the copy. Under the regulations, a transfer of copyright rights will occur if the transferee obtains any of the following:

1. The right to make copies of the computer program to distribute to the public, for sale, or other transfer of ownership, or by rental, lease or lending;

2. The right to prepare derivative computer programs based upon the copyrighted program;

3. The right to make a public performance of the program; or
4. The right to publicly display the program.

Reg. § 1.861–18(c)(2).

If there has been a transfer of copyright rights, the issue is whether the transfer is a sale, generating gain or loss, or a license, generating royalty income. The transaction will be a sale or exchange if, taking into account all of the facts and circumstances, all substantial rights in the copyright have been transferred. The principles under Section 1222 relating to capital gains and losses and Section 1235 relating to the sale or exchange of patents may be applied when determining whether all substantial rights have been transferred. Reg. § 1.861–18(f)(1). In particular, T.D. 8785 states that the all substantial rights test set forth in Reg. § 1.1235–2(b) generally reflects case law on this issue and so provides an appropriate standard for the test. 1998–2 C.B. at 499.

If the transferee acquires a copy of a computer program, but does not acquire any of the rights listed above, the transaction is characterized as a transfer of a copyrighted article. A copyrighted article is a copy of a computer program from which the work can be perceived, reproduced or otherwise communicated. Reg. § 1.861–18(c)(3). Further, the electronic transfer of software can constitute the transfer of copyrighted articles. Reg. § 1.861–18(g)(2). Once it has been determined that there has been a transfer of a copyrighted article, an analysis of the facts and circumstances, including the intent of the parties as evidenced by their agreement and conduct, may lead to the conclusion that the transaction involves the provision of services. Reg. § 1.861–18(d). If not, the issue then becomes whether there has been a sale or a lease of the copyrighted article. The transaction will be a sale or exchange if, taking into account all of the facts and circumstances, the benefits and burdens of ownership have been transferred. Reg. § 1.861–18(f)(2). If a transaction does not constitute a sale or exchange because insufficient benefits and burdens of ownership of the copyrighted article have been transferred, it will be classified as lease generating rental income. Reg. § 1.861–18(f)(2).

Specific source rules apply to the income derived from transactions in computer programs. Income from the sale or exchange of a copyright right will be sourced under the rules that apply to personal property sales. § 865; Reg. § 1.861–18(f)(2). Income from the sale of copyrighted articles where the computer program constitutes purchased inventory property will be U.S.- or foreign-source income, depending upon where title passes. §§ 861(a)(6), 862(a)(6); Reg. § 1.861–18(f)(2). On the other hand, income from the sale of copyrighted articles where the computer program constitutes noninventory personal property will be U.S.- or foreign-source income, depending upon the residence of the seller. § 865; Reg. § 1.861–18(f)(2). Finally, income from either the leasing of a computer program or the licensing of a copyright in a computer program will be U.S.- or foreign-source income, depending upon where the property is located in the case of rents and the place where the property is used in the case of royalties. §§ 861(a)(4), 862(a)(4); Reg. § 1.861–18(f)(1)(2).

An analysis of the facts and circumstances, including the intent of the parties as evidenced by their agreement and conduct, may lead to the conclusion that the transaction involves the provision of services. If so, the source rules for compensation apply. The facts and circumstances include the intent of the parties as to the ownership of the copyright and how the risks of loss are allocated. Reg. § 1.861–18(d).

A provision of knowhow will occur if information respecting a computer program relates to computer programming techniques, is furnished under conditions preventing unauthorized disclosure and is considered "property subject to trade secret protection." Reg. § 1.861–18(e). In such transactions, the issue is whether there has been a sale or a license of the property interest.

Notice that the source rules applicable to the transactions may be materially different under the respective potential characterizations of the transaction, and they may generate quite different answers to the source question. Moreover, if the income is deemed to be attributable to the provision of services, the task of determining where the services were actually rendered by the corporation may be very challenging. Finally, as will be seen in the following chapters, different forms of income are often treated quite differently under tax treaties.

The application of source rules to electronic commerce transactions is just one area of international concern to tax administrators and practitioners. While discussion of such issues has been widespread, definitive answers have not yet been developed under U.S. law and practice. The OECD has established a number of Technical Advisory Groups ("TAGs") that have undertaken to examine different tax issues arising from the use of electronic commerce in the international context and in particular under tax treaties. One such TAG report included a list of 28 transactions in which the characterization of income was determined by members of the TAG. OECD, Technical Advisory Group on Treaty Characterization of E–Commerce Payments (2001). See ¶ 12,090.

H. SPECIAL RULES

[¶ 2180]

1. STATUTORY PROVISIONS

Section 863(c) prescribes rules for determining the source of income derived from international transportation using vessels and aircraft. Usually 50 percent is U.S.-source income and 50 percent is foreign-source income for international transportation beginning or ending in the United States. This allocation will generally result in the inclusion as U.S.-source income of profits in fact generated when the vessel or aircraft is outside of the territorial limits of the United States. Rules in effect prior to 1986 based allocations in many cases on the location of the vessel or aircraft during its journey. The change was intended to increase U.S. tax levies by increasing taxes in some cases on foreign persons and reducing foreign tax credits in some cases for U.S. persons.

Modern technology has sometimes resulted in the creation of new statutory source rules. Section 863(d) specifies rules for determining the source of income derived from certain space and ocean activities. Generally, such income is U.S.-source for a U.S. citizen, resident alien or U.S. corporation. Such income is foreign-source for foreign persons. Section 863(e) prescribes rules for determining the source of income from international communications activities. For U.S. persons, 50 percent of such income is U.S.-source and 50 percent is foreign-source. For foreign persons, the income is usually foreign-source unless it is attributable to a U.S. office.

[¶ 2185]

2. NONSTATUTORY SOLUTIONS

When the Code does not prescribe source rules, they have been developed by the IRS and the courts. In such instances, the "theory" or the "policy" reflected by the statutory rules is often cited as the basis for determining the source of the income in question. The following materials relate to forms of income for which statutory rules have not been adopted.

[¶ 2190]

a. Scholarships, Prizes and Awards

Even though the recipient is normally expected to undertake academic work to qualify for a scholarship, the IRS has apparently determined that it is not analogous to compensation, and there is no Code provision that directly applies to determine its source. As in any case in which there is no statutory source rule, the basic premises of the Code rules must be applied to create one. The regulations provide generally that the source of income from scholarships, fellowships, grants, prizes and awards will be determined by the status of the payor rather than the recipient. Reg. § 1.863–1(d). Such payments by U.S. persons are thus treated, if taxable, as U.S.-source income. Such payments by foreign persons are treated as foreign-source income.

The rationale for the regulations seems to reflect a decision that such payments are more similar to interest, another form of income in which the status of the payor determines source. However, if a U.S. person awards a scholarship to a foreign person for study outside of the United States, the payment is regarded as foreign-source income. Reg. § 1.863–1(d)(2)(iii). Can the results provided by these regulations be explained in conceptual terms? Note that foreign students will not be taxed on assistance provided from home even if they do all of their academic work in the United States. Is the result of the regulations intended to avoid deterring foreign students who might choose to study in the United States?

[¶ 2195]

b. Alimony

Certain alimony payments are treated as items of gross income under Section 71. There is no statutory source rule. Can the principles reflected in the materials set forth in this Chapter be applied to fashion an appropriate rule?

Several analogies seem possible. No person would ever receive alimony income without having committed to join in a marriage. Should the source of alimony, therefore, be determined by the rule for compensation income? On the other hand, the domicile of the marriage is significant for many legal purposes. In fact, the marriage is regarded as a "community" in some states. Should the place of domicile be regarded as the source of alimony income? Finally, the person paying the alimony normally has a legal obligation to do so. Is such an obligation analogous to that of a borrower who is legally obliged to pay interest on a loan?

The following Ruling provides an analytical response by the IRS. Note that the taxpayer which is the subject of the Ruling is an estate that is both a foreign person and a foreign resident for U.S. income tax purposes. The recipient of the alimony is a nonresident alien. However, the payments are in fact being made from assets held in the United States.

[¶ 2200]

REVENUE RULING 69–108

1969–1 C.B. 192.

Advice has been requested whether, under the circumstances described below, periodic payments made by the United States ancillary administrator of a nonresident alien estate to a nonresident alien individual are income from sources within the United States and therefore subject to withholding tax under section 1441 * * *.

Decedent, a citizen of the United States, was a resident and domiciliary of a foreign country at the time of his death. Approximately one-half of the assets of his estate were located outside the United States. The decedent's sister was appointed sole executrix of her deceased brother's estate in accordance with foreign law, and she is administering the foreign assets. The United States assets are being administered by an ancillary administrator in the United States. The estate is a nonresident alien estate for Federal income tax purposes but is subject to Federal tax on income from sources within the United States in the same manner as a nonresident alien individual.

Under the terms of a settlement agreement, entered into by the decedent during his lifetime with his former wife, and incident to their divorce, the nonresident alien estate is required to pay to the former wife, a nonresident alien, a certain amount annually for 20 years for her support and maintenance. The ancillary administrator located in the United States was authorized by the court to pay the annual installments to the former wife in accordance with the settlement agreement, less the amount, if any, required to be withheld for income tax purposes. These amounts qualify as periodic payments within the meaning of section 71(a) * * *.

Section 1441(a) * * * provides, in part, that all persons in whatever capacity acting, making payment of fixed or determinable annual or periodical income (to the extent such income is gross income from sources within the United States) to a nonresident alien must, generally, withhold 30 percent of such income. Amounts described in section 71(a) * * * are fixed or determinable annual or periodical income. Rev. Rul. 54–53, C.B. 1954–1, 156.

In the case of *Walter A. Howkins v. Commissioner*, 49 T.C. 689 (1968), the Tax Court of the United States held that certain alimony payments paid by a resident alien individual to his former wife, a nonresident alien individual, from a bank account in the United Kingdom were from sources within the United States. The court stated, in pertinent part, that although the Code does not contain a comprehensive general rule or set of rules for determining the "source" of an item of income, a number of source-of-income rules, now contained in sections 861 through 864 * * *, have been provided for certain common classes of income. While alimony is not among the categories of income for which a statutory source-of-income rule is available, the rules that are set forth in the Code show, for the most part, that Congress thought of the "source" of an item of income in terms of the place where the income was "produced." Interest payments, like alimony, however, involves an obligation, usually to make periodic payments over a period of time, that is not incurred in exchange for property or services. In enacting section 861(a)(1) * * *, Congress turned to the residence of the obligor, the situs of the debt, as the place where the income is produced, and thus the source of the income.

In *A.C. Monk & Co., Inc. v. Commissioner*, 10 T.C. 77 (1948) at p. 82, a case in which a domestic corporation was required to withhold a tax on interest paid to a nonresident alien individual in spite of the fact that the interest payments were made from a foreign bank account and were derived from foreign income, the court stated:

> "* * * This obligation has its source in the obligor, and thus the source of the payment of the obligation is the residence of obligor. There the right of payment arises and there the right may be

enforced. The only qualification is that the payment be actually made by the resident obligor or on its behalf and pursuant to its obligation. * * * ''

It follows, then, that the alimony obligation creates a debt running from the estate, in the instant case, to the former wife as each successive payment matures. Thus, the residence of the estate should control the determination of the geographic source of periodic alimony payments just as it controls the source of income paid on an interest-bearing obligation.

Accordingly, the described periodic payments made by the United States ancillary administrator of the nonresident alien estate to the decedent's former wife, a nonresident alien, are not from sources within the United States and, therefore, are not subject to the withholding of tax at the source under section 1441 * * *.

[¶ 2205]

c. Banking and Financial Services

The more intangible forms of income production raise many different issues of tax policy and administration. The rules for determining the source of interest income are clearly specified in the Code. The following case addresses the complexities of source determinations with respect to income other than interest derived from the provision of banking and financial services. Its somewhat complex facts also provide useful information about common forms of financing international trade and investment transactions.

[¶ 2210]

BANK OF AMERICA v. UNITED STATES

United States Court of Claims, 1982.
680 F.2d 142.

KASHIWA, JUDGE:

* * *

Plaintiff is an Edge Act corporation organized and existing under the laws of the United States * * *. The Edge Act amended the Federal Reserve Act in 1919 to allow national banks to participate in international banking through qualified subsidiaries. These subsidiaries, such as plaintiff, are domestically organized corporations which are permitted to offer international banking services. As an Edge Act corporation, plaintiff is only permitted to transact international business and therefore is actively involved in financing of international trade. The financing of international trade often occurs through the issuance of short-term loans, confirmed letters of credit, and the issuance of banker's acceptances. We are concerned here with the commissions charged by the plaintiff for confirmed letters of credit, banker's acceptances, and negotiations in connection with export letters of credit. These commissions were paid to the plaintiff in the years 1958 through 1960 by foreign banks located in Germany, France, Guatemala, and Singapore.

The transactions at issue involve commercial letters of credit issued by a foreign bank on behalf of a foreign purchaser for the benefit of an American exporter. Such a transaction begins with an agreement by an American exporter to sell goods to a foreign purchaser. The foreign purchaser then requests a commercial letter of credit from a foreign bank. A commercial letter of credit is a mechanism whereby trade is facilitated; it is a document issued by a bank on behalf of its customer. This document commits the bank to pay the beneficiary of the letter when certain terms have been met. By issuing a letter of credit, a bank has substituted its credit for that of its customer. The bank issuing the letter of credit is commonly referred to as the opening bank. An opening bank will only issue a letter of credit when it has evaluated its customer's credit and found it satisfactory. Thus, the foreign bank issues the letter of credit for the benefit of the American seller if it finds the foreign purchaser creditworthy. The terms of such a letter typically include some of the terms of the sales agreement between the merchants. By issuing such a letter of credit, the foreign opening bank agrees to pay the American seller a specified amount when the American seller meets the terms of the letter of credit. The foreign opening bank, in turn, expects its customer, the foreign importer, to reimburse it.

The letter of credit the opening bank issues may be one of two different types known as sight and usance (or time) letters of credit. The beneficiary of a sight letter of credit is entitled to payment once it is determined he has met the terms of the letter. The beneficiary of a usance letter of credit, on the other hand, is not entitled to payment immediately upon the determination he has met the terms of the letter but, instead, will be entitled to payment at a specified time in the future. Plaintiff's transactions in the years in question involve both sight and usance letters of credit. A draft is the specific document that directs payment be made to the beneficiary. There are both sight and time drafts.

Any letter of credit a foreign bank issues on behalf of a foreign purchaser for the benefit of an American exporter can be advised by the plaintiff as a courtesy to the foreign bank. When a letter of credit is *advised* by the plaintiff, plaintiff simply informs the American beneficiary of the letter that a letter of credit has been issued in his favor and forwards the letter. The plaintiff does not undertake any credit commitment and so informs the letter's beneficiary. Uniform Customs & Practice for Commercial Documentary Credits Fixed by the Thirteenth Congress of the International Chamber of Commerce, Article 6 (effective January 1, 1952) (hereinafter UCP). See generally U.C.C. § 5–103. During the years 1958 through 1960, no fee was charged by the plaintiff for advisement.

Alternatively, a foreign bank can request that plaintiff *confirm* a sight letter of credit. If plaintiff agrees to confirm a sight letter of credit, it not only advises the letter but it irrevocably commits itself to pay the face amount of the letter. Payment is only made if the beneficiary has met the terms of the letter of credit. UCP, Article 5. Under ordinary circumstances, plaintiff is reimbursed by the foreign bank for paying the draft. Whether or not plaintiff agrees to confirm a letter of credit depends upon its evaluation and credit analysis of the opening bank. When plaintiff does agree to confirm, it notifies the beneficiary. At the time of notification, plaintiff becomes obligated to pay the beneficiary regardless of any changes that might take place affecting the ability of the opening bank to reimburse the plaintiff. Subsequent to notification, a beneficiary can present the letter of credit and supporting documents for payment at any time.

After plaintiff has paid the amount of the draft to the beneficiary, it will ordinarily debit the foreign bank's account. Occasionally, a foreign bank will prepay the amount of the draft. When prepayment occurs, plaintiff usually waives the confirmation commissions. During the years 1958 through 1960, plaintiff charged the opening foreign bank a commission for confirmation of 1/20 of 1 percent of the face amount of the draft for each calendar quarter or fraction thereof the draft was outstanding. If this amount was less than $2.50, a minimum commission of $2.50 was charged. Confirmation commissions are charged the opening bank upon confirmation.

A foreign bank can also request that plaintiff *negotiate* a letter of credit. This can be done with either advised or confirmed letters of credit. Negotiation is the process by which the beneficiary's papers are checked to see whether they meet the terms of the letter of credit. This process takes place at the offices of the plaintiff in the United States. The papers are then forwarded to the opening bank which independently checks the papers. Neither bank inspects the merchandise. In cases involving confirmed letters of credit, negotiation is always required. A separate commission was charged for negotiation of 1/10 of 1 percent of the face amount of the draft. If this amount was less than $5, a minimum of $5 was charged. With confirmed letters of credit, the negotiation commission is charged at the time the sight draft is honored.

The third type of commission we are concerned with is *acceptance* commissions. Acceptance financing can be used to obtain money directly, to finance the storage of goods, to refinance sight letters of credit, and to finance export/import trade. The acceptance commissions involved in this case were paid to plaintiff by foreign banks as a result of plaintiff's acceptance of time drafts drawn pursuant to usance letters of credit issued by those foreign banks or pursuant to lines of credit extended by plaintiff to the foreign banks. When a foreign bank requests plaintiff's involvement in acceptance, plaintiff first undertakes a credit analysis of the foreign bank. If plaintiff agrees, the following procedures take place.

In circumstances involving usance letters of credit, when the beneficiary presents the letter of credit and accompanying documents to the plaintiff, plaintiff examines the documents to see whether they conform to the terms of the letter of credit. If the documents conform, plaintiff places its acceptance stamp upon the draft. By placing its stamp upon the draft, plaintiff obligates itself to pay the face amount of the draft on the day the draft becomes due. Once the plaintiff's acceptance is stamped, the draft becomes a money market obligation and is freely tradeable. Plaintiff is obligated to pay any holder in due course on the date the draft becomes due.

Customarily, the foreign bank pays the plaintiff the face amount of the time draft on the day preceding the date of its maturity. This normally is done by debiting the account of the foreign bank. Whether or not the foreign bank makes the payment, plaintiff is obligated to pay the holder in due course of the draft. The acceptance commission charged by the plaintiff would vary from 1.5 percent to 2.5 percent per year of the face amount of the draft, depending upon the creditworthiness of the foreign bank.

In circumstances involving lines of credit, these lines of credit are first established by plaintiff for its customer, the foreign bank, after a thorough credit evaluation is conducted by the plaintiff. Typically, such lines of credit provide a ceiling dollar amount for direct loans, letters of credit, and banker's acceptances. A foreign bank with such a line of credit can ask the plaintiff to refinance a letter of credit. In that situation, the foreign bank requests plaintiff to provide financing in the form of a draft of a sufficient amount to reimburse the plaintiff for its payment of the original letter of credit. The present discounted value of this draft is equivalent to the face amount of the original draft. Plaintiff then accepts the newly issued draft. Upon its acceptance, the draft is immediately discounted and the proceeds used to reimburse the plaintiff for payment of the original draft. Under this type of financing, the foreign bank pays the plaintiff the same acceptance commissions it pays in acceptance transactions involving usance letters of credit. The foreign bank also pays the plaintiff the amount of the discount. The commission and the discount together approximate the interest charge the foreign bank would have paid if it had obtained a direct loan.

* * *

It is well settled that sections 861 through 863 and their predecessors were not intended to be all inclusive. * * * When an item of income is not classified within the confines of the statutory scheme nor by regulation, courts have sourced the item by comparison and analogy with classes of income specified within the statutes. * * *

The parties agree that to determine what class of income the commissions fall within or may be analogized to we must look to the substance of the transaction. * * * The Government takes the position that plaintiff is paid by the opening banks for services. If so, personal services are sourced under sections 861(a)(3) and 862(a)(3) where those services are performed. The Government contends the plaintiff performed the services relevant to the commissions at its offices in the United States. Thus, under the Government's theory the commissions are sourced as income from United States sources. The plaintiff, on the other hand, contends it is not being paid for personal services but instead for something similar to a loan (the use of its credit). Thus, plaintiff claims its income may be sourced by analogy to interest. Interest under sections 861(a)(1) and 862(a)(1) is in general sourced by the residence of the obligor. * * * Since the commissions in this case were paid by foreign banks, the plaintiff takes the position the income is foreign source. The trial judge found neither the plaintiff's nor the Government's analysis adequate. He found the substance of the transaction to be the plaintiff's promise to pay regardless of any change in circumstances, i.e., the assumption of risk of the foreign bank's default. Since the foreign bank and the risks associated with it are located abroad, the trial judge found the commissions to be foreign source.

We do not fully agree with any single analysis proposed. Instead, to properly determine the source of the various commissions, we hold that each type of commission must be examined separately.

* * *

We first consider acceptance commissions. As we have explained, the acceptance commissions at issue are paid by foreign banks to the plaintiff under two circumstances. The first is as a result of plaintiff's acceptance of time drafts drawn pursuant to usance letters of credit; the second is as a result of the acceptance of drafts drawn against a line of credit extended by plaintiff to the foreign bank. In either circumstance what occurs is similar to a loan transaction. In a direct loan a lender uses its credit resources to intermediate between investors who have money available and borrowers who need money. With direct loans a lender will assume the credit risk of the borrowers to its investors. Similarly, in the acceptance financing transactions at issue the plaintiff acts as an intermediate between the holder of the acceptance draft and the foreign bank. The plaintiff assumes the credit risk of the foreign bank and assures the draft's holder of its payment. The plaintiff on the day it accepts a time draft guarantees to the holder that it will pay the full amount of the draft at maturity at a specified date in the future. This promise is made regardless of any change in circumstances that may cause the foreign bank to default. The significance of the plaintiff's guarantee is evidenced by the fact the accepted draft is freely tradeable on the market. In *Helvering v. Stein*, 115 F.2d 468 (4th Cir.1940), an income tax case that also involved a sourcing issue, the Fourth Circuit treated a transaction involving banker's acceptances as a loan transaction. The court said, "[we] do not think the use of drafts instead of promissory notes in these transactions goes beyond the form of the transaction." *Id.* at 472. Similarly, we find the use of banker's acceptances in the transactions at issue cannot mask their essence. The essence of the transactions, like that of a direct loan, is the use of plaintiff's credit.

The commissions charged the foreign banks by the plaintiff include elements covered by the interest charges made on direct loans. The evidence established that interest typically covers credit risk, credit administration, and cost of funds. * * * If we examine an acceptance financing transaction, we find the commissions charged cover credit risk and credit administration. A holder of an accepted draft may present his draft for payment or trade it on the market at any time. If he does so prior to maturity, he will receive not the value of the draft at maturity but its discounted value. The discounted value is equivalent to the value at maturity less the time value of the money (cost of funds). Typically, the discount plus the acceptance commission will approximate interest charges made on direct loans. It is thus apparent that acceptance commissions cover the cost to the plaintiff of credit administration and credit risk. This notion is reinforced by the fact plaintiff varied its acceptance commissions from 1.5 percent to 2.5 percent dependent upon the creditworthiness of its customer. *Cf. Sumitomo Bank, Ltd. v. Commissioner*, 19 B.T.A. 480 (1930) (compensation received by a Japanese bank with a New York agency on transactions involving banker's acceptances was treated as interest).

We recognize the plaintiff performed services for the foreign banks as part of the acceptance transactions; e.g., advising the letter of credit and making the actual payment of money. We also realize foreign banks without United States branches cannot perform some of these services and require an agent in the United States to do that. We find, however, these functions are not the predominant feature of the transactions. Instead, the predominant feature of these transactions is the substitution of plaintiff's credit for that of the foreign banks. No one would question that lenders in making direct loans also perform personal services. Yet, Congress in section 861(a)(1) and 862(a)(1) has determined that all interest will be sourced under those sections and not as personal services under sections 861(a)(3) and 862(a)(3). We find acceptance commissions to be similar.

In *Block v. Pennsylvania Exchange Bank*, 253 N.Y. 227, 230–231, * * * (1930), then Chief Judge Cardozo said:

> * * * "The central function of a commercial bank is to substitute its own credit, which has general acceptance in the business community for the individual's credit, which has only limited acceptability." * * * A bank "manufactures credit by accepting the business paper of its customers as security in exchange for its own bank credit in the form of a deposit account." * * * "It stands ready to exchange its own

> credits for those of its customers." * * * Whatever is an appropriate and usual incident to this substitution or exchange of credits, instead of being foreign to the functions and activities of banking, is in truth of their very essence. It is the end for which a bank exists. * * *

We therefore hold that for the reasons discussed the acceptance commissions are sourced by analogy to interest under the provisions of sections 861(a)(1) and 862(a)(1). Interest should be used because it furnishes the closest analogy in the statutory sourcing provisions, although (as the trial judge held) the acceptance commissions here cannot be directly equated with interest. Since interest is sourced by the residence of the obligor and the obligors in all instances were foreign banks, we find the acceptance commissions are foreign source income.

* * *

We next consider confirmation commissions. In confirmation the plaintiff advises a sight letter of credit *and* adds to it its own obligation to pay the sight draft when the terms of the letter have been met. The plaintiff irrevocably commits itself to pay the draft at the time it notifies the beneficiary of the letter of credit that it has confirmed the letter. The beneficiary may present the letter and accompanying document to the plaintiff for payment at any time thereafter. The account of the foreign bank is ordinarily not debited until the sight draft is presented and paid. Thus, from the moment of confirmation the plaintiff has made an enforceable promise to pay regardless of any change in the foreign bank's financial condition. As in acceptance and loan transactions, the plaintiff here has acted as an intermediate, has assumed the risk of default of the foreign bank, and has assured the draft's holder of payment.

The services involved in confirmation are little different from those in advisement where no charge is made. The only service provided by plaintiff in confirmation that was not provided in advisement is the actual payment of dollars. It is important to note the plaintiff usually waived the confirmation commissions when a foreign bank prepaid the amount of the draft. Thus, it is apparent what plaintiff was really charging for was not the services performed but the substitution of its own credit for that of the foreign bank. The predominant feature of the confirmation transactions was the substitution of plaintiff's credit for that of the foreign banks. The services performed were subsidiary to this. Therefore due to the similarities between a confirmation and a loan transaction, we hold that the confirmation commissions should be sourced by analogy to interest. Again we point out that interest should be used because it furnishes the closest analogy in the statutory sourcing provisions, although confirmation commissions cannot be directly equated with interest. Since the obligors were all foreign banks, we hold the confirmation commissions are income from without the United States.

* * *

Finally, we consider negotiation commissions. The analysis here is somewhat different. Negotiation is simply the process by which the plaintiff checks to see whether the documents the beneficiary presents conform to the terms of the letter of credit. A separate commission is charged for negotiation of advised letters of credit and confirmed letters of credit. Where negotiation commissions are charged for advised letters of credit, we find the commissions are charged for personal services. In those situations there is no assumption of any credit risk by the plaintiff. The plaintiff does not make any payments to the beneficiary of the letter of credit. The only risk present is that the plaintiff will improperly check the documents. No analogy can possibly be drawn to a loan situation. Since the negotiation commissions charged with advised letters of credit are clearly being charged for personal services, we hold they should be sourced as personal services.

Plaintiff contends, however, in instances where letters of credit are confirmed it must negotiate to protect itself from making payment to a party who has not met the terms of the letter of credit. Plaintiff therefore argues the risks of the confirmation process are dominant and should control the sourcing of the negotiation commissions. Although we agree plaintiff requires negotiation with confirmed letters of credit, we cannot agree the character of confirmation controls that of negotiation. Plaintiff's own method of structuring these transactions militates against its argument. Plaintiff does not charge just one fee for confirmation and negotiation but makes two separate charges at two separate points in time. It charges negotiation commissions when it completes the actual negotiation process. In addition, the negotiation commissions are twice that of confirmation commissions. We therefore cannot conclude the services of negotiation are so minor they are merely a part of the confirmation process. When a foreign bank pays the plaintiff a commission for negotiation, it is paying the plaintiff to perform the physical process of checking documents and nothing more.

We therefore hold negotiation is a personal service and negotiation commissions are therefore sourced under sections 861(a)(3) and 862(a)(3). Personal services are sourced where the services are performed. Plaintiff performed negotiation at its offices in the United States. Thus, negotiation commissions are income from sources within the United States.

* * *

In conclusion, we hold the acceptance and confirmation commissions at issue are income from sources without the United States and the negotiation commissions are income from sources within the United States. * * *

[¶ 2211]

NOTES

1. In Container Corp. v. Commissioner, 134 T.C. No. 5 (2010), a U.S. subsidiary paid fees to a Mexican parent corporation for providing a guaranty of the subsidiary's debts to unrelated U.S. lenders. There were no statutory source rules applicable to such payments. The IRS argued that the fees were analogous to interest. As the subsidiary was a U.S. resident, the fees would be considered to be U.S.-source income subject to a withholding tax under the regime discussed in Chapter 4. Citing the *Bank of America* decision, the Tax Court held that the guaranty was more like a service. As the guaranty was provided in Mexico, the fee was foreign-source income not subject to U.S. tax.

The Tax Court decision prompted some criticism, and Congress responded late in 2010 by establishing a new statutory source rule for debt guaranty fees. As a result, fees paid by a U.S. resident or corporation for the guarantee of the indebtedness of the resident or corporation will be treated as U.S.-source income. Fees paid by a foreign person will also be treated as U.S.-source income if the indebtedness is or is deemed to be effectively connected with the conduct of a U.S. trade or business by the foreign person. § 861(a)(9). Other such fees paid by a foreign person are treated as foreign-source income. § 862(a)(9).

2. Rev. Rul. 2009–14, 2009–1 C.B. 1031, dealt with several tax consequences for a U.S. person who had purchased a life insurance contract from the insured, a U.S. citizen, and who subsequently received death benefit payments from a U.S. insurance company. The Ruling noted that "The Code does not specify the source of income resulting from the payment of death benefits pursuant to a term life insurance contract. * * * . Consequently, the source of such income is determined by comparison and analogy to classes of income that are specified within the statute. * * * In the current situation, [the insured] is a United States citizen residing in the United States, and [the insurance company] * * * is a domestic corporation. [The taxpayer's] * * * income is from sources within the United States." The ruling did not specify which analogy was used to reach the decision.

[¶ 2215]

PROBLEMS

1. Southcal, a U.S. corporation, borrows $10 million from the Brussels office of a Belgian bank. During each of the preceding five years, 85 percent of the income of Southcal was from sources outside the United States and was attributable to the active conduct of business in Belgium. The remaining 15 percent of Southcal's income was from U.S. sources. Interests payments are made in U.S. dollars to the account of the Belgium lender maintained in a bank in New York. What is the source of the interest paid to the Belgium bank? How, if at all, would your answer change if all interest payments were made directly to the Brussels office of the lender? How, if at all, would your

answer change if all of the shares of Southcal were owned by residents of Belgium?

2. Labelle, a French corporation, is engaged in the cosmetic business in France and the United States. The U.S. business is conducted through a branch. During each of the preceding four years, 35 percent of the gross income of Labelle was effectively connected with its U.S. business. If Labelle pays a dividend to its sole shareholder, a French holding company, is there any basis for characterizing all or a portion as U.S.-source income?

3. Galaxy, a U.S. corporation engaged in the engineering business, performed services under a contract with a Canadian corporation. The employee of Galaxy who performed the services spent 25 working days in Canada and 50 working days in the United States. Because the work in the United States was largely routine supervision of drafting of plans while the work in Canada demanded a high degree of creativity and presence above the Arctic Circle, Galaxy charged $50,000 for the work in Canada and $50,000 for the work in the United States. Assume that Galaxy would like to maximize the amount of income treated as foreign-source because the income will be exempt from Canadian tax, and Galaxy has other income that generates excess foreign tax credits (see ¶ 5230). How much of the gross income for services can Galaxy treat as foreign-source gross income?

4. Cosmos, a U.S. corporation engaged in the manufacture, sale and leasing of computer equipment, has a Paris branch office engaged in marketing its computers in Europe. The Paris branch leases a computer to the Paris branch office of a German company. What is the source of the rental income?

5. Bolivar, a Panamanian corporation, owns a U.S. patent. Bolivar grants a nonexclusive license under the patent to Trimingham, a Bermuda corporation, in exchange for a royalty equal to three percent of the net sales by Trimingham of products incorporating the patented invention. What is the source of the royalty paid by Trimingham to Bolivar?

6. Suncare, a wholly owned U.S. sales subsidiary of Soin de Soleil, a French corporation, purchases a variety of skin care products from unrelated U.S. suppliers and sells them at a profit to unrelated distributors in Europe. Suncare also manufactures cosmetics in the United States and sells them to unrelated distributors in Europe. Finally, Suncare purchases a computer from an unrelated U.S. supplier and resells it at a profit to Soin de Soleil, which will use the computer in its treasurer's office in Paris. Title on all of the sales passes from Suncare to the purchaser at the international airport in France when the goods arrive. What is the source of the income realized by Suncare from these transactions?

7. Fabulous, a U.S. corporation, sells all of its rights to a German patent to Erfurt A.G. ("Erfurt"), a German corporation, for $1 million, payable in ten equal annual installments with interest at ten percent on the deferred payments. Title is passed to Erfurt in Germany. The patent had an original cost basis of $400,000 and had been subject to total amortization adjustments of $200,000, all of which had been deducted in calculating German-source

taxable income. What is the source of the gross income realized? If the sales price is cast in the form of a "royalty" of five percent of the net sales by Erfurt of products incorporating the patented invention, what is the result? Suppose Fabulous sells its German trademark "Fabulair" and associated goodwill to Erfurt for $5 million payable in five equal annual installments with interest of ten percent on the deferred payments. What is the source of the income realized?

8. Assume the same facts as in the first three sentences of Problem 7, except that the German patent is one of many foreign patents the exploitation of which is handled by a licensing branch office of Fabulous located in Frankfurt, Germany. The gain on the sale of the German patent to Erfurt is exempt from German tax. What is the source of the income realized? If the patent sold were inventory property, would the result change? If the patent were sold for a royalty-like price, would the result change?

9. Suppose that Fabulous had purchased trucks for $400,000 which were used solely in the transportation of inventory purchased in different parts of the United States to U.S. customers. All transportation expenses, including depreciation deductions of $200,000 in respect of the trucks, were applied to reduce U.S.-source income. Fabulous then resells the used trucks for $410,000, thereby realizing income of $210,000, to a foreign purchaser that took title to the trucks in Peru. What is the source of the income realized on the sale of the trucks?

10. United States Tool Corp., a U.S. corporation, sells all of the stock of its wholly owned German subsidiary, Modern Tool A.G., to an unrelated German corporation for $50 million cash, which produces a gain of $40 million. All negotiations occur and the sale contract is executed in Germany. Title to the stock passes to the purchaser in Germany, and the purchase price is paid in Germany. Modern Tool A.G. has been actively engaged in business in Germany and France for the last 10 years and has received approximately 60 percent of its gross income from France and 40 percent from Germany each year. Is the gain foreign-source income?

11. Jackson, a U.S. citizen, took the grand tour of Europe. While in Paris, Jackson used his card, issued by a New York banking corporation, to get $1,000 in cash from an ATM on the Left Bank. The New York bank had no French branch. However, pursuant to a standard contract, the ATM was operated by a French bank that was in turn reimbursed by the New York bank. The New York bank charged a "service fee" of $10 for the transaction. What is the source of the service fee to the New York bank?

12. U.S. Systems, a U.S. corporation, produces electronic toys in the United States. A portion of the production is sold through a branch in Europe to retailers for $300 per unit. The cost of production is $100 per unit. Some of the toys are sold directly by U.S. Systems to independent distributors for $250 per unit. How much of the income from each unit sold to a European retailer will be treated as foreign-source income? How, if at all, would your answer change if sales were made directly to distributors at $150?

13. HiTech, a U.S. corporation, owns the copyright in a computer program for "All Out War," a popular realistic game. HiTech copies the program onto disks that are inserted into boxes covered with a wrapper containing a "shrink-wrap license." The license is stated to be perpetual, but no modification of the program is permitted. The programs are sold extensively throughout Europe. Purchasers are allowed to use the program on their own computers, and may make and sell one copy of the program subject to the same limitations. After HiTech receives an order by telephone or electronic mail, the computer programs are shipped directly to customers from warehouses maintained by HiTech in New York and Ireland. Does HiTech realize U.S.- or foreign-source income from the transactions? How, if at all, would your answer change if the computer programs were transmitted electronically to purchasers after HiTech receives payment effected electronically by charging a credit card?

14. Consider the case of a nonresident alien who is planning to write a book in his home office and hopes to reach the U.S. market by concluding a contract with a U.S. publisher. At least three arrangements would be possible:

—The author could agree to write the book in return for royalties geared to U.S. sales and allow the publisher to obtain the U.S. copyright.

—The author could write the book, obtain the U.S. copyright and license it to the publisher in return for royalties geared to U.S. sales.

—The author could write the book, obtain the U.S. copyright and sell it to the publisher for a fixed price.

What is the characterization of the payments that would be received under each of these alternatives? What is the source of income under each?

[¶ 2220]

I. SOURCE RULES FOR DEDUCTIONS

Under a variety of Code provisions, it is necessary to identify what deductions should be taken against foreign- and U.S.-source gross income to determine foreign- and U.S.-source taxable income. These rules are often referred to as the source rules for deductions. For example, as indicated in the introductory materials of Chapter 1 and discussed in Chapter 3, foreign persons will be taxed on the net income of a U.S. trade or business. It is necessary in such instances to determine what expenses are sufficiently related to the trade or business to warrant deductibility for U.S. tax purposes. The foreign tax credit limitation provisions, discussed in Chapters 5 and 7, require the calculation of taxable income from foreign sources in various categories to determine the maximum allowable credit for foreign taxes against U.S. tax otherwise imposed on foreign-source taxable income. In that context, it is also necessary to determine what deductible expenses are properly allocable to foreign and U.S. sources.

[¶ 2225]

1. GENERAL RULES

The statutory rules for determining the source of deductions are cast in rather general terms. Section 861(b) states that "[f]rom the items of gross income specified * * * as being income from sources within the United States there shall be deducted the expenses, losses, and other deductions properly apportioned or allocated thereto and a ratable part of [such items] * * * which cannot definitely be allocated to some item or class of gross income." Sections 862(b) and 863(a), respectively, provide similar formulations for allocating deductions to foreign- and to mixed foreign- and U.S.-source income. In addition to the general prescriptions, there are special statutory rules for the allocation of interest expenses and certain research and development costs.

The rather noncontroversial formulation reflected in the basic Code provisions does not fully reflect the conceptual and practical complexities involved in implementing the allocation function. The most important vehicle for the allocation rules is the lengthy and complicated regulations beginning at Reg. § 1.861–8. These regulations have been subject to frequent debate and review and have been modified on a number of occasions.

The basic thrust of the regulations is that amounts of deductions must usually, if possible, be charged against U.S.-source and foreign-source gross income on a basis that turns on the factual relationship between the income and the expenses. A simple ratable division of a deduction based on the amount of foreign- and U.S.-source gross income will usually not suffice, "[e]xcept for deductions, if any, which are not definitely related to gross income." Reg. § 1.861–8(a)(2). Deductions that are generally considered not to be definitely related to gross income include real estate taxes on a personal residence, medical expenses and alimony. Reg. § 1.861–8(e)(9). A simple ratable apportionment to all gross income can be made for such deductions. But for virtually all income-related, or business, deductions the determination is made on the basis of the relevant facts. The regulations prescribe a two-step method for making this determination.

Allocation. The particular deduction in question must be factually attributed to some "class of gross income" specified in Reg. § 1.861–8(a)(3)—at this point on a worldwide basis. The classes enumerated in the regulations track the listing of income categories in Section 61. For example, deductions for salaries or other compensation related to managing income-producing real property may be attributed to rents, which would be the "class of gross income." If such deductions were attributable to licensing activities that generate royalties, royalties would be the "class of gross income." When deemed to be "definitely related" to the "class of gross income," the deduction is allocated to that class. The language may imply a more sound and accurate determination than is necessarily the case.

Apportionment. The deduction that has been allocated to a class of gross income must next be apportioned between the appropriate statutory grouping of that class of gross income under the applicable Code provision and the residual grouping. Reg. § 1.861–8(a)(4). The nature of a taxpayer's particular situation will determine the category of taxable income that must be calculated under the relevant section of the Code, which the regulations call the "operative section." The regulations label the gross income in the class that must be identified under the operative section as the "statutory grouping" and all other gross income as the "residual grouping." For example, in the case of a foreign corporation engaged in a U.S. trade or business, the operative section is Section 882(a) and the statutory grouping is gross income effectively connected with the U.S. business; the residual grouping is all other gross income.

A deduction is apportioned by attributing the deduction to gross income (within the class to which the deduction has been allocated) that is in one or more statutory groupings and to gross income (within the class) that is in the residual grouping. Temp. Reg. § 1.861–8T(c)(1) cautions that such attribution "must be accomplished in a manner which reflects to a reasonably close extent the factual relationship between the deduction and the grouping of gross income."

This approach assumes that the taxpayer must have some factual basis on which to make the apportionment. The regulation lists some relevant bases and factors to be considered:

(i) Comparison of units sold attributable to the statutory grouping and attributable to the residual grouping;

(ii) Comparison of the amount of gross sales or receipts;

(iii) Comparison of costs of goods sold;

(iv) Comparison of profit contribution;

(v) Comparison of expenses incurred, assets used, salaries paid, space utilized and time spent that are attributable to the activities or properties giving rise to the class of gross income; and

(vi) Comparison of the amount of gross income in the statutory grouping with the amount in the residual grouping.

Temp. Reg. § 1.861–8T(c)(1).

The regulations prescribe specific rules for certain expenses. The special rules applicable to interest and research and experimentation are discussed in the materials that follow. Specific rules have also been prescribed for stewardship expenses, legal and accounting fees, income taxes and net operating losses. Reg. § 1.861–8(e)(4), (5), (6), and (8). Charitable contributions were formerly considered to be not definitely related to gross income. However, under current regulations, the deduction for charitable contributions is considered to be definitely related and allocable to all of the U.S.-source gross income of the taxpayer. As a result, the deduction is apportioned between or among the statutory groups of U.S.-source gross income on that basis. Reg. § 1.861–8(e)(12).

[¶ 2230]

2. INTEREST EXPENSES

The proper allocation of interest expenses has been a particularly troublesome issue. Because money is a fungible commodity and because taxpayers can finance business and investment transactions in so many ways, there has been great concern about the possibility of arranging interest allocations to achieve substantial reductions in income tax liabilities. The basic premise of the current allocation rule is that because money is fungible most loans in a financial or economic sense contribute to the financing of all of a taxpayer's activities and assets. Thus, all interest expenses are considered to be factually related to all income-producing activities and assets of the taxpayer. Temp. Reg. § 1.861–9T(a). Therefore, with exceptions noted below, interest is allocated to all gross income as a class.

Section 864(e)(2) provides that "[a]ll allocations and apportionments of interest expense shall be made on the basis of assets rather than gross income." Moreover, to prevent corporations in an affiliated group from locating borrowings in particular corporations as a means of manipulating the way in which the interest deductions are allocated and apportioned, Section 864(e)(1) requires that taxable income under the operative section be determined by allocating and apportioning interest expense as if all members of the group are a single corporation.

Under the asset method, the taxpayer apportions interest expense to the statutory grouping of gross income identified under the operative Code section on the basis of the average total value of assets within the grouping for the tax year. Temp. Reg. § 1.861–9T(g)(1)(i). The taxpayer may use either the tax book value or the fair market value of assets in determining asset values for this purpose. Temp. Reg. § 1.861–9T(g)(1)(ii). The average book or market value is computed for the year on the basis of values of assets at the beginning and end of the year. Temp. Reg. § 1.861–9T(g)(2)(i). A taxpayer may elect to determine the tax book value of tangible property solely for purposes of the allocation of interest expense by using the alternative method of depreciation set forth in Section 168(g). Reg. § 1.861–9(i). The result for many taxpayers will be that the depreciation in respect of such property will be less, and often substantially less, than the depreciation deductions actually taken by the taxpayer using the accelerated cost recovery system generally provided by Section 168. As a result, the relevant properties will have a higher adjusted basis for purposes of the allocation. The election will be beneficial to taxpayers when it increases the amount of interest allocable to U.S.-source, rather than foreign-source, income, thereby enlarging the potential foreign tax credit. See ¶¶ 5215 et. seq.

The apportionment methods can be demonstrated with a simple example. Excalibur, a U.S. corporation, earns all of its income through the sale of razor blades. Most sales occur in the United States, but some income is derived through a branch office in England. During the tax year Excalibur had deductible interest expense of $5,000. The company assets producing U.S.-source income had a tax basis of $90,000 and a fair market value of $150,000. Those assets producing foreign-source income had a tax basis of $10,000 and a fair market value of $50,000.

If Excalibur chooses to use the tax book value method, $500 ($5,000 x $10,000/$100,000) of the interest expense will be allocated to foreign-source income. If Excalibur chooses to use the fair market value method, $1,250 ($5,000 x $50,000/$200,000) of the interest expense will be allocated to foreign-source income. The remainder will be allocated to U.S.-source income.

There are three exceptions to the rule that interest deductions must be allocated and apportioned on the basis of asset values. The first relates to a nonrecourse borrowing that is used to finance the acquisition, construction or improvement of specific property. If, under the tests contained in the regulations, a borrowing is "qualified nonrecourse indebtedness," the interest deductions are directly allocable solely to the gross income generated by the property acquired, constructed or improved with the proceeds of the borrowing. Temp. Reg. § 1.861–10T(b)(1). The second exception provides that interest expense incurred on funds borrowed in connection with certain "integrated financial transactions" is directly allocated to the income generated by the investment funded with the borrowing. Temp. Reg. § 1.861–10T(c). The third exception provides special allocation rules to be used in calculating the limitations on the foreign tax credit for a U.S. shareholder that incurs substantially disproportionate indebtedness in relation to the indebtedness of its controlled foreign corporations. Temp. Reg. § 1.861–10T(e). When an exception is applicable so that the interest expense is allocated directly, the assets relating to the loan are removed from the allocation formula used for the remaining interest expenses.

In 2004 Congress amended the authorization for the promulgation of regulations to implement the methods of allocating interest expense in several ways. Section 864(e)(7)(B) extends the authority for the direct allocation of interest expense incurred to carry out an integrated financial transaction to any interest or interest-type income derived "in other circumstances where such allocation would be appropriate to carry out the purposes of this subsection * * *." The 2004 legislation also authorized the promulgation of regulations to prevent "assets or interest expense from being taken into account more than once * * *" § 864(e)(7)(F).

Under current law, the allocation of interest expense to U.S.- and foreign-source income by a domestic corporation is based upon the assets of all of the domestic corporations included in an "affiliated group," which is generally defined to include corporations eligible for inclusion in a consolidated return. § 864(e)(1) and (2). Prior to 2011 foreign corporations, although affiliated, were not generally includible in an "affiliated group." Congress was concerned that the omission of affiliated foreign corporations in the application of the source rules for interest income had resulted in an excessive allocation of interest expense to foreign-source income, thereby limiting foreign tax credits and creating internationally competitive disadvantages for U.S. businesses. The legislation adopted in 2004 included a new Section 864(f) responding to such concern by authorizing taxpayers to elect to include foreign affiliated corporations that would be treated as members of an affiliated group for purposes of allocating and apportioning interest expenses of domestic members of the group.

Under present law certain financial institutions are excluded from the affiliated group for purposes of the interest allocation. Although financial institutions are treated separately, the 2004 legislation also provides a onetime "financial institution group" election that expands the present-law bank group. § 864(f)(4)(C). Further, at the election of the common parent of the pre-election worldwide affiliated group, the interest expense allocation rules are applied separately to a subgroup of the worldwide affiliated group consisting of all corporations that are part of the present-law bank group and all "financial corporations." § 864(f)(5)(C). For this purpose a corporation is a financial corporation if at least 80 percent of its gross income is financial services income that is derived from transactions with unrelated persons. Items of income are disregarded if a principal purpose for the transaction is to qualify any corporation as a financial corporation.

The effective date for elections under the 2004 provisions has been extended on several occasions. Under current law, elections must be made for the first taxable year starting after 2020. As with many elective provisions, the election if made must continue unless it is revoked with the consent of the IRS. § 864(f)(6).

A separate regulation determines the interest deduction for U.S. branches of foreign corporations. These provisions are analyzed at ¶ 3140.

The regulations provide special rules for individual taxpayers. Business interest expense is apportioned by a method based upon business asset comparisons. Qualified residence and deductible personal interest expenses are allocated by a method based upon gross income comparisons. Temp. Reg. § 1.861–9T(d).

[¶ 2235]

PROBLEMS

In the following problems, assume that all foreign assets generate foreign-source general limitation income. See Temp. Reg. § 1.861–9T(g).

1. Global World, a U.S. corporation, has interest expense for the tax year of $200,000, no portion of which is directly allocable to identified property under the regulations. Global World's worldwide assets have an adjusted basis of $5,000,000 and a value of $10,000,000, of which assets having an adjusted basis of $4,000,000 and a value of $6,000,000 generate U.S.-source income. How much of the interest expense is apportioned to U.S.-source income?

2. International Products, Ltd., a U.S. corporation, has an office and several factories in Brazil and operates branches in Colombia and the United States. During the tax year, the company pays interest of $1,050,000, of which $50,000 is attributable to a nonrecourse loan used to finance the construction of a small factory in Brazil. The adjusted basis of the corporation's assets, which are worth $41,000,000, is $21,000,000, of which $5,000,000 is attributable to assets worth $5,000,000 in Colombia and $5,000,000 is attributable to assets worth $20,000,000 in the United States. The small factory in Brazil has an adjusted basis of $1,000,000 and is worth $1,000,000. All other assets are located in Brazil. How much interest is apportioned to the corporation's U.S.-source income?

[¶ 2240]

3. RESEARCH AND EXPERIMENTATION EXPENSES

The proper allocation and apportionment of research and development (or experimentation) expenses has also been a difficult conceptual issue because the fruits of the research effort may contribute to the production of both U.S.- and foreign-source income and because there may be no easy way to estimate the amount of research and development expense allocable to each category of income at the time expenditures are incurred and deductions are calculated. Taxpayers have pressed for the smallest possible allocation of such deductions against foreign-source income to maximize foreign-source taxable income and, therefore, the allowable foreign tax credit under the applicable foreign tax credit limitations. The Treasury and the IRS have pressed in the opposite direction.

The regulations dealing with research and experimental expenditures have been the object of extensive discussion and debate. The results are now reflected in Reg. § 1.861–17. These regulations provide that research and development expenses are related to gross income from product categories and are to be allocated to income based upon such categories. Relevant product categories are determined by reference to a Standard

Industrial Classification system ("SIC"). For purposes of the apportionment requirements discussed below, sales of a product category by corporations controlled by the taxpayer, including foreign corporations, are generally included. Reg. § 1.861–17(c)(3).

If a taxpayer undertakes research to meet legal requirements imposed by a government entity and that research is not reasonably expected to generate more than de minimis income outside that government's jurisdiction, then the research deductions are allocated solely to the geographic source that includes that jurisdiction. Reg. § 1.861–17(a)(4). Such an allocation might arise, for example, if the taxpayer undertook research at the insistence of the U.S. Food and Drug Administration on a drug that was not to be marketed abroad.

After allocations of expenditures to meet legal requirements have been made, fifty percent of the remaining expenses are first apportioned to income from the geographic source where more than half of the taxpayer's research and development activities were performed (the "statutory grouping"). Reg. § 1.861–17(b)(1)(i). This is "the place of performance" apportionment.

The remaining, or residual, expenses are then apportioned to U.S.- and foreign-source income by a ratio based upon a comparison of total foreign-source sales in the relevant SIC product group to the total worldwide sales in that SIC product group. This apportionment is called the "sales method." Reg. § 1.861–17(c)(1).

The regulations also allow the taxpayer to elect to apportion expenses, other than those attributable to legal necessity, under a gross income method instead of the sales method. Under the gross income method, the place of performance apportionment is 25 percent, meaning that the remaining expenses to be allocated by formula will be larger. Reg. § 1.861–17(b)(1)(ii). Taxpayers electing the gross income method will apportion residual research expense according to the relative amounts of gross income from U.S. and foreign sources for each product group. Reg. § 1.861–17(d). Moreover, there is a limitation on the use of the gross income method. The amounts apportioned to U.S.- and foreign-source income cannot be less than 50 percent of the amounts determined under the sales method. Reg. § 1.861–17(d)(2)(ii). If the limitation is applicable to an electing taxpayer, the amounts apportioned will be 50 percent of the amount that would be apportioned under the sales method of apportionment. Reg. § 1.861–17(d)(3).

An election of either the sales or a gross income method is binding for five years and may not be changed without the consent of the IRS. After five years, a new election can be made that will be binding for another five years. Reg. § 1.861–17(e).

It should be noted that on several occasions Congress adopted statutory rules for effecting the allocation of research and experimental expenditures. The last statutory formulation, although no longer applicable, is still reflected in the Code. § 864(g). It provided generally for the allocation of half of qualified expenses to foreign source income, except for expenses allocated directly to a country because the expenditure was required to satisfy legal requirements. This formula was regarded as favorable to many U.S. corporations because it allowed for a relatively smaller allocation of deductions to foreign-source income, thereby enlarging the availability of foreign tax credits under various limitation provisions, discussed in Chapters 5 and 7. Because of the controversial nature of the issue and the enormous amounts involved for taxpayers and the Treasury, further legislative attention to the issue is possible.

[¶ 2245]

J. REFLECTIONS ON SOURCE RULES

The various rules for determining the source of income and deductions discussed in this Chapter derive from an attempt to identify the place, meaning whether inside or outside of the United States, in which the income was produced or to which the deduction is applicable. Generally the focus has been on the situs of economic activity generating various items of income. It may seem premature to reflect at this point on the appropriateness of the source rules. After all, they do not exist in a vacuum. The rules have been designed in part to advance a variety of tax policy decisions relating to both U.S. and foreign taxpayers. The focus on the geographic locus of economic activity seems sometimes tempered by the desire to advance tax policy objectives. Nevertheless, it is appropriate to consider whether the source rules reflect a coherent set of economic and financial principles.

There are some interesting applications of the source rules suggesting that other criteria could be used. The U.S. lawyer who works in a New York office for a client in Argentina on a project in Brazil has U.S.-source income even though the value of the legal work is attributable to the Brazilian project and benefits the client in Argentina. Loans made to a foreign borrower will create foreign-source interest even though the money loaned may have been saved from earnings in the United States. An investor residing in Israel who buys on the New York Stock Exchange through a U.S. broker stock in a U.S. corporation having no foreign activities and pays for the stock with a check drawn on a New York bank account will have foreign-source income if the stock is sold for a gain, but will have U.S.-source income if the corporation pays a dividend. Are there any fundamental economic or other principles underlying the existing source rules? If you were designing the appropriate source rules, would the same results obtain?

Rapidly evolving technology, such as electronic commerce and new forms of financing, sometimes strains existing source rules. Can the principles reflected by the existing source rules provide adequate certainty and coherence? Or should Congress prescribe new statutory source rules to deal with such situations?

Finally, should taxpayers be able easily to organize and implement transactions to advance tax-avoidance objectives by manipulating the formalities of the source rules? Should the passage-of-title test, for example, be replaced in the Code by one that emphasizes the economic substance of the transaction, as suggested in Reg. § 1.861–7(c), if title is passed outside of the United States for the primary purpose of tax avoidance?

CHAPTER 3

FOREIGN PERSONS: U.S. TRADE OR BUSINESS INCOME

■ ■ ■

[¶ 3000]

A. INTRODUCTION

As indicated in the summary description in Chapter 1, the way in which foreign persons will be taxed in the United States depends generally on whether income derives from U.S. sources and whether the income that is taxed derives from the conduct of a U.S. trade or business or from passive investment arrangements. As a general rule, a nonresident alien or foreign corporation that conducts a U.S. trade or business will be subject to the usual (individual or corporate) U.S. tax rates on *net* (i.e., taxable) income "effectively connected with the conduct of a trade or business within the United States." §§ 871(b)(1) and 882(a)(1). Tax treaties generally provide, however, that such income will not be taxed unless attributable to a "permanent establishment" maintained by the foreign person in the United States. Under prior law, the so-called "force of attraction doctrine" provided that any foreign person operating a U.S. trade or business was taxed at the usual rates on all U.S.-source net income. However, under present law, that doctrine has been substantially limited. If the foreign corporation or nonresident alien receives U.S.-source income that is not "effectively connected" with the U.S. trade or business, a different taxing regime usually applies that may result in the imposition of a flat tax of 30 percent (or lesser treaty rate) on gross income.

While the conceptual distinction between the conduct of a trade or business and the ownership of investment properties is familiar, a number of complex issues of factual analysis and legal interpretation inhere in its implementation. This Chapter explores the way in which profits from the conduct of a U.S. trade or business are taxed. Chapter 4 deals with the taxation of nonbusiness U.S.-source income realized by foreign persons.

The threshold question raised by the materials in this Chapter is, thus, whether the foreign person is engaged in a U.S. business. This inquiry may involve examining U.S. activities carried on directly by the foreign person or U.S. activities carried on by employees, agents or other representatives of the foreign person. If the foreign person is operating a U.S. trade or business, another question arises if a tax treaty is in effect between the United States and the country in which the foreign person is a resident. Under such tax treaties, a foreign person's trade or business income will not be subject to U.S. tax unless the income is attributable to a "permanent establishment" of the foreign person in the United States.

[¶ 3005]

B. U.S. TRADE OR BUSINESS

The term "trade or business" is used throughout the Internal Revenue Code in many different contexts. Regardless of the consequences of its application, the term is almost always employed to describe the process of producing or seeking to produce income from actively engaging in business activities, as distinguished from merely owning income-producing property. Compare, e.g., §§ 162 and 212. Since the term "trade or business" is used in different contexts in the U.S. income tax system, an important element of its meaning as applied to international transactions will derive from interpretations and applications having no international element.

The classic examples of a trade or business are situations in which the taxpayer is engaged in the marketing of goods or services. Thus, the manufacture and sale of automobiles is a trade or business; but the ownership of shares of a company that manufactures and sells automobiles is generally not a trade or business (unless the taxpayer is a broker-dealer in securities).

The term "trade or business within the United States" is not defined in the Code, although certain statutory prescriptions apply in specific instances dealing with the performance of services and trading in securities and commodities. § 864(b). As applied to foreign persons, a U.S. trade or business will be found to exist if there are regular, continuous and considerable business activities in this country. Isolated or sporadic transactions will not usually be construed as the conduct of a trade or business.

The regulations state that "[w]hether or not [a foreign taxpayer] is engaged in trade or business within the United States shall be determined on the basis of the facts and circumstances in each case." Reg. § 1.864–2(e). While such a proposition is difficult to contest, the value of its guidance is obviously limited. One is left, therefore, primarily to the legacy of interpretation of the concept in the context of other provisions of the Code and a modest accumulation of judicial decisions and rulings interpreting the term in the international context. For example, in the domestic context the Supreme Court has held that mere investing, including the active management of one's own investments, however extensive, does not constitute a trade or business. Higgins v. Commissioner, 312 U.S. 212 (1941).

Even though there may be no particular situs of the economic activity, a foreign person may be found to have conducted a U.S. trade or business because of a "considerable" volume of "regular" and "continuous" activity in the United States. The imprecise nature of these tests creates a substantial challenge to taxpayers seeking to avoid establishing a U.S. trade or business. One group of tax experts has proposed that trade or business profits should in general only be taxed when they derive from the conduct of a trade or business through a fixed place of business in the United States. See Federal Income Tax Project—International Aspects of United States Income Taxation—Proposals on United States Taxation of Foreign Persons and of Foreign Income of United States Persons 90 (A.L.I. 1987). The proposal is similar to the approach used in virtually all income tax treaties, which generally limit the taxation of trade or business profits to situations in which a foreign person operates through a "permanent establishment" in the other treaty country. See U.S. Model Treaty (Appendix A), Art. 7, discussed at ¶ 3165.

[¶ 3010]

1. PERFORMANCE OF PERSONAL SERVICES

Section 864(b) provides that "the performance of personal services within the United States at any time within the taxable year" generally constitutes the conduct of a U.S. trade or business. There is, however, a de minimis exception for a nonresident alien who is present within the United States not more than 90 days during the tax year and receives no more than $3,000 as compensation for working in the United States for a foreign person, entity or office. § 864(b)(1). This provision effectively reiterates the provisions of Section 861(a)(3) creating a de minimis exception to the usual source rules applicable to personal service income. The modest $3,000 cap, which has been in place for many years, greatly reduces the contemporary significance of the exception.

The effect of Section 864(b) and the related source rule is to allow a foreign business person to come to the United States, perhaps for a business meeting, without fear of being subjected to U.S. income taxes. The conditions of the exception have been strictly applied. A nonresident alien who receives a dollar too much or stays a day too long will be treated as conducting a U.S. trade or business, and all of the resulting compensation will be treated as effectively connected to that trade or business. Rev. Rul. 69–479, 1969–2 C.B. 149. In Rev. Rul. 64–184, 1964–1 C.B. 323, a U.S. corporation operated a facility for dry docking and ship repair. The corporation hired on a temporary basis ("usually less than two months") foreign crew members who were employees of foreign shipowners and who were only temporarily in the United States with their ship. The IRS ruled that the exception was not available since the services, although perhaps benefitting and being effectively paid by the foreign shipowner, were being performed for the U.S. corporation and not for the foreign shipowner.

Most tax treaties have a substantially more liberal exemption for personal service income. See ¶ 3190.

[¶ 3015]

2. TRADING IN STOCKS, SECURITIES OR COMMODITIES

If trading by foreign investors on U.S. securities and commodities markets through U.S. brokers were regarded as a U.S. trade or business, all profits derived therefrom might be taxed in the United States. Concerned that the threat of substantial U.S. taxes would deter foreign investors from trading on U.S. markets and using U.S. brokers, Congress created several safe harbor provisions to eliminate the risk.

Section 864(b)(2)(A) provides a broad safe harbor to assure that foreign persons may trade in stocks and securities on U.S. markets without establishing a U.S. trade or business. A foreign person, including a dealer, may trade in stocks or securities through a resident broker, commission agent, custodian or other independent agent without establishing a U.S. trade or business. This safe harbor will not be available to a taxpayer, whether corporate or individual, who maintains an office or other fixed place of business in the United States "through which or by the direction of which" the stock or securities transactions are effected. § 864(b)(2)(C).

A foreign investor may *trade for the investor's own account* either directly or through employees, resident brokers, commission or other agents (whether or not "independent") or custodians. Further, and most importantly for the brokerage community in the United States, when the foreign person is trading for its own account, even the exercise of discretionary authority by a U.S. employee, broker, agent or custodian will not be treated as a U.S. trade or business. This safe harbor is not available to dealers in stocks or securities because they are regularly engaged in the purchase and sale of stocks and securities for profit. Reg. § 1.864–2(c)(2)(iv).

A similar, but slightly different, safe harbor was created to allow foreign persons to trade on U.S. commodities exchanges using U.S. brokers without fear of creating a U.S. trade or business. § 864(b)(2)(B). The foreign person, including dealers, may trade in commodities of a kind customarily traded on an organized commodity exchange if the transaction is of a kind customarily consummated on such an exchange and use a resident broker, commission or other independent agent or custodian without establishing a U.S. trade or business. This safe harbor will not be available to a taxpayer, whether corporate or individual, who maintains an office or other fixed place of business in the United States "through which or by the direction of which" the commodities transactions are effected. § 864(b)(2)(C).

Except for commodities dealers, *trading for the taxpayer's own account* in such commodities and in such transactions either directly or by using employees, resident brokers, commission agents or custodians or other agents (whether or not "independent") will not be treated as a U.S. trade or business even if the employee, broker, agent or custodian has discretionary authority to effect transactions. § 864(b)(2)(B)(ii).

It should be noted that the failure to satisfy the specific requirements of a safe harbor provision does not necessarily require the conclusion that a U.S. trade or business has been established. Whether the foreign person has established a U.S. trade or business will then be determined by the general principles discussed in the ensuing portions of this Chapter.

[¶ 3020]

3. OTHER SITUATIONS

The absence of a comprehensive definition in the Code or regulations of a "U.S. trade or business" and the emphasis of the regulations on the facts and circumstances of each situation underline the importance of judicial decisions and revenue rulings determining the existence or nonexistence of a U.S. trade or business. As with any determination that depends upon an analysis of facts and circumstances, bright lines are sometimes hard to find. The question is when business activities carried on in the United States are enough to be regarded as "regular," "continuous" and "considerable." Also, the U.S. activities must rise to the level of a "business" and be central to the derivation of profit. See Pinchot v. Commissioner, 113 F.2d 718 (2d Cir.1940). Note that a *foreign* "trade or business" will not necessarily become a "*U.S.* trade or business" as a result of isolated transactions in the United States. Note further that the facts and circumstances test includes no requirement that the foreign person conduct the U.S. trade or business out of an office or other fixed place in the United States.

The general approach is represented by the materials that follow. The court is applying a "facts and circumstances" test. The lengthy summary of arguably relevant facts in the *Continental Trading* case is, therefore, essential to an understanding of the court's conclusion. Note that in this case the taxpayer wished to be treated as the operator of a U.S. trade or business so that U.S. taxes would be applied on net, rather than gross, income. Because much of the taxpayer's income consisted of dividends, the taxpayer would have benefitted substantially from the dividends-received deduction as well as interest and other deductions.

[¶ 3025]

a. General Approach

CONTINENTAL TRADING, INC. v. COMMISSIONER

United States Court of Appeals, Ninth Circuit, 1959.
265 F.2d 40, cert. denied, 361 U.S. 827.

[The taxpayer was a Panamanian corporation organized in 1947 with a principal office in Mexico City. It filed U.S. income tax returns for 1948, 1949 and 1950 based upon the assertion that it was operating a U.S. trade or business. Accordingly, it took various deductions in determining its U.S. tax liability. The IRS contended that the taxpayer did not conduct a U.S. trade or business and was not, therefore, entitled to deductions.

The taxpayer qualified to do business as a foreign corporation in Nevada. It "used for its American address that of the Reno, Nevada, company that acted as its resident agent." Turnbow, a U.S. citizen with an office in Oakland, California, served as the president of the taxpayer. The name of the taxpayer appeared on the office door and a building listing in Oakland, but it paid no rent.

The taxpayer "represented the incorporation of part of the vast holdings of Axel Wenner–Gren," an internationally famous billionaire financier who held substantial amounts of stock in the Electrolux and Servel corporations, both U.S. corporations, as well as sizable and diverse holdings in Mexican and other foreign enterprises. Prior to the incorporation of the taxpayer, Wenner–Gren borrowed large sums from American lending institutions for use outside the United States. After incorporation, the taxpayer assumed Wenner–Gren's liabilities to various banks, having acquired his stock in Electrolux and Servel. The stock was in turn pledged as security for the loans. As of the beginning of 1948, the taxpayer had assumed such debt to the Bank of America of $1,100,000, to Central Hanover Bank and Trust Company of New York of $480,000 and to Teleric, Inc. of $926,000.

The taxpayer had no paid employees in the United States during the three tax years in question, although Turnbow received $1,500 monthly during the last six months of 1950 for his services to the taxpayer. The taxpayer maintained no books of account in the United States, although Turnbow's secretary in Oakland kept records consisting of bank statements, check books and documents pertaining to transactions in the United States. At the end of 1948, the only assets of the taxpayer in the United States were the Electrolux and Servel stock and two bank accounts.

According to the facts set forth in the decision, the taxpayer reported income from sources within the United States for 1948 of $817,791.30

(dividend income of $823,635.50 from Electrolux and Servel less losses on property sales of $5,844.11), for 1949 of $605,635.10 (dividends of $602,125.20 and other income of $3,509.90) and for 1950 of $446,863.19 (dividends of $441,624 and sales income of $5,239.19). The taxpayer reported that more than 50 percent of its gross income for those years derived from foreign sources.

During each of the three tax years, the taxpayer made payments of principal and interest on outstanding debt. In 1948 it also borrowed from the Bank of America $1,000,000, which Wenner–Gren used in the acquisition of Mexican telephone companies, and $1,850,000, which it used in part to repay prior Wenner–Gren debt to the bank. In 1949 it secured and repaid short-term advances from Turnbow, borrowed from the Bank of America $1,700,000, which it used to liquidate loans to the same bank, and sold 55,000 shares of Servel stock, using the proceeds to repay other loans to that bank. In 1950, it borrowed $2,000,000 from Central Hanover Bank, repaid $1,700,000 to the Bank of America, transferred funds to accounts in Mexico City and later repaid $2,000,000 to Central Hanover. In its negotiations with Central Hanover, the taxpayer "represented itself as a Panamanian corporation, doing business in foreign countries."]

POPE, CIRCUIT JUDGE:

* * *

It will be noted that the activities described * * * all relate to the corporation's investment in the stock of other corporations, the collection of dividends and the borrowing of money, some of which was used to acquire Mexican companies and some of which was used by Wenner–Gren. The taxpayer's filed returns stated that its principal activity was "Investment", and such a term would appear to describe the activities just listed.

On the basis of these facts, taken alone, there cannot be any question but that the petitioner corporation was not "engaged in trade or business" within the meaning of [the Code] * * *. While the Internal Revenue Code did not specifically define "trade or business", yet the decisions have definitely established that where those terms are used elsewhere in the income tax laws, they do not include such activities as those here described.

The leading case on this point arose out of a taxpayer's effort to deduct the expenses of managing his investments in stocks and bonds as expenses incurred "in carrying on any trade or business" under the provisions of [the taxing statute] * * *. The Board of Tax Appeals upheld the Commissioner's refusal to permit the deduction. Said the Supreme Court: "The petitioner merely kept records and collected interest and dividends from his securities, through managerial attention for his investments. No matter how large the estate or how continuous or extended the work required may be, such facts are not sufficient as a matter of law to permit the courts to reverse the decision of the Board." Higgins v.

Commissioner, 312 U.S. 212, 218 * * *. Since that decision it is fair to say that it is settled law that the mere management of investments and the collection of rents, interest, and dividends is insufficient to constitute the carrying on of a trade or business.

* * *

This brings us to a consideration of some other activities of the petitioner,—activities referred to by the Tax Court as "isolated and noncontinuous" transactions. These were of three kinds: (1) In July, 1948, petitioner purchased a carload of dry milk fat from Kraft Foods Company for $46,212.75 and sold it one month later through one of Turnbow's companies for $40,248. (2) As an accommodation to a Mexican corporation petitioner purchased, in 1950, equipment for that corporation for which it was reimbursed without profit. (3) In all three years petitioner bought tin cans for milk products which were needed by Supply, one of Turnbow's companies. The Tax Court summarized these can transactions as follows: "In each year, the only other activity reported by petitioner was represented by nominal amounts of income resulting from transactions relating to cans used by Supply. In 1948, such reported income amounted to $120.64; in 1949, $3,509.90; in 1950, $5,239.19." The first such can purchase occurred in December, 1948. Turnbow or Supply put in the order, but in petitioner's name. It paid for the cans and turned the cans to Supply for a five percent increase over the price it paid. This December 1948 transaction was repeated 37 times in 1949 and on 48 occasions in 1950. Said the Tax Court: "There was no business purpose connected with the can transactions engaged in by petitioner. It never used its Nevada office in these operations. It carried no inventory of cans and ordered no cans other than those used by Supply. In every instance in which Supply acquired cans in this way, it paid petitioner within 10 days of petitioner's payment to Western. After 1950, Supply recommenced ordering and purchasing of cans directly from Western."

We think it was within the competence of the Tax Court to find that these facts were insufficient to show that petitioner was engaged in trade or business within the United States. The court found these milk fat, equipment and milk can transactions, because they were "of an isolated and noncontinuous nature", and because they were "dictated not by a business objective but purely by a desire to save taxes," did not amount to activities sufficient to bring petitioner within the definition of * * * [the Code]. Wholly apart from any question of "business purpose", it seems plain that whether these milk fat, milk can transactions were properly to be regarded, in the light of the corporation's whole enterprise, as casual or incidental transactions, was a question of fact. And further, whether as such, those transactions served to change an otherwise "non-trade or business" corporation into one * * * is also a question of fact.

* * *

[W]e think the Tax Court's holding that casual or incidental transactions (such as these milk fat and milk can matters) are not sufficient to show the corporation to be "engaged in trade or business," was within the fair meaning of the statute.

* * *

[¶ 3030]

NOTES

1. In InverWorld, Inc. v. Commissioner, 71 T.C.M. (CCH) 3231 (1996), the taxpayer, InverWorld, Ltd. ("LTD"), was an investment management and financial services company organized under the laws of the Cayman Islands to serve a Mexican clientele. LTD owned all the stock of InverWorld Holdings, Inc. ("Holdings"), a U.S. corporation. Holdings owned all the stock of InverWorld, Inc. ("INC"), also a U.S. corporation. INC maintained LTD's client account files in the United States, provided investment advice to LTD pursuant to a written agreement and performed bookkeeping services for LTD. INC also purchased investment instruments on behalf of LTD clients. LTD did not file any U.S. or foreign returns for the years at issue. One question before the court was whether LTD, either directly or indirectly through its agent, INC, engaged in trade or business activities in the United States within the meaning of Section 864(b). The court held that it did and discussed the modest interpretive authority on this issue:

> In *European Naval Stores Co., S.A. v. Commissioner*, 11 T.C. 127 (1948), the Court addressed whether the taxpayer, a foreign corporation, was "engaged in trade or business within the United States" within the meaning of section 231(b) of the 1939 Code, as amended. In interpreting former section 231(b), the Court held that the "question as to what activities of a taxpayer constitute the carrying on of a business is one of fact." * * * The Court in *European Naval Stores* indicated that the phrase "engaged in trade or business within the United States" refers to profit-seeking activities that are sufficiently regular, continuous, and extensive to constitute "carrying on a trade or business" within the meaning of section 162. The Court added:
>
>> The meaning of the phrases "engaged in business," "carrying on business," and "doing business" were defined by the Circuit Court of Appeals for the Third Circuit in *Lewellyn v. Pittsburgh, B. & L.E.R. Co.*, 222 Fed. 177. It was stated therein that, "The three expressions, either separately, or connectedly, convey the idea of progression, continuity, or sustained activity. 'Engaged in business' means occupied in business; employed in business. 'Carrying on business' does not mean the performance of a single disconnected business act. It means conducting, prosecuting, and continuing business by performing progressively all the acts normally incident thereto, and likewise the expression 'doing business', when employed as descriptive of an

occupation, conveys the idea of business being done, not from time to time, but all the time. * * * ''. * * *

In *Scottish Am. Inv. Co., Ltd. v. Commissioner*, 12 T.C. 49 (1949), the Court addressed whether the taxpayers, foreign investment trusts, were, by virtue of maintaining a U.S. office, ''engaged in trade or business within the United States'' within the meaning of section 231(b) of the 1939 Code, as amended. The Court examined ''the real business of * * * [the taxpayers], the doing of what they were principally organized to do in order to realize profit''. * * * In *Scottish American*, the Court decided that the taxpayers' real business was ''the cooperative management in Scotland of British capital'' and that ''the business activities of the American office were merely helpfully adjunct.'' * * * Additionally, the Court stated that, ''In cases such as these * * * [regarding whether the taxpayer is engaged in trade or business within the United States], it is a matter of degree, based upon both a quantitative and a qualitative analysis of the services performed, as to where the line of demarcation should be drawn.'' * * * In *Scottish American*, the Court decided that the factors to be examined were the ''character'' of the activities performed in the U.S. office, ''the purpose for which the office * * * [was] established'', and, to a lesser extent, ''the volume of the activities''. * * *

In *Spermacet Whaling & Shipping Co. S/A v. Commissioner*, 30 T.C. 618 (1958), the Court addressed whether the taxpayer, a foreign corporation, was ''engaged in trade or business within the United States'' within the meaning of section 231(b) of the 1939 Code, as amended. In interpreting former section 231(b), the Court stated:

> We have consistently held that before a taxpayer can be found to be ''engaged in trade or business within the United States'' it must, during some substantial portion of the taxable year have been regularly and continuously transacting a substantial portion of its ordinary business in this country. * * * [* * * (citing, inter alia, *European Naval Stores Co., S.A. v. Commissioner, supra*, and *Scottish American Investment Co. v. Commissioner, supra*).]

After summarizing the test pursuant to former section 231(b), the Court concluded that the taxpayer was not ''engaged in any substantial, regular, or continuous ordinary business activity in the United States.'' * * *

Petitioners contend that LTD's ''real business'' was ''to render investment advice to clients in Mexico.'' Accordingly, petitioners argue that all of the activities relating to LTD's business occurred in Mexico: LTD's clients were solicited and advised by Mexican-based promoters in Mexico, their accounts were opened and approved in Mexico, clients changed their investment portfolios in consultation with their Mexican promoter, and the spread (where applicable) was negotiated in Mexico. Petitioners contend that INC performed merely ministerial activities in the United States and did not render any investment advice to clients in Mexico. On those premises, petitioners conclude that LTD's ''real business"—even if INC's activities were imputed to LTD—did not occur in the United States.

We disagree. Contrary to petitioners' argument, we believe that the term "performance of personal services within the United States" for purposes of section 864(b) does not require that LTD itself perform such "personal services" in order to be engaged in "trade or business within the United States."

We first look to the "real business" of the taxpayers, the "doing of what * * * [the taxpayers] were principally organized to do in order to profit". * * * LTD is a corporation organized pursuant to the laws of the Cayman Islands. Based on the record, we believe that the "real business" of LTD, the doing of what LTD was "principally organized to do in order to realize profit", was to enable Mexican nationals to invest their capital in non-Mexican financial markets. LTD's "real business" was not merely to render investment advice to clients in Mexico, as petitioners contend. During each of the years in issue, LTD's income consisted of four major categories: Management fees, interest income, currency transactions fees, and other fees and commissions. LTD's income, therefore, was derived from effecting, primarily in the United States, transactions in financial markets. Accordingly, we conclude that LTD's "real business" was providing Mexican nationals with access to non-Mexican financial markets and that such business was conducted primarily in the United States.

In *Scottish Am. Inv. Co. v. Commissioner,* * * * the Court made "a quantitative and a qualitative analysis of the services performed". Quantitatively, LTD performed a substantial number of services in the United States. LTD maintained a client clearing account at Frost Bank in San Antonio in which it collected deposits from clients. During the years in issue, LTD had approximately the following number of client accounts: 257 during 1985, 434 during 1986, 557 during 1987, 870 during 1988, and 1,131 during 1989. Not all client accounts were actively traded. Nonetheless, we conclude that the number of LTD's client accounts, and, as a corollary, the number of services performed in the United States for such accounts, during each of the years in issue, can be characterized as quantitatively substantial.

Qualitatively, LTD performed substantial services in the United States. Directly and through its agent INC, LTD provided investment management services and marketed investment products. The purpose for which LTD was established was to provide access to non-Mexican financial markets, and LTD conducted such business primarily in the United States. We therefore conclude that LTD's activities in the United States during each of the years in issue can be characterized as qualitatively substantial.

In sum, we conclude that LTD "engaged in * * * substantial, regular, or continuous ordinary business activity in the United States." * * * We find that LTD's activities in the United States, conducted directly or through agents, included: Receiving client funds, monitoring interest

> rates, effecting trades, collecting and disbursing dividends and interest, maintaining customer account information, and valuing portfolios. Accordingly, we conclude that, during the years in issue, LTD was "engaged in business in the United States" * * *. Consequently, we hold that LTD was "engaged in the active conduct of a banking, financing, or similar business in the United States" * * *. A fortiori, we hold that LTD was engaged in "trade or business within the United States" pursuant to section 864(b) for its taxable years June 30, 1985 through 1989.

71 T.C.M. (CCH) at 3237–28 to –30.

2. In Pasquel v. Commissioner, 12 T.C.M. (CCH) 1431 (1954), the taxpayer was a citizen and resident of Mexico who advanced moneys to a U.S. shipbuilder to enable the purchase of several ships in the United States. The ships were purchased in the United States and resold. The parties divided the profits equally. The court, citing the discussion in *European Naval Stores*, rejected the IRS argument that the taxpayer had participated in a U.S. trade or business on the ground that the transaction was a "single and isolated" event that was not "sufficiently regular, continuous and extensive."

[¶ 3035]

b. Effect of Agency Arrangements

While the use of agents or representatives within the United States by a foreign person does not necessarily establish a U.S. trade or business, such a result may obtain even though the foreign person is not present and has no employees in the United States. The determination will depend upon the functions and activities performed by people and entities within the United States on behalf of the otherwise absent foreign person and in some cases the relationship between the foreign person and the people and entities undertaking the functions and activities.

[¶ 3040]

REVENUE RULING 70–424

1970–2 C.B. 150.

* * *

M, a foreign corporation, and *Q*, a domestic corporation, entered into an agreement under which *M* conveyed to *Q* the sole agency for the sales of its products in the United States. *Q* agreed to make sales of such products within the United States and not to make sales of the same kind of products of any other company except on express permission from *M*. *Q* further agreed not to make sales of *M*'s products to purchasers domiciled outside the United States or to any competitor to *M* without consent of *M* and not to take a financial interest in any competitor of *M*. It is also provided that *Q* will secure yearly contracts which will be subject to the approval of *M*. *Q* assumes the full responsibility for the sales of *M*'s product and acts as guarantor. However, *M* agreed to share equally with *Q* any loss incurred up to a specified amount in any one year during the life of the agreement. Under the agreement *Q* is to receive a commission based on a graduated percentage of the selling price of the products.

Held, the arrangement is one of ordinary principal and agent through which *M* carries on its activities in the United States and thus is engaged in trade or business within the United States. *M* is, therefore, subject to the provisions of section 882 * * *.

* * *

[¶ 3045]

NOTE

Compare the Ruling to Section 864(c)(5), which determines when the office of an agent will be regarded as the office or fixed place of business of a foreign principal. A distinction is made for a "general commission agent, broker, or other agent of independent status acting in the ordinary course of his business," whose office will not be attributed to a foreign principal. § 864(c)(5)(A). However, if such an agent acts "exclusively, or almost exclusively" for the foreign principal, the agent will not be classified as "independent" if all of the facts and circumstances warrant such a conclusion. Reg. § 1.864–7(d)(3)(iii).

The distinction between an independent agent acting in the ordinary course of business and other agents is also reflected in many tax treaties. See, e.g., Art. 5(6) of the U.S. Model Treaty. Again, the activities of such an agent are not imputed to the foreign principal for purposes of determining whether there is a permanent establishment in the United States. The distinction, which was not discussed in the Ruling, raises interesting conceptual questions. If the acts taken within the United States by agents on behalf of foreign principals produce income, why should the status of the agent, as defined in these provisions, affect the taxability of the foreign principal?

[¶ 3050]

HANDFIELD v. COMMISSIONER

United States Tax Court, 1955.
23 T.C. 633.

* * *

ARUNDELL, JUDGE: The principal question in this proceeding is whether the petitioner, a nonresident Canadian, was engaged in business in the United States during the year in controversy. The determination of this question depends upon the nature of the arrangement which the petitioner had for selling in this country an item which he manufactured in Canada.

The petitioner manufactures a novelty item called Folkards which is a kind of postal card. He had a contract with the American News Company by which the latter distributed his cards to newsstands in the United States where they were sold to the public. The petitioner contends that the American News Company purchased the cards from him for resale. He further contends that the sale occurred in Canada when the cards were placed in transportation and at that time he surrendered all his right, title, and interest in the cards to the News Company.

The respondent contends that the arrangement between the petitioner and the News Company provided for an agency relationship, and that the News Company was petitioner's exclusive distributor in the United States.

The nature of the contract between petitioner and the News Company is to be determined from the intention of the parties. * * * We have an extremely meager record on which to make that determination. At the trial, the parties were cautioned that the record was quite ambiguous for a decision on a question of some importance. Nevertheless, we have been left with only the bare agreement between the petitioner and the News Company and a few stipulated facts from which to determine the nature of the arrangement.

It will be observed that the agreement between the petitioner and the News Company nowhere says that the News Company *buys* or will buy the Petitioner's cards or that the company is or will be obligated for any definite number of cards or in any definite amount. The contract uses the word "sale" twice. In each instance it is clear that the word refers to transactions with the public, not between the petitioner and the News Company. Thus, the contract states, "If * * * the *sale* in any city should be unsatisfactory, we will pick up stock from dealers, and return it to you * * *." * * * And, also, that the News Company "reserves the right to withdraw them [the cards] from *sale* without notice" when copyright or patent infringement is threatened. * * * The contract speaks of its purpose as confirmation of "arrangements recently discussed *for the exclusive distribution through our Company*" in the United States where it is "mutually agreed to put these [cards] out." * * * The contract specifies the rate at which the News Company will be billed for the cards, the rate at which the cards will be billed to the "trade," and the retail price at which the cards will be sold. But, payments were to be made "on the basis of actual check-ups of dealers' stocks sixty days *after distribution*, and every thirty days thereafter." * * * The contract stated that all cards were "fully returnable" and that transportation on shipments to and from the United States was to be paid by the petitioner and that he would allow credit on all unsold cards, regardless of condition.

The contract gave exclusive rights to the News Company "to *distribute* Folkards in the United States" and, as noted above, the News

Company could "pick up stock from dealers and return it" after it "mutually agreed to discontinue the *distribution*" in any city. * * *

The foregoing language raises some doubt whether the News Company actually sells the cards to the public or whether it acts as a distributor to newsdealers who sell to the public. We do not have enough information in the record to make any findings concerning the relationship between the News Company and the dealers. In our view of the case, it is immaterial precisely what that relationship may be because, as will appear below, the important relationship is that between the petitioner and the News Company.

Petitioner visited the United States occasionally to check on his arrangement with the News Company and during the period in issue, he was in the country for a total of 24 days on four different visits. However, he had an employee in the United States whom he paid to visit the various outlets of the News Company checking to insure that the cards were being properly displayed and retailed.

From all the provisions of the contract and all the information on the operations of the petitioner in relation to it that are in this record, we think that the arrangement between the petitioner and the News Company was one in which the News Company was his agent in the United States. We think that the cards were shipped on consignment to the News Company for sale to the public. All the aspects of the agreement point to this interpretation of the contract and none are inconsistent with this interpretation.

The features of the contract which are particularly persuasive in bringing us to the interpretation we have placed on it are: The News company does not obligate itself to buy any definite amount of merchandise from petitioner and it is obligated only to account for the merchandise which has been sold; all merchandise unsold may be returned; the petitioner will pay the transportation on the cards to and from Canada and give full credit for all cards unsold regardless of their condition; the agreement controls the retail price; and it gives the News Company the right to discontinue merchandising the cards when they move slowly or when they infringe copyright or patent provisions. All these, taken together, we think indicate that the arrangement was an agency relationship in the form of a contract of consignment. * * *

Of such an arrangement, one court has said (*In re Taylor*, (E.D.Mich., 1931) 46 F.2d 326, 328):

> A contract of consignment * * * imposes no obligation upon the consignor to sell or upon the consignee to buy any property, and it effects no sale or transfer of title, conditional or absolute, from consignor to consignee. It merely creates a bailment between the consignor as bailor and the consignee as bailee, of property of the bailor, with authority in the bailee as his agent to sell such property

to third persons and with the duty to account to him for the proceeds of any such sale. On such a sale the title passes, not from the consignor to the consignee as in a contract of conditional sale, but from the consignor as owner, through the consignee as his agent, to the purchaser. In the absence of such a sale the consignee may return the property to the consignor without liability for the purchase price thereof.

* * *

The News Company, under its contract with petitioner, was an "agent" in the United States with a "stock of merchandise" from which it regularly filled orders for the public. * * * It follows, then, that he was engaged in business within the United States in the year in issue and the income from his operations in this country is subject to taxation * * *.

* * *

[¶ 3055]

NOTES

1. The *Handfield* decision involves in part an application of the United States–Canada Tax Treaty. The effect of treaty provisions on foreign persons who might be conducting a U.S. trade or business is discussed at ¶ 3165. For purposes of this case, it is sufficient to observe that a foreign person may have a U.S. trade or business without having a "permanent establishment." However, U.S. tax treaties, such as that with Canada, generally provide that the foreign person may not be taxed on trade or business income unless there is a "permanent establishment" in the United States to which the income is attributable. The court also concluded that Handfield had such a permanent establishment as defined in the U.S.-Canada Tax Treaty then in effect.

2. The activities of all agents (whether dependent or independent) in the United States on behalf of foreign principals are generally imputed to the foreign principals for purposes of determining whether it is engaged in a U.S. trade or business. However, in certain situations when the taxable income of the U.S. trade or business depends upon the existence of an "office or other fixed place of business within the United States," the operation of such an *office* by an *independent* agent will not be imputed to the foreign principal even though its *activities* in the United States will be imputed. Is there a reason for the distinction? As indicated previously, under Article 5(6) of the U.S. Model Treaty, a permanent establishment operated by an independent agent is not imputed to a foreign principal from the treaty country. Some commentators contend that it is inappropriate to attribute the activities of an independent agent to a foreign principal for purposes of determining whether a U.S. trade or business is being conducted by the foreign principal.

[¶ 3060]

c. Partnerships, Trusts and Estates

The results of partnership operations are attributed to the respective partners for federal income tax purposes. If a partnership conducts a trade or business in the United States, each partner (whether limited or general) will be deemed to be conducting the U.S. trade or business. § 875(1). The income or loss attributable to a foreign partner will, therefore, be treated under the rules discussed in this Chapter. The same results obtain for a member of a limited liability company that is taxed under the partnership rules. If a trust or estate conducts a U.S. trade or business, its beneficiaries are deemed to be conducting a U.S. trade or business and will be taxed under the rules discussed in this Chapter when effectively connected income is distributed. § 875(2). Whether a U.S. trade or business is being conducted will be determined by the standards that have been developed for application to foreign corporations and nonresident aliens.

[¶ 3065]

UNITED STATES v. BALANOVSKI

United States Court of Appeals, Second Circuit, 1956.
236 F.2d 298, cert. denied, 352 U.S. 968 (1957).

CLARK, CHIEF JUDGE:

* * *

Defendants Balanovski and Horenstein were copartners in the Argentine partnership, Compania Argentina de Intercambio Comercial (CADIC), Balanovski having an 80 per cent interest and Horenstein, a 20 per cent interest. Balanovski, an Argentinian citizen, came to the United States on or about December 20, 1946, and remained in this country for approximately ten months, except for an absence of a few weeks in the spring of 1947 when he returned to Argentina. His purpose in coming here was the transaction of partnership business; and while here, he made extensive purchases and sales of trucks and other equipment resulting in a profit to the partnership of some $7,763,702.20.

His usual mode of operation in the United States was to contact American suppliers and obtain offers for the sale of equipment. He then communicated the offers to his father-in-law, Horenstein, in Argentina. Horenstein, in turn, submitted them at a markup to an agency of the Argentine Government, Instituto Argentino de Promocion del Intercambio (IAPI), which was interested in purchasing such equipment. If IAPI accepted an offer, Horenstein would notify Balanovski and the latter would accept the corresponding original offer of the American supplier. In the meantime IAPI would cause a letter of credit in favor of Balanovski to be opened with a New York bank. Acting under the terms of the letter of credit Balanovski would assign a portion of it, equal to CADIC's purchase price, to the United States supplier. The supplier could then draw on the New York bank against the letter of credit by sight draft for 100 per cent invoice value accompanied by (1) a commercial invoice billing Balanovski, (2) an inspection certificate, (3) a nonnegotiable warehouse or dock receipt issued in the name of the New York bank for the account of IAPI's Argentine agent, and (4) an insurance policy covering all risks to the merchandise up to delivery F.O.B. New York City. Then, if the purchase was one on which CADIC was to receive a so-called quantity discount or commission, the supplier would pay Balanovski the amount of the discount. These discounts, paid after delivery of the goods and full payment to the suppliers, amounted to $858,595.90, constituting funds which were delivered in the United States.

After the supplier had received payment, Balanovski would draw on the New York bank for the unassigned portion of the letter of credit, less 1 per cent of the face amount, by submitting a sight draft accompanied by (1) a commercial invoice billing IAPI, (2) an undertaking to ship before a certain date, and (3) an insurance policy covering all risks to the merchandise up to delivery F.A.S. United States Sea Port. The bank would then deliver the nonnegotiable warehouse receipt that it had received from the supplier to Balanovski on trust receipt and his undertaking to deliver a full set of shipping documents, including a clean on board bill of lading issued to the order of IAPI's Argentine agent, with instructions to notify IAPI. It would also notify the warehouse that Balanovski was authorized to withdraw the merchandise. Upon delivery of these shipping documents to the New York bank Balanovski would receive the remaining 1 per cent due under the terms of the letter of credit. Although Balanovski arranged for shipping the goods to Argentina, IAPI paid shipping expenses and made its own arrangement there for marine insurance. The New York bank would forward the bill of lading, Balanovski's invoice billing IAPI, and the other documents required by the letter of credit (not including the supplier's invoice billing Balanovski) to IAPI's agent in Argentina.

Twenty-four transactions following substantially this pattern took place during 1947. Other transactions were also effected which conformed to a substantially similar pattern, except that CADIC engaged the services of others to facilitate the acquisition of goods and their shipment to Argentina. And other offers were sent to Argentina, for which no letters of credit were opened. Several letters of credit were opened which remained either in whole or in part unused. In every instance of a completed transaction Balanovski was paid American money in New York, and in every instance he deposited it in his own name with New York banks. Balanovski never ordered material from a supplier for which he did not have an order and letter of credit from IAPI.

Balanovski's activities on behalf of CADIC in the United States were numerous and varied and required the exercise of initiative, judgment, and executive responsibility. They far transcended the routine or merely clerical. Thus he conferred and bargained with American bankers. He inspected goods and made trips out of New York State in order to buy and inspect the equipment in which he was trading. He made sure the goods were placed in warehouses and aboard ship. He tried to insure that CADIC would not repeat the errors in supplying inferior equipment that had been made by some of its competitors. And while here he attempted "to develop" "other business" for CADIC.

Throughout his stay in the United States Balanovski employed a Miss Alice Devine as a secretary. She used, and he used, the Hotel New Weston in New York City as an office. His address on the documents involved in the transactions was given as the Hotel New Weston. His supplier contacted him there, and that was the place where his letters were typed and his business appointments arranged and kept. Later Miss Devine opened an office on Rector Street in New York City, which he also used. When he returned to Argentina for a brief time in 1947 he left a power of attorney with Miss Devine. This gave her wide latitude in arranging for shipment of goods and in signing his name to all sorts of documents, including checks. When he left for Argentina again at the end of his 10–month stay, he left with Miss Devine the same power of attorney, which she used throughout the balance of 1947 to arrange for and complete the shipment of goods and bank the profits.

* * *

The district court held that CADIC was not engaged in a trade or business within the United States * * *, but that each of the partners was liable for certain taxes because Balanovski as an individual was so engaged in business and therefore taxable * * *, while Horenstein received "fixed or determinable annual or periodical gains, profits, and income" * * *. We, on the contrary, hold that the partnership CADIC was engaged in business in the United States and that hence the two copartners were taxable for their share of its profits from sources within the United States. * * *

CADIC was actively and extensively engaged in business in the United States in 1947. Its 80 per cent partner, Balanovski, under whose hat 80 per cent of the business may be thought to reside, was in this country soliciting orders, inspecting merchandise, making purchases, and (as will later appear) completing sales. While maintaining regular contact with his home office, he was obviously making important business decisions. He maintained a bank account here for partnership funds. He operated from a New York office through which a major portion of CADIC's business was transacted. * * *

We cannot accept the view of the trial judge that, since Balanovski was a mere purchasing agent, his presence in this country was insufficient to justify a finding that CADIC was doing business in the United States. We need not consider the question whether, if Balanovski (an 80 per cent partner) were merely engaged in purchasing goods here, the partnership could be deemed to be engaged in business, since he was doing more than purchasing. Acting for CADIC he engaged in numerous transactions wherein he both purchased and sold goods in this country, earned his profits here, and participated in other activities, pertaining to the transaction of business. Cases cited in support of the proposition that CADIC was not engaged in business here are quite distinguishable. * * *

* * *

[¶ 3070]

NOTES

1. In Rev. Rul. 91–32, 1991–1 C.B. 107, the IRS ruled that gain or loss realized by a foreign partner from the disposition of an interest in a partnership that conducted a U.S. trade or business is considered to be effectively connected with the U.S. trade or business. If the partnership has both effectively connected income property and other property, only the portion of gain attributable to property used in the U.S. trade or business will be deemed to be effectively connected.

2. Subchapter S corporations, like partnerships, are generally not subject to tax. Their shareholders are taxed on their share of corporate income. However, foreign investors cannot use Subchapter S corporations because a corporation with nonresident alien or corporate shareholders does not qualify for the election. § 1361(b). Accordingly, the operation of a trade or business in the United States by a U.S. corporation will never be attributed to its foreign shareholders solely because of their equity interests.

3. A partnership operating a U.S. trade or business in which effectively connected income is allocable to foreign persons is subject to a withholding obligation under Section 1446. This requirement is discussed more fully at ¶ 4175.

[¶ 3075]

d. Banking

Not all lenders are commercial banks. The regulations prescribe particular tests for determining whether a foreign person is conducting a banking business within the United States. Reg. § 1.864–4(c)(5). They provide that the foreign person will be deemed to be conducting a "banking, financing, or similar business in the United States" if the foreign person is engaged in a trade or business here and if the activities consist of "any one or more of the following activities carried on, in whole or in part, in the United States in transactions with persons situated within or without the United States:"

1. Receiving deposits of funds from the public;

2. Making personal, mortgage, industrial or other loans to the public;

3. Purchasing, selling, discounting or negotiating for the public on a regular basis notes, drafts, checks, bills of exchange, acceptances or other evidences of indebtedness;

4. Issuing letters of credit to the public and negotiating drafts drawn under those letters of credit;

5. Providing trust services for the public; or

6. Financing foreign exchange transactions for the public.

The fact that the taxpayer is subjected to banking and credit laws of a foreign country is relevant but is not determinative of whether there is a U.S. trade or business.

[¶ 3080]

e. Management of Real Property

The ownership and rental of real property does not necessarily constitute a trade or business. However, the tax planning objective of the foreign person owning real property in the United States may be to assure that the arrangement is treated as a U.S. trade or business so that U.S. taxes will be imposed only on net income. The taxpayer thereby benefits from the considerable deductions ordinarily available in respect of real property investments.

[¶ 3085]

LEWENHAUPT v. COMMISSIONER

United States Tax Court, 1953.
20 T.C. 151, aff'd per curiam, 221 F.2d 227 (9th Cir.1955).

[The taxpayer, a Swedish Count, was a citizen and resident of Sweden during and before the tax year. The case arose because the IRS sought to tax long-term capital gains realized by the taxpayer from the sale of real property located in the United States. Under the then applicable law, such gain would not be subject to U.S. tax unless effectively connected with a U.S. trade or business.

The taxpayer asserted two alternative arguments in support of the conclusion that the gain was not subject to U.S. tax. The first was that the United States–Sweden Tax Treaty exempted such gains. The court rejected that argument. The second was that the taxpayer had not been engaged in a U.S. trade or business during the tax year of the sale.]

* * *

HARRON, JUDGE: * * *.

* * *

The issue here is whether the petitioner's activities with respect to certain parcels of improved real estate constituted engaging in a trade or business. The petitioner, during the taxable year, did not trade in, or realize gain from the sale or exchange of, securities or commodities. At the beginning of the taxable year, the petitioner owned United States securities of an approximate value of $100,000. His only security transactions during the taxable year were the purchase of additional securities with part of the proceeds from the sale of the Modesto real property, which gave rise to the capital gain in question. The respondent's argument on brief that petitioner failed to show that his security transactions did not constitute engaging in business is without merit. * * *

Whether the activities of a nonresident alien constitute engaging in a trade or business in the United States is, in each instance, a question of fact. The evidence and record before us establish, and we have found as a fact, that the petitioner's activities during the taxable year connected with his ownership, and the management through a resident agent, of real property situated in the United States constituted engaging in a business. The petitioner, prior to and during the taxable year, employed LaMontagne as his resident agent who, under a broad power of attorney which included the power to buy, sell, lease, and mortgage real estate for and in the name of the petitioner, managed the petitioner's real properties and other financial affairs in this country. The petitioner, during all or a part of the taxable year, owned three parcels of improved, commercial real estate. The approximate aggregate fair market value of the three properties was $337,000. In addition, the petitioner purchased a residential property, and through his agent, LaMontagne, acquired an option to purchase a fourth parcel of commercial property, herein referred to as the El Camino Real property, at a cost of $67,500. The option was exercised and title to the property conveyed to the petitioner in January 1947.

LaMontagne's activities, during the taxable year, in the management and operation of petitioner's real properties, included the following: executing leases and renting the properties, collecting the rents, keeping books of account, supervising any necessary repairs to the properties, paying taxes and mortgage interest, insuring the properties, executing an option to purchase the El Camino Real property, and executing the sale of the Modesto property. In addition, the agent conducted a regular correspondence with the petitioner's father in England who held a power of attorney from petitioner identical with that given to LaMontagne; he submitted monthly reports to the petitioner's father; and he advised him of prospective and advantageous sales or purchases of property.

The aforementioned activities carried on in the petitioner's behalf by his agent, are beyond the scope of mere ownership of real property, or the receipt of income from real property. The activities were considerable, continuous, and regular and, in our opinion, constituted engaging in a business. * * *

* * *

[¶ 3090]

REVENUE RULING 73-522

1973-2 C.B. 226.

Advice has been requested whether a nonresident alien individual is considered to be engaged in trade or business within the United States during the taxable year, within the meaning of section 871 * * * under the circumstances described below. * * *

The taxpayer, a nonresident alien individual who has not elected to treat real property income as income effectively connected with the conduct of a trade or business within the United States pursuant to section 871(d) * * *, did not, except as described below, engage in any activity within the United States during the taxable year * * *.

The taxpayer owned rental property situated in the United States that was subject to long-term leases each providing for a minimum monthly rental and the payment by the lessee of real estate taxes, operating expenses, ground rent, repairs, interest and principal on existing mortgages, and insurance in connection with the property leased. The leases are referred to as "net leases" and were entered into by the taxpayer on December 1, 1971. The taxpayer visited the United States for approximately one week during November 1971 for the purpose of supervising new leasing negotiations, attending conferences, making phone calls, drafting documents, and making significant decisions with respect to the leases. This was his only visit to the United States in 1971. The leases were identical in form (net leases) to those applicable to the properties owned by the taxpayer prior to December 1, 1971, and were entered into with lessees unrelated to each other or to the taxpayer.

Section 871(a)(1) * * * imposes for each year a tax of 30 percent of the amount received from sources within the United States by a nonresident alien individual as income in the form of items enumerated, but only to the extent that the amount so received is not effectively connected with the conduct of a trade or business within the United States.

Section 871(b)(1) * * * provides for the imposition of a tax on a nonresident alien individual engaged in trade or business in the United States during the taxable year * * * on his taxable income that is effectively connected with the conduct of a trade or business within the United States.

Court decisions involving nonresident alien individual owners of real estate in the United States have developed a test for determining when such individuals are engaged in trade or business within the United States as a result of such ownership. These cases hold that activity of nonresident alien individuals (or their agents) in connection with domestic real estate that is beyond the mere receipt of income from rented property, and the payment of expenses incidental to the collection thereof, places the owner in a trade or business within the United States, provided that such activity is considerable, continuous, and regular. * * *

In the instant case the taxpayer's only activity in the United States during the taxable year * * * was the supervision of the negotiation of leases covering rental property that he owned during that year. No other activity was necessary on the part of the lessor in connection with the properties because of the provisions of the net leases. The taxpayer's supervision of the negotiation of new leases is not considered to be beyond the scope of mere ownership of real property or the mere receipt of income from real property since such activity was sporadic rather than continuous (that is a day-to-day activity), irregular rather than regular, and minimal rather than considerable.

Accordingly, the taxpayer in the instant case is not considered to be engaged in trade or business within the United States during the taxable year ended December 31, 1971, within the meaning of section 871 * * *. See *Evelyn M.L. Neill*, 46 B.T.A. 197 (1942), wherein the operation of one parcel of real estate by the lessee did not result in the owner being considered to be engaged in trade or business. Compare *Adolf Schwarcz*, 24 T.C. 733, *acq*. 1956–1, C.B. 5, wherein an owner operating one parcel of rental property in all its aspects was considered to be engaging in trade or business.

* * *

[¶ 3092]

f. Electronic Commerce

The rapid evolution of electronic commerce and the Internet has generated many difficult conceptual issues. Since a foreign person can be found to be conducting a U.S. trade or business without having a fixed place of business in the United States, an obvious question is when and how business activities undertaken on the Internet affecting the U.S. economy will be deemed to constitute a U.S. trade or business. The U.S. Treasury in a study focused on international tax issues raised by electronic commerce suggested that existing principles should be used to resolve issues presented by new forms of commerce:

> [T]he principle of neutrality between physical and electronic commerce requires that existing principles of taxation be adapted to electronic commerce, taking into account the borderless world of cyberspace. An advantage of an approach based on existing principles, in addition to neutrality, is that such an approach is suitable for adaptation as an international standard. Existing principles are, in broad outline, common to most countries' tax laws.

U.S. Treas. Dep't, Selected Tax Policy Implications of Global Electronic Commerce 20 (1996).

Suppose that a foreign corporation regularly and continuously undertakes to effect a substantial quantity of sales to customers in the United States through Internet advertising and sales on a web site that is maintained by an independent Internet service provider in the United States. Could such an arrangement support the conclusion, applying general principles reflected in the materials set forth in this Chapter, that the foreign corporation is engaged in a U.S. trade or business?

[¶ 3095]

4. ELECTION TO TREAT REAL ESTATE INVESTMENT AS TRADE OR BUSINESS

If a foreign person derives rental income from U.S. real property that is not effectively connected with a U.S. trade or business, the gross amount of the rental income is taxed at the flat rate of 30 percent under the rules described in Chapter 4. Because real property rental income ordinarily is attended by substantial deductions for such items as maintenance, depreciation, taxes and mortgage interest, a tax on gross rental income could create substantial tax burdens even when the property generates a net loss. The Code, however, provides relief by permitting a foreign person to elect to be treated as if it were engaged in a U.S. trade or business with respect to all of its U.S. real property held for the production of income, even if the person is not in fact so engaged. §§ 871(d) and 882(d). Such an election, which binds the foreign person in all subsequent years (unless the IRS consents to revocation of the election), enables the foreign person to be taxed with respect to its net income from real property, thereby utilizing available deductions.

In Rev. Rul. 91–7, 1991–1 C.B. 100, the IRS ruled that a nonresident alien or foreign corporation that derived no income from U.S. real property during a tax year could not make the election. As a result, taxes, interest and carrying charges were not deductible and could not be capitalized under Section 266 so that they could be applied against rental income that might be realized in future years.

C. DETERMINING AMOUNT TO BE TAXED

[¶ 3100]

1. INCOME ITEMS—THE "EFFECTIVELY CONNECTED" PRINCIPLE

In earlier times, any foreign person that conducted a trade or business in the United States would be taxed at the usual rates on all U.S.-source income, whether or not connected to the trade or business. However, this so-called "force-of-attraction" doctrine was largely replaced in 1966 by a mechanism that maintains the distinction between the treatment of income from the active conduct of business and passive income unrelated to the business. Under current law, only income that is actually related to the conduct of the U.S. trade or business will generally be taxed at the usual individual or corporate rates. However, there are limited circumstances in which other U.S.-source income will be taxed as if it were actually connected to the U.S. trade or business.

The key test is whether the item of income in question is "effectively connected" with the U.S. trade or business. Section 864(c)(3) provides that:

> "[a]ll income, gain, or loss from sources within the United States (other than income, gain, or loss to which paragraph (2) applies) shall be treated as effectively connected with the conduct of a trade or business within the United States."

The effect of the paragraph 2 reference (which is Section 864(c)(2)) is to exclude from the trade or business taxing regime most items of U.S.-source investment income and capital gains that are not effectively connected with the trade or business. Such items, when taxed, are in general subject to the taxing regime described in Chapter 4, under which withholding taxes are imposed on gross income. When there is a question whether such items are effectively connected with the U.S. trade or business, Section 864(c)(2) prescribes some factors for analysis:

1. Did the income, gain or loss derive from assets used in or held for use in the conduct of the trade or business (the "asset-use test")?

2. Did the activities of the trade or business constitute a material factor in the realization of the income, gain or loss (the "business-activity test")?

In applying these factors, the Code provides that due regard must be given to whether the income, gain or loss was accounted for through the trade or business.

The "asset-use test" is employed to determine the functional relationship between the assets giving rise to income or loss and the operation of the U.S. trade or business. The regulations indicate that a direct relationship between the asset and the U.S. trade or business will be found only if the asset is held to meet the present needs of that trade or business and not its anticipated future needs. For example, an asset is considered as needed in the trade or business conducted in the United States if the asset is held to meet the operating expenses of that trade or business. Conversely, an asset is considered as not needed in the trade or business conducted in the United States if the asset is held for the purpose of providing for future diversification into a new trade or business, expansion of trade or business activities conducted outside of the United States, future plant replacement or future business contingencies. Reg. § 1.864–4(c)(2)(iv)(a). Further, the regulations establish a presumption that there is a direct relationship between the holding of an asset giving rise to the realization of income and a U.S. trade or business if the asset was acquired with funds generated by the trade or business, the income from the asset is retained or reinvested in that trade or business and personnel present in the United States and actively involved in the conduct of the trade or business exercise significant management and control over the investment of the asset. Reg. § 1.864–4(c)(2)(iv)(*b*).

The "business-activities test" is used to distinguish the active conduct of a business from the normal supervisory functions of an investor. The relevant factors include whether the activities of such a trade or business were a material factor in the realization of the income, gain or loss. § 864(c)(2)(B). The regulations provide that the "business-activities test" is of primary significance where dividends or interest are derived by a dealer in stocks or securities, gain or loss is derived from the sale or exchange of capital assets in the active conduct of a trade or business by an investment company, royalties are derived in the active conduct of a business consisting of the licensing of patents or similar intangible property or service fees are derived in the active conduct of a service business. Reg. § 1.864–4(c)(3)(i).

A vestige of the force-of-attraction doctrine remains in the Code. Any items of U.S.-source income not covered by Section 864(c)(2) will be attributed to the U.S. trade or business even absent an actual connection with that trade or business. § 864(c)(3). As a result, U.S.-source income from the sale of inventory by a foreign person conducting a U.S. trade or business will be taxed as effectively connected income even though there is no actual connection with the U.S. trade or business. For example, a foreign person engaged in the sale of one inventory product within the United States through a U.S. trade or business must include in taxable income the gain or loss realized from an isolated sale within the United States of other inventory property not related to the production and marketing of the first. As another example, a foreign person conducting a U.S. trade or business because of the performance of services in the United States would be taxed on the isolated sale of inventory in the United States even though the inventory sale was not related to the performance of services. A foreign person electing to treat U.S. real estate investment as a trade or business (as discussed at ¶ 3095) will, however, be taxed only upon income from real property. Reg. § 1.871–10(b)(1).

All "effectively connected" income will be combined for purposes of determining the foreign person's U.S. tax liability. If the foreign person is conducting more than one trade or business venture within the United States, the results of all will be combined in the tax calculation. This means that losses generated by one U.S. trade or business can be applied against income generated by another.

The following Ruling reflects the attempt to determine whether certain banking income is effectively connected with the U.S. branch of a foreign bank. Although it applies regulations specially directed to the banking industry, it demonstrates the type of linkage which results in the conclusion that income is effectively connected with a U.S. trade or business.

[¶ 3105]

REVENUE RULING 86–154

1986–2 C.B. 103.

ISSUE

Whether, in the situations described below, securities held by a United States branch of a foreign bank and recorded on its books are attributable to the United States branch or to the home office.

FACTS

P, a foreign corporation whose home office is located in foreign country *X*, is actively engaged in the conduct of the banking business within the United States within the meaning of section 1.864–4(c)(5)(i) of the * * * Regulations through *B* and *C*, *P*'s United States branch offices. *B* has in its possession and has recorded on its books interest bearing securities of related and unrelated United States corporations evidencing funds advanced by *B* to these borrowers. Typically, the branch offices' participation in the loan acquisition process varies and is described in the situations presented below.

Situation 1: Unrelated Party Loans

B has full-time permanent employees who are account officers. These account officers contact financial officers of medium size United States companies. Through scheduled appointments, the account officers propose terms to prospective customers, and, if a customer is interested in the terms being offered, the customer executes a credit application. *B* transmits the credit application to *C*, which is staffed with personnel particularly capable of performing credit analysis, security evaluation, and other research functions. *C*'s findings are forwarded to *B*. The account officer incorporates *C*'s findings into a loan package which is forwarded to a credit committee composed of officers from *B* and *C*. The credit committee generally approves or rejects the loan package. In some cases, the committee will suggest modification of terms, in which case further negotiation by the account officer with the customer is necessary. Once the customer has agreed to terms and those terms are approved by the credit committee, *B* prepares the loan documentation and forwards it to the customer for signature. After the customer has signed, *B* funds the loan.

Situation 2: Related Party Loans

P has a wholly-owned United States subsidiary, *S*, which is actively engaged in equipment leasing and related services. *S* is in need of additional funding for expansion of its operations. The home office of *P* reviews *S*'s expansion plans, evaluates the customer orders and the credit worthiness of the customers' future receivables, and approves the loan. *P* funds the loan through *B*, by increasing *B*'s capital and having *B* loan the funds to *S*. *B* actually disperses the funds to *S*. As evidence of the loan, *S* executes a promissory note in favor of *B*. *B* services the loan throughout its term.

Situation 3: Loan Participations

An unrelated foreign multinational corporation, *Z*, is solicited by *P*'s home office and negotiates with that office for lines of credit that far exceed the funding capability of an individual branch such as *B*. In cases where *P* has approved such a large line of credit, it does so in anticipation that its various branches will participate in the funding of the loan. Regarding *B*'s participation, *P*'s home office forwards the loan documentation to *B* and instructs *B*, subject to *B*'s normal credit analysis and other loan review procedures, to fund a part of the loan to *Z*. *Z*'s wholly-owned domestic subsidiary contacts *B* for purposes of obtaining the designated loan amount. With the benefit of the information contained in the prior loan documentation forwarded from *P*, an independent global credit analysis is not performed by *B*. However, an account officer of *B* negotiates with *Z*'s United States subsidiary for the necessary collateral which is standard under *B*'s loan practices. *C* performs a thorough credit analysis of *Z*'s domestic subsidiary, evaluates the collateral and confirms to *B* that the collateral is adequate to secure the loan. *B* funds the loan.

LAW AND ANALYSIS

* * *

Section 1.864–4(c)(5)(ii) and (iii) of the regulations provides special rules for determining whether income from securities is effectively connected with the active conduct of a banking, financing, or similar business within the United States. Subdivision (ii) requires the securities be acquired in the course of conducting specified activities, or, the securities consist of particular types. In addition, the securities must be considered attributable to a United States office through which the banking, financing, or similar business is carried on.

Subdivision (iii) provides that a security is attributable to a United States office only if such office actively and materially participates in soliciting, negotiating, or performing other activities required to arrange the acquisition of the security. However, a United States office need not have been the only active participant in arranging the acquisition of the security.

HOLDING

Situation 1

The activities of *B* and *C* are considered to be active and material with respect to the acquisition of the security. *B* or *C* solicited and negotiated the loan, performed the credit analysis and loan review, and approved the loan. These factors demonstrate that *P*'s branch office operation had the requisite authority and capability to make the loan and in fact performed all material functions with respect to the making of the loan. Accordingly, the interest income from the security held by *B* is considered effectively connected with the active conduct of a banking and finance business in the United States.

Situation 2

B did not actively and materially participate in the acquisition of the loan merely because it funded the loan. All essential functions in connection with the loan were performed by *P*'s home office. Therefore, the interest income received with respect to the security evidencing the related party loan to *Z* is not effectively connected with the active conduct of the banking, financing, or similar business within the United States. The Service will closely scrutinize loans made to related parties to determine whether a United States branch office actively and materially participates in arranging the acquisition of the securities. Absent facts clearly indicating active and material participation by a United States branch office including contemporaneous written evidence documenting such participation, it will be presumed that the office did not actively and materially participate.

Situation 3

B's and *C*'s activities are considered active and material. Although *P*'s home office solicited and negotiated the overall line of credit, *B* negotiated the collateral for the loan and *C* performed an independent credit analysis and evaluation of the collateral prior to the granting of the loan. The fact that *P*'s home office also actively and materially participated in the acquisition does not affect this result.

[¶ 3110]

2. COMPENSATION INCOME

Section 864(c) and Sections 871 and 881 appear to overlap when applied to compensation for the performance of personal services. Such compensation is listed in Sections 871(a)(1)(A) and 881(a)(1). However, Section 864(b) specifically provides that the performance of personal services within the United States generally constitutes a trade or business. Compensation is, therefore, always taxed to the recipient at normal rates as effectively connected income, and expenses connected with the activity may be deducted. Moreover, certain personal deductions and exemptions may be available. Even though the taxpayer is entitled to such deductions, special withholding rules are imposed on the payor by Sections 1441 et seq. These rules are discussed at ¶ 4160.

[¶ 3115]

3. DEFERRED INCOME AND LOOK-BACK RULES FOR CERTAIN PROPERTY DISPOSITIONS

Section 864(c)(6) provides that deferred payments of income items, such as those that might result from an installment sale, will be treated as effectively connected with a U.S. trade or business if they would have been so treated in the year the transaction giving rise to the income was effected. In some cases, therefore, a foreign person will be subject to tax at the usual rates on income items during a year in which no U.S. trade or business is in fact being conducted.

Under Section 864(c)(7), property formerly used in a U.S. trade or business continues to be so treated if it is disposed of within ten years after the cessation of such use. The result is that gain will be taxed as if the property were still being used in connection with the U.S. trade or business. This rule is intended to deny taxpayers the opportunity to dispose of inventory acquired in connection with a U.S. trade or business or to enjoy deductions from the depreciation or amortization of U.S. trade or business property and then in both instances avoid U.S. tax by selling the property after the U.S. trade or business has been terminated.

[¶ 3120]

4. CERTAIN FOREIGN-SOURCE INCOME

On several occasions in this and earlier chapters it has been noted that foreign persons are unlikely to have a U.S. income tax liability if there is no U.S.-source income. Section 864(c)(4)(A) confirms the principle that foreign-source income will generally not be treated as effectively connected with a U.S. trade or business. However, several exceptions are prescribed which can result in the subjection of foreign-source income to U.S. taxation.

Foreign-source income, gains and losses may be deemed to be effectively connected (and therefore included in the determination of the taxable income of the U.S. trade or business) if the foreign person "has an office or other fixed place of business within the United States to which [the item of] income, gain, or loss is attributable." The regulations define "an office or other fixed place of business" as a fixed facility in which a foreign individual or corporation engages in a trade or business. Reg. § 1.864–7. If the foreign person not infrequently uses another's office, the office will be considered to be that of the foreign person. Reg. § 1.864–7(b)(2). The office of an agent will create this result if the agent is not independent and either has and regularly exercises authority to negotiate and conclude contracts in the name of the foreign principal or maintains a stock of merchandise belonging to the foreign principal from which orders are regularly filled on the principal's behalf. Reg. § 1.864–7(d). Income is "attributable" to a U.S. office or fixed place of business if the facility is a "material factor" in the realization of the income and if the income is realized in the ordinary course of the trade or business carried on through it. § 864(c)(5)(A). The office or fixed place of business in the United States will not be considered to be a material factor "unless [it] provides[s] a significant contribution to, by being an essential economic element in, the realization of the income, gain, or loss." Reg. § 1.864–6(b)(1).

The effect of these provisions is to raise the possibility that foreign-source income will be taxed to foreign persons. However, as indicated below, the circumstances in which this result can obtain are very narrowly defined.

The exception will apply to foreign-source rents or royalties for the use of intangible properties derived in the active conduct of a trade or business. § 864(c)(4)(B)(i). Thus, if the U.S. branch of a foreign corporation operates a research facility in the United States and markets the technology that it develops, even foreign-source royalties attributable thereto will be treated as effectively connected income.

The exception will apply to foreign-source dividends or interest derived from the conduct through an office or other fixed place of business in the United States of a banking, financing or similar business or received by a corporation whose principal business is trading in stocks or securities for its own account. § 864(c)(4)(B)(ii). Thus, if the New York branch of a foreign bank should make a loan to a foreign resident, the interest will be treated as effectively connected income.

Income from sales of inventory outside of the United States by a foreign person may also be characterized as effectively connected to the taxpayer's U.S. trade or business. First, Section 865(e)(2) provides that, contrary to the usual rule, under certain circumstances, sales of inventory may be considered to be U.S.-source income even though title passes outside of the United States. Such income will thus be effectively connected income under Section 864(c)(3). Such a result obtains if the sales are attributable to an office or fixed place of business in the United States unless the inventory property is sold for use, disposition or consumption outside the United States and a foreign office or foreign fixed place of business of the taxpayer materially participates in the sale. This rule will apply for foreign corporations and most nonresident aliens.

If a nonresident alien has a tax home in the United States and is, therefore, treated as a "U.S. resident" under Section 865(g)(1)(A)(i)(II), the exception to the source rule for inventory does not apply. However, in such a situation (which would almost never apply because an alien with a tax home in the United States would likely be treated as a resident of the United States for tax purposes), foreign-source income from inventory sales will nevertheless be deemed to be attributed to the U.S. trade or business if it is derived through an office or fixed place of business in the United States maintained by the taxpayer, unless the inventory is sold for use, consumption or disposition outside the United States and a foreign office or foreign fixed place of business of the taxpayer has participated materially in the sale. § 864(c)(4)(B)(iii).

It should be noted that income from the foreign sales of inventory will not be treated as effectively connected with a U.S. trade or business as long as a foreign office or fixed place of business has participated materially in the sale. It would seem, therefore, that U.S. tax on foreign sales could be avoided in many, if not most, circumstances.

Whether there is an office or other fixed place of business within the United States may depend on arrangements between the foreign person and its agents functioning within the United States. § 864(c)(5)(A). As mentioned previously, a distinction is made for these purposes in respect of an "independent agent acting in the ordinary course of business" and other agents. The office of such an independent agent will not be treated as a fixed place of business for the foreign person even if the agent "has authority to negotiate and conclude contracts in the name of his principal, and regularly exercises that authority, or maintains a stock of goods from which he regularly fills orders on behalf of his principal." Reg. § 1.864–7(d)(2).

The 2004 JOBS Act added language intended to assure that certain foreign-source income deemed to be effectively connected with a U.S. trade or business will not escape such characterization through the use of various contractual or other arrangements. Section 864(c)(4) now provides that "Any income or gain which is equivalent to any item of income or gain described in clause (i), (ii), or (iii) shall be treated in the same manner as such item for purposes of this subparagraph." The new provision is intended to increase the amount of foreign-source income that will be deemed to be effectively connected with a U.S. trade or business.

[¶ 3125]

REVENUE RULING 75–253

1975–1 C.B. 203.

* * *

The taxpayer, a foreign subsidiary of a United States commercial bank, is incorporated in country *M*, and is in the business of making loans to organizations doing business in less developed countries. The taxpayer has offices in country *M* and in the United States. The taxpayer's United States office handles the negotiation and acquisition of the securities involved in the loan transactions. The United States office presents interest coupons for payment and presents all securities for payment at maturity. It maintains complete photocopy files of the taxpayer's outstanding loans as well as records indicating dates of maturity of and interest payments on the securities. The only business activities of the taxpayer's office in country *M*, which had a skeleton staff, consisted of receiving and storing the original securities and giving pro forma approval of the loans.

Section 864(c)(4) * * * provides, in part, that interest income from sources without the United States shall be treated as effectively connected with the conduct of a trade or business within the United States by a foreign corporation if such corporation has an office or other fixed place of business within the United States to which such income is attributable and such income is derived in the active conduct of banking, financing, or similar business within the United States.

Section 1.864–5(a) of the * * * Regulations provides, in part, that foreign source income realized by a foreign corporation engaged in a trade or business in the United States shall be treated as effectively connected with such trade or business only if the foreign corporation has in the United States an office or other fixed place of business to which such income is attributable in accordance with section 1.864–6.

Section 1.864–6(b)(2)(ii)(*b*) of the regulations provides, in part, that the determination as to whether foreign source interest income derived by a foreign corporation in the active conduct of a banking, financing, or similar business in the United States shall be treated as effectively connected with the active conduct of that business, shall be made by applying the principles of paragraph (c)(5)(ii) of section 1.864–4.

Section 1.864–4(c)(5)(ii) of the regulations states, in part, that United States source interest income derived by a foreign corporation in the active conduct of a banking, financing, or similar business in the United States shall be treated as effectively connected with the conduct of that business only if the securities giving rise to such interest income are attributable to the United States office through which such business is carried on and were acquired in a certain manner or consist of certain types of securities.

Section 1.864–4(c)(5)(iii)(*a*)(2) of the regulations states, in part, that for the purposes of section 1.864–4(c)(5)(ii) a security shall be deemed to be attributable to a United States office only if such security is or was held in the United States by or for such office and recorded on its books or records as having been purchased or acquired by such office or for its account.

The reference to the principles of section 1.864–4(c)(5)(ii) of the regulations in section 1.864–6(b)(2)(ii)(*b*) does not mean that the provisions of section 1.864–4(c)(5)(iii)(*a*)(*2*) will determine whether foreign source income is effectively connected with a United States banking, financing, or similar business. Section 1.864–4(c)(5)(iii)(*a*)(*2*) provides a standard for determining whether United States source interest income received by foreign banks of financing companies through the efforts of their United States offices will be taxed a flat rate under section 881 * * * or at graduated rates under section 882 in order to enable such taxpayers to conduct business within the United States with some certainty as to the tax consequences of their activities.

However, in the case of foreign source interest income earned by foreign banks or financing companies in the United States, the question is not whether such interest is to be taxed at ordinary or flat rates, but whether said interest is to be taxed by the United States at all. Therefore, section 1.864–4(c)(5)(iii)(*a*)(*2*) applies only in the case of United States source income that is to be treated as effectively connected with a United States banking, financing, or similar business with the result that foreign source income (interest, dividends, etc.) may be effectively connected with the active conduct of a United States banking, financing, or similar business despite the wording of section 1.864–4(c)(5)(iii)(*a*)(*2*). A foreign corporation cannot, for example, avoid the taxation of effectively connected foreign source income simply by holding securities outside the United States.

In the instant case, the taxpayer is engaged in the active conduct of a banking, financing, or similar business in the United States within the meaning of section 864(c)(4) * * *. Moreover, since the taxpayer's United States office performed all the significant tasks relating to the negotiation and acquisition of the securities, with the sole exception of storage of the securities, the interest income derived from the securities is attributable to the taxpayer's United States office within the meaning of the regulations under section 864.

Accordingly, foreign source interest income derived by the taxpayer from the securities is effectively connected with the conduct of a trade or business within the United States under section 864(c)(4) * * *.

[¶ 3130]

NOTE

Is the imposition of a U.S. tax on foreign-source income of a foreign person under Section 864(c)(4) within the jurisdictional limitations of customary international law? See ¶ 1070.

5. DEDUCTIONS AND CREDITS APPLICABLE TO EFFECTIVELY CONNECTED INCOME

[¶ 3135]

a. Business Credits and Deductions

In determining the taxable income of a foreign person engaged in a U.S. trade or business, gross income effectively connected with the U.S. business is reduced by deductions for expenses that are connected with that effectively connected income. §§ 873(a) and 882(c)(1). In addition, deductions for charitable gifts under Section 170 are allowed for a foreign corporation whether or not the gifts are connected with income effectively connected with a U.S. business. § 882(c)(1)(B).

After the tentative U.S. tax is calculated on taxable income effectively connected with the U.S. business, credits may be available against the tentative tax. These may include a foreign tax credit. Section 906(a) accords to a nonresident alien or a foreign corporation engaged in a U.S. trade or business foreign tax credits under Sections 901 and 902 for foreign taxes imposed on income that is effectively connected with the U.S. trade or business. However, because the foreign tax credit is generally available only in respect of foreign-source income and foreign persons are taxable on foreign-source income only in the limited circumstances set forth in Section 864(c)(4), it is very seldom used by nonresident aliens and foreign corporations. Section 906(b) provides, moreover, that foreign income taxes imposed on U.S.-source income of a foreign person because of nationality or residence of the taxpayer will not be eligible for the foreign tax credit. However, Section 877(b) allows a taxpayer subject to U.S. tax under the expatriation provisions to take a credit in respect of foreign income taxes imposed on the income subject to tax only by reason of Section 877. The foreign tax credit provisions are discussed in Chapters 5 and 7.

Under Sections 874(c) and 882(c)(2), a foreign person is entitled to deductions and credits only if it files an accurate U.S. income tax return showing its total U.S.-source income. A foreign taxpayer that fails to file such a return may be taxed on the basis of gross income from U.S. sources. Reg. §§ 1.873–1(a), 1.882–4(a)(2). In Swallows Holding, Ltd. v. Commissioner, 515 F.3d 162 (3d Cir.2008), the court sustained the validity of the regulations requiring that deductions be reflected in a timely filed tax return. In doing so, the court reversed a Tax Court decision holding that the regulations constituted an invalid assertion of rule-making authority. 126 T.C. 96 (2006). If the foreign taxpayer takes the position that a treaty preempts usual Code provisions to the taxpayer's benefit, it must be disclosed on a tax return or in some other form acceptable to the IRS. § 6114. However, the IRS has waived certain disclosure requirements in some circumstances. Reg. § 301.6114–1(c).

The generally applicable rules for determining the deductible expenses that may be allocated and apportioned to effectively connected gross income are set forth in Reg. § 1.861–8 and Temp. Reg. § 1.861–8T, discussed at ¶ 2220. If a foreign person receives U.S.-source income that is effectively connected with a U.S. trade or business and other U.S.-source income that is taxed under the regime discussed in Chapter 4, it may be necessary to allocate expenses between the two categories of U.S.-source income because deductions are only available against the effectively connected income. Such an allocation might arise, for example, if state taxes are imposed on a foreign corporation by methods that include both forms of income. See, e.g., Rev. Rul. 87–64, 1987–2 C.B. 166, which requires such apportionment of a state income tax that is imposed on both the business and investment income of a foreign corporation.

[¶ 3140]

b. Interest Deductions

The method of allocating interest payments to the U.S. trade or business of a foreign corporation has been a source of concern that over time has produced a number of approaches. The concern derives from the recognition that money is a peculiarly fungible commodity and that loan arrangements can be tailored to avoid taxes by allocating interest expenses in one direction or another.

The current approach is specified by Section 864(e)(2), which provides that "[a]ll allocations and apportionments of interest expense shall be made on the basis of assets rather than gross income." The basic principle derives from the perception that loan proceeds, in effect, help to finance all of the assets and activities of a corporation. Accordingly, a comparison of asset values is an appropriate way to determine the amount of interest expense properly allocable to the U.S. trade or business.

Because the generally applicable rules for allocating and apportioning interest deductions, discussed at ¶ 2230, can produce unreasonable results for foreign persons engaged in business in the United States, special rules for allocating interest deductions in this situation have been promulgated in Reg. § 1.882–5. The regulation allows a deduction for interest booked in the United States. However, in accordance with the mandate of Section

864(e)(2), the regulations use comparative asset values to effect an appropriate allocation. The following "three-step process" is prescribed:

(1) Determine annually the average value of all "U.S. assets" of the corporation, i.e., assets producing effectively connected income or loss. The "value" of such assets may be either book value for tax purposes or fair market value. The taxpayer must, however, use the same valuation method for every tax year unless the IRS consents to a change. Reg. § 1.882–5(b).

(2) Determine the amount of liabilities connected with the U.S. trade or business by multiplying the asset value determined in Step One by one of two alternative ratios: either a fixed ratio of 50 percent (93 percent in the case of a "banking, financing, or similar business") or an "actual ratio" determined by a comparison of average worldwide liabilities to the average value of worldwide assets. While a taxpayer may elect to use either ratio, it cannot change in subsequent years without the consent of the IRS. Reg. § 1.882–5(c).

(3) The final allocation of interest deductions can then be made according to one of two alternative methods:

(a) *Adjusted U.S.-booked liabilities method.* Compare the amount of U.S.-connected liabilities determined in Step Two to the average total liabilities "shown on the books" of the U.S. trade or business. If the amount shown on the books is equal to or exceeds the amount of U.S.-connected liabilities determined in Step Two, the allocable interest expense deduction is the interest paid or accrued on the books of the branch multiplied by the "scaling ratio." The scaling ratio is the ratio between U.S.-connected and U.S.-booked indebtedness. Reg. § 1.882–5(d)(4). If the amount of U.S.-connected liabilities determined in Step Two exceeds the average of liabilities shown on the books of the U.S. trade or business, the allocable interest expense deduction will be the sum of the interest expense shown on the books of the U.S. trade or business and the amount of the excess of U.S.-connected liabilities times the average interest rate on U.S. dollar liabilities for the tax year shown on the books of offices and branches of the foreign corporation outside the United States. Reg. § 1.882–5(d)(5).

(b) *Separate currency pools method.* The allocable interest expense deductions will be the sum of separate allowed interest deductions determined for each currency in which the taxpayer has borrowed. Reg. § 1.882–5(e). The amount for each currency is the product of: (1) a fraction, in which the numerator is the amount determined in Step Two and the denominator is the average total amount of liabilities (in all currencies) shown on the books of the U.S. trade or business, (2) the average total liabilities shown on the books of the U.S. trade or business denominated in a particular currency and (3) the taxpayer's average worldwide interest rate for the particular currency.

Once a taxpayer has selected one of the two methods for use in Step Three, that method must be used in future years unless the IRS consents to a change.

In addition to the deduction available under the formula, a direct allocation may be made of interest attributable to nonrecourse indebtedness secured by U.S. branch property and "integrated financial transactions" attributable to the branch. Reg. § 1.882–5(a)(1)(ii). The requirements for transactions allowing a direct allocation are set forth at Temp. Reg. § 1.861–10T(b) and (c).

The regulations contain examples of the way in which the alternative approaches will apply. A careful review of the examples will help in addressing the Problem that follows.

[¶ 3145]

PROBLEM

Community Autos A.G. ("Community") is a German corporation engaged in the manufacture of automotive parts. All of Community's operating facilities are located in Europe except for a factory in the United States. During the tax year, Community has average worldwide liabilities of $10 million on which interest at the average rate of 10 percent is paid. Average total liabilities of $2 million are reflected on the books of the U.S. operation, on which interest of $280,000 (14 percent) is paid. The average fair market value of all of Community's assets is $50 million. These assets have a book value for tax purposes of $40 million. The average fair market value of Community's assets in the United States (all of which are connected with the operation of the factory) is $10 million. These assets have a book value of $5 million. All liabilities appearing on the books of the U.S. operation are U.S. dollar obligations. All other liabilities are also in U.S. dollars.

What is the maximum interest deduction that may be taken against the effectively connected income of the U.S. branch, assuming that no prior elections have been made? Would your answer change if the debt not related to the U.S. operation had been established in a foreign currency?

[¶ 3150]

6. PERSONAL DEDUCTIONS

Nonresident aliens engaged in a U.S. trade or business may deduct, in addition to expenses effectively connected with the U.S. trade or business, casualty losses in respect of property located within the United States, charitable contributions and a personal exemption. § 873(b). More generous personal exemptions are permitted if the taxpayer is a resident of Mexico or Canada. § 873(b)(3).

[¶ 3155]

PROBLEMS

1. African Art Traditions, Ltd. ("Traditions") is a long-established, family-owned company organized and operated in a West African country to purchase art objects produced by artists and craftsmen in West Africa and sell them to tourists visiting the country. Traditions has never sold such objects in the United States. However, the scion of the family has recently returned to the home office of Traditions after completing study in the United States that included courses in sales and marketing. He has convinced his family that West African art could generate big volume sales at substantial profit in many of the more chic stores in the United States.

Members of the family have invited U.S. department store buyers to the home office to discuss the potential market for West African art in the United States. As a result of these discussions, the family has determined to start exporting art to the United States, aiming at substantial sales to a limited number of stores (20 or 25). They are considering a number of possibilities:

a. Have no representation in the United States. Sell only to U.S. department store buyers who visit the home office or other countries in the region where Traditions has agents. In addition, sell to U.S. buyers who order by phone, fax, mail or on the Internet.

b. Have a Traditions officer visit the United States annually for three or four months to travel throughout the country promoting and selling the art to department stores and accepting orders, which would be forwarded for approval to the Traditions home office. Traditions would have no warehouse, office or other fixed place of business in the United States. Art would be shipped from the home office directly to the customer.

c. Have a permanent sales office, but no warehouse, in the United States staffed with Traditions personnel. Art objects would be shipped from the home office directly to the customer.

d. Have Traditions set up no sales office in the United States, but retain under contract an independent sales agent that has a U.S. office and employees who will organize marketing efforts and conduct sales campaigns in the United States.

e. Authorize an independent sales agent, in addition to the activities described in d., to solicit, negotiate and accept orders for art in the name and on behalf of Traditions.

f. Have Traditions establish a shop on Fifth Avenue in New York that would maintain a modest inventory. The shop would sell directly to customers, fill orders by mail, fax or on the Internet received from customers in certain Central and South American countries and accept orders from customers in Asian countries that would be forwarded to and filled by shipments directly from the home office to the customers. All sales would be under commercial terms prescribed by the home office. However, employees in New York would have the power to decide whether or not to accept and fill all orders.

Traditions would much prefer to operate under method a., but business exigencies may dictate the use of one of the other methods. In each case consider whether it matters to your analysis if title to the art objects passes outside or within the United States. You have been retained primarily to offer U.S. tax advice. The only income taxes imposed in Traditions' home country are on oil production and mining. The family has become quite accustomed to receiving its income without fiscal erosion and would like to keep it that way. Advise them.

2. How, if at all, would your answers in Problem 1 be modified if Traditions also hired craftsmen as employees to produce art objects for the corporation at its headquarters?

D. EFFECT OF TAX TREATY PROVISIONS

[¶ 3160]

1. INTRODUCTION

Most foreign investment and other business activity in the United States has derived from individuals and entities in countries with which the United States has concluded bilateral tax treaties. As indicated in Chapter 1, no analysis of U.S. income tax provisions relating to international transactions is complete until the impact of any applicable treaty has been fully analyzed. The following materials explore the ways in which treaties affect the U.S taxation of foreign persons engaged in a U.S. trade or business. It should be noted that tax treaties may impose lesser taxes than would be imposed under the Code, but treaties will generally not increase the U.S. tax burdens of a foreign person.

[¶ 3165]

2. U.S. TRADE OR BUSINESS INCOME—THE "PERMANENT ESTABLISHMENT" PROVISION

A foreign person is subject to the usual individual or corporate tax rates on net income effectively connected with a trade or business in the United States. However, as suggested by the prior materials, there is uncertainty as to how much activity is necessary to establish a U.S. trade or business. The tests use such imprecise terms as "continuous," "regular," and "considerable." Such tests admit the possibility that an employee or agent could move about the country engaging in enough activities for a long enough time that a U.S. trade or business will have been established.

Tax treaties usually provide more predictability in the determination of when income from U.S. trade or business activities will be taxed to the foreign person. They generally provide that "business profits" will not be taxed within the United States unless the taxpayer carries on a U.S. trade or business through a "permanent establishment to which the profits are attributable." Article 7 of the U.S. Model Treaty provides an example of such a provision and treaty language implementing it.

Article 5 of the U.S. Model Treaty provides a description of circumstances in which a permanent establishment will be found. Article 5(1) explains that a permanent establishment generally means a fixed place of business through which the business is undertaken. Article 5(2) specifies that a permanent establishment includes a place of management, a branch, an office, a factory, a workshop, a mine, an oil or gas well, a quarry or any other place of extracting natural resources. However, the treaty expressly permits foreign persons to undertake rather substantial activities through a fixed place of business without being deemed to have a permanent establishment. To be treated as a permanent establishment, a threshold level of business activity generally must be carried on in the fixed place. If the business activities are only "preparatory or auxiliary," the place will not be deemed to be a permanent establishment. Article 5(4) lists certain "preparatory or auxiliary" activities to include, for example, use solely for storage, display or delivery of goods, solely for the purchase of goods or solely for the collection of information. Article 5(3) allows a foreign person to pursue for up to 12 months certain specified activities that would otherwise constitute a permanent establishment without being deemed to have created a permanent establishment.

The consequences of using agents to conduct activities are also addressed in detail. Article 5(5) provides that an agent who acts on behalf of the foreign enterprise and who "has and habitually exercises [within the country] an authority to conclude contracts that are binding on the enterprise" may constitute a permanent establishment of that enterprise even if the agent does not conduct the activities through a fixed place of business. However, there will be no permanent establishment attributable solely to carrying on business through a "broker, general commission agent, or any other agent of independent status, provided that such persons are acting in the ordinary course of their business as independent agents." U.S. Model Treaty, Art. 5(6). The IRS has ruled that a U.S. subsidiary of a foreign corporation can be an independent agent. Accordingly, the presence of the U.S. subsidiary "is by itself no basis to hold that the parent corporation has a permanent establishment." Rev. Rul. 76–322, 1976–2 C.B. 487, 488.

The following two cases explore the meaning of "permanent establishment" in two quite different contexts. The first is a relatively simple case involving one man's work. The second requires an analysis of the role of an agent in a complex transaction. Note in the second case the importance of whether an agent is of "independent" status.

[¶ 3170]

SIMENON v. COMMISSIONER

United States Tax Court, 1965.
44 T.C. 820.

[This case turned on whether Georges Simenon, the author of the Inspector Maigret mysteries, had a permanent establishment in the United States during any part of the year 1955 within the meaning of the United States–France Tax Treaty then in force. Under that treaty all of Simenon's royalty income from the United States during the year would be exempt from U.S. tax if he had no permanent establishment. On the other hand, if Simenon had a permanent establishment in the United States for even a part of the year 1955, he would be taxable on the entire year's royalties.]

HARRON, JUDGE: * * *.

* * *

Petitioner converted part of his house at Shadow Rock Farm to the use of an office. He reported on his 1955 return that 50 percent of this property was used for his business and took depreciation on that basis; and that furniture and fixtures acquired in 1954 were devoted 100 percent to business use, and he took depreciation on that basis. Respondent has not questioned those deductions and petitioner still adheres to them. He purchased the Shadow Rock Farm property in November 1950. According to Schedule C–1 in his 1955 return, he had taken depreciation deductions on part of his house for 4 years prior to 1955 in the total sum of $10,765.41, which indicates that he began in 1951, for income tax purposes, to treat the use of part of his house as a conversion to business uses. Lacking evidence to the contrary, the inference and conclusion are that petitioner used part of his house for business purposes, hence as an office, for 4 years prior to 1955 and that such use continued in 1955 to March 19. Other evidence from which such inference may be drawn consists of business correspondence and contracts with his publishers in which his address is both Shadow Rock Farm and Lakeville, Conn. The fact that petitioner regarded 50 percent of the use of his house as devoted to his business is significant. He did not introduce evidence to explain the meaning of his classification of 50 percent of his residence as devoted to business use, or to negate the inference that such use constituted maintaining an office and fixed place of business. * * * There is nothing in the treaty definition of "permanent establishment," insofar as it includes an "office," which would serve to exclude from the term "office" an office at the taxpayer's residence, provided it was devoted to petitioner's business. We are unable to find any merit in petitioner's contention that the office at petitioner's residence cannot be regarded as his "permanent establishment" in the United States within the treaty definition of that term and its meaning in article 7.

The treaty definition of "permanent establishment" is a fairly broad and inclusive one in which there is the catchall term "and other fixed place of business." The term "business" has a broad meaning, which has been defined as including "that which occupies the time, attention, and labor of men for the purpose of livelihood or profit." *Flint v. Stone Tracy Co.*, 220 U.S. 107, 171. * * * In *Kerns Wright*, 31 T.C. 1264, 1267, affirmed per curiam 274 F.2d 883, we observed, in effect, that where a taxpayer has the intent and makes the effort to engage in writing, with some continuity, for the purpose of producing income and a livelihood, his writing activities can qualify as a trade or business. Continuous or repeated activity in the literary field, coupled with a reasonable expectation of making a profit, is convincing evidence of an intent to engage in writing as a business or profession. * * *

* * *

* * * In fact, petitioner took the position in his 1955 return that he was engaged in a business during part of 1955, in the United States, as an author. He reported on Schedule C, income from his business in excess of $40,000, and he took "business deductions" in excess of $12,000 for wages, depreciation, legal and accounting fees ($1,484), business entertainment, publicity photographs, auto expenses, 50 percent of the utilities at his house, 50 percent of building maintenance, stationery and printing, and postage; and he also included a U.S. self-employment tax of $126. The evidence indicates that petitioner's general occupation and business activities as a professional author had been carried on in the United States for several years before 1955, and that what he did in the period January 1 to March 19, 1955, was a continuation of the same activities which previously had been carried on with regularity and continuity for the purpose of producing a livelihood, income, and profits. Although petitioner's testimony is rather limited, having been taken in deposition form in Paris, France, in response to written interrogatories and cross-interrogatories, his testimony shows that he wrote stories and novels for publication, for the purpose of obtaining income and profits, and that his income from royalties received from U.S. publishers and from the sale of motion-picture rights in his literary works was substantial in each of the years 1952 through 1954. Moreover, there are in evidence items of business correspondence with Doubleday and contracts with publishers which indicate that petitioner did much more than just think out plots and write stories in the whole process of earning royalties through granting publication and reproduction rights. Petitioner was concerned about proper translations of his works into English, the skill of translators engaged by the publisher and their charges, condensations of his stories for magazine publication, and innumerable tasks to be performed by himself in connection with his

publisher's procedures in handling and preparing his "manuscripts" for publication. Petitioner's contracts with his publishers, which are detailed and long, contain reservations, and requirements that the publisher must consult the author about various matters. Petitioner retained various rights relating to other media of reproduction of his stories than publication, such as cinema rights, and television and dramatic rights. In other words, petitioner promoted the sale of his various rights in addition to his work as a writer. His literary properties were, like merchandise (however commercial the comparison is), for sale in all forms, and the market in which his interests in his literary works was sold was a wide one, which included many more prospective buyers than just the publishers of books, such as Doubleday, Appleton, and Prentice–Hall. The evidence indicates that petitioner was concerned with and participated in publicity about himself, as a successful author, and about his works, and the promotion aspects of selling to others his various rights in the products of his highly skilled and talented efforts. All of these facets of petitioner's activities as an author represented his carrying on of a business. It is understood that petitioner's literary works are widely recognized as having a high degree of literary value. But the whole activity of marketing them was nevertheless a commercial activity. Petitioner has not established the negative proposition that he did no more than seclude himself in the ivory tower of his house in Connecticut writing out plots and typing manuscripts, completely detached and disassociated from the crass and practical activities of dealing in the business matters incident to the circulation, purchase, and production of his stories; and the evidence establishes that he engaged in carrying on business activities. As for the period in issue, January 1 to March 19, 1955, the evidence shows that petitioner negotiated and entered into a new contract, with Doubleday, before departing from the United States. We are unable to accept as reasonable or realistic petitioner's argument that his activities as an author were confined and limited to making up an outline of a story and then retiring to his office in his home to typewrite his story, and were restricted to "the act of creativity which produces masterpieces of literature"; and that petitioner's "workshop is wherever he happens to be."

* * *

* * * Upon the record in this case, we are not able to conclude that petitioner's office in his house was not his fixed place of business, prior to 1955 and up to March 19 or 20, 1955, when he departed. Petitioner may have been able to, and probably did, develop plots for his stories while sitting out in a park or driving through the country, all of which is immaterial under the particular question. And he probably did part of his business negotiations in the office of a prospective publisher or producer. On the other hand, it appears that it was ordinary, necessary, and appropriate in relation to his author-business for him to have a fixed place of business, in view of the regularity, continuity, and extent of his

business activities as an author who wrote for profit, undertook to sell rights in his literary products, and maintained more or less continuous contacts with his publisher, publishers, and others with whom he transacted his author-business. * * *

* * *

[¶ 3175]

THE TAISEI FIRE AND MARINE INSURANCE CO., LTD. v. COMMISSIONER

United States Tax Court, 1995.
104 T.C. 535 (acq.).

[The taxpayers are Japanese property and casualty insurance companies that wrote reinsurance through Fortress Re, Inc., a U.S. corporation operating in the United States. The IRS contended that the taxpayers had a permanent establishment, as defined by the United States–Japan Tax Treaty, because of their relations with and the activities of Fortress Re, Inc. in the United States.]

TANNENWALD, JUDGE: * * *.

* * *

Under the Convention Between the United States of America and Japan * * * (hereinafter referred to as the U.S.-Japan convention or convention), the commercial profits of a Japanese resident are exempt from U.S. Federal income tax, unless such profits are attributable to a U.S. permanent establishment. Convention, art. 8(1). The relevant provisions of the convention whereby a Japanese resident will be deemed to have a U.S. permanent establishment due to the activities of an agent are as follows:

> (4) A person acting in a Contracting State on behalf of a resident of the other Contracting State, other than an agent of an independent status to whom paragraph (5) of this article applies, shall be deemed to be a permanent establishment in the first-mentioned Contracting State if such person has, and habitually exercises in the first-mentioned Contracting State, an authority to conclude contracts in the name of that resident, unless the exercise of such authority is limited to the purchase of goods or merchandise for that resident.
>
> (5) A resident of a Contracting State shall not be deemed to have a permanent establishment in the other Contracting State merely because such resident engages in industrial or commercial activity in that other Contracting State through a broker, general commission agent, or any other agent of an independent status, where such broker or agent is acting in the ordinary course of his business.

Initially, it is undisputed that Fortress had the authority, which it exercised, to conclude contracts on behalf of petitioners, so that unless Fortress is "a broker, general commission agent, or any other agent of an independent status" within the meaning of article 9(5), petitioners will be deemed to have U.S. permanent establishments. The parties are in agreement that Fortress was not a "broker" or "general commission agent", and respondent concedes that Fortress was acting in the ordinary course of its business when acting on behalf of petitioners. Thus, the issue before us is whether, during the years at issue, Fortress was an "agent of an independent status" in respect of each petitioner. In this connection, we note that neither petitioners nor respondent has argued that any petitioner should be treated differently from any other petitioner in resolving this issue.

BACKGROUND

The U.S.-Japan convention itself does not define an "agent of an independent status". In applying a treaty definition, "Our role is limited to giving effect to the intent of the Treaty parties." *Sumitomo Shoji America, Inc. v. Avagliano*, 457 U.S. 176, 185 (1982) * * *. Beyond the literal language, we must examine the treaty's "purpose, history and context." *Crow v. Commissioner*, 85 T.C. at 380.

Our examination shows that the relevant provisions of the convention are not only based upon, but are duplicative of, Article 5, comments 4 and 5, of the 1963 O.E.C.D. Draft (Model) Convention (hereinafter referred to as the 1963 model). * * * While the 1963 model itself provides no more definition than the convention, the model is explained in part by a commentary, which states in pertinent part:

> 15. *Persons who may be deemed to be permanent establishments must be strictly limited to those who are dependent, both from the legal and economic points of view,* upon the enterprise for which they carry on business dealings (Report of the Fiscal Committee of the League of Nations, 1928, page 12). Where an enterprise has business dealings with an independent agent, this cannot be held to mean that the enterprise itself carries on a business in the other State. In such a case, there are two separate enterprises.
>
> * * *
>
> 19. Under paragraph 4 of the Article, only one category of dependent agents, who meet specific conditions, is deemed to be permanent establishments. All independent agents and the remaining dependent ones are not deemed to be permanent establishment. Mention should be made of the fact that the Mexico and London Drafts * * * and a number of Conventions, do not enumerate exhaustively such dependent agents as are deemed to be permanent establishments, but merely give examples. In the interest of preventing differences of interpretation and of furthering international economic

relations, it appeared advisable to define, as exhaustively as possible, the cases where agents are deemed to be "permanent establishments".

* * *

20. * * * In the Mexico and London Drafts and in the Conventions, brokers and commission agents are stated to be agents of an independent status. Similarly, business dealings carried on with the co-operation of any other independent person carrying on a trade or business (e.g. a forwarding agent) do not constitute a permanent establishment. Such independent agents must, however, be acting in the ordinary course of their business. * * *

* * *

The special problems which can arise in the case of insurance companies dealing by means of intermediaries or variously qualified representatives shall be further studied. (Commentary to Art. 5 of the 1963 model.)

Based on the above, petitioners argue that the test of independent status is one of both legal and economic dependence and that, if we find that Fortress was either legally or economically independent of petitioners, it will necessarily follow that Fortress was not a permanent establishment. Respondent argues that comment 15 erroneously phrased the standard in terms of "dependence" and the conjunctive "and" instead of the disjunctive "or", thus allowing either legal or economic independence to satisfy the requirement for independent status. * * * The basis for this argument is that comment 15 of the 1963 model expressly refers to the Report of the Fiscal Committee of the League of Nations (1928), the commentary to which states: "The words 'bona-fide agent of independent status' are intended to imply absolute *independence, both from the legal and economic points of view*" (emphasis supplied) * * *. Indeed, the commentary to the OECD model was changed in the 1977 revision so that both legal and economic independence is necessary. Comment 36 to the OECD Revised Model Double Taxation Convention on Income and Capital—1977 (hereinafter referred to as the 1977 model); see also comment 37 to Art. 5 of the OECD Model Tax Convention on Income and on Capital (1992). Generally, we would have reservations about interpreting a convention, ratified in 1971, on the basis of a commentary, adopted in 1977, that contradicts the literal language of the commentary in effect at the time of ratification. However, in light of the extensive analysis by the previously cited commentators and the confirmation of such analysis by our own research, we are persuaded that the criteria in the later commentary reflects the original intention of the commentary to the 1963 model and that the 1963 model should be interpreted as having a disjunctive ("or") meaning.

We note, however, that if we focus, as the parties have ultimately done, on the test for legal and economic independence set forth in comment 37 to Article 5 of the 1977 model, as applied to the facts herein, the issue of disjunctive versus conjunctive reading of the 1963 model fades into the background. That comment provides:

> 37. Whether a person is independent of the enterprise represented depends on the extent of the obligations which this person has vis-a-vis the enterprise. Where the person's commercial activities for the enterprise are subject to detailed instructions or to comprehensive control by it, such person cannot be regarded as independent of the enterprise. Another important criterion will be whether the entrepreneurial risk has to be borne by the person or by the enterprise the person represents. * * *

It is obvious that the tests of "comprehensive control" and "entrepreneurial risk," as the determinants of legal and economic independence, involve an intensely factual inquiry, which does not lend itself to the articulation of a "definitive statement that would produce a talisman for the solution of concrete cases." *Commissioner v. Duberstein*, 363 U.S. 278, 284–285 (1960).

Petitioners suggest that guidance can be found in the factors used in distinguishing employees from independent contractors. * * * We think the employee versus independent contractor analogy is of limited use. The fact that petitioners herein are clearly not employees (indeed, respondent does not contend that they are) and therefore would be considered independent contractors does not answer the question before us, namely, whether they are the kind of independent contractors who should be held to be "agent(s) of an independent status". Nor are we prepared to accept respondent's argument that the quoted phrase should be given a narrow scope by virtue of the ejusdem generis rule in that it was intended to encompass only those agents who exhibited characteristics associated with a "broker" or "commission agent". We think that the generality of the phrase "agent of an independent status" was intended to have an expansive rather than a confining scope, particularly since the words "broker" and "commission agent" themselves lack specificity. Respondent's reliance on *Fleming (H.M. Inspector of Taxes) v. London Produce Co.*, 1 W.L.R. 1013, 2 All E.R. 975 (Ch.Div.1968), is misplaced. In that case the language, to which the doctrine of ejusdem generis was applied, was totally different ("In this subsection, 'broker' *includes* a general commission agent" (emphasis added)).

Against the foregoing background, we turn to the determination of Fortress' legal and economic independence.

LEGAL INDEPENDENCE

The relationship between Fortress and petitioners is defined by the management agreement that Fortress entered into separately with each petitioner. Petitioners have no interest in Fortress, and no representative of any of the petitioners is a director, officer, or employee of Fortress. The agreements grant complete discretion to Fortress to conduct the reinsurance business on behalf of petitioners. * * *

Respondent agrees that Fortress had independence with respect to day-to-day operations, but then argues that its actions were restricted by gross acceptance limits and limits on net premium income. However, even if there were such restrictions, they would not necessarily constitute control. The gross acceptance limit and net premium income both relate to the total exposure of petitioners, and even an independent agent only has authority to perform specific duties for the principal. It is freedom in the manner by which the agent performs such duties that distinguishes him as independent.

In any event, the record is clear that the gross acceptance limits were set by Fortress as part of its strategy to limit risk through diversification. Fortress advised petitioners of the gross acceptance limits for informational purposes and changed the limits without the advice or consent of petitioners. Fortress refused to put gross acceptance limits in the management agreements in order to retain flexibility. Respondent implies that the limit forced Fortress to enter into many small contracts instead of being able to enter into a few large contracts, but the pattern is consistent with Fortress' strategy of limiting risk through diversification, a strategy which Fortress was clearly in a position to implement through a plethora of available contracts.

As to net premium income, there were no limits under the terms of the management agreements. If one of petitioners sought to lower its net premium income from U.S. sources, Fortress' advice was to cede a greater share to Carolina Re, operating in Bermuda. Petitioners could also terminate agreements with their other U.S. agents. Respondent places great weight on the estimates of net premium income Fortress provided to petitioners before each management year, but the estimates are clearly that, and nothing more, and were greatly exceeded for at least one of the years at issue. While Fortress was aware that at times petitioners wanted only to absorb a certain amount of net premium income, Fortress did not change its business to accommodate their concerns.

Respondent further argues there were restrictions on Fortress' corporate affairs not reflected in the agreements that gave petitioners comprehensive control of Fortress. As evidence, respondent relies on Fortress' consultations with petitioners in regard to the request of Dai Tokyo to become a client of Fortress, and to Fortress' intent to include Carolina Re in the reinsurance program. Respondent also points out that Fortress reported to petitioners more regularly than required by the agreements. However, these are actions of a company seeking to maintain good relations with longstanding clients, rather than one seeking approval. With respect to the Dai Tokyo and Carolina Re situations, Fortress had already made its decision before consulting with petitioners. *Lewenhaupt v. Commissioner*, 20 T.C. 151, 162–163 (1953), affd. per curiam 221 F.2d

227 (9th Cir.1955), cited by respondent, not only involved a different test, i.e., whether the taxpayer was engaged in business in the United States through an agent, but involved continuous activity in managing U.S. real estate owned by the taxpayer which went beyond mere ownership or receipt of income. It is clearly distinguishable.

Respondent further argues that petitioners exercised "comprehensive control" over Fortress by acting as a "pool". However, there is no evidence that petitioners acted in concert to control Fortress. In only rare and isolated instances did petitioners communicate with one another regarding Fortress. Further, there are references to a "pool" throughout the history of Fortress, which period covers relationships with 17 separate U.S. and Japanese insurance companies. The inferences respondent would have us draw from the fact that petitioners are all from Japan and that petitioners are among the participants in regular industry conferences in Japan are simply insufficient to establish the existence of control by a "pool".

In a similar vein, we reject respondent's attempt to construct control from the fact that, during the years at issue, Fortress' activities were confined to the reinsurance it underwrote on behalf of petitioners. Pointing to Article 2(2) of the U.S.-Japan convention, respondent attempts to support her position by drawing upon the phrase "other agent of independent status" in section 864(c)(5)(A) and the regulation thereunder, section 1.864–7(d)(3), Income Tax Regs. See S.Rept. 89–1707 (1966) * * *. Obviously, the statute simply repeats the phrase used in the convention. The regulations suggest two elements to be considered. The first is ownership or control, section 1.864–7(d)(3)(ii), Income Tax Regs., which the regulation specifically states is not determinative. The second, section 1.864–7(d)(3)(iii), Income Tax Regs., is whether the agent acts "exclusively, or almost exclusively, *for one principal*," (emphasis added) in which event "the facts and circumstances of a particular case shall be taken into account in determining whether the agent, while acting in that capacity, may be classified as an independent agent." Assuming without deciding that these regulations, implementing a particular statute, should be accorded interpretative effect in respect of a treaty provision, it has no application herein where we have concluded that Fortress acted separately in respect of each of four petitioners and where respondent concedes that Fortress was acting in the ordinary course of its business, a position that seems inconsistent with both the "pool" and "exclusively" concepts. Moreover, we note that the number of principals for whom Fortress acted varied over the years and that, even during the years before us, Fortress carried on a substantial amount of activity in handling claims, etc., for several other insurance companies.

Finally, we note that all four petitioners, while not their primary business, did have reinsurance departments. Thus, petitioners had the ability to give detailed instructions to Fortress, yet they did not.

As an agent, Fortress had complete discretion over the details of its work. As an entity, Fortress was subject to no external control. In sum, Fortress was legally independent of petitioners.

ECONOMIC INDEPENDENCE

Fortress is owned solely by Mr. Sabbah and his family and Mr. Kornfeld. There was no guarantee of revenue to Fortress, nor was Fortress protected from loss in the event it had been unable to generate sufficient revenue. Fortress has management agreements with four separate clients, whereby any one of them can leave on 6 months' notice. If one of petitioners did end its relationship, Fortress would bear the burden of finding a replacement to subscribe to that client's share of reinsurance contracts.

Respondent argues that Fortress bore no entrepreneurial risk because its operating expenses were covered by a management fee, and because it was guaranteed business due to the creditworthiness of the reinsurers on whose behalf it acted, petitioners.

While the management agreements provided that Fortress earned a percentage of the gross premiums written which effectively covered Fortress' operating expenses, this did not mean that Fortress bore no risk. Fortress had to acquire sufficient business to produce the gross premiums. Further, it appears that this provision of the agreements is normal for an underwriting manager. That respondent's argument on this point misses the mark is illustrated, for example, by a large mutual fund that charges an annual management fee to cover operating expenses. Clearly, the mutual fund company would not be considered dependent on its thousands of investors. Under these circumstances, even with as few as four investors, Fortress cannot be considered dependent on petitioners to pay its operating expenses.

Nor do we agree with respondent's argument that Fortress is able to secure profitable reinsurance contracts only because its clients are petitioners. Although Fortress needs clients with a certain minimum capital to conduct its business, any of hundreds of other insurance companies worldwide would be adequate substitutes. Also, it cannot be denied that Fortress had access to the reinsurance contracts it considered good, in part because of Fortress' relationships and reputation in the industry. In fact, it appears that Fortress' access to profitable reinsurance contracts, as well as its experience and ability to choose profitable reinsurance contracts, attracted petitioners to Fortress, and would attract other insurance companies if Fortress needed another client to take a share of the contracts.

Finally, we think that the amount of Fortress' profits is significant. * * * For the 3 years in issue, Fortress was paid over $27 million. This is not the kind of sum paid to a subservient company. In addition, petitioners were in effect forced to share reinsurance profits with Carolina Re, an entity owned by the same people who owned Fortress, by permitting Fortress to cede reinsurance to Carolina Re even though Carolina Re was not as well known or financially secure as other potential quota share reinsurers.

CONCLUSION

In sum, during the years at issue, Fortress was both legally and economically independent of petitioners, thus satisfying the definition of an agent of an independent status under Article 9 of the U.S.-Japan convention.

Two further items deserve comment. First, petitioners point to a decision of the Federal Republic of Germany Tax Court at Bremen * * * regarding the application of the independent agent provision of the Germany–Netherlands Treaty to a German insurance agent. A Dutch company had engaged a German firm as its representative and principal agent and signed a standard form granting power of attorney to the German firm enabling the German firm to conclude contracts on behalf of the Dutch company. The German firm acted as an independent insurance agent for numerous domestic and foreign insurance companies. The court held the Dutch company did not have a permanent establishment in Germany by virtue of the performance of the German insurance agent. While the result reached in the German case is consistent with that which we reach herein, we think that its utility herein is limited by the clearly distinguishable facts. Nor does *De Amodio v. Commissioner*, 34 T.C. 894 (1960), affd. on other grounds 299 F.2d 623 (3d Cir.1962), provide petitioners with any sustenance. There, a resident of Switzerland owned U.S. rental property which was managed and operated through local real estate agents. We determined that the agents fell within the term "broker" or "independent agent", in the income tax convention between the United States and Switzerland, but the discussion is limited.

Second, we note that, in the commentary to the OECD's 1977 model, it is stated that an insurance company could do "large-scale business in a State without being taxed in that State on their profits arising from such business." Comment 38 to Art. 5 of 1977 model; see also comment 21 to Art. 5 of 1963 model. The commentary goes on to suggest that contracting states may want to contemplate that an insurance company will be "deemed to have a permanent establishment in the other State if they collect premiums in that other State through an agent established there", other than a dependent agent. Comment 38 to Art. 5 of 1977 model. However, the commentary notes that such a provision is not in the model and its inclusion should depend upon the factual and legal situation involved. Comment 38 to Art. 5 of 1977 model * * *.

The Convention between the United States of America and the Kingdom of Belgium for the Avoidance of Double Taxation and the Prevention of Fiscal Evasion with Respect to Taxes on Income, July 9,

ADTPF FR4In

1970 * * * (hereinafter referred to as the U.S.-Belgium convention), does include such an insurance provision. It provides that the independent agent provision "shall not apply with respect to a broker or agent acting on behalf of an insurance company if such broker or agent has, and habitually exercises, an authority to conclude contracts in the name of that company." U.S.-Belgium convention, Art. 5(6). Finally, we note that it was decided not to include reinsurance within the coverage of this provision. Technical Explanation by Treasury Department on the Convention Between the U.S. and Belgium for the Avoidance of Double Taxation and the Prevention of Fiscal Evasion with Respect to Taxes on Income, signed July 9, 1970 * * *. From the foregoing it appears that the resolution of the issue of the existence of an agent of independent status in the insurance arena turns, at least in part, upon the presence of a specific treaty provision. * * *

Given the absence of any provision dealing with insurance or reinsurance in the U.S.-Japan convention, our holding herein that Fortress is not a permanent establishment of petitioners is consistent with the approach suggested by the OECD model and the application thereof in the U.S.-Belgium convention.

* * *

[¶ 3180]

NOTES

1. It may not seem unusual that interpretations of the "permanent establishment" provisions used in other U.S. tax treaties are applied in this case. The relative paucity of interpretations of the meaning of "permanent establishment" under U.S. law and practice, however, also led Judge Tannenwald to consider analyses developed under the OECD Model Treaty and a decision of a foreign court dealing with a treaty to which the United States is not a party. Compare the OECD analysis to the U.S. Treasury's views with respect to the permanent establishment language in Article 5 of the U.S. Model Treaty set forth in the Technical Explanation (Appendix B). The permanent establishment concept is further examined in the context of planning exports from the United States in Chapter 11.

2. New transactions, particularly in an era of rapidly changing technology, often impose pressures on established lines of analysis. The ease of electronic communications has created new issues to be addressed with traditional formulations. Many governments and organizations have been considering the tax implications of electronic commerce. One of the questions is whether, when and where electronic commerce conducted primarily on the

Internet can create a permanent establishment. The OECD has undertaken a serious examination of this issue. The commentary adopted to accompany the provisions of the OECD Model Convention dealing with permanent establishments included the following observation:

> [A]n Internet web site, which is a combination of software and electronic data, does not in itself constitute tangible property. It therefore does not have a location that can constitute a "place of business" as there is no "facility such as premises or, in certain instances, machinery or equipment" * * * as far as the software and data constituting that web site is concerned. On the other hand, the server on which the web site is stored and through which it is accessible is a piece of equipment having a physical location and such location may thus constitute a "fixed place of business" of the enterprise that operates that server.

¶ 42.2 of Commentary on Article 5 of the OECD Model Tax Convention.

[¶ 3185]

3. U.S. TAX LIABILITY ON OPERATION OF PERMANENT ESTABLISHMENTS

All items of income attributable to the permanent establishment will be included in its gross income. Article 7 of the U.S. Model Treaty reflects the approach used in treaties to determine the extent to which income will be attributable and taxed to a permanent establishment. Article 7(2) provides that the income so attributable will be the business profits that the permanent establishment "might be expected to make if it were a distinct and independent enterprise engaged in the same or similar activities under the same or similar conditions." Further, treaties usually provide explicitly that gains from the sale of personal property attributable to a U.S. permanent establishment and gains from the disposition of the establishment may be taxed in the United States. See U.S. Model Treaty, Art. 13(3).

Other U.S.-source income not attributable to a permanent establishment may be taxable under the withholding tax rules, as possibly modified by the terms of the applicable treaty. See ¶ 4050.

In general, the business profits of a resident of a treaty country will be taxable only in that country unless the business is undertaken through a permanent establishment in the other country. Once the taxpayer is conducting business through a permanent establishment, only the income attributable thereto may be taxed in the country where the profits are being generated. U.S. Model Treaty, Art. 7(1).

Article 7(2) provides that the profits attributable to a permanent establishment include only those derived from the assets or activities of the permanent establishment. This approach is consistent with the "asset use" and "business activities" analysis authorized under Section 864(c)(2). See U.S. Model Treaty, Technical Explanation, Art. 7(2).

The treaty requires a determination of the net income of a permanent establishment. Its gross income is reduced by allowable deductions. Tax treaties typically provide that deductions allowable in determining the net income of the permanent establishment are those "incurred for purposes of the permanent establishment" and include "a reasonable allocation of executive and general administrative expenses, research and development expenses, interest, and other expenses incurred for the purposes of the enterprise as a whole * * *, whether incurred in the [country] in which the permanent establishment is situated or elsewhere." U.S. Model Treaty, Art. 7(3). The provisions of U.S. law should generally apply in determining what constitutes a "reasonable allocation" for these purposes. For example, the interest allocations set forth in the regulations are applicable to determining interest expense attributable to the business profits of a permanent establishment. Reg. § 1.882–5(a)(2).

A foreign person may have more than one permanent establishment in the United States. Income and losses from all such permanent establishments of a taxpayer will be combined to determine the U.S. income tax liability. As a result, losses generated by one may offset income produced by another.

While transactions between a branch and a home office or between two branches of a corporation are not normally recognized under U.S. tax law, the treaty treats each permanent establishment as a "distinct and independent" enterprise and permits as a deduction "expenses that are incurred for the purpose of the permanent establishment, including executive and general administrative expenses so incurred, whether in the [United States] * * * or elsewhere." U.S. Model Treaty, Art. 7(2) and (3).

The issue of allocating expenses to the income of an enterprise is often very complex. A number of situations have arisen in which foreign taxpayers from treaty countries have opposed the application of formulaic allocations on the ground that the allocation formula was inconsistent with applicable treaty provisions, resulting in a higher U.S. tax liability than was guaranteed under the treaty. As reflected by the court's discussion in the case that follows, the taxpayer challenge constitutes a direct attack on the validity of allocation formulae set forth in the Code and regulations.

[¶ 3187]

NATIONAL WESTMINSTER BANK, PLC v. UNITED STATES

United States Court of Federal Claims, 1999.
44 Fed. Cl. 120.

TURNER, JUDGE. * * *

I

The essential facts are simple and undisputed.

Plaintiff (NatWest) is a United Kingdom corporation engaged in a wide range of banking, financial and related activities throughout the world, including the United States. NatWest's offices and business outlets in this country, through which its United States operations are conducted, are collectively called the U.S. Branch.

Banking operations of the U.S. Branch are supported by the world-wide capital of NatWest. If the U.S. Branch were a subsidiary corporation rather than an integral part of NatWest, it would, as both a legal and practical matter, be required to maintain capital reserves which are unnecessary as a result of its branch relationship with NatWest.

Typically, the U.S. Branch obtains the funds to conduct its banking operations by borrowing from NatWest's headquarters office or from other branches of NatWest (e.g., the Hong Kong branch), as well as from other banks and lending institutions having no relationship with NatWest. In turn, funds so acquired by the U.S. Branch are lent to its customers, thereby generating interest income. There may be occasions when the U.S. Branch lends funds to other branches of NatWest.

Concerning any such borrowing and lending transactions which are intra-corporate, the lending headquarters or branch would "charge" interest on its loans to the U.S. Branch, and the U.S. Branch would "charge" interest on its loans to other units of NatWest, just as if each branch were unrelated to NatWest. The books of account of the U.S. Branch (and of other units within NatWest) would reflect both interest income received from other branches and interest expense paid pursuant to such inter-branch transactions just as if they resulted from transactions with unrelated commercial banks.

Plaintiff's U.S. tax returns for the years at issue, 1981–87, reflected such interbranch transactions in the calculation of income and expense, and resulting taxable profit, attributable to the U.S. Branch as if it were a separate business entity.

Upon audit, the Internal Revenue Service disallowed a portion of the interest expense reflected on the books of the U.S. Branch and insisted that the allowable interest deduction for calculation of profit attributable to the U.S. Branch be determined in accordance with the formula set out in Treas. Reg. § 1.882–5 * * *. This disallowance resulted in higher taxes which plaintiff paid and now seeks to recover.

II

A

Plaintiff asserts that application of Treas. Reg. § 1.882–5 to plaintiff's U.S. Branch operations violates the [United States–United Kingdom] Treaty. Defendant argues that the regulation is consistent with the Treaty. The parties agree that, in the circumstances of this case, if Treas. Reg. § 1.882–5 is inconsistent with the Treaty, the Treaty will control. * * * As suggested by its title, the purpose of the Treaty is to avoid, with respect to residents (including resident corporations) of each Contracting State, taxation of particular items of income by both Contracting States. The general rule adopted to achieve this purpose is that the income of a resident of one Contracting State, even though connected to obligations or activities in the other, is taxed only by the Contracting State of residence. The several exceptions to this general rule (one of which concerns business profits) are specifically addressed in the Treaty.

With respect to business operations, the general principle espoused in the Treaty is that business profits also shall be taxed only by the country of residence, unless the enterprise carries on business in the other state through a "permanent establishment" located in the other state. A "permanent establishment," as defined in the Treaty, Article 5(1) & (2), is "a fixed place of business through which the business of an enterprise is wholly or partly carried on" and includes a branch and an office.

The parties agree that the U.S. Branch of plaintiff is such a "permanent establishment" and that business profits of plaintiff attributable to the U.S. Branch are subject to United States income taxation. Further, the parties agree that Treas. Reg. 1.882–5 was duly adopted pursuant to lawful authority.

B

The parties' core disagreement concerns whether the regulation is inconsistent with the Treaty and thus inapplicable to the U.S. Branch. Thus, the provisions of the Treaty dealing with the business profits of a permanent establishment become critical to resolution of this case. Those provisions are found in Article 7 (Business Profits) which states, in pertinent part:

> (1) The business profits of an enterprise of a Contracting State [e.g., United Kingdom] shall be taxable only in that State unless the enterprise carried on business in the other Contracting State [United States] through a permanent establishment situated therein. If the enterprise [e.g., plaintiff] carries on business as aforesaid, the business profits of the enterprise may be taxed in that other State [United

States] but only so much of them as is attributable to that permanent establishment.

(2) Subject to the provisions of paragraph (3), where an enterprise of a Contracting State [e.g., United Kingdom] carries on business in the other Contracting State [United States] through a permanent establishment situated therein [e.g., U.S. Branch], there shall in each Contracting State be attributed to that permanent establishment the profits which it might be expected to make if it were a distinct and separate enterprise engaged in the same or similar activities under the same or similar conditions and dealing wholly independently with the enterprise of which it is a permanent establishment.

(3) In the determination of the profits of a permanent establishment [e.g., U.S. Branch], there shall be allowed as deductions those expenses which are incurred for the purposes of the permanent establishment, including a reasonable allocation of executive and general administrative expenses, research and development expenses, interest, and other expenses incurred for the purposes of the enterprise as a whole . . . , whether incurred in the State in which the permanent establishment is situated or elsewhere.

C

While the parties agree that Article 7 of the Treaty insures that the U.S. Branch must be treated for tax purposes as if it were a separate enterprise, they disagree over whether, in calculating profits attributable to the U.S. Branch, intra-corporate "loan" transactions between U.S. Branch and other non-U.S. units of plaintiff may be treated as transactions between separate entities. (Of course, this litigation directly concerns only the interest deduction for calculating taxable income of the U.S. Branch, not interest income from such transactions.)

In practical terms, the precise, narrow issue for resolution at this juncture in the proceedings is whether, in the determination of the interest expense deduction for the U.S. Branch, the interest expense reflected in its books of account—with appropriate adjustments, if necessary, to reflect imputation of adequate capital and arm's-length, market interest rates in intra-corporate "borrowing" transactions—may be used in calculating plaintiff's U.S. tax liability, or whether, with respect to interest expense, the defendant may require use of a formulary approach, such as that in Treas. Reg. § 1.882–5, which disregards intra-corporate "lending" transactions reflected in the books of account.

Resolution of this disagreement requires interpretation of the Treaty and Treas. Reg. § 1.882–5.

III

We first explore sources bearing on a proper interpretation of the critical Treaty terms, beginning with the text of Article 7.

Article 7(1) starts with the presumption that with respect to a U.K. corporation such as plaintiff, no business profits whatever may be taxed by the United States unless the corporation carries on business in this country through a permanent establishment. Article 7(1) then provides that if there is a permanent establishment such as the U.S. Branch, only profits attributable to that permanent establishment may be taxed by the United States.

Article 7(2), building on the foundation that only profits attributable to the permanent establishment may be taxed, provides that there shall be attributed to a permanent establishment such as the U.S. Branch the profits "which it might be expected to make *if it were a distinct and separate enterprise* engaged in" the same business activity "and *dealing wholly independently with the enterprise of which it is a permanent establishment*." (Emphasis added.) Fundamentally, profits are derived by deducting expenses from gross income.

This Treaty paragraph is made subject to Article 7(3) which provides for an additional deduction to determine taxable profits of the permanent establishment, to wit, "a reasonable allocation of executive and general administrative expenses, research and development expenses, interest, and other expenses incurred for the purposes of the enterprise as a whole . . ." wherever incurred. Thus, in addition to deductions for expenses shown on its own books reflecting its separate operations, a permanent establishment may deduct a reasonable portion of home-office expense. The face of Article 7, then, would appear to provide in the context of this case that, to determine taxable income of the U.S. Branch, the U.S. Branch is to be regarded as an independent, separate entity dealing at arm's length with other units of NatWest as if they were wholly unrelated, except that the U.S. Branch may deduct, in addition to its "own" expenses, a reasonable allocation of home office expense. Words such as "distinct" and "separate" and the phrase "dealing *wholly* independently" (emphasis added) would appear to permit no other interpretation.

Contemporaneous commentaries and reports generally support this interpretation.

IV

A 1977 report of the United States Department of the Treasury concerning the then-proposed Treaty said with respect to paragraph 2 of Article 7 that the United States (as one of the "Contracting States") "will attribute to the permanent establishment such profits as it would reasonably be expected to derive if it were an independent entity. . . . " Treasury Department Technical Explanation of the United States and United Kingdom Income Tax Treaty, March 9, 1977 at 16. This was the Treasury's contemporaneous understanding while the Treaty draft was under consideration but before adoption.

With respect to paragraph 3 of Article 7, the Treasury report said: "[E]xpenses, wherever incurred, which are reasonably connected with profits attributable to the permanent establishment, . . . will be allowed as deductions in determining the business profits of the permanent establishment." *Id.*

The Report of the Senate Committee on Foreign Relations, dated April 25, 1978, concerning its consideration and favorable recommendation of the Treaty, in explanation of Article 7 stated:

> The profits of a permanent establishment are to be determined on an arm's-length basis. Thus, there is to be attributed to it the . . . commercial profits which would reasonably be expected to have been derived by it *if it were an independent entity* engaged in the same or similar activities under the same or similar conditions and *dealing at arm's-length with the resident of which it is a permanent establishment.* * * *

V

The United States and the United Kingdom (together with Canada, Turkey and most western European countries) have been members of the Organization for Economic Co–Operation and Development (OECD) since 1961. * * * International double taxation was recognized by the OECD as an obstacle to the development of economic relations between member countries. In an effort to enhance economic development, the OECD, in 1963, published a Draft Double Taxation Convention on Income and Capital (OECD Document).

The OECD Document, prepared by the OECD's Fiscal Committee and approved by its Council, was proposed for adoption by member countries. * * * The U.S.-U.K. Treaty on double taxation is based on the OECD Document.

The drafters of the OECD Document, as stated therein,

> set out to establish a series of Articles which could be easily interpreted and applied in spite of the differences in national taxation laws and economic interests. The Articles . . . provide a means of settling on a uniform basis the most common problems of double taxation. In certain cases, supplementary provisions or solutions for special questions have been specified or outlined in the Commentaries on the Articles.

OECD Document, ¶ 6 at 10.

Although the entire OECD Document is designated a draft "Convention," the convention (treaty) proposed for adoption by member countries constitutes only a part of the document. The full document includes introductory and explanatory material concerning its history, terms, interpretation and implementation, OECD Document at 7–32, an Annex I consisting of the actual proposed (model) tax treaty (also called the "Draft

Convention"), *Id.* at 36–58,and an Annex II consisting of "Commentaries on The Articles of the Draft Convention," *Id.* at 60–164. (The document also includes the decisions of the OECD Council pertaining to implementation of the OECD Document, *Id.* at 167–68.)

The initial explanatory material of the OECD Document and the Commentaries in Annex II thereof are important and helpful in determining the probable mutual understanding of countries which used the Document as the basis for a tax treaty. This was intended by the drafters of the OECD Document. Thus, explanatory material in the OECD Document is appropriate for use in divining probable intent of countries adopting treaties based thereon.

The OECD Document, specifically addressing the Commentaries and their intended use, states:

> For each of the Articles in the Convention there is a detailed Commentary which is *designed to illustrate or interpret the provisions.* ...Although the present Commentaries are not designed to be annexed in any manner to the Conventions to be signed by Member countries, which alone constitute legally binding international instruments, *they can nevertheless be of great assistance in the application of the Conventions and, in particular, in the settlement of eventual disputes.*

OECD Document, ¶ 34 at 18 (emphasis added).

The Commentaries on the Articles of the Draft Convention, OECD Document, Annex II, are presumed to have been in the minds of the negotiators when they drafted the Treaty; consequently, they are persuasive in resolving disputed interpretations.

VI

The text of the OECD Document, in the course of providing an overview of the Draft Convention, says concerning Article 7:

> Article 7 ... formulates the basic principle which must govern the calculation of the profits of the permanent establishment, namely that the permanent establishment *must be treated as an enterprise distinct and separate from the head office of the enterprise.* It settles the question of the expenses which *must* be allowed as deductions in computing the profits of the permanent establishment....

OECD Document, ¶ 14 at 12 (emphasis added).

Time and again throughout the Commentary on Article 7, OECD Document at 79–89, one finds affirmation of the concept that where the books of account of a permanent establishment are, with adjustments, adequate to determine the profits (gross revenues less expenses) of the permanent establishment as a separate entity, then those books should be used (and presumably not some substituted formula).

The Commentary pertaining to Article 7(2) provides:

> This paragraph [i.e., Article 7(2)] *contains the central directive on which the allocation of profits to a permanent establishment is intended to be based*. The paragraph incorporates the view ... that the profits to be attributed to a permanent establishment are those which that permanent establishment would have made if, *instead of dealing with its head office, it had been dealing with an entirely separate enterprise under conditions and at prices prevailing in the ordinary market*. Normally, this would be the same profit that one would expect to be reached by the ordinary processes of good business accountancy. In the great majority of cases, therefore, *trading accounts of the permanent establishment*—which are commonly available if only because a well-run business organization is normally concerned to know what is the profitability of its various branches—*will be used by the taxation authorities concerned to ascertain the profit properly attributable to that establishment*.... [W]here there are such accounts, they will naturally form the starting point for any processes of adjustment in case adjustment is required to produce the amount of properly attributable profits.... *[I]t is always necessary to start with the real facts of the situation as they appear from the business records of the permanent establishment and to adjust as may be shown to be necessary the profit figures which those facts produce.*

OECD Document at 82, Commentary on Article 7, ¶ 10 (emphasis added).

That adjustments to reflect "arm's length" prices are contemplated in the application of Article 7(2) of the Treaty is made clear by paragraphs 11 and 12 of the Commentary on Article 7 which state:

> 11. Even where a permanent establishment is able to produce proper accounts which purport to show the profits arising from its activities, it may still be necessary for the taxation authorities of the country concerned to rectify those accounts, in accordance with the general directive laid down in paragraph 2 [of Article 7]. Adjustment of this kind may be necessary; for example, because goods have been invoiced from the head office to the permanent establishment at prices which are not consistent with this directive, and profits have thus been diverted from the permanent establishment to the head office, or vice versa.
>
> 12. In such cases, it will usually be appropriate to substitute for the prices used ordinary market prices for the same or similar goods supplied on the same or similar conditions.... Clearly many special problems ... [pertaining to adjustment of prices applied to intracorporate exchanges] may arise in individual cases but *the general rule should always be that the profits attributed to a permanent establishment should be based on that establishment's accounts insofar as accounts are available which represent the real facts of the situation.*

OECD Document at 82–83, Commentary on Article 7, ¶¶ 11 & 12 (emphasis added).

Paragraph 21 of the Commentary on Article 7, applicable to paragraph 7(3) of the model treaty, provides as follows:

> 21. It is usually found that there are, or there can be constructed, adequate accounts for each part . . . of an enterprise so that profits and expenses, adjusted as may be necessary, can be allocated to a particular part of the enterprise with a considerable degree of precision. This method of allocation is . . . to be preferred in general wherever it is reasonably practicable to adopt it.

OECD Document at 86, Commentary on Article 7, ¶ 21.

Paragraph 22 of the Commentary on Article 7 actually pertains to paragraph 7(4) of the model treaty which does not appear in the Treaty at issue. However, language of this Commentary paragraph is helpful to an understanding of the general tenor of Article 7 concerning intra-corporate dealings and further illustrates the intent of provisions for "separate enterprise" treatment:

> 22. It has in some cases been the practice to determine the profits to be attributed to a permanent establishment not on the basis of separate accounts or by making an estimate of arm's length profit, but simply by apportioning the total profits of the enterprise by reference to various formulae. Such a method differs from those envisaged in paragraph 2 of the Article [7], since it contemplates not an attribution of profits on a separate enterprise footing, but an apportionment of total profits. . . .

OECD Document at 86, Commentary on Article 7, ¶ 22.

VII

One would suppose that the clear wording of paragraph 2 of Article 7—especially in combination with paragraphs 10, 11 and 12 of the Commentary on Article 7 emphasizing use of a permanent establishment's books of account even with respect to intra-corporate transactions—would apply to all transactions between a permanent establishment and its parent enterprise giving rise to items of income and expense. However, as emphasized by defendant, paragraphs 14 and 15 of the Commentary on Article 7, OECD Document at 83–84, provide that despite the literal wording of paragraph 2, there are several exceptions to a strict interpretation of the "wholly independent/separate enterprise" concept.

Paragraphs 14 and 15 of the Article 7 Commentary provide:

> 14. *Apart from what may be regarded as ordinary expenses*, there are some classes of payments between permanent establishments and head offices which give rise to special problems, and it is convenient to deal with them at this point. The next five paragraphs discuss three specific cases of this kind and give solutions for them. . . .

> 15. The first of these cases relates to interest, royalties and other similar payments made by a permanent establishment to its head office in return for money loaned, or patent rights conceded, by the latter to the permanent establishment. *In such a case, it is considered that the payments should not be allowed as deductions in computing the permanent establishment's taxable profits.* (Equally, such payments made to a permanent establishment by the head office should be excluded from the computation of the permanent establishment's taxable profits.) *It is, however, recognised that special considerations apply to payments of interest made by different parts of a financial enterprise (e.g., a bank) to each other on advances, etc., (as distinct from capital allotted to them), in view of the fact that making and receiving advances is narrowly related to the ordinary business of such enterprises....*

OECD Document at 83–84 (emphasis added).

Although these Commentary paragraphs provide that certain intra-corporate interest charges "should not be allowed as deductions in computing the permanent establishment's taxable profits," we conclude for several reasons that such provision was not intended to apply to banks and other financial institutions whose ordinary business is the borrowing and relending of money.

First, the language of paragraph 14 begins: "Apart from what may be regarded as ordinary expenses, there are some classes of [intra-corporate] payment ... which give rise to special problems.... " The intra-corporate interest payments involved in this case are, for a banking enterprise such as plaintiff, the most ordinary of expenses. The very business of banking is the borrowing and relending of funds. Consequently, it is presumed that what follows the opening clause concerning intra-corporate lending transactions is not intended to be applicable to banking enterprises but rather to manufacturing and other non-financial operations.

This interpretation is reinforced by wording in paragraph 15 of the Commentary pertaining, *inter alia*, to "payments made by a permanent establishment to its head office in return for money loaned ... by the latter to the permanent establishment." After then stating that such payments should *not* be allowed as deductions "in computing the permanent establishment's taxable profits," the Commentary paragraph provides:

> It is, however, recognised that *special considerations apply* to payments of interest made by different parts of a financial enterprise (e.g., a bank) to each other on advances, etc., (as distinct from capital allotted to them), in view of the fact that making and receiving advances is narrowly related to the ordinary business of such enterprises.

OECD Document at 83–84, Commentary on Article 7, ¶ 15 (emphasis added).

Although the "special considerations apply" language of the quoted sentence is somewhat cryptic and leaves room for defendant to argue, as it does, that the exception to the general thrust of paragraph 15 does not unequivocally say that intra-corporate interest payments by a permanent establishment of a banking enterprise *must* be allowed, it is concluded that the principal provision of paragraph 15 pertaining to intra-corporate loan transactions was intended for application to non-financial enterprises and not to banks. Given the nature of the ordinary business of banks, this interpretation is consistent both with the language of Article 7 Commentary paragraphs 14 and 15, viewed as a whole, and with other Treaty provisions and Commentaries, whereas a contrary interpretation would be highly inconsistent.

VIII

The foregoing examination of Article 7 of the Treaty, pre-ratification reports of the Treasury Department and the Senate, and Commentaries intended to assist in interpretation leads to the conclusion that the Treaty contemplates that a foreign banking corporation in the position of plaintiff will be subjected to U.S. taxation only on the profits of its U.S. branch and that such profits should be based on the books of account of such branch maintained as if the branch were a distinct and separate enterprise dealing wholly independently with the remainder of the foreign corporation, provided that the financial records of the branch, especially those reflecting intra-corporate lending transactions, are subject to adjustment as may be necessary for imputation of adequate capital to the branch and to insure use of market rates in computing interest expenses. In addition to normal deductible expenses reflected on the books of the branch, as adjusted, there shall be allowed in the determination of the profits of the U.S. Branch a reasonable allocation of general and administrative expenses incurred for the purposes of the foreign enterprise as a whole.

We next consider whether Treas. Reg. § 1.882–5 is consistent with this interpretation of the Treaty.

IX

Section 882(c)(1) of the Internal Revenue Code states:

> [T]he proper apportionment and allocation of the deductions ... [allowable in the determination of tax on the income of foreign corporations engaged in business within the United States] shall be determined as provided in regulations prescribed by the Secretary.

Treas. Reg. § 1.882–5 is the regulation prescribed by the Secretary for determining a foreign corporation's interest expense deduction. The regulation, by its terms, applies to all foreign corporations with income from business operations in the United States but applies to no purely domestic corporations.

The regulation makes no distinction between businesses of countries with which the U.S. has entered a treaty, like the one at issue, to avoid double taxation, and enterprises of those countries with which no such treaty exists. (Further, the regulation applies to all foreign corporations engaged in U.S. business regardless of the nature of the business; for present purposes we need only be aware that it unquestionably applies to banking corporations.)

The regulation was amended in 1996, although the general scheme remained the same as that described below. In this opinion we quote from and cite to the original 1981 version in effect during the 1981–87 tax years in issue.

A

Treas. Reg. § 1.882–5 applies a complex formula to all foreign corporations with U.S. branches and, in very general terms, operates as follows: Before application of the formula, the regulation requires that all interbranch lending/borrowing transactions be disregarded: "Assets, liabilities, and interest expense amounts resulting from loan or credit transactions of any type between the separate offices or branches of the same foreign corporation are disregarded." Treas. Reg. § 1.882–5(a)(5). The formula then uses a three-step process to determine the interest deduction allowable to off-set income from U.S. operations.

The first step requires the calculation of the amount of the assets of the U.S. branch of a foreign corporation (but excludes from the total any funds resulting from interbranch borrowing).

The second step requires a calculation of liabilities of the U.S. operation (but, again, excluding from the total any "obligations" arising from interbranch borrowing). This calculation begins with establishment of a ratio which must be either a fixed percentage (95 percent for banks and similar financial enterprises or 50 percent for other businesses) or the ratio of the foreign corporation's actual worldwide liabilities to its actual worldwide assets (i.e., the foreign corporation's capital ratio). The resulting fraction or fixed percentage is then multiplied by the assets calculated in step one; the resulting amount is presumed to be the liabilities of the foreign corporation's U.S. operation.

The third step of the formula is the determination of the actual allowable interest expense deduction with respect to the U.S. operation. The foreign taxpayer is given a choice of two methods to determine its actual allowable interest expense deduction, both of which begin by comparing the "presumed" liabilities computed in step two with actual liabilities of the U.S. branch to third parties (thus disregarding interbranch borrowing). This comparison determines whether the foreign corporation will be permitted to deduct interest in excess of that shown on the books of the U.S. branch as paid to third parties. If the "presumed" liabilities exceed the liabilities to third parties, as is usually the case,* * * the taxpayer is allowed to deduct (in addition to that paid to third parties) interest on the portion of the liabilities computed in step two which exceeds the actual liabilities to third parties, but the rates to determine such additional interest will be average rates incurred on various liabilities of the foreign corporation having no direct relation to the U.S. branch.

Keeping in mind that Treas. Reg. § 1.882–5 purports to control the interest expense deduction for the U.S. operations of all foreign corporations, whether or not U.S. operations are the subject of a tax treaty like the one in issue, it is intended to accomplish (1) imputation or allocation of capital to the U.S. branch, (2) application of arm's length interest rates for intra-corporate borrowing and (3) prevention of improper, intentional shifting of income away from the U.S. branch merely to avoid United States income taxation.

Defendant argues that the regulation, with respect to interest expense, treats all U.S. branches of foreign enterprises as separate entities and merely uses the regulation's formulary approach as an effective yet simple means to allocate capital, adjust charges for intra-corporate "borrowing" and insure correction of any improper manipulation among branches of the foreign enterprise to shift income for tax avoidance.

We find that rather than treating the U.S. branch of foreign enterprises as separate entities, the regulation plainly treats each U.S. branch as a unit of a worldwide enterprise and, thus, is inconsistent with the "separate entity" provision of Article 7(2) of the Treaty.

B

Stated broadly, Treas. Reg. § 1.882–5 is inconsistent with Article 7 of the Treaty for two reasons. First, the regulation, in the computation of the interest expense deduction, disregards all interbranch transactions, even for banking operations (although a portion of a U.S. branch's interbranch borrowing will typically be restored in step three of the deduction calculation). Second, the regulation computes liabilities (in step two), and from that figure the ultimate interest deduction (in step three), on the basis of worldwide assets and worldwide liabilities of the entire foreign enterprise, rather than determining the interest deduction on the basis of the separate, independent operations of the U.S. branch.

The regulation simply disregards, as an initial matter and before application of the interest expense formula, all "[a]ssets, liabilities, and interest expense amounts resulting from loan or credit transactions of any type between the separate offices or branches of the same foreign corporation." Treas. Reg. § 1.882–5(a)(5). This plainly violates the separate entity/wholly independent provision of Article 7, paragraph 2 of the Treaty, especially as interpreted in light of paragraphs 10, 11 and 12 of the Commentary on Article 7, OECD Document at 82–83. This initial requirement of the regulation affects every step of its formula.

The first step of the formula requires calculation of the assets of the U.S. branch, but without the assets appearing on the books of the branch which result from interbranch transactions. This is contrary to the separate entity/wholly independent provision of Article 7.

The second step requires a calculation of liabilities, but not the liabilities actually shown on the books of the branch; instead, step two requires application to the assets figure a fixed percentage (an assumed capital ratio) or the actual capital ratio of the entire foreign enterprise (determined, of course, on the basis of the worldwide operations of the foreign enterprise). This also is contrary to the separate entity/wholly independent provision of Article 7.

The third step, involving the determination of the actual interest deduction amount, begins by comparing the "presumed" liabilities computed in step two with actual liabilities of the U.S. branch to third parties (thus disregarding interbranch borrowing shown on the books of the branch). If the "presumed" liabilities exceed the liabilities to third parties, the taxpayer may deduct, in addition to interest paid to third parties, a deemed interest on the portion of the "presumed" liabilities which exceeds the actual liabilities to third parties, but the rates to determine such additional interest are average worldwide rates incurred in various other worldwide transactions of the foreign corporation unrelated to the U.S. branch. Use of the "presumed" liability figure is, as explained above, inconsistent with Article 7. Further, requiring the use of worldwide average rates of the foreign enterprise and not permitting use of borrowings and rates shown on the branch's books of account, both adjusted as may be necessary, are plainly inconsistent with the separate entity/wholly independent provision of Article 7.

In sum, insofar as the U.S. branch of a banking corporation is concerned, Treas. Reg. § 1.882–5 is fundamentally incompatible with paragraphs 2 and 3 of Article 7 of the Treaty.

X

The defendant had occasion in 1989 to consider the same issue presented by the parties' cross-motions and held, in Revenue Ruling 89–115, that "Articles 7(2) and 7(3) of the [Treaty] . . . cannot be interpreted to allow [a foreign banking corporation such as NatWest] . . . to allocate and apportion interest in a manner other than that mandated by [Treas. Reg.] section 1.882–5." Rev. Rul. 89–115, 1989–2 C.B. 130 * * *. (The revenue ruling was concerned only with application of the Treaty to the U.S. permanent establishment of a banking corporation, as are we in our consideration of the regulation and the revenue ruling.)

Of course, based on the foregoing discussion, we disagree with the conclusion in Revenue Ruling 89–115. We believe that it misinterprets both paragraphs 2 and 3 of Article 7 of the Treaty. However, in our view, its fundamental flaw is in its preliminary position that the Treaty does not provide (for banking corporations) "a specific rule for the allocation of interest expense to the profits of a permanent establishment." On the contrary, Article 7, paragraphs 2 and 3, especially when interpreted in light of the Commentary pertaining thereto, clearly contemplate that interest expense with respect to the permanent establishment of a bank shall be allocated as any other significant deductible expense, particularly for a bank whose very business is the borrowing and lending of money. We believe it is clear that this allocation should be as shown on the books of account of the permanent establishment, with necessary adjustments, as if the permanent establishment were "a distinct and separate enterprise . . . dealing wholly independently with" the foreign enterprise.

XI

A

Based on the foregoing, plaintiff is entitled to a ruling that Treas. Reg. § 1.882–5 is inconsistent with the "separate entity" treatment provided by Article 7 of the Treaty. * * *

* * *

[¶ 3188]

NOTES

1. Notice 2005–53, 2005–2 C.B. 263, stated that treaties with the United Kingdom and Japan allow banks from those countries to use an "alternative approach" to the determination of the interest deduction attributable to U.S. branches. Reg. § 1.882–5 need not apply.

2. A special rule requiring the allocation of a minimum amount of net investment income to the U.S. operations of a foreign insurance company is set forth in Section 842(b) of the Code. Under this provision, such an insurance company is required to report the greater of its actual "effectively connected" income or the "effectively connected" income determined under the Section 842(b) formulary method. A Canadian insurance company challenged the application of the statutory minimum on the ground that it was inconsistent with the provisions of the applicable United States–Canada Tax Treaty with respect to the determination of profits appropriately attributable to a permanent establishment. Article 7(2) of the Treaty provided that " * * * there shall * * * be attributed to [a] * * * permanent establishment the profits which it might be expected to make if it were a distinct and separate enterprise engaged in the same or similar activities under the same or similar conditions." The taxpayer argued that the treaty provision did not contemplate the application of the minimum income allocations set forth in the Code. The Tax Court held in favor of the taxpayer, applying the treaty even though it "may give an economic advantage to Canadian insurance companies operat-

ing through a permanent establishment in the United States * * * . [O]ur view is that [the taxpayer's] * * * interpretation * * * best carries out the intent of the United States and Canada as set forth in the Canadian Convention and satisfies the purpose of article VII * * * to attribute income to a permanent establishment based on its real facts * * * ." North West Life Assurance Co. of Canada v. Commissioner, 107 T.C. 363 (1996).

3. Do the decisions in the *National Westminster Bank* and *North West Life Assurance Co. of Canada* cases suggest that the method prescribed in the regulations for allocating interest expenses is inaccurate or inappropriate? If so, can you think of a reason why multinational corporations have not lobbied to replace the formula set forth in the regulations with an approach similar to those asserted by the foreign banks?

[¶ 3190]

4. EXCEPTION FOR CERTAIN PERSONAL SERVICES

The source of personal service income is the place where the services are rendered. § 861(a)(3). The performance of personal services in the United States usually constitutes a U.S. trade or business. § 864(b). However, tax treaties generally provide exemptions from U.S. tax for nonresident aliens who work temporarily in the United States that are broader than the de minimis exception established by the Code and discussed at ¶ 3010.

Most treaties currently in force for the United States include a specific provision dealing with nonresident aliens who work as independent contractors in the United States. Such treaties generally exempt compensation income from U.S. tax if the nonresident alien has no fixed base that is regularly available for such work. For example, Article 14 of the 1996 U.S. Model Treaty provided:

> Income derived by an individual who is a resident of [the treaty partner] * * * in respect of the performance of personal services of an independent character shall be taxable only in [the treaty partner] * * * , unless the individual has a fixed base regularly available to him in [the United States] * * * for the purpose of performing his activities.

A different formulation is reflected in the current U.S. Model Treaty, however. Under the current Model, the taxability of a nonresident alien independent contractor will be determined under the permanent establishment provisions of Articles 7 and 5. Thus, if the independent contractor has no permanent establishment in the United States, compensation income derived from work in the United States will not be taxed.

In Rev. Rul. 2004–3, 2004–1 C.B. 486, the taxpayer was a German resident who was a partner in a German service partnership which conducted business through an office in the United States. The German partner worked only at the partnership office in Germany. Partnership services were provided by a U.S. partner in the United States. The IRS held that the German partner was subject to U.S. tax on the partner's allocable share of partnership profits attributable to the partnership's U.S. activities. Moreover, it held that Article 14 of the U.S.-Germany Tax Treaty (exempting certain income compensation of independent contractors) did not apply to exempt the German partner from U.S. tax because the German partner was deemed to have a fixed place of business in the United States because of the partnership office.

Article 14 of the U.S. Model Treaty provides an exemption for compensation income paid to a nonresident alien employee for work in the United States if the employee is present for not more than 183 days during the calendar year in which the services are rendered, the remuneration is not paid by or for a resident employer and the remuneration is "not borne by" a permanent establishment or fixed base of the foreign employer in the United States.

Article 16 of the U.S. Model Treaty limits the exemptions created by Articles 5, 7 and 14 in the case of "Artistes and Sportsmen." Such foreign persons may be taxed on their compensation from working in the United States except when the amount of receipts, including reimbursed expenses, does not exceed $20,000 for the tax year. Article 15 of the U.S. Model Treaty authorizes the imposition of an income tax on fees paid to a director of a U.S. corporation who is a resident of the treaty partner and who renders services in the United States. In both instances, a tax may be authorized even though the individual taxpayer is not providing services through his or her permanent establishment.

While a ship or aircraft for some legal purposes is considered to be an extension of the territory of the country in which it is registered, Article 15(3) of the U.S. Model Treaty provides that only the state of his or her residence may tax a crew member employed as a member of the regular complement of a ship or aircraft operated in "international traffic."

[¶ 3195]

5. OTHER TREATY PROVISIONS AFFECTING U.S. TRADE OR BUSINESS INCOME

A number of other types of exemptions commonly found in tax treaties are reflected by provisions in the U.S. Model Treaty. To reflect international law and practice, Article 19 exempts income earned from the performance of services in the United States of a governmental nature for the treaty country by a citizen thereof. To facilitate international educational opportunities, Article 20 provides that payments received from abroad for maintenance, education or training by students and trainees who are in the United States for the purpose of "full-time education or training" will not be subject to U.S. tax. Such exemption applies for only one year in the case of an apprentice or business trainee. Article 20(2) also provides an annual exemption of $9,000 (adjusted periodically) for personal service income of an eligible student or trainee.

Although all foreign persons may elect to treat investments in U.S. real estate as a U.S. trade or business under Sections 871(d) and 882(d), Article 6(5) of the U.S. Model Treaty also provides that residents of the treaty country may elect to compute taxable income from real estate on a net basis and have it treated as a permanent establishment. The election, once made, is binding unless the IRS agrees to its revocation. Article 13(1) of the U.S. Model Treaty provides in effect that gains realized by a nonresident alien or foreign corporation from the alienation of U.S. real property or from stock in a company the property of which consists principally of U.S. real property may be taxed in the United States whether or not the foreign investor is in fact conducting a U.S. trade or business. This provision effectively sanctions the tax imposed by Section 897, which is discussed at ¶ 4185.

[¶ 3200]

6. RELATION OF TREATY AND CODE PROVISIONS

Although a tax treaty will never increase the U.S. tax liability of a foreign person under the Code, there are some circumstances in which the generally applicable rules may produce certain results that are more favorable than the treaty. The foreign person may generally choose not to exercise treaty rights. However, as reflected in the following Ruling, a taxpayer may not normally elect to have some U.S. business activities treated under a treaty and other U.S. business activities treated under the Code.

[¶ 3205]

REVENUE RULING 84–17

1984–1 C.B. 308.

ISSUE

Whether a taxpayer can elect the provisions of the United States–Polish People's Republic [Tax Treaty] * * * with respect to the taxability of business gain that is in part attributable to a permanent establishment and in part not attributable thereto, while in the same taxable year elect provisions of the * * * Code with respect to a nonattributable business loss.

FACTS

In Rev. Rul. 81–78, 1981–1 C.B. 604, a Polish corporation (the taxpayer) markets two entirely different products in the United States through separate and unrelated business activities. One business activity, the manufacturing and marketing of product *a* both in the United States and abroad, constitutes a permanent establishment in the United States within the meaning of Article 6 of the Convention. The profits attributable to the activity of the permanent establishment are taxable by the United States under Article 8(1) of the Convention. The profits attributable to the second business activity, the manufacturing of the product *b* in Poland and the sale of the product through an independent contractor in the United States and abroad, are not taxable under the Convention by the United States since the activity does not constitute a permanent establishment in the United States.

Assume that the facts of Rev. Rul. 81–78 apply in the subsequent taxable year. In addition to the manufacture and sale of products *a* and *b*, the taxpayer manufactures product *c* in its home office in Poland and sells the product through another independent contractor in the United States. The manufacture and sale of product *c* are wholly independent of the taxpayer's operations through the permanent establishment in the United States and from the sale of product *b* in the United States through an independent contractor. In the taxable year in question, the taxpayer has gain from the manufacture and sale of product *a* through the permanent establishment, gain on the sale of product *b*, and a loss from the sale of product *c* in the United States. The gain or loss from the sale of products *b* and *c* in the United States is not attributable to a permanent establishment in the United States, but, like the income from the sale of product *a*, is effectively connected with the conduct of a trade or business in the United States within the meaning of sections 882(a) and 864(c)(3) [because of the limited application of the force-of-attraction doctrine] * * *.

The taxpayer claimed the provisions of the Convention with respect to the gain-producing activities, involving products *a* and *b*, so that the gain from the permanent establishment was subject to United States income taxation and the gain from the sale of product *b* was exempt from United States income taxation. The taxpayer claimed the provisions of the Code with respect to the loss producing activity so that the loss from the sale of product *c* was used to offset the product *a* gain from the permanent establishment in determining the taxpayer's United States income tax liability.

LAW AND ANALYSIS

Section 882(a) * * * provides that a foreign corporation engaged in a trade or business within the United States during the taxable year shall be taxable as provided in section 11 * * * on its taxable income that is effectively connected with the conduct of a trade or business within the United States.

Section 864(c)(3) * * * provides that all income, gain, or loss from sources within the United States (other than income, gain, or loss to which section 864(c)(2) applies) shall be treated as effectively connected with the conduct of a trade or business within the United States.

Section 894(a) * * * provides that income, to the extent required by any treaty obligation of the United States, shall be exempt from taxation * * *.

Article 5(2)(a) of the Convention prevents the United States from construing the Convention to restrict in any manner any deduction allowed by the laws of the United States in the determination of the tax that the United States imposes.

The Technical Explanation of the Convention * * * states that the rule of Article 5(2)(a) reflects the principle that a convention should not increase the tax burden on residents of the Contracting States.

Article 8(1) of the Convention provides that the profits of an enterprise of a Contracting State, in this case Poland, will be taxable only by Poland unless the enterprise carries on business in the other Contracting State, in this case the United States, through a permanent establishment situated therein; if the enterprise carries on business as aforesaid, only the profits of the enterprise that are attributable to the permanent establishment may be taxed by the United States.

The provisions of the Convention dealing with business profits indicate an intent to subject Polish businesses to United States income taxation only on profits attributable to a permanent establishment in the United States. All nonattributable profits are to be taxed only by Poland. This intent is further evidenced by a statement in the report of the Senate Foreign Relations Committee describing the general objectives of the Convention. The Committee stated that ordinarily business income is not taxable in the source country, in this case the United States, unless the taxpayer has a fixed place of business there; if there is only a temporary or minimal presence in the source country, the conventions typically provide for taxation exclusively by the residence country, in this case Poland. S. Ex. Rep. No. 94–15, 94th Cong., 1st Sess. 1 at 7–8 (1975) * * *.

The intent under the Convention—that the United States will only tax business profits of a Polish enterprise that are attributable to a trade or business conducted by such enterprise in the United States—would be thwarted if losses not attributable to a permanent establishment in the United States are offset against gain attributable to a permanent establishment in the United States. Further, such an offset would require the inconsistent treatment (during a taxable year) of nonattributable gain and loss—such gain being exempt under the Convention and such loss being deductible under the Code. Accordingly, the product *c* nonattributable loss cannot be used to offset the product *a* gain attributable to the United States permanent establishment because the provisions of the Convention have been claimed with respect to the product *a* and product *b* gain.

However, Article 5(2)(a) allows the taxpayer the option to use the provisions of the Code to determine the tax liability with respect to the sales activities for products *a*, *b*, and *c* if this results in a lower tax liability than that obtained using the provisions of the Convention with respect to all of those sales activities. If the Code provisions are used, the effectively connected product *c* loss can be used to offset the effectively connected gain from products *a* and *b* in determining the taxpayer's United States income tax liability.

HOLDING

The taxpayer must use the provisions of the Convention with respect to the taxability of the product *c* nonattributable loss for the taxable year in question because those provisions are used with respect to the taxability of the gain from products *a* and *b*.

If, for the taxable year, the taxpayer desires to use the provisions of the Code with respect to the taxability of the product *c* loss, the provisions of the Code must also be used with respect to the taxability of the gain from products *a* and *b*.

* * *

[¶ 3210]

7. PARTNERSHIPS AND TRUSTS

The tax consequences of operating a permanent establishment through a partnership or trust (or a limited liability company treated as a partnership) will generally be attributed to partners and beneficiaries according to the usual rules therefor as if each partner and beneficiary had the permanent establishment.

[¶ 3215]

REVENUE RULING 90–80

1990–2 C.B. 170.

* * *

Situation 1

A, a calendar year taxpayer, is a citizen and resident of the United States. *B* is a citizen and resident of *FC*, a foreign country that has an income tax convention with the United States (the Convention) identical with the draft United States Model Income Tax Convention of 1981.

On January 1, 1989, *A* and *B* entered into a written agreement (the Agreement) under which *A* and *B* will each contribute $10,000 to fund barter transactions in the United States. *A* will use the cash to purchase goods and services within the United States from sellers who have an oversupply of goods and services, and will then barter those goods and services for others with the intent of making a profit. The Agreement provides that *A* and *B* are jointly and severally liable for obligations arising under these barter transactions, and also, that any disputes arising between *A* and *B* under the Agreement will be governed by *FC* law. Further, under the Agreement, either party can terminate the venture at will and neither *A* or *B*'s interest can be transferred.

The Agreement allocates two-thirds of all profits and losses to *A* and one-third to *B*. In order to be able to distribute profits in cash, *A* will from time to time exchange some of the bartered goods and services for cash.

A will maintain an office in the United States to conduct the barter transactions and to store the goods obtained thereby. *A* will not trade in stocks, securities or commodities within the meaning of section 864(b)(2) * * *.

In January of 1989, *A* purchased goods and services from United States sellers with the $20,000. During the year, *A* entered into a large number of separate barter transactions. *A* did not exchange any goods or services for cash. The profit from all 1989 transactions was $90,000.

Situation 2

D, a citizen and resident of *FC* (described in *Situation 1*), wished to invest $20,000 in the United States. On January 1, 1989, *D* entered into a written agreement (the Agreement) with *C*, a citizen and resident of the United States. The Agreement gives *C* the authority to negotiate and conclude barter transactions in *D*'s name. *C* will act only on behalf of *D* in these transactions, will be under *D*'s management and control, and will have no other employment during 1989.

Acting under the Agreement, *C* maintained an office and performed bartering activities identical to those of *A* in *Situation 1*. After paying *C* for his services, *D* made a profit of $70,000 on the 1989 barter transactions.

* * *

Situation 1

The arrangement between *A* and *B* is a partnership (the Partnership) for United States tax purposes. *A* and *B* have contributed cash to conduct a profit-making activity; the profits and losses from that activity will be divided between them; they will be jointly and severally liable for obligations arising from the activity; the venture may be terminated at will by either party; and there is no free transferability by *A* or *B* of either of their interests. *See* section 7701(a)(2) * * * and section 301.7701–2(a)(1), (2), and (3) of the * * * Regulations.

Under Article 5 of the Convention, the Partnership has a permanent establishment in the United States by virtue of *A*'s barter activities performed in the United States on behalf of the Partnership and the United States office that *A* uses to conduct the barter transactions.

Article 5(1) of the Convention provides that the term "permanent establishment" means a fixed place of business through which the business of an enterprise is wholly or partly carried on. Article 5(2)(c) provides that the term "permanent establishment" includes an office.

Article 5(5) of the Convention provides, in part, that notwithstanding the provisions of paragraph 1 and 2, where a person—other than an agent of an independent status—is acting on behalf of an enterprise and has, and habitually exercises, in a Contracting State an authority to conclude contracts in the name of the enterprise, that enterprise shall be deemed to have a permanent establishment in that State in respect of any activities which that person undertakes for the enterprise. *A*'s activities performed on behalf of the Partnership are those of a general agent and therefore, come within the purview of Article 5(5).

Since the Partnership has a permanent establishment in the United States under Article 5 of the Convention, *B* is also treated as having a permanent establishment in the United States. [I]n *Donroy, Ltd. v. United States*, 301 F.2d 200 (9th Cir.1962), the court held that the general partner in a United States limited partnership was the general agent of the limited partners in the partnership, and that the office or permanent establishment of the partnership was the office of each of the partners—whether general or limited—for purposes of Article XI of the United States–Canadian Income Tax Convention of 1942. The decision in the *Donroy* case was recently relied upon by the Tax Court in *Unger v. Commissioner*, T.C.M. 1990–15. In that case, a Canadian limited partner in a United States limited partnership was found to have a permanent establishment in the United States because, under the first Protocol to the United States–Canadian Income Tax Convention of 1942, the limited partnership had a permanent establishment in the United States by virtue of its offices in Boston and its general partners' acting as its agents. * * * Also, Rev. Rul. 85–60, 1985–1 C.B. 187, held that income, received by a nonresident alien beneficiary of a foreign trust that is a limited partner in a U.S. partnership (which has a permanent establishment in the U.S.), is included in gross income of the beneficiary under section 871(b) * * * and is not exempt from federal income tax under an income tax treaty because the beneficiary is considered to be in receipt of business profits attributable to that partnership's permanent establishment. *See also*, section 875(1) * * *.

Under section 702 * * *, *B*'s distributive share of the Partnership's 1989 income is $30,000 (one-third of $90,000). Since *B* is treated as having a permanent establishment in the United States for the taxable year 1989, *B*'s distributive share of the business profits of the Partnership that are attributable to the permanent establishment are taxable in the United States under Article 7(1) of the Convention. Article 7(1) provides that the profits of an enterprise of a Contracting State shall be taxable only in that State unless the enterprise carries on business in the other Contracting State through a permanent establishment situated therein. Article 7(1) further provides that if the enterprise carries on business as aforesaid, the business profits of the enterprise may be taxed in the other State but only so much of them as is attributable to that permanent establishment.

The $30,000 profit is attributable to *B*'s permanent establishment and is therefore subject to United States taxation. Thus, *B* is subject to tax under section 871(b) * * * on its $30,000 distributive share of the profits from the barter transactions. Under Section 871(b), *B*'s taxable income will be taxable as provided in section 1, or 55.

The Partnership, *A* and *B* must each file 1989 United States tax returns.

Situation 2

C has and habitually exercises in the United States the authority to conclude barter contracts and transactions in *D*'s name. *C* is not an independent agent because *C* has no other employment during 1989 and is under *D*'s management and control. Therefore, under Article 5 of the Convention, *D* has a permanent establishment in the United States in 1989 by virtue of the activities *C* undertakes for *D* and the office maintained by *C* for the purpose of conducting *D*'s barter transactions.

Since *D* is treated as having a permanent establishment in the United States, under Article 7(1) of the Convention, the 1989 business profits of *D* that are attributable to its United States permanent establishment are taxable in the United States. The $70,000 profit that *D* derived from the barter transactions is attributable to *D*'s United States permanent establishment, and thus, those profits are subject to tax under section 871(b) * * *. Under section 871(b), *D*'s taxable income will be taxable as provided in section 1 or 55.

D must file a 1989 United States tax return.

HOLDING

Situation 1

For 1989, *B* is subject to tax under section 871(b) * * * on its $30,000 distributive share of the profits from the barter transactions.

Situation 2

For 1989, *D* is subject to tax under section 871(b) * * * on its $70,000 profit from the barter transactions.

[¶ 3220]

NOTES

1. The court of appeals affirmed the *Unger* decision, rejecting the taxpayer's contention that, because his investment in the limited partnership was passive, he should not properly be deemed to have a permanent establishment in the United States under the United States–Canada Tax Treaty. Unger v. Commissioner, 936 F.2d 1316 (D.C.Cir.1991).

2. In Rev. Rul. 91–32, 1991–1 C.B. 107, the IRS ruled that the gain or loss realized by a foreign partner resident in a treaty country from the disposition of an interest in a partnership conducting a U.S. trade or business through a permanent establishment would be treated as attributable to the permanent establishment. If the partnership has property attributable to the permanent establishment and other property, only the portion of gain attributable to the property used in the permanent establishment will be taxed.

3. The terms of tax treaties do not generally vary the usual rule that the characterization for U.S. tax purposes of a business entity will be governed by U.S. law. For example, in Rev. Rul. 76–435, 1976–2 C.B. 490, a German taxpayer was a partner in a U.S. limited partnership. The IRS ruled that the entity was properly characterized under the then applicable regulations as an "association" taxable as a corporation. Accordingly, its distributions were taxed as corporate dividends, and applicable withholding taxes were imposed.

[¶ 3225]

PROBLEMS

1. Revisit the Traditions Problems at ¶ 3155. Would your responses be modified if the U.S. Model Treaty were in effect between the United States and Traditions' country of incorporation and operation?

2. Consider the following variations on the Traditions situation if the U.S. Model Treaty were in effect between the United States and Traditions' country of incorporation and operation:

a. Suppose that Traditions sells art it purchases from local artists and craftsmen in the United States through traveling sales employees in the United States who operate from hotel rooms across the country and solicit orders on Traditions' standard conditions of sale. All sales orders are accepted at Traditions' home office. Traditions maintains no sales office in the United States. Would Traditions be subject to U.S. income tax?

b. How would your response to a. be affected if Traditions has a warehouse and showroom in Chicago at which art is displayed and from which deliveries are made to customers?

c. How would your response to b. be affected if the art consisted of carvings that, while held in the U.S. warehouse, were painted, labeled and packaged for sale by an independent third party?

d. How would your response to a. be affected if Traditions also maintains a separate office in New York which conducts U.S. market research and directs U.S. advertising?

e. Suppose that the employees described in a. operate out of the Traditions warehouse described in b. and that the employees have the power, which is regularly exercised, to solicit, negotiate and conclude sales contracts with U.S. department stores. Would Traditions be subject to U.S. income tax?

3. How would the case of *Handfield v. Commissioner*, at ¶ 3050, be decided under the U.S. Model Treaty?

4. Medtech Inc. ("Medtech") is a Delaware corporation with its headquarters in New York and operations in many countries. Sam Spode is a medical sleuth specializing in tracking down the origin of strange diseases. He is a citizen and resident of Costa Rica, a country with which the United States has concluded a tax treaty congruent with the provisions of the U.S. Model Treaty. Medtech would like to hire Sam either as an independent consultant or as a regular employee. In either event Sam would continue to maintain his Costa Rican residence and would spend no more than 100 days working in the United States in any year. Would it make any difference to Sam's U.S. tax position whether he was an independent consultant or a regular employee of Medtech?

5. Sally Suarez is an associate in a law firm in Panama, of which she is a citizen and resident. She comes to New York to work on the acquisition of a Panamanian corporation by a U.S. corporation, which is a client of her firm. She spends 30 consecutive days in New York working on the deal and living in a fancy hotel. She receives compensation from the law firm of $10,000 for the time spent working in New York. The firm, which has no office in the United States, collects fees of $30,000 from the U.S. corporation as a result of the work of Suarez in New York. Assuming that the U.S. Model Treaty is in force between Panama and the United States, are either Suarez or the firm subject to U.S. income tax on the amounts they receive? Would the U.S. tax consequences be altered if the law firm had an office in New York and Suarez did most of her work on the deal in that office?

6. Global History, Ltd. ("Global History") is a corporation organized under the laws of India where its headquarters and principal operations are located. Global History has acquired the right to publish electronically 100,000 volumes of history books in many different languages. Its operations in the United States are effected through a web site maintained in this country by an independent service provider. All advertising in the United States is on the web site. When customers in the United States wish to acquire an electronic version of a history book, an order is placed through the web site and payment is tendered electronically by a credit card acceptable to Global History. When the order and payment are confirmed at headquarters in India, the book is "shipped" electronically to the customer in the United States. During recent years, Global History has sold an average of 100,000 volumes producing gross revenues of $2,500,000. Is Global History conducting a U.S.

trade or business? If the U.S. Model Treaty were in force between the United States and India, would Global Business have a permanent establishment in the United States?

[¶ 3230]

E. BRANCH PROFITS TAX

Until 1987, there was a difference in the tax burden on foreign corporations that operated through a branch in the United States and foreign corporations that chose to operate through a U.S. subsidiary. The net income of the U.S. branch was taxed at the usual corporate rates under the principles discussed in this Chapter. Of course, the net income of a U.S. subsidiary was also taxed at the usual corporate rates. However, there was a substantially different tax consequence to the foreign parent when it sought to repatriate profits from the U.S. enterprise. Branch profits could be repatriated with no tax because no income was realized as a result of the repatriation. Dividends paid by a U.S. subsidiary were subject to a withholding tax of 30 percent under the Code or to a lesser rate (as little as five percent) under applicable tax treaties.

In an attempt to equalize the tax treatment of using U.S. subsidiaries and branches, Section 884 was adopted as part of the Tax Reform Act of 1986. Section 884 imposes a withholding tax, called a "branch profits tax," of 30 percent on the deemed remittance of profits by a U.S. branch of a foreign corporation.

The branch profits tax is an interesting departure from some traditional federal income tax concepts. The movement of assets among the branches of a single corporate taxpayer is not usually regarded as a taxable event. In fact, when related domestic corporations file consolidated returns, intercompany transactions are not regarded as taxable events. The branch profits tax, however, specifically treats the deemed repatriation of already taxed profits from the United States by a foreign corporation as an occasion to impose a second tax. Has the foreign corporation realized income in such a circumstance?

Regardless of whether the creation of an income tax on the movement of assets by a taxpayer is consistent with the concept of income realization, there are special problems in imposing a withholding tax on branch remittances. Because both are part of the same entity, branches do not declare and pay dividends to the home office. Accounts and transactions may run between the branch and the home office very much as they run between two departments of the same corporation that are located across the hall from one another.

Section 884 describes the tax base as the "dividend equivalent amount," which is defined as the "effectively connected earnings and profits" with certain adjustments. It is intended to be the functional equivalent of earnings distributed as dividends by a subsidiary either out of current earnings not invested in subsidiary assets or out of accumulated earnings withdrawn from such investment. The amount taxed is reduced, therefore, by any increase in the branch equity. Conversely, the amount of earnings taxed is increased by a reduction of branch equity but not in excess of effectively connected earnings and profits accumulated at the end of the prior tax year. Branch equity is measured by the adjusted basis of branch assets less liabilities connected with the branch. In effect, this leaves a base of distributed profits, subject to certain definitions and exceptions. § 884(d)(1) and (2).

Under prior law, a "second dividend tax" was imposed upon foreign shareholders receiving dividends from foreign corporations when at least 25 percent of the corporation's gross income for a prescribed base period derived from U.S. sources. When the branch profits tax was established, the second dividend tax was not applied to dividends paid out of earnings and profits attributable to tax years in which the foreign corporation was subject to the branch profits tax. The second dividend tax has been completely repealed for distributions made after 2004 even though such dividends may be regarded as U.S.-source income under Section 861(a)(2)(B). §§ 871(i)(2)(D), 881(d).

Because the branch profits tax was new, U.S. tax treaties in force at the time of its adoption contained no reference to it. Because the rationale for the branch profits tax was to reduce differences between the use of U.S. subsidiaries and U.S. branches, the Code itself provides that tax treaty provisions can modify, reduce or eliminate the branch profits tax. See, e.g., U.S. Model Treaty, Arts. 10(8) and 10(2)(a). Under Section 884(e)(2), even if a treaty does not mention the branch profits tax, the rate of that tax shall be limited to the rate of U.S. withholding tax provided by the treaty for dividends from a wholly owned U.S. subsidiary. Treaties concluded since the enactment of the branch profits tax authorize its imposition.

Section 884(e) also attempts to limit avoidance of the branch profits tax by "treaty shopping"—the exploitation of treaty benefits by taxpayers who have little or no relationship with the treaty partner except as shareholders in corporations organized therein. The application of any treaty provisions modifying the branch profits tax is restricted to a corporation that is a "qualified resident" of the treaty country. For purposes of these rules, the foreign corporation will not be a qualified resident if 50 percent or more of the value of its stock is owned by individuals who are not residents of the treaty country and are not U.S. citizens or residents, or if 50 percent or more of its income is used to meet liabilities to persons who are not resident in the treaty country and are not U.S. citizens or residents. The foreign corporation will, however, be a qualified resident if its stock is primarily and regularly traded on an established securities market in the treaty country, if it is wholly owned (directly or indirectly) by a corporation organized in the treaty country whose stock is so traded or if it is the wholly owned subsidiary of a U.S.

corporation the stock of which is primarily and regularly traded on an established securities market in the United States. § 884(e)(4).

The branch profits tax also applies to certain interest paid by or allocated to the branch. Interest paid by the branch is treated as U.S.-source interest. If interest deductions allocated to the branch (pursuant to Reg. § 1.882–5) exceed the amount of interest actually paid by the branch, the excess is treated as U.S.-source interest paid by the branch to the foreign corporation, which is subject to the applicable withholding tax, as if the branch were a wholly owned U.S. subsidiary. § 884(f)(1). If the constructive interest arising under these provisions involves a corporation that is a qualified resident of a treaty country, treaty benefits for interest will apply. Article 11 of the U.S. Model Treaty provides that interest paid to a resident of the treaty country is generally exempt from U.S. tax.

The operation of the branch profits tax can be demonstrated in a simple example. El Dorado, Inc. ("El Dorado"), a foreign corporation, has net equity (adjusted basis of branch assets less branch liabilities) in its U.S. branch at the end of tax year 1 of $450,000. El Dorado has effectively connected earnings and profits (effectively connected net income less U.S. income taxes) for tax year 2 of $100,000. The company acquired an additional $50,000 of U.S. assets during tax year 2 bringing its U.S. net equity at the end of tax year 2 to $500,000.

El Dorado's dividend equivalent amount is equal to its effectively connected earnings and profits reduced by the amount of its increase in U.S. net equity ($100,000 − $50,000). Its dividend equivalent amount for tax year 2 is, therefore, $50,000. A branch profits tax of $15,000 will have to be paid in addition to the U.S. income tax on the tax year 2 taxable income of the branch.

If El Dorado's U.S. net equity were reduced in tax year 2 by $50,000, its effectively connected earnings and profits would be increased by the amount of the reduction subject to the limitations discussed. The dividend equivalent amount for tax year 2 in this case would be $150,000 ($100,000 + $50,000), and a branch profits tax of $45,000 would be due.

If El Dorado is a qualified resident of a country with which the U.S. Model Treaty is in effect, the branch profits tax is five percent of the dividend equivalent amount as a result of Section 884(e) and Article 10(2)(a) of the treaty.

The application of the branch profits tax with respect to interest arises in situations in which interest actually paid by the branch is less than the amount of interest allocated to the branch under applicable provisions of the Code and regulations. Suppose for example that the U.S. branch of El Dorado actually paid interest of $5,000 but was able to deduct interest of $6,000 as a result of the allocation provisions described in ¶ 3140. The $5,000 payment would be treated as U.S.-source interest to the lender invoking whatever tax consequences would generally apply to such payments. The excess interest deduction of $1,000 would be treated as if it were paid by a U.S. subsidiary to a foreign parent corporation in respect of a loan from the parent. The $1,000 payment would be subject to a withholding tax of 30 percent unless otherwise provided by an applicable treaty.

The branch profits tax applies only to foreign corporations. Would the application of the branch profits tax to a foreign corporation that is a qualified resident of a treaty country be a violation of the nondiscrimination clause of a treaty containing the language of Article 24 of the U.S. Model Treaty?

[¶ 3235]

PROBLEMS

1. Rastaco, a Jamaican corporation engaged in the production and sale of musical recordings, operates a branch in Miami. The branch's "U.S. net equity," as defined in Section 884(c)(1), was $1 million as of the end of the prior tax year. During the current tax year, the Miami branch had taxable income effectively connected with its U.S. business of $1 million and a U.S. income tax liability of $350,000. During the course of the year, the corporation purchased a new recording studio in Miami for $2 million. The purchase was financed by a cash payment of $200,000, made from a corporate account in Jamaica, and from a loan of $1.8 million from a Florida bank secured by a mortgage on the studio building. At the end of the current tax year, the fair market value of assets held by the Miami branch (including the recording studio) had increased by $3 million. The adjusted basis of assets held by the Miami branch had, however, increased by only $2.3 million. Rastaco incurred no other liabilities during the current tax year relating to the Miami branch operation. The Miami branch remitted $200,000 in cash to the head office in Jamaica on September 30 of the current tax year. What, if any, is the dividend equivalent amount for the current tax year?

2. How would your answer to Problem 1 change if the adjusted basis of assets held by the Miami branch had increased by only $2 million? By $2.5 million? How much tax would be owed in each instance?

3. Suppose that the Miami branch of Rastaco had paid interest of $10,000 during the year to various unrelated creditors, but that it properly deducted interest of $15,000 in determining its effectively connected income on the basis of the interest allocation rules. Would there be an additional branch profits tax? How much?

4. How, if at all, would your answers to Problems 1, 2 and 3 be affected if the U.S. Model Treaty were in force between the United States and Jamaica?

[¶ 3240]

F. EXCEPTIONS BASED UPON FOREIGN POLICY CONSIDERATIONS

Sections 892 and 895 relieve foreign governments, foreign central banks and international organizations from income taxes imposed on certain investments and deposits in the United States. Specifically, foreign governments and international organizations are exempt from tax on income from investments in the United States in stocks, bonds or other domestic securities and financial instruments held in the execution of governmental financial or monetary policy and from U.S. banks. § 892(a)(1) and (b). This broad exclusion is partially a reflection of the requirements of the international law doctrine of foreign sovereign immunity and the immunities provided by treaty to certain international organizations. See, e.g., Convention on the Privileges and Immunities of the United Nations of February 13, 1946, 21 U.S.T. 1418, at Section 7. It also reflects a desire to encourage foreign states and international organizations to invest and operate in the United States and to use U.S. banks.

Taxes nevertheless will be imposed on income derived directly or indirectly from commercial activities undertaken in the United States by foreign governmental entities. § 892(a)(2). This practice is consistent with the modern notion of restrictive sovereign immunity, under which business ventures operated by governments and/or governmental agencies do not enjoy the immunities established under international law to protect governmental actions from the legal process of other countries. See Foreign Sovereign Immunities Act of 1976, 28 U.S.C.A. § 1605. The distinction between governmental and commercial activities has been addressed in a number of cases. For example, in Qantas Airways Ltd. v. United States, 97–1 U.S.T.C. ¶ 50,344 (Fed.Cl.1997), aff'd without opinion, 98–2 U.S.T.C. ¶ 50,859 (Fed.Cir. 1998), the court held that operating an airline was a commercial activity so Qantas was not entitled to the exemption under Section 892 even though the airline was wholly owned by the Government of Australia.

Section 893 excludes from U.S. taxable income compensation paid to certain alien employees of foreign governments and international organizations by such entities even though the services are performed in the United States. This exclusion reflects in part the practice of diplomatic immunity, the requirements of treaties creating the international organizations and reciprocal governmental arrangements. See Vienna Convention on Diplomatic Relations of April 18, 1961, 23 U.S.T. 3227, at Article 34. Certain income, including that produced from the conduct of a trade or business in the United States not related to the performance of the employee's official duties, is not excluded. Further, Section 893(c) denies the exclusion to an employee of a controlled commercial entity of a foreign government or to an employee of a foreign government whose services are rendered "in connection with a commercial activity (whether within or outside the United States)."

Section 893(a)(3) conditions the exclusion upon the reciprocal provision of exemptions to U.S. government employees performing similar services in the foreign country. Section 893(b) provides that the Secretary of State "shall certify the names of foreign countries which grant equivalent exemptions to" U.S. government employees. However, in Abdel–Fatah v. Commissioner, 134 T.C. No. 10 (2010), the court held that the State Department certification requirement was not a condition for the exemption claim by a foreign employee of the Embassy of the United Arab Emirates. As the taxpayer satisfied the requirements set forth in Section 893(a), he was entitled to the exemption despite the lack of a State Department certification.

[¶ 3245]

PROBLEMS

1. The Government of South Africa has been capitalizing on the interest of investors in gold by marketing gold coins in the United States. The coins constitute legal tender in South Africa. The gold coins, however, sell for a price in dollars that is substantially in excess of both the dollar cost to produce them and the dollar equivalent of the South African currency in which they are denominated. The coins are marketed by an office of the South Africa Ministry of Export in New York, where a substantial inventory of coins is maintained. Sales are made at retail outlets and by mail. The Government of South Africa has asked you to determine whether there is any U.S. income tax liability associated with these activities. Is South Africa subject to U.S. income taxes? Is it necessary for South Africa to invoke the special exemption provisions to avoid tax? Do those provisions apply in favor of South Africa?.

2. John Johnson, Ambassador of a small Caribbean nation to the United States, receives a salary from his government of $100,000, which he supplements by providing consulting services to companies interested in opportunities in his country. As a result, he receives $50,000 from meeting with clients in various Caribbean resorts and $50,000 from meeting with clients in Washington, D.C. Does Johnson owe any U.S. income taxes?

CHAPTER 4

FOREIGN PERSONS: NONBUSINESS U.S.–SOURCE INCOME

■ ■ ■

A. BASIC MECHANISM

[¶ 4000]

1. TAX ON GROSS INCOME

As discussed in Chapter 3, U.S.-source income that is effectively connected with a U.S. trade or business will be taxable to foreign persons at the usual individual or corporate rates. Appropriate deductions and credits will apply in the determination of U.S. tax liabilities.

Most of the forms of U.S.-source income received by foreign persons that are not effectively connected with a U.S. trade or business will be subject to a flat tax of 30 percent on the gross amount of the income received. Sections 871(a) (for nonresident aliens) and 881(a) (for foreign corporations) impose the 30–percent tax on "interest * * * dividends, rents, salaries, wages, premiums, annuities, compensations, remunerations, emoluments, and other fixed or determinable annual or periodical gains, profits, and income." This enumeration is sometimes referred to as "FDAP income." The collection of such taxes is effected primarily through the imposition of an obligation on the person or entity making the payment to the foreign person to withhold the tax and pay it over to the IRS. The tax collected is, therefore, often referred to as a "withholding tax." In fact, however, the recipient of the income is the taxpayer. The obligation imposed on the payor to withhold tax is intended to assure its collection.

The result is a combination of two basic taxing regimes. Many items of U.S.-source FDAP income are taxed at the statutory rate of 30 percent. However, items of such income that are effectively connected with a U.S. trade or business will be taxed under the rules discussed in Chapter 3. Moreover, certain other items of FDAP income are exempted from any U.S. tax even though deriving from U.S. sources.

The complete taxing structure is more complex. Certain items of U.S.-source capital gains that are neither FDAP income nor connected with a U.S. trade or business will be taxed under the withholding tax regime. As indicated in the previous Chapter, other gains not in fact connected with a U.S. trade or business will be taxed (under some special rules) as if they were. Certain gains in respect of timber, coal and iron ore governed by special rules are also subject to the 30–percent tax. §§ 871(a)(1)(B) and 881(a)(2).

As in the case of U.S. trade or business income, tax treaties modify the statutory provisions. The most significant modification effected by tax treaties with respect to FDAP income that is not attributable to a permanent establishment is the reduction or elimination of the statutory withholding tax.

The law is still evolving. Concerns with respect to capital-import neutrality, horizontal equity and federal revenues have produced legislation intended to increase the U.S. income tax burdens on certain foreign investors. Other proposals to increase taxes on foreign persons have also been debated in recent sessions of the Congress.

[¶ 4005]

2. RATIONALE FOR TAX ON GROSS INCOME

This is one of the few circumstances in which a tax on gross income is imposed as part of the U.S. income tax laws. Although it constitutes a significant departure from normal income tax policy, the withholding mechanism applied to items of gross income paid to foreign persons is used by most countries.

The rationale for the imposition of a gross income tax derives less from sound tax theory than from the realities of a limited power to enforce tax laws. As indicated earlier (see ¶ 1080), countries do not usually open the doors of their courthouses for foreign tax collection efforts even by friendly other countries. This creates practical problems of administration when an income tax liability accrues in respect of investment income realized by a foreign investor who is outside of the country. The investment itself may be the only asset within the jurisdictional reach of the taxing government, and it may have been liquidated or removed by the time the taxing authorities learn of the unpaid liability.

The withholding tax thus provides a useful response to a practical dilemma. The obligation to withhold tax, as described at ¶ 4120, is imposed on persons and entities that are normally within the United States and are, therefore, subject to the broad range of IRS collection powers.

The flat tax on gross income serves to simplify the administration of the withholding mechanism. While the person or entity making the payment and withholding the tax may be within the potential grasp of the IRS, that person is not likely to possess much information about the tax circumstances of the foreign taxpayer who is receiving the item of income. The reliance on the withholding mechanism to collect the tax, therefore, militates against the use of a complicated formula of deductions, exemptions and progressive rates. The result is the flat tax on gross income that, at least theoretically, is intended to approximate the tax burden on net income that would be borne by the foreign person in question if it were feasible to take account of allowable deductions.

The success of the theoretical attempt to equate tax burdens is open to obvious question. The 30–percent flat rate existed at times when the maximum marginal rates of U.S. tax for individuals were 91 percent, 70 percent and 50 percent. The maximum stated marginal rate of tax on an individual's *net income* is 35 percent through 2010, but an increase is possible. Although it changed from time to time, the maximum tax rate for corporations during the decades prior to 1986 ranged from 46 to 52 percent. The maximum nominal rate on the net income of corporations is now 35 percent, but an increase is also possible. Yet the flat-rate withholding tax continues to be 30 percent for both individual and corporate taxpayers. That rate could now reflect only the crudest attempt to equalize tax burdens. There is obviously little room to accommodate any costs of producing the items of income in question.

As indicated previously, the withholding tax rates are often negotiated with other countries through the bilateral tax treaty process. The usual result is a withholding rate for at least some items of FDAP income not attributable to a permanent establishment of less than 30 percent. Under many treaties, the withholding tax on interest and royalties is wholly eliminated. Some recently concluded treaties also exempt dividend payments to corporate shareholders in certain instances. Perhaps the continued 30–percent rate is best explained as a mutual starting point for such treaty negotiations.

[¶ 4010]

B. WHAT IS FDAP INCOME?

The Code defines FDAP income by specifically listing a series of income forms that are usually of a recurring nature, such as interest, dividends, rents and royalties. The gross amount of such payments, when from U.S. sources but not effectively connected with a U.S. trade or business, is clearly subject to the 30–percent tax. The statutory definition adds the encompassing (but not defined) phrase "and other fixed or determinable annual or periodical" income. The regulations emphasize the need for caution in applying such everyday terms as "annual" or "periodical": "The fact that a payment is not made annually or periodically does not * * * prevent it from being fixed or determinable annual or periodical income * * *." Reg. § 1.1441–2(b)(1)(ii).

The following cases address some interesting questions about the meaning of the statutory language. The *Wodehouse* case considers whether a single payment can be "annual or periodical." The *Central de Gas de Chihuahua* case considers whether a tax administered through the establishment of a withholding requirement on payments can apply when no payment in fact has been made.

[¶ 4015]

COMMISSIONER v. WODEHOUSE

Supreme Court of the United States, 1949.
337 U.S. 369.

[P.G. Wodehouse, the popular author who created the Jeeves series, received a lump-sum payment from a U.S. publisher for "an exclusive serial or book right throughout the United States in relation to a specified original story * * * ready to be copyrighted." The applicable Code provisions were similar to those now in force and the taxpayer argued, inter alia, that (1) the payment received was not a royalty but rather the proceeds of a sale of a property interest in a copyright and (2) payment was made in a lump sum and, therefore, was not "fixed or determinable annual or periodical gains, profits, and income * * *." The Court, however, upheld the IRS on both issues.]

JUSTICE BURTON delivered the opinion of the Court.

* * *

Once it has been determined that [the transaction was not a sale and that] the receipts of the respondent would have been required to be included in his gross income for federal income tax purposes if they had been received in annual payments, or from time to time, during the life of the respective copyrights, it becomes equally clear that the receipt of those same sums by him in single lump sums as payments in full, in advance, for the same rights to be enjoyed throughout the entire life of the respective copyrights *cannot,* solely by reason of the consolidation of the payment into one sum, render it tax exempt. No Revenue Act can be interpreted to reach such a result in the absence of inescapably clear provisions to that effect. There are none such here.

The argument for the exemption was suggested by the presence in [current Sections 871 and 881] * * * of the words "annual" and "periodical." If read apart from their text and legislative history and supplemented by the gratuitous insertion after them of the word "payments," they might support the limiting effect here argued for them. However, when taken in their context, and particularly in the light of the legislative history of those Acts, and the interpretation placed upon them by the Treasury Department and the lower courts, they have no such meaning. Those words are merely generally descriptive of the character of the gains, profits and income which arise out of such relationships as those which produce readily withholdable interest, rents, royalties and salaries, consisting wholly of income, especially in contrast to gains, profits and income in the nature of capital gains from profitable sales of real or personal property.

In the instant case, each copyright which was to be obtained had its full, original life of 28 years to run after the advance payment was received by the author covering the use of or the privilege of using certain rights under it. Fixed and determinable income, from a tax standpoint, may be received either in annual or other payments without altering in the least the need or the reasons for taxing such income or for withholding a part of it at its source. One advance payment to cover the entire 28–year period of a copyright comes within the reason and reach of the Revenue Acts as well as, or even better than, two or more partial payments of the same sum.

* * *

[¶ 4020]

NOTES

1. Justice Frankfurter, joined by two other Justices, dissented on the ground that the transaction was a sale and not a licensing agreement. 337 U.S. at 401. If the transaction had been characterized by the majority as a sale, the lump-sum payment could not have been properly characterized as a royalty. Note, however, that gains from the sale of intellectual property in situations where payments are contingent on "productivity, use, or disposition of the property interest" will be treated under rules analogous to the royalty rules and, in such cases, be subject to withholding tax even though not included in the statutory definition of FDAP income. §§ 871(a)(1)(D), 881(a)(4).

2. In Commissioner v. Raphael, 133 F.2d 442 (9th Cir.), cert. denied, 320 U.S. 735 (1943), a lump-sum payment of interest was held to be subject to the withholding tax.

3. In Rev. Rul. 73–522, 1973–2 C.B. 226, the U.S. tenant of a foreign landlord was required under the terms of the leasehold to pay applicable real estate taxes. The IRS ruled that such payments were properly characterized as additional rents subject to the withholding tax. Note that the foreign landlord could not deduct the real estate taxes in determining his U.S. income tax liability unless he was actually engaged in a U.S. trade or business or elected to be treated as so engaged. See ¶ 3095.

4. In Rev. Rul. 2004–75, 2004–2 C.B. 109, the IRS considered whether U.S. tax applies to annuity payments by U.S. life insurance companies to nonresident aliens when insurance policies and annuities had been sold by foreign branches of the insurance companies. The Ruling addressed two issues: whether income from such contracts derived from U.S. sources and, if so, whether it was FDAP income to which the withholding tax applied. Noting

that there is no statutory source rule applicable to annuity payments, the Ruling identified appropriate analogies among the statutory source rules:

> Income received under a life insurance or annuity contract under section 72 is an investment return on the cash value of the contract and is analogous to (1) interest on a debt obligation, (2) dividends on a stock, and (3) earnings and accretions on pension fund assets. Thus, the source of that income is determined in the same manner as the source of interest, dividends and earnings and accretions on pension fund assets. Under sections 861(a)(1) and (2), interest or dividends are U.S. source when the obligor or corporation, respectively, is domestic. Earnings and accretions on pension fund assets are also U.S. source when the pension trust is domestic. * * * Accordingly, income received under a life insurance or annuity contract is U.S. source when the issuer of the contract is a domestic corporation.

Id. at 110. Noting that "payments from annuity contracts are specifically listed as a type of FDAP income in section 871(a)(1)(A)," the Ruling concluded that " * * * both annuity payments and withdrawals made from the cash value of the contract, * * * [are] FDAP income. Accordingly, when such income is received by nonresident alien individuals, it generally is subject to 30% tax and withholding * * *."

5. The 2004 JOBS Act included a provision that is intended to defend against the use of U.S. holding companies by foreign corporations to avoid U.S. withholding taxes on dividend distributions by U.S. corporations. Section 332(d) treats distributions upon the liquidation of certain domestic corporations to certain foreign shareholders as dividends instead of the proceeds of the disposition of the stock of the U.S. corporation. Such treatment is prescribed when there is a distribution to a foreign corporation in complete liquidation of an "applicable holding company." As a result, while gains on the sale or disposition of such stock would in most instances be treated as foreign-source income not subject to U.S. tax, the application of the source rules for dividends will generally treat the distributions as U.S.-source dividend income subject to the withholding tax regime. An "applicable holding company" is a U.S. corporation which is a common parent of an affiliated group whose stock is directly owned by the distributee foreign corporation and substantially all of whose assets consist of stock in other members of the affiliated group. The provision applies, however, only if the U.S. corporation has not been in existence at all times during the five years preceding the liquidation date. An "affiliated group" is defined by Section 1504(a) without regard to Section 1504(b)(2) and (4).

6. Various techniques had evolved for effectively converting dividend income into gain from the sale of stock or some other form that would avoid the withholding tax. For example, gain realized from the sale of stock in a U.S. corporation by a foreign person will usually be treated as foreign-source income under the residence-of-seller rule. Suppose that a foreign shareholder sells shares in a U.S. corporation immediately prior to a dividend distribution and contracts to repurchase the shares after the dividend has been distributed. In effect, the potential U.S.-source income created by a dividend distribu-

tion will have been largely converted into foreign-source income. Section 871(m) was adopted in 2010 to defend against such avoidance techniques. Under that provision, "dividend equivalent payments" will be taxed as if they were a dividend. The tax will apply to:

(1) Any substitute dividend made pursuant to a securities lending or a sale-repurchase transaction that (directly or indirectly) is contingent upon, or determined by reference to, the payment of a dividend from sources within the United States;

(2) Any payment made pursuant to a specified notional principal contract that (directly or indirectly) is contingent upon, or determined by reference to, the payment of a dividend from sources within the United States; and

(3) Any other payment determined by the IRS to be substantially similar to such payments.

[¶ 4025]

CENTRAL DE GAS DE CHIHUAHUA, S.A. v. COMMISSIONER

United States Tax Court, 1994.
102 T.C. 515.

[In this case, the IRS has exercised its considerable power under Section 482 to recalculate the tax consequences of transactions between related corporations to reflect arm's length standards. Section 482 is analyzed in Chapter 8. The taxpayer argues that the 30–percent tax on gross rental income, normally collected through the withholding mechanism, could not apply because no payment had in fact been made.]

TANNENWALD, JUDGE: * * *.

* * *

During 1990, petitioner (a Mexican corporation) rented a fleet of tractors and trailers to another Mexican corporation, Hidro Gas de Juarez, S.A. (hereinafter Hidro). Hidro did not pay rent for the equipment. Petitioner and Hidro were under common control within the meaning of section 482. The rented equipment was used to transport liquified petroleum gas from points within the United States to the Mexican border area where it was sold to Pemex, the Mexican Government-operated oil company, for distribution in Mexico.

Petitioner did not file a Federal income tax return for 1990. Respondent, acting under section 482, allocated to petitioner the amount of $2,320,800 as the fair rental value of the equipment for 1990 (which the parties now agree should be $1,125,000) and determined that petitioner was liable for the 30–percent tax imposed by section 881 on that amount, which is the primary position respondent asserts herein. Respondent also determined in the deficiency notice and asserts herein, as an alternative position in the event that we should grant petitioner's motion, i.e., hold that the section 881 tax does not apply, that petitioner is liable for tax under section 882 on income effectively connected with the conduct of trade or business within the United States. Similarly, petitioner has reserved the right, in the event that we grant respondent's motion, i.e., hold that the section 881 tax does apply, to contend that only a portion of the agreed rental value should be allocated to the use of the equipment within the United States and other matters relating to the nature of the relationship between petitioner and Hidro. The parties are in agreement that our disposition of the motions herein will facilitate resolution of the matters reserved.

The pertinent provisions of the Code upon which the positions of the parties are based are section 881(a) and section 1442(a), the latter section incorporating a portion of section 1441(a).

* * *

Petitioner argues that, in order for section 881(a) to apply, there must be an actual payment of the income item and that the allocation of rent to petitioner from Hidro under section 482 does not satisfy that requirement. Respondent counters with the assertion that there is no requirement of actual payment under section 881 and that the allocation of rent to petitioner under section 482 provides a sufficient basis for imposing the 30–percent tax under that section. For the reasons hereinafter set forth, we agree with the respondent.

In marshaling support for their positions, the parties have viewed section 881, on one hand, and sections 1441 and 1442, on the other, as being mirror images of each other. In this context and in the absence of authority dealing with the issue whether actual payment is required for section 881 to apply, they have pointed to cases dealing with such requirement under sections 1441 and 1442 and comparable provisions of the Internal Revenue Code of 1939.

Petitioner relies on *L.D. Caulk Co. v. United States*, 116 F.Supp. 835 (D.Del. 1953). In that case, the issue was the obligation of the plaintiff to withhold tax, under section 143 of the Internal Revenue Code of 1939 (the predecessor of sections 1441 and 1442) on royalties payable to nonresident aliens at a time when payment of such royalties was blocked under U.S. law. The District Court articulated a thorough analysis of the obligation to withhold under such circumstances and concluded that, at least where the item of income could not have been legally paid, no such obligation existed. We think *Caulk* is clearly distinguishable from the situation herein where there was no legal impediment to the payment of rent by Hidro to petitioner. The same caveat was expressed in *Southern Pacific Co. v. Commissioner*, 21 B.T.A. 990, 994 (1930), also relied upon by petitioner, which likewise involved the obligation to withhold in respect of blocked income and is therefore distinguishable. In a similar vein, we find petitioner's reliance on several of respondent's revenue rulings beside the point. The rulings involve clearly distinguishable circumstances, for the most part the measure of excise taxes on discounted payments, and in any event are not binding upon us. * * *

Respondent relies on *Casa De La Jolla Park v. Commissioner*, 94 T.C. 384 (1990). That case also involved the obligation to withhold under section 1441(a) in a situation where interest was owed by petitioner therein to a nonresident alien who in turn owed money to a Canadian bank. Petitioner caused the amount of the interest it owed to be remitted to the Canadian bank to be applied against the sums due the bank from the nonresident alien. We held that petitioner in that case had an obligation to withhold. In so doing, we interpreted section 1441(a) as not necessarily requiring payment. We think *Casa De La Jolla Park* does not furnish respondent the degree of support which she attaches to it. In the first place, there was payment although it was indirect. In the second place, the case dealt with the obligation to withhold and not with the issue of liability for the tax as such, which is the situation we have before us. Under these circumstances, we see no reason for us to pursue that question of how far the obligation to withhold attaches to an item of income allocated by respondent under section 482. * * *

We think that the parties' use of the mirror image concept is misguided. Section 881 imposes a liability for tax, and sections 1441 and 1442 provide a method for collecting that tax. * * * Thus, the former section and the latter two sections serve distinctly separate purposes. Consequently, we are not persuaded that, even if actual payment is required for withholding under sections 1441 and 1442 (an issue we expressly do not decide herein), it necessarily follows that the same requirement should apply in determining the import of the word "received" in section 881. Indeed, the District Court, in *L.D. Caulk Co. v. United States*, 116 F.Supp. at 840 n. 9, upon which petitioner heavily relies, indicated a similar view.

Petitioner does not question the broad authority of respondent to allocate income under section 482. Moreover, petitioner does not question the authority of respondent to "create" income by an allocation between related entities—a question which was the subject of conflicting views until resolved in respondent's favor. * * * To be sure, the existence of such authority was articulated in the context of provisions in the section 482 regulations for a correlative adjustment to the income of the entity from which the income is allocated. See sec. 1.482–1(d)(4), Income Tax Regs. The fact that such an adjustment may not have any effect on Hidro for the taxable year before us since Hidro is a foreign corporation which does not appear to be subject to U.S. tax for such year is irrelevant; the adjustment is deemed made and conceivably could affect Hidro's U.S. tax liability in a subsequent year. *Id.*

Petitioner asserts that section 482 does not confer upon respondent the authority to "create" a payment. We think this position begs the question to be resolved. There can be no doubt that the authority of respondent to allocate income encompasses the conclusion that such allocation "creates" a deemed payment. Any other view would render such an allocation nugatory in a host of situations implicating the application of section 482 even where only domestic corporations are involved. Indeed, petitioner carefully refrains from pushing its rationale that far, seeking only to apply the requirement of actual payment to the language of section 881. In this context, the question is whether a deemed payment constitutes "an amount received" under section 881. We think it does. A holding that actual payment is required could significantly undermine the effectiveness of section 482 where foreign corporations are involved. Such a view would permit such corporations to utilize property in the United States without payment for such use and thereby avoid any liability under section 881. We are not impressed with petitioner's argument that equating a deemed payment under section 482 with "an amount received" under section 881 would constitute a license to respondent to run wild in the arena of allocations under section 482 between foreign corporations under common control. Although respondent's authority under section 482 is extremely broad, it is not open ended and a taxpayer will always be able to challenge an allocation as not permitted by law and/or not correct in amount.

Similarly, we are not impressed with petitioner's attempt to characterize the allocated fair rental value of the equipment as a constructive dividend to the parent of Hidro and petitioner and a nontaxable contribution of capital to petitioner. Petitioner's reliance on Rev.Rul. 78–83, 1978–1 C.B. 79, is misplaced. Aside from the fact that the ruling is not binding upon us, * * * it simply does not apply to the instant situation. The facts of that ruling were that sums due one subsidiary were actually paid to another subsidiary. Thus, there was an actual transfer of property, which is the hallmark of cases involving both the allocation of intercorporate payments and the consequent presence of a constructive dividend. * * *

The long and the short of the matter is that we hold that the word "received" in section 881 includes the fair rental value of the equipment even though the amount thereof was not actually received by petitioner from Hidro. We are reinforced in this holding by the fact that Congress has clearly indicated when it wished to refer to actual receipts. * * * We reject petitioner's attempt to derive sustenance from the fact that, under sections 881(c) and 871(a)(1)(C), original issue discount element of portfolio interest is generally not subject to the tax until paid or the obligation is sold or exchanged. If anything, the fact that Congress found it necessary to include a payment requirement for original issue discount indicates that such a requirement was not intended to apply to the phrase "amount received" in section 881(a).

* * *

[¶ 4027]

NOTE

A practical problem arises when interest takes the form of original issue discount because the arrangement does not lend itself to the easy implementation of a withholding obligation. U.S. tax law generally requires that deductions and income be accrued in such situations. However, the practical problem arises because no payment may be made from which the payor may withhold a tax. Congress has, therefore, prescribed a special rule for taxing original issue discount from U.S. sources that is not effectively connected with a U.S. trade or business. §§ 871(a)(1)(C), 881(a)(3). No U.S. tax will be imposed on the basis of the accrual alone. Rather, the 30–percent tax will be imposed when the financial benefit of the original issue discount is actually realized through a payment or otherwise. This may arise in two circumstances. First, when the obligation is paid, the amount of the original issue discount accruing during the period that the foreign person held the obligation will be subject to tax. Second, if the foreign person sells or exchanges the obligation, the amount of the original issue discount accruing during the period during which the obligation was held is subject to the 30–percent tax. However, the special rule will not apply to original issue discount obligations if the instrument matures not more than 183 days from the issuance date or in the case of obligations that are generally tax exempt under Section 103. § 871(g)(1)(B).

[¶ 4030]

C. UNTAXED ITEMS OF U.S.–SOURCE FDAP INCOME

Most items of U.S.-source FDAP income will be taxed to a foreign recipient either on a net income basis if the income is effectively connected with a U.S. trade or business as described in Chapter 3 or under the 30–percent withholding tax described in this Chapter. There are, however, instances in which such income will not be taxed when it is not effectively connected with a U.S. trade or business.

1. CERTAIN U.S.–SOURCE INTEREST

[¶ 4035]

a. Interest on Certain Bank Accounts

To encourage foreign persons to use U.S. banks and savings institutions, Sections 871(i)(2)(A) and 881(d) exempt interest earned on certain deposits from the 30–percent tax even though the interest is treated as U.S.-source income.

[¶ 4040]

b. Portfolio Interest

For many years, U.S. corporations wishing to borrow overseas could exploit the provisions of certain tax treaties (in particular the treaty then in force with the Netherlands Antilles) to avoid the 30–percent withholding tax on interest payments. In 1984, Congress effectively removed the incentive to use the treaty structure in many instances by eliminating the 30–percent tax on interest from "portfolio debt investments." §§ 871(h) and 881(c). As a result of the exclusion, most interest payments to foreign persons on publicly traded debt securities that are either registered obligations or are bearer obligations that are subject to certain arrangements specified in Section 163(f)(2)(B) (designed to assure that interest is payable only outside of the United States to foreign persons) will not be subject to the withholding tax. However, as a result of legislation enacted in 2010, bearer obligations issued after March 18, 2012, will no longer qualify as a portfolio debt investment.

Eligible debt securities include bonds and other debt issued by the U.S. government. Note that the exemption will in most instances reduce interest costs to U.S. borrowers, including the U.S. government, because foreign lenders will usually base lending decisions on an after-tax return. The portfolio interest exemption extends to original issue discount on obligations that satisfy the qualification criteria.

Not all interest payments will be excluded even if they meet the qualification requirements for debt obligations described above. In particular, interest paid by a U.S. corporation to an individual or entity that owns at least ten percent of the voting power of the corporation is not eligible for the exemption. §§ 871(h)(3) and 881(c)(3)(B). Interest received by a controlled foreign corporation from a related person is not eligible. § 881(c)(3)(C). Further, interest on nongovernmental obligations paid to banks on an extension of credit made pursuant to a loan agreement is not exempt. § 881(c)(3)(A).

Portfolio interest will not include certain interest payments that are contingent. §§ 871(h)(4), 881(c)(4). Such interest payments will be subject to the withholding tax unless exempt from withholding under a treaty. Interest is treated as contingent under these provisions, and therefore subject to tax, if the amount of the interest is determined by reference to receipts, sales or cash flow, income or profits or changes in property value of the debtor or a person related thereto. Interest will also be deemed to be contingent if it is dependent upon dividend or partnership distributions by the debtor or a related person. "Related person" is defined by reference to Sections 267(b) and 707(b)(1) and includes any person who enters into an arrangement for a purpose of avoiding the contingent-interest rule.

[¶ 4042]

c. Interest Paid by 80–20 Corporations

Interest paid by U.S. corporations is generally characterized as U.S.-source income. However, as described briefly at ¶ 2005, interest paid by certain U.S. corporations was treated as foreign-source income if more than 80 percent of the gross income of the corporation over a base period (three years preceding the year of the payment) consisted of foreign-source income attributable to the conduct of foreign trade or business. The effect of the modification of the source rule on foreign persons was to eliminate any withholding tax on the interest paid to unrelated foreign lenders and to limit the amount of withholding tax imposed on interest paid to related foreign lenders.

Congress enacted legislation in 2010 to limit substantially the favorable tax treatment of interest paid by such "80–20 corporations" for tax years beginning in 2011. Under the new rules, interest payments by U.S. corporations will generally be treated as U.S.-source income. However, the legislation included several provisions effectively grandfathering at least a portion of the old regime by exempting certain interest payments from the withholding tax. Withholding taxes will not be imposed on the payment of interest on "existing debt" owed by qualified corporations unless such interest is paid to a related party. This provision would not apply, however, if there is a significant modification in the terms of the debt. Education, Jobs and Medicaid Assistance Act of 2010, § 217(d)(2). Moreover, a portion of interest on new debt issued by a corporation that qualified under the 80–20 test for the last year prior to 2011 and that continues so to qualify will be not be subject to the withholding tax as long as the corporation does not initiate a substantial line of new business. If the debtor corporation qualifies under the grandfathering provisions, the portion of interest on new debt not subject to the withholding tax will be determined by the percentage of the debtor corporation's total gross income that is attributable to foreign-source active business income. § 871(i)(2)(B)(ii) and (*l*).

[¶ 4045]

2. CERTAIN DIVIDENDS

Dividends paid by a U.S. corporation are U.S.-source income. § 861(a)(2)(A). However, prior to the enactment of legislation in 2010, if a U.S. corporation earned 80 percent or more of its gross income from foreign sources as a result of the active conduct of a foreign trade or business, a portion of its dividend was not subject to the withholding tax. §§ 871(i)(2)(B) and 881(d). The untaxed portion was determined by the percentage of the gross income of the corporation for a base period that derived from all foreign sources. The base period was the three years ending with the close of the tax year preceding the dividend payment. For example, if 90 percent of such gross income of the U.S. corporation derived from foreign sources during the base period, only ten percent of the corporation's dividends was subject to the withholding tax. The exception was obviously based upon the fact that the exempted dividends derive from extensive business activities in other countries.

Legislation adopted in 2010 also substantially eliminated this dividend exception for 80–20 corporations. However, the legislation included a grandfathering provision that applied to some dividends. For dividends to be treated under this provision, the corporation had to be qualified as an 80–20 company for its last tax year prior to 2011 and continue so to qualify for each year thereafter under slightly revised rules. The qualification requirement has been modified for years beginning in 2011 so that 80 percent of the gross income of the corporation must consist of active foreign business income. § 871(i)(2)(B)(ii) and (*l*)(1)(B). If the corporation so qualifies, a portion of dividend payments will not be subject to the withholding tax. The portion so treated will be determined by the percentage of the corporation's total gross income attributable to foreign-source active business income. § 871(i)(2)(B)(i) and (*l*)(2).

The 2004 JOBS Act effectively exempted from the withholding tax regime dividends paid by foreign corporations to foreign shareholders even though such dividends may be regarded as U.S.-source income under Section 861(a)(2)(B). §§ 871(i)(2)(D), 881(d). The adoption of the branch profits tax generally eliminated the need for such a withholding tax. See ¶ 3230.

[¶ 4046]

3. CERTAIN WAGERING INCOME

The 2004 JOBS Act included a provision that exempts from taxation gross income derived by a nonresident alien "from a legal wagering transaction initiated outside the United States in a parimutuel pool with respect to a live horse race or dog race in the United States." § 872(b)(5). The exemption applies even though the winnings may be regarded as U.S.-source income and even though the wagers may have been placed in (although initiated outside) the United States. Such lucky (or skilled) nonresident alien taxpayers join those who win from "blackjack, baccarat, craps, roulette, or big–6 wheel" and are not taxed. § 871(j).

[¶ 4047]

NOTES

1. In Barba v. United States, 2 Cl.Ct. 674 (1983), the taxpayer was a nonresident alien who frequently visited Nevada gambling casinos. The court held that the withholding tax applied to all of the taxpayer's winnings. It rejected the taxpayer's argument that the term "amount received," as used in Section 871(a), authorized a subtraction for gambling losses. Barba may have been lucky too soon. Congress adopted Section 871(j) in 1988. Note that slot

machine winnings are not included in the exception. How would the IRS enforce a 30–percent tax on gross winnings at the slot machines?

2. In The International Lotto Fund v. Virginia State Lottery Department, 20 F.3d 589 (4th Cir.1994), an Australian trust won a state lottery worth almost $28 million. Seeking to avoid the imposition of the withholding tax, it sued the Lottery Department in the U.S. district court and obtained an injunction requiring the payment of the full amount of the jackpot. The court of appeals reversed the decision on the ground that it was contrary to Section 7421(a) of the Code, known as the "Anti–Injunction Act." The court therefore did not have jurisdiction to consider the argument of the Fund that the winnings were business profits (rather than FDAP income) that were exempt from tax under the United States–Australia Tax Treaty because the trust maintained no permanent establishment in the United States. What result should obtain if a court had jurisdiction to consider the issue?

D. EFFECT OF TREATIES ON WITHHOLDING TAXES

[¶ 4050]

1. WITHHOLDING TAX ON FDAP INCOME

Tax treaties generally provide for the reduction or elimination of withholding taxes on specified items of U.S.-source FDAP income that are not attributable to a permanent establishment in the United States. Of course, such income attributable to a U.S. permanent establishment is included in determining the net income that will be taxed at the usual rates.

Because each treaty results from separate bilateral negotiations, the extent to which the taxes are reduced varies substantially among the treaties currently in force between the United States and other countries. The U.S. Model Treaty (Appendix A) reflects the kinds of reductions commonly found in actual treaties. The withholding taxes on interest (Article 11) and royalties (Article 12) are generally eliminated. The withholding tax on dividends is reduced generally to 15 percent. If the foreign shareholder is a corporation that owns at least ten percent of the U.S. corporation, however, the tax is usually only five percent. U.S. Model Treaty, Art. 10. In some treaties concluded in recent years, certain dividend payments have been exempted from the withholding tax. See, e.g., United States–Japan Treaty, Art. 10(3), which came into force in 2004; March 8, 2004 Protocol to United States–Netherlands Treaty; June 1, 2006 Protocol to United States–Germany Treaty; November 27, 2006 Protocol to United States–Belgium Treaty; and December 1, 2008, Protocol to United States–New Zealand Treaty.

Article 17 eliminates the withholding tax for pensions, annuities, social security payments and alimony payments. Article 17(5) provides that child support payments will not be taxable in either country. Of course, under Section 71(c) of the Code, child support does not constitute gross income, so that the withholding tax would not apply even absent a treaty.

Some tax treaties also relieve residents of the other country from the imposition of specified U.S. withholding obligations on payments that they make. Under such treaties, for example, a foreign corporation would not be required to withhold tax on interest or dividend payments even in circumstances in which the Code might impose withholding requirements on such payments by foreign corporations. See, e.g., United States–Netherlands Tax Treaty, Art. 12.

Treaty benefits will depend upon the residence of the taxpayer and the form of income involved. For example, in U.S. v. Brown, 348 F.3d 1200 (10th Cir. 2003), a Qualified Settlement Fund ("QSF") was established in the United States as part of the resolution of litigation arising from a securities fraud claim. All of the beneficiaries were citizens of Germany. The United States–Germany Treaty exempts German residents from taxes on capital gains and certain other investment income. The beneficiaries contended that such income realized by the QSF should be exempt because they would bear the economic burden of the tax. The court held, however, that the QSF was itself a taxable domestic entity, and that the treaty was inapplicable.

In Abeid v. Commissioner, 122 T.C. 404 (2004), there was a dispute as to the form of the income. The taxpayer was a resident of Israel who won a lottery sponsored by the State of California. As a result of the purchase of a one dollar ticket, he was entitled to 20 annual payments of $722,000. The taxpayer contended that there should be no U.S. tax because Article 20 of the United States–Israel Tax Treaty exempts certain annuities from taxes imposed by the source country. The court, however, rejected the argument and explained its decision in the following way:

> We therefore hold that the payments petitioner received from the California State Lottery were not an annuity within the meaning of the U.S.-Israel Income Tax Treaty because the payments did not arise from the exchange of adequate and full consideration; rather, they were the result of winning a wager. Thus, the sums were not paid "under an obligation to make the payments *in return for* adequate and full consideration" (emphasis added) within the meaning of Article 20(5) of the treaty.

Id. at 412. The court further noted that the treaty "is silent with respect to gambling winnings."

[¶ 4055]

2. "SHOPPING" FOR TREATY BENEFITS

Historically, under most of the treaties that have come into force, a corporation organized under the laws of a contracting state was entitled to the benefits of applicable treaty provisions. If investors did not reside in a treaty country, the relative ease of corporate organization and operation often led tax planners to establish corporate vehicles in third countries to take advantage of the benefits of a treaty between the third country and the country in which income would be earned. The practice is characterized by tax administrators and practitioners as "treaty shopping."

A typical structure involved the establishment by a U.S. corporation of a "finance subsidiary" in a country with which the United States had a treaty exempting interest from U.S. withholding tax. The finance subsidiary would issue bonds on foreign markets or, in some cases, borrow directly from foreign lenders. Interest payments on the bonds would be subject to no withholding tax under the laws of the jurisdiction in which the finance subsidiary had been organized. The proceeds of that loan would in turn be reloaned to the U.S. parent, and the U.S. withholding tax on interest would be eliminated under the treaty.

A similar advantage might be sought by a foreign investor from a nontreaty country contemplating an equity investment in the United States. By effecting the investment through a holding company organized in a country with which the United States had a tax treaty, the withholding tax on dividends might be substantially reduced.

[¶ 4060]

3. DEFENSES AGAINST TREATY SHOPPING ABUSES

Such treaty shopping arrangements have been well-known and widely practiced. In time they generated a variety of responses by U.S. tax officials intended to prohibit or limit the exploitation of third-country treaties beyond the scope contemplated by the United States when establishing the treaty relationship.

[¶ 4065]

a. Invoking Judicial Doctrines

The IRS has sought to defend against treaty-shopping abuse in some cases by arguing that the financing corporation interposed between the "true" borrower and the lender or lenders should be disregarded because it is without substance. The IRS has, however, been uniformly unsuccessful in such attempts. The failure of the IRS argument is largely attributable to the test originated by the Supreme Court in Moline Properties, Inc. v. Commissioner, 319 U.S. 436, 438–39 (1943), under which the taxpayer need only establish that the corporation was formed for a business purpose *or* carried on business activity in order to be respected as a separate entity for tax purposes. In Bass v. Commissioner, 50 T.C. 595 (1968), the Tax Court rejected the use of the IRS argument to deny benefits to a Swiss corporation under the United States–Switzerland Tax Treaty. The court held that the questions of whether a corporation has been organized for a business purpose or carries on sufficient business activity to require its recognition as a separate entity for tax purposes are questions of fact. In this case the court concluded that the documentary evidence and testimony assembled by the taxpayer "demonstrated that the corporation was managed as a viable concern, and not as simply a lifeless facade." 50 T.C. at 602.

As indicated in the following case, the IRS has enjoyed somewhat greater success with its alternative argument that the foreign corporation interposed in the treaty country should be treated as a mere conduit not entitled to the benefits of the treaty.

[¶ 4070]

AIKEN INDUSTRIES, INC. v. COMMISSIONER

United States Tax Court, 1971.
56 T.C. 925 (acq.).

[Aiken Industries, the petitioner, was a U.S. corporation. Aiken Industries owned 100 percent of the stock of MPI, which was also a U.S. corporation. ECL, a Bahamian corporation, owned 99.997 percent of the stock of Aiken Industries and all of the stock of CCN, an Ecuadoran corporation. CCN became the owner of 100 percent of Industrias, a new corporation organized in Honduras.]

QUEALY, JUDGE: * * *.

* * *

In April 1963, MPI borrowed $2,250,000 from ECL and issued its 4–percent sinking fund promissory note in recognition of the debt. In March 1964, Industrias was incorporated under the laws of Honduras with all of its stock being held by CCN. ECL then transferred the note of MPI to Industrias in exchange for nine of the latter's notes. Each of the nine notes was payable on demand, each note was for the same principal amount of $250,000, and each carried the same 4–percent annual interest rate.

Generally, section 1441(a) requires "all persons, in whatever capacity acting," to withhold taxes on payment of any items of income specified in section 1441(b) to "any nonresident alien individual" or to "any foreign partnership." Section 1441(b) designates interest as one of the items of income subject to section 1441(a). Section 1442(a) requires a tax of 30 percent to be "withheld at the source in the same manner and on the same items of income" as established in section 1441 if there is a payment of any of the designated income items to a foreign corporation "subject to taxation."

Under this statutory framework, MPI ordinarily would have been required to withhold tax on the interest which is paid to Industrias. However, during 1964 and 1965, there was in force a "United States–Honduras Income Tax Convention" (the convention was terminated on December 31, 1966) to provide for "the avoidance of double taxation and the prevention of fiscal evasion with respect to taxes on incomes." Article IX of the convention provided that interest paid by a United States corporation to a Honduran corporation not having a permanent establishment in the United States was to be exempt from United States tax.

On the basis of the convention, MPI claimed exemption from the withholding provision applicable to United States source income paid to foreign corporations, and having ostensibly conformed to the literal requirements of the withholding regulations prescribed under the convention, MPI did not withhold tax.

The question for decision is whether the convention was applicable to the facts and circumstances of this case so as to exempt MPI from the requirements of withholding income tax on interest payments which it made to a foreign corporation, or whether petitioner, as successor by merger to MPI, is now liable for such taxes.

The respondent argues that the organization of Industrias and its existence as a corporate entity should be disregarded for tax purposes. He concludes that ECL should be deemed the true owner and recipient of the interest in question with the consequence that petitioner is now liable for the failure of MPI to withhold income tax.

Petitioner claims that an exemption from withholding flows from the exemption from taxation for interest found in article IX of the convention which provides in pertinent part:

> "Interest * * * from sources within one of the contracting States received by a * * * corporation or other entity of the other contracting State not having a permanent establishment within the former State * * * shall be exempt from tax by such former State."

In support of its claim for exemption from taxation under article IX, petitioner argues that Industrias conformed to the definition of a corporation established by article II, section (1)(g), in that it was "a corporation or other entity formed or organized in Honduras or under the laws of Honduras" and that it was therefore a corporation for purposes of article IX. On this basis, the petitioner concludes that Industrias cannot be disregarded as a corporate entity and that the interest paid to Industrias by MPI was exempt from United States taxation under article IX thus relieving MPI of its duty to withhold income tax on such interest.

* * *

* * * [A]ll treaties made under the authority of the United States are to be the supreme law of the land and superior to domestic tax laws. *Cook v. United States,* 288 U.S. 102 (1933). This concept has been expressly recognized in section 894(a) which, during the years in question, provided:

> * * * Income of any kind, to the extent required by any treaty obligation of the United States, shall not be included in gross income and shall be exempt from taxation under this subtitle.

Consequently, neither the courts nor the taxing authorities may establish definitions for terms contained in a treaty contrary to those definitions expressly set forth in that treaty. Where the formal requirements of a definition established by a treaty are met, the benefits flowing from a treaty as the result of conforming to such formal definitional requirements cannot be denied by an inquiry behind those formal requirements. * * *

Article II, the definitional article of the convention, provides in section (1)(g):

> (g) The term "Honduran enterprise" means an industrial or commercial or agricultural enterprise or undertaking carried on by a resident of Honduras * * * or a fiduciary of Honduras or by a Honduran corporation or other entity; the term "Honduran corporation or other entity" means a corporation or other entity formed or organized in Honduras or under the laws of Honduras.

Article II, section (1)(f), is structured in the same manner with "United States" standing in place of "Honduras" or "Honduran" as the case may be.

The term "corporation" is nowhere defined in the convention in its own right, and in article II, sections (1)(f) and (1)(g), the definition of a corporation of a contracting State appears in the definition of an "enterprise" of such contracting State. However, in the absence of any indication to the contrary, it is clear that in defining the term "corporation" for one purpose, the contracting States intended that definition to apply in other contexts as well. Consequently, we are convinced that the term "corporation," as utilized in article IX, refers to a corporation or other entity formed or organized in one of the contracting States or under the laws of one of the contracting States.

Thus, Industrias, being a corporation organized under the laws of Honduras and conforming to the specific definition of "Honduran corporation" established by article II, section (1)(g), of the convention, was a "corporation or other entity" of one of the contracting States within the meaning of article IX. Therefore, the convention prevents us from ignoring the corporate entity as such. * * *

However, while we agree with the petitioner that Industrias was a "corporation" for purposes of article IX, and that it therefore cannot be disregarded, we do not agree with the petitioner's conclusion that this factor alone was sufficient to qualify the interest in question for the exemption from taxation granted by article IX. Rather, we must determine whether the transaction in question conforms to the other requirements established by article IX.

In seeking to give substance to the terms of article IX which establish those requirements, we are free under article II, section (2), of the convention, to assign to those terms "not otherwise defined" by the convention the meanings which would normally attach to such terms under our laws "unless the context otherwise requires." In so doing, we recognize that the fact that the actions taken by the parties in this case were taken to minimize their tax burden may not by itself be utilized to deny a benefit to which the parties are otherwise entitled under the convention. See *Gregory v. Helvering*, 293 U.S. 465, 469 (1935). And we are aware of the necessity for liberal construction in determining the applicability of the convention. * * *

However, "To say that we should give a broad and efficacious scope to a treaty does not mean that we must sweep within the Convention what are legally and traditionally recognized to be * * * taxpayers not clearly within its protections." *Maximov v. United States,* [373 U.S. 49 (1963)] at 56. In deciding whether a given taxpayer in a specific instance is protected by the terms of a treaty, we must "give the specific words of a treaty a meaning consistent with the genuine shared expectations of the contracting parties," and in so doing, it is necessary to examine not only the language, but the entire context of agreement. *Maximov v. United States*, 299 F.2d 565, 568 (C.A.2, 1962), affd. 373 U.S. 49 (1963).

Applying these principles, we find that the interest payments in question were not "received by" a corporation of a contracting State (herein a Honduran corporation) within the meaning of article IX of the convention. As utilized in the context of article IX, we interpret the terms "received by" to mean interest received by a corporation of either of the contracting States as its own and not with the obligation to transmit it to another. The words "received by" refer not merely to the obtaining of physical possession on a temporary basis of funds representing interest payments from a corporation of a contracting State, but contemplate complete dominion and control over the funds.

The convention requires more than a mere exchange of paper between related corporations to come within the protection of the exemption from taxation granted by article IX of the convention, and on the record as a whole, the petitioner has failed to demonstrate that a substantive indebtedness existed between a United States corporation and a Honduran corporation.

In this case, ECL transferred the $2,250,000 4–percent sinking fund promissory note of MPI to Industrias in exchange for nine notes of Industrias with each of those notes payable on demand, each with the same principal amount of $250,000, and each with the same 4–percent interest rate. In essence, Industrias acquired the $2,250,000 4–percent sinking fund promissory note of MPI by giving nine notes totaling $2,250,000 at 4–percent interest. Industrias obtained exactly what it gave up in a dollar-for-dollar exchange. Thus, it was committed to pay out exactly what it collected, and it made no profit on the acquisition of MPI's note in exchange for its own.

In these circumstances, where the transfer of MPI's note from ECL to Industrias in exchange for the notes of Industrias left Industrias with the same inflow and outflow of funds and where MPI, ECL, and Industrias were all members of the same corporate family, we cannot find that this transaction had any valid economic or business purpose. Its only purpose was to obtain the benefits of the exemption established by the treaty for interest paid by a United States corporation to a Honduran corporation. While such a tax-avoidance motive is not inherently fatal to a transaction, * * * such a motive standing by itself is not a business purpose which is sufficient to support a transaction for tax purposes. * * *

In effect, Industrias, while a valid Honduran corporation, was a collection agent with respect to the interest it received from MPI. Industrias was merely a conduit for the passage of interest payments from MPI to ECL, and it cannot be said to have received the interest as its own. Industrias had no actual beneficial interest in the interest payments it received, and in substance, MPI was paying the interest to ECL which "received" the interest within the meaning of article IX. Consequently, the interest in question must be viewed as having been "received by" an entity (ECL) which was not a "corporation or other entity" of one of the contracting States involved herein, and we therefore hold that the interest in question was not exempt from taxation by the United States under article IX of the convention.

* * *

[¶ 4075]

b. Invoking Administrative Authority

The Netherlands Antilles was a favorite jurisdiction for many years because it was one of the few tax havens with which the United States had a tax treaty (albeit the old treaty with the Netherlands that had been effectively inherited at the time the Netherlands Antilles gained independence). The applicable treaty provided that the United States could impose no withholding tax on interest payments to a Netherlands Antilles corporation, and included very favorable provisions governing royalties, rents and dividends. In fact, the literature of tax planning was marked with descriptions of arrangements characterized as a "Dutch Sandwich" (in one version a Netherlands corporation inserted between a U.S. corporation and a foreign lender; in a tastier version a Netherlands Antilles corporation owned by a Netherlands corporation that was owned by a Netherlands Antilles corporation) or an "open face Dutch sandwich" (Netherlands Antilles corporation owned a Netherlands corporation that in turn owned a U.S. subsidiary).

Because of the extensive exploitation of the Netherlands Antilles treaty by taxpayers, and its attendant publicity, the U.S. Treasury took several steps to close the treaty door. The exemption from U.S. withholding tax of interest on portfolio debt investments was intended in part to eliminate the need for such devices, at least in connection with foreign borrowing by U.S. corporations. Moreover, the treaty with the Netherlands Antilles was terminated. Prior to its termination, however, the IRS acted to deny treaty benefits for certain finance subsidiary arrangements, particularly those arranged in the Netherlands Antilles. The following Ruling was a key weapon in the attack.

[¶ 4080]
REVENUE RULING 84–152

1984–2 C.B. 381.

ISSUE

Whether the exemption provided by Article VIII(1) of the United States–Netherlands Income Tax Convention (the Convention) [which, as indicated, had been made effective with respect to the Netherlands Antilles at the time of its independence], * * * is applicable to interest payments made by a domestic corporation to an Antilles corporation under the circumstances described below.

FACTS

P, a corporation organized under the laws of Switzerland, owns 100 percent of the stock of *S*, a corporation organized under the laws of the Antilles and engaged in business there. *P* also owns 100 percent of the voting stock and voting power of *R*, a domestic corporation engaged in manufacturing in the United States.

R required a significant increase in working capital for purposes of upgrading its production capabilities. On August 1, 1984, *P* agreed to lend to *S* an amount approximating the funds required by *R* at an annual interest rate of 10 percent. *S* shortly thereafter reloaned the proceeds of this loan to *R* at an annual interest rate of 11 percent. *S* is not sufficiently liquid to make the loan to *R* out of funds other than those obtained from *P*.

Thereafter, *R* made timely interest payments to *S*, and *S* made timely interest payments to *P*. Any excess revenue after expenses with respect to the financing arrangement was retained by *S*. Neither *R* nor *S* was thinly capitalized. * * *

Neither *P* nor *S* is engaged in a trade or business within the United States through a permanent establishment.

LAW AND ANALYSIS

Section 881(a)(1) * * *, except as provided in the portfolio interest exemption in new subsection (c), * * * generally imposes a 30 percent tax on any interest received by a foreign corporation from sources within the United States, to the extent such interest is not effectively connected with the conduct of a trade or business within the United States. Section 1442(a) provides generally that such tax is to be deducted and withheld at the source of the income.

Under section 881(c) * * *, the 30 percent tax under section 881(a)(1) or (3) is not imposed on portfolio interest received by a foreign corporation from sources within the United States.

Section 881(c)(3)(B) * * * provides, in part, that for purposes of that subsection the term "portfolio interest" shall not include any portfolio interest which is received by a 10–percent shareholder (within the meaning of section 871(h)(3)(B)).

* * *

Section 894(a) * * * provides that income of any kind, to the extent required by any treaty obligation of the United States, shall not be included in gross income and shall be exempt from income taxation.

Article VIII(1) of the Convention, as extended to the Antilles, provides generally that interest (other than mortgage interest) derived from sources within the United States by a resident or corporation of the Antilles not engaged in a trade or business in the United States through a permanent establishment shall be exempt from United States tax.

* * *

Article VII(1) of the United States–Switzerland Income Tax Convention (Swiss Treaty) * * * provides that the tax imposed by the United States on interest derived from sources within the United States by a resident or corporation of Switzerland not having a permanent establishment in the United States shall not exceed 5 percent.

Under the facts presented here, in order for the interest exemption under Article VIII(1) of the Convention to apply to interest paid by *R*, such interest must be "derived ... by" *S* from *R*. The words "derived ...

by'' refer not merely to *S*'s temporarily obtaining physical possession of the interest paid by *R*, but to *S*'s obtaining complete dominion and control over such interest payments. * * * In substance, *S*, while a valid Antilles corporation, never had such dominion and control over *R*'s interest payments but rather was merely a conduit for the passage of *R*'s interest payments to *P*. The primary purpose for involving *S* in the borrowing transaction was to attempt to obtain the benefits of the Article VIII(1) interest exemption for interest paid in form by *R*, a domestic corporation, to *S*, an Antilles corporation, thus, resulting in the avoidance of United States tax. This use of *S* lacks sufficient business or economic purpose to overcome the conduit nature of the transaction, even though it can be demonstrated that the transaction may serve some business or economic purpose. * * * Thus, for purposes of the interest exemption in Article VIII(1) of the Convention, the interest payments by *R* will be considered to be ''derived . . . by'' *P* and not by *S*.

Section 881(c) * * * does not apply to the interest payments by *R* because *P* owns 100 percent of the voting stock and voting power of *R*, and is considered to derive the interest paid by *R*. See section 881(c)(3)(B).

HOLDING

Under the facts of this case, the interest payments by *R* are not exempt from taxation by the United States under Article VIII(1) of the Convention, as extended to the Antilles. Further, such interest payments will be subject to a 5 percent United States withholding tax under Article VII(1) of the Swiss Treaty.

* * *

[¶ 4085]

NOTES

1. Compare the facts and the analysis of the Ruling to the facts and the analysis in the *Aiken* case. Would the Ruling be sustained if challenged in court?

2. The IRS issued a companion ruling at the same time holding that the United States–Netherlands Antilles Treaty benefits were not applicable when a U.S. parent uses an Antilles subsidiary to issue bonds to foreign parties and then lends the proceeds to a U.S. subsidiary. Rev. Rul. 84–153, 1984–2 C.B. 383. The issuance of the two rulings reportedly sent shock waves through the Eurobond market among holders of debt that had been financed through Netherlands Antilles financing corporations. Implicitly acknowledging that the rulings went beyond the holding in *Aiken,* the IRS later announced that they would only be applied prospectively.

3. The IRS cited *Aiken Industries* in support of its unsuccessful challenge to a financing arrangement involving a borrowing by a Netherlands

Antilles finance subsidiary interposed to exploit the United States–Netherlands Antilles Tax Treaty in Northern Indiana Public Service Co. v. Commissioner, 105 T.C. 341 (1995). The court, however, held that the finance subsidiary could be recognized as the borrower because the arrangement had been established to borrow money from unrelated lenders for relending to the taxpayer. The court distinguished *Aiken Industries* by noting that significant earnings were generated by the finance subsidiary's financing activity. The court explicitly rejected the argument that the finance subsidiary was inadequately capitalized. The Tax Court decision was affirmed. 115 F.3d 506 (7th Cir.1997).

4. The decision in *Northern Indiana Public Service* was distinguished in Del Commercial Properties, Inc. v. Commissioner, 251 F.3d 210 (D.C.Cir. 2001). The issue arose in a very complicated series of transactions, which were described by the court in the following way:

> Del Commercial Properties, Inc. * * * is an Illinois corporation whose principal place of business is in Ontario, Canada. It is a fourth-tier subsidiary of an affiliated group of corporations ("the Affiliated Group") whose common parent is DL Shekels Holdings Ltd. Delcom Financial, Ltd. is a second-tier subsidiary in the Affiliated Group. Delcom Financial is a Canadian corporation that owns 100% of the outstanding stock of Delcom Holdings, Ltd., another Canadian corporation. In turn, Delcom Holdings owns 100% of Delcom Cayman, Ltd. (a corporation organized in the Cayman Islands), which owns 100% of the outstanding stock of Delcom Antilles, N.V. (a corporation organized in the Netherlands Antilles). Delcom Antilles owns 100% of the outstanding stock of Del Investments Netherlands B.V. ("Del BV"), a corporation organized in the Netherlands.
>
> From 1990 through 1993, appellant's principal business was leasing industrial real estate it owned in the United States. In 1990, when appellant needed funding to refinance and improve some of its American properties, one of DL Shekels's first-tier subsidiaries, Tridel Corporation, arranged the following financing scheme: On July 18, 1990, the Royal Bank of Canada loaned $18 million (in U.S. dollars) to Delcom Financial. That same day, Delcom Financial made two unsecured interest-bearing loans to Delcom Holdings. One of those loans (the one directly relevant to this case) was for $14 million. Delcom Holdings then contributed "about $14 million to Delcom Cayman for common shares of stock." * * * On the same day, "Delcom Cayman contributed about $14 million to Delcom Antilles and received common shares of stock in that entity. Later on that same date, Delcom Antilles contributed about $14 million to Del BV and received common stock in that entity." * * *
>
> The following day, July 19, appellant borrowed $14 million from Del BV. That same day, appellant "guaranteed repayment of a portion of amounts owed by Delcom Financial to Royal Bank" and authorized Royal Bank to place a mortgage on its real property in the U.S. * * * Appellant also agreed to provide Royal Bank with "annual financial statements, to insure its real property, to assign the insurance policies to Royal Bank, to

defer paying dividends to shareholders, and to use the proceeds from any sales of real property to make payments on the $14 million Royal Bank loan." * * *

Id. at 211.

Interest payments were exempt from the withholding tax under the United States–Netherlands Treaty. However, interest payments were subject to a 15 percent withholding tax under the United States–Canada Treaty. The Tax Court had applied the step transaction doctrine to conclude that the 15 percent withholding tax was applicable. The court of appeals described the step-transaction doctrine as one in which "a particular step in a transaction is disregarded for tax purposes if the taxpayer could have achieved its objective more directly, but instead included the step for no other purpose than to avoid U.S. taxes." Id. at 213. After reviewing the details of the related transactions and the evidence that had been proffered at trial, the court of appeals concluded that the Tax Court analysis was not clearly erroneous.

5. Legislation enacted in 2010 for the first time codified an "economic substance doctrine." Section 7701(*o*) characterizes the provision as a "clarification" of the doctrine. Debate about the rationale for codification was not focused on issues of treaty shopping. However, the scope of the broad language used in the "clarification" could arguably be applied to certain transactions involving treaty shopping.

[¶ 4090]

c. Treaty Provisions

Treaties concluded more recently between the United States and new treaty partners and recently revised treaties with long-standing treaty partners have included provisions intended to defend against unacceptable forms of treaty shopping. Article 22 of the U.S. Model Treaty provides an example of such a provision. The purpose is obviously to restrict the treaty benefits to individuals and corporations having clear and substantive connections with the treaty country. For example, the treaty benefits would not be available to a corporation organized in a treaty country that is wholly owned by a citizen and resident of another country unless the corporation were actively engaged in a trade or business in the treaty country. Are the limitations appropriate? Do they provide an adequate defense against potential abuse of treaty arrangements? Are they unnecessarily complex? The 2004 JOBS Act directed the Treasury to consider these questions. The results of the study are set forth in U.S. Treas. Dep't, Report to The Congress on Earnings Stripping, Transfer Pricing and U.S. Income Tax Treaties (Nov. 2007).

[¶ 4095]

d. Anti–Conduit Regulations

Congress in 1993 added Section 7701(*l*), which authorizes the promulgation of regulations allowing for the "recharacterization" of multiple-party financing transactions as a transaction directly among any two or more of the parties to it if such characterization "is appropriate to prevent avoidance of any tax * * *." The IRS has implemented this authority by issuing so-called "anti-conduit" regulations. The principal result when the new regulations apply is that intermediate entities ("conduits") are disregarded in determining U.S. taxes on international financing arrangements, which may include loans, leases and licenses. The U.S. tax result will then be determined as if the loan were made directly from the foreign lender to the U.S. borrower. The definitional provisions governing the application of the anti-conduit rules are found principally in Reg. §§ 1.881–3 and –4.

The key factors that will trigger the exercise of power by the IRS to recharacterize conduit entities are:

—The participation of the intermediate entity or entities reduces the tax imposed by Section 881,

—Such participation is "pursuant to a tax avoidance plan," and either

—The intermediate entity is related to the financing or financed entity or would not have participated in the financing arrangement but for the fact that the financing entity engaged in the transaction with the intermediate entity.

Reg. § 1.881–3(a)(4).

The regulations also identify the factors that will determine whether there is a tax-avoidance purpose:

—Is there a "significant reduction" in the tax otherwise imposed under Section 881?

—Did the conduit have the ability to make the advance without advances from the related financing entity?

—What was the period of time between the respective transactions?

—Did the financing transactions occur in the ordinary course of business of the related entities?

Reg. § 1.881–3(b)(2).

The regulations also establish a rebuttable presumption in favor of the taxpayer if the conduit entity "performs significant financing activities with respect to the financing transactions forming part of the financing arrangement." Such activities might include the earning of rents and royalties from the active conduct of a trade or business or active risk management by the intermediate entity. Reg. § 1.881–3(b)(3).

The effect of invoking the anti-conduit regulations is that the payments will be deemed to be paid directly by and to the entities other than the conduit, usually the financing and financed entity. The role of the conduit will be disregarded. If these provisions were invoked in the case of a finance subsidiary, for example, the interest payment by a U.S. corporation that borrowed money from a foreign lender through the use of a financing subsidiary in a tax treaty country would be treated as if the interest were paid directly to the foreign lender. The treaty would not apply, and the 30–percent withholding tax would be imposed unless the "true" lender were a resident of another treaty country where withholding rates on interest were reduced or eliminated. The borrower is required to withhold the appropriate amount under the recharacterized transaction. Reg. §§ 1.1441–3(g) and –7(f). Special recordkeeping requirements have been established to assist in administering the rules. Reg. §§ 1.881–4 and 1.6038A–3(b)(5). The anti-conduit regulations specifically authorized by Congress effectively replaced the 1984 rulings discussed previously although the rationale of the rulings continues to be applied by the IRS. See Rev. Rul. 95–56, 1995–2 C.B. 322.

Suppose that the anti-conduit regulations are applied in respect of a transaction in which the financing subsidiary is organized in a country with which the U.S. Model Treaty applies. Does the language of Article 22 of the U.S. Model Treaty authorize the application of the anti-conduit rules in respect of such a corporation? See Reg. § 1.881–3(a)(3)(ii)(C). Would their application violate the obligations of the United States under the U.S. Model Treaty? If so, does Section 7701(*l*) represent another treaty override?

[¶ 4100]

e. Reflections on Treaty Shopping

A judgment about the validity of concern with treaty shopping and the appropriateness of the response thereto requires consideration of the reasons for the problem. The principal focus of treaty shopping activities is on the provisions of tax treaties in which source countries surrender revenues, usually by waiving or reducing withholding taxes on FDAP income (although the substitution of the permanent establishment standard under a treaty for the trade or business test can also result in material revenue losses to the source country). The loss of revenue is presumably recompensed by the reciprocal nature of the treaty provisions. When foreign income taxes are reduced for U.S. persons, potential foreign tax credits are similarly reduced. As a result, U.S. tax revenues will increase unless the taxpayer has excess credits from other transactions that can reduce U.S. taxes on the income not taxed abroad because of the treaty. See Chapters 5 and 7.

Situations that came to be characterized as "treaty shopping" test the structure of the deal between the treaty countries by impinging upon the calculation of costs and benefits contemplated in the normal reciprocal flow of transactions by residents of the two countries. Another possible response to treaty shopping could obviously be to emphasize the right of the source country to tax and the treaty commitment of the country of residence to mitigate double taxation. In other words, the source country would be allowed to impose statutory withholding taxes and the treaty partner (country of residence) would be left to deal with the loss of tax revenues. Would this approach resolve all treaty shopping concerns?

[¶ 4102]

f. Treaties and Hybrid Entities

Issues involving "hybrid entities" arise in a number of different contexts in the taxation of international transactions. A hybrid entity is one that is characterized as a corporation in one jurisdiction and as a transparent entity in another. For example, an entity organized in a foreign country may be treated as a corporation under the laws of that country, but may be treated as a partnership under U.S. tax law. The reverse situation (often called a "reverse hybrid") may also obtain in which an entity is treated as a corporation under U.S. tax law, but as a transparent entity under the laws of a foreign country. Such situations may lead to opportunities for cross-border arbitrage in which the tax laws of the different countries are exploited for multiple advantage in ways that may be deemed excessive. The increased frequency of such situations is at least in part attributable to the check-the-box regulations that permit taxpayers in many instances to choose how certain business entities will be characterized for U.S. tax purposes. See ¶¶ 1223 and 13,035 et seq.

The existence of hybrid entities may impact upon the administration of income tax treaties. For example, suppose that a foreign entity is treated as a partnership for U.S. tax purposes. It is organized in Country A, with which the United States has no income tax treaty. One of the partners, Partner X, is a citizen and resident of Country B, with which the United States has a tax treaty that is identical to the U.S. Model Treaty. However, the entity is treated as a corporation under the laws of Country A and Country B. The foreign entity, organized in Country A, realizes U.S.-source interest income, a portion of which is allocable under U.S. law to Partner X. U.S.-source interest payments to corporations organized in Country A are subject to a withholding tax of 30 percent. U.S.-source interest payments to Partner X, as a resident of Country B, would be exempt from tax under the treaty with Country B. Should a portion of the interest payments be exempt from U.S. tax under the treaty?

Section 894(c) expressly limits the availability of treaty benefits in certain hybrid situations and authorizes the promulgation of regulations to defend against perceived treaty abuse in other hybrid situations.

Section 894(c)(1) denies treaty benefits for income derived through a partnership or other entity treated as transparent for U.S. tax purposes in certain situations even though the partner is a resident of a foreign treaty country. The application of the provision depends largely upon the law of the treaty country. Withholding tax reductions or exemptions provided in a treaty will be denied to a partner (or interest holder), even if the entity is treated as a partnership or other transparent entity under U.S. tax law, if the item of income is not treated under the tax law of the treaty country as income of the partner, the treaty itself contains no provision addressing its applicability in the case of income derived through a partnership and the foreign treaty country does not tax the distribution of such item of income from the partnership to the partner. In the example described above, since Partner X is not subject to tax in Country B (the treaty country) on income realized by the entity (because it is treated as a corporation under the laws of Country B), Section 894(c)(1) applies and Partner X is not entitled to the treaty exemption for interest payments from U.S. sources.

Section 894(c)(2) authorizes the promulgation of regulations

> as may be necessary or appropriate to determine the extent to which a taxpayer to which * * * [Section 894(c)(1)] does not apply shall not be entitled to benefits under any income tax treaty of the United States with respect to any payment received by, or income attributable to any activities of, an entity organized in any jurisdiction (including the United States) that is treated as a partnership or is otherwise treated as fiscally transparent * * * [under the Code] and is treated as fiscally nontransparent for purposes of the tax laws of the jurisdiction of residence of the taxpayer.

Extensive regulations have been promulgated under the authority of Section 894(c)(2). The regulations clarify the application of treaty benefits in a number of situations. If the entity is classified as a partnership under U.S. tax law, the availability of treaty benefits will normally depend upon whether the entity is classified as a transparent entity under the laws of its place of organization and, if so, whether the laws of the place of residence of an interest holder in the foreign entity treat that entity as a transparent entity. If the entity is not classified as a transparent entity in the foreign country in which it is organized, the taxpayer will be treated as the entity itself and any treaty benefits applicable to a resident of the country of organization will be available. Treaty benefits will also be available when there is a treaty between the United States and the interest holder's country and the laws of that country characterize the entity as a fiscally transparent entity. In any case, an item of income paid directly to a type of entity specifically identified in a treaty as a resident of a treaty country is treated as derived by a resident of the treaty jurisdiction entitled to treaty benefits. Reg. § 1.894–1(d)(1).

The regulations further provide that treaty benefits will not be available to foreign interest holders of an entity classified as a corporation under U.S. law, even though the entity may be classified as a transparent entity under the laws of a treaty country (the reverse hybrid situation). Reg. § 1.894–1(d)(2)(i). Income items paid by an domestic entity classified as a corporation under U.S. law will be treated as income to interest holders regardless of the classification of the entity under foreign law and the character of the income will be determined by applying U.S. legal standards. As such, the foreign interest holder may be subject to tax, but will be entitled to any treaty benefits that might apply. If the foreign interest holder is a transparent entity under the laws of its place of organization, the tax consequences of such payments, including the possible availability of treaty benefits, will depend upon the identity of the partners or members of the foreign entity. Reg. § 1.894–1(d)(2)(ii)(A).

Special regulations address certain situations in which a payment is made from a domestic entity to a related reverse hybrid entity (treated as a corporation under U.S. law but transparent under foreign law), which in turn makes a payment to a related foreign interest holder. For these purposes, a person (individual or entity) is treated as related by reason of the ownership requirements of Sections 267(b) or 707(b)(1) except that "at least 80 percent" applies instead of "more than a 50 percent." When such a situation obtains, payments from the reverse hybrid entity will be treated as a dividend even if it is not so characterized by the parties.

The regulations can be demonstrated by a relatively simple example. A reverse hybrid entity receives dividend payments from a related U.S. corporation. The reverse hybrid entity then in turn makes payments, such as interest, to a foreign related interest holder that would be deductible to the reverse hybrid entity itself. Note that the concern arises because the reverse hybrid entity (treated as a corporation for U.S. tax law) is making a payment that reduces its U.S. income tax liability, but the payment is not taxed in the foreign country (where it is treated as a transparent entity) to the interest holder. In such instances, the regulations require that the portion of the payment from the reverse hybrid entity to the foreign interest holder attributable to the dividend received from the related U.S. corporation be characterized as a dividend. As such, the payment is not deductible by the hybrid entity. Further, while treaty benefits may be available, dividends are more likely to be taxed under treaty provisions than interest payments. Reg. § 1.894–1(d)(2)(ii)(B). Payments to unrelated foreign interest holders are not affected by the regulations.

[¶ 4105]

PROBLEMS

1. Olson and Johnson are wealthy investors who were born and raised in Sweden. Each owns half of International Lenders, Ltd. ("ILL"), a corporation organized and headquartered in Stockholm. ILL makes equity investments and loans all over the world. Several years ago, ILL loaned $100 million to the American Fish Company ("AmFish"), a U.S. corporation that operates solely in the United States. AmFish pays interest annually of $10 million on debt that does not qualify as a portfolio investment. The principal of the loan

is to be paid at the end of ten years. Assume that the U.S. Model Treaty applies between Sweden and the United States. Are interest payments by AmFish to ILL subject to the U.S. withholding tax?

2. Does your answer in Problem 1 change if Olson retires and moves to Brazil, a country with which the United States has no tax treaty?

3. How, if at all, does your answer in Problem 1 change if Olson and Johnson sell all of their stock to Superrich Corp., a corporation organized and operated in Brazil?

4. How, if at all, does your answer in Problem 1 change if Olson and Johnson decide to list and sell all of their ILL shares on the stock exchange in Sweden?

5. How would your answer to Problem 4 change if they list and sell 75 percent of the shares, most of which are acquired by residents of a country having no tax treaty with the United States?

6. How would your answer to Problem 1 change if 75 percent of the shares are sold by Olson and Johnson directly to residents of countries that have no tax treaty with the United States?

7. Amcar, a U.S. corporation, has negotiated to borrow $20 million from a bank in Norway. The interest rate demanded by the bank is "eight percent, net of U.S. taxes." Assume there is no tax treaty between the United States and Norway. Amcar owns a subsidiary, Partsub, established and operated in Sweden that manufactures several small parts imported into the United States for use in Amcar's manufacturing operation. The Norwegian bank agrees to loan the $20 million to Partsub at a net interest of eight percent. Partsub in turn loans $20 million to Amcar at nine percent per annum. Assume that the U.S. Model Treaty applies between Sweden and the United States. Do U.S. withholding taxes apply to any interest payments?

8. Would your answer in Problem 7 change if Amcar guaranteed the loan to Partsub?

9. Would your answer in Problem 7 change if Partsub were established just before the loan agreements were signed and had not yet undertaken any other activity?

E. GAINS FROM SALE OF PROPERTY NOT EFFECTIVELY CONNECTED WITH A U.S. TRADE OR BUSINESS

[¶ 4110]

1. CERTAIN CAPITAL GAINS

Historically there have been substantial opportunities for foreign persons to derive income from the U.S. economy without being subjected to U.S. tax, which some would characterize as a gap or loophole in the structure of taxing U.S.-source income. Gains from the sale of property are not treated as FDAP income. Reg. § 1.1441–2(b)(2)(i). Capital gains realized by foreign persons from the sale or disposition of assets not effectively connected with a U.S. trade or business have not generally been taxed even when they derive from U.S. sources.[1] Section 871(a)(2) provides, however, that such gains will be subject to the 30–percent tax if they are realized by a nonresident alien who was present in the United States for at least 183 days during the taxable year. The impact of this exception is marginal because, under current law, such presence would usually mean that the alien would be treated as a resident (subject to U.S. tax at usual rates on worldwide income). See § 7701(b) and ¶ 1185. If a treaty applies, capital gains not attributable to a permanent establishment, even though from U.S. sources, are generally not subject to U.S. tax unless they arise directly or indirectly from the ownership of U.S. real property. See, e.g., U.S. Model Treaty, Art. 13.

Some opportunities for foreign taxpayers to realize untaxed income from the U.S. economy have generated a legislative response. For example, gain from the sale of intellectual property, such as U.S. patents and trademarks, will not be considered to be exempt capital gain in situations in which payments to the seller are contingent on the exploitation of the property interest. Because such payments are similar to those used in determining royalty income under licensing agreements, such gain will be subject to the 30–percent withholding tax if it is derived from U.S. sources. §§ 871(a)(1)(D) and 881(a)(4). Legislation passed in 1980 to tax certain capital gains attributable to investments in real property in the United States is analyzed at ¶ 4185.

[¶ 4115]

2. GAINS FROM SALE OF INVENTORY PROPERTY

In most instances, the profits from the sale of inventory in the United States will be related to the conduct of a trade or business here. However, if the frequency and implementation of sales do not reflect a continuous, regular and considerable enterprise under the rules reflected at ¶ 3020, there will be no U.S. trade or business. Gains from such sales will not be taxed even though they derive from U.S. sources unless the taxpayer is conducting an unrelated U.S. trade or business and Section 864(c)(3) applies. If a tax treaty applies, there will be no U.S. tax on U.S.-source inventory sales by a foreign person not attributable to a permanent establishment in the United States. See ¶ 3165. In no event will income from the sale of inventory in the United States by a foreign person be subject to the withholding tax regime.

---

1. Under prior law, gain from the sale of U.S. personal property, including stock of U.S. corporations, was more likely to be treated as U.S.–source income. Under current law, however, source is sometimes determined by the taxpayer's residence. See, e.g., § 865(a). When the taxpayer is a foreign person, therefore, even gain from the sale of U.S. property, other than U.S. real property interests, is likely to be foreign-source income. Whether U.S.- or foreign-source income, no U.S. tax generally applies.

F. WITHHOLDING MECHANISM

[¶ 4120]

1. GENERAL RULE

Sections 1441 and 1442 establish the basic withholding mechanism for implementing the 30-percent tax on FDAP income. The scope and reach of the withholding requirements are substantial. They apply to "all persons, in whatever capacity acting * * * having the control, receipt, custody, disposal, or payment of any of the items of income specified * * *" in Sections 1441(a) (for nonresident aliens and foreign partnerships) and 1442(a) (for foreign corporations).

The withholding requirement is imposed for payments to nonresident aliens, foreign partnerships and foreign corporations. The items of income subject to withholding generally track the language of Sections 871 and 881 listing FDAP income, but a few exceptions have been made. No withholding is required of the payor for an item of income (other than compensation for personal services) that is effectively connected with the conduct of a U.S. trade or business by a nonresident alien or foreign partnership "and which is included in the gross income of the recipient under section 871(b)(2) for the taxable year." § 1441(c)(1). No withholding is required on payments to foreign corporations that are engaged in a U.S. trade or business "if the [IRS] determines that the requirements of [withholding] impose an undue administrative burden and that the collection of the tax imposed by section 881 * * * will not be jeopardized." § 1442(b).

Payors of FDAP income to foreign persons must pay close scrutiny to the withholding requirements before concluding that withholding is not required. The regulations under Sections 1441 et seq. establish strict procedures, intended to assure that the foreign person is not liable for the tax or that applicable tax liabilities will be paid, which must be satisfied before a withholding agent is relieved of the obligation to withhold. See, e.g., Reg. § 1.1441–4.

[¶ 4125]

a. Amounts Subject to Withholding

The withholding requirements of Sections 1441 and 1442 may require withholding substantially in excess of the actual tax liability attributable to the item of gross income. For example, withholding will be required in respect of income exempt from U.S. tax or subject to tax at lesser rates unless certification requirements intended to confirm entitlement to such benefits have been satisfied. In Rev. Rul. 72–87, 1972–1 C.B. 274, the IRS concluded that withholding under Section 1441 was required on a distribution by a domestic corporation to a nonresident alien "even though some or all of such distribution may be treated as gain from the sale or exchange of property * * *." In the wake of criticism of that ruling, however, regulations now in effect provide an avenue of relief for a corporation from the withholding obligation in respect of corporate distributions not treated as a dividend. Reg. § 1.1441–3(c).

In Rev. Rul. 85–193, 1985–2 C.B. 191, the IRS held that a domestic bank was required to withhold 30 percent on the gross amount of interest payments made to nonresident aliens and foreign corporations even though the taxpayers had purchased the debt at a price that reflected the principal plus interest accrued to the date of purchase, thereby realizing interest income that was less than the gross amount paid by the bank.

[¶ 4140]

b. Foreign Withholding Agents

The withholding requirements apply to the "persons * * * having the control, receipt, custody, disposal, or payment of any of the items" of U.S.-source FDAP income. As demonstrated in some of the problems at ¶ 2215, a foreign person may be in control of such an income item. When the withholding requirements are applied to such foreign persons, is there a violation of the jurisdictional limitations of international law discussed at ¶ 1070?

[¶ 4145]

REVENUE RULING 80–362

1980–2 C.B. 208.

ISSUE

Are royalties paid for the use of a patent in the United States, under the circumstances described below, subject to United States tax?

FACTS

A, a citizen and resident of a country other than the United States or the Netherlands, licenses the United States rights on a patent to *X*, a Netherlands corporation. *X* is a bona fide corporation unrelated to *A*. *X* agrees to pay *A* a fixed royalty each year in return for the patent license. *X* relicenses the patent to *Y*, a United States corporation, for use in the United States. *Y* agrees to pay *X* royalties based on the number of units produced by *Y* each year under the patent. *X*'s fixed royalty to *A* is not contingent upon the receipt of royalties from *Y*. *A*'s royalty income is not effectively connected with the conduct of a trade or business within the United States within the meaning of section 871(b) * * *.

Article IX(1) of the United States–Netherlands Income Tax Convention * * *, as amended by the United States–Netherlands Supplementary Income Tax Convention * * * provides that royalties paid to a resident or corporation of the Netherlands shall be exempt from tax by the United States. There is no income tax convention between *A*'s country of residence and the United States.

LAW AND ANALYSIS

Section 861(a)(4) * * * provides that royalties for the privilege of using a patent in the United States are treated as income from sources within the United States.

Section 871(a)(1)(A) * * * imposes a tax of 30 percent of the amount received from sources within the United States by a nonresident alien individual as interest, dividends, rents, salaries, wages, premiums, annuities, compensations, remunerations, emoluments, and other fixed or determinable annual or periodical gains, profits, and income.

Section 1.871–7(b) of the * * * Regulations provides that royalties, including royalties for the use of a patent, constitute fixed or determinable annual or periodical income to which the 30–percent tax rate imposed by section 871(a)(1)(A) applies.

Section 1441(a) * * * provides that all persons, in whatever capacity acting, having the control, receipt, custody, disposal or payment of any of the items of income specified in section 1441(b) (to the extent that any of such items constitute gross income from sources within the United States), of any nonresident individual shall deduct and withhold from such items a tax equal to 30 percent thereof.

Section 1.1441–2(a) of the regulations provides that royalties are included in the items of income enumerated under section 1441(b) * * *.

In the present factual situation, the royalties from *Y* to *X* are exempt from United States tax under Article IX(1) of the Convention. However, the royalties from *X* to *A* are not exempt from taxation by the United States because there is no income tax convention between *A*'s country of residence and the United States providing for such an exemption. Since the royalties from *X* to *A* are paid in consideration for the privilege of using a patent in the United States, they are treated as income from sources within the United States under section 861(a)(4) * * * and are subject to United States income taxation under section 871(a)(1)(A).

HOLDING

Royalties paid by *X* to *A* are subject to United States tax at the 30–percent rate pursuant to section 871(a)(1)(A) * * *. *X*, under section 1441(a), is required to withhold from the royalties paid to *A* a tax equal to 30 percent of such royalties.

[¶ 4150]

NOTES

1. The situation analyzed in the Ruling is sometimes referred to as the problem of "cascading royalties" because each royalty payment would be defined by the Code to be U.S.-source income subject to the withholding tax unless exempted by an applicable treaty.

2. The facts set forth in the Ruling demonstrate a shortcoming of any gross income tax. In the Ruling, the initial licensee is exempt from the U.S. tax by an applicable treaty. If no treaty applied, however, a heavy tax burden would result. Note that the initial licensee's profit from the acquisition of the right to use the patents is the difference between the royalties it receives and the royalties it paid. Because expenses are not deductible in the application of the withholding tax regime, a 30–percent tax on gross royalties could produce a tax in excess of the net profit. If the royalty payments effectively emanating from the economic activity in the United States are subject to no U.S. tax, what is the policy justification for imposing the withholding tax in such situations? Can the result be properly characterized as another example of a response to treaty shopping?

3. As indicated previously, some tax treaties effectively exempt foreign persons from specified U.S. withholding tax obligations in circumstances where the Code would require withholding on payments they make.

[¶ 4151]

SDI NETHERLANDS B.V. v. COMMISSIONER

United States Tax Court, 1996.
107 T.C. 161.

[The taxpayer ("SDI Netherlands") was the licensee of a Bermuda corporation ("SDI Bermuda") of worldwide rights to use computer software. SDI Netherlands in turn licensed those rights for use in the United States to a U.S. corporation ("SDI USA"). SDI Netherlands received royalties from SDI USA as well as from other licensees. SDI Netherlands paid specified percentages of the royalties it received from its licensees to SDI Bermuda. SDI Netherlands, SDI USA and SDI Bermuda were members of a group of corporations under common control. One issue before the court was whether a portion of the royalties paid by SDI Netherlands to SDI Bermuda attributable to the use of technology protected in the United States could avoid characterization as U.S.-source royalty income because of the prior payment of royalties by SDI USA to SDI Netherlands.]

TANNENWALD, JUDGE: * * *

* * *

There can be no dispute that the royalty payments received by petitioner from SDI USA constitute U.S. source income and were received by petitioner as such within the meaning of section 1442(a). * * * However, royalties paid by SDI USA to petitioner are exempt from taxation by virtue of section 894 and article IX of the United States–Netherlands Income Tax Convention [of 1948, as amended] * * *. See also sec. 894. There is no comparable U.S. treaty exemption that would apply to royalty payments from petitioner to SDI Bermuda.

The parties have locked horns on several aspects of the application of the statutory provisions in light of the impact of the U.S.-Netherlands treaty exemption: (1) Whether the royalties paid by petitioner to SDI Bermuda constitute income "received from sources within the United States by" SDI Bermuda and are thus subject to withholding under section 1441(a); (2) whether petitioner can be considered a "withholding agent"; * * *

For reasons hereinafter set forth, we resolve the first issue in petitioner's favor with the result that it is unnecessary for us to address the remaining issues. Before proceeding with our analysis of the first issue, however, it is important to note that respondent does not question the existence of petitioner as a valid Netherlands corporation or the application of the treaty exemption insofar as the payments by SDI USA to petitioner are concerned. Similarly, respondent does not attack the arrangements under which petitioner had a license of the worldwide rights and SDI USA had a license of the U.S. rights, although respondent does ask us to take into account the close relationship of the various corporations involved. * * *

Rather, respondent focuses her argument solely on the proposition that, since the royalties paid by SDI USA to petitioner were U.S. source income, they retained that character as part of the royalties paid by petitioner to SDI Bermuda and, as a matter of law, constitute income "received from sources within the United States by" SDI Bermuda under section 881(a). Respondent contends that the fact that such royalties were combined with non-U.S. source royalties received by petitioner to determine the amount of royalties payable by petitioner to SDI Bermuda does not preclude the tracing of the royalties received by petitioner from SDI USA to U.S. sources. To implement such tracing, respondent simply applies the percentage specified in the worldwide license agreement between petitioner and SDI Bermuda and utilized in computing the amount of the required payment by petitioner to SDI Bermuda. To support her contention that such an allocation is permissible, respondent cites [a number of cases] * * *. In all of these cases, however, the payments, upon which a withholding tax was imposed, were directly from a U.S. payor, and the U.S. withholding tax was imposed on that payor. None of them address the situation involved herein, where there is a second licensing step under which royalties are being paid and upon which the U.S. withholding tax is sought to be imposed. Thus, these cases provide no guidance in respect of whether the U.S. source characterization of the royalties paid by SDI USA to petitioner flows through to the royalties paid by petitioner to SDI Bermuda.

Petitioner argues that the royalties paid by SDI USA to petitioner and exempt from tax under the U.S.-Netherlands treaty became merged with the other royalties received by petitioner from non-U.S. sources and consequently lost their character as U.S. source income. Petitioner submits that, while the royalty payments from SDI USA may be U.S. source income, its royalty payments to SDI Bermuda were made on a separate and independent basis. With respect to the payments to SDI Bermuda, petitioner contends that they were made pursuant to a worldwide licensing agreement between two foreign corporations, and as such do not constitute income "received from sources within the United States" so that no withholding is required under section 1442(a).

Pertinent authority on the issue before us is sparse. Indeed respondent relies solely on Rev. Rul. 80–362, 1980–2 C.B. 208, for her "flow-through" position. In Rev. Rul. 80–362, A, a resident of a country other than the United States and The Netherlands, licensed the rights to a U.S. patent to X, a Netherlands corporation. X agreed to pay a fixed royalty each year to A. X relicensed those rights to Y, a U.S. corporation, for use in the United States. In ruling that X was liable for a withholding tax under section 1441, the ruling states:

> In the present factual situation, the royalties from Y to X are exempt from United States tax under Article IX(1) of the Convention. However, the royalties from X to A are not exempt from taxation by the United States because there is no income tax convention between A's country of residence and the United States providing for such an exemption. Since the royalties from X to A are paid in consideration for the privilege of using a patent in the United States, they are treated as income from sources within the United States under section 861(a)(4) of the Code and are subject to United States income taxation under section 871(a)(1)(A). [Rev. Rul. 80–362, 1980–2 C.B. at 208–209.]

We are not persuaded that Rev. Rul. 80–362 * * * provides any significant support for respondent's position herein. It fails to reflect any reasoning or supporting legal authority. This circumstance is particularly relevant in applying the usual rule that, in any event, revenue rulings are not entitled to any special deference. * * *

At this point, we note that respondent has not argued that petitioner was a mere conduit or agent of SDI USA in paying royalties to SDI Bermuda or that SDI Bermuda was the beneficial owner of the royalties petitioner received from SDI USA so that the U.S.-Netherlands treaty exemption should not apply. * * * Presumably such an argument would have produced a situation where SDI USA rather than petitioner would have been targeted by respondent as the taxpayer liable for the withholding tax under section 1442(a). * * *

Although *Aiken Industries, Inc. v. Commissioner* * * * and *Northern Indiana Public Service Co. v. Commissioner* * * * involved the conduit concept, we think they provide some guidance for our disposition of the instant case. We take this view because the flow-through characterization concept is, in a very real sense, the conduit concept albeit in a somewhat different garb, i.e., whether the U.S. source income is being received as such, because of the status of the paying entity in one case and the status of the subject matter of the payment in the other.

In *Aiken Industries, Inc. v. Commissioner,* * * * back-to-back loans, in the identical amounts of principal and rates of interest, were made between a U.S. corporation and a related corporation organized under the laws of the Republic of Honduras, and between the Honduran corporation and its indirect parent. Respondent argued that the Honduran corporation should be disregarded for tax purposes, and that the parent corporation should be deemed the true owner and recipient of the interest payment from the U.S. corporation. We held the Honduran corporation to be a mere conduit for the passage of interest payments and imposed withholding tax liability on the U.S. corporation.

In *Northern Indiana Public Service Co. v. Commissioner,* * * * the taxpayer, a domestic corporation, organized a finance subsidiary incorporated in Curacao under the Commercial Code of the Netherlands Antilles (to which the U.S.-Netherlands treaty applied), for the purpose of issuing notes in the Eurobond market. The finance subsidiary borrowed $70 million at 17–1/4 percent interest in that market and lent that amount to the taxpayer at 18–1/4 percent interest. Respondent argued that the finance subsidiary should be ignored and that the taxpayer was liable for withholding taxes under section 1441 on the interest payments to the foreign Eurobond holders. Finding that the finance subsidiary engaged in substantive business activity that resulted in significant earnings, we held that the finance subsidiary was not a mere conduit or agent.

We think the within situation falls more within the ambit of *Northern Indiana* than *Aiken Industries*. In the latter case, there was an identity both in terms and timing between the back-to-back loans, as well as a close relationship between the parties involved. In the former case, although there was a clear connecting purpose between the borrowing and lending transactions, i.e., to obtain the benefit of the exemption from the withholding tax on interest under the U.S.-Netherlands treaty, there were differences in terms, i.e., in the interest rate (albeit not large); and a close relationship between all the parties was not present since the borrowings by the finance subsidiary were from unrelated parties.

In the instant case, there was a close relationship between the parties. However, although respondent asks us, in passing, to take that relationship into account, she does not pursue the matter to the point where she contends that it is a significant factor. Given the fact that respondent recognizes the existence of all of the parties as valid corporate entities and does not attack the bona fides of the license agreements between SDI USA and petitioner, on the one hand, or petitioner and SDI Bermuda, on the other, we are not disposed to allow the close relationship element to control our decision.

The facts of the matter are that the two license agreements had separate and distinct terms and that petitioner had an independent role as the licensee from SDI Bermuda and the licensor of the other entities, including but not limited to SDI USA. The schedules of royalty payments provided for a spread, not unlike the spread involved in *Northern Indiana*, which compensated petitioner for its efforts. Like the finance subsidiary in *Northern Indiana*, petitioner engaged in licensing activities from which it realized substantial earnings. In fact, on a percentage basis, it earned between 5 and 6 percent, compared to the 1 percent earned by that finance subsidiary in *Northern Indiana*. Under the circumstances herein, we think these arrangements should be accorded separate status with the result that, although the royalties paid by petitioner to SDI Bermuda were derived from the royalties received by petitioner from SDI USA, they were separate payments.

We find support for our conclusion herein in that respondent's view of the law could cause a cascading royalty problem, whereby multiple withholding taxes could be paid on the same royalty payment as it is transferred up a chain of licensors.* * * But for the U.S.-Netherlands treaty, the royalty payments from SDI USA could be subject to withholding tax twice under respondent's reasoning herein.

Respondent argues that only one withholding tax is being sought herein. However, this ignores the fact that, by treaty, the United States agreed to forgo taxing royalties and to allow them to be taxed by The Netherlands. Whether or not The Netherlands actually taxed the royalties is irrelevant.

Respondent also implies that she would use her discretion not to apply more than one level of withholding tax on multiple transfers of income that originated as U.S. source income. We think this places an improper exercise of discretion in respondent's hands. To avoid the imposition of interest and additions to tax as determined by respondent herein, each payor in the chain might well feel compelled to file returns and pay withholding taxes. * * * We are not disposed to conclude, in the absence of any legislative expression on the subject, that Congress intended the statutory provisions to permit "cascading" with the question of relief left to the mercy of respondent.

We hold that the payments by petitioner with respect to which respondent seeks to impose liability for the 30-percent withholding tax herein were not "received from sources within the United States by" SDI Bermuda under sections 881(a), 1441(a), and 1442(a). * * *

[¶ 4152]

NOTE

Does the *SDI Netherlands* decision make it clear how and when royalties derived from intellectual property used in the United States will not be treated as U.S.-source income? Why did Judge Tannenwald choose not to include Section 861(a)(4), which clearly prescribes the source rules applicable to royalties, in the list of relevant Code sections set forth in the last paragraph of the portion of the decision reproduced here? Would you favor the adoption of legislation to eliminate the problem of "cascading royalties?" If so, what language would you propose to resolve the matter? In the light of the decision in *SDI Netherlands*, is a legislative response necessary?

[¶ 4155]

c. Responsibilities of Withholding Agents

A potential withholding agent will generally be responsible for determining the existence of a withholding obligation. Withholding agents are persons having "control, receipt, custody, disposal, or payment" of an item of income realized by a foreign person. Reg. § 1.1441–7(a)(1). This may present difficulties for a withholding agent that does not have detailed information about the payee. Suppose, for example, that a U.S. corporation having some foreign shareholders declares a dividend. How does it know whether the withholding obligation applies?

The regulations establish an elaborate system of documentation and certification that must be satisfied to avoid the withholding requirements. See Reg. §§ 1.1441–1 et seq. The regulations reflect IRS concern that withholding taxes are being avoided through the use of agents in whose name stock shares and other properties are registered. Responsibility for determining the applicability of the withholding requirements is placed squarely upon the individual or entity making the payment: "A withholding agent must withhold 30–percent of any payment of an amount subject to withholding made to a payee that is a foreign person unless it can reliably associate the payment with documentation upon which it can rely to treat the payment as made to a payee that is a U.S. person or as made to a beneficial owner that is a foreign person entitled to a reduced rate of withholding." Reg. § 1.1441–1(b)(1). The regulations set forth a complex series of reporting and certification requirements and also opportunities intended to make it easier for withholding agents to determine the extent of their obligations in respect of various payees. Under the regulations, payments made to U.S. persons will not be subject to withholding "absent actual knowledge or reason to know otherwise" that a foreign taxpayer is involved if a withholding agent relies on the methods described in the regulations in determining whether the recipient of a payment is a U.S.

person and therefore not subject to withholding. Reg. § 1.1441–1(d)(1). For example, a withholding agent can rely upon certain forms of documentation to justify not withholding:

1. Documentation that the beneficial owner is a U.S. person and, therefore, not subject to the withholding regime. This can be provided by a Form W–9 signed by the beneficial owner that includes his/her Social Security Number or EIN. Reg. § 1.1441–1(d).

2. Documentation that the owner is an exempt foreign beneficial owner under one of several statutory provisions, including a representation that the income is effectively connected with a U.S. trade or business. Reg. § 1.1441–1(e).

3. Documentation that the foreign payee has assumed withholding responsibilities, such as foreign banks that can agree with the IRS to become "qualified intermediaries." Reg. § 1.1441–1(e)(5).

[¶ 4160]

2. WITHHOLDING IN RESPECT OF COMPENSATION INCOME

If a nonresident alien is an employee working within the United States, normal wage withholding provisions will apply to the compensation income. Otherwise, the 30–percent withholding requirement of Section 1441 continues to obtain (with exceptions noted in the following Ruling) for items of compensation received by a nonresident alien for working in the United States as an independent contractor. Note that the withholding requirement will apply even though the income is (under Sections 864(b) and 864(c)(2)) effectively connected with the trade or business of providing personal services and even though the taxpayer has reported the income as required by Section 871(b). A lower withholding rate of 14 percent is, however, prescribed in respect of certain payments to nonresident aliens temporarily within the United States primarily as students. § 1441(a).

The withholding mechanism in the instance of a nonresident alien's compensation income thus differs from that which normally applies for most items of FDAP income with respect to which the tax rate is 30 percent and the withholding satisfies exactly the applicable tax liability. In the case of compensation income, the tax liability cannot be determined without reference to allowable deductions and exemptions and application of the progressive rates set forth in Section 1 of the Code. The nonresident alien is expected to file a return and either pay the additional taxes owed or obtain a refund of excess withholdings.

[¶ 4165]

REVENUE RULING 70–543

1970–2 C.B. 173.

Advice has been requested regarding the filing of Form 4224 (a statement for use by a nonresident alien individual or fiduciary, foreign partnership, or foreign corporation in claiming exemption from withholding of tax on income effectively connected with the conduct of a trade or business in the United States) by a nonresident alien individual conducting a trade or business in the United States. Three typical situations are described below.

Situation (1). A, a pugilist, is a self-employed nonresident alien individual who has contracted to engage in a prize fight in the United States during the taxable year. *A* pays the salaries of his handlers, pays commissions to his agent, and has other allowable expenses.

Situation (2). B, a professional golfer, is a nonresident alien individual who enters various professional golfing tournaments in the United States during the taxable year. *B* pays the fees of his caddies, incurs traveling expenses, and has other allowable expenses.

Situation (3). C is a nonresident alien individual who is an owner and operator of a stable of racing horses in his native country. During the taxable year *C* enters some of his horses in one or more races to be held in the United States in either flat or harness races, or both. *C* employs jockeys to ride his horses in flat races; however, *C* may drive his own sulky in harness races. *C* pays the jockeys' fees, entrance fees, stable and other allowable expenses.

It has been established that the nonresident alien individual in each of the above situations is engaged in trade or business in the United States and that the income from such self-employment is not excluded in whole or in part from gross income under section 61 * * * by any tax convention to which the United States is a party.

Section 871(b) * * * provides that a nonresident alien individual engaged in trade or business within the United States is taxable at graduated rates * * * on taxable income which is effectively connected with the conduct of such trade or business within the United States. The imposition of the 30 percent tax rate on gross income under section 871(a) * * * is therefore not applicable to such income.

Section 1441(a) * * * provides, in pertinent part, for the withholding at the source of Federal income tax at the rate of 30 percent on items of fixed and determinable annual or periodical gains, profits, or income from sources within the United States paid to a nonresident alien or foreign partnership, except as otherwise provided in section 1441(c) * * *.

Section 1441(c)(1) * * * provides that no deduction or withholding under section 1441(a) * * * is required in the case of any item of income (other than compensation for personal services) which is effectively connected with the conduct of a trade or business within the United States and which is included in the gross income of the recipient under section 871(b)(2) * * * for the taxable year. Section 1441(c)(4) * * * provides that regulations may be promulgated to exempt compensation for personal services from deduction and withholding under section 1441(a) * * *.

Section 1.1441–4(a)(1) of the * * * Regulations provides, in pertinent part, that no withholding is required under section 1441 * * * in the case of any item of income if such income is effectively connected with the conduct of a trade or business within the United States by the person entitled to such income and is includible in his gross income under section 871(b)(2) * * * and if he has filed the statement prescribed by section 1.1441–4(a)(2) of the regulations. Such statement may be made on Form 4224 (statement claiming exemption). This section of the regulations does not exempt from withholding compensation for personal services performed by a nonresident alien individual and the instructions on Form 4224 explicitly state that such Form is not to be filed for compensation for personal services performed by a nonresident alien individual.

Section 1.1441–4(b) of the regulations, however, exempts from withholding under section 1441 * * * that compensation for personal services performed by a nonresident alien individual which (1) is subject to withholding at graduated rates under section 3402 * * *; (2) would be subject to withholding at graduated rates but for section 3401(a) * * * (other than section 3401(a)(6)) * * *; (3) is paid to certain Mexican and Canadian residents; or (4) is exempt from tax by reason of a provision of the Code or a tax convention to which the United States is a party. Section 1.1441–4(b)(2) of the regulations sets forth the information which must be included in the statement claiming exemption from withholding based on a claimed exemption from Federal income tax, and further states that no particular form is prescribed for such statement. Although with respect to exemption from withholding provided by section 1.1441–4(b)(1)(i) through (iii) no statement is required to be filed by the person entitled to the compensation referred to therein, the withholding agent, in connection with the filing of annual information returns, Forms 1042S, must file a brief statement as to the authority for his failure to withhold. See section 1.1461–2(c)(2)(ii) of the regulations.

Section 3401 and section 3402 * * * apply to remuneration for services performed by an employee for an employer and hence have no application to compensation paid for personal services where such an employment relationship does not exist. Section 31.3401(a)(1) of the * * * Regulations. See also section 6015(i)(2) * * * which provides, in effect, that a nonresident alien individual is required to file a declaration of estimated tax on income (other than compensation for personal services subject to deduction and withholding under section 1441) * * * which is effectively connected with the conduct of a trade or business in the United States.

In view of the above sections of the Internal Revenue Code and the regulations prescribed thereunder, the compensation for personal services performed by a self-employed nonresident alien individual is not exempt from withholding at the 30 percent rate under section 1441 * * * if such compensation is not otherwise exempt from Federal tax and is gross income effectively connected with the conduct of a trade or business within the United States under section 871(b)(2) * * *.

The conclusions set forth below apply the foregoing principles to the factual situations presented above.

Situation (1). The purse received by *A* for participation in the prize fight is compensation for personal services as a self-employed nonresident alien individual. The exemptions from withholding provided by section 1.1441–4(b) of the regulations are not applicable. Accordingly, it is held that the purse received for such prize fight during the taxable year is subject to withholding at 30 percent even though *A* will be taxable at graduated rates on the amount of his taxable income under section 871(b) * * *. *A* may not file Form 4224 or any other statement to claim exemption from withholding of tax.

Situation (2). The amounts received by *B* during the year as prizes for participation in various golfing tournaments are compensation for personal services as a self-employed nonresident alien individual. Accordingly, these amounts are subject to withholding at 30 percent even though *B* will be taxable at graduated rates on the amount of his taxable income under section 871(b) * * *. *B* may not file Form 4224 or any other statement to claim exemption from withholding of tax.

Situation (3). The amounts received by *C* as winner's purses are not compensation for personal services as that term is used in section 1441(c)(1) * * *. It is immaterial whether the purses are won when *C* drives the sulky himself in a harness race or hires a professional jockey in a flat race. * * *

Accordingly, it is held that *C* is exempt from withholding of tax under section 1441 * * * on the amount of the winner's purses provided a Form 4224 or an equivalent statement is filed with the withholding agent in accordance with section 1.1441–4(a)(2) of the regulations.

* * *

[¶ 4170]

NOTE

While Section 1442(a) imposes the withholding requirements on compensation payments to a foreign corporation for services rendered in the United States, withholding is waived if the foreign corporation files a "withholding certificate" with the withholding agent asserting that the income is effectively connected with a U.S. trade or business. Reg. § 1.1441–4(a). The withholding certificates or other information provided to a withholding agent need not be filed by the agent with the IRS. Reg. § 1.1461–1(b). This relaxation of the withholding requirement is explicitly authorized by Section 1442(b) and presumably reflects greater confidence by Congress and the U.S. Treasury that U.S. income tax obligations will be satisfied by foreign corporations operating branches in the United States.

[¶ 4175]

3. WITHHOLDING IN RESPECT OF PARTNERSHIPS

As indicated at ¶ 3060, the income of a partnership engaged in a U.S. trade or business will be attributable to a foreign partner and will be taxed as if the foreign partner were conducting the U.S. trade or business under the regime described in Chapter 3. § 875(1). Section 1446 nevertheless imposes a withholding obligation on the share of partnership net income that is effectively connected with a U.S. trade or business allocable to a foreign partner. The result is that the partnership must withhold an amount equal to the product of the allocable share of such income attributable to the foreign partner and the maximum marginal tax rates specified in Sections 1 (for individuals) and 11 (for corporations), except that a lower rate may be applied for capital gains allocable to a noncorporate foreign partner. Reg. § 1.1446–3(a)(2)(ii). Note that, unlike other situations in which withholding obligations apply when payments are made, the partnership is required to withhold the appropriate amount whether or not the foreign partner's share of income is actually distributed. The tax so withheld will be treated as a distribution to the foreign partner to whom the withholding applies. Reg. § 1.1446–3(d)(2)(v).

As in the case of nonresident alien compensation income, the effect is the establishment of a withholding obligation that does not equal the income tax liability of the taxpayer. That liability may depend on other income, deductions and credits available to the taxpayer that are not reflected in the partnership calculations because they relate to other U.S. trades or businesses and the effective tax rate of the foreign partner. The foreign partner is required to file the appropriate income tax return in which the amount withheld by the partnership will be credited against any U.S. income tax liability.

[¶ 4180]

4. BRANCH PROFITS TAX

Foreign corporations operating a branch in the United States will be subject to an additional 30–percent (or lesser treaty rate) tax on branch earnings not invested in branch assets or withdrawn from such investment. § 884. The rationale for the tax derives from the regime of taxation prescribed for dividend income from U.S. sources described in this Chapter. Moreover, the rules for its implementation are derived from the withholding requirements imposed on U.S.-source dividends not connected with a U.S. trade or business. A detailed discussion of the branch profits tax is set forth at ¶ 3230.

[¶ 4182]

5. WITHHOLDING REQUIREMENTS AS A DEFENSE AGAINST TAX EVASION

Concerned with the extent to which U.S. persons were reportedly evading U.S. income tax laws through foreign accounts and entities, Congress in 2010 enacted a vigorous regime of reporting intended to strengthen the ability to defend against such practices. The Foreign Account Tax Compliance Act (called "FATCA"), when it becomes effective in 2013, effectively compels the disclosure of information by foreign financial institutions that will identify U.S. persons involved in such practices. See §§ 1471–1474. The principal means of implementing the new regime is through the imposition of a 30–percent withholding tax on dividends, interest and certain other payments to the foreign financial institutions unless they provide information with respect to U.S. account holders. § 1471(a).

The information required to be reported, which is intended to identify the U.S. persons holding a beneficial interest in the accounts, is set forth in Section 1471(c). The information is required of any "United States account," which is defined to be "any financial account which is held by one or more specified United States persons or United States owned foreign entities." § 1471(d)(1). The U.S. persons so specified are listed in Section 1473(3). Section 1471(d)(5) applies the FATCA requirements to foreign entities that:

1. Accept deposits in the ordinary course of a banking or similar business;

2. Hold financial assets for the account of others as a substantial portion of its business; or

3. Are engaged primarily in the business of investing, reinvesting, or trading in securities, partnership interests or commodities.

If the information reporting requirements are not satisfied, Section 1473(1)(A) applies the withholding requirement to:

1. Any payment of interest (including any original issue discount), dividends, rents, salaries, wages, premiums, annuities, compensations, remunerations, emoluments and other fixed or determinable annual or periodical gains, profits and income, if such payment is from sources within the United States; or

2. Any gross proceeds from the sale or other disposition of any property of a type which can produce interest or dividends from sources within the United States.

However, the withholding requirement does not apply to income that is taxed under the U.S. trade or business tax regime discussed in Chapter 3. § 1473(1)(B).

Section 1471(b) provides that the reporting requirements are deemed to have been satisfied if the institution agrees to obtain relevant information, comply with verification and due diligence procedures that may be required, report relevant information on an annual basis and deduct and withhold a 30-percent tax on "passthru payments" made to a "recalcitrant account holder or other foreign financial institution which does not meet [these] * * * requirements." Further, the institution must agree to comply with requests for additional information about such accounts.

The withholding tax imposed under the FATCA regime applies in addition to the withholding requirements imposed by Sections 1441 et seq. The primary objective of the regime, however, is not to collect additional withholding tax revenues, but rather to defend against tax evasion by U.S. persons.

G. TREATMENT OF GAINS FROM U.S. REAL PROPERTY

[¶ 4185]

1. BACKGROUND

As indicated at ¶ 4110, capital gains from U.S. sources not effectively connected with a U.S. trade or business are not generally subject either to the 30-percent withholding tax or to the usual taxes on net income. As foreign investment in the United States grew dramatically during the 1970s, many legislators began to express concern that foreign investors were benefiting from an unfair competitive advantage over American-owned enterprises because of the broad opportunity for foreign taxpayers to avoid U.S. taxes. These concerns were magnified in the wake of the petroleum crises of the 1970s, which adversely affected the U.S. balance of payments, reduced the value of the U.S. dollar and provided enlarged opportunities for foreign investors to acquire real property in the United States at very favorable prices.

Focus and debate on the capital gains "loophole" for foreign investors evoked a series of proposals that would effectively increase the U.S. tax on the earnings of foreign investors. Some of the most unrestrained debate was directed to the fear that foreign interests were "buying up America itself" (not really such bad news to domestic owners of property whose value had risen as a result of increased foreign demand). In 1980, Congress acted on these particular concerns by adopting Section 897 (in legislation called the Foreign Investment in Real Property Tax Act or "FIRPTA," a term often still used by tax practitioners), which narrowed considerably the chance for foreign taxpayers to realize untaxed income from real estate investments in the United States.

[¶ 4190]

2. PRIOR LAW

To understand fully the purposes and structure of Section 897, it is useful to examine the situation existing at the time of its enactment. Prior to 1981, income derived by foreign persons from the sale or other disposition of real property in the United States could be arranged in such a way as to minimize or completely avoid U.S. income tax. The first step was to assure that the real estate was taxed as a U.S. trade or business, either by qualifying for such treatment directly or electing so to be treated, so that rental income would be taxed on a net basis. The second step was effected by arrangements to assure that gains from the sale of the U.S. real estate were not deemed to be effectively connected with the conduct of a U.S. trade or business and, hence, not taxable.

Over years of imaginative tax planning, a number of techniques had been developed by which foreign investors would be taxed only on current net income (if any) from real property, rather than on 30 percent of gross rentals, but nevertheless could avoid tax on the eventual gain realized upon disposition of the property. These devices included the use of installment sales provisions under which gains reported in years after the sale were not deemed effectively connected to a U.S. trade or business, the exploitation of provisions which at that time allowed corporations to distribute appreciated property to shareholders without being taxed on the appreciation in the value of the property, the nonrecognition of gain in like-kind exchanges and certain treaties that allowed an annual election to treat real estate investments as a U.S. trade or business. The desire to eliminate these well known techniques accounts for many of the specific elements, and some of the complexities, of Section 897.

[¶ 4195]

3. EFFECTS OF SECTION 897

Section 897 was designed to counteract the use of the various techniques that had been developed to avoid income tax on the disposition of U.S. real property. Section 897 provides that gain or loss realized by nonresident aliens or foreign corporations on the disposition of U.S. real property interests will be treated generally as if such gain or loss were effectively connected with a U.S. trade or business. In some instances, the tax will also apply to gains on the sale of stock in U.S. corporations that hold 50 percent or more of specified assets in the form of U.S. real property. While gain from the sale of stock in a foreign corporation will not be taxed, the foreign corporation is taxed if and when it sells U.S. real property interests or distributes such interests to its shareholders.

While the rationale for most of the elements of FIRPTA will be self-explanatory, it should be noted that a number of other legislative changes made since the adoption of FIRPTA would themselves have reduced or eliminated some of the avenues by which foreign investors had been able to avoid U.S. income taxes on U.S. real estate profits. As a result, FIRPTA now applies to a number of situations which today would not provide avenues for tax avoidance.

[¶ 4200]

4. TAX ON GAIN FROM U.S. REAL PROPERTY INTERESTS

Section 897 imposes a tax on gain realized upon the disposition of a "U.S. real property interest." A U.S. real property interest is defined to include "an interest in real property (including an interest in a mine, well, or other natural deposit) located in the United States." § 897(c)(1)(A)(i). It also includes certain leasehold interests, options to acquire real property and "associated personal property," such as movable walls. § 897(c)(6)(A) and (B). A U.S. real property interest does not include an "interest solely as a creditor * * * in real property." Reg. § 1.897–1(d)(1). However, a loan in which the lender has a direct or indirect right to share in the increase in value or the proceeds of the disposition of property will not be regarded as an interest solely as a creditor. Reg. § 1.897–1(d)(2). The tax applies even to gain accrued prior to the adoption of Section 897.

Nonresident aliens and foreign corporations are subject to tax on net gains from the disposition of U.S. real property interests under Sections 871(b) and 882, respectively, as though the gains and losses were effectively connected with a U.S. trade or business. § 897(a)(1). However, a nonresident alien may be taxed under the alternative minimum tax rates of Section 55 if that would produce a tax higher than the regular tax. § 897(a)(2).

[¶ 4205]

5. TAX ON SALE OF STOCK IN U.S. CORPORATION

U.S. real property interest is also defined to include any interest (other than an interest solely as a creditor) in a U.S. corporation unless the foreign person holding such interest establishes that the U.S. corporation was at no time during the five years ending on the date of the disposition a U.S. real property holding corporation. § 897(c)(1)(A)(ii). A "U.S. real property holding corporation" is defined to include any corporation (whether domestic or foreign), the fair market value of whose U.S. real property interests equals or exceeds 50 percent of the sum of the fair market value of (1) its U.S. real property interests, (2) its interests in real property located outside the United States and (3) any other of its assets that are used or held for use in a trade or business. § 897(c)(2). Since the test depends on comparative asset values, note that a corporation could become a U.S. real property holding corporation, even though it did not modify its asset holdings, simply as a result of fluctuating property values.

U.S. real property interests will not include any class of stock of a corporation that is regularly traded on an established securities market, except in the case of a person owning more than five percent of such a class of stock during the relevant time period. § 897(c)(3). Constructive ownership rules are prescribed by Section 897(c)(6)(C) in applying the five-percent test. If a taxpayer owns, directly or indirectly, more than five percent of such stock, the stock of the corporation may be a U.S. real property interest.

Various statutory rules ensure that characterization of a U.S. corporation as a U.S. real property holding corporation cannot be avoided by having the corporation hold a U.S. real property interest through a foreign corporation, a partnership, trust or estate or any corporation (or chain of corporations) that it controls. § 897(c)(4). Look-through rules apply so that a corporation will be treated as owning a proportionate share of assets held by the partnership, trust or estate. § 897(b)(2)(B). Reg. § 1.897–2(e)(2). If a corporation holds a "controlling interest" (i.e., 50 percent or more of the fair market value of all classes of stock) of another corporation, the controlling corporation is treated as holding a portion of each of the assets of the controlled corporation equal to the percentage of the fair market value of the controlled corporation's stock held by the controlling corporation. § 897(c)(5)(A). Thus, a corporation that owns no U.S. real property may be a U.S. real property holding corporation because of the real property owned by its affiliates.

Gains realized from the disposition of an interest in a U.S. corporation that constitutes a U.S. real property holding corporation is generally taxed at the same rate and under the same rules as the disposition of direct holdings in U.S. real property. The entire amount of gain realized from the sale of stock in a domestic U.S. real property holding corporation is subject to tax, regardless of the portion attributable to the U.S. real property interests that it holds. However, Section 897 will not apply to the sale or other disposition of the stock if the corporation holds no U.S. real property interest at the time of the disposition and if all U.S. real property interests held by the corporation during the five years prior to the disposition (which made the corporation itself a U.S. real property holding corporation) have been transferred by the corporation in transactions in which the full amount of gain was recognized. § 897(c)(1)(B).

The tax imposed by Section 897 is due even, for example, in the case of a sale of stock of a domestic U.S. real property holding corporation between two nonresident aliens (or foreign corporations) when all the negotiations for the transaction and the transaction itself take place outside the United States. Note that in such a case the gain would not be regarded as U.S.-source income but for the special rule established in Section 861(a)(5).

A foreign corporation may be a U.S. real property holding corporation. However, stock in a foreign corporation will not be classified as a U.S. real property interest unless it elects to be treated as a U.S. corporation. See ¶ 4220. Sale of the stock of a foreign corporation is not, therefore, usually taxable under Section 897. It is assumed, however, that purchasers of stock in a foreign corporation owning appreciated U.S. real property interests will pay less for the stock because of the U.S. taxes that will eventually be imposed when the foreign corporation disposes of those interests.

[¶ 4210]

6. ANTI-AVOIDANCE MEASURES

In addition to taxing certain gains even though they are not in fact connected with a U.S. trade or business, Section 897 establishes a series of rules intended to defend against various potential techniques and devices that might avoid its intended effect.

[¶ 4215]

a. Dispositions of Interests in Foreign Corporations and Distributions by Foreign Corporations

Ordinarily, the sale or other disposition of shares in a foreign corporation that owns a U.S. real property interest is not subject to U.S. taxation. Instead, the foreign corporation must recognize gain and pay U.S. tax when it distributes a U.S. real property interest to any of its shareholders, whether by way of dividend, liquidation or redemption of stock. The foreign corporation is generally obligated to pay tax on the amount equal to the excess of the fair market value of the U.S. real property interest at the time it is distributed over its adjusted basis. § 897(d)(1). Such a gain will be taxed as if it were effectively connected with the conduct of a U.S. trade or business.

[¶ 4220]

b. Election by Foreign Corporation to Be Treated as U.S. Corporation

Many tax treaties between the United States and other countries have nondiscrimination clauses that prohibit the United States from treating a permanent establishment of a foreign corporation in the United States less favorably than domestic corporations carrying on the same activities. See ¶ 1280. Section 897(i) permits a foreign corporation having a permanent establishment in the United States that is protected by a nondiscrimination clause in a tax treaty to elect to be treated as a U.S. corporation for purposes of Sections 897, 1445 (withholding requirements) and 6039C (reporting requirements). One result of such an election would be that the sale of real property by the electing foreign corporation would not invoke Section 897.

[¶ 4225]

c. Nonrecognition Provisions

The various nonrecognition provisions of the Code generally have no application to transactions covered by Section 897. Exceptions to this rule apply (1) in the case of an exchange of a U.S. real property interest for an interest, the sale of which would be subject to U.S. taxation, and (2) to the extent nonrecognition provisions are made applicable by regulations. § 897(e); see Temp. Reg. §§ 1.897–5T and –6T. The following Ruling deals with a situation in which the IRS concludes that the nonrecognition provisions of Section 351 will not undermine the implementation of Section 897.

[¶ 4230]

REVENUE RULING 84–160

1984–2 C.B. 125.

FX is a corporation organized under the laws of a foreign country (*FC*), which does not have an income tax treaty with the United States. *FX* holds 100 percent of the stock of corporation *S*, a domestic corporation. *S* is engaged in real estate development and has determined that it constitutes a U.S. real property holding corporation as defined in section 897(c)(2) * * *. Therefore, the stock of *S* constitutes a U.S. real property interest pursuant to section 897(c)(1). For business purposes *FX* wishes to interpose a holding company between itself and *S*. Therefore, on December 1, 1984, in a transaction qualifying for nonrecognition under section 351, *FX* transfers all of the shares of *S* to *H*, a corporation newly organized in the United States, solely in exchange for the stock of *H*. Because the shares of *S* are the only assets of *H*, *H* constitutes a U.S. real property holding corporation as defined in section 897(c)(2).

LAW AND ANALYSIS

Under section 897(a) * * *, a foreign corporation's gain or loss from the disposition of a U.S. real property interest is treated as if the foreign corporation were engaged in a trade or business within the United States and as if the gain or loss were effectively connected with the trade or business. Section 897 applies to dispositions made after June 18, 1980.

Section 897(e) * * * provides that except to the extent otherwise provided in section 897(d) and section 897(e)(2), any nonrecognition provision shall apply for purposes of section 897 to a transaction only in the case of an exchange of a United States real property interest for an interest the sale of which would be subject to taxation under this chapter, i.e., chapter 1 of the Code. Section 897(e)(2) provides that the Secretary shall prescribe regulations (which are necessary or appropriate to prevent the avoidance of Federal income taxes) providing the extent to which nonrecognition provisions shall, and shall not, apply for purposes of section 897, and the extent to which the transfers of property in reorganizations and changes in interest in, or distributions from, a partnership, trust, or estate, shall be treated as sales of property at fair market value. Section 897(e)(3) defines the term "nonrecognition provision" as meaning any provision of this title, i.e., the Internal Revenue Code, for not recognizing gain or loss.

Section 897(e) * * * is intended to preserve otherwise-available nonrecognition in cases where it is clear that gain inherent in a U.S. real property interest will remain subject to U.S. taxation. In the present case, *FX* has exchanged, in a transaction qualifying for nonrecognition under section 351, one U.S. real property interest for another U.S. real property interest, the sale of which will be clearly subject to U.S. taxation. Therefore, *FX* is entitled to receive nonrecognition treatment pursuant to section 897(e) * * *.

HOLDING

In accordance with section 897(e) * * *, in the above fact situation, the nonrecognition provision will apply for purposes of section 897.

* * *

7. ENFORCEMENT MECHANISMS

[¶ 4235]

a. Adoption of Withholding to Replace Reporting

A vigorous debate at the time of the adoption of Section 897 attended the establishment of a withholding obligation. When it was originally adopted, no additional withholding requirements were imposed. Enforcement was to be based on a rather complex system of information-reporting requirements designed to identify foreign owners (rather than sellers) of a U.S. real property interest. Temporary and proposed regulations were issued, pursuant to a legislative mandate, implementing the reporting requirements. However, they were widely criticized for imposing a burdensome and unworkable reporting system. Among the many seemingly intractable problems was identifying owners of bearer shares of foreign corporations. Final regulations were never issued.

The absence of a clear and effective reporting system meant that the tax regime established by Section 897 in its original form was susceptible to relatively easy evasion. Since the tax was not normally due until a tax return was filed after the end of the year in which a sale or other disposition had occurred, a foreign person could sell U.S. real estate, remove the proceeds from the United States and (once beyond the jurisdiction of the United States) pay no tax on the sale.

A withholding tax mechanism was eventually established by the Tax Reform Act of 1984. Section 1445 requires that, when a foreign person disposes of a U.S. real property interest, the "transferee" must withhold ten percent of the amount realized by the transferor on the disposition and pay it to the U.S. Treasury. A transferee includes "any person, foreign or domestic, that acquires a U.S. real property interest by purchase, exchange, gift, or any other transfer." Reg. § 1.1445–1(g)(4).

Since it applies to the proceeds of the disposition and not to the income realized on the disposition, Section 1445 provides another example of the imposition of a withholding obligation for an amount not necessarily equal to the income tax liability. In fact, the withholding obligation is imposed on gross receipts rather than gross income. Any tax imposed on a foreign person under Section 897 in excess of amounts withheld remains the liability of the foreign investor. The foreign person is entitled to recover any portion of the tax withheld that exceeds the actual tax liability, but must file a refund claim to do so.

The amount to be withheld on the sale by a foreign investor of a U.S. real property interest generally is the lesser of ten percent of the "amount realized" or the transferor's "maximum tax liability." The amount realized equals the cash and fair market value of other property received and any liability assumed by the transferee or to which the property was subject. Thus, the withholding obligation may exceed the cash paid by the transferee. The maximum tax liability alternative would come into play when the seller's maximum tax is less than ten percent of the proceeds of the sale, and depends upon a certification by the IRS, as discussed below.

[¶ 4240]

b. Exceptions to Withholding Requirements

The purpose of the withholding requirement is obviously to assure compliance by the taxpayer. There are, therefore, a series of exceptions designed to deal with circumstances in which the tax is not payable or collection of the applicable tax liability seems assured. Withholding is not required:

1. By the transferee of property if the transferor furnishes an affidavit stating that the transferor is not a foreign person and setting forth the transferor's taxpayer identification number. § 1445(b)(2).

2. On the disposition of an interest in a U.S. corporation if the corporation furnishes an affidavit stating that it is not and has not been a U.S. real property holding corporation during the five-year or shorter base period specified in Section 897(c)(1)(A)(ii). § 1445(b)(3).

3. If the transferee receives a "qualifying statement" from the IRS that the transferor is exempt from tax or that adequate arrangements to secure payment of the tax or acceptable arrangements to pay the tax have been made. § 1445(b)(4).

4. If the transferee is going to use the property as a residence and the amount realized by the transferor on the disposition does not exceed $300,000. § 1445(b)(5).

5. On a disposition of shares of a class of stock regularly traded on an established securities market. § 1445(b)(6). This exemption has been expanded to cover certain dispositions of classes of stock and other interests that are not traded on established markets if the issuing corporation has at least one class of stock that is so traded. Reg. § 1.1445–2(c)(2).

Section 1445(c) also provides that the amount withheld need not exceed the amount of the income tax liability deriving from the transaction and authorizes a determination by the IRS of the correct taxable amount. This authorization reflects the practical realities of the situation. It is highly unlikely that the purchaser of the real property interest would have any way of determining the amount of income tax, if any, payable by the transferor on the transaction.

[¶ 4245]

c. Corporate Distributions

A foreign corporation is required to withhold tax on a distribution of a U.S. real property interest when gain on the distribution is recognized by the corporation under Section 897. For example, withholding by a foreign corporation is required when the corporation distributes a U.S. real property interest to shareholders in a liquidating distribution. Under rates in effect through 2010, the amount of tax to be withheld is 35 percent of the foreign corporation's gain. Withholding is at the maximum nominal corporate rate rather than at the lower ten-percent rate because the corporation is itself the taxpayer. § 1445(e)(2).

Withholding is required by a U.S. corporation that is a U.S. real property holding corporation when the corporation distributes property to a foreign shareholder in a liquidation or stock redemption. The same requirement applies if the corporation was a U.S. real property holding corporation during the base period specified in Section 897(c)(1)(A)(ii). The amount to be withheld is generally ten percent of the gross amount of the distribution. § 1445(e)(3).

[¶ 4250]

d. Partnerships, Trusts and Estates

U.S. partnerships, trusts and estates are required to withhold tax in respect of the share of gain attributable to a foreign partner or foreign beneficiary of any amount realized by the entity upon a disposition of a U.S. real property interest. § 1445(e)(1). The withholding rate will generally be 35 percent. Reg. § 1.1445–5(c). However, the withholding rate may be reduced to 15 percent with respect to certain capital gains distributions, reflecting the lower rates applicable to long-term capital gains. § 1445(e)(1). These rates in effect through 2010 may be increased.

Every U.S. or foreign partnership, trust or estate is generally required to withhold ten percent of the fair market value of a U.S. real property interest distributed to a foreign partner or foreign beneficiary if the distribution would be taxable. § 1445(e)(4). Also, a transferee of a partnership interest or of a beneficial interest in a trust or estate may be generally required to withhold ten percent of the amount realized on the disposition. § 1445(e)(5).

[¶ 4255]

e. Information–Reporting Requirement

The 1984 Act generally repealed the information reporting requirements that had originally been established to implement Section 897. However, it authorizes the Treasury to require reporting by foreign persons holding direct investments in U.S. real property interests. For this purpose, a foreign person will be treated as holding a direct investment in a U.S. real property interest during any calendar year if the foreign person did not engage in a U.S. trade or business at any time during the calendar year and the fair market value of the U.S. real property interest held directly by the person at any time during the year was $50,000 or more. § 6039C. No regulations have as yet been issued under this provision.

[¶ 4260]

8. EFFECT OF TREATIES

Article 13 of the U.S. Model Treaty provides that gains realized from the alienation of real property in the United States or of a "U.S. real property interest" (which would include stock in a corporation the assets of which consist principally of U.S. real property) may be taxed in the country where the property is located. This formulation effectively authorizes the application of Section 897.

The relationship between treaties and the Code is discussed at ¶ 1295. As indicated in that discussion, one of the most notable exercises of the treaty override authority occurred with the enactment of the Section 897. Many treaties then in force provided that a host government would impose no taxes on certain capital gains not effectively connected with a U.S. trade or business. Because Section 897 imposes a tax not only on gains realized on sales of U.S. real estate itself but also on gains realized from the sale of stock in certain U.S. corporations owning U.S. real estate, the legislation was inconsistent with such treaty provisions. Under U.S. practice, the later-in-time legislation would be applied by U.S. courts even though its application would constitute a violation of U.S. treaty commitments. The 1980 legislation, therefore, provided for the continued application of existing treaties for four years during which time it was expected that the Treasury would negotiate amendments explicitly to permit the application of Section 897.

H. FINANCING THE U.S. ENTERPRISE

[¶ 4265]

1. ROLE OF DEBT AND EQUITY

A foreign investor deciding to operate through a separately incorporated entity in the United States is presented with the usual incentives to use debt rather than equity. Interest is deductible; dividends are not. The repayment of principal provides an avenue for repatriating cash without incurring an income tax; redemption of stock may involve dividend consequences. While the withholding tax normally applies to dividends as well as to interest, many U.S. treaties exempt interest payments, but not dividends, from the tax.

There is a long history of situations in which the distinction between debt and equity has been the object of challenge by the IRS under what is sometimes referred to as the "thin capitalization doctrine." The following factors, set forth in Section 385 when it was adopted in 1969, were to have been the cornerstone of extended regulations intended to provide additional predictability with respect to the matter:

1. Whether there is a written unconditional promise to pay on demand or on a specified date a sum certain in money in return for an adequate consideration, and to pay a fixed rate of interest;

2. Whether there is subordination to or preference over other indebtedness;

3. The ratio of debt to equity;

4. Whether there is convertibility into the stock of the corporation; and

5. The relationship between debt and stock holdings.

While attempts to issue regulations have failed, the factors set forth in Section 385 and in a plethora of judicial decisions relating to U.S corporations are used to address the same question for foreign investment in the United States.

Should the IRS successfully treat putative "debt" as substantive equity, the usual consequences will obtain. Both the "interest" payments and the repayments of "principal" will be treated as corporate distributions taxable as dividends to the extent that they are deemed to come from earnings and profits. As dividends, they will not be deductible, and the withholding tax of 30 percent (or lower rate mandated by a tax treaty) will apply.

[¶ 4270]

2. "EARNINGS–STRIPPING" PROVISIONS

As indicated in the foregoing section, there are strong tax incentives to use debt to finance foreign investment in the United States. There are limitations on the deductibility of interest payments that may apply even if the debt is not recharacterized as equity under the thin capitalization doctrine. Section 163(j), which is usually referred to as the "earnings-stripping provision," limits the magnitude of interest deductions in certain situations when payments are made to related taxpayers who have no U.S. income tax liability. The limits would, therefore, apply on loans made by foreign shareholders to a corporation in circumstances where a tax treaty exempts interest payments from U.S. withholding tax.

Section 163(j)(1) disallows a deduction for what is labeled "disqualified interest," which is defined as interest paid directly or indirectly to a related person if no U.S. tax is imposed. § 163(j)(3)(A). A related person for purposes of Section 163(j)(4) is any person who is related to the taxpayer within the meaning of Section 267(b) or Section 707(b)(1). The disallowance is limited to the portion of disqualified interest equal to the corporation's "excess interest expense." § 163(j)(1)(A).

"Excess interest expense" is defined as the excess (if any) of the corporation's net interest expense over 50 percent of the corporation's adjusted taxable income (calculated without deductions for interest, net operating losses, depreciation, amortization or depletion) plus any carried-over excess limitation from a prior year. § 163(j)(2)(B). Excess limitation is the excess (if any) in the current year of 50 percent of the corporation's adjusted taxable income over its net interest expense. § 163(j)(2)(B)(iii).

Disallowance of interest deductions under Section 163(j) can occur only if the corporation has both excess interest expense for the year and a debt-equity ratio as of the end of the year that exceeds 1.5 to 1 based on the adjusted basis of assets. § 163(j)(2)(A) and (C).

If the U.S. withholding tax on interest paid by a U.S. corporation to a foreign person is reduced by an applicable tax treaty from 30 percent to a lower rate or to zero, the interest is treated as tax exempt to the extent of the reduction. § 163(j)(5)(B). For example, if the withholding rate is reduced from 30 percent to ten percent, two thirds of the interest payments are treated as exempt.

Foreign corporations that have items of income, gain, loss or deductions that are effectively connected with the conduct of a U.S. trade or business are subject to the earnings-stripping rules in the same manner as U.S. corporations. Proposed regulations under Section 163(j) provide detailed special rules describing how such a corporation is to allocate its debt, equity, income and expenses between its U.S. and foreign businesses for purposes of the earnings-stripping rules. Under the proposed regulations, the amount of interest deemed paid by the U.S. branch of a foreign corporation to a related person includes (1) interest payments reflected on the books of the U.S. branch that are made to a related person and (2) the corporation's "excess interest," as determined for purposes of the branch profits tax. See ¶ 3230 and Prop. Reg. § 1.163(j)–8(d).

"Disqualified interest" includes interest paid to unrelated lenders in respect of loans subject to a "disqualified guarantee" made by a related foreign person in certain situations. § 163(j)(3)(B) and (6)(D). A "disqualified guarantee" encompasses any form of credit support, including a commitment to make a capital contribution to the debtor or otherwise maintain its financial viability, or an arrangement reflected in a "comfort letter," whether or not legally enforceable. Further, if the guarantee is contingent upon the occurrence of an event, the disqualified interest provisions will apply as if the event had occurred. § 163(j)(6)(D)(iii).

The disqualified guarantee rule is subject to two significant exceptions. First, a guarantee is not a disqualified guarantee if the debtor owns a controlling interest (at least 80 percent of the vote and value of a corporation or at least 80 percent of the profits and capital interests of a partnership) in the guarantor. § 163(j)(6)(D)(ii)(II). Second, a guarantee is not a disqualified guarantee if, under certain circumstances to be identified by regulation, the interest on the guaranteed loan would have been subject to a "net-basis" tax rather than a gross withholding tax had it been paid to the related guarantor rather than the unrelated party lender. § 163(j)(6)(D)(ii)(I). This exception will come into play, for example, when the foreign guarantor conducts a U.S. trade or business and interest on a hypothetical loan by the foreign person to the guarantor, similar to the actual guaranteed loan, would have been taxed as income effectively connected with the conduct of that U.S. trade or business.

The operation of Section 163(j) may be demonstrated in a simple example. Suppose that NA Inc. is a U.S. corporation wholly owned by Forco, a foreign corporation. During the tax year, NA Inc. has adjusted taxable income of $1,000, pays interest to Forco of $700 which is exempt from tax by treaty and fails the debt-equity ratio test. NA Inc. has excess interest expense of $200 ($700 interest paid less 50 percent of adjusted taxable income, or $500). Accordingly, NA Inc. may deduct only $500. The remaining $200 of excess interest is carried over as disqualified interest to the ensuing year when its deductibility will depend upon the application of Section 163(j) in that year.

While Section 163(j) may apply to restrict the interest deduction in certain domestic situations such as financial arrangements with exempt organizations, one of the primary targets of the provision was interest paid to foreign investors exploiting treaty benefits. Is Section 163(j) a violation of the nondiscrimination provisions of treaties containing language similar to that set forth in Article 24 of the U.S. Model Treaty?

A number of proposals have been advanced during recent years for strengthening the earnings stripping provisions. Although the focus on these proposals had been magnified by reports that earnings stripping had been used to enlarge the U.S. tax benefits achieved by so-called "corporate inversions," discussed in Chapter 10, Congress did not include any modification of the earnings-stripping rules in the 2004 JOBS Act. However, Section 424 of the Act required that the Treasury "conduct a study of the effectiveness of the provisions" of the Code applicable to earnings stripping which would include the following elements:

1. The effectiveness of section 163(j) in preventing the shifting of income outside the United States;

2. Whether any deficiencies of such provisions place U.S.-based business at a competitive disadvantage relative to foreign-based business;

3. The impact of earnings stripping activities on the U.S. tax base;

4. Whether laws of foreign countries facilitate stripping of earnings out of the United States;

5. Whether changes to the earning stripping rules would affect jobs in the United States.

See U.S. Treas. Dep't, Report to The Congress on Earnings Stripping, Transfer Pricing and U.S. Income Tax Treaties (Nov. 2007).

[¶ 4275]

I. TAX PLANNING CONSIDERATIONS FOR INBOUND TRANSACTIONS

The materials discussed in Chapters 3 and 4, along with the source rules discussed in Chapter 2, together reflect the ways in which foreign persons may be taxed in the United States. The basic elements of the picture obviously derive from the fundamental difference in the methods of taxing investment income and trade or business income. Tax planning for economic activities by foreign individuals and corporations in the United States will often require an analysis of both approaches and a careful evaluation of their comparative costs and advantages.

A foreign corporation considering an investment in a business in the United States can choose either to undertake the U.S. activity through a U.S. branch or to organize a U.S. subsidiary corporation or a foreign subsidiary (that would have a U.S. branch). Although efforts have been made to equalize the U.S. income tax burden with respect to the alternative methods, a number of differences are still possible.

Income realized from transactions by the U.S. branch of a foreign corporation will generally produce effectively connected income that is subject to tax at the normal corporate rates. Moreover, the 30–percent branch profits tax may also apply. See ¶ 3230. When the branch is liquidated and the assets sold, all gains will be effectively connected with the U.S. trade or business and will be taxed accordingly.

The use of a U.S. or foreign subsidiary by a foreign corporation may provide a means of avoiding taxes when and if the U.S. operation is sold or liquidated. In circumstances in which the assets owned by the subsidiary corporation do not consist primarily of U.S. real properties, the sale of stock, whether in a U.S. or a foreign subsidiary, will usually not be taxed. Even if its assets consist primarily of U.S. real property interests, gain on the sale of the stock of a foreign subsidiary will not be taxed by the United States. In either event, however, the value of the shares of the foreign corporation may be diminished by potential U.S. taxes on the eventual disposition of the subsidiary's appreciated assets.

The use of a separate corporation can serve to simplify the analysis of tax consequences. So long as the formalities of corporate separateness are observed, the nature of problems relating to the allocation of income and deductions is somewhat modified. Although use of a separate corporation obviates the need to allocate income and expenses as is required in the case of a branch operation, questions regarding transfer pricing may be raised by the IRS when it appears that prices charged and paid in transactions between related corporations do not reflect fair market values. See generally Chapter 8.

[¶ 4280]

PROBLEMS

The Problems that follow are intended to bring together many of the considerations raised by the materials in this and the prior two chapters. In each instance analyze the result under the usual sources of U.S. income tax law; then, consider whether your answer would be modified if the U.S. Model Treaty were in force with respect to the transaction.

1. Dickens, a citizen and resident of the United Kingdom, occasionally purchases and sells securities on the New York and American Stock Exchanges. He effects his transactions through a stockbroker in New York City, who is instructed by telephone from London. During the tax year, Dickens made 20 purchases and 15 sales. He received dividends during the year of $30,000 from his shares. He realized gains of $200,000 and losses of $100,000 from transactions involving the shares. Dickens wishes to know the extent of any U.S. income tax liability. Advise him.

2. In Problem 1 would Dickens' U.S. taxes be reduced if he had realized losses of $230,000?

3. The broker in Problem 1 has recently suggested that Dickens give him discretionary authority to buy and sell "to exploit fast-breaking market conditions." Would such an arrangement affect your earlier responses?

4. Carlson, a citizen and resident of Denmark, is a commodities dealer operating in Copenhagen. During the tax year, Carlson, by e-mail from her home office, purchased several carloads of wheat. She took title to the wheat in Minneapolis. The wheat was sold to the government of India, FOB New York City, where the wheat was placed aboard a Liberian flag vessel. Carlson has never been to the United States. While she has occasionally purchased U.S. commodities in the past, this is her sole transaction in the United States during the current year. Does she have any potential U.S. income tax liability?

5. Rosario, a corporation organized in Argentina, sells consumer products to retailers in the main cities of that country. Rosario has no office in the United States. Rosario sales representatives in Argentina send orders to a purchasing agent in New York. The purchasing agent purchases the products from U.S. manufacturers in Rosario's name. The products are shipped to Miami and delivered to vessels bound for Argentina. Orders are accepted in Argentina. Title to the goods is transferred to customers at the port of destination. However, the customers have agreed contractually to insure against all losses attributable to shipwreck, fire and accident while the goods

are in transit. The Argentine customers make payment to an account maintained by Rosario in Switzerland. Does Rosario have any liability for U.S. taxes? Would your answer differ if the purchasing agent is properly characterized as an "independent agent"?

6. Empire, Ltd. ("Empire"), is a German corporation engaged in the sale of machinery parts to various customers throughout Europe. For many years Empire purchased the parts from Colonial Ohio Corp. ("Colonial"), an Ohio corporation, in Youngstown, Ohio. Although Empire has no U.S. office, it took title to the parts in Youngstown, transported the parts to Europe and made delivery to its European customers. The two companies are each wholly owned by a Swiss holding company. Does Empire have any U.S. income tax liability? Should the relationship between Empire and Colonial affect the analysis?

7. The method of operation in Problem 6 has recently changed. Empire now arranges sales between Colonial and the European customers. The parts are delivered FOB Youngstown where title passes to the customers, who then pay all shipping costs. Empire receives a 20–percent commission from Colonial whenever customer payments are received. Does Empire have any U.S. income tax liability? Should the prior arrangement between the corporations affect the analysis?

8. Mimi Manon is a well-known soprano from France. While visiting Los Angeles for one week several years ago, Manon made a highly acclaimed recording which broke sales records around the world. Manon has returned to her home in France, where she receives monthly checks equal to ten percent of the gross revenues produced by worldwide record sales in accordance with a written contract between Manon and the U.S. recording company. The contract describes such payments as "royalties." Does Manon have any U.S. income tax liability? Does the recording company have any obligation to withhold?

9. Hawthorne, a U.S. citizen, moved from his home in Connecticut to Peru to accept an important assignment from the South American subsidiary of the U.S. shipping company for which Hawthorne has worked for many years. Hawthorne is committed to a five-year tour of duty in Peru. During his first year in Peru, Hawthorne met and married Anna, a citizen of Peru who had never visited the United States. Since Peru is a community property jurisdiction, Hawthorne takes the position based on early decisions dealing with community property jurisdictions within the United States that half of his income is not subject to U.S. taxes. The IRS disagrees.

Section 879 now provides a clear answer to this case by attributing the income to the spouse rendering the services. How would U.S. tax have been imposed for tax years prior to the effective date of Section 879? While Section 879 was greeted without enthusiasm by Hawthorne, other U.S. citizens were pleased with the amendment. Is there a class of U.S. taxpayers who might have benefitted from the change?

10. Hawthorne has returned to Connecticut, but Anna has remained in Peru. Pursuant to a divorce decree properly entered by a court in Peru, Hawthorne sends Anna $1,000 per month as alimony and $500 per month as

child support. Also, Hawthorne pays interest of $10,000 per year to a small neighborhood bank in Peru on a personal loan. Advise Hawthorne with respect to any liability that he might have to withhold U.S. taxes on any of these payments. How much should Hawthorne withhold when he repays the principal of the loan to the bank?

11. Horatio, a citizen and resident of Ireland, is an equal partner with Imogene, a U.S. citizen, in a consulting firm operating out of a Miami office and serving clients located in Florida. Under the terms of the partnership agreement, Horatio and Imogene are to share equally in profits and losses. During the course of the year, Horatio devotes 100 days to the venture, but works primarily at home in Dublin and communicates with his partner and his clients by telephone, fax and Internet. In fact Horatio is actually in the United States only ten days during the year. During the year the partnership earns net income of $200,000, all of which derives from the provision of consulting services by the partnership to clients in the United States. All of the partnership income is reinvested in the business and none is distributed to the partners. Horatio has no other economic involvement in the United States. To what extent, if at all, will Horatio be subject to U.S. income taxes for the year?

12. Leonardo and Verdi, citizens and residents of Italy, purchased some undeveloped farm land in Iowa for $1 million. They have leased the land to a tenant farmer who completely manages the agricultural use of the land, pays all real estate taxes (which amount to $80,000 annually) and pays an annual rental of $100,000. How should Leonardo and Verdi minimize their U.S. income tax liabilities in respect of the leasehold arrangements?

13. After a number of years Leonardo and Verdi have decided to sell the land and are delighted to have received an offer of $10 million for the property. Will they be taxed on the gain realized from the sale? Could they have avoided U.S. tax on the gain if they had not elected to minimize U.S. taxes in Problem 12?

14. Romano, a citizen and resident of Colombia, invested $6 million in Knickerbocker, a wholly owned U.S. corporation. Knickerbocker acquired an apartment building in New York for $2 million, purchased $2 million of stock in small holdings of publicly traded U.S. companies and invested $2 million in a fancy art gallery operated in rented space on Fifth Avenue that produced no U.S. real property income. Although the art gallery has been subject to an annual lease with no right of renewal, it has been operated at the same location since its establishment. After only five years, Knickerbocker was worth $100 million and Romano has decided to sell the company. Determine how much, if any, of Romano's gain will be subject to U.S. income taxes in the circumstances described below. Assume that the property values indicated in each case represent the maximum values during the five years since Knickerbocker was organized.

a. The apartment building is worth $60 million; the stock is worth $20 million; the gallery assets are worth $20 million.

b. The apartment building is worth $40 million; the stock is worth $40 million; the gallery assets are worth $20 million.

c. The apartment building is worth $40 million; the stock is worth $20 million; the gallery assets are worth $40 million.

d. The apartment building is worth $100 million, but is subject to a mortgage of $80 million which secures loans to Knickerbocker used to finance art inventory purchases and executive bonuses; the stock is worth $40 million; the gallery assets are worth $40 million.

15. If Knickerbocker were a corporation organized in the Cayman Islands, in which of the circumstances described in Problem 14 would Romano be subject to U.S. income tax on the sale of stock in the corporation?

16. Blue Water Resorts Inc. ("Blue Water"), a U.S. corporation whose shares are not publicly traded, operates resort hotels in many countries of the Caribbean, but does not operate in the United States. By the end of Year 1, Blue Water owned real property in various other countries with an adjusted basis of $10,000,000 and a value of $30,000,000. In Year 2, Blue Water acquired American Paradise Co. ("Paradise"), a Bahamas corporation that operated resort properties in Florida. In fact all of the assets of Paradise consisted of real property in the United States. The value of the Paradise real property, which was also the purchase price paid by Blue Water for the stock, was $40,000,000, but the adjusted basis of the real property to Paradise was only $5,000,000. In early Year 3, Casino, a nonresident alien of the United States, realized a profit of $1,000,000 from the sale of shares in Blue Water. Is the gain realized by Casino subject to U.S. income tax?

17. American Products, Inc. ("American") is a U.S. corporation that is wholly owned by International Investors, Ltd. ("IIL"), a Swiss corporation. The net worth of American at the end of its first year of operation, based upon the adjusted basis of its assets, is $1,000,000. At the beginning of the year, IIL loaned American $2,800,000 for five years at an annual interest rate of ten percent. American paid interest of $280,000 during the year which, because of the tax treaty in force between the United States and Switzerland, was not subject to a U.S. withholding tax. No principal payments were made during the year. American's net income for U.S. tax purposes for the year (which was reduced by depreciation deductions of $20,000 and the interest payment as well as other allowable deductions) is $200,000. American has no interest income and no interest expense other than the payment to IIL. What is the effect of the provisions of Section 163(j) on American's taxable income for the year?

18. The U.S. Treasury is concerned with the international implications of increasing electronic commerce. It has retained you to consider issues relating to the U.S. taxation of foreign persons. In particular you have been asked what, if any, special source rules are necessary for electronic commerce and whether there are criteria for increasing the predictability of when penetration of the U.S. market by electronic commerce will and should constitute a U.S. trade or business. In connection with the second issue, you have been asked whether it is justifiable to conclude that a U.S. trade or

business is being conducted because of a web site using a server in the United States if there are no other manifestations of a presence in this country. Prepare a report explaining your conclusions.

[¶ 4285]

J. TAX PLANNING PROBLEMS

The following problem situations present an opportunity to address many of the issues raised in Chapters 1 through 4 from the perspective of counsel endeavoring to assist a client by organizing affairs in a way that minimizes income tax burdens.

1. Ricardo Moreno, a practicing attorney and financial adviser, is a citizen and resident of Colombia. Moreno represents a group of extremely wealthy citizens of Latin American countries who have sought his legal and financial advice. They seek forms of investment that would be relatively safe from political risk.

Moreno has proposed that members of the group invest in real estate in the United States. His plan is based on the organization of a corporation in Panama ("PANCO") that would be exempt from Panamanian income taxes for income earned outside of Panama. His clients would buy stock in PANCO. PANCO would in turn invest in real estate ventures, either directly or through other corporations engaged in real estate activities, in the United States.

Moreno proposes that PANCO be organized and operated by a service company to be established in another tax haven jurisdiction, the Cayman Islands ("CAYCO"). CAYCO, which will be owned solely by Moreno, would be responsible for effecting transactions in the stock of PANCO and for making investment decisions on the part of PANCO. CAYCO would be paid commissions by PANCO for performing both services. The amount of the commissions would be based on the magnitude of new investment by PANCO and by the rate of earnings generated by the investment decisions that are made.

Sometimes PANCO would purchase stocks or bonds of publicly traded real estate companies. In that event CAYCO would implement its investment decisions on behalf of PANCO by directing orders to a New York brokerage house, which would execute purchases and sales for the account of PANCO. PANCO would obtain direct title for the new real estate ventures that it undertakes.

Moreno has been told "by someone at a cocktail party" that there is no U.S. tax on non-U.S.-source income and that capital gains will not be taxed even if they arise from U.S. sources. Accordingly, he is convinced that neither PANCO nor CAYCO need bear any U.S. income tax liability. He would, however, like to have you confirm these conclusions or indicate any problems that might arise in achieving a tax-free operation. There is no tax treaty in force between the United States and either Colombia, Panama or the Cayman Islands.

2. Abdul Ibrahim, a citizen and resident of Nigeria, owns a Nigerian corporation that produces jute. Ibrahim sat next to a senior partner of your firm on a recent transatlantic flight and learned that your firm is proud of its expertise in the taxation of international trade and investment. Ibrahim, impressed with what he learned, told your senior partner that he wishes to use some of the jute produced in Nigeria to manufacture carpeting in factories to be operated in the southeastern part of the United States. Ibrahim has arranged to visit your firm next week to discuss the best way of structuring his U.S. operation. Your senior partner has asked you to be responsible for the meeting. You should begin to prepare by listing the questions that you would like to ask Ibrahim about his plans, hopes and expectations.

3. Assume that your meeting with Ibrahim has taken place and that you have learned some additional information about his plans that may be relevant to your development of an appropriate legal structure to advance his interests.

Ibrahim has indicated that he expects to invest $5 million in the U.S. operation. He does not intend to purchase any real estate because of the costs involved, and has found a suitable site available for leasing. The $5 million is necessary to meet startup costs and to cover any losses that might occur during the first year or two of operation. While he is not totally confident in his predictions, he believes that the U.S. operation will turn a profit of $2 million annually, beginning in the third year of operation. After that point, Ibrahim believes that he will need to reinvest about $1 million in the expansion of the U.S. operation. He expects to invest the remaining profits by purchasing stocks and bonds in Europe, Asia and the United States.

Unless there are adverse tax consequences, Ibrahim would like to spend as much time as possible each year in the United States and intends to travel on a nonimmigrant visa that will allow him to make multiple trips into the country to deal with business matters. He believes in the stability of the U.S. government and economy and would like to reinvest at least half of the profits of the U.S. operation in this country.

Ibrahim will be coming today for his second meeting. Be prepared to advise him with respect to the U.S. income tax aspects of his business and personal plans.

K. SOME REFLECTIONS ON THE TAXATION OF FOREIGN PERSONS

[¶ 4290]

1. GENERAL CONSIDERATIONS

The materials in Chapters 2, 3 and 4 together reflect the extent to which foreign persons will be liable for U.S. income taxes. The appropriateness of these provisions is subject to almost constant debate. One view is that the taxing regimes in place in the United States effectively deter foreign investors from coming into the U.S. economy. Advocates of this view urge that taxes be reduced to provide foreign investors an additional incentive to invest in the United States and generate the economic advantages of increased investment.

The extent to which such tax reductions would in fact increase foreign investment is rather difficult to estimate. Other factors, such as the value of the U.S. dollar, the availability of financial services, the quality of the labor force and posture of industrial relations and perceptions of risk of loss from political actions, are also very important to an investor considering investment alternatives among competing countries. There is, moreover, the usual difficulty of devising a tax incentive that does not begin by subsidizing many investors for doing exactly what they would have done even if the incentive had not been established.

Another view of U.S. practice is that the tax burdens imposed on foreign investors have been too low and have created a tilted "playing field" favoring foreign interests at the expense of domestic enterprise, thereby compromising the achievement of capital-import neutrality. Capital gains, even from U.S. sources, have historically not usually been taxed unless they have been effectively connected with a U.S. trade or business. Moreover, the source rules have been modified during recent years so that gain realized by foreign persons from the sale of investments in U.S. corporations will usually not be treated as U.S.-source income. Treaty provisions have been used to reduce or eliminate taxes imposed by the statutory regime.

The perception that some foreign persons may be undertaxed in the United States led to the adoption of Section 897 in 1980. Other proposals to increase the tax burden on foreign investors by taxing additional capital gains from U.S. investments have not been adopted. Should any U.S.-source income go untaxed? Should profits from dealing in U.S. stocks and securities be included as U.S.-source income and be taxed? Are the answers to these questions affected by whether new foreign investment in the United States exceeds new investment abroad by U.S. investors, thereby helping to offset the U.S. international trade deficit? In the light of rapidly changing economic circumstances and the realities of ongoing budget debates, it is unlikely that such questions have yet been put to rest by the legislative process.

In some cases foreign persons have been saved from potential tax. The safe harbor provisions invite foreign investors to trade in U.S. stocks and commodities using U.S. brokers without risk of U.S. tax on gains. The portfolio interest exemption was established in part to reduce the cost of borrowing to U.S. corporations. If such measures reflect sound economic policy, should they be expanded by exempting other forms of income derived by foreign persons from the U.S. economy?

Another question is presented by the decision to reduce dramatically the application of the force-of-attraction principle. The effect is to subject some foreign taxpayers to both of the taxing regimes. It is likely, though not certain, that the U.S. taxes of such foreign taxpayers are higher than if the force-of-attraction principle had been retained. Such a result could derive from several factors. Items of U.S.-source FDAP income are subject to a gross income tax of 30 percent rather than a tax on net income at possibly lower or only slightly higher rates. Further, losses that might be realized from the operation of a U.S. trade or business do not reduce the amount of unconnected FDAP income subject to tax. Recall that the rationale for the withholding tax on gross income is based upon a desire to assure that the tax is collected from foreign persons who may have no assets in the United States. The withholding technique is not generally applied to income deriving from a U.S. trade or business because of the substantial likelihood that there are identifiable properties within the country connected with the trade or business that would be subject to IRS collection efforts if tax liabilities are not satisfied. If the foreign person has such properties in the United States, is there a sound policy reason for continuing to impose a gross income tax on any element of U.S.-source income?

Are the rules sufficiently clear to allow foreign investors to understand in advance the exact U.S. tax liabilities that may arise from business activities or investment in the U.S. economy? The question of when business activities are sufficient to establish a U.S. trade or business may be particularly difficult to answer. Treaties substitute the more concrete test of a "permanent establishment" before tax liabilities accrue. If the standard is widely accepted and if predictability could be enhanced, should the permanent establishment standard be enacted for all taxpayers?

As reflected in the foregoing discussion, considerations of horizontal equity are invoked with respect to many of the issues raised by the rules for taxing foreign persons. Note that it is very difficult, perhaps even impossible, to apply the considerations characterized as vertical equity. In addition to the usual issues arising because corporate income taxes are effectively borne by many taxpayers having different incomes, only a portion of income received by nonresident aliens and foreign corporations usually comes within the taxing jurisdiction of the United States.

[¶ 4295]

2. TREATY ISSUES

Both treaty parties are generally entitled under applicable norms of international law to tax the income from the transactions addressed by the terms of the treaty. The tax imposed by one party is usually based on the fact that the income is derived from transactions that occurred, or from property that is located, within the country. The tax imposed by the other is based on the residence or nationality of the taxpayer. While protecting against double taxation as a general rule, the provisions of the treaties dealing with FDAP income and certain compensation reflect a preference for the country asserting a tax on the basis of nationality or residence. The substitution of the permanent establishment provisions for the trade or business tests also limits taxes payable to the country in which income is sourced.

This should be distinguished from the result that obtains because of the operation of the foreign tax credit, as reflected in Chapters 5 and 7, by which the country of residence effectively cedes primary taxing power to the country of source. Is there a rational basis for selecting between the two jurisdictional rationales?

The answer to the question may not matter very much to the governments of the treaty partners so long as there is true reciprocity, not only in the terms of the treaty, but in the economic effects of those provisions. If both treaty parties forego approximately the same amount of tax revenues, each will benefit accordingly. Should the Treasury Department suspend or terminate treaties in circumstances in which they produce net revenue losses over time to the United States? If not, why not?

The assumption of reciprocal costs and benefits is unlikely to obtain in relations between rich and poor countries. Waiving the right to tax income according to source, for example, reduces the taxes collected from foreign investors. It is almost certain that the amount of foreign investment from the rich to the poor country will substantially exceed investment flow in the opposite direction. The reciprocal application of treaty provisions in such a case obviously does not produce a reciprocal result. The poor country will be giving up much more badly needed tax revenue than the wealthy country. What treaty provisions should be devised to create true reciprocity? Because of these considerations, the United Nations has developed a different model treaty for use between developed and developing nations.

There is, nevertheless, an obvious advantage of treaty relationships for developing countries that have difficulty in applying their tax laws to multinational enterprises. The provisions for cooperation in tax administration and the sharing of taxpayer information can be particularly valuable in such situations.

The present Treasury approach to tax treaties with developing countries is to soften the provisions that limit source country taxing jurisdiction. In the permanent establishment provisions, the time limit for a construction site or installation project to be considered a permanent establishment may be made shorter than in developed country treaties. Perhaps a more important softening may come in the so-called "force-of-attraction" principle. Virtually all U.S. treaties since the early 1960s have limited the taxation of business profits to those attributable to a permanent establishment. A full force-of-attraction principle, suggested by some developing countries, would allow taxation of all domestic-source income of the enterprise by a country in which the enterprise had a permanent establishment—whether or not the income was actually attributable to the permanent establishment.

Treaties with developing countries may allow higher withholding rates on dividends, interest and royalties than do treaties with wealthier countries. As to royalties, both the OECD and the Treasury models specify exclusive royalty taxation in the country of residence, and almost all U.S. treaties with developed countries so provide. The treaties with developing countries, on the other hand, tend to allow withholding on royalties by the source state. This practice is reflected in the terms of the United States–India Tax Treaty, which provides for withholding rates of 15–20 percent on dividends (Article 10), 10–15 percent on interest (Article 11) and 15–20 percent on royalties (Article 12).

[¶ 4300]

3. REPRISE: INDUSTRIA REVISITED

In Chapter 1, before being tainted with information about the evolution of U.S. tax policy and practice, you were asked to design a system for taxing the income of "outsiders" to Industria. See ¶ 1030. Has the United States created a good prototype for your system? In what ways would you modify U.S. practice if you were in fact reporting to the Government of Industria?

CHAPTER 5

INTRODUCTION TO OUTBOUND INTERNATIONAL TAXATION; THE FOREIGN TAX CREDIT AND OTHER METHODS FOR MITIGATING THE DOUBLE TAXATION OF U.S. PERSONS

■ ■ ■

[¶ 5000]

A. INTRODUCTION

As discussed in Chapter 1, the United States generally taxes U.S. persons, including U.S. corporations, on their worldwide incomes at the usual tax rates set forth in Sections 1 and 11, subject to a foreign tax credit for creditable foreign taxes. However, as discussed below and later in this Chapter, the Code contains several exceptions to this principle. Under one such exception in Section 911, if certain requirements are met, a U.S. individual may elect to exclude a limited amount of foreign compensation income from gross income, without regard to whether a foreign country chooses to tax such income.[1]

Decision whether to use a branch or a foreign subsidiary to conduct business abroad. One of the key decisions for a U.S. corpora-

1. The 2004 JOBS Act created another exception to this principle for the shipping industry, providing a new elective, preferential tax regime for U.S. and foreign corporations with respect to their qualifying international shipping income. See §§ 1352–1359. If a corporation so elects, the corporation will pay tax at the maximum corporate tax rate on its "notional shipping income," which is based on the net tonnage of the corporation's qualifying vessels (i.e., vessels documented under U.S. law and used exclusively in transporting goods or passengers between a place in the United States and a foreign place or between foreign places). This special regime, if elected, takes the place of the normal corporate tax that would be imposed on the electing taxpayer's actual international shipping income. Because an electing taxpayer's notional shipping income will normally be less than the taxpayer's qualifying international shipping income, this regime has the effect of providing a partial exclusion from U.S. tax for such income. No deductions or credits are allowed with respect to income that is taxed under this regime. An electing corporation pays its usual corporate income tax on the remaining portion of its taxable income that does not fall within this alternative tax regime (or, in the case of a foreign corporation, the remaining portion of its taxable income that is subject to U.S. tax under Sections 881 and 882).

tion that is planning to conduct business abroad is whether to use an unincorporated branch or a foreign subsidiary to conduct the foreign business. There are numerous nontax factors that affect this decision, including various foreign investment laws that may favor use of a local country subsidiary and the fact that a foreign subsidiary may provide the U.S. parent corporation with limited liability concerning the subsidiary's activities. There are various tax factors that affect this decision as well.

One important tax factor is the phenomenon of international tax deferral. If a U.S. person uses a foreign subsidiary to conduct business abroad and does not run afoul of the anti-deferral regimes discussed in Chapter 6, the foreign earnings of the subsidiary will not be subject to U.S. tax (i.e., the U.S. tax is "deferred") unless and until they are distributed to the U.S. parent corporation as a dividend or the U.S. parent corporation sells its stock in the foreign subsidiary. By contrast, the foreign earnings of an unincorporated branch are treated as the income of the U.S. corporation (since the branch is not a separate taxpayer for U.S. tax purposes) and current U.S. tax is imposed on such earnings, but with a foreign tax credit for any creditable foreign taxes imposed on such income. The availability of deferral with respect to foreign-source income earned through a foreign subsidiary is obviously most important in low-tax or no-tax foreign countries, because the amount of residual U.S. income tax that is deferred is greater. By contrast, if the U.S. person will be conducting operations in high-tax foreign countries, then there is little or no U.S. residual tax to be deferred since the foreign tax credit for the foreign country's taxes will offset the U.S. income tax on the foreign-source income.

Another important tax factor is the ability of the taxpayer to deduct currently losses incurred in the international business or investment activity. If the U.S. corporate taxpayer anticipates that deductible expenses will exceed the gross income from the international venture, then the taxpayer may choose to use a branch, rather than a subsidiary, at least for the early years of the venture. The losses of a taxpayer's branch operation are deductible on the taxpayer's own tax return because the branch is not treated as a separate taxpayer for U.S. tax purposes. By contrast, the losses of a taxpayer's foreign subsidiary may not be deducted by the taxpayer because the subsidiary is treated as a separate taxpayer. Note that if a U.S. taxpayer uses a branch to conduct foreign business operations when the operations are producing deductible losses and then switches to a foreign subsidiary form of doing business when the income exceeds the deductible expenses from operations, the branch loss recapture rules in Section 367(a)(3)(C) may require the taxpayer to report taxable gain on its transfer of the branch assets to the foreign subsidiary to the extent of the prior branch losses deducted. See ¶ 10,095.

There are many other tax and nontax factors that are relevant to the branch-versus-subsidiary decision. These factors are discussed in Chapter 13.

Foreign tax credit regime in U.S. law and the alternative methods of mitigating international double taxation. The exercise of taxing jurisdiction by the nations of the world inevitably raises the issue of double taxation of income generated by international transactions. The issue of double taxation is generally regarded as the most pervasive and challenging problem in international taxation. Virtually all countries tax on the bases of territorial source and residence. Many, including the United States, also tax on the basis of nationality of a corporation, frequently the country under the laws of which the corporation is incorporated. The United States is one of the very few countries that also taxes individuals on the basis of their citizenship, regardless of their place of residence or domicile. The United States generally taxes the worldwide income of U.S. citizens, resident aliens and corporations, including income from foreign sources. Accordingly, it is very common for two countries to tax the same income, one on the basis of source, the other on the basis of residence or nationality.

Without some adjustment, the assertion of concurrent taxing jurisdiction by two countries would greatly inhibit international investment, technology transfer and other transactions. As discussed in Chapter 1, there are a number of approaches to mitigating the impact of international double taxation. One unilateral approach, advanced by proponents of the national neutrality standard for analyzing international tax rules, is to allow only a deduction for foreign taxes imposed by the country of source. The premise underlying this approach is that foreign taxes are merely a cost of a taxpayer's choosing to do business in another country. However, since a deduction only generates tax savings equal to the taxpayer's tax rate multiplied by the amount of the deduction, the deduction method will mitigate, but not eliminate, double taxation. Thus, under the deduction approach, a potential tax disincentive to engaging in international transactions continues to exist. The United States generally does not favor this remedy for the double taxation problem, although it has adopted this approach in a number of limited circumstances.

A second unilateral approach is for the country of residence to grant a dollar-for-dollar credit against the tax it would otherwise impose for each dollar of source country tax that has been paid on the income earned there. Under this foreign tax credit approach, if the country of source tax is not more than the country of residence tax, the effective overall tax burden after the foreign tax credit is equal to the country of residence tax. This approach to mitigating international double taxation is the unilateral approach generally favored by the United States and by proponents of the capital-export neutrality standard for analyzing international tax rules. The taxpayer's decision whether to invest in the United States or abroad is not affected by income tax considerations because the taxpayer pays the same total (U.S. and foreign) income tax regardless of the source of income. Note, however, that to fully implement capital-export neutrality, the United States would have to allow a foreign tax credit for all foreign income taxes, even those in excess of the U.S. rate of tax on the foreign income, which effectively would allow the foreign tax credit to offset U.S. taxes on U.S.-source income. The United States, however, limits the foreign tax credit to the U.S. tax (before credit) on the taxpayer's foreign-source income because the credit is intended only to mitigate double taxation. Once the U.S. tax on foreign-source income has been eliminated, there can be no "double" tax.

A third unilateral approach is for the country of residence to adopt a territorial or exemption system of taxation and exempt foreign-source income from its tax. Under the exemption approach, there is no double taxation because only the country of source imposes tax. Proponents of this approach, adopting the capital-import neutrality standard for evaluating international tax rules, and, more recently, the capital-ownership neutrality standard, argue that it is the most efficient method of taxing international transactions because it enhances the ability of citizens, residents and corporations of the country of residence to compete in the country of source. Moreover, proponents of this approach argue that it is simpler than other approaches, such as the foreign tax credit, which require complex definitional rules and limitation rules. The extent of that alleged simplicity may be illusory, however, because the exemption approach places great pressure on both the source-of-income rules (discussed in Chapter 2) and the transfer pricing rules (discussed in Chapter 8), two areas of tremendous complexity. Under an exemption system, a taxpayer has an incentive to engage in tax planning maneuvers that change the source of income to a low-tax foreign jurisdiction (and thereby eliminate any tax in the residence country) and to shift income to low-tax foreign jurisdictions by selling goods and services and transferring technology at artificially low transfer prices to foreign subsidiaries formed in tax haven countries. Furthermore, if the country of source imposes no taxes or only very low taxes, then the exemption approach creates a tax incentive for taxpayers to locate their investments and business activities abroad at the expense of the domestic economy and worldwide economic efficiency. Consequently, to date, the United States uses or has used this approach in only a limited number of situations, including the foreign earned income exclusion for individuals under Section 911 and the special provisions relating to Puerto Rico and other U.S. possessions under Sections 931 through 936.[2] In recent years, however, the capital-import neutrality and capital-ownership neutrality proponents have had the ear of Congress and various commentators have characterized the enactment of the 2004 JOBS Act, with its weakening of the foreign tax credit limitations, as a significant U.S. tax policy shift in the direction of capital-import neutrality. In addition, in recent years, the Joint Committee Staff and President Bush's

2. Although Section 936 was structured as a tax credit, rather than an exclusion or exemption, it had the same effect as an exclusion or exemption—it eliminated the U.S. tax that would otherwise be owed on certain qualifying income earned in U.S. possessions and Puerto Rico. In 1996, Congress repealed the Section 936 credit for new claimants and phased out the credit for existing claimants over a ten-year period.

Advisory Panel on Federal Tax Reform have developed serious exemption proposals and the fact that major trading partners of the United States (i.e., Australia, Canada, Japan and the United Kingdom) have recently adopted territorial systems has increased the pressure on the U.S. Congress and the Executive Branch to seriously consider such proposals (notwithstanding their deficiencies noted above).

As discussed earlier in this book, a fourth, bilateral device for mitigating international double taxation is the income tax treaty. The primary purpose of a tax treaty is to provide relief from double taxation of income from international transactions. All tax treaties concluded between the United States and another country contain a reciprocal agreement to mitigate double taxation by reducing or eliminating the tax otherwise imposed by the source country on specified types of income realized by a resident (which may include a citizen and domestic corporation) of the other treaty partner. As a result of the saving clause that is found in all modern U.S. treaties, the United States reserves the right to tax U.S. citizens, residents and corporations as if the treaty did not exist. Thus, tax treaties generally do not reduce a U.S. person's U.S. taxes on income from international transactions (except to the extent that the treaty allows a credit for foreign taxes that otherwise would not meet the U.S. tax rules for creditable taxes or in certain other limited ways discussed at ¶ 5380). Instead, a tax treaty mitigates international double taxation on a U.S. person by reducing or eliminating the foreign treaty partner's taxes on certain income earned by the U.S. person from sources in the foreign treaty country.

The remainder of this Chapter first examines the features of the foreign tax credit system. This discussion includes consideration of who may qualify to use foreign tax credits, the requirements that must be met by a foreign levy to qualify as a creditable tax for purposes of the foreign tax credit and certain foreign levies presenting special problems. Also included in these materials is a discussion of the "indirect" credit under Section 902 (available to a U.S. corporation owning at least ten percent of the voting stock of a foreign corporation for foreign taxes paid by the foreign corporation) and an introduction to the foreign tax credit limitations in Section 904. (A more detailed examination of the foreign tax credit limitations is deferred until Chapter 7 because they rely heavily on definitions in the controlled foreign corporation provisions discussed in Chapter 6.) This Chapter then considers an example of the exemption approach used in U.S. tax law to mitigate international double taxation—Section 911, which excludes from gross income a portion of certain U.S. individual taxpayers' foreign compensation income. This Chapter concludes with an examination of the role of tax treaties in mitigating the double taxation burden of U.S. persons.

[¶ 5005]

B. THE FOREIGN TAX CREDIT: OVERVIEW

As discussed throughout this book, a fundamental principle of the U.S. international tax system is that the United States taxes U.S. citizens, resident aliens and corporations on worldwide income. Although such an extraterritorial extension of taxing jurisdiction is consistent with international norms, it has the consequence of subjecting U.S. persons to potential double taxation on foreign-source income—once by the country of source (which has primary jurisdiction to tax under international norms) and once by the United States as the country of residence or nationality. Without an appropriate adjustment, such double taxation would seriously inhibit international trade and investment. Although there are a number of devices for mitigating this double taxation burden, the primary unilateral device used by the United States is the foreign tax credit, which has been part of the U.S. tax law since 1918.[3] In concept, the foreign tax credit is simple: the country of residence or nationality allows a dollar-for-dollar credit against its taxes for income taxes paid to the country of source, thus acknowledging that primary taxing jurisdiction over the foreign income lies with the country of source.

Suppose Acme Shoes ("Acme"), a Delaware corporation, which typically earns $10 million a year in the United States, established a branch operation (not a subsidiary) in Mexico. In year 1, the branch earned $1 million and Acme paid a 30–percent Mexican income tax, or $300,000, on the branch's Mexican income. Acme, as a U.S. corporation, is taxable in the United States on its worldwide income. Assuming a 35–percent U.S. tax rate, Acme's U.S. tax bill before credit would be $3,850,000 ([$10 million U.S. income + $1 million Mexican income] × 35 percent). However, under Section 901, Acme would be allowed a credit for the Mexican income tax of $300,000, which would reduce the U.S. tax to $3,550,000. In the language of international tax, this credit is called the "direct credit" because the U.S. taxpayer (Acme) itself paid the Mexican tax that gives rise to the credit.

Notice that, in effect, Acme has paid $350,000 total tax on its Mexican income ($300,000 to Mexico and $50,000 to the United States). (In tax parlance, the United States collects a residual tax of $50,000 on Acme's foreign-source income.) This total rate, 35 percent, matches exactly the higher rate of the two countries. Most policy analysts would say that this is the way the foreign tax credit should work; it should eliminate double taxation but should not lower the overall rate below that of either one of the countries involved.

3. The taxpayer may elect annually between a credit under Sections 27 and 901 or a deduction under Section 164 for all creditable foreign income taxes. But a deduction is preferable only in unusual cases. See ¶ 5275.

In this simple example, in which Acme conducted its foreign operations through an unincorporated branch, achieving this goal was straightforward and obvious. But, as discussed below, it is not always so. Should a credit be available, for example, if Acme had run its Mexican operation through a wholly owned Mexican subsidiary, which, in year 1, had paid a dividend to Acme of $700,000? The answer is not obvious. On the one hand, the Mexican subsidiary is a separate foreign taxpayer not subject to U.S. tax because it has no U.S.-source income and is not conducting a U.S. trade or business. Moreover, Acme is not normally subject to U.S. tax on the foreign earnings of its Mexican subsidiary until those earnings are repatriated through distributions or otherwise. On the other hand, a failure to provide the U.S. parent corporation with any foreign tax credit for foreign taxes paid by its Mexican subsidiary would lead to a serious tax disparity in the treatment of foreign branches and foreign subsidiaries.

huh?

The answer devised by Congress in 1918 and modified many times since involves an "indirect" or "deemed paid" foreign tax credit for the U.S. parent corporation under Section 902. When the subsidiary's earnings are distributed to the U.S. parent as a dividend and a U.S. tax liability arises for the first time, Section 902 treats the U.S. parent corporation as if it had paid a share of the foreign taxes actually paid by the foreign subsidiary. Sections 901 and 27 then allow the U.S. parent corporation to obtain a foreign tax credit for such taxes, subject to the limitations in Section 904. This provision is designed to achieve rough parity of treatment, for foreign tax credit purposes, between U.S. corporations operating abroad through foreign subsidiaries and those operating abroad through unincorporated foreign branches.[4] A U.S. corporation will be eligible to claim an indirect credit if it owns at least ten percent of the foreign corporation's voting stock.

[¶ 5010]

C. TAXPAYERS THAT MAY USE FOREIGN TAX CREDITS

The primary beneficiaries of the direct credit are U.S. citizens, corporations and resident aliens.[5] § 901(a)-(c). The direct credit is available only for foreign income taxes paid or accrued directly by the taxpayer.

---

4. In fact, because the U.S. parent corporation has both the benefit of deferral of U.S. tax on the foreign earnings of its foreign subsidiary and the availability of an indirect foreign tax credit under Section 902 if and when those earnings are distributed to it, something better than tax parity is accorded to the U.S. corporation conducting foreign operations through a foreign subsidiary.

5. However, under Section 901(c), the foreign tax credit is not available to a resident alien in certain cases in which the resident alien's country of citizenship refuses like treatment to U.S. citizens. Nonresident alien individuals and foreign corporations may also use the direct credit under certain limited circumstances. §§ 901(b)(4) and 906, discussed at ¶ 3135. Further, in the case of a nonresident alien taxpayer who was a former U.S. citizen or resident alien and who was subject to U.S. tax under Section 877 (see ¶ 1195), Section 877(b) allowed the taxpayer a foreign

As illustrated in the Acme example above, the result of the direct credit is that the taxpayer effectively bears the burden of only a single income tax: the higher of the foreign tax or the U.S. tax on the income concerned. The basic operation of the direct credit is simple. It principally applies in four situations:

1. ***The corporate branch.*** When a U.S. corporation conducts its business in a foreign country directly (rather than through a foreign corporation), it is said to have a branch. Foreign income taxes incurred by the branch are, of course, paid directly by the U.S. corporation and therefore qualify for the direct credit.

2. ***Individual earnings.*** Individual U.S. citizens or resident aliens who earn income abroad and pay foreign income taxes may credit those taxes against their U.S. income tax.

3. ***Withholding taxes.*** Both individuals and corporations may pay withholding taxes to foreign countries on dividends, interest, royalties and certain other payments of income sourced in the taxing country. These taxes are normally creditable by the recipient of the payment if they qualify as creditable taxes. In some cases, however, the foreign withholding provisions have been such that it was not clear whether the tax was borne by the foreign payor or the U.S. recipient. And since the direct credit is available only to taxpayers who have borne the tax, the credit has sometimes been lost. Biddle v. Commissioner, 302 U.S. 573 (1938); cf. *Nissho Iwai American Corp. v. Commissioner*, at ¶ 5115. Today the language of withholding provisions usually makes clear that although the payor withholds the tax from the payment and pays it to the foreign tax authority, the withholding is for the account of and on behalf of the payee and, therefore, the direct credit is available. In this context, the payee is the "taxpayer" and is entitled to take the foreign tax credit for the withholding taxes under what is sometimes called the "technical taxpayer rule." See Reg. § 1.901–2(f).

4. ***Earnings through a partnership or S corporation.*** U.S. citizens, resident aliens and corporations that earn income abroad through an ownership interest in an entity treated as a partnership for federal income tax purposes (including a limited liability company treated as a partnership for federal tax purposes) may claim a direct credit for their distributive shares of the foreign income taxes paid by the entity. Similarly, U.S. citizens and resident aliens who earn income abroad through a stock interest in a Subchapter S corporation may claim a direct credit for their pro rata shares of the foreign income taxes paid by the S corporation. A partnership or S corporation is not a taxpaying entity for federal income tax purposes (with certain exceptions, in the case of an S corporation). Instead, the partnership's or S corporation's income, expenses and creditable

tax credit for qualifying foreign taxes paid on income that was subject to U.S. tax solely by reason of Section 877.

foreign taxes flow through to the owners of the entity (i.e., the partners of the partnership or the shareholders of the S corporation).

Earnings through a foreign subsidiary. As mentioned above, in addition to the direct credit available to the foreign branch operation, Section 902 allows an indirect credit to a U.S. corporation owning at least ten percent of the voting stock of a foreign corporation and receiving dividends from the foreign corporation. Section 902 treats the U.S. corporation as if it had paid the same proportion of the foreign corporation's foreign income taxes as the amount of the dividend bears to the foreign corporation's undistributed earnings. See ¶¶ 5135 et seq.

Earnings through a "hybrid entity." As discussed at ¶ 4102, a hybrid entity is an entity that is treated as a corporation for U.S. tax purposes and as a fiscally transparent entity or a non-entity (often referred to as a "disregarded entity") for foreign tax purposes, or vice versa. Although hybrid entities have been part of international transactions for many years, the check-the-box entity classification regulations, discussed in Chapters 1 and 13, have made the creation of such entities much easier. Under the current entity classification rules of U.S. law, a taxpayer generally can elect whether to treat an entity as a corporation or a fiscally transparent entity, unless the entity is a "per se" corporation under the regulations that is required to be treated as a corporation for U.S. tax purposes.

Under the "technical taxpayer rule" in Reg. § 1.901–2(f)(1), the taxpayer "on whom foreign law imposes legal liability" for a foreign tax is treated as paying the foreign tax for foreign tax credit purposes, even if another party remits such tax to the foreign country. This has led to some tax planning devices in which a U.S. taxpayer conducts business abroad through a reverse hybrid foreign entity—a foreign entity that the taxpayer elects to treat as a corporation for U.S. tax purposes but that is treated as a fiscally transparent entity for foreign tax law purposes. Under the foreign tax law, therefore, the income of the entity is treated as the income of the U.S. taxpayer and the U.S. taxpayer has the legal liability for the foreign taxes on such income. For U.S. tax purposes, however, the foreign corporation is treated as a separate entity earning the income and since it is a foreign taxpayer, U.S. tax on such income is deferred until such income is distributed as a dividend to the U.S. taxpayer or the U.S. taxpayer sells its ownership interest in the foreign corporation. Yet, the U.S. taxpayer will receive a direct foreign tax credit under Section 901 for the foreign taxes on such income because the U.S. taxpayer has legal liability for such taxes under the technical taxpayer rule. The income is, thus, separated from the foreign taxes for U.S. tax purposes and the credit for such taxes is accelerated and can be used to offset the U.S. residual tax on other low-taxed foreign income of the U.S. taxpayer.[6] This can be

6. This technique of offsetting foreign tax credits arising from one type of foreign income against the residual U.S. tax on low-taxed foreign income of a different type is often referred to as "cross-crediting." It is discussed in more detail later in this Chapter and in Chapter 7.

viewed as another example of the cross-border tax arbitrage problem that has been discussed at various points throughout this book.

Example. Cathy, a U.S. citizen, has $1,000 of foreign-source business income that is subject to no foreign tax in Country A, the low-tax country in which it is earned. Assuming that Cathy has paid no foreign taxes on any other income and assuming a 35–percent U.S. tax rate on Cathy's income, Cathy will owe $350 of U.S. income tax on the $1,000 of foreign-source income. However, suppose that Cathy also owns all of the equity interests in a foreign entity that is treated as fiscally transparent for foreign tax purposes (under the laws of Country B, the jurisdiction in which the entity is organized) but that Cathy elects to treat as a foreign corporation for U.S. tax purposes—a so-called reverse hybrid entity. The entity earns $1,000 of foreign business income, which is subject to a foreign tax of $350 (i.e., a 35 percent tax). Under the tax law of Country B, Cathy is treated as legally liable for the tax on the income of the fiscally transparent entity and, under the technical taxpayer rule in the U.S. tax regulations, Cathy is treated as paying $350 of foreign taxes for Section 901 purposes. However, the entity's $1,000 of income is the income of the foreign corporation, a separate taxpayer for U.S. tax purposes, not Cathy's income. So Cathy may credit the $350 of foreign taxes imposed on the entity's Country B income against the U.S. residual tax of $350 on the $1,000 of foreign business income in Country A, thus eliminating the U.S. tax on such income. However, regulations proposed in 2006 (if adopted as final regulations) and Section 909, enacted in 2010 and discussed below, would use different approaches to change the result in this Example. Because this Example involves a foreign tax credit splitting event in which the foreign income taxes have been separated from the associated foreign-source income, Section 909 prevents Cathy from taking the foreign income taxes into account for U.S. tax purposes until she takes into account the related income.

In Guardian Industries Corp. v. United States, 477 F.3d 1368 (Fed. Cir. 2007), the Federal Circuit affirmed a decision by the Court of Federal Claims and held that a U.S. corporation was entitled to a direct credit under Section 901 for Luxembourg taxes paid by one of its "subsidiaries," a hybrid entity that was treated as a disregarded entity for U.S. tax purposes and as a corporation for Luxembourg tax purposes. The taxes were imposed on the taxable income of the U.S. corporation's group of Luxembourg operating subsidiaries that had been consolidated for Luxembourg tax purposes and the income of such foreign subsidiaries was not subject to current U.S. tax because it constituted foreign-source income of separate foreign taxpayers, the foreign subsidiaries. The court held that the U.S. corporation was entitled to the credit because, under Luxembourg law, the disregarded entity had sole liability for the taxes imposed with respect to the consolidated group's taxable income and, for U.S. tax purposes, the taxes paid by the disregarded entity were to be treated as paid by the U.S. parent corporation. Thus, the foreign tax credit was available to the U.S. corporation for foreign taxes on earnings of the foreign operating subsidiaries on which U.S. tax was deferred indefinitely. This case demonstrates the potential for absurd results that arises from strict application of the technical taxpayer rule in Reg. § 1.901–2(f).

In REG–124152–06, 2006–2 C.B. 368, the Treasury and the IRS proposed changes to the technical taxpayer rule in Reg. § 1.901–2(f). These proposed regulations would retain the general principle in the current regulations that a foreign tax is considered paid by the person who has legal liability for the tax under foreign law. However, these proposed regulations would clarify application of the legal liability rule in cases where foreign law imposes tax on the income of one person but requires another person to actually remit the tax. REG–124152–06 explains that the "proposed regulations make clear that foreign law is considered to impose legal liability for income tax on the person who is required to take such income into account for foreign tax purposes even if another person has the sole obligation to remit the tax * * *." 2006–2 C.B. at 369; see Prop. Reg. § 1.901–2(f)(1)(i). Moreover, these proposed regulations would clarify the application of the legal liability rule to foreign consolidated-type regimes in which the group members do not have joint and several liability in the U.S. sense for the group's foreign tax and require that the foreign tax be apportioned among all the group members *pro rata, i.e.,* in proportion to each group member's portion of the group's combined net income as computed under foreign law. See Prop. Reg. § 1.901–2(f)(2)(i). If adopted in the final regulations, these rules would change the result in in the Example above and in a case like *Guardian Industries*. See Prop. Reg. § 1.901–2(f)(6), Ex. 6.

Moreover, as mentioned in the Example above, in 2010, Congress enacted Section 909, which is aimed at transactions that split foreign taxes from the income to which they relate. This provision takes a different approach to dealing with this issue than would the 2006 proposed regulations described above. It essentially adopts a matching rule that attempts to prevent a taxpayer from separating creditable foreign taxes (whether under Section 901 or the indirect credit provisions of Sections 902 and 960) from the associated foreign-source income. Stated generally, Section 909 provides that when there is a foreign tax credit splitting event concerning a foreign income tax paid or accrued by a taxpayer, the foreign income tax is not taken into account for federal income tax purposes and, therefore, is not creditable until the tax year in which the related income is taken into account by the taxpayer. This legislation changes the result in the Example above and in a case like *Guardian Industries*.

Taxes must be creditable taxes. To qualify for the direct credit under Section 901 or the indirect credit under Section 902, a foreign levy must meet the standards for creditability set forth in Sections 901 and 903 and the regulations issued under those provisions. This Chapter now turns to that key issue. Keep in mind that the amount of foreign taxes meeting the standards for creditability that can actually be taken as a credit in any tax year is subject to the limitations in Section 904, which are introduced later in this Chapter and examined in more detail in Chapter 7.[7]

D. CREDITABLE TAXES (SECTIONS 901 AND 903)

[¶ 5015]

1. INTRODUCTION

Section 901(a) and (b) provides the credit for foreign "income, war profits, and excess profits taxes" to taxpayers who elect to credit rather than deduct these taxes. The central requirement for creditability is that the foreign tax be a tax on "income" (or "profits"). The fundamental purpose of the credit is to prevent or minimize double taxation of income that is subject to tax in at least one foreign country in addition to the United States. It is evidently for this straightforward reason that the credit is available only for foreign taxes imposed on income. Other foreign taxes, such as excise taxes, sales taxes, turnover taxes, property taxes, taxes on payroll, taxes on capital or net worth and taxes on gifts and legacies, may be deductible by a U.S. taxpayer, if they meet the requirements of Section 164, but are not creditable.[8]

Over the years and in a large number of cases and rulings, it has not always been easy to determine whether or not a foreign levy is a tax on income. The basic doctrine is that a foreign levy must come within the U.S. meaning of an income tax to qualify for the credit, regardless of the label placed on the levy by the foreign government that imposes it. Biddle v. Commissioner, 302 U.S. 573 (1938). In 1983, after long effort and much public discussion, the Treasury promulgated comprehensive regulations under Section 901. These regulations involved a number of conceptual

---

7. The basic purpose of Section 904 is to prevent the foreign tax credit from reducing a taxpayer's U.S. tax on U.S.-source income. Section 904 also contains a limitation that is applied separately to different categories of foreign-source income for the purpose of preventing a taxpayer from crediting foreign taxes imposed on one type of high-taxed foreign income against U.S. taxes imposed on another type of low-taxed foreign income.

8. On a more theoretical level, Elisabeth A. Owens has suggested that the "the chief determinative factor in deciding whether a tax qualifies for the credit should be whether or not the tax is shifted or passed on by the person paying the tax." E. Owens, The Foreign Tax Credit 83 (1961). The idea is that the purpose of the foreign tax credit is to avoid double taxation. To the extent that the taxpayer on whom the foreign tax is imposed is able to raise the prices of its products or services commensurately and pass on the tax to its customers, as is often the case with foreign sales and excise taxes, the taxpayer does not bear the burden of the foreign tax, no double taxation occurs and no foreign tax credit need be allowed for such taxes. By contrast, Ms. Owens concludes that there is "a justification in terms of tax incidence for the largest part of credit relief which is granted for foreign income taxes" because, in her view, such income taxes are not shifted or passed on and do reduce the taxpayer's net return after tax. Id. at 85. In practice, however, it is often very difficult to determine the incidence of a particular tax and, therefore, tax incidence is not a practical standard for deciding whether a particular foreign tax is creditable and is not, in fact, a factor cited in the cases, regulations or rulings.

shifts that rendered a substantial portion of the then existing body of rulings and case law obsolete.

The regulations start with the proposition, stated in Reg. § 1.901–2(a)(1), that:

> A foreign levy is an income tax if and only if—
>
> (i) It is a tax; and
>
> (ii) Its predominant character is that of an income tax in the U.S. sense.

The regulations go on to define an income tax in considerable detail. Foreign taxes on business and investment earnings which are substantially like the U.S. income tax—that is, based on net income or profits—will qualify even if, for example, some income items taxed or deductions allowed are not exactly the same. But a tax imposed wholly on a base not considered income under the U.S. Code will generally not be an income tax. These regulations are basic to an understanding of the foreign tax credit and are worthy of careful study.

The scope of the creditable income tax under Section 901 is expanded somewhat by Section 903, which provides that the term "income tax" includes a tax "in lieu of" an income tax. Although Section 903 has not been subject to many interpretations by the courts, the central idea—that of a substitute tax—is clear. A tax *in addition to* the general income tax will not qualify. Thus, Reg. § 1.903–1(b)(1) requires that "the tax in fact operates as a tax imposed in substitution for, and not in addition to, an income tax or a series of income taxes otherwise generally imposed." See ¶ 5075.

[¶ 5020]

2. CREDITABILITY OF SUBNATIONAL FOREIGN TAXES

Foreign taxes that are income taxes in the U.S. sense will qualify for the foreign tax credit whether the taxes are imposed by the national government or by a political subdivision of the foreign country. By contrast, taxes paid to state or local governments within the United States are allowed only as a deduction. This disparity in the U.S. tax treatment of foreign and U.S. subnational taxes may create an incentive for U.S. persons to shift investment abroad. It is, therefore, inconsistent with the capital-export neutrality standard.

> *Example.* DC, a U.S. corporation, can earn $100 before any taxes from either a U.S. or foreign investment. Assume that the rate of U.S. federal income tax is 35 percent and the rate of income tax imposed by the national government of the foreign country is 20 percent. Assume further that a state in the United States and a local govern-

ment in the foreign country both impose an income tax of 10 percent. On an investment in the United States, DC pays $31.50 of U.S. federal tax (35 percent multiplied by $90 ($100 − $10)) and $10 to the state government in the United States, resulting in an effective rate of 41.5 percent and leaving DC with $58.50 after tax. On a foreign investment, DC pays $18 of tax to the foreign national government (20 percent multiplied by $90 ($100 − $10)) and $10 of tax to the foreign local government. After DC takes a foreign tax credit of $28, DC must pay $7 in tax to the United States and is left with $65 after tax. Thus, DC has a tax incentive to shift profitable operations to the foreign country.

There are at least two obvious ways that Congress could eliminate this bias in favor of foreign investment. First, Congress could replace the credit for foreign subnational income taxes with a deduction for such taxes, which would be consistent with national neutrality. Alternatively, Congress could replace the deduction for state and local taxes with a credit for state and local taxes. See Staff of Joint Comm. on Tax'n, 102d Cong., 1st Sess., Factors Affecting the International Competitiveness of the United States, at 254–55 (1991).

3. WHEN IS A FOREIGN LEVY A TAX?

[¶ 5025]

a. Introduction: Creditable Tax or Royalty?

As mentioned above, to be creditable for U.S. tax purposes, a foreign levy must be a "tax," as determined under U.S. legal principles. The regulations define a "tax" as a compulsory payment under a foreign country's authority to levy taxes. Penalties, fines, interest, customs duties and similar obligations are not taxes within this definition. Reg. § 1.901–2(a)(2)(i).

One issue of significant controversy and importance in this area concerns a U.S. taxpayer's payments to a foreign country that may result in economic benefits for the taxpayer. To what extent are such payments "taxes" for purposes of the foreign tax credit provisions rather than normal business expenses for which only a deduction is available? Of particular concern are payments by a U.S. taxpayer to mineral-producing nations that may be royalties masquerading as creditable foreign taxes. It is in the financial interest of both the taxpayer and the foreign government to maximize the portion of the payment treated as a creditable tax. As the following discussion illustrates, the IRS, the courts and the Congress have struggled with this issue over the years.

[¶ 5030]

REVENUE RULING 55–296

1955–1 C.B. 386, revoked by Rev. Rul. 78–63, 1978–1 C.B. 228.

The Government of Saudi Arabia by Royal Decree * * *, dated November 4, 1950, imposed a general income tax on incomes of individuals and corporations [that] applies to all persons except those specifically exempted. By Royal Decree * * *, dated December 27, 1950, the Government of Saudi Arabia imposed an additional tax on every company registered or required to be registered in accordance with the Decree for the Registration of Companies and engaged in the production of petroleum or other hydrocarbons in the Kingdom of Saudi Arabia. *Held*, both the general income tax and the additional tax imposed under the foregoing Decrees come within the United States concept of an income tax and are allowable as a credit against United States income tax * * *, subject to the [foreign tax credit] limitations * * *.

[¶ 5035]

b. Aftermath of the Saudi Arabian Ruling

In 1974, Tax Analysts & Advocates, a public interest organization that promotes tax reform, petitioned the IRS to revoke both the Saudi Arabian ruling above and Rev. Rul. 68–522, 1968–2 C.B. 306, which had held a surtax paid to Libya under the Libyan Petroleum Law to be creditable. It later sued for revocation in district court, but the suit was dismissed for lack of standing. Tax Analysts & Advocates v. Blumenthal, 566 F.2d 130 (D.C.Cir.1977), aff'g Tax Analysts & Advocates v. Simon, 390 F.Supp. 927 (D.D.C.1975), cert. denied, 434 U.S. 1086 (1978). The following excerpt, taken from the petition to the IRS as published in 2 Tax Notes 19 (1974), clearly sets forth the issue of whether these "taxes" imposed by Saudi Arabia and other oil-producing countries were creditable foreign income taxes or disguised royalties:

> According to the opening statement of Senator Frank Church, Chairman of the Senate Foreign Relations Subcommittee on Multinational Corporations, at the January 30, 1974 Subcommittee Hearing on International Oil Companies and United States Foreign Policy, the Treasury Department, in the summer of 1950, at the urging of the Department of State, agreed to treat payments denominated as "income taxes" and made to Middle East oil producing nations by United States oil companies as taxes qualifying for the foreign tax credit under Section 901.
>
> As a result of this decision, a pattern developed pursuant to which the principal oil producing nations in the Middle East, North Africa and South America promulgated a series of formal income tax

statutes which appeared to impose net income taxes on United States companies producing oil in these foreign nations. In 1955 and 1968, the Internal Revenue Service published rulings that the "income taxes" paid respectively to Saudi Arabia and Libya on oil production income were creditable taxes. In addition, it is understood that in this post–1950 period, the IRS has issued numerous private, unpublished rulings to U.S. oil companies that payments denominated as income taxes made to the other principal OPEC nations also were creditable taxes under Section 901.

Whatever the merits and correctness of these rulings when they first were issued, it is evident that as important changes have occurred in the method of calculating the "tax" revenues due the principal OPEC nations, the nature of the payments has been transformed so that presently they clearly are not creditable taxes under either Section 901 or Section 903 * * *.

Presently, amounts paid by United States oil companies to the principal OPEC nations are divided artificially into two categories—a relatively small amount denominated as a "royalty" and a larger amount denominated as an "income tax." The "royalty" payment is the number of barrels produced during the relevant period by a company holding a concession multiplied by a low percentage, generally 12–15% of the posted price for each barrel. The larger part, the "income tax," in general, is the number of barrels of oil produced by a company holding a concession multiplied by a per barrel cost equal to a fixed percentage (around 55–60%) of the posted price reduced by the per barrel production costs and the royalty payment.

The mechanics of the calculation of the OPEC government per barrel revenue is illustrated by the following example based upon the $7.00 "government take" and $11.65 posted price now in effect for the benchmark Persian Gulf crude produced in Saudi Arabia—Arabian light 34° API:

Posted price	$11.65	per barrel
Royalty	(1.46)	
Production cost	(0.12)	
Profit before tax	$10.07	
Tax at 55%	5.54	
Government take	7.00	(Royalty plus tax)
Tax paid cost	7.12	

The posted price, which in some countries is called the "tax reference price," is an arbitrary value established by an oil producing nation for a barrel of its crude oil for the purpose of computing the revenues owed that country by the oil companies. For the past several years, posted prices have been set substantially in excess of the actual market price or market value of the crude oil, thereby resulting in payments by the oil companies far in excess of 55% or 60% of their actual net income from the production of the oil on which the payments are made.

* * *

It should be noted that if, in the example on the previous page, production company after tax profit per barrel of the benchmark crude is assumed to be $0.50 (i.e., that each barrel of Arabian light crude can be sold for $7.62 without taking shipping costs into account), the producing company would be paying Saudi "income taxes" at a rate of over 91% of its taxable income, i.e., $5.54 of tax on $6.04 of pre-tax income ($5.54 plus $0.50).

The $7.00 per barrel revenues are collected by the Saudi government on a monthly basis. Thus, any expenses which enter into the deductible production costs also must be calculated on a monthly basis. Although the Saudi Arabian tax statute applicable to oil production income appears to provide numerous deductions from gross income for items such as capital expenditures and other drilling and exploration costs, the deductions available for production costs apparently are so small compared to the total oil company income calculated on the posted price per barrel basis, that in the recent past, even substantial changes in the gross amount of such deductions would, at a maximum, only alter the deductible per barrel production costs by a negligible amount—a few pennies at most.

However, the language of the December 23, 1973 OPEC press release quoted earlier with respect to the announced $7.00 per barrel Persian Gulf "government take" failed to mention any possibility that these governments would accept anything less than $7.00 per barrel for oil taken under concession agreements. Yet such a result would occur if oil company production costs increased after the posted price was set, and such costs were allowed under local OPEC tax law to reduce taxable income, and therefore to reduce government take. Thus, the mandatory $7.00 per barrel language strongly implies that the principal OPEC nations now will not allow unforeseen high production costs to reduce their receipts below the specified per barrel government revenues. This press release very likely may have signaled the elimination of the last remnants of the system which permitted production costs to even minimally affect the revenues paid the principal OPEC nations. In effect, the principal OPEC nation "income taxes" may have changed from almost fixed per barrel charges to pure fixed per barrel costs.

Since October 1973, posted price increases, such as the $11.65 price set for Persian Gulf crude after January 1, 1974, have been made unilaterally by the principal OPEC nations without prior consent of the concession-holding Western oil companies. This current practice of unilateral posted price increases was preceded by a period in which posted prices were determined by protracted negotiations between the OPEC nations and the international oil companies. The Libyan negotiations of 1970–71 apparently served as the prototype for other OPEC/oil company negotiations during 1970–1973. A recently released chronology of these Libyan negotiations indicates that different oil companies holding oil concessions within Libya each engaged in separate negotiations with the Libyan government. As a result of separate agreements, different concession holders paid taxes at different rates. For example, on December 28, 1970, while the prevailing rate of "tax" paid by oil companies in Libya was 54/55% of the posted price, Aquitaine still was paying "tax" at a 50% rate while Occidental Petroleum was paying "tax" at 58%. Certainly, imposition of "taxes" at different rates on similarly situated taxpayers is inconsistent with the application of true national income taxes; it is much more consistent with royalty negotiations.

* * *

* * * Although the principal OPEC nations denominate the payments required to be made to them by oil companies as "income taxes," this foreign terminology by itself obviously does not allow the payments to be treated as creditable taxes under Section 901 or 903 if they in fact are not taxes at all.

Since the OPEC countries both own the land where exceptionally valuable oil fields have been discovered and are also sovereign states, they have the option to collect revenues either in their capacity as sovereigns exercising their rights of taxation, or as ordinary owners of property from which they can collect rents or royalties, or as both. Although the OPEC nations denominate the revenues they collect in connection with the use of these oil producing lands largely as "income taxes," in fact, as the following analysis will show, they have chosen to collect all their revenues in connection with the oil production in a form which has only the elements of royalties. As such, these revenue payments are not taxes at all, and, therefore, cannot be credited under either Section 901 or 903.

In past years, the dual function of the oil producing nations as sovereign states and valuable oil property owners raised the problem in the minds of many persons outside the Treasury Department whether the amounts denominated as their income taxes were, in fact, royalties. Although no firm conclusions were reached in the past as to the exact nature of these amounts, events beginning with the 1970 Libyan negotiations described earlier in the petition have made clear that these payments now clearly constitute royalties and not taxes.

The fact that the principal OPEC nations divide their oil payment "takes" into amounts denominated as "taxes" and "royalties" does not mean, as is argued by representatives of the U.S. oil companies, that the amounts denominated as taxes must be true creditable taxes. The general OPEC royalty rate is 12–15% of the posted price, which is comparable to the predominant royalty rates paid to lessors on oil properties located in the United States. However, the cost of producing oil in the Middle East and North Africa is many times cheaper than the cost of producing oil in the United States. Under basic economic theory, profits stemming from efficient oil properties accrue to the owner of the mineral rights. Therefore, these efficient foreign wells should command very high royalty rates—not the minimal 12–15% currently charged. By comparison, when lease bonuses are spread over expected oil fields from U.S. offshore wells, the effective royalty rates, calculated on prices expected in early 1973, are about 50%; and these wells are much more costly and less productive than those of the Persian Gulf.

* * *

The OPEC revenues denominated as income taxes actually take the form of royalties because they are per barrel payments unrelated to the income or gross receipts of the oil company concession holder. As described earlier in this petition, amounts received by the principal OPEC nations presently treated as creditable income taxes are determined by reference to an artificial posted price. This price, in turn, is fixed by the OPEC nations by reference to the amount of total revenue ("income tax" plus royalty) each principal OPEC nation has determined it should receive per barrel of crude oil produced under concession agreements by foreign oil companies. Since the posted price is unrelated to the actual market price of the crude oil, the posted price is unrelated to the actual gross receipts received by the oil companies for their crude oil production. Thus, since the purported "income taxes" are a fixed percentage of this artificial price minus certain fixed costs (the amount denominated as a "royalty") and other costs which can vary, if at all, a minimum amount per barrel, the "taxes" in fact are fixed or almost fixed per barrel costs. This is obviously the form of a royalty rather than a net income, gross income, or gross receipts tax.

* * *

Apart from being denominated as "income taxes," the payments made to the principal OPEC nations by the international oil companies in connection with their oil production activities no longer have anything in common with true income taxes. In this context, the old riddle traditionally attributed to Abraham Lincoln would appear relevant:

"If you call a tail a leg, how many legs has a dog?"

"Five?"

"No; calling a tail a leg don't *make* it a leg."

Similarly, a foreign government, merely by calling a royalty an "income tax," does not make the royalty a creditable income tax.

[¶ 5040]

IRS NEWS RELEASE IR-1638

July 14, 1976.

* * *

The Internal Revenue Service has further considered whether foreign taxes paid or incurred by taxpayers engaged in extracting mineral resources owned by foreign governments are eligible for the U.S. foreign tax credit.

* * * [T]he IRS was asked to state specific circumstances under which a foreign tax credit would be allowed against U.S. income tax under section 901 * * * where a levy is imposed by a foreign government owning minerals extracted by U.S. taxpayers.

If a foreign government owns mineral resources and the taxpayer has an economic interest in such minerals in place, a foreign tax will not be recognized as a tax for U.S. Federal income tax credit purposes, unless that government also requires payment of an appropriate royalty or other consideration for the property that is commensurate with the value of the concession. Such royalty or other consideration must be calculated separately and independently of the foreign tax. Satisfaction of such royalty by the U.S. taxpayer must be independent of the discharge of any foreign tax liability.

In order for a foreign tax to be creditable under section 901, it must qualify in substance and form as an income tax under U.S. concepts. Generally, in the absence of other factors which have contrary implications, payments to a foreign government owning the minerals in place extracted by the U.S. taxpayer will be treated as a creditable income tax if all of the following characteristics are present.

(1) The amount of income tax is calculated separately and independently of the amount of the royalty and of any other tax or charge imposed by the foreign government.

(2) Under the foreign law and in its actual administration, the income tax is imposed on the receipt of income by the taxpayer and such income is determined on the basis of arm's length amounts. Further, these receipts are actually realized in a manner consistent with U.S. income taxation principles.

(3) The taxpayer's income tax liability cannot be discharged from property owned by the foreign government.

(4) The foreign income tax liability, if any, is computed on the basis of the taxpayer's entire extractive operations within the foreign country.

(5) While the foreign tax base need not be identical or nearly identical to the U.S. tax base, the taxpayer, in computing the income subject to the foreign income tax, is allowed to deduct, without limitation, the significant expenses paid or incurred by the taxpayer. Reasonable limitations on the recovery of capital expenditures are acceptable.

The purpose of this News Release is to state the current IRS position regarding a levy imposed by a foreign government owning minerals extracted by U.S. taxpayers, in which all of the characteristics listed above are present. Any departure from these characteristics may jeopardize the qualification of the levy as a creditable income tax. There is no intent to state any position with respect to what taxes may constitute "in lieu of" taxes under section 903 * * *.

* * *

[¶ 5045]

NOTE

This News Release was an opening gun in a campaign by the IRS and the Treasury to clarify and tighten the rules as to "dual capacity" taxpayers, that is, taxpayers who have a commercial relationship with a foreign government in addition to being taxpayers. A typical example of a dual capacity taxpayer is, of course, an oil or a mining company operating under a foreign government concession. But many other cases exist, such as a private business buying supplies or renting a building from a foreign government.

As reflected in the News Release, the IRS position was that a given payment to a foreign government had to be classified on an all-or-nothing basis. Either it was a qualifying income tax in its entirety, or it was not. See also Rev. Rul. 76–215, 1976–1 C.B. 194, in which payments under production-sharing agreements between a U.S. oil company and the government of Indonesia were held not to qualify as creditable taxes but to constitute royalties. The other shoe dropped when the IRS issued Rev. Rul. 78–63, 1978–1 C.B. 228. Revenue Ruling 78–63 revoked both the 1955 Saudi ruling above and the 1968 ruling which had held the surtax paid to Libya under the Libyan Petroleum Law to be creditable. The IRS reasoned that an "income tax in the United States sense is not one that is intentionally structured to tax artificial or fictitious income" (1978–1 C.B. at 230) and concluded that both the Saudi and Libyan taxes were based on receipts determined with reference to an arbitrarily determined posted price, which was a fictitious price set above the market price that an unrelated purchaser would pay. (Note that Revenue Ruling 78–63 was later declared obsolete by the IRS after it issued the revised 1983 regulations discussed in the next paragraph.)

Taxpayers, principally the U.S.-based international oil companies, urged the IRS and the Treasury to accept the view that payments by dual capacity taxpayers to foreign governments may consist at least in part of creditable income taxes. Three sets of proposed and temporary regulations were issued in subsequent years as the controversy continued.

[¶ 5050]

c. 1983 Regulations

In 1983, final regulations were promulgated which set forth the basic requirements that must be met by a foreign levy to be creditable. The regulations concede that payments made to a foreign government by a U.S.-based natural resources corporation may be divided between a creditable income tax component and a non-creditable royalty component (which normally will be deductible under Section 162), but require the taxpayer to bear the burden of proving the appropriate allocation. The problem for a taxpayer in this situation (called a "dual capacity taxpayer" in the regulations) is how to carry its burden of identifying and segregating the portion of the payment that qualifies as a creditable tax under the standards articulated in the regulations. The starting point is Reg. § 1.901–2(a)(2):

> (2) *Tax*—(i) *In general.* A foreign levy is a tax if it requires a compulsory payment pursuant to the authority of a foreign country to levy taxes. A penalty, fine, interest, or similar obligation is not a tax, nor is a customs duty a tax. Whether a foreign levy requires a compulsory payment pursuant to a foreign country's authority to levy taxes is determined by principles of U.S. law and not by principles of law of the foreign country. * * * Notwithstanding any assertion of a foreign country to the contrary, a foreign levy is not pursuant to a foreign country's authority to levy taxes, and thus is not a tax, to the extent a person subject to the levy receives (or will receive), directly or indirectly, a specific economic benefit (as defined in [Reg. § 1.901–2(a)(2)(ii)(B)]) from the foreign country in exchange for payment pursuant to the levy. Rather, to that extent, such levy requires a compulsory payment in exchange for such specific economic benefit. If, applying U.S. principles, a foreign levy requires a compulsory payment pursuant to the authority of a foreign country to levy taxes and also requires a compulsory payment in exchange for a specific economic benefit, the levy is considered to have two distinct elements: a tax and a requirement of compulsory payment in exchange for such specific economic benefit. In such a situation, these two distinct elements of the foreign levy (and the amount paid pursuant to each such element) must be separated. No credit is allowable for a payment pursuant to a foreign levy by a dual capacity taxpayer (as defined in [Reg. § 1.901–2(a)(2)(ii)(A)]) unless the person claiming such credit establishes the amount that is paid pursuant to the distinct element of the foreign levy that is a tax. * * *

Reg. § 1.901–2A provides methods by which a dual capacity taxpayer can meet its burden of proving the amount that is truly a tax. Reg. § 1.901–2A(c)(2) outlines the facts and circumstances method and Reg. §§ 1.901–2A(c)(3), 1.901–2A(d) and 1.901–2A(e) permit use of a safe harbor formula.[9]

[¶ 5055]

PROBLEM

Try out the safe harbor formula in Reg. § 1.901–2A on this case. Taxpayer, a U.S. mining corporation operating in Country X, has $1,000 of gross receipts and $500 of mining costs. It mines government land but pays no royalty to the government. It pays a levy to the Country X government of $300. (Because Taxpayer is subject to the Country X mining tax, it is not subject to the generally imposed Country X income tax.) The tax rate in Country X "applicable in computing tax liability under the general tax" is 33⅓ percent of net income. See Reg. § 1.901–2A(e)(3). How much of the $300 payment will be considered a creditable tax? How do the regulations treat that part of the $300 payment that is not a tax? See Reg. § 1.901–2A(b)(1). Do you think the result in this case makes sense?

[¶ 5060]

4. IS THE "PREDOMINANT CHARACTER" OF THE FOREIGN TAX THAT OF AN "INCOME TAX IN THE U.S. SENSE"?

The centerpiece of the law on whether a foreign tax qualifies as a creditable tax under Section 901 is the requirement in Reg. § 1.901–2(a)(1)(ii) that "[t]he predominant character of [the] tax is that of an income tax in the U.S. sense." Reg. § 1.901–2(a)(3)(i), in turn, provides that a foreign tax will meet this requirement only if the "tax is likely to reach net gain [in the] normal circumstances in which it applies." Reg. § 1.901–2(b)(1) amplifies this requirement by stating that the net gain test is met if, based on the predominant character of the tax, it meets the three requirements set out in Reg. § 1.901–2(b)(2) through (4): (i) the

9. In addition to the general rules on creditability of foreign taxes in the regulations discussed above, there are special rules in the Code concerning foreign income taxes arising in connection with foreign oil and gas and other mineral activities. These Code provisions reflect continuing congressional concern about foreign tax credit abuses involving foreign taxes paid to mineral-producing nations. Section 901(e) reduces the amount of creditable foreign taxes on foreign mineral income if a taxpayer claims percentage depletion under Section 613 with respect to such income. Section 901(f) prevents a taxpayer from obtaining a foreign tax credit for any foreign taxes paid to a foreign country in connection with the purchase and sale of oil or gas extracted in that country if (1) the taxpayer does not have an economic interest in the oil and gas (within the meaning of the depletion rules in Section 611) and (2) either the purchase or sale is at a price that differs from the fair market value of the oil or gas. Section 907 contains special limitations on the creditability of foreign oil and gas extraction taxes and certain foreign taxes on "foreign oil related income."

realization requirement, (ii) the gross receipts requirement and (iii) the net income requirement.

Realization requirement. To meet the realization requirement under Reg. § 1.901–2(b)(2), the foreign tax must be imposed upon, or subsequent to, a realization event under the Code or upon a number of events before a realization event under U.S. tax concepts. One of the listed prior events is the physical transfer, processing or export of readily marketable property. This rule accommodates foreign taxes triggered by the export from a foreign producing country of a commodity, such as crude oil, by an integrated producer. A realization event for purposes of the Code may not occur in the case of an integrated oil producer until products are sold to distributors or to customers at the gas station.

Gross receipts requirement. To meet the gross receipts requirement under Reg. § 1.901–2(b)(3), the starting point for calculating the foreign tax must be *actual* gross receipts or gross receipts calculated in a way that is not likely to overstate them (as the OPEC posted price discussed at ¶ 5035 had done).

Net income requirement. A foreign tax meets the net income requirement under Reg. § 1.901–2(b)(4), if it allows (i) recovery of significant actual costs and expenses (including capital expenditures) attributable under reasonable principles to gross receipts *or* (ii) recovery of costs and expenses under a method producing a result that approximates or exceeds significant actual costs and expenses. For this purpose, Reg. § 1.901–2(b)(4)(i) treats a foreign tax law as allowing recovery of significant costs and expenses even if it uses different timing rules than the timing rules in the Code, "unless the time of recovery is such that under the circumstances there is effectively a denial of such recovery."

Note that the references to "predominant character" in the regulations imply some flexibility in applying U.S. standards in characterizing foreign taxes for purposes of the creditable foreign tax requirement. A foreign tax law need not be identical to the U.S. income tax system to meet these requirements.

The regulations contain rules on combining or separating foreign levies for purposes of determining whether the levies are creditable foreign taxes. If the levies are combined, then the test for determining whether the levy is an income tax in the U.S. sense is applied to the base of the combined levy as a whole. If the levies are separated, then the base of each levy is tested separately to see whether the levy qualifies as an income tax; thus, some of the levies may be creditable and others not creditable. See Reg. § 1.901–2(d).

The following case arose before the current 1983 final regulations became effective but it enunciates a test that was essentially adopted in those regulations.

[¶ 5065]

BANK OF AMERICA NATIONAL TRUST & SAVINGS ASS'N v. UNITED STATES

United States Court of Claims, 1972.
459 F.2d 513, cert. denied, 409 U.S. 949 (1972).

[The taxpayer bank conducted its banking business, inter alia, in Thailand, Argentina and the Philippines. Each country had a general, admittedly creditable, income tax which the taxpayer paid. However, in each country the taxpayer was also subject to a tax on gross income from its banking business. The Thailand business tax was typical: it provided specified rates on the "gross takings" of the banking business and defined gross takings as "(a) interest, discounts, fees or service charges, and (b) profit, before the deduction of any expense, from the exchange, purchase or sale of currency, issuance, purchase or sale of notes or foreign remittances."]

DAVIS, JUDGE:

* * *

* * * The problem, then, is whether such imposts on gross banking income, of this character, are "income taxes" under the foreign tax credit (§ 901(b)(1))—"income taxes" as we use that term in the federal system under our own revenue laws. * * *

There is consensus on certain basic principles, in addition to the rule that the United States notion of income taxes furnishes the controlling guide. All are agreed that an income tax is a direct tax on gain or profits, and that gain is a necessary ingredient of income. * * * Only an "income tax", not a tax which is truly on gross receipts, is creditable.

We can also put aside as irrelevant to this case the frequent controversy whether the foreign tax is a direct income tax or a privilege, excise, or similar tax which happens to be measured by income. The Thailand, Philippine, and Argentine bank taxes, whether or not they were "income taxes" for foreign tax credit purposes, were admittedly direct levies and not franchise, privilege, or excise taxes. But they were not imposed upon and limited to net gain.

The trial commissioner and the taxpayer say that this kind of direct gross income tax is nevertheless allowable under § 901(b)(1) because, in their view, gross income taxation (apparently any type of gross income tax) falls under the United States concept of an income tax. They emphasize that the Supreme Court has suggested that the Sixteenth Amendment extends the federal taxing power to gross income * * *; that several federal taxing provisions are levied on gross income; that prior court decisions under the foreign tax credit have permitted use of certain foreign gross income assessments; and that Internal Revenue Service rulings have upheld the crediting of some foreign taxes levied on gross income. The generalization the plaintiff and the trial commissioner draw is that all gross income taxes (as distinguished from gross receipts levies) come within § 901(b).

For the reasons elaborated in this and the succeeding sections of this opinion, we cannot accept the position that all foreign gross income taxes, no matter whether or not they tax or seek to tax profit or net gain, are covered by that provision. True, the Supreme Court has indicated, somewhat cursorily, that Congress may impose gross income taxes, but the full ramifications of that observation are as yet unknown since Congress has not yet sought in its income tax legislation to disregard net gain entirely. On the contrary, from 1913 on, Congress has always directed the domestic levy at some net gain or profit, and for almost 60 years the concept that the income tax seeks out net gain has been inherent in our system of taxation. That is the "well-understood meaning to be derived from an examination of the [United States] statutes which provide for the laying and collection of income taxes"—the basic test set forth in Biddle v. Commissioner of Internal Revenue, 302 U.S. 573, 579 * * * (1938), for determining whether a foreign tax is an "income tax" under the foreign tax credit.

Similarly, it comports better with the dominant purpose of the credit to avoid or minimize double taxation of income * * * to refer to the actual system historically utilized by Congress in imposing domestic income taxes rather than to some potential and unused, though constitutionally permissible, scheme of gross income taxation. Where the gross income levy may not, and is not intended to, reach profit (net gain), allowance of the credit would serve only haphazardly to avoid double taxation of net income, since only the United States tax—under the concept followed since 1913—would necessarily fall upon such net gain. There would not then be any significant measure of commensurability between the two imposts (except by chance).[8] * * *

We do not, however, consider it all-decisive whether the foreign income tax is labeled a gross income or a net income tax, or whether it specifically allows the deduction or exclusion of the costs or expenses of realizing the profit. The important thing is whether the other country is attempting to reach some net gain, not the form in which it shapes the income tax or the name it gives. In certain situations a levy can in reality be directed at net gain even though it is imposed squarely on gross income. That would be the case if it were clear that the costs, expenses, or

8. In seeking to reduce double taxation, Congress has not required that the foreign income tax be levied at the same rate as the United States income tax. The limitation on the credit established by § 904 * * * can serve to prevent, to a certain degree, the off-setting of the foreign tax where there is no parallel income subject to domestic tax. But if foreign gross income levies were automatically creditable there would still be very many situations in which the § 904 limitation would permit a credit despite the absence of any comparable taxable income under our income tax law.

losses incurred in making the gain would, in all probability, always (or almost so) be the lesser part of the gross income. In that situation there would always (or almost so) be some net gain remaining, and the assessment would fall ultimately upon that profit.

For instance, it is almost universally true that a wage or salary employee does not spend more on expenses incident to his job than he earns in pay. A foreign tax upon the gross income of an employee from his work should therefore be creditable by the employee under § 901(b)(1) despite the refusal of the other jurisdiction to permit deduction of job-related expenses. The reason is, of course, that in those circumstances the employee would always (or almost always) have some net gain and, accordingly, the tax, though on gross income, would be designed to pinch net gain in the end—and would in fact have that effect. In those circumstances, a loss (excess of expenses over profit) is so improbable, and some net gain is so sure, that the tax can be placed on gross income without any real fear or expectation that there will be no net gain or profit to tax.

* * *

This has been the underlying theory, as we see it, of the decisions, rulings, and legislation which both parties invoke. Sometimes the phrasing of the opinions and rulings has been overly broad or too narrow, but in each instance the core of the holding harmonizes with the principle that a direct income tax is creditable, even though imposed on gross income, if it is very highly likely, or was reasonably intended, always to reach some net gain in the normal circumstances in which it applies—otherwise the gross income tax is not creditable.

* * *

Domestic taxes: There are some minor federal income taxes imposed on gross income—plaintiff urges them strongly as analogies or exemplars—but here, too, we judge that Congress has used a gross income levy only in those instances in which it seemed clear that costs and expenses within this country (or affecting the production of the income in this country) would not wipe out net gain.

Sections 871 and 1441 * * * imposed a tax on certain non-business gross income of nonresident aliens from investments, compensation, etc. The assumption is, as we understand it, that such nonresident taxpayers, not engaging in business here, are very unlikely to have expenses which will reduce to zero their net gains from the taxed items. A like assumption underlies § 881(a)(1) imposing a 30 percent tax on the gross income from similar investment sources in this country by a foreign corporation "but only to the extent the amount so received is not effectively connected with the conduct of a trade or business within the United States." For a foreign corporation connected with United States business, § 882 imposes the tax on taxable income, after deductions related to the United States activities (with the exception that charitable contributions need not be so related).

The normal expectation is, of course, that taxpayers engaging in business can and may well suffer losses in some years.

Plaintiff points out that the portion of the social security tax imposed by § 3101 on wages received by resident employees, and paid by the employee, is an income tax on gross income. * * * Again, it seems clear that the legislative assumption was that it would be rare for an employee to spend so much of his own money in producing his wages that all net gain would be eliminated.

This review of the pertinent judicial decisions and Internal Revenue Service rulings, as well as of comparable gross income levies in the federal income tax system, persuades us that the term "income tax" in § 901(b)(1) covers all foreign income taxes designed to fall on some net gain or profit, and includes a gross income tax if, but only if, that impost is almost sure, or very likely, to reach some net gain because costs or expenses will not be so high as to offset the net profit. * * *

* * *

Do the three foreign taxes we are now discussing (Thailand Business Tax, Type 1 and Type 2; Philippines Tax on Banks; Buenos Aires Tax on Profit–Making Activities) meet this test? * * * [T]here is little difficulty in concluding that they do not.

Each of the taxes is levied on gross income from the banking business and allows no deductions for the costs or expenses of producing the income. Any taxpayer could be liable whether or not it operated at a profit during the year. The only question is whether it is very unlikely or highly improbable that taxpayers subject to the impost would make no profit or would suffer a loss. Plaintiff has presented no proof to this effect and does not very strongly urge that proposition. Obviously, it and the other institutions subject to the taxes had substantial costs in their banking business, salaries and rent being the major items. The covered banks must also have had bad debts and defaults, and these would have to be taken into account in calculating annual net gain.

The three taxes were each imposed on banks generally, not merely on the successful ones. Banks do suffer losses in certain years, especially newly established banks, and some have even been known to fail. There is no reason to believe that banks in Thailand, the Philippines, and Argentina are any different. Nor can one say on this record that the three governments felt that net gain would always (or nearly so) be reached by these special banking levies, or that they designed these particular taxes to nip such net profit. Each of the three jurisdictions had a general net income tax (comparable to ours, and admittedly creditable) which the Bank of America and other banks had to pay. That was the impost intended to reach net gain.

We cannot say, therefore, that there was only a minimal risk that the combination of a bank's expenses plus its bad debt experience (and other losses) would outbalance its net gain or profits in any particular year—or that the foreign countries so considered. * * *

The result is that the plaintiff is not entitled to recover * * *.

[¶ 5070]

NOTES

1. How would the *Bank of America* case be decided under the current regulations? See Reg. § 1.901–2(b)(1), (4)(i) and (iv), Ex. 1, and the discussion at ¶ 5095.

2. In order for a foreign tax to satisfy the "net income" test in the regulations, Reg. § 1.901–2(b)(4)(i) requires that computation of the base of the tax (1) allows recovery of significant costs and expenses attributable to the gross receipts or (2) provides an allowance "computed under a method that is likely to produce an amount that approximates, or is greater than, recovery of such significant costs and expenses." The following cases illustrate how this requirement has been applied by the courts.

In Texasgulf, Inc. v. Commissioner, 172 F.3d 209 (2d Cir.1999), aff'g 107 T.C. 51 (1996), the court held that the Ontario Mining Tax ("OMT") met the net income test in the Section 901 regulations and was a creditable income tax. The OMT did not allow a taxpayer to deduct investment interest, cost depletion and royalties paid for production of a mine on privately owned land even if such expenses were attributable to gross receipts included in the base of the OMT. The OMT did, however, allow a taxpayer to deduct a processing allowance with a sliding scale percentage based on which processing assets a taxpayer owned and where they were located. At issue was whether the OMT was not a creditable tax because it neither allowed recovery of nor effectively compensated for significant expenses attributable to gross receipts included in the OMT base. The taxpayer presented industry data and return-by-return data to show that the processing allowance adequately compensated for significant non-allowed costs, although the IRS attempted to argue that such data was irrelevant to the creditability issue. The Second Circuit and Tax Court both upheld the taxpayer's argument on this issue. The Second Circuit noted that only 33 percent of the tax returns in the industry showed nonrecoverable expenses in excess of the processing allowance, and, that of the income tax returns that reflected OMT liability, only 16 percent showed nonrecoverable expenses in excess of the processing allowance. Thus, the court of appeals concluded that the taxpayer had satisfied its burden of proving that it was effectively compensated for nonrecoverable costs under the OMT.

In Exxon Corp. v. Commissioner, 113 T.C. 338 (1999) (acq.), the Tax Court held that the United Kingdom's Petroleum Revenue Tax ("PRT") was a creditable income tax under Section 901. The IRS argued that the tax was not creditable under Section 901 because the PRT did not allow a taxpayer to deduct interest expense in computing the base of the tax. However, following the approach used in the *Texasgulf* case, the Tax Court looked to expert witness testimony, industry data and other evidence to find that certain allowances available under the PRT effectively and adequately compensated Exxon for the expenses disallowed under the PRT. Accordingly, the court held that the PRT met the net income test in the regulations and was a creditable tax.

[¶ 5075]

5. FOREIGN TAXES "IN LIEU OF" INCOME TAXES (SECTION 903)

The essence of the term "tax paid in lieu of a tax on income" is the requirement that the foreign tax be imposed as a substitute for, and not as an addition to, a generally applicable income tax. So long as the substitution test is met, the reason the substitute tax was imposed makes no difference. Often the substitute tax will be imposed to obviate the administrative difficulties involved in imposing a tax on net income, but this need not be so in order for the substitute tax to qualify for creditability under Section 903. In any event, it is immaterial that the base on which the tax is imposed has nothing to do with net income. Indeed, Reg. § 1.903–1(a) provides that the base of the substitute tax "may, for example, be gross income, gross receipts or sales, or the number of units produced or exported."

Reg. § 1.903–1(b)(1), moreover, provides that: "A comparison between the tax burden of * * * [the substitute tax] and the tax burden that would have obtained under the generally imposed income tax is irrelevant." Thus, in assessing the creditability of a substitute tax under Section 903, it does not matter whether the U.S. taxpayer's tax burden under the substitute tax is greater or less than what the taxpayer's burden would have been under the generally imposed income tax. On the other hand, the "in lieu of" regulations incorporate the general requirements of the Section 901 regulations relating to, inter alia, dual capacity taxpayers, soak-up taxes and creditable amounts. Reg. § 1.903–1(a).

[¶ 5080]

6. SOAK–UP TAXES

According to the regulations, a foreign levy is a creditable income tax or tax "in lieu of" an income tax only to the extent that it is not dependent on the availability of a foreign tax credit in the taxpayer's home country. A foreign tax that is conditioned on the ability of the taxpayer to claim a foreign tax credit at home is usually called a "soak-up" tax and is not creditable. Reg. § 1.901–2(c). The concern here is that a foreign country will take advantage of the U.S. foreign tax credit system and impose a tax only when it comes out of the pocket of the U.S. Treasury.

[¶ 5085]

REVENUE RULING 87-39

1987-1 C.B. 180.

ISSUE

Is the Uruguayan withholding tax on dividends and profits * * * a creditable tax under section 901 or 903 * * *?

FACTS

* * * [A new Uruguayan law] imposes a 30 percent tax, withheld at the source of payment, on Uruguayan source dividends and profits paid or credited to non-Uruguayan shareholders. However, the tax is imposed only if the country of the recipient's domicile allows the tax to be credited against the recipient's domestic income tax liability. The Uruguayan tax authorities require any dividend recipient who claims to be exempt from the tax to present a translated certification from its country of domicile that the tax will not be creditable in that country.

LAW AND ANALYSIS

Section 901 * * * provides that a credit is allowed against United States income tax for the amount of any income, war profits, and excess profits taxes paid or accrued to any foreign country. Section 1.901–2(a)(3) of the * * * Regulations provides that a foreign levy is an income tax for this purpose only if it is a tax, and if the predominant character of that tax is an income tax in the United States sense. Section 1.901–2(a)(3)(ii) provides that the predominant character of a foreign tax is that of an income tax in the United States sense only to the extent that liability for the tax is not dependent on the availability of a credit for the tax against income tax liability to another country. Section 1.901–2(c) provides that liability for foreign tax is dependent on the availability of a credit for the tax against income tax liability to another country to the extent that the foreign tax would not be imposed but for the availability of such a credit.

Section 903 * * * extends the credit available under section 901 to taxes paid in lieu of income taxes. Section 1.903–1(a)(1) of the regulations provides that a foreign levy is a tax in lieu of an income tax only if it is a tax, and if it meets the "substitution requirement" of section 1.903–1(b). Section 1.903–1(b)(2) provides that a foreign tax meets the substitution requirement only to the extent that liability for the tax is not dependent on the availability of a credit for the tax against income tax liability to another country. Accordingly, if a foreign country imposes a withholding tax only if a credit for the tax is available from the recipient's country of domicile, the tax is not creditable under section 901 or 903.

HOLDING

The Uruguayan withholding tax on dividends and profits * * * is not a creditable tax under section 901 or 903 * * *, since it is imposed only if a credit for the tax is available from the recipient's country of domicile. * * *

[¶ 5090]

NOTES

1. In Rev. Rul. 2003–8, 2003–1 C.B. 290, the IRS ruled that certain Costa Rican withholding taxes were not creditable under Section 903 because they were soak-up taxes. Under Costa Rican law, the Costa Rican Tax Administration was given authority to provide a total or partial exemption from the taxes if the recipient of the income subject to tax is not granted a credit for these taxes by the country in which the taxpayer operates or resides.

2. Is there any foundation in the text of the Code for denying the creditability of soak-up taxes?

3. How should a soak-up tax be characterized? Should it be regarded as an effort by the foreign country to use the U.S. tax credit system to shift revenues from the United States to the foreign country with no cost to the U.S. taxpayer? Alternatively, could it be regarded as an effort by the foreign country to avoid having its policy of attracting foreign capital by granting a tax exemption from being frustrated by the U.S. foreign tax credit system? Is it relevant to this issue that international tax principles accord the primary right to tax to the country of territorial source? Could it be argued that this right implies as well the primary right of that state to exempt domestic-source income from tax? If so, the soak-up tax might be regarded by the source country as a justifiable mechanism to discourage the cancellation of the exemption it seeks to accord by the operation of the foreign tax credit regime to which the foreign investor is subject. A more widely used mechanism to avoid cancellation of tax exemptions accorded by the source country is the tax-sparing credit, which has been adopted by a substantial number of capital-exporting countries (but not the United States) in tax treaties with developing countries. See ¶ 5210.

[¶ 5095]

7. GROSS INCOME TAXES AND WITHHOLDING TAXES

As discussed in Chapter 4, a standard feature of international taxation is the imposition of withholding taxes on the gross amounts of payments such as interest, dividends, rents and royalties (which would be characterized as fixed or determinable annual or periodical income under Sections 871(a)(1)(A) and 881(a)(1) of the Code) paid by domestic persons to foreign persons. Because of the difficulty of auditing the deductions of the foreign recipient properly chargeable against such categories of income, withholding taxes are nearly always imposed on gross income. In addition, countries with limited fiscal auditing resources may impose taxes on gross income of domestic persons and foreign persons engaged in domestic business because they are much simpler to audit than taxes imposed on net income (an example would be the taxes on gross income from banking imposed in the *Bank of America* case, at ¶ 5065).

A number of policy issues could be raised concerning the treatment of gross income taxes under the foreign tax credit regime. Should gross income taxes be creditable? Does the absence of deductions make any conceptual difference so far as allowance of a credit is concerned? Is a gross income tax less likely to result in double taxation than a net income tax? Is the incidence of a gross income tax different than the incidence of a net income tax? Can a gross income tax be passed on more easily than a net income tax?

Before the Section 901 regulations were issued in 1983, the Treasury regarded the standard withholding taxes on the interest, royalties and dividends of nonresidents as income taxes under Section 901. In the case of dividends this seemed appropriate because dividend income would almost always exceed the costs of earning it. In other cases, however, it strained the principle that an income tax was a tax on net income. The IRS glossed over the strain by concluding, as in the Tanzania ruling below, at ¶ 5100, that "[t]he thrust of these United States [withholding] tax provisions is realistically directed against net gain." This conclusion is hard to justify when applied, for example, to the foreign interest income of banks because the cost of funds loaned and other business expenses may exceed the interest income. See the *Bank of America* case, at ¶ 5065.

Under the regulations, foreign gross basis withholding taxes on income items such as interest, dividends, rents and royalties, of a type similar to taxes imposed by the United States under Sections 871(a)(1)(A) and 881(a)(1), are generally creditable as "in lieu of" taxes under Section 903. See Reg. §§ 1.901–2(b)(4)(i), 1.903–1(a) and 1.903–1(b)(3), Exs. 1, 2 and 3. Other foreign taxes on gross income or gross receipts may be creditable as foreign income taxes under Section 901 but only "in the rare situation where [the] tax is almost certain to reach some net gain in the normal circumstances in which it applies because costs and expenses will almost never be so high as to offset gross receipts or gross income, * * * and the rate of the tax is such that after the tax is paid persons subject to the tax are almost certain to have net gain." Reg. § 1.901–2(b)(4)(i). Consider how the withholding taxes involved in the following Ruling would be treated under the current regulations.

[¶ 5100]
REVENUE RULING 78–234

1978–1 C.B. 237, declared obsolete by Rev. Rul. 84–172, 1984–2 C.B. 315.

Advice has been requested whether the withholding tax imposed by the Republic of Tanzania under section 49(1) of the East African Income

Tax Management Act, 1958 (Management Act), * * * is an income tax for which credit is allowable under section 901 * * *.

* * * As applicable to Tanzania, section 49(1) of the Management Act, imposes a withholding tax on dividends, interest, royalties, and management or professional fees paid to a nonresident person not having a permanent establishment in Tanzania. The general effect of the permanent establishment provision of section 49(1) with respect to dividends, interest, and royalties is that the tax imposed by section 49(1) would not be imposed on any income that would be considered, under United States principles, to be connected with the conduct of a business in Tanzania. [The Tanzanian Income Tax Act] provides that the rate of nonresident withholding tax under section 49(1) shall be 12½ percent of the gross amount payable in respect of dividends, 12½ percent of the gross amount payable in respect of interest, 20 percent of the gross amount payable in respect of royalties, and 20 percent of the gross amount payable in respect of "management or professional fees." Section 2(d) of the Management Act * * * defines the term "management or professional fees" as any payment made to any person, other than a payment made to an employee of the person making the payment, in consideration for any services of a managerial, technical, professional or consultancy nature, whether payment is on a fixed sum or calculated on the basis of profits or otherwise.

* * *

The tax imposed by section 49(1) of the Management Act is not an integrated, indivisible, or unified tax since dividends, interest, royalties, and management or professional fees each form a separate tax base on which a tax is separately computed. * * * The determination whether the tax is imposed on realized net gain must therefore be made separately with respect to dividends, interest, royalties, and management or professional fees.

Applying this general test to the tax imposed by section 49(1) of the Management Act on gross management or professional fees leads to the conclusion that the tax is not the substantial equivalent of an income tax in the United States sense. The tax is levied on business income since performing personal services is classified as a trade or business. *See* section 864(b) of the Code. In general, a tax on business income will not reach net gain unless it allows for the deduction of the generally significant expenses related to the production of such income. * * * Section 49(1), of the Management Act levies a tax on the gross amount of management or professional fees derived from the conduct of a trade or business in Tanzania without allowing for the deduction of the expenses attributable to the production of that income. Because these expenses may be substantial, a tax imposed by a tax law that does not permit their deduction is not almost certain of falling on net gain. Furthermore, the tax may be imposed when the taxpayer has incurred a loss in its business of performing professional or management service.

Accordingly, the tax imposed by section 49(1) of the Management Act on the gross amount of management and professional fees is not the substantial equivalent of an income tax and, therefore, is not creditable under section 901 * * *.

The separate taxes imposed by section 49(1) of the Management Act on the gross amount of dividends, interest, and royalties do not, in fact, allow for deductions. Certain foreign taxes on gross dividends, interest, and royalties have been held to qualify as income taxes in the United States sense. * * * Additionally, similar taxes have long been imposed by the United States on dividends, interest, and royalties paid to nonresident aliens and foreign corporations (that are not effectively connected with the conduct of a trade or business in the United States) as a basic part of the United States income tax system. *See* sections 871(a)(1)(A) and 881(a)(1) * * *. The thrust of these United States tax provisions is realistically directed against net gain. * * * Accordingly, the taxes imposed by section 49(1) of the Management Act on the gross amount of dividends, interest, and royalties qualify as income taxes available for credit within the meaning of section 901 * * *.

[¶ 5105]

8. FOREIGN TAXES MUST BE ACTUALLY PAID AND MUST BE A COMPULSORY PAYMENT

The Treasury and IRS are justifiably concerned that the foreign tax credit system provides an incentive for U.S. taxpayers to collude with foreign persons to design transactions in which the foreign person purports to withhold an amount of foreign tax in excess of the amount that is actually due and payable to the foreign country. Under this scheme, the foreign person pockets the excess foreign tax and the U.S. taxpayer obtains a foreign tax credit for nonexistent foreign taxes. Even though the additional foreign tax withheld produces extra taxable income for the U.S. taxpayer, every such dollar of tax is creditable against U.S. income tax (if the scheme works). For example, if the U.S. taxpayer is in the 35–percent tax bracket, every dollar of fictional foreign tax produces an additional dollar of taxable foreign income. That additional dollar of income, in turn, creates 35 cents of additional U.S. tax liability and one dollar of additional U.S. tax benefit in the form of the U.S. foreign tax credit, resulting in a net benefit to the U.S. taxpayer of 65 cents. See, e.g., Continental Illinois Corp. v. Commissioner, 998 F.2d 513, 516–17 (7th Cir.1993), cert. denied, 510 U.S. 1041 (1994).

To forestall such abuses, the regulations contain strict requirements for proving that a foreign tax has been actually paid; failure to meet these requirements is likely to result in loss of the taxpayer's foreign tax credit. The regulations require that a taxpayer submit "the receipt for each * * * [foreign] tax payment." Reg. § 1.905–2(a)(2). If the taxpayer shows to an

IRS district director's satisfaction that "it is impossible to furnish a receipt for such foreign tax payment," the district director may "in his discretion" accept as secondary evidence of payment "a photostatic copy of the check, draft, or other medium of payment showing the amount and date thereof, with certification identifying it with the tax claimed to have been paid, together with evidence establishing that the tax was paid for taxpayer's account as his own tax on his own income." Reg. § 1.905–2(b). The courts generally have upheld the IRS's strict application of these regulations. See, e.g., Continental Illinois Corp. v. Commissioner, 998 F.2d 513, 516–17 (7th Cir.1993), cert. denied, 510 U.S. 1041 (1994) (Judge Posner stating that "it is a foreign tax credit that the Internal Revenue Code allows, not a foreign fraud credit").

Furthermore, to qualify for the foreign tax credit, the taxpayer's payment to a foreign country must be a "compulsory payment" within the meaning of Reg. § 1.901–2(e)(5). An amount paid to a foreign government is not a compulsory payment to the extent that it exceeds the amount of the taxpayer's liability under foreign law for tax. An amount paid to the foreign country does not exceed the amount of the taxpayer's liability if the taxpayer determines the amount paid "in a manner that is consistent with a reasonable interpretation and application of the substantive and procedural provisions of foreign law (including applicable tax treaties) in such a way as to reduce, over time, the taxpayer's reasonably expected liability under foreign law for tax, and if the taxpayer exhausts all effective and practical remedies * * * to reduce, over time, the taxpayer's liability for foreign tax * * *." Id. The basically sensible idea here is that the United States will not grant a foreign tax credit to a U.S. taxpayer for amounts paid to a foreign country in excess of the amount required under the foreign country's tax laws.

In 2008, the Treasury and the IRS issued temporary regulations regarding the application of the "compulsory payment" rule in Reg. § 1.901–2(e)(5) to situations in which a taxpayer claiming the foreign tax credits is a party to a "structured passive investment arrangement." Temp. Reg. § 1.901–2T(e)(5)(iv) treats a foreign payment attributable to such as an arrangement as a noncompulsory payment that is not a creditable foreign tax. The Treasury and Service explain the rationale for these temporary regulations in T.D. 9416, 2008–2 C.B. 1142:

> * * * These complex arrangements are intentionally structured to create a foreign tax liability when, removed from the elaborately engineered structure, the basic underlying business transaction generally would result in significantly less, or even no, foreign taxes. The parties use these arrangements to exploit differences between U.S. and foreign law in order to permit a person to claim a foreign tax credit for the purported foreign tax payments while also allowing the counterparty to claim a duplicative foreign tax benefit. The person claiming foreign tax credits and the counterparty share the cost of the

purported foreign tax payments through the pricing of the arrangement.

[¶ 5110]

9. FOREIGN TAXES INVOLVING REFUNDS, REBATES AND SUBSIDIES

The regulations quite logically provide that an amount paid to a foreign country is not a creditable foreign tax "to the extent that it is reasonably certain that the amount will be refunded, credited, rebated, abated, or forgiven." Reg. § 1.901–2(e)(2)(i). In other words, since the taxpayer is not out of pocket for the amount to be refunded or rebated, there is no double taxation and no foreign tax credit is appropriate. Furthermore, Section 901(i) and Reg. § 1.901–2(e)(3) provide that a tax is not a creditable foreign income tax to the extent that the foreign country uses the tax directly or indirectly to provide a subsidy to the taxpayer, certain related persons or any party to the transaction or a related transaction.

The following case considers the validity of an earlier temporary regulation that was issued before Section 901(i) was added to the Code. The case involves "net loan" transactions in which the creditor and the borrower agree that payments of principal and interest under the loan contract will be made net of any applicable foreign taxes. In effect, the borrower agrees to assume the burden of the foreign withholding taxes imposed on the creditor's interest income. For federal income tax purposes, absent any issue of subsidies or whether the tax has in fact been paid, the U.S. creditor is treated as receiving interest income in the amount of the net interest paid, increased ("grossed up") by the amount of foreign taxes paid to the foreign country by the debtor on the creditor's behalf. The U.S. creditor then may obtain a foreign tax credit for the foreign taxes, subject to the limitations in Section 904. These net loan transactions have been commonly used by U.S. banks (and the banks in other developed countries) in making loans to borrowers in developing countries.

[¶ 5115]

NISSHO IWAI AMERICAN CORP. v. COMMISSIONER

United States Tax Court, 1987.
89 T.C. 765.

JACOBS, JUDGE: * * *.

* * *

This case concerns the amount of foreign tax credit, if any, which may be claimed with respect to Brazilian taxes withheld on interest income received by petitioner as a result of a loan to a Brazilian borrower. The borrower was contractually obligated to absorb all Brazilian taxes required to be paid with respect to the interest income (i.e., petitioner was to receive the interest free of all Brazilian taxes). During the years involved, the borrower received a subsidy from the Brazilian Government equal to a percentage of the taxes withheld.

The issues to be resolved are: (1) whether petitioner is legally liable for Brazilian withholding taxes paid by the Brazilian borrower; and if so, then (2) whether such subsidy reduces the amount of the foreign tax credit allowable to petitioner pursuant to section 901 * * *.

FINDINGS OF FACT

* * *

Nissho Iwai American Corp. (hereinafter referred to as petitioner or NIAC) is a corporation organized and existing under the laws of the State of New York. * * *

Petitioner is a wholly owned subsidiary of Nissho Iwai Corp. (hereinafter referred to as NIC), a Japanese corporation. NIC is a large trading company, having numerous subsidiaries and branches.

During the years in issue, petitioner was engaged in the business of importing and exporting a wide variety of products, including metals and metal products, machinery, textiles, lumber, chemicals, foodstuffs, fuels, and general merchandise. It also engaged in making loans in the United States and abroad.

On January 27, 1978, petitioner entered into a loan agreement with Companhia Nipo–Brasileira de Pelotizacao–Nibrasco (hereinafter referred to as Nibrasco), a corporation organized and existing under the laws of the Federal Republic of Brazil. The loan agreement provided that NIAC would lend Nibrasco $20 million dollars U.S. (the loan) on or before February 17, 1978 (the remittance date). Nibrasco agreed to repay the principal of the loan in six semi-annual installments, the first of which was due 30 months from the remittance date and the last of which was due 60 months from the remittance date. The amount of the first installment was $3.5 million and the amount of each of the remaining five installments was $3.3 million.

The loan agreement provided that Nibrasco would pay interest semi-annually; the first interest payment was due six months after the remittance date. The rate of interest fluctuated; it was based on the rate quoted to the Industrial Bank of Japan, Ltd., London Branch, for the offering of dollars by prime banks in the London interbank eurodollar market for deposit for the applicable 6–month period.

All payments of principal and interest were to be made by means of telegraphic transfer to NIAC's bank account in New York, in U.S. dollars.

All payments of principal and interest were to be free and clear of, and without deduction for, any taxes imposed by Brazil.

The loan was subject to the approval of the Brazilian government and the obtaining of a certificate of registration by the Banco Central do Brasil (hereinafter referred to as the Central Bank).[5] Nibrasco also agreed to pay NIAC an administration fee of $200,000 within 10 days after the issuance of the certificate of registration. On February 17, 1978, NIAC caused $20 million to be transferred to Nibrasco's Brazilian bank. The U.S. dollars were subsequently converted into Brazilian currency.

The Central Bank issued a registration certificate with respect to the loan on March 31, 1978. Nibrasco timely paid the administration fee, as well as all required installments of principal and interest.

Brazil imposes a 25–percent withholding tax on interest paid by Brazilian borrowers on loans to foreign entities. Foreign loans to Brazilian borrowers fall into two categories—gross loans and net loans. The difference between a gross loan and a net loan is that in the former the quoted interest rate is a gross rate which does not guarantee the lender a fixed rate of return after deduction of the withholding tax, whereas in the latter the interest quoted is net of the withholding tax. Because of this difference, most of the foreign loans made to Brazilian borrowers during the years in issue were net loans, as was the NIAC–Nibrasco loan.

Evidence of payment of the withholding tax is a pre-condition for the payment of interest to a foreign lender.[6] Under Brazilian law, payment of the tax is made by submitting a Documento de Arrecadacao de Receitas Federais (hereinafter referred to as a DARF) and the amount of tax to a Brazilian bank.

Nibrasco maintained a bank account at Banco America de Sul, S.A. (hereinafter referred to as the bank). For each interest payment made to NIAC during the years in issue, Nibrasco prepared a DARF indicating the amount of the interest payment and the 25–percent withholding tax due thereon and submitted it to the bank. Thereafter, the bank debited Nibrasco's account for the amount of tax due.

On July 31, 1975, Brazilian Decree–Law No. 1411 was issued which inter alia granted the National Monetary Council[7] authority to reduce the

5. Brazil imposes restrictions on the receipt and exchange of foreign currency. By law, all foreign currency loans must be approved and registered with the Central Bank. Once prior approval for the loan is obtained, the funds are remitted in foreign currency by the lender to the borrower via a bank in Brazil where the foreign currency is converted into Brazilian currency by means of an exchange contract. Pursuant to the exchange contract, the borrower "sells" the foreign currency to the Brazilian bank for Brazilian currency at the official rate of exchange periodically set by the Central Bank. To effect payment of interest and principal on the payment date the borrower must "purchase" the foreign currency from a Brazilian bank at the official rate of exchange and the Brazilian bank then makes such payment to the lender. The certificate of registration permits the borrower to "purchase" the foreign currency.

6. The borrower cannot purchase foreign currency and remit it to the lender without establishing that the withholding tax has been paid.

7. The National Monetary Council is a Government agency responsible for economic programs. It acts through the Central Bank.

income tax on interest paid to non-Brazilian persons or to grant a monetary benefit (i.e., a subsidy) to the Brazilian borrower. The subsidy is payable only when payment of income tax on the interest is "actually made, and never in an amount higher than the collected tax." Pursuant to Decree-Law No. 1411, on August 5, 1975, a subsidy was granted to certain borrowers (including Nibrasco) equal to 85 percent of the income tax withheld.[8] The amount of the subsidy was reduced from 85 percent to 50 percent, effective July 27, 1979, and remained at 50 percent until December 9, 1979. From December 10, 1979, to May 12, 1980, the amount of the subsidy was 95 percent. From May 13, 1980, to June 30, 1985, the amount of the subsidy was 40 percent until its elimination on July 1, 1985.

The Brazilian borrower (here, Nibrasco) automatically receives a credit from his bank (i.e., the tax-collecting bank) in the amount of the subsidy at the time of payment of the withholding tax; however, the credit is subject to the approval of the Central Bank. Mechanically, the tax-collecting bank credited the account of the National Treasury for the entire tax due and simultaneously debited (reduced) the account of the National Treasury for the amount of the subsidy. The effect of this accounting procedure was that the National Treasury was credited only with the amount by which the withholding tax exceeded the subsidy.

During the years in issue, the payments made and received by NIAC and Nibrasco, and NIAC's treatment of the transaction for Federal tax purposes, were as follows:

(1) *Date of interest payment*	(2) *Amount received by NIAC*	(3) *Amount of withholding tax collected*	(4) *Amount of income reported on NIAC's tax returns*	(5) *Percentage of subsidy*	(6) *Amount of subsidy to Nibrasco*
8/17/79	$1,225,520	$408,466	$1,633,986	50%	$204,233
2/17/80	1,265,000	421,624	1,686,624	95	400,543
8/17/80	1,605,138	534,992	2,140,131	40	213,997
2/17/81	1,012,000	288,693	1,300,683	40	115,477

Note: Column (4) equals column (2) plus column (3);
Column (6) equals column (3) multiplied by column (5).

* * *

In the notice of deficiency, respondent reduced the amount of claimed foreign tax credit for both years in issue by 85 percent, except for the

8. On Oct. 24, 1974, Brazilian Decree-Law No. 1351 was issued which permitted the National Monetary Council to reduce temporarily the withholding income tax due on interest payable to foreign creditors. On the same day (i.e., Oct. 24, 1974), the National Monetary Council decided to temporarily reduce from 25 percent to 5 percent the withholding income tax on interest on loans registered at the Central Bank. On Aug. 5, 1975, the National Monetary Council revoked this temporary withholding income tax reduction. We recognize that on the same date (Aug. 5, 1975), the withholding tax reduction was revoked (which had the effect of increasing the withholding tax) and a Government subsidy to the borrower was instituted.

foreign tax credit claimed with respect to the August 17, 1979, payment which respondent allowed under the grandfather clause set forth in Rev. Rul. 78–258, 1978–1 C.B. 239, 241. Respondent disputes petitioner's entitlement to the additional $48,650 of foreign tax credit. By the amendments to his answer to the petition, respondent seeks increased deficiencies claiming that none of the Brazilian foreign tax credits are allowable because petitioner was not legally liable for the Brazilian tax.

OPINION

At the outset, it should be noted that this case involves the unusual situation in which a taxpayer seeks to recognize income. The reason for this is because attached to the recognition of income is the potential availability of a foreign tax credit; and taxwise, the foreign tax credit is worth more than the detrimental recognition of the income.

Section 901 allows a domestic corporation to claim as a credit against its Federal income tax (subject to certain limitations not applicable herein) the amount of any income taxes paid on behalf of the taxpayer to a foreign country. Sec. 4.901–2(a), Temporary Income Tax Regs. * * *.[13]

* * *

A foreign tax is creditable only if the taxpayer is legally liable under foreign law for the tax. Sec. 4.901–2(g), Temporary Income Tax Regs. However, legal liability for a tax and the obligation to pay the tax are not necessarily the same. For example, under a withholding system, legal liability for the tax and the obligation to pay the tax are different. The Federal wage withholding system illustrates this difference—the employer is the person obligated to withhold the tax and to pay the withheld tax to the Government; the employee is the person legally liable for the tax.

Under Brazilian law, interest paid to foreign lenders (i.e., lenders residing or domiciled abroad) is subject to an income tax at the rate of 25 percent. The Brazilian borrower is required to withhold that percentage from each payment of interest; as a practical matter, the interest payment cannot be made unless and until the Brazilian withholding tax is paid. Respondent argues that the Brazilian withholding tax is a tax upon the payment, rather than receipt, of interest. We disagree.

U.S. tax law is the standard for deciding whether a foreign levy is a creditable income tax. *Biddle v. Commissioner*, 302 U.S. 573 (1938). After reviewing translations of the applicable Brazilian law, it is our opinion that the tax is on the receipt of the interest. The tax is imposed on the foreign lender; the Brazilian borrower is simply the person required to pay

13. In November 1980, the Internal Revenue Service issued temporary regulations which set forth requirements for, and limitations on, the amount of foreign tax credit. These temporary regulations, sec. 4.901–2 et seq., generally were made applicable to taxable years ending after June 15, 1979. Final regulations under sec. 901 were made effective for taxable years beginning after November 14, 1983. [The final regulations are contained in Reg. § 1.901–2(e)(1) and (3). The provisions are essentially the same as the temporary regulations.]

the tax on behalf of the foreign lender. Accordingly, we believe that the Brazilian withholding tax per se is potentially creditable to the lender. See sec. 4.901–2(a), Temporary Income Tax Regs.; *Gleason Works v. Commissioner*, 58 T.C. 464 (1972). We now turn to the amount of the Brazilian withholding tax which is creditable.

Section 4.901–2(f), Temporary Income Tax Regs. (relating to amount of income tax paid or accrued), provides:

> (f) *Amount of income tax paid or accrued*—(1) *In general.* A credit is allowed under section 901 for the amount of income tax * * * that is paid or accrued to a foreign country, subject to the provisions of this paragraph (f). The amount of income tax paid or accrued is determined separately for each taxpayer.
>
> * * *
>
> (3) *Subsidies*—(i) *General rule.* An amount is not income tax paid or accrued to a foreign country to the extent that—
>
> (A) The amount is used directly or indirectly by [a] country to provide a subsidy by any means (such as through a refund or credit) to the taxpayer; and
>
> (B) The subsidy is determined directly or indirectly by reference to the amount of income tax, or the base used to compute the income tax, imposed by the country on the taxpayer.
>
> (ii) *Indirect subsidies.* A foreign country is considered to provide a subsidy to a person if the country provides a subsidy to another person that—
>
> (A) Is owned or controlled, directly or indirectly, by the same interests that own or control, directly or indirectly, the first person; or
>
> (B) Engages in a business transaction with the first person, but only if the subsidy received by such other person is determined directly or indirectly by reference to the amount of income tax, or the base used to compute the income tax, imposed by the country on the first person with respect to such transaction. * * *

Respondent contends that if petitioner is legally liable for the Brazilian tax, that portion of the tax which was returned to Nibrasco by way of the subsidy is not creditable. Respondent relies on section 4.901–2(f)(3), Temporary Income Tax Regs., for this position. Petitioner argues that this regulation is invalid and requests that we follow what have been termed the "Mexican railroad car rental" cases. * * * We agree with respondent.

The temporary regulations in effect during both years in issue provide that, for purposes of creditability, amounts of tax paid or accrued to a foreign country do not include amounts used directly or indirectly as a subsidy to either the taxpayer or a person who is engaged in a business transaction with the taxpayer where the subsidy is determined directly or indirectly by reference to the amount of income tax, or the base used to compute the income tax, imposed by the country on the taxpayer. Here, the amount of the subsidy received by Nibrasco is clearly based on the amount of the withholding tax.

These regulations were promulgated under the Treasury's general rule-making power as authorized by section 7805(a). As stated by the Supreme Court, Treasury regulations "must be sustained unless unreasonable and plainly inconsistent with the revenue statutes." *Commissioner v. South Texas Lumber Co.*, 333 U.S. 496, 501 (1948), and they "should not be overruled except for weighty reasons." *Bingler v. Johnson*, 394 U.S. 741, 750 (1969). We recognize that the regulations involved are temporary, not final, regulations; nevertheless, we believe that they are entitled to the same weight as the final regulations.[16] * * *

The position set forth in the temporary regulations, in our opinion, is not unreasonable. The purpose of the foreign tax credit is to reduce international double taxation. See *American Chicle Co. v. United States*, 316 U.S. 450 (1942). Here, no double taxation occurred; in fact, because petitioner's loan with Nibrasco was a net loan, petitioner was not "out of pocket" for any of the Brazilian taxes. As far as petitioner is concerned, its receiving credit for the Brazilian taxes in any amount essentially constitutes a windfall. The question to be resolved is how much of a windfall petitioner is to receive.

Here, Nibrasco absorbed the entire amount of the Brazilian withholding tax on behalf of petitioner. Simultaneous with the payment of the tax, Nibrasco received a subsidy from the Brazilian Government based on the amount of tax paid. Petitioner argues that an amount collected as a tax does not "lose its status as such by virtue of the fact that the taxing authority (foreign or domestic) allocates that amount to a specific program." While in general we agree with petitioner's argument, in the situation involved herein, payment of the tax and receipt of the subsidy are in lockstep. Common sense dictates that payment of the tax and receipt of the subsidy be viewed together in determining the amount of foreign taxes creditable for purposes of section 901. If we accept payment of the Brazilian tax as one transaction and receipt of the subsidy as another, we would ignore the true unity of the transaction and elevate form over substance; this we shall not do.

* * *[17]

---

16. It is to be noted that the final regulations (Treas. Reg. sec. 1.901–2(e)(3)) provide that a subsidy accorded in connection with foreign taxes reduces the creditability of such taxes.

17. We note that sec. 1204 of the Tax Reform Act of 1986, Pub. L. 99–514 * * *, codifies the position set forth in the temporary and final regulations. The applicable Senate Finance Committee report provides:

"A Treasury regulation denies a foreign tax credit for foreign taxes used directly or indirectly as a subsidy to the taxpayer. Absent this rule, the Treasury would, in effect, bear the cost of tax subsidy programs instituted by foreign countries for the direct or indirect benefit of their residents and certain nonresidents. The committee is informed that some U.S. lenders and

[¶ 5120]

NOTES

1. Section 901(i) now specifically denies credits for any foreign taxes used to provide subsidies. This provision was enacted as part of the Tax Reform Act of 1986 and was intended to codify the rule embodied in the temporary regulation sustained by the Tax Court.

2. Note that the current regulations under Section 901(i) and the prior temporary regulations upheld in the *Nissho Iwai* case define certain amounts of tax as non-creditable subsidies without reference to the degree of actual economic benefit conferred upon the taxpayer. As stated by Judge Posner in Continental Illinois Corp. v. Commissioner, 998 F.2d 513, 519–20 (7th Cir. 1993), cert. denied, 510 U.S. 1041 (1994):

> "Subsidy" is a tricky concept. It is by no means clear that the Brazilian tax rebate [i.e., the pecuniary benefit program also at issue in *Nissho Iwai*] subsidized, in the sense of conferring an actual benefit upon, American net lenders like Continental [and NIAC]. * * * Indeed, insofar as the interest rate had been fixed in the loan contract before the rebate was instituted, only the borrowers benefited; for we noted at the outset that the difference between a net and a gross loan is that a net loan allocates the risk and benefit of any change in the tax rate to the borrower because the lender's return is specified net of tax. Even if not frozen by the contract the interest rate might not rise by the amount of the subsidy. It is true that the subsidy would make the borrowers more eager to take out foreign loans and that an increase in demand usually results in an increase in price, but the increase in demand need not be proportionally equal to the increase in price and it would be tempered here by competition among the foreign lenders; also, Brazil imposed ceilings on interest rates. Figuring out who gets how much of the benefit of a subsidy is like figuring out who really pays a tax, since the nominal taxpayer has an incentive to shift it as best he can forward or backward. It all depends on contract terms and on conditions of demand and supply.
>
> The IRS regulation * * * elides a difficult factual inquiry by deeming the taxpayer subsidized if the country subsidizes a person with whom the

---

other U.S. taxpayers take tax return positions that are inconsistent with this rule. The committee does not believe that foreign tax credits should be allowed for foreign taxes which, while ostensibly borne by a U.S. taxpayer, are effectively rebated by the levying country by means of a government subsidy to the taxpayer, a related party, a party to a transaction with the taxpayer, or a party to a related transaction. To eliminate any uncertainty in this area, the committee believes that the Treasury regulation rule disallowing foreign tax credits for taxes used as a subsidy should be clarified and codified. [S. Rept. 99–313 at 307 (1986) * * *.]"

The Senate Finance Committee report also states:

"The committee is aware that the validity under current law of a ruling predating Treas. Reg. sec. 1.901–2(e)(3) that embodies its substance is being challenged in litigation pending in the U.S. Tax Court. No inference should be drawn from the committee's action as to the validity or invalidity of the regulation or ruling for years prior to the effective date of the bill [foreign taxes paid or accrued in taxable years beginning after December 31, 1986]. [S. Rept. 99–313 at 325 (1986) * * *.]"

> taxpayer "engages in a business transaction," provided the subsidy "is determined directly or indirectly by reference to the amount of income tax . . . imposed by the country on [that] person with respect to such transaction." * * * Just as the IRS must be given leeway in deciding what proof to require that a tax has actually been paid, so it must be given leeway in deciding when a rebate to a foreign business partner of a U.S. taxpayer should be deemed a subsidy to the taxpayer, disentitling [the taxpayer] to a foreign tax credit. The IRS can hardly be faulted for having chosen a bright-line approach in preference to interminable investigation of the mysteries of public finance, much as the latter approach might appeal to the legal, accounting, and economic-consulting communities. * * *

3. Three courts of appeals have upheld the validity of the prior temporary regulations on subsidies in cases involving various U.S. banks and the same Brazilian pecuniary benefit program at issue in the *Nissho Iwai* case. See Norwest Corp. v. Commissioner, 69 F.3d 1404 (8th Cir.1995), cert. denied, 517 U.S. 1203 (1996); Continental Illinois Corp. v. Commissioner, 998 F.2d 513 (7th Cir.1993), cert. denied, 510 U.S. 1041 (1994); Citizens & Southern Corp. v. Commissioner, 919 F.2d 1492 (11th Cir.1990) (per curiam). One other court of appeals, the Federal Circuit, in a rather strangely reasoned opinion, has held that the prior temporary regulations were invalid because they were inconsistent with earlier definitive court rulings by the Court of Claims (a predecessor court of the Federal Circuit) that it viewed as stare decisis on the subsidy issue. See Bankers Trust New York Corp. v. United States, 225 F.3d 1368 (Fed.Cir.2000), rev'g 36 Fed. Cl. 30 (1996).

4. In Riggs Nat'l Corp. v. Commissioner, 107 T.C. 301 (1996), rev'd on another ground, 163 F.3d 1363 (D.C.Cir.1999), the Tax Court upheld the prior temporary regulations on subsidies in yet another case involving a U.S. bank and the Brazilian pecuniary benefit program at issue in the *Nissho Iwai* case. The borrower in *Riggs* was the Central Bank of Brazil, an entity that is exempt from tax under Brazilian law. However, the U.S. bank had obtained a favorable private letter ruling from the Brazilian Minister of Finance that the Central Bank of Brazil was required to pay the tax obligations assumed from the lenders in the net loan transaction. The Tax Court, nevertheless, upheld the argument of the IRS that under Brazilian law a tax-immune borrower such as the Central Bank was not obligated to pay the tax on the interest income, and, hence, the tax payments on the interest income were voluntary and not creditable. On appeal, the D.C. Circuit reversed the Tax Court on the ground that the IRS's theory that the tax payments by the Central Bank were voluntary payments violates the act of state doctrine (163 F.3d at 1365–69). On remand, the Tax Court held that the taxpayer bank failed to establish, through credible direct or secondary evidence, that the withholding taxes in issue were in fact paid by the Central Bank on the taxpayer's behalf. Accordingly, under Section 905(b), the Tax Court disallowed the taxpayer's foreign tax credits for the years in issue. Riggs Nat'l Corp. v. Commissioner, 81 T.C.M. (CCH) 1023 (2001). This second Tax Court decision was, in turn,

also reversed by the D.C. Circuit, with the court of appeals concluding that the Brazilian taxes were withheld and paid by the Central Bank. 295 F.3d 16 (D.C. Cir. 2002). This led to a third Tax Court decision in which, on remand, the court held that in determining the taxpayer's creditable amount under Section 901, the Brazilian withholding taxes paid by the Central Bank had to be reduced by the pecuniary benefit received by the Central Bank. Riggs Nat'l Corp. v. Commissioner, 87 T.C.M. (CCH) 1276 (2004). This third Tax Court decision was affirmed sub nom. by the D.C. Circuit in PNC Fin. Servs. Group, Inc. v. Commissioner, 503 F.3d 119 (D.C. Cir. 2007).

5. In the following case, the Seventh Circuit considered the application of the indirect subsidy rules in the context of a complicated transaction between a U.S. oil company and an instrumentality of the Saudi Arabian government.

[¶ 5122]

AMOCO CORP. v. COMMISSIONER

United States Court of Appeals, Seventh Circuit, 1998.
138 F.3d 1139.

WOOD, CIRCUIT JUDGE:

The Internal Revenue Code permits U.S. taxpayers who have paid the equivalent of income taxes to foreign governments to credit those amounts against their U.S. taxes, with certain limitations. * * *[1] We must decide in this case whether Amoco was entitled to claim credits derived from some of its operations in the Arab Republic of Egypt ("ARE" or "Egypt"). This would be complex enough if all we had to do was ascertain what the law of Egypt was and whether Amoco's tax payments to the Egyptian authorities met the criteria of § 901, but those questions begin rather than end our inquiry. As the following account of the facts indicates, we must also consider the effect of Egypt's decision to use a wholly owned corporate entity for its critically important oil business, as well as the significance of certain mistakes that entity made in handling the Egyptian taxes on its transactions with Amoco.

I

Amoco Corporation, formerly Standard Oil Company (Indiana), through its affiliate the Amoco Egypt Oil Company (all of which we refer to as "Amoco"), has been active in crude oil and natural gas exploration and production in Egypt since the 1960s. Under the Egyptian Constitution and implementing Egyptian law, the ARE owns all the country's natural resources, including its oil and gas. Within the executive branch of the

1. The 1954 code as amended applies to this case, and unless otherwise indicated statutory citations * * * are to it. The current code differs in only one relevant way from that applicable to this litigation. Section 901(i) was enacted in 1986 and is applicable to tax years beginning after December 31, 1986. * * * The 1991 amendments to Treas. Reg. § 1.901–2, implementing § 901(i), * * * also do not apply.

government, the Ministry of Petroleum and Mineral Resources is responsible for the management of Egypt's mineral resources. Affiliated with the Ministry is the Egyptian General Petroleum Corporation (EGPC), which was initially created in 1958 pursuant to Egyptian Law No. 167 of 1958, and later reconstituted under the same name by Egyptian Law No. 20 of 1976. According to the 1976 statute, EGPC is "a Public Authority endowed with an independent juristic personality, engaged in developing and properly utilizing the petroleum wealth and in supplying the country's requirements of the various petroleum products." EGPC is the entity through which the government organizes oil concession agreements with outside companies.

EGPC is wholly owned by the ARE and controlled by the Egyptian Government. Upon its dissolution, all of its assets must revert to the state. The chair of its board of directors is appointed by decree of the President of the Republic, and the remaining members are appointed by decree of the Prime Minister on the recommendation of the Minister of Petroleum and Mineral Resources. Resolutions of the Board must be forwarded to the Minister for ratification, amendment, or cancellation. Notwithstanding these close ties to the Government, EGPC has an independent budget prepared in the same manner as a commercial budget, and it is subject to Egyptian income tax. Its funds bear the oxymoronic label "privately owned State funds." Except for certain reserves, however, its after-tax surplus (if any) each year is turned over to the public treasury, and in the (as of yet hypothetical) event there were a deficit the treasury would be responsible for it.

When Amoco began its Egyptian oil operations in the early 1960s, it negotiated agreements with EGPC that set forth the terms under which it would do business. Over the course of its first decade in Egypt Amoco entered into three such concessions: the Western Desert Concession Agreement (October 1963), the Gulf of Suez Concession Agreement (February 1964), and the Western Desert and Nile Valley Concession Agreement (September 1969). Under these agreements, Amoco was generally required to pay for all preliminary exploration costs, up to a specified amount, after which Amoco and EGPC split both production costs and crude oil revenues on a 50–50 basis. Each entity paid its own Egyptian income taxes, and in addition each paid royalties and other miscellaneous charges imposed by the government. (These and all other concession agreements in Egypt are technically laws, and before becoming effective are ratified by the legislature and signed by the Egyptian President.) Amoco's exploration efforts were richly rewarded in February 1965, when it struck the El Morgan field in the Gulf of Suez. Production from that field, the largest oil find in Egypt to date, began in February 1967.

Eager to secure for itself a greater share of the benefits from its oil, the Government of Egypt in 1970 began entering into a different type of concession agreement with oil companies. The new agreements used a production-sharing format rather than the 50–50 income-sharing approach of Amoco's early agreements. Under these production-sharing agreements, EGPC holds the concession to explore for and produce petroleum while its foreign partners act as contractors, bearing the cost of all exploration, development, and production activities in return for a negotiated share of the production. Part of the contractor's share is earmarked for the recovery of costs.

Several oil companies entered into production-sharing agreements with EGPC between 1970 and 1974. In 1974, Amoco and EGPC entered into three production-sharing agreements, which related to oil fields not covered by Amoco's earlier income-sharing agreements. In early 1975, Amoco and EGPC began discussing converting the three existing 50–50 income-sharing agreements into a single production-sharing agreement that came to be called the Merged Concession Agreement, or MCA. The Tax Court's opinion contains a detailed description of these negotiations. See *Amoco Corp. v. Commissioner*, 71 T.C.M. (CCH) 2613 * * * (1996). Amoco and EGPC devoted considerable attention in those negotiations to the creditability of Amoco's Egyptian taxes for U.S. tax purposes. Amoco wanted to pay its own Egyptian taxes. EGPC, in contrast, preferred that the transaction be arranged so that Amoco would remain responsible for its own taxes, but EGPC would pay Amoco's taxes out of EGPC's share of the oil produced. (By thus structuring the agreement EGPC would itself sell the oil allocated to taxes, thus obtaining foreign currency.)

The MCA was initialed by the parties in November, 1975, was ratified by the Egyptian Government in February, 1976 (Law No. 15 of 1976), and was effective retroactive to July 1, 1975. In the final draft, Amoco and EGPC agreed that Amoco would be entitled to up to 20% of the crude oil produced as a reimbursement for the costs of exploration, production, and related operations. EGPC and Amoco would share the remaining 80% of production in varying percentages, between 85 and 87% for EGPC and 13 to 15% for Amoco. Out of its share of production, EGPC had to pay the Government of Egypt a royalty of 15% of the total quantity of petroleum produced and saved from the concession; Amoco had no direct royalty obligation to the Egyptian government. Article IV(f) of the MCA addressed the subject of taxes, and stated in pertinent part:

> 1. AMOCO shall be subject to Egyptian Income Tax Laws and shall comply with the requirements of the A.R.E. Law in particular with respect to filing returns, assessment of tax, and keeping and showing of books and records.
>
> * * *
>
> 3. EGPC shall assume, pay and discharge, in the name and on behalf of AMOCO, AMOCO's Egyptian Income Tax out of EGPC's share of the Crude Oil produced and saved and not used in operations under

> Article VII. All taxes paid by EGPC in the name and on behalf of AMOCO shall be considered taxable income to AMOCO.
>
> * * *
>
> 6. In calculating its A.R.E. income taxes, EGPC shall be entitled to deduct all royalties paid by EGPC to the GOVERNMENT and AMOCO's Egyptian Income Taxes paid by EGPC on AMOCO's behalf.

As often happens with international agreements, the English version of the text was not the only one, nor the only authentic one. In the Arabic version of Article IV(f), paragraph 6, which appears if anything to be slightly more authoritative, the Arabic word "minha," meaning "therefrom," appeared immediately after the Arabic words "an takhssim," meaning "to deduct." The term "minha" literally means "from it or her." The Arabic word for taxes is a feminine noun, "daraa 'ib'," while the Arabic word for income is a masculine noun, "al-dakhl." This brief excursion into Arabic helps to explain why, in later years, EGPC took the position that Article IV(f), para. 6, allowed it to credit against its Egyptian taxes the full amount of the taxes it was paying on Amoco's behalf, even though the English version of the text sounds as if Amoco's Egyptian taxes were to be taken as a deduction against EGPC's income. In any event, at the time no one appears to have noticed the linguistic ambiguity. (The Egyptian Government eventually concluded that the MCA authorized only deductions, the Tax Court so held, and the Commissioner does not challenge that interpretation on appeal.)

It was not long after the MCA took effect that Amoco got wind of the fact that EGPC was interpreting the agreement to allow it to take a credit against its own Egyptian taxes for the payments it was making on Amoco's behalf. The issue arose no later than September 1980, during the course of discussions between the parties about possible amendments to the agreement. At the same time, Amoco was seeking rulings from the IRS about the creditability of its Egyptian taxes if the agreement were changed in certain ways. In the end, no changes were made in the Egyptian agreement that affected its tax provisions, and it was not until April 1988 that Amoco verified once and for all that EGPC was indeed taking credits for its payments. Amoco then informed the Commissioner of this fact.

Numerous officials in the Egyptian government, both high and low, also became involved in the question of the tax consequences of the MCA. In the end, the key actor turned out to be one Ahmed Ismail, a tax inspector in the Petroleum Section of the Department of Tax on Joint Stock Companies of the Egyptian Tax Department. In December 1989, Ismail conducted his first audit of EGPC for the 1983–84 tax return. That audit did not challenge EGPC's claimed tax credits for royalties or foreign partner taxes, but Ismail apparently changed his mind when he reviewed EGPC's 1984–85 tax return, and challenged the credits for that year. Ismail continued to monitor EGPC's returns; tax assessment forms sent out for later years do not indicate an allowance of a tax credit for foreign partner taxes, and Ismail testified that the credit was in fact disallowed. Eventually, higher Egyptian tax authorities concluded that under Egyptian law EGPC was not entitled to take a credit for the royalties and foreign partner taxes (including Amoco's). The Minister of Petroleum and Mineral Resources, Dr. Hamdi El Banbi, knew that the change in treatment would have "some" unfavorable impact on EGPC, but by 1992, the Ministers of Finance and Petroleum had worked out an agreement whereby EGPC's tax credits for the contested items would be disallowed for all tax years still open under the law. Given the applicable Egyptian statute of limitations, adjustments were made for taxable periods ending June 30, 1981, and thereafter.

In the meantime, Amoco had been taking a foreign tax credit on its U.S. tax returns in the amount its tax receipts from EGPC indicated had been paid to the Government of Egypt on Amoco's behalf. Our concern at this point is with four tax years: 1979 and 1980, because they were closed under Egyptian law by the time the Egyptian authorities implemented the change from a credit to a deduction, and 1981 and 1982. The Commissioner, in its notice of deficiency and before the Tax Court, argued that Amoco was not entitled to any credits for these latter two years. On appeal the Commissioner concedes that some credit should be granted, but urges us to remand to the Tax Court to determine how much credit Amoco is entitled to, taking into account the changes in the foreign exchange rate (and presumably also the time-value of money) between the time these taxes were credited against Amoco's U.S. taxes and the time when EGPC eventually revised its Egyptian tax filings, in 1992. We do not need to reach the issues specific to the 1981 and 1982 tax years unless we find that Amoco's foreign tax credits for the 1979 and 1980 years were invalid, since holding those earlier credits valid would necessarily imply that the full 1981 and 1982 credits taken by Amoco were also valid.

Relying on the 1983 foreign tax credit regulations and on the "safe harbor" method for determining which tax credits were allowable, see Treas. Reg. § 1.901–2A(e) (1983), Amoco included the Egyptian taxes allegedly paid by EGPC as income, and then claimed the following combination of credits and deductions on its U.S. taxes:

Year	Egyptian Taxes Allegedly Paid	U.S. Tax Credit	U.S. Tax Deduction
1979	$304,015,893	$215,414,631	$ 88,601,262
1980	$498,086,280	$459,881,927	$ 38,204,353
1981	$557,873,428	$383,993,639	$173,879,789
1982	$453,586,679	$308,490,749	$145,095,933

When the dust settled, the IRS took the position that Amoco's claimed foreign tax credits from those years had to be disallowed, on the theory that EGPC's now unreviewable act of taking a credit against its own Egyptian taxes meant that in effect nothing had been paid on Amoco's behalf. The IRS accordingly issued a notice of deficiency to Amoco on June 18, 1992, challenging Amoco's calculations for the 1979 to 1982 tax years, and listing the following amounts:

Year	Deficiency
1980	$109,618,203
1981	$200,848,534
1982	$155,776,311
TOTAL	$466,243,048

(No deficiency was alleged for the 1979 tax year, because Amoco's claimed tax credits for that year were carried forward. The Commissioner's calculated deficiencies do not match the credits initially claimed by Amoco both because of this carryover and because the Commissioner reduced Amoco's income by the tax amounts allegedly paid by EGPC. As noted above, the Commissioner now concedes that some part of the credits claimed for the 1981 and 1982 tax years should have been allowed.)

Amoco responded to this unwelcome missive by filing a petition in the Tax Court contesting the proposed deficiencies. After a two-week trial, the Tax Court found that Amoco was entitled to the credits it had claimed.

II

Under I.R.C. § 901(b)(1), United States citizens and domestic corporations are generally allowed to claim tax credits against their U.S. income taxes in "the amount of any income, war profits, and excess profits taxes paid or accrued during the taxable year to any foreign country or to any possession of the United States[.]" The Treasury has issued regulations defining in greater detail which foreign taxes can support a tax credit under § 901(b)(1). In this case, the parties agree, the 1983 version of Treas. Reg. § 1.901–2 * * * controls. (While this regulation was issued after the tax years in question, Amoco elected to have it apply under § 1.901–2(h)(2) (1983).) Under that regulation, even if foreign taxes were nominally paid, under some circumstances the U.S. taxpayer is nonetheless not entitled to claim a credit on its U.S. tax return:

> **(e) Amount of income tax that is creditable.—(1) In general.** Credit is allowed under section 901 for the amount of income tax (within the meaning of paragraph (a)(1) of this section) that is paid to a foreign country by the taxpayer. The amount of income tax paid by the taxpayer is determined separately for each taxpayer.
>
> **(2) Refunds and credits.—(i) In general.** An amount is not tax paid to a foreign country to the extent that it is reasonably certain that the amount will be refunded, credited, rebated, abated, or forgiv-

en. It is not reasonably certain that an amount will be refunded, credited, rebated, abated, or forgiven if the amount is not greater than a reasonable approximation of final tax liability to the foreign country.

* * *

(3) Subsidies.—(i) General rule. An amount is not an amount of income tax paid by a taxpayer to a foreign country to the extent that—

(A) The amount is used, directly or indirectly, by the country to provide a subsidy by any means (such as through a refund or credit) to the taxpayer; and

(B) The subsidy is determined, directly or indirectly, by reference to the amount of income tax, or the base used to compute the income tax, imposed by the country on the taxpayer.

(ii) Indirect subsidies. A foreign country is considered to provide a subsidy to a taxpayer if the country provides a subsidy to another person that—

(A) Owns or controls, directly or indirectly, the taxpayer or is owned or controlled, directly or indirectly, by the taxpayer or by the same persons that own or control, directly or indirectly, the taxpayer, or

(B) Engages in a transaction with the taxpayer, but only if the subsidy received by such other person is determined, directly or indirectly, by reference to the amount of income tax, or the base used to compute the income tax, imposed by the country on the taxpayer with respect to such transaction.

Subsection (f) of the same regulation makes it clear that the person on whom the foreign law imposes liability for the tax is the "taxpayer" in question, even if another person actually remits the tax to the foreign revenue authority. Treas. Reg. § 1.901–2(f).

Our case turns on the question whether the income taxes EGPC paid on Amoco's behalf were "taxes paid to a foreign country" within the meaning of § 901(b)(1) and the implementing Treasury Regulations, or if, by force of Treas. Reg. § 1.901–2(e)(2) or (3), those amounts paid do not qualify as "tax paid to a foreign country" either because it was reasonably certain that the monies would be refunded or credited, or because the amounts were indirect subsidies to Amoco. Whether a taxpayer is entitled to foreign tax credits is a question we decide by applying principles of domestic tax law. *Cf. United States v. Goodyear Tire & Rubber Co.*, 493 U.S. 132 * * * (1989); *Biddle v. Commissioner*, 302 U.S. 573, 578 * * * (1938). That is not to say that the foreign law is irrelevant, of course; it means only that the ultimate U.S. tax consequences of a particular set of rights and obligations established under foreign law remains a question of U.S. law.

The Tax Court decided that Treas. Reg. § 1.901–2(e)(2) did not deprive Amoco of the right to take a foreign tax credit in this case, because the credit of the Egyptian taxes paid on Amoco's behalf had been made to EGPC rather than to Amoco itself, which meant that Amoco had in fact paid these taxes within the meaning of the regulation. It also concluded that the tax credits to EGPC were not an indirect subsidy to Amoco, because for this purpose EGPC had to be treated as part of the Egyptian government, and it made no sense to say that the Egyptian government was providing a subsidy to itself (*i.e.* EGPC). If the credits were not a subsidy to EGPC, then no party engaged in a transaction with Amoco received the kind of subsidy that would deprive Amoco of its foreign tax credits. The Commissioner naturally urges us to reverse the Tax Court on both counts. Furthermore, she also asks us, assuming we agree with her on these points, to remand the case for a determination of the time as of which EGPC should be deemed to have paid Amoco's Egyptian taxes, and a recalculation of the foreign tax credit Amoco is entitled to based on the adjusted value of EGPC's payments.

A. *Refund or Credit: Treas. Reg. § 1.901–2(e)(2)*

The critical question in determining whether Treas. Reg. § 1.901–2(e)(2) deprives a taxpayer of the right to take a credit for "tax[es] paid to a foreign country" is whether the amount was "reasonably certain" to be refunded, credited, or similarly returned to the taxpayer. We agree with the Tax Court that, under all the circumstances, it was not reasonably certain that the Egyptian Finance Ministry would allow a full credit to EGPC (on its own Egyptian tax returns) for EGPC's payments of Amoco's taxes. The language of Article IV(f)(6) of the MCA was at best ambiguous about the way in which EGPC was to treat these payments: the English version appears to contemplate deductions from income, while the Arabic version may have suggested credits. Given this ambiguity, the Tax Court carefully examined the negotiations leading up to the MCA and the parties' course of dealing under the agreement, and came to the conclusion that Amoco Egypt thought the MCA provided a deduction, EGPC was unsure whether it could take a credit or a deduction, and the Government of Egypt had no view on the matter. *Amoco v. Commissioner*, *supra*, 71 T.C.M. (CCH) at 2632–33. Had the parties intended to allow EGPC to take a credit, the court believed the agreement would have been more explicit.

In addition, the court took into account the actual decision of the Egyptian Tax Department (ETD) when it formally reviewed EGPC's returns in 1992. As noted above, the ETD concluded that EGPC was not entitled to take a credit for the taxes it was paying on Amoco's behalf. The consequence of this decision was that EGPC had to pay the back taxes it owed, going back as far as the Egyptian statute of limitations would permit. The Tax Court concluded, and we agree, that a taxpayer could not be "reasonably certain" that it would receive a credit or refund when the governing law did not entitle it to one. *Id.* at 2635. Indeed, if the ETD had begun reviewing EGPC's returns a few years earlier, it would have been entitled to reopen the remaining years at issue in this case. One cannot say that a taxpayer is reasonably certain to obtain a refund or credit just because the taxpayer hopes that the revenue authorities will fail to notice an error until the period of limitations has run. As the Tax Court commented, "[t]he expiration of the period of limitations does not substantively legitimatize the barred action; it simply reflects an inability to enforce the obligation that would otherwise exist." *Id.*

The Tax Court also found that, even had there been a refund or credit to EGPC as defined in the regulation, this refund could not be attributed to Amoco. Treas. Reg. § 1.901–2(e)(2) does not contain an "indirect refund" rule analogous to the indirect subsidy concept in § 1.901–2(e)(3), and no one disputes the fact that the ETD did not refund or credit Amoco's Egyptian tax account for as much as a single Egyptian pound. The Commissioner argues at length that the Tax Court cannot be correct, because it is easy to envision circumstances in which a third party pays foreign tax on behalf of a U.S. taxpayer and then receives a refund of that same payment. We do not disagree that this kind of situation can arise, but it seems to us that this is precisely what the indirect subsidy rule of § 1.901–2(e)(3) was designed to cover. The Commissioner loses nothing by proceeding under subsection (3) of her own regulation, rather than subsection (2), and subsection (3) explicitly includes refunds and credits as types of subsidies. See Treas. Reg. § 1.901–2(e)(3)(i)(A). We therefore agree with the Tax Court that the absence of any refund to the U.S. taxpayer provides an alternate ground for rejecting the applicability of § 1.901–2(e)(2) in this case.

B. *Indirect Subsidies: § 1.901–2(e)(3)*

The more difficult question is whether, even if Amoco's payments did not count as foreign tax payments under the refund regulation, the credits EGPC enjoyed for the closed years were an indirect subsidy to Amoco. On the face of the regulation, this appears to be a strong argument for the Commissioner. First, under this regulation it is clear that a subsidy to another person can be attributed to the U.S. taxpayer, where the other person "[e]ngages in a transaction with the taxpayer" and the subsidy is somehow computed by reference to the amount of the tax or tax base in question. Here, EGPC engaged in a transaction with Amoco, and the subsidy it received (the tax credits) was measured precisely by the amount of tax EGPC was paying on Amoco's behalf to the ETD. "Q.E.D.," says the Commissioner: Amoco received an indirect subsidy because its business partner, EGPC, in effect paid no taxes on its account to the Egyptian government. The Commissioner analogizes this to the Brazilian tax cases, in which this court and a number of other courts found an indirect subsidy to the extent that a fixed percentage of the taxes on interest income paid by Brazilian borrowers was rebated by the government to those borrowers. See *Norwest Corp. v. Commissioner*, 69 F.3d 1404 (8th Cir.1995); *Continental Illinois Corp. v. Commissioner*, 998 F.2d 513 (7th Cir.1993); *Bankers Trust New York Corp. v. United States*, 36 Fed. Cl. 30 (1996); *Nissho Iwai American Corp. v. Commissioner*, 89 T.C. 765 * * * (1987). The fact that Amoco may have received no economic benefit from the credits EGPC enjoyed (which appears to be the case) is of no importance. See *Norwest*, 69 F.3d at 1408–09; *Continental Illinois*, 998 F.2d at 519–20.

The Tax Court found that the indirect subsidy rule did not apply for a more basic reason. It agreed with Amoco that the EGPC was part of the Egyptian government, and thus by definition it was incapable of receiving a subsidy from itself. It found some support for this notion in Treas. Reg. § 1.901–2(e)(3)(ii), which indicates that indirect subsidies to the U.S. taxpayer occur when a foreign nation provides a subsidy to *another* person. EGPC, recall, is wholly owned and controlled by the Egyptian government; it is affiliated with the Petroleum Ministry; all of its directors are appointed by the government; and their resolutions are subject to the approval of the Minister of Petroleum. Although it has an independent budget, it turns its profits over to the public treasury, and if it were to experience losses the treasury would absorb them. All of that indicated to the Tax Court that no meaningful difference exists between EGPC and the government itself. Amoco argues further on appeal that one should not speak of a "subsidy" unless or until funds move from the government out into the private sector.

Support for Amoco's reading comes from Treas. Reg. § 1.901–2(f)(2)(ii) (Example 3), which clarifies that were a party to enter into a contract with a foreign government directly, whereby that government agreed to assume any tax liability owed itself, the party would remain eligible for foreign tax credits. The Commissioner has attempted to counter this point by referring us to the 1991 regulations, especially Treas. Reg. § 1.901–2(e)(3)(iv) (Example 4) (1991), though it acknowledges those regulations are not applicable to the tax years in question. In this instance we decline to defer to Example 4. It is technically inapplicable, and we note that it was drafted during the pendency of this case and bears the marks of a litigating position. * * * (Were the regulation applicable we would consider it despite this latter concern, as it was promulgated through notice-and-comment rulemaking. * * *)

The question of how to treat state-owned enterprises or instrumentalities is exceedingly complicated. The one thing that can be said with confidence, however, is that the Supreme Court has eschewed bright-line rules in favor of a more functional approach to the matter. As an initial matter, we think it overstates the case to say that EGPC has no separate identity from the Government of Egypt. As the Supreme Court pointed out in *First National City Bank v. Banco Para El Comercio Exterior de*

Cuba, 462 U.S. 611 * * * (1983) ("*Bancec*"), governments often create instrumentalities to carry out specific purposes:

> A typical government instrumentality, if one can be said to exist, is created by an enabling statute that prescribes the powers and duties of the instrumentality, and specifies that it is to be managed by a board selected by the government in a manner consistent with the enabling law. The instrumentality is typically established as a separate juridical entity, with the powers to hold and sell property and to sue and be sued. Except for appropriations to provide capital or to cover losses, the instrumentality is primarily responsible for its own finances. The instrumentality is run as a distinct economic enterprise; often it is not subject to the same budgetary and personnel requirements with which government agencies must comply.

Id. at 624 * * *. Nevertheless, although the Court also said that principles of comity normally require foreign governments to respect the separate existence of the instrumentalities of other States, * * *, in *Bancec* itself the Court chose to look beyond Bancec's separate juridical personality to the Government of Cuba, which in turn permitted Citibank to obtain a setoff against the amounts the plaintiff Bancec claimed were due to it under a letter of credit. * * *

Whether one is looking at an instrumentality of a foreign government, which is suable in U.S. court under the provisions and limitations of the Foreign Sovereign Immunities Act of 1976 (FSIA), 28 U.S.C. §§ 1330, 1602–1611, or one is looking at an instrumentality of the U.S. government, the kind of legal issue presented and the context of the suit has been more important than the label "governmental" or "non-governmental." Thus, for example, in *Lebron v. National Railroad Passenger Corp.*, 513 U.S. 374 * * * (1995), the Supreme Court decided that the National Railroad Passenger Corporation, commonly known as Amtrak, was part of the Government for purposes of the First Amendment to the U.S. Constitution, notwithstanding language in the enabling legislation that expressly said that the corporation was "not . . . an agency or establishment of the United States Government." *Lebron*, 513 U.S. at 391 * * *, quoting 45 U.S.C. § 541 (1994), since recodified to 49 U.S.C. § 24301(a)(3) ("[Amtrak] is not a department, agency, or instrumentality of the United States Government."). The statute creating Amtrak assigned it particular governmental goals; six of its eight externally named directors were appointed directly by the President, and the government's control was essentially perpetual.

Nevertheless, for other purposes the statutory declaration that Amtrak is not an agency or instrumentality of the United States continues to have force. This court held in *Hrubec v. National Railroad Passenger Corp.*, 49 F.3d 1269 (7th Cir.1995), that employees of Amtrak are not "employees of the United States" for purposes of the statute punishing unauthorized disclosures of an individual's income tax return, 26 U.S.C.

§ 7431. And Amtrak is not alone; the Red Cross, for example, is intermittently viewed to be a part of the government. * * *

Given this general approach to government instrumentalities, we do not find dispositive the fact that the Treasury Regulations on which the Commissioner relies define the term "foreign country" to mean "any foreign state, ... and any political subdivision of any foreign state.... " Treas. Reg. § 1.901–2(g)(2). Persons familiar with the FSIA will notice immediately the difference between that definition and the definition that governs the amenability of foreign governments to suit in U.S. court, which says "[a] 'foreign state', except as used in section 1608 of this title, includes a political subdivision of a foreign state or an agency or instrumentality of a foreign state as defined in subsection (b)." 28 U.S.C. § 1603(a). An agency or instrumentality, in turn, is an entity that is a separate legal person, either an organ of the foreign state or one of its political subdivisions or a majority of whose shares is owned by the foreign state or a political subdivision, and which is neither a citizen of a State of the United States nor of a third country. 28 U.S.C. § 1603(b). Thus, if the question before us were whether EGPC itself could be sued in U.S. court, the answer would certainly be that it could be sued only under the FSIA, with the attendant protections and rules the FSIA provides for suits against foreign sovereigns.

Since that is not the question, however, we must decide whether an indirect subsidy to an instrumentality of a foreign government is functionally a transfer within the government itself, even though "instrumentalities" are not included in the regulatory definition of the term "foreign country." Even more narrowly, we must decide whether EGPC's status as an instrumentality of the Egyptian government means that the credit given against its own taxes deprives Amoco of its foreign tax credit. We need not decide whether it is impossible in all circumstances for a government to grant a subsidy to one of its wholly or majority owned enterprises, because issues relating to subsidies arise in other contexts as well. * * * It is enough here to focus on the question of tax law that is presented.

Amoco argues that the odd situation here, where the benefit conferred on EGPC is a fluke of the operation of Egypt's statute of limitations, cannot give rise to a "subsidy" for purposes of § 1.901–2(e)(3), because Egypt's action was inadvertent. The dictionary definition of "subsidy," it reminds us, normally implies some kind of intentional disbursement. See Black's Law Dictionary 1428 (6th ed.1990) ("[a] grant of money made by government in aid of the promoters of any enterprise ... in which the government desires to participate, or which is considered a proper subject for government aid"); Webster's Third New International Dictionary 2279 (1993) ("1. something *intended* to aid, support or comfort; 2. a *grant* or *gift* of money or other property made by way of financial aid") (emphasis added, first definition considered archaic). It seems to us that we must go beyond the dictionary level of analysis to resolve such an important question. Amoco may be right that the term "subsidy" often implies an intention to confer a benefit, but it does not always carry that meaning. We note, for example, that the World Trade Organization's Agreement on Subsidies and Countervailing Duties defines a subsidy very broadly, as "a financial contribution by a government or any public body within the territory of [that country]," which includes a direct transfer of funds, potential direct transfers of funds or loan guarantees, forgiveness of required payments (including tax credits), and provision of goods or services, as long as a benefit is thereby conferred on the recipient. See Agreement on Subsidies and Countervailing Measures, Article 1, § 1.1, Apr. 15, 1994, Marrakesh Agreement Establishing the World Trade Organization, Annex 1A * * *. Although we express no view on the question, one could argue that the Agreement includes both deliberate and inadvertent subsidies. More importantly, we are exceedingly reluctant to embrace a definition of "subsidy" for tax purposes that would require the IRS to show in every case that the public body in question "intended" to confer a benefit. That kind of inquiry is notoriously difficult to conduct, and without far stronger support than we find here, it is better avoided. * * *

We return, therefore, to the twin facts that EGPC is an instrumentality of the Egyptian government (though not "the country" itself) and that it was the sole entity that received the benefit of the (erroneous) tax credit. In our view, both of these facts are relevant to the question of characterization we face: under all the circumstances, should EGPC be treated as part of the government of Egypt, or as a separate and distinct entity? Under EGPC's corporate structure, as described above, it is perfectly clear that any benefit to EGPC is a benefit to the government of Egypt, and vice versa: EGPC's profits go straight to the treasury, and it would never feel any losses, because the treasury would absorb them. EGPC is therefore not subject to conditions of demand and supply in the same way an ordinary taxpayer is.

EGPC's financial relationship with the government is significant when we consider the reason that lies behind the IRS's choice of a bright-line rule for indirect subsidies, under which the indirect subsidy will prevent a taxpayer from taking the foreign tax credit even if the business partner who received the subsidy directly does not pass along any of the benefit to the taxpayer. We pointed out in *Continental Illinois* that a rule requiring the IRS to figure out in every case who gets how much of the benefit of a subsidy would lead to "interminable investigation of the mysteries of public finance." 998 F.2d at 520. This is because the task would involve figuring out how much of the benefit was retained by the direct recipient of the subsidy and how much was passed on to the U.S. taxpayer. * * * Here, however, the opposite problem looms just as large. If the government itself agrees to assume any tax liability owed, the U.S. party remains eligible for foreign tax credits. Treas. Reg. § 1.901–2(f)(2)(ii) (Example 3). How are we to tell under the particular relationship that obtains between the government of Egypt and EGPC how much of Amoco's tax liability was actually assumed by EGPC and how much was absorbed by the government? The government of Egypt can receive a greater amount of EGPC's taxes today (if EGPC deducts Amoco's tax payment) and a smaller amount of profit at the end of the year, or it can receive slightly less today (if EGPC takes a credit) and more profit at the end of the year. One way or the other, however, the economic reality of this transaction is identical to that of Example 3, and differs from a case in which a government confers a benefit on a business partner of the taxpayer that does not have EGPC's characteristics.

From an economic standpoint, Amoco was paying its taxes to the government of Egypt, no matter how many hands the money later passed through. The percentage of production to which Amoco was entitled under the MCA was less than it otherwise would have been, to account for the fact that EGPC would be responsible for Amoco's Egyptian taxes. Recall that Amoco was entitled to 20% of the crude oil produced as reimbursement for its costs of exploration, production, and related operations, and the remaining 80% was split between EGPC and Amoco approximately 85% to 15%. The latter split reflected EGPC's responsibility for royalties on the oil produced and for Amoco's taxes. Further, Amoco's declared income to both the Egyptian and U.S. government was "grossed up," that is included as additional income EGPC's tax payments on Amoco's behalf, and the MCA noted this requirement and noted that Amoco owed Egyptian income taxes on these payments.

In a sense, Amoco paid its Egyptian taxes as soon as it turned over the oil it produced to EGPC as an agent for the Egyptian government. EGPC was then required to turn the payment over to the ETD, which it did. The ETD documented the amounts of the payments, which Amoco then used as evidence of the amount of the foreign tax credit to which it was entitled on its U.S. tax returns. Whether the ETD later sent the money back to EGPC, or shuttled it to the Suez Canal, or used it on Nile River preservation efforts, means nothing from Amoco's point of view. We are obviously not saying that Amoco could have estimated the amounts of its tax payments directly from the production sharing agreement or otherwise disregarded the formal act of paying the ETD. We are making the far different point that Amoco unquestionably bore the economic burden of the taxes imposed on its operations by Egypt. This means that it does no violence to the tax laws to construe them as allowing Amoco to take the foreign tax credit under these circumstances.

Our decision to treat EGPC and the Egyptian government as a single entity in this situation is no different from the way U.S. law occasionally treats the United States and its individual agencies. For example, when monies are owed to an individual by one agency, and the individual has debts to another, the different agencies may set off the debts owed by one agency against claims that another agency has. * * * We therefore hold that for tax purposes the Government of Egypt and EGPC should be treated here as a unitary entity, even if in other contexts it would be appropriate to recognize EGPC as a separate corporate body.

C. *Computation of Dollar Value of Taxes*

Given our resolution of the Commissioner's principal claim in Amoco's favor, we also reject the Commissioner's argument that a remand is necessary to allow the Tax Court to compute the extent to which the dollar value of EGPC's 1992 and 1993 payments of back Egyptian taxes on its own account corresponds to the value of the foreign tax credits Amoco claimed on its U.S. tax returns. The Commissioner has never disputed that EGPC paid Amoco's taxes to the ETD in each year when they were due. EGPC's later payments simply resolved its own tax situation under Egyptian law. For the reasons we have already set forth, this internal Egyptian governmental issue does not affect Amoco's foreign tax credits.

For these reasons, we AFFIRM the judgment of the Tax Court.

[¶ 5123]

NOTE

The IRS argued in the *Amoco* case that no tax had in fact been paid on behalf of Amoco. The Seventh Circuit cited Reg. § 1.901–2(f)(2)(ii), Ex. 3, in rejecting that argument. Is that regulation example consistent with the requirement that a tax must actually be paid?

[¶ 5125]

10. DENIAL OF FOREIGN TAX CREDITS FOR INTERNATIONAL POLITICAL POLICY PURPOSES

As discussed in Chapter 1, tax policy considerations do not always determine the content of U.S. tax rules. The international tax provisions of the Code have been modified in several ways to implement economic sanctions against other countries. For example, Section 901(j) denies foreign tax credits for taxes paid to any foreign country—

(i) the government of which the United States does not recognize, unless such government is otherwise eligible to purchase defense articles or services under the Arms Export Control Act,

(ii) with respect to which the United States has severed diplomatic relations,

(iii) with respect to which the United States has not severed diplomatic relations but does not conduct such relations, or

(iv) which the Secretary of State has, pursuant to section 6(j) of the Export Administration Act of 1979, as amended, designated as a foreign country which repeatedly provides support for acts of international terrorism.[10]

Under Section 901(j)(5), which was added to the Code in 2000, the denial of the foreign tax credit with respect to a foreign country will not apply if two conditions are met. First, the President determines that a waiver of the denial of the foreign tax credit is in the national interest of the United States and will expand the trade and investment opportunities for U.S. companies in the foreign country. Second, not less than 30 days before granting the waiver of the foreign tax credit denial, the President must report to Congress the intention to grant the waiver and the reasons for granting the waiver.

As of October 1, 2005, the countries covered by the Section 901(j) tax credit denial were Cuba, Iran, North Korea, Sudan and Syria. See Rev. Rul. 2005–3, 2005–1 C.B. 334. Although Iraq had been removed from the list in 1982, it was returned to the list in the Fall of 1990, soon after it invaded Kuwait, and then was removed again in June 2004, soon after the fall of the regime of Saddam Hussein. Section 901(j) also denied credits for taxes paid to South Africa during the period from January 1, 1988, through July 10, 1991, the date the Executive Branch certified that South Africa met the requirements of the Comprehensive Anti–Apartheid Act of 1986. Vietnam was on the list until July 21, 1995, when the United States reestablished diplomatic relations with it.

Finally, under Section 908(a), foreign tax credits otherwise allowable may be reduced if a U.S. taxpayer has participated in or cooperated with certain international boycotts. The international boycott rules are discussed in Chapter 14.

Note that a U.S. taxpayer may be able to deduct under Section 164 foreign taxes that are not creditable by reason of the special rules in Sections 901(j) and 908, if the requirements of Section 164 are met. See §§ 901(j)(3); 908(b); 164(a).

[¶ 5130]

PROBLEMS

1. Galaxy Inc. ("Galaxy"), a U.S. corporation, is engaged in the business of rendering engineering and project management services in Country A. Galaxy also licenses certain Country A patents to clients for use in connection with projects in which Galaxy is involved. Country A has no generally applicable income tax. It does, however, impose a withholding tax of 20

10. The income from any of the countries covered by Section 901(j) is subject to a separate foreign tax credit limitation to prevent taxes paid on income from other countries from being cross-credited against the U.S. tax on income from the covered countries. For the general discussion on the separate limitations on the foreign tax credit, see ¶ 5245. The income of any U.S. corporation receiving dividends or Subpart F inclusions from a controlled foreign corporation is not grossed up by taxes treated as non-creditable under Section 901(j).

percent on gross royalties and a withholding tax of 25 percent on gross fees for services rendered in Country A when such royalties and fees are paid by residents of Country A to foreign persons. The gross royalties and gross service fees are independent tax bases on which each withholding tax is separately computed. No deductions are permitted. Galaxy receives royalties and engineering and project management fees from clients in Country A from which the 20 and 25 percent taxes are withheld, respectively. Are the withholding taxes creditable by Galaxy?

2. Would the results in Problem 1 be different if Country A has a generally applicable income tax that is not imposed on royalties and fees paid by Country A residents to foreign persons, which are subject to the withholding taxes described?

3. The government of Country B imposes an income tax of 30 percent on the net income realized from sources within Country B by foreign persons engaged in business there. Domestic persons (including Country B corporations) are not subject to the income tax. Cosmos Corporation, a U.S. corporation, is engaged in Country B in the business of mining and exporting copper ore through a wholly owned subsidiary organized under the laws of Country B. As a Country B corporation, the subsidiary is exempt from the income tax, but it pays an export tax of $1,000 per ton of the copper ore exported. No portion of this levy is paid in exchange for a specific economic benefit from the government of Country B. No deductions are permitted in calculating this tax, and $1,000 per ton is a rate that is fixed without reference to the market value of the exported copper. Is the export tax creditable?

4. Would the results in Problem 3 be different if Cosmos Corporation were engaged in the business described through a branch in Country B (rather than through a Country B subsidiary) and the branch were subject to the export tax rather than to the income tax?

5. Orbit Corporation ("Orbit"), a U.S. corporation, has established in Country C a branch office that coordinates the export sales throughout Africa of Orbit products manufactured by Orbit in the United States. Since the office is not actually engaged in the sales transactions, which are handled by Orbit's export division in New York, no revenue appears on the books of the Country C branch; only the expenses of the office are reflected on its books. Country C has a generally applicable income tax. Recognizing, however, the difficulty of determining the proper amount of the net export income attributable to the Country C branch office, the Country C tax authorities issue a ruling to the effect that the branch will be taxed on the assumption that the gross income of the office will equal 120 percent of the expenses of the office. This assumed income less the actual expenses of the office will be subject to the generally applicable Country C income tax of 35 percent. Will the resulting Country C tax be creditable?

6. Sun Incorporated, a U.S. corporation, owns 5,000 acres of undeveloped land in Country D, but is not engaged in business in Country D and has no income (under U.S. concepts) from Country D sources. Country D has a generally applicable tax imposed on net income at a rate of 30 percent. Under

Country D tax law, an owner of real estate is deemed to realize the imputed rental value of any real estate to the extent that the imputed rental value exceeds the actual rental income (if any) received. Costs and expenses attributable to the imputed rent are allowed as a deduction in computing the base of the Country D tax. Accordingly, the 30–percent Country D tax is imposed on an imputed rental value from Sun Incorporated's land equal to $50,000 per year, less the costs and expenses attributed to the imputed rent. Is this tax creditable?

7. Would the results in Problem 6 be different if the United States had severed diplomatic relations with Country D?

8. Katherine, a U.S. citizen and resident, is employed for eight months in Country E by a Country E corporation and earns $90,000 during that period. She also owns shares of stock in several Country E corporations, which trade on the Country E stock exchange and have increased in total value by $50,000 during the current year. Under the tax laws of Country E, a taxpayer's net income from all business and investment activities is subject to a tax rate of 25 percent. Net income from the sale of property, including stock, is subject to this tax when the property is sold or exchanged. The definition of net income for purposes of this tax is similar to the definition of taxable income in Section 63 of the Code, except that no personal deductions or exemptions are allowable. In determining the amount of a taxpayer's income from the trade or business of being an employee, gross wages are includible in income and no deductions for the expenses attributable to the wage income are allowable.

In addition, the aggregate net appreciation in the fair market value of all shares of stock in Country E corporations held by a taxpayer at the end of the tax year is subject to a tax of ten percent. The adjusted basis of the stock for purposes of the 25–percent tax on net income is adjusted upward in an amount equal to the net appreciation in the value of the stock that was subject to this ten-percent stock appreciation tax.

During the current year, Katherine pays the 25–percent tax on her compensation income and the ten-percent tax on the appreciation in her stock in the Country E corporations. Are these Country E taxes creditable?

9. Lunar Inc. ("Lunar"), a U.S. corporation, is engaged in manufacturing widgets in Country F through a branch located there. Under its contract with the government of Country F, Lunar must pay tax to Country F equal to the greater of (i) $100 per item produced or (ii) the maximum amount creditable by Lunar against its U.S. tax liability for that year with respect to income from its operations in Country F. Lunar is exempted from Country F's otherwise generally imposed income tax. Lunar produces 500 widgets during the tax year and the maximum amount creditable by Lunar against its U.S. tax liability for the year is $75,000. If Lunar had been subject to Country F's generally imposed income tax, it would have paid a tax to Country F of $40,000. How much, if any, of the $75,000 tax paid by Lunar to Country F will be creditable?

10. How would your answer in Problem 9 differ if Lunar had produced 1,000 widgets (and, thus, had to pay Country F a tax of $100,000 ($100

multiplied by the 1,000 widgets produced) because that amount exceeded the $75,000 maximum amount creditable by Lunar against its U.S. tax liability for the year)?

11. How would your answer in Problem 9 differ if Lunar would have paid $80,000 in tax to Country F if it had been subject to the generally imposed income tax?

12. Foreclosure Bank Corporation ("Foreclosure"), a U.S. banking corporation, lends money to Foreign Development, Inc., a development bank in Country G, a foreign country. Foreign Development, Inc. relends the borrowed funds to various Country G corporations. Country G imposes a 30-percent withholding tax of $300,000 on the $1,000,000 of interest paid by Foreign Development, Inc. to Foreclosure, which Foreign Development, Inc. withholds from the interest payments to Foreclosure. (This withholding tax applies to Foreclosure's interest income instead of the generally imposed Country G net income tax.) Country G credits 60 percent of the tax to an account of Foreign Development, Inc. on the date the tax is withheld and requires Foreign Development, Inc. to transfer the credited amount to the various Country G corporations that had borrowed funds from Foreign Development, Inc. Is the $300,000 withholding tax on the interest income creditable by Foreclosure?

13. How would your answer in Problem 12 differ if the Country G corporations that had borrowed the funds from Foreign Development, Inc. were wholly owned by the Country G government?

14. In year 1, XYZ Manufacturing Corporation ("XYZ"), a U.S. corporation, receives $1,000,000 of interest income from a borrower who is resident in Country H, a foreign country. Country H has an income tax law that imposes a tax of 30 percent ($300,000) on the gross amount of such interest income and requires Country H debtors to collect the tax through withholding. However, a tax treaty between Country H and the United States provides that Country H may not tax interest received by a U.S. resident at a rate in excess of five percent. A U.S. resident may claim the benefit of the treaty only by applying for a refund of the excess withheld amount (25 percent of the gross amount of interest income) after the end of the tax year. XYZ does not file a timely claim for refund of the $250,000 excess withheld amount. To what extent is the Country H tax paid by XYZ creditable?

15. How would your answer in Problem 14 differ if it is not clear whether XYZ is eligible for the treaty reduction because under the loan agreement the amount of XYZ's interest income is, in part, contingent on the Country H borrower's net profits for the year and the Country H treaty provision on interest income does not apply to certain types of contingent interest? XYZ has been advised by counsel that efforts to invoke the competent authority process have been fruitless and that securing the benefits of the treaty provision would probably involve costly litigation to establish XYZ's entitlement to such benefits. Accordingly, XYZ decides not to pursue the refund claim.

[¶ 5133]

E. ELECTION AND ACCOUNTING RULES FOR FOREIGN TAX CREDITS

For each tax year, a taxpayer may claim a foreign tax credit for all creditable foreign taxes paid or accrued for the year, or, alternatively, claim a deduction under Section 164 for all such taxes. Under a special statute of limitations in Section 6511(d)(3)(A), a taxpayer generally has ten years from the due date for the return for the tax year in which the taxes were paid or accrued to make or change this election. See § 901(a); Reg. § 1.901–1(d).

Section 905(a) allows a taxpayer to elect to use the accrual method of tax accounting for purposes of determining when foreign taxes may be credited, regardless of the taxpayer's general tax accounting method. In other words, a cash method taxpayer may elect to use the accrual method for foreign tax credit purposes. Once made, the election applies for all subsequent years. Section 905(c) requires a taxpayer using the accrual method for foreign tax credit purposes to make adjustments in certain situations where (1) the amount of the foreign taxes accrued differs from the amount of such taxes actually paid, (2) the accrued taxes are not paid within two years after the close of the tax year to which the taxes relate, or (3) the taxes are partially or wholly refunded.

What if a taxpayer using the accrual method for foreign tax credit purposes contests its tax liability for a tax year and does not pay the foreign taxes until several years after the tax year to which they relate? The law is well-established that the foreign tax is still accruable for the tax year to which the taxes relate but that the taxpayer must make the accrual, retroactively, when the contest is finally resolved and the amount of the taxpayer's foreign tax liability is finally determined. To obtain the benefit of the foreign tax credit in this situation, the taxpayer must redetermine its U.S. tax liability for the tax year to which the taxes relate and must file a claim for refund within ten years of the due date of the federal income tax return for the year to which the contested foreign taxes relate. See, e.g., Rev. Rul. 84–125, 1984–2 C.B. 125. For example, suppose that ABC Manufacturing Corporation ("ABC"), a U.S. corporation that uses the accrual method for foreign tax credit purposes, contests liability for certain foreign taxes imposed by Country X that relate to year 1. In year 3, the contest is finally resolved by a court in Country X holding that ABC is liable in full for the foreign taxes. If ABC has elected to credit foreign taxes for year 1, ABC must accrue the taxes for year 1 by amending its year 1 return, redetermining its year 1 tax liability to reflect the increased foreign tax credit and filing a refund claim in year 3 for its reduced year 1 federal income tax liability.

F. INDIRECT CREDIT (SECTION 902)

[¶ 5135]

1. INTRODUCTION

In addition to the direct credit available to the foreign branch operation, Section 902 allows an indirect credit. This provision effectively allows a U.S. corporation receiving a dividend from a foreign corporation to credit a portion of the foreign corporate income tax paid by the foreign corporation if the U.S. corporation meets a voting stock ownership test with respect to the foreign corporation. Specifically, Section 902(a) provides that the corporate shareholder should be "deemed to have paid" the same proportion of the foreign corporation's post–1986 foreign income taxes as the amount of the dividend bears to the foreign corporation's post–1986 undistributed earnings. As a consequence of the statutory terminology, the indirect credit is often referred to as the "deemed paid" credit.

Section 902 is in a sense the international counterpart of Section 243, which mitigates the double taxation of domestic intercorporate dividends by allowing a dividends-received deduction to a U.S. corporation receiving a dividend from another U.S. corporation.[11] The broad intent of the indirect credit is to place a U.S. corporation conducting foreign operations through a foreign subsidiary on a basis roughly comparable to a U.S. corporation conducting operations through a foreign branch for foreign tax credit purposes. Because the U.S. corporation is allowed to defer U.S. tax on the foreign earnings of the foreign corporation until they are distributed or otherwise repatriated to the United States, however, a tax bias exists in favor of using a foreign subsidiary to conduct the operations abroad when the foreign corporate tax is less than the U.S. corporate tax.

The indirect credit is not limited to cases involving wholly owned or majority owned foreign subsidiaries. It is available when the U.S. corporation owns at least ten percent of the voting stock of the foreign corporation at the time of the dividend distribution and therefore is commonly thought of as applying in cases in which the U.S. corporation has a "direct investment" in the foreign corporation. Direct investment means an investment that involves some substantial measure of control or influence over the enterprise in which the investment is made and contrasts with a portfolio or passive investment. In a variety of international tax provisions

11. The dividends-received deduction is generally not available with respect to dividends received by a U.S. corporation from a foreign corporation. See § 243(a). However, if a U.S. corporation receives a dividend from a ten-percent-or-more-owned foreign subsidiary that has income effectively connected with the conduct of a U.S. trade or business, Section 245 allows the U.S. corporation a 70–, 80– or 100–percent dividends-received deduction to the extent that the dividend is attributable to earnings from income effectively connected with a U.S. trade or business. To the extent that Section 245 applies, no foreign tax credit is allowable to the U.S. corporation for foreign taxes attributable to the dividend paid out of the earnings and profits attributable to the effectively connected income. § 245(a)(8).

of the Code, the threshold for a direct investment is a ten-percent interest in the voting stock of a foreign corporation.[12]

The operation of the indirect credit may be illustrated by the following examples, which assume a 35–percent U.S. corporate tax rate.

> *Example 1.* Simplex, a Delaware corporation, has a wholly owned subsidiary organized under the laws of Country X (X–Sub). In its first year of operation X–Sub earns $100,000 in Country X, pays a 30–percent Country X income tax of $30,000 and pays a dividend to Simplex of $70,000.

> *Step 1.* Determine the amount of foreign income taxes deemed paid by Simplex. § 902(a). This is the portion of the foreign income taxes paid by X–Sub which "the amount of such dividends (determined without regard to Section 78) bears to * * * such foreign corporation's post–1986 undistributed earnings." Thus, the numerator is the actual amount of the dividend (not grossed up under Section 78 by the amount of foreign taxes deemed to be paid with respect to that dividend under Section 902(a)). The denominator is X–Sub's post–1986 undistributed earnings ($100,000 less the Country X corporate tax ($30,000) attributable to those earnings).

$$\frac{\text{Dividend}}{\text{X–Sub post–1986 earnings}} \times \text{Country X tax} = \text{amount deemed paid}$$

$$\frac{\$70{,}000}{\$70{,}000} \times \$30{,}000 = \$30{,}000$$

> *Step 2.* Gross up the amount of the dividend of $70,000 by adding to it an amount equal to the $30,000 of taxes deemed paid under Section 902(a). § 78. This is the amount includible in the income of Simplex on which the tentative U.S. tax is based. This gross-up is needed to avoid giving Simplex both a deduction and a credit for the 30–percent Country X tax and to create congruity with the credit that would have been available if Simplex had operated its business through a branch in Country X.

$$\underset{\text{(Step 1)}}{\text{Dividend + taxes deemed paid}} = \text{amount on which U.S. tax before credit will be computed}$$

$$\$70{,}000 + \$30{,}000 = \$100{,}000$$

12. See, for example, the definition of U.S. shareholder in Section 951(b) for purposes of the controlled foreign corporation provisions discussed in Chapter 6 and for purposes of the Section 904(d)(3) look-through rules discussed in Chapter 7.

Step 3. Compute the tentative U.S. tax on the grossed-up amount (before credit).

$100,000 × 35% = $35,000 (U.S. tax on dividend before credit)

Step 4. Credit the Section 902(a) deemed paid amount against the U.S. tax on the grossed-up amount. The result is the net U.S. tax payable by Simplex.

U.S. tax on grossed-up amount	$35,000
less § 902(a) deemed paid amount	– 30,000
net U.S. tax	5,000

Notice that this comes out "right." The total tax bill on the $100,000 of Country X earnings is $35,000: $30,000 to Country X and $5,000 to the United States. Thus, the total rate is 35 percent, the same as the U.S. rate.

The process is the same if the dividend recipient is less than a 100–percent shareholder or if less than all of the earnings after tax are paid out. Thus:

Example 2. Simplex owns 50 percent of X–Sub, which earns $100,000 in Country X, pays a 30–percent Country X income tax and pays a total dividend of $70,000. Simplex receives one half the dividend, or $35,000.

Step 1. Determine the amount of Country X tax deemed paid:

$$\frac{\$35{,}000}{\$70{,}000} \times \$30{,}000 = \$15{,}000$$

Step 2. Gross-up of dividend:

$35,000 + $15,000 = $50,000

Step 3. Tentative U.S. tax on the grossed-up amount (before credit):

$50,000 × 35% = $17,500

Step 4. Apply credit to reach net U.S. tax:

U.S. tax on grossed-up amount	$17,500
less § 902(a) deemed paid amount	– 15,000
net U.S. tax	2,500

Example 3. Simplex owns 50 percent of X–Sub, which earns $100,000 in Country X, pays a 30–percent Country X income tax and pays a total dividend of $35,000. Simplex receives one half the dividend, or $17,500.

Step 1. Amount deemed paid:

$$\frac{\$17{,}500}{\$70{,}000} \times \$30{,}000 = \$7{,}500$$

Step 2. Gross-up of dividend:

$$\$17{,}500 + \$7{,}500 = \$25{,}000$$

Step 3. Tentative U.S. tax on the grossed-up amount (before credit):

$$\$25{,}000 \times 35\% = \$8{,}750$$

Step 4. Apply credit to reach net U.S. tax:

U.S. tax on grossed-up amount	$8,750
less § 902(a) deemed paid amount	– 7,500
net U.S. tax	1,250

It is, of course, very common for the foreign country to have both an income tax on subsidiary profits and a withholding tax on dividends paid to nonresidents. Here the dividend recipient is entitled to a combination of the direct and indirect credits:

Example 4. Assume the following figures for X–Sub:

Income	$100,000
Country X tax (30%)	30,000
Earnings after tax	70,000
Dividend	20,000
Withholding on dividend (5%)	1,000

Simplex, a Delaware corporation, is a 50–percent shareholder of X–Sub and therefore receives cash in hand of $9,500, that is, a gross dividend of $10,000 less $500 withholding.

Simplex income (grossed up)	$14,286*
Tentative U.S. tax (35%)	5,000
Direct credit	500
Indirect credit	4,286*
Total credit	4,786
Net U.S. tax	214

* The amount of Country X tax deemed paid is $\frac{\$10{,}000}{\$70{,}000} \times \$30{,}000 = \$4{,}286$.

As indicated above, the Section 902 credit is available only to U.S. corporations owning at least ten percent of the voting stock of the foreign corporation. Voting common stock or voting preferred stock will qualify for this purpose provided that the U.S. corporation owns at least ten percent of the foreign corporation's total voting stock; nonvoting common stock will not qualify. There are no constructive ownership or stock attribution rules that apply in determining whether the U.S. corporation meets the ten-percent-voting stock threshold. Thus, if a U.S. corporation owns five percent of the voting stock of a foreign corporation and a wholly owned U.S. subsidiary of the U.S. corporation also owns five percent of the voting stock of the same corporation, neither the U.S. parent corporation nor its wholly owned U.S. subsidiary will qualify for the Section 902 credit with respect to the foreign corporation. See, e.g., First Chicago NBD Corp. v. Commissioner, 135 F.3d 457 (7th Cir.1998), aff'g 96 T.C. 421 (1991); Rev. Rul. 85–3, 1985–1 C.B. 222. U.S. citizens and resident aliens do not qualify for the indirect credit in Section 902; nor does a U.S. corporation that has elected to be taxed as an S corporation under Section 1361(a). § 1373(a); Reg. § 1.902–1(a)(1).

A U.S. corporation should qualify for the indirect credit in Section 902 if it holds a ten-percent-or-greater voting stock interest in the foreign corporation through a U.S. general partnership. For example, in Rev. Rul. 71–141, 1971–1 C.B. 211, the IRS treated a general partnership as an aggregate of its partners (the so-called aggregate theory of partnership taxation) and held that two U.S. corporations owning 50–percent interests in a U.S. general partnership that, in turn, owned 40 percent of the voting stock of a foreign corporation both qualified for the Section 902 credit with respect to the foreign corporation. However, under pre–2004 law, it was somewhat unclear whether Revenue Ruling 71–141 extended to stock held by a foreign general partnership, a domestic or foreign limited partnership or a domestic or foreign limited liability company, if such an entity elects to be classified as a partnership for federal income tax purposes.

The 2004 JOBS Act clarified the eligibility requirements for the indirect credit by adding Section 902(c)(7) to the Code, which provides that stock owned directly or indirectly by or for a partnership is treated as owned proportionately by its partners. This provision should apply to any entity classified as a partnership for U.S. tax purposes. The statute gives the Treasury and the IRS authority to issue regulations providing rules to account for special partnership allocations of dividends, credits and other incidents of stock ownership in determining proportionate ownership for purposes of this rule. The House Ways and Means Committee Report states that Congress intended that no inference be drawn from this change about the application of then existing law. H.R. Rep. No. 548, pt. 1, 108th Cong., 2d Sess. 195 (2004).

[¶ 5140]

PROBLEMS

1. Kowe Chips, Incorporated ("Kowe Chips"), is a Delaware corporation engaged in the manufacture and sale of computer chips and other hi-tech products associated with computers. During the past several years, the corporation has begun to export extensively. It now finds that its manufacturing capacity is being fully used and that a new plant must be constructed. It is considering a site in Maryland and a site in Greece.

There are a number of nontax considerations that will affect the decision; but there are several tax considerations that may be relevant. Kowe Chips is paying U.S. corporate income taxes at a rate of 35 percent. The corporate state income tax in Maryland is ten percent. Kowe Chips pays no Delaware state income tax on income earned outside of Delaware.

The national corporate income tax in Greece is 20 percent and the local Greek province corporate income tax is ten percent. There is also a withholding tax of ten percent imposed on dividends paid by a Greek corporation to a foreign parent corporation. Kowe Chips is permitted to operate as a branch in Greece. In that event, the Greek national income tax of 20 percent and the Greek province tax of ten percent will apply to the net income earned by the branch operation. There would be no withholding taxes on repatriated profits. The Greek province tax of ten percent is deductible in computing the base of the Greek national income tax.

Kowe Chips expects to invest $5 million in the new site development whether it is in Maryland or Greece. It has asked you to prepare an analysis of the tax considerations that would attend the alternatives which it is considering.

2. X Corporation, a U.S. corporation, and Betty, a U.S. citizen, have formed a general partnership under the laws of the State of California. (Betty owns no stock in X Corporation.) X Corporation and Betty each owns a 50–percent interest in all capital, profits and losses of the partnership. The partnership in turn owns 20 percent of the voting stock of FC Corporation, a foreign corporation. The partnership has properly elected to be classified as a partnership for federal tax purposes under the check-the-box entity classification regulations. Assuming that FC Corporation makes a dividend distribution to the partnership, will the partnership, X Corporation or Betty be eligible for the indirect credit with respect to a proportionate share of the foreign income taxes paid by FC Corporation?

3. Would your answer in Problem 2 differ if instead of forming a general partnership X Corporation and Betty formed a limited liability company under the laws of the State of California, the limited liability company has properly elected to be classified as a partnership for federal tax purposes and the limited liability company owns the 20–percent voting stock interest in FC Corporation?

4. Y Corporation, a U.S. corporation, owns ten percent of the voting common stock (the only class of voting stock outstanding) and five percent of the nonvoting preferred stock of Foreign Subsidiary, Inc., a foreign corporation. During the current year, Foreign Subsidiary, Inc. pays dividends on the nonvoting preferred stock, but pays no dividends on the voting common stock. Is Y Corporation eligible for the indirect credit for the current year with respect to the foreign income taxes paid by Foreign Subsidiary, Inc.? See Rev. Rul. 79–74, 1979–1 C.B. 242 (holding that dividends received for Section 902 purposes include dividends on both voting stock and nonvoting stock of a foreign corporation if the U.S. corporation receiving the dividends owns at least ten percent of the voting stock of the foreign corporation).

[¶ 5145]

2. INDIRECT CREDIT THROUGH MULTIPLE TIERS

The indirect credit is available to the U.S. parent corporation on dividends paid up from a foreign sub-subsidiary to a subsidiary and then to the parent. § 902(b)(2). It is also available on dividends paid up through the chain from a foreign sub-sub-subsidiary. In each case the recipient of a dividend is deemed to have paid an appropriate amount of the underlying corporate tax of the payor of the dividend. The deemed-paid amount is then counted as part of the taxes paid by the recipient when it, in turn, pays a dividend to the next level. At each level there must be ownership of at least ten percent of the voting stock of the next level subsidiary. Moreover, in a two-tier case the first level ownership percentage multiplied by the second level ownership percentage must equal at least five percent and in a three-tier case the percentages of the first, second and third levels, all multiplied together, again must equal at least five percent. § 902(b)(2)(B). Thus, in a three-tier case, 50 percent ownership at the first level, 20 percent at the second level and 50 percent at the third level would just qualify. 50% × 20% × 50% = 5%.

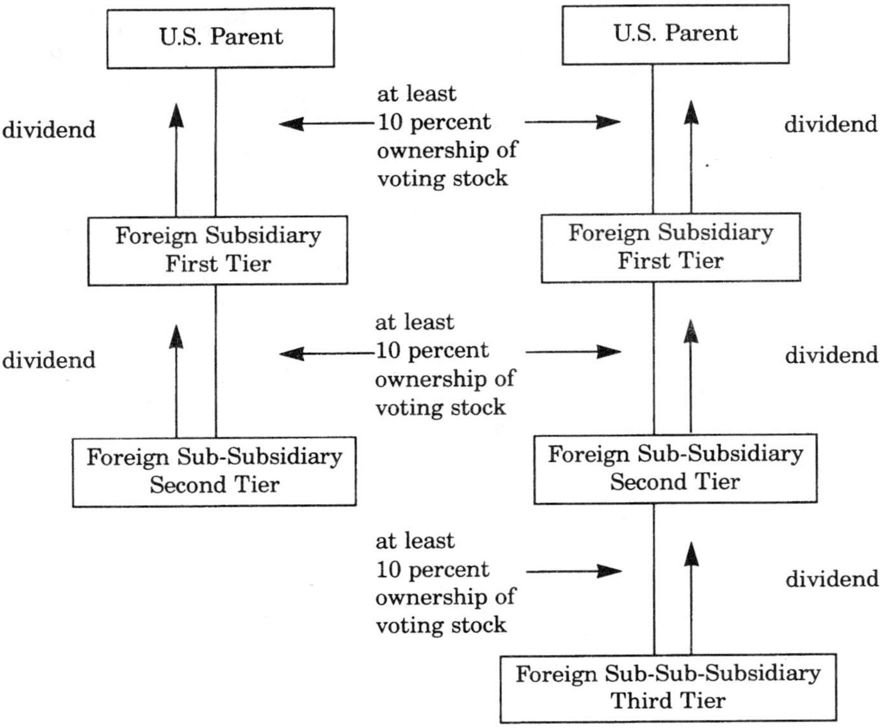

Illustrations of the credit computations under Section 902 are in Reg. § 1.902–1(f).

Under current law, the Section 902 credit is also available with respect to foreign subsidiaries below the third tier in a chain of foreign subsidiaries of a U.S. parent corporation but only if the foreign subsidiary is a controlled foreign corporation (as defined in Section 957) and the U.S. parent corporation is a United States shareholder (as defined in Section 951(b)) in such foreign corporation. These concepts are discussed in detail in Chapter 6. In such a case, the Section 902 indirect credit calculation will take into account taxes paid by a fourth-tier, fifth-tier or sixth-tier foreign subsidiary only with respect to periods during which the foreign subsidiary was a controlled foreign corporation. § 902(b)(2). At each level there must be ownership of at least ten percent of the voting stock of the next lower level foreign subsidiary. Moreover, in a multiple-tier case the percentages of all the levels, multiplied together, must equal at least five percent. § 902(b)(2)(B). No indirect credit will ever be allowed with respect to dividends and foreign taxes paid by a foreign subsidiary below the sixth tier in a chain of foreign corporations. § 902(b)(2)(B)(iii).

3. DETERMINATION OF EARNINGS, FOREIGN TAXES AND DIVIDENDS FOR CALCULATING THE INDIRECT FOREIGN TAX CREDIT

[¶ 5150]

a. Introduction

When a U.S. corporation receives a dividend from a foreign corporation in which it owns at least ten percent of the voting stock, Section 902(a) provides that the indirect credit is calculated by the following formula:

$$\text{Indirect Credit} = \frac{\text{Amount of dividend (not grossed up under Section 78)}}{\text{Foreign corporation's post-1986 undistributed earnings}} \times \text{Foreign corporation's post–1986 foreign income taxes}$$

The concept underlying this formula is that each dividend distribution from the foreign corporation to the U.S. corporation from the pool of post–1986 earnings carries with it a proportionate amount of the post–1986 foreign income taxes.

The numerator of the Section 902(a) fraction is determined in accordance with the usual rules in Section 316 for determining when a distribution from a U.S. corporation is treated as a dividend. Reg. § 1.902–1(a)(11). Specifically, the earnings and profits of the foreign corporation are divided into (1) current earnings (earnings and profits as of the close of the current tax year unreduced by any distributions made during the year) and (2) accumulated earnings (a cumulative pool of earnings and profits from March 1, 1913, through the end of the year before the distribution). A distribution is treated as a dividend to the extent that it is paid out of either current earnings or accumulated earnings. Furthermore, a distribution will be treated as a dividend if it is covered by earnings in the current year, however large an accumulated deficit there may be in earnings through the end of the prior year. Current and accumulated earnings and profits are calculated and allocated among distributees under U.S. tax law rules.[13]

In determining the denominator of the Section 902 fraction, there was uncertainty before the Tax Reform Act of 1986 as to whether earnings

13. Under those rules, current earnings and profits are calculated at the close of the corporation's tax year and allocated retroactively and ratably among all who were recipients of distributions during the year. By contrast, accumulated earnings and profits are allocated to the corporation's distributions in chronological order until they are exhausted.

must be calculated under U.S. or foreign rules. This uncertainty was resolved for pre–1987 years in favor of U.S. rules by the Supreme Court's decision in the *Goodyear Tire & Rubber* case, at ¶ 5165. The 1986 Act has reached a similar result for post–1986 years by making a specific reference to Section 964(a) in Section 902(c)(1). Section 964(a) provides that earnings and profits (or deficits) of a foreign corporation are to be "determined according to rules substantially similar to those applicable to domestic corporations." The regulations under Section 964 contain some detailed rules for computing earnings and profits, which allow some leeway by providing that adjustments must be made to the accounts of the foreign corporation only if they are material. Reg. § 1.964–1. While in general earnings and profits of a U.S. corporation are calculated by using only straight-line depreciation, Section 312(k)(4) exempts from this restriction the calculation of earnings and profits of a foreign corporation that, for the tax year, derives less than 20 percent of its gross income from U.S. sources. In addition, the amount of any illegal bribe, kickback or other payment (within the meaning of Section 162(c)) is not to be taken into account to decrease earnings or increase a deficit. These are payments that would be unlawful under the Foreign Corrupt Practices Act of 1977 if the payor were a U.S. person. § 964(a). Note that in calculating a foreign corporation's post–1986 undistributed earnings, reduction is made for foreign income taxes paid or accrued by the corporation, regardless of whether the taxes are creditable for Section 902 purposes. Reg. § 1.902–1(a)(9)(iii).

Before 1987, the earnings of a foreign corporation for purposes of computing the Section 902 foreign tax credit were calculated year by year and were matched with foreign taxes paid or accrued each year. If a dividend exceeded the earnings of the current year, the excess of the dividend was deemed to be paid out of the after-tax accumulated earnings of the preceding year. If the remaining portion of the dividend exceeded the after-tax accumulated earnings of the preceding year, the dividend was treated as paid from accumulated earnings of the next preceding year and so on until the dividend had been completely covered by accumulated earnings to the extent available. A separate Section 902 calculation of the deemed-paid credit had to be made for each year to which a portion of the dividend was allocated, using the taxes paid and the accumulated earnings of that year.

The 1986 Act changed to a perpetual pool system. Section 902(c)(1) creates a continuing pool of post–1986 earnings to which new earnings are added and from which distributed earnings are removed. Section 902(c)(2) creates a continuing pool of foreign income taxes to which new taxes paid are added and from which taxes used as a credit are removed.[14] The appropriate indirect tax credit for each post–1986 dividend is calculated by reference to the content of these two cumulative pools. § 902(a). Note, however, that the pools start in 1987. When a distribution exceeds the post–1986 earnings pool and must draw on pre–1987 earnings and taxes, the old system calling for year-by-year matching of earnings and taxes must be used.

On a more technical level, the "post–1986 undistributed earnings" of a foreign corporation are the total earnings for years starting in 1987 through the end of the tax year in which a dividend is distributed, undiminished by any dividend distributions made during that year. § 902(c)(1); Reg. § 1.902–1(a)(9)(i). Dividend distributions do reduce the pool of earnings taken into account in subsequent years. Reg. § 1.902–1(a)(9)(i). Moreover, the corporation's pool of post–1986 foreign income taxes are reduced to reflect the portion of the taxes deemed paid with respect to such dividends for purposes of computing Section 902 credits in subsequent tax years. Reg. § 1.902–1(a)(8)(i).[15] The same pooling mechanism applies to dividends paid by second- and third-tier foreign corporations (and by fourth-tier, fifth-tier and sixth-tier foreign corporations if they constitute controlled foreign corporations and the U.S. parent corporation is a United States shareholder in those foreign corporations).

To take a simple illustration, assume that Gamma S.A., a corporation organized under the laws of Country M, is a wholly owned subsidiary of American Gamma Corporation, a U.S. corporation. Gamma S.A.'s post–1986 undistributed earnings (after payment of foreign income taxes) and foreign income taxes paid for the years 1 through 3 were as follows:

---

14. Consistent with creditable tax requirements under the direct credit in Section 901, only creditable taxes meeting the requirements of Section 901 or 903 are part of a foreign corporation's pool of post–1986 foreign income taxes for purposes of calculating the Section 902 credit. See §§ 902(c)(2)(A), (c)(4)(A); 901; 903; Reg. § 1.902–1(a)(7). Moreover, Section 909, enacted in 2010, applies in the case of a foreign tax credit splitting event relating to foreign income tax paid or accrued by a Section 902 corporation (i.e., a transaction in which creditable foreign income taxes paid or accrued by the Section 902 corporation are separated from the associated foreign income). Under that provision, such foreign tax is not taken into account for purposes of Section 902 or 960, or for purposes of determining the Section 902 corporation's earnings and profits under Section 964(a), until the year in which the related income is taken into account for U.S. tax purposes by the Section 902 corporation itself or a U.S. corporation that meets the Section 902 ownership requirements with respect to the Section 902 corporation. Thus, if Section 909 applies to a foreign tax paid by a Section 902 corporation, the corporation's pool of foreign income taxes is not increased by such tax nor are its earnings and profits reduced by such tax until the year in which the related income is taken into account for U.S. tax purposes.

15. Dividends paid by the foreign corporation to foreign shareholders or to U.S. shareholders who are not eligible to claim the Section 902 credit nonetheless do reduce the foreign corporation's pool of post–1986 undistributed earnings. Reg. § 1.902–1(a)(9)(i). Moreover, the foreign corporation's pool of post–1986 foreign income taxes is reduced by the foreign income taxes deemed paid with respect to such dividends (i.e., dividends paid to foreign shareholders or to U.S. shareholders who are not eligible to claim the Section 902 credit). Reg. § 1.902–1(a)(8)(i).

	After–Tax Post–1986 Undistributed Earnings	*Foreign Income Taxes*
Year 1	$100,000	$ 30,000
Year 2	$200,000	$ 60,000
Year 3	$300,000	$ 90,000
Pools as of Dec. 31 of Year 3	$600,000	$180,000

Gamma S.A. paid a dividend of $400,000 to American Gamma Corporation on December 1 of year 3. The indirect foreign tax credit calculation under Section 902(a) is as follows:

$$\frac{\$400{,}000}{\$600{,}000^{[17]}} \times \$180{,}000^{[16]} = \$120{,}000$$

The U.S. tax is calculated as follows:

	Dividend		*Section 78 Gross-up*		
Dividend grossed-up under § 78	$400,000	+	$120,000	=	$520,000
Tentative U.S. tax (35% × $520,000)				=	$182,000
Less indirect credit				=	$120,000
U.S. tax					$ 62,000

Gamma S.A.'s post–1986 undistributed earnings as of January 1 of year 4, would be $200,000, and its foreign income taxes pool would be $60,000.

It is important to note that the pooling of post–1986 earnings and taxes applies only to earnings and taxes that arise during or after the first tax year in which a U.S. corporation holds at least a ten-percent voting stock interest in the foreign corporation. § 902(c)(3)(A). Accordingly, if, for example, a U.S. corporation acquires ten percent or more of the stock of a previously independent foreign corporation during 1999, the pooling of earnings and taxes does not begin until 1999. All pre–1999 earnings and taxes will be subject to the pre–1987 year-by-year matching of earnings and taxes. § 902(c)(3) and (c)(6)(A); Reg. § 1.902–1(a)(13). Those pre–1986 Act rules for calculating the Section 902 credit are now contained in Reg. § 1.902–3 and, by reason of this special effective date rule for the pooling system in the statute and regulations, these rules will remain relevant law for the indefinite future.

---

16. The foreign income taxes pool as of December 31 of year 3. § 902(c)(1).

17. The earnings pool as of December 31 of year 3 undiminished by the distribution. § 902(c)(1).

[¶ 5155]

b. Reasons for Adoption of Perpetual Pools of Post–1986 Earnings and Taxes

The reasons for abandoning the year-by-year matching of dividends with accumulated profits and taxes in favor of the perpetual cumulative pools approach adopted for post–1986 years are explained as follows in Staff of Joint Comm. on Tax'n, 100th Cong., 1st Sess., General Explanation of the Tax Reform Act of 1986, at 868–70 (1987):

> Prior law affected the availability of the deemed-paid credit when a foreign corporation's effective foreign tax rate changed for any reason (for example, where foreign tax rates rose as a result of the end of a "tax holiday" or otherwise or where foreign tax rates declined). It was frequently advantageous under prior law for foreign subsidiaries, where possible, to accumulate their earnings in years in which their effective foreign tax rate was low and distribute their earnings to U.S. parent corporations in years in which their effective foreign tax rate was high, rather than distributing their earnings on an annual basis with more constant dividends. Since, for purposes of computing the foreign taxes attributable to a dividend, the dividend was deemed distributed out of the subsidiary's earnings and profits for the current year first, drawing with it the foreign taxes with respect to those earnings, and then was treated as being derived from each preceding year, the distribution of dividends only in high tax years yielded a higher foreign tax credit than the average foreign taxes actually paid by that foreign subsidiary over a period of years. This result did not and does not occur in the case of a direct branch operation, since all branch income is subject to U.S. tax currently and foreign taxes eligible for the credit are taken into account currently.
>
> Prior law thus provided opportunities for the so-called "rhythm method" of dividend distributions from foreign subsidiaries. For example, suppose a U.S. parent corporation had two foreign subsidiaries and the foreign tax rate for each could be significantly lowered in one year at the cost of an increased rate in the next year, through timing the allowance of deductions and the recognition of income. Matters could be arranged so that the high and low tax years of the subsidiaries alternated, and the U.S. parent corporation took the dividends it needed each year from the particular subsidiary that in that year had a high effective foreign rate.
>
> In addition, when a foreign subsidiary had profits (subject to foreign tax) in some years and deficits in other years and did not distribute all its earnings currently, a portion of the foreign tax may never have been creditable. For example, although there may have been no foreign tax in a year in which a deficit occurred, the foreign law may not have provided for a reduction in the foreign taxes paid in earlier profitable years (that is, the foreign country may not have allowed a loss carryback). In such a case, even if the subsidiary paid out all its net after-tax earnings at the end of the several years, the IRS took the position that less than all the foreign taxes paid over

those years could be eligible for the credit. This was because the deficit was in some cases viewed as eliminating accumulated profits for the prior years in which the foreign taxes were paid, thus reducing the total amount of creditable taxes. See Rev. Rul. 74–550, 1974–2 C.B. 209. In a branch situation in which foreign income is taxed currently, this loss of foreign tax credits generally would not occur.

Congress recognized that there are difficulties in equating the foreign tax credit results of operation through a subsidiary and a branch, principally because of the deferral that is generally available to a subsidiary. However, Congress believed that in some instances steps to provide more similar results in the two cases were desirable. The Act adopts an approach, on a prospective basis, that computes the deemed-paid foreign tax credit of a U.S. shareholder with reference to the post-effective date accumulated foreign taxes and pool of accumulated earnings and profits (including all earnings and profits of the current year in the pool).

In summary, this pooling approach was intended to have two results. It was intended to alleviate the situation described above in which deemed-paid foreign tax credits were lost as a result of a deficit in a foreign corporation's earnings and profits. More importantly, Congress intended to limit the ability of taxpayers to claim a deemed-paid credit that reflects foreign taxes higher than the average rate over a period of years, by averaging the high tax years and the low tax years of the foreign corporation in determining the foreign taxes attributable to the dividend.

[¶ 5160]

c. U.S. Rules Used in Calculating Earnings in the Section 902 Denominator

An issue addressed by the Supreme Court in the *Goodyear Tire & Rubber* case, presented below, is whether the effect of a foreign corporation's losses on its earnings should be determined under U.S. or foreign rules for the purpose of calculating indirect foreign tax credits. The Court's opinion focuses on the term "accumulated profits," which is used in the formula for calculating the indirect foreign tax credit for years before 1987. The denominator in the Section 902 fraction for these years is accumulated profits minus foreign taxes. This is the functional equivalent of "undistributed earnings" used in the denominator of the post–1986 calculation.

The Tax Court's decision in *Vulcan Materials*, which follows the *Goodyear Tire & Rubber Co.* case, looks at a different issue involving the effects of foreign law on the calculation of the Section 902 credit. The question in *Vulcan Materials* is whether the term "accumulated profits," used in the denominator of the pre–1987 version of the Section 902 fraction, includes the portion of a Saudi Arabian corporation's profits not taxed. Under Saudi Arabian tax law, only the portion of a Saudi Arabian corporation's profits attributable to non-Saudi shareholders was subject to the Saudi income tax. Is the Tax Court's decision in *Vulcan Materials* consistent with the Supreme Court's decision in *Goodyear Tire & Rubber Co.*?

[¶ 5165]

UNITED STATES v. GOODYEAR TIRE & RUBBER CO.

Supreme Court of the United States, 1989.
493 U.S. 132.

JUSTICE MARSHALL delivered the opinion of the Court.

In this case, we must decide whether "accumulated profits" in the indirect tax credit provision of the Internal Revenue Code of 1954, * * * § 902 * * *, are to be measured in accordance with United States or foreign tax principles. We conclude that "accumulated profits" are to be measured in accordance with United States principles.

I

Goodyear Tyre and Rubber Company (Great Britain) Limited (Goodyear G.B.) is a wholly owned subsidiary of Goodyear Tire and Rubber Company (Goodyear), a domestic corporation. Goodyear brought this suit seeking a refund of federal income taxes collected for the years 1970 and 1971. During those years, Goodyear G.B. filed income tax returns in, and paid taxes to, the United Kingdom and the Republic of Ireland. Goodyear G.B. also distributed dividends to Goodyear, its sole shareholder. Goodyear reported these dividends on its federal tax return, as required by [§§ 301, 316]. Goodyear thereafter sought credit for a portion of the foreign taxes paid by Goodyear G.B. in the amount specified in § 902.[1]

Section 902 provides a parent of a foreign subsidiary with an "indirect" or "deemed paid" credit on its domestic income tax return to reflect foreign taxes paid by its subsidiary. The credit protects domestic corporations that operate through foreign subsidiaries from double taxation of the same income: taxation first by the foreign jurisdiction, when the income is earned by the subsidiary, and second by the United States, when the income is received as a dividend by the parent. In some circumstances, a foreign subsidiary may choose to distribute only a portion of its available profit as a dividend to its domestic parent. For that reason, a domestic parent cannot automatically claim credit for all foreign taxes paid by its subsidiary: § 902 limits a domestic parent's credit to the amount of tax paid by the subsidiary attributable to the dividend issued. The foreign tax

1. Section 902(a) provides:

"For purposes of this subpart, a domestic corporation which owns at least 10 percent of the voting stock of a foreign corporation from which it receives dividends in any taxable year shall—

(1) to the extent such dividends are paid by such foreign corporation out of accumulated profits (as defined in subsection (c)(1)(A)) of a year for which such foreign corporation is not a less developed country corporation, be deemed to have paid the same proportion of any income, war profits, or excess profits taxes paid or deemed to be paid by such foreign corporation to any foreign country or to any possession of the United States on or with respect to such accumulated profits, which the amount of such dividends (determined without regard to section 78) bears to the amount of such accumulated profits in excess of such income, war profits, and excess profits taxes (other than those deemed paid)...." * * *

deemed paid by the domestic parent is calculated by multiplying the total foreign tax paid (T) by that portion of the subsidiary's after-tax accumulated profits (AP − T) that is actually issued to the domestic parent in the form of a taxable dividend (D).[2]

In 1973, Goodyear G.B. reported a net loss on its British tax return and carried back that loss to offset substantial portions of its 1970 and 1971 income. Based on the 1973 carried-back losses, British taxing authorities recalculated Goodyear G.B.'s income and tax liability for the years 1970 and 1971. Goodyear G.B. thereafter received a refund of a substantial portion of its 1970 and 1971 foreign tax payments.

In response to the refunds, and pursuant to § 905(c) * * * which permits redetermination of the foreign tax credit whenever "any tax paid is refunded in whole or in part," the Commissioner * * * recalculated the indirect tax credit available to Goodyear for the tax years 1970 and 1971. The Commissioner lowered the foreign taxes paid (T) to reflect the refund. He refused, however, to lower accumulated profits (AP) for those years to reflect British tax authorities' redetermination of Goodyear G.B.'s income. The deductions that created, for British tax purposes, the 1973 loss would not have been allowable in the computation of United States income tax if Goodyear G.B. had been a United States corporation filing a United States return. * * * In the Commissioner's view, accumulated profits are to be calculated in accordance with United States tax principles; accordingly, the Commissioner regarded Goodyear G.B.'s 1970 and 1971 accumulated profits as unaffected by the deductions allowed under British law.

In view of the reduced amount of Goodyear's tax deemed paid, the Commissioner assessed substantial tax deficiencies for the tax years 1970 and 1971. Goodyear paid the deficiencies and, following the IRS' denial of its administrative refund claim, brought this action in the United States Claims Court, averring that foreign tax law principles govern the calculation of "accumulated profits" in § 902's tax credit. Calculating "accumulated profits" in accordance with British tax law principles, Goodyear maintained that Goodyear G.B.'s after-tax accumulated profits for 1970 and 1971 were insufficient to cover the dividends paid in those years. In such a circumstance, § 902 requires that, for the purpose of computing the indirect credit, the excess of the dividend be deemed paid out of the after-tax accumulated profits of the preceding year. If in that year the remaining portion of the dividend exceeds the after-tax accumulated profits, the remainder of the dividend is allocated or "sourced" to the next most recent year, until the dividend is exhausted. Thus, Goodyear argued that the dividends it received from Goodyear G.B. in 1970 and 1971 should have been sourced to prior tax years, 1968 and 1969, until Goodyear

2. The formula for calculating the § 902 credit is as follows:

$$\text{Credit} = \begin{matrix}\text{Foreign}\\ \text{Taxes Paid}\\ \text{(T)}\end{matrix} \times \left(\frac{\text{Dividends (D)}}{\text{Accumulated Profits (AP) minus Foreign Taxes (T)}} \right)$$

G.B.'s after-tax accumulated profits covered the dividends. Through this sourcing mechanism, Goodyear would, in computing its domestic tax liability for the dividends issued by Goodyear G.B., receive credit for a portion of the foreign taxes paid by Goodyear G.B. in 1968 and 1969. Because Goodyear G.B. paid substantial foreign taxes in those tax years, allocation of the dividend to those years would yield a tax deemed paid by Goodyear in excess of £1 million, over four times greater than the tax the Commissioner deemed paid. If the term "accumulated profits" is defined in accordance with domestic tax principles, as the Commissioner advocated, the dividends issued in 1970 and 1971 are fully exhausted by the accumulated profits of those years, resulting in a tax deemed paid of £247,124.

The Claims Court rejected Goodyear's claim. * * * Viewing the statutory definition of "accumulated profits" in § 902(c)(1)(A) as inconclusive, * * * the court turned to the purposes underlying § 902 and found that they favored calculation of "accumulated profits" in accordance with United States tax concepts * * *. The Court of Appeals for the Federal Circuit reversed. * * * The court held that the "plain meaning" of § 902 "requires [accumulated profits] to be determined under foreign law." * * * The court also held that the fundamental congressional purpose underlying § 902, "elimination of international double taxation," * * * would be defeated if the taxes paid by a foreign subsidiary, but not its accumulated profits, were calculated in terms of foreign law. * * *

The Court of Appeals' decision has important consequences for the calculation of the indirect tax credit of domestic parents that have received dividends from their subsidiaries abroad. To clarify the operation of the § 902 credit in the tax years to which it applies,[4] we granted certiorari, * * * and now reverse.

II

Our starting point, as in all cases involving statutory interpretation, "must be the language employed by Congress." * * * We find that the text of § 902 does not resolve whether "accumulated profits" are to be calculated in accordance with foreign or domestic tax concepts.

It is true, as the Court of Appeals emphasized, that §§ 902(a)(1) and 902(c)(1)(A) link "accumulated profits" to the foreign tax imposed on the subsidiary. The link is forged by describing the foreign tax as that tax imposed "on or with respect to" accumulated profits. The provisions also,

4. Calculation of the indirect credit for tax years beginning after 1986 is governed by the amended version of § 902 established by the Tax Reform Act of 1986 * * *. The amended version substantially overhauls the method of calculating the credit and removes the controversy regarding the definition of "accumulated profits." The current version of § 902(c)(1) replaces "accumulated profits" with "undistributed earnings," which are defined as the "earnings and profits of the foreign corporation (computed in accordance with sections 964 and 986)." Section 964(a) in turn provides that "the earnings and profits of any foreign corporation ... shall be determined according to rules substantially similar to those applicable to domestic corporations." * * *

however, link "accumulated profits" to "dividends" by describing "accumulated profits" as the pool from which the "dividends" are issued. Section 316(a), in turn, makes clear that domestic principles control whether a payment is a "dividend" subject to domestic tax. On the basis of this link, a leading treatise has concluded that "[a]ccumulated profits of the foreign corporation ... are, in general, equated with earnings and profits of the foreign corporation and are determined in accordance with domestic law principles." B. Bittker & J. Eustice, Federal Income Taxation of Corporations and Shareholders ¶ 17.11, p. 17–44 (5th ed. 1987) ("Adoption of these principles has the virtue of correlating the denominator of the § 902 computation with the definition of dividends (the numerator), thus avoiding the possible distortions that could arise if different definitional approaches were used for the numerator and denominator of the § 902 fraction"). Because § 902 relates "accumulated profits" both to the foreign tax paid by the subsidiary, calculated in accordance with foreign law, and to the dividend issued by the subsidiary, calculated in accordance with domestic law, we are unpersuaded that the statutory language is dispositive. We must therefore look beyond the statute's language to the legislative history, purposes, and operation of the indirect tax credit.

III

A

The history of the indirect credit clearly demonstrates that the credit was intended to protect a domestic parent from double taxation of its income. Congress first established the indirect tax credit in § 240(c) of the Revenue Act of 1918, * * * permitting a domestic parent to receive a credit for a portion of the foreign taxes paid by its subsidiary during the year in which the subsidiary issued a dividend to the parent. This Court subsequently described the purpose of § 240(c) as protection against double taxation. *American Chicle Co. v. United States*, 316 U.S. 450, 452 (1942) * * *.

The legislative history of the indirect credit also clearly reflects an intent to equalize treatment between domestic corporations that operate through foreign subsidiaries and those that operate through unincorporated foreign branches. In § 238(e) of the Revenue Act of 1921, * * * Congress amended § 240(c) to permit a domestic corporation to claim credit for taxes its subsidiary paid in years other than those in which the dividend was issued. Prior to the amendment, a domestic corporation could not receive credit for foreign taxes paid on distributed income if its subsidiary issued the dividend out of income earned in prior years, * * * because § 240(c) limited the credit to taxes paid by the subsidiary "during the taxable year" in which the dividend was issued. The amendment corrected this deficiency by relating the credit to the accumulated profits out of which the dividends were paid.

In defending the amended version of the indirect credit, one sponsor described the purpose of the credit as securing, for domestic corporations that receive income in the form of dividends from foreign subsidiaries, the same sort of deduction available to domestic corporations that receive income from foreign branches. 61 Cong. Rec. 7184 (1921).[5] This goal of equalized treatment is reflected as well in testimony regarding the amendment before the Senate Committee on Finance, in which a spokesperson for the Department of the Treasury described the proposal as intended "to give this American corporation about the same credit as if conducting a branch." Hearings on H.R. 8245 before the Senate Committee on Finance, 67th Cong., 1st Sess., pt. 2, p.389 (1921). More recently, the Senate Report on the 1962 amendments to the indirect credit confirms Congress' intent to treat foreign branches and foreign subsidiaries alike in terms of the tax credits they generate for their domestic companies. See S. Rep. No. 1881, 87th Cong., 2d Sess., 66–67 (1962) * * *.

B

Given these purposes, we now turn to the operation of the indirect tax credit. Goodyear contends that the failure to calculate accumulated profits in terms of foreign law subjects domestic corporations that receive dividends from their foreign subsidiaries to double taxation. This undesirable result occurs, in Goodyear's view, because calculation of accumulated profits in accordance with domestic principles may disconnect the relationship in § 902's formula between accumulated profits and the foreign tax paid by the subsidiary. A subsidiary incurs foreign tax liability in proportion to its foreign defined income. To recover foreign taxes paid by its subsidiary, a domestic parent's dividend must be allocated or sourced to years in which its subsidiary paid foreign tax. If, however, accumulated profits are defined in domestic terms, the dividends of a domestic parent may be allocated to years in which the subsidiary paid little or no tax. In such a scenario, the parent may not be credited with foreign taxes paid by its subsidiary. To avoid this mismatching of accumulated profits and foreign tax, Goodyear contends that accumulated profits should be determined in accordance with the same principles that govern the imposition of the tax: those found in foreign law.

The Government contests Goodyear's characterization of this case as one of "double taxation." In the Government's view, the dividends received by Goodyear should not be allocated to prior years because to do so would permit Goodyear to avoid taxation altogether on domestically defined income that its subsidiary earned in 1970 and 1971. Under

5. Senator Smoot stated:

"[A] foreign subsidiary is much like a foreign branch of an American corporation. If the American corporation owned a foreign branch, it would include the earnings or profits of such branch in its total income, but it would also be entitled to deduct from the tax based upon such income any income or profits taxes paid to foreign countries by the branch in question. Without special legislation, however, no credit can be obtained where the branch is incorporated under foreign laws."

domestic rules, Goodyear G.B. earned sufficient income in 1970 and 1971 to cover the dividends it issued to Goodyear in those years. That British taxing authorities recognized little income in those years should not, in the Government's view, prevent the United States from recognizing the substantial income attributable to those years under domestic rules. According to the Government, the foreign tax paid in 1968 and 1969 by Goodyear G.B.—the years to which Goodyear seeks to source its dividends—relates to income that Goodyear G.B. chose not to distribute during those years as dividends to Goodyear. To credit Goodyear with taxes paid on undistributed income, the Government concludes, would be inequitable because it would provide domestic parents that operate through foreign subsidiaries favorable treatment vis-à-vis domestic corporations that use foreign branches.

Goodyear attempts to avoid the force of the Government's analysis by exploring hypothetical situations in which the calculation of accumulated profits in accordance with domestic rules presents a more plausible claim of double taxation than does this case. For example, if a subsidiary earns an equal amount of income under foreign and domestic rules, but those rules regard the income as being earned in different years, the domestic parent would be credited with a lower portion of the tax paid by the subsidiary if domestic timing rules govern. This result appears anomalous because the same credit should be available where foreign and domestic tax principles recognize equal amounts of income and the amount of tax paid remains constant. The effect of the divergence in foreign and domestic tax principles is particularly clear when a subsidiary pays a substantial foreign tax in a given year and the amount of income recognized under domestic rules in that year is zero. In such a circumstance, *none* of the tax paid by the subsidiary can be credited to the parent because a dividend cannot be sourced to a year in which there are no accumulated profits.

Goodyear's hypotheticals persuade us that if accumulated profits are calculated according to domestic tax principles, situations can arise in which § 902's statutory goal of avoiding double taxation will be disserved. Equally persuasive, however, is the Government's claim that defining accumulated profits in terms of foreign tax principles can unfairly advantage domestic parents that operate through foreign subsidiaries over companies operating through unincorporated branches. Thus, no definitional approach to "accumulated profits" uniformly and unqualifiedly satisfies the dual purposes underlying the indirect credit.

C

We nonetheless believe that the Government's interpretation of "accumulated profits" is more faithful to congressional intent. Our view is informed first and most significantly by our assessment that the risk of double taxation outlined by Goodyear is less substantial than the risk of unequal treatment cited by the Government. Defining "accumulated profits" in accordance with domestic tax concepts results in double taxation only when a dividend is sourced to a year in which domestic tax concepts recognize little or no income and yet a subsidiary pays substantial foreign tax. Goodyear offers no basis for the suggestion that such mismatching commonly occurs.

Goodyear's approach, on the other hand, leads to unequal tax treatment of subsidiaries and branches whenever the foreign taxing authority calculates income more or less generously than the United States. A domestic corporation must pay tax on all income of a foreign branch that is recognized under domestic law. Under Goodyear's interpretation, a domestic corporation may in some cases receive credit for taxes paid on income that, under domestic rules, the parent never received. This result is difficult to square with the express congressional purpose of ensuring tax parity between domestic corporations that operate through foreign subsidiaries and those that operate through foreign branches.

The Government's approach is also supported by administrative interpretations of § 902. In defining the credits available against foreign tax under the predecessor to § 902, the Commissioner stated that "[i]t is important in establishing the amount of the accumulated profits that it be based as a fundamental principle upon all income of the foreign corporation available for distribution to its shareholders *whether such profits be taxable by the foreign country or not.*" I.T. 2676, XII–1 Cum. Bull. 48, 50 (1933)(emphasis added). The Commissioner's approach requires a domestic assessment of income for the purposes of calculating accumulated profits. The Commissioner's position is reflected as well in a formal regulation promulgated by the Treasury in 1965, Treas. Reg. § 1.902–3(c)(1) * * *, which defines "accumulated profits" under § 902(a)(1) as "the sum of [t]he earnings and profits of [the foreign subsidiary] for such year, and [t]he foreign income taxes imposed on or with respect to the gains, profits, and income to which such earnings and profits are attributable." Defining a subsidiary's "accumulated profits" as its "earnings and profits" reflects an intent to calculate accumulated profits according to domestic principles, because "earnings and profits" in this context is a domestic tax concept.

Lastly, we find support for the Government's position in the statutory canon adopted in *Biddle v. Commissioner*, 302 U.S. 573, 578 (1938), that tax provisions should generally be read to incorporate domestic tax concepts absent a clear congressional expression that foreign concepts control. This canon has particularly strong application here where a contrary interpretation would leave an important statutory goal regarding equal tax treatment of foreign subsidiaries and foreign branches to the varying tax policies of foreign tax authorities.

IV

"Accumulated profits," as that term appears in § 902's indirect tax credit, should be calculated in accordance with domestic tax principles. The judgment of the Court of Appeals is therefore reversed * * *.

* * *

— Stop

[¶ 5170]

VULCAN MATERIALS CO. v. COMMISSIONER

United States Tax Court, 1991.
96 T.C. 410 (nonacq.), aff'd without published opinion, 959 F.2d 973 (11th Cir.1992).

TANNENWALD, JUDGE: Respondent determined a deficiency in petitioner's 1984 Federal income tax in the amount of $133,679. The sole issue for decision is the amount of Saudi Arabian taxes that petitioner should be deemed to have paid under section 902 [the pre–1986 Act version of Section 902] for the purpose of determining its foreign tax credit.

* * *

Petitioner is a domestic corporation with its principal corporate offices in Birmingham, Alabama. * * *

Petitioner was a member of a Saudi Arabian partnership (Saudi partnership) which began operations in Saudi Arabia in 1976. The other original partners in the Saudi partnership included Trading & Development Company (Tradco), a Saudi Arabian company; Shepherd Construction Co., Inc. (Shepherd); * * * and Dalton Rock Products Co. (Dalton). Shepherd * * * and Dalton were U.S. corporations unrelated to Vulcan or Tradco by ownership through 1984. Tradco was wholly owned by a Saudi Arabian national at all times from 1976 through, and including, 1984. * * *

The Saudi partnership's operations consisted of the production of construction materials under a contract with the Arabian American Oil Company (Aramco) and the operation of a Saudi Arabian quarry under a contract with Tradco. * * *

* * *

In 1979, the business and assets of the Saudi partnership were transferred to Tradco–Vulcan Company, Limited (TVCL), a corporation organized and existing under the laws of Saudi Arabia, in exchange for shares in TVCL. The shares of TVCL were issued to the partners in the Saudi partnership in proportion to their partnership interests. TVCL's shareholders and their interests at the time of its initial organization and through the years in issue were as follows:

Shareholder	*Percentage interest*
Vulcan	48%
Shepherd	10
Dalton	10
Tradco	32

At all relevant times since its formation, TVCL has continued to carry on the same lines of business as the partnership.

Saudi Arabia Royal Decree No. 17/2/28/3321 (1950), as amended, contains the income tax laws of Saudi Arabia. The Saudi Arabian income tax laws are not applicable to the income of Saudi Arabian nationals and Saudi Arabian corporations wholly owned by Saudi Arabian nationals. Rather, such Saudi Arabian nationals and corporations are required by Islamic law, the Shari'ah, to pay a tax called the Zakat. In the case of a Saudi Arabian corporation wholly owned by Saudi Arabian nationals, the Zakat was calculated in 1984 and for all relevant prior years as a flat-rate percentage of the net equity of the corporation less its net fixed assets; for 1984, the Zakat percentage was 1.25.

Saudi Arabian income tax laws impose an income tax on a "mixed corporation" (i.e., a Saudi Arabian corporation owned in part by Saudi Arabian nationals and in part by non-Saudi Arabian nationals) with respect to that portion of the corporation's net profits attributable to the ownership interest of non-Saudi Arabian shareholders. The portion of the net profits attributable to the non-Saudi Arabian shareholders is determined by reference to the percentage ownership interests of the non-Saudi Arabian shareholders as reflected by their stock ownership. The requirements of the Shari'ah are satisfied by imposing the Zakat on the Saudi Arabian shareholders' interests in the net equity of the corporation less its net fixed assets. Dividends paid by Saudi Arabian corporations, whether to Saudi Arabian or non-Saudi Arabian shareholders, are not subject to any further Saudi Arabian tax.

TVCL has always maintained profit accounts and paid dividends from those accounts to its shareholders. TVCL allocated and distributed its profits to a particular shareholder as follows:

> The pre-Saudi Arabian tax profits of such corporation are allocated to each shareholder, both Saudi Arabian and non-Saudi Arabian, on the basis of each shareholder's proportionate share interest in the corporation. Each shareholder's share of profits is then reduced by the Saudi Arabian tax. In the case of the Saudi Arabian shareholder, its share of the pre-corporate income tax profits is reduced by the Zakat tax paid on the basis of its shareholder interest. In the case of the non-Saudi Arabian shareholders, each such shareholder's share of pre-corporate income tax profits is reduced by its proportionate share of the Saudi Arabian corporate income tax paid on the basis of that non-Saudi Arabian shareholder's interest. As a result of the above calculation, there is a profit account for each shareholder. Each profit account is further reduced by the dividends paid to each shareholder.

The above profit accounts indicated an allocation to Tradco of 32 percent of the pre-tax profits of TVCL reduced by the Zakat and by previous distributions to Tradco, and an allocation to the three U.S. shareholders of their respective shares of TVCL's pre-tax profits (i.e., petitioner—48 percent, Shepherd—10 percent, and Dalton—10 percent) reduced by the Saudi Arabian income taxes and by previous distributions to such shareholders. All dividends through 1984 were in proportion to the balances in the shareholders' profits accounts at the end of the month preceding the declaration of the dividend.

In 1984, TVCL, which used the calendar year as its taxable year, paid dividends to petitioner aggregating 1,327,405 riyals, of which 557,924 riyals were paid in the first 60 days of 1984 and, under section 902(c)(1), were considered as paid out of the 1983 profits of TVCL, and 769,481 riyals were paid later in the year out of its 1984 profits. TVCL's pre-income tax profits for 1983 and 1984, calculated pursuant to U.S. tax principles but stated in Saudi Arabian currency, were 20,902,753 and 10,436,790 riyals, respectively. TVCL credited 68 percent of such pretax amounts (i.e., 14,213,872 and 7,097,017 riyals, respectively) to the profit accounts of its U.S. shareholders in proportion to their ownership interests, and the balance thereof to the profit account of Tradco. TVCL's Saudi Arabian corporate income taxes for the 2 years were 6,883,191 and 4,267,909 riyals, respectively, all of which TVCL charged against the profit accounts of the U.S. shareholders in proportion to their relative share interests. The applicable conversion rates for Saudi Arabian income taxes paid for the 2 years were 3.46 and 3.53 riyals to the dollar, respectively.

On its 1984 Federal corporate income tax return, petitioner claimed a section 902 deemed paid credit for Saudi Arabian income taxes for each of the 2 years 1983 and 1984 by using a fraction, the numerator of which was the amount of the dividends paid to petitioner out of the profits of such year and the denominator of which was the portion of TVCL's pre-tax profits for the year that was allocated to the U.S. shareholders, reduced by TVCL's Saudi Arabian income taxes for each year, as follows (expressed in riyals):

1983

Saudi tax	6,883,191
Dividend	557,924
Pre-tax profits allocated to U.S. shareholders	14,213,872

Computation of allowable section 902 credit:

$$6{,}883{,}191 \times \frac{557{,}924}{14{,}213{,}872 - 6{,}883{,}191} = 523{,}866$$

1984

Saudi tax	4,267,909
Dividend	769,481
Pre-tax profits allocated to U.S. shareholders	7,097,017

Computation of allowable section 902 credit:

$$4{,}267{,}909 \times \frac{769{,}481}{7{,}097{,}017 - 4{,}267{,}909} = 1{,}160{,}816$$

In his notice of deficiency, respondent calculated petitioner's deemed paid credit for Saudi Arabian taxes paid by TVCL in the same manner as petitioner had on its 1984 return, except in one major aspect. In the denominators of the fractions, respondent included all of TVCL's pre-income tax profits for the year, including amounts allocated by it to Tradco. Thus, respondent's calculations were as follows (expressed in riyals):

1983

Saudi tax	6,883,191
Dividend	557,924
Pre-tax profits allocated to U.S. shareholders	20,902,753

Computation of allowable section 902 credit:

$$6{,}883{,}191 \times \frac{557{,}924}{20{,}902{,}753 - 6{,}883{,}191} = 273{,}924$$

1984

Saudi tax	4,267,909
Dividend	769,481
Pre-tax profits allocated to U.S. shareholders	10,436,790

Computation of allowable section 902 credit:

$$4{,}267{,}909 \times \frac{769{,}481}{10{,}436{,}790 - 4{,}267{,}909} = 532{,}362$$

On its 1984 Federal corporate income tax return, petitioner claimed that $477,533 of the Saudi Arabian income taxes paid by TVCL with respect to its 1983 and 1984 profits was allowable as a deemed paid credit using the previously described calculation. On the other hand, respondent, using his own calculation, determined that $229,980 was the deemed paid credit allowable to petitioner and disallowed $247,553 in foreign tax credits claimed by petitioner. As a collateral adjustment, pursuant to section 78, respondent decreased petitioner's income by the same amount.

* * *

[Under Section 902], petitioner's credit for the income taxes paid by TVCL is determined by application of the following formula:

$$\text{Foreign income taxes deemed paid} = \text{Foreign income taxes paid} \times \frac{\text{Dividends received by petitioner from TVCL}}{\text{Accumulated profits of TVCL minus foreign income taxes paid by TVCL}}$$

The parties are in agreement as to the amount of the foreign taxes paid and of the dividends received. Their dispute centers on the meaning of the term "accumulated profits." Petitioner contends that the proper figure is the amount of the profits of TVCL upon which the Saudi Arabian income tax was imposed, i.e., 68 percent of the total accumulated profits of TVCL, the portion of the profits allocable to all U.S. shareholders. Respondent contends that the proper figure is the total accumulated profits of TVCL. For the reasons hereinafter set forth, we agree with petitioner.

Initially, we need to dispose of the applicability of *United States v. Goodyear Tire & Rubber Co.*, 493 U.S. 132 (1989), in which the Supreme Court determined that "accumulated profits" were to be determined in accordance with U.S. rather than foreign tax rules. Applying that standard, the Supreme Court refused to permit the taxpayer to take into account a loss of its British subsidiary attributable to deductions which were allowed under British tax law but would not have been allowed under U.S. law. * * *

Respondent contends that *Goodyear* precludes us from taking into account the fact that under Saudi Arabian law the income taxes were imposed only on a portion of TVCL's accumulated profits. We think respondent misconceives the scope of *Goodyear*. There is no question that, under *Goodyear*, the determination of TVCL's accumulated profits turns upon the application of U.S. tax rules, and petitioner does not contend otherwise. The question before us is not how TVCL's accumulated profits are to be determined but whether, pursuant to section 902, all or only a pro rata portion of such profits so determined are to be included in the denominator of the formula.

The fact that the Supreme Court in *Goodyear* put its stamp of approval on the position of respondent set forth in I.T. 2676, XII–1 C.B. 48, 50 (1933), * * * does not, as respondent argues, support his view of *Goodyear*. In that ruling, respondent stated:

> It is important in establishing the amount of the accumulated profits that it be based as a fundamental principle upon all income of the foreign corporation available for distribution to its shareholders, whether such profits be taxable by a foreign country or not. * * *

It is clear, however, that respondent's ruling was directed at the methodology for calculating "income" for purposes of the deemed foreign tax credit and, in fact, the Supreme Court itself described respondent's statement precisely that way. *United States v. Goodyear Tire & Rubber Co.*, [*supra*].

Turning to the question before us, we start out by examining the applicable statutory provisions because, if they are unambiguous, we are not permitted, except in rare and unusual situations, to depart from the statutory language. * * * Respondent contends that the language of [the pre–1986 Act version of] section 902 mandates that the total accumulated profits of TVCL be used. We are not convinced such is the case. The phraseology of section 902(a) and (c)(1) * * * relates the taxes paid to "the accumulated profits of such foreign corporation from which such dividends were paid" (sec. 902(a)) and specifies that "accumulated profits" should be determined without reduction by the taxes "imposed on or with respect to such profits" (sec. 902(c)(1)). Similarly, we are not persuaded that the terminology of section 1.902–1(e)(1), Income Tax Regs., requires us to conclude that the statutory provisions are as all-encompassing as respondent maintains. That terminology states that, in determining the accumulated profits of a foreign corporation, there shall be included "The earnings and profits of such corporation for such year." The use of the word "The" is not necessarily equivalent of "the entire" or "all." We recognize that respondent has ruled in accordance with the position he takes herein. Rev. Rul. 87–14, 1987–1 C.B. 181. However, the ruling is devoid of any analysis; it simply announces its conclusion and cites the pertinent statutory provisions and regulations. Moreover, we note that the position taken in this ruling is inconsistent with the approach respondent adopted in explaining the methodology to be used in calculating the foreign tax credit under the United States–United Kingdom Income Tax Convention * * *. Granted that the interpretation of a treaty is not equivalent to the interpretation of a statutory provision, we think that there is sufficient commonality involved to cause us not to give particular weight to respondent's ruling, which clearly is not binding upon us. * * *

In short, we think that the statutory and regulatory provisions are sufficiently unclear to permit us to examine the objectives of the foreign tax credit. * * * Those objectives, so recently articulated in *United States v. Goodyear Tire & Rubber Co.*, *supra*, have, since the inception of the foreign tax credit in 1918, been avoiding double taxation and affording a U.S. corporation operating through a foreign subsidiary the same credits as if it were conducting a branch operation in the foreign country. * * * In terms of those objectives, we are satisfied that petitioner should prevail.

There can be no question that if TVCL had been conducted as a branch, only petitioner's share of the profits would have been taken into account, and that it would have received a direct credit for the foreign taxes paid, and respondent does not contend otherwise. Similarly, if accumulated profits are not limited to the profits which were the subject of the Saudi Arabian income tax and in which petitioner shared, petitioner will not be entitled to the full credit for the Saudi Arabian taxes imposed on its share of those profits and, to that extent, double taxation will result. Indeed, the logical result of respondent's position is that if the share of TVCL's profits allocable to U.S. shareholders were not subject to any Saudi Arabian income tax but only the share allocated to the Saudi Arabian shareholders were the base for imposing such tax, the U.S. shareholders would be entitled to a foreign tax credit under section 902 even though they suffered no economic burden from such income tax. Such a result would be bizarre to say the least, as respondent himself has recognized in setting forth examples of situations which he claims would be abusive by permitting the U.S. tax burden to be manipulated through the establishment of separate shareholder accounts for accumulated profits, and the foreign income taxes attributable thereto, simply to suit the U.S. shareholders' purpose. But the situation here is not simply the result of the establishment of separate accounts by the parties in interest; it is founded on the stipulated structure of the Saudi Arabian tax law.

Respondent also seeks to counteract petitioner's position by an analysis which aggregates the Saudi Arabian income tax and the Zakat tax (which is a non-creditable type of tax) and then allocating the resulting tax burden among TVCL's shareholders, in order to sustain his claim that petitioner is not really exposed to a double tax burden under respondent's approach. This analysis mixes apples and pears. In *United Dyewood Corp. v. Bowers*, 44 F.2d 399 (S.D.N.Y.1930), affd. per curiam 56 F.2d 603 (2d Cir.1932), a British subsidiary of the taxpayer was subject to British income tax on the average of 3 years of taxable income and to an excess profits tax on the current year's taxable income. Respondent maintained that both amounts of taxable income and both amounts of British taxes should be aggregated for the purpose of computing the taxpayer's deemed foreign tax credit. That position was rejected, and respondent was required separately to compute the credits for each of the taxes.

The sourcing of accumulated profits has been utilized in various other contexts. Thus, Rev. Rul. 69–440, 1969–2 C.B. 46, uses the sourcing method of earnings and profits to allocate distributions among various classes of stock in order to determine what portion should constitute dividends under section 316 in respect of each class. The determination of "dividends" under section 316 is applicable to a comparable determination under section 902(a), see sec. 1.902–1(a)(6), Income Tax Regs., and has been applied to source accumulated profits to the appropriate taxable year for the purpose of calculating the foreign tax credit. See *Champion International Corp. v. Commissioner*, 81 T.C. at 431–432. Additionally, in providing the U.S. Senate with an explanation of the operation of the deemed foreign tax credit in respect of United Kingdom taxes, respondent utilized the separate proportionate interest approach utilized by petitioner herein. See Technical Explanation of the United States–United Kingdom Income Tax Convention, 1980–1 C.B. 455, 472–476. See also *Xerox Corp. v. United States*, 14 Cl.Ct. 455. Respondent is, of course, correct that this explanation was not an interpretation of section 902 as such but was presented in the specific context of a negotiated agreement. Admittedly, the foregoing examples of sourcing are distinguishable, but we believe they provide useful analogies in resolving the issue before us. In this connection, we note that, while the economic burden of the foreign income tax is irrelevant for determining who is liable for such tax, see, e.g., *Biddle v. Commissioner*, 302 U.S. 573 (1938), it is an important element in determining how that liability should be apportioned under section 902 among the parties in interest.

The long and short of the matter is that "no definitional approach to 'accumulated profits' uniformly and unqualifiedly satisfies the dual purposes underlying the indirect credit." See *United States v. Goodyear Tire & Rubber Co.*, 493 U.S. at [143]. Such being the case, the question before us is which interpretation of that term as discussed by the parties herein "is more faithful to congressional intent." [*Id.*] Our view is that petitioner's interpretation of the phrase "accumulated profits," rather than that of respondent, best carries out that intent. We so hold.

* * *

[¶ 5175]

NOTES

1. The *Vulcan Materials* decision involved interpretation of the term "accumulated profits" in the denominator of the pre–1986 Act Section 902 calculation. The current version of Section 902(a) replaces the term "accumulated profits in excess of [foreign taxes]" in the denominator of the Section 902 fraction with the term "post–1986 undistributed earnings," but the Tax Court's reasoning arguably applies under current law.

2. In an attempt to reverse *Vulcan Materials*, revised regulations under Section 902, issued in 1997, provide that special allocations of accumulated profits and taxes to particular shareholders, whether required or permitted under foreign law or a shareholder agreement, will be disregarded in determining post–1986 undistributed earnings and pre–1987 accumulated profits that are distributed in a tax year starting after 1986. Reg. § 1.902–1(a)(9)(iv) and (10)(ii).

[¶ 5180]

PROBLEMS

1. ABC Manufacturing, Inc., a U.S. corporation, owns 40 percent of the stock of FC, Inc. ("FC"), which was incorporated under the laws of Country Y. The other 60 percent of FC's stock is owned by unrelated foreign persons. During the first three years of operations (all post–1986 years), FC had the following amounts of pre-tax earnings from operations abroad and paid the following amount of foreign income taxes to Country Y on those earnings:

	Before-Tax Earnings	*Foreign Income Taxes*
Year 1	$100,000	$ 30,000
Year 2	$400,000	$120,000
Year 3	$400,000	$150,000

FC broke even during year 4 and paid no foreign income taxes during that year. In year 4, FC paid ABC Manufacturing, Inc. a dividend of $200,000. The dividend was subject to a gross-basis, Country Y withholding tax of $30,000.

Determine the amount of ABC Manufacturing, Inc.'s direct and indirect credits under Sections 901 and 902.

2. Would you answer in Problem 1 change if the tax laws of Country Y were such that it imposed income taxes on the earnings of FC only with respect to the portion of net profits attributable to the ownership interest of non-Country Y shareholders? Assume that one-third of FC's stock is owned by Country Y shareholders, so that the $300,000 of Country Y foreign income taxes were imposed on a base of only $600,000 of FC's income (i.e., the two-thirds of the before-tax income not attributable to Country Y shareholders).

3. You are the chief negotiator for Country M in working out the terms of an investment by Acme International ("Acme"), a U.S. corporation. The investment will be made through Subsid Ltd., a wholly owned subsidiary of Acme, which is incorporated in Country M. The pro forma financial statements of Subsid Ltd. show profits of $1 million per year and dividend distributions to Acme of $700,000 per year. To the extent its cash flow is greater than $700,000 per year Acme will reinvest the balance in Country M.

Country M has a tax of 22 percent on corporate profits and a withholding tax on dividends of ten percent. The tax law of Country M defines corporate profits or income in the same way as does U.S. tax law.

a. So far the negotiations have been proceeding on the assumption that the standard Country M tax rates of 22 percent on profits and ten percent withholding on dividends will apply to the project. Should you try to negotiate something different? As a matter of Country M law you can provide for special tax rates on this project. Is there any way you can raise the rates without costing Subsid Ltd. or Acme any more? (Assume a U.S. tax rate of 35 percent.)

b. Compare results, raising the Country M corporate tax rate to 25 percent.

c. Now compare results, leaving the Country M corporate tax rate at 22 percent, but raising the withholding rate to 15 percent.

4. Parent ("P"), a domestic U.S. corporation, owns 100 percent of Sub ("S"), a foreign corporation, which, in turn, owns 100 percent of Sub–Sub ("SS"), another foreign corporation. SS, in turn, owns 100 percent of Sub–Sub–Sub ("SSS"), a third foreign corporation.

In year 1, SSS has income (all from foreign sources) of $300, pays foreign income tax of $100 and pays a dividend of $100 to SS. In year 1, SS has regular income (all from foreign sources) of $300 in addition to the $100 dividend from SSS, pays foreign income tax of $120 and pays a dividend of $140 to S. Also in year 1, S has regular income (all from foreign sources) of $175 in addition to the $140 dividend from SS. S pays foreign income tax of $75 and pays a dividend to P of $180.

Compute P's U.S. tax assuming a rate of 35 percent. Is this a sensible result?

5. LN Corporation, a U.S. corporation, owns all the stock of Foreign Sub 1, a foreign corporation. Foreign Sub 1 in turn owns 20 percent of the voting stock of Foreign Sub 2, also a foreign corporation. LN Corporation also owns ten percent of the nonvoting common stock of Foreign Sub 2 but owns no voting stock in Foreign Sub 2. During the current year, Foreign Sub 2 pays dividends on its nonvoting common stock, but pays no dividends on its voting stock. Is LN Corporation eligible for a Section 902 indirect foreign tax credit for the current year with respect to the foreign income taxes paid by Foreign Sub 2? See Rev. Rul. 74–459, 1974–2 C.B. 207, 208 (holding that the Section 902 credit is not available to a U.S. parent corporation receiving a dividend directly from a second-tier foreign corporation because the U.S. corporation owned only nonvoting stock of the second-tier corporation; IRS reasoned that the Section 902 credit is "contingent upon distribution [of a dividend] through the chain of corporations possessing voting stock ownership in the distributing corporation").

[¶ 5185]

d. Foreign Currency Conversion

Foreign taxes for which an indirect foreign tax credit is taken will normally be paid, and earnings and profits of a foreign corporation will normally be measured, in a foreign currency (its "functional currency"). The result is that conversion into U.S. dollars will be required to calculate the tentative U.S. tax and the available foreign tax credit in connection with a particular dividend distribution. Section 986 contains the rules for translating foreign taxes and a foreign corporation's earnings and profits into U.S. dollars. These translation matters are discussed at ¶¶ 9115–9120.

[¶ 5190]

e. Effect of Deficits in Post–1986 Undistributed Earnings or Pre–1987 Accumulated Profits

The regulations provide rules for computing foreign taxes deemed paid under Section 902 when there are deficits in a foreign corporation's post–1986 undistributed earnings or pre–1987 accumulated profits (determined under the pre–1986 Act version of Section 902). Reg. § 1.902–2(a)(1) provides that if there is a deficit in post–1986 undistributed earnings of a first-, second- or third-tier foreign corporation and the foreign corporation makes a dividend distribution to shareholders, the deficit is carried back to the most recent pre-effective date tax year of the first-, second- or third-tier corporation with positive accumulated profits determined under the pre–1986 Act version of Section 902 (i.e., the most recent tax year of the corporation with positive accumulated profits for which the pre–1986 Act version of Section 902 applies in computing the indirect credit). The amount carried back reduces the deficit in the foreign corporation's pool of post–1986 undistributed earnings, but any foreign income taxes paid with respect to those earnings are not carried back to a tax year starting before 1987 (or a later year if the special effective date of Reg. § 1.902–1(a)(13) applies) and do not reduce the foreign corporation's pool of post–1986 foreign taxes.

Reg. § 1.902–2(b)(1) provides that if there is a deficit in pre–1987 accumulated profits (determined under the pre–1986 Act version of Section 902) of a first-, second- or third-tier foreign corporation as of the end of its last pre-effective date tax year, that deficit is carried forward to the first tax year of the foreign corporation starting after 1986 (or later year if the special effective date of Reg. § 1.902–1(a)(13) applies). The deficit carried forward is included in and reduces the foreign corporation's post–1986 undistributed earnings. However, foreign income taxes paid with respect to pre-effective date years are not carried forward. Reg. § 1.902–2(b)(2) clarifies that if a foreign corporation has a deficit in Section 902 accumulated profits at the end of its last pre-effective date year (i.e., its last tax year governed by the pre–1986 Act rules for calculating the Section 902 credit), then, unless there is an adjustment (such as a refund of foreign taxes) that restores earnings to a positive amount in a pre-effective date tax year, the foreign corporation will never be able to pay a dividend out of pre-effective date earnings and profits and will never be able to claim a credit for taxes deemed paid under Section 902 for any foreign income taxes remaining in pre-effective date years. See INTL–933–86, 1995–1 C.B. 959, 962; T.D. 8708, 1997–1 C.B. 137, 140.

If a foreign corporation has a positive amount of current earnings, but has a deficit in the post–1986 undistributed earnings by reason of losses in years before the year of the dividend, a dividend paid to a ten-percent U.S. corporate shareholder will produce dividend income to the shareholder but will not carry any deemed paid foreign taxes with it. See Reg. § 1.902–2(b)(3), Ex. 2(iii). This result occurs because a distribution made to a shareholder in a year when the distributing corporation has current earnings and profits (sometimes called a "nimble dividend") is treated as a dividend under Sections 301(c)(1) and 316(a)(2), notwithstanding the existence of a deficit in the corporation's accumulated earnings. Yet, under the formula prescribed by Section 902, the distributing foreign corporation must have a positive amount of post–1986 undistributed earnings in order for a dividend to carry with it foreign taxes of the foreign corporation.

The rules in these revised regulations under Section 902, issued in 1997, concerning the carryforward and carryback of deficits between post–

1986 and pre–1987 earnings and profits, were first enunciated in the following IRS Notice, which provides several examples showing the application of these rules. Other examples illustrating the application of these rules are now contained in Reg. §§ 1.902–2(a)(2), Exs. 1–3 and 1.902–2(b)(3), Exs. 1–2.

[¶ 5195]

IRS NOTICE 87–54

1987–2 C.B. 363.

This notice provides guidance relating to several aspects of the amendments made to the foreign tax credit rules by the Tax Reform Act of 1986 (the "Act") * * *. The rules contained in this notice will be incorporated in regulations to be issued under the Act. Taxpayers may rely on the rules provided herein for the purposes specified until regulations are issued. [As discussed above, the regulations were issued in 1997 and did incorporate the rules set forth in this Notice. See Reg. § 1.902–2.]

Specifically, this notice provides guidance with respect to the carryforward and carryback of deficits between post–1986 and pre–1987 earnings and profits, and the foreign currency issues with respect thereto, for purposes of computing the deemed-paid foreign tax credit of section 902 * * *.

* * *

The examples in * * * this notice assume that: (1) all earnings and profits and deficits in earnings and profits are attributable to the taxpayer's general limitation category (section 904(d)(1)(I)) [Section 904(d)(1)(B), for tax years starting after 2006]; (2) the foreign corporation's earnings and profits and related tax amounts are computed in the corporation's foreign functional currency ("u"), which did not change from pre–1987 to post–1986 taxable years; and (3) the foreign income taxes attributable to post–1986 taxable years have been translated into U.S. dollars at the exchange rate as of the date of payment, as required by [a prior version of] section 986(b).

(a) *Carryback of deficits from post–1986 earnings and profits to pre–1987 earnings and profits for purposes of section 902* * * *. In computing the section 902 deemed-paid foreign tax credit for dividends paid in a taxable year of the foreign corporation in which there is a deficit in the post–1986 undistributed earnings pool, the deficit is carried back to pre-effective date taxable year(s). The amount carried back will reduce the earnings and profits of such pre-effective date taxable year(s) for purposes of calculating the deemed-paid credit and will be removed from the pool of post–1986 undistributed earnings. * * *

* * *

(b) *Carry forward of deficits from pre–1987 earnings and profits to post–1986 earnings and profits for purposes of section 902.* In computing the section 902 deemed-paid foreign tax credit for dividends paid in a taxable year of the foreign corporation beginning after the effective date of the Act, the amount of a deficit in earnings and profits (or after-tax accumulated profits) of the foreign corporation accumulated as of the end of the last pre-effective date taxable year is carried forward and included in the post–1986 undistributed earnings pool. Such amount is carried forward as of the first day of the foreign corporation's first taxable year beginning after December 31, 1986. The following examples illustrate this rule.

Example 3

CALENDAR TAXABLE YEAR SHARE-HOLDER AND FOREIGN CORP.	CURRENT E & P/ AFTER-TAX ACCUMULATED PROFIT (DEFICITS)	CURRENT PLUS ACCUMULATED E & P	POST-'86 UNDISTRI-BUTED EARNINGS POOL	FOREIGN INCOME TAXES (ANNUAL)	POST-'86 POOL OF FOREIGN INCOME TAXES	DEC. 31 DISTRI-BUTIONS
1984.......	25u	25u		20u		–0–
1985.......	(100u)	(75u)		5u		–0–
1986.......	(25u)	(100u)		–0–		–0–
1987.......	200u	100u	100u	$100	$100	–0–
1988.......	100u	200u	200u	$50	$150	200u
1989.......	100u	100u	100u	$50	$50	–0–

Under section 316(a), the 1988 dividend distribution of 200u represents all the earnings and profits (current plus accumulated) of the foreign corporation and is made out of the post–1986 undistributed earnings pool. The denominator of the section 902 fraction for the 1988 distribution is 200u (the post–1986 undistributed earnings of 300u reduced by the 100u accumulated deficit carried forward from 1986), and the section 902 credit is $150. *Cf.* Rev. Rul. 87–72 * * *. None of the foreign income taxes associated with pre–1987 tax years will be carried forward and included in the post–1986 pool of foreign income taxes.

If a dividend is paid out of current earnings and profits and there is a deficit in current plus accumulated earnings and profits, then the results will be modified.

Example 4

CALENDAR TAXABLE YEAR SHARE-HOLDER AND FOREIGN CORP.	CURRENT E & P/ AFTER-TAX ACCUMULATED PROFIT (DEFICITS)	CURRENT PLUS ACCUMULATED E & P	POST-'86 UNDISTRI-BUTED EARNINGS POOL	FOREIGN INCOME TAXES (ANNUAL)	POST-'86 POOL OF FOREIGN INCOME TAXES	DEC. 31 DISTRI-BUTIONS
1986.......	(100u)	(100u)		–0–		–0–
1987.......	150u	50u	50u	$120	$120	100u
1988.......	(150u)	(200u)	(200u)	–0–	–0–	–0–
1989.......	100u	(100u)	(100u)	$50	$50	100u
1990.......	250u	50u	50u	$100	$150	50u
1991.......	–0–	–0–	–0–	–0–	–0–	–0–

Under these facts, the 1987 distribution of 100u is considered a dividend in its entirety (as a result of current earnings and profits in 1987 of 150u). The denominator of the section 902 fraction is 50u (the post–1986 undistributed earnings pool of 150u reduced by the 100u accumulated deficit carried forward from 1986). * * * Although the dividend is 100u, because the section 902 credit cannot exceed the taxes actually paid or deemed paid by the foreign corporation, the numerator of the section 902 fraction cannot exceed the denominator of the fraction; thus, the numerator of the fraction for 1987 is limited to 50u, and the section 902 [credit] is 50u/50u multiplied by $120, or $120.

After determination of the section 902 credit for 1987, the 1987 nimble dividend of 100u reduces the current earnings and profits for 1987 of 150u to 50u, which is added to the accumulated earnings and profits of (100u) from the previous year. At the end of 1987 (after the distribution), the corporation has a deficit of (50u) in accumulated earnings and profits.

In 1989, the 100u distribution will be taxed as a dividend because there are current earnings and profits in 1989 of 100u. The post–1986 undistributed earnings pool for 1989 is (100u), which is the sum of (50u) (the deficit in accumulated earnings and profits at the end of 1987), plus (150u) (the deficit in current earnings and profits for 1988), plus 100u (the current earnings and profits for 1989). Because there is a deficit in the corporation's post–1986 pool of undistributed earnings and profits, [the] foreign income taxes of $50 will not be creditable in 1989. The taxes will, however, remain in the pool of post–1986 foreign income taxes not previously credited. The 100u dividend in 1989 eliminates the current earnings and profits of 100u for that year; therefore, at the end of 1989 (after the distribution), accumulated earnings and profits are exactly what they were at the end of 1988, that is (200u), which is the sum of (50u) (the deficit in accumulated earnings and profits at the end of 1987) plus (150u) (the deficit in current earnings and profits for 1988).

Since there are 250u of current earnings and profits in 1990, the 50u distribution in that year will be taxed as a dividend. The post–1986 undistributed earnings pool for 1990 is 50u which equals the total of (200u) (the post–1986 undistributed earnings pool at the end of 1989, after the 1989 distribution), plus 250u (the current earnings and profits for 1990). Thus, the section 902 credit is 50u/50u times $150 (the pool of foreign income taxes not previously credited), or $150.

[¶ 5200]

PROBLEMS

1. Alexandra Corporation, a U.S. corporation, owns all the stock of Foreign Subsidiary Corp., a foreign corporation incorporated under the laws of Country Z. (Alexandra Corporation acquired the stock in Foreign Subsidiary Corp. before 1987.) Foreign Subsidiary Corp. has a deficit of $200,000 in

pre–1987 accumulated profits (as determined under the pre–1986 Act version of Section 902) and has $50,000 of income taxes paid to Country Z during pre–1987 tax years, which were not deemed paid with respect to dividends paid by Foreign Subsidiary Corp. in prior years. Foreign Subsidiary Corp. broke even during the current year (a year after 1986), but has post–1986 undistributed earnings of $400,000 and post–1986 foreign income taxes of $80,000. During the current year, Foreign Subsidiary Corp. distributes a cash dividend of $100,000 to Alexandra Corporation. How much foreign tax will be deemed paid by Alexandra Corporation under Section 902(a)?

2. Cosmos Corporation, a U.S. corporation, establishes a wholly owned foreign subsidiary in Brazil, Cosmos Brazilia S.A. ("Cosmos Brazilia"), on January 1 of year 1 (a tax year governed by the post–1986 Act version of Section 902). Cosmos Brazilia has a loss of $200,000 in year 1 and a loss of $100,000 in year 2. In year 3, it has earnings of $400,000, on which it pays foreign income tax of $200,000, and it makes a distribution of $200,000. How much will be treated as a dividend and how much foreign tax will be deemed paid under Section 902(a)?

[¶ 5205]

f. Lingering Questions and Possible Reforms

Although the perpetual pools of earnings and taxes represent a significant step in the direction of simplification, some problems remain. The perpetual pool of earnings and taxes applies only to calculating indirect tax credits. In determining whether a distribution must be treated as a dividend, the matching of the distribution first against current earnings and profits and then against accumulated earnings and profits, as required by Section 316, is still applicable. As the above problems on the effect of deficits on the calculation of the Section 902 credit illustrate, anomalies can result when the two systems do not mesh.

Moreover, the perpetual pooling approach of post–1986 Section 902 has been criticized for its complexity and for the compliance burden that it has created by requiring, in effect, that records of a foreign corporation's earnings and taxes "be retained indefinitely for all post–1986 years." U.S. Treas. Dep't, International Tax Reform: An Interim Report 28 (Jan. 1993). That 1993 Treasury Report contained (at pp. 28–29) discussion of several alternative approaches for dealing with the abuses that arose under the pre–1987 version of Section 902:

> An alternative solution would be to create "moving pools" of several years. This suggestion would both mitigate the potential for manipulation and limit the period of time for which records must be kept. However, the continual addition and subtraction of taxable years from the moving pools could introduce a new element of complexity by virtue of the need to account for distributions and

current inclusions.[64] In addition, special rules would be required for situations in which distributions exceeded the earnings in the moving pool, although these rules could be similar to the existing rules for coordination of pre-1987 and post-1986 pools. If the pooling period were sufficiently long, these rules would not apply for most taxpayers.

[Another] possibility would be to limit the number of years for which earnings and taxes included in eternal pools could be subject to audit, e.g., to five years. Thus, for example, if a taxpayer established its pools of post-1986 earnings and taxes in 1987 (and made a distribution in 1987) and the IRS had not adjusted the amounts of 1987 earnings and taxes by 1993, those amounts could not be adjusted in any subsequent year. This approach could reduce the recordkeeping burden associated with the current rules, because, at some point, amounts of earnings and taxes for a particular year would no longer be open to question. It might also be somewhat simpler than the moving pools approach, because it would not require the continual addition and subtraction of taxable years.

[Yet another] option would be to return to the [pre-1986 Act year-by-year] method but add a general anti-abuse rule that would permit the IRS to apply a multi-year pooling rule in the abuse cases. This approach could be more difficult to administer and enforce by virtue of its reliance on the IRS' ability to identify instances of manipulation. All of these suggestions deserve further consideration, however, in light of the frequency of taxpayer complaints with regard to the "eternal pools" of existing law.

[¶ 5210]

G. TAX-SPARING CREDITS

Many developing countries have adopted special tax incentive regimes, called "tax holidays," to attract foreign investment. These tax holidays reduce or eliminate the income tax liability of the foreign investor for a specified period of years. The net effect of such a holiday when provided to U.S. investors must be considered in the light of the mechanism for calculating the foreign tax credit under U.S. tax law. Because uncollected foreign taxes are not creditable to a U.S. investor, a tax holiday in the developing country results in increased tax collections by the IRS from the U.S. investor (i.e., the United States will collect its usual tax on the income earned by the U.S. investor in the developing country and, hence, the tax holiday inures to the benefit of the U.S. Treasury, not

64. For example, if five-year pools were chosen, it would be necessary in the sixth taxable year to subtract the first taxable year from the pool. If the corporation in question has made a distribution, or if a portion of its earnings have been subject to current inclusion, then some portion of the earnings distributed or currently included must be allocated to the first taxable year and the first year's earnings reduced by that amount before deletion from the moving pool. This process would have to be repeated each year.

the U.S. investor). Accordingly, the U.S. investor will be indifferent about whether to conduct business in the United States or in the developing country with the tax holiday because the investor will pay U.S. taxes at the usual rates in either case and, thus, the incentive effect of the tax holiday will have been substantially undercut or eliminated altogether.

A device to mitigate such results, called "tax-sparing credits," has been adopted by a substantial number of capital-exporting countries either under their domestic law or, more typically, in tax treaties with developing countries. The basic premise of tax-sparing credits is that the capital-exporting country provides the taxpayer with a foreign tax credit, not only for foreign income taxes actually paid but also for foreign income taxes that would have been paid if the developing country had not provided a tax holiday for the taxpayer (i.e., a foreign tax credit is granted for the foreign tax waived or "spared").

To illustrate, assume that a U.S. corporation, which has an effective U.S. tax rate of 35 percent, earns $100 of business income through a permanent establishment in Country X, a developing country. Assume further that, in the absence of any tax holiday granted by Country X, the U.S. corporation would have to pay an income tax of $25 to Country X. The Country X tax would be creditable for U.S. tax purposes and would reduce the corporation's U.S. tax liability on the $100 of business income by $25, resulting in a residual U.S. tax liability of $10 to the United States (i.e., tentative tax of $35 reduced by the foreign tax credit of $25) and a total tax liability of $35 ($25 to Country X and $10 to the United States). If Country X grants a tax holiday that exempts business income from the Country X income tax for a specified number of years and the United States does not provide a tax-sparing credit, the U.S. corporation's Country X tax liability will be reduced from $25 to 0, but its U.S. tax liability will increase from $10 to $35. Thus, in the absence of a tax-sparing credit, the Country X tax holiday results in no decrease in the total tax liability of the U.S. corporation (i.e., the total tax liability is still $35) but instead results in a $25 increase in tax collections by the United States. Accordingly, the U.S. corporation has no real tax incentive to invest in Country X instead of in the United States. By contrast, if the United States granted a tax-sparing credit for the taxes waived by Country X by reason of the tax holiday, the U.S. corporation would have a U.S. tax liability of only $10 to the United States, save $25 in taxes by reason of conducting its business in Country X and have a tax incentive to invest in Country X.

Although the governments of many developed countries (e.g., Denmark, France, Germany, Japan, Norway, Sweden and the United Kingdom) have provided for tax-sparing credits in one form or another in tax treaties with developing countries, the U.S. Senate has rejected tax-sparing credits on those occasions when they have been included in tax treaties presented for approval. As a matter of treaty policy, the United States generally takes the position that U.S. income tax treaties should not reduce the taxing jurisdiction of the United States over a U.S. person's foreign-source income any more than is necessary to eliminate double taxation of such income.[18] Moreover, the OECD has issued a report identifying "a number of concerns that put into question the usefulness of the granting of tax sparing relief by OECD Member countries," including (1) the vulnerability of tax sparing to taxpayer abuse; (2) the effectiveness of tax sparing as a tool to provide foreign aid and promote economic development; and (3) "general concerns with the way in which tax sparing may encourage countries to use tax incentives." See OECD, Tax Sparing—A Reconsideration 41–42 (1998).

The resistance of the United States to tax-sparing credits has been based on a number of considerations. First, tax-sparing credits reward investment abroad in developing countries offering the tax holidays at the expense of investment in the United States (and, although probably of less concern to U.S. policymakers, in other foreign countries not providing such tax holidays). In other words, tax-sparing provisions violate the principle of capital-export neutrality and serve as a tax incentive for U.S. persons to export capital abroad to developing countries. Second, the United States believes that developing countries should not be encouraged to provide tax holidays because the loss of tax revenues may not be worth the additional investment attracted thereby. Third, the United States is concerned that the practice of offering tax holidays leads poor, developing countries to compete with one another to give up badly needed tax revenues to the detriment of all such countries. Fourth, the United States is not enthusiastic about surrendering any tax revenues to other countries.

In response to these concerns, leaders of developing countries are likely to note that they have not asked the United States to determine the effectiveness of their economic and fiscal policies and that they view the U.S. concerns as unwanted economic paternalism. Further, leaders of developing countries are not necessarily enthusiastic about helping the United States address its revenue needs by allowing it to impede the effectiveness of their tax holidays. More importantly, based on the principle of capital-import neutrality, proponents of tax-sparing credits would argue that the absence of tax-sparing credits in the United States places the U.S. investor at a competitive disadvantage in conducting business in the developing country offering the tax holiday as compared with investors from capital-exporting countries that have adopted tax-sparing provisions or a territorial or exemption system of taxation.

---

18. The United States did provide in its domestic tax law a tax-sparing credit of sorts in Section 936. Section 936 allowed a credit for the U.S. income tax attributable to certain active-business income and certain qualified passive investment income earned by U.S. corporations operating in U.S. possessions and Puerto Rico. However, in 1996, Congress repealed the Section 936 credit for new claimants and phased out the credit for existing claimants over a ten-year period.

It should be noted that the U.S. investor, even in the absence of a tax-sparing credit in the U.S. tax law, often may have another means available to substantially retain the benefits of the developing country's tax holiday. If the U.S. investor uses a foreign subsidiary corporation (instead of an unincorporated branch) to conduct the business in the developing country, the U.S. investor may be able to defer any U.S. tax on the earnings generated in the developing country by not distributing its earnings. The foreign-source earnings of a foreign corporation controlled by U.S. shareholders are generally not subject to U.S. tax unless and until they are distributed to the U.S. shareholders or the U.S. shareholder sells the stock in the foreign corporation (i.e., the U.S. tax is "deferred"). This concept of deferral is central to tax planning involving the use of U.S.-owned foreign corporations to conduct international transactions. As discussed in Chapter 6, the U.S. tax law contains a number of exceptions to the deferral principle under which certain undistributed foreign-source income of foreign corporations is taxed to their U.S. shareholders. But as long as the U.S. investor operating through the foreign corporation can avoid these anti-deferral rules, the U.S. investor can defer the payment of the U.S. tax on the income earned in the developing country and thereby substantially reduce the effective U.S. tax on such income (i.e., in present value terms, a tax to be paid many years in the future is substantially less than the same tax to be paid in the current year). Such deferral effectively results in retention of the benefits of the tax holiday notwithstanding the general failure of the United States to adopt tax-sparing provisions.

[¶ 5215]

H. INTRODUCTION TO FOREIGN TAX CREDIT LIMITATIONS

After the U.S. taxpayer has identified foreign income taxes that qualify as creditable under the direct credit of Section 901 or the indirect credit of Section 902, the potentially creditable foreign taxes are totaled. The amount that may actually be claimed as a credit for the tax year is subject to the limitations in Section 904. Foreign income taxes in excess of the applicable limitations cannot be credited in the taxpayer's current tax year but may be carried back and carried over to certain other tax years (as discussed at ¶ 5225).

[¶ 5220]

1. PURPOSE OF LIMITATIONS

As discussed in Chapter 1, a pure capital-export neutrality approach to mitigating international double taxation would require that a full foreign tax credit for foreign taxes be allowed without any limitation. Under this approach, foreign taxes paid at rates higher than the U.S. rate on total foreign-source income would effectively reduce U.S. taxes on U.S.-source income, which would be similar in effect to a refund of the "excess" foreign taxes. However, allowing a credit for foreign taxes in excess of the U.S. rate would result in an erosion of the core component of the U.S. tax base—U.S.-source income. Stated differently, if the United States allowed the foreign tax credit to offset U.S. tax on U.S.-source income, it would be ceding primary taxing jurisdiction over U.S.-source income to foreign countries. Thus, since 1921, limitations on the foreign tax credit have been a part of the U.S. international tax system. See U.S. Treas. Dep't, International Tax Reform: An Interim Report 18 (Jan. 1993); Staff of Joint Comm. on Tax'n, 102d Cong., 1st Sess., Factors Affecting the International Competitiveness of the United States, at 123–24 (1991).

The purpose of the limitations is to prevent taxes imposed by foreign jurisdictions with higher effective tax rates than U.S. rates from offsetting U.S. tax on income from U.S. sources. Accordingly, the thrust of the limitations is to limit the credit that may be taken for foreign taxes to the amount of U.S. tax that otherwise would be imposed on a U.S. taxpayer's foreign-source taxable income. When the limitation is computed on an "overall" or worldwide basis, as in Section 904(a), the calculation is as follows:

$$\text{Foreign tax credit limitation} = \frac{\text{Foreign-source taxable income}}{\text{Worldwide taxable income}} \times \text{U.S. tax on worldwide taxable income (before foreign tax credit)}$$

The heart of the limitation calculation is the limitation fraction and, in particular, its numerator—taxable income from sources without the United States. If the top effective U.S. tax rate on a U.S. taxpayer's taxable income is 35 percent, the limitation calculated on an overall basis will not, roughly speaking, exceed 35 percent of a U.S. taxpayer's foreign-source taxable income.

The above calculation is only the basic limitation. As a result of tax changes made over a number of years, the limitation is no longer a single overall limitation. For tax years starting before 2007, Section 904(d)(1) required that the Section 904(a) limitation be applied separately to seven categories—often called "baskets"—of income and an eighth residual category of income—often called the "general" limitation category—which included all remaining foreign-source income. For tax years starting after 2006, the 2004 JOBS Act has reduced the number of baskets in Section 904(d) to two: a passive category income basket and a general category income basket.

The limitations on the foreign tax credit and particularly the general category income limitation of Section 904(d)(1)(B) are the principal focal points for the tax planning of international transactions and investments by U.S. taxpayers. The overall objective is to plan and implement such transactions and investments in a way that will minimize foreign income taxes that will exceed the applicable limitations and therefore not be creditable against the U.S. taxpayer's U.S. tax burden. In many foreign countries in which U.S. taxpayers have made and are likely to make major investments, corporate and individual income tax rates exceed the top effective corporate and individual rates in the United States. Consequently, the potential for generating excess foreign tax credits and the need for tax planning to permit use of the excess credits are ubiquitous features of the international tax landscape. The goal of the international tax planner is to generate foreign-source taxable income subject to low or no foreign taxes to include in the numerator of the limitation fraction and thereby absorb the excess foreign tax credits arising from high foreign taxes imposed on other foreign-source taxable income in the numerator of the limitation fraction.

It makes sense to introduce some tax terminology here. If a U.S. taxpayer has a greater amount of limitation in a particular basket than the creditable taxes in that basket, the taxpayer is said to be in an "excess limitation" position. By contrast, if a U.S. taxpayer has creditable taxes in excess of the applicable limitation basket, the taxpayer is said to be in an "excess credit" position.

[¶ 5225]

2. CARRYOVERS OF EXCESS CREDITS

Under current law, as revised by the 2004 JOBS Act, foreign tax credits in excess of the applicable limitation for any tax year may be carried back to the immediately preceding tax year and carried forward ten years, in chronological order, starting with the immediately preceding year. § 904(c). (Under pre–2004 Act law, the carryback period was two years and the carryforward period was only five years.) The excess credits will be usable in any year to which they are carried only to the extent that they and the creditable foreign taxes for that year do not exceed the Section 904 limitations applicable to that year. Thus, if having foreign tax credits in excess of the available limitations is not an isolated or periodic but a chronic phenomenon, the carryover of excess credits will be of no use. The tax planner's challenge is then to try to develop foreign-source taxable income subject to a lower tax than the U.S. effective rate (or, best of all, to no foreign tax) that can be included in the numerator of the applicable limitation fraction.

[¶ 5230]

3. EFFECT OF OVERALL LIMITATION: HOMOGENIZATION OF FOREIGN INCOME AND TAXES

The key aspect of the Section 904(a) overall limitation fraction is that high-taxed foreign-source income can be mixed in the numerator with foreign-source income that is subject to a low or to no foreign tax. The items of foreign income are blended, and the foreign taxes thereon are averaged. Through this homogenization of foreign income and taxes the tax planner may be able to blend in the numerator of the limitation fraction high-taxed foreign income with lower-taxed foreign income, the result being that, while the foreign tax on *some* of the income would exceed the applicable limitation (e.g., the 35–percent U.S. tax on that income), the average of the foreign taxes on the total of the blended income will not; thus, the aggregate foreign taxes will be fully creditable. This result reflects a foreign tax credit system that goes well beyond its core purpose of mitigating international double taxation.

The averaging possibilities of the limitation were most extensive when the only Section 904 limitation was a single limitation calculated on an overall basis. In those halcyon days for the tax planner, the Section 904(a) limitation lumped together all income from high-tax jurisdictions with all income from low-tax or tax-free jurisdictions in determining the numerator of the limitation fraction, and the resulting limitation applied to the aggregate of a taxpayer's direct and indirect credits for income taxes paid to all foreign countries for the taxable year. Taxpayers used the averaging mechanism of the overall foreign tax credit limitation to improve their foreign tax credit position by structuring international transactions and investments whenever possible in a way that generated foreign-source income that was subject to little or no foreign tax. Inclusion of this low-taxed or tax-free foreign-source income in the numerator of the limitation fraction increased the taxpayer's overall foreign tax credit limitation with little or no increase in foreign tax. Thus, in effect, credits for foreign taxes imposed on other foreign-source income that would otherwise exceed the limitation could be used to offset the taxpayer's potential U.S. tax liability on the low-taxed or tax-free foreign-source income. Stated differently, the overall limitation permits a U.S. taxpayer to "cross-credit" the high foreign taxes imposed on some foreign-source income against the U.S. taxes that would otherwise be imposed on other foreign-source income that is subject to low or no foreign taxes.

Example. A U.S. corporation has U.S.-source income of $100 and income of $100 from sources in Country A, which has an effective corporate tax rate of 45 percent and thus imposes a tax of $45 on the $100 of Country A income. Assume an effective U.S. corporate income tax rate of 35 percent. Since the limitation on the foreign tax credit is \$35 (100/200 × the pre-foreign tax credit U.S. tax liability of \$70), \$10 of the Country A income tax cannot be credited. If, however, the corporation makes an investment in Country B, which has an effective tax rate of 20 percent, and earns income of \$100 from Country B subject to Country B tax of \$20, the total foreign income taxes of \$65 paid to Country A and Country B will be creditable since the limitation will be \$70 (200/300 × the pre-foreign tax credit U.S. tax liability of \$105).

Thus, through the averaging mechanism of the overall limitation, the U.S. corporation in effect uses otherwise excess credits for the Country A taxes to offset most of the U.S. tax that would otherwise apply to the income from Country B. Credits with respect to the Country A taxes in excess of the limitation that would apply to that income considered alone are cross-credited against the U.S. tax that would apply if the Country B income were the only foreign-source income involved. If the corporation had only \$100 of Country B income, the Country B tax would be \$20 and the residual U.S. tax, after the credit for the Country B tax of \$20, would be \$15. However, as a result of the cross-crediting permitted under the averaging mechanism of the overall limitation, \$10 of that U.S. residual tax is offset by the credit for the Country A tax. The residual tax payable to the United States is reduced to \$5, and all of the potential tax credits generated by the Country A tax are absorbed.

The example illustrates that, as a result of cross-crediting under an overall limitation, the foreign tax credit does more than eliminate double taxation of the income from Country A (which is accomplished by the credit's offsetting of all of the U.S. tax on that income); it also reduces the U.S. residual tax on the income from Country B below what it would be if a credit were available only for the Country B tax on that income. It also reduces it below the tax of \$35 that would apply to \$100 of income from an investment in the United States. Consequently, a U.S. taxpayer with foreign-source income carrying excess foreign tax credits has an incentive to make a new investment in a low-tax or no-tax foreign country rather than in the United States. A single overall limitation on foreign tax credits is generally more favorable to taxpayers than other types of more narrowly focused limitations because it permits maximum scope for tax planning aimed at making the most of averaging or cross-crediting of foreign taxes.

[¶ 5235]

4. POLICY ARGUMENTS FOR AND AGAINST THE OVERALL LIMITATION

The averaging or cross-crediting of effective foreign tax rates under an overall limitation on the foreign tax credit raises a number of policy concerns. First, as illustrated in the example above, the averaging permitted under the overall limitation encourages U.S. taxpayers with operations in a high-tax foreign country to make investments in a low-tax foreign country, rather than in the United States, so that the otherwise excess credits from the high-tax operations reduce the U.S. tax otherwise due on the taxpayer's income from those investments. The distortion of economic decisions resulting from this phenomenon is exacerbated when effective U.S. tax rates are reduced significantly below the rates in most other countries (as occurred with the enactment of the Tax Reform Act of 1986).

Second, the averaging permitted under the overall limitation permits some foreign countries to maintain high tax rates without suffering the negative consequences of losing U.S. investment. Under an overall limitation, a U.S. taxpayer with operations in a low-tax country is able to invest in a high-tax foreign country without bearing the full cost of the high foreign tax. In effect, the overall limitation results in the U.S. Treasury bearing the burden of the high foreign taxes on U.S. taxpayers to the extent it loses all or part of its residual tax on the low-tax or tax-free foreign income.

By contrast, proponents of the overall limitation argue that restrictions on averaging harm the ability of U.S. taxpayers to compete with taxpayers from foreign countries with exemption or territorial systems of taxation which provide an exemption for foreign-source income. Such systems necessarily permit an averaging of foreign tax rates since the taxpayer's total tax burden on income from foreign operations is the total of the foreign taxes imposed on that income. Proponents of the overall limitation also argue that the overall limitation is consistent with the reality of the integrated nature of U.S. multinational operations abroad. In addition, those proponents maintain that arguments that averaging encourages U.S. taxpayers to make investments in low-tax or no-tax foreign jurisdictions are overstated since nontax considerations often dominate such decisions (except, perhaps, in the case of easily movable passive investments that generate interest, dividends or income from active trading operations). Moreover, proponents of the overall limitation argue that attempts to limit averaging inevitably increase the complexity of the calculation of the foreign tax credit limitation and, therefore, the U.S. tax system. Finally, proponents of the overall limitation point out the overall limitation is consistent with the basic purpose of the foreign tax credit limitation, which is to prevent foreign tax credits from being used to offset U.S. tax on U.S.-source income.

For tax policymakers, the question then becomes whether and how to narrow the overall limitation in the light of these competing policy arguments. If one's objective were to eliminate all averaging, then the foreign tax credit limitation would have to be calculated separately with respect to each item of foreign-source income. This item-by-item approach, however, is not administratively workable since it would require a taxpayer to identify each item of foreign-source gross income and the deductions properly allocable to it, to separate out the foreign tax on each such item and then to calculate the U.S. tax liability on each item of income, a process of considerable complexity. Once one accepts that an item-by-item approach is not feasible, one has to accept that some averaging and cross-crediting of foreign tax rates will occur and then ask what types of restrictions should be placed on such averaging in the light of the competing policy concerns (discussed above).

[¶ 5240]

5. NARROWING THE OVERALL LIMITATION WITH A PER–COUNTRY LIMITATION

One approach to narrowing the overall limitation that has been used in some prior years is calculating the foreign tax credit limit on a per-country basis. The per-country limitation prevents the cross-crediting of taxes imposed by one country to reduce the U.S. tax on income from other countries, thus preserving the residual U.S. tax on such income. For example, under a per-country limitation, the foreign tax credits allowed for creditable taxes paid to Country A for a taxable year would be calculated as follows:

$$\text{Foreign tax credit limitation} = \frac{\text{Taxable income from Country A}}{\text{Worldwide taxable income}} \times \text{U.S. tax on worldwide taxable income (before foreign tax credit)}$$

One possible criticism of the per-country limitation, however, is that it allows a U.S. taxpayer to claim a foreign tax credit for taxes paid to one country even though the taxpayer has losses in other foreign countries. For example, suppose that a taxpayer has income of $100 from Country A on which it pays a Country A tax of $45 and a loss of $100 from Country B. Under the per-country limit, the taxpayer will be able to take a foreign tax credit for the $35 tax paid to Country A (i.e., the taxpayer's foreign-source taxable income from Country A multiplied by the assumed U.S. tax rate of 35 percent) even though its net taxable foreign-source income is zero. By contrast, under an overall limitation, the numerator of the limitation fraction (worldwide foreign-source taxable income) would be zero and no foreign tax credit would be available to the taxpayer. Thus, in this situation, the per-country limitation produces a more favorable result for the taxpayer than the overall limitation and provides the taxpayer with a foreign tax credit in a situation where there is no international double taxation to mitigate.

The history of the foreign tax credit system has been marked by vacillation between the overall and per-country limitations. From 1921 through 1932, the foreign tax credit was subject to an overall limitation. From 1932 until 1954, the foreign tax credit was subject to the lesser of an overall limitation or a per-country limitation. From 1954 until 1960, the credit was subject to only a per-country limitation. During the period from 1960 to 1975, taxpayers had the best of both worlds and could choose whichever of the two limitations was more favorable. Between 1976 and 1986, the foreign tax credit was generally subject to an overall limitation, but certain types of income (e.g., passive interest income) were subject to separate limitations. In 1985, as part of the ongoing tax reform debate, the Reagan Administration proposed a mandatory per-country foreign tax credit limitation. In the Tax Reform Act of 1986, Congress rejected that proposal and instead enacted the expanded separate basket limitations in Section 904(d), which, in turn, have been reduced to two baskets by the 2004 JOBS Act.

[¶ 5245]

6. NARROWING THE OVERALL LIMITATION WITH LIMITATIONS BASED ON TYPE OF INCOME (SECTION 904(d))

As noted above, the homogenizing and cross-crediting effects of a single foreign tax credit limitation calculated on an overall basis provide a benefit beyond the elimination of double taxation and offer a strong incentive for taxpayers to arrange their international transactions and investments to take maximum advantage of them. Even before opting broadly for separate limitation calculations for various categories of foreign-source income in the 1986 Act, Congress had reduced the opportunities for cross-crediting foreign taxes on high-taxed foreign income against the U.S. tax on low-taxed or tax-free foreign income by requiring that certain types of income be subject to separate limitation calculations. For example, most passive interest from foreign sources was subject to a separate limitation calculation. Before this change, U.S. taxpayers with excess foreign tax credits could simply shift interest-bearing bank deposits to foreign banks and the interest, on which there was often no foreign tax, could be blended in the numerator of the single overall limitation calculation with the income generating the excess foreign tax credits. A special limitation also applied to the credit for foreign taxes imposed on oil and gas extraction income and on certain categories of export-related income that are discussed in Chapter 11.

The use of separate basket limitations involves a cost in terms of increased complexity. For each separate limitation calculation, it is necessary to identify the foreign-source gross income concerned, the deductions to be allocated and apportioned against that income and the foreign taxes imposed on that income.

The 1986 Act extended the separate basket limitation concept to segregate for limitation purposes eight categories of income that were excluded from the remaining overall or general limitation. The income in each basket and the foreign taxes attributable to it were subject to a limitation separately calculated as follows:

$$\text{Foreign tax credit limitation} = \frac{\text{Foreign-source taxable income in applicable basket}}{\text{Worldwide taxable income}} \times \text{U.S. tax on worldwide taxable income (before foreign tax credit)}$$

The eight separate basket limitations and the general basket limitation were listed in the prior version of Section 904(d)(1). Those basket limitations applied separately to:

(1) passive income;

(2) high withholding tax interest;

(3) financial services income;

(4) shipping income;

(5) in the case of a corporation, dividends from each noncontrolled Section 902 corporation, for tax years starting before 2003 (for tax years starting after 2002, different rules applied, as described below);

(6) dividends from a domestic international sales corporation ("DISC") or former DISC;

(7) taxable income attributable to foreign trade income of a foreign sales corporation ("FSC");

(8) certain distributions from a FSC or former FSC; and

(9) all other income ("general" or residual basket).

As more fully explained below, each of the separate limitations of former Section 904(d)(1)(A) through (H), as distinguished from the general or residual limitation of former Section 904(d)(1)(I), had generally been applied to a particular category of income for one or more of the following reasons: (1) the income's source can be readily manipulated, e.g., in the case of passive income, by moving to a foreign country the investment that generates dividend or interest income; (2) the income typically bears little or no foreign tax, e.g., interest and international shipping income; or (3) the income bears a rate of foreign tax that is relatively high, e.g., high withholding tax interest and dividends carrying direct and indirect credits in excess of the U.S. maximum corporate tax rate.

The first basket, created by Section 904(d)(1)(A), covers passive income, which includes "foreign personal holding company income" as defined in Section 954(c) for purposes of the controlled foreign corporation provisions in Subpart F (which are discussed in Chapter 6). Section 954(c)(1) defines this term generally to include income items such as dividends, interest, royalties, rents and annuities, as well as gains exceeding losses from the sale or exchange of property giving rise to such income or not giving rise to any income. Section 954(c)(1) also includes certain other items within the definition of foreign personal holding company income. However, as discussed at ¶ 6085, Section 954(c)(2) and (3) contains several exclusions from the general definition of foreign personal holding company income that also generally apply for purposes of defining the passive income limitation in Section 904(d)(1)(A). In addition, former Section 904(d)(2)(A)(iii) excluded certain categories of what would otherwise be foreign personal holding company income from passive income for purposes of the Section 904(d)(1)(A) limitation. (For tax years starting after 2006, the exclusions from the passive income category are in Section 904(d)(2)(B)(iii).) The excluded categories included export financing interest, high-taxed income, foreign oil and gas extraction income and any income included in another basket of Section 904(d)(1).

The rationale for the passive income basket was explained as follows in Staff of Joint Comm. on Tax'n, 100th Cong., 1st Sess., General Explanation of the Tax Reform Act of 1986, at 863 (1987) ("General Explanation of the 1986 Act"):

> In general, passive income earned abroad by U.S. persons * * * tends to bear little or no foreign tax. Also, many forms of passive income are manipulable as to source. The incentive at the margin to place new investments abroad rather than at home, if the taxpayer has excess foreign tax credits that can be used to shelter additional foreign income from U.S. tax, is of particular concern in the case of passive investments, which often can quickly or easily be made in low or no tax foreign countries.

High withholding tax interest was placed in a separate basket under former Section 904(d)(1)(B). Moreover, in the case of a noncontrolled Section 902 corporation, no foreign tax credit could be taken by the U.S. corporate shareholder for foreign withholding taxes paid by the foreign corporation in excess of five percent on any interest it earned. Former § 904(d)(2)(E)(ii). The rationale for this basket was explained by the Joint Committee Staff as follows:

> A number of foreign countries, particularly developing countries, impose gross withholding taxes on interest earned by nonresident lenders that significantly exceed the general income taxes that would be imposed on the associated net interest income were it taxed on a net basis. In the case of U.S. lenders, these gross withholding taxes often far exceed the pre-credit U.S. tax on the net interest income as well. When, under prior law, a gross withholding tax equaled the pre-credit U.S. tax, the U.S. lender paid no U.S. tax on loan proceeds

> associated with interest subject to the withholding tax under the United States' generally applicable foreign tax credit rules. When a gross withholding tax exceeded the pre-credit U.S. tax, the U.S. lender was subject to a negative rate of U.S. tax on the foreign loan transaction (as other U.S. taxpayers operating abroad sometimes are on other foreign transactions) to the extent that the lender used the excess foreign tax credits to reduce its U.S. tax liability on other income, derived from the same foreign country or from other sources outside the United States, that was subject to little or no foreign tax. Income from domestic loans, by contrast, generally is subject to full U.S. tax. As a result of the foreign tax credit mechanism, the U.S. Treasury, in effect, bore the burden of those high levels of foreign tax on foreign loans.
>
> Congress was concerned, moreover, that the available evidence suggested that the economic burden of high foreign gross withholding taxes on interest falls largely, in the typical situation, on the foreign borrower rather than on the U.S. lender. To the extent that is the case, the prior rules allowing a full foreign tax credit for high foreign taxes on interest paid to U.S. lenders provided an incentive for some U.S. lenders to make foreign loans rather than domestic loans that would otherwise be equally attractive, and to make otherwise uneconomical foreign loans. The higher the applicable foreign tax on interest was, the larger the U.S lender's foreign tax available for credit was and, thus, the greater the incentive could be. Congress was particularly concerned that foreign countries seeking to attract U.S. capital might have been encouraged by the prior law rules to increase rather than to decrease their gross withholding taxes on interest paid to U.S. persons. * * *
>
> In light of the above, Congress believed that interest received by U.S. persons that bears a foreign withholding tax (or other tax determined on a gross basis) of 5 percent or more should be subject to a separate foreign tax credit limitation. Congress subjected such interest to a separate limitation, rather than directly disallowing foreign tax credits for gross interest taxes in excess of net U.S. tax, because some argued that such disallowance could have violated income tax treaties. Congress chose to apply the separate limitation to interest subject to a 5–percent or greater gross-basis tax, instead of to interest taxed on a gross basis at a net rate greater than the net U.S. rate, in the interest of administrative simplicity. The [1986] Act's approach may be theoretically inferior to the latter approach, but avoids the necessity of computing the net U.S. tax on particular interest payments to determine allowable foreign tax credits.

General Explanation of the 1986 Act, at 864–65.

Former Section 904(d)(1)(C) created a separate basket limitation for financial services income. The rationale for that limitation was explained by the Joint Committee Staff as follows:

> Income earned in a financial services business, by its nature, is relatively movable; it may sometimes be shifted to low tax jurisdictions where excess credits from unrelated high tax business operations could, under prior foreign tax credit limitation rules, shelter it from U.S. tax. As a practical matter, it is sometimes not possible to differentiate passive investment from bona fide financial services activity. The exception from separate limitation treatment under prior law for interest derived in the conduct of a banking, financing, or similar business gave manufacturing companies with substantial excess credits, for example, an incentive to establish or acquire banking- (or other financial services-) type entities in low tax jurisdictions to generate low tax income to be sheltered by those excess credits. Congress was concerned that the foreign tax credit rules created too great an incentive for businesses to divert their resources into such entities abroad for tax purposes.

General Explanation of the 1986 Act, at 863–64.

Former Section 904(d)(1)(D) created a separate basket limitation for shipping income. The rationale for that basket limitation was explained by the Joint Committee Staff as follows:

> Congress also understood that shipping income frequently is not taxed by any foreign country or is subject to very limited foreign tax. Under the overall limitation of prior law, U.S. multinational entities with excess foreign tax credits from other business activities could earn such shipping income free of U.S. tax as well: their excess credits could shelter the shipping income from U.S. tax.

General Explanation of the 1986 Act, at 864.

One of the separate baskets, former Section 904(d)(1)(E), as in effect for tax years starting before 2003, could actually be many baskets. It mandated a separate limitation calculation for the dividends of each noncontrolled foreign corporation paid to a ten-percent U.S. corporate shareholder that may claim an indirect foreign tax credit under Section 902.[19] The rationale for this basket was explained by the Joint Committee Staff as follows:

> Congress concluded that, for several reasons, dividends paid by "noncontrolled section 902 corporations" (dividends eligible for the section 902 deemed-paid credit, paid by foreign corporations out of earnings and profits generated when the corporations were not con-

19. Note that a noncontrolled Section 902 corporation is sometimes referred to as a "10/50 company" or a "10/50 foreign corporation" because it is a foreign corporation with at least one ten-percent-or-more U.S. corporate shareholder but is not a controlled foreign corporation by reason of having more than 50 percent of the total voting power or value of its stock owned by ten-percent-or-more U.S. shareholders.

> trolled foreign corporations) should be subject to a separate limitation on a corporation-by-corporation basis. First, and most importantly, application of a look-through rule to dividends from noncontrolled section 902 corporations is not appropriate under the view, generally adopted by Congress in connection with this tax reform legislation, that it is frequently appropriate to allow cross-crediting of taxes paid by one unit of a worldwide business against income earned by another unit of that business. In the case of controlled foreign corporations, Congress adhered to this general view, on the theory that in many cases, whether one unit or another of a multinational enterprise is considered to earn income in a business (and whether any particular unit is considered to earn income in one country rather than another) makes little economic difference, so long as the income from that business generally inures to the benefit of the same person. Because of this general view, and because of concerns about the difficulty of administration, Congress declined to adopt the [Reagan] Administration's proposal to reimpose a per-country limitation on the foreign tax credit. In the case of foreign corporations that are not controlled foreign corporations, however, Congress did not believe that there is sufficient identity of interest with U.S. shareholders to treat nonmajority ownership positions as units of a worldwide business. Accordingly, Congress did not believe it is appropriate to allow cross-crediting of taxes from nonmajority interests against income derived from controlling interests or vice versa, or of taxes from one nonmajority interest against income of another nonmajority interest. In rejecting the application of a single separate limitation to all dividends received by a taxpayer from noncontrolled section 902 corporations collectively, Congress was concerned, in addition, that such an approach would permit the cross-crediting of taxes with respect to earnings from foreign companies that were not parts of a single economic unit. Congress believed that a company-by-company limitation, by eliminating the possibility that any of these companies' dividends will be taxed twice, still achieves the goal of the foreign tax credit of preventing double taxation.

General Explanation of the 1986 Act, at 867–68.

However, as discussed in more detail at ¶ 7030, the Taxpayer Relief Act of 1997 and the 2004 JOBS Act changed the treatment of dividends (and the associated foreign taxes) from noncontrolled section 902 corporations for purposes of the foreign tax credit limitation, with respect to tax years starting after 2002. Under this change, the look-through rule in Section 904(d)(4) applies to dividends from a noncontrolled Section 902 corporation. Under this look-through rule, the determination of the foreign tax credit limitation categories into which the dividend falls depends on the limitation categories into which the noncontrolled Section 902 corporation's earnings and profits fall. For example, if all of the noncontrolled Section 902 corporation's earnings and profits are attributable to foreign business income falling within the general category income limitation in Section 904(d)(1)(B), then a dividend paid by the corporation to a U.S. corporate shareholder owning at least ten percent of its voting stock is treated as falling within the general category income limitation. The reasons for this change are discussed at ¶ 7030.

The most important basket was the last, the residual basket of former Section 904(d)(1)(I), which was usually designated the general limitation basket (the term used in the Section 904 regulations). This is what remains of the overall limitation as it was before separate basket limitations made their appearance, but it still includes much international business income, such as income from manufacturing, sales of inventory and rendering of services.[20] It also includes passive income, such as dividends, passive rents and passive royalties, that is kicked out of the passive income basket under the high-tax kickout in former Section 904(d)(2)(A)(iii)(III) and (d)(2)(F) (for tax years starting after 2006, Section 904(d)(2)(B)(iii)(II) and (d)(2)(F)) because the income bears a foreign tax that is in excess of the highest U.S. tax rate that could be imposed on such income. The general category basket has been enlarged by the 2004 JOBS Act, as discussed below at ¶ 5250. It therefore remains the focus of most of the tax planning efforts of U.S.-based multinationals.

Note that export financing interest—interest derived from financing the exports of the taxpayer or related persons—received special treatment for purposes of the basket limitations in Section 904(d). Such interest was excluded from the separate limitations for passive income, high withholding tax interest and financial services income; thus, such interest fell within the general limitation. As explained by the Joint Committee Staff, the rationale for that special treatment was that "Congress was concerned that the [1986] Act might have the effect of reducing the pre-enactment availability of export financing in some cases, which could, in turn, have a negative impact on the volume of exports." General Explanation of the 1986 Act, at 865.

[¶ 5250]

7. POLICY REVERSAL FOR POST-2006 TAX YEARS: JOBS ACT CREATES A TWO-BASKET LIMITATION SYSTEM

In 2004, Congress changed policy course and accepted the claims of U.S. multinational corporations and their advisers and lobbyists that the foreign tax credit limitation system in Section 904 was too complex and impeded the "competitiveness" of U.S. corporations in the global economy. See H.R. Rep. No. 548, pt. 1, 108th Cong., 2d Sess. 190 (2004).

20. A 1993 Treasury Report estimated that approximately 75 percent of all foreign-source income falls within the general limitation category. U.S. Treas. Dep't, International Tax Reform: An Interim Report 20 (Jan. 1993).

Accordingly, as mentioned earlier, the JOBS Act reduced the number of foreign tax credit limitation categories or "baskets" in Section 904(d)(1) to two: a passive category income basket and a basket for all other or "general" category income basket (i.e., the residual basket).

As under the pre-JOBS Act law, passive income is defined to include "foreign personal holding company income" as defined in Section 954(c), i.e., income received or accrued by any person of a kind that would be foreign personal holding company income within the meaning of Section 954(c) if it were received by a controlled foreign corporation. § 904(d)(2)(A)(i) and (B)(i) and Temp. Reg. § 1.904–4T(b)(2)(i)(A). Section 954(c)(1) defines this term to include income items such as dividends, interest, royalties, rents and annuities, as well as gains exceeding losses from the sale or exchange of property giving rise to such income or not giving rise to any income. Section 954(c)(1) also includes certain other items within the definition of foreign personal holding company income. However, as discussed at ¶ 6085, Section 954(c)(2) and (3) contains several exclusions from the general definition of foreign personal holding company income, and those exclusions generally apply for purposes of defining the passive category income limitation in Section 904(d)(1)(A). In addition, Section 904(d)(2)(B)(iii) excludes two categories of what would otherwise be foreign personal holding company income from passive income for purposes of the Section 904(d)(1)(A) limitation. The excluded categories are export financing interest and high-taxed income (i.e., passive income on which the foreign taxes imposed exceed the highest U.S. tax that can be imposed on the income) in a provision that is sometimes referred to as the "high-tax kickout." As more fully explained at ¶ 7010, the export financing interest exception is one of the tax preferences in the Code intended to encourage exports and the high-taxed income exception is intended to prevent U.S. taxpayers from cross-crediting high foreign taxes on some types of passive income against the residual U.S. tax liability on most other types of passive income that bear little or no foreign tax.

The JOBS Act delayed the effective date for this change to tax years starting after 2006; thus, most of the prior law rules in Section 904(d) remained in effect for 2005 and 2006. When this change to Section 904(d) became effective in 2007, income that previously fell within one of the other seven baskets is included either in the passive category income basket or in the general category income basket. For example, shipping income generally falls into the general category income basket; high withholding tax interest income falls into the passive category income basket or the general category income basket, depending on the circumstances. See H.R. Rep. No. 548, pt. 1, 108th Cong., 2d Sess. 190 (2004). Under Section 904(d)(2)(A)(i) and (d)(2)(B)(v), dividends from a DISC or former DISC, taxable income attributable to certain foreign trade income and certain distributions from a FSC or former FSC constitute "specified passive income" and fall into the passive category income basket. Section 904(d)(2)(C)(i) generously treats financial services income as general category income in the case of a member of a financial services group or any person predominantly engaged in the active conduct of a banking, insurance, financing or similar business. The statute also directs the Treasury and the IRS to issue regulations specifying the treatment of financial services income received or accrued by partnerships and other pass-through entities that are not members of a financial services group. § 904(d)(2)(C)(iii).

Notice that the 2004 JOBS Act changes to Section 904(d) do not eliminate the export financing interest income exception to the passive category income basket, an exception that is of questionable policy merit and adds complexity to the foreign tax credit limitation system. The JOBS Act changes also do not eliminate the often-criticized high-tax kickout from the passive income basket, a source of considerable complexity in the application of the foreign tax credit limitation rules. Needless to say, the JOBS Act changes to the foreign tax credit rules are hardly a coherent approach to international tax reform and simplification.

The JOBS Act added to the Code a special transitional rule to deal with the carryover of creditable foreign taxes paid or accrued in tax years starting before 2007. Foreign taxes paid or accrued in pre–2007 tax years that are carried forward to a later tax year are included either in the passive category income basket or in the general category income basket for the tax year to which carried, as appropriate. § 904(d)(2)(K)(i); Temp. Reg. § 1.904–2T(i)(1). Creditable foreign taxes paid or accrued in tax years starting after 2006 that are carried back to pre–2007 tax years are allocated to the pre–2007 baskets under regulations issued by the Treasury and the IRS. See Temp. Reg. § 1.904–2T(i)(2).

The JOBS Act also added new Section 904(d)(2)(H)(i) to the Code, which treats creditable foreign taxes that are imposed on amounts that do not constitute income under U.S. tax principles as imposed on general category income. (This statutory provision confirms the treatment that applied under the pre-JOBS Act law under Reg. § 1.904–6(a)(1)(iv).) An example of a foreign tax that would qualify under this provision is a creditable foreign tax imposed on the imputed rental value of owner-occupied housing that is taxable under a foreign country's income tax laws but is not subject to U.S. tax. This provision is generally effective for tax years starting after 2006. Moreover, at the taxpayer's election, any such taxes that are paid or accrued in tax years starting in 2005 and 2006 are treated as imposed either on general limitation income or on financial services income under the pre–2007 multi-basket system. § 904(d)(2)(H)(ii). As a policy matter, it is not clear why such foreign taxes should be creditable or deductible at all for federal income tax purposes since the taxes are imposed on income that is not taxable under U.S. principles and, thus, no possibility of double taxation is present. In any event, it is difficult to describe this provision as a simplification measure.

Finally, the JOBS Act made one change to the foreign tax credit rules that has retroactive effect, as discussed above. The look-through rule in Section 904(d)(4) applicable to dividends received by a U.S. corporation from a noncontrolled Section 902 foreign corporation was extended retroactively for tax years starting after 2002, to apply to all such dividends regardless of when the earnings were accumulated from which the dividends are paid. Such dividends are placed in each foreign tax credit basket in proportion to the ratio of the noncontrolled Section 902 foreign corporation's earnings and profits attributable to income in that basket to total earnings and profits.

The net result of these changes to the foreign tax credit rules is substantially increased cross-crediting opportunities for U.S. taxpayers and further reduction of the residual U.S. tax on low-taxed foreign-source income (unless the income falls within the passive income basket). The following example provides a simple illustration of how the two limitation categories currently in force work to limit a taxpayer's allowable foreign tax credit.

> *Example*. During the current year, DC Manufacturing, Inc., a U.S. corporation, has $200,000 of interest income from a bank account it maintains in Country Z, a foreign country. DC Manufacturing, Inc. pays no foreign taxes on this bank account interest. DC Manufacturing, Inc. also has $100,000 of interest income on a loan it made to an unrelated foreign borrower in Country Y, a second foreign country. Country Y imposes a withholding tax of ten percent on this interest (i.e., $10,000 of foreign withholding tax). DC Manufacturing, Inc. also earns $200,000 of net income from a manufacturing operation in yet another foreign country, Country F (all of which is foreign-source income). Country F imposes a 50–percent income tax of $100,000 on this income. DC Manufacturing, Inc. also has $500,000 of net income from its manufacturing operations in the United States, all of which is U.S.-source income. Assume that DC Manufacturing, Inc. pays U.S. tax at a flat 35–percent rate on its taxable income. Thus, DC Manufacturing, Inc. has worldwide taxable income of $1,000,000 and a pre-foreign tax credit U.S. tax liability of $350,000.
>
> The $200,000 of bank account interest is passive category income, within the meaning of Section 904(d)(2)(A)(i) and (B), and falls within the passive category income limitation in Section 904(d)(1)(A). Under current law, the $100,000 of interest on the loan to the foreign debtor also is passive category income, within the meaning of Section 904(d)(2)(A)(i) and (B), and, thus, falls within the passive category income limitation. There is $10,000 of foreign tax falling within this category. The limitation fraction for this category is:

$$\frac{\text{Foreign-source taxable income in passive category (\$300,000)}}{\text{Worldwide taxable Income (\$1,000,000)}} \times \text{35\% U.S. tax on worldwide taxable income (\$350,000)} = \$105,000$$

Thus, all $10,000 of the foreign taxes falling within this limitation category is currently creditable.

The $200,000 of foreign manufacturing net income does not fall within the passive category income basket in Sections 904(d)(1)(A), and, thus, falls within the general category income limitation in Section 904(d)(1)(B). There is $100,000 of foreign taxes falling within this category. The limitation fraction for this category is:

$$\frac{\text{Foreign-source taxable income in general category (\$200,000)}}{\text{Worldwide taxable Income (\$1,000,000)}} \times \text{35\% U.S. tax on worldwide taxable income (\$350,000)} = \$70,000$$

Thus, only $70,000 of the foreign taxes falling within this limitation category is currently creditable and the remaining $30,000 is subject to the carryback and carryforward provisions of Section 904(c).

This discussion of the separate basket limitations in Section 904(d), as in effect for tax years starting after 2006, and the problems at ¶ 5280 are intended as only an introduction to the subject. Detailed consideration of the contours of these limitation provisions is deferred until Chapter 7, after you have had an opportunity in Chapter 6 to study the controlled foreign corporation provisions on which many of the definitions in Section 904(d) are based. Chapter 7 also covers several other more advanced topics involving the foreign tax credit limitations.

[¶ 5253]

8. 2010 SHIFT IN POLICY COURSE

In 2010, Congress, at the urging of the Obama Administration, modified its recent policy course and enacted several foreign tax credit "reforms" aimed at tightening somewhat the foreign tax credit provisions in several situations in which Congress thought that the existing rules were being used in inappropriate ways. These provisions did not constitute fundamental international tax reform. Rather, they consisted of five narrowly targeted provisions aimed at mitigating specific perceived abuses. First, as discussed at ¶ 5010, the 2010 legislation contained rules in new Section 909 aimed at preventing the separation of creditable foreign taxes from the associated foreign-source income. Second, the 2010 legislation contained new Section 901(m) of the Code which denies a foreign tax credit with respect to foreign-source income not subject to U.S. income tax by reason of a "covered asset acquisition," which is defined to include, for example, a qualified stock purchase to which Section 338(a) applies. Third, as more fully explained at ¶ 7042, in new Section 904(d)(6), a separate foreign tax credit limitation is applied to each income item of a U.S. taxpayer that is treated as U.S.-source income under U.S. tax law without regard to a U.S. tax treaty but as foreign-source income under a U.S. tax treaty if the taxpayer chooses the benefits of the treaty. Fourth, in new Section 960(c), the 2010 legislation limits the amount of foreign taxes deemed paid with respect to inclusions under the anti-deferral provisions of Section 956, discussed in Chapter 6. Fifth, the 2010 legislation modified the corporate affiliation rules in Section 864(e)(5) relating to the rules for allocating and apportioning interest expense in Section 864 and the regulations under Sections 861 and 864 (discussed in Chapter 2). Under the statutory amendment, a foreign corporation may be treated as a member of an affiliated group with one or more domestic corporations for interest allocation and apportionment purposes, if certain requirements are met. This provision, thus, tightens up the interest allocation and apportionment rules by increasing the amount of a U.S. multinational corporate group's interest expense that must be allocated and apportioned to foreign-source income for foreign tax credit limitation purposes. Finally, as also discussed in Chapter 2, the 2010 legislation terminated the special source rule in former Section 861(a)(1) and (c) for interest income received from a resident alien individual or an 80/20 domestic corporation, subject to certain grandfathering provisions. Under this statutory amendment, interest income received from a resident alien individual or an 80/20 domestic corporation would generally be treated as U.S.-source income, not foreign-source income, regardless of the percentage of the resident alien individual's or domestic corporation's gross income that is derived from one or more active foreign businesses. Whatever the merits of these provisions in terms of mitigating abuses and increasing revenue for the U.S. government, they obviously add another degree of complexity to an already highly complex and incoherent international tax regime.

[¶ 5255]

9. USE OF U.S. TAX LAW RULES (INCLUDING SOURCE RULES)

Foreign-source taxable income for purposes of the numerator of each foreign tax credit limitation fraction is determined in accordance with the rules prescribed in the Code for calculating taxable income and for determining the source of that income. Thus, in determining relevant amounts of taxable income, U.S. rules, not foreign law rules, apply with respect to items includible in income and allowable exclusions and deductions. Also, in determining whether the taxable income can be considered to be from a foreign source so as to be includible in the numerator of the limitation fraction, the U.S. source-of-income rules, discussed in Chapter 2, are determinative. Indeed, for U.S. taxpayers, it is in the context of foreign tax credit limitation calculations that the source rules occupy center stage. These include both the rules for determining the source of gross income and the rules under the Section 861 regulations for calculating the portion of deductible expenses and losses to be allocated and apportioned against foreign-source gross income in determining foreign-source *taxable* income, which is included in the numerator of each separate limitation fraction. Because of the way in which these limitations are applied, the tax planning objective of U.S. taxpayers is to maximize the amount of their gross income that is treated as derived from foreign sources and minimize the amount of their deductions that is allocable to that foreign-source income.

When the U.S. rules with respect to items includible in income or allowable as deductions or the U.S. source rules are inconsistent with the applicable foreign rules, as they frequently are, serious foreign tax credit anomalies may result.

Example. Acme, Inc. ("Acme"), a Delaware corporation, has $1,000 of taxable income from Argentina and $19,000 of taxable income from the United States—according to U.S. source rules. Argentina allows fewer deductions or considers items to be income that are not so classified under U.S. rules. Consequently, under Argentine rules, Acme has $2,000 of taxable income from Argentine sources. If the Argentine income tax rate is 35 percent, Argentina will impose tax of $700 (35 percent of $2,000). But, the United States applies U.S. rules in determining the components of the limitation formula. Thus, assuming that Acme is subject to a U.S. tax rate of 35 percent and that Acme has no other foreign-source taxable income, the limitation will be:

$$\frac{\text{Foreign-source taxable income (\$1,000)}}{\text{Worldwide taxable income (\$20,000)}} \times \text{35\% U.S. tax on worldwide taxable income (\$7,000)} = \$350$$

The remaining $350 of Argentine tax will not be creditable in the current tax year.

[¶ 5260]

PROBLEM

Freda, a U.S. citizen who practices law as a sole proprietor in New York City, performs legal services in the United States for a major Brazilian corporate borrower in connection with negotiation and documentation of a loan made by a consortium of U.S. banks. Under Brazilian source-of-income rules, the fee of $50,000 charged by Freda and paid by the Brazilian corporation is considered to be Brazilian-source income and is therefore subjected to a 30–percent Brazilian withholding tax of $15,000. Freda has no other foreign-source income for the year. Will this withholding tax be creditable?

[¶ 5265]

10. SPECIAL RULES FOR CAPITAL GAINS

Section 904(b) contains special rules for handling capital gains in the numerator of the Section 904 limitation fractions. These rules require that foreign-source capital gains be netted with capital losses and that adjustment be made for the fact that long-term capital gains may be taxed at a preferential rate. These rules must be applied separately for each limitation basket.

With respect to capital losses, Section 904(b)(2)(A) states that foreign-source taxable income is to include gain from the sale or exchange of capital assets only to the extent of "foreign source capital gain net income." The effect of this rule and the intricate implementing definitional provisions is to ensure that any foreign-source capital gains included in the numerator of the applicable Section 904 limitation fraction will be reduced by foreign-source capital losses. Thus, Section 904(b)(2)(A) limits the amount of foreign-source taxable capital gain income that is included in the numerator of the fraction of the appropriate basket limitation to the excess of foreign-source capital gains over foreign-source capital losses (or, if less, the excess of capital gains over capital losses). The foreign-source capital gain net income included in the numerator of a particular basket must be reduced by any net U.S.-source capital loss allocable to that basket.

In years in which there is a "capital gain rate differential," Section 904(b)(2)(B) is applied in lieu of Section 904(b)(2)(A). While the mechanics are complex, the purpose is to reduce the amount of foreign-source capital gain net income includible in the numerator of the Section 904 limitation fraction for the basket concerned by an amount necessary to adjust for the fact that a preferential rate of tax is imposed on long-term capital gains. Since, under current law, only individuals may enjoy a preferential rate of taxation on such gains, Section 904(b)(2)(B) currently applies only to individuals.

Recall from Chapter 1 that tax legislation in 2003 added Section 1(h)(11), which applies the preferential tax rates for capital gains to "qualified dividend income." If certain requirements are met, dividends received by an individual from a foreign corporation may constitute qualified dividend income. Section 1(h)(11)(C)(iv) provides that rules similar to those in Section 904(b)(2)(B) will apply to this "dividend rate differential." Under a sunset rule, Section 1(h)(11) will expire for tax years starting after 2010, unless Congress extends the effective date or makes permanent the provision.

[¶ 5270]

11. DE MINIMIS EXEMPTION FROM THE LIMITATION FOR CERTAIN INDIVIDUAL TAXPAYERS

To simplify the foreign tax credit rules for many individual taxpayers with only a small amount of foreign taxes and foreign-source income, the Taxpayer Relief Act of 1997 added to the Code a de minimis exemption from the foreign tax credit limitations in Section 904(k). Under this provision, an individual taxpayer is exempt from the foreign tax credit limitation in Section 904 if three conditions are met. First, the taxpayer must have creditable foreign taxes of no more than $300 for the tax year ($600 for married taxpayers filing a joint return). Second, the taxpayer must not have any foreign-source gross income other than qualified passive income. Qualified passive income is passive income (as defined for purposes of the basket limitations in Section 904(d), with one modification) that is shown on a payee statement furnished to the taxpayer. Third, the taxpayer must elect to have this de minimis rule apply.

[¶ 5275]

12. CREDIT V. DEDUCTION

A taxpayer who does not elect to credit foreign income taxes for a particular tax year is entitled to deduct them in calculating U.S. taxable income. The choice is available year by year but must be made on an all-or-nothing basis each year; all potentially creditable foreign income taxes for the year must be treated as creditable or deductible. Stated differently, if a taxpayer chooses to credit foreign taxes to any extent in a tax year, the taxpayer generally cannot deduct any foreign income taxes for that year.[21]

21. § 275(a)(4)(A). There are a few exceptions to this rule, which apply to certain foreign taxes that the Code does not allow to be credited. For example, Section 901(j), discussed at ¶ 5125, disallows any foreign tax credit for taxes paid to certain blacklisted countries. Section 901(j)(3) allows a taxpayer to deduct such taxes notwithstanding the taxpayer's use of the foreign tax credit for other foreign taxes. A taxpayer may also deduct certain foreign taxes incurred in connection with the purchase and sale of oil and gas that are not creditable by reason of Section

Once an election to credit foreign taxes has been made, any excess taxes over the applicable limitation can only be carried back and carried forward as a credit; the excess cannot be deducted in a year to which it is carried.

In most cases, it is clearly more advantageous for a taxpayer to credit rather than deduct foreign taxes because the credit is a dollar-for-dollar offset against U.S. tax, while a deduction of a dollar is worth only as much as the taxpayer's marginal U.S. tax rate multiplied by a dollar (in the case of a high-income U.S. taxpayer, often 35 cents under current law). However, in some cases, the Section 904 limitations on the foreign tax credit may permit so little credit to be taken that a deduction is more valuable than a credit. The carryback and carryforward of excess credits from a particular year may provide relief but will not do so if the taxpayer's excess tax credit position is chronic. For example, if a taxpayer's only income on which it pays foreign income taxes is treated as U.S.-source income under U.S. tax law rules and the taxpayer has no other foreign-source income, the Section 904 limitations will prevent a taxpayer from taking any foreign tax credit for such taxes. Moreover, if the taxpayer pays no U.S. tax because it has an operating loss, neither a credit nor a deduction will be of value in the current year; however, the deduction may be of more potential value as an addition to a net operating loss carryover under Section 172, which can be carried back two years and carried forward 20 years, than as an excess foreign tax credit carryover, which can be carried back only one year and carried forward only ten.

[¶ 5280]

PROBLEMS

1. Terry Trade is an unmarried U.S. citizen who lives in the United States. During the current tax year, Terry receives $140,000 of net income from a retailing business conducted as a sole proprietorship. All of the sales transactions producing this income involve sales of inventory property. $50,000 of this income is attributable to sales of inventory within the United States, $50,000 is attributable to sales within Country C and $40,000 is attributable to sales within Country D. Terry's personal services are not a material income-producing factor in the retailing business. Terry also receives $10,000 of interest income from a bank account in a Country D bank.

During the year, Terry pays an income tax to Country C of 20 percent ($10,000) on the net income from the retailing business conducted within Country C. Terry also pays an income tax to Country D of 50 percent ($20,000) on the net income from the retailing business conducted within Country D. Country D imposes no income tax on interest income earned by nonresident individuals.

Assume that Terry's effective U.S. tax rate is 28 percent and ignore any standard deduction or personal exemption deduction to which Terry may be

901(f) and taxes that are not creditable by reason of the international boycott rules of Section 908 (discussed in Chapter 14).

entitled. How much foreign tax will Terry be allowed to credit against her U.S. income tax?

2. During the current year, Martha, a U.S. citizen and unmarried individual, has $99,500 of income from performing personal services in the United States and $500 of foreign-source dividends from a foreign corporation (which were subject to a foreign withholding tax of $210) in which Martha held a very small stock interest. Assume that Martha's effective U.S. tax rate is 28 percent and ignore any standard deduction or personal exemption to which Martha may be entitled. How much foreign tax will Martha be allowed to credit against her U.S. income tax?

3. Gardtrac Inc. ("Gardtrac"), a Delaware corporation, makes small garden tractors in its plant in Bridgeport, Connecticut. It also has three foreign operations. It has a branch in Argentina that owns a residential apartment building in Buenos Aires. The building is managed by an unrelated local apartment management company. Gardtrac has no employees in Argentina. It also owns 40 percent of the stock of Braztrac S.A., a Brazilian corporation that makes small garden tractors. (The remaining 60 percent of Braztrac's stock is owned by unrelated foreign persons.) All Braztrac's income (or loss) is sourced in Brazil and is derived from the manufacture and sale of tractors. Finally, Gardtrac has a branch of its garden tractor business in Colombia. All income (or loss) of the branch is sourced in Colombia.

Gardtrac's results in the current tax year were as follows:

—The Buenos Aires apartment building had a net profit of $100,000. Gardtrac paid $10,000 of income tax to Argentina.

—Braztrac paid a dividend of $65,000 to Gardtrac on the last day of the tax year. Braztrac had $325,000 of post–1986 undistributed earnings and paid $175,000 of post–1986 foreign income taxes.

—The Colombia branch had a net profit of $100,000. Gardtrac paid $45,000 of income tax to Colombia.

—Gardtrac had taxable income of $700,000 from its U.S. operations, all sourced in the United States.

Assume that Gardtrac's effective U.S. tax rate is 35 percent and that the tax year is one that begins after 2006. How much foreign tax will Gardtrac be allowed to credit against its U.S. income tax?

4. How would your answer in Problem 3 change if the facts are the same as above, except that Gardtrac's employees (instead of a management company) actively manage the apartment building in Argentina?

5. How would your answer in Problem 3 change if the facts are the same as above, except that Braztrac's income is derived 80 percent from the manufacture and sale of small garden tractors in Brazil and 20 percent from income on its investment assets (i.e., income that would constitute foreign personal holding company income within the meaning of Section 954(c) if Braztrac were a controlled foreign corporation)?

I. ANTI–ABUSE LIMITATIONS ON THE FOREIGN TAX CREDIT

[¶ 5285]

1. ADMINISTRATIVE ACTION

As discussed in more detail in Chapter 7, despite the rationale for the Section 904(d)(1) separate basket regime (whether that regime consists of nine, eight or two baskets), there continue to be opportunities for cross-crediting of high foreign taxes against the U.S. taxes that would otherwise be imposed on income in the same basket subject to low or no foreign taxes. The opportunities are greatest, of course, within the general category income limitation basket, but they are also present in connection with income in other baskets, including the passive category income basket. Another aspect of the cross-crediting regime is presented when a U.S. corporation has available excess foreign tax credit limitation with respect to foreign-source income in a particular basket that exceeds the foreign taxes on such income. In such a case there is an incentive to engage in transactions that will generate foreign tax credits with respect to the income in the excess limitation basket in order to offset the residual U.S. tax that would otherwise be imposed on such income. The IRS has become increasingly concerned about transactions it finds abusive that are designed to generate foreign tax credits in order to reduce the residual U.S. tax on foreign-source income falling into particular Section 904(d)(1) baskets. This concern is reflected in IRS Notice 98–5, set forth in part below and since withdrawn by IRS Notice 2004–19, which is also set forth in part below.

IRS Notice 98–5 identified and illustrated two categories of abusive transactions. The first category consists of transactions involving transfers of foreign tax liability through the acquisition of an asset (e.g., stock or debt obligations issued by a foreign corporation or foreign intangible property rights) that generates an income stream (e.g., dividends, interest or royalties) subject to foreign gross basis taxes—typically withholding taxes. This category is illustrated by Examples 1 through 3 in the Notice and by the *Compaq Computer* case, at ¶ 5310.

The second category of abusive transactions consists of cross-border tax arbitrage transactions that permit duplicate tax benefits granted by the United States and a foreign country to separate persons with respect to the same taxes or income. This category is illustrated by Examples 4 and 5 of IRS Notice 98–5. The common thread in the two categories is the acquisition of foreign tax credits in a transaction that either produces no economic gain or a gain that is insubstantial in relation to the U.S. foreign tax credits expected to result from the transaction.

[¶ 5290]

IRS NOTICE 98-5

1998-1 C.B. 334, withdrawn by IRS Notice 2004-19, 2004-1 C.B. 606.

I. BACKGROUND

* * *

Multinational corporations that are subject to relatively low rates of tax on their foreign-source income may be in an excess limitation position. Generally, such taxpayers may properly use credits for foreign taxes imposed on high-taxed foreign income to offset residual U.S. tax on their low-taxed foreign income. Treasury and the Service are concerned, however, that such taxpayers may enter into foreign tax credit-generating schemes designed to abuse the cross-crediting regime and effectively transform the U.S. worldwide system of taxation into a system exempting foreign-source income from residual U.S. tax.

This result is clearly incompatible with the existence of the detailed foreign tax credit provisions and cross-crediting limitations enacted by Congress. No statutory purpose is served by permitting credits for taxes generated in abusive transactions designed to reduce residual U.S. tax on low-taxed foreign-source income. The foreign tax credit benefits derived from such transactions represent subsidies from the U.S. Treasury to taxpayers that operate and earn income in low-tax or zero-tax jurisdictions. The effect is economically equivalent to the tax sparing benefits for U.S. taxpayers that Congress and the Treasury have consistently opposed in the tax treaty context because such benefits are inconsistent with U.S. tax principles and sound tax policy.

II. ABUSIVE ARRANGEMENTS

Treasury and the Service have identified two classes of transactions that create potential for foreign credit abuse. The first class consists of transactions involving transfers of tax liability through the acquisition of an asset that generates an income stream subject to foreign gross basis taxes such as withholding taxes. Transactions described in this class may include acquisitions of income streams. Through securities loans and similar arrangements involving such transactions, foreign tax credits are effectively purchased by a U.S. taxpayer in an arrangement where the expected economic profit from the arrangement is insubstantial compared to the foreign tax credits generated.

The second class of transactions consists of cross-border tax arbitrage transactions that permit effective duplication of tax benefits. Duplicate benefits result when the U.S. grants benefits and, in addition, a foreign country grants benefits (including benefits from a full or partial imputation or exemption system, or a preferential rate for certain income) to separate persons with respect to the same taxes or income. These duplicate benefits generally can result where the U.S. and a foreign country treat all or part of a transaction or amount differently under their respective tax systems. In abusive arrangements involving such transactions the U.S. taxpayer exploits these inconsistencies where the expected economic profit is insubstantial compared to the foreign tax credits generated.

The following are examples of abusive arrangements within the scope of this notice.

Example 1

On June 29, 1998, *US*, a domestic corporation, purchases all rights to a copyright for $75.00. The copyright will expire shortly and the only increase expected to be received with respect to the copyright is a royalty payable June 30, 1998. The gross amount of the royalty is expected to be $100.00. The royalty payment is subject to a 30–percent Country X withholding tax. On June 30, 1998, *US* receives the $100.00 royalty payment, less the $30.00 withholding tax. *US* reasonably expects to incur a $5.00 economic loss (having paid $75.00 for the right to receive a $70.00 net royalty payment), but expects to acquire a $30.00 foreign tax liability. In this example, *US* has effectively purchased foreign tax credits in a transaction that was reasonably expected to result in an economic loss.

Example 2

On June 29, 1998, *US*, a domestic corporation, purchases a foreign bond for $1096.00 (including accrued interest). The foreign bond provides for annual interest payments of $100.00 payable June 30 of each year. The interest payments are subject to a 4.9–percent Country X withholding tax. On June 30, 1998, *US* receives a $95.10 interest payment on the bond (net of a $4.90 Country X withholding tax). On July 4, 1998, *US* sells the bond for $1001.05. Because the value of the bond is not reasonably expected to appreciate due to market factors, *US* reasonably can expect only a $0.15 economic profit (the $1001.05 sales price and the $95.10 net interest coupon, less the $1096.00 purchase price) and expects to acquire a $4.90 foreign tax liability. In this example, *US* has effectively purchased foreign tax credits in a transaction with respect to which the reasonably expected economic profit is insubstantial in relation to expected U.S. foreign tax credits. No implication is intended as to whether the interest described in this example will constitute high withholding tax interest under section 904(d)(2)(B).

Example 3

F, an entity that does not receive a tax benefit from foreign tax credits, wishes to acquire a foreign bond with a value of $1000.00 that provides for annual interest payments of $100.00. The interest payments are subject to a 4.9–percent Country X withholding tax. Instead of purchasing the bond, *F* invests its $1000.00 elsewhere and enters into a three-year notional principal contract (NPC) with *US*, an unrelated domestic corporation. Under the terms of the NPC, *US* agrees to make an annual payment to *F* equal to $96.00 and *F* agrees to make an annual payment to *US* equal to the product of $1000.00 and a rate calculated based on LIBOR. In addition the parties agree that, upon termination of the NPC, *US* will make a payment to *F* based on the appreciation, if any, in the value of the foreign bond, and *F* will make a payment to *US* based on the depreciation, if any, in the value of the foreign bond. In order to hedge its obligations under the NPC, *US* purchases the bond for $1000.00. Assume that, in connection with the purchase of the foreign bond, *US* incurs or maintains an additional $1000.00 of borrowing at an interest rate equal to the LIBOR-based rate provided for in the NPC.

At the time *US* enters into this agreement, *US* reasonably expects to incur an annual $0.90 economic loss each year under the arrangement (the $95.10 net interest payment on the bond plus the LIBOR-based amount received from *F* under the NPC, less the sum of the $96.00 payment to *F* under the NPC and the LIBOR-based amount associated with the $1000.00 borrowing incurred or maintained in order to acquire the foreign bond). In this example, *US* has effectively purchased foreign tax credits in a transaction that was reasonably expected to result in an economic loss.

Example 4

US, a domestic corporation, forms *N*, a Country X corporation, by contributing $10.00 to the capital of *N* in exchange for the only share of *N* common stock. *N* borrows $90.00 from *F*, a Country X individual related to *US*, at an annual interest rate of 7.5 percent, and *N* purchases preferred stock of an unrelated party with a par value of $100.00 or a bond with a face amount of $100.00. *US* reasonably expects the preferred stock or bond to pay dividends or interest at an annual rate of 10 percent. Alternatively, rather than purchasing preferred stock or the bond, *N* lends $100.00 to *US* at an annual interest rate of 10 percent.

Country X treats the *F* loan as an equity investment and does not allow a deduction for *N*'s interest expense. Country X imposes an individual income tax and a corporate income tax of 30 percent. Country X thus is expected to impose a $3.00 corporate income tax each year on *N*. Country X has an imputation system, under which dividends from Country X corporations are excluded from the gross income of Country X individuals. (A similar result could be achieved if the dividends are wholly or partially exempt from Country X tax due to a consolidated return or group relief regime, a dividend-received deduction, or an imputation credit.)

At the time *US* enters into this arrangement, *US* reasonably expects that *N* will have annual earnings and profits of $0.25 ($10.00 dividend or interest income from the preferred stock or bond (or $10.00 interest income from the loan to *US*), less $6.75 interest expense and $3.00 foreign tax liability). *US* expects that each year *N* will pay a $0.25 dividend to *US* and *US* will claim a $3.00 foreign tax credit for taxes deemed paid under section 902. In this example, *US* has entered into an arrangement to exploit the inconsistency between U.S. and Country X tax laws in order to generate foreign tax credits in a transaction with respect to which the reasonably expected economic profit is insubstantial in relation to expected U.S. foreign tax credits.

Example 5

US, a domestic corporation, forms *N*, a Country X entity. *US* contributes $100.00 to the capital of *N* in exchange for a 100–percent ownership interest. *N* borrows $900.00 from *F*, an unrelated Country X corporation, at an annual interest rate of 8 percent, and *N* purchases preferred stock of an unrelated party with a par value of $1000.00 that *US* reasonably expects to pay dividends at an annual rate of 10 percent. The dividends are subject to a Country Y 25–percent withholding tax.

Country X treats the *F* loan as an equity investment in *N* and treats *N* as a partnership. Consequently, *F* claims a foreign tax credit in Country X for 90 percent of the withholding tax paid by *N*. Under U.S. law, the *F* loan is respected as debt and *N* is regarded as a separate entity (a partnership with only one partner). See Reg. § 301.7701–3(a) and § 301.7701–3(b)(2)(C). Thus, *US* claims a U.S. foreign tax credit for the taxes paid by *N* and the tax benefit of the foreign taxes paid by *N* are effectively duplicated.

At the time *US* enters into this arrangement, *US* reasonably expects an annual profit of $3.00 ($100.00 dividend income, less $72.00 interest expense and $25.00 foreign tax liability) and an annual foreign tax credit of $25. In this example, *US* has entered into an arrangement to exploit the inconsistency between U.S. and Country X tax laws in order to generate foreign tax credits in a transaction with respect to which the reasonably expected economic profit is insubstantial in relation to expected U.S. foreign tax credits.

III. REGULATIONS TO BE ISSUED PURSUANT TO THIS NOTICE

Regulations will be issued to disallow foreign tax credits for taxes generated in abusive arrangements such as those described in Part II above. These regulations will be issued under the authority of some or all of the following sections of the Internal Revenue Code of 1986: section 901, section 901(k)(4), section 904, section 864(e)(7), section 7701(1), and section 7805(a).

In general, these regulations will disallow foreign tax credits in an arrangement such as those described in Part II above from which the reasonably expected economic profit is insubstantial compared to the value of the foreign tax credits expected to be obtained as a result of the arrangement. The regulations will emphasize an objective approach to calculating expected economic profit and credits, and will require that the determination of expected economic profit reflect the likelihood of realizing both potential gain and potential loss (including loss in excess of the taxpayer's investment). Thus, under the regulations, expected economic profit will be determined without regard to executory financial contracts (*e.g.*, a national principal contract, forward contract, or similar instrument) that do not represent a real economic investment or potential for profit or that are not properly treated as part of the arrangement. Further, the regulations will require that expected economic profit be determined over the term of the arrangement, properly discounted to present value.

It is expected that the regulations in general and any test relying on a comparison of economic profit and credits in particular would be applied to discrete arrangements. The utility of a test comparing profits and credits depends upon the proper delineation of the arrangement to be tested. If necessary to effectuate the purposes of the regulations, a series of related transactions or investments may be treated as a single transaction or investment or may be treated as separate arrangements. The proper grouping of transactions and investments into arrangements will depend on all relevant facts and circumstances.

For example, a series of transactions involving a purchase and resale might be treated as a single arrangement. Similarly, an investment together with related hedging and financing transactions, *e.g.*, a borrowing, an investment, and an asset swap designed to limit the taxpayer's economic exposure with respect to the investment, might be treated as a single arrangement. In addition, if a controlled foreign corporation, as part of its business, enters into a buy-sell transaction involving a debt instrument, that buy-sell transaction could be treated as a separate arrangement.

In general, reasonably expected economic profit will be determined by taking into account foreign tax consequences (but not U.S. tax consequences). However, it is inappropriate in the context of the U.S. foreign tax credit system to allow foreign tax credits with respect to abusive arrangements simply because the arrangements generate substantial foreign tax savings. Accordingly, the regulations will provide that the calculation of expected economic profit will not include expected foreign tax savings attributable to a tax credit or similar benefit allowed by a foreign country with respect to a tax paid to another foreign country.

In general, expected economic profit will be determined by taking into account expenses associated with an arrangement, without regard to whether such expenses are deductible in determining taxable income. For example, in determining economic profit, foreign taxes will be treated as an expense. In addition, interest expense (and similar amounts, including borrowing fees, "in lieu of" payments, forward contract payments, and notional principal contract payments) generally will be taken into account in determining expected economic profit only to the extent that the indebtedness or contract giving rise to the expense is part of the arrangement.

In addition, the regulations will provide special rules that will operate to deny credits for foreign taxes generated in abusive arrangements involving asset swaps or other hedging devices (including rules that allocate interest expense to an arrangement in certain cases other than pursuant to a tracing approach). For example, an arrangement involving a purchase of a foreign security coupled with an asset swap that is designed to hedge substantially all of the taxpayer's risk of loss with respect to the security for the duration of the arrangement generally will constitute an abusive foreign tax credit arrangement even if the taxpayer has not incurred indebtedness for the specific purpose of acquiring the asset. However, the regulations will not treat arrangements involving debt instruments as abusive solely because the taxpayer diminishes its risk of interest rate or currency fluctuations, unless the taxpayer also diminishes its risk of loss with respect to other risks (*e.g.*, creditor risk) for a significant portion of the taxpayer's holding period. * * *

Under the foregoing principles, the regulations will not disallow foreign tax credits merely because income from the arrangement is subject to a high foreign tax rate. Treasury and the Service anticipate that credits for taxes paid to a high-tax jurisdiction will not be subject to disallowance under the regulations absent other indicia of abuse.

The regulations generally will not disallow a credit for withholding taxes on dividends if the holding period requirement of section 901(k) is satisfied. However, the regulations will operate to determine whether foreign tax credits with respect to cross-border tax arbitrage arrangements (as described in Part II, above) will be disallowed, even if such credits arise with respect to withholding taxes on dividends and the section 901(k) holding period is satisfied. In addition, the regulations generally will apply to determine whether credits should be disallowed with respect to qualified taxes (as defined in section 901(k)(4)(B)) that are not subject to the general section 901(k) holding period rule. For example, the regulations may disallow credits with respect to gross basis taxes paid or accrued with respect to certain arrangements involving equity swaps and equity buy-sell transactions entered into by securities dealers even if such credits would not have been disallowed under section 901(k) pursuant to section 901(k)(4). See section 901(k)(4)(C).

IV. EFFECTIVE DATE OF REGULATIONS ISSUED PURSUANT TO THIS NOTICE

The regulations to be issued with respect to arrangements of the kind described in Part II above generally will be effective with respect to taxes paid or accrued on or after December 23, 1997, the date this notice was issued to the public. The effective date of the regulations issued pursuant to this notice, however, will not limit the application of other principles of existing law to determine the proper tax consequences of the structures or transactions addressed in the regulations.

* * *

VI. OTHER FOREIGN TAX CREDIT GUIDANCE

Treasury and the Service are considering issuing other guidance to ensure that foreign tax credits are allowed to U.S. taxpayers in a manner consistent with the overall structure of the Code and the intent of Congress in enacting the credit. For example, Treasury and the Service are considering issuing additional regulations under section 904(d)(2)(B)(iii) to address abusive transactions involving high withholding taxes. Treasury and the Service are also considering whether additional approaches may be necessary to identify abuses in the case of foreign gross basis taxes generally.

In addition, Treasury and the Service are considering various approaches to address structures (including hybrid entity structures) and transactions intended to create a significant mismatch between the time foreign taxes are paid or accrued and the time the foreign-source income giving rise to the relevant foreign tax liability is recognized for U.S. tax purposes. For such structures and transactions, Treasury and the Service are considering either deferring the tax credits until the taxpayer recognizes the income, or accelerating the income recognition to the time at which the credits are allowed (*e.g.*, by allocating the credits or the income under section 482).

Finally, Treasury and the Service are concerned about credits claimed in transactions described in Part II above, with respect to assets or income streams that are hedged pursuant to portfolio hedging strategies and with respect to hedges entered into with respect to assets or income streams that the taxpayer holds without diminished risk of loss for a significant period of time.

In general, regulations addressing these other foreign tax credit issues will be effective no earlier than the date on which proposed regulations (or other guidance such as a notice) describing the tax consequences of the arrangements are issued to the public. The effective date of any such regulations will not, however, affect the application of other principles of existing law to determine the proper tax consequences of the structures or transactions addressed in the regulations.

* * *

[¶ 5295]

IRS NOTICE 2004–19

2004–1 C.B. 606.

PURPOSE

The purpose of this Notice is to describe the approach that the Treasury Department and the Internal Revenue Service (IRS) are using to address transactions involving inappropriate foreign tax credit results and to withdraw Notice 98–5 * * *, because Treasury and the IRS do not intend to issue regulations in the form described in that notice.

BACKGROUND

Notice 98–5 announced that Treasury and IRS intended to issue regulations that would apply an economic profit test to address abusive tax-motivated transactions that generate foreign tax credits that can be used to reduce residual U.S. tax on other foreign source income. Part II of Notice 98–5 describes two classes of transactions that create the potential for foreign tax credit abuse. The first class includes transactions that effectively transfer a foreign tax liability through the acquisition of an asset that generates an income stream subject to foreign gross basis taxes such as withholding taxes. The second class includes cross-border tax arbitrage transactions that effectively permit the duplication of tax benefits. Notice 98–5 contemplated that regulations would apply an economic profit test to disallow credits for foreign taxes generated in an arrangement such as those described above if the reasonably expected economic profit were determined to be insubstantial compared to the value of the foreign tax credits expected to be obtained as a result of the arrangement. Notice 2003–76, [2003–2 C.B. 1181] and its predecessors identified transactions that are the same as or substantially similar to transactions described in Part II of Notice 98–5 as listed transactions for purposes of the tax shelter disclosure, registration, and list maintenance requirements of § 1.6011–4 of the * * * Regulations and §§ 301.6111–2 and 301.6112–1 of the * * * Regulations.

DISCUSSION

Treasury and the IRS do not intend to issue regulations in the form described in Notice 98–5. Accordingly, Notice 98–5 is withdrawn. Consistent with this withdrawal, Notice 2003–76 is modified by eliminating the reference to Notice 98–5 in the identification of listed transactions. Accordingly, transactions will not be considered listed transactions for purposes of §§ 1.6011–4(b)(2), 301.6111–2(b)(2), and 301.6112–1(b)(2) solely because they are the same as or substantially similar to the transactions or arrangements described in Part II of Notice 98–5. No inference is intended, however, as to whether such transactions are otherwise subject to the disclosure requirements of section 6011, the registration requirements of section 6111, or the list maintenance requirements of section 6112.

Treasury and the IRS remain concerned about transactions that involve inappropriate foreign tax credit results. The tax benefits claimed in these transactions are inconsistent with the purposes of the foreign tax credit provisions, including the foreign tax credit limitation of section 904, which are intended to reduce or eliminate double taxation of income.

The IRS will continue to scrutinize abusive transactions that are designed to generate foreign tax credits. In appropriate circumstances, the IRS will challenge the claimed tax consequences of such transactions under the following principles of existing law: the substance over form doctrine, the step transaction doctrine, debt-equity principles, section 269, the partnership anti-abuse rules of § 1.701–2, and the substantial economic effect rules of § 1.704–1.

Treasury also has proposed legislative changes to address transactions involving inappropriate foreign tax credit results. Section 901(k), which was enacted in 1997, disallows a credit for certain foreign taxes paid with respect to a dividend if the recipient of the dividend does not meet certain holding period requirements or is under an obligation to make related payments with respect to substantially similar or related property. The Administration's FY 2005 Budget includes a proposal to expand section 901(k) to apply to foreign taxes with respect to income or gain other than dividends (such as interest, rents, and royalties), disallowing a credit for foreign withholding taxes if the recipient of the income or gain does not meet certain holding period requirements with respect to the asset generating the income or is under an obligation to make related payments with respect to substantially similar or related property. [As discussed below at ¶ 5315, this proposal was enacted as new Section 901(*l*) in the 2004 JOBS Act.] * * *

The Administration's FY 2005 Budget also includes a proposal for broad regulatory authority to address transactions that involve inappropriate separation of foreign taxes from the related foreign income in cases where foreign taxes are imposed on any person with respect to income of an entity. The regulations that would be issued under this proposed authority may provide for the disallowance of a credit for all or a portion of the foreign taxes or for the allocation of the foreign taxes among the participants in the transaction in a manner that is more consistent with the underlying economics of the transaction. The Administration's FY 2005 Budget proposal to expand existing regulatory authority is intended to provide additional mechanisms for Treasury and the IRS to address the second class of transactions described in Notice 98–5 as well as other abusive transactions involving foreign tax credits.

Treasury and the IRS will use existing authority under section 901 and other provisions of the Code to address transactions or structures that produce inappropriate foreign tax credit results. The 2004 business plan for published guidance includes regulations addressing the allocation of foreign taxes by a partnership under section 704. In particular, the regulations will address situations involving special allocations of foreign taxes among the partners that are inconsistent with the allocation of the related foreign income. Treasury and the IRS expect to issue these regulations shortly. [As discussed at ¶ 5300, these regulations were issued in temporary and proposed form in 2004 and in final form in 2006. See

Reg. § 1.704–1(b)(4)(viii).] Treasury and the IRS also are working on guidance under section 901 concerning the application of the legal liability rule of § 1.901–2(f) in certain circumstances, including, for example, in the case of consolidated tax reporting systems in foreign countries. These regulations are intended to provide rules that make the allocation of foreign taxes imposed on the combined income of two or more persons more consistent with each person's respective share of the foreign income to which the tax relates. [As noted at ¶¶ 5010 and 5300, these regulations were issued in proposed form in 2006. In addition, in 2010, Congress enacted Section 909, which is aimed at transactions that split foreign taxes from the income to which they relate. See ¶¶ 5010 and 5315.]

Notice 2004–20, [2004–1 C.B. 608] * * *, identifies as a listed transaction for purposes of the tax shelter disclosure, registration, and list maintenance regulations a purported stock acquisition that is intended to generate credits for foreign taxes paid on gain that is not subject to tax in the United States. That notice provides that the IRS will challenge the purported foreign tax credit results where a domestic corporation purportedly acquires the stock of a foreign target corporation, makes a 338 election, and then, pursuant to a prearranged plan, sells all or substantially all of the target corporation's assets in a transaction that generates a taxable gain for foreign tax purposes (but not for U.S. tax purposes). [As noted at ¶¶ 5253 and 5315, Section 901(m), enacted in 2010, disallows a foreign tax credit in such a "covered acquisition."] * * *

In addition, Treasury and the IRS are working on modifications to the tax shelter disclosure regulations of § 1.6011–4(b) (identifying transactions subject to the disclosure requirements) to ensure that the regulations require appropriate reporting of potentially abusive transactions involving foreign tax credits. In particular, Treasury and the IRS are considering revisions to the tax shelter disclosure regulations to require reporting of transactions that effectively separate foreign taxes from the related foreign income, including transactions that create a mismatch in the timing of recognition for U.S. tax purposes of foreign taxes and the related foreign income.

* * *

[¶ 5300]

NOTES

1. As predicted in IRS Notice 2004–19, temporary regulations under Section 704(b) were issued in 2004 and final regulations were issued in 2006 concerning the allocation of a partnership's creditable taxes among its partners. The regulations provide that special allocations of creditable foreign taxes cannot have substantial economic effect and, therefore, creditable for-

eign taxes must be allocated in accordance with the partners' interests in the partnership. However, the regulations contain a safe harbor under which an allocation of a creditable foreign tax is treated as in accordance with the partners' interests in the partnership if the partnership agreement provides for the allocation of creditable foreign tax in proportion to the partners' distributive shares of partnership income to which the tax relates and certain other requirements are met. Reg. § 1.704–1(b)(4)(viii)(*a*). As discussed in IRS Notice 2004–19, these regulation provisions are designed to prevent abuse of the foreign tax credit provisions by U.S. taxpayers using special partnership allocations of creditable foreign taxes to claim foreign tax credits that are not matched by an allocation of partnership income subject to U.S. income tax to which the taxes relate.

2. As discussed in more detail at ¶ 5010, the Treasury and the IRS in 2006 issued proposed regulations aimed at transactions in which creditable foreign taxes are split from the income to which they relate (sometimes called "foreign tax credit splitter transactions"). Those proposed Section 901 regulations would treat the person who is required to take the income into account under foreign law as the one upon whom foreign law imposes legal liability for the tax for purposes of the so-called technical taxpayer rule in Reg. § 1.901–2(f)(1). Legislation enacted in 2010 deals with this issue in a different way and, in the case of a foreign tax credit splitting event, defers the foreign tax credit for the foreign taxes paid or accrued by the taxpayer until the year when the related foreign income is taken into account for federal income tax purposes. See § 909.

[¶ 5305]

2. USE OF JUDICIAL DOCTRINES IN LITIGATION

Another approach used by the government to combat abusive transactions in the foreign tax credit area is to attack such transactions under the judicial doctrines such as the economic-substance, business-purpose and sham-transaction doctrines. In the following case, the IRS was successful in using such an approach in the Tax Court, but ultimately lost the case in the court of appeals. Which court had it right in this case?

[¶ 5310]

COMPAQ COMPUTER CORP. v. COMMISSIONER

United States Court of Appeals, Fifth Circuit, 2001.
277 F.3d 778.

EDITH H. JONES, CIRCUIT JUDGE.

In this case, Compaq Computer Corporation engaged in a foreign stock transaction involving the purchase and resale of American Depository Receipts (ADRs). The Tax Court held that because the ADR transaction lacked economic substance, the transaction should be disregarded for federal income tax purposes. * * * The Eighth Circuit recently decided the same question and concluded as a matter of law that ADR transactions of the sort at issue here have economic substance and a business purpose. We agree with the Eighth Circuit's conclusion and reverse.

BACKGROUND

The facts are stated in the opinion of the Tax Court and are set out only briefly here. An ADR is a trading unit, issued by a trust, that represents ownership of stock in a foreign corporation. Foreign stocks are customarily traded on U.S. stock exchanges using ADRs. An ADR transaction of the kind at issue in this case begins with the purchase of ADRs with the settlement date at a time when the purchaser is entitled to a declared dividend—that is, before or on the record date of the dividend. The transaction ends with the immediate resale of the same ADR with the settlement date at a time when the purchaser is no longer entitled to the declared dividend—that is, after the record date. In the terminology of the market, the ADR is purchased "cum dividend" and resold "ex dividend."

Twenty–First Securities Corporation, an investment firm specializing in arbitrage transactions, proposed to Compaq that Compaq engage in an ADR transaction. Compaq's assistant treasurer, James Tempesta, and treasurer, John Foster, had a one-hour meeting with Twenty–First to discuss this possibility. After a discussion among Tempesta, Foster, and Compaq's chief financial officer, Darryl White, it was decided to go forward with an ADR transaction. Tempesta did not perform a cash-flow analysis before agreeing to the transaction. His investigation of the transaction and of Twenty–First was limited to telephoning a reference and reviewing a Twenty–First spreadsheet analyzing the transaction.

The securities chosen for the transaction were ADR shares of Royal Dutch Petroleum Company. Compaq knew little or nothing about Royal Dutch other than generally available market information. Without involving Compaq, Twenty–First chose both the sizes and prices of the trades and the identity of the company that would sell the ADRs to Compaq.

On September 16, 1992, Twenty–First, acting on Compaq's behalf, bought ten million Royal Dutch ADRs from the designated seller, which was another client of Twenty–First. Twenty–First immediately sold the ADRs back to the seller. The trades were made in 46 separate New York Stock Exchange (NYSE) floor transactions—23 purchase transactions and 23 corresponding resale transactions—of about 450,000 ADRs each and were all completed in a little over an hour. Any trader on the floor was able to break up any of these transactions by taking part or all of the trade; but none, it appears, did. Because the trades were completed at market prices, no trader had an incentive to break up the transaction. The aggregate purchase price was about $887.6 million, cum dividend. The aggregate resale price was about $868.4 million, ex dividend. Commissions, margin account interest, and fees were about $1.5 million. Pursuant to special NYSE settlement terms, the purchase trades were formally settled on September 17. Pursuant to regular NYSE terms, the resale trades were settled on September 21. Compaq used a margin account with Bear Stearns & Co., a well known securities brokerage firm. Compaq was the shareholder of record of the ADRs on the dividend record date and was therefore entitled to a gross dividend of about $22.5 million. About $3.4 million in Netherlands tax was withheld from Compaq's dividend by Royal Dutch and paid to the Netherlands government. The net dividend, about $19.2 million, was paid directly to Compaq.

On its 1992 U.S. income tax return, Compaq reported about $20.7 million in capital losses on the purchases and resales, about $22.5 million in gross dividend income, and a foreign tax credit of about $3.4 million for the Netherlands tax withheld from the gross dividend. Compaq used the capital loss to offset part of a capital gain of about $231.7 million that Compaq had realized in 1992 from the sale of stock in another company.

The Commissioner sent a notice of deficiency to Compaq for its federal income taxes that cited, among other things, the Royal Dutch transaction. Compaq filed a petition in the Tax Court for redetermination of the deficiencies and of an accuracy-related penalty for negligence asserted for 1992 under * * * § 6662. Concluding that the transaction should be disregarded for U.S. income tax purposes, the court upheld the deficiencies and the negligence penalty. The court disallowed the gross dividend income, the foreign tax credit, and the capital losses reported by Compaq on its tax return. Compaq then argued that it should at least be allowed to deduct the out of pocket losses—commissions, margin account interest, and fees—that it had incurred in the course of the transaction, but the court held that the expenses could not be deducted. Compaq appealed.

STANDARD OF REVIEW

This court reviews the Tax Court's conclusions of law de novo and its factual findings for clear error. * * * The Tax Court's determinations of mixed questions of law and fact are subject to de novo review. * * * In particular, "legal conclusion[s]" that transactions are shams in substance are reviewed de novo. * * * This is true even though the Tax Court has characterized some of its determinations as "ultimate findings of fact." * * *

DISCUSSION

"[W]here ... there is a genuine multiple-party transaction with economic substance which is compelled or encouraged by business or regulatory realities, is imbued with tax-independent considerations, and is not shaped solely by tax-avoidance features that have meaningless labels attached, the Government should honor the allocation of rights and duties effectuated by the parties." *Frank Lyon Co.*, 435 U.S. at 583–84 * * *. * * * The Government has stipulated that aside from its contention that the Royal Dutch transaction lacked economic substance, it has no objection to how Compaq chose to report its tax benefits and liabilities concerning the transaction.

In *Rice's Toyota World, Inc. v. Comm'r*, 752 F.2d 89 (4th Cir. 1985), the court held that after *Frank Lyon Co.*, it is appropriate for a court to engage in a two-part inquiry to determine whether a transaction has economic substance or is a sham that should not be recognized for income tax purposes. "To treat a transaction as a sham, the court must find that the taxpayer was motivated by *no business purposes* other than obtaining tax benefits in entering the transaction, and that the transaction has *no economic substance* because no reasonable possibility of a profit exists." *Id.* at 91 (emphasis added). *See id.* ("[S]uch a test properly gives effect to the mandate of the Court in *Frank Lyon* that a transaction cannot be treated as a sham unless the transaction is shaped *solely* by tax avoidance considerations.") (emphasis added). Other courts have said that business purpose and reasonable possibility of profit are merely factors to be considered in determining whether a transaction is a sham. *See, e.g., ACM Partnership v. Comm'r*, 157 F.3d 231, 247 (3d Cir. 1998) ("[T]hese distinct aspects of the economic sham inquiry do not constitute discrete prongs of a 'rigid two-step analysis,' but rather represent related factors both of which inform the analysis of whether the transaction had sufficient substance, apart from its tax consequences, to be respected for tax purposes.") (citation omitted) * * *. Because we conclude that the ADR transaction in this case had both economic substance and a business purpose, we do not need to decide today which of these views to adopt.

The Tax Court reasoned that Compaq's ADR transaction had neither economic substance nor a non-tax business purpose. The court first concluded that Compaq had no reasonable opportunity for profit apart from the income tax consequences of the transaction. The court reached this conclusion by employing a curious method of calculation: in computing what it called Compaq's net "cash flow" from the transaction, the court assessed neither the transaction's pre-tax profitability nor its post-tax profitability. Instead, the court assessed profitability by looking at the transaction after Netherlands tax had been imposed but before considering U.S. income tax consequences. The court subtracted Compaq's $20.7 million in capital losses, not from the $22.5 million gross dividend, but from the $19.2 million net dividend. The court then ignored the $3.4 million U.S. foreign tax credit that Compaq claimed corresponding to the $3.4 million Netherlands tax. Put otherwise, in determining whether the ADR transaction was profitable, the court treated the Netherlands tax as a cost of the transaction, but did not treat the corresponding U.S. tax credit as a benefit of the transaction. The result of this half pre-tax, half after-tax calculation was a net loss figure of roughly $1.5 million.

The court rejected Compaq's argument that it had a profit prior to the assessment of tax.

> [Compaq] used tax reporting strategies to give the illusion of profit, while simultaneously claiming a tax credit in an amount (nearly $3.4 million) that far exceeds the U.S. tax (of $640,000) attributed to the alleged profit, and thus is available to offset tax on unrelated transactions.... By reporting the gross amount of the dividend, when only the net amount was received, petitioner created a fictional $1.9 million profit as a predicate for a $3.4 million tax credit.

113 T.C. at 222. The court said that the intention and effect of the transaction were to capture a tax credit, not substantive ownership of Royal Dutch ADRs, and that the transaction had been arranged so as to minimize the risks associated with it. * * *

As for Compaq's business purpose, the Tax Court concluded that Compaq was motivated only by the expected tax benefits of the ADR transaction. Among other things, the court said, Compaq had not engaged in a businesslike evaluation of the transaction. * * *

The Tax Court's decision is in conflict with *IES Indus., Inc. v. United States*, 253 F.3d 350 (8th Cir. 2001). In *IES*, the court held as a matter of law that an ADR transaction identical to this one was not a sham transaction for income tax purposes. Undertaking the two-part inquiry set out in *Rice's Toyota World*, 752 F.2d at 91–92, the court declined to decide whether a transaction would be a sham if either economic substance or business purpose, but not both, was present. * * * Instead, the court concluded that both economic substance and business purpose were present in the transaction before it.

Turning first to economic substance, the court rejected the argument that the taxpayer purchased only the right to the net dividend, not the gross dividend. "[T]he economic benefit to IES was the amount of the *gross* dividend, before the foreign taxes were paid. IES was the legal owner of the ADRs on the record date. As such, it was legally entitled to retain the benefits of ownership, that is, the dividends due on the record date." [253 F.3d] at 354. The court said that the part of the gross dividend withheld as taxes by the Dutch government was as much income to the taxpayer as the net dividend remaining after taxes. The court relied on the venerable principle, articulated in *Old Colony Trust Co. v. Comm'r*, 279 U.S. 716, 729 * * * (1929), that "[t]he discharge by a third person of an obligation to him is equivalent to receipt by the person taxed." In *Old Colony Trust Co.*, the Supreme Court held that when an employer pays an employee's income taxes, the payment of the taxes constitutes income to the employee. * * *

The *IES* court saw no reason why the *Old Colony Trust Co.* principle should not apply to the payment of foreign tax by withholding. "The foreign corporation's withholding and payment of the tax on IES's behalf is no different from an employer['s] withholding and paying to the government income taxes for an employee: the full amount before taxes are paid is considered income to the employee." *IES*, 253 F.3d at 354.

When the full amount of the gross dividend was counted as income to the taxpayer, the transaction resulted in a profit to the taxpayer. *See id.*

As for business purpose, the court said that "[a] taxpayer's subjective intent to avoid taxes ... will not by itself determine whether there was a business purpose to a transaction." *Id.* at 355. * * * The court rejected the Government's argument that because the ADR transaction carried no risk of loss, it was a sham. The court noted that some risk, minimal though it may have been, attended the transaction. That the taxpayer had tried to reduce the risks did not make it a sham. "We are not prepared to say that a transaction should be tagged a sham for tax purposes merely because it does not involve excessive risk. IES's disinclination to accept any more risk than necessary in these circumstances strikes us as an exercise of good business judgment consistent with a subjective intent to treat the ADR trades as money-making transactions." *IES*, 253 F.3d at 355.

The court further noted that the ADR transactions had not been conducted by alter egos or by straw entities created by the taxpayer simply for the purpose of facilitating the transactions. Instead, "[a]ll of the parties involved ... were entities separate and apart from IES, doing legitimate business before IES started trading ADRs and (as far as we know) continuing such legitimate business after that time." *Id.* Each individual ADR trade was an arm's-length transaction. * * *

We agree with the *IES* court and conclude that the Tax Court erred as a matter of law by disregarding the gross amount of the Royal Dutch dividend and thus ignoring Compaq's pre-tax profit on the ADR transaction. We add the following comments.

First, as to economic substance: the Commissioner does not explain why the *Old Colony Trust Co.* principle does not apply here. That the tax was imposed by the Netherlands rather than by the United States, or that it was withheld rather than paid at the end of the tax year, is irrelevant to how the part of the dividend corresponding to the tax should be treated for U.S. income tax purposes. Pre-tax income is pre-tax income regardless of the timing or origin of the tax. *See Old Colony Trust Co.*, 279 U.S. at 729, 49 S. Ct. at 504 ("It is ... immaterial that the taxes were directly paid over to the government [by the taxpayer's employer, rather than by the taxpayer].") * * * Because Compaq was entitled to payment of the dividend as of the record date, Compaq was liable for payment of tax on the dividend; accordingly, the payment of Compaq's Netherlands tax obligation by Royal Dutch was income to Compaq. * * * See * * * Treas. Reg. § 1.901–2(f)(1) ("The person by whom tax is considered paid for purposes of [the foreign tax credit provisions of the Revenue Code] is the person on whom foreign law imposes legal liability for such tax, even if another person (e.g., a withholding agent) remits such tax."); Treas. Reg. § 1.901–2(f)(2)(i) ("Tax is considered paid by the taxpayer even if another party to a direct or indirect transaction with the taxpayer agrees, as a part of the transaction, to assume the taxpayer's foreign tax liability."). Indeed, the Commissioner admitted in this case that according to generally accepted accounting principles, the entire amount of Compaq's gross dividend must be reported as income. If the $3.4 million had been paid to the United States (whether by withholding or at the end of the tax year) instead of the Netherlands, there would have been no argument that this money was not income to Compaq. It follows that the gross Royal Dutch dividend, not the dividend net of Netherlands tax, should have been used to compute Compaq's pre-tax profit.

The Tax Court also erred by failing to include Compaq's $3.4 million U.S. tax credit when it calculated Compaq's after-tax profit. * * * This omission taints the court's conclusion that the "net economic loss" from the transaction after tax was about $1.5 million. If the effects of tax law, domestic or foreign, are to be accounted for when they subtract from a transaction's net cash flow, tax law effects should be counted when they add to cash flow. To be consistent, the analysis should either count all tax law effects or not count any of them. To count them only when they subtract from cash flow is to stack the deck against finding the transaction profitable.[6] During this litigation, the I.R.S. has consciously chosen to try to stack the deck this way. *See* I.R.S. Notice 98–5 * * * ("In general, reasonably expected economic profit will be determined by taking into account foreign tax consequences (but not U.S. tax consequences) [of transactions].... In general, expected economic profit will be determined by taking into account expenses associated with an arrangement, without regard to whether such expenses are deductible in determining taxable income. For example, in determining economic profit, foreign taxes will be treated as an expense."). The Commissioner, however, has provided no reason to endorse its approach and ignore *Old Colony Trust Co.* That the Government would get more money from taxpayers does not suffice.

To un-stack the deck and include the foreign tax credit in calculating Compaq's after-tax profit from the Royal Dutch transaction does not give Compaq a windfall. The purpose of the Revenue Code's foreign tax credit provisions is to reduce international double taxation. * * * Compaq reported its gross Royal Dutch dividend income to both the United States and the Netherlands. Without the tax credit, Compaq would be required to pay tax twice—first to the Netherlands through withholding on the gross dividend, and then to the United States—on the same dividend income. Taking the tax credit into account, Compaq owed roughly $644,000 more in worldwide income tax liability as a result of the transaction than it

6. The Tax Court's assertion that "if we follow [Compaq]'s logic, ... we would conclude that [Compaq] paid approximately $4 million in worldwide income taxes on ... $1.9 million in profit" suffers from the same flaw. 113 T.C. at 222. When Compaq's $3.4 million U.S. tax credit is counted in the calculation, Compaq's net worldwide tax liabilities arising from the transaction amount only to $644,000. In addition, the assertion ignores the fact that only about $644,000 of the $4 million was paid on Compaq's $1.9 million pre-tax profit. The rest of the $4 million was not paid on the profit; rather, the tax was paid (to the Netherlands) on the gross amount of the Royal Dutch dividend.

would have owed had the transaction not occurred. Although the United States lost $2.7 million in tax revenues as a result of the transaction, that is only because the Netherlands gained $3.4 million in tax revenues.

If the effects of the transaction are computed consistently, Compaq made both a pre-tax profit and an after-tax profit from the ADR transaction. Subtracting Compaq's capital losses from the gross dividend rather than the net dividend results in a net pre-tax profit of about $1.894 million. Compaq's U.S. tax on that net pre-tax profit was roughly $644,000. Subtracting $644,000 from the $1.894 million results in an after-tax profit of about $1.25 million. The transaction had economic substance.

Second, as to business purpose: even assuming that Compaq sought primarily to get otherwise unavailable tax benefits in order to offset unrelated tax liabilities and unrelated capital gains, this need not invalidate the transaction. *See Frank Lyon Co.*, 435 U.S. at 580 * * * ("The fact that favorable tax consequences were taken into account by Lyon on entering into the transaction is no reason for disallowing those consequences. We cannot ignore the reality that the tax laws affect the shape of nearly every business transaction.") (footnote omitted) * * *; *Helvering v. Gregory*, 69 F.2d 809, 810 (2d Cir. 1934) (Hand, J. Learned) ("Any one may so arrange his affairs that his taxes shall be as low as possible; he is not bound to choose that pattern which will best pay the Treasury; there is not even a patriotic duty to increase one's taxes."), *aff'd*, 293 U.S. 465 * * *.[8] Yet the evidence in the record does not show that Compaq's choice to engage in the ADR transaction was solely motivated by the tax consequences of the transaction. Instead, the evidence shows that Compaq actually and legitimately also sought the (pre-tax) $1.9 million profit it

8. In particular, the fact that Compaq had a large unrelated capital gain in 1992 does not mean that Compaq had an impermissible motive in seeking to engage in the transaction. The capital gain, of course, made it possible for Compaq to obtain an otherwise unavailable tax benefit from the ADR transaction by offsetting its $20.7 million in capital losses from the transaction against the gain [under Section 1211(a) of the Code]. * * * If Compaq had had no capital gain whatsoever in 1992, it would still have had to pay tax on the gross amount of its $22.5 million dividend from Royal Dutch, which—in the absence of a capital gain against which to offset its capital losses—would have resulted in a substantial after-tax loss to Compaq. * * * Put otherwise, the availability of a capital gain against which to offset the capital losses from the ADR transaction was a necessary precondition to the profitability of the transaction on an after-tax basis. A sensible taxpayer would have engaged in such a transaction only if it had a capital gain against which to offset the capital losses that the taxpayer knew would result from the transaction. All this is unremarkable and is no evidence that Compaq had an impermissible motive.

According to the Commissioner, tax-exempt organizations with no use for U.S. income tax credits have an incentive to loan out their ADRs to non-tax-exempt persons in transactions of the kind at issue in this case. The non-exempt persons can use the capital losses and tax credits resulting from ADR transactions to offset unrelated capital gains and tax liabilities. The fact that the differing tax attributes of investors make ADRs more valuable for some investors than for others does not deprive ADR transactions of economic substance for purposes of the tax laws. The possible benefits from ADR transactions for investors with unrelated capital gains and tax liabilities are analogous to the benefits that taxpaying investors (especially investors with high incomes), but not tax-exempt persons, get from the purchase of tax-exempt bonds with lower yields than the pre-tax yields available from non-exempt bonds. * * * In both instances the benefits would not exist were it not for the investors' individual tax attributes.

would get from the Royal Dutch dividend of approximately $22.5 million less the $20.7 million or so in capital losses that Compaq would incur from the sale of the ADRs ex dividend.

Although, as the Tax Court found, the parties attempted to minimize the risks incident to the transaction, those risks did exist and were not by any means insignificant. The transaction occurred on a public market, not in an environment controlled by Compaq or its agents. The market prices of the ADRs could have changed during the course of the transaction (they in fact did change * * *); any of the individual trades could have been broken up or, for that matter, could have been executed incorrectly; and the dividend might not have been paid or might have been paid in an amount different from that anticipated by Compaq. * * * The absence of risk that can legitimately be eliminated does not make a transaction a sham * * *; but in this case risk was present. In light of what we have said about the nature of Compaq's profit, both pre-tax and post-tax, we conclude that the transaction had a sufficient business purpose independent of tax considerations.[9]

Because the Royal Dutch ADR transaction had both economic substance and a non-tax business purpose, it should have been recognized as valid for U.S. income tax purposes. This court's decisions applying the economic substance doctrine to disregard various transactions are not to the contrary. Without enumerating all of the decisions, we mention some to give a flavor of the differences between the facts at issue in the decisions and in this case. In *Freytag v. Comm'r*, 904 F.2d 1011 (5th Cir. 1990), * * * this court affirmed a Tax Court decision disallowing losses allegedly incurred as a result of investments in a commodity straddle program. The taxpayers' investment agent had "absolute authority over the pricing and timing of the transactions" at issue, which "occurred in [a] self-contained market of its own making." 904 F.2d at 1016. In *Merryman*, a business partnership was disregarded for tax purposes because "the formation and role of the partnership served no other purpose except tax avoidance;" a number of facts found by the Tax Court indicated that the partnership lacked economic reality and was a mere formality. *See* [873 F.2d] at 881–83. In *Killingsworth*, this court affirmed a Tax Court decision concluding that a scheme of option hedge or option straddle transactions lacked economic substance. We relied on Revenue Code section 108, a provision that is not relevant to this case, and noted that the transactions "appear[ed] to be devoid of profit making potential." 864 F.2d at 1218. In *Holladay*, this court affirmed the Tax Court's decision to

9. In *IES*, the court noted the Tax Court's assertion in this case that in light of Compaq's limited investigation of the risks of the Royal Dutch transaction, Compaq had had no non-tax business purpose in agreeing to the transaction. 253 F.3d at 355. Even if we agreed with the Tax Court that Compaq had not adequately investigated the risks, it would not make a difference to the outcome of this case. Though Compaq could have done more to evaluate the risks of the transaction, the process it used does not alone prove a lack of business purpose for a transaction that had real risks. It should also be noted that in this case, as in *IES*, the taxpayer declined to go forward with all of the transactions that Twenty–First had proposed. * * *

disallow half of certain tax benefits that an agreement between two joint venturers allocated to only one of the venturers. The allocation had no valid non-tax business purpose. 649 F.2d at 1180. * * *

In this case, by contrast, the ADR transaction had both a reasonable possibility of profit attended by a real risk of loss and an adequate non-tax business purpose. The transaction was not a mere formality or artifice but occurred in a real market subject to real risks. And, as has been discussed, the transaction gave rise to a real profit whether one looks at the transaction prior to the imposition of tax or afterwards.

For the foregoing reasons, the Tax Court erred as a matter of law in disallowing Compaq's identification of gross dividend income, a foreign tax credit, and capital losses associated with the Royal Dutch ADR arbitrage transaction. It is unnecessary to reach the alternative arguments for reversal offered by Compaq: first, that the statutory foreign tax credit regime implicitly displaces the economic substance doctrine; and second, that a 1997 amendment to the foreign tax credit scheme, which added what is now Internal Revenue Code § 901(k), implies that ADR transactions that took place before the amendment are to be recognized for tax purposes. Because we reverse the Tax Court's decision concerning the underlying transaction, it follows that the court erred in imposing the negligence penalty and that the court's holding that Compaq was not entitled to deduct its out of pocket losses becomes superfluous.

The decision of the Tax Court is REVERSED.

[¶ 5315]

3. STATUTORY ANTI–ABUSE PROVISIONS

In 1997, to deal with certain tax-avoidance transactions involving the foreign tax credit and dividends on corporate stock, Congress added Section 901(k) to the Code. This provision generally denies a shareholder any direct or indirect foreign tax credits with respect to a dividend on stock in a corporation if a shareholder has not held the stock for a minimum period during which the shareholder is not protected from risk of loss. For dividends on common stock, the minimum holding period is 16 days within the 31–day period starting 15 days before the ex-dividend date. In the case of preferred stock, the stock must be held for 46 days within the 91–day period starting 45 days before the ex-dividend date. Furthermore, the provision generally denies a shareholder any foreign tax credits, regardless of the shareholder's holding period for the stock, to the extent that the shareholder has an obligation to make payments (whether through a short sale or otherwise) related to the dividend with respect to substantially similar or related property. There are several exceptions to this foreign tax credit disallowance rule, including one for foreign tax credits with respect to dividends received by securities dealers engaged in the active conduct of a foreign securities business. Congress explained the policy underlying Section 901(k), as follows:

> Although present law imposes a holding period requirement for the dividends-received deduction for a corporate shareholder (sec. 246), there is no similar holding period requirement for foreign tax credits with respect to dividends. As a result, some U.S. persons have engaged in tax-motivated transactions designed to transfer foreign tax credits from persons that are unable to benefit from such credits (such as a tax-exempt entity or a taxpayer whose use of foreign tax credits is prevented by the limitation) to persons that can use such credits. These transactions sometimes involve a short-term transfer of ownership of dividend-paying shares. Other transactions involve the use of derivatives to allow a person that cannot benefit from the foreign tax credits with respect to a dividend to retain the economic benefit of the dividend while another person receives the foreign tax credit benefits.

H.R. Rep. No. 148, 105th Cong., 1st Sess. 545 (1997).

The 2004 JOBS Act added Section 901(*l*) to the Code, which provides a minimum holding period rule for income other than dividends. Under this rule, no foreign tax credit will be allowed for any withholding tax on any item of income or gain with respect to any property (1) if the property is held by the recipient of the income item for 15 days or less during the 31–day period starting on the date that is 15 days before the date on which the right to receive payment of the income item arises or (2) to the extent that the recipient of the income item is under an obligation (whether under a short sale or otherwise) to make related payments with respect to positions in substantially similar or related property. This minimum holding period requirement does not apply to "any qualified tax with respect to any property held in the active conduct in a foreign country of a business as a dealer in such property." The statute also gives the Treasury and the IRS the authority to provide other exceptions by regulation where application of this minimum holding period is not necessary to carry out its purposes.

In 2010, Congress added two additional statutory foreign tax credit anti-abuse provisions to the Code. First, new Section 901(m) disallows any foreign tax credit for otherwise creditable foreign income taxes attributable to income or gain from a "covered asset acquisition" that is not subject to U.S. tax. A covered asset acquisition includes, for example, a qualified stock purchase to which Section 338(a) applies. Second, as discussed in more detail at ¶ 5010, new Section 909 deals with so-called foreign tax credit splitter transactions in which a taxpayer splits creditable foreign taxes from the income to which they relate in order to exploit cross-crediting opportunities. Section 909 operates by deferring any foreign tax credit for the foreign taxes paid or accrued until the income to which they relate is taken into account for U.S. income tax purposes.

Finally, in 2010, Congress also codified the economic-substance doctrine in new Section 7701(*o*). Under this provision, for any transaction to which the economic substance doctrine is relevant, the transaction shall be treated as having economic substance only if (1) the transaction changes in a meaningful way (apart from federal income tax effects) the taxpayer's economic position, and (2) the taxpayer has a substantial purpose (other than federal income tax effects) for entering into the transaction. For purposes of determining whether a transaction meets these two requirements, the potential for profit of a transaction is taken into account "only if the present value of the reasonably expected pre-tax profit from the transaction is substantial in relation to the present value of the net tax benefits that would be allowed if the transaction were respected." Fees and other expenses are to be taken into account as expenses for purposes of determining pre-tax profit and the provision directs the Treasury and the IRS to issue regulations "requiring foreign taxes to be treated as expenses in determining pre-tax profit in appropriate cases." There is a strict liability penalty in Section 6662(b)(6) and (i) imposed on a transaction that lacks economic substance within the meaning of Section 7701(*o*). The penalty is 20 percent of the underpayment attributable to the disallowance of the claimed tax benefits or 40 percent of such underpayment if the transaction is not adequately disclosed on the taxpayer's return. No reasonable cause exception is available to the imposition of this penalty. § 6664(c)(2), (d)(2). Would these new statutory provisions have affected the result in *Compaq*, if they had applied to the tax year in issue in that case?

[¶ 5320]

PROBLEM

Atlas Manufacturing Co. ("Atlas"), a Delaware corporation, which is engaged in the manufacture and sale of widgets in the United States, has received substantial dividends from its wholly owned manufacturing subsidiary, R Co., organized in Country C. All of the income of R Co. is from the manufacture and sale of widgets in Country C, and the dividends, which are the only foreign-source income of Atlas, have been free of Country C corporate income tax and withholding tax as a result of a five-year Country C tax holiday.

Atlas has learned that it may be able to purchase a Country C patent owned by an unrelated U.S. corporation, Sierra Inc., covering an invention that would be helpful to R Co. in its manufacturing operations. This patent is currently the subject of a five-year license from its U.S. owner to another Country C corporation, which has one more year to run. Thereafter the patent will have a remaining life of eight years. The existing license calls for a "balloon" royalty payment of $5 million in the last year. This payment will be subject to a Country C withholding tax of $2 million (40 percent of the gross payment). Atlas will buy the Country C patent subject to the license from

Sierra Inc. and will therefore receive the royalty payment of $5 million. Will Atlas be entitled to claim a foreign tax credit for the $2 million of Country C withholding tax against the residual U.S. tax that would otherwise be imposed on the dividends it will receive from R Co.?

J. TAX EXEMPTION FOR CERTAIN U.S. TAXPAYERS LIVING AND WORKING ABROAD (SECTION 911)

[¶ 5325]

1. THE EXCLUSION AND ITS HISTORY

Because U.S. citizens and resident aliens are taxable by the United States on worldwide income, the probability of taxation by two (or more) countries on foreign earnings is relatively high. As discussed earlier in this Chapter, the most direct response (and the one generally favored by the United States) to the problem of international double taxation is the foreign tax credit. As an alternative to the foreign tax credit, however, certain U.S. citizens and resident aliens who live and work abroad may elect under Section 911 to exclude a portion of their foreign earnings from U.S. tax.

The magnitude of the exclusion and the rules by which it is applied have varied over time. Although often criticized by tax policy commentators, special tax benefits have been accorded to U.S. persons working abroad continuously since 1926. Until 1978 the form of the benefit was an exclusion from gross income of certain amounts of earned income (meaning compensation income and *not* investment income) from foreign sources. During previous periods, the maximum amount of income that could be excluded was changed several times, ranging from $15,000 to $35,000. The criteria for qualification also varied somewhat but generally depended on either the establishment of a bona fide foreign residence or simple presence abroad for specified periods of time.

Following some years of controversy and intense scrutiny, the Foreign Earned Income Act of 1978 radically altered the U.S. approach. Instead of an income exclusion, relief was provided for certain extra expenses required by living and working overseas. The 1978 legislation created a general deduction for a cost-of-living differential and other deductions for children's primary and secondary school expenses, home leave travel expenses and excess housing costs. The linkage of tax benefits to actual additional cost burdens would seem to be appropriate tax policy (assuming one is going to provide any tax relief in this area). However, the resulting legislation was very complicated, was very difficult for the overseas taxpayer to apply and produced many anomalous results. These factors, coupled with the fact that it narrowed benefits previously enjoyed by many taxpayers, evoked a strong protest from multinational corporations and Americans working overseas.

The Economic Recovery Tax Act of 1981 enlarged dramatically the benefits available under Section 911. As enacted in 1981, Section 911 would have eventually excluded both foreign earned income as high as $95,000 per year and a housing allowance. As part of the base-broadening compromises leading to the adoption of the Tax Reform Act of 1986, however, the maximum exclusion was cut back to $70,000 annually plus a housing allowance. In the Taxpayer Relief Act of 1997, Congress reversed course yet again and increased the cap on the foreign earned income exclusion to $72,000 for 1998, $74,000 for 1999, $76,000 for 2000, $78,000 for 2001, and $80,000 for 2002 and later years (with the $80,000 cap to be adjusted for inflation in each year after 2007). In 2006, as part of the Tax Increase Prevention and Reconciliation Act of 2005, Congress amended Section 911(b)(2)(D) to provide that the inflation adjustments to the $80,000 exclusion amount were to start in each year after 2005, instead of 2007, a taxpayer-friendly amendment. Yet, that same legislation contained changes to the determination of the exclusion or deduction for housing costs in Section 911(c) that generally have the effect of reducing the amount of such exclusion or deduction as compared with prior law. The 2006 legislation also contained a new stacking rule in Section 911(f), which provides that any income of an electing taxpayer in excess of the exclusion amount in Section 911 is taxed by applying to that excess income the marginal rates that would have applied if the individual had not elected Section 911.

Interestingly, the Section 911 exclusion is available to all U.S. citizens (and to certain resident aliens) who meet the eligibility criteria. These criteria are not specifically related to the policy rationales for the exclusion (discussed below). Eligible taxpayers need not actually have incurred any of the unusual financial burdens cited by proponents of the exclusion to obtain the exclusion. Moreover, although Section 911 is intended in part to mitigate double taxation, the exclusion is available to a qualifying U.S. individual regardless of whether any foreign tax is imposed on the individual's foreign earnings.

[¶ 5330]

2. POLICY ARGUMENTS FOR AND AGAINST THE EXCLUSION

The issue of whether special tax benefits should be provided to U.S. taxpayers working abroad has been vigorously debated for more than 85 years. Proponents of the Section 911 exclusion often argue for an even broader exclusion than the one in the current Code, asserting that the limited exclusion in current law does not fully achieve the policy objectives intended by the provision. Opponents of the exclusion, including most traditional tax policy analysts, generally argue for its complete elimination on grounds of horizontal and vertical equity, economic efficiency/neutrality and complexity. The major arguments for and against the Section 911 exclusion are summarized here.[22]

First, proponents of the exclusion argue that the tax burdens and extra living costs imposed on U.S. taxpayers working abroad make it more expensive for U.S. businesses to use such U.S. employees abroad. In many cases, the argument goes, the U.S. business must reimburse the U.S. employee for the extra tax costs and extra living costs of working abroad, resulting in an increased cost to the U.S. business, which often is passed through to the customers of the business in the form of higher prices. The higher prices, in turn, may mean that the U.S. business may not be able to effectively compete with its foreign competitors from countries which exempt foreign earned income from tax who will be able to charge a lower price for the same goods or services offered by the U.S. business. This argument essentially focuses on the role of Section 911 in helping make U.S. businesses competitive in the international marketplace and recognizes that, in many (if not most) cases, the ultimate beneficiaries of the Section 911 exclusion are the employers of the U.S. worker, who are able to pay lower total compensation to the U.S. worker than if the exclusion were not available. It was one of the major reasons cited in the legislative history of the 1981 Act for reinstating a broadened Section 911 exclusion. See, e.g., H.R. Rep. No. 201, 97th Cong., 1st Sess. 59–60 (1981).

However, in response to this argument, one might well question why the U.S. tax system should be providing a tax subsidy to U.S. businesses that results in an understatement of the true costs of operating abroad, thereby providing a tax incentive for U.S. businesses to shift operations from the United States to a foreign country in violation of the capital-export neutrality tax policy criterion. Moreover, Section 911 may distort the workings of the free market by causing U.S. citizens and resident aliens to accept overseas employment in situations in which they would not have done so in the absence of this tax preference. Furthermore, Section 911 is not limited to U.S. employees of U.S. employers, but can apply to an otherwise qualifying U.S. citizen or resident alien who works for a foreign employer. In such a case, the U.S. tax system is, in effect, providing a tax subsidy to foreign businesses who employ U.S. workers abroad, thus providing an incentive (by allowing them to pay lower compensation to the U.S. worker who can exclude the income from U.S. tax) for those foreign businesses to invest in business operations in some

22. This discussion is drawn from the following sources: H.R. Rep. No. 201, 97th Cong., 1st Sess. 59–60 (1981); Staff of Joint Comm. on Tax'n, 97th Cong., 1st Sess., General Explanation of the Economic Recovery Tax Act of 1981, at 43 (1981); 1 J. Kuntz & R. Peroni, U.S. International Taxation ¶ B1.04[1] (1992); Kingson, "A Somewhat Different View," 34 Tax. Law. 737 (1981); Maiers, "The Foreign Earned Income Exclusion: Reinventing the Wheel," 34 Tax Law. 691 (1981); Sobel, "United States Taxation of Its Citizens Abroad: Incentive or Equity," 38 Vand. L. Rev. 101 (1985).

foreign country instead of in the United States—certainly a strange use of the U.S. tax system.

Focusing on a different aspect of this argument in favor of the Section 911 exclusion, i.e., the extra tax burden incurred by U.S. workers overseas, it is unclear why a Section 911 exclusion is needed to compensate U.S. individuals working abroad for the extra tax costs incurred thereby. Under the foreign tax credit system used by the United States, there generally should be no extra tax burden. The U.S. person generally should receive a foreign tax credit for any foreign income taxes paid on the foreign earnings, thus resulting in a residual U.S. tax only to the extent that the U.S. income taxes on the foreign earnings exceed the foreign income taxes on such earnings.

A second related argument advanced by proponents of the Section 911 exclusion is that, in the absence of a Section 911 exclusion, the increased costs borne by U.S. businesses employing U.S. workers abroad would cause those businesses to cut back foreign operations or replace U.S. workers in key executive positions with foreign nationals who are not taxed by their countries of nationality. The foreign nationals, the argument goes, would be more likely to purchase goods from their own countries rather than from the United States, thus reducing the potential foreign market for U.S. goods. This was another one of the major reasons advanced by Congress in the legislative history of the 1981 Act for reinstating a broadened Section 911 exclusion. See, e.g., H.R. Rep. No. 201, 97th Cong., 1st Sess. 60 (1981) (which cited no data in support of this claim). This seems a questionable argument at best, one that is inconsistent with the fact of the truly global marketplace in which all goods are sold today. Is it really true that Americans generally prefer American goods (think of American tastes in cars, clothing, jewelry and wine) or that foreign nationals generally prefer foreign goods (think of worldwide demand for American jeans, hamburgers and other types of fast food)?

Opponents of the Section 911 exclusion make three basic arguments against the exclusion (in addition to the argument discussed above that Section 911 violates capital-export neutrality). First, like many other tax preferences in the Code, Section 911 violates horizontal equity by removing an item of economic income from the tax base. U.S. workers who work in the United States must pay tax on their entire compensation income, while those who work abroad receive exclusions for up to $80,000 of foreign earnings (in 2002 and later years, but adjusted for inflation for years after 2005) plus a generous housing cost amount. Proponents of Section 911 counter this argument by pointing out that U.S. workers abroad face higher living costs, face less favorable living conditions and receive fewer services from the U.S. government than do U.S. workers living and working in the United States. Thus, proponents of Section 911 argue that horizontal equity principles are not violated because U.S.

workers living and working in the United States and those living and working abroad are not comparable.

Second, opponents of the Section 911 exclusion argue that the exclusion violates vertical equity principles because (like all exclusion or deduction provisions) the value of the exclusion in terms of tax savings varies with the taxpayers' marginal tax rates, i.e., a high-income taxpayer receives a greater benefit than does a low-income taxpayer.[23] Further, high-income taxpayers working in executive or professional positions are in the types of jobs that are more likely to involve a foreign work assignment and these taxpayers have the social status and income level that make it more likely that they will be able to meet the eligibility requirements for Section 911 by becoming assimilated into the foreign society. Proponents of the Section 911 exclusion counter these arguments either by minimizing the importance of vertical equity in analyzing the tax system or by pointing out that the vertical equity concerns are reduced in part by the cap on the basic exclusion ($80,000 in 2002 and later years, but adjusted for inflation for years after 2005).

Finally, opponents of the Section 911 exclusion point out that Section 911 makes the tax system more complex by adding yet another tax preference with its own detailed requirements that must be interpreted by courts and administered by the IRS. One need only look at the authorities in this Chapter (interpreting, for example, the bona fide residence test for eligibility for the exclusion) to see that Section 911 does indeed add complexity to the tax system. Many proponents of capital-import neutrality would likely counter this argument by agreeing that Section 911 is needlessly complex and should be repealed but only as part of a major revision of the U.S. international tax system to adopt a territorial or exemption system of taxing foreign-source income.

[¶ 5335]

3. AMOUNT OF THE EXCLUSION—FOREIGN EARNED INCOME WITHIN A SPECIFIED EXCLUSION AMOUNT

Section 911 provides an exclusion from gross income of "foreign earned income" not in excess of the "exclusion amount" for the year. § 911(b)(2)(A). Section 911(b)(2)(D)(i) now provides that the exclusion amount for calendar year 2002 and thereafter is $80,000. The $80,000 exclusion amount is to be adjusted for inflation for calendar years after 2005. § 911(b)(2)(D)(ii). Thus, as a result of inflation adjustments, the exclusion amount for 2011 is $92,900.

Foreign earned income is defined by Section 911(d)(2)(A) to include, inter alia, "wages, salaries, or professional fees" resulting from the

23. A tax reform study prepared by the Staff of Joint Committee of Taxation contained a proposal to impose a "stacking rule" under which a taxpayer's other income, after deductions, would be stacked on top of the Section 911 exclusion amounts to arrive at the taxpayer's appropriate marginal tax rate bracket in Section 1. See Staff of Joint Comm. on Tax'n, 109th Cong., 1st Sess., Options to Improve Tax Compliance and Reform Tax Expenditures, at 176–77 (2005). This proposal was enacted into law in 2006. See § 911(f), discussed at ¶ 5370.

performance of services. Since the earned income must be "foreign," the services must be rendered outside of the United States. See ¶ 2025. Compensation income derived from working within the United States and investment income from any source do not qualify for the benefits of Section 911.

A question arises when profits are derived from the conduct of a trade or business "in which both personal services and capital are material income-producing factors." In such a case, no more than 30 percent of the taxpayer's share of the net profits from the business may be considered to be earned income. § 911(d)(2)(B). The following case demonstrates an approach to determining whether capital is a material income-producing factor in a business.

[¶ 5340]

ROUSKU v. COMMISSIONER

United States Tax Court, 1971.
56 T.C. 548.

FEATHERSTON, JUDGE: * * * [Petitioner Rousku was a U.S. citizen and bona fide resident of Canada.] The only issue presented for decision is whether, within the meaning of section 911, capital was a material income-producing factor in an automobile body repair business which petitioner George Rousku conducted in Canada.

* * *

Petitioner's business consists primarily of the repair of automobiles which have been involved in collisions. Repairs of this nature require the use of equipment and machinery such as air compressors, welding equipment, grinders, sanders, and body jacks. Air filters and paint-spraying equipment are also used for repainting the repaired automobiles. In addition, in some instances petitioner purchases and sells parts, such as bumpers, fenders, panels, and the like, which are used in making repairs.

During 1967, petitioner employed five licensed workmen to assist him in his business. While petitioner personally performed some shop services, his work consisted primarily of estimating the cost of repair work, supervising other workers in the body shop, allocating work to the several employees, and inspecting the completed repairs prior to delivery to the customers. During the year in issue he kept his business open 5½ days each week, but he personally averaged 10 to 12 hours of work, 7 days a week. This overtime and weekend work consisted mainly of making estimates for customers and doing his recordkeeping.

During 1967, petitioner's equipment and tools for his repair operations had a book value of $4,023. His purchases of parts for automobile repairs amounted to $61,420.19 during the year; he carried an average inventory of parts in the amount of $2,500. In April 1967, petitioner bought the building in which his shop was located for $38,000, making no downpayment; his monthly payments on the purchase price are $125 plus interest. Prior to the purchase, he had paid rent in the amount of $125 per month.

During 1967, petitioner had gross receipts totaling $121,253.50, of which $55,037.61 was attributable to labor and $66,215.89 was attributable to the sale of materials. He paid wages of $38,674.63, realizing a gross profit from labor of $16,362.98. The cost of sales of materials amounted to $56,150.44, leaving a gross profit from this source of $10,065.45. His net profit from all sources was $8,775.07.

Respondent, in his notice of deficiency, allowed as an exclusion from taxable income, 30 percent of the income from the automobile body business, stating that petitioner was engaged in a trade or business in which both personal services and capital are material income-producing factors.

* * *

Respondent contends that petitioner's body shop business is one in which capital is a material income-producing factor, and that, therefore, petitioner's exclusion is limited to 30 percent of his net profits from the business. Petitioner argues that the income from his business is derived principally from labor, and that capital is not a material income-producing factor.

The issue as to whether a trade or business is one in which "both personal services and capital are material income-producing factors" has arisen under several statutes and in a variety of factual settings. * * * The question is fundamentally factual in nature. Capital is a material income-producing factor if a substantial portion of the gross income of the business is attributable to the employment of capital in the business conducted by the enterprise. Moreover, capital is ordinarily a material income-producing factor if the operation of the business requires substantial inventories or substantial investments in plant, machinery, or other equipment. On the other hand, capital is not a material income-producing factor where the gross income of the enterprise consists principally of fees, commissions, or other compensation for personal services. * * * If capital is "utilized merely to pay the cost of salaries, wages, office space, and general business expenses, it is not a material income-producing factor but is only incidental to the production of the income." * * *

Turning to the facts of the present case, even though substantial amounts of personal services are involved in petitioner's business, we think capital was a material income-producing factor. During 1967, his total charges for materials ($66,215.89) exceeded his total charges for labor ($55,037.61). Compared with gross income in the amount of $16,362.98 from labor charges, his gross income from the sale of materials and parts was $10,065.45, nearly 40 percent of the total. A substantial portion of petitioner's gross income was, therefore, derived from the sale of automobile parts. Petitioner's machinery and equipment had a book value of $4,023, and he carried an inventory of parts, which averaged about $2,500. While these amounts may appear to be small compared with the capital employed in many business endeavors, they must be related to petitioner's net operating profit from his business, the amount of only $8,775.07.

We note also that petitioner committed himself in April of 1967 to purchase the building used for his business at a cost of $38,000. While he made no downpayment on the building and his monthly payments approximated his prior rent, the record does not contain the details as to the other terms of the building purchase or the prior rental arrangements. We note that a valuable leasehold, as well as the ownership of the quarters used for a business, may constitute part of the capital employed in producing income. * * *

We recognize that no definite percentage ratio of gross income derived from capital sources to total income can be fixed at an exact point as a key to deciding when capital is a material income-producing factor. Moreover, the extent to which capital actually contributes materially to the production of income in a business like that of petitioner's is at best an approximation. * * * It is clear, however, that petitioner could not have produced his income without the capital needed for his garage space and his equipment. Nor could he have earned his income without parts needed for repair work. From the manner in which he conducted his business, we think it apparent that it basically involves merchandising as well as the performance of personal services. The capital employed by petitioner was not merely incidental to his personal services but contributed materially to the production of his income. We think his business was the kind of activity for which the * * * gross income exclusion was designed.

* * *

[¶ 5345]

NOTES

1. In Cook v. United States, 599 F.2d 400 (Ct.Cl.1979), the taxpayer was a bona fide foreign resident sculptor who produced his work in a studio in Rome. Profits from the sale of his commissioned and uncommissioned works were held to be earned income rather than income from the sale of personal property. However, the resulting exclusion applied to his gross (rather than net) income received from the sale of art.

2. Under Sections 861(a)(3) and 862(a)(3), the place where services are performed will determine whether the earned income is "foreign." The situs of the payor and the place of payment are irrelevant. See ¶ 2025. In Rev. Rul. 72–423, 1972–2 C.B. 446, the IRS ruled that the salary paid to an individual

for management services performed for his U.S. bank could be excluded under Section 911 because the services were conducted from abroad by mail and telephone.

3. Where a taxpayer eligible for the benefits of Section 911 works both within and without the United States, the income must be allocated between U.S. and foreign sources. In Rev. Rul. 77–167, 1977–1 C.B. 239, the IRS ruled that compensation paid to an airline pilot should be allocated according to the hours devoted to preflight and in-flight services actually performed within and without the United States even though the pilot's compensation was based only on actual flight time.

In Cini v. Commissioner, 67 T.C. 857 (1977), the U.S. citizen-taxpayer resided in France. He was employed as an executive to oversee the operations of several foreign subsidiaries of Johns–Manville Corp. The taxpayer often spent time in the United States in connection with his responsibilities. He was paid a salary plus a bonus based on the profitability of the foreign subsidiaries. The Tax Court held that his total compensation had to be allocated according to the time spent within and without the United States; the portion of the compensation allocable to U.S. sources did not qualify for the Section 911 exclusion. The bonus was not entirely foreign income simply because it was measured by the profits of foreign subsidiary corporations.

4. Amounts paid by the United States or a U.S. agency to an employee of the United States or a U.S. agency do not qualify for the Section 911 exclusion. § 911(b)(1)(B)(ii). Thus, for example, the Section 911 exclusion does not apply to the salaries of U.S. employees stationed at U.S. embassies abroad. The policy for this provision is to prevent U.S. government employees stationed abroad from obtaining a double benefit—exclusion from U.S. tax under Section 911 and exemption from foreign tax because of the practice followed by most countries of not taxing employees of another sovereign.

5. Section 911(b)(2)(A) and (D) limit the amount of the exclusion for foreign earned income in Section 911(a)(1) to a specified dollar amount ($80,000 for 2002 and later years, but adjusted for inflation for calendar years after 2005; as a result of inflation adjustments, the amount for 2011 is $92,900). This limit is designed to prevent abuse of the exclusion by highly paid entertainers, athletes, business executives or professionals who otherwise might move abroad to escape U.S. tax on their foreign earned income. See H.R. Rep. No. 201, 97th Cong., 1st Sess. 60 (1981).

The exclusion amount limit has to be prorated on a daily basis for a year in which the taxpayer meets the qualification requirements in Section 911(d)(1) (discussed below) for only part of the year. See Reg. § 1.911–3(d)(2). Thus, for example, if a taxpayer meets the qualification requirements in Section 911(d)(1) for the period from January 1 of 2002 through January 31 of 2005, the taxpayer has a full $80,000 limit for each of years 2002, 2003 and 2004 but a limit of only $6,792 (31/365 multiplied by $80,000) for 2005.

For purposes of applying the exclusion amount limit, foreign earned income is considered earned in the tax year in which the individual performed the services that gave rise to the income. Thus, if income is earned one year and received in another year, the income must be attributed to the year in which earned for purposes of applying the limit. See § 911(b)(2)(B); Reg. § 1.911–3(e)(1). This attribution rule, however, does not change the time for reporting the income as gross income to the extent that it does not qualify for the Section 911 exclusion (i.e., a cash method taxpayer will report the income in the tax year in which it is actually or constructively received).

6. Section 911(b)(1)(B)(iv) excludes from the definition of foreign earned income any income received after the close of the first tax year following the tax year in which the services were performed that gave rise to the income. Thus, for example, if a taxpayer who qualifies for the exclusion performs the services in 2009, but does not receive the income until 2011 or a later year, the income will not be a foreign earned income for Section 911 purposes. The reason is that Section 911 is intended to serve as an inducement for U.S. persons to work abroad and Congress saw no reason "to provide this special inducement long after the period in which the employment occurred." H.R. Rep. No. 1447, 87th Cong., 2d Sess. 55 (1962). Amounts received as a pension or annuity under a retirement plan are excluded from the definition of foreign earned income for essentially the same reason. § 911(b)(1)(B)(i) and (iii).

[¶ 5350]

4. AMOUNT OF EXCLUSION—HOUSING COSTS

In addition to the foreign earned income exclusion of Section 911(a)(1), Section 911(a)(2) allows exclusion of the "housing cost amount." Under current law, as amended in 2006, this is defined by Section 911(c)(1) to be reasonable foreign housing expenses in excess of a base housing subtraction amount equal to 16 percent of the exclusion amount (computed on a daily basis) in Section 911(b)(2)(D) ($80,000 for calendar years 2002 through 2005; $92,900 for calendar year 2011, as adjusted for inflation) multiplied by the number of the electing individual's number of days of bona fide foreign residence or physical presence in one or more foreign countries, as the case may be. (Under prior law, the base housing subtraction amount was 16 percent of the salary of U.S. government employees at the GS–14 (step 1) level.) Moreover, under current law, as also amended in 2006, the housing cost amount is subject to a limitation of 30 percent of the exclusion amount (computed on a daily basis) in Section 911(b)(2)(D). § 911(c)(2)(A). The Treasury and the IRS, however, are authorized to issue guidance that adjusts the 30–percent housing cost limitation based on geographic differences in housing costs relative to housing costs in the United States. § 911(c)(2)(B). (This 30–percent limitation is based on the U.S. Department of Housing and Urban Development's standard for what is considered maximum affordable housing.) Thus, for example, for years in which the Section 911(b)(2)(D) exclusion amount is $80,000, the base housing subtraction amount is $14,800 (i.e., $80,000 multiplied by 16 percent) and the 30–percent limitation on the housing cost amount is $24,000 (i.e., $80,000, multiplied by 30 percent), assuming foreign residence or days of physical presence by the electing individual on all days in the year. If an employer paid $40,000 for an electing employee's housing for such a year, the housing cost amount would be $25,200 (i.e., $40,000 minus $14,800), but, because of the 30–percent limitation, the maximum amount of the employee's housing expenses that could be excluded from gross income would be $24,000.

In some such cases, however, the employee will be able to exclude the entire $40,000. The payment of the $40,000 housing expense by the employer will itself be "foreign earned income" to the employee. See § 911(c)(4)(D). Accordingly, so long as the total of the employee's salary and housing expense allowance does not exceed the $80,000 maximum foreign earned income exclusion for 2005, for example, both can be totally excluded from gross income. The base housing subtraction amount and the 30-percent limitation on housing costs apply only when the maximum foreign earned income exclusion is exceeded and it becomes necessary to rely on the housing cost exclusion. The total amount of the two exclusions combined cannot exceed the total of the individual's foreign earned income for the year. § 911(d)(7).

When a taxpayer's foreign earned income is income from self-employment, the housing cost amount is allowed as a deduction. The deduction is calculated in the same manner as the exclusion in the case of an employee (Reg. § 1.911–4(e)) but cannot exceed a limit equal to the excess of the individual's earned income over the amount of the Section 911(a)(1) foreign earned income exclusion for the year. § 911(c)(4)(B). Section 911(c)(4)(C) provides that an amount not allowed as a deduction by reason of the limit can be carried over to the succeeding taxable year—a one-year carryover. If in that year it fits within the limit, it may then be allowed as a deduction. There is no comparable provision in Section 911 with regard to an exclusion of income.

From a tax policy standpoint, one interesting question is why there should be an exclusion for housing costs when one of the justifications for the basic $80,000 foreign earned income exclusion (for 2002 and later years, but adjusted for inflation for calendar years after 2005) is to compensate U.S. taxpayers living and working abroad for their increased living costs. Opponents of Section 911 might well argue that the exclusion for the housing cost amount duplicates the exclusion for foreign earned income in this respect and thereby undercuts the policy justifications for the $80,000 foreign earned income exclusion. Proponents of Section 911 would undoubtedly argue that the basic $80,000 foreign earned income exclusion is insufficient to fully compensate U.S. workers abroad for their increased living costs so that a housing cost exclusion is also necessary.

Another interesting policy question is why there should be an exclusion when such housing costs would not meet the criteria of Section 119, which defines the general exclusion for employer-provided housing. There are at least two possible responses. One response is that certain living costs for those working abroad should perhaps be characterized as particularly attributable to the foreign work so that the taxpayers are, in a very general sense, living on the business premises of the employer, living there for the convenience of the employer and required to live there as a condition of this particular employment (the criteria for excludible housing contained in Section 119). The other, more plausible, response is that Section 911 (including the exclusion for certain housing costs) is primarily a result of effective legislative representation by U.S. enterprises operating abroad and their employees. In other words, the exclusion of the housing cost amount is yet another tax subsidy granted to U.S. persons who work abroad (and their employers).

[¶ 5355]

5. WHO IS ELIGIBLE FOR THE EXCLUSION?

There are two alternative ways to qualify for the exclusion of Section 911. The exclusion applies to U.S. citizens who are "bona fide resident[s] of a foreign country or countries for an uninterrupted period which includes an entire taxable year." § 911(d)(1)(A). Under the regulations and case law (including the *Jones* case, set forth below), the test for determining bona fide residence under Section 911(d) is the facts-and-circumstances test under Section 871 that was formerly used (before the enactment of Section 7701(b) in 1984) for determining whether an alien was a resident of the United States for tax purposes. Reg. §§ 1.871–2(b), (c) and –5. Thus, the "objective" tests in Section 7701(b) used under current law to determine whether an alien is a U.S. resident do not apply for this purpose. Reg. §§ 1.911–2(c) and 301.7701(b)–1(a). While the requisites of bona fide residency status are not prescribed in the Code, any taxpayer who submits to a taxing authority of a foreign country a statement that he or she is not a resident and is as a result exempt from its tax will not qualify. § 911(d)(5). This provision is aimed at preventing a taxpayer from taking inconsistent positions concerning his or her foreign residence with the U.S. and foreign taxing authorities.

The exclusions of Section 911 also apply to U.S. citizens and resident aliens who are present in a foreign country or countries during at least 330 full days in any period of 12 consecutive months. § 911(d)(1)(B). No day in which any part is spent in the United States (for whatever reason) can contribute to the 330 days required by the test. But, a day spent in any foreign country or no country (perhaps at sea) will count towards the 330–day target.

In either instance, the taxpayer must have a "tax home" in a foreign country. § 911(d)(1). A tax home is defined by Section 911(d)(3) to be the place from which traveling expenses are deductible under Section 162(a)(2), provided that the taxpayer's abode is not in the United States.

In the following case, the court considers whether the taxpayer qualifies for the Section 911 exclusion by reason of the bona fide residence test. The court also considers whether the taxpayer's tax home is in a foreign country and whether the taxpayer's abode is in the United States.

[¶ 5360]

JONES v. COMMISSIONER

United States Court of Appeals, Fifth Circuit, 1991.
927 F.2d 849.

GOLDBERG, CIRCUIT JUDGE:

* * *

I. FACTS AND PROCEEDINGS BELOW

When George H. Jones ("Jones") retired from the air force in 1970, he entered into an employment agreement with International Air Service Company, Ltd. ("IASCO"), a California corporation in the business of furnishing flight crew personnel to aircraft operators. Pursuant to a contract between IASCO and Japanese Air Lines Co., Ltd. ("JAL"), Jones was assigned exclusively to JAL, flying out of Tokyo, Japan. While in Japan on this initial assignment, Taxpayers and their four children resided in a rented house in Japan.

Jones served with JAL, based in Tokyo, from 1971 through March 1972. On March 31, 1972, JAL furloughed Jones. Jones moved his family and belongings back to San Antonio, Texas, so he could attempt to obtain interim employment. On January 1, 1973, JAL recalled Jones to active duty and reassigned him to JAL's Tokyo base. Although he then moved back to Tokyo, his wife remained in San Antonio so that their son could graduate from high school, after which time Mrs. Jones and their youngest daughter anticipated joining Jones in Tokyo. During both his first and second assignment in Tokyo, Jones' flights consisted of routes within Japan and between Japan and Asia.

In March 1974 JAL reassigned Jones to Anchorage, Alaska, its only base located in the United States. Therefore, after Taxpayers' son graduated from high school in San Antonio, Mrs. Jones and Taxpayers' youngest daughter also moved to Anchorage. Taxpayers' youngest daughter only lived in Anchorage until she left for college. After moving to Anchorage, Mrs. Jones began a career for the first time. She eventually went to work for a newly-formed bank and worked directly for the chairman of the bank.

On March 3, 1980, and continuing through the years in issue, JAL transferred Jones back to Tokyo. Although Mrs. Jones had the opportunity to move to Tokyo as well, she decided to remain in Anchorage and pursue her own career until Jones' expected retirement in 1988. She continued to occupy the townhome that Taxpayers' jointly owned in Anchorage. Taxpayers filed joint United States income tax returns for the years in question, 1981, 1982, and 1983.

When he moved back to Tokyo, Jones moved into the Hotel Nikko Narita (the "Hotel"), where he stayed until his retirement in 1988. Jones apparently elected to stay at the Hotel instead of renting an apartment or a house for reasons of convenience, economy, and the society of other JAL crewmembers who also lived in the Hotel. He checked into and out of the Hotel in accordance with his schedule, and left his personal belongings in storage at the Hotel when he was away.

Although Taxpayers tried to see each other as frequently as possible, Jones was only able to fly on JAL with discount tickets for approved vacation periods. Unlike many domestic air carriers, JAL did not allow its flight crew members the privilege of flying free anytime a seat was available. This same policy applied to Mrs. Jones.

Although Jones did not own an automobile in Japan during the years in issue, he had renewed his Japanese driver's license so that he could occasionally borrow a car or rent a car when his family came to visit him. Jones also maintained his Alaska driver's license and two cars in the United States were co-titled in his name. Although he did not maintain a bank account in Japan and held no Japanese-based credit cards, he did maintain joint bank accounts with his wife in Alaska and San Antonio, and held U.S.-based credit cards. During the years in question, Jones was registered to vote in Alaska and voted absentee in United States elections.

Jones held a commercial multi-entry visa, renewable every four years, which allowed him to stay in Japan a maximum of three years per entry. The only limitation was a requirement that he leave Japan at least once every three years. Since his profession dictated frequent trips outside Japan, this was not a problem for Jones.

Jones paid both Japanese and United States income taxes for the years at issue. Jones' Japanese income tax returns were prepared at his expense by a Japanese accountant in Japan. After moving to Japan, Jones received a dividend check, representing a 1981 payment under the Alaska Permanent Fund Distribution Program. Because entitlement was based on Alaskan residence, Jones returned the check, explaining that he was no longer an Alaska resident.

During the years in issue, JAL assigned Jones to flights which were either intercontinental between Japan and the United States, or intracontinental segments of such international flights within Japan and the United States. Jones had no control over which flights he was scheduled to fly. During the relevant period, Jones spent less than 165 nights a year in Japan. Since Anchorage was JAL's only U.S. base, and one of the normal stopover cities on Japan/U.S. routes, Jones' job required that he be in

Anchorage frequently. When overnight in Anchorage, Jones stayed in the townhouse co-owned by Taxpayers.

During the years in issue, Jones did not have extensive contact with Japanese culture. He did visit a local Japanese doctor for medical attention and he participated in certain recreational activities, including jogging and playing golf. Jones socialized with co-workers also living at the Hotel and occasionally drove into Tokyo for dinner and entertainment.

On Taxpayers' joint 1981 federal income tax return, they claimed a deduction of $5,590 under [former] Section 913 * * *. On their 1982 and 1983 joint returns, Taxpayers claimed exclusions of $76,050 and $81,272, respectively, under Section 911 * * *. The Commissioner issued a statutory notice of deficiency determining deficiencies in each year resulting from, among other items, the disallowance of taxpayer's Section 913 deduction in 1981, and their Section 911 exclusions in 1982 and 1983. The Taxpayers timely filed a petition with the tax court for a redetermination of these deficiencies. The tax court held that Jones was not a bona fide resident of Japan during the applicable period and therefore was not entitled to section 913 deductions and section 911 exclusions. Jones now appeals this decision.

II. DISCUSSION

The Tax Court's conclusion regarding Jones' residency is a conclusion of law or at least a determination of a mixed question of law and fact. As such, it is reviewable de novo and this court may freely substitute its judgment for that of the tax court. * * *

The only issue this court must address is whether Jones was a "qualified individual" within the meaning of sections 913 and 911 * * *. To be entitled to the deduction available under Code Section 913[2] for certain expenses while living abroad, and the exclusion available under Code Section 911[3] of foreign earned income, a taxpayer had to have a tax home in a foreign country and demonstrate (1) that he had either been a "bona fide resident" of a foreign country for an uninterrupted period including an entire taxable year (the "bona fide residency test"), or (2)

2. Section 913 * * *, as in effect in 1981, permitted a deduction for certain expenses incurred by a taxpayer living abroad. Section 913 allowed the taxpayer to deduct a cost-of-living differential, hardship area deduction, and housing, schooling, and home leave travel expenses. § 913(b). This deduction could not, however, exceed taxpayer's net foreign source earned income while his tax home was in a foreign country. § 913(c).

3. As part of the Economic Recovery Tax Act of 1981, Congress repealed Code Section 913 for tax years after 1981 and replaced it with a revised section 911. * * * Congress completely revised section 911 for tax years after 1981, replacing the existing system of a deduction for excess living costs with an exclusion for foreign earned income and providing for an individual's election to exclude a portion of his income and his housing costs. § 911(a). It allows a "qualified individual" living abroad to exclude foreign earned income from gross income of up to $75,000 in 1982 and $80,000 in 1983. § 911(a)(1). [The Tax Reform Act of 1986 reduced the cap on the exclusion to $70,000 and the Taxpayer Relief Act of 1997 increased the cap over a period of years to reach $80,000 for 2002 and later years. The $80,000 exclusion amount is adjusted for inflation for calendar years after 2005.]

that he had been physically present in a foreign country for a certain period of time (the "physical presence test"). *See* §§ 913(a)(1) and 911(d)(1)(A); 26 C.F.R. §§ 1.913–1, 1.911–2(a); *see also Lemay v. Commissioner*, 837 F.2d 681, 682 (5th Cir.1988). Jones concedes that he does not meet the "physical presence test." Therefore, Jones must show that his tax home was in Japan and that he was a bona fide resident of Japan during the applicable period.

Since the tax court below only addressed the issue of whether Jones was a bona fide resident of Japan, we will begin our discussion with that inquiry. Neither section 913 nor section 911 defines the term "bona fide resident." Residence is an elusive expression peculiarly related to the facts in any given case. * * * As the Ninth Circuit succinctly stated, "residence . . . has an evasive way about it, with as many colors as Joseph's coat." *Weible v. United States*, 244 F.2d 158, 163 (9th Cir.1957). This court must determine residence in light of congressional intent, which was to encourage foreign trade by encouraging foreign employment for citizens of the United States, and to place them in an equal position with citizens of other countries going abroad who are not taxed by their own countries. * * *

For purposes of sections 913 and 911, the test of a taxpayer's bona fide residence in a foreign country is the test of alien residence established in Code Section 871. *Richard v. Commissioner*, 55 T.C.M. (CCH) 864 (1988); *see also* [Reg.] §§ 1.913–2(b), 1.911–2(c). Treasury Regulation Section 1.871–2(b) provides in pertinent part that:

> An alien actually present in the United States who is not a mere transient or sojourner is a resident of the United States for purposes of the income tax. . . . One who comes to the United States for a definite purpose which in its nature may be promptly accomplished is a transient; but, if his purpose is of such a nature that an extended stay may be necessary for its accomplishment, and to that end the alien makes his home temporarily in the United States, he becomes a resident, though it may be his intention at all times to return to his domicile abroad when the purpose for which he came has been consummated or abandoned.

* * * Residence is therefore much less than domicile which requires an intent to make a fixed and permanent home. *Dawson v. Commissioner*, 59 T.C. 264, 270 (1972) ("it is possible to be a bona fide resident of one country while retaining one's domicile in another").

When determining whether a taxpayer was a bona fide resident of a foreign country, courts consider a number of objective factors, first enunciated in *Sochurek v. Commissioner*, 300 F.2d 34 (7th Cir.1962). These factors include:

(1) intention of the taxpayer;

(2) establishment of his home temporarily in the foreign country for an indefinite period;

(3) participation in the activities of his chosen community on social and cultural levels, identification with the daily lives of the people and, in general, assimilation into the foreign environment;

(4) physical presence in the foreign country consistent with his employment;

(5) nature and duration of his employment; whether his assignment abroad could be promptly accomplished within a definite or specified time;

(6) assumption of economic burdens and payment of taxes to the foreign country;

(7) status of resident contrasted to that of transient or sojourner;

(8) treatment accorded his income tax status by his employer;

(9) marital status and residence of his family;

(10) nature and duration of his employment; whether his assignment abroad could be promptly accomplished within a definite or specified time;

(11) good faith in making his trip abroad; whether for purpose of tax evasion.

Sochurek, 300 F.2d at 38. While all these factors may not be present in every situation, those appropriate should be properly considered and weighed. *Id.* A taxpayer must offer "strong proof" of bona fide residence in a foreign country to qualify for the foreign earned income exclusion under section 911. *Schoneberger v. Commissioner*, 74 T.C. 1016, 1024 (1980).

In upholding the Commissioner's assessment, the tax court seemed to place particular emphasis on the fact [that] Jones chose to live in the Hotel, rather than renting an apartment or a home in Japan, and the fact that Jones' wife chose to live in Anchorage, rather than give up her job and move to Japan with her husband. The tax court also noted that Jones had a number of ties to the United States, while he remained relatively unassimilated into the Japanese community. The tax court's analysis, however, overlooks the other *Sochurek* factors.

First, the tax court failed to consider Jones['] intent. Jones obviously intended to become a resident of Japan and therefore he accordingly returned to the State of Alaska a dividend check which was based on Alaskan residence. A taxpayer's intent plays perhaps the most important part in determining the establishment and maintenance of a foreign residence. *Dawson*, 59 T.C. at 268.

Jones established his home in Japan, presumably for the remainder of his career. Jones' job as a pilot was ongoing and both JAL and Jones intended Jones to live and work in Japan until his retirement. Therefore, Jones['] purpose for being in Japan was of such a nature that an extended stay was necessary. Due to his flight schedule, JAL required his physical presence in Japan and such presence was consistent with his employment.

In addition, Jones argues that he should not be penalized because the economic realities of Japan lead him to choose to live in the Hotel, instead of renting an apartment or buying a home. The Commissioner and the tax court seemed bothered by the apparent temporary nature of a hotel, but it is not necessary for a taxpayer to establish a fixed, permanent place of abode in order to be a "resident" of a foreign country. * * *

Furthermore, Jones was apparently only away from his home in Japan when his business required it, or when he was on vacation. The fact that Jones was able to stay at his home in Anchorage during flights was merely fortuitous and should not be held against Jones. If JAL had not previously based Jones in Anchorage, Taxpayers would not have owned property there. In addition, if JAL had scheduled Jones to fly only Asian trips, as he had done when he was previously assigned to Japan, Jones would not have had occasion to layover in Anchorage. Nevertheless, business and vacation trips to the United States should not affect Jones['] residency. *See, e.g., Schoneberger v. Commissioner*, 74 T.C. 1016, 1025 (1980) (taxpayer's employment as a pilot flying international flights "required that, wherever his residence was, he would spend substantial amounts of time away from it"); *Weible v. United States*, 244 F.2d 158, 166–67 (9th Cir.1957) (frequent trips to the United States did not affect taxpayer's status as a foreign resident where on each visit it was his intention to return to Spain).

Jones paid resident Japanese income taxes. Jones' Japanese income tax returns were prepared at his expense by a Japanese accountant. Both JAL and IASCO viewed Jones as a resident of Japan for Japanese income tax purposes. In fact, JAL required IASCO to withhold Japanese income taxes from Jones' payroll checks. The last *Sochurek* factor also arguably supports Jones' claim to bona fide residency because the Commissioner has never suggested that Jones took the job in Japan for the purposes of tax evasion. * * *

Both in his briefs and during oral argument, the Commissioner seemed to rely heavily on the fact that Jones' wife did not move to Japan during his last assignment to Tokyo. The Commissioner seems to argue that Taxpayers should be punished because Mrs. Jones chose to stay in Anchorage and pursue a career, rather than move to Japan with her husband. When JAL reassigned Jones to Japan in 1980, Taxpayers' children were all away at school or married. For the first time in a number of years, Mrs. Jones was free to devote herself to a career. She would most likely not have been able to find comparable employment if she had joined her husband in Japan.

We are besieged with cases and statistics and erudite writing about the necessity for the equalization of rights and opportunities for men and women in our society. It would be strange indeed if the Congress of the United States which has legislated frequently and ardently for the equality of the sexes, should in the field of taxation find that a woman who desires to establish herself in the field of business, and her husband who obviously encouraged her, should be penalized because she is pursuing something which the Congress thinks is in the interest of our nation and its economy. Penalizing Taxpayers for Mrs. Jones' decision in no way furthers the clearly enunciated legislative purpose behind sections 913 and 911 of encouraging foreign employment of United States' citizens.

Although Jones' admittedly did not learn to speak Japanese and was relatively unassimilated into the Japanese culture, the majority of *Sochurek* factors support Jones' contention that he was a bona fide resident of Japan during the relevant period. Jones was not a mere transient or sojourner in Japan. Even though he intended to eventually return to his domicile in the United States after he retired from JAL, his purpose for being in Japan required him to remain there for at least eight years. Although Jones may have felt a little like a sojourner in a foreign land, as Moses did after he left Egypt and fled to Midian,[4] under the applicable modern day tax statutes we are required to classify him as a bona fide resident of Japan, and not a mere transient or sojourner.

Sections 913 and 911 speak to the modern age; neither were quilled in antiquity. Today, husbands and wives, men and women, have the right to separate careers. With respect to Jones' tax residence, he was neither a domiciliary nor a transient. He was a resident of Japan. The Code clearly could have used the word domicile or transient; neither of these are strange to our congressional enactments and legislation. Instead, the Code speaks in terms of residence. Since we find that Jones was a bona fide resident of Japan during the relevant time period, we reverse the tax court.

TAX HOME

Because the tax court determined that Jones was not a bona fide resident of Japan, it did not reach the question of whether Jones' tax home was in Japan. As we stated earlier, however, in order to qualify for the tax benefits available pursuant to sections 913 and 911, the taxpayer must prove both that he was a bona fide resident of a foreign country and that his tax home was in a foreign country. The term "tax home" was defined in Code Section 913(j)(1)(B) for Taxpayers' 1981 tax year and in Code Section 911(d)(3) for Taxpayers' 1982 and 1983 tax years. Both of these sections defined "tax home" as follows:

> The term "tax home" means, with respect to any individual, such individual's home for purposes of § 162(a)(2) (relating to traveling

4. 4 Exodus 2:22.

> expenses while away from home). An individual shall not be treated as having a tax home in a foreign country for any period for which his abode is within the United States.

* * * Treasury Regulation Section 1.911–2(b) sets forth the general rule that a taxpayer's tax home is at his principal place of business or employment. However, both sections 913 and 911, and the regulations promulgated pursuant to them, provide the overriding exception that if an individual's *abode* is in the United States, then he is legally incapable of establishing that his tax home is in a foreign country. *See Lemay v. Commissioner*, 837 F.2d 681, 683 (5th Cir.1988).

The term "abode" was not defined by the 1978 Foreign Earned Income Act which added the abode limitation. * * * According to the Taxpayers, the only indication of legislative intent is found in a House Ways and Means Committee report:

> [A] taxpayer is ineligible for the deduction for excess foreign living costs for any period for which his abode is in the United States. For example, a taxpayer who lives in Detroit, Michigan, but commutes daily to work in Windsor, Ontario, would ordinarily have his tax home in Windsor, but nevertheless would be ineligible for the deduction for excess foreign living costs.

H.R. Rep. No. 1463, 95th Cong., 2d Sess. 10 (1978) * * *. This excerpt seems to indicate that the Congressional purpose in adding the abode limitation was to make these tax benefits available only to those individuals who actually incurred increased living expenses while living abroad. * * *

Recently the tax court has had an opportunity to discuss the abode limitation, and this court has affirmed at least two of these opinions. *See Lemay v. Commissioner*, 53 T.C.M. (CCH) 862 (1987), aff'd, 837 F.2d 681 (5th Cir.1988); *Bujol v. Commissioner*, 53 T.C.M. (CCH) 762 (1987), *aff'd without published opinion*, 842 F.2d 328 (5th Cir.1988). In these cases, this court has adopted the following definition of abode:

> "Abode" has been variously defined as one's home, habitation, residence, domicile, or place of dwelling. Black's Law Dictionary 7 (5th ed. 1979). While an exact definition of "abode" depends upon the context in which the word is used, it clearly does not mean one's principal place of business. Thus, "abode" has a domestic rather than a vocational meaning, and stands in contrast to "tax home"....

Lemay, 837 F.2d at 683. In both *Lemay* and *Bujol*, this court denied the taxpayer the tax benefits found in sections 913 and 911, finding that their abode remained in the United States. Both of these cases involved taxpayers who worked in the oil industry and worked primarily on offshore oil rigs. In both instances, the taxpayer/employee commuted to and from the foreign jurisdiction for a brief and fixed period of time, typically twenty-eight days at work and twenty-eight days off. The taxpayer's family did not accompany them due to the living conditions. Further, the taxpayer's commuting and living expenses while abroad were paid for by the employers.

In denying benefits, this court analyzed the taxpayer's familial, economic and personal ties to the foreign workplace and compared these with the taxpayer's ties to his home in the United States. *Lemay*, 837 F.2d at 684; *Bujol*, 53 T.C.M. (CCH) at 764. This court, and the tax court below, focused on the regularity with which the taxpayer returned to his home in the United States and to the minimal contact the taxpayer had with the culture and society of the foreign country in which they worked. *Id.*

The facts in this case can easily be distinguished from oil rig and compound worker cases, such as *Lemay* and *Bujol*. In those cases, when the taxpayers were on duty on oil rigs or in the oil field compounds, they slept in employer-provided housing, ate employer-provided meals and returned home to the United States after each work period on employer-provided flights. In addition, the taxpayer's family was not allowed to join him abroad. These taxpayers were not incurring any costs associated with living abroad; rather, they were essentially commuting on a regular basis from their homes in the United States.

In contrast, Jones had to pay for his vacation travel to the United States. Jones also paid for his meals and his housing while abroad. Jones also incurred the additional cost of paying Japanese income taxes. In addition, Mrs. Jones had the opportunity to move to Japan if she had so desired, but she elected to keep her job in Anchorage for her own personal reasons. Therefore, Jones' abode was in Japan and not in the United States, and his tax home was also in Japan during the relevant period.

III. CONCLUSION

We are compelled to conclude that the tax court erred as a matter of law. Taxpayers have established that Jones was a bona-fide foreign resident of Japan and had his tax home in Japan during the years in question. Therefore, the tax court decision is REVERSED and REMANDED with direction to the tax court to expunge the deficiency assessed and enter judgment for the Taxpayers.

[¶ 5365]

NOTES

1. Courts have held that to be a bona fide resident, rather than merely a transient or sojourner, in a foreign country, the taxpayer's intent to stay in the foreign country must either be indefinite or in connection with the performance of a project requiring an extended stay. Thus, a taxpayer who moves abroad for a specific purpose that involves a short, fixed period of time will probably fail the bona fide residence test. See, e.g., Jones v. Kyle, 190 F.2d 353 (10th Cir.), cert. denied, 342 U.S. 886 (1951); Ferrer v. Commissioner, 50 T.C. 177 (1968), aff'd per curiam, 409 F.2d 1359 (2d Cir.1969).

2. The *Jones* court minimizes the importance of the taxpayer's failure to become assimilated into the Japanese culture, treating that fact as merely one equal factor in determining whether the taxpayer is a bona fide resident of Japan under the multi-factor *Sochurek* test. By contrast, the IRS and some other courts have placed greater emphasis on this factor in determining whether the bona fide residence test has been met. See, e.g., Schoneberger v. Commissioner, 74 T.C. 1016 (1980). Which approach better effectuates the legislative policies underlying Section 911?

3. Under the terms of Section 911(d)(1), a U.S. citizen may qualify for the Section 911 exclusions by meeting either the bona fide residence test or the physical presence test, while resident aliens may only qualify by meeting the physical presence test. However, in Rev. Rul. 91–58, 1991–2 C.B. 340, the IRS ruled that under the nondiscrimination article of U.S. income tax treaties (applied without regard to the saving clause), resident aliens who are nationals of foreign countries with which the United States has entered into an income tax treaty may qualify for Section 911 by meeting either the physical presence test or the bona fide residence test. Note that, under current law, it is possible for an alien to be a U.S. resident under one of the "objective" tests in Section 7701(b), but still qualify as a bona fide resident of a foreign country under the facts-and-circumstances test used in determining residence under Section 911.

4. Under certain conditions, Section 911(d)(4) waives the eligibility requirements of Section 911(d)(1) for an individual who was a bona fide resident or was physically present in a foreign country but left that country during a period for which the Treasury Secretary (in consultation with the Secretary of State) determines that individuals had to leave because of war, civil unrest or other similar conditions. To qualify for this special relief provision, the individual must have established residency or been physically present in the foreign country on or before the date that the individual was required to leave the country and must show that but for the adverse conditions the individual could reasonably have been expected to meet the eligibility requirements. Congress enacted this provision in 1980 to help taxpayers residing in Iran who suddenly and unexpectedly had to leave that country in 1978 by reason of the fall of the government of the Shah of Iran.

5. Under Section 911(d)(8), an individual who is present in a country with respect to which travel restrictions are in effect will not qualify under Section 911 with respect to such country if the individual's travel is in violation of law. As of October 1, 2005, the only country currently subject to Section 911(d)(8) was Cuba. See Rev. Rul. 2005–3, 2005–1 C.B. 334. This provision attempts to coordinate tax policy and foreign relations and defense policy by imposing a tax penalty on travel in violation of the travel restrictions. Is this an appropriate use of the federal tax system?

[¶ 5370]

6. COST OF THE EXCLUSION ELECTIONS AND NEW STACKING RULE IN SECTION 911(f)

Section 911(d)(6) disallows any exclusion, deduction or credit that is allocable to income excluded under Section 911(a). The purpose of this disallowance rule is to prevent taxpayers from obtaining a double tax benefit—tax-free income under Section 911 and an exclusion, deduction or credit for amounts allocable to such income. The most important effect of this provision is to disallow any foreign tax credit for foreign taxes allocable to amounts excluded by Section 911. The taxpayer must, therefore, compare the relative advantages of the exclusion and the foreign tax credit discussed earlier in this Chapter. This provision also prevents, for example, a taxpayer from deducting business expenses under Section 162 or moving expenses under Section 217 to the extent those expenses are allocable to foreign earned income excluded under Section 911. Reg. § 1.911–6 contains rules for allocating the taxpayer's deductible expenses and foreign taxes to determine how much of the taxpayer's deductions and credits are disallowed by Section 911(d)(6).

Under a new "stacking" rule in Section 911(f), enacted in 2006, if an individual elects the Section 911 exclusion, any taxable income in excess of the amount excluded under Section 911 is taxed, for both regular tax and alternative minimum tax purposes, by applying the marginal tax rates that would have applied if the individual had not made the Section 911 exclusion election. For example, an individual with $80,000 of foreign earned income that is excluded under Section 911 and $70,000 of other taxable income, will be subject to income tax at the rate or rates in Section 1 (as adjusted for inflation) that apply to taxable income in the range of $80,000 to $150,000, not at the rate or rates that apply to taxable income of $70,000.

[¶ 5375]

PROBLEMS

1. Clemens is a middle-level executive of the National Shipping Company ("Company"). He has been working at the corporate headquarters in New York City for ten years. During that period, he has often been required to travel to Europe to deal with agents and customers of the Company. The Company has decided to send Clemens to London to open an office. Clemens, a U.S. citizen, is delighted about the prospects of living and working abroad, but he is concerned about the tax consequences.

At the present time, Clemens is receiving a salary of $85,000 per year. However, he also receives a bonus based upon the Company's performance, which has ranged between $5,000 and $25,000 during the past few years. The Company has agreed to increase Clemens' salary to $90,000, continue his entitlement to the annual bonus and pay $20,000 per year for his "overseas living expenses." Clemens expects this amount to just cover his rent for a fashionable Georgian home in London.

Clemens is being assigned to England for an indefinite period. The length of his stay will depend upon the success of his branch operation and Clemens' reaction to living abroad. He has been advised by United Kingdom counsel not to become a resident of the United Kingdom for tax purposes. If he remains in a visitor's status, he will be taxable in the United Kingdom only with respect to the salary that he actually receives in England. Clemens estimates that he will need to bring about $30,000 each year into England to cover his personal expenses. This amount (and only this amount) will be subject to a U.K. income tax of about 40 percent.

Clemens will be required to travel outside of the United Kingdom in various European countries about 60 days each year. He also will be required to return to New York City periodically to meet with other Company officials.

Assume that the exclusion amount is $80,000.

a. Advise Clemens with respect to the tax consequences of his transfer to London.

b. How would your answer differ if Clemens were employed by a U.K. corporation?

c. How would your answer differ if a portion of Clemens' compensation package was paid in shares of the Company's stock?

2. Jennifer, a U.S. citizen and a cash method, calendar year taxpayer, is an attorney who specializes in international business transactions. She works as a senior associate for a Miami law firm. She took a leave of absence from the law firm and moved to Paris to get a broader exposure to sophisticated international business transactions and because she thought it would be an interesting experience. While in France, she engaged in legal work as an independent contractor, but continued to do some work for the Miami law firm.

When Jennifer first moved to Paris (on October 1 of year 1), she went there with the idea that she would return to the United States sometime within the next two or three years, but with no definite plan to return at any particular time. From October 1 of year 1 through March 31 of year 3, Jennifer lived in a house in Paris that she rented on a month-to-month basis pursuant to a written lease. She retained her voting registration, car registration and driver's license in Florida. She opened several bank accounts in France, although the bulk of her investment assets remained in the United States. She obtained an international driver's license. Her fiance, Matthew, also a U.S. citizen, remained in the United States where he worked as a business executive. She had many friends in Paris and had an aunt, uncle and three cousins who lived in France, but all of Jennifer's remaining relatives (including her parents and siblings) remained in the United States. She kept most of her own furniture in storage in Miami (using rental furniture in her Paris home) and rented out her Miami home to various tenants during her stay in France. She paid income taxes to France on her French earnings but her French income tax liability was quite small.

During her stay in France she returned to the United States four times: November 14 through November 23 of year 1, to work on several matters for the Miami law firm; February 2 through February 5 of year 2, to attend business meetings relating to legal matters that she was handling for her French clients; July 1 through July 26 of year 2, to visit family and friends; and December 22 through December 29 of year 2, for a personal skiing vacation in Colorado. Jennifer permanently moved back to the United States on April 1 of year 3.

During year 2, Jennifer received compensation for her legal services in the amount of $140,000. $20,000 related to legal services performed by Jennifer in the United States in year 2 for clients of the Miami law firm. $10,000 related to legal services performed by Jennifer in France in year 1 for U.S. clients of the Miami law firm but for which payment was not received by Jennifer until year 2. $25,000 related to work performed in the United States in year 2 for her own French clients. $85,000 related to legal services performed by Jennifer in France in year 2 (of which $20,000 represented payment to Jennifer for legal work performed in France for U.S. clients of the Miami law firm). In year 2, Jennifer paid $24,000 for her housing costs in Paris.

a. Is Jennifer eligible to elect the exclusions in Section 911 for year 1, year 2 and year 3?

b. Assuming for purposes of this part of Problem 2 that Jennifer is eligible to elect the exclusions and the exclusion amount is $80,000, how much may Jennifer elect to exclude under Section 911 for year 2?

3. Fred Jones wrote a book during year 1 and year 2 while he was a bona fide resident of Brazil. Assume that he rendered half of the services in writing the book in year 1 and the other half of the services in year 2. He receives a lump-sum payment of $200,000 from his publisher in year 2. He owns his own home in Brazil and has annual housing expenses of $15,000. Assume that the exclusion amount is $80,000. How much of the $200,000 could he elect to exclude? Would the result be different if the $200,000 were received in year 3?

4. Mary Smith is a U.S. citizen who is a bona fide resident of, and whose tax home is located in, Brazil for the entire taxable year. All of her income described below is from Brazilian sources. Study carefully Reg. §§ 1.911–3 and –4, including the examples. How much may Mary elect to exclude under Section 911 on the assumptions that she performs no services in the United States, the exclusion amount is $80,000 and on the following further alternative assumptions?

a. She is an employee and receives for the year a salary of $65,000 as well as housing furnished by her employer having an annual rental value of $13,000.

b. She is an employee who receives a salary of $75,000, is furnished housing by her employer worth $15,000 and pays housing expenses of $8,000.

c. She is self-employed in a business in which capital is *not* a material income-producing factor. She earns a profit of $90,000 and pays $23,000 for her own housing.

d. In the following year, after the facts in Problem 4.c. have taken place, she continues to be self-employed in the same business, receives compensation of $120,000 and pays $21,000 for her housing.

e. She is self-employed in a business in which capital is a material income-producing factor. She earns a profit of $90,000 and pays $18,000 for her own housing.

f. She is an employee, receives a salary of $135,000 and is furnished housing by her employer worth $25,000.

g. She is an employee, receives a salary of $90,000 and is furnished housing by her employer worth $70,000.

[¶ 5380]

K. THE ROLE OF TAX TREATIES IN MITIGATING THE DOUBLE TAXATION OF U.S. PERSONS

As discussed in the prior chapters, the primary purpose of U.S. tax treaties is to provide relief from the double taxation of income earned in international transactions. The effect of the treaty provisions is to obtain the reciprocal commitment of each of the treaty partners to mitigate double taxation by reducing or eliminating the tax on income realized by a resident (which may include a citizen and domestic corporation) of the other treaty partner.

As discussed at ¶ 1270, as a result of the saving clause that is found in all modern U.S. tax treaties, the United States reserves the right to tax its citizens, residents and domestic corporations as if the treaty did not exist. Accordingly, the principal significance of the treaties for the U.S. citizen, resident alien or corporation is not that they reduce U.S. taxes, but rather that they reduce or eliminate the foreign taxes on various types of income (including, for example, interest, royalties, dividends and income from certain sales operations not attributable to a permanent establishment) from sources within the other country. These reductions are of great importance to many U.S. corporations that are in an excess foreign tax credit position because certain foreign-source income that bears a reduced level of foreign tax or no foreign tax under a tax treaty enables the U.S. corporation to absorb excess foreign tax credits otherwise generated by high-taxed foreign income.

A saving clause typically excepts a number of treaty provisions from its application. See, e.g., U.S. Model Treaty, Art. 1(5). Thus, a U.S. tax treaty may reduce the U.S. tax liability of a U.S. person in the following ways:

(1) ***Relief from double taxation article.*** A U.S. tax treaty typically contains a relief from double taxation article in which the United States agrees to allow its residents and citizens a foreign tax credit for income taxes paid to the treaty country. In this treaty article, the United States also typically agrees to allow a U.S. company, which owns at least ten percent of the voting stock of a foreign company resident in the treaty country and receives dividends from that company, a foreign tax credit for treaty country income taxes paid by the foreign company with respect to profits out of which the dividends are paid. Article 23 of the U.S. Model Treaty states that these treaty credits are allowed in accordance with the provisions and limitations of U.S. law, thus incorporating the source rules, foreign tax credit limitations and other provisions of U.S. tax law.

Those provisions and limitations, however, may be modified in certain ways specified in the treaty. Thus, a U.S. tax treaty may allow a foreign tax credit for taxes of the treaty partner that would not otherwise meet the standards for creditability under the Code and regulations. Furthermore, a treaty may provide source rules more favorable than the Code rules, which apply for purposes of calculating the foreign tax credit limitations with respect to taxes imposed by the treaty country. As more fully explained at ¶ 7042, however, in 2010, Congress enacted Section 904(d)(6), which applies a separate foreign tax credit limitation to each income item of a U.S. taxpayer that is treated as U.S.-source income under U.S. tax law without regard to a U.S. tax treaty but as foreign-source income under a U.S. tax treaty if the taxpayer chooses the benefits of the treaty.

(2) ***Nondiscrimination article.*** Notwithstanding the saving clause, a resident alien may use the nondiscrimination article in a tax treaty to attack U.S. tax law provisions that discriminate on the basis of citizenship (as discussed below in the Note after the *Filler* case at ¶ 5390).

(3) ***Associated enterprises article.*** A U.S. person may be able to use the treaty provision dealing with associated enterprises to require the United States to make a correlative reduction in a U.S. person's U.S. tax liability to reflect a transfer pricing adjustment made by the foreign treaty partner (see Chapter 8).

(4) ***Definitions and procedural rules.*** Treaties typically contain various special definitions and procedural rules, including the competent authority procedures, which U.S. persons may use for certain U.S. tax purposes.

(5) ***Other provisions.*** There are a few other treaty provisions that may be excepted from the saving clause, such as those relating to

social security and private pensions, which allow U.S. persons to reduce their U.S. taxes under specially defined circumstances.

See Federal Income Tax Project—International Aspects of United States Income Taxation II—Proposals on United States Income Tax Treaties 230–31 (A.L.I. 1992); J. Kuntz & R. Peroni, U.S. International Taxation ¶¶ 4.22, 4.04[2] (1992).

In the following case, a U.S. citizen residing and working in France is facing a double tax on some of his service income because both the United States and France seek to tax the income. The United States and France had entered into a tax treaty in which both agreed to mitigate double taxation by some appropriate mechanism and which applied to the case. But, to obtain such relief, the taxpayer had to seek relief in the right forum in the right country. As you read this case, consider what the taxpayer might have done differently to achieve his objective of double taxation relief. Is there any relief available to the taxpayer in this case?

[¶ 5385]

FILLER v. COMMISSIONER

United States Tax Court, 1980.
74 T.C. 406.

RAUM, JUDGE: * * * During 1972 and 1973, [Herbert Filler, the petitioner] was a bona fide resident of France, employed there by "IBM-Europe." In the determination of the deficiencies, the Commissioner made certain uncontested adjustments in the total compensation received by petitioner in each year. Furthermore, the Commissioner recomputed the foreign tax credit with respect to the income taxes paid to France for each year. The recomputations thus made are not in dispute, except to the extent that the foreign tax credit is, in effect, reduced by reason of the Commissioner's treatment of a portion of petitioner's compensation as U.S. source income. * * *

During each of the years in issue, petitioner spent 5 days in the United States on business, and the parties have stipulated that he thus had U.S. source compensation for his services in the amounts of $1,108 and $1,157 for the years 1972 and 1973, respectively. There is no dispute that petitioner paid income taxes to France on the total amount of compensation received by him in those years, including the portions allocable to his services in the United States. Also, petitioners do not appear to contest the correctness, under our internal revenue laws, of the Commissioner's recomputation of the foreign tax credit.

The sole issue raised in the pleadings is that petitioner is being subjected to double taxation on the portions of his income allocated to U.S. sources in violation of the Income Tax Treaty between the United States and France, and in particular article 25 thereof. United States–France Convention with respect to taxes on income and property, July 28, 1967

* * * (as amended by the United States–France Income Tax Protocol, Oct. 12, 1970 * * *) hereinafter sometimes referred to as the convention or 1967 convention. [A new United States–France Income Tax Treaty went into effect in 1995.] We hold * * * that the substantive provisions of the convention, properly construed, do not affect the operation of our Internal Revenue Code in the circumstances of this case, and instead call for the application of the French income tax law in such manner as to avoid double taxation.

* * *

* * * *The substantive provisions of the convention.*—The materials before us appear to indicate that petitioner initially sought a reduction in his French taxes to obtain relief from double taxation, but the French authorities denied such relief, relying upon article 15 of the convention. Article 15, which is set forth below to the extent pertinent,[6] would indeed support that conclusion if it stood alone. Although paragraph (1) of that article does empower the United States generally to tax the compensation of a French resident for services performed in the United States, paragraph 2(a) effectively takes that power away here since petitioner was not present in the United States for a period exceeding 183 days in each of the years 1972 and 1973. However, article 15 does not stand alone, and its effect is completely eliminated here by the savings clause in paragraph (4)(a) of article 22,[8] since petitioner is a United States citizen.

Although many foreign countries tax their residents on their worldwide income, the United States taxes its citizens, as well as its residents,

6.

ARTICLE 15

DEPENDENT PERSONAL SERVICES

(1) Salaries, wages, and other similar remuneration paid to a resident of a Contracting State for labor or personal services shall be taxable only in that State unless such labor or personal services were performed in the other Contracting State. Remuneration received for labor or personal services performed within such other State may be taxed by such other State.

(2) Notwithstanding the provisions of paragraph (1), remuneration derived by a resident of a Contracting State in respect of an employment exercised in the other Contracting State shall not be taxable in such other State if:

(a) The recipient is present in the other State for a period or periods not exceeding in the aggregate 183 days in the fiscal year concerned,

(b) The remuneration is paid by, or on behalf of, an employer who is not a resident of the other State, and

(c) The remuneration is not borne by a permanent establishment which the employer has in the other State.

* * *

8.

ARTICLE 22

GENERAL RULES OF TAXATION

(4)(a) The United States may tax its citizens and residents as if the present Convention had not come into effect.

(i) This provision shall not affect the rules laid down in Article 20 (Social Security Payments), Article 23 (Relief from Double Taxation), and Article 24 (Nondiscrimination). * * *

on their worldwide income. * * * Accordingly, the United States insists on the inclusion of a "savings clause" in its tax treaties; the effect of this clause is to reserve the right of the United States to tax its citizens and residents on the basis of the provisions of the Internal Revenue Code without regard to the provisions of the treaty. * * * Paragraph 4(a) of article 22 is just such a savings clause, which preserves the right of the United States to tax its own citizens in accordance with its own laws. * * * Since the savings clause does not include article 15 among the articles which take precedence over the savings clause, the savings clause has the effect of providing that the source of income allocation rules found in the Internal Revenue Code are applicable to U.S. citizens, rather than the provisions of article 15. These code provisions and the related regulations clearly indicate that petitioner's compensation for services performed in the United States is U.S. source income. See sec. 861(a)(3) * * *; sec. 1.861–4(b), Income Tax Regs. Accordingly, article 15 of the convention does not exempt such compensation from tax by the United States.

It is true that the savings clause does not affect the convention rules on relief from double taxation, found in article 23.[9] However, a fair reading of this provision indicates that petitioner is entitled to a tax credit from France, and not the United States, in respect of compensation for services performed in the United States. Under article 23, the United States is required to provide a tax credit only for the "appropriate amount" of French taxes paid; and this "amount" is strictly limited so as not to be in excess of the U.S. tax on French source income. The report of the Senate Committee on Foreign Relations recommending that the

9.

ARTICLE 23

RELIEF FROM DOUBLE TAXATION

Double taxation of income shall be avoided in the following manner:

(1) The United States shall allow to a citizen, resident, or corporation of the United States as a credit against its tax specified in paragraph (1) of Article 1 the appropriate amount of income taxes paid to France. Such appropriate amount shall be based upon the amount of French tax paid but shall not exceed that portion of the United States tax which net income from sources within France bears to the entire net income.

(2) In the case of France:

(a) Income other than that mentioned in paragraph (b) below shall be exempt from the French taxes mentioned in paragraph (1) of Article 1 while the income is, by reason of the Convention, taxable in the United States.

(b) As regards income taxable in both Contracting States in accordance with the provisions of this Convention, France shall allow to a resident of France receiving such income from United States sources a tax credit corresponding to the amount of tax levied in the United States. Such tax credit, not exceeding the amount of French tax levied on such income, shall be allowed against taxes mentioned in paragraph (1)(b)(i) of Article 1 of this Convention, in the bases of which such income is included.

(c) Notwithstanding the provisions of paragraphs (a) and (b), French tax may be computed on income chargeable in France by virtue of this Convention at the rate appropriate to the total of the income chargeable in accordance with French law.

* * *

Senate give its advice and consent to ratification of the treaty explains that although specific reference in the treaty was not made to the foreign tax credit provisions in the Code, in order that subsequent statutory modifications would not alter the effect of the convention, a per-country limitation on the amount of the credit was to be applied under the convention. * * * It is reasonable to infer that since the convention contemplated the use of a per-country limitation (as was then provided in section 904(a)(1) * * *), it was also assumed that the related Code sections determining the source of income (including section 861(a)(3)) would also be applicable, as those source of income provisions are necessary for application of a per-country limitation on the credit. Moreover, the convention itself provides that terms not otherwise defined are to be applied by the United States in accordance with United States law;[11] this provision would appear to require use of U.S. source of income rules, at least where the treaty fails to adequately define the source of income, as is the case here.[12] Thus, it seems clear that in article 23 of the convention, the United States consented only to provide a foreign tax credit on income attributable to sources in France, as determined under the source of income rules of the Internal Revenue Code, and not to income from United States sources. At the same time, France, in article 23(2)(b), consented to provide a tax credit against French taxes for U.S. income taxes on income from sources within the United States.

It would thus appear that under the convention, relief from double taxation is available here only as a credit against the French tax. To be sure, we are aware that petitioner has already sought such relief and it was denied by the French authorities in reliance upon article 15. But we think they erred in this respect * * *. Perhaps petitioner may seek reconsideration by the French authorities in the application of their own law as modified by the convention. And as a last resort, he may be able to present his case to the French competent authority, thereby initiating the international administrative procedure established by article 25, in respect of which this Court has no jurisdiction. However, we express no opinion as to such courses of action.

* * *

11.

ARTICLE 2

GENERAL DEFINITIONS

(2) As regards the application of the Convention by a Contracting State any term not otherwise defined shall, unless the context otherwise requires, have the meaning which it has under the laws of that Contracting State relating to the taxes which are the subject of the Convention.

* * *

12. Source of income rules are provided for dividends, interest, royalties, and capital gains. 1967 Convention, art. 9(4), 10(6), 11(6), 12(1) * * *. The 1967 Convention otherwise does not define the sources of other types of income, such as income from the performance of personal services. * * *

[¶ 5390]

NOTE

The meaning of the language of a saving clause in a tax treaty has sometimes been confused by a nondiscrimination provision in the treaty. A series of issues arose, for example, with respect to the application of the Section 911 exclusion for certain foreign-source earned income at a time when the exclusion was available to U.S. citizens but not to resident aliens (before the Foreign Earned Income Act of 1978 amended Section 911 to provide that a resident alien could qualify for the exclusion by meeting the physical presence test). The interaction of the saving clause and the nondiscrimination article in various treaties created an ambiguous situation. The saving clause preserved the right of the United States to impose the usual taxes on residents; but the nondiscrimination article indicated that residents who were citizens of certain treaty partners should receive all benefits available to U.S. citizens. The IRS eventually ruled that "in the absence of a specific treaty provision or a provision of the regulations under the treaty to the contrary, the nondiscrimination clause in a particular income tax treaty will be applied without regard to the savings clause in such treaty." Rev. Rul. 72–330, 1972–2 C.B. 444, 445. Rev. Rul. 91–58, 1991–2 C.B. 340, 341, discussed in Note 3 at ¶ 5365, declared Rev. Rul. 72–330 obsolete, but reaffirmed its principle that the nondiscrimination article will generally be applied without regard to the saving clause in a tax treaty. See also U.S. Model Treaty, Art. 1(5)(a).

[¶ 5395]

PROBLEM

J.J. Morse is an independent oil consultant. She is a citizen of the United States but has been for many years a resident of an oil-producing country located in the Middle East (a foreign country that, for purposes of this Problem, has in effect a treaty with the United States that is identical to the U.S. Model Treaty). She performs almost all of her work and has her only home in that foreign country. Her husband and children spend virtually all their time in that foreign country. During year 1, she was engaged by a Texas corporation to do some consulting work on an oil production problem near Houston, Texas. She spent 30 days in the United States, all on the Houston oil consulting job. Will Morse be taxable in the United States on the fee received for that job? See U.S. Model Treaty, Arts. 1(4), 1(5), 4(1), 5, 7 and 23.

Assume that Morse is taxable in the United States. Assume also, for purposes of this Problem, that Morse is taxable in her foreign country of residence on the Houston consulting fee because that country taxes the worldwide income of its residents and has a foreign tax credit system like that of the United States. Will Morse be allowed a tax credit against her U.S. tax for a portion of the tax paid to her foreign country of residence? Will Morse be allowed a tax credit against the tax in her foreign country of residence for all or a portion of the tax paid to the United States?

Chapter 6

The Controlled Foreign Corporation Provisions and Other Anti-Deferral Regimes

■ ■ ■

[¶ 6000]

A. INTRODUCTION AND OVERVIEW OF THE ANTI-DEFERRAL REGIMES

As discussed in Chapters 1 and 5, a U.S. person that conducts business or invests abroad directly is taxed currently by the United States on the foreign income, but is entitled to a foreign tax credit under Section 901 for foreign taxes imposed on such income. By contrast, a U.S. person that conducts business or invests abroad through a foreign corporation generally pays no U.S. income tax on the foreign corporation's foreign-source earnings unless and until such earnings are distributed to the U.S. person or the U.S. person disposes of the foreign corporation's stock. The U.S. tax law generally respects the foreign corporation as a separate entity and, as discussed in Chapters 3 and 4, the foreign corporation itself is seldom subject to U.S. tax on its foreign-source income. If the U.S. person locates the foreign corporation's business or investments in a foreign country with a tax rate below the U.S. rate, the U.S. person enjoys tax savings in the amount by which the U.S. rate exceeds any current foreign taxes imposed. Thus, in the jargon of international taxation, the foreign corporation's foreign earnings enjoy "deferral" of U.S. taxes until they are repatriated to the United States by distributions or otherwise.[1] Given the time value of money, this deferral of the U.S. tax may produce significant tax savings for the U.S. person and substantially reduce the *effective* rate

1. Upon distribution of the foreign corporation's earnings to the U.S. person, U.S. income tax will be imposed. At that time, the U.S. person may be entitled to both a direct credit under Section 901 for any withholding taxes imposed on the distribution and, in the case of a U.S. corporation owning ten percent or more of the foreign corporation's voting stock, an indirect credit under Section 902 for any foreign taxes that were imposed on the distributing foreign corporation's earnings out of which the distribution was made.

of U.S. tax on the U.S. person's share of the foreign corporation's earnings.

This concept of deferral is one of the fundamental principles of the U.S. system for taxing international transactions and is a major reason that U.S. corporations operating or investing abroad often do so through a foreign subsidiary rather than directly through a branch. However, this deferral principle violates the capital-export neutrality standard because the U.S. person operating through a foreign corporation abroad in a low-tax country is paying less overall (U.S. and foreign) current tax than a U.S. person conducting a business or investing either in the United States or abroad directly through a branch. Thus, if not limited in some way, this deferral principle serves as an incentive for U.S. taxpayers to move their operations and investments abroad to low-tax or tax-free foreign countries as a tax-avoidance maneuver to the detriment of the U.S. Treasury and worldwide economic efficiency. Stated differently, this principle of deferral could cause a U.S. person to favor foreign investments in low-tax foreign countries with pre-tax returns substantially below those of comparable U.S. investments. See, e.g., U.S. Treas. Dep't, International Tax Reform: An Interim Report 7 (Jan. 1993). It also distorts choice-of-entity decisions regarding international business ventures because it favors the foreign subsidiary form of business operation over operation through an unincorporated branch or partnership. The deferral principle also distorts investment decisions by encouraging U.S. shareholders to retain and invest abroad the deferred foreign earnings, rather than repatriate them to the United States as dividend distributions and trigger U.S. income tax on the dividend. This phenomenon is sometimes referred to as the "lock-out problem" or the "repatriation tax barrier."

To deal with the perceived abuses arising from the misuse of this deferral principle, Congress over the years created four sets of complex and somewhat overlapping anti-deferral regimes directed at U.S. persons earning income through foreign corporations. These anti-deferral regimes represented exceptions to the general rule of deferral: (1) the foreign personal holding company provisions (former Sections 551–558); (2) the controlled foreign corporation rules of Subpart F (Sections 951–964) and the related provisions in Section 1248; (3) the rules for foreign investment companies (former Section 1246) and electing foreign investment companies (former Section 1247); and (4) the passive foreign investment company provisions (Sections 1291–1298). In addition, two penalty tax regimes of general application could also apply to foreign corporations: the accumulated earnings tax (Sections 531–537) and the personal holding company tax (Sections 541–547).

The first regime specifically aimed at limiting deferral by U.S. persons earning income through foreign corporations was the foreign personal holding company provisions (former Sections 551 through 558). These provisions were enacted in 1937 to prevent the avoidance of U.S. income tax by a concentrated group of U.S. individuals through channeling passive investment income and certain other income into a foreign corporation (sometimes referred to as an "incorporated pocketbook"), typically established in a "tax haven" foreign country. They also were intended to prevent U.S. taxpayers from converting ordinary investment income into capital gain by accumulating investment income in a foreign corporation and then selling the stock of or liquidating the corporation. See H.R. Rep. No. 1546, 75th Cong., 1st Sess. 15–16 (1937). The approach taken to deal with these abuses was to impose constructive dividend treatment on the U.S. persons owning stock in a foreign personal holding company.[2] Accordingly, every U.S. person (i.e., a U.S. citizen, resident alien, corporation, partnership, trust or estate) that owned stock in the foreign personal holding company, no matter how small the stock interest, had to include in gross income its pro rata share of the company's undistributed income, thus eliminating the benefits of deferral for such shareholders. A foreign personal holding company was defined with reference to both a stock ownership test (more than 50 percent of the vote or value of the foreign corporation's stock had to be owned, directly or indirectly, by five or fewer U.S. individuals) and a gross income test (a specified percentage, either 60 or 50 percent, of the corporation's gross income had to consist of passive investment income and certain other types of income, defined as "foreign personal holding company income"). Because of these definitional rules, the foreign personal holding company provisions did not apply to many foreign corporations, particularly those owned by U.S. corporations (rather than U.S. individuals).

The use of foreign base companies by U.S. corporations enjoyed a surge of popularity in the years from 1950 to 1962. Generally, the primary purpose for establishing such companies was the desire to minimize the overall (foreign and U.S.) tax burden on the income generated by international business operations. Important tax savings were achieved by U.S. corporations through the use of foreign base companies to perform a variety of roles, including, for example:

(1) holding stock in foreign operating subsidiaries;

(2) serving as licensor or lessor to independent or affiliated foreign licensees or lessees;

(3) handling export sales from, or import purchases into, the United States and other countries;

(4) supplying technical, managerial or other services to independent or affiliated foreign companies;

(5) making loans to independent or affiliated foreign borrowers; and

(6) conducting insurance and reinsurance operations.

---

2. This approach avoided the imposition of a U.S. tax on the foreign-source income of a foreign corporation. The domestic personal holding company provisions in Sections 541 through 547 formerly imposed a penalty tax on such companies that failed to distribute personal holding company income.

Typically, the foreign base company was a wholly owned subsidiary of the U.S. parent corporation and was organized in a tax haven country, such as Switzerland, Bermuda, Panama, the Bahamas or Liberia. In such countries, foreign-source corporate income and accumulated profits were subject to little or no tax. Furthermore, because, before enactment of Subpart F in 1962, the foreign-source income of a foreign corporation could not generally be taxed in the United States, the income received by a foreign base company (from foreign sources) was not subject to U.S. tax unless and until it was remitted, as dividends or otherwise, to the U.S. parent corporation.[3] Thus, the accumulated earnings of foreign base companies enjoyed deferral of the U.S. corporate tax. The difference between the foreign tax burden (if any) borne by the foreign base company and the then U.S. corporate tax rate of as high as 52 percent represented a tax saving which increased the pool of funds available to the base company that could be reinvested outside the United States. The tax saving through deferral of the U.S. tax was tantamount to an interest-free loan from the U.S. Treasury to the U.S. parent corporation (or to its foreign base company). It could be viewed as an indirect subsidy by the U.S. government to U.S. multinational corporations' business and investment activities abroad.

In 1961, the Kennedy Administration proposed a complete end of deferral of U.S. tax on the income of foreign corporations controlled by U.S. persons, except with respect to certain income from investments in underdeveloped countries. The basic concern of the Administration was expressed in the following excerpt from President John F. Kennedy's 1961 Tax Message to Congress, at 107 Cong.Rec. 6458 (1961):

> * * * Profits earned abroad by American firms operating through foreign subsidiaries are, under present tax laws, subject to U.S. tax only when they are returned to the parent company in the form of dividends. In some cases, this tax deferral has made possible indefinite postponement of the U.S. tax; and, in those countries where income taxes are lower than in the United States, the ability to defer the payment of U.S. tax by retaining income in the subsidiary companies provides a tax advantage for companies operating through overseas subsidiaries that is not available to companies operating solely in the United States. * * *
>
> The undesirability of continuing deferral is underscored where deferral has served as a shelter for tax escape through the unjustifiable use of tax havens such as Switzerland. Recently more and more

3. This statement assumes, as was usually the case, that the foreign base company did not meet the definition of a foreign personal holding company because either or both the stock ownership and income tests for meeting that definition were not met. The foreign base company often was owned entirely or largely by a single, widely held U.S. corporate parent and most of its income might not have met the definition of foreign personal holding company income in former Section 553.

> enterprises organized abroad by American firms have arranged their corporate structures—aided by artificial arrangements between parent and subsidiary regarding intercompany pricing, the transfer of patent licensing rights, the shifting of management fees, and similar practices which maximize the accumulation of profits in the tax haven—so as to exploit the multiplicity of foreign tax systems and international agreements in order to reduce sharply or eliminate completely their tax liabilities both at home and abroad.

President Kennedy recommended that:

> * * * legislation be adopted which would * * * tax each year American corporations on their current share of the undistributed profits realized in that year by subsidiary corporations organized in economically advanced countries. This current taxation would also apply to individual shareholders of closely held corporations in those countries. * * *
>
> * * *
>
> [Under this proposal, tax deferral would have generally continued for income from investment in underdeveloped countries, except that President Kennedy also recommended] elimination of the tax haven device anywhere in the world, even in the underdeveloped countries, through the elimination of tax deferral privileges for those forms of activities, such as trading, licensing, insurance, and others, that typically seek out tax haven methods of operation. There is no valid reason to permit their remaining untaxed regardless of the country in which they are located.

Proponents of the Kennedy Administration's proposal invoked the capital-export neutrality standard and argued that eliminating deferral would remove an unwarranted incentive in the tax system for U.S. persons to move their business activities and investments to foreign countries (particularly tax haven countries). Opponents of ending or reducing deferral invoked the capital-import neutrality standard and argued that retaining deferral was necessary in order to enable U.S. multinational corporations to compete effectively with their foreign competitors in the international business arena.

As a compromise between these competing arguments, Congress enacted the Subpart F provisions in 1962. These provisions use the constructive dividend technique previously used in the foreign personal holding company provisions with respect to foreign corporations controlled by five or fewer U.S. individuals. A controlled foreign corporation was defined solely with reference to a stock ownership test, which required that more than 50 percent of the corporation's voting power (under current law, voting power *or* value) be owned by U.S. shareholders. However, under Subpart F, only U.S. persons holding a ten-percent-or-greater interest in the foreign corporation's voting power count in determining whether the foreign corporation is a controlled foreign corporation and only such shareholders are subject to constructive dividend treatment. Moreover, such constructive dividend treatment applies only with respect to certain categories of the foreign corporation's undistributed foreign-source income, generally income that is both relatively movable from one taxing jurisdiction to another and subject to low foreign tax rates. The general rule of deferral remains with respect to other foreign-source income earned by a U.S. person through a foreign corporation, unless one of the other anti-deferral regimes in the Code applies.

The controlled foreign corporation and foreign personal holding company provisions did not eliminate all possibilities for accumulating passive income in a tax haven corporation. For example, a publicly owned foreign investment company would normally not meet the definition of controlled foreign corporation (because there are no ten-percent U.S. shareholders) or the definition of foreign personal holding company (because five or fewer U.S. individuals would not control it). Congress was concerned that U.S. persons owning shares of a widely held foreign investment company could allow passive income of the foreign investment company to accumulate, thereby avoiding current dividend taxation, and eventually sell their shares at the favorable rates applicable to long-term capital gain. Accordingly, in 1962, in the same legislation containing the Subpart F provisions, Congress enacted the foreign investment company provisions of former Section 1246. These provisions treated gain from the sale of shares in a foreign investment company, of which U.S. persons owned 50 percent or more of the voting power or value of the stock, as ordinary income rather than capital gain. In 1962, Congress also enacted former Section 1247, which permitted a foreign investment company to avoid application of Section 1246 by electing, before 1963, to have its shareholders taxed on their shares of the current ordinary income and capital gains of the company substantially like shareholders in a U.S. regulated investment company.

In the case of a U.S. person owning a small interest in a widely held "offshore" investment company not controlled by U.S. persons, the controlled foreign corporation, foreign personal holding company and foreign investment company rules did not prevent the accumulation of income of the foreign investment company in a tax haven free of tax. The passive foreign investment company ("PFIC") provisions were enacted as part of the Tax Reform Act of 1986 to close this loophole. In these provisions, a different technique for eliminating the benefits of deferral was adopted. Instead of treating the U.S. shareholder as having received a share of the undistributed income of the foreign investment company for the tax year as a constructive dividend, the PFIC provisions eliminate the economic benefit of deferral by imposing additional U.S. tax when the U.S. person owning stock in the PFIC disposes of the PFIC stock at a gain or receives an unusually large distribution from the PFIC. That is, when a U.S. person disposes of stock in a PFIC at a gain or receives a so-called "excess distribution" from a PFIC, the U.S. tax imposed at that time is increased by an interest charge based on the value of the tax deferral. This treatment generally applies to any U.S. person who is a shareholder in a PFIC, however small the interest. Alternatively, a U.S. person owning stock in a PFIC can elect to pay current U.S. tax on the PFIC's earnings under so-called "qualified electing fund" rules. § 1293(a). As a third alternative, if the stock in the PFIC is "marketable stock," the U.S. person owning stock in the PFIC can elect to mark the stock to market at the end of the year. Under this method, the U.S. person includes in ordinary income the excess of the fair market value of the PFIC's stock at the end of the tax year over the U.S. person's adjusted basis in it or takes an ordinary deduction for the excess of the U.S. person's adjusted basis in the PFIC's stock over its fair market value at the end of the tax year (subject to a limitation). § 1296(a).

The PFIC provisions were aimed at ending deferral on income earned by a U.S. person through a foreign corporation the income of which consists largely of passive investment income or the assets of which are predominantly passive investment assets. Thus, a PFIC is defined as any foreign corporation if at least 75 percent of its gross income is passive income or if at least an average of 50 percent of its assets (by value or, in certain cases, by adjusted basis) produce passive income. § 1297(a). Unlike the other anti-deferral regimes, the PFIC provisions do *not* contain any stock ownership test that focuses on the percentage of stock owned by U.S. persons; thus, the PFIC provisions may apply to a foreign corporation in which U.S. persons own in total only a small percentage of the outstanding stock. Note that although the PFIC provisions were aimed particularly at U.S. persons holding stock in offshore investment funds, they may apply to U.S. persons holding stock in any foreign corporation, even one engaged in an active foreign business such as manufacturing, for any tax year in which the corporation derives enough passive income or owns enough passive assets to meet the definition of a PFIC.

As the above overview suggests, each of the four principal anti-deferral regimes in effect before 2004 had its own rules concerning the definition of the foreign corporations that fell within its scope, the types of income of the foreign corporation as to which the benefits of deferral were eliminated or reduced, the mechanism used to eliminate or reduce the benefits of deferral and whether a U.S. person had to own some specified minimum percentage of stock (e.g., ten percent) to trigger the anti-deferral mechanism. The same foreign corporation could have fallen within the scope of more than one of these anti-deferral regimes. To deal with this overlap, the Code contained provisions that coordinated the application of these regimes. Moreover, in 1997, Congress eliminated one key overlap between these anti-deferral regimes. The PFIC provisions no longer apply to a U.S. person owning stock in a PFIC during periods after 1997 when the U.S. person is a "United States shareholder" (as defined in Section 951(b)) in a PFIC that also meets the definition of a "controlled foreign corporation" in Section 957; however, the PFIC provisions continue to apply to other U.S. persons owning stock in such a PFIC. § 1297(e).

Reversal of policy course; 2004 JOBS Act reduction in the number of anti-deferral regimes. In 2004, Congress concluded that "the overlap among the various anti-deferral regimes results in significant complexity usually with little or no ultimate tax consequences." H.R. Rep. No. 548, pt. 1, 108th Cong., 2d Sess. 205 (2004). Moreover, by 2004, taking its cue from the U.S. multinational community and its legion of corporate lobbyists, Congress had clearly become more enamored with capital-import neutrality as a guiding economic efficiency model. Accordingly, the 2004 JOBS Act repealed the foreign personal holding company provisions in former Sections 551 through 558 and the foreign investment company provisions in former Sections 1246 and 1247. The JOBS Act also exempted foreign corporations from the application of the personal holding company tax in Section 541, which seldom applied to foreign corporations as a practical matter. Thus, the JOBS Act reduced the number of anti-deferral regimes in the Code that apply to foreign corporations in which U.S. persons own stock from six to three: the controlled foreign corporation provisions of Subpart F (the most important of these anti-deferral regimes), the PFIC rules and the accumulated earnings tax. However, as discussed at ¶ 6365, as a practical matter, the accumulated earnings tax regime rarely applies to a foreign corporation.

Temporary repatriation tax reduction. In another policy move in the direction of capital-import neutrality, the 2004 JOBS Act made an additional change in the international tax deferral area, albeit only on a temporary basis. This change rewarded those U.S. multinationals that had been the most successful in deferring U.S. tax on foreign-source income earned through foreign subsidiaries and retaining those earnings abroad. The provision—Section 965—provided a temporary, elective 85–percent dividends-received deduction for certain cash dividends received from controlled foreign corporations by a U.S. corporation that is a U.S. shareholder (as defined in Section 951(b)) of those corporations. As discussed above, a U.S. person (including a U.S. corporation) that earns income abroad through a foreign corporation can defer payment of the U.S. residual tax on its share of the foreign corporation's foreign earnings until those earnings are repatriated to the United States (provided that none of the anti-deferral regimes applies to such earnings). Congress was concerned that "the residual U.S. tax imposed on the repatriation of foreign earnings can serve as a disincentive to repatriate these earnings." H.R. Rep. No. 548, pt. 1, 108th Cong., 2d Sess. at 146 (2004). The thought was that the repatriation tax served to "lock out" earnings that would be reinvested in the United States but for the existence of the repatriation tax.[4] Congress believed that a temporary cut in the repatriation tax would

4. Of course, the ultimate source of this lock-out is the deferral principle itself and Congress could eliminate the tax disincentive to repatriate earnings to the United States by eliminating

"stimulate the U.S. domestic economy by triggering the repatriation of foreign earnings that otherwise would have remained abroad." Id. The committee reports accompanying enactment of Section 965 stressed that "this is a temporary economic stimulus measure," id., although some policy commentators were skeptical both of the soundness of the policy rationale for the provision and the likelihood that it would end up being only temporary.

Section 965 was effective, at the election of the taxpayer, for either the taxpayer's last tax year starting before the date of enactment of the JOBS Act (i.e., October 22, 2004) or the taxpayer's first tax year starting during the one-year period that began on the date of enactment. § 965(f). This 85–percent dividends-received deduction in Section 965 was subject to a number of limitations, which made some U.S. multinational corporations hesitant to elect to use the provision. Some capital-import neutrality proponents have argued that this provision should be enacted again on a temporary basis or even made a permanent part of the Code, but Congress has rejected these arguments to date.

Other countries' approach to the deferral issue. The United States was the first country to attempt to use specifically targeted legislative provisions to deal with tax haven abuses arising from the deferral principle. Initially, the U.S. efforts to narrow the deferral principle were criticized by some European commentators as representing an unreasonable extension of U.S. taxing jurisdiction that in substance, if not in form, conflicted with the principle, embodied in the vast majority of international income tax treaties, that the separate legal existence of a foreign corporation must be respected. In time, however, other industrialized countries followed the lead of the United States and adopted special legislative regimes to deal with tax haven abuses. Although these anti-tax haven regimes have, broadly speaking, a similarity of purpose, they differ significantly from country to country in both scope and operation.

Scope of this Chapter. This Chapter first discusses the controlled foreign corporation provisions in Subpart F, and the related provisions in Sections 1248 and 1249, both because these provisions have the most significant impact on international tax planning and because an in-depth understanding of these provisions helps one understand the need for other anti-deferral regimes in the Code. Next, this Chapter examines the passive foreign investment company provisions, the principal other remaining anti-deferral regime in the Code. The Chapter then looks briefly at the very limited role of the accumulated earnings tax in dealing with the abuses that arise from the deferral principle and the various reporting requirements that apply to foreign corporations owned by U.S. persons. Finally, the Chapter concludes with a policy discussion of alternatives to the current anti-deferral regimes in the Code.

---

altogether the deferral of U.S. tax on income earned by a U.S. person through a controlled foreign corporation.

B. OVERVIEW OF CONTROLLED FOREIGN CORPORATION PROVISIONS

[¶ 6005]

1. INTRODUCTION

The fundamental changes effected by the Revenue Act of 1962 in the taxation of foreign base companies and contained in Subpart F of the Code apply only to "United States shareholders" (hereinafter "U.S. shareholders") of "controlled foreign corporations." Under the prevailing view in 1962, problems concerning a proper jurisdictional basis under international law and conflicts with U.S. tax treaty obligations might have been presented if an attempt had been made to tax the controlled foreign corporation as such (i.e., as if it were a foreign branch). Consequently, the 1962 Act adopted the mechanism of taxing the U.S. shareholders on their pro rata shares of the controlled foreign corporation's undistributed income as if those shares of income had been distributed as dividends. However, only certain specified types of the controlled foreign corporation's income—known collectively as "Subpart F income"—are generally subject to this constructive dividend treatment.

[¶ 6010]

2. DEFINITIONS OF U.S. SHAREHOLDER AND CONTROLLED FOREIGN CORPORATION

The original 1962 Act version of Section 957(a) defined a "controlled foreign corporation" as a foreign corporation of which more than 50 percent of the total combined voting power of all classes of stock entitled to vote was owned, directly, indirectly or constructively under the Section 958 ownership rules, by "U.S. shareholders" on any day during the foreign corporation's tax year. Section 951(b) defined a "U.S. shareholder" as a U.S. citizen, resident alien, corporation, partnership, trust or estate owning, directly, indirectly or constructively under the ownership rules of Section 958, ten percent or more of the total combined voting power of all classes of stock of a foreign corporation. Thus, only those U.S. shareholders owning ten percent or more of the voting power were to be taken into account in determining whether a foreign corporation was a controlled foreign corporation, and a foreign corporation would fall within the definition only if more than 50 percent of the total combined voting power of all classes of its stock were owned directly, indirectly or constructively by such ten-percent U.S. shareholders.

These definitions were intended to ensure that a U.S. taxpayer holding merely a portfolio (i.e., less than ten percent) interest in a foreign corporation would not have to pay current U.S. tax on the taxpayer's pro rata share of the undistributed earnings of the foreign corporation even though the taxpayer lacked the voting power needed to force distribution of those earnings. Such voting power apparently was also thought to be absent when the U.S. persons holding ten-percent-or-more voting stock interests did not hold as a group more than 50 percent of the corporation's voting power.[5]

Congress later became concerned that the 1962 definition of controlled foreign corporation based solely on ownership of the corporation's voting power was being manipulated by taxpayers. For example, a foreign corporation would issue to foreign investors preferred stock that carried at least 50 percent of the voting power but participated in corporate earnings only to the extent of its fixed preferred dividend and its right to receive a fixed preferred distribution upon redemption of the stock or liquidation of the corporation. By using this device, the foreign corporation's U.S. shareholders who held all of the common stock that carried the other 50 percent of the voting power were in some cases able to avoid having the foreign corporation classified as a controlled foreign corporation even though the common stock they owned had a value representing much more than 50 percent of the total value of the corporation's outstanding stock. See *CCA, Inc. v. Commissioner*, at ¶ 6045. To prevent such avoidance techniques, the Tax Reform Act of 1986 broadened the definition of controlled foreign corporation to include a foreign corporation if more than 50 percent of either the *value* of all of the outstanding stock *or* the *total combined voting power* is owned by U.S. shareholders. § 957(a). However, the definition of a U.S. shareholder based solely on ownership of at least ten percent of the foreign corporation's voting power was *not* changed by the 1986 Act.

The test of controlled foreign corporation status is applied on a year-by-year basis. Thus, a foreign corporation may be a controlled foreign corporation in some tax years and not in others.

It is important to note that, as a result of tax changes enacted in 1986 dealing with limitations on the foreign tax credit, under current law U.S. taxpayers do not always seek to avoid controlled foreign corporate status for foreign corporations in which they invest. By reason of the look-through rules in Section 904(d)(3), which apply for foreign tax credit limitation purposes, controlled foreign corporate status may achieve a more favorable tax result than does noncontrolled foreign corporate status

5. Furthermore, it could be argued that requiring that U.S. persons holding at least ten percent of the voting power own a majority of the foreign corporation's stock as the definitional standard for controlled foreign corporation status is appropriate since the Subpart F rules are based in part on the analogy of a controlled foreign corporation to a foreign branch of a U.S. corporation. The analogy breaks down when the foreign corporation does not have a majority of U.S. shareholders. See Federal Income Tax Project—International Aspects of United States Income Taxation—Proposals on United States Taxation of Foreign Persons and of Foreign Income of United States Persons 233–34 (A.L.I. 1987). Of course, if this branch analogy were extended to its logical conclusion, all of the controlled foreign corporation's income should be subject to current U.S. income tax at the U.S. shareholder level, as it would if it were earned through a branch.

(for which a narrower look-through rule in Section 904(d)(4) applies). See ¶¶ 6255 and 7085.

[¶ 6015]

3. U.S. SHAREHOLDERS' CURRENT INCLUSIONS OF SUBPART F INCOME AND OF EARNINGS INVESTED IN U.S. PROPERTY

Not all undistributed income of a controlled foreign corporation is taxed to a U.S. shareholder under Subpart F. The 1962 legislation was aimed primarily at the tax advantages previously enjoyed by foreign base companies accumulating certain types of income that were relatively easy to shift to them from related U.S. corporations. Accordingly, as noted above, the U.S. shareholder is generally required to include in gross income for U.S. tax purposes its pro rata share of only certain types of undistributed income of the controlled foreign corporation (collectively called "Subpart F income"). If a foreign corporation is a controlled foreign corporation for an uninterrupted period of at least 30 days during the tax year, each U.S. shareholder of the corporation (as defined in Section 951(b)), who owns stock in the corporation on the last day in the year on which it is a controlled foreign corporation, must include in gross income a pro rata share of the corporation's Subpart F income. § 951(a)(1)(A)(i). The U.S. shareholder's pro rata share is determined with reference to the percentage of the corporation's stock owned by the shareholder on that last day of the year and the portion of the tax year during which the corporation was a controlled foreign corporation. In addition, if the U.S. shareholder acquired the stock during the year, the pro rata share is reduced by a portion of the dividends paid to the shareholder's predecessor in interest during the year. § 951(a)(1) and (a)(2), discussed at ¶ 6065. Foreign shareholders and U.S. persons owning stock in a controlled foreign corporation but not meeting the definition of a U.S. shareholder in Section 951(b) are *not* subject to tax under Subpart F. Thus, U.S. persons not having a large enough stock interest to meet the definition of a "U.S. shareholder" continue to obtain the tax benefit of deferral of U.S. income tax on such earnings unless one of the other anti-deferral regimes applies.

In addition to requiring that the U.S. shareholder include in income a pro rata share of the controlled foreign corporation's Subpart F income for the tax year, the 1962 provisions required that a U.S. shareholder include in income pro rata shares of certain amounts withdrawn by the controlled foreign corporation from favored investment[6] and the earnings of the

6. Specifically, the U.S. shareholder was required to include as a constructive dividend its pro rata share of the corporation's previously excluded Subpart F income withdrawn from investments in less developed countries (determined under former Section 955(a)(3) as in effect before its repeal by legislation enacted in 1975) and from foreign base company shipping operations for the year. § 951(a)(1)(A)(ii) and (iii). To encourage U.S. investment in less developed countries, Congress included in the original definition of "foreign base company income," the most

controlled foreign corporation invested in U.S. property (Sections 951(a)(1)(B) and 956). As more fully discussed at ¶ 6200, the theory behind the latter category of constructive dividend treatment was that when undistributed earnings of a controlled foreign corporation were invested in certain property in the United States (e.g., debt obligations issued by a U.S. shareholder), the U.S. shareholder has realized the economic value of the earnings. As a consequence, the earnings should be treated as if they had been distributed to the U.S. shareholder even though the earnings were not Subpart F income.[7] Thus, if a controlled foreign corporation invests its non-Subpart F earnings in U.S. property, the invested earnings are subject to current taxation by the U.S. shareholders. Finally, the 1962 legislation provided that if the U.S. shareholder sold or exchanged in a taxable transaction stock in a controlled foreign corporation, gain recognized may be treated as an ordinary income dividend, not as capital gain, to the extent of the shareholder's pro rata share of all of the post–1962 undistributed earnings of the controlled foreign corporation attributable to periods during which the stock sold or exchanged was held by the shareholder while the corporation was a controlled foreign corporation. § 1248(a), discussed at ¶ 6245.

Note that amounts included in a U.S. shareholder's income under Section 951(a)(1) are treated as ordinary income, regardless of the character of the controlled foreign corporation's underlying income (capital gain or ordinary income) giving rise to the inclusion under Section 951.[8] Note also that since Subpart F does *not* treat a controlled foreign corporation as a pass-through entity with respect to its U.S. shareholders, net losses

important component of Subpart F income, a provision excluding dividends and interest from and gains on sale or liquidation of certain "qualified investments in less developed countries" to the extent of any increase for the tax year in such "qualified investments in less developed countries." Former § 954(b)(1). Such reinvested amounts are taxable to the U.S. shareholder only upon withdrawal from a qualifying investment. Even though the exclusion has been repealed, this treatment continues to apply to Subpart F income excluded before repeal of the exclusion when that income is withdrawn by the controlled foreign corporation from investment in less developed countries.

7. Legislation enacted in 1993 amended Section 951(a) to restrict further the benefit of deferral of U.S. tax on undistributed earnings that were not reinvested in active business assets. Under the 1993 legislation, U.S. shareholders of a controlled foreign corporation were required to include in income their pro rata share of the accumulated post-September 30, 1993 earnings and current-year earnings of the corporation to the extent those earnings were invested in what were called "excess passive assets." These were passive (rather than active business) assets that exceeded 25 percent of the corporation's total assets. Former §§ 951(a)(1)(C) and 956A. In 1996, however, after intense lobbying pressure by U.S. multinational corporations, Congress repealed former Section 956A, effective for tax years of foreign corporations starting after 1996.

8. Amounts included in a U.S. shareholder's gross income under Section 951(a)(1) are not treated as dividends for Section 1(h)(11) purposes (which contains preferential rates of tax for individual shareholder's "qualified dividend income"). Accordingly, inclusions under Section 951(a)(1) cannot constitute "qualified dividend income" for Section 1(h)(11) purposes. By contrast, actual distributions of non-previously taxed earnings from a controlled foreign corporation to its individual U.S. shareholders and amounts treated as dividends under Section 1248(a) may constitute "qualified dividend income" if the controlled foreign corporation is a "qualified foreign corporation" and the other requirements of Section 1(h)(11) are met. See IRS Notice 2004–70, § 4, 2004–2 C.B. 724, 726. Section 1(h)(11) will expire for tax years starting after 2010, unless it is extended or made permanent by Congress in new legislation.

incurred by a controlled foreign corporation do *not* flow through to the U.S. shareholders. By contrast, if a U.S. corporation conducts its operations abroad through a branch, it reports the income and deductions of the branch on its own return. Thus, the character of the income as capital gain or ordinary income is preserved and any net losses from the foreign business operations of the branch are deductible on the U.S. corporation's U.S. income tax return. The same results obtain for a U.S. corporation's distributive share of the income or losses from participating in a partnership through which foreign operations are carried on.

[¶ 6020]

4. INDIRECT FOREIGN TAX CREDITS, PREVIOUSLY TAXED INCOME RULES AND BASIS ADJUSTMENTS

If the U.S. shareholder is a U.S. corporation that actually owns at least ten percent of the controlled foreign corporation's voting stock, the U.S. shareholder's inclusion in gross income of the Subpart F income (or the earnings invested in U.S. property) carries with it an indirect or "deemed paid" credit under Section 960 for foreign income taxes attributable to the earnings deemed distributed under Section 951. Under Section 78, the U.S. shareholder's Subpart F inclusion is increased (in international tax jargon, "grossed up") by the controlled foreign corporation's foreign taxes deemed paid by the U.S. shareholder. Moreover, Section 962 allows an individual U.S. shareholder who actually owns at least ten percent of the controlled foreign corporation's voting stock and who elects to be taxed at U.S. corporate rates on the income taxed under Subpart F to obtain the benefit of the Section 960 indirect credit.

Subpart F is not intended to be a system of double taxation. Section 951 typically requires a U.S. shareholder to be taxed currently on the pro rata share of all or some portion of the controlled foreign corporation's earnings even though the controlled foreign corporation has not made any actual distribution to the shareholder. Thus, to avoid double taxation of the U.S. shareholder's share of the controlled foreign corporation's earnings, actual distributions from the corporation to a U.S. shareholder are tax-free to the extent attributable to amounts already taxed under Section 951(a). § 959(a).[9] Similar tax-free treatment applies to constructive distributions under Section 951(a)(1)(B) resulting from an investment of the controlled foreign corporation's earnings in U.S. property under Section

9. Note that a controlled foreign corporation's earnings and profits, as determined under Sections 964(a) and 312, are not reduced by its U.S. shareholders' Section 951 inclusions because such inclusions are not "dividends" for Section 312 purposes. Instead, the reduction in earnings and profits occurs when the controlled foreign corporation pays out as dividends the previously taxed earnings that are excludible under Section 959(a). See § 959(d). Thus, stated differently, actual dividends paid by a controlled foreign corporation to its shareholders reduce the corporation's earnings and profits, even if they are excludible from gross income under Section 959(a).

956 to the extent those constructive distributions are attributable to amounts already taxed as a Subpart F income inclusion under Section 951(a)(1)(A). For a particular tax year, amounts includible under Section 951(a)(1) are determined before the tax consequences of an actual distribution are determined. Under ordering rules that are generally favorable to taxpayers, actual distributions by a controlled foreign corporation are deemed to come first out of earnings previously taxed under Subpart F and out of other earnings only thereafter. § 959(c). These ordering rules increase the likelihood that both actual distributions and constructive distributions under Sections 951(a)(1)(B) and 956 will receive tax-free treatment under Section 959.

A U.S. shareholder's basis in the controlled foreign corporation's stock is increased by the amounts included in gross income under Section 951(a) as if the amounts had been distributed to the shareholder and then transferred back to the corporation as a contribution to capital. § 961(a). This basis adjustment is necessary to prevent double taxation of the controlled foreign corporation's previously taxed (and undistributed) income when a U.S. shareholder disposes of the corporation's stock.[10] However, to prevent a U.S. shareholder from obtaining a double tax benefit from the corporation's previously taxed income, when previously taxed income is distributed to the shareholder tax-free under Section 959, the tax-free portion of the distribution reduces the shareholder's basis in the stock. § 961(b)(1). If the tax-free portion of the distribution exceeds the shareholder's basis in the stock, the excess is treated as gain from sale or exchange of the stock. § 961(b)(2).

[¶ 6025]

5. COMPONENTS OF SUBPART F INCOME

The definition of "Subpart F income" has five components. The most important component is "foreign base company income." The other four components are: (1) income from certain insurance activities defined in Section 953, (2) certain international boycott-related income, (3) certain illegal bribes, kickbacks or other payments to government officials, employees or agents and (4) income from certain ostracized foreign countries to which Section 901(j) applies (see ¶ 5125). § 952(a).

Under current law, the "foreign base company income" component of Subpart F income, in turn, has four components: (1) "foreign personal

10. There is no basis increase for the Section 78 gross-up to reflect the foreign taxes deemed paid under Section 960 by a U.S. shareholder of the controlled foreign corporation. This makes sense because the U.S. shareholder is receiving a foreign tax credit for such amounts and allowing a basis increase as well would result in an inappropriate double benefit from the same amount of taxes. Moreover, Section 961(a) does not apply to an amount included in gross income by reason of the Section 78 gross-up because by its terms the basis increase in Section 961(a) applies only to "the amount required to be included in [the U.S. shareholder's] gross income under section 951(a)."

holding company income," (2) "foreign base company sales income," (3) "foreign base company services income" and (4) "foreign base company oil related income." § 954(a).[11] In determining the amount of each component of foreign base company income, the gross amount of income in each is reduced by the deductions properly allocable to such income.

As is more fully discussed at ¶¶ 6085 et seq., foreign personal holding company income is elaborately defined in Section 954(c). It includes, with some specific exceptions, such items of passive income as dividends, interest, royalties, rents, annuities, certain gains from commodity transactions, income from notional principal contracts, gains from sales of property producing passive income or no income and foreign currency gains. It also includes amounts received under certain personal service contracts involving a 25–percent-or-more shareholder. Congress recognized that passive investments typically are easily movable from one country to another and that a taxpayer's decision concerning the location of such investments is often highly responsive to tax considerations. Thus, it viewed ending deferral on passive income as necessary to remove an incentive for U.S. shareholders to transfer such investments to controlled foreign corporations located in tax haven countries.

The primary target of the foreign base company sales income and foreign base company services income components of Subpart F income is business income from transactions in which the controlled foreign corporation is being used by its U.S. shareholders largely as a conduit for diverting income from the United States to a low-tax or no-tax foreign country in which the foreign corporation is organized.[12] These provisions are designed to reach U.S. shareholders who divert sales income to a foreign base company located in a low-tax or no-tax foreign country that is neither the origin or destination of the products sold and who deflect services income to a foreign base company located in a low-tax or no-tax foreign country that is not the place where the services are performed. Accordingly, most types of active business income deriving from substantial business activities of the controlled foreign corporation in the country in which it is organized do not fall within the definition of Subpart F income. See, e.g., Federal Income Tax Project—International Aspects of United States Income Taxation—Proposals on United States Taxation of Foreign Persons and of Foreign Income of United States Persons 178–79 (A.L.I. 1987) (hereinafter "ALI International Taxation Study").

11. Under prior law, the "foreign base company income" component of Subpart F income also included "foreign base company shipping income," as defined in former Section 954(f). However, in another bow to capital-import neutrality and to the political clout of the international shipping industry, in the 2004 JOBS Act, Congress repealed this element of foreign base company income. This change was effective for tax years starting after 2004.

12. In this context, the Subpart F regime serves as a backstop to the transfer pricing rules under Section 482 (discussed in Chapter 8) by reducing the incentive for a U.S. parent corporation to use aggressive intercompany transfer pricing to shift income to a foreign base company subsidiary located in a tax haven.

The following simple examples illustrate the central focus of the foreign base company component of the Subpart F provisions.

Example 1. DC, a U.S. corporation, organizes a wholly owned foreign subsidiary, FC1, in Country X, a tax haven foreign country that imposes no tax on passive income. Before 1962, DC transfers some of its passive investments to FC1, thereby deferring any U.S. tax on the future income from such investments, until the income is distributed to DC or DC sells the FC1 stock. Under Subpart F, however, such passive investment income falls within the definition of "foreign personal holding company income" in Section 954(c) (as discussed at ¶¶ 6085 et seq.). Consequently, DC will be subject to current U.S. tax under Section 951 on such income as if it had been distributed as a dividend.

Example 2. DC also organizes a wholly owned foreign sales subsidiary, FC2, in Country Y, another tax haven foreign country. DC manufactures widgets at a cost of $40 per widget. In connection with its widget export business, DC sells widgets to FC2 for $50 per widget. FC2, in turn, sells the widgets to foreign customers in Country Z, another foreign country, for $100 per widget (their actual retail value in the global marketplace), and passes title to the widgets in Country Y. FC2 pays no tax to Country Y or Country Z on these sales. Under Subpart F, the $50 of income earned by FC2 on these sales involving DC's widgets falls within the definition of "foreign base company sales income" in Section 954(d) (as discussed at ¶ 6140). Consequently, DC will be subject to current U.S. tax under Section 951 on such income as if it had been distributed as a dividend.

Example 3. DC also organizes a wholly owned foreign services subsidiary, FC3, in Country Y. DC owns a hospital located in Country Z and engages FC3 to manage that hospital. FC3 pays little or no tax to Country Y or Country Z on the services income that it receives from DC for managing the hospital. Under Subpart F, the income earned by FC3 from the hospital management services will fall within the definition of "foreign base company services income" in Section 954(e) (as discussed at ¶ 6145). Consequently, DC will be subject to current U.S. tax under Section 951 on such income as if it had been distributed as a dividend.

Over the years from 1962 through the mid–1990s, taxpayers sought to obtain tax savings by using controlled foreign corporations to conduct activities to produce additional types of income that did not fall within any of the original component definitions of foreign base company income. Controlled foreign corporations have consistently been a focal point of tension between creative, and sometimes adventuresome, taxpayers, on one side, and congressional concerns over protecting the revenue and the fairness of the tax system, on the other. To meet new perceived abuses, Congress had progressively expanded the definitions of the categories of foreign base company income (especially foreign personal holding company income) and added new categories. That expansion, however, seemed to cease in 1996. Since that time, Congress has proceeded to reduce the reach of Subpart F by enacting new exceptions to the definition of foreign base company income. In 2004, however, Congress did add a new category of foreign base company income to the statute, when it repealed the foreign personal holding company provisions in former Sections 551 through 558 and added the following item to the list of income items that are treated as foreign personal holding company income for Subpart F income purposes: amounts received by a controlled foreign corporation under certain personal service contracts involving a 25–percent-or-more shareholder of the corporation. See § 954(c)(1)(H).

Four other provisions relating to the determination of a controlled foreign corporation's Subpart F income should be mentioned here. First, Section 954(b)(3)(A) contains a de minimis rule under which a controlled foreign corporation with relatively little foreign base company income is treated as having no such income. See ¶ 6160. Second, Section 954(b)(3)(B) contains a full-inclusion rule under which all of the gross income of a controlled foreign corporation is treated as foreign base company income if the corporation has actual gross foreign base company income in excess of 70 percent of its total gross income. See ¶ 6160. Third, Section 952(c)(1) generally limits a controlled foreign corporation's Subpart F income for a tax year to its earnings and profits for that year. See ¶ 6080. Fourth, Section 952(b) excludes from Subpart F income any U.S.-source income that is effectively connected with a U.S. trade or business and subject to full U.S. income tax. See ¶ 6075.

C. DEFINITION OF CONTROLLED FOREIGN CORPORATION

[¶ 6030]

1. APPLICATION OF INDIRECT AND CONSTRUCTIVE OWNERSHIP RULES UNDER SECTION 958

In determining whether a U.S. person meets the Section 951(b) definition of a U.S. shareholder and whether a foreign corporation meets the Section 957(a) definition of a controlled foreign corporation, Section 958 applies direct, indirect and constructive ownership rules to determine stock ownership in the foreign corporation. Stock ownership under all three types of rules counts for purposes of determining whether a shareholder is a "U.S. shareholder" and whether a foreign corporation is a "controlled foreign corporation."

Section 958(a)(1) provides the direct ownership rules for determining stock ownership for such purposes. Section 958(a)(2) provides indirect ownership rules to determine beneficial ownership of shares when a foreign entity is interposed between the U.S. person and the foreign corporation. Specifically, stock of a foreign corporation owned, in turn, by another foreign corporation or by a foreign partnership, trust or estate is deemed to be owned proportionately by the latter's shareholders, partners or beneficiaries. There is no minimum threshold of ownership interest in the foreign corporation necessary to trigger the application of this indirect ownership rule involving foreign entities. Thus, if a foreign partnership with four equal partners owns four percent of the stock of a foreign corporation, each partner is treated under Section 958(a)(2) as owning one percent of the stock of the foreign corporation (i.e., one-fourth of the partnership's four-percent stock interest in the corporation). Likewise, if a U.S. person owns ten percent of the stock of a foreign corporation that owns 25 percent of a second foreign corporation's stock, the U.S. person is treated as owning 2.5 percent of the stock of the second foreign corporation under Section 958(a)(2).

Section 958(b) applies (with several modifications for Subpart F purposes) the constructive ownership rules of Section 318(a). These constructive ownership rules of Section 318(a) require attribution of stock between certain family members and between corporations, partnerships, trusts and estates, on the one hand, and their shareholders, partners or beneficiaries, on the other. § 318(a)(1)-(3). (In the case of corporation-to-shareholder attribution or shareholder-to-corporation attribution, a minimum threshold of stock ownership must be met for the attribution rule to be applied. § 318(a)(2)(C), (a)(3)(C).) Those constructive ownership rules also treat a person with an option to acquire stock as owning such stock. § 318(a)(4). Section 318(a)(5) contains certain operating rules for determining constructive stock ownership, and those operating rules apply for purposes of Section 958(b). However, Section 958(b) makes the following four modifications to the Section 318(a) constructive ownership rules:

(1) In applying the family constructive ownership rules in Section 318(a)(1), Section 958(b)(1) provides that stock owned by a nonresident alien individual shareholder will not be attributed to a U.S. citizen or resident alien. Note that the members of a family for purposes of Section 318(a)(1) include only a person's spouse, children, grandchildren and parents.

(2) In applying the entity-to-owner constructive ownership rules in Section 318(a)(2), Section 958(b)(2) provides that if a partnership, estate, trust or corporation owns more than 50 percent of the combined voting power of a corporation, it will be treated as owning all of the voting stock of the corporation.

(3) Section 318(a)(2)(C) treats stock owned by a corporation as owned proportionately by its shareholders, but only if the shareholders meet a minimum threshold of stock ownership in the corporation.

For Subpart F purposes, Section 958(b)(3) reduces that threshold from 50 percent to ten percent.

(4) Section 318(a)(3)(C) requires attribution of stock owned by a partner of a partnership, a beneficiary of a trust or estate or 50–percent-or-more shareholder of a corporation to the partnership, trust, estate or corporation. However, Section 958(b)(4) provides that stock owned by a foreign person (i.e., nonresident alien individual, foreign corporation, foreign partnership or foreign trust or estate) will not be attributed to a U.S. person under Section 318(a)(3)(C).

For purposes of any one determination, in applying the direct, indirect and constructive ownership rules in Section 958(a) and (b), the same stock cannot be counted twice (i.e., the same stock cannot be attributed twice to the same person under different indirect ownership or attribution rules or to two different persons under the same or different indirect ownership or attribution rules). However, stock that may be owned by a person under more than one of these rules, or by more than one person, is treated as "owned under that attribution rule which imputes to the person, or persons, concerned the largest total percentage of such stock." Reg. § 1.958–2(f)(2).

The following problems are intended to introduce the application of these indirect and constructive ownership rules.

[¶ 6035]

PROBLEMS

1. Zeus S.A. is a Swiss corporation that has 1,000 shares of a single class of stock outstanding, of which 460 shares are owned by Jupiter Corp., a widely held U.S. corporation, and the remaining 540 shares are owned in equal amounts (i.e., 90 shares each) by six individuals who are U.S. citizens and who are not related to one another by family or business relationships. Is Zeus a controlled foreign corporation?

2. If the facts are the same as in Problem 1, but the number of individual shareholders is reduced from six to five (owning 108 shares each), is Zeus a controlled foreign corporation?

3. The facts are the same as in Problem 1, except that one of the shareholders of Zeus is not an individual but a U.S. investment partnership which owns 90 shares of Zeus directly. One of the individuals who owns 90 shares of Zeus directly also owns a five-percent interest in the profits and capital of the partnership. Is Zeus a controlled foreign corporation?

4. If the facts are the same as in Problem 1, except that two of the individuals are husband and wife, is Zeus a controlled foreign corporation?

5. Would your answer in Problem 4 change if the wife is a nonresident alien?

6. If the facts are the same as in Problem 1, except that two of the individuals are brother and sister, is Zeus a controlled foreign corporation?

7. If the facts are the same as in Problem 1, except that one of the individuals also owns 50 percent of the stock of Jupiter Corp., is Zeus a controlled foreign corporation?

8. Would your answer in Problem 7 change if that individual owns ten percent of the Jupiter Corp. stock?

9. Would your answer in Problem 7 change if that individual owns five percent of the Jupiter Corp. stock?

10. The facts are the same as in Problem 1, except that of the 1,000 shares of Zeus stock outstanding, 410 shares are owned by Jupiter Corp. and 90 shares are owned by a U.S. citizen who also owns three percent of the shares of Juno B.V., a Dutch corporation that owns 500 Zeus shares. Is Zeus a controlled foreign corporation?

[¶ 6040]

2. VOTING–POWER OR VALUE TEST

Both of the following cases concern whether the foreign corporation at issue is a "controlled foreign corporation." Both cases were decided under the definition of controlled foreign corporation in effect before the Tax Reform Act of 1986. As discussed above, the 1986 Act amended Section 957(a) by adding to the preexisting test based on U.S. shareholders (as defined in Section 951(b)) owning more than 50 percent of the total voting power of the foreign corporation's stock, an *alternative* test based on U.S. shareholders owning more than 50 percent of the total value of the foreign corporation's stock.[13] Thus, under current law, a foreign corporation will be treated as a controlled foreign corporation if the U.S. shareholders own more than 50 percent of *either* the total voting power *or* total value of the corporation's stock.

[¶ 6045]

CCA, INC. v. COMMISSIONER

United States Tax Court, 1975.
64 T.C. 137 (nonacq.).

WILES, JUDGE: * * *. The only remaining issue for decision is whether a Swiss corporation is determined to be a controlled foreign corporation within the meaning of section 957(a).

13. A different definition of "controlled foreign corporation" applies to foreign corporations engaging in certain insurance activities. See §§ 953 and 957(b).

FINDINGS OF FACT

* * *

Controls Co. of America (hereinafter referred to as old CCA) was organized under Delaware law on January 29, 1953. * * *

* * *

On or about June 23, 1958, old CCA organized a Swiss corporation known as Control AG (hereinafter referred to as AG) with the principal office at Zug, Switzerland, as a wholly owned subsidiary. From the date of incorporation to November 30, 1963, old CCA owned beneficially all of AG's issued and outstanding capital stock, which, as of the close of business November 29, 1963, consisted of 800 common shares having a par value of 1,000 Swiss francs per share. For purposes of compliance with the requirements of Swiss corporate law, 1 share of AG common stock stood in the name of each of the persons elected by old CCA as a director of AG during their respective terms of office.

The articles of incorporation of AG that were in effect from June 23, 1958, to November 30, 1963 (hereinafter referred to as the 1958 articles), provided for a board of directors consisting of not less than three nor more than five members who were required to be shareholders. Although the 1958 articles referred to the board as a board of directors, the governing body in Swiss corporations is generally referred to as a board of administrators and the articles of incorporation as amended, in effect, on and after November 30, 1963, did so refer to the governing body of AG. The 1958 articles provided that the managing director had the power to bind a corporation singly but that members of the board had the power to bind the corporation only jointly. The 1958 articles also provided that in case of a tie the vote of the chairman is decisive. The 1958 articles stated that the duration of the corporation is perpetual. With regard to transfers of stock the 1958 articles provided as follows:

> The Corporation keeps a stock register book in which the names and addresses of the shareholders are entered. Only persons registered in the stock register book are recognized as shareholders by the Corporation. The registration shall be certified on the same certificate by a member of the Board of Directors. The Board of Directors may refuse the registration of a shareholder without having to state a reason.

* * *

AG was initially created for the purpose of exporting old CCA's products from the United States. On May 1, 1959, old CCA entered into an agreement with AG whereby the latter was granted the exclusive right to use (and permit others to use) in any country except the United States, Canada, or the Netherlands, "the designs, technical know-how and manufacturing information and processes of [old] CCA." The agreement also granted AG the exclusive right (including the right to license others) under patents listed in the agreement. * * * The agreement further provided AG the exclusive use, within Switzerland, of trademarks listed in the agreement and those which are acquired by old CCA during the life of the agreement. * * * AG then expanded with manufacturing plants in other European countries. The operation of these subsidiaries was financed by a small investment by AG and by loans from AG which in turn were subordinated to loans of local banks in each of the countries.

* * *

Upon passage of the Revenue Act of 1962 (hereinafter referred to as the 1962 Act), representatives of old CCA became concerned with the possible adverse effects of the controlled foreign corporation provisions on its European operations. Old CCA contacted its attorneys and accountants in order to determine if it could comply with the Revenue Act of 1962 and still take advantage of the tax-deferral provisions. Upon advice of counsel, old CCA decided to "decontrol" AG. In a board of directors meeting of old CCA held on September 24, 1963, reorganization of the European operation was discussed * * *. * * * On October 28, 1963, a letter from * * * [the] secretary of old CCA * * * contained a consent to action by the members of old CCA's board of directors without a meeting to establish the following program:

> Basically, the program involves transferring stock equities from Controls Aktiengesellschaft (Controls A.G., the Swiss company) to Controls Maatschappij Europa N.V. and then issuing a new preferred stock by Controls A.G. with 50% of the voting power. This will leave ownership of all of our operating companies in Holland which is owned 100% by Controls Company and leave Controls Company with 50% control of the Swiss service company.

Between October 14, 1963, and November 5, 1963, old CCA contacted various European brokers with regard to placement of the proposed issue of preferred stock. Correspondence to these brokers from A. E. Kornhauser (hereinafter referred to as Kornhauser), treasurer of old CCA, indicated that the primary concern of old CCA in issuing the preferred stock was conformity with the Revenue Act of 1962. Letters to some brokers also stated that the preferred stock must be sold to investors not related in business to old CCA and which cannot be deemed to be under their influence. "In other words, they should be bona fide long-term investors." In a letter dated October 14, 1963, to a European broker, Kornhauser stated that:

> In view of the short time that we have to place these shares, we have decided that if it becomes necessary in order to satisfy our prospective investors with respect to the safety of principal and continuity of income, Controls Company of America will provide a right or put to the investor to sell his shares to Controls company of America at par plus accrued dividends.

In a letter dated November 5, 1963, Kornhauser told another broker that "any formal agreement on the part of the preferred shareholders to sell their shares to Controls Company or its designee would in effect give us a call on the issue." He therefore indicated that any such provision should be removed. During this same period, old CCA sought investment in the proposed preferred stock issue by a United States institutional investor to the extent of a 9–percent interest, so that such investor would not be classified as a United States shareholder under provisions of the 1962 Act.

On November 8, 1963, AG transferred to Controls Maatschappij Europa N.V. (hereinafter referred to as CME), a wholly owned Dutch subsidiary of old CCA, for 6,029,804.75 Swiss francs, all of its stock in * * * [five European manufacturing subsidiaries]. The transfer of the manufacturing subsidiaries from AG to CME was not a simple or routine transaction. The decision to make this transfer had been reached in mid-October and had to be completed within 6 weeks. Clearance had to be obtained from the Swiss and Dutch tax authorities and the corporate and tax laws of England, France, Italy, Holland, Switzerland, Argentina, and Brazil had to be reviewed. The cost of the transfer was approximately $30,000–$35,000.

On November 29, 1963, the board of administrators of AG resolved to increase the capital stock of AG by issuing 800 6–percent preferred nominative shares of 1,000 Swiss francs par value each, fully paid. Each share of common stock and each share of preferred stock was entitled to one vote. This resolution was approved by the shareholders of AG on November 30, 1963. Swiss Credit Bank and Bank und Finanz–Institut A.G., Swiss corporations, each subscribed to 400 shares of the preferred stock of AG, and by November 30, 1963, had placed said shares with the University of Wisconsin Trust and four Swiss corporations. * * *

From November 30, 1963, through July 11, 1968, the only classes of stock of AG authorized, issued, and outstanding were 800 shares of common stock and 800 shares of preferred stock, both classes having a par value per share of 1,000 Swiss francs. Each share of common stock and each share of preferred stock was entitled to one vote. From November 30, 1963, through July 11, 1968, the 800 shares of common stock of AG were beneficially owned by old CCA or new CCA. The AG preferred stock was owned at all times only by persons who are not United States shareholders and the ownership of such stock may not be attributed under any provision of the [Code] to old CCA or new CCA or to any other person.

AG's articles of incorporation were amended on November 30, 1963 (hereinafter referred to as 1963 articles), by public deed at a special meeting of shareholders. Articles of incorporation of a Swiss company commonly contain a provision giving the chairman of the board of administrators the power to break a tie vote; however, the 1963 articles contained no such provision. With regard to transfer of shares of stock, the 1963 articles provided as follows:

> The Corporation shall maintain a stock register in which the names and addresses of the shareholders are entered. Only persons

registered in the stock register shall be recognized as shareholders by the Corporation. The registration of a shareholder in the stock register shall be certified on the share or the share certificate by the signature of a member of the Board of Administrators. The Board of Administrators' approval is required for each registration, and it may refuse to register a new shareholder without indicating any reason for such refusal.

The 1963 articles provided for a 10–member board of administrators, 5 each to be nominated by the common and preferred shareholders. Under Swiss law, if an administrator retired, resigned, or otherwise ceased to be an administrator, the same class of stock that nominated him would nominate his successor.

* * *

After November 30, 1963, AG's board consisted of 10 members. Five of such members were appointed by and represented the common shareholders. [The other five were appointed by the preferred shareholders.] * * *

Under provisions of Swiss law the authority of anyone, including a member of a Swiss company's board of administrators, to represent the company and to exercise executive powers is founded on "signature power" as evidenced by registry in the Swiss commercial register. All the members of AG's board of administrators representing the preferred stock had joint signature power. That is, any two of the members of AG's board of administrators acting jointly had the executive power to represent AG vis-à-vis the outside world. Any restrictions of these powers would be void as regards bona fide third parties unless they were entered in the commercial register. No such restrictions were entered in the commercial register.

Under Swiss law, any restriction on the voting rights of shareholders of a Swiss company or on their right to be represented by proxy will not be recognized unless such provision is contained in the articles of incorporation. The 1963 articles contained no provision restricting the voting rights of shareholders except for a requirement that obligated both common and preferred shareholders to vote for each group's nominee to the board of administrators. This obligation was unconditional "provided that there are no important reasons to the contrary." Also under Swiss law, preferred shares of a Swiss company rank equally in all respects with common shares of a Swiss company except as provided in the articles of incorporation.

On December 1, 1963, AG and old CCA entered into a licensing agreement for all countries of the world except North, Central, and South America, Australia, Malaysia, New Zealand, Formosa, Hong Kong, Japan, Korea, Okinawa, and the Netherlands. The agreement provided that AG was granted the exclusive right to use (and permit others to use) "the designs, technical know-how and manufacturing information and processes of [old] CCA." The agreement also granted AG the exclusive right to use (and grant sublicenses using) patents listed in the agreement and to use, within Switzerland, patents listed in the agreement. The agreement was to remain in effect until December 31, 1968, and from year to year thereafter unless terminated by either party after a default or through written notice given 90 days prior to the expiration of the original term or renewal period. The agreement between old CCA and AG could not be assigned, in whole or in part, by either party without the prior written consent of the other party.

On February 23, 1966, [new CCA was formed] * * * for the purpose of acquiring the business and substantially all the assets of old CCA. * * *

The transfer of the common shares of AG from old CCA to [new CCA] * * * was approved by the board of administrators at a meeting held on April 29, 1966. Present at the meeting were all five board members who represented the preferred shareholders. * * * [Only two] members representing the common shareholders * * * were present at the meeting.

Under Swiss law, the board of administrators of a Swiss company exercises powers ordinarily exercised by both the board of directors and officers of a United States corporation. Under provisions of Swiss law, shareholders of a Swiss company can only receive dividends if the meeting of shareholders declares dividends.

During the period November 30, 1963, through July 11, 1968, AG held its ordinary shareholders meeting annually, except for an additional special shareholders meeting held on August 22, 1966. Although under Swiss law a board of administrators may delegate the management and representation of the company to a board member or members or third parties, AG's board made no such delegation. As a result, the right of management and representation of AG rested jointly with all members of the board.

There were no express agreements, written or oral, between the parties involved with respect to the manner in which the preferred stockholders would vote their stock. There were no express understandings or other kind of agreements between the parties with regard to any preferred shareholder refraining from voting his stock in the manner his judgment and interests dictated.

During the period November 30, 1963, through July 11, 1968, there were five regular shareholders meetings and one special shareholders meeting. With the exception of the University of Wisconsin Trust, the preferred shareholders were represented through proxy by members of the board who represented the preferred shareholders. On three occasions, the University of Wisconsin Trust was represented through proxy by Peter D. Lederer, an attorney for the law firm which represented old CCA. During the shareholders meetings, the preferred shareholders' representative raised many questions with regard to the operation of the business of AG, ranging from the effect of a request by President Johnson for American corporations to decrease the value of financing foreign operations from United States sources to the future use of office space by AG. During this same period, the board of administrators met on five separate occasions. At two meetings, the preferred and common stockholders were equally represented. At one meeting, representatives of the preferred shareholders outnumbered the representatives of the common shareholders five to two. At two meetings, representatives of the common shareholders outnumbered representatives of the preferred shareholders four to three. The board, on several occasions, also acted on matters unanimously by virtue of circulated correspondence.

From November 30, 1963, through July 11, 1968, the only classes of stock authorized, issued, and outstanding were 800 shares of common stock and 800 shares of preferred stock. Each class of stock has par value of 1,000 Swiss francs per share. Paid-in capital of the stock of AG was 800,000 ($186,047) Swiss francs for each class of stock.

OPINION

Section 951 provides that a United States shareholder of a "controlled foreign corporation" must include in its income its pro rata share of the controlled foreign corporation's "subpart F income" regardless of whether that income has been distributed to the shareholder. There is no dispute in this case as to the amount of AG's income or that all such income was subpart F income. Also there is no question that petitioners were United States shareholders within the meaning of section 951(b). Consequently, the only issue for decision is whether AG was a "controlled foreign corporation" during the taxable years in issue within the meaning of section 957(a).

Section 957(a) defines the term "controlled foreign corporation" as any foreign corporation of which more than 50 percent of the total combined voting power of all classes of stock entitled to vote is owned by United States shareholders on any day during the taxable year of such corporation.

Petitioners argue that since legal ownership of more than 50 percent of the total combined voting power of all classes of stock of AG entitled to vote was in the hands of non-United States shareholders, AG is not a controlled foreign corporation within the definition of section 957(a). Respondent contends that by virtue of all surrounding facts and circumstances, petitioners, in effect, retained more than 50 percent of the voting power of AG.

A mere technical compliance with section 957(a) is not sufficient to exclude petitioners from its application. *Hans P. Kraus*, 59 T.C. 681 (1973), affd. 490 F.2d 898 (2d Cir.1974); *Garlock, Inc.*, 58 T.C. 423 (1972), affd. 489 F.2d 197 (2d Cir.1973), cert. denied 417 U.S. 911 (1974). The 50–

percent test of section 957(a) was intended to exclude from the definition of controlled foreign corporation only those foreign corporations which are not subject to the dominion and control of the United States shareholders. *Garlock, Inc.*, *supra* at 433. We must determine whether the substance of the transaction in this case was that which the statute intended, specifically, a meaningful ownership of at least 50 percent of the voting power of AG by non-United States shareholders.

Section 1.957–1(b)(2), Income Tax Regs., provides in part that "Any arrangement to shift formal voting power away from United States shareholders of a foreign corporation will not be given effect if in reality voting power is retained." * * *

After a comprehensive analysis of the evidence in this case we are of the opinion that the petitioners divested themselves of meaningful voting power in AG.

The 6–percent preferred stock of AG was issued without substantial restriction except that transfer was subject to approval by the board of administrators. This restriction, however, appears to be reasonable for several reasons. First, the common stock was also subject to the same restriction. Second, the restriction appears to be reasonable to insure that at least 50 percent of the voting power of AG remained in the hands of non-United States shareholders. Furthermore, the restriction of nontransfer without approval of the board of administrators was merely a carryover from the 1958 articles of incorporation. In other words, this restriction appears to be merely an extension of old corporate rules to cover the new issuance of preferred stock. Finally, in this case the transfer of preferred stock by preferred stockholders was approved by the board on the only two occasions when transfers were requested. This is in sharp contrast with the situation in the *Kraus* case in which the preferred stock was subject to several substantial restrictions while the common stock was issued without any restrictions at all.

The board of directors was evenly split between representatives of the common and preferred stockholders during the entire period and there were no provisions for breaking deadlocks. In fact, any provisions to prevent deadlocks were purposely avoided by the parties. We also deem as significant the powers which the representatives of the preferred shareholders possessed under Swiss law. These included: (1) The power to vote on dividends to be declared, which included dividends to the common shareholders; (2) to vote on transfer of registration of common stock; and (3) the power to alter the course of corporate events by use of the "signature power" which could have bound the corporation. Respondent does not contest the presence of these powers but argues that they are irrelevant because in reality the preferred shareholders had no reason to ever use such powers because they possessed only the limited right to a fixed dividend. We recognize that the preferred shareholders had a more limited interest to protect than the common shareholders and that this was one factor in both the *Garlock* and *Kraus* cases. None the less, we are not prepared to state that the preferred shareholders possessing such wide powers were not disposed to use such powers to protect the interest they did have. Neither of the taxpayers in *Kraus* or *Garlock* possessed such wide powers. See also *Estate of Edwin C. Weiskopf*, 64 T.C. 78 (1975) [excerpted at ¶ 13,125]. Moreover, the interests of the common shareholders in those cases were buttressed by restrictions on redemption or reacquisition of the preferred stock which inured strictly to the benefit of the common shareholders. In other words, there were significant strings tied to any action which the preferred shareholders would take.

The parties have argued at great length with regard to the question of whether the preferred shareholders actively participated in the corporate affairs of the corporation. This Court in the *Kraus* case specifically relied on the fact that "the evidence does not indicate any active participation in the management of (the company) by the preferred shareholders." In the *Garlock* case this Court relied on the "manipulation and selection" of the board of directors "as negativing any shift of control from the taxpayers." The evidence in this case shows a continued participation by the representatives of the preferred shareholders in the affairs by virtue of their activities on the board of directors and at the shareholder meetings. As noted by this Court in the *Kraus* case, a highly successful corporation is apt to sell its shares to persons who are indisposed to question corporate policy. The minutes of the corporate shareholders meetings of AG, however, show that the representatives of the preferred shareholders took an active part in considering various questions with regard to the activities of AG. These questions ranged from the use of office space by AG within Switzerland to the question of pressure being applied by President Johnson on United States corporations with regard to investments in foreign countries. What was lacking in [the] *Weiskopf*, *Kraus*, and *Garlock* cases was any real opportunity to alter the course of events by the preferred shareholders. In this case the preferred shareholders had, by virtue of the powers which they possessed, a real opportunity to alter the course of events of the corporation if they desired to do so. Their participation in the shareholders meeting also showed that the preferred shareholders were interested in protecting the interest which they did possess in the corporation.

Prior to the issuance of the preferred stock in AG old CCA had AG transfer its ownership interest in other foreign manufacturing corporations to a third foreign corporation, CME. Representatives of old CCA testified that this was done in order to insure that the 50–percent voting power given up to the preferred shareholders would not interfere in any way with the activities of these manufacturing corporations. We view this transfer as some indication that petitioners viewed the issuance of the preferred stock as a threat to their unfettered control over AG. After such transfer AG's business activities consisted of licensing technology to CCA subsidiaries, as well as to third parties, and technical service, assistance, and sales activities in Europe and the Middle East.

The overall arrangement also shows that old CCA intended to divest itself of 50 percent of the voting power of AG in order to meet the provisions of the Revenue Act of 1962. This factor, however, does not "taint" the transfer per se. In *Hans P. Kraus*, *supra* at 693, this Court stated:

> We have no doubt that the effects of being classified as a controlled foreign corporation have caused many U.S. shareholders to divest themselves of enough voting power to avoid section 957(a). There is clearly nothing improper about such a purpose for the divestiture.

Old CCA attempted to so divest itself by issuing preferred stock with 50 percent of the voting power of AG to non-United States shareholders.

The aggregate effect of the factors considered above indicates that old CCA did divest itself of dominion and control of AG. There were no substantial restrictions placed upon the preferred stock that were not also placed upon the common stock. Nor were there any provisions made whereby old CCA would reacquire the stock of the preferred shareholders should they desire to sell the stock. Furthermore, a board of directors that was equally divided between preferred and common shareholders was established and the members of that board were given very significant powers which could have been used by both the common and the preferred shareholders to alter the course of events of the corporation. The preferred stock was sold to nonrelated shareholders whose representatives at the shareholders meetings and the board of directors took an active part in the consideration of AG's business. Old CCA retained no significant strings which could have been used by it to require the preferred shareholders to vote with it regarding questions of AG's business. This is in sharp contrast to the cases in which this Court has found that United States shareholders retained dominion and control over the foreign corporation. See *Estate of Edwin C. Weiskopf*, *supra*; *Hans P. Kraus*, *supra*; *Garlock, Inc.*, *supra*. We recognize that, as in the *Kraus* case, the amount paid by the preferred shareholders for their stock was less than 50 percent of the net worth of AG. This fact alone, in light of the other factors present in this case, is not sufficient to classify AG as a controlled foreign corporation.

We hold that under the facts and circumstances of this case, old CCA successfully divested itself of 50 percent of the voting power of AG. Therefore, AG is not considered to be a controlled foreign corporation within the provisions of section 957(a).

* * *

[¶ 6050]

KOEHRING CO. v. UNITED STATES

United States Court of Appeals, Seventh Circuit, 1978.
583 F.2d 313.

WOOD, CIRCUIT JUDGE:

The question presented in this appeal is whether the district court erred in finding that a foreign corporation partially owned by the Koehring Company was a "controlled foreign corporation" within the meaning of Section 957 * * *. We affirm.

The facts as found by the district court in its unreported opinion are as follows: Koehring Company (taxpayer) is a Wisconsin corporation engaged in the manufacture of heavy construction equipment. In 1959 Koehring acquired a Panamanian corporation which it renamed Koehring Overseas Corporation (KOS). KOS was thereafter operated as a wholly-owned subsidiary responsible for the overseas marketing of Koehring products in the western hemisphere. Under the provisions of the Internal Revenue Code (IRC or Code) prevailing at that time, KOS's profits were not taxed to Koehring until remitted to the parent corporation in the form of a dividend. However, in 1962 Congress debated adding provisions to the IRC which would have taxed the undistributed income of certain controlled foreign corporations. This change was a matter of concern to Koehring officials, who made their views known to members of Congress. Nevertheless, in October of 1962 Congress added the provisions of Subpart F to the Code which would have required Koehring to pay taxes on KOS's undistributed earnings.

In 1963 Koehring entered into an arrangement designed to take KOS out of the ambit of Subpart F by transferring voting control of KOS to Newton Chambers, an English corporation, also engaged in the manufacture of construction machinery. On or about September 3, 1963, Newton Chambers acquired 44,000 shares of newly issued 8% cumulative voting preferred stock with a par value of $10 per share. This represented 55% of the outstanding KOS stock entitled to a vote. Koehring retained 36,000 voting shares of $10 par value common stock, representing the remaining 45% of the voting shares.

At the time of the sale, Newton Chambers and Koehring enjoyed a long standing business relationship, which began shortly after World War II. At that time Koehring gave Newton Chambers a license to manufacture certain equipment designed by Koehring and to market the products in an exclusive territory encompassing much of the eastern hemisphere. In subsequent years Newton Chambers was gradually relieved of portions of its exclusive territory, largely because of its alleged lack of diligence in promoting sales of the Koehring products. This and related problems were the subject of ongoing discussions between the two companies beginning in 1958. Both corporations wanted to improve the international marketing of their products. One of the ideas discussed was the concept of a jointly-owned international marketing subsidiary.

In 1962 Koehring acquired an interest in a French company which it renamed Koehring–Brissonneau. Since Koehring–Brissonneau was engaged in marketing Koehring products in continental Europe, Newton Chambers' chairman, Sir Peter Roberts, protested that the licensing agreement between Koehring and Newton Chambers was being violated and renewed his suggestion of a joint marketing subsidiary. More specifically, his letter suggested that Newton Chambers acquire an equity interest in KOS and that KOS should be the means of coordinating the "international impact of Koehring."

In the spring and summer of 1963, Koehring and Newton Chambers discussed various cross-investment plans. On July 5, 1963, Newton Chambers applied for exchange control approval for the acquisition of the $400,000 worth of KOS preferred stock. Newton Chambers was to acquire the KOS stock on September 1, 1963, but with a right to force redemption of the shares at a premium after June 30, 1968. In December of 1963 Koehring–Waterous, Koehring's Canadian subsidiary, was to invest $400,000 in an issue of 5% redeemable, non-voting preferred stock to be issued by Ransomes & Rapier, Ltd., a Newton Chambers subsidiary. However, in August of 1963, Koehring discovered that under Panamanian law KOS preferred could not be issued at less than par value, which meant that Newton Chambers would have to invest $440,000 rather than $400,000. At the same time, the amount that Koehring was to invest in Ransomes & Rapier was increased by $40,000. In the end, by February of 1964 Koehring–Waterous had purchased 143,000 shares of Newton Chambers preferred stock for $440,000 (instead of the Ransomes & Rapier preferred) and Koehring itself had purchased 325,000 shares of Ransomes & Rapier common stock for approximately $2,400,000 and 100,000 shares of Ransomes & Rapier preferred for 63,272 pounds. Newton Chambers purchased the 44,000 shares of KOS preferred which the district court found to be subject to an agreement that Newton Chambers would be allowed to withdraw its investment on one year's notice.

In September 1963, a new KOS Board of Directors was constituted; three directors being elected by Newton Chambers and two by Koehring. In January 1964, Sir Peter Roberts became Chairman. The district court found that between October 25, 1963, and November 1967 there were ten board meetings and two stockholders meetings. Of the two stockholders meetings, one was adjourned for lack of a quorum and no Newton Chambers representatives attended the other. Of the ten board meetings, no Newton Chambers directors participated in six, one of which had to be adjourned for lack of a quorum. One of the four directors meetings attended by Newton Chambers directors was that at which Sir Peter Roberts was elected Chairman. At each of the others the primary actions were found by the district court to be of a passive nature more consistent with the theory that KOS was an instrumentality of Koehring than that it was a joint international sales subsidiary actively dominated by Newton Chambers. The court also made the following finding:

> The actions of the Newton–Chambers directors was such as would be expected of sham directors whose real interest lay in protecting the Newton–Chambers stake in KOS. On April 1, 1965, Sir Peter Roberts urged that KOS keep $440,000 in the bank to protect the preferred shareholder's investment. On September 16, 1966, Sir Peter Roberts acquiesced in surrendering to Koehring–Brissonneau the European territory and former non-British African colony territory. In November 1967, the Newton–Chambers directors successfully opposed declaring a dividend on the common stock.

After Newton Chambers acquired majority control of KOS there were remarkably few changes in KOS operations. Newton Chambers did not attempt to replace existing management, which was closely identified with Koehring, with executives more loyal to Newton Chambers. KOS continued to sell only Koehring products until 1967, when it began selling a few Newton Chambers products on a trial basis at the suggestion of Koehring's president. No Newton Chambers directors were authorized to draw checks on behalf of KOS, even though at least two Koehring directors who were not officers of KOS were so authorized. Moreover, Newton Chambers referred to its control over KOS as being "nominal" in the minutes of the Board of Directors meeting on September 11, 1963 (Exhibit G), and stated that its investment in KOS was "nominal" in its 1963 annual report.[1]

On the basis of the above facts, the Internal Revenue Service claimed that for the tax year ending November 30, 1964, KOS was a "controlled foreign corporation" of Koehring as defined by Section 957 * * * and that its "Subpart F" income was therefore taxable to Koehring under Section 951 even though not yet distributed as a dividend to Koehring. * * *

I.

Subpart F of the IRC was enacted in order to deter United States taxpayers from using related foreign base companies located in tax haven countries to accumulate earnings that could have been accumulated just as easily in the United States. By requiring the United States taxpayer to include in his current taxable income his share of the current foreign base company income of foreign corporations controlled by him, Subpart F removes the tax deferral benefits of such off-shore earnings accumulations. For the purposes of this subpart, Section 957(a) * * * defines a "controlled foreign corporation" (hereinafter CFC) as "any foreign corporation of which more than 50 percent of the total combined voting power

1. The finding with respect to the Board meeting was not made by the district court. The reference in the annual report merely indicated that the investment was nominal from an accounting point of view for consolidation purposes.

of all classes of stock entitled to vote is owned ... by United States shareholders...." Not surprisingly, the Treasury Regulations relating to Section 957 require that in certain circumstances the nominal distribution of voting power will be ignored when it is not consistent with the reality of control. Of particular relevance to the case at bar are the two parts of Regulation § 1.957–1(b)(2). The first part of that regulation provides:

> (2) Shifting of formal voting power. Any arrangement to shift formal voting power away from United States shareholders of a foreign corporation will not be given effect if in reality voting power is retained. The mere ownership of stock entitled to vote does not by itself mean that the shareholder owning such stock has the voting power to such stock for purposes of section 957. For example, if there is any agreement, whether express or implied, that any shareholder will not vote his stock or will vote it only in a specified manner, or that shareholders owning stock having not more than 50 percent of the total combined voting power will exercise voting power normally possessed by a majority of stockholders, then the nominal ownership of the voting power will be disregarded in determining which shareholders actually hold such voting power, and this determination will be made on the basis of such agreement.

Here, the IRS argues that the nominal control of KOS was transferred by Koehring to Newton Chambers pursuant to an implied agreement which effectively permitted Koehring to continue to exercise operating control over its marketing subsidiary. The second part of Regulation 1.957–1(b)(2) sets forth the "tri-test" which is to be applied where there are separate classes of voting stock:

> [W]here United States shareholders own shares of one or more classes of stock of a foreign corporation which has another class of stock outstanding, the voting power ostensibly provided such other class of stock will be deemed owned by any person or persons on whose behalf it is exercised or, if not exercised, will be disregarded [1] *if the percentage of voting power of such other class of stock is substantially greater than its proportionate share of the corporate earnings,* [2] *if the facts indicate that the shareholders of such other class of stock do not exercise their voting rights independently or fail to exercise such voting rights, and* [3] *if a principal purpose of the arrangement is to avoid the classification of such foreign corporation as a controlled foreign corporation under section 957.* (Emphasis added.)

The IRS also argues that the facts of the present case come within the tri-test and that Newton Chambers' nominal voting control should therefore be disregarded.

On appeal, Koehring does not challenge the validity of the above regulations,[4] but rather their applicability to the facts of this case. They

4. The Regulation has been upheld in other cases. See, *e.g. Garlock, Inc. v. Commissioner*, 489 F.2d 197, 201 (2d Cir.1973).

argue that there was no agreement that Newton Chambers would abstain from exercising its power to control the operations of KOS, but that, quite to the contrary, it was made clear to Koehring at the time that the stock purchase was being negotiated that Newton Chambers would exercise its majority power in its own interests should there be a conflict.[5] They also argue that the tri-test is not applicable. It is not strongly urged that the arrangement with Newton Chambers did not have as a principal purpose the avoidance of KOS being classified as a CFC. Nor is there a substantial challenge to the district court's conclusion that Newton Chambers' ownership of the separate class of stock carried with it a percentage voting power that was substantially greater than its proportionate share of KOS's earnings.[6] However, Koehring does forcefully disagree with the district court on the question of whether Newton Chambers exercised its voting rights independently within the meaning of the second branch of the tri-test.

II.

Koehring has graphically demonstrated that the voting preferred issued to Newton Chambers here was subject to fewer formal restrictions than the stock issued to the foreign shareholders in other cases in which a transfer of control has been found to be illusory. *See Garlock, Inc. v. Commissioner*, 489 F.2d 197 (2d Cir.1973), *aff'g* 58 T.C. 423, *cert. denied*, 417 U.S. 911 * * * (1974); *Kraus v. Commissioner*, 490 F.2d 898 (2d Cir.1974), *aff'g* 59 T.C. 681 (1973); *Estate of Weiskopf*, 64 T.C. 78 (1975), *aff'd*, 538 F.2d 317 * * * (2d Cir.1976). The formal restrictions found in those cases included restrictions on the transferability of the shares, call provisions, provisions giving the stockholders the right to force redemption of their shares, etc. In addition, in each of those cases there was a 50–50 division of voting rights between the U.S. shareholders and foreign shareholders. In the present case, Newton Chambers acquired shares representing 55% of the total voting shares, and there was an absence of formal restrictions on transfer, call features, or charter provisions permitting Newton Chambers to force redemption of its shares.[7] Formal restrictions on the transferability of the stock issued to the foreign shareholders might be useful to the U.S. shareholder where the foreign shareholder has been chosen because of his lack of interest in exercising its voting power.

5. Koehring's concern with the tax consequences of Subpart F was manifest even before that section was enacted. Moreover, the record is replete with evidence which demonstrates that, even if there were some business reasons for Newton Chambers to make an investment in KOS, the transaction was timed and structured the way that it was largely because of Koehring's desire to avoid the tax consequences of Subpart F.

6. The issue of preferred stock gave Newton Chambers 55% of the total voting rights, yet less than 10% of the average annual earnings.

7. The district court found that Newton Chambers had the right to withdraw with one year's notice—a finding that Koehring attacks as clearly erroneous. We do not interpret the district court's finding to be that there was a formal right to force redemption attached to the preferred shares, but rather that the right to withdraw was part of the "understanding" between Koehring and Newton Chambers.

In such a case, the restrictions on transfer could prevent the shares from falling into unfriendly hands. Formal provisions giving the foreign shareholders a "put" on their stock would make it more attractive for them to invest money in a corporation which they realize will be controlled in fact by the U.S. shareholder, by giving them an enforceable means of withdrawing their investment without loss. A provision giving the corporation the right to call the shares issued to the foreign shareholders would allow the U.S. shareholder to protect its control by forcing out the foreign shareholders if they should try to take their nominal voting rights seriously. A 50–50 split of the voting rights combined with other formal features or circumstances giving the U.S. shareholder a modicum of additional leverage can insure that the latter will retain effective control even if the foreign shareholders were to try to exercise their full voting power. Thus, the presence of one or more of these features tends to support a finding that the U.S. shareholder has arranged things in such a way that he has not actually divested himself of effective control. This does not mean that an absence of such formal restrictions militates against a finding that an apparent transfer of a majority of the voting rights merely hides an elaborate and subtle arrangement for retaining operational control. In the present case, this purpose was allegedly accomplished by an informal side agreement between Newton Chambers and Koehring rather than by more visible tinkering with the nature of the legal rights formally transferred to the English company.

III.

Koehring's version of Newton Chambers' investment in KOS might be paraphrased as follows. Koehring and Newton Chambers have had a long-standing, cooperative relationship in the production and marketing of heavy construction equipment, with the primary component being Newton Chambers' license to manufacture and market Koehring-designed equipment in large areas of the globe. Desiring even further integration of the interests of the two companies, it was decided that Newton Chambers would take a controlling equity position in KOS as a first step in turning KOS into a joint-marketing subsidiary for the products of both companies. This was done by issuance of KOS preferred to Newton Chambers, which then used its voting power to elect a majority of the board of directors. Newton Chambers proceeded to use this majority to protect its interests as a preferred shareholder and to promote the transformation of KOS into a joint-sales subsidiary selling both Koehring and Newton Chambers products. Independently, Koehring made an equity investment in the Newton Chambers group in order to more closely link the interests of the two companies in the eastern hemisphere.

The IRS sees the situation differently. After the passage of Subpart F, Koehring was anxious to find some means of shielding KOS's profits from the taxman, but without losing operating control of its subsidiary. It was decided to transfer nominal control to Newton Chambers, a company that

Koehring could trust and which was sympathetic to Koehring's tax plight. Because of the long-standing working relationship between the two companies and Newton Chambers' continuing dependence on Koehring under the license agreement, Newton Chambers would have little incentive to try to use its nominal control over KOS to make operating changes against Koehring's wishes. Because Newton Chambers was short of cash, an arrangement was made for a cross-investment by Koehring in the Newton Chambers group of companies, thus giving Newton Chambers nominal control of KOS for a zero net investment. In order to compensate Newton Chambers for the risks and inconveniences of taking nominal control of KOS, the dividend rates on the two issues of preferred involved in the cross-investments were adjusted so as to give Newton Chambers a net gain. Both investors were also given the right to withdraw should the need arise. Although there was no formal redemption feature on the KOS stock, there was an informal understanding to this effect. After the transfer of nominal control, the Newton Chambers directors would occasionally appear to participate in the running of KOS, but effective operational control remained in Koehring's hands. An occasional action was taken to protect Newton Chambers' minimal financial interest in KOS, such as the setting up of a cash reserve for the redemption of Newton Chambers' preferred stock, but this was apparently a part of the original agreement between Koehring and Newton Chambers. Thus, what might have otherwise been construed as evidence of Newton Chambers' independent use of its control position to protect its own limited interests was actually part of the prearranged consideration for its willingness to help Koehring out with its tax problem.

The district court appears to have accepted the second version of events and we cannot say that the record is inconsistent with its findings. We also agree that the nature of the agreement between Koehring and Newton Chambers was such that Newton Chambers' nominal control of KOS should be disregarded for the tax year in question. By retaining operational control coupled with a 100% interest in the earnings of KOS after allowance for the limited preferred dividend, Koehring continued to enjoy the tax deferral benefits of off-shore earnings accumulation of the type that Subpart F was intended to eliminate. * * *

Koehring first contends that the district court's finding that Newton Chambers' KOS investment was conditioned on a cross-investment by Koehring is clearly erroneous. They point out that the Koehring–Waterous investment in Newton Chambers did not occur until six months after Newton Chambers acquired the KOS preferred stock. We agree that there is nothing in the record which indicates that Koehring was legally bound to make a subsequent investment in the Newton Chambers group, but the facts give rise to a strong inference that there was an understanding that Koehring–Waterous would make such an investment in order to provide Newton Chambers with the funds for its investment in KOS. * * *

* * *

Koehring itself suggests that whether or not the Newton Chambers investment in KOS was conditioned on a cross-investment in the Newton Chambers group is irrelevant with regard to the question of whether there was an agreement that Newton Chambers would not independently exercise its control over KOS. We cannot fully agree. Although there may be instances when there are clear business reasons for cross-investments between two companies, when the circumstances suggest that one investment is being undertaken to provide the investee with the funds for the reciprocal transaction, there is support for the view that the second transaction is not really being undertaken in order to gain operating control. * * *

* * *

Koehring also makes a multi-pronged attack on the district court's finding that Newton Chambers failed to independently exercise control over KOS. It is pointed out that Newton Chambers used its majority voting power at a number of stockholders meetings to do what majority stockholders normally do—i.e., elect a majority of the Board of Directors. It is suggested that the inquiry should end there and that there is no reason to examine whether these directors proceeded to exert independent control at the director level in furtherance of the interests of Newton Chambers. We do not believe that the investigation need be so limited. In *Garlock* and *Kraus* the courts relied in part on the failure of the foreign shareholders to use their representatives on the Board to try to influence corporate policies. The tax court in *CCA, Inc. v. Commissioner*, 64 T.C. 137 (1975), seemed somewhat more reluctant to examine the actual actions of the representatives of the foreign shareholders where they had "by virtue of the powers which they possessed, a real opportunity to alter the course of events of the corporation if they desired to do so." 64 T.C. at 152. Yet if the foreign shareholders use their voting power to elect directors who are their representatives in name only because of an implied agreement that they will permit the U.S. shareholders to determine operating policy, it can hardly be said that the foreign shareholders are voting their shares independently. Where, as here, there are other factors suggesting the existence of such an agreement, it is only reasonable that the actual actions of the directors elected by the foreign shareholder be examined to see whether they are consistent or inconsistent with the existence of such an agreement.

* * * We agree with taxpayer that the record with regard to Newton Chambers' participation in the shareholder meetings—primarily consisting of the election of a majority of the Board of Directors—does not in itself present strong evidence of an agreement to permit Koehring to retain control. The one exception was the October 25, 1965, shareholders meeting where Newton Chambers gave a proxy to vote its shares to Mr. F. C. Chambers (not associated with Newton Chambers), a Koehring nominee. This is scarcely a means of assuring that its shares would be voted

independently. However, the record of Newton Chambers' participation in the directors meetings is a somewhat different story. Of the 13 such meetings held between September 30, 1963 and November 1967, six were held by unanimous consent.[9] Of the remainder, Newton Chambers failed to arrange for the presence of enough of its representatives to assure majority control in five.[10] In light of this record we cannot say that it was clearly erroneous for the district court to conclude that had Newton Chambers really been interested in dominating the affairs of KOS, the pattern of the participation of its representatives in the directors meetings would have been different.

Even stronger evidence of an implied agreement to leave operational control of KOS in Koehring's hands can be found in the actual actions and omissions of the Newton Chambers directors at the Board of Directors level. Although at the time of the "transfer of control," KOS was staffed entirely by employees closely identified with Koehring, Newton Chambers made no personnel changes. Although certain non-officer Koehring directors were given the power to draft checks for KOS, none of the Newton Chambers directors were given this power. Nor is there any record of a significant effort being made to restructure KOS into a joint international sales subsidiary, although that was Newton Chambers' avowed aim in taking control of KOS. KOS continued to market only Koehring-produced equipment until 1967, when at the suggestion of Koehring's president a small number of products produced by Newton Chambers were marketed on a trial basis. Moreover, at the September 16, 1966, directors meeting the Newton Chambers directors acquiesced in the transfer of a portion of the KOS sales territory to Koehring–Brissonneau, in spite of Newton Chambers' previous consternation with the expansion of Koehring–Brissonneau in Newton Chambers' backyard. The district court was clearly reasonable in concluding that this is hardly the record of a determined effort to turn KOS into an active joint-sales subsidiary during the years in question, although it is quite possible that such was the eventual goal of Koehring and Newton Chambers. This assessment is also in agreement with the following report given to the Newton Chambers board on September 9, 1963 (Exhibit G):

> The Company would gain *nominal control* of Koehring Overseas Corporation of Panama, an export company formed to sell Koehring products overseas, by nominating three Directors on that Company's Board. This association would, in all probability, lead to the formation

9. Koehring suggests that no inference can be drawn from the fact that these meetings took place by means of the unanimous consent device. While this is formally true, when the unanimous consent mechanism is used primarily to "rubber stamp" proposals originated by Koehring concerning modifications of the profit sharing and retirement plans jointly run by Koehring and KOS, such meetings can scarcely be cited as prime examples of Newton Chambers' use of its majority voting power to dominate the affairs of KOS.

10. These five consisted of the two meetings at which it is conceded that the Newton Chambers directors were outnumbered by the Koehring representatives and the three meetings where the two were equal in number.

of an International Company comprising all Companies with whom Koehring were [sic] associated throughout the world. (Emphasis added.)

Lastly, Koehring argues that the district court made certain findings of fact with regard to the actions of the Newton Chambers directors which negate any finding that Newton Chambers failed to independently exercise its voting rights. The first of such findings is the district court's statement that the Newton Chambers directors caused the creation of a cash reserve for the redemption of the preferred stock. This is an action which was concededly more in Newton Chambers' interest than in Koehring's. In fact, absent other evidence of an informal agreement to leave operating control in the U.S. shareholders' hands, such an action might constitute substantial evidence that the foreign shareholders are voting their shares independently within the meaning of the second branch of the tri-test. See *CCA, Inc.*, *supra*. However, in the present case the evidence suggests that an action such as this was contemplated by the agreement between Koehring and Newton Chambers. It is understandable that in the process of enticing Newton Chambers into taking an equity position in KOS an understanding would arise that certain provisions would be made for the protection of the latter's limited investment. A number of protections were written into the KOS charter, including provisions depriving the common shares of their votes should a certain number of preferred dividends be passed, or should the net asset of KOS fall below a certain value. An additional protection was Newton Chambers' "right" to bring about a redemption of its stock, discussed above. In order to make this protection an effective one, Koehring apparently agreed that KOS would maintain sufficient funds to redeem the preferred stock, or at least that Newton Chambers would be allowed to use its voting power to see that such a result was achieved. That this was a part of the prearrangement between Koehring and Newton Chambers is suggested by the fact that even before Newton Chambers elected a majority of the KOS directors, Koehring had Koehring–Waterous modify a note representing a loan to KOS to make further payments of principal by KOS subject to the consent of the preferred shareholders (Exhibit No. 39). This offered further protection to Newton Chambers with respect to KOS's cash position. Thus, what might otherwise have been seen as an assertion of its majority control by Newton Chambers contrary to the interests of Koehring must here be seen more as a part of the agreed consideration granted Newton Chambers for its willingness to participate in the arrangement to prevent KOS from being classified as a CFC.

The second, and more troubling, finding of fact pointed out by Koehring is the district court's observation that the Newton Chambers directors twice successfully opposed the declaration of a dividend on the common stock. A finding that the U.S. taxpayer was unable to force the declaration of a dividend on its stock in spite of the full exertion of its effective power during a tax year for which the IRS sought to impose

Subpart F taxability would raise a substantial question as to the applicability of Subpart F. Koehring has pointed to certain portions of the legislative history of Subpart F which suggest that Congress was concerned with the fairness and constitutionality of taxing U.S. shareholders who are not able to bring about a distribution of the earnings of the foreign corporation in order to pay the tax. However, that problem is not squarely presented by this case. Here, the two instances in which a Koehring director's proposal for the declaration of a dividend on the common stock never made it to a vote, after Sir Peter Roberts spoke out against the idea, occurred approximately two and three years after the close of the tax year which is the subject of this suit. * * * In any case, we do not believe that the district court's finding leads to the conclusion that Koehring was without power to cause a dividend to be declared on the KOS common stock during the tax year before this court, and therefore need not decide whether the classification of KOS as a CFC for that tax year would have been precluded on such a basis.

We cannot agree with Koehring's argument that a finding that KOS was [a] CFC in this case is inconsistent with the decision in *CCA, Inc. v. Commissioner*, 64 T.C. 137 (1975). Although the record of the foreign shareholders' exercise of their voting power was hardly stronger there than in this case, in *CCA, Inc.* the tax court found an absence of any agreement between the U.S. and foreign shareholders regarding the voting of the latter's shares. Although it might be argued that it is incongruous to tax a U.S. shareholder who gives away nominal control of a foreign subsidiary but who retains operating control under an implied agreement, while a second taxpayer who gives away nominal control but who retains practical control because of the dispersal of the ownership of the foreign-held stock or other nonconsensual circumstances escapes taxation, the existence of an agreement brings the former situation more forcefully within traditional sham doctrine principles with regard to the transfer of control.[13] * * *

The kind of implied agreement that the IRS suggests existed in this case is somewhat amorphous and flexible. There is much evidence in the record that suggests that Koehring and Newton Chambers were honestly considering ways in which their interests might be further enmeshed, including the possibility of a joint sales subsidiary. It may even be the case that for tax years subsequent to those under consideration here a real effort was made to turn KOS into such an entity.[14] If KOS were to begin to market Newton Chambers products in significant quantities, Newton Chambers would have much more important interests to protect by exertion of its nominal control position than those stemming from its ownership of the KOS preferred. In short, at some point it is possible that

13. We do not mean to imply that we would necessarily agree with the tax court's analysis in *CCA, Inc.* if a similar situation were presented to us.

14. In fact, the minutes of the 1966 and 1967 directors meetings suggest an increasingly active participation by Sir Peter Roberts in the policy-making deliberations of the Board.

the operations of KOS would in fact have taken on the mantle of the kind of partnership allegedly envisaged by the parties. However, the record here suggests that, at the very least, the timing of Newton Chambers' investment in KOS was dictated by Koehring's Subpart F concerns and that the transaction was structured accordingly. Whatever may have been the long run potential for treating KOS as a joint venture, there is strong evidence here that there was no intention of divesting Koehring of operating control in the short run.

* * *

[¶ 6055]

PROBLEMS

1. What were the key facts in *CCA, Inc.* that led the Tax Court to conclude that the foreign corporation was not a controlled foreign corporation? Did the directors representing the holders of the preferred stock in *CCA, Inc.* have any material economic incentive to exercise their voting and other rights independently of the directors representing the holders of the common stock? How important should the absence of any such incentive be in determining whether voting rights are independently exercised by the preferred shareholders?

2. Can the Seventh Circuit's decision in *Koehring* be reconciled with the Tax Court's decision in *CCA, Inc.*? Was there a material difference between the manner in which the voting rights were exercised by the preferred shareholders in the two cases? Was there a basis in *CCA, Inc.* for concluding that there was an implied agreement that operating control would remain in the U.S. shareholder?

3. The *CCA, Inc.* case was decided under the 1962 Act definition of controlled foreign corporation based exclusively on more than 50 percent of the total combined voting power of the foreign corporation. Would the *CCA, Inc.* case have been decided differently under the current definition?

4. In the light of the current definition of a controlled foreign corporation, is it still possible to decontrol a foreign corporation by selling voting preferred stock to unrelated foreign persons? Would it be possible to give characteristics to the preferred stock that would enable it to continue to be worth at least 50 percent of the value of the foreign corporation's stock as the earnings of the foreign corporation (and possibly the value of its assets such as goodwill) increase over time? If this could not be done, would the foreign corporation become a controlled foreign corporation as soon as the value of the preferred stock fell below 50 percent of the total value of the corporation's stock? If you sought to use voting preferred stock to avoid classification of a foreign corporation as a controlled foreign corporation, what terms would you recommend for the preferred stock and what further steps would you recommend be taken in connection with establishing its value, the control arrangements and the exercise by the preferred shareholders (or their representatives

on the board) of their voting and other rights? See the additional materials, beginning at ¶ 13,120, which discuss the circumstances under which a joint venture in which a U.S. corporation owns only 50 percent of the voting stock may be classified as a controlled foreign corporation because of the control arrangements and other circumstances extraneous to the ownership of voting stock.

[¶ 6060]

3. STAPLED–STOCK CORPORATIONS AND RELATED ISSUES

Before the Tax Reform Act of 1984, some publicly owned U.S. corporations attempted to decontrol their controlled foreign corporations, which were typically wholly owned foreign subsidiaries, by distributing the stock of the controlled foreign corporations pro rata to the shareholders of the U.S. corporations. This transaction produced a taxable dividend to the shareholders; but after the transaction, because the stock of the foreign corporation would then be owned pro rata by the public shareholders of the U.S. parent corporation, it was expected that the foreign corporation would no longer be classified as a controlled foreign corporation (more than 50 percent of the voting power and value no longer being owned by ten-percent U.S. shareholders). Consequently, the foreign corporation would no longer be subject to the provisions of Subpart F. To maintain common control of the distributing U.S. corporation and the foreign corporation, the latter's stock certificates would be stapled to or paired with (e.g., by being printed on the back of) the stock certificates of the U.S. corporation. The result was that a given shareholder could dispose of the holdings in the foreign corporation and the U.S. corporation (the former parent corporation of the former controlled foreign corporation) only as a unit; the stock of the two corporations could not be sold independently. Typically, managements of the stapled-stock corporations were identical or closely related. Although some authority appeared to support the validity of this method of decontrol of a foreign corporation, other authority indicated that the courts might treat the split-off foreign corporation as still controlled by its former U.S. parent corporation.

Congress concluded that stapling of corporate stock was an improper tax-avoidance device that undercut the fairness of the tax system. As stated in Staff of Joint Comm. on Tax'n, 98th Cong., 2d Sess., General Explanation of the Revenue Provisions of the Deficit Reduction Act of 1984, at 455 (1984):

> * * * Stapling of a taxable entity with a nontaxable entity was a particularly serious problem. In such a case, the shareholders (who were the same for both corporations) generally preferred profits to be realized in the nontaxable entity rather than in the taxable entity.

Congress believed that to permit the use of such a transparent device would have weakened the integrity of the tax system.

Transfer pricing.—Shareholders of stapled stock may have had no business reason to complain if their taxable entity undercharged their nontaxable entity for goods or services. If stock is not stapled, by contrast, the shareholders of a company can sue its management (in a shareholders' derivative suit) if the company undercharges another entity. Although the United States has the right to correct improper transfer prices between related parties (sec. 482), this is a complicated and difficult issue.

The problem of transfer pricing also arises on stapling of a U.S. corporation with a foreign corporation operating in a low-tax jurisdiction or in a tax haven. * * *

Stapled foreign entities.—Stapling may also allow avoidance of the anti-tax-haven rules and the anti-boycott rules. Improper avoidance of these rules may occur if a stapled foreign entity is widely held, because the rules apply in cases of relatively concentrated ownership. * * *

To combat these abuses, the 1984 Act added Section 269B to the Code. Section 269B(a) provides generally that when a foreign and a U.S. corporation are stapled entities, the foreign corporation will be treated as a U.S. corporation subject to U.S. income tax on its worldwide income.[14] Stapled entities are defined as any group of two or more entities if more than 50 percent in value of the beneficial ownership in each of them consists of "stapled interests."[15] Stapled interests are defined as two or more interests if, by reason of form of ownership, restrictions on transfer or other terms or conditions in connection with the transfer of one of such interests, the other interests are also transferred or required to be transferred. § 269B(c)(2) and (3).

Even if a foreign corporation and a U.S. corporation are stapled entities, the foreign corporation will not be treated as a U.S. corporation if both corporations are foreign-owned. § 269B(e)(1). This test will be met if less than 50 percent of the total combined voting power and value of each corporation is owned directly or indirectly (after applying Sections 958(a)(2) and (3) and 318(a)(4)) by U.S. persons. § 269B(e)(2).

The stapled-stock provision generally overrides treaties. § 269B(d). However, in the case of entities stapled on June 30, 1983, and treated as

---

14. Note that the anti-abuse device adopted in Section 269B, taxing the foreign corporation itself currently on worldwide income, was rejected by Congress for general use in Subpart F in part because of concerns with the appropriateness under international law and U.S. tax treaties of imposing U.S. tax on the foreign-source income of foreign corporations.

15. The recharacterization of a foreign corporation as a U.S. corporation will be treated as a reorganization that is subject to the rules of Section 367. In addition, the unstapling of a foreign corporation (e.g., by removing a requirement that its shares trade in tandem with those of a U.S. corporation) that had been treated as a U.S. corporation under Section 269B will be treated as a reorganization that is subject to the rules of Section 367. See generally Chapter 10.

residents of treaty partners on that date, the provision does not deny treaty benefits to which they were entitled on that date, so long as the entities remain entitled to such benefits under the applicable treaty. For example, a treaty may provide that a corporation incorporated under the laws of the treaty partner is not taxable in the United States on industrial or commercial profits unless it has a U.S. permanent establishment to which the profits are attributable. In such a case, a foreign corporation stapled to a U.S. corporation on June 30, 1983, is entitled to applicable treaty benefits. Section 269B will not treat it as a U.S. corporation unless and until the treaty is renegotiated to eliminate benefits for stapled companies.

Under the standard rules governing consolidated returns in Section 1504, a foreign corporation treated as a U.S. corporation because it is stapled to a U.S. corporation generally is not eligible to file a consolidated return with its U.S. sister corporation because there is no common parent corporation. The inability to consolidate in this situation prevents taxpayers from using the stapled-stock rules to their advantage (for example, by using losses of a stapled foreign corporation). See Staff of Joint Comm. on Tax'n, 98th Cong., 2d Sess., General Explanation of the Revenue Provisions of the Deficit Reduction Act of 1984, at 458 (1984).

"Corporate inversion" transactions. During the period from 1994 through 2004, the Treasury Department and Congress became concerned with so-called "corporate inversion" transactions in which a publicly held U.S. corporation with foreign subsidiaries (which were controlled foreign corporations) would become a subsidiary of an existing foreign subsidiary or a newly formed foreign subsidiary through a stock or asset exchange intended to come within the corporate reorganization provisions (but in which some or all of the U.S. shareholders' gains on the restructuring transaction may be subject to tax under the rules in Section 367). After the transaction, the former shareholders of the U.S. parent corporation would own stock of a foreign corporation that is not a controlled foreign corporation because no more than 50 percent of its voting power or value would be owned by ten-percent-or-greater U.S. shareholders. Thus, the inversion transaction could provide substantial U.S. tax savings that exceeded any shareholder-level tax on the inversion transaction itself by allowing the restructured U.S. multinational group with a foreign parent to avoid the Subpart F rules as well as to engage in various "base stripping transactions" in which the now U.S. subsidiary makes deductible payments (such as interest or royalties) to the foreign parent. The foreign parent often is organized in a low-tax or no-tax foreign country that may have a favorable tax treaty with the United States under which those payments are subject to little or no U.S. withholding tax.

As discussed at ¶ 10,088, to deal with the perceived abuses arising from such transactions, in the 2004 JOBS Act, Congress enacted several new provisions that attempt to solve this problem. Under one of these provisions, Section 7874, a foreign corporation may be treated as a U.S. corporation for federal income tax purposes, if certain requirements are met, thus denying the U.S. multinational group the intended tax benefits to be obtained from the inversion transaction.

Proposal to change rules for determining corporate residence. As mentioned in Chapter 1, in a report issued in 2005, the Staff of the Joint Committee on Taxation proposed new rules for determining the residence of publicly traded foreign entities. Under these proposed rules, a publicly traded foreign-incorporated entity's residence would be based on the location of its primary management and control. For this purpose, a corporation's place of primary management and control is "where the executive officers and senior management of the corporation exercise day-to-day responsibility for the strategic, financial and operational policy decision making for the company (including direct and indirect subsidiaries)." See Staff of Joint Comm. on Tax'n, 109th Cong., 1st Sess., Options to Improve Tax Compliance and Reform Tax Expenditures, at 179–80 (2005). This proposal constitutes a more comprehensive solution to the tax policy issues raised by the stapled-stock and corporate inversion transactions.

Unlike the current law rules for determining corporate residence, however, the proposed rules would create uncertainty concerning the residence of publicly traded foreign-incorporated entities for U.S. tax purposes. Thus, these proposed rules would be more difficult for the IRS to administer than the current law rules, thereby resulting in increased administration costs for the IRS. Moreover, by compromising "the clarity and consistency of current law," as the Joint Committee Staff acknowledges that this proposal would do, this proposal also would likely increase compliance and tax planning costs for taxpayers. Id. at 181. These detrimental effects of the proposal would be offset by the benefits of the proposal in preserving the U.S. tax base. Id.

D. SOME MECHANICS OF SUBPART F INCOME INCLUSIONS

[¶ 6065]

1. DETERMINATION OF U.S. SHAREHOLDER'S PRO RATA SHARE

As mentioned earlier, inclusion of the Subpart F income of a controlled foreign corporation in the gross income of its U.S. shareholders under Section 951(a)(1) occurs only if the corporation is a controlled foreign corporation for an uninterrupted period of 30 days or more during its tax year. If this test is met, every person who is a U.S. shareholder of the corporation (as defined in Section 951(b)) and who owns stock on the last day of the tax year on which the foreign corporation is a controlled foreign corporation must include its pro rata share of the corporation's Subpart F income in gross income for the tax year in which or with which the tax year of the corporation ends. (Note that a controlled foreign corporation's tax year is determined under the special rules in Section 898, which require a controlled foreign corporation to use as its tax year the tax year of its majority U.S. shareholder, if it has one. See ¶ 6360.)

A U.S. shareholder's pro rata share is determined by going through a *hypothetical* dividend distribution of the controlled foreign corporation's Subpart F income on the last day of its tax year on which it meets the controlled foreign corporation definition. Specifically, a U.S. shareholder's pro rata share of Subpart F income is the amount of the distribution that the U.S. shareholder would have received with respect to the stock owned in the controlled foreign corporation if, on the last day of its tax year on which it was a controlled foreign corporation, the corporation had distributed pro rata to all of its shareholders a dividend in an amount equal to the Subpart F income for the year. However, if the corporation was a controlled foreign corporation for only part of its tax year, the U.S. shareholder's pro rata amount is reduced proportionately. § 951(a)(2)(A). For example, if a foreign corporation is a controlled foreign corporation for only 100 days during a taxable year with 365 days, its U.S. shareholders will have to include only 100/365 of their pro rata shares of the corporation's Subpart F income for the year.

Furthermore, if the U.S. shareholder acquired the stock in the controlled foreign corporation during the year of the Subpart F inclusion, the pro rata amount is reduced by a portion of the dividends received by the U.S. shareholder's predecessor in interest during that year. § 951(a)(2)(B). This latter amount includes a portion of any gain by the predecessor in interest on the disposition of the controlled foreign corporation's stock that was treated as a deemed dividend under Section 1248 (discussed at ¶ 6245).

As discussed at ¶ 6030, stock owned directly, indirectly and constructively under the rules of Section 958(a) and (b) is taken into account in determining whether a shareholder owns or is deemed to own the requisite ten percent of the voting power of the controlled foreign corporation's stock to be treated as a U.S. shareholder. However, Section 951(a)(2)(A) specifies that the U.S. shareholder's pro rata share of the controlled foreign corporation's undistributed Subpart F income that is currently included in gross income under Section 951(a)(1)(i) is determined only with respect to the stock the shareholder owns directly or indirectly (under the rules in Section 958(a)(2)) through other foreign corporations, foreign partnerships, foreign trusts or foreign estates in which the shareholder has a beneficial interest. Stated differently, the constructive ownership rules in Section 958(b), which apply in determining whether a U.S. person meets the ten-percent-voting-power threshold for U.S. shareholder status and whether a foreign corporation meets the definition of a controlled foreign corporation, do not apply in determining the U.S. shareholder's pro rata share of the corporation's undistributed income. See also Reg. § 1.958–1(a) (second sentence).

Example. DC, a U.S. corporation, owns 45 percent of the only class of stock (voting stock) of FC, a foreign corporation that has Subpart F income for the year. C, a U.S. citizen, owns 5 percent of FC's stock. The other 50 percent of FC's stock is owned by FP, a foreign partnership. C owns 10 percent of DC's stock and has a 5–percent partnership interest in FP. (The remainder of DC's stock is widely held by persons unrelated to C and the remaining partners in FP are nonresident aliens who are unrelated to C.)

For purposes of determining whether DC and C are U.S. shareholders and whether FC is a controlled foreign corporation, all stock owned directly, indirectly and constructively under Section 958 is taken into account. Thus, in determining whether C is a U.S. shareholder, C's actually owned shares (5 percent), indirectly owned shares through FP, the foreign partnership (2.5 percent, i.e., 50 percent multiplied by 5 percent) and constructively owned through DC (4.5 percent, i.e., 45 percent multiplied by 10 percent) are taken into account. Consequently, C is treated as owning 12 percent of FC and is a U.S. shareholder, and FC is a controlled foreign corporation under Section 957 because U.S. shareholders (DC and C) own more than 50 percent of its voting stock.

However, C must include in gross income only 7.5 percent of FC's Subpart F income (assuming that the percentages of stock ownership are maintained throughout the tax year). Section 951(a)(2)(A) defines the U.S. shareholder's share of Subpart F income as the amount that would have been distributed with respect to stock that the shareholder owns within the meaning of Section 958(a). Section 951(a)(2)(A) thus incorporates the indirect ownership rules of Section 958(a)(2), but not the constructive ownership rules of Section 958(b). Accordingly, in determining C's pro rata share of FC's Subpart F income, C's 5 percent of FC owned directly and 2.5 percent of FC owned indirectly through FP under Section 958(a)(2) are taken into account, but C's 4.5 percent of FC owned constructively under the attribution rules of Section 958(b) is not taken into account. These rules for determining pro rata share avoid double-counting of any of the 45-percent interest in FC owned by DC. Of course, DC must include in its own gross income 45 percent of FC's Subpart F income.

In the case of a controlled foreign corporation with more than one class of stock outstanding, the regulations contain rules for allocating the corporation's Subpart F income and earnings and profits among the different classes of stock for purposes of determining its U.S. shareholders' pro rata shares. These regulations include special rules governing such allocation where the controlled foreign corporation's board of directors has the discretionary power to allocate its earnings among the different classes of stock. See Reg. § 1.951–1(e).

Under the rules for determining a U.S. shareholder's pro rata share, Subpart F income of a lower-tier controlled foreign corporation owned only indirectly by the U.S. shareholder may be includible in the shareholder's income. In this situation, the Subpart F income of the lower-tier controlled foreign corporation is treated as if it were received directly by the U.S. shareholder rather than as if it flowed up through the intervening entities and was homogenized or blended with their earnings. This method of taxation is often referred to as the "hopscotch" method because the Subpart F income of the lower-tier controlled foreign corporation hopscotches over the intervening foreign corporations directly to the U.S. shareholder. As previously noted, the Subpart F income carries an indirect foreign tax credit under Section 960 for the foreign corporate tax on the income deemed distributed from the lower-tier controlled foreign corporation. Thus, the foreign tax credit hopscotches to the U.S. shareholder along with the Subpart F income to which it is attributable, and it does not affect the foreign tax credit computations for dividends paid or deemed paid by the intervening foreign corporations. Moreover, the amount of the U.S. shareholder's income inclusion under Section 951 will be grossed up by the foreign taxes deemed paid by the shareholder under Section 960.

> *Example*. DC, a U.S. corporation, owns 70 percent of the only class of voting stock of FS1, a foreign corporation that has no Subpart F income for the year. (FS1 has no nonvoting stock.) FS1, in turn, owns 80 percent of the only class of voting stock of FS2, a foreign corporation that has Subpart F income for the year. (FS2 also has no nonvoting stock.) Under the constructive ownership rules of Section 958(b)(2), DC is deemed to own 100 percent of the stock of FS1, which, in turn, is deemed to own 100 percent of the stock of FS2; hence, FS2 is a controlled foreign corporation. Under the indirect ownership rules of Section 958(a)(2), DC is treated as owning 56 percent (70 percent multiplied by 80 percent) of FS2's voting stock, and, under Section 951(a)(1)(A)(i), DC must include in its gross income 56 percent of the undistributed Subpart F income of FS2 (assuming that the percentages of stock ownership are maintained throughout the tax year). Under Section 961(a), DC will increase its basis in the FS1 stock by the amount of this Section 951(a)(1)(A) inclusion. In addition, DC will be entitled to an indirect credit under Section 960 for the foreign corporate tax paid by FS2 with respect to the Subpart F income deemed distributed to DC. Under Section 78, the amount of DC's income inclusion under Section 951 will be increased (i.e., "grossed up") by the amount of foreign taxes of FS2 deemed paid by DC under Section 960.[16] When FS2 makes a distribu-

16. As noted at ¶ 6020, the U.S. shareholder does not obtain an increase in basis under Section 961(a) for the amount of the Section 78 gross-up to reflect the taxes deemed paid under

tion to FS1, Section 959(b) will exclude such distribution from FS1's gross income to the extent it is attributable to the amount previously included in DC's income under Section 951(a).

Solely for purposes of determining the amount of the Subpart F inclusion of a U.S. shareholder of an upper-tier controlled foreign corporation from gain on the disposition of the stock of a lower-tier controlled foreign corporation, the upper-tier controlled foreign corporation's basis in the stock of the lower-tier controlled foreign corporation is to be increased, under regulations to be issued by the Treasury, by income inclusions of earnings that were not later distributed by the lower-tier controlled foreign corporation. § 961(c).

Example. DC, a U.S. corporation, owns all of the stock of FS1, a foreign corporation. FS1, in turn, owns all of the stock of FS2, also a foreign corporation. FS1 is a controlled foreign corporation. FS2 also is a controlled foreign corporation because DC is treated as owning all of the stock of FS2 under the indirect ownership rules of Section 958(a)(2). DC is a U.S. shareholder (as defined in Section 951(b)) with respect to both corporations.

During year 1, FS2 earns $100 of Subpart F income, which DC must include in its gross income under Section 951(a)(1)(A). During year 2, FS2 earns $50 of Subpart F income, which DC also must include in its gross income under Section 951(a)(1)(A). (DC will increase its basis in the FS1 stock by the $100 and $50 inclusions under Section 951(a)(1)(A). § 961(a).) In year 3, FS1 disposes of FS2's stock and recognizes $400 of income on the disposition (all of which is foreign personal holding company income under Section 954(c), and, hence, Subpart F income). Under regulations to be issued by the Treasury under Section 961(c), DC's inclusion under Section 951(a)(1)(A) in year 3 will be reduced by $150 (i.e., from $400 to $250) to reflect the prior income inclusions by DC with respect to FS2 that had not been distributed as dividends to FS1 prior to FS1's sale of the FS2 stock. The effect of this adjustment will be to allow FS1 to increase its basis in the FS2 stock by the $150 of Subpart F income previously included in gross income by DC. See H.R. Conf. Rep. No. 220, 105th Cong., 1st Sess. 620–21 (1997).

Subpart F income partnership blocker transactions. In some cases, taxpayers have set up ownership structures that attempt to prevent the U.S. parent corporation at the top of the chain of ownership from having a Section 951(a) inclusion with respect to some lower-tier controlled foreign corporation. For example, suppose that a DC, a U.S. corporation, sets up the following structure (sometimes called a "Subpart F income partnership blocker transaction"). DC owns all of the stock of

Section 960. Instead, the U.S. shareholder receives a foreign tax credit for such amount under Section 960 and allowing both a credit and basis increase for the same amount would result in a double tax benefit for the U.S. shareholder.

FC1 and FC2, both controlled foreign corporations. FC1 and FC2, in turn, each owns 50 percent of DP, a U.S. partnership, which, in turn, owns all of the stock of FC3, also a controlled foreign corporation. FC3 earns Subpart F income, which would definitely trigger an income inclusion under Section 951(a) for DC if DP had not been interposed between FC1/FC2 and FC3 in the chain of ownership of the stock of FC3. DC argues, however, that it has no inclusion under Section 951(a) with respect to FC3 because DP is the first U.S. person in the chain of ownership of FC3. In IRS Notice 2009–7, 2009–1 C.B. 312, the Treasury and the IRS stated their belief that DC's position on this issue is contrary to the purpose and intent of Section 951. Accordingly, in IRS Notice 2009–7, the Treasury and the IRS identified this "partnership blocker" transaction (and other similar transactions) as a "transaction of interest" for purposes of the tax shelter disclosure requirements of Sections 6111 and 6112. Moreover, in IRS Notice 2010–41, 2010–1 C.B. 715, the Treasury and the IRS indicated that they intended to issue regulations that would, if certain conditions are met, classify an otherwise U.S. partnership as a foreign partnership solely for purposes of identifying the U.S. shareholders of a controlled foreign corporation that are required to include in gross income amounts determined under Section 951(a) with respect to such corporation. Thus, under these regulations, DP in the transaction described above would be classified as a foreign partnership and DC would have to include FC3's Subpart F income in its gross income under Section 951(a) because it would be treated as owning all of FC3's stock under the direct and indirect ownership rules of Section 958(a). Specifically, IRS Notice 2010–41 stated that the regulations to be issued would treat a U.S. partnership as foreign solely for purposes of Section 951(a) if the following three conditions were met:

(1) The partnership is a U.S. shareholder of a foreign corporation that is a controlled foreign corporation (within the meaning of Section 957(a) or 953(c));

(2) If the partnership were treated as a foreign partnership, that foreign corporation would still be a controlled foreign corporation; and

(3) If the partnership were treated as a foreign partnership, at least one U.S. shareholder of the controlled foreign corporation both (i) would be treated under Section 958(a) as indirectly owning stock of the controlled foreign corporation that is owned by the partnership that is indirectly owned by a foreign corporation, and (ii) would have to include an amount in gross income under Section 951(a) with respect to the controlled foreign corporation.

Indirect credit under Section 960. Section 960(a) incorporates the rules of Section 902 to determine whether a U.S. shareholder of a controlled foreign corporation is entitled to claim an indirect credit with respect to inclusions under Section 951(a) and to calculate the amount of the indirect credit. Consequently, to qualify for an indirect foreign tax credit under Section 960, a U.S. corporation must actually own at least ten percent of the first-tier controlled foreign corporation's voting stock. The foreign entity indirect ownership rules in Section 958(a)(2) and the constructive ownership rules in Section 958(b) do not apply for this purpose.

Under a change made by the Taxpayer Relief Act of 1997, an indirect credit is now available with respect to a foreign corporation below the third tier in a chain of foreign corporations owned indirectly by a U.S. corporation if the foreign corporation is a controlled foreign corporation (as defined in Section 957) and the U.S. corporation is a U.S. shareholder (as defined in Section 951(b)) in such lower-tier foreign corporation. In such a case, the indirect credit calculation will take into account taxes paid by a fourth-tier, fifth-tier or sixth-tier foreign corporation with respect to periods during which the foreign corporation was a controlled foreign corporation. § 902(b)(2). At each level there must be ownership of at least ten percent of the voting stock of the next lower level foreign corporation. Moreover, in a multiple-tier case the percentages of stock ownership at all the levels, multiplied together, must equal at least five percent. § 902(b)(2)(B). Thus, for example, in a four-tier case, 50–percent ownership at the first level, 40–percent at the second level, 50–percent at the third level and 50–percent at the fourth level would just qualify, assuming that each foreign corporation has sufficient other U.S. shareholders to meet the definition of a controlled foreign corporation and that the domestic corporate parent owns directly, indirectly or constructively under Section 958 enough stock in the fourth-tier subsidiary to be a U.S. shareholder in that subsidiary (i.e., 50% × 40% × 50% × 50% = 5%). Note that no indirect credit will be allowed with respect to dividends and foreign taxes paid by a foreign corporation below the sixth tier in a chain of foreign corporations. § 902(b)(2)(B)(iii). The result is that Subpart F inclusions of earnings of controlled foreign corporations below the sixth tier of foreign corporations will not carry with them indirect foreign tax credits.

Finally, as discussed in Chapter 5, Section 909, enacted in 2010, applies in the case of a foreign tax credit splitting event relating to foreign income tax paid or accrued by a Section 902 corporation (i.e., a transaction in which creditable foreign taxes paid or accrued by the Section 902 corporation are separated from the associated foreign income). Under that provision, such foreign tax is not taken into account for purposes of Section 902 or 960, or for purposes of determining the Section 902 corporation's earnings and profits under Section 964(a), until the year in which the related income is taken into account for U.S. tax purposes by the Section 902 corporation itself or a U.S. corporation that meets the Section 902 ownership requirements with respect to the Section 902 corporation. The statute defines "Section 902 corporation" for this purpose to mean any foreign corporation with respect to which one or more U.S. corporations meets the ownership requirements of Section 902(a) or (b), and, thus, can include a controlled foreign corporation. § 909(d)(5). Thus, if Section 909 applies to a foreign tax paid by a Section 902 corporation, the corporation's pool of foreign taxes is not increased by such tax nor are its earnings and profits reduced by such tax until the year in which the related income is taken into account for U.S. tax purposes.

[¶ 6070]

PROBLEMS

1. On January 1 of year 1, Sam, a nonresident alien individual, Molly, also a nonresident alien individual, and Widgets, Inc., a U.S. corporation, organize a new foreign corporation, Foreign Base Company, Inc., under the laws of Ireland. Sam contributes $30,000 cash to the new foreign corporation and receives 30 shares of its stock, Molly also contributes $30,000 and receives 30 shares of stock and Widgets, Inc. contributes $40,000 and receives 40 shares of stock. On August 8 of year 1, Molly acquires a green card and becomes a lawful permanent resident of the United States.

Foreign Base Company, Inc. has net income (after payment of foreign income taxes) of $400,000 for year 1. One half of this amount (i.e., $200,000) constitutes Subpart F income within the meaning of Section 952. (Foreign Base Company, Inc. paid $80,000 in foreign income taxes to Ireland on its pre-foreign tax net income of $480,000. None of Foreign Base Company, Inc.'s income was subject to U.S. tax under Section 881 or 882.) Foreign Base Company, Inc. makes no dividend distributions during year 1.

What are the tax consequences to the shareholders of Foreign Base Company, Inc. for year 1 under the Subpart F provisions?

2. On April 1 of year 2, Foreign Base Company, Inc. makes a dividend distribution of $15,000 cash to Sam, $15,000 cash to Molly and $20,000 cash to Widgets, Inc. Foreign Base Company, Inc. breaks even from operations during year 2 and has no net income for the year. What are the U.S. tax consequences to the shareholders of Foreign Base Company, Inc. on account of this dividend distribution?

[¶ 6075]

2. EXCLUSION OF U.S. TRADE OR BUSINESS INCOME

As mentioned earlier, Subpart F income does not include any item of U.S.-source income that is effectively connected with the conduct by the controlled foreign corporation of a trade or business within the United States. The exclusion does not apply, however, to any item of income that is exempt from U.S. tax (or is subject to a reduced rate of U.S. tax) under an applicable tax treaty. § 952(b). However, an exemption or reduction by treaty of the controlled foreign corporation's potential branch profits tax liability under Section 884 does not prevent this exclusion from applying to the corporation's U.S. trade or business income. The theory underlying this exclusion is that constructive dividend treatment to a U.S. shareholder with respect to a controlled foreign corporation's undistributed income is not warranted to the extent that the income has been subjected to a net-basis U.S. tax at usual rates under Section 882 at the corporate level. Note that this exclusion does not apply to any item of U.S.-source income that is not effectively connected with a U.S. trade or business, regardless of whether such income has been subjected to a gross-basis, 30–percent U.S. tax at the corporate level.

> *Example.* DC, a U.S. corporation, owns all the stock of FC, a foreign corporation that is a controlled foreign corporation. FC earns $100 of U.S.-source interest income that is effectively connected with the conduct of FC's trade or business in the United States under Section 864(c)(2) and is subject to U.S. income tax under Sections 882 and 11 of $35. Such income, even though it meets the definition of "foreign personal holding company income" in Section 954(c) is not Subpart F income by reason of the exclusion in Section 952(b).
>
> If, however, such income were exempt from U.S. income tax under the business profits article of a U.S. income tax treaty, because FC has no permanent establishment in the United States to which the income is attributable, the exclusion in Section 952(b) would not apply and the $100 of income would constitute Subpart F income under Section 954(c). By contrast, if FC were subject to tax on the income under Section 882, but exempted from the branch profits tax under Section 884 by reason of U.S. income tax treaty provision, the exclusion in Section 952(b) would still apply, and the $100 would not constitute Subpart F income.

[¶ 6080]

3. LIMIT ON SUBPART F INCOME BASED ON CURRENT EARNINGS AND PROFITS

Consistent with the treatment of the U.S. shareholder's pro rata share of Subpart F income as a constructive dividend of sorts, Section 952(c)(1)(A) limits a controlled foreign corporation's Subpart F income to its current earnings and profits (as computed under the rules in Section 964(a) and its regulations). Stated differently, the corporation's Subpart F income for the year is reduced to the amount of its current earnings and profits, thus reducing the amount of the current inclusions to its U.S. shareholders under Section 951(a)(1)(A). Under this rule, a controlled foreign corporation's current losses from an activity that would not generate Subpart F income may reduce its current earnings and profits, and hence, its Subpart F income.

If, however, in a later tax year, the corporation has an excess of current earnings and profits over Subpart F income, Section 952(c)(2) may recharacterize that excess as Subpart F income to the extent of the prior reductions in Subpart F income. Consequently, the U.S. shareholders may have additional current inclusions of income under Section 951(a) in the later year as a result of this recharacterization rule.

> *Example.* DC, a U.S. corporation, owns all the stock of FC, a foreign corporation that is a controlled foreign corporation. During the current year, FC has foreign base company sales income of $100 (determined under Section 954), but its current earnings and profits (as calculated under Section 964) is $80. Thus, Section 952(c)(1)(A) limits FC's Subpart F income to $80 for year 1 and DC would include the $80 in gross income under Section 951(a)(1)(A).
>
> In year 2, FC has foreign base company sales income of $75 (determined under Section 954) and its current earnings and profits are $85. Under the recharacterization rule in Section 952(c)(2), the $10 excess of current earnings and profits of $85 over the Subpart F income of $75 is recharacterized as Subpart F income. Thus, FC is treated as having Subpart F income of $85 and DC must include the $85 in gross income under Section 951(a)(1)(A).
>
> In year 3, FC has foreign base company sales income of $50 (determined under Section 954) and its current earnings and profits are $80. Under the recharacterization rule in Section 952(c)(2), only $10 of the $30 excess of current earnings and profits of $80 over the Subpart F income of $50 is recharacterized as Subpart F income. This is because the total amount recaptured under Section 952(c)(2) ($10 in year 2 and $10 in year 3) cannot exceed the reduction of Subpart F income in year 1 by reason of the limit in Section 952(c)(1)(A) (i.e., $20).

Accumulated deficits in a controlled foreign corporation's earnings and profits from prior tax years generally do not reduce its Subpart F income for the current tax year, except to the limited extent provided in Section 952(c)(1)(B). Moreover, a deficit of one controlled foreign corporation generally may not be used to reduce the Subpart F income of a related controlled foreign corporation. This limitation prevents taxpayers from sheltering passive investment income from U.S. tax by moving the passive investments into a controlled foreign corporation with prior deficits. Congress also wanted to restrict loss trafficking by preventing deficits in earnings and profits incurred by a foreign corporation before its acquisition by a U.S. corporation from sheltering post-acquisition Subpart F income of the foreign corporation from tax and by preventing a controlled foreign corporation from reducing its Subpart F income with deficits of related controlled foreign corporations attributable to different activities. See Staff of Joint Comm. on Tax'n, 100th Cong., 1st Sess., General Explanation of the Tax Reform Act of 1986, at 972 (1987).

Under Section 952(c)(1)(B), a controlled foreign corporation's accumulated deficits in earnings and profits from certain activities in prior tax years may reduce only its Subpart F income from similar activities in the current tax year. Specifically, under Section 952(c)(1)(B)(i), the amount of Subpart F income includible by a U.S. shareholder for any tax year and attributable to a "qualified activity" is reduced by the shareholder's pro rata share of any "qualified deficit." A "qualified deficit" is a deficit in earnings from a prior year after 1986 "attributable to the same qualified activity as the activity giving rise to the income being offset." § 952(c)(1)(B)(ii). The five "qualified activities" are those giving rise to (1) foreign base company oil-related income, (2) foreign base company sales income, (3) foreign base company services income, (4) in the case of a qualified insurance company, insurance income or foreign personal holding company income or (5) in the case of a qualified financial institution, foreign personal holding company income. § 952(c)(1)(B)(iii). Thus, the foreign personal holding company income of a controlled foreign corporation that is not a qualified insurance company or financial institution cannot be reduced by prior deficits.

Moreover, a controlled foreign corporation may elect to reduce its Subpart F income attributable to a "qualified activity" by a deficit in earnings and profits of another related foreign corporation attributable to the same activity, but only if the related corporation is a "qualified chain member." A "qualified chain member" is a foreign corporation organized under the laws of the same country as the controlled foreign corporation and which either (i) is a wholly owned subsidiary (directly or through one or more corporations other than the common parent) of the controlled foreign corporation or (ii) owns (directly or through one or more corporations other than the common parent) all the stock of the controlled foreign corporation. § 952(c)(1)(C). The purpose of this provision is to allow U.S. taxpayers conducting business abroad through a group of affiliated foreign corporations a "reasonable measurement for their taxable income from foreign operations." H.R. Rep. No. 795, 100th Cong., 2d Sess. 260 (1988).

E. DEFINITION OF FOREIGN BASE COMPANY INCOME

1. FOREIGN PERSONAL HOLDING COMPANY INCOME

[¶ 6085]

a. Interest, Dividends, Rents, Annuities, Royalties and Gains From the Sale of Property Producing Such Income

The first major category of foreign base company income is "foreign personal holding company income," defined in Section 954(c). It includes most types of passive income, such as interest, dividends, rents, annuities, royalties and gains from the sale of stock, securities or other property that produces interest, dividends, rents, annuities or royalties. § 954(c)(1)(A) and (c)(1)(B)(i).

Exceptions for certain income arising in active business activities. Other provisions narrow the foreign personal holding company definition in Section 954(c)(1) by providing that certain income normally regarded as passive income is not foreign personal holding company income for purposes of the controlled foreign corporations provisions when it arises in connection with the conduct of an active business. Specifically, foreign personal holding company income does not include *rents and royalties* received from a person who is *not a related person*[17] and derived from the active conduct of a trade or business (sometimes called the "active-business-unrelated-person exception"). § 954(c)(2)(A).[18] In addition, interest derived in the conduct of a banking business that constitutes export financing interest as defined in Section 904(d)(2)(G) is excluded from foreign personal holding company income, whether received from a related or unrelated person. § 954(c)(2)(B). The rationale for these exceptions is that income of the specified types, which arises in active business activities, is much less likely to be used in tax-avoidance arrangements.

Exceptions for certain income received from related persons. Certain passive income received from a related person incorporated in the same country as the controlled foreign corporation is excluded from foreign personal holding company income (an exception sometimes called the "same-country-related person exception"). Specifically, foreign personal holding company income does not include *dividends and interest* received from a *related person* (as defined in Section 954(d)(3)) that is organized under the laws of the same foreign country as the controlled foreign corporation and that has a substantial part of its assets used in its trade or business located in that country. § 954(c)(3)(A)(i). The rationale for this exception is that since the controlled foreign corporation would not have had Subpart F income if it conducted the business itself (because the business is being conducted in its country of incorporation), its use of a subsidiary to conduct the business in that country is not a tax-avoidance device. Thus, the dividends and interest it receives from the subsidiary should not be Subpart F income.

In addition, *rents and royalties* received from a *related person* (whether or not incorporated in the same jurisdiction) are excluded from foreign personal holding company income if these amounts are received for the use of property within the country in which the controlled foreign corpora-

17. The "related person" concept is important under a number of Code provisions. It is defined in Section 954(d)(3), discussed at ¶ 6155.

18. The 2004 JOBS Act added a new sentence at the end of Section 954(c)(2)(A), which provides a ten-percent safe harbor rule for purposes of determining whether a lessor's income "from leasing an aircraft or vessel in foreign commerce" is derived in the active conduct of a trade or business, and, thus, if the lessee is an unrelated person, may be excluded from foreign personal holding company income for Subpart F purposes under the "active-business-unrelated-person" exception. Under this safe harbor rule, the exception will apply (and the lease income will not be foreign personal holding company income) if the active leasing expenses are at least ten percent of the profit on the lease.

tion is incorporated. § 954(c)(3)(A)(ii). The rationale for this exception is that the controlled foreign corporation is engaged in genuine business activity (and is not being utilized merely as an income diversion device) if it is incorporated in the same country in which the leased or licensed property is being used, despite the fact that the rents or royalties are being paid to it by a related person. See ALI International Taxation Study, at 256–57.

However, these exceptions for interest, rents and royalties received from a related person do not apply to the extent such payments reduce the Subpart F income of the related payor corporation or create or increase a deficit that under Section 952(c) may reduce the Subpart F income of the payor corporation or another controlled foreign corporation. § 954(c)(3)(B). Such interest, rents and royalties will therefore be included in the recipient corporation's foreign personal holding company income. The policy is that Congress wanted to prevent a group of related controlled foreign corporations from using these exceptions to reduce the group's total Subpart F income through deductible intercompany payments that reduce one group member's Subpart F income without increasing another group member's Subpart F income because of the same-country-related-person exceptions.

Another exception to the same-country-related-person exception of Section 954(c)(3)(A)(i) covers dividends received by a controlled foreign corporation that are attributable to earnings and profits accumulated by a foreign distributing corporation during periods before the controlled foreign corporation receiving the dividend acquired the distributing corporation's stock (either directly or indirectly through a chain of one or more subsidiaries, each of which qualified as a same-country corporation). § 954(c)(3)(C). Such dividends do not qualify for the exception in Section 954(c)(3)(A)(i) and will therefore be included in the recipient corporation's foreign personal holding company income. This provision appears to be aimed at preventing a U.S. shareholder from shifting the pre-acquisition earnings of an acquired foreign corporation to another controlled foreign corporation through dividend distributions that would otherwise be excluded from Subpart F income under the same-country-related-person exception.

Look-through rule exception for certain payments received or accrued from a related controlled foreign corporation. Section 954(c)(6) provides another important, but temporary, exclusion from the definition of foreign personal holding company income. Dividends, interest, rents and royalties received by a controlled foreign corporation from another controlled foreign corporation that is a related person are excluded to the extent such income is attributable or properly allocable to income of the related person that is neither Subpart F income nor income treated as effectively connected with the conduct of a trade or business in the United States. (This provision is sometimes referred to as "the look-through rule for certain payments between related controlled foreign corporations.") Interest income for purposes of this provision includes factoring income that is treated as income equivalent to interest for purposes of Section 954(c)(1)(E) (discussed at ¶ 6110). Rules similar to the rules of Section 904(d)(3)(C) and (D) (discussed at ¶¶ 7085 et seq.) apply for purposes of determining whether payments are attributable or properly allocable to neither Subpart F income or effectively connected income of the payor corporation. The initial guidance on the allocation issues is in IRS Notice 2007–9, §§ 3, 5, 6, 2007–1 C.B. 401, 402–03. This exclusion from foreign personal holding company income does not apply to interest, rents or royalties to the extent such income creates or increases a deficit that under Section 952(c) may reduce the Subpart F income of the payor corporation or another controlled foreign corporation. § 954(c)(6)(B). (The deficit rules in Section 952(c) are discussed at ¶ 6080.) This look-through rule is not elective and applies to any payments that meet its requirements. See IRS Notice 2007–9, § 2, 2007–1 C.B. 401, 402. The following Example illustrates the application of this provision:

Example. DC, a U.S. corporation, owns all of the stock of FC1, incorporated in Country C. FC1, in turn, owns all of the stock of FC2, incorporated in Country D. FC1 and FC2 are both controlled foreign corporations (within the meaning of Section 957(a)). As its primary source of income, FC2 purchases machinery parts from DC (which DC manufactures in the United States) and resells the machinery parts to customers in Country D, realizing net income from such sales. This income is not foreign base company sales income. Although FC2 is purchasing the parts from DC, a related person, FC2 is reselling the machinery parts to customers in Country D, its country of incorporation. See § 954(d)(1)(B). When FC2 pays a dividend to FC1 out of such earnings and profits that are attributable to FC2's non-Subpart F income, the dividend payment will not constitute foreign personal holding company income in FC1's hands under the look-through rule exception in Section 954(c)(6). Thus, DC will not have a Section 951(a) inclusion by reason of such dividend payment to FC1.

The statute authorizes the Treasury and the IRS to issue rules designed to prevent abuse of the purposes of this provision. § 954(c)(6)(A). IRS Notice 2007–9, § 7, 2007–1 C.B. 401, 403–04, gives examples of the types of transactions that the Treasury and the IRS believe are abusive in this respect. One example is a transaction that reduces "income from the U.S. income tax base by having the net effect of creating a deduction of a payment, accrual, or loss of a person subject to U.S. tax without a corresponding inclusion in the subpart F income of the CFC recipient, where such inclusion would have resulted in the absence of" Section 954(c)(6). Id. at § 7(b), 2007–1 C.B. at 404.

As indicated above, this exclusion applies only to dividends, interest, rents or royalties received or accrued by a controlled foreign corporation from another controlled foreign corporation that is a related person within the meaning of Section 954(d)(3) (discussed at ¶ 6155). A payor controlled foreign corporation is a related person of the recipient controlled foreign corporation if the payor corporation controls the recipient corporation, is controlled by the recipient corporation or is controlled by a controlled foreign corporation that is controlled by the same person or persons that control the recipient controlled foreign corporation. Control for this purpose means ownership, directly or indirectly, of more than 50 percent of the corporation's stock (by vote or value).

The purpose of Section 954(c)(6) is to allow U.S. multinational corporations to reinvest their active earnings where it makes the most business sense to do so without incurring an immediate current tax under the Subpart F rules. Congress believed that most countries allowed their multinational corporations "to redeploy active foreign earnings with no additional tax burden" and that this exception to the foreign personal holding company income rules would "enable U.S. companies to make more sales overseas, and thus produce more goods in the United States." H.R. Rep. No. 304, 109th Cong., 1st Sess. 45 (2005).

This provision was enacted as part of the Tax Increase Prevention and Reconciliation Act of 2005 and was first effective for tax years starting after 2005 and before 2009. Legislation enacted in 2007 and 2008 made changes to this provision and extended its effective date to tax years starting before 2010. It remains to be seen whether Congress will further extend this provision to 2010 and later years.

Exception for certain gains or losses from stocks or securities held as dealer property. Gains and losses from the sale or exchange of stock or securities are not taken into account in determining foreign personal holding company income if the stock or securities are held by the controlled foreign corporation primarily for sale to customers in the ordinary course of its business within the meaning of Section 1221(a)(1) (so-called "dealer property"). § 954(c)(1)(B). In such a case, the stock and securities transactions are not viewed as passive in nature.

Section 964(e). Gain recognized by a controlled foreign corporation on the sale or exchange of stock in another foreign corporation is included in the controlled foreign corporation's gross income as a dividend to the same extent that it would have been treated as a dividend under Section 1248(a) (discussed at ¶ 6245) if the controlled foreign corporation were a U.S. person. § 964(e)(1). This deemed dividend may constitute foreign personal company income under Section 954(c)(1)(A) and trigger an income inclusion under Section 951(a)(1)(A) by the U.S. shareholders of the controlled foreign corporation. This deemed dividend also may carry foreign taxes deemed paid under Section 960. Note that the same-country-related-person exception in Section 954(c)(3)(A)(i) does not apply to this deemed dividend. § 964(e)(2). Note also that this provision does not affect the determination of whether the foreign corporation whose stock is sold meets the definition of a controlled foreign corporation. § 964(e)(1).

Example. DC, a domestic corporation, owns all the stock of FC1, which is a controlled foreign corporation. FC1, in turn, owns all the stock of FC2, which is also a controlled foreign corporation. DC has owned all the stock of FC1 during the entire period that FC1 has owned all the stock of FC2. FC2 has earnings and profits of $200. During the current year, FC1 sells all the stock of FC2 to an unrelated buyer and recognizes $200 of gain on the sale. If FC1 had been a U.S. person, Section 1248(a) would have treated all $200 of FC1's gain on the sale of the FC2 stock as a dividend. Accordingly, under Section 964(e)(1), FC1's gain on the sale of FC2 stock is included in FC1's gross income as a dividend, and, thus, constitutes foreign personal holding company income under Section 954(c)(1)(A) that will trigger an income inclusion by DC under Section 951(a)(1)(A). This dividend also will carry foreign taxes of FC2 deemed paid under Section 960.

Finally, for purposes of Section 964(e), a controlled foreign corporation is treated as having sold or exchanged stock in a foreign corporation if, under any income tax provision in the Code, the controlled foreign corporation is treated as having gain from the sale or exchange of the stock in the foreign corporation. § 964(e)(3). As discussed above, this gain may be treated as deemed dividend to the controlled foreign corporation under Section 964(e)(1), which, in turn, constitutes foreign personal holding company income under Section 954(c)(1)(A). For example, suppose that a controlled foreign corporation distributes to its U.S. shareholder stock that the controlled foreign corporation owns in another foreign corporation. If the controlled foreign corporation recognizes gain under Section 311(b) as if the stock were sold to the U.S. shareholder for its fair market value, the controlled foreign corporation is treated as having sold or exchanged the stock for purposes of Section 964(e) and the recognized gain may be treated as a deemed dividend to the corporation under Section 964(e)(1). See H.R. Rep. No. 148, 105th Cong., 1st Sess. 529 (1997).

Reverse hybrid entities. As discussed at ¶ 13,040, the IRS issued IRS Notice 98–11, 1998–1 C.B. 433, and temporary and proposed regulations dealing with reverse hybrid entities used as a device for avoiding Subpart F. A reverse hybrid entity is an entity treated as a separate taxable entity under foreign law but as a pass-through entity for U.S. tax law purposes. In IRS Notice 98–35, 1998–2 C.B. 34, the IRS withdrew Notice 98–11 and announced its intention to withdraw the temporary and proposed regulations covering hybrid transactions. The IRS also announced its intention to issue another set of proposed regulations concerning hybrid transactions that would not be finalized before 2000. In July 1999, the IRS re-issued these regulations in proposed form, but with a proposed delayed effective date of five years after publication of the regulations in final form in the Federal Register. These proposed regulations are not likely to be issued in final form without further congressional direction in the hybrid branch area and it is unlikely that the current Congress will enact legislation supporting the issuance of these regulations. In fact, Section 954(c)(6), enacted in 2006 and discussed above, allows taxpayers to achieve substantially the same tax benefits as the hybrid branch arrangement but through favorable tax treatment of dividend, interest, rent and royalty payments made between two related controlled foreign corporations.

[¶ 6090]

b. Related Person Factoring Income

When a seller of goods or services takes back from the buyer a receivable (a promise to pay in the future) in exchange therefor and then sells the receivable to a third party (a "factor") at a discount, the seller's income on the sale of the goods or services is reduced by the amount of that discount. Upon collection or sale of the receivable, the factor realizes income equal to the difference between the amount paid for the receivable and the amount received by the factor on collection or sale of the receivable.

In most respects, a factoring transaction is a financing transaction in which the factor has acquired a loan to the obligor-buyer represented by the receivable and the discount earned by the factor is functionally the equivalent of interest. By structuring the transaction as the factoring of a receivable rather than as a loan, however, the parties could plan around the controlled foreign corporation provisions. In cases in which the factored receivable arose from a sale by a U.S. taxpayer, the U.S. tax base was directly reduced, and the U.S. tax was often not replaced by a significant foreign tax because the factoring activity was conducted by a controlled foreign corporation in a tax haven. Some taxpayers also sought to use factoring transactions instead of direct loans to the U.S. taxpayer to circumvent the provisions that treat certain investments in U.S. property by a controlled foreign corporation as a constructive distribution. § 956, discussed at ¶ 6200.

Under Section 864(d)(1), any income (whether as discount, stated interest or in some other form) arising from a trade or service receivable acquired directly or indirectly by a foreign corporation from a related person[19] is treated as if it were interest on a loan to the obligor-buyer under the receivable. The related person may be either a foreign person or a U.S. person. This rule applies only for purposes of the Subpart F rules and the foreign tax credit limitations. § 864(d)(2). In applying this rule, the source rules of Sections 861 and 862 apply as though the income from a trade or service receivable were interest on a loan to the obligor-buyer under the receivable.

A trade or service receivable is defined as an account receivable or other evidence of indebtedness initially arising out of either (1) the disposition of property described in Section 1221(a)(1) (generally inventory or property held by the taxpayer primarily for sale to customers in the ordinary course of a trade or business) or (2) the performance of services by a person who is a related person with respect to the person who earns income from the satisfaction or disposition of the receivable or evidence of indebtedness. § 864(d)(3). Income from a receivable is subject to the rule of Section 864(d)(1) whenever the receivable or an interest in the receivable has been assigned to a foreign corporation by a related person.

Moreover, a loan by a controlled foreign corporation for the purpose of financing the purchase of goods or services of a related party is treated like the acquisition by the foreign corporation of the purchaser's receivable. § 864(d)(6). This rule is intended to prevent taxpayers from restructuring transactions to avoid the impact of the related person factoring rule. Thus, either the purchase of a trade or service receivable by a controlled foreign corporation from a related person or a loan by the controlled foreign corporation to a related person's customer generally produces the same unfavorable tax result.

Related person factoring income is subject to tax if it is earned by any controlled foreign corporation with earnings and profits. Therefore, related person factoring income does not benefit from certain exceptions to the Subpart F rules. § 864(d)(5)(A). For example, the income will be taxed to the U.S. shareholders without regard to the general less-than-five-percent de minimis exception from foreign base company income (Section 954(b)(3)(A), discussed at ¶ 6160).[20] In addition, factoring income does not benefit from the same-country-related-person interest exception of Section 954(c)(3)(A)(i) or the export financing interest exception of Section 954(c)(2)(B), discussed at ¶ 6085.

---

19. "Related person" is defined broadly to include not only related persons as defined for the purpose of the Section 267 loss disallowance rule but also ten-percent U.S. shareholders and persons related to ten-percent U.S. shareholders. § 864(d)(4). This broad definition of related person prevents tax-free related person factoring by foreign corporations owned by several U.S. persons.

20. Factoring income will nonetheless count as foreign base company income in determining whether under Section 954(b)(3) less than five percent or more than 70 percent of total gross income is gross foreign base company income. Assume, for example, that four percent of the gross income of a controlled foreign corporation is related person factoring income, four percent is foreign base company services income and 92 percent is not foreign base company income. The services income, as well as the factoring income, will be treated as foreign base company income.

These rules treating related person factoring income as interest income will not apply if three requirements are met. First, both the controlled foreign corporation and the related person must be formed in the same foreign country. Second, the related person must have a substantial part of its assets used in its trade or business in that country. Third, if the related person had collected the receivable, its income from collection would not have been foreign base company income or income effectively connected with the conduct of a U.S. trade or business. § 864(d)(7).

[¶ 6095]

c. Income From Foreign Currency Gains

Another component of foreign personal holding company income for Subpart F purposes is the excess of foreign currency gains over foreign currency losses (as defined in Section 988(b)) attributable to any Section 988 transaction. § 954(c)(1)(D). This provision incorporates concepts contained in Section 988 dealing with foreign currency gains, discussed at ¶ 9030. An exception is provided for hedging and other transactions that are directly related to the business needs of the controlled foreign corporation. Congress added income from foreign currency gains to the definition of foreign personal holding company income in 1986 because such gains had become more frequent with floating exchange rates and it believed that such gains represent "the type of income that can easily be routed through a controlled foreign corporation in a tax haven jurisdiction." Staff of Joint Comm. on Tax'n, 100th Cong., 1st Sess., General Explanation of the Tax Reform Act of 1986, at 966 (1987).

[¶ 6100]

d. Income From Commodity Transactions

Foreign personal holding company income also includes the excess of gains over losses from transactions (including futures, forward contracts and similar transactions) in any commodities. § 954(c)(1)(C). An exception is provided for certain commodities gains or losses arising out of commodity hedging transactions (as defined in Section 954(c)(5)(A)). An additional exception is provided for transactions (not limited to hedging transactions) that occur in the active business of a foreign corporation substantially all of the commodities of which are property within the meaning of Section 1221(a)(1), (2) or (8). This exception is intended to apply only to foreign corporations actively engaged in commodities businesses, not those primarily engaged in such financial transactions as the trading of futures. A third exception is provided for certain commodities gains or losses that are foreign currency gains or losses attributable to Section 988 transactions (discussed at ¶ 9030).

[¶ 6105]

e. Gains From Sale of Property Producing Passive Income or No Income and Certain Other Property

Also included in the definition of foreign personal holding company income are the excesses of gains over losses from sales or exchanges of three other types of property. As mentioned at ¶ 6085, the first type is property that gives rise to three categories of passive (foreign personal holding company) income: (1) most dividends and interest (other than property which gives rise to income qualifying for the active banking or financing exception in Section 954(h) or property which gives rise to income qualifying for the active insurance income exception in Section 954(i), discussed below at ¶ 6135); (2) rents and royalties other than active business rents and royalties from unrelated persons; and (3) annuities. § 954(c)(1)(B)(i); Reg. § 1.954–2(e)(1)(i)(A). Under this provision, gain from the sale of dividend-producing stock or interest-producing debt instruments will normally be foreign personal holding company income (unless an exception applies). In addition, gain from the disposition of a patent that gave rise to active business royalties from an unrelated person would not be foreign personal holding company income, but gain from the sale of a patent licensed to a related person for use in another country would be. An exception is provided for gains and losses from the sale or exchange of inventory property or other property held primarily for sale to customers in the ordinary course of the controlled foreign corporation's business. § 954(c)(1)(B); Reg. § 1.954–2(e)(1)(ii).

The second type is property "which does not give rise to any income." § 954(c)(1)(B)(iii); Reg. § 1.954–2(e)(1)(i)(C). With certain specified exceptions, this type of property "includes all rights and interests in property (whether or not a capital asset)." Reg. § 1.954–2(e)(3). For example, gain on the sale of diamonds held for investment purposes is foreign personal holding company. Gain from the sale of unimproved land located in a foreign country and held for investment also is foreign personal holding company income.

The statute and regulations provide three exceptions to this second type of property. First, property that gives rise to passive income is not within this provision, but instead is within Section 954(c)(1)(B)(i) (discussed above); Reg. § 1.954–2(e)(3)(i). Second, an exception is provided for gains and losses from the sale or exchange of inventory property or other property held primarily for sale to customers in the ordinary course of the controlled foreign corporation's business. § 954(c)(1)(B); Reg. § 1.954–2(e)(1)(ii). Without this exception, for example, many types of inventory gains and losses could be treated as gains and losses from the sale of non-income producing property and the excess of the gains over the losses would be foreign personal holding company income under Section

954(c)(1)(B)(iii). Third, the regulations provide an exception for the following types of trade or business property of the controlled foreign corporation:

(1) Tangible property (other than real property) that is used in the controlled foreign corporation's business and that is of a character that would be subject to depreciation under Sections 167 and 168, Reg. § 1.954–2(e)(3)(ii);

(2) Real property not giving rise to rental or similar income, "to the extent used or held for use in the controlled foreign corporation's trade or business," Reg. § 1.954–2(e)(3)(iii);

(3) Intangible property, goodwill and going concern value "to the extent used or held for use in the controlled foreign corporation's trade or business," Reg. § 1.954–2(e)(3)(iv);

(4) Notional principal contracts (defined at ¶ 6115), Reg. § 1.954–2(e)(3)(v); and

(5) Other property excepted in published guidance by the IRS, Reg. § 1.954–2(e)(2)(vi).

The third type of property is an interest in a trust, partnership or REMIC (a specialized pass-through regime). § 954(c)(1)(B)(ii); Reg. § 1.954–2(e)(1)(i)(B). The check-the-box entity classification regulations at Reg. §§ 301.7701–2 through –4 determine whether the entity in which the controlled foreign corporation has sold an interest is a "trust" or "partnership" for purposes of this provision. These regulations are discussed briefly at ¶ 1223 and in more detail at ¶¶ 13,035 et seq.

The statute contains two exceptions to this third type of property. First, an exception is provided for inventory property or other property held primarily for sale to customers in the ordinary course of the controlled foreign corporation's business. § 954(c)(1)(B). Second, the 2004 JOBS Act added Section 954(c)(4) to the Code, which contains a look-through rule that applies to a controlled foreign corporation's sale of an interest in a partnership in which the corporation owns at least 25 percent of the capital or profits interest. Under this look-through rule, the controlled foreign corporation is treated as selling a proportionate share of the assets of the partnership, and, thus, the controlled foreign corporation's sale of the partnership interest will be treated as Subpart F income only to the extent that the sale of a proportionate share of the partnership assets attributable to the partnership interest would constitute Subpart F income. See H.R. Rep. No. 548, pt. 1, 108th Cong., 2d Sess. 204 (2004).

For example, suppose that a controlled foreign corporation owns a 25–percent interest in a partnership and sells the partnership interest at a gain of $100,000. Suppose further that a sale of the partnership assets would result in Subpart F income with respect to 50 percent of the partnership's assets. Under the look-through rule in Section 954(c)(4), $50,000 (i.e., 50 percent of $100,000) of the gain realized by the controlled foreign corporation on the sale of the partnership interest would be characterized as Subpart F income.

For purposes of measuring the controlled foreign corporation's ownership interest in a partnership to determine whether the 25–percent ownership threshold has been met, the statute provides that if the controlled foreign corporation is a shareholder of a corporation or a partner of a partnership, the controlled foreign corporation is treated as owning directly its proportionate share of any capital or profits interest that such corporation or partnership holds directly or indirectly. The statute also provides that if, under constructive ownership rules similar to the Section 958(b) rules, a controlled foreign corporation is treated as owning a capital or profits interest in a partnership, then the controlled foreign corporation will be treated as owning such interest directly for purposes of this partnership sales provision.

If the controlled foreign corporation does not meet the 25–percent ownership threshold in the partnership, the controlled foreign corporation's gain from the sale of the partnership interest generally will continue to be treated as foreign personal holding company income under Section 954(c)(1)(B)(ii), without regard to the partnership's underlying assets or activities.

"Check and sell" planning maneuvers using the check-the-box entity classification regulations. Suppose that a U.S. corporation owns all the stock of a foreign holding corporation, which, in turn, owns all of the stock of another foreign corporation that owns all assets used in a trade or business. These assets are of a type that would not constitute property that gives rise to passive income under Section 954(c)(1)(B)(i) or property "which does not give rise to any income" under Section 954(c)(1)(B)(iii) by reason of the exception in Reg. § 1.954–2(e)(3)(ii) through (iv) if they were sold by the lower-tier corporation. However, the foreign country in which the lower-tier foreign operating corporation is located might well impose a tax on the sale of the lower-tier corporation's assets. If the foreign holding corporation sells the stock of the lower-tier foreign corporation to a purchaser, the foreign country is not likely to impose tax on the stock sale gain. However, the gain from the sale of the stock will be foreign personal holding company income either under Section 954(c)(1)(B)(i) (i.e., gain from the sale of property producing passive dividend income) or Section 954(c)(1)(B)(iii) (i.e., gain from the sale of property producing no income), thus resulting in an inclusion to the U.S. parent corporation under Section 951(a)(1)(A)(i). Instead, the foreign holding corporation agrees to sell the lower-tier foreign corporation to a purchaser but, just before sale, the lower-tier foreign corporation files an election under the check-the-box entity classification regulations (discussed at ¶¶ 1223 and 13,035 et seq.) to be treated as a disregarded entity. (The lower-tier foreign corporation is an "eligible entity," meaning that it may elect corporate or noncorporate status for U.S. tax purposes under the check-the-box regulations. This election generally will have no effect for foreign tax purposes and a foreign country is likely to respect the form of this transaction as sale of stock in the lower-tier foreign corporation.) The taxpayer will argue that the lower-tier foreign corporation's assets come within the exception in Reg. § 1.954–2(e)(3)(ii) through (iv) and, thus, the gain on the sale of the assets is not foreign personal holding company income. In response, the government will argue that the deemed sale of the lower-tier foreign corporation's operating assets does not constitute a sale of property used or held for use in the foreign holding company's trade or business and, thus, even if the transaction is respected as a sale of assets (rather than stock), the gain from the sale of the assets is foreign personal holding company income.

In Dover Corp. v. Commissioner, 122 T.C. 324 (2004), the Tax Court held that this transaction was to be treated for U.S. tax purposes as a sale of operating assets of a disregarded entity and that the disregarded entity election resulted in a deemed Section 332 liquidation of the lower-tier foreign corporation into the foreign holding corporation. Consequently, the foreign holding company succeeded to the tax attributes of the lower-tier corporation under Section 381. Furthermore, the court held that the assets used in the business of the deemed liquidated subsidiary retained their status as assets used in the same business by what, as a result of the deemed liquidation, became the deemed branch of the foreign holding company. Thus, the foreign holding company's gain from the sale of those operating assets to the purchaser was not foreign personal holding company income under Section 954(c)(1)(B)(iii).

This decision upholds a taxpayer's creative use of the check-the-box entity classification regulations to convert what would have been an item of Subpart F income currently taxable to the U.S. parent corporation into an item of income that is not currently subject to U.S. income tax. It can also be viewed as another example of a cross-border tax arbitrage transaction in which a taxpayer exploits differences in U.S. and foreign country tax treatment of the entity conducting the business here (i.e., it is a foreign corporation for foreign tax purposes but a disregarded entity for U.S. tax purposes—a reverse hybrid entity). Does this planning maneuver constitute an abuse of the tax system that impairs the effectiveness and frustrates the underlying purpose of the Subpart F rules or a proper application of the elective, check-the-box entity classification rules, which were created by the Treasury and the IRS through exercise of their regulatory authority? Should the tax system allow the use of such a technique when, as is typically the case, the election to treat a single-owner foreign entity as a disregarded entity (i.e., a branch) for U.S. tax purposes has no nontax economic consequences? Note that the Staff of the Joint Committee on Taxation has recommended that Congress enact a statutory rule that would require an organization to be treated as a corporation for U.S. tax purposes if it is a separate business entity organized under foreign law and has a single member. See Staff of Joint

Comm. on Tax'n, 109th Cong., 1st Sess., Options to Improve Tax Compliance and Reform Tax Expenditures, at 183 (2005), excerpted at ¶ 13,055. Would such proposed legislation solve the tax policy issue raised by the *Dover* case?

[¶ 6110]

f. Income Equivalent to Interest

Before 1986, U.S. taxpayers continued to use controlled foreign corporations to shelter passive interest-type income from current U.S. tax by rearranging offshore investments so that the interest-like income they generated was not traditional interest income. To combat these devices, Congress extended the definition of Subpart F foreign personal holding company income to include income equivalent to interest. § 954(c)(1)(E). This includes, for example, income from commitment fees for loans actually made.

[¶ 6115]

g. Income From Notional Principal Contracts

The definition of "foreign personal holding company income" was expanded in 1997 to include net income from notional principal contracts. However, income, gain, deduction or loss from a notional principal contract entered into for the purposes of hedging an item of income falling within one of the other categories of foreign personal holding company income described above is included in that category and not taken into account under this provision. § 954(c)(1)(F). Congress made this change because it believed that net income from notional principal contracts was economically equivalent to other types of income included in the definition of foreign personal holding company income. H.R. Rep. No. 148, 105th Cong., 1st Sess. 543 (1997).

Reg. §§ 1.446–3(c)(1)(i) and 1.863–7(a)(1) define a "notional principal contract" as a financial instrument providing "for the payment of amounts by one party to another at specified intervals calculated by reference to a specified index upon a notional principal contract amount in exchange for specified consideration or a promise to pay similar amounts." Interest rate swaps, currency swaps, interest rate caps, interest rate floors and other similar agreements are notional principal contracts under this definition. Reg. § 1.446–3(c)(1)(i). For example, suppose that DC, a U.S. corporation, enters into an interest rate swap contract with FC, an unrelated foreign corporation. Under the contract, DC must pay FC fixed rate dollar amounts, and FC must pay DC floating rate dollar amounts, each of which is determined solely by reference to a notional dollar denominated principal amount that is specified in the contract. This contract constitutes a notional principal contract. See Reg. § 1.863–7(d), Ex.

[¶ 6120]

h. Payments in Lieu of Dividends in Certain Securities Lending Transactions

The definition of foreign personal holding company income includes payments in lieu of dividends that are made under an agreement to which Section 1058 applies. § 954(c)(1)(G). Section 1058 applies to an agreement relating to a transfer of securities if (i) the agreement provides for the return to the transferor of securities identical to the securities transferred; (ii) the agreement requires that payments be made to the transferor of securities equivalent to all interest, dividends and other distributions that the owner of the securities is entitled to receive during the period starting with the transfer of the securities by the transferor and ending with the transfer of identical securities back to the transferor; (iii) the agreement does not reduce the risk of loss or opportunity for gain of the transferor of the securities in the transferred securities; and (iv) meets any other requirements provided by the Treasury in regulations. § 1058(b). Congress believed such payments to be economically equivalent to dividends. See H.R. Rep. No. 148, 105th Cong., 1st Sess. 543 (1997).

[¶ 6125]

i. Certain Personal Services Contract Income

As discussed at ¶ 6000, the 2004 JOBS Act repealed the foreign personal holding company rules, including former Section 553(a)(5), which applied to certain personal services contract income. To fill a perceived gap in the anti-deferral rules as a result of this change, the JOBS Act added Section 954(c)(1)(H), which treats personal services contract income of a type formerly covered by now-repealed Section 553(a)(5) as foreign personal holding company income for Subpart F purposes. This provision applies to amounts received under a personal services contract (or from the disposition of the contract) if (i) the controlled foreign corporation is to furnish the personal services; (ii) some person other than the corporation has the right to designate the individual who is to perform the services or the individual who is to perform the services is designated in the contract; and (iii) at some time during the tax year, 25 percent or more in value of the corporation's outstanding stock is owned, directly or indirectly, by or for the individual who has performed, will perform or may be designated to perform the services.

[¶ 6130]

j. Exception for Regular Dealers

A statutory provision applicable to regular dealers excepts the following items from the definition of foreign personal holding company income: income, gain, deduction or loss from transactions (including hedging transactions and transactions involving physical settlement) entered into in the ordinary course of a business of a controlled foreign corporation as a regular dealer in property, forward contracts, options, notional principal contracts or other similar financial instruments (including notional principal contracts and instruments referenced to commodities). This exception, however, does not apply to dividends, interest, royalties, rents and annuities falling within Section 954(c)(1)(A), income equivalent to interest falling within Section 954(c)(1)(E) or payments in lieu of dividends falling within Section 954(c)(1)(G). § 954(c)(2)(C)(i). If the controlled foreign corporation is a dealer in securities, any interest, dividend, interest equivalent amount or dividend equivalent amount from a transaction (including a hedging transaction) entered into in the ordinary course of the dealer's trade or business as a dealer in securities is excepted from the definition of foreign personal holding company income if the income from the transaction is attributable to activities of the dealer in the country of incorporation of the controlled foreign corporation. § 954(c)(2)(C)(ii).

[¶ 6135]

k. Exception for Certain Active Financing and Insurance Income

The Taxpayer Relief Act of 1997 provided temporary exceptions from the definition of foreign personal holding company income for (1) certain income derived in the active conduct of a banking, financing or similar business by a controlled foreign corporation predominantly engaged in the active conduct of such a business or (2) certain income received from an unrelated person and derived from specified investments made by a qualified insurance company. See former § 954(h). President Clinton canceled these provisions in 1997, using the Line Item Veto Act. The Supreme Court, however, held that the Line Item Veto Act was unconstitutional. See Clinton v. City of New York, 524 U.S. 417 (1998). Tax legislation enacted in 1998 and 1999 modified these exceptions by placing the exception for insurance income in its own subsection and extended the exceptions through tax years starting before 2002. §§ 953(e) and 954(h), (i). Subsequent legislation enacted in 2002 through 2008 further modified these exceptions and extended them through tax years starting before 2010. It remains to be seen whether Congress will further extend these temporary exceptions. Under a change made to Section 954(h) by the 2004 JOBS Act, a controlled foreign corporation may qualify for the exception even though the banking or financing activity is performed by employees of a related person, if certain requirements are met.

[¶ 6140]

2. FOREIGN BASE COMPANY SALES INCOME

The second major category of foreign base company income is "foreign base company sales income." The definition of such income includes both a "related person" test and a two-pronged "geographical" test that must be met. It is defined as income derived from the purchase and sale of personal property (1) if the property is either purchased from (or on behalf of) a related person or sold to (or on behalf of) a related person and (2) if the property purchased is manufactured, produced, grown or extracted outside of the country where the controlled foreign corporation is organized and the property also is sold for use, consumption or disposition outside that country. § 954(d)(1)(A) and (B).[21] S. Rep. No. 1881, 87th Cong., 2d Sess. 84 (1962), explained these two requirements as follows:

> The sales income with which [Subpart F] is primarily concerned is income of a selling subsidiary (whether acting as principal or agent) which has been separated from manufacturing activities of a related corporation merely to obtain a lower rate of tax for the sales income. This accounts for the fact that this provision is restricted to sales of property, to a related person, or to purchases of property from a related person. Moreover, the fact that a lower rate of tax for such a company is likely to be obtained only through purchases and sales outside of the country in which it is incorporated, accounts for the fact that the provision is made inapplicable to the extent the property is manufactured, produced, grown, or extracted in the country where the corporation is organized or where it is sold for use, consumption, or disposition in that country. Mere passage of title or the place of the sale are not relevant in this connection.

Note that this definition does not require any finding of a tax-avoidance purpose for the transaction.

Foreign base company sales income includes income generated by such trading activity whether the controlled foreign corporation buys and resells the property or merely acts as a sales agent or representative in return for a sales commission.

Foreign base company sales income includes only sales income from the purchase and sale of personal property that is not manufactured,

21. The 1993 Act amended the definition of foreign base company sales income to include any income (whether in the form of profits, commissions, fees or otherwise) derived in connection with (1) any sale of unprocessed timber which is a softwood cut in the United States or (2) the milling of such timber outside the United States. § 954(d)(4). Congress was concerned that allowing deferral on such income tended to "accelerate the removal of old-growth forests" and encouraged the export of raw logs, causing "American milling jobs to be exported overseas." S. Prt. No. 103–37, 103d Cong., 1st Sess. 209 (1993).

produced or constructed by the controlled foreign corporation. The controlled foreign corporation, however, will not be treated as having manufactured, produced or constructed personal property that it sells merely because the property sold is in a different form than when it was purchased. Instead, under the current regulations, which were substantially revised in late 2008, a controlled foreign corporation will be treated as having manufactured, produced or constructed personal property only if it meets one of three tests through the activities of its employees with respect to the property. Reg. § 1.954–3(a)(4)(i).

Under the first such test, if personal property sold by the controlled foreign corporation is substantially transformed by the foreign corporation before sale, the property sold by the controlled foreign corporation is treated as manufactured, produced or constructed by such corporation. Reg. § 1.954–3(a)(4)(ii). This involves an analysis of the surrounding facts and circumstances. For example, the transformation of wood pulp to paper, steel rods to screws and bolts and fish into canned fish are all substantial transformations of the property purchased that constitute manufacturing or production of property for purposes of this first test. See Reg. § 1.954–3(a)(4)(ii), Exs. 1–3.

Under the second such test, if purchased property is used as a component part of personal property that is sold, the sale of the property will be treated as the sale of a manufactured product, rather than a sale of the component parts, if the selling corporation's assembly or conversion of the component parts into the final product involves activities that are both substantial in nature and generally considered to be the manufacture, production or construction of property. This is a substantive test the application of which is dependent on the facts and circumstances of the particular case. Reg. § 1.954–3(a)(4)(iii).

However, for purposes of this second test, the regulations contain a safe-harbor rule under which the controlled foreign corporation's operations with respect to the purchased product will be treated as manufacturing if its conversion costs (direct labor and factory burden) account for 20 percent or more of the total cost of goods sold for the product. In any event, packaging, repackaging, labeling or minor assembly will not be treated as the manufacture, production or construction of property for Section 954(d)(1) purposes. Reg. § 1.954–3(a)(4)(iii), and the *Fischbein* case, at ¶ 11,095.

Under the third such test, the "substantial contribution" test, which was not in the prior version of these regulations, the property is being manufactured by an unrelated person under a contract manufacturing or similar arrangement. In order to meet this test, two requirements must be met. First, the manufacturing, production and construction activities being undertaken with respect to the property before its sale must be such that if those activities had been undertaken by the corporation before sale through the activities of its employees, the product would have been treated under one of the first two tests as having been manufactured, produced or constructed by the controlled foreign corporation. Second, the surrounding facts and circumstances must show that the controlled foreign corporation makes a substantial contribution through the activities of its employees to the manufacture, production or construction of the personal property. Reg. § 1.954–3(a)(4)(iv)(*a*). The regulations provide a list of some of the activities that will be considered in determining whether the controlled foreign corporation will be treated as making a substantial contribution, including the overview and direction of the manufacturing or production activities or processes by the unrelated person, material or vendor selection and control of manufacturing related logistics. Reg. § 1.954–3(a)(4)(iv)(*b*). No one factor is determinative and the weight that will be given to the performance of any quantum of any activity will vary with the facts and circumstances of each taxpayer's particular business. Reg. § 1.954–3(a)(4)(iv)(*c*).

The "substantial contribution" test in the most recent version of the regulations represents an attempt by the Treasury and the IRS to resolve a vigorous controversy concerning whether the manufacturing, production or construction activities of an unrelated contract manufacturer can be taken into account for purposes of determining whether the controlled foreign corporation has manufactured, produced or constructed the personal property it is selling. Because of the proliferation of cross-border manufacturing operations by controlled foreign corporations that outsource manufacturing to unrelated contract manufacturers located in multiple countries, this change results in an important pro-taxpayer narrowing of the definition of foreign base company sales income. See the discussion at ¶¶ 11,120–11,125.

Even if the controlled foreign corporation manufactures the products it sells, income generated by sales operations handled through a branch operating outside of the country in which the controlled foreign corporation is incorporated will be treated as foreign base company sales income under certain circumstances. That result will occur if the combined effect of the tax treatment accorded the branch by the country of incorporation of the controlled foreign corporation and the country in which the branch is established is to treat the branch substantially the same as if it were a wholly owned subsidiary corporation of the controlled foreign corporation organized in the country in which it carries on its trade or business. § 954(d)(2), Reg. § 1.954–3(b) and Temp. Reg. §§ 1.954–3T(b), (e)-(g), discussed at ¶ 11,100.

[¶ 6145]

3. FOREIGN BASE COMPANY SERVICES INCOME

The third major category of foreign base company income is "foreign base company services income," which is defined as income derived from the performance of technical, managerial, engineering, architectural, scientific, skilled, industrial, commercial or similar services, if such services are performed for (or on behalf of) a related person and if they are performed outside the country in which the controlled foreign corporation is organized. § 954(e)(1).[22] Again, only if both a "related person" test and a "geographical" test are met will services income fall within the definition. Is there a link between foreign base company sales and services income that makes these tests appropriate? S. Rep. No. 1881, 87th Cong., 2d Sess. 84 (1962), explained: "As in the case of sales income, the purpose here is to deny tax deferral where a service subsidiary is separated from manufacturing or similar activities of a related corporation and organized in another country primarily to obtain a lower rate of tax for the service income." Note that, as is generally true of foreign base company sales income and the other elements of the foreign base company income component of Subpart F income, this definition does not require any finding of a tax-avoidance purpose for the transaction.

The regulations provide examples of when services performed by a controlled foreign corporation will be treated as performed for, or on behalf of, a related person. Under those examples, a controlled foreign corporation is treated as performing services for, or on behalf of a related person, where (i) it is paid or reimbursed by the related person for performing the services; (ii) it performs services which a related person was obligated to perform; (iii) it performs services with respect to property sold by a related person and the performance of such services is a condition or a material term of the sale; or (iv) a related person has provided substantial assistance to the performance of the services. Reg. § 1.954–4(b)(1).

For purposes of the substantial assistance test in (iv) above, the regulations define "assistance" by a related person as including "direction, supervision, services, know-how, financial assistance (other than contributions to capital), and equipment, material, or supplies." Reg. § 1.954–4(b)(2)(ii)(*a*). For such assistance by a related person to the controlled foreign corporation to be considered "substantial," the regulations require either (1) that the assistance furnished provide the corporation "with skills which are a principal element in producing the income from the performance of" services by the corporation or (2) the cost to the corporation of the assistance furnished by the related person equals at least 50 percent of the corporation's total cost of performing the services that it performs. Reg. § 1.954–4(b)(2)(ii)(*b*). The regulations contain several other requirements relating to application of this substantial assistance

22. Excluded from the definition is income derived in connection with the performance of services that are directly related to (1) the sale or exchange by the controlled foreign corporation of property manufactured, produced, grown or extracted by it and that are performed before the time of the sale or exchange or (2) an offer or effort to sell or exchange such property. § 954(e)(2). Such income is excluded because it has a close connection with sales income that is not itself Subpart F income.

test. See Reg. § 1.954–4(b)(2)(ii)(*c*)-(*e*). The purpose of the "substantial assistance" rules in the regulations is to characterize income as foreign base company services income if it is "received by a CFC [controlled foreign corporation] from rendering services to an unrelated person where in rendering those services a related person substantially contributes to the CFC's performance of such services in a manner that suggests that the CFC, rather than the related party, entered into the contract to obtain a lower rate of tax on the service income." IRS Notice 2007–13, 2007–1 C.B. 410, 411.

In 2007, the Treasury and the IRS noted that there had been a substantial expansion in the reach of the global services economy since 1968, when the "substantial assistance" regulations had been published, and that U.S. multinational corporations providing services outside the United States "currently have globally integrated businesses with support capabilities for unrelated customer projects in different geographic locations, largely based on factors such as expertise and cost efficiencies." Id. Further, the Treasury and the IRS acknowledged that unless these regulations are amended to take into account the global business structures that had developed since 1968, taxpayers might be forced "to change the way they do business or structure their operations in [the] light of the substantial assistance rules, even if such a structure would be less efficient from a business perspective by, for example, requiring a taxpayer to duplicate a full service infrastructure in each country." Id. Accordingly, IRS Notice 2007–13 (2007–1 C.B. at 411–12) announced the following:

> The Treasury Department and the IRS will amend Treas. Reg. § 1.954–4(b)(1)(iv) and (b)(2)(ii) and the examples thereunder. Treas. Reg. § 1.954–4(b)(1)(iv) as amended will provide that services performed by a CFC in a case where substantial assistance by a related United States person or persons (as the term is defined in section 957(c) * * *) contributes to the performance of such service will constitute "services which are performed for, or on behalf of, a related person." Treas. Reg. § 1.954–4(b)(2)(ii) as amended will provide that "substantial assistance" consists of assistance furnished (directly or indirectly) by a related United States person or persons to the CFC if the assistance satisfies an objective cost test. The subjective "principal element" test will no longer apply to determine substantial assistance. For purposes of the objective cost test, the definition of the term "assistance" will include, but will not be limited to, direction, supervision, services, know-how, financial assistance (other than contributions to capital), and equipment, material, or supplies provided directly or indirectly by a related United States person to a CFC.
>
> The cost test will be satisfied if the cost to the CFC of the assistance furnished by the related United States person or persons equals or exceeds 80 percent of the total cost to the CFC of performing the services. The term "cost" will be determined after taking into

account adjustments, if any, made under section 482 * * *. Taxpayers may apply the cost test either by demonstrating that the assistance provided, directly or indirectly, by related United States persons is below the 80 percent cost threshold, or, alternatively, by demonstrating that the cost of the services provided by the CFC itself, and/or by a related CFC, is more than 20 percent of the total cost to the CFC of performing the services. For this purpose, services provided by a CFC itself are not assistance provided "indirectly" by a related United States person (or persons). However, employees, officers, or directors of the CFC who are concurrently employees, officers, or directors of a related United States person during a taxable year of the CFC will be considered employees, officers or directors solely of the related United States person for such taxable year for purposes of this notice.

The Taxpayer Relief Act of 1997 provided a temporary exception from the definition of foreign base company services income for (1) certain income derived in the active conduct of a banking, financing or similar business by a controlled foreign corporation predominantly engaged in the active conduct of such a business or (2) certain income received from an unrelated person and derived from specified investments made by a qualified insurance company. See former § 954(e)(2)(C) and (h). As described at ¶ 6135, President Clinton cancelled this provision in 1997, using the Line Item Veto Act, but the Supreme Court subsequently held the Act to be unconstitutional. Tax legislation enacted in 1998 and 1999 modified this exception and extended the application of the exception through tax years starting before 2002. §§ 953(e)(10) and 954(e)(2), (h) and (i). Subsequent legislation enacted in 2002 through 2008 further modified this exception and extended it through tax years starting before 2010. It remains to be seen whether Congress will further extend this temporary exception to 2010 and later years.

[¶ 6150]

4. FOREIGN BASE COMPANY OIL RELATED INCOME

Finally, foreign base company income includes "foreign base company oil related income," defined as "foreign oil related income" (within the meaning of Section 907(c)(2) and (3)) of a foreign corporation, if it is a "large oil producer" for the tax year. Excluded from the definition is income derived from a source within a foreign country in connection with (1) oil or gas that was extracted from an oil or gas well located therein or (2) oil, gas or a primary product of oil or gas that is sold by the foreign corporation or a related person for use or consumption within such country or is loaded in such country on a vessel or aircraft as fuel for such vessel or aircraft. § 954(g)(1). A large oil producer is any corporation if, for the current or preceding tax year, the average daily production of foreign crude oil and natural gas of the related group (as defined in Section 954(g)(2)(C)) of which the corporation is a part equaled at least 1,000 barrels. § 954(g)(2).

[¶ 6155]

5. DEFINITION OF "RELATED PERSON" (SECTION 954(d)(3))

As discussed above, the definition of "related person" in Section 954(d)(3) is an important element of a number of significant components of foreign base company income, the central target of the Subpart F regime. This term is also used in other places in the Code, such as the passive foreign investment company provisions, which are discussed later in this Chapter. An individual, corporation, partnership, trust or estate that controls or is controlled by a controlled foreign corporation is a "related person" with respect to the controlled foreign corporation. § 954(d)(3)(A). In addition, a corporation, partnership, trust or estate that is controlled by the same persons or persons that control a controlled foreign corporation is a "related person" with respect to the controlled foreign corporation. § 954(d)(3)(B).

For purposes of this definition of related person, control means, in the case of a corporation, direct or indirect ownership of more than 50 percent of the total voting power *or* value of the stock of the corporation. In the case of a partnership, trust or estate, control means direct or indirect ownership of more than 50 percent (by value) of the beneficial interests in the partnership, trust or estate. In measuring ownership for purposes of applying this definition, rules similar to the indirect and constructive ownership rules in Section 958 (see ¶ 6030) apply. § 954(d)(3).

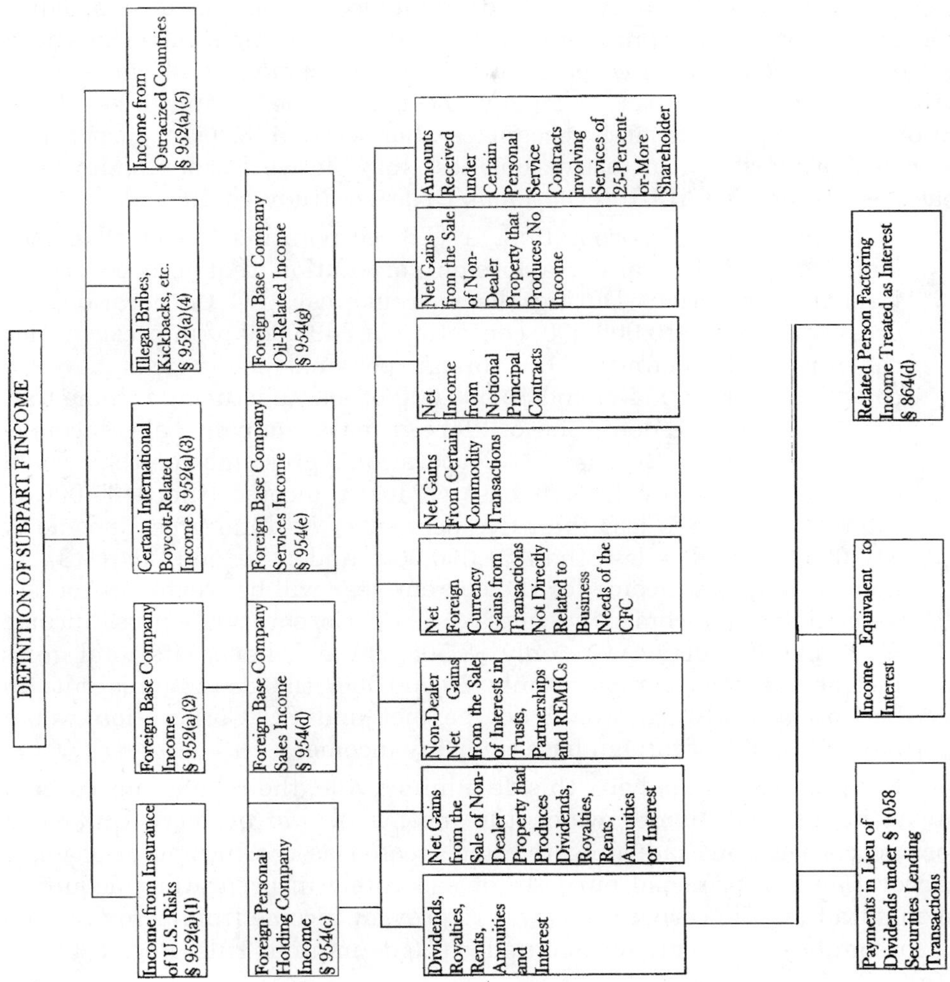

6. SPECIAL RULES

[¶ 6160]

a. De Minimis and Full–Inclusion Rules

De minimis rule. Gross income of a controlled foreign corporation that would otherwise fall within the scope of foreign base company income is not treated as foreign base company income for the tax year if the sum of it and the corporation's gross insurance income, if any, represents less than the smaller of (1) five percent of the total gross income of the controlled foreign corporation or (2) $1 million. Thus, a controlled foreign corporation may realize a de minimis amount of foreign base company income, such as some interest, without that income being treated as Subpart F income that is currently included in the gross income of its U.S.

shareholders. § 954(b)(3)(A). This de minimis rule is aimed at avoiding the disproportionate administrative burden of subjecting U.S. shareholders of controlled foreign corporations with small amounts of what would otherwise be foreign base company income to the complexities of the Subpart F regime. It also recognizes that even a foreign corporation engaged primarily in an active business may derive incidental items of passive income. See ALI International Taxation Study, at 198–99.

Example. DC Corporation, a U.S. corporation, owns all of the stock of FC Corporation, a foreign corporation that is a controlled foreign corporation. During the current year, FC Corporation has gross income of $10,000,000, consisting of $495,000 of interest income that meets the definition of "foreign personal holding company income" in Section 954(c) and $9,505,000 of manufacturing income that does *not* meet the definition of "foreign base company sales income" in Section 954(d). Because FC Corporation's gross income that would otherwise constitute foreign base company income (the $495,000 of interest income) is less than five percent of its total gross income of $10,000,000 and is less than $1,000,000, under Section 954(b)(3)(A), none of its gross income for the current year will be treated as foreign base company income. By contrast, if FC Corporation's gross income from manufacturing were only $8,505,000 and, hence, its total gross income for the year were only $9,000,000, the de minimis rule in Section 954(b)(3)(A) would not be met and FC Corporation would have $495,000 of foreign base company income.

For purposes of applying this de minimis rule, the regulations contain an anti-abuse rule under which the income of two or more controlled foreign corporations is aggregated and treated as the income of a single corporation if a principal purpose for separately incorporating, acquiring or maintaining the corporations was to prevent income from being treated as foreign base company income under the de minimis rule. Reg. § 1.954–1(b)(4).

Full-inclusion rule. On the other hand, if the controlled foreign corporation's gross foreign base company income (and the gross insurance income) for the tax year exceeds 70 percent of its total gross income, all of the gross income of the controlled foreign corporation will be treated as foreign base company income (or insurance income). § 954(b)(3)(B). This full-inclusion rule is aimed at avoiding the administrative difficulties of separating tainted and untainted income when the bulk of the foreign corporation's income is tainted and is premised on the assumption that complete termination of deferral is justified when most of the corporation's income is tainted income. See ALI International Taxation Study, at 201.

Example. DC Corporation, a U.S. corporation, owns all of the stock of FC Corporation, a foreign corporation that is a controlled foreign corporation. During the current year, FC Corporation has gross income of $1,000,000, consisting of $701,000 of sales income that meets the definition of "foreign base company sales income" in Section 954(d) and $299,000 of manufacturing income that does not meet the definition of "foreign base company sales income" in Section 954(d). Because FC Corporation's gross income that constitutes foreign base company income is more than 70 percent of its total gross income of $1,000,000, under the full-inclusion rule in Section 954(b)(3)(B), all of its gross income for the current year will be treated as foreign base company income. By contrast, if FC Corporation's gross income meeting the definition of foreign base sales company income for the current year were only $699,000 and its manufacturing gross income were $301,000, the full-inclusion rule would not apply and only $699,000 of its gross income would be foreign base company income.

Even if the full-inclusion rule in Section 954(b)(3)(B) applies in a given year to treat all of a controlled foreign corporation's gross income as foreign base company income, that does not end the process of determining the controlled foreign corporation's foreign base company income under Section 954(a). First, any item of gross income that is subject to high foreign taxes within the meaning of Section 954(b)(4) (as discussed in the next paragraph) is excluded from foreign base company income, notwithstanding Section 954(b)(3)(B).[23] Second, as discussed at ¶ 6175, any deductions that are properly allocable to the controlled foreign corporation's foreign base company income reduce such income under Section 954(b)(5).

[¶ 6165]

b. Exception for High-Taxed Income

An item of income of a controlled foreign corporation that would otherwise be tainted foreign base company income will not be tainted if it was subject to an effective foreign tax rate greater than 90 percent of the maximum U.S. corporate tax rate specified in Section 11. Thus, under current law, if the item of income of a controlled foreign corporation is subject to a foreign tax of more than 31.5 percent (i.e., 90 percent of 35 percent), it will not be foreign base company income. § 954(b)(4). This exception applies after reducing the income by deductions (including taxes) that are allocable to the income under Section 954(b)(5) (discussed at ¶ 6175). This exception is based on the theory that if an item of income is subject to a foreign tax rate substantially equivalent to or greater than the U.S. rate, there is little U.S. tax advantage gained by routing the

23. Note, however, that Section 954(b)(3)(B) applies before applying Section 954(b)(4); thus, items of foreign base company income that eventually will be excluded from foreign base company income under Section 954(b)(4) generally are still taken into account in determining whether the controlled foreign corporation has sufficient foreign base company gross income to meet the more-than-70-percent threshold in Section 954(b)(3)(B). Reg. § 1.954-1(d)(1).

income through a controlled foreign corporation and, therefore, little reason to impose current U.S. tax on the U.S. shareholders under Subpart F. Staff of Joint Comm. on Tax'n, 100th Cong., 1st Sess., General Explanation of the Tax Reform Act of 1986, at 983 (1987). Unlike the high-taxed income exception of the pre–1986 Act law, which used a subjective, tax-reduction-motive standard, Section 954(b)(4) of current law does not require a determination of the taxpayer's motive for entering into a transaction. Congress viewed the subjective standard of prior law as administratively unworkable.

The regulations require the controlling U.S. shareholders of a controlled foreign corporation to make an election in order for this high-taxed-income exception to apply. Reg. § 1.954–1(d)(1)(i). The election is binding on all of the U.S. shareholders of the controlled foreign corporation. Reg. § 1.954–1(d)(5).

This high-taxed-income exception applies after the de minimis rule in Section 954(b)(3)(A). Thus, items of foreign base company income that qualify for this exception are still treated as foreign base company income for the purpose of applying the de minimis tests in Section 954(b)(3)(A). This high-taxed-income exception also applies after the full-inclusion rule in Section 954(b)(3)(B). Reg. § 1.954–1(d)(1). Thus, items of foreign base company income qualifying for this exception generally are treated as foreign base company income for purposes of applying the full-inclusion rule and can cause non-foreign base company income to be treated as foreign base company income under the full-inclusion rule. The regulations, however, contain a special rule that applies if the high-taxed-income election is made and more than 90 percent of the controlled foreign corporation's gross foreign base company income and gross insurance income is attributable to income items qualifying for the high-taxed-income exception. If this special rule applies, the controlled foreign corporation's non-foreign base company income that would be treated as foreign base company income only by reason of the full-inclusion rule will be excluded from Subpart F income. Reg. § 1.954–1(d)(6).

Example. FC, a controlled foreign corporation, has $10,000 of portfolio dividend income and $145,000 of interest income that are foreign personal holding company income within the meaning of Section 954(c). FC also has $45,000 of manufacturing income that is not foreign base company income. Under the full-inclusion rule of Section 954(b)(3)(B), because FC's gross foreign base company income of $155,000 exceeds 70 percent of FC's total gross income of $200,000, all of its gross income, including the $45,000 of non-foreign base company income, would normally be treated as foreign base company income.

If, however, FC's interest income is subject to an effective foreign tax rate of 32 percent, the $145,000 of interest income will qualify for the high-taxed-income exception in Section 954(b)(4) and FC's income qualifying for the high-taxed-income exception will constitute more than 90 percent of its gross foreign base company income of $155,000. Accordingly, if FC has the high-taxed-income election in effect, the $45,000 of manufacturing income will be excluded from Subpart F income treatment under the regulation provision. The $145,000 of interest income is excluded from foreign base company income under the high-taxed-income exception in Section 954(b)(4). The $10,000 of portfolio dividend income is foreign personal holding company income under Section 954(c) and will *not* be excluded from foreign base company income under the de minimis rule in Section 954(b)(3)(A) because the de minimis rule applies before the high-taxed-income exception. See Reg. § 1.954–1(d)(7), Exs. 1 and 5.

Suppose instead that FC's gross income consisted of $20,000 of portfolio dividend income that is foreign personal holding company income under Section 954(c) and is subject to an effective foreign tax rate of less than 31.5 percent; $135,000 of interest income that is foreign personal holding company income under Section 954(c) and is subject to an effective foreign tax rate of 32 percent and $45,000 of manufacturing income that is *not* foreign base company income and is subject to an effective foreign tax rate of less than 31.5 percent. FC's interest income qualifying for the high-taxed-income exception of $135,000 would not constitute more than 90 percent of its gross foreign base company income of $155,000 and the special regulation provision would not apply. Under the full-inclusion rule in Section 954(b)(3)(B), which is applied before the high-taxed-income exception in Section 954(b)(4), FC's foreign base company income of $155,000 exceeds 70 percent of its total gross income of $200,000. Accordingly, all $200,000 of the FC's gross income is treated as foreign base company income under the full-inclusion rule. The $135,000 of interest income, however, is excluded from foreign base company income by reason of the high-taxed-income exception in Section 954(b)(4) if FC has the high-taxed-income election in effect. FC's remaining gross income of $65,000 is foreign base company income.

[¶ 6170]

c. Relief for Blocked Earnings

Under Section 964(b), no earnings and profits of a controlled foreign corporation will be subjected to constructive dividend treatment under Subpart F if they cannot be distributed because of currency or other restrictions imposed by the laws of the foreign country. This relief provision is based on the idea that it is unfair to treat the U.S. shareholders of a controlled foreign corporation as receiving a constructive distribution of the corporation's Subpart F income when the corporation could not actually distribute it.

[¶ 6175]

7. FOREIGN BASE COMPANY INCOME REDUCED BY CERTAIN DEDUCTIONS

To determine a controlled foreign corporation's foreign base company income, the corporation's gross income in each of the four categories of foreign base company income is reduced by the deductions (including taxes) that are properly allocable to such income. § 954(b)(5). Thus, the rules for allocating and apportioning deductions, discussed in Chapter 2, are important in this area as well. Note that deductions are ignored in applying the de minimis rule in Section 954(b)(3)(A) and the full-inclusion rule in Section 954(b)(3)(B), both of which are based on the controlled foreign corporation's gross income.

Section 954(b)(5) contains a special allocation rule for any interest paid or accrued by a controlled foreign corporation to one of its U.S. shareholders (or to any other controlled foreign corporation related to a U.S. shareholder). Notwithstanding the general rules for allocating interest deductions, such interest is allocated first to the corporation's foreign personal holding company income which is passive income to the extent thereof. See ¶ 7100.

[¶ 6180]

8. CHARACTERIZING INCOME EARNED THROUGH PARTNERSHIPS

Consider how the tax law should treat a controlled foreign corporation that is a partner in a partnership which earns income that would be foreign base company income if earned directly by the corporation. Should the controlled foreign corporation's distributive share of such partnership income be treated as foreign base company income? The answer to this question may depend, in part, on whether, for purposes of this issue, the partnership is treated as an aggregate of its partners (the so-called "aggregate theory" of partnership taxation) or as an entity distinct from its partners (the so-called "entity theory" of partnership taxation).

In Rev. Rul. 89–72, 1989–1 C.B. 257, a partnership purchased machines from the U.S. parent corporation of a controlled foreign corporation and sold the machines for use outside the country in which the controlled foreign corporation was incorporated. The controlled foreign corporation owned a 25–percent interest in the partnership. If the controlled foreign corporation had earned the income from the sales directly, the income would have been foreign base company sales income. Accordingly, the IRS held that the controlled foreign corporation's distributive share of that partnership income was foreign base company sales income, citing Section 702 and its regulations in support of this conclusion. The IRS conclusion seems consistent with the purposes of Subpart F since it prevents U.S. shareholders of controlled foreign corporations from using a partnership to circumvent the provisions of Subpart F.

Former Section 954(f)(2), before its repeal in 2004, however, contained an explicit rule concerning one type of foreign base company income earned by a partnership—foreign base company shipping income. Under that rule, "foreign base company shipping income" included a partner's distributive share of partnership income attributable to foreign base company shipping income. The existence of the very specific rule in former Section 954(f)(2) for one type of foreign base company income seemed to undercut the IRS's conclusion in Rev. Rul. 89–72 because it would be unnecessary if the IRS's more broadly based approach were clearly the law. See J. Kuntz & R. Peroni, U.S. International Taxation ¶ B3.05[11] (1992).

The issue of how to treat income earned through a partnership for Subpart F purposes also was considered in Brown Group, Inc. v. Commissioner, 77 F.3d 217 (8th Cir.1996), rev'g 104 T.C. 105 (1995). In that case, Brown Group International, a U.S. corporation and wholly owned subsidiary of another U.S. corporation, Brown Group, Inc., owned all the stock of Brown Cayman, Ltd., a Cayman Islands corporation. Brown Cayman, Ltd., in turn, owned an 88–percent interest in Brinco, a Cayman Islands partnership. Brown Group International imported footwear from Brazil and other countries for sale in the United States. During the tax years in issue, Brinco acted as a purchasing agent for Brown Group International with respect to footwear manufactured in Brazil and was paid commissions by Brown Group International. Those commissions would have been foreign base company sales income under Section 954(d) if earned directly by Brown Cayman, Ltd. The issue in the case was whether Brown Cayman, Ltd.'s distributive share of Brinco's commissions was foreign base company sales income.

The Tax Court, in its first opinion in this case, respected Brinco as an entity (applying the entity theory of partnership taxation) and held that since the commission income earned by the partnership was not Subpart F income in the hands of the partnership, it retained such character at the partner level and could not be Subpart F income to its controlled foreign corporate partner. The court rejected Revenue Ruling 89–72 as incorrect and declined to follow the Ruling. However, the Tax Court later granted the government's motion for reconsideration in the case and withdrew this first opinion.

In its second opinion in the case, written by Judge Halpern, the Tax Court held that Brown Cayman, Ltd.'s distributive share of Brinco's commission income was foreign base company sales income under Section 954(d)(1) and that Brown Group International had to include such Subpart F income in its gross income under Section 951. In this opinion, the Tax Court majority undertook both a technical analysis of the partnership provisions of Subchapter K and of the Subpart F provisions and a policy analysis of those provisions. The Tax Court concluded that Brinco had to separately state items of income, such as commission income, that could constitute foreign base company in the hands of the partner "[t]o give effect to Section 702(a)(7) * * * and to avoid frustrating the purpose of Congress in enacting subpart F." 104 T.C. at 114. The court reasoned:

> It is important to keep in mind the method that Congress chose to meet its objectives: subpart F imposes a conduit scheme with regard to subpart F income. Subpart F income is taxed currently to U.S. shareholders notwithstanding that no distribution of such income is made. * * * The parallel with subchapter K is obvious. Congress chose to minimize (perhaps even eliminate) the entity character of the [controlled foreign corporation] in order to tax U.S. shareholders as if they had earned directly the subpart F income earned by the [corporation]. It would be ironic, indeed, if one could defeat the clearly expressed intent of Congress to tax the income from the activities involved here by engaging in those activities [through] a form of doing business that not only is taxed on a conduit basis but whose non-tax-law character often resembles an aggregate of persons doing business together (as mutual agents) rather than an entity.

Id. at 114–15. For purposes of characterizing Brown Cayman, Ltd.'s share of Brinco's commission income under Subpart F, the court thus concluded that "Brown Cayman should be put into the shoes of Brinco for determining whether Brown Cayman was earning commission income on sales by third parties to International." Id. at 119. There were several concurring opinions in the case as well as a vigorous dissent by Judge Jacobs, who had written the withdrawn, original opinion in the case.

On appeal, the Eighth Circuit reversed the Tax Court and held that Brown Cayman, Ltd.'s distributive share of the partnership's commission income could not be treated as Subpart F income under the version of the statute in effect for the tax years at issue because the income was not Subpart F income in the hands of the partnership. Thus, the character of the income as non-Subpart F income carried through to the partners, including Brown Cayman, Ltd. The Eighth Circuit criticized the Tax Court's decision as having erroneously ignored the partnership entity in characterizing the partnership's income for Subpart F purposes and adopted the reasoning and holding of Judge Jacobs's dissenting Tax Court opinion. In the Eighth Circuit's view, Section 702(b) of the partnership tax provisions requires that partnership income be characterized at the partnership level and retain its character in the hands of the partners.

The decisions of the Tax Court and Eighth Circuit in this case remain important with respect to the broader issue of whether the aggregate or entity approach should generally be used in characterizing a partner's distributive share of a partnership's income for various Code and regulation provisions, including those relating to international taxation. The decisions, however, have much less continuing importance with respect to the application of Subpart F to partnership transactions of the type at issue in the case. First, the so-called "loophole" used by the taxpayer in the case to avoid Subpart F has since been closed by an amendment to Section 954(d)(3) that broadened the definition of "related person" to include not only partnerships that control controlled foreign corporations but also partnerships that are controlled by controlled foreign corporations or by their parent corporations. Under the current statute, therefore, Brinco's commission income would be foreign base company sales income under Section 954(d) without regard to the approach generally used in characterizing income earned by a partnership.

Second, the Treasury and the IRS issued anti-abuse regulations under Section 701 that permit the IRS, inter alia, to "treat a partnership as an aggregate of its partners in whole or in part as appropriate to carry out the purpose of any provision of the Internal Revenue Code or regulations." Reg. § 1.701–2(e)(1). Thus, under current law, the IRS could use these partnership anti-abuse regulations to attack the transaction at issue in the *Brown Group* case.

Finally, in IRS Notice 96–39, 1996–2 C.B. 209, 210, the IRS announced that it disagreed with the Eighth Circuit's decision in the *Brown Group* case because it viewed that decision as contrary to the purposes of Subpart F. The IRS also stated that it intended to issue regulations under Subpart F confirming "its position that whether a CFC [controlled foreign corporation] partner's distributive share of partnership income is subpart F income generally is determined at the CFC partner level." Before the effective date of these regulations, the IRS "will rely on principles and authorities under subpart F and subchapter K to apply the aggregate approach," including the partnership anti-abuse regulations.

In 2002, the Treasury and the IRS issued final regulations dealing with the characterization of the distributive share of partnership income of a partner that is a controlled foreign corporation. These regulations sought to overturn the rule enunciated in the Eighth Circuit's decision in the *Brown Group* case. They generally apply the aggregate theory of partnership taxation for Subpart F purposes and require that the determination of whether a controlled foreign corporation partner's share of partnership income is foreign base company income be made at the partner level as if the controlled foreign corporation partner had received the income directly. See Reg. § 1.952–1(g)(1). Moreover, for purposes of applying the definitions of foreign base company income in Section 954, the regulations require that the determinations of whether a related person is involved in a transaction and the country where an entity is formed or activities occur be made at the controlled foreign corporation partner level. Reg. § 1.954–1(g)(1). The regulations contain the following additional specific rules:

1. The exceptions to foreign base company income treatment in Section 954(c) based on whether the controlled foreign corporation is engaged in the active conduct of a trade or business will apply to a controlled foreign corporation partner's distributive share of partnership income only if the exception would have applied if the controlled foreign corporation had earned the partnership income directly, determined by taking into account only the activities of and the property owned by the partnership and not the separate activities or property of the controlled foreign corporation or any other person. Reg. § 1.954–2(a)(5)(ii).

2. For purposes of determining whether purchase and sales transactions between a partnership and a controlled foreign corporate partner involving personal property meet the related person test in the foreign base company sales income rules in Section 954(d), the regulations treat a transaction between the controlled foreign corporation and the partnership as a transaction with an entity that is a related person if—

> (1) the "controlled foreign corporation purchased such personal property from (or sold it to the partnership on behalf of), or sells such personal property to (or purchases it from the partnership on behalf of), a related person with respect to the controlled foreign corporation (other than the partnership)," as defined in Section 954(d)(3); or
>
> (2) the branch rule in Section 954(d)(2) (discussed at ¶ 11,100) applies to treat as foreign base company sales income the controlled foreign corporation's income from selling to the partnership (or a third party) personal property that the controlled foreign corporation has manufactured, where the partnership purchases personal property from (or sells personal property on behalf of) the controlled foreign corporation.

Reg. § 1.954–1(g)(2).

3. For purposes of determining whether a controlled foreign corporation partner's distributive share of partnership income is foreign base company sales income, the property sold by the partnership will be treated as manufactured by the controlled foreign corporation in its country of incorporation only if the manufacturing exception would have applied to exclude the income from the definition of foreign base company sales income if the controlled foreign corporation had received the income directly. Only the activities of and the property owned by the partnership and not the separate activities of the controlled foreign corporation or any other person are to be taken into account in making such a determination. Reg. § 1.954–3(a)(6).

4. For purposes of determining whether a controlled foreign corporation partner's distributive share of partnership income is foreign base company services income (within the meaning of Section 954(e)), a controlled foreign corporation's distributive share of a partnership's services income will be treated as deriving from services performed for or on behalf of a related person if two conditions are met. First, the partnership is a related person with respect to the controlled foreign corporation within the meaning of Section 954(d)(3). Second, in connection with the services performed by the partnership, the controlled foreign corporation, or a person that is "related person" of the controlled foreign corporation, provides assistance that would have constituted substantial assistance contributing to the performance of the services if provided to the controlled foreign corporation by a related person. Reg. § 1.954–4(b)(2)(iii). This "substantial assistance" rule is discussed at ¶ 6145.

Recall, as discussed in more detail at 6105, the 2004 JOBS Act added new Section 954(c)(4) to the Code, which applies a look-through rule to determine the extent to which a controlled foreign corporation's gain from the sale of an interest in a partnership in which the corporation owns at least 25 percent of the capital or profits interest will be treated as foreign personal holding company income for Subpart F purposes.

Recall also, as discussed in more detail at ¶ 6065, in IRS Notice 2010–41, 2010–1 C.B. 715, the Treasury and the IRS announced that they planned to issue regulations aimed at "Subpart F income partnership blocker transactions." In these transactions, a U.S. partnership typically is interposed between upper-tier controlled foreign corporations in which a U.S. person owns sufficient stock to constitute a U.S. shareholder of those corporations (within the meaning of Section 951(b)) and a lower-tier controlled foreign corporation that earns Subpart F income in an attempt to prevent the U.S. shareholder of the upper-tier controlled foreign corporations from having a gross income inclusion under Section 951(a) with respect to the Subpart F income earned by the lower-tier controlled foreign corporation. The regulations to be issued would prevent this result by treating the U.S. partnership as a foreign partnership for Section 951(a) purposes if certain conditions are met, thus insuring that the U.S. shareholder is treated as owning its proportionate share of the lower-tier controlled foreign corporation's stock for Section 951(a) purposes.

[¶ 6185]

9. SUBPART F AND THE "NEW" ECONOMY

The following excerpt from a Treasury study of Subpart F discusses the challenges to the Subpart F rules created by the growth of services income as a part of the U.S. economy and by electronic commerce.

[¶ 6190]

U.S. TREASURY DEPARTMENT, THE DEFERRAL OF INCOME EARNED THROUGH U.S. CONTROLLED FOREIGN CORPORATIONS: A POLICY STUDY

68, 70, 75–81 (Dec. 2000).

CHAPTER 6

CHALLENGES TO SUBPART F: ENTITY CLASSIFICATION, SERVICES AND ELECTRONIC COMMERCE

I. Introduction

* * * The nature of business is also changing. Subpart F was designed and enacted in the 1960s when the foreign business paradigm was a manufacturing plant. Since that time, however, services activities have grown significantly as a percentage of the overall U.S. economy, and this growth appears likely to continue. The treatment of services under subpart F is already posing a number of challenges to subpart F. Further, it is possible now to perceive some of the challenges to subpart F that will be posed by electronic commerce.

* * *

As noted above, services activities are a significantly greater contributor to the overall U.S. economy today than when subpart F was originally enacted, and this growth in services activities seems likely to continue.[9] Subpart F was designed principally to deal with manufacturing industries operating in high-tax, developed countries, rather than with service industries. The treatment of services is already posing a number of challenges to subpart F. * * *

* * *

IV. The Challenges To Subpart F Posed By Electronic Commerce

A. General

The previous section noted the difficulties of applying subpart F to the provision of services generally. The ability of taxpayers to provide services (as well as goods) over the Internet and through other electronic media will present further challenges to the current subpart F regime. None of these challenges is entirely new. The increased commercial use of the telephone, radio, television, and facsimile has contributed to a trend in

9. Services employment has grown steadily relative to manufacturing employment. In 1950, the ratio of manufacturing employment to services employment was 57 percent. In 1962, it was 48 percent, declining to 41 percent by 1970 and to 18 percent by 1999. Economic Report of the President Transmitted to the Congress February 2000, together with the Annual Report of the Council of Economic Advisers 358–59 (2000).

which the physical location of the provider of goods and services is less significant and more difficult to determine.

Subpart F must be evaluated by considering where this trend might lead and what challenges it poses. For example, as the Treasury observed in its 1996 report on electronic commerce:

> If CFCs can engage in extensive commerce in information and services through Web sites or computer networks located in a tax haven, it may become increasingly difficult to enforce Subpart F.... because it may be difficult to verify the identity of the taxpayer to whom foreign base company sales income accrues and the amount of such income. It may be necessary to revise Subpart F or the regulations thereunder to take these new types of transactions into account.[25]

In addition to enforcement challenges, electronic commerce and its underlying technologies also have implications for the content and scope of the substantive subpart F rules. This section briefly considers, through examples, whether the current subpart F regime is capable of achieving its objectives in a world in which electronic commerce and new technologies seem sure to play a large role.

B. Specific Issues

1. Location of Activities

Electronic commerce may present challenges to the subpart F rules to the extent that such rules look to where transactions or activities take place. For example, the technologies underlying electronic commerce make possible new sorts of services, such as Internet access, and make easier the remote provision of other services, such as remote database access, video conferencing and remote order processing. With respect to all such services, it is difficult to assign a place of performance, a factor that is relevant with respect to certain subpart F rules. Similarly, it may be difficult to ascertain a place of use, consumption or disposition (another factor relevant in the application of certain subpart F rules) with respect to the sale of digitizable products, such as images and computer software, delivered electronically.

New technologies increase opportunities for CFCs to be incorporated in low- or no-tax jurisdictions. These technologies increase the ease with which employees of a CFC can be located outside the CFC's jurisdiction of incorporation, and increase the ease with which certain products and services can be provided to a CFC. They also allow CFCs to provide services to customers located outside their jurisdiction of incorporation with relative ease. As discussed in the examples later in this chapter, these developments together increase opportunities for CFCs to earn income that may not be subpart F income.

---

25. U.S. Treasury, *Selected Tax Policy Implications of Global Electronic Commerce* § 7.3.5 (1996) ("Treasury E–Commerce Report").

2. Classifying Income

Electronic commerce also may pose challenges to the extent subpart F has different rules for different types of income. For example, under certain circumstances it may be unclear whether payments for digitized products are treated as payments for a good, a right or a service.[28] As discussed in the examples below, results under subpart F may differ significantly depending on how the payment is classified.

C. Examples of Potential Effects of Electronic Commerce on Subpart F

The following examples illustrate the ways in which electronic commerce and its underlying technologies may present challenges to subpart F. In most cases, the planning techniques described in these examples are available in both the electronic commerce and traditional commerce context. However, because the technologies underlying electronic commerce allow these techniques to be accomplished more easily and effectively than in traditional commerce, these techniques have now become more generally available.[29]

1. Offshore Development, Production, And Sale And Licensing Of Goods

The relocation of activities can be used as a subpart F planning technique. As previously noted, income is foreign base company sales income (FBCSI) if it is derived from the sale of property that (a) is purchased from, or on behalf of, or sold to, or on behalf of, a related person and (b) is both manufactured and sold for use outside the CFC's country of organization. Thus, if a CFC purchases copies of software from its parent that the parent has developed and produced in the United States, the income of the CFC from the sales of such software for use outside its country of incorporation would be FBCSI in its entirety.[30] Suppose, however, that the parent restructures so that its software development and production activities are conducted within the CFC, rather than the parent. Income from the sale of software manufactured by the CFC and sold by the CFC to unrelated persons will not necessarily give rise to subpart F income, even with respect to sales for use outside

28. Treasury has provided guidance with respect to the proper characterization of payments for one type of digitized product, computer programs. Treas. Reg. § 1.861–18 provides that a transfer of a computer program is treated as: (a) the transfer of a copyright right; (b) the transfer of a copyrighted article; (c) the provision of services; or (d) the provision of know-how, based on all the facts and circumstances of the transaction.

29. The examples below assume that the CFC is located in a low-tax jurisdiction and that the United States does not have an income tax treaty with that jurisdiction. The United States is actively engaged in discussions at the OECD on electronic commerce issues arising under income tax treaties, including jurisdictional issues (e.g., whether certain activities give rise to a permanent establishment) and issues relating to the appropriate characterization of activities and income.

30. This example is not intended to comment on what constitutes the manufacture of software.

the CFC's country of incorporation.[31] Thus, by restructuring its operations, which in this case may mean no more than having software development personnel transferred on paper from the parent to the CFC, the parent company may isolate offshore at least some of the profit from the sale of the software.

The extent to which a U.S. parent could achieve deferral in such a manner, however, would depend on where the software development and production and sales of the software were taking place. If the CFC's development and production activities were kept within the United States, the CFC may be considered engaged in a U.S. trade or business. If so, the CFC would be subject to tax in the United States on the income effectively connected with the conduct of that business.[32] Regular and continuous sales of the software into the United States by the CFC would also likely create a U.S. trade or business. However, sales outside the United States of software developed and produced by the CFC within the United States likely would not generate income taxable by the United States under either subpart F or the U.S. trade or business rules, except to the extent that either the branch rule applies or any such income were deemed to be effectively connected to any U.S. trade or business of the CFC (for example, the U.S. software development). Assuming the CFC's sales income was not effectively connected income, U.S. tax on income not subject to the branch rule would be deferred. Further, as noted previously, the technologies underlying electronic commerce make it easier to locate software development activities outside the United States, through the use, for example, of "virtual migrants" [i.e., overseas programmers who telecommute from various foreign countries].

Moreover, it may be possible to prevent regular and continuous sales of the software into the United States by the CFC from being treated as a U.S. trade or business. If the CFC advertised its products in the United States and had an agent in the United States that maintained a stock of inventory from which it regularly filled orders for the public, the CFC likely would be engaged in a U.S. trade or business. If, however, the CFC advertised solely on the Web and digitally delivered its products to U.S. customers, then it is less clear that the CFC is engaged in a trade or business within the United States. If the CFC is not engaged in a U.S. trade or business under those circumstances, even income from sales into

31. If the CFC conducts its software manufacturing activities within its country of incorporation, the income would be excluded from subpart F income because the FBCSI rules do not apply where manufacture occurs within the CFC's country of incorporation. If the CFC conducts the manufacturing activities through a branch located in a separate tax jurisdiction, the income may be excluded from subpart F income under the manufacturing exception of Treas. Reg. § 1.954–3(a)(4) unless the branch rule applies. (The branch rule will treat the sales income as FBCSI if the CFC conducts the sales and manufacturing activities in separate tax jurisdictions and the sales income is subject to a significantly lower tax rate than it would have been in the jurisdiction where the manufacturing occurs. *See* Treas. Reg. § 1.954–3(b).)

32. This U.S. source effectively connected income, however, is excluded from subpart F income. *See* I.R.C. § 952(b).

the United States could be isolated offshore (at least to the extent that inclusions are not required under section 956).

Finally, the above example also assumes that the sale of the software will be regarded as the sale of a good. If instead the CFC is considered to license the software to customers, then the CFC would be considered to receive royalties, not sales proceeds, and the royalties would not be considered subpart F income if the CFC "has developed, created, or produced, or has acquired and added substantial value to" the software and if the CFC is "regularly engaged in the development, creation or production of, or in the acquisition of and addition of substantial value to" the software. Thus, it may be possible for a CFC that purchases software from its parent and adds substantial value to the software by, for example, customizing the software for unrelated licensees, to receive royalties that are not subpart F income. In addition, even if a CFC/licensor does not develop, or add substantial value to, the property it licenses, the CFC may nevertheless exclude the royalties from subpart F income if it licenses the property as a result of performing marketing functions.[35]

2. Offshore Provision of Services to Unrelated Third Parties

If the sale of the software is characterized not as the sale of a good or as a license but rather as the provision of services, a different set of rules will apply. Income from the provision of services is foreign base company services income if the services are performed for or on behalf of a related person outside the CFC's country of incorporation.[36] If the CFC purchases software from its U.S. parent, but, instead of selling the software to a third party, either provides services to unrelated third parties making use of the software or, in the alternative, transfers the software to the unrelated third party in the form of services, the income the CFC receives likely would not be foreign base company services income.[37] If the sale of the software had been characterized as the sale of a good, however, it would have been foreign base company sales income because the income was derived from the purchase of software, which was manufactured outside the CFC's country of incorporation, from a related person, the U.S. parent, and sold for use outside the CFC's country of incorporation.[38]

35. This exception applies only if the CFC/ licensor "through its own officers or staff of employees located in a foreign country, [maintains and operates] an organization in such country that is regularly engaged in the business of marketing, or of marketing and servicing, the licensed property and that is substantial in relation to the amount of royalties derived from the licensing of such property." Treas. Reg. § 1.954–2(d)(1)(ii).

36. I.R.C. § 954(e). In addition, if a related person provides the CFC with substantial assistance contributing to the performance of the services, the services will be treated as performed for or on behalf of a related person. *See* Treas. Reg. § 1.954–4(b)(1)(iv).

37. This example assumes that the parent is not rendering substantial assistance to the CFC within the meaning of Treas. Reg. § 1.954–4(b)(1)(iv).

38. It may be difficult to manipulate the rules to change the classification from the sale of goods to the provision of services with respect to computer programs, because Treasury Regulations clarify the distinction between the sale of goods and the provision of services in the context of computer software. Treas. Reg. § 1.861–18(d) provides that whether the transfer of a computer program is treated as the provision of services or otherwise "is based on all the facts and

Problems arising from the distinction between the provision of a good and a service are not limited to computer programs and may in fact be more acute with respect to digitizable products other than software. Consider, for example, a reference work, such as a legal treatise or set of court cases, that previously would have been sold only as a set of bound volumes. The sale of the bound volumes would have resulted in sales income. Today, a potential purchaser might be able to choose between a set of bound volumes, a set of CD–ROMs and an on-line database. The sale of the CD–ROMs may be characterized as the sale of a good. However, a taxpayer may take the position that income arising from the provision of access to an on-line database should be considered the provision of a service. If so, taxpayers may claim that sales by a CFC to unrelated third parties of access to an on-line database the CFC purchases from its parent would not generate subpart F income because the services are not performed for or on behalf of a related person.[40] Similar issues may be implicated with respect to the provision of other services such as telecommunications services and Internet access.

3. Offshore Provision of Services to Related Parties within the Country of Incorporation

Electronic commerce and its underlying technologies make it possible to set up CFC offshore service centers to provide services to related parties.[41] Foreign base company services income [under Section 954(e)] includes income from services performed for or on behalf of a related person only if the services "are performed outside the country under the laws of which the controlled foreign corporation is organized." Thus, under the current subpart F rules, depending on how the place where services are performed is determined, taxpayers may claim that formation of such offshore service centers to service related parties may not generate subpart F income. For example, assume a U.S. corporate vendor of goods over the Internet establishes a CFC in Country A to process customer orders and arrange for product delivery outside of Country A through the use of the CFC's computer software and servers and other equipment located within Country A. The U.S. corporate vendor pays CFC a fee for

---

circumstances of the transaction" including "the intent of the parties . . . as to which party is to own the copyright rights in the computer program and how the risks of loss are allocated between the parties." For example, the regulations provide that, if a developer of computer programs agrees to provide upgrades of the program when they become available, the developer is not treated as providing services to its customers. Treas. Reg. § 1.861–18(h), Ex. 12. In contrast, if the person commissioning the creation of the program bears all of the risk of loss associated with its creation and will own all of the copyright rights in the underlying program when it is completed, the developer is treated as providing services. Treas. Reg. § 1.861–18(h), Ex. 15. With respect to the provision of other digitizable products, the distinction between the provision of a good and the provision of a service may not be as clear.

40. As under the prior example, the foreign base company services income [definition] would nevertheless apply if the parent were rendering substantial assistance to the CFC within the meaning of Treas. Reg. § 1.954–4(b)(1)(iv).

41. This example assumes that income that was previously earned by people performing certain functions (e.g., accepting orders) can now be "earned" by machines performing the same functions.

performing these processing and product delivery services. Unless it is determined that the services are performed outside Country A, the U.S. vendor may be able to use such an arrangement to isolate offshore income associated with the processing and delivery function with no corresponding income inclusion under subpart F.

As communication equipment becomes more efficient and reliable, the relationship between the service provider's location and the service consumer's location will be further weakened. For example, increased use of the Internet, as well as intranets, e-mail and video conferencing, will make it easier to provide services across vast distances. That increases the possibility that rules that are premised on the coincidence of the service provider's and service customer's locations may no longer be adequate.

D. Summary of Possible Effects of Electronic Commerce on Subpart F

Many of the issues identified in this section (e.g., classifying and locating activities and associated income) are not unique to CFCs engaged in electronic commerce. As noted above, some of the same issues arise, for example, with respect to CFCs that provide financial services and businesses involved in more "traditional" activities, such as the development and manufacturing of tangible goods. Electronic commerce and new technologies do, however, affect the ease with which structures that are not contemplated by the rules of subpart F can be used. Furthermore, they affect the interaction between subpart F and the more general international taxation rules, such as the general source of income rules and the definition of a U.S. trade or business.

As planning opportunities become more generally known, offshore companies may become the operating vehicles of choice for many newly formed electronic commerce companies. In addition, many U.S. electronic commerce companies are relatively new. Therefore, it may be possible for them to move offshore without incurring a significant tax liability. These developments, taken together, may pose greater challenges to subpart F in the future.

V. Conclusions Relating to Challenges to Subpart F

* * * [S]ubpart F was intended to address a systemic problem in the U.S. tax system that created inequity and caused tax base erosion. Many of the specific rules of subpart F, however, may no longer operate effectively. In addition, weaknesses in these rules are exacerbated by the new entity classification rules, which have facilitated the creation of hybrid entities. The growth in service industries is creating new issues that may be difficult to resolve without adding considerable complexity to the subpart F rules. The challenges that will be posed by electronic commerce and the Internet are only just beginning to emerge. Thus, although the policies underlying subpart F may be as important (or more important) today as they were in 1962 (when subpart F was enacted), new

developments are already challenging the effectiveness of subpart F, and these challenges seem likely to increase in the future.

[¶ 6195]

PROBLEMS

1. Consider whether income earned by Matterhorn, S.A. ("Matterhorn"), a Swiss corporation, of which 100 percent of the total combined voting power of all classes of stock is owned by USM Corp. ("USM"), a U.S. corporation, would constitute "foreign base company income" under the following circumstances:

a. Matterhorn acquires by license from USM rights to all European patents owned by the latter. Matterhorn sublicenses these patents in return for royalties to 12 independent licensees in countries outside Switzerland.

b. Would your answer in Problem 1.a. change if the patents were acquired originally by Matterhorn covering inventions developed by its own technicians?

c. Matterhorn receives $200,000 of dividends and $100,000 of interest from each of two wholly owned subsidiaries, which are organized under the laws of, and have all of their assets and operations in, Belgium and Switzerland, respectively. Of the gross income of the Belgian subsidiary for the tax year, $800,000 consists of income from the manufacture and sale of machine tools in Belgium and $200,000 consists of passive interest income. Of the gross income of the Swiss subsidiary, $600,000 consists of income from the manufacture and sale of electronic instruments in Switzerland and $400,000 consists of interest income that is foreign personal holding company income.

d. Matterhorn sells gold coins of numismatic value at a gain to an independent dealer in Switzerland. The coins were purchased by Matterhorn in Antwerp, Belgium, ten years before as an investment.

e. Matterhorn sells at a gain all rights to a group of Swiss patents (purchased from USM three years ago) to Eiger, S.A., a Swiss corporation, which is engaged in the manufacture and sale of consumer products in Switzerland, which is also a wholly owned subsidiary of Matterhorn and which had previously paid royalties to Matterhorn for the use of these patents.

f. Matterhorn purchases from USM golf balls manufactured by USM in the United States. Matterhorn packages them and sells them to independent distributors outside of Switzerland.

g. Would it make a difference in Problem 1.f. if Matterhorn sold only to independent distributors in Switzerland?

h. Would it make a difference in Problem 1.f. if Matterhorn bought the golf balls from an independent U.S. manufacturer (instead of USM)?

i. Would it make a difference in Problem 1.f. if Matterhorn bought the component material for the golf balls from USM and used that component material to manufacture the golf balls in Switzerland? What additional facts would you need to know to answer this question?

j. Would it make a difference in Problem 1.i. if Matterhorn bought the component material for the golf balls from USM and had the golf balls manufactured by AB Corporation, an unrelated corporation, under a contract manufacturing arrangement? AB Corporation performs the manufacturing activities with respect to the golf balls outside of Switzerland. Matterhorn's employees do not engage in any significant oversight or direction of AB Corporation's manufacturing activities with respect to the golf balls.

k. Would it make a difference in Problem 1.j. if Matterhorn's employees engage in product design and quality control of the golf balls and control manufacturing logistics with respect to the golf balls? What additional facts would you need to know to answer this question?

l. Matterhorn purchases products manufactured by a German corporation and a Dutch corporation and resells these products to independent customers in European countries other than Switzerland. USM owns 49 percent and 51 percent, respectively, of the value and the total combined voting power of all classes of stock of the German and Dutch corporations. Assume that the applicable corporate income tax rates in Germany would be 40 percent, in the Netherlands would be 38 percent and in Switzerland would be 20 percent. (Does the application of the definition of "foreign base company sales income" in Section 954(d) to these facts imply a broader scope for the provision than is justified by policy considerations?)

m. Would it make a difference in Problem 1.l. if USM owned 50 percent of the voting power and value of the stock of the German corporation?

n. Would it make a difference in Problems 1.l. and 1.m. if, instead of purchasing and reselling for its own account the output of the German and Dutch companies, Matterhorn acted as a sales agent, receiving a commission for its services?

o. Matterhorn renders, in return for fees, technical and engineering services to independent customers in European countries outside Switzerland.

p. Would your answer in Problem 1.o. change if Matterhorn renders the services in Switzerland for a Dutch manufacturing corporation, of which all the voting stock is owned by USM?

q. Matterhorn's gross income consists of two components—$9.6 million is in the form of services income as described in Problem 1.o., and $400,000 is in the form of fees paid by USM for services rendered to the European customers of USM outside Switzerland.

r. How would your answer in Problem 1.q. change if the amount of Matterhorn's services income as described in Problem 1.o. totaled $2.5 million and Matterhorn's income from fees paid by USM for services rendered to European customers of USM outside Switzerland totaled $7.5 million?

s. Would your answers in Problems 1.q. and 1.r. change if Matterhorn's services income is subject to an effective rate of Swiss and other foreign income taxes of 32 percent?

t. Matterhorn is a 60–percent partner of Partnership X, organized under the laws of Belgium. What result to Matterhorn under Section 954(c) if Partnership X receives interest income that would have met the definition of foreign personal holding company income in Section 954(c)(1)(A) if it had been received directly by Matterhorn?

2. USM sells products it manufactures in the United States to unrelated foreign and U.S. customers who agree in a written installment debt obligation to pay the purchase price in installments over a period of five years. USM sells the installment obligations to Matterhorn for less than the unpaid principal balance on the obligations. Matterhorn either collects the obligations at maturity at face value or sells them to an unrelated party for more than it paid USM for them but less than their face value. What are the tax consequences of these transactions under Sections 864(d), 951(a)(1)(A) and 954(c)?

3. Would your answer in Problem 2 change if Matterhorn loaned the funds directly to the unrelated foreign customers who used them to buy the products from USM for cash?

4. EastLaw, Inc., a U.S. corporation, has developed an on-line legal research database. EastLaw, Inc. owns all of the stock of Foreign Base Company, S.A., a corporation formed under the laws of Bermuda, a low-tax country. Foreign Base Company, S.A. purchases access to the legal research database from EastLaw, Inc. and then sells access to the database to various unrelated third-party customers located in foreign countries outside of Bermuda. Is the income that Foreign Base Company, S.A. earns from these sales of access to the database foreign base company income?

5. Nile, Inc., a U.S. corporation, sells computers and electronic equipment over the Internet. Nile, Inc. owns all of the stock of Tax Avoidance, Ltd., a corporation organized under the laws of the Netherlands Antilles, another low-tax country. Tax Avoidance, Ltd. processes customer orders for Nile, Inc. and arranges for product delivery to customers of Nile, Inc. in return for a fee paid to it by Nile, Inc. Tax Avoidance, Ltd.'s employees perform all of their work for Nile, Inc. in the Netherlands Antilles but the customers of Nile, Inc. for whom the work is performed are located in foreign countries outside of the Netherlands Antilles. Is the fee paid to Tax Avoidance, Ltd. by Nile, Inc. foreign base company income?

F. EARNINGS INVESTED IN U.S. PROPERTY

[¶ 6200]

1. OVERVIEW

In connection with enacting Subpart F, Congress concluded that if any controlled foreign corporation loaned its accumulated earnings that were not Subpart F income to its U.S. shareholder, effective repatriation of the earnings to the United States had occurred and, consequently, the transaction should be treated as a constructive dividend. This treatment was based on the theory that, because the U.S. shareholder had use of the money loaned to it, it could reasonably be treated as if it had received the funds as a dividend even though it had an unconditional obligation to repay the principal of the loan. This result also obtained if the earnings of the controlled foreign corporation were used to buy stock of the U.S. shareholder.

> *Example.* On January 1 of last year, DC, a U.S. corporation, formed a wholly owned foreign subsidiary, FC, which is a controlled foreign corporation. FC is engaged in a foreign business that generated $100,000 of net income during last year (its first year of operation), none of which was Subpart F income within the meaning of Section 952. On February 1 of last year, FC made a bona fide loan of $10,000 to DC and such loan remained outstanding at the end of the year. The loan from FC to DC is treated as an investment of FC's earnings in U.S. property (within the meaning of Section 956(c)(1)(C) and (c)(2)). Consequently, under Sections 951(a)(1)(B) and 956, DC must include $10,000 in gross income as if FC had distributed that amount to DC. The same result would obtain if, on February 1, FC had paid $10,000 to purchase stock in DC. See § 956(c)(1)(B) and (c)(2).

Section 956 was the vehicle for producing these results, but its sweep is far broader than the treatment of loans to, and equity investments in, the U.S. shareholder as constructive dividends. Indeed, constructive dividend treatment under Sections 951(a)(1)(B) and 956 extends to a broad range of investments in U.S. property by the controlled foreign corporation that may represent no benefit to the U.S. shareholder. While the basic thrust of Section 956 is clear, the mechanics are complex.

In 1993 and 1996, Congress made various changes in the rules of Sections 951(a)(1)(B) and 956 relating to the constructive dividend treatment of earnings invested in U.S. property.[24] Under the revised scheme, the amount includible in a U.S. shareholder's income as a result of the

24. To enhance comprehension of the authorities interpreting Section 956, we have replaced the pre–1993 designations of subsections of Section 956 with the current designation as in effect after the 1993 and 1996 legislation. Those replacements are in brackets within the cases and rulings.

controlled foreign corporation's investment in U.S. property is the *lesser* of—

(1) the excess (if any) of (i) the U.S. shareholder's pro rata share of the average amounts of U.S. property held directly or indirectly by the controlled foreign corporation as of the close of each quarter of the tax year, over (ii) the amount of earnings and profits attributable to amounts that previously resulted in an inclusion for investment of earnings in U.S. property (or that would have if they had not been previously taxed as Subpart F income) with respect to the U.S. shareholder, or

(2) the U.S. shareholder's pro rata share of the "applicable earnings" of the controlled foreign corporation.

§ 956(a). The amount taken into account with respect to any property is the adjusted basis of the property as determined for purposes of computing earnings and profits, reduced by any liability to which the property is subject.

"Applicable earnings" for this purpose means the sum of the controlled foreign corporation's (1) earnings and profits accumulated in prior tax years and (2) earnings and profits for the current tax year. This amount is reduced by (1) distributions made during the year and (2) accumulated earnings and profits previously included in the gross income of U.S. shareholders on account of investments of the earnings in U.S. property. § 956(b)(1).

Items of property acquired by the controlled foreign corporation before the first day the corporation was treated as a controlled foreign corporation, are disregarded in determining the investment of earnings in U.S. property. However, the total amount of property disregarded may not exceed the portion of the applicable earnings of the controlled foreign corporation accumulated during periods before that first day. § 956(b)(2). Moreover, a special rule applies if the corporation ceases to be a controlled foreign corporation during the tax year. § 956(b)(3).

To prevent double taxation, however, an amount of earnings invested in U.S. property is not taxable under Sections 951(a)(1)(B) and 956 to the extent that it is attributable to earnings and profits previously taxed under Subpart F. See § 959(a), discussed at ¶ 6240.

Foreign tax credit consequences of Section 956. One paradoxical aspect of Section 956 is that U.S.-based multinational corporations may deliberately cause their controlled foreign corporations to lend funds to their U.S. parent corporations or otherwise make investments in U.S. property to trigger constructive dividends in connection with their foreign tax credit planning. Like other Subpart F constructive dividend inclusions, those resulting under Sections 951(a)(1)(B) and 956 carry with them, pursuant to Section 960, indirect foreign tax credits for the foreign corporate taxes imposed on the earnings deemed distributed. Subpart F constructive dividends have a potential advantage over actual dividends distributed by a controlled foreign corporation in that no foreign withholding tax is typically imposed (because there is no actual dividend distribution). Thus, in many cases, it will be useful in connection with foreign tax credit planning to cause a Section 956 inclusion by having the controlled foreign corporation lend funds to its U.S. parent rather than have it pay an actual dividend because the foreign withholding tax, which may exceed the applicable foreign tax credit limitation, will not be imposed.

Section 960(c), enacted in 2010, imposes a limitation on the use of Section 956 for foreign tax credit planning purposes. That provision limits the amount of a foreign corporation's foreign income taxes deemed to have been paid under Sections 902 and 960 with respect to a U.S. corporation's gross income inclusion under Section 951(a)(1)(B) to the amount of foreign income taxes that would have been deemed to have been paid If cash in an amount equal to such inclusion had been distributed to the domestic corporation. Stated differently, Section 960(c) limits the foreign tax credits allowed on a deemed dividend under Section 951(a)(1)(B) to the amount of foreign tax credits that would have been allowed on a cash dividend of the same amount.

This limit is applied by comparing the foreign taxes deemed paid with respect to the U.S. shareholder's inclusion under Section 956 (the "tentative credit") to the hypothetical amount of foreign taxes the U.S. shareholder would have been deemed to have paid if cash in an amount equal to the Section 956 inclusion had been distributed through the chain of ownership that starts with the foreign corporation that holds the investment in U.S. property and ends with the U.S. shareholder (the "hypothetical credit"). If the hypothetical credit is less than the tentative credit, then Section 960(c) limits the amount of foreign taxes deemed paid with respect to the Section 956 inclusion to the hypothetical credit. Note, however, that to the extent an actual distribution would be subject to foreign income or withholding tax, such taxes are not taken into account in computing the hypothetical credit. This provision can be illustrated with the following Example drawn from Staff of Joint Comm. on Tax'n, Technical Explanation of the Revenue Provisions of H.R. 5982, The "Small Business Tax Relief Act of 2010," 111th Cong., 2d Sess., at 25–26 (JCX–43–10; July 30, 2010):

> *Example.* DC, a U.S. corporation, owns all of the stock of FC1, a controlled foreign corporation organized in Country X. FC1 has post–1986 undistributed earnings of $400 and post–1986 foreign income taxes of $20. FC1, in turn, owns all of the stock of FC2, a controlled foreign corporation organized in Country Y. FC2 has post–1986 undistributed earnings of $200 and post–1986 foreign income taxes of $100. FC2 makes a loan to DC that triggers a Section 956 inclusion of $200. The tentative credit with respect to such inclusion is $100 ($200/$200 × $100).

The hypothetical distribution of cash of $200 from FC2 to FC1 would increase FC1's current earnings and profits from $400 to $600 and increase FC1's foreign income taxes from $20 to $120. This hypothetical distribution results in a dividend of $200 that is non-Subpart F income of FC1 under the Subpart F look-through rule in Section 954(c)(6). Although Country Y would impose a five-percent withholding tax on an actual distribution from FC2 to FC1 (i.e., a withholding tax of $10 in this case), this amount is not taken into account in calculating the hypothetical credit. The $200 hypothetical distribution from FC1 to DC would result in a dividend of $200, on which DC would be deemed to have paid $40 in foreign income taxes ($200/$600 × $120). Because the hypothetical credit of $40 is less than the tentative credit of $100, Section 960(c) limits DC's foreign income taxes deemed paid with respect to its Section 956 inclusion to $40.

2. DEFINITION OF U.S. PROPERTY

[¶ 6205]

a. Generally

Section 956(c) defines U.S. property to include four basic types of property acquired after 1962. First, U.S. property includes tangible property located in the United States. § 956(c)(1)(A). Second, U.S. property includes stock of a U.S. corporation. § 956(c)(1)(B). Third, U.S. property includes obligations of U.S. persons. § 956(c)(1)(C). Fourth, U.S. property includes any right to use patents, knowhow, copyrights or similar property in the United States. § 956(c)(1)(D).

Certain assets are specifically excluded from the definition of U.S. property. For example, obligations of the United States, money or deposits with banks (as specifically defined for this purpose) or certain corporations that are more than 80 percent owned by certain bank holding companies or financial holding companies are excluded. § 956(c)(2)(A). Export property is excluded, as is any obligation of a U.S. person arising in connection with the sale or processing of property if the amount of the obligation outstanding at any time of the year does not exceed the amount which would be ordinary and necessary to carry on the trade or business of both the other party to the sale or processing transaction and the U.S. person if the transaction had occurred between unrelated persons. § 956(c)(2)(B) and (C). Also excluded are the stock or obligations of a U.S. corporation which is neither a U.S. shareholder (as defined in Section 951(b)) of the controlled foreign corporation nor a U.S. corporation, 25 percent or more of the total combined voting power of which is owned by such U.S. shareholders in the aggregate. § 956(c)(2)(F). Transportation equipment used predominantly outside the United States and a number of other assets are excluded as well. § 956(c)(2)(D), (E) and (G)–(J). In addition, under certain circumstances, the Treasury and the IRS will allow a taxpayer to elect to exclude certain short-term obligations from the definition of "obligation" for Section 956 purposes. See, e.g., Notice 2008–91, 2008–2 C.B. 1001; Notice 2009–10, 2009–1 C.B. 419; Notice 2010–12, 2010–1 C.B. 326.

The 2004 JOBS Act added two more items to the list of property that is excluded from the definition of "U.S. property" in Section 956(c)(2). First, Section 956(c)(2)(K) provides that securities will not be treated as U.S. property if they are acquired and held by a controlled foreign corporation in the ordinary course of its business as a securities dealer. For this exception to apply, however, the controlled foreign corporation must (1) account "for the securities as securities held primarily for sale to customers in the ordinary course of business"; and (2) dispose of the securities (or the securities mature while held by the controlled foreign corporation) "within a period consistent with the holding of securities for sale to customers in the ordinary course of business."

Second, Section 956(c)(2)(L) provides that an obligation issued by a U.S. person will not be treated as U.S. property provided that (1) the issuer is not a U.S. corporation; (2) the issuer is not a U.S. shareholder (within the meaning of Section 951(b)) of the controlled foreign corporation; and (3) the issuer is not a partnership, estate or trust in which the controlled foreign corporation (or any related person within the meaning of Section 954(d)(3)) is a partner, beneficiary or trustee immediately after the controlled foreign corporation's acquisition of the obligation.

The issue of what constitutes a bank for purposes of Section 956(c)(2)(A), as in effect before its amendment by the 2004 JOBS Act, was the subject of litigation. In The Limited, Inc. v. Commissioner, 113 T.C. 169 (1999), rev'd, 286 F.3d 324 (6th Cir.2002), WFNNB, a U.S. subsidiary of The Limited, was a credit card bank that issued private-label credit cards to customers of its parent corporation. To meet its liquidity needs, WFNNB borrowed funds from various sources, including a large amount under a line of credit from Limited Service Corp., another affiliated corporation of The Limited. MFE, a controlled foreign corporation and fourth-tier Netherlands Antilles subsidiary of The Limited, purchased eight certificates of deposit from WFNNB. WFNNB transferred the proceeds from sale of the certificates of deposit to Limited Service Corp. to reduce the outstanding balance under its line of credit from Limited Service. At issue in the case was whether MFE's purchase of the certificates of deposit from WFNNB constituted an investment of earnings in U.S. property, triggering a constructive dividend to The Limited, its U.S. parent, under Section 956. The taxpayer argued that the certificates of deposits were not investments in U.S. property because they were "deposits with persons carrying on the banking business" within the meaning of the pre-JOBS Act version of Section 956(c)(2)(A). The Tax Court carefully examined the legislative history of Subpart F in interpreting the meaning of the exception for "deposits" in Section 956(c)(2)(A). The court held in favor of the government and concluded (113 T.C. at 186–88):

> From the context of the term "the banking business" we infer that Congress meant a group of activities carried on to aid the domestic business activities of controlled foreign corporations. For example, section 956[(c)](2)(B) and (C) except, from the definition of U.S. property, property that is purchased for export and loans to U.S. sellers or processors of the controlled foreign corporation's property. We believe that a person carrying on the banking business, for purposes of section 956[(c)](2)(A), must, at the very least, provide banking services useful to a controlled corporation engaging in business activities in the United States. Our conclusion that Congress had a group of business-facilitating activities in mind is bolstered by the tax-writing committees' stated belief that the exceptions to the definition of U.S. property were for "normal commercial transactions without intent to permit the funds to remain in the United States indefinitely." * * *
>
> * * *
>
> WFNNB is a special-purpose institution that is not of much use to a foreign business customer seeking banking services except as the issuer of a private-label credit card or as the recipient of large deposits of funds that are not needed immediately. Those are insufficient services for us to conclude that WFNNB was "carrying on the banking business" as Congress used that phrase in section 956[(c)](2)(A).

On appeal, the Sixth Circuit used a so-called "plain meaning" approach to interpreting Section 956(c)(2)(A) and reversed the Tax Court's decision in the case, thus providing a significant victory for the corporate taxpayer that had designed a clever end-run around the provisions of Section 956. See 286 F.3d 324 (6th Cir.2002). However, the 2004 JOBS Act clarified and narrowed the definition of a banking business for Section 956(c)(2)(A) purposes and thereby effectively overturned the Sixth Circuit's decision in *The Limited* for post-2004 years. Under revised Section 956(c)(2)(A), U.S. property does not include obligations of the United States, money or deposits with either (1) any bank (as defined by the Bank Holding Company Act of 1956) or (2) any corporation that is not a bank but with respect to which a bank holding company (as defined by the Bank Holding Company Act) or a financial holding company (as defined by that Act) owns directly or indirectly more than 80 percent of the vote or value of its stock. The House Conference Committee Report stated that no inference was intended to be drawn from this change concerning the meaning of the phrase "carrying on the banking business" under prior law. H.R. Conf. Rep. No. 755, 108th Cong., 2d Sess. 625 (2004).

[¶ 6210]

b. Special Rules for Pledges and Guarantees by Controlled Foreign Corporations and for Pledges of Stock by U.S. Shareholders

Section 956(d) may treat a controlled foreign corporation as holding the obligation of a U.S. person if the corporation is a pledgor or guarantor of the obligation. Moreover, as the following materials demonstrate, the government has attempted to use Section 956(d) to treat a controlled foreign corporation as owning an obligation of its U.S. shareholder if the shareholder pledges stock possessing a significant portion of the total voting power of the corporation as security for the obligation and if certain other circumstances are present. Do the Treasury and the IRS have sufficient statutory authority for their attempt to extend the scope of Section 956(d)?

[¶ 6215]

LUDWIG v. COMMISSIONER

United States Tax Court, 1977.
68 T.C. 979 (nonacq.).

FEATHERSTON, JUDGE: * * * [T]he sole issue remaining for decision is whether a controlled foreign corporation wholly owned by petitioner Daniel K. Ludwig was a guarantor, within the meaning of section 956[(d)], of petitioner's obligations to a group of lending banks, with the result that income was realized by petitioner under section 951.

FINDINGS OF FACT

* * *

In June 1963, petitioner entered into an agreement with Phillips Petroleum Co. (hereinafter Phillips), providing for the purchase by petitioner from Phillips of 1,340,517 shares of stock of Union Oil Co. (hereinafter Union Oil). These shares represented Phillips' entire holding in Union Oil, and amounted to approximately 15 percent of Union Oil's total outstanding stock. The purchase price was $75 per share, or a total of $100,538,775.

* * *

In order to pay for the 1,340,517 shares of Union Oil, petitioner arranged to borrow the entire amount of the purchase price from three banks—Chase Manhattan Bank (Chase Manhattan), Chemical Bank New York Trust Co. (Chemical Bank), and Bank of America National Trust & Savings Association (Bank of America). Chase Manhattan served as agent for the lending banks in negotiating the loan agreement with petitioner.

All negotiations as to the terms and conditions of the loan agreement (other than those concerning the amount of participation of each of the lending banks) were conducted by Chase Manhattan as agent for the lending banks.

Part of the negotiation of the agreement involved the collateral to be used to secure the loan. Under Regulation U, Federal Reserve Board, 12 C.F.R., Part 221 (1963) (hereinafter Regulation U), a loan of this type (for the purchase of a security listed on a national securities exchange) was required to be secured by collateral having a value of at least twice the amount of the loan. Petitioner offered and the banks accepted as collateral the 1,340,517 shares of Union Oil stock to be acquired by petitioner with the loan proceeds, plus 1,000 shares of Oceanic Tankships, S.A. (Oceanic).

Oceanic was a Panamanian corporation which, during 1963, had 1,000 shares of stock outstanding, all of which were owned by petitioner. During the taxable year 1963, Oceanic's assets consisted primarily of all of the outstanding stock of Universe Tankships, Inc. (Universe), a Liberian corporation engaged principally in the business of owning and operating oceangoing vessels. As of December 31, 1963, Oceanic had accumulated earnings and profits of $5,092,318. At the time Chase Manhattan agreed to accept the stock of Oceanic as collateral for petitioner's loan, it determined that such stock had a value at least equal to its book value of approximately $200 million. Thus, the total collateral for the loan (the Union Oil stock plus the Oceanic stock) was valued by the lending banks at approximately $300 million.

In order to protect the value of the Oceanic stock held as collateral, the banks required of petitioner certain negative covenants restricting his absolute control over the assets and liabilities of Oceanic and Universe during the term of the loan. These restrictions were set forth in the loan agreement and included, in part, the borrower's covenants not to cause Oceanic or Universe to do any of the following without the consent of the lenders:

(1) Borrow money, except in connection with shipping operations;

(2) Pledge assets as collateral, except as to borrowings in connection with shipping operations;

(3) Guarantee, assume, or become liable on the obligation of another, or invest in or lend funds to another, except to the extent of $40 million total;

(4) Merge or consolidate with any other corporation;

(5) Sell or lease (other than in the ordinary course of business) or otherwise dispose of any substantial part of its assets;

(6) Transfer any shares of any controlled subsidiary;

(7) Pay or secure any amount owing by Oceanic or Universe to petitioner;

(8) Pay any dividends, except in such amounts as may be required to make interest or principal payments on petitioner's loan from the lending banks.

The principal purpose of these negative covenants was to protect the lenders against possible actions by petitioner, as the controlling stockholder of Oceanic and (through Oceanic) Universe, which could diminish the value of the Oceanic stock held as collateral. This kind of protection was critical in satisfaction of Regulation U requirements concerning the value of collateral. With the protection of the negative covenants the lending banks could look to the value of the Oceanic stock as their source of recovery in the event of default in repayment by petitioner. In the event of such default the banks expected to be able to sell the pledged Union Oil and/or Oceanic stock to satisfy their claims.

In July 1963, the loan agreement was concluded and petitioner issued personal promissory notes to the lending banks as follows:

Chase Manhattan	$50,269,387.50
Chemical Bank	40,000,000.00
Bank of America	10,269,387.50
Total	100,538,775.00

In that same month, petitioner completed his purchase of the Union Oil stock.

During 1963 through 1965, the board of directors of Oceanic held meetings and kept minutes of these meetings. Such minutes do not reflect any discussion of or reference to petitioner's purchase of Union Oil stock or the loan agreement pursuant to which his Oceanic stock was pledged as collateral.

* * *

ULTIMATE FINDING OF FACT

Oceanic was not a guarantor of petitioner's obligations to the lending banks.

OPINION

Under section 951(a)(1)(B), a United States shareholder of a controlled foreign corporation is required to include in gross income his pro rata share of such corporation's increase in earnings invested in United States property during the taxable year. Section 956(a)(1) [as worded before the 1993 Act] provides that the amount of the earnings of a controlled foreign corporation invested in United States property for the taxable year is the aggregate amount of such property held, directly or indirectly, at the close of the taxable year but only to the extent that the amount thereof would have constituted a dividend if such amount had been distributed during the year. See sec. 1.956–1(a), Income Tax Regs.

Section 956[(c)](1)(C) provides that the term "United States property" includes an obligation of a "United States person." Thus, if a controlled foreign corporation makes a loan to its shareholder, a United States person, the obligation to repay the loan is United States property and the shareholder thereby realizes income under section 951. Section 956[(d)] goes further and provides that a controlled foreign corporation shall be considered as holding an obligation of a United States person if such corporation is, under regulations issued by the Secretary of the Treasury, a "guarantor" of such obligation.

In the instant case, petitioner was a United States shareholder of a controlled foreign corporation, Oceanic. As of December 31, 1963, that corporation had accumulated earnings and profits of $5,029,318 which, if distributed to petitioner, would have constituted a dividend. In that year, petitioner pledged his Oceanic stock to the lending banks in connection with the Union Oil stock purchase. Respondent contends that Oceanic thereby became a "guarantor," within the meaning of section 956[d], of petitioner's obligation to the lending banks. On this theory, respondent maintains, petitioner realized taxable income under section 951 to the extent of Oceanic's undistributed earnings and profits of $5,029,318.

We do not agree.

Section 956[(d)], on which respondent relies, is as follows:

> For purposes of subsection (a), a controlled foreign corporation shall, under regulations prescribed by the Secretary or his delegate, be considered as holding an obligation of a United States person if such controlled foreign corporation is a pledgor or guarantor of such obligation.

Neither the Code nor the related regulations define the term "guarantor" for purposes of section 956[(d)]. In the absence of any such specific technical definition, the term should be given its normal and customary meaning. * * * Black's Law Dictionary defines "guarantor" as one who makes a guaranty, and defines "to guaranty" as follows (Black's Law Dictionary, 833 (rev. 4th ed. 1968)):

> To undertake collaterally to answer for the payment of another's debt or the performance of another's duty, liability, or obligation; to assume the responsibility of a guarantor; to warrant.

This Court had occasion to define the term "guaranty" in *Perry v. Commissioner*, 47 T.C. 159, 163 (1966), affd. 392 F.2d 458 (8th Cir.1968), as follows:

> "an undertaking or promise on the part of one person which is collateral to a primary or principal obligation on the part of another,

> and which binds the obligor to performance in the event of nonperformance by such other, the latter being bound to perform primarily." 24 Am. Jur., Guaranty, sec. 2, p. 873–874.

See also *Underwood v. Commissioner*, 63 T.C. 468, 475 (1975), affd. 535 F.2d 309 (5th Cir.1976). * * *

Two essential elements in the nearly uniform definitional language of these cases are (1) an undertaking or promise on the part of the guarantor and (2) a liability of the guarantor to make payment if the primary obligor fails to do so. Both of these critical elements are missing in the instant situation. The alleged guarantor, Oceanic, did not undertake or promise anything. Oceanic took no action whatsoever in connection with petitioner's debt to the lending banks. In the event that petitioner had failed to pay his obligation, Oceanic's pledged stock might have been sold to another, but Oceanic would have had no liability to make any payment. Thus, Oceanic can hardly be considered to have made a guaranty within the usual meaning of that term.

This being the case, section 951 is not applicable, unless the word "guarantor" as used in section 956[(d)] has a unique meaning and consequence beyond its normal usage. This is, in effect, what respondent would have us hold in this case. Although this issue has not previously been litigated, respondent's position has been spelled out in a revenue ruling which was adopted after the notice of deficiency was issued in the instant case.[4] Rev. Rul. 76–125, 1976–1 C.B. 204, concluded that a stock pledge transaction, almost identical in form to the instant one, had the same effect of indirect repatriation of the controlled foreign corporation's income as if such corporation had itself guarantied the controlling stockholder's obligation. The following language from Rev. Rul. 76–125, *supra* at 204–205, sets forth the rationale on which respondent relies:

> The purpose of section 956 of the Code is to terminate the tax deferment privilege with respect to the earnings of controlled foreign corporations when such earnings are directly or indirectly repatriated. S. Rep. No. 1881, 87th Cong., 2d Sess. 80, 87–88 (1962) * * *, states, in part, "Generally, earnings brought back to the United States are taxed to the shareholders on the grounds that this is substantially the equivalent of a dividend being paid to them." Consistent with the intent of section 956, section 956[(d)] is interpreted to hold that use of the assets or credit of a controlled foreign corporation as collateral for an obligation of a United States person shall be considered a repatriation of earnings.
>
> The loan agreement in the instant case indicated it was the intention of the parties that if *A* [the U.S. controlling stockholder] defaulted on the loan *X*'s [the controlled foreign corporation's] assets

4. This 1976 ruling was issued in the year following the year in which the notice of deficiency was issued to petitioners in this case (1975). The courts have not looked with favor upon bootstrapping revenue rulings issued shortly prior to the initiation of litigation. * * *

> * * * would be available to answer for the debt of *A*. Thus, although the agreement was signed by *A* for himself only, the net effect of the agreement was the same as a guaranty by *X* of the loan to *A*. Under section 956[d] of the Code, *X* must therefore be considered as holding *A*'s obligation, which is defined as United States property under section 956[(c)](1)(C).

The premise of this ruling is that the loan agreement indicated it was the "intention" of the parties that if the controlling United States shareholder defaulted on the loan the foreign corporation's assets would be available to answer for the debt. There is no evidence of any such "intention" in the instant case. To the contrary, the loan agreement gave the lending banks the remedies normally associated with pledge foreclosures.[5] Sale of the pledged asset is the remedy ordinarily followed in case of default and foreclosure. It seems clear that, under usual principles of law applicable to the disposition of collateral for a loan, the banks could not have directly liquidated Oceanic; they would first have had to acquire the Oceanic stock as a purchaser on a foreclosure sale. See footnote 5. We find no basis for questioning the testimony of the officer of Chase Manhattan who negotiated the loan that had the banks foreclosed the pledge they would have sold Oceanic's stock and, further, that to have attempted to liquidate Oceanic and sell its assets would have been impracticable.[6] Thus, this crucial premise on which the ruling is based is lacking in the instant case.

Moreover, Rev. Rul. 76–125, *supra* at 205, incorrectly reasons that "although the agreement was signed by * * * [the United States shareholder] for himself only, the net effect of the agreement was the same as a guaranty." Had Oceanic guarantied the bank loans in the manner described in section 956[(d)], it would have subjected itself to a contingent liability to pay the loans if petitioner defaulted. In those circumstances and in case of petitioner's default, the banks could have sued Oceanic for the unpaid balance of the notes and enforced their rights as creditors of Oceanic. Section 956[(d)] treats such use of the controlled foreign corporation's credit as an indirect repatriation of funds sufficient to trigger the realization of income under section 951.

---

5. Under the terms of the loan agreement, the lending banks' principal remedies were substantially as follows:

(1) The lending banks could sell the pledged collateral at public or private sale after giving the borrower 10 days' written notice of their intention to make such sale; or

(2) The lending banks could proceed by a suit in law or equity to foreclose the pledge and sell the pledged collateral under a judgment or decree of a court; and

(3) The lending banks were required to apply the proceeds of any sale of the pledged collateral to the payment of selling expenses, interest on the loan, and principal on the loan; any surplus to be paid to the borrower.

6. The Chase Manhattan officer testified:

"The idea of liquidating (Oceanic) is nothing less than outrageous. Think of the troubles that you'd have in going through trying to get a new Board of Directors and everything else. You don't try to make life complicated for yourself. You get rid of it (the pledged stock) and get your loan paid. Period."

However, the stock pledge in the instant case had no such current or future effect upon Oceanic's assets and liabilities. Oceanic assumed no liability, contingent or otherwise, to pay petitioner's loans. In case of petitioner's default on the bank loans, the banks might have foreclosed the pledge and sold the Oceanic stock. But the new owner purchasing at the foreclosure sale would have acquired stock with the same value as it would have had if no pledge had occurred. The banks would have had no remedy against Oceanic. Thus, the net effect of the stock pledge was not the same as a guaranty.

That petitioner realized a benefit from owning and pledging his Oceanic stock to secure the bank loans does not mean that Oceanic's earnings were invested in United States property within the meaning of section 951. Neither that section nor section 956[(d)] reaches every benefit derived from the ownership of stock in a controlled foreign corporation. In a real sense, the owner of such stock gains financially from every increase in its value, including increases attributable to an accumulation of earnings. Such value increases may so enhance his net worth as to enable him to borrow more money than he could have borrowed otherwise. But such an economic benefit does not trigger the realization of income. The owner realizes income under sections 951 and 956(a)(1) only when the controlled foreign corporation's earnings are invested in United States property. Neither a pledge of the controlled foreign corporation's stock to secure a shareholder's loan nor the listing of such stock on a balance sheet as evidence to support a loan, constitutes an investment of earnings in United States property. Only by reason of section 956[(d)] does the controlled foreign corporation's guaranty of its shareholder's indebtedness constitute such an investment in United States property, and the language of that section does not include a pledge of the controlled corporation's stock.

Respondent attempts to minimize this distinction between a shareholder's pledge of the corporation's stock and the corporation's guaranty of the loan by arguing that the ultimate basis of the lender's security in either case is the underlying assets of the corporation (and, thus, the shareholder-borrower indirectly utilizes these assets). Respondent relies heavily upon the negative covenants (detailed in our Findings) in petitioner's loan agreement in which petitioner is required, as controlling stockholder, to refrain from certain actions with respect to Oceanic's operations and net worth during the term of the loan. Respondent interprets these negative covenants as intended to preserve the assets of the corporation for access by the lenders in the event of petitioner's default.

However, the record amply demonstrates that covenants of this character, restricting the borrowing of funds, the sale of certain assets, or payment of dividends and forbidding gratuitous guaranties, are not at all uncommon. A breach of the restrictions or prohibitions ordinarily constitutes an event of default which permits acceleration of the loan. The

Chase Manhattan officer who arranged the loan explained that unless "the loan is so strong that you don't need the protection of the collateral at all, it (inclusion of negative covenants in a loan agreement) is almost a necessity." He further testified that the negative covenants included in the instant loan agreement were less restrictive than those usually found in an agreement of this kind.

The purpose of the negative covenants in the instant case was not, as respondent argues, to enable the lending banks, in the event of petitioner's default, to enforce their claim against Oceanic or its assets. Their purpose was to protect the value of the pledged Oceanic stock as security for the loans. As pointed out in our Findings, the loan was made subject to the provisions of Regulation U which required the banks to make certain at all times that the value of all the pledged security was at least twice the amount of the loan. As discussed above, the recourse of the lenders in the event of petitioner's default would have been to sell the pledged Oceanic stock, not to attempt to recover through direct access to Oceanic's assets.

We think Rev. Rul. 76–125, *supra*, and respondent's position in this case attempt to stretch the statute and regulations to cover a situation with which they do not deal. True, the legislative history of subpart F in which sections 951 and 956 appear makes it quite clear that one of its objectives is to tax United States shareholders of controlled foreign corporations on the indirect repatriation of income earned by such corporations but not distributed as dividends (and in many instances, not subjected to tax by the jurisdiction of incorporation). S. Rept. 1881, 87th Cong., 2d Sess. (1962), * * *; H. Rept. 1447, 87th Cong., 2d Sess. (1962) * * *. As noted above, an obvious form of such indirect repatriation would be a loan from the controlled foreign corporation to its controlling stockholder(s). This is dealt with specifically in section 956[(c)](1)(C) * * *.

Less directly, the controlling stockholders could derive nearly identical benefits by borrowing funds from another source and having the loan guarantied by the controlled foreign corporation or secured by a pledge of such corporation's assets. Such use of the credit or assets of the controlled foreign corporation indirectly effects a repatriation of available earnings. Section 956[(d)] was enacted specifically to cover these more subtle forms of indirect repatriation. S. Rept. 1881, *supra* * * *.

But section 956[(d)] says nothing about pledging the stock of the controlled foreign corporation. Moreover, although that section specifically authorizes the Secretary or his delegate to prescribe regulations for its detailed application, the present regulations do not contain any provisions expanding the guaranty concept to include a pledge of the controlled foreign corporation's stock. Indeed, the regulations dealing with the treatment of pledges and guaranties, in substance, follow the statute. They are cast in terms which assume that "pledgor" and "guarantor" have their normal meaning except that one example explains that the guarantor concept includes an agreement by the controlled foreign corporation to buy the note at maturity if the United States person does not repay the loan. Sec. 1.956–2(c)(1), Income Tax Regs.

Another regulation, defining the term "acquired," provides that property which is an obligation of a United States person "with respect to which a controlled foreign corporation is a pledgor or guarantor" shall be considered acquired when "such corporation assumes liability as a pledgor or guarantor." Sec. 1.956–2(d)(1)(b), Income Tax Regs. A corporation does not assume a liability as pledgor or guarantor unless it is a party to the transaction. Thus, the regulation contemplates that section 956[(d)] is applicable only where the guarantor—the controlled foreign corporation—is a party to the transaction, not when its stock is merely pledged.[8]

While we are aware that in most cases the value of stock as collateral will be based at least in some part upon the value of the underlying corporate assets (including undistributed income), the extent of the importance of such assets will vary from case to case. In many instances, the going-concern value of the company or the market value of the stock in the public securities market will have more significance than the value of the company's assets. In fact, it is conceivable that stock could be used as collateral in a case where the corporation has no significant tangible assets (or has liabilities substantially offsetting or exceeding the amount of its assets). Thus, the extent to which the stockholder of a controlled foreign corporation derives a benefit from the assets of the corporation is much less certain in the case of a pledge of stock than in the case of a direct commitment of its assets or credit by the corporation. We think that was the rationale followed by the draftsman of section 956 in stopping short of including the stock pledge transaction. Had Congress intended to cover the stock pledge arrangement, it could have, and would have, done so. * * *

Whether this distinction explains the omission of the stock pledge type of transaction from section 956[(d)] or whether the omission was an oversight, we can find no basis for respondent's expansive interpretation of that section in the statutory language, its legislative history, or the implementing regulations. If the draftsman's handiwork fell short of fully accomplishing the objectives sought, it must be left to Congress to repair such shortfall. Accordingly, we hold that petitioner did not realize gross income under section 951 by reason of his pledge of his Oceanic stock as collateral for his loan from the lending banks.

* * *

8. Regulations promulgated pursuant to specific grant of authority in the applicable Code section are ordinarily given great weight by the courts. * * * Conversely, this Court has been reluctant to sustain expansive interpretations of statutory language by the Commissioner when, as here, such interpretations have not been promulgated in regulations despite such a specific grant of interpretive regulatory authority. * * * Had the Secretary or his delegate, charged with responsibility for drafting the applicable regulation, thought sec. 956[(d)] was applicable when a controlled foreign corporation's stock was pledged, the regulation would have said so. Failure to include such a provision in the regulation suggests that the Secretary or his delegate thought the statute would not accommodate that interpretation.

[¶ 6220]

NOTE

After the Tax Court's decision in the *Ludwig* case, the Treasury and IRS issued the following proposed regulation amendment to Reg. § 1.956–2:

§ 1.956–2. **Definition of United States Property.—**

* * *

(c) *Treatment of pledges and guarantees*—(1) *General rule.* * * *

(2) *Indirect pledge or guarantee.* If the assets of a controlled foreign corporation serve at any time, either directly or indirectly, as security for the performance of an obligation of a United States person, then, for purposes of paragraph (c)(1) of this section, the controlled foreign corporation will be considered a pledgor or guarantor of that obligation. * * *

(3) *Facilitation of borrowing.* If the assets of a controlled foreign corporation do not serve as security for the performance of an obligation of a United States person under paragraph (c)(2) of this section, but the controlled foreign corporation otherwise facilitates a loan to, or borrowing by, that person, the corporation will be considered a pledgor or guarantor of the obligation of a United States person under paragraph (c)(1) of this section. For example, where the assets of a controlled foreign corporation serve as an inducement, consideration, compensating balance, or other accommodation for the extension of a loan to, or the continued carrying of a preexisting loan by, a United States person, the corporation will be considered to have facilitated a loan to, or borrowing by, that person. * * *

* * *

(5) *Illustrations.* The following examples illustrate the application of this paragraph (c):

* * *

Example (5). A, a United States person, owns all of the stock of Y, a controlled foreign corporation. United States person A and controlled foreign corporation Y both use the calendar year as a taxable year. Y Corporation is engaged in providing working capital and funds for the expansion of A's business both in the United States and abroad through its various affiliates. In recent years, A has experienced financial difficulties as a result of its United States operations. On December 15, 1976, Y Corporation makes a deposit in an unrelated domestic financial institution in the amount of $100,000. Shortly thereafter, A borrows $100,000 from the same financial institution. The rate of interest earned by Y on its deposit and the rate of interest charged A on its loan differ by a fraction of 1 percent. Although the deposit by Y Corporation was nominally designated a demand deposit, the funds were not withdrawn by Y until A repaid the amount it had borrowed. Since the facts indicate that Y facilitated the loan to A, a U.S. person, under paragraph (c)(3) of this section Y will be considered a pledgor or guarantor of the obligation of A. Y Corporation would likewise be considered a pledgor or guarantor if Y's deposit followed, rather than preceded, the loan to A. * * *

* * *

The final regulations were amended on August 6, 1980, by T.D. 7712, 1980–2 C.B. 226, which omitted the paragraph on "facilitation of borrowing" and Example 5. Reg. § 1.956–2(c)(2), as amended, provides:

> (2) *Indirect pledge or guarantee.* If the assets of a controlled foreign corporation serve at any time, even though indirectly, as security for the performance of an obligation of a United States person, then, for purposes of paragraph (c)(1) of this section, the controlled foreign corporation will be considered a pledgor or guarantor of that obligation. For this purpose the pledge of stock of a controlled foreign corporation will be considered as the indirect pledge of the assets of the corporation if at least 66⅔ percent of the total combined voting power of all classes of stock entitled to vote is pledged and if the pledge of stock is accompanied by one or more negative covenants or similar restrictions on the shareholder effectively limiting the corporation's discretion with respect to the disposition of assets and the incurrence of liabilities other than in the ordinary course of business. This paragraph (c)(2) applies only to pledges and guarantees which are made after September 8, 1980. For purposes of this paragraph (c)(2) a refinancing shall be considered as a new pledge or guarantee.

Should the final regulations be sustained as a reasonable interpretation of the statute? Was it necessary or appropriate for the Treasury and the IRS to omit the paragraph on "facilitation of borrowing" and Example 5 of the proposed regulations from the amendment as adopted?

[¶ 6225]

3. INDIRECT OWNERSHIP OF U.S. PROPERTY THROUGH A PARTNERSHIP

How does Section 956 apply when a controlled foreign corporation is a partner in a partnership which owns property that would constitute U.S. property if held directly by the controlled foreign corporation? The following Revenue Ruling provides the IRS's answer to this question. As you read the Ruling, think about whether the reasoning of the Eighth Circuit in the *Brown Group* case (discussed at ¶ 6180) undercuts the IRS's conclusion.

[¶ 6230]

REVENUE RULING 90–112

1990–2 C.B. 186.

ISSUE

Does a controlled foreign corporation hold "United States property" within the meaning of section 956 * * * when it is a partner in a partnership that owns real property located in the United States?

FACTS

S, a wholly owned Country *X* subsidiary of *P*, a domestic corporation, is a controlled foreign corporation (CFC) as defined in section 957 * * *. *S* reports its income on a calendar year basis. *S* is not engaged in any United States business activity and does not earn any income that is effectively connected with a United States trade or business. *PRS*, an entity classified as a partnership for United States federal tax purposes, is organized under the laws of Country *X*. *S* owns a 25 percent interest in the capital and profits of *PRS*, which it purchased in 1987. The remaining 75 per cent interest in *PRS* is owned by an unrelated Country *X* corporation. In 1988, *PRS* purchased undeveloped land in the United States. The land is not subject to any mortgages or other liabilities.

LAW AND ANALYSIS

Under section 956(a) [as worded before the 1993 Act] * * *, the amount of earnings of a CFC invested in United States property at the close of any taxable year is the aggregate amount of such property held, directly or indirectly, by the CFC at the close of the taxable year, to the extent that such amount would have constituted a dividend if it had been distributed. Under section 956[(c)](1), "United States property" is defined as any tangible property located in the United States. "Tangible property" includes undeveloped land. See section 1.956–2(a)(*l*)(i) of the * * * [r]egulations.

Section 956 * * *, and the regulations thereunder, do not specifically address the treatment of a CFC's investment in United States property through a partnership. Whether a CFC partner is treated as holding, on the last day of its taxable year, a portion of the United States property owned by the partnership depends upon whether the partnership is viewed as an "entity" separate from its partners or as an "aggregate" of its partners for purposes of section 956. There is no exclusive rule as to when a partnership will be treated as an entity or as an aggregate for purposes outside of subchapter K. The resolution depends upon which approach is more appropriate to the specific Code section involved. *See, e.g.*, Rev. Rul. 89–72, 1989–1 C.B. 257, (a CFC's distributive share of income from a non-controlled partnership is treated as foreign base company sales income, if it would have been treated as such had it been realized directly by the CFC). * * *

For purposes of section 956 * * *, a CFC is considered to hold United States property if it holds the property directly or indirectly. *See* section 956(a)(1). This rule is a specific application of the general principle that section 956 is concerned with the substance of a transaction and not merely its form. *See* Rev. Rul. 89–73, 1989–1 C.B. 258. The House Report on the Revenue Act of 1962, which adopted section 956, stated that an objective of that section was "to prevent the repatriation of income to the United States in a manner which does not subject it to U.S. taxation." H.R. Rep. No. 1447, 87th Cong., 2d Sess. (1962), at 58 * * *. While taxpayers with excess foreign tax credits may desire to trigger a section 956 inclusion, it is still appropriate to construe section 956 in a manner consistent with this statement under these facts.

The purpose of section 956 * * * would be frustrated if it were construed not to reach the United States property held by a CFC through a partnership. Thus, in the context of section 956, it is appropriate to apply the aggregate view of a partnership so that the United States property of the CFC includes United States property held by the CFC through a partnership. This result applies section 956 according to the substance of the arrangement, without regard to whether the form of the ownership is direct or indirect.

Therefore, for purposes of section 956 * * *, *S* is considered to hold on the last day of its 1988 taxable year, a 25 percent interest in the undeveloped land that is owned by *PRS* on such date. The amount taken into account, for purposes of section 956, with respect to *S*'s 25 percent interest in the undeveloped land will be 25 percent of *PRS*'s adjusted basis in the land, limited by *S*'s total basis in *PRS*. See Section 1.956–1(e)(1) of the regulations. The result would be the same if *PRS* were a domestic partnership. * * *

HOLDING

Real property located in the United States that is owned by a partnership in which a controlled foreign corporation is a partner constitutes United States property held by the CFC for purposes of section 956[(c)] * * *.

[¶ 6235]

PROBLEMS

1. Delft, a Dutch corporation, all of the voting stock of which is owned by Eurotile, Inc., a U.S. corporation, is engaged in manufacturing and selling plastic kitchen utensils in the Netherlands. Consider the possible U.S. tax consequences if a portion of Delft's surplus earnings is loaned to Eurotile, Inc. or is invested in stock of an unrelated corporation listed on the New York

Stock Exchange. What are the U.S. tax consequences if Delft purchases from an unrelated party the exclusive right to use, manufacture and sell in the United States an invention protected by a U.S. patent for the life of the patent?

2. Review the facts of the alternative transactions in Problems 2 and 3 at ¶ 6195. What are the tax consequences of those transactions under Sections 951(a)(1)(B) and 956?

[¶ 6240]

G. PREVIOUSLY TAXED INCOME AND ORDERING RULES

Unlike actual dividends, income inclusions by U.S. shareholders under Section 951 do not reduce the controlled foreign corporation's earnings and profits within the meaning of Sections 312, 316 and 964 of the Code (which are used in determining whether distributions from a corporation to its shareholders will be taxed as dividends to the shareholders). Accordingly, to prevent U.S. shareholders from being taxed twice on the same income, earnings and profits of a controlled foreign corporation that have been included in the income of U.S. shareholders as a constructive distribution under Section 951(a) are excluded from the shareholders' gross income when those earnings are actually distributed.[25] Furthermore, amounts of a controlled foreign corporation's earnings and profits that would be taxed to the U.S. shareholders as a constructive distribution under Section 951(a)(1)(B) because they were invested in U.S. property are excluded from the shareholders' gross income to the extent that they are attributable to amounts that have previously been included in the income of U.S. shareholders under Section 951(a). § 959(a).[26]

Any actual or constructive distributions excluded from gross income under this provision generally do not carry indirect foreign tax credits under Section 960 for foreign taxes deemed paid by a U.S. corporation in any prior tax year. §§ 959(d) and 960(a)(2). This common-sense rule prevents the same foreign taxes from being treated as deemed paid twice for purposes of Sections 902 and 960—once in the earlier year when the U.S. shareholder had an income inclusion under Section 951 and a second time when the controlled foreign corporation makes a tax-free distribution of the previously taxed income under Section 959. However, a distribution excluded under Section 959(a) may carry indirect credits for foreign taxes

---

25. Amounts excluded from a U.S. shareholder's gross income as previously taxed income under Section 959 do not constitute dividends for Section 1(h)(11) purposes. Accordingly, such amounts cannot constitute "qualified dividend income" for Section 1(h)(11) purposes. See IRS Notice 2004–70, § 4.03, 2004–2 C.B. 724, 726. Section 1(h)(11) will expire for tax years starting after 2010 unless it is extended or made permanent by Congress in new legislation.

26. For purposes of the previously taxed income rules in Section 959, amounts included in gross income as a dividend under Section 1248 (discussed at ¶ 6245) are treated as if they had been included in prior years as Subpart F income. § 959(e).

not deemed paid by the U.S. corporation for any prior tax year that are attributable to the accumulated profits out of which the distribution is made. § 960(a)(3).

For purposes of determining the amount of an *actual distribution* by a controlled foreign corporation that is not taxable because it represents previously taxed income, the earnings distributed are attributed to the following categories in the following order: (1) to earnings and profits that were required in prior years to be included as investments in U.S. property and as investments in excess passive assets (before repeal of the excess passive assets rules for tax years after 1996), allocated to each category on a pro rata basis, (2) to earnings and profits that were required in prior years to be included as Subpart F income and (3) to other earnings and profits. § 959(c). Under these rules, the amount of earnings treated as previously included in income of the U.S. shareholder on account of the investment of earnings in U.S. property or excess passive assets includes not only earnings that resulted in inclusion, but also earnings that would have resulted in inclusion but for being attributable to earnings that had been previously taxed as Subpart F income.

To determine the amount of a *constructive inclusion* on account of an investment in U.S. property, a special rule applies for purposes of determining amounts that are excluded from income because they represent previously taxed earnings. Amounts that would be included in income as investments in U.S. property are attributed to the following categories of earnings in the following order: (1) to retained earnings required to be included as Subpart F income, and (2) to other earnings and profits. § 959(f)(1). For purposes of applying these rules, actual distributions are taken into account before constructive distributions under Section 951(a)(1)(B). § 959(f)(2).

Suppose that a U.S. shareholder includes an amount in income under Section 951(a) with respect to a lower-tier controlled foreign corporation (e.g., the U.S. shareholder owns stock in an upper-tier controlled foreign corporation that, in turn, owns stock in a lower-tier controlled foreign corporation and the U.S. shareholder's indirect interest in the lower-tier controlled foreign corporation's voting stock is at least ten percent). See ¶ 6065. Section 959(b) will exclude from the upper-tier controlled foreign corporation's gross income a distribution to it from the lower-tier controlled foreign corporation to the extent the distribution is attributable to earnings and profits that have already been included in the U.S. shareholder's gross income under Section 951(a). This prevents the U.S. shareholder from being taxed twice on the same amount.

Under the previously taxed income rules, the retained earnings of the controlled foreign corporation that are treated as having been previously included in income of a U.S. shareholder include the retained earnings that were previously included in income of another U.S. person that is a predecessor in interest to the U.S. shareholder. § 959(a).

As discussed above, Section 959 treats a distribution of previously taxed income to a U.S. shareholder as excludible from gross income; accordingly, such a distribution does not produce foreign-source income for the U.S. shareholder for purposes of the foreign tax credit limitation in Section 904. Thus, absent a special rule, if a foreign country imposes a withholding tax on the distribution that is a creditable tax, the Section 904 limitation might prevent the U.S. shareholder from obtaining a foreign tax credit for the withholding tax. However, Section 960(b) increases the Section 904 foreign tax credit limitation for the year of the distribution if certain requirements are met, which may help the U.S. shareholder in obtaining a credit for the withholding tax.

Suppose that a U.S. shareholder receives an actual dividend distribution and a Subpart F inclusion in the same year. What ordering rules apply in determining the extent to which the actual dividend distribution is taxable or excludible under Section 959? Does the actual dividend distribution reduce the U.S. shareholder's Section 951(a) inclusion? To what extent do the Subpart F inclusion and actual dividend distribution reduce the controlled foreign corporation's earnings and profits?

> *Example*: DC, a domestic corporation, owns all the stock of FC, a foreign corporation that is a controlled foreign corporation. During year 1, FC has Subpart F income of $200, earnings and profits of $400 and pays an actual dividend of $100. Assume that FC pays no foreign taxes on its income. DC must include $200 in gross income as ordinary income under Section 951(a)(1)(A)(i). (Note that the actual dividend paid to DC does not reduce DC's inclusion under Section 951(a)(1)(A)(i) because there was no part of year 1 during which DC did not own (within the meaning of Section 958(a)) the stock of FC.) Under the ordering rules in Section 959(c), DC would exclude the actual dividend of $100 from gross income under Section 959, because the distribution represents earnings and profits attributable to amounts that DC previously included in income under Section 951(a). The actual dividend would reduce FC's earnings and profits from $400 to $300. (Note that DC's Section 951(a) inclusion did not itself trigger a reduction of FC's earnings and profits.) See Reg. §§ 1.951–1(b)(1) and –1(b)(2), Exs. and 1.959–1(b) and –1(b), Ex.

[¶ 6245]

H. GAINS FROM CERTAIN SALES OR EXCHANGES OF STOCK IN CONTROLLED FOREIGN CORPORATIONS (SECTION 1248)

Before the addition to the Code of Section 1248 in 1962, U.S. shareholders could "cash in" on and realize the economic benefit of the accumulated earnings of a controlled foreign corporation at long-term capital gains tax rates. The capital gain result could be accomplished by selling stock of the foreign corporation at a price that would reflect the accumulated earnings of the controlled foreign corporation. It could also be achieved by liquidating the foreign corporation. In either event, the excess of the amount realized upon the sale or liquidation by the U.S. shareholder over the basis in the stock interest disposed of was usually taxed as long-term capital gain. By contrast, if the U.S. shareholder had repatriated the foreign earnings through dividend distributions, the earnings would have been taxed as ordinary income. At the time that Section 1248 was enacted, the capital gain preference for both individual and corporate taxpayers was quite substantial.

Section 1248 prevents this result by, under specified circumstances, treating the gain recognized on sale or exchange (or through liquidation or redemption) of the U.S. shareholder's stock as a dividend to the extent that the gain reflects the shareholder's interest in post–1962 undistributed earnings attributable to the stock sold or exchanged. By converting what would otherwise be long-term capital gain into ordinary income, Section 1248 eliminated one of the major advantages once presented in operating through a controlled foreign corporation. This is especially true when individual ten-percent U.S. shareholders not entitled to the indirect foreign tax credit are involved, although the provision has reduced significance in the light of the fact that the "qualified dividend income" of noncorporate taxpayers is taxed (at least for tax years starting before 2011) at preferential capital gains tax rates.[27]

In the case of a U.S. corporate shareholder, however, dividend treatment under Section 1248 is frequently more favorable than capital gain treatment because dividends under Section 1248 carry indirect foreign tax credits for foreign taxes paid with respect to the earnings deemed distributed. Reg. § 1.1248–1(d). Additionally, realization of dividend income under Section 1248 by a sale of stock or liquidation of a controlled foreign corporation typically has the advantage of avoiding the foreign withholding tax usually imposed on actual dividends; gain on a sale of stock or a liquidation is usually exempt from withholding tax. If the credit for the withholding tax would not be usable because it exceeds the applicable foreign tax credit limitation (discussed in Chapters 5 and 7), avoiding the tax may represent a real saving. Thus, under current law, in the light of the absence of a capital gain rate preference for corporate taxpayers and the availability of an indirect foreign tax credit, Section 1248 in many cases is more of a benefit for U.S. corporations than a burden.

Not all U.S. persons owning stock in all foreign corporations are swept into the Section 1248 net. The provision applies only to U.S.

27. Section 1(h)(11) will expire for tax years starting after 2010 unless it is extended or made permanent by Congress in new legislation. Amounts treated as dividends under Section 1248(a) may constitute "qualified dividend income" for purposes of the preferential tax rates in Section 1(h)(11) if the controlled foreign corporation is a "qualified foreign corporation" and the other requirements of Section 1(h)(11) are met. See IRS Notice 2004–70, § 4, 2004–2 C.B. 724, 726.

persons who owned or were considered to have owned (under the rules of Section 958) ten percent or more of the voting power of the foreign corporation at any time during the five-year period before the sale or exchange when the corporation was a controlled foreign corporation (within the meaning of Section 957). This means that Section 1248 can apply even though a foreign corporation is not a controlled foreign corporation at the time that the shareholder sells the corporation's stock if the corporation met the definition of a controlled foreign corporation at any time during the five years before the stock sale at a time when the selling shareholder met the definition of a "U.S. shareholder" in Section 951(b). See Reg. § 1.1248–1(a)(5), Ex. 1. It also means that Section 1248 can apply to a U.S. person's sale of stock in a foreign corporation even if the U.S. person does not at the time of sale meet the definition of a "U.S. shareholder" in Section 951(b) if the U.S. person met that definition at any time during the five years before the sale of the stock at a time when the foreign corporation was a controlled foreign corporation. See Reg. § 1.1248–1(a)(5), Ex. 2.

If these conditions are met, the gain realized must be included in the gross income of the shareholder as a dividend to the extent of the earnings and profits[28] of such corporation attributable to the stock sold or exchanged that were accumulated after 1962 during periods in which (1) such stock was held by the shareholder and (2) the corporation was a controlled foreign corporation.[29] Any gain in excess of the amount treated as a dividend under Section 1248 may qualify for long-term capital gain treatment under the normal Code rules that determine the character of gain from the sale of stock.

If the selling shareholder is an individual and the stock sold is a capital asset held for more than one year in the selling shareholder's hands, Section 1248(b) limits the *tax* attributable to the deemed dividend under Section 1248(a) to the sum of two amounts. The first amount is the selling shareholder's pro rata share of the excess of the U.S. taxes that would have been paid by the foreign corporation if it were a U.S. corporation on its income attributable to periods after 1962 during which the stock sold or exchanged had been held by the selling shareholder, over the foreign income taxes paid by the foreign corporation on such income. The second amount is the tax that would result by including in gross income as long-term capital gain an amount equal to the excess of the deemed dividend included in the selling shareholder's income under Sec-

28. Section 1248(d)(4) provides that any item of gross income of the foreign corporation treated as income effectively connected with a U.S. trade or business is not included in the earnings and profits to be taken into account. The statute also provides that earnings included in income by a shareholder under other sections (e.g., Sections 951 and 1293) are not subject to Section 1248 dividend treatment. § 1248(d)(1) and (6).

29. The U.S. shareholder bears the burden of showing the amount of the earnings and profits of the foreign corporation to be taken into account; if this burden is not met, the entire gain from the sale or exchange is treated as a dividend. § 1248(h).

tion 1248(a), over the first amount. The calculation of this limitation is illustrated at Reg. § 1.1248–4(b)(2), Exs. 1 and 2.

Unlike actual dividends, amounts treated as a deemed dividend to the selling shareholder under Section 1248 do not reduce the controlled foreign corporation's earnings and profits at the time of recognition of the Section 1248 deemed dividend. See Rev. Rul. 90–31, 1990–1 C.B. 147. To prevent double taxation of the same amounts, Section 959 treats the amount of the deemed dividend under Section 1248 as previously taxed earnings and profits (i.e., as if the Section 1248 deemed dividend had been included in income under Section 951(a)(1)(A)) and, thus, not taxable on a later distribution. § 959(e). Accordingly, as the IRS held in Revenue Ruling 90–31, the controlled foreign corporation's earnings and profits are decreased by the amount previously included in the gross income of the transferor shareholder as a Section 1248 deemed dividend at the time of actual distribution of the previously taxed income amount that is attributable to such deemed dividend and nontaxable under Section 959(a) and (e).

There are some ways in which a U.S. shareholder may be able to avoid Section 1248 dividend treatment. For example, an individual shareholder may be able to avoid Section 1248 by retaining the stock until death. At that point its tax basis to the legatee is stepped up to its fair market value under Section 1014 without tax on the inherent gain (possibly other than for 2010, by reason of the one-year repeal of the federal estate tax). Accordingly, the legatee may sell or exchange the stock immediately without realizing any gain that could be subject to Section 1248. In addition, a shareholder who cannot sell or exchange stock without dividend treatment may, in some cases, be able to benefit from the share of the accumulated earnings by borrowing and pledging the stock as collateral. See *Ludwig v. Commissioner*, at ¶ 6215.

[¶ 6250]

PROBLEM

Heavy Metal Manufacturing, Inc. ("Heavy Metal"), a U.S. corporation, owns 80 percent of the stock of Foreign Base Company, Inc., a controlled foreign corporation within the meaning of Section 957(a). The other 20 percent of Foreign Base Company, Inc.'s stock is owned by Mary, a U.S. citizen. Heavy Metal and Mary have owned all of the stock of Foreign Base Company, Inc. since its incorporation in 1987. Since that time, Foreign Base Company, Inc. has $1,200,000 of net earnings from foreign business and investment activities on which it has paid foreign income taxes of $120,000. Only $200,000 of that income and $20,000 of the foreign income taxes paid on the income are attributable to amounts that have been previously included in Heavy Metal's and Mary's gross incomes under Section 951 by reason of the income being Subpart F income. Foreign Base Company, Inc. has not made any dividend distributions to Heavy Metal or Mary.

During the current year, Heavy Metal sells one fourth of its stock interest in Foreign Base Company, Inc. (i.e., a 20–percent stock interest in Foreign Base Company, Inc.), in which Heavy Metal has an adjusted basis of $50,000, for $300,000 (its fair market value at the time of sale). Mary sells all of her stock in Foreign Base Company, Inc., in which she has an adjusted basis of $50,000, for the same price, $300,000. What are the federal income tax consequences to Heavy Metal and Mary on account of these stock sales? (Do *not* attempt to compute the Section 1248(b) limitation on Mary's tax liability. Assume that no foreign country imposes any income tax on these stock sales.)

[¶ 6255]

I. EFFECT OF CONTROLLED FOREIGN CORPORATION STATUS ON CALCULATION OF U.S. SHAREHOLDER'S FOREIGN TAX CREDITS

Under the separate basket and look-through rules for determining foreign tax credit limitations enacted in 1986 and substantially revised in later years, important foreign tax credit consequences may turn on whether a foreign corporation is classified as a controlled foreign corporation. As discussed more fully in Chapter 7, income inclusions by a U.S. shareholder under Section 951(a)(1) and dividends, interest, rents and royalties received by a U.S. shareholder from a controlled foreign corporation are subject to the separate foreign tax credit limitations (e.g., most importantly that for passive income) in accordance with look-through rules set forth in Section 904(d)(3). These look-through rules treat the controlled foreign corporation in effect as a conduit. They take into account the extent to which the income of the payor controlled foreign corporation is itself subject to one or more of these separate limitations. See ¶ 7085. Thus, broadly speaking, if 25 percent of the earnings of the payor foreign corporation consisted of active business income that would be subject to the Section 904(d)(1)(B) general category income limitation, 25 percent of an income inclusion under Section 951(a)(1) or a dividend, interest, royalty or rent payment made by the controlled foreign corporation to its U.S. shareholder generally would be subject to the general category income limitation.

By contrast, for tax years starting before 2003, dividends from each "non-controlled Section 902 foreign corporation," as defined in former Section 904(d)(2)(E), had to be included in the separate Section 904(d)(1)(E) basket limitation, as in effect under prior law, and were not included in the general limitation of former Section 904(d)(1)(I). Before 2003, no look-through rule applied to characterizing, for foreign tax credit limitation purposes, dividends, interest, rents and royalties paid by a foreign corporation which was not a controlled foreign corporation because the U.S. shareholders owned in the aggregate only 50 percent or less of its stock.

As discussed in Chapters 5 and 7, the 2004 JOBS Act repealed the separate basket limitation in Section 904(d)(1)(E) for dividends from noncontrolled Section 902 corporations, effective retroactively for tax years starting after 2002. Under the JOBS Act, the look-through rule in Section 904(d)(4) applies to determine the foreign credit limitation basket into which dividends from noncontrolled Section 902 corporations will fall. Under that look-through rule, the dividend income will be placed into the appropriate foreign tax credit limitation basket in proportion to the ratio of the (1) the portion of the foreign corporation's earnings and profits attributable to income in that basket, to (2) the foreign corporation's total earnings and profits. Note, however, that unlike the look-through rules in Section 904(d)(3), the look-through rule in Section 904(d)(4) for noncontrolled Section 902 corporations applies only to dividends received from such corporations, and not to interest, rent or royalties paid by the corporation. Thus, the look-through rules in Section 904(d)(3) for controlled foreign corporations are still more advantageous than the look-through rule applicable to noncontrolled Section 902 corporations. In addition, the JOBS Act reduced the number of foreign tax credit limitation baskets in Section 904(d) from eight (formerly nine) to two, effective for tax years starting after 2006, and thereby made the look-through rules in Section 904(d)(3) less significant for 2007 and later years.

[¶ 6260]

J. SALES AND EXCHANGES OF PATENTS AND OTHER INDUSTRIAL PROPERTY RIGHTS TO CONTROLLED FOREIGN CORPORATIONS (SECTION 1249)

Before the enactment of Section 1249 in 1962, many U.S. corporations owning valuable foreign patents and knowhow used foreign licensing base companies in effect to convert what would otherwise have been royalty income taxable as ordinary business income into proceeds of sale taxable as long-term capital gain. This device was sometimes called a patent and knowhow "bailout." In cases in which for business reasons the U.S. corporation was unwilling to make a sufficiently unrestricted grant of foreign patent and knowhow rights to independent licensees to qualify the royalties received as the proceeds of a sale of rights, the rights were sold outright by the U.S. corporation to its wholly owned foreign base company for payments equal to a substantial percentage (for example, 50 percent) of the royalty income to be realized by the base company from licenses to independent licensees. The latter licenses would contain the restrictions desired from a business point of view that would have prevented the licenses from qualifying as sales if the licenses had run directly from the U.S. parent corporation to the independent foreign licensees. A substantial portion (50 percent in our example) of the royalty income earned by the base company that was paid as purchase price to the U.S. parent was thus converted into long-term capital gain. Section 1249 put the damper on such arrangements by treating gain realized on the transfer by sale or exchange of "a patent, an invention, model, or design (whether or not patented), a copyright, a secret formula or process, or any other similar property right" to a foreign corporation as ordinary income if the transferor is a U.S. person that owns more than 50 percent of the foreign corporation's voting power. The indirect and constructive ownership rules in Section 958 (discussed at ¶ 6030) apply in determining stock ownership for this purpose. § 1249(b).

K. PASSIVE FOREIGN INVESTMENT COMPANY PROVISIONS

[¶ 6265]

1. INTRODUCTION

The Tax Reform Act of 1986 added the passive foreign investment company ("PFIC") to the panoply of statutory inroads on the deferral principle. See §§ 1291 through 1298. The objective of the PFIC provisions is to deprive a U.S. taxpayer of the economic benefit of deferral of U.S. tax on the taxpayer's share of the undistributed income of a foreign investment company that has predominantly passive income, however small the individual or aggregate interests of U.S. persons in the company may be. Congress concluded that achieving this objective was necessary to eliminate the advantage previously enjoyed by U.S. shareholders in foreign investment funds not controlled by U.S. persons, who were not taxed on current income of the fund, over U.S. shareholders investing in domestic investment funds, who were.

Although the PFIC provisions were aimed particularly at U.S. persons holding stock in foreign investment funds, they have a much broader impact than their legislative background would suggest. The PFIC provisions may apply to any U.S. person holding stock in any foreign corporation, even one engaged in an active foreign business such as manufacturing, for any tax year in which the corporation derives enough passive income or owns enough passive assets to meet the definition of a PFIC. However, under a change made in 1997 to eliminate an overlap between the Subpart F and PFIC rules, the PFIC rules do not apply to a U.S. person owning stock in a foreign corporation during periods after 1997 when the U.S. person meets the definition of a "U.S. shareholder" in Section 951(b) and the corporation meets the definition of a "controlled foreign corporation" in Section 957(a). The PFIC rules do, however, continue to apply to other U.S. persons owning stock in such a foreign corporation if it meets the definition of a PFIC in Section 1297.

The PFIC provisions contain three sets of rules with three different mechanisms for ending or recapturing the benefits of deferring U.S. income tax on the foreign earnings of PFICs:

(1) ***Current inclusion under qualified electing fund election.*** Under one set of rules, which apply to PFICs that are "qualified electing funds," the electing U.S. persons holding stock in the PFIC include currently in gross income their pro rata shares of the PFIC's earnings. Moreover, these U.S. persons may elect to defer payment of the tax, subject to an interest charge, on the portion of the PFIC's earnings not currently received.

(2) ***Current taxation under mark-to-market election.*** Under a second set of rules, if the stock of a PFIC is "marketable stock," a U.S. person owning stock in the PFIC may elect to mark to market the value of the PFIC's stock each year. If this election is made, the U.S. person includes in gross income the excess of the fair market value of the PFIC's stock at the end of the year over the U.S. person's adjusted basis in the stock. Alternatively, if U.S. person's basis in the PFIC's stock exceeds the fair market value of the stock at the end of the year, the U.S. person is allowed to deduct such excess (subject to a limitation).

(3) ***Deferral of tax, but with an interest charge, until sale of PFIC stock or "excess distribution" is received.*** Under the third set of rules, which applies to PFICs that are not qualified electing funds and for which the U.S. person owning stock in the PFIC cannot make a mark-to-market election or has not made such an election, the U.S. persons holding stock in the PFIC pay tax when they receive a distribution from the PFIC or sell their shares of PFIC stock, but also must pay an interest charge attributable to the value of the tax deferral when they receive an unusually large distribution (called an "excess distribution") or have gain from the disposition of the PFIC stock.

2. DEFINITION OF PFIC

[¶ 6270]

a. Basic Definition

A foreign corporation is a PFIC if at least 75 percent of its gross income is passive income ("income test") or the average percentage of its assets producing passive income or held for the production of such income is at least 50 percent ("asset test"). § 1297(a).

For purposes of the income test, passive income is defined in Section 1297(b) as income of a kind that would be foreign personal holding company income under Section 954(c), subject to four exceptions. The first two exceptions relate to income from the active conduct of a banking or insurance business. § 1297(b)(2)(A) and (B). The third covers interest, dividend, rent or royalty income received from a related person[30] to the extent that such income is properly allocable (under regulations) to income of such related person that is not passive income. § 1297(b)(2)(C). The fourth covers certain export trade income of an export trade corporation discussed at ¶ 11,140. § 1297(b)(2)(D).

As a general rule, the asset test for determining whether a foreign corporation meets the definition of a PFIC is applied by using the value of the corporation's assets. § 1297(f)(1). However, Congress recognized that many foreign corporations hold assets (such as tangible or intangible business assets) that are difficult to value. Thus, to ameliorate the administrative burden of such valuation issues for both taxpayers and the IRS, the statute allows a foreign corporation to elect to apply the PFIC asset test using the adjusted bases of its assets (as determined for earnings and profits purposes) in lieu of their value. Once made, an election to use adjusted bases may be revoked only with the IRS's consent. However, a publicly traded corporation is required to use the value of its assets in applying the asset test and cannot make the election to use adjusted bases. § 1297(f)(1)(A), (f)(2). Moreover, a PFIC that is also a controlled foreign corporation but is not publicly traded is required to use the adjusted bases of its assets in applying the asset test for PFIC status, with no option to use the value of its assets. § 1297(f)(2)(A). Congress required that a controlled foreign corporation measure its assets by their adjusted bases because such measurement was well established under Section 956 and Congress saw no good reason to allow a different method to be used for purposes of the PFIC asset test. See S. Prt. No. 103–37, 103d Cong., 1st Sess. 169 (1993).

Congress believed that it was appropriate for a foreign corporation to take into account, for purposes of applying the PFIC asset test, certain tangible property that it used in an active business but did not own. See S. Prt. No. 103–37, 103d Cong., 1st Sess. 169 (1993). Thus, certain leased properties are treated as assets held by the foreign corporation for purposes of the PFIC asset test. This rule applies to tangible personal property with respect to which the foreign corporation is the lessee under a lease with a term of at least 12 months. The amount taken into account with respect to leased property for purposes of applying the asset test is the unamortized portion of the present value of the payments under the lease. However, property leased by a corporation is not taken into account in testing for PFIC status under the asset test if either the lessor is a related person (as that term is defined in Section 954(d)(3)) with respect

30. "Related person" is as defined in Section 954(d)(3) (applied by substituting "foreign corporation" for "controlled foreign corporation"). § 1297(b) (last sentence). See ¶ 6155 (discussing the definition of "related person" in Section 954(d)(3)).

to the lessee, or a principal purpose of leasing the property was to avoid the PFIC provisions. § 1298(d).

Note that the tests for determining whether a foreign corporation is a PFIC are applied on a year-by-year basis. Thus, a foreign corporation may be a PFIC in some tax years and not in others.

[¶ 6275]

b. Special Rules Applicable to Controlled Foreign Corporations

In the case of a foreign corporation that is a controlled foreign corporation (within the meaning of Section 957(a)), the adjusted basis of the corporation's assets for purposes of the PFIC asset test is modified to take into account certain research and experimental expenditures and certain payments for the use of intangible property (as defined in Section 936(h)(3)(B)) that is licensed to the controlled foreign corporation. First, the aggregate adjusted basis of the total assets of the controlled foreign corporation is increased by the total amount of research and experimental expenditures made by the controlled foreign corporation in the current tax year and the two most recent prior tax years. § 1298(e)(1). Congress provided this special rule for research and experimental expenditures in recognition that such expenditures "enhance the corporation's ability to generate active business income over an extended period." See S. Prt. No. 103–37, 103d Cong., 1st Sess. 169 (1993).

Second, the aggregate adjusted basis of the total assets of the controlled foreign corporation is increased by an amount equal to three times the total payments made during the tax year to unrelated persons and related U.S. persons for the use of intangible property with respect to which the controlled foreign corporation is a licensee and which the controlled foreign corporation uses in the active conduct of its trade or business. Payments made to related foreign persons are not taken into account. In addition, payments made by a controlled foreign corporation for the use of intangible property are disregarded if a principal purpose of licensing the intangible property was to avoid the PFIC rules. § 1298(e)(2). This special rule was enacted because Congress believed it was appropriate for a controlled foreign corporation to take into account, for purposes of applying the PFIC asset test, certain intangible property that it used in an active business but did not own. See S. Prt. No. 103–37, 103d Cong., 1st Sess. 169 (1993).

[¶ 6280]

c. Look–Through Rule for 25–Percent-or-More Owned Subsidiaries and Special Rule for Certain Stock in 25–Percent-or-More Owned U.S. Corporations

For purposes of the PFIC income and asset tests, a look-through rule applies to a foreign corporation that owns, directly or indirectly, at least 25 percent (by value) of the stock of another corporation, whether U.S. or foreign. This rule is intended to prevent foreign corporations that own subsidiaries primarily engaged in active business from being classified as a PFIC. Under this rule, the foreign corporation is treated as owning its proportionate share of the other corporation's assets and as receiving directly its proportionate share of the other corporation's income in determining whether the foreign corporation is a PFIC. Moreover, in applying the PFIC tests to the foreign corporation, amounts such as dividends and interest received from the 25–percent-or-more-owned subsidiary are eliminated from the foreign corporation's income for purposes of the income test, and the foreign corporation's stock or debt investment in the subsidiary is eliminated from the foreign corporation's assets for purposes of the asset test. § 1297(c).

Another special rule may apply for purposes of determining whether a foreign corporation is a PFIC if (i) the foreign corporation owns at least 25 percent (by value) of the stock of a U.S. corporation, and (ii) the foreign corporation is subject to accumulated earnings tax in Section 531 (discussed at ¶ 6365) or waives any U.S. treaty benefits which would otherwise prevent the application of the tax. Under this special rule, for purposes of applying the PFIC tests to the foreign corporation, any "qualified stock" held by the 25–percent-or-more-owned U.S. subsidiary is treated as an asset which does not produce passive income (and is not held for the production of passive income) and any amount included in income with respect to the stock is not treated as passive income. Thus, in applying the look-through rule that applies to 25–percent owned corporations, the foreign corporation is treated as owning a nonpassive asset, through its U.S. subsidiary, if this special provision applies. § 1298(b)(8)(A). "Qualified stock" is stock in a C corporation which is a U.S. corporation and which is not a regulated investment company or real estate investment trust. § 1298(b)(8)(B). This rule attempts to reduce the potential disparity in tax treatment of U.S. individual shareholders who hold U.S. stock investments through a U.S. holding company and those who hold such investments through a foreign holding company.

[¶ 6285]

d. Special Rules for Start–Up Year and Corporations Changing Businesses

A foreign corporation is not treated as a PFIC during the first tax year that it has gross income (called the "start-up year") if three requirements are met. First, no predecessor of the corporation was a PFIC. Second, the corporation establishes to the satisfaction of the IRS that it will not be a PFIC for either of the first two tax years after the start-up year. Third, the corporation is not in fact a PFIC for either of the first two years after the start-up year. § 1298(b)(2). This exception recognizes that even a foreign corporation that will be engaged primarily in an active foreign business may have predominantly passive income during its first year of operation.

A foreign corporation that is changing businesses is not treated as a PFIC for a tax year if three requirements are met. First, neither the corporation nor any predecessor was a PFIC. Second, the corporation establishes to the satisfaction of the IRS that (i) substantially all of its passive income for the tax year is attributable to the proceeds from disposition of one or more active trades or businesses, and (ii) it will not be a PFIC for either of the first two tax years after such tax year. Third, the corporation is not in fact a PFIC for either of such two tax years. § 1298(b)(3). This exception recognizes that a foreign corporation that is primarily engaged in an active foreign business may have predominantly passive income in a year when it is changing from one active business to another.

[¶ 6290]

e. Continuing Taint of PFIC Status for Some Shareholders' Stock

The determination of whether a foreign corporation is a PFIC under the above rules is made on a year-by-year basis. Consequently, a corporation may be a PFIC in some tax years and not in others. However, a special rule in Section 1298(b)(1) provides that a foreign corporation's status as a PFIC for even a single tax year may continue to taint the shareholders' stock even if the corporation does not meet the PFIC definition in any other tax year. Under that rule, stock held by a taxpayer will be treated as stock in a PFIC if, at any time during the taxpayer's holding period for such stock, the corporation (or any predecessor) was a PFIC which was not a qualified electing fund. Thus, a taxpayer subject to this rule faces the Section 1291 interest charge on deferred taxes when the shareholder disposes of the corporation's stock or receives an "excess distribution."

There are two ways that a taxpayer can purge the stock of its PFIC taint and thereby avoid this rule. First, the taxpayer can prevent the application of Section 1298(b)(1) by electing qualified electing fund treatment with respect to the PFIC during all of the time that the shareholder holds the stock. Second, the taxpayer can purge the stock of its PFIC taint by electing to recognize gain on the last day of the last tax year on which the corporation was a PFIC as if the stock had been sold for its fair market value on that day.

[¶ 6295]

f. Overlap Between Controlled Foreign Corporation and PFIC Provisions

As discussed above, a foreign corporation may meet both the definition of a "controlled foreign corporation," as defined in Section 957, and a PFIC, as defined in Section 1297(a). However, Section 1297(e)(1), added to the Code in 1997, provides that a foreign corporation will not be treated as a PFIC with respect to a shareholder during the "qualified portion" of the shareholder's holding period for the stock in the corporation. The "qualified portion" of the holding period is the portion of the shareholder's holding period after 1997, during which the shareholder is a "U.S. shareholder" (as defined in Section 951(b)) and the corporation is a controlled foreign corporation (as defined in Section 957). § 1297(e)(2). Thus, a U.S. shareholder that is subject to current inclusion under the Subpart F rules with respect to stock in a PFIC is not also subject to the PFIC rules with respect to such stock. This means, for example, that the U.S. shareholder of a PFIC that is also a controlled foreign corporation will be able to continue to defer U.S. tax on the earnings of the controlled foreign corporation that are not Subpart F income, because the provisions of Subpart F will not provide constructive dividend treatment for such earnings and the PFIC provisions will not apply to the shareholder by reason of Section 1297(e). However, the PFIC provisions continue to apply to other U.S. persons owning stock in the PFIC who are not U.S. shareholders (within the meaning of Section 951(b)).

If a shareholder is not subject to the PFIC provisions by reason of Section 1297(e)(1) and then ceases to qualify for such treatment either because the shareholder is no longer a U.S. shareholder (as defined in Section 951(b)) or the PFIC is no longer a controlled foreign corporation, the shareholder's holding period for the stock, for purposes of the PFIC rules, is treated as starting immediately after such cessation. § 1297(e)(3)(A). However, if a U.S. person owning stock in a PFIC is subject to the rules applicable to PFICs that are not qualified electing funds before it is eligible for the special rule in Section 1297(e)(1), the stock held by the shareholder continues to be treated as PFIC stock. The U.S. person may purge the stock of its PFIC taint and obtain the benefit of this holding period rule by making an election under Section 1298(b)(1) to recognize gain on the stock and paying tax and an interest charge on such gain. § 1297(e)(3)(B); see also H.R. Rep. No. 148, 105th Cong., 1st Sess. 534 (1997).

The special rule in Section 1297(e)(1) does not apply to stock treated as owned by a person under Section 1298(a)(4) by reason of the person having an option to acquire such stock, unless that person shows that the stock is owned (within the meaning of Section 958(a)) by a U.S. shareholder (as defined in Section 951(b)) who is not exempt from U.S. income tax. § 1297(e)(4).

[¶ 6300]

3. TAX AND INTEREST CHARGE ON DISPOSITION OF PFIC STOCK OR ON RECEIPT OF "EXCESS DISTRIBUTIONS"

In the case of a PFIC that is not a qualified electing fund, the advantage of deferral in a PFIC is removed by requiring U.S. persons owning shares in a PFIC to pay U.S. tax plus an interest charge based on the value of the tax deferral at the time the shareholder disposes of the PFIC stock at a gain or receives an "excess distribution" from the PFIC. § 1291(a)(1) and (2). An excess distribution is any current year distribution in respect of the PFIC stock to the extent that it represents a ratable portion of the total distributions on the stock during the year that are in excess of 125 percent of the average amount of distributions in respect of the stock during the three prior years. § 1291(b). The excess distribution is deemed to be earned ratably over the shareholder's holding period for the stock. § 1291(a)(1)(A).[31] In the case of a disposition of stock, the entire gain recognized on the disposition is treated as an excess distribution. § 1291(a)(2). The following example, based on an example in Staff of Joint Comm. on Tax'n, 100th Cong., 1st Sess., General Explanation of the Tax Reform Act of 1986, at 1027–28 (1987), illustrates the calculation of an excess distribution.

> *Example.* On January 1 of year 1, Samantha, a U.S. citizen, acquires 1,000 shares of stock in FC, a foreign corporation that is a passive foreign investment company. She acquires another 1,000 shares of FC stock on January 1 of year 2. (FC uses a calendar year as its tax year.) During years 1 through 5, Samantha receives the following distributions from FC:

31. Distributions (including excess distributions) from a PFIC are not qualified dividend income for Section 1(h)(11) purposes because Section 1(h)(11)(C)(iii) excludes PFICs from the definition of a qualified foreign corporation. See IRS Notice 2004–70, § 7.01, 2004–2 C.B. 724, 727. Section 1(h)(11) will expire for tax years starting after 2010 unless it is extended or made permanent by Congress in new legislation.

Date of Distribution	*Amount of Distribution*
Dec. 31 of year 1	$ 500
Dec. 31 of year 2	$1,000
Dec. 31 of year 3	$1,000
Dec. 31 of year 4	$1,000
Apr. 1 of year 5	$1,500
Oct. 1 of year 5	$ 500

Under Section 1291, none of the distributions received before year 5 are excess distributions since the amount of each distribution with respect to a share of stock is 50 cents. However, with respect to the distributions during year 5, the total distribution with respect to each share of stock is $1, resulting in a total excess distribution with respect to each share of 37.5 cents ($1 minus 62.5 cents (1.25 multiplied by 50 cents)).

Accordingly, the total excess distribution for the FC tax year ending December 31 of year 5 is $750 (37.5 cents per share multiplied by 2,000 shares). This excess distribution must be allocated ratably between the two distributions during year 5. Thus, $562.50 (75 percent of the excess distribution, i.e., $750 multiplied by $1,500/$2,000) is allocated to the April 1 distribution and $187.50 (the remaining 25 percent of the excess distribution, i.e., $750 multiplied by $500/$2,000) is allocated to the October 1 distribution. These amounts are then ratably allocated to each block of stock outstanding on the relevant distribution date. For the distribution on April 1 of year 5, $281.25 of the excess distribution is allocated to the block of stock acquired on January 1 of year 1 and $281.25 is allocated to the block of stock acquired on January 1 of year 2. The $187.50 excess distribution on October 1 of year 5 is also allocated evenly between the two blocks of stock outstanding on the date of the distribution. Finally, the excess distribution is allocated ratably to each day in Samantha's holding period for each block of stock in accordance with Section 1291(a)(1).

The U.S. tax due in the year of disposition (or year of receipt of an excess distribution) is the sum of (1) the U.S. tax computed using the highest rate of U.S. tax for the shareholder (without regard to other income or expenses the shareholder may have) on income attributed to prior years (called "the aggregate increases in taxes" in Section 1291(c)(1)), plus (2) interest imposed on the deferred tax (i.e., on the aggregate increases in taxes), plus (3) the U.S. tax on the gain attributed to the year of disposition (or year of receipt of the distribution) and to years in which the foreign corporation was not a PFIC (for which no interest is due). §§ 1291(a), (c). (Items (1) and (2) together are called the "deferred tax amount" in Section 1291.) Item (2), the interest charge on the deferred tax, is computed for the period starting on the due date for the prior tax year to which the gain on distribution or disposition is attributed and ending on the due date for the current tax year in which the distribution or disposition occurs. Interest is computed by using the rates and method that apply under Section 6621 for underpayments of tax for such period. § 1291(c)(3).

The amount of the excess distribution allocated to the year of disposition (or receipt) and to the part of the U.S. person's holding period before the first day of the first tax year of the corporation after 1986 in which it was a PFIC is treated as ordinary income. § 1291(a)(1)(B). The portions of distributions that are not characterized as excess distributions are subject to tax in the current year under the normal rules of the Code.

Distributions from a PFIC to a U.S. corporation are eligible for the deemed paid foreign tax credit under Section 902, but the taxpayer must navigate the computational complexities of Section 1291(g). For purposes of claiming any withholding tax as a foreign tax credit, the total amount of the distribution, including any excess distribution amount, is included in gross income in the year of receipt.

Except as otherwise provided in the regulations, a taxpayer that uses any stock in a PFIC as security for a loan is treated as having disposed of the stock. § 1298(b)(6). Thus, the Section 1291 rules may apply to such a deemed disposition.

To the extent provided in the regulations, if a U.S. person transfers stock in a PFIC, Section 1291(f) will override otherwise applicable nonrecognition provisions and require the U.S. person to recognize as gain from the sale or exchange of the stock the excess of the fair market value of the stock over the U.S. person's basis in the stock. The Section 1291 rules will apply to such gain.

[¶ 6305]

4. TREATMENT OF "QUALIFIED ELECTING FUNDS"

"Qualified electing funds" are treated in a different manner. Every U.S. person who owns stock in a PFIC and who has elected qualified electing fund treatment with respect to that PFIC must currently include in gross income the person's pro rata share of the PFIC's current earnings and profits. § 1293. However, shareholders in qualified electing funds may elect to defer U.S. tax on amounts included in income for which no current distributions have been received, but must pay an interest charge on the deferred tax. § 1294.

A shareholder who has elected qualified electing fund treatment includes in gross income the shareholder's pro rata share of the fund's ordinary earnings for the year as ordinary income and the pro rata share of the fund's net capital gain for the year as long-term capital gain. § 1293(a)(1).[32] Thus, unlike current inclusions treated as constructive

32. Amounts included in a PFIC shareholder's gross income under Section 1293(a) are not qualified dividend income for Section 1(h)(11) purposes because Section 1(h)(11)(C)(iii) excludes PFICs from the definition of a qualified foreign corporation. See IRS Notice 2004–70, § 7.01, 2004–2 C.B. 724, 727.

dividends under Subpart F, the qualified electing fund rules allow the shareholder to retain the long-term capital gain character of income derived at the PFIC level. A shareholder's pro rata share is the amount which would have been distributed with respect to the shareholder's stock if, on each day during the fund's tax year, the fund had distributed to the shareholder a pro rata share of that day's ratable share of the fund's ordinary earnings and net capital gains for that year. § 1293(b). The shareholder includes in gross income its pro rata share of the fund's earnings for the shareholder's tax year in which or with which the tax year of the fund ends. § 1293(a)(2).

The election to have a PFIC treated as a qualified electing fund is made at the U.S. shareholder level on a shareholder-by-shareholder basis rather than at the PFIC level. Some shareholders may elect, while others may not. The shareholder election, however, is available only if the PFIC complies with information-disclosure requirements, which include supplying information needed to determine the PFIC's ordinary earnings and net capital gain. Once made, a taxpayer may revoke the qualified electing fund election only with the consent of the IRS. § 1295.

To prevent double taxation, distributions by a PFIC to a U.S. person that has elected qualified electing fund treatment are excluded from gross income under Section 1293(c) to the extent they are paid out of earnings and profits which the person has already included in income under Section 1293(a). To prevent double taxation of amounts already included in gross income when a U.S. person sells the stock of the PFIC that is a qualified electing fund, the U.S. person's basis in the PFIC stock is increased by amounts included in gross income under Section 1293(a). The U.S. person's basis is then decreased by distributions that are excluded from gross income under Section 1293(c). § 1293(d).

In the case of amounts included in income from a qualified electing fund by a U.S. corporation owning at least ten percent of the PFIC's voting stock, foreign tax credits are allowed to the same extent as, and under rules similar to those that apply to, constructive dividends from controlled foreign corporations. § 1293(f).

[¶ 6310]

5. COORDINATION OF SECTION 1291 RULES WITH QUALIFIED ELECTING FUND RULES

The deferred tax and interest charge rules in Section 1291 do not apply to a U.S. person if the PFIC was a qualified electing fund with respect to that person for each of the corporation's tax years (1) that started after 1986 and for which it was a PFIC and (2) that included any part of the U.S. person's holding period. § 1291(d)(1). Under this rule, a U.S. person's gain from disposition of a PFIC's stock and receipt of excess distributions from a PFIC *will* be subject to the Section 1291 rules if for any tax year after 1986 the corporation is a PFIC but not a qualified electing fund with respect to that U.S. person.

However, if a U.S. person owns stock in a PFIC which was not a qualified electing fund for prior tax years but has now become a qualified electing fund, a special election in Section 1291(d)(2)(A) allows the U.S. person to purge the stock of the Section 1291 taint for later tax years. The U.S. person may make this election only for the first tax year in which the PFIC becomes a qualified electing fund with respect to the U.S. person. Under the election, the U.S. person recognizes gain on the first day of the first tax year that the PFIC becomes a qualified electing fund as if the U.S. person's PFIC stock had been sold for its fair market value on that day. This gain is subject to the deferred tax and interest charge rules in Section 1291. The U.S. person's adjusted basis in the PFIC stock is increased by the recognized gain and the U.S. person is treated as having a new holding period for the stock. Thereafter, the U.S. person is taxed under the qualified electing fund rules. § 1291(d)(2)(C).

An alternative election for purging the Section 1291 taint is available to a U.S. person that owns stock in a controlled foreign corporation that is a PFIC and that becomes a qualified electing fund. Under the alternative election, the U.S. person includes in gross income as a dividend its share of the corporation's earnings and profits accumulated after 1986 and during the period the U.S. person held the stock while the corporation was a PFIC. This dividend is treated as a distribution for purposes of the Section 1291 excess distribution rules. § 1291(d)(2)(B). The U.S. person's basis in the PFIC stock is increased by the amount of the dividend and the U.S. person is treated as having a new holding period in the stock. Thereafter, the U.S. person is taxed under the qualified electing fund rules. § 1291(d)(2)(C).

[¶ 6315]

6. MARK-TO-MARKET ELECTION FOR MARKETABLE PFIC STOCK

There is an alternative mechanism for ending deferral with respect to a U.S. person's income earned through a PFIC. Under Section 1296, a U.S. person owning stock in a PFIC may elect to mark to market the stock of a PFIC if it is "marketable stock." Under this provision, if the fair market value of the stock in the PFIC at the end of the tax year exceeds the U.S. person's adjusted basis in the stock, the U.S. person includes in income the amount of such excess.[33] § 1296(a)(1); Reg. § 1.1296–1(c)(1). If

33. Amounts included in a PFIC shareholder's gross income under Section 1296 are not qualified dividend income for Section 1(h)(11) purposes because Section 1(h)(11)(C)(iii) excludes PFICs from the definition of a qualified foreign corporation. See IRS Notice 2004–70, § 7.01, 2004–2 C.B. 724, 727.

the U.S. person's adjusted basis in the PFIC's stock exceeds the fair market value of the stock at the end of the tax year, the U.S. person is entitled to a deduction equal to the lesser of (i) the amount of such excess or (ii) the "unreversed inclusions" with respect to the stock. § 1296(a)(2); Reg. § 1.1296–1(c)(3). The "unreversed inclusions" are the excess of the prior inclusions in income under this election over the prior deductions taken under this election. § 1296(d); Reg. § 1.1296–1(a)(3). Once made, the election applies to the tax year for which it is made and all later tax years unless (i) the stock ceases to be marketable stock, or (ii) the election is revoked with the consent of the IRS. § 1296(k).

Amounts included in income under this mark-to-market election and any gain on the sale of marketable stock in a PFIC with respect to which the election is made are treated as ordinary income. Any amounts deducted under this mark-to-market election and any loss on the sale of the marketable stock in a PFIC with respect to which the election is made are treated as an ordinary loss that is deductible in computing adjusted gross income. In the case of losses from the sale of stock, this characterization rule is limited to the extent that the loss does not exceed the "unreversed inclusions" with respect to the stock; any loss in excess of this amount is characterized under the normal rules regarding capital gains and losses. § 1296(c)(1); Reg. § 1.1296–1(c)(2) and (4). The source of any amount included in income or allowed as a deduction under this mark-to-market election is determined in the same manner as if it were gain or loss from the sale of stock in the PFIC. § 1296(c)(2); Reg. § 1.1296–1(c)(6).

The shareholder adjusts the basis of the stock in the PFIC to reflect the amounts included in income or deducted under this election. Thus, the shareholder's basis in the PFIC stock is increased to reflect income inclusions under the election and is decreased to reflect deductions under the election. § 1296(b).

This election applies only to stock in a PFIC that meets the definition of "marketable stock" in Section 1296(e). To qualify as marketable stock, Section 1296(e)(1)(A) provides that the stock in the PFIC must be regularly traded on either (i) a national securities exchange that is registered with the Securities and Exchange Commission, (ii) the national market system established under the Securities Exchange Act of 1934, or (iii) an exchange that the IRS determines "has rules sufficient to ensure that the market price represents a legitimate and sound fair market value." H.R. Rep. No. 148, 105th Cong., 1st Sess. 535 (1997); see Reg. § 1.1296–2(a)–(c). To the extent provided in regulations, marketable stock also includes stock in a foreign corporation that is comparable to a U.S. regulated investment company and issues stock which is offered for sale or is outstanding and is redeemable at its net asset value. § 1296(e)(1)(B); Reg. § 1.1296–2(d). In addition, to the extent provided in regulations, marketable stock includes any option on stock that meets any of the above three definitions. § 1296(e)(1)(C). Finally, marketable stock also includes any stock in a PFIC owned directly or indirectly by a U.S. regulated investment company. § 1296(e)(2); Reg. § 1.1296–2(f)(1).

A controlled foreign corporation that owns stock in a PFIC that is marketable is treated as a U.S. person that may make the mark-to-market election. Amounts includible by the controlled foreign corporation in its income under the election are treated as foreign personal holding company income for Subpart F purposes and amounts deductible by the controlled foreign corporation under the election are treated as deductions allocable to foreign personal holding company income. § 1296(f); Reg. § 1.1296–1(g)(2). The source of these income or deduction amounts is determined by reference to the controlled foreign corporation's "actual residence." H.R. Rep. No. 148, 105th Cong., 1st Sess. 536 (1997). Reg. § 1.1296–1(g)(2)(i) treats a controlled foreign corporation as a foreign person for purposes of applying the source rules in Reg. § 1.1296–1(c)(6).

Stock owned, directly or indirectly, by a foreign partnership, foreign trust or foreign estate is treated as owned proportionately by its partners or beneficiaries. U.S. persons treated as owning PFIC stock under this constructive ownership rule may make the mark-to-market election in Section 1296. Any disposition of PFIC stock in this situation is treated as a disposition of the stock by the U.S. person who is treated as the owner of the stock under the constructive ownership rule. § 1296(g). The basis adjustments for the income inclusions and deductions under the election apply to the basis of the PFIC stock in the hands of the foreign partnership, foreign trust or foreign estate, but only for purposes of applying the PFIC rules to the tax treatment of the constructive owner (i.e. the partner or beneficiary of the entity owning the PFIC stock). Similar basis adjustments are made to the basis of the property by reason of which the U.S. person is treated as owning the PFIC stock. § 1296(b)(2).

The statute contains a special basis rule for PFIC stock acquired from a decedent and for which a Section 1296 election was in effect on the date of the decedent's death. The person acquiring the stock from the decedent will obtain an initial basis equal to the lesser of (1) the decedent's adjusted basis in the stock immediately before his or her death or (2) the basis determined under Section 1014 (other than for 2010, by reason of the one-year repeal of the federal estate tax). § 1296(i); Reg. § 1.1296–1(d)(4).

The statute has a transition rule for an individual becoming a U.S. person in a tax year starting after 1997. Solely for purposes of Section 1296, the adjusted basis of any marketable stock in a PFIC (before any adjustments made under this election) owned by the individual on the first day of such tax year will be treated as the greater of (i) the fair market value of the stock on such day, or (ii) the individual's adjusted basis in the stock on such day. § 1296(*l*); see Reg. § 1.1296–1(d)(5).

[¶ 6320]

7. COORDINATION OF SECTION 1291 RULES WITH THE MARK–TO–MARKET ELECTION

The rules of Section 1291 generally do not apply to a shareholder for tax years for which a mark-to-market election under Section 1296 is in effect. § 1291(d)(1). If Section 1291 does apply to a shareholder and the shareholder had an election in effect under Section 1296 for any prior tax year, the shareholder's holding period is treated as starting on the first day of the first tax year starting after the last tax year for which the Section 1296 election applied. § 1291(a)(3)(A). The statute, however, contains a coordination rule that applies if a taxpayer makes a mark-to-market election for stock in a PFIC that is not a qualified electing fund at any time after the start of the taxpayer's holding period for the stock. See § 1296(j). The purpose of this rule is to prevent the taxpayer from avoiding the interest charge under Section 1291 on deferred amounts attributable to tax years before the mark-to-market election in Section 1296. H.R. Rep. No. 148, 105th Cong., 1st Sess. 536 (1997).

[¶ 6325]

8. RULES FOR ATTRIBUTING STOCK OWNERSHIP

In determining stock ownership for purposes of the PFIC provisions, a U.S. person is treated as owning its proportionate share of the stock of a PFIC owned by any partnership, trust or estate in which the U.S. person is a partner or beneficiary. In addition, if a U.S. person owns 50 percent or more in value of a foreign corporation's stock, the U.S. person is deemed to own its proportionate share of stock of a PFIC owned by the foreign corporation. However, notwithstanding this foreign corporation attribution rule, a U.S. person that owns stock in an upper-tier PFIC is treated as owning its proportionate share of any lower-tier PFIC stock owned by the upper-tier PFIC, regardless of that U.S. person's ownership percentage in the upper-tier PFIC. Moreover, the regulations may treat any person that has an option to acquire stock as owning such stock. These attribution rules apply to the extent that the effect is to treat a PFIC's stock as owned by a U.S. person and generally do not apply to treat stock owned by a U.S. person as owned by any other person. § 1298(a).

If a U.S. person is treated as owning stock in a PFIC under these attribution rules, the regulations may treat any disposition of the PFIC stock (whether by the U.S. person or the actual owner of the stock) that results in the U.S. person being treated as no longer owning the stock as a disposition by the U.S. person. In addition, the regulations may treat any distribution of money or other property to the actual holder of the stock as a distribution to the U.S. person. § 1298(b)(5).

If a U.S. person is treated, under these attribution rules, as owning stock in a PFIC that is a qualified electing fund, amounts included in the U.S. person's income under Section 1293(a) and distributions received by the U.S. person tax-free under Section 1293(c) will be applied to adjust the basis of the U.S. person's property that gave rise to the attributed stock ownership in the PFIC. § 1293(d). For example, if a U.S. person is a partner in a partnership that owns PFIC stock, Section 1293(a) current income inclusions will increase, and Section 1293(c) tax-free distributions will reduce, the U.S. person's basis in the partnership interest.

[¶ 6330]

PROBLEMS

1. Compare the PFIC provisions with the Subpart F provisions. What circumstances would be covered by the PFIC provisions that would not be covered by the Subpart F provisions? Which is the best conceptual approach to dealing with the tax abuses that arise from the deferral of U.S. income tax on a U.S. person's share of passive income earned through a foreign corporation? Which is the most practical anti-deferral approach from the viewpoint of effective tax administration?

2. Tax Avoidance, Inc., a corporation incorporated under the laws of the Cayman Islands, has one class of stock outstanding, voting common, which is owned by the following shareholders: 40 shares by U.S. Parent, Inc., a publicly held U.S. corporation; 12 shares by Sam, a U.S. citizen; 15 shares by Angelina, a nonresident alien, who is Sam's sister; 9 shares by Wolfgang, a nonresident alien; 18 shares by Foreign Venture, a foreign partnership with two equal partners, Alexandra, a U.S. resident alien, and Foreign Business, Inc., a publicly held foreign corporation; 5 shares by USA, Inc., a publicly held U.S. corporation; and 1 share by John, a U.S. citizen. Except as otherwise indicated in the prior sentence, assume that the parties in this Problem are unrelated to each other and own no stock in any corporation except as expressly indicated.

During the current year, Tax Avoidance, Inc. has $10 million of income having the following character: $4 million in foreign-source dividends and interest from unrelated persons; $1.5 million in capital gains from the sale of foreign investment securities; $1 million in income from a foreign business, which constitutes foreign base company sales income (within the meaning of Section 954(d)); and $3.5 million in income from an active foreign business, which does not constitute foreign base company income (within the meaning of Section 954). Assume, for simplicity, that Tax Avoidance, Inc. has no allowable deductions for the year with respect to this income.

During the current year, Tax Avoidance, Inc.'s assets consist of the following: assets that are used to conduct its trade or business activities, which have an average value of $60 million and average adjusted bases of $30 million; and assets producing passive income or held for the production of passive income, which have an average value of $50 million and average adjusted bases of $30 million.

a. Is Tax Avoidance, Inc. a controlled foreign corporation for the current year?

b. Is Tax Avoidance, Inc. a PFIC for the current year?

c. Do any of Tax Avoidance, Inc.'s shareholders have inclusions under Section 951(a)(1)(A)?

d. How would the PFIC provisions apply to Tax Avoidance, Inc.'s shareholders under these facts?

e. How would your answer in Problem 2.d. change if Tax Avoidance, Inc.'s stock were regularly traded on a national securities exchange?

[¶ 6335]

L. REPORTING REQUIREMENTS AND OTHER MISCELLANEOUS PROVISIONS

Congress has recognized that the provisions of Subpart F and the other anti-deferral regimes can be enforced effectively only if affected U.S. taxpayers are required to supply to the IRS a substantial amount of information concerning the organization and operation of foreign corporations in which those U.S. taxpayers own equity interests. Accordingly, the Code contains extensive reporting and recordkeeping requirements with respect to foreign corporations.

[¶ 6340]

1. REQUIREMENT FOR FILING OF INFORMATION RETURN BY OFFICERS, DIRECTORS AND FIVE-PERCENT SHAREHOLDERS OF A FOREIGN CORPORATION UPON THE OCCURRENCE OF CERTAIN EVENTS

Section 6046 requires the filing of a Form 5471 return within 90 days after the happening of certain events, such as the organization, reorganization or acquisition of shares of a foreign corporation. A return is required from each U.S. person who is an officer, director or owner of ten percent or more in the voting power or value of the stock of a foreign corporation, if at least ten percent in the voting power or value of the corporation's stock is owned by a U.S. person. The return is required when a U.S. person acquires enough stock in such foreign corporation to meet the ten-percent threshold, increases his or her stock interest by at least ten percentage points or disposes of an interest so as to cease to be a ten-percent shareholder or when the foreign corporation is reorganized. See Reg. § 1.6046–1 (issued before Congress raised the threshold from five percent to ten percent in 1997).

Constructive ownership rules apply in determining stock ownership for purposes of this provision. § 6046(c). Provision is made for joint filing, so as to avoid unnecessary duplication of information when more than one person has an interest in the same foreign corporation. A civil penalty of $10,000 is imposed unless failure to file is due to reasonable cause. If the failure to report continues for more than 90 days after notification by the Treasury, an additional $10,000 penalty applies for each 30–day period (or fraction of such period) during which the failure continues after the initial 90–day period. The total increase in penalties that can be imposed is limited to $50,000. § 6679. Criminal penalties may also apply. § 7203.

[¶ 6345]

2. REQUIREMENT FOR FILING OF ANNUAL INFORMATION RETURN BY U.S. PERSONS WHO CONTROL A FOREIGN CORPORATION

Section 6038 requires an annual information return (Form 5471) to be filed by every U.S. person who is in control of a foreign corporation. Control is defined as ownership of stock (including that attributed by application of certain constructive ownership rules) representing more than 50 percent of the value or voting power of a foreign corporation. The information required includes annual accounting statements (profit and loss and balance sheet), as well as a description of various types of transactions with related parties. Reg. § 1.6038–2(f). Returns are required for the fiscal years of foreign corporations ending with or within the tax year of the U.S. person, and, so long as one person files the required information, other stockholders may not need to file. A civil penalty involving loss of foreign tax credits may be imposed in the event of a failure to supply the required information. The amount of credits that may be lost in respect of any failure is limited to the greater of $10,000 or the income of the foreign corporation in question. § 6038(c). In addition, there is a civil penalty of $10,000 for a failure to supply information, which may be increased if the failure continues. If the failure to report continues for more than 90 days after notification by the Treasury, an additional $10,000 penalty applies for each 30–day period (or fraction of such period) during which the failure continues after the initial 90–day period. The total increase in penalties that can be imposed is limited to $50,000. § 6038(b). Criminal penalties may also apply. § 7203. U.S. persons holding at least a ten-percent interest in controlled foreign partnerships are subject to the same reporting requirements.

[¶ 6350]

3. RECORDKEEPING REQUIREMENTS FOR U.S. SHAREHOLDERS OF CONTROLLED FOREIGN CORPORATIONS

Section 964(c) requires U.S. shareholders (as defined in Section 951(b)) of controlled foreign corporations to keep, and produce upon audit, records sufficient to permit the IRS to verify for each tax year such matters as: (1) the controlled foreign corporation's Subpart F income and (2) the earnings invested by such corporation in U.S. property under Section 956. Reg. § 1.964–3. Records must further be maintained to permit verification by the IRS of the amounts of the various components of Subpart F income discussed earlier in this Chapter. Reg. § 1.964–4.

[¶ 6355]

4. INFORMATION–REPORTING REQUIREMENTS RELATING TO A PFIC

Every U.S. person who, on the last day of a passive foreign investment company's tax year, owns at least five percent in value of the company's stock must report to the IRS such information as the regulations may require. § 1291(e).

Unless otherwise provided in the regulations, under a new reporting requirement added to the Code in 2010, each U.S. person who is a shareholder of a passive foreign investment company must file an annual report containing such information as the Treasury and the IRS may require. § 1298(f). Moreover, an individual who is a passive foreign investment company shareholder may also be required to file an annual report under Section 6038D, also added in 2010. That provision requires an individual with an interest in a "specified foreign asset" to disclose certain information for a tax year if the total value of all such assets exceeds $50,000 (or such higher amount as may be prescribed by the Treasury and the IRS). It is expected that the Treasury and the IRS will issue guidance limiting duplicative reporting under these two new reporting provisions.

[¶ 6360]

5. REQUIRED TAX YEAR FOR CONTROLLED FOREIGN CORPORATION

Section 898 applies to a controlled foreign corporation if any U.S. shareholder owns (directly, indirectly through another foreign entity or under the applicable attribution rules) more than 50 percent of the voting power or value of the corporation's stock. Section 898 generally requires such a controlled foreign corporation to use the same tax year as its majority U.S. shareholder. § 898(a), (b) and (c)(1)(A). The purpose of this provision is to prevent a majority U.S. shareholder of a controlled foreign corporation from deferring the tax on its Subpart F inclusions by having the foreign corporation adopt a tax year that differs from the majority U.S. shareholder's tax year. Section 898(c)(2) allows a foreign corporation to elect to adopt a tax year that starts one month earlier than the tax year of its majority U.S. shareholder, thus effectively allowing a majority U.S. shareholder to obtain a one-month deferral of the tax on Subpart F inclusions.

[¶ 6365]

M. ACCUMULATED EARNINGS TAX

Another penalty tax of general application that may also apply to a foreign corporation is the accumulated earnings tax under Sections 531 through 537, although its application to foreign corporations is infrequent as a practical matter. The accumulated earnings tax applies at the corporate level in addition to any regular corporate income taxes. It is imposed on a corporation, whether U.S. or foreign, "formed or availed of for the purpose of avoiding the income tax with respect to its shareholders * * * by permitting earnings and profits to accumulate instead of being * * * distributed." §§ 531 and 532(a). The fact that the corporation is "a mere holding or investment company" is prima facie evidence of the purpose to avoid the income tax with respect to its shareholders. § 533(b). The fact that earnings and profits are permitted to accumulate beyond the reasonable needs of the business is determinative of the proscribed tax-avoidance purpose unless the corporation can prove to the contrary by a preponderance of the evidence. § 533(a). The purpose of this tax is to prevent a corporation from avoiding shareholder-level taxes on accumulated earnings in excess of reasonable business needs by, in effect, forcing it to make distributions to avoid the tax.

Under current law, the accumulated earnings tax is imposed at a rate of 15 percent of the corporation's "accumulated taxable income." § 531.[34] Section 535 defines this term as the corporation's taxable income (with certain adjustments) for the tax year reduced by the sum of (1) dividends paid during the year and (2) a minimum accumulated earnings credit of $250,000 ($150,000, for certain corporations performing services). For a foreign corporation, accumulated taxable income includes only income from U.S. sources and income effectively connected with a U.S. trade or business. § 882(b). Thus, as a practical matter, a foreign corporation can

34. This rate is the same as the preferential tax rate imposed on high-income taxpayers' "qualified dividend income" under Section 1(h)(11), which was enacted in 2003. The preferential tax rates on qualified dividend income in Section 1(h)(11) will expire for tax years starting after 2010 and the accumulated earnings tax rate will again become the highest rate of tax under Section 1(c) of the Code (i.e., 35 percent under current law; 39.6 percent for tax years starting after 2010 if the tax rate cuts enacted in 2001 are allowed to expire), unless Congress extends the effective date or makes permanent the rules in Section 1(h)(11).

have problems under Section 531 only when it accumulates taxable income from U.S. sources or effectively connected with a U.S. trade or business in excess of $250,000.

The accumulated earnings tax applies to the U.S.-source income of a foreign corporation if any of its shareholders is subject to income tax on its dividend distributions by reason of being (1) a U.S. citizen or resident alien, (2) a nonresident alien subject to withholding tax on dividends distributed by the corporation or (3) a foreign corporation in which any person described in (1) or (2) directly or indirectly owns an interest. Thus, the penalty tax may be imposed even on a foreign corporation wholly owned by nonresident aliens to enforce payment of the dividend-withholding tax.

U.S. persons cannot use two or more tiers of foreign corporations to avoid the accumulated earnings tax on certain U.S. income. This device had been used by some corporations organized in tax havens as investment funds to invest in portfolio securities of U.S. corporations. The pattern was for a two-tiered corporate structure to be used. A foreign parent corporation owned by the fund shareholders would establish a wholly owned foreign subsidiary, which would purchase the U.S. securities. The subsidiary would claim that it was not subject to the accumulated earnings tax because it distributed all of its earnings to its parent. The parent would claim that it was not subject to the tax because all of its income was from sources outside the United States.

To defeat this device, Congress enacted a special source rule that applies for purposes of the accumulated earnings tax to certain dividends and interest received by a "U.S.-owned foreign corporation." If ten percent or more of the earnings and profits of any foreign corporation for any tax year are derived from U.S. sources or are effectively connected with the conduct of a U.S. trade or business, then any distribution received (directly or indirectly) by a U.S.-owned foreign corporation out of those earnings and profits is treated as derived by the recipient corporation from U.S. sources. That is, the earnings retain their U.S. source or U.S. connection in the hands of the recipient (upper-tier) foreign corporation, so that they may be subject to the accumulated earnings tax. A similar rule applies to interest paid by a lower-tier foreign corporation. If the payor corporation meets the ten-percent earnings and profits threshold, interest that it pays to a U.S.-owned foreign corporation out of U.S.-source earnings is U.S.-source income for purposes of the accumulated earnings tax. § 535(d)(1).

"U.S.-owned foreign corporation" is defined by cross-reference to Section 904(h)(6), discussed at ¶ 7160, to mean any foreign corporation in which 50 percent or more of the total voting power or total value of the stock is held directly or indirectly by U.S. persons. § 535(d)(2). This provision applies to closely held and publicly held foreign corporations alike.

The Code contains one rule for coordinating the accumulated earnings tax with the other anti-deferral regimes discussed earlier in this Chapter. That rule provides that a passive foreign investment company is not subject to the accumulated earnings tax. § 532(b)(4). There is no similar provision governing the relationship between the accumulated earnings tax provisions and the controlled foreign corporation provisions, so the accumulated earnings tax apparently may apply to a controlled foreign corporation. However, to the extent that the U.S. shareholders of a controlled foreign corporation are taxed on their shares of the corporation's Subpart F income, the accumulated earnings tax should not apply to the corporation because it is not being used to avoid shareholder-level taxes. Moreover, for purposes of determining a controlled foreign corporation's accumulated taxable income, Section 535(b)(10) allows the corporation to deduct the amount of its income for the tax year that is included in a U.S. shareholder's gross income under Section 951(a).

[¶ 6370]

N. POLICY DISCUSSION OF ALTERNATIVES TO THE CURRENT ANTI-DEFERRAL REGIMES

As has been discussed throughout this Chapter, the complex and somewhat incoherent anti-deferral regimes of current law reflect an uneasy compromise between a strict application of the capital-export neutrality standard, which would suggest completely ending deferral of U.S. tax on income earned by a U.S. person through a foreign corporation, and a strict application of the capital-import neutrality standard, which would suggest that few or no limits be placed on such deferral. Moreover, Subpart F, the most important of those regimes, was enacted in 1962, when international trade was a smaller part of the U.S. and world economies and the makeup of industry was different than it is today. Service industries and modern technologies play a much more important role in today's U.S. and world economies than they did in 1962; accordingly, as discussed at ¶ 6190, Subpart F may not be properly designed to deal with the modern economy. In response to the perceived unsatisfactory state of current law, various alternative ways of dealing with the deferral issue have been proposed. One of the authors of this book and two co-authors have proposed ending deferral completely by treating a foreign corporation as a pass-through entity with respect to its U.S. shareholders. See, e.g., Peroni, Fleming, Jr. & Shay, "Getting Serious About Curtailing Deferral of U.S. Tax on Foreign Source Income," 52 SMU L. Rev. 455 (1999). By contrast, one leading industry group, the National Foreign Trade Council, has argued the Subpart F rules should be weakened to ensure that U.S. multinationals will be competitive in the global marketplace. See National Foreign Trade Council, Inc., The NFTC Foreign

Income Project: International Tax Policy for the 21st Century—Part One: A Reconsideration of Subpart F (1999). The NFTC argued (at page xxi) that:

> Changes in the international economic environment, as well as refinements in the theory of international taxation, support a shift in the balance of U.S. international tax policy towards competitiveness and away from capital export neutrality. This could be accomplished by narrowing the scope of subpart F to portfolio income, for which the theory of capital export neutrality remains valid. A secondary benefit from such a shift in policy would be a major simplification of U.S. tax rules, as the subpart F rules are a source of substantial complexity and tax controversy. Such a shift would tend to harmonize U.S. tax rules with those of other major industrial countries which either exempt foreign direct investment from home country tax or target their anti-deferral more narrowly on portfolio-type income.

The following excerpts discuss several possible alternatives to the anti-deferral rules of current law. The first excerpt is from a 2000 Treasury study of the anti-deferral regimes of current law and the various alternative ways of dealing with the deferral problem. The second excerpt is from a tax reform report issued by the Staff of the Joint Committee on Taxation in 2005, which proposes a dividend exemption system as a possible replacement for the United States' current "worldwide" system for taxing international income.

[¶ 6375]

U.S. TREASURY DEPARTMENT, THE DEFERRAL OF INCOME EARNED THROUGH U.S. CONTROLLED FOREIGN CORPORATIONS: A POLICY STUDY

82–99 (Dec. 2000).

CHAPTER 7

CRITERIA AND OPTIONS FOR CHANGE

I. Introduction

This chapter considers options for reforming or replacing the current subpart F regime. The fundamental goals of international tax policy provide the appropriate criteria for analyzing these options. These fundamental goals of international tax policy are (1) meeting our revenue needs in an equitable manner, (2) promoting economic welfare, (3) minimizing compliance and administrative burdens, and (4) conforming with international norms to the extent possible. In addition, as in 1962 when subpart F was enacted, one should also consider whether any policy option would place undue burdens on the competitive position of U.S. companies. To determine how these goals should be implemented in the specific context of subpart F, this chapter relies upon the analysis and conclusions set out in the prior chapters of this study. No specific recommendations about the reform or replacement of subpart F, however, are being made at this time.

II. Criteria for Evaluating Changes to Subpart F

A. Equity

A core objective of any tax system is to raise the revenue necessary to fund government functions and services. A perception of unfairness can undermine the willingness of taxpayers to comply voluntarily with a tax system.[2] For a tax system to raise revenue effectively, taxpayers must believe that the tax burden is being equitably distributed. Taxation on the basis of worldwide income is grounded in the equitable principle that the tax burden should be imposed equally on all income, without regard to its source.

Chapter 1 noted that the worldwide taxing jurisdiction of the United States generally subjects the income from domestic and foreign investment of U.S. citizens and residents to the same tax burden and provides a foreign tax credit to alleviate double taxation. The foreign tax credit generally prevents U.S. persons from being unfairly penalized for earning foreign income. Under current law, however, U.S. businesses continue to be able to limit worldwide taxation of their foreign income to some extent by separately incorporating their foreign operations in a foreign tax jurisdiction. To the extent that this arrangement subjects the income from those foreign operations to a lower tax burden than the income of a U.S. citizen or resident that conducts activities entirely in the United States or conducts foreign activities in branch form, equity concerns arise. As discussed in Chapter 2, this basic inequity was one of the principal reasons that the Kennedy Administration advocated an end to deferral.

Although narrower than the original Kennedy Administration proposal, subpart F was intended to reduce this potential inequity by limiting the ability of taxpayers to reduce or eliminate taxes on income from foreign investment. The subpart F regime operates through specific rules that are intended to tax passive income on a current basis and to prevent the deflection of income to low-tax jurisdictions. Chapter 5 discussed some of the rules of this regime that may no longer operate effectively. One example is the foreign personal holding company income rules, which have been made less effective by hybrid transactions. Hybrid transactions allow taxpayers to exploit the differences between U.S. and foreign entity classification to deflect income from a high-tax country to a low-tax country and to reduce or avoid the overall tax on their foreign income. Chapter 5 also noted that the foreign base company sales income provisions, which are intended to prevent the shifting of sales income to low-tax

---

2. The goal of equity is related to the goal of efficiency, discussed below. Over the long-term, differing treatment of businesses operating solely in the United States and U.S.-based businesses operating in foreign jurisdictions may not result in unequal treatment of shareholders (who are free to invest wherever they can get the highest after-tax rate of return), but it could result in a sub-optimal allocation of investments between the United States and foreign countries.

jurisdictions, might be circumvented through contract manufacturing arrangements. Chapter 6 [excerpted at ¶ 6190] described how changes in the U.S. and world economies are posing challenges to subpart F and noted that these challenges are likely to increase in the future. For example, subpart F generally does not deal with services industries in any detail, and where subpart F does provide rules (i.e., for financial services income), those rules may be inadequate to deal with issues relating to the mobility of enterprise and the mobility of income and may not adequately distinguish between active and passive income.

To promote the goal of equity, income from domestic investment and income from foreign investment should be subject to a similar tax burden. To further this goal, some form of anti-deferral regime is necessary to prevent U.S. taxpayers from using tax avoidance techniques involving foreign corporations to lower the tax on their income from foreign investment. In particular, to prevent the shifting of passive income to low-tax jurisdictions, such an anti-deferral regime should recognize, as Congress did over 60 years ago when it enacted the foreign personal holding company regime, that foreign passive income should be taxed on a current basis. Further, any such anti-deferral regime should eliminate inappropriate distinctions between business conducted in corporate form and business conducted in other forms, such as through partnerships and disregarded entities.

B. Efficiency

Another important tax policy objective is economic efficiency or the promotion of economic welfare. Generally, global economic welfare is promoted when resource allocation decisions are based solely on which investments are expected to be the most productive.

Chapter 3 concluded that, whether the goal is to maximize global or U.S. economic welfare, it is generally beneficial to reduce disparities in tax rates that cause investment income earned in foreign countries to be taxed at lower rates than investment income earned in the United States. Chapter 3 also concluded that capital export neutrality, which requires structuring taxes so that they are neutral and do not cause investors to favor either domestic or foreign investment, is probably the best policy for promoting economic welfare. Chapter 3 found the efficiency effect of the subpart F foreign-to-foreign related party rules (even when these rules operate as intended) to be uncertain.

Thus, to further the goal of promoting economic welfare, it appears that income from foreign investment should be taxed at the same rate as income from U.S. investment. To the extent that deferral of foreign income does not result in such tax treatment, it is likely to be inefficient from an economic perspective. It may be preferable, however, for an anti-deferral regime to deal directly with tax disparity, rather than using proxies such as the current foreign-to-foreign related party rules.

C. Simplicity and Administrability

Promoting simplicity and administrability is another important tax policy goal. There are a number of different aspects of this goal. On a basic level, simplicity can mean that rules are drafted simply. Rules that are drafted simply, however, may not always be adequate to address complex situations and thus might undermine administrability. Therefore, a balance must be struck. In general, however, simple tax rules facilitate voluntary compliance and minimize administrative costs for taxpayers and government. Further, overly complex rules may create "traps for the unwary," which could penalize poorly advised taxpayers.[5]

Chapter 6 noted that the business model upon which the foreign base company sales and services provisions of subpart F are designed—relatively immobile manufacturing operations in high-tax foreign countries—no longer represents the norm. Rather, the United States is shifting toward a more service-based economy and one in which business income and income-producing activities are increasingly mobile. As a result, new issues are arising with respect to the mobility of income, the mobility of business enterprise, and the distinction between active and passive income. Chapter 6 also noted that other economic developments, particularly the rapid growth of electronic commerce, may give rise to numerous interpretative issues for which the current subpart F regime provides no clear answers. Specifically, electronic commerce and new technologies can affect the ease with which structures that are not contemplated by the rules of subpart F can be used. Furthermore, they can affect the interaction between subpart F and the more general international taxation rules, such as the general source of income rules and the definition of a U.S. trade or business.

To further the goal of promoting simplicity and administrability, an anti-deferral regime should provide a clear, simple and coherent distinction between passive and active income (if the necessity for such a distinction cannot itself be eliminated). To address the increasing mobility of business activities, alternatives to rules based on the location of business activities may be more appropriate. Further, in general, an anti-deferral regime should avoid rules that rely heavily on the form in which transactions are structured. Such rules are often not flexible enough to keep pace with changing business practices. Attempts to modify the rules to address these changing business practices may increase complexity (and may nevertheless fail to address the changes in an adequate and fair manner). For example, to avoid income classification issues that result from the changing nature of business, to the extent possible an anti-deferral regime should avoid separate sets of rules for different types of income.

5. In this respect, the goal of simplicity is closely related to the goal of equity. That is, to the extent that the tax system avoids penalizing poorly advised taxpayers or rewarding those who engage in sophisticated tax planning techniques, the overall tax burden is apportioned more fairly among all taxpayers.

D. International Norms

To promote the tax policy goal of conforming with international norms, countries should, to the extent possible, adopt broad tax policies that harmonize with the tax policies generally in use internationally. The adoption by one country of tax policies that deviate significantly from international norms can lead to double taxation or double non-taxation. Further, rules that are inconsistent with those generally in use internationally tend to increase administrative burdens.

Chapter 4 noted that, as more countries have eliminated foreign exchange controls, they have found it necessary to adopt anti-deferral measures to prevent tax base erosion and to reduce the effect of harmful tax competition. It also noted that the trend among countries is to enact controlled foreign corporation (CFC) legislation or tighten existing CFC legislation. Because the United States was the first country to enact CFC legislation, it has had the longest experience with the strengths and weaknesses of its regime.

This study indicates that limiting deferral through an anti-deferral regime is consistent with international norms, and reforming an existing anti-deferral regime to limit deferral in an appropriate and effective manner is also consistent with international norms. Although the United States should continue to set the standard for an appropriate anti-deferral regime, any anti-deferral regime should, to the extent possible, be designed in a manner that minimizes any disharmony with international norms. This [will] help prevent double taxation, double non-taxation and increased administrative burdens.

E. Competitiveness

Multinational competitiveness measures the ability of U.S. firms headquartered in the United States with production facilities abroad to compete in foreign markets with residents of the host country and other multinational firms based elsewhere. In 1962, when subpart F was enacted, Congress considered the effect of any anti-deferral rules on the competitiveness of U.S. multinationals. Thus, in evaluating any policy options regarding subpart F, one should still consider any potential effects on competitiveness.

Chapter 4 noted, however, that multinational competitiveness is measured by many factors, only a portion of which relate to the tax burden imposed on a business. In addition, Chapter 4 noted that the available data provide no reliable basis for concluding that subpart F has had a significant effect on multinational competitiveness. Chapter 4 also indicates that our major trading partners all have anti-deferral regimes. Thus, while there is no direct way to measure the extent to which subpart F has affected multinational competitiveness, it appears that foreign multinationals are subject to rules that are similar in effect to our subpart F rules. In addition, as noted in Chapter 4, the United States, as a general matter, is agreed by almost any measure to be one of the most competitive countries in the world.

Finally, Chapter 4 found that policies that enhance the ability of a particular firm to compete may not necessarily promote overall economic welfare. As a result, because multinational competitiveness may conflict with tax policy goals such as economic efficiency or equity, the effects on multinational competitiveness, if any, should not be considered in isolation, but should be weighed against the possible positive effects of implementing the option (such as promoting economic efficiency).

III. Alternatives

A. General

This section briefly outlines three alternative options to the current subpart F regime for taxing foreign income and evaluates them against the principles described immediately above. Because of the difficulty in measuring how any specific anti-deferral regime would affect multinational competitiveness, this section will not attempt to analyze this issue separately for each option. As noted above, any potential effects of any policy option regarding subpart F on multinational competitiveness would need to be considered in light of the possible positive effects of implementing the option (such as any improvements in economic efficiency or administrability).

The options described below clearly do not (and are not intended to) represent the entire range of possibilities.[6] They merely illustrate certain routes that might be explored. In addition, for each option, numerous implementation alternatives are possible. Although some of these alternatives are briefly mentioned, the study does not attempt to examine them in detail.

Option 1 is the repeal of deferral. This could be done in a number of ways. However, the result in all cases would be to subject foreign income to current U.S. taxation. Option 2 would tax all active foreign income currently, but at a lower rate of tax than the normal U.S. rates. There would be no subsequent tax upon repatriation. Option 3 would retain most

---

6. * * * One option that is not discussed in this chapter is the adoption of a territorial system of taxation. As noted in the introduction to this study, in its purest form, a territorial system completely exempts both the active and passive foreign income of its residents and provides no foreign tax credit. Few countries, and no major trading partners of the United States, have such a complete exemption system. More common is a partial exemption system under which, by treaty or statute, branch profits and subsidiary dividends are exempted and other foreign source income, e.g., royalty income, is included in gross income with a credit to offset the foreign tax imposed on this income. Countries that use a partial exemption system, such as France, have nevertheless found it necessary to adopt a CFC regime to prevent base erosion. Thus, an exemption system is not necessarily an alternative to the implementation of an anti-deferral regime. An analysis of the merits of an exemption system as compared to a worldwide system of taxation with a foreign tax credit more appropriately belongs in the context of an examination of methods to avoid double taxation and is therefore beyond the scope of this study. For an example of a paper examining the merits of a dividend exemption system, see Harry Grubert and John Mutti, Dividend Exemption Versus the Current System for Taxing Foreign Business Income (Dec. 6, 1999) (unpublished paper).

of the current subpart F rules, with the exception of the foreign-to-foreign related party rules. To reduce tax disparity, however, Option 3 would include an effective tax rate test for active income, which would require a U.S. shareholder of a CFC to include in income the income of the CFC that was not otherwise treated as subpart F income if the effective rate of foreign tax on this income were less than a certain percentage. Under all options, income from passive investment would continue to be subject to current U.S. tax at full U.S. rates.

These options thus represent a range of alternatives that could be considered to reform or replace the current subpart F rules. Option 1 would clearly represent a tightening of the current anti-deferral regime. Options 2 and 3 may, depending on the specific parameters chosen, represent either a tightening or a relaxation compared to the current anti-deferral rules.[7]

B. Option 1: Repeal of Deferral

1. Description of Option

There are at least three methods by which deferral could be ended: the full inclusion method, the branch method, and the domestic corporation method. Under any of these methods, the income of controlled foreign corporations would be subject to current U.S. taxation. The differences between the methods, however, might yield somewhat different tax results. Each method is briefly described below.

a. Full Inclusion Method

The full inclusion method would operate in a manner similar to the current subpart F regime except that all of the net income of the CFC, and not just certain targeted income, would be includible on a current basis in the gross income of U.S. shareholders as a deemed dividend. As under the current regime, a net loss of the CFC could not be used to reduce the U.S. shareholders' income. In general, the full inclusion method would achieve significant simplification over the current subpart F regime. Because all of the income of the CFC would be includible on a current basis, this method would permit the repeal of certain provisions that classify subpart F

7. Another approach that could be considered would be to strengthen the effectiveness of the foreign-to-foreign related party rules. [S]trengthening the effectiveness of these rules would have an uncertain effect on economic welfare, but would help protect the U.S. tax base by minimizing the incentive for capital to leave the United States in favor of lower-taxed foreign investment opportunities.

Alternatively, consideration could be given to relaxing or repealing the foreign-to-foreign related party rules and making no other significant changes to current subpart F. This approach would, however, decrease equity between U.S. taxpayers with significant foreign investments and those without such investments. Further, by relaxing the current anti-deferral rules, this approach would be out of step with developments in many other countries (which, as previously noted, have either recently enacted or recently tightened existing CFC legislation). This approach would also retain much of the complexity of the current subpart F regime while eviscerating the rules that were designed to prevent excessive tax disparity. Accordingly, unlike the options presented in this chapter, such an approach does not appear to be a useful alternative to the current regime.

income into different types (e.g., insurance income under section 953 and foreign personal holding company income and foreign base company income under section 954). Other rules, however, would continue to be needed to prevent earnings from being taxed again when actually distributed to the U.S. shareholders, although such rules could be made significantly simpler than the current rules under section 959.

The full inclusion method would also lessen the current form-based distinction between branches and subsidiaries. However, unlike the branch method (described below), the full inclusion method would continue to treat the CFC as a separate entity. Therefore, under this method, net income would continue to be determined at the CFC level and the amount of the inclusion would be subject to an earnings and profits limitation. Thus, as under the current regime, rules to calculate net income and earnings and profits of the CFC would be necessary. A determination would have to be made about whether income would be calculated on a consolidated basis or continue to be calculated on a CFC-by-CFC basis as under current law or, for example, on a QBU-by-QBU[9] basis.

b. Branch Method

The branch method would treat a CFC as though it were a branch or transparent entity when it was wholly-owned by a single U.S. shareholder and as a partnership or flow-through entity when it was owned by multiple U.S. shareholders. Unlike the current subpart F regime, there would be no need for rules to prevent the double taxation of previously taxed income because the CFC would not be treated as a separate taxable entity. Rather, the U.S. shareholders would be treated as earning the income. Thus, unlike the current regime under which net losses are not included in the income of the U.S. shareholders, the U.S. shareholders would take into account both the income and losses of the CFC. Rules would be required for apportioning income, losses, deductions and credits among unrelated U.S. owners of the CFC. Since actual branches are entitled to the benefits of tax treaties, arguably a CFC taxed under the branch method also should be entitled to treaty benefits to avoid double taxation. Achieving that result, however, may require some renegotiation of our existing tax treaties.

c. Domestic Corporation Method

The domestic corporation method would treat a CFC as though it were a domestic corporation for all purposes of the Internal Revenue Code. Under this method, the CFC itself, rather than its U.S. shareholders, would be taxed in the United States on its worldwide income. This method would allow for the complete repeal of subpart F. An elective version of this regime currently applies to certain CFCs that are insurance

9. A qualified business unit ("QBU") is "any separate and clearly identified unit of a trade or business of a taxpayer which maintains separate books and records." I.R.C. § 989.

companies. Further, an elective version that would apply to all CFCs has been formally proposed in the past. This method might also require renegotiation of our tax treaties. Issues raised by this method include: whether controlled foreign entities should be allowed to consolidate with affiliated domestic corporations; whether there should be recapture of earnings or gain (and loss) recognition when the corporation is treated as becoming "domestic"; and other issues similar to those involving the "domestication" of a foreign entity under a state domestication statute.

2. Summary Evaluation of Option 1

In terms of the policy principles set forth above, ending deferral would do the most to promote equity among U.S. taxpayers by ensuring that taxpayers could not limit taxation of foreign income by separately incorporating their foreign operations. This would further the equitable principle that a similar tax burden should be imposed on all income, without regard to its source. Among all of the options considered, ending deferral would also be likely to have the most positive long-term effect on economic efficiency and welfare because it would do the most to eliminate tax considerations from decisions regarding the location of investment. Because of the foreign tax credit limitation, taxpayers expecting to be in an excess credit position would still have a disincentive to invest in countries where they would be subject to a rate of tax that was higher than the rate of tax imposed in the United States.[12] Depending on the method chosen, ending deferral could provide considerable simplification as compared to the current subpart F rules. There would be no need, for example, to distinguish between different types of foreign income (active vs. passive, manufacturing vs. sales, etc.). In addition, many of the other technical rules of operation of subpart F could also be eliminated. Further, if consolidation of foreign operations were an element of this regime, intragroup transactions could be ignored, which would also represent a simplification of the current rules.

With regard to the policy objective of conforming to international norms, very few other countries, and no major U.S. trading partners, have completely eliminated deferral. Ending deferral would thus set the U.S. regime apart from the regimes of its major trading partners. As noted above, however, most major U.S. trading partners now have some form of an anti-deferral regime, and some of these countries have moved recently to tighten their existing regimes. Further, a U.S. regime that completely eliminates deferral generally would operate harmoniously with the tax laws of other countries. For example, ending deferral generally would not lead to international double taxation because of the availability of the

12. The effects of any disincentive to invest in high-tax jurisdictions would presumably be mitigated to some extent because, within each foreign tax credit basket, some "cross crediting" of foreign taxes may occur. That is, the disadvantage of high-tax countries in attracting capital would be lessened somewhat since U.S. companies with investments in low-tax countries could offset the U.S. tax on income earned in these countries with the taxes paid to the high-tax countries.

foreign tax credit to offset foreign taxes on the income subject to current U.S. tax.[13]

C. Option 2: Foreign Income Currently Includible But Subject to a Lower Rate of Tax

1. Description of Option 2

This option is similar to the full inclusion method, discussed under Option 1, in that it would operate in a manner similar to the current subpart F regime but would require the U.S. shareholders to currently include all of the net income of the CFC in gross income as a deemed dividend.[14] Under Option 2, however, the portion of the deemed distribution that was attributable to the active foreign income of the CFC would be subject to a lower rate of U.S. tax.[15] This could be done in a number of ways. For example, active foreign income could be subject to a lower rate of U.S. tax (determined as a percentage of either the U.S. shareholder's marginal rate or the maximum U.S. rate), with foreign tax credits, or the foreign income could be subject to an even lower rate of tax, without foreign tax credits. This latter option would represent more significant simplification because it would narrow the scope of the foreign tax credit.

If foreign tax credits were allowed, calculations of income and tax could be made under the current system on a CFC-by-CFC basis or on a QBU or groupwide basis. The portion of the deemed distribution that was attributable to passive income of the CFC would continue to be subject to U.S. tax at the U.S. shareholder's marginal rate. Foreign taxes paid on passive income could either be creditable against U.S. tax or deductible from taxable income. As under the full inclusion method of Option 1, there would be no further tax upon the earnings when they were subsequently distributed to the U.S. shareholders.

2. Summary Evaluation of Option 2

As discussed above, to enhance equity among U.S. taxpayers, the disparity between the tax burden borne by domestic income (or income from foreign branch operations) and that borne by income earned through a foreign corporation should be reduced. Accordingly, the extent to which this option promotes the goal of equity would depend upon the rate at which the tax on foreign income is set. To the extent that this option reduces tax disparity compared to the current subpart F regime (which would depend on the rate of tax imposed on foreign income), it would enhance economic efficiency.

---

13. The domestic corporation method, however, may raise questions under current international norms (generally reflected in treaties) relating to the consequences of classification of an entity as foreign or domestic.

14. This option could also be designed using the branch method or the domestic corporation method described above in the discussion of Option 1.

15. A decision to subject foreign income to a lower rate of tax would only be made to address the concerns of those who believed that an outright end to deferral would impose too great a burden on multinational competitiveness. As previously noted, however, this section does not attempt to evaluate the effect of any of these proposals on multinational competitiveness.

This option would promote the goal of simplicity by eliminating the tax and reporting requirements on repatriated income. Further, if consolidation of foreign operations were an element of this regime, intra-group transactions could be ignored, which would also represent a simplification of the current rules. In other respects, however, this option would not promote simplification. To prevent the "exportation" of income or the "importation" of losses, rules would continue to be needed to determine when income was foreign or domestic. Because passive income would continue to be subject to tax at regular U.S. rates, it would be necessary to distinguish adequately between active and passive income. The variant of this option that lowers the rate but eliminates the foreign tax credit could be viewed as inconsistent with international norms and could require renegotiation of some U.S. tax treaties.

D. Option 3: Retain Current Subpart F, But End Foreign-To-Foreign Related Party Rules and Add Effective Tax Rate Test Rule Preventing Tax Disparity

1. Description of Option 3

Under this option, current subpart F would be retained but modified by repealing the foreign-to-foreign related party rules. Thus, the foreign base company sales and services rules would not include income earned in connection with sales to, from, or on behalf of related foreign persons and services performed for or on behalf of related foreign persons.[16] Further, foreign personal holding company income would not include dividends, interest, rents and royalties received from related foreign corporations whether or not the payments were from a corporation organized in, or for the use of property in, the same foreign country as the CFC. In general, the other categories of subpart F income would remain unchanged and other subpart F rules would continue to operate (e.g., investments in U.S. property under section 956, previously taxed income rules under section 959, earnings and profits limitation under section 952(c), computation of net income under section 954(b)(5)).

To address the issue of tax disparity, and to counterbalance any adverse effects of the repeal of the foreign-to-foreign related party rules, an effective tax rate test would be added so that a U.S. shareholder would be required currently to include in income, as a deemed dividend, the income of the CFC that was not otherwise treated as subpart F income if the effective rate of foreign tax on this income were less than a certain percentage. In effect, this rule would create a new category of subpart F income defined based on the effective tax rate imposed on the income rather than the type of activity that produced the income. (It may be appropriate to extend this effective tax rate test to the income of foreign

16. The foreign base company sales and services rules would continue to include income earned in connection with sales to, from, or on behalf of related U.S. persons and services performed for or on behalf of related U.S. persons if the income otherwise fits within the definition of foreign base company sales or services income.

branches of U.S. corporations and partnerships.) It would have to be determined whether the effective tax rate was to be calculated on a CFC, QBU, or foreign groupwide basis. To determine the effective tax rate, a test similar to the one used in the regulations under section 954(b)(4) could be adopted.[17]

Alternatively, rather than full inclusion if the effective tax rate test were not met, U.S. shareholders might be required to make an equalizing payment of tax to the United States sufficient to bring the effective tax rate on the foreign income up to the threshold rate (with a credit for foreign taxes as well as for the equalization payment upon repatriation of the foreign income).[18] A similar alternative would be an actual or deemed minimum distribution regime, under which taxpayers would be required to make distributions (or pay tax on deemed distributions) from a CFC unless the effective tax rate on the income of the CFC equaled or exceeded a certain percentage.[19]

2. Summary Evaluation of Option 3

As with Option 2, the extent to which this option would enhance equity among U.S. taxpayers would depend on the level at which the effective tax rate was set. If the effect of this option were to decrease the disparity between the taxation of U.S. income and foreign income, equity would be enhanced. Similarly, economic efficiency would be enhanced if the effect of this option were to decrease the disparity between rates of taxation on U.S. income and foreign income, because taxpayers would have less of an incentive to locate in low-tax countries for tax reasons.

Current subpart F conforms with international norms. The addition of an effective tax rate test, which other countries have also employed, would also conform with international norms.[20] It is unlikely, however, that this option would significantly promote the goal of simplicity. The current subpart F regime is complicated, and retaining much of the current regime would mean retaining much of its complexity. Although elimination of the foreign-to-foreign related party rules could eliminate some complexity, calculating an effective tax rate could add complexity. Because the portion of the U.S. shareholder's subpart F inclusion attributable to passive income would continue to be subject to tax at regular U.S. rates, the distinction between active and passive income would need to be retained.

17. See Treas. Reg. § 1.954–1(d)(2) (effective tax rate determined as the ratio of the U.S. dollar amount of foreign taxes on an item of income to the U.S. dollar amount of the item of income).

18. For example, if the effective tax rate of the unit were 10 percent and the effective tax rate threshold were 25 percent, then an equalization payment of 15 percent would be currently payable by the U.S. taxpayer. Upon subsequent repatriation, the 10 percent of foreign tax and 15 percent of equalization payment would both be creditable (subject to foreign tax credit limitation rules, etc.)[.]

19. Subpart F previously contained a minimum distribution regime. This regime was repealed in 1975. * * *

20. For example, * * * Japan uses an effective tax rate test.

E. Other Reforms

As already noted, the options described above represent only a sampling of possible reforms to subpart F. Many other reforms could be considered, some of which could be incorporated into one or more of the options described above. For example, as suggested above, the calculations of foreign taxes paid under Option 2 or the effective foreign tax rate under Option 3 could be made on a foreign groupwide basis (rather than on an entity-by-entity basis). To avoid the formalistic distinctions that currently characterize subpart F (and facilitate avoidance of its rules), the rules could be amended to provide that all foreign entities, regardless of how they would otherwise be classified for U.S. tax purposes, would be subject to identical treatment under subpart F. Alternatively, clearer, more rational rules could be provided with respect to the treatment of non-corporate entities (e.g., partnerships and branches) under subpart F.

In addition, other fundamental changes to the U.S. anti-deferral regime could be considered, similar to the approaches that have been adopted in other countries. For example, some countries apply some form of a "list" approach to the taxation of foreign income. Under a "negative" list approach, income earned by an entity incorporated and/or resident in any of the jurisdictions on the list is currently taxable to the entity's shareholders. Under a mirror image of such an approach, a "positive" list approach, if an entity is resident in or incorporated in any of the jurisdictions on the list, non-passive income of such an entity would automatically qualify for deferral.[21] Other intermediate alternatives could involve combining a list of jurisdictions with an effective tax rate test, with the result that income earned by an entity in a jurisdiction on the list would only qualify for deferral if the income was subject to a specified minimum rate of tax.

Other possible reforms relate to the basic active/passive distinction that is currently used in subpart F. For example, rather than specifying types of income that do not qualify for deferral, rules could be provided that would specify when income would be considered "active" and would thereby qualify for deferral. Alternatively, certain types of income could presumptively qualify for deferral, while other types would qualify only if certain tests (focused on the activity involved in earning the income) were met. Another alternative would determine whether income was actively earned based on the ratio of the income to the costs properly associated with earning that income.

Each of these reforms, as well as numerous others not discussed, could be considered to amend the existing subpart F regime. Each such reform should be evaluated under the general international tax policy

---

21. Australia considered a negative listing approach but ultimately rejected it in favor of a positive listing approach, in part because of the perceived administrative and informational burden of maintaining a list of jurisdictions to be included on a negative list. * * *

principles set forth at the beginning of this chapter and the analysis and conclusions of this study.

IV. Conclusion on Options for Change

Although no specific recommendations for reform or replacement of subpart F are being made in this study, any subsequent reform of subpart F should be guided by the fundamental goals of international tax policy discussed in this chapter. To promote the goal of equity, the tax system should evenly apportion the tax burden between income from domestic and foreign investment. Because of its mobility and susceptibility to tax avoidance, foreign passive income should be taxed on a current basis. Equity concerns, as well as concerns of simplicity and administrability, also indicate that an anti-deferral regime should avoid inappropriate distinctions between business conducted in corporate form and business conducted in non-corporate form. To further the goal of economic efficiency, it is generally beneficial to reduce tax disparity between income from U.S. investment and income from foreign investment. To promote simplicity and administrability, an anti-deferral regime should provide a clear, simple and coherent distinction between passive and active income (if such a distinction is necessary), and should use a more comprehensive approach in targeting income subject to the anti-deferral rules. To address the increasing mobility of businesses, rules should, to the extent possible, not be based on the location of business activities. Although the tax policy goal of consistency with international norms can be met by a broad range of anti-deferral regimes, any such regime should avoid rules that may lead to international double taxation or double non-taxation or radically increase administrative burdens.

CHAPTER 8
RESTATEMENT OF CONCLUSIONS

I. Conclusions

A. Background to Subpart F

To place subpart F in a broad historical context, Chapter 1 considered developments in the tax laws from 1913 until the enactment of subpart F. As part of this analysis, Chapter 1 considered the extent to which the need for anti-deferral rules was the result of certain structural features of the U.S. tax system. The chapter concluded that subpart F was not a unique response to a specific set of tax avoidance problems that are no longer of concern. Rather, subpart F was, more generally, one in a series of measures addressing tax avoidance problems caused by a structural tension in the tax system. This tension is caused by the incompatibility of certain fundamental features of the U.S. tax system, principally the current taxation of worldwide income and the treatment of corporations as taxpayers and legal persons separate from their owners. These incompatible features are still a fundamental part of the U.S. tax system.

B. The Intent of Subpart F

Having placed subpart F in a broad historical context, the study next considered the specific legislative intent of subpart F. Chapter 2 concluded that the aims of subpart F were to prevent tax haven abuse, to prevent passive foreign income from escaping current U.S. taxation, to promote equity between U.S. taxpayers doing business overseas and those doing business in the United States, and to promote economic efficiency without unduly harming competitiveness.

Chapter 2 noted that the original 1961 proposal of the Kennedy Administration to end deferral completely was modified in 1962 because of concerns about the competitiveness of U.S.-owned foreign corporations. Nevertheless, Congress ultimately determined that U.S. taxpayers should not be able to use tax-avoidance techniques to obtain a wide disparity between domestic and foreign tax rates. The relative importance that Congress gave to preserving competitiveness is unclear, however, because in 1962 U.S. multinationals generally conducted their active foreign businesses in high-tax jurisdictions and tax haven devices were the primary cause of significant disparities between U.S. and foreign tax rates. The rules as enacted intended to address such tax haven devices. Congress heard testimony from the Administration indicating that enactment of the tax haven rules would largely preserve the benefits of the Administration's original proposal, although the Administration warned that limiting its proposal in this manner would likely result in increased complexity. Consequently, Congress may have believed that, by ending deferral only in the tax haven context and with respect to passive income, it was addressing the Administration's equity and efficiency goals without unduly harming competitiveness.

C. Economic Welfare and the Taxation of Foreign Income

Chapter 3 examined economic research discussing the best way to tax foreign income. In particular, Chapter 3 asked whether global or national economic welfare would be improved by allowing foreign income to be taxed at a lower rate than domestic income. The chapter summarized numerous economic analyses concerning this question and concluded that capital export neutrality is probably the best policy when the goal is to maximize global economic welfare. Further, whether the goal is to maximize global economic welfare or national economic welfare, Chapter 3 concluded that there appears to be little reason to abandon the conclusion that foreign investment income should be taxed no lower than domestic investment income.

After examining the broader issues, the chapter then examined the foreign-to-foreign related party rules. The chapter concluded that the current subpart F foreign-to-foreign related party rules (even if fully effective) have an uncertain effect on economic welfare.

D. Competitiveness and the Taxation of Foreign Income

Chapter 4 considered the issue of multinational competitiveness. The chapter first noted that promoting multinational competitiveness may conflict with the goal of promoting economic welfare. It then attempted to evaluate the effect of subpart F on competitiveness and concluded that the available data do not provide a reliable basis for evaluating whether subpart F has had a significant effect on multinational competitiveness. Although some have attempted to use statistics selectively in an attempt to show a decline in U.S. competitiveness, there is no convincing evidence of such a decline, nor is there convincing evidence regarding what impact, if any, subpart F may have had on these figures. Further, there are many other statistics that appear to show, generally, that the U.S. economy is highly competitive.

Chapter 4 also noted that the U.S. tax regime imposes a lower overall tax burden than that imposed in many other OECD countries. The chapter further determined that most developed countries did not need anti-deferral rules to discourage tax motivated offshore investments in 1962 because they maintained exchange controls that allowed them to monitor foreign direct investment. As these countries have eliminated or relaxed exchange controls within the last two decades, there has been a corresponding increase in CFC legislation to prevent tax base erosion. Thus, the current trend in other countries is to implement, or strengthen existing, CFC regimes.

E. How Effective is Subpart F?

Chapter 5 examined whether subpart F is effectively fulfilling its original goals discussed at length in (Chapter 2 and summarized above). The chapter concluded that subpart F may in some cases not be doing what it was intended to do. This is because it may now be possible to avoid some important provisions of subpart F, due in part to the proliferation of hybrid entities and the use of contract manufacturing and other arrangements. Therefore, it may be possible in some cases to deflect income to low-tax jurisdictions and earn passive income in low-tax jurisdictions without triggering subpart F.

F. Challenges to Subpart F: Entity Classification, Services and Electronic Commerce

Chapter 6 [excerpted at ¶ 6190] considered three major challenges to the effectiveness of subpart F: the entity classification rules of the Internal Revenue Code, the growth of services in the global economy and electronic commerce. Some of these already have had an effect on subpart F; all of them have the potential to have still greater effect in the future. The chapter concluded that a number of the assumptions underlying subpart F are no longer valid. For example, the rules of subpart F are based on the assumption that relatively immobile manufacturing activities in high-tax foreign countries are the typical active foreign business operations of U.S. multinationals. Further, subpart F assumes that these multinationals generally will conduct their active foreign businesses in jurisdictions with effective tax rates similar to U.S. rates. As such, subpart F deals with the problem of economic inefficiency caused by a disparity between U.S. and foreign tax rates by attempting to ensure that U.S. tax is imposed upon transactions that have the effect of stripping income out of high-tax jurisdictions into low-tax jurisdictions.

However, Chapter 6 concluded that an immobile manufacturing plant as the primary model for an active foreign subsidiary may be obsolete and that targeting related party transactions may no longer be an effective way to address tax disparity. First, the entity classification rules, and, particularly the check-the-box regulations, have greatly facilitated the formation of hybrids, which make many of the related party rules less effective. Second, because the rules preventing income stripping are largely focused on corporation-to-corporation transactions, they do not (even apart from the issue of hybrids) take into account the differing tax treatment of branches, joint ventures, partnerships, and other structures. Third, subpart F may not currently be adequate to prevent services industries from deflecting income to low-tax jurisdictions and otherwise exacerbating tax disparity, in part because of the difficulty in distinguishing between active and passive income in a services industry and the difficulty of defining the location of services. Finally, the growth of electronic commerce is likely to increase and place subpart F under greater pressure for a number of reasons, including the difficulty in identifying the location of activities, the difficulty of identifying the nature of the income arising from transactions, and the increased ease with which offshore activity can be undertaken.

G. Considering Options for Change

Chapter 7 discussed several options for the reform of subpart F. Although the chapter made no specific recommendations, it noted that any subsequent reform of subpart F should be guided by the fundamental goals of international tax policy as those goals were developed from the conclusions of this study. Thus, Chapter 7 concluded, generally, that to further the goal of equity, an anti-deferral regime should contribute to the even apportionment of the tax burden between income from domestic and foreign investment, it should tax passive income on a current basis, and it should avoid inappropriate distinctions between the conduct of business in corporate form and the conduct of business in non-corporate form. To promote the goal of economic efficiency, an anti-deferral regime generally should reduce the tax disparity between income from U.S. and foreign investment. To promote simplicity and administrability, an anti-deferral regime should provide a clear, simple and coherent distinction between passive and active income, and should use a more comprehensive approach in targeting income subject to the anti-deferral rules. To promote the goal of consistency with international norms, a broad range of anti-deferral regimes are possible, although any such regime should avoid rules that may lead to international double taxation or double non-taxation or that radically increase administrative burdens. Chapter 7 also noted that the impact of an anti-deferral regime on multinational competitiveness is a relevant factor but should not be considered in isolation, as it may conflict with the fundamental policy goals of equity and efficiency.

II. Summary of Conclusions

Subpart F was intended to address problems arising from incompatible features of U.S. tax law. These features are still incompatible and still in place. The problems they create still exist, and the need to address these problems is perhaps greater than ever. Because of changes in other areas of the law and changes in the nature of business, however, in significant ways subpart F may not effectively address these problems, and it may become less effective in the future.

A careful review of the economic literature reveals that capital export neutrality, which provides that U.S. and foreign income should be taxed at the same rates, is probably the best policy when the goal is to maximize economic welfare (although the foreign-to-foreign related party rules of subpart F may not be maximally efficient in all cases). Therefore, preventing significant tax disparity should remain an important goal.

An anti-deferral regime continues to be needed to prevent significant disparity between the rates of tax on U.S. and foreign income, thereby promoting efficiency, preserving the tax base and promoting equity.

* * *

[¶ 6380]

STAFF OF JOINT COMMITTEE ON TAXATION, OPTIONS TO IMPROVE TAX COMPLIANCE AND REFORM TAX EXPENDITURES

109th Cong., 1st Sess.
186–97 (Comm. Print 2005).

VI. INTERNATIONAL PROVISIONS

* * *

D. Adopt a Dividend Exemption System for Foreign Business Income

Present Law

"Worldwide" vs. "territorial" taxation of business income

The tax systems of the world generally reflect two basic approaches to the taxation of cross-border business income, often referred to as "worldwide" and "territorial" approaches. Under a pure worldwide tax system, resident corporations are taxable on their worldwide income, regardless of source, and the potential double taxation arising from overlapping source-country and residence-country taxing jurisdiction is mitigated by allowing a foreign tax credit. In contrast, under a pure territorial tax system, a country taxes only income derived within its borders, irrespective of the residence of the taxpayer. Thus, foreign-source income earned by a resident corporation is exempt from tax under a pure territorial tax system.

Each type of system may be said to promote a particular conception of economic efficiency. A pure worldwide tax system promotes capital export neutrality, a norm that holds that tax considerations should not influence a taxpayer's decision of whether to invest at home or abroad. Under a pure worldwide tax system, the after-tax return to an otherwise equivalent investment does not depend on whether the investment is made at home or abroad, since in either case the income from the investment generally will be subject to tax at the residence-country rate. Thus, investment-location decisions are governed by business considerations, instead of by tax law. A pure territorial system, on the other hand, promotes capital import neutrality, a norm that holds that all investment within a particular source country should be treated the same, regardless of the residence of the investor. Thus, if a residence country adopts a pure territorial system, residents of that country, when investing abroad in a particular source jurisdiction, will not receive a lower after-tax return than other investors by virtue of their country of residence.

In a world with diverse tax systems and rates, it is impossible fully to achieve both capital import neutrality and capital export neutrality at the same time. For example, suppose a source country offers a lower tax rate on a particular investment than the U.S. rate on a similar investment in the United States. Capital export neutrality would dictate that the United States impose a residual residence-based tax on the foreign investment at a level sufficient to make a U.S. investor indifferent on an after-tax basis between the two investment locations; however, doing so would violate capital import neutrality, as a U.S. investor in the source country would earn a lower after-tax rate of return compared to non-U.S. investors in the same source country, to the extent that such investors' residence countries did not assert a similar residual tax on the income. As long as different countries maintain different tax systems and rates, the two goals will remain in tension with each other.

The tax systems of all large, industrialized countries may be said to reflect varying compromises between these competing goals. Accordingly, no large, industrialized country employs a pure worldwide or pure territorial system. Existing systems may be accurately characterized as predominantly worldwide or territorial, but all systems share at least some features of both the worldwide and territorial approaches. Thus, systems commonly described as "worldwide" in fact include many territorial-type elements that promote capital import neutrality, such as indefinite deferral of tax on most types of foreign business income earned through foreign subsidiaries in the case of the United States. Similarly, systems commonly described as "territorial" include many worldwide-type features that promote capital export neutrality, such as residence-country taxation of passive income earned through foreign subsidiaries in lower-tax countries.

Many countries tax resident corporations on a predominantly territorial basis by exempting dividends received from foreign subsidiaries from residence-country tax.[415] This exemption typically applies only where the parent company's ownership in the subsidiary exceeds a certain threshold (commonly five to 10 percent), and the exemption may be total or partial (e.g., only 95 percent, or 60 percent, of qualifying dividends might be exempted, as a proxy for disallowing expenses allocable to exempt income). A number of restrictions generally apply, in order to limit the exemption to certain categories of income (e.g., active business income) and to address concerns about shifting income to lower-tax countries in order to avoid tax. These exemption systems generally do impose tax on foreign-source royalties and portfolio-type income.

The U.S. system: worldwide, deferral-based taxation of foreign business income

The United States employs a "worldwide" tax system, under which domestic corporations generally are taxed on all income, whether derived in the United States or abroad. Income earned by a domestic parent corporation from foreign operations conducted by foreign corporate subsidiaries generally is subject to U.S. tax when the income is distributed as a dividend to the domestic corporation. Until such repatriation, the U.S. tax on such income generally is deferred, and U.S. tax is imposed on such income when repatriated.

However, under anti-deferral rules, the domestic parent corporation may be taxed on a current basis in the United States with respect to certain categories of passive or highly mobile income earned by its foreign subsidiaries, regardless of whether the income has been distributed as a dividend to the domestic parent corporation. The main anti-deferral provisions in this context are the controlled foreign corporation ("CFC") rules of subpart F and the passive foreign investment company ("PFIC") rules.

A foreign tax credit generally is available to offset, in whole or in part, the U.S. tax owed on foreign-source income, whether earned directly by the domestic corporation, repatriated as a dividend from a foreign subsidiary, or included in income under the anti-deferral rules. The foreign tax credit generally is limited to the U.S. tax liability on a taxpayer's foreign-source income, in order to ensure that the credit serves its purpose of

415. These systems are often referred to as "participation exemption" systems.

mitigating double taxation of foreign-source income without offsetting the U.S. tax on U.S.-source income.

The foreign tax credit limitation is applied separately to different types of foreign-source income, in order to reduce the extent to which excess foreign taxes paid in a high-tax foreign jurisdiction can be "cross-credited" against the residual U.S. tax on low-taxed foreign-source income. For example, if a taxpayer pays foreign tax at an effective rate of 40 percent on certain active income earned in a high-tax jurisdiction, and pays little or no foreign tax on certain passive income earned in a low-tax jurisdiction, then the earning of the untaxed (or low-tax) passive income could expand the taxpayer's ability to claim a credit for the otherwise uncreditable excess foreign taxes paid to the high-tax jurisdiction, by increasing the foreign tax credit limitation without increasing the amount of foreign taxes paid. This sort of cross-crediting is constrained by rules that require the computation of the foreign tax credit limitation on a category-by-category basis. Thus, in the example above, the rules would place the passive income and the active income into separate limitation categories, and the low-tax passive income would not be allowed to increase the foreign tax credit limitation applicable to the credits arising from the high-tax active income. A significant degree of cross-crediting may be achieved within a single limitation category, however. For example, a high-tax dividend from a CFC and a low-tax royalty from another CFC may both fall into the general limitation category, with the result that potential excess credits associated with the dividend effectively may reduce the residual U.S. tax owed with respect to the royalty.

Reasons for Change

It has long been recognized that the worldwide, deferral-based system of present law distorts business decisions in a number of ways. By establishing repatriation as the system's principal taxable event, the worldwide, deferral-based system creates incentives in many cases to redeploy foreign earnings abroad instead of in the United States, thereby distorting corporate cash-management and financing decisions. At the same time, basing the system on repatriation renders the payment of U.S. tax on foreign-source business income substantially elective in many cases, because repatriation itself is elective. By maintaining deferral indefinitely, a taxpayer may achieve a result that is economically equivalent to 100–percent exemption of income, with no corresponding disallowance of expenses allocable to the exempt income, provided that the taxpayer does not repatriate the earnings or run afoul of subpart F or other anti-deferral rules.[422] In addition, taxpayers that repatriate high-tax earnings may be able to use excess foreign tax credits arising from these repatriations to

422. In addition, in some cases taxpayers may enter into transactions that are substantially equivalent to repatriations economically, but that are intended to escape taxation as such. Section 956 imposes limits on this practice with respect to many of the nearest repatriation equivalents.

offset the U.S. tax on lower-tax items of foreign-source income, such as royalties received for the use of intangible property in a low-tax country.

For these reasons, in many cases, the present-law "worldwide" system actually may yield results that are more favorable to the taxpayer than the results available in similar circumstances under the "territorial" exemption systems used by many U.S. trading partners, as these systems generally fully tax foreign-source royalties and portfolio-type income, and often exempt less than 100 percent of a dividend received from a subsidiary, as a proxy for disallowing expenses allocable to the exempt income. At the same time, however, the potential for taxation under the U.S. system by reason of either repatriation or application of the highly complex U.S. anti-deferral rules arguably forces U.S.-based multinationals to contend with a greater degree of complexity, and to engage in a greater degree of tax-distorted business planning, than many of their foreign-based counterparts resident in countries with exemption systems.

The present-law system thus creates a sort of paradox of defects: on the one hand, the system allows tax results so favorable to taxpayers in many instances as to call into question whether it adequately serves the purposes of promoting capital export neutrality or raising revenue; on the other hand, even as it allows these results, the system arguably imposes on taxpayers a greater degree of complexity and distortion of economic decision making than that faced by taxpayers based in countries with exemption systems, arguably impairing capital import neutrality in some cases.

The Congress recognized and addressed some of these problems in AJCA [2004 JOBS Act], but significant problems remain. Replacing the worldwide, deferral-based system with a dividend exemption system arguably would mitigate many of these remaining problems, while generally moving the system further in the direction charted by the Congress in 2004.

Description of Proposal

Overview

Under the proposed dividend exemption system, income earned abroad by foreign subsidiaries of U.S. parent corporations would fall into one of two categories: (1) passive and other highly mobile income, which would be taxed to the U.S. parent on a current basis under subpart F; or (2) all other income—i.e., active, less-mobile income not subject to subpart F—which would be exempt from U.S. tax and thus could be repatriated free of any tax impediment. The deferral and repatriation tax at the heart of the present-law system would be eliminated, and the foreign tax credit system would serve a more limited function than it does under present law.

CFC-parent dividends exempt from tax

A U.S. corporation that holds 10 percent or more of the stock of a CFC would exclude from income 100 percent of the dividends received from the CFC. This exclusion would be mandatory, and no foreign tax credits would arise with respect to foreign taxes attributable to the excluded dividend income (including both corporate-level income taxes and dividend withholding taxes). In addition, a special rule would provide that no subpart F inclusions would be created as a dividend moves up a chain of CFCs, to the extent that the dividend is attributable to a 10 percent or greater direct or indirect interest in the dividend-paying CFC owned by the U.S. parent. This rule would ensure that dividends could be repatriated from lower-tier CFCs without losing the benefit of dividend exemption, and it also would make it easier to redeploy CFC earnings in different foreign jurisdictions without triggering subpart F, thus promoting neutrality as to the decision of how to dispose of CFC earnings.

Under the dividend exemption system, CFC earnings would constitute a predominantly tax-exempt stream of income for the U.S. parent corporation. Accordingly, deductions for interest and certain other expenses incurred by the U.S. corporation would be disallowed to the extent allocable to exempt (non-subpart-F) CFC earnings. These allocations would be made as the earnings are generated, as opposed to when they are distributed. Thus, for expense allocation purposes, CFC earnings would be treated as giving rise to foreign-source income as they are earned.

Interest expense would first be allocated between U.S. and foreign-source income under rules similar to those of present law, including the interest allocation changes made by AJCA. The amount of interest expense allocated to foreign-source income under these rules then would be further allocated between exempt CFC earnings and other foreign-source income on a pro rata basis, based on assets. Research and experimentation expenses would first be allocated between U.S. and foreign-source income under rules similar to those of present law. The amount of research and experimentation expenses allocated to foreign-source income then would be further allocated first to taxable royalties and similar payments (e.g., cost-sharing or royalty-like sale payments) to the extent thereof, then to CFC earnings to the extent thereof (with this amount divided on a pro rata basis between exempt CFC earnings and non-exempt CFC earnings), and then finally to other foreign-source income. General and administrative expenses would be allocated to exempt CFC earnings in the same proportion that exempt CFC earnings of the group bears to overall earnings of the group. Other expenses, such as stewardship expenses, may be directly allocable to exempt CFC earnings in some cases. With respect to all of these categories of expenses, as under present law, it will be necessary for the Treasury Department to provide detailed expense allocation rules by regulation.

Other foreign-source income fully taxed

Non-dividend payments from the CFC to the U.S. corporation (e.g., interest, royalties, service fees, income from intercompany sales) would be fully subject to tax, and this tax generally would not be offset by cross-crediting as it often is under present law. In addition, dividends from non-CFCs, or from CFCs with respect to which the U.S. corporation is not at least a 10–percent shareholder, would be fully subject to tax.

Anti-avoidance rules retained

Subpart F would be retained in its current form. Thus, notwithstanding the general rule of dividend exemption, a U.S. corporation that holds a 10–percent or greater stake in a CFC would still face current income inclusion when the CFC earns certain types of passive or highly mobile income. As under present law, a subpart F inclusion would carry with it a credit for any foreign taxes associated with the subpart F income. The PFIC rules also would be retained in their current form.

Treatment of gain or loss on sale of CFC stock

A U.S. corporation's gain on the sale of CFC stock would be excluded from income to the extent of undistributed exempt earnings. Any excess of gain over this amount would be taxable, even though some of this gain may relate to appreciation of assets that would have generated exempt income.[425] Deductions for losses on the sale of CFC stock would be disallowed.

Foreign branches

Foreign branch income would be exempt to the same extent as it would be if earned by a CFC, under rules that would treat foreign trades or businesses conducted directly by a U.S. corporation as CFCs for all Federal tax purposes. Thus, subpart F would apply to branch operations, branch losses would not flow directly onto a U.S. corporation's tax return,

425. Allocating gain between appreciation of assets that produce exempt income and those that produce non-exempt income, while perhaps attractive in theory, would be highly complex and would introduce difficult issues of valuation into the system.

and transactions between the U.S. corporation and the foreign branch would be subject to the full range of rules dealing with intercompany transactions. Except as provided in regulations, all trades or businesses conducted predominantly within the same country would be treated as a single CFC for this purpose. The Treasury Secretary would be given regulatory authority to issue the rules necessary to place branches and CFCs on an equal footing for these purposes.

Transition and collateral issues

Transition

The exemption system would apply only with respect to CFC earnings generated after the effective date, thus requiring ongoing separate tracking of earnings pools. With respect to pre-effective-date earnings, the present-law system would continue to apply in all respects. Dividends would be treated as coming first from exempt, post-effective-date earnings and then from pre-effective-date earnings.

Collateral change to subpart F

The deemed-repatriation rules of section 956 would be repealed, as these rules are merely a backstop to the present-law repatriation tax, which would be eliminated under the proposed system. (However, as indicated above, these and all other relevant rules of present law would continue to apply to pre-effective-date earnings.)

Collateral changes to the foreign tax credit

The foreign tax credit would remain in place with respect to: (1) income that is included on a current basis under the subpart F or PFIC rules; and (2) other foreign-source income that is not eligible for exemption (e.g., dividends received on a portfolio investment in a foreign corporation, foreign-source royalty income earned directly by the U.S. corporation).

The indirect foreign tax credit of section 902 would be repealed, except insofar as it applies to subpart F inclusions. This rule would eliminate the indirect foreign tax credit for noncontrolled section 902 corporations ("10–50 companies"). A foreign tax credit generally would remain available with respect to withholding taxes imposed on dividends received from 10–50 companies, as these dividends generally would remain subject to U.S. tax under the proposal. However, a U.S. corporation would be allowed to elect to treat its investment in a 10–50 company as an investment in a CFC for Federal tax purposes, thus rendering the investment both eligible for dividend exemption and subject to subpart F. Thus, the U.S. corporation effectively would choose between treating the 10–50 investment as a portfolio-type investment or as a direct, CFC-type investment.

The separate limitation categories of section 904 would be repealed, and thus the foreign tax credit limitation would apply on an overall basis. By removing most foreign business income from the foreign tax credit system altogether, most high-tax foreign-source income would be removed from the computation, greatly reducing the potential for cross-crediting relative to present law. Under these conditions, it would no longer be necessary to apply the limitation on a separate-category basis.

No change would be made to the export source rule under section 863(b), but the benefits of this rule would be significantly reduced or eliminated in most cases, in view of the narrowed scope of the foreign tax credit and the likelihood that most taxpayers will be in excess-limitation positions under the new system (because most high-tax foreign income will be exempted, leaving mostly low-tax or untaxed foreign-source income in the foreign tax credit system).

Treaties

The proposed system would require the renegotiation of existing income tax treaties, which are premised on the assumption that the United States will continue to operate a worldwide tax system. For example, existing treaties generally require the United States to allow foreign tax credits for foreign corporate income taxes and dividend withholding taxes under certain circumstances. These treaties would have to be revised to reflect the conversion from a credit mechanism to an exemption mechanism.

Effective Date

The proposal is generally effective for taxable years of foreign corporations beginning after the date of enactment, and for taxable years of U.S. shareholders with or within which such taxable years of such foreign corporations end. The rules dealing with foreign branches are effective for taxable years of U.S. corporations beginning after the date of enactment.

Discussion

As described above, the present-law deferral system arguably imposes on taxpayers a greater degree of complexity and distortion of economic decision making than that faced by taxpayers based in countries with exemption systems, arguably impairing capital import neutrality in some cases. At the same time, the system allows tax results so favorable to taxpayers in many instances as to call into question whether it adequately serves the purposes of promoting capital export neutrality or raising revenue. Although the Congress recognized and addressed some of these problems in AJCA, significant problems remain. Replacing the worldwide, deferral-based system with a dividend exemption system arguably would mitigate many of these remaining problems, while generally moving the system further in the direction charted by the Congress in 2004.

For example, recognizing that deferral-based taxation created an impediment to repatriating certain foreign earnings, the Congress in 2004 provided a temporary window during which foreign earnings could be repatriated at a reduced rate of tax. This legislation reduced the tax impediment to repatriating existing earnings, but as a temporary provision, it left this impediment in place with respect to future earnings. Indeed, to the extent that taxpayers may expect the provision to be adopted again as a fiscal stimulus response to a future downturn, they may be even less likely to repatriate earnings at full tax cost after the temporary window than they were before the window. Adopting a dividend exemption system would remove the repatriation disincentive permanently, in a manner generally consistent with steps that the Congress has already taken on a temporary basis.

More broadly, the Congress made a number of changes to the international tax provisions of the Code that will promote greater capital import neutrality. Most significantly in this regard, the foreign tax credit rules were amended in a number of ways in order to reduce the burden on U.S. taxpayers of the foreign tax credit limitation.[426] More limited changes were made outside the foreign tax credit area, but these changes also generally moved the system in the direction of greater capital import neutrality.[427] Adopting a dividend exemption system would further pro-

426. See AJCA secs. 401 (interest allocation), 402 (overall domestic loss), 403 (noncontrolled sec. 902 corporations), 404 (reduction of number of separate limitation categories), 406 (treatment of deemed royalties), and 417 (extension of carryover period). These changes promote capital import neutrality in the long run, as they reduce the U.S. residence-country tax burden imposed on the cross-border income of U.S. taxpayers. More directly, these changes also may be viewed as promoting capital export neutrality, because they reduce the impact of the foreign tax credit limitation. The foreign tax credit limitation, while necessary to preserve full U.S. taxing jurisdiction with respect to U.S.-source income, impairs capital export neutrality by allowing investments in high-tax foreign jurisdictions to be subjected to a greater aggregate tax burden than comparable investments in the United States.

427. See, e.g., AJCA secs. 407 (dealer exceptions to deemed repatriation rules), 412 (subpart F treatment of CFC sales of partnership interests), 414 (subpart F treatment of commodities transactions), 415 (subpart F treatment of aircraft leasing and shipping income), and 416 (subpart F active financing exception).

mote capital import neutrality in many cases, as U.S. corporations no longer would need to contend with the possibility of residual U.S. taxation with respect to most types of foreign business income. Adopting a dividend exemption system also would specifically promote the Congress's demonstrated goal of further simplifying the foreign tax credit regime, as the regime would be rendered inapplicable to most foreign business income, which would simply be exempt from U.S. tax under the system. Application of the foreign tax credit regime on a more limited basis would reduce the amount of income and activity subject to these complex rules, and would allow further simplifying changes to be made to them, including the elimination of separate limitation categories.

While the Congress made sweeping changes to the foreign tax credit regime in 2004, the Congress made no similarly sweeping changes with respect to the anti-deferral regimes. The complexity of these regimes, the distortions that they produce, and their diminishing effectiveness in promoting capital export neutrality are all problems that remain to be solved. The seriousness of these problems, and the appropriateness of various possible solutions, are not significantly affected by moving to a dividend exemption system. Under either type of system, effective regimes are needed to prevent the avoidance of tax through shifting income into low-tax jurisdictions, without unduly interfering with the operation of nontax-motivated business structures. Accordingly, the desirability of various proposals that the Congress may wish to consider in this area is largely independent of the question of whether to adopt a dividend exemption system or to retain the present-law worldwide, deferral-based system—in either case, certain categories of passive or highly mobile foreign income must be defined and subjected to immediate U.S. tax.[428]

Although moving from the present-law system to a dividend exemption system broadly promotes capital import neutrality, such a move also should serve to promote capital export neutrality in a few respects. For example, in cases in which indefinite deferral and cross-crediting of high-tax dividends with low-tax royalties may produce results more advantageous to a taxpayer than the results available under a typical dividend exemption system, capital export neutrality may be improved by shifting to dividend exemption. In addition, the disallowance of deductions for interest and overhead expenses allocable to exempt income may have the

428. There are several proposals dealing with subpart F that the Congress may wish to consider, either in conjunction with this proposal or as freestanding proposals. One such proposal would be to limit taxpayers' ability to use disregarded entities to avoid what would traditionally have been subpart F income * * *. Other possible proposals include repeal of the foreign base company sales and services income rules, which arguably are outmoded and distort business decision making, and yet appear to be ineffective as a practical matter in promoting capital export neutrality and reinforcing the transfer pricing rules. Another possible proposal would be to make permanent the active financing exception of sections 954(h) and (i) and 953(e), in order to promote greater certainty and stability in the tax law.

effect of promoting capital export neutrality, although this effect would be offset to some extent by exemption itself.[429]

Thus, like any other system, the proposed system would result in a compromise between these two efficiency norms, but arguably a better compromise, involving less complexity and fewer distortions than the present-law system. On the other hand, the continued need for provisions like subpart F and the inter-company pricing rules means that significant complexity will remain, and the transition from the present-law system to the proposed system will create significant complexities of its own.

Some have expressed a concern that switching from a deferral system to an exemption system might cause U.S. investment to flow out of the United States and into lower-tax countries, because permanent exemption is thought to be significantly more attractive than the deferral available under present law. While such an incentive may arise in certain circumstances, there is little evidence that this would generally be the case. First, as discussed above, the indefinite deferral available under present law is in many cases no worse a tax result for taxpayers than the tax results available under a dividend exemption system. Second, as long as the exemption system maintains anti-avoidance provisions of present law, such as subpart F and the transfer pricing rules of sections 482 and 367(d), problems of tax avoidance should be similar under both types of system.[431] Third, the disallowance of deductions for expenses allocable to exempt income should serve as a brake on any incentive to move investments and activities offshore, as the exemption achieved by such a shift may come at a cost of greater deduction disallowance.

Economists who have studied how moving to a dividend exemption system might affect the location incentives of U.S. corporations find no definitive evidence that incentives would be significantly changed. Two recent studies examine how the incentive to invest in low-tax locations abroad would be affected if the United States were to move to a dividend exemption system similar to the one described here.[432] In both studies, the authors consider dividend exemption systems that impose allocation rules similar to those of present law so that some portion of deductions for interest and overhead expenses incurred by the U.S. parent company and allocated to exempt foreign income are disallowed as deductions from U.S. taxable income. One study concludes that under dividend exemption, the

429. Even if a dividend exemption system is not adopted, some would favor allocating certain expenses to CFC earnings and deferring deductions for the expenses so allocable during the period that the U.S. tax on the CFC earnings is deferred.

431. To the extent that permanent exemption is more favorable than the indefinite-but-restricted deferral available under present law, an exemption system may place somewhat more pressure on some of these rules, thus making it somewhat more important to remedy existing defects in the design and administration of those rules.

432. Harry Grubert and John Mutti, *Taxing International Business Income: Dividend Exemption versus the Current System,* Washington, D.C., American Enterprise Institute (2001) ("Grubert and Mutti"); and Rosanne Altshuler and Harry Grubert, "Where Will They Go if We Go Territorial? Dividend Exemption and the Location Decisions of U.S. Multinational Corporations," *National Tax Journal,* Vol. LIV, No. 4 (December 2001) ("Altshuler and Grubert").

effective tax rate on U.S. investment in low-tax locations would actually increase relative to the system in place prior to AJCA.[433] Although active foreign business income would avoid U.S. residual taxation, the loss of the ability to shield U.S. tax on foreign royalties through cross-crediting and to claim deductions for overhead and interest expense at home (or in other high-tax locations) results in higher tax burdens in low-tax locations. The second study presents hypothetical effective tax rates for incremental investment by a U.S. taxpayer in a low-tax subsidiary abroad under the U.S. tax system in place prior to AJCA and under dividend exemption with expense allocation rules.[434] This study also finds that the tax burden of investing in low-tax countries may increase under dividend exemption. In addition, the study uses two other approaches to investigate how location decisions may change under dividend exemption: a comparison of foreign direct investment patterns for the United States and for two countries which exempt dividends received from foreign affiliates resident in countries with which they have tax treaties (Germany and Canada) and an empirical analysis of the extent to which residual U.S. taxes on low-tax foreign earnings impact the location decisions of U.S. corporations. Neither approach yielded results that would suggest that location decisions would be significantly altered if the United States were to exempt dividends from residence country taxation.

[¶ 6385]

NOTES

1. The OECD has devoted considerable resources to the issue of harmful tax competition among countries. In 1998, the Council of Ministers of the OECD adopted a report on the issue, Harmful Tax Competition: An Emerging Global Issue (hereinafter "OECD Report"). In the OECD's view, a country's tax practices constitute harmful tax competition when they are designed to erode the tax base of other countries. The OECD Report identifies two categories of harmful tax competition: tax havens and harmful preferential tax regimes. Tax havens are countries that impose nominal or no effective rates of income tax and that have other features such as a lack of transparency in the operation of their legislative, administrative or legal process, a lack of effective information exchange with other governments and a lack of a requirement of substantial activities for transactions to be treated as arising in the country. Harmful preferential tax regimes are countries that offer nominal or no rates of income tax on certain types of income (through such devices as tax holidays) that are insulated from domestic taxpayers through a variety of means (sometimes called "ring-fenced" regimes) and that have other features such as a lack of transparency in their legislative, administrative or legal process and a lack of effective information exchange with other governments. The OECD Report contained a number of recommendations,

433. Grubert and Mutti.

434. Altshuler and Grubert.

including a recommendation that countries enact controlled foreign corporation and passive foreign investment company regimes as means of combating harmful tax competition. The OECD Report also created a Forum on Harmful Tax Practices, which evaluates the tax regimes of countries, analyzes the effectiveness of measures taken to combat harmful tax competition and produces and updates a list of tax haven and preferential tax regimes. The purpose of the list is to focus attention on the listed countries and to encourage those countries to change their tax regimes.

Critics of the OECD's efforts claim that the OECD is attempting to set minimum tax rates and will thereby impede innovation in countries' tax systems and discourage countries from lowering their tax rates. In addition, some critics argue that the OECD, most of the member countries of which are industrialized wealthy countries, is attempting to undermine developing countries' ability to attract investment capital by preventing them from offering tax incentives to foreign investors.

2. In Chapter 1, before having the opportunity to study the U.S. foreign tax credit system, the foreign earned income exclusion and the anti-deferral regimes, you were asked to design a system for taxing the income of Industrian individuals and entities from working, conducting business or investing abroad. How do the U.S. rules fare as a prototype for the system that you would design to mitigate international double taxation and to deal with the deferral issue? Would you place greater emphasis on the traditional equity and efficiency (i.e., capital-export neutrality) concerns, or, instead, on concerns about the impact of your system on the competitiveness of Industrian enterprises operating abroad (i.e., capital-import neutrality)? How would capital-ownership neutrality concerns affect your conclusions? In what ways would you modify the U.S. rules if you were in fact reporting to the Government of Industria? Would you recommend adoption of an exemption system along the lines suggested in the Joint Committee Staff's tax reform report? Would adoption of such an exemption system result in significant simplicity and efficiency gains or instead result in increased complexity and significant efficiency losses? How would adoption of such an exemption system fare under an equity analysis?

CHAPTER 7

FOREIGN TAX CREDIT LIMITATIONS: SEPARATE BASKETS, LOSSES AND LOOK-THROUGH RULES

■ ■ ■

[¶ 7000]

A. INTRODUCTION

This Chapter will examine some of the special rules that are used in calculating the separate limitations on the foreign tax credit under Section 904(d)(1). In particular, the focus here will be on (i) the definitions of the categories or "baskets" of income subject to separate application of the Section 904(a) limitation, (ii) the treatment of foreign- and U.S.-source losses and (iii) the look-through rules that apply in specified circumstances. These look-through rules apply when a U.S. shareholder receives interest, royalties, rents or dividends or is deemed to receive a constructive Subpart F inclusion from a controlled foreign corporation, when a controlled foreign corporation receives interest, royalties, rents or dividends from another controlled foreign corporation and when a U.S. corporation receives dividends from a noncontrolled Section 902 corporation.

[¶ 7005]

B. DEFINITIONS OF THE SEPARATE CATEGORIES OF INCOME UNDER SECTION 904(d)(1)

For the reasons discussed in Chapter 5, Congress decided in 1986 to reduce the opportunities for cross-crediting excess foreign tax credits generated by foreign-source income subject to high foreign taxes against the U.S. tax otherwise imposed on low-taxed or tax-free foreign-source income. The method selected was to require that the limitation of Section 904(a) be applied separately to eight (formerly nine) principal categories (or "baskets" as they are often called) of foreign-source income that were identified in subparagraphs (A) through (I) of the former version of Section 904(d)(1). (Subparagraph (E) was repealed for post-2002 years.) As a result of the 2004 JOBS Act, the number of Section 904(d)(1) baskets is reduced from eight to two—an expanded passive category income basket, Section 904(d)(1)(A), and the general category income basket, Section 904(d)(1)(B)—effective for tax years starting after 2006. In addition, separate limitations are applied to two specialized categories of income. Section 907(a) applies a separate limitation to foreign oil and gas taxes, and Sections 865(h), 904(d)(6) and 904(h) apply separate limitations to certain types of income that would otherwise be treated as U.S.-source but are treated as foreign-source under an applicable tax treaty. The limitations applicable to treaty-resourced income are discussed at ¶ 7042.

The separate basket regime requires that the foreign tax credit be calculated separately for each type of foreign-source income included in a particular category or basket. The foreign tax credit for each income category is subject to the Section 904(a) limitation calculated as follows:

$$\frac{\text{Foreign-source taxable income in relevant category}}{\text{Worldwide taxable income}} \times \text{U.S. tax on worldwide income} = \text{Limitation applicable to category}$$

This separate limitation approach prevents foreign taxes that exceed the U.S. effective tax on taxable income in one limitation category or basket from offsetting the U.S. tax on taxable income that is included in another category or basket.

The separate baskets take precedence over the general category income basket. Any income that does not fall into a separate basket automatically falls into the general category income limitation basket, which, therefore, can be thought of as a residual limitation basket. This basket (hereinafter simply the "general limitation basket") was identified in former Section 904(d)(1)(I) for tax years starting before 2007 and is identified in Section 904(d)(1)(B) for tax years starting thereafter.[1]

Both the definitions of the categories of foreign-source income subject to separate application of the Section 904(a) limitation and the look-through rules under Sections 904(d)(3) and 904(d)(4) that apply to certain income received by a U.S. person from a foreign corporation rely heavily on concepts used in the controlled foreign corporation provisions. For that reason, examination in detail of the definitions of the income placed in

1. A special rule deals with the carryover of taxes paid or accrued in tax years starting before 2007. Taxes paid or accrued in pre-2007 tax years that are carried forward to a subsequent tax year are included either in the passive income or in the general limitation basket, as appropriate, for the tax year to which carried. § 904(d)(2)(K)(i). Carrybacks of creditable income taxes for tax years starting after 2006 are to be allocated to pre-2007 baskets under Temp. Reg. § 1.904-2T(i)(2).

separate baskets and of the look-through rules has been postponed until the controlled foreign corporation provisions, discussed in Chapter 6, have been reviewed.

The separate basket limitations apply to the total of direct foreign tax credits under Sections 901 and 903 and indirect foreign tax credits under Sections 902 and 960 related to the total amount of taxable income included in each of the limitation baskets. In addition, Section 1291(g) applies similar limitations to excess distribution taxes on distributions from a passive foreign investment company ("PFIC").

To apply the separate foreign tax credit limitations, the taxpayer must take the following steps for each basket:

(1) Determine the amount of gross income included in the basket;

(2) Allocate and apportion deductions to that gross income to determine taxable income in the basket and

(3) Identify all direct and indirect foreign tax credits attributable to that taxable income.

In addition, in appropriate cases, it will be necessary to take one or more of the following steps:

(1) Apply the look-through rules of Section 904(d)(3) to interest, rents, royalties, dividends and Subpart F inclusions from controlled foreign corporations;

(2) Apply the look-through rule of Section 904(d)(4) to certain dividends received by a U.S. corporation from noncontrolled Section 902 corporations;

(3) Make the adjustments for any preferential rate of tax on capital gains discussed at ¶ 5265;

(4) Apply the rules for carryback or carryover of excess foreign tax credits discussed at ¶ 5225;

(5) Make the adjustments for U.S.-source or foreign-source losses discussed at ¶¶ 7055 et seq.

It should be emphasized that the separate limitation basket regime reduces, but by no means eliminates, the opportunities for cross-crediting excess foreign tax credits generated by some high-tax foreign-source income against the U.S. tax otherwise imposed on other foreign-source income subject to a low or no foreign tax. Cross-crediting opportunities are most extensive within the general limitation basket, which is therefore a principal focus of international tax planning.

[¶ 7010]

1. PASSIVE INCOME

The Section 904(d)(1)(A) passive category income basket (hereinafter called simply "the passive income basket") includes income that would be foreign personal holding company income under Section 954(c) if it were received by a controlled foreign corporation. § 904(d)(2)(A). In many cases, the recipient of the passive income will be a U.S. person, not a controlled foreign corporation, but the Section 954(c) definition is applied as if the U.S. person were a controlled foreign corporation. Reg. § 1.904–4(b)(1)(i)(A).

Because it incorporates by reference the Section 954(c) definition of foreign personal holding company income, passive income will generally include such items of income as dividends, interest, royalties and rents. It also includes gains from the sale or exchange of property (other than inventory) that produces foreign personal holding company income or that produces no income. § 954(c)(1)(B). In addition, passive income includes certain foreign currency gains, gains from certain commodities transactions, certain income that is equivalent to interest, income from notional principal contracts, certain payments made in lieu of dividends and amounts received under certain personal service contracts involving a 25-percent shareholder. § 954(c)(1)(C)-(H). For tax years starting after 2006, the passive income basket includes some categories of income previously included in other separate baskets, such as (i) high withholding tax interest and (ii) financial services income not earned by a specified financial services entity.

The principal exceptions to the Section 954(c) definition of foreign personal holding company income in the controlled foreign corporation context also apply to the definition of passive income for purposes of Section 904(d)(1)(A). The same-country-related-person exceptions of Section 954(c)(3)(A) for certain dividends, interest, rents and royalties also exclude them from passive income if received by a controlled foreign corporation. Passive income generally does not include royalties or rents derived in the active conduct of a trade or business whether received from related or unrelated persons. Temp. Reg. § 1.904–4T(b)(2)(iii)(A). Moreover, the regulations provide that, for purposes of the Section 904(d)(1)(A) limitation, royalties or rents will be deemed to be derived in the active conduct of a business if the active-business test is met by any one of an affiliated group of corporations (within the meaning of Section 1504(a) without regard to Section 1504(b)). For purposes of this affiliated group rule, the regulations define affiliated group to include only U.S. corporations and controlled foreign corporations in which U.S. members of the group own, directly or indirectly, at least 80 percent of the stock (by voting power and value). Temp. Reg. § 1.904–4T(b)(2)(iii)(B).[2]

Reflecting the ongoing efforts of Congress to encourage U.S. exports (the efficacy of which is a matter of some debate), Section 904 contains a number of provisions that accord favored treatment to export financing interest. One of these excludes export financing interest received by a U.S. person from the definition of passive income with the result that such excluded interest generally falls into the general limitation basket. § 904(d)(2)(B)(iii)(I). "Export financing interest" is defined to include interest from financing the sale or other disposition of property if the property (i) is for use or consumption outside the United States, (ii) is manufactured, produced, grown or extracted in the United States by the taxpayer or a related person and (iii) not more than 50 percent of its fair market value is attributable to imported products. § 904(d)(2)(G); Reg. § 1.904–4(h)(1)(i). However, income derived by a U.S. person (or a controlled foreign corporation) on an export trade or service receivable acquired from a related person does not qualify for the export financing interest exception, and thus is passive income, because it constitutes related person factoring income under Section 864(d)(1). For a similar reason, interest received by a controlled foreign corporation on loans to finance purchases of inventory or services of a related person under Section 864(d)(6) is passive income. However, such interest received by a U.S. person can qualify as export financing interest and be included in the general limitation basket. Temp. Reg. § 1.904–4T(h)(3)(i) and (ii). See ¶ 11,235.

High-taxed income, as defined in Section 904(d)(2)(F), is also excluded from passive income. § 904(d)(2)(B)(iii)(II). This exclusion is sometimes referred to as the "high-tax kickout." It results in moving the excluded high-taxed income to the general limitation basket to preclude cross-crediting the high foreign tax against the U.S. tax otherwise imposed on low-taxed or tax-free income in the passive income basket. Income falls within the high-taxed income exclusion if the foreign taxes it bears exceed the highest rate of U.S. individual or corporate tax, as the case may be. § 904(d)(2)(F). In determining whether foreign-source income is high-taxed income, gross foreign-source income must be reduced by deductions properly allocated and apportioned to it. See Reg. § 1.904–4(c)(2)(ii). In the case of dividends received from a foreign corporation, the foreign taxes taken into account include both withholding tax potentially creditable under Section 901 or Section 903 and corporate income tax potentially creditable under Section 902 or Section 960.

Dividends from a domestic international sales corporation ("DISC") or former DISC and certain distributions from a former foreign sales corporation ("FSC") are included in "specified passive income," which in

2. For purposes of the controlled foreign corporation provisions, rents and royalties from related persons derived in the active conduct of business would not be excluded from foreign personal holding company income under Section 954(c)(2)(A). In addition, the active-business test must be met by the controlled foreign corporation itself. See ¶ 6085.

turn is included in the passive income basket. § 904(d)(2)(A)(i) and 904(d)(2)(B)(v). Financial services income is treated as general limitation income in the case of a specified financial services entity. § 904(d)(2)(C). Otherwise, such income is passive income.

[¶ 7015]

2. HIGH WITHHOLDING TAX INTEREST

High withholding tax interest is interest that is subject to a foreign tax of at least five percent imposed on the gross amount thereof. If earned in tax years starting before 2007, such interest was included in the former Section 904(d)(1)(B) separate basket. Former § 904(d)(2)(B)(i). Typically, such a tax will be withheld at the source; but even if the tax was not withheld by the payor and was paid by the U.S. taxpayer, the separate basket limitation applied.

For tax years starting before 2007, high withholding tax interest was placed in a separate basket because a five-percent tax on gross interest is likely to represent a very high tax on the *net* amount of interest earned by a bank or other lending institution after expenses (including interest paid on the lending institution's borrowings) are deducted from the gross interest income subject to the five-percent foreign tax. If the interest were not subject to a separate limitation, this high tax on net interest income could be cross-credited against the U.S. tax otherwise applicable to foreign-source interest that is often exempt from foreign income tax. Such an exemption may be available under local law, and, in any event, is often provided by the terms of a tax treaty between the United States and a foreign country in which the borrower resides.

For tax years starting after 2006, high withholding tax interest is no longer placed in a separate basket; in most cases, it falls into the enlarged passive income basket, thus expanding the cross-crediting opportunities for foreign taxes on such income.

[¶ 7020]

3. FINANCIAL SERVICES INCOME

For tax years starting before 2007, financial services income was subject to a separate limitation under former Section 904(d)(1)(C) because often it could be shifted quite easily to a low-tax or tax-free foreign jurisdiction. Such shifting enabled U.S. corporations to cross-credit excess credits generated by high-taxed foreign income against the U.S. tax otherwise imposed on low-taxed or tax-exempt foreign-source financial services income. Before the 1986 Act, even U.S. manufacturing corporations were establishing captive banking and financing entities in tax havens in order to assist in absorbing excess foreign tax credits.

Only a person "predominantly engaged in the active conduct of a banking, insurance, financing or similar business" or a member of a financial services group (each herein a "financial services entity") can include financial services income in the general limitation basket. § 904(d)(2)(C)(i). A financial services group means any affiliated group (as defined in Section 1504(a) excluding paragraphs (2) and (3) of Section 1504(b)) which is so engaged. § 904(d)(2)(C)(ii). A person will be treated as a financial services entity if at least 80 percent of its gross income consists of "active financing income." Reg. § 1.904–4(e)(3)(i). Active financing income includes a long list of types of income from financial operations. The list includes, for example, interest on loans, income from transactions involving negotiable instruments and letters of credit, income from trust services, income from underwriting the issuance of securities, income earned by broker-dealers from securities and commodities transactions and income from investment advisory services. Reg. § 1.904–4(e)(2).

Once a person has been identified as a financial services entity, the following three categories of its income are included in financial services income:

(1) income from an active banking, financing or similar business, Section 904(d)(2)(D)(ii)(I),

(2) certain insurance-related income, Section 904(d)(2)(D)(ii)(II) and (III) and

(3) passive income, even if it would otherwise be excluded from passive income as high-taxed income, Section 904(d)(2)(D)(i)(II).

For tax years starting after 2006, Section 904(d)(2)(C)(i) treats financial services income as general limitation income in the case of a financial services entity. Other financial services income is passive income. Regulations prescribe the treatment of financial services income received or accrued by partnerships and other pass-through entities that are not members of a financial services group. Reg. § 1.904(e)(3)(iii).

[¶ 7025]

4. SHIPPING INCOME

For tax years starting before 2007, a separate basket under former Section 904(d)(1)(D) was provided for shipping income because it is often subject to a low or to no foreign tax. If such income were included in the general limitation basket, it could be used to absorb excess foreign tax credits generated by other general limitation income subject to high foreign taxes.

"Shipping income" was income of a kind that would have been "foreign base company shipping income," as defined in former Section 954(f), if such income were received by a controlled foreign corporation. Former § 904(d)(2)(D). It included income from the use, hiring or leasing for use of an aircraft or vessel in foreign commerce, dividends from a foreign corporation attributable to foreign base company shipping income and income from space and ocean activities. Former § 954(f). Section 954(f) was repealed by the 2004 JOBS Act (thereby ending the exposure of shipping income to constructive dividend treatment under Subpart F).

For tax years starting after 2006, shipping income is no longer included in a separate basket but is generally included in the Section 904(d)(1)(B) general limitation basket.

[¶ 7030]

5. DIVIDENDS FROM NONCONTROLLED SECTION 902 CORPORATIONS

Until 2003, the Section 904(d) separate limitation rules drew a fundamental distinction between the treatment of dividends from a controlled foreign corporation and those from a noncontrolled foreign corporation.

As noted in Chapter 6 and further discussed at ¶ 7085, actual dividends and constructive dividend inclusions under Subpart F, as well as interest, rents and royalties, received by a U.S. shareholder from a controlled foreign corporation are classified for foreign tax credit limitation purposes under look-through rules prescribed by Section 904(d)(3). The broad effect of these rules is that the determination of the limitation basket into which actual or constructive dividends, interest, rents and royalties received by a U.S. shareholder from a controlled foreign corporation fall depends on the classification of the underlying income received by the foreign corporation. Thus, if all of the income of the controlled foreign corporation is active-business income that falls into the Section 901(d)(1)(B) general limitation basket, any dividends and constructive dividend inclusions under Subpart F, interest, rents and royalties received from the controlled foreign corporation by a U.S. shareholder will also fall into the general limitation basket. With respect to income in that basket, high foreign taxes can be cross-credited against the U.S. tax otherwise applicable to income subject to a low or to no foreign tax.

The rationale for this look-through treatment is that controlled foreign corporations within a U.S.-based multinational group could be regarded as parts of a single economic unit and could be treated substantially as if they were foreign branches of the U.S. parent corporation. If a U.S. corporation operated in foreign countries exclusively through foreign branches (rather than through controlled foreign subsidiaries), income earned by the branches would be classified for limitation basket purposes in accordance with the types of income earned by the branches themselves and cross-crediting of foreign taxes within each limitation income basket would be permitted. The Section 904(d)(3) look-through rules treat actual and constructive dividends, interest, rents and royalties from a controlled foreign corporation in the hands of a U.S. shareholder broadly in the same manner as income earned by foreign branches by treating the controlled foreign corporation, in effect, as a conduit for purposes of the foreign tax credit limitations.

Congress was not, however, prepared in 1986 to treat noncontrolled foreign corporations as if they were branches for foreign tax credit limitation purposes. On the contrary, for them, it adopted a stringent regime under which dividends received by a U.S. corporation from *each* noncontrolled Section 902 corporation had to be placed in a separate limitation basket under since-repealed Section 904(d)(1)(E). Thus, excess foreign tax credits carried along with dividends from a noncontrolled Section 902 foreign corporation could not be cross-credited against the U.S. taxes otherwise imposed on any other foreign-source income, not even dividends from another noncontrolled Section 902 corporation. Moreover, the Section 904(d)(3) look-through rules did not and still do not apply to interest, rents or royalties paid to a U.S. shareholder by a foreign corporation that is not a controlled foreign corporation.

The separate basket for dividends from each noncontrolled Section 902 corporation applied only to a U.S. corporation receiving a dividend from a foreign corporation in which the U.S. corporation owned at least ten percent of the voting stock, provided that at the time of the distribution the foreign corporation was not a controlled foreign corporation (as defined in Section 957(a)) in which the U.S. corporation was a U.S. shareholder (as defined in Section 951(b)). Thus, a noncontrolled Section 902 corporation is typically a foreign corporation of which the U.S. corporation owns between 10 and 50 percent of the stock, sometimes called a "10/50 foreign corporation" or simply a "10/50 company."

Placing dividends from each noncontrolled Section 902 corporation in a separate foreign tax credit limitation basket caused a loss of foreign tax credits to U.S. corporations for foreign taxes imposed on such dividends at rates exceeding the effective U.S. rate. Congress later concluded that this denial of the look-through treatment that is available for dividends from controlled foreign corporations to 10/50 foreign corporations created a serious disincentive for U.S. corporations to invest in foreign joint venture corporations in which they would own 50 percent or less of the equity. In the Taxpayer Relief Act of 1997, Congress responded to this perceived problem by extending look-through treatment comparable to that applied to controlled foreign corporations to dividends received by a U.S. corporation from 10/50 foreign corporations (including those that are PFICs) under Section 904(d)(4), but this liberalization was to be effective only for dividends paid out of earnings and profits accumulated in a tax year starting after 2002. However, the 2004 JOBS Act retroactively extended the Section 904(d)(4) look-through rule to all dividends received by a U.S. corporation from a 10/50 foreign corporation regardless of when the earnings were accumulated from which the dividends are paid. This rule applies to all dividends received in tax years starting after 2002.

As a result of the liberalizations enacted in 1997 and 2004, high foreign taxes on dividend inclusions from a 10/50 foreign corporation may be cross-credited against the U.S. tax otherwise imposed on a low-taxed dividend from another such corporation when both dividends are included in the general limitation basket under the Section 904(d)(4) look-through rule.

The Staff of the Joint Committee on Taxation explained the reasons for these liberalizing changes as follows:

> The Congress found that the prior-law rule that subjects the dividends received from each so-called 10/50 company to a separate foreign tax credit limitation imposes a substantial record-keeping burden on companies and has the additional negative effect of discouraging minority-position joint ventures abroad. Indeed, the Congress was aware that recent academic research suggests that the present-law requirements may distort the form and amount of overseas investment undertaken by U.S.-based enterprises. The research findings suggest that the prior-law limitation "greatly reduces the attractiveness of joint ventures to American investors, particularly ventures in low-tax foreign countries. Aggregate data indicate that U.S. participation in international joint ventures fell sharply after [enactment of the limitation of prior law] in 1986. The decline in U.S. joint venture activity is most pronounced in low-tax countries * * *. Moreover, joint ventures in low-tax countries use more debt and pay greater royalties to their U.S. parents after 1986, which reflects their incentives to economize on dividend payments." [Footnote omitted.]
>
> The Congress believed that the joint venture can be an efficient way for American business to exploit its know-how and technology in foreign markets. If the prior-law limitation was discouraging such joint ventures or altering the structure of new ventures, the ability of American business to succeed abroad could be diminished. The Congress believed it is appropriate to modify the prior-law limitation to promote simplicity and the ability of American business to compete abroad.

Staff of Joint Comm. on Tax'n, 105th Cong., 1st Sess., General Explanation of Tax Legislation Enacted in 1997, at 302 (1997).

[¶ 7035]

NOTE

Is it sound tax policy to encourage investments by U.S. corporations in 10/50 foreign corporations in low-tax countries? If the reasons for liberalizing the foreign tax credit limitation rules for dividends from 10/50 foreign corporations are persuasive, it seemed odd for Congress in the 1997 Act to have postponed their effectiveness until 2003. While the postponement presumably resulted from efforts not to increase the then existing budget deficit, it had the collateral effect of giving Congress an opportunity to rethink the issue yet again before the liberalized rules became law. The rethinking resulted in a further liberalization enacted in the 2004 JOBS Act.

[¶ 7040]

6. CERTAIN EXPORT-RELATED INCOME

For tax years starting before 2007, because foreign-source dividends from a domestic international sales corporation (DISC) or a former DISC frequently bear no foreign tax, they were placed in the separate former Section 904(d)(1)(F) basket to prevent their absorbing excess foreign tax credits generated by other foreign-source income. The same purpose motivated the establishment of a separate basket for taxable income attributable to "foreign trade income" (i.e., gross income attributable to foreign trading gross receipts) of a FSC. Former § 904(d)(1)(G). In addition, and again for the same reason, distributions from a FSC or a former FSC out of earnings attributable to "foreign trade income" (or certain interest or carrying charges) were placed in a separate basket. Former § 904(d)(1)(H). However, the FSC regime was repealed on November 15, 2000, and FSC treatment of existing FSCs generally ended on January 1, 2002. The extraterritorial income exclusion regime that replaced the FSC regime provided that no foreign tax credit would be allowed with respect to excluded extraterritorial income (which was exempt from U.S. tax). Former § 114(d). The extraterritorial income exclusion was repealed by the 2004 JOBS Act, subject to generous transitional rules that permitted substantial benefits in 2005 and 2006, and in some cases beyond. See ¶ 11,230.

For tax years starting after 2006, under Section 904(d)(2)(A)(i) and (B)(v), dividends from a DISC or former DISC, and distributions attributable to certain foreign trade income or certain interest or carrying charges of a former FSC constitute "specified passive income" and are included in the passive income basket. § 904(d)(2)(B)(v).

[¶ 7042]

7. SEPARATE LIMITATION FOR CERTAIN ITEMS OF INCOME RESOURCED UNDER TREATIES

As more fully discussed at ¶ 7160, under section 904(h), a special sourcing rule is applied for foreign tax credit limitation purposes to certain amounts, including certain Subpart F and PFIC inclusions, dividends and interest, received from a U.S.-owned foreign corporation that are attributable to the U.S.-source income of that foreign corporation. Such amounts, which would otherwise be treated as foreign-source, are treated as U.S.-source. A U.S.-owned foreign corporation ("USOFC") is a foreign corporation that is at least 50–percent owned directly (or indirectly under Sections 958(a)(2) and (3) and 318(a)(4)) by vote or value by U.S. persons. § 904(h)(6). This special sourcing rule is intended to prevent a taxpayer from increasing its applicable foreign tax credit limitation by routing what would otherwise be U.S.-source income through a foreign affiliate, thereby converting it into foreign-source income. Interest subject to the special sourcing rule generally includes interest paid or accrued by a USFOC, to a U.S. shareholder (as defined in Section 951(b)) or to a related person (as defined in Section 267(b)) to such shareholder if such interest is properly allocable to U.S.-source income of the USOFC. § 904(h)(3). The amount of a dividend subject to the special sourcing rule, is the U.S.-source ratio of any dividend paid or accrued by a USOFC, which is determined by dividing the corporation's U.S.-source earnings and profits by its total earnings and profits. § 904(h)(4). Under a de minimis rule, interest and dividends are exempt from the special sourcing rule if less than ten percent of the USOFC's earnings and profits (unreduced under Section 904(h)(3) determined without regard to paragraph (C) thereof) is from U.S. sources. § 904(h)(5). A Subpart F inclusion or a PFIC inclusion from a qualified electing fund is treated as U.S-source to the extent it is attributable to U.S.-source income of a USOFC. § 904(h)(1) and (2).

Under a coordination rule contained in Section 904(h)(10), if any amount derived from a USOFC would be treated as U.S.-source under the foregoing special sourcing rule, but a U.S. treaty obligation would treat such income as foreign-source and the taxpayer chooses the benefit of this coordination rule, the income is treated as a foreign-source and is exempt from the special sourcing rule. However, such income and the associated foreign creditable taxes are subject to a separate foreign tax credit limitation under Sections 902, 904, 907 and 960.[3] The coordination rule does not apply to amounts derived from a foreign branch or a disregarded entity.

A similar special sourcing rule applies to gain from the sale of stock of a foreign corporation or an intangible as defined in Section 865(d)(2), which would otherwise be U.S.-source. If such gain would be treated as foreign-source under an applicable tax treaty and the taxpayer chooses the benefit of the treaty, the income is treated as foreign-source. In this case, also, the foreign-source income must be placed in a separate foreign tax credit limitation basket under Sections 902, 904, 907 and 960. § 865(h).

In legislation enacted in 2010, new Section 904(d)(6) generalizes the above treaty resourcing rule to apply to all income (not covered by the foregoing rules) that would otherwise be U.S.-source but that would be treated a foreign-source under an applicable treaty. If the taxpayer elects

3. A Subpart F inclusion under Section 951(a)(1) is treated as a dividend under the special sourcing rule only if dividends paid by each controlled foreign corporation (the stock of which is taken into account in determining whether the shareholder is a U.S. shareholder in the USOFC), if paid to the U.S. shareholder, would be treated as foreign-source under an applicable tax treaty. § 904(h)(10)(B).

the benefit of the treaty, the income is included in a separate foreign tax credit limitation basket under Sections 902, 904, 907 and 960.

[¶ 7045]

8. GENERAL LIMITATION BASKET

For tax years starting before 2007, foreign-source income that was not included in one of the seven separate baskets identified in subparagraphs (A) through (H) (excluding the repealed subparagraph (E)) of former Section 904(d)(1) fell into the former Section 904(d)(1)(I) general limitation basket. Thus, active foreign-source business income, other than financial services income and shipping income, fell into the general limitation basket.

For tax years starting after 2006, nearly all active business income is included in the Section 904(d)(1)(B) general limitation basket. For example, it now includes (i) shipping income and (ii) financial services income received by a qualifying financial services entity. In addition, Section 904(d)(2)(H)(i) treats creditable foreign taxes that are imposed on amounts that do not constitute income under U.S. tax principles as imposed on general limitation income. An example of a foreign tax that would qualify under this provision is a creditable foreign tax imposed on stock dividends that are taxable under a foreign country's income tax law but are not subject to U.S. tax by reason of Section 305. Consequently, as noted above, this basket is the focus of a great deal of foreign tax credit planning aimed at structuring transactions and investments abroad so that they will generate general limitation income that is subject to a low foreign tax or no foreign tax and that therefore can absorb excess foreign tax credits generated by general limitation income subject to high foreign taxes. As discussed in Section D below, the importance of the general limitation basket is greatly enhanced by look-through rules that apply to actual dividends or constructive Subpart F inclusions, interest, rents and royalties received by a U.S. shareholder from a controlled foreign corporation and to dividends received by U.S. corporations from 10/50 foreign corporations.

[¶ 7050]

9. ELECTIVE SIMPLIFYING RULES

In 1997, Congress made an effort to reduce the complexity of applying the separate limitation regime to individuals who receive a limited amount of foreign-source investment income. As discussed at ¶ 5270, the Act allows individuals with no more than $300 ($600 in the case of married persons filing jointly) of creditable foreign taxes, and no foreign-source income other than passive income, to elect to be exempted from the foreign tax credit limitation rules. § 904(k)(2). An individual making this election is not entitled to any carryover of excess foreign taxes to or from a tax year to which the election applies. Reg. § 1.904(j)–1(b). For purposes of the election, passive income generally is defined to include all types of income that is foreign personal holding company income, as defined in Section 954(c), plus income inclusions from PFICs, provided that the income is shown on a payee statement furnished to the individual. § 904(k)(3)(A).

Another step in the direction of simplification taken in the 1997 Act was the addition of an election to use a simplified foreign tax credit limitation calculation for purposes of the alternative minimum tax ("AMT"). Before the change, the foreign tax credit limitation fraction for AMT purposes used the ratio of foreign-source AMT taxable income to worldwide AMT taxable income, even though the differences between AMT and regular taxable income are relevant primarily to U.S.-source income. Use of this fraction required a separate allocation and apportionment of deductions to determine foreign-source AMT taxable income. Under the 1997 amendment, taxpayers may elect to use as their AMT foreign tax credit limitation fraction, foreign-source regular (rather than AMT) taxable income divided by worldwide AMT taxable income. § 59(a)(3).

[¶ 7055]

C. TREATMENT OF LOSSES

The operation of the separate basket limitations can be complicated by the existence of foreign-source losses in one or more of the income baskets or a U.S.-source loss. At least three situations should be distinguished. First, foreign-source losses in one or more of the foreign tax credit limitation baskets (i.e., the excess of properly allocable and apportionable deductions over income in such basket(s)) may exceed the total foreign-source income in other basket(s) for the tax year so that there is an overall foreign loss for the tax year. Second, there may be a loss in one or more, but not all, of the limitation baskets that offsets some, but not all, of the foreign-source income in other baskets. Third, there may be a U.S.-source loss while there is foreign-source income in one or more of the limitation baskets. To permit implementation of the Section 904(f) rules on losses, which apply only for purposes of determining the Section 904 limitations, losses (as well as income) must be accounted for on a basket-by-basket basis.

[¶ 7060]

1. OVERALL FOREIGN LOSS

If a U.S. corporation has an overall foreign-source loss for the tax year, that loss will reduce the corporation's worldwide taxable income and, therefore, its U.S. tax. This means, of course, that the foreign-source loss has reduced U.S.-source income. In the following year, however, if the foreign operation shows a profit and pays a foreign tax, nothing in the basic limitation formula prevents a credit because the limitation is calculated on an annual basis. This is unfair to the U.S. Treasury. The U.S. tax on U.S.-source income was reduced because of the foreign loss; the United States should be able to tax subsequent foreign profits at least up to the amount of the prior loss without a foreign tax credit that reduces the U.S. tax.

Assume the following facts for a U.S. corporation with a foreign branch operation and assume that Section 904(f) does not exist.

	Foreign income	*Foreign tax (40%)*	*U.S. income*	*U.S. tax (35%) after credit*
Year 1	$(1,000)	0	$2,000	$350
Year 2	$1,000	$400	$2,000	$700[4]

This seems an improper result. Over the two-year span, the taxpayer has $4,000 of U.S.-source income, $4,000 of worldwide income and zero foreign-source income but pays only $1,050 of U.S. tax. If the U.S. tax were imposed on $4,000 of income, the tax would be $1,400. Thus, the foreign tax credit is effectively reducing the U.S. tax on U.S.-source income.

Section 904(f)(1) attempts to correct this anomaly. Its approach is to "recapture" the overall foreign loss in Year 1 by resourcing in subsequent years an amount of foreign-source income equal to the amount of the prior loss as U.S.-source income. This resourcing has the effect of reducing in those subsequent years the numerator of the applicable Section 904 limitation fraction. Specifically, in subsequent years, the taxpayer must treat an amount of foreign-source income as U.S.-source income equal to the lesser of

(1) the amount of the previously unrecaptured overall foreign loss in prior tax years or

(2) 50 percent (or such larger percentage as the taxpayer may choose) of the foreign-source taxable income for the year.

Thus, under Section 904(f)(1), the result in year 2, if the taxpayer elects to recapture 100 percent of the prior loss, is:

	Foreign income after resourcing	*Foreign tax*	*U.S. income*	*U.S. tax*
Year 2	0	$400	$3,000	$1,050

This seems the proper result because now, over the two-year span, the taxpayer pays a total U.S. tax of $1,400, or 35 percent of its $4,000 of worldwide income.

4. This amount is the tentative U.S. tax on $3,000 ($1,050) less the creditable portion of the foreign tax ($350).

Under Section 904(f)(3), overall foreign loss not previously recaptured is also recaptured if property used in a trade or business outside the United States is disposed of at a gain. In this case, 100 percent of the gain (up to the amount of the overall foreign loss not previously resourced) is resourced as U.S.-source income.

To the extent that the foreign tax system in which the loss was incurred permits a net operating loss carryforward, Section 904(f) does not result in any detriment to the U.S. taxpayer. Reverting to the prior example, if the foreign tax system permits a carryforward of the loss from year 1 to year 2, no foreign income tax would be payable in year 2 and no question of a foreign tax credit for that year would arise. Under Section 904(f)(1)-(3), the pinch comes if the foreign country in which the loss is incurred does not provide a loss carryforward or if the loss is incurred in one country and the subsequent income realized in another, in which case, of course, no loss carryforward would be available.

[¶ 7065]

2. FOREIGN LOSSES IN PARTICULAR BASKETS

In enacting the separate basket limitation regime in the 1986 Act, Congress determined that losses in separate limitation baskets and the general limitation basket should not be used to reduce U.S.-source taxable income before all foreign-source taxable income in all baskets is totally offset by the losses. The foreign tax credit would otherwise be effectively inflated and would reduce, in the loss year and possibly permanently, the U.S. tax on U.S.-source income. To avoid this result, Section 904(f)(5)(A) and (B) provides that separate limitation basket foreign losses are to be allocated to and thus reduce separate limitation basket incomes proportionately and are to reduce U.S.-source taxable income only to the extent that the aggregate foreign losses exceed the aggregate amount of separate limitation foreign-source incomes for the tax year.

The allocation of loss in one limitation basket to another basket reduces the residual U.S. tax otherwise due on income in the latter basket in the event that the income is subject to a relatively low or no foreign tax. On the other hand, if the loss is allocated to relatively high-taxed foreign-source income in the other basket, it may result in additional excess foreign tax credits generated by income in that basket. Section 904(f)(5)(C) mitigates these consequences. When, in a tax year after the loss year, income is earned in the basket that had the loss in a prior year, that income is recharacterized as income in the basket previously reduced by the loss allocation.

To illustrate, suppose a loss in the general limitation basket is allocated to the passive income basket and thus reduces passive income

re-am nxt pg

that was subject to relatively high foreign taxes. By reducing the applicable foreign tax credit limitation, the loss allocation may give rise to additional excess foreign tax credits generated by income in the passive income basket. The subsequent treatment of income in the general limitation basket as foreign-source income in the passive basket may increase the foreign tax credit limitation for the latter basket in the year or years when the recharacterization occurs. This may permit credits for what would otherwise be excess foreign tax credits. If a loss in the general limitation basket is allocated to income in the passive income basket that bore little or no foreign tax, by reducing the amount of taxable income the allocation will have the effect of decreasing the U.S. tax liability in the loss year. The subsequent recharacterization of additional general limitation income as passive income bearing little foreign tax may result in a recovery of some or all of the previously foregone U.S. tax revenue in the year or years when the recharacterization occurs.

[¶ 7070]

3. U.S.-SOURCE LOSSES

Section 904(f)(5)(D) requires that a U.S.-source loss for any tax year be allocated among (and thus reduce) foreign-source income in separate limitation baskets on a proportionate basis. Assume, for example, that a U.S. corporation has a $100 U.S.-source loss, $150 of net foreign-source general limitation income and $50 of net foreign-source passive income in a given tax year. Under Section 904(f)(5)(D), $75 of the U.S. loss reduces general limitation income and $25 of the U.S. loss reduces passive income. For foreign tax credit limitation purposes, then, the corporation has (disregarding other deductions) $75 of general limitation income and $25 of passive income for the tax year. This rule applies after any foreign losses have been allocated among the foreign income baskets in which the taxpayer earns income.

However, for tax years starting before 2007, if an overall U.S.-source loss reduced foreign-source income, there was no rule correlative to the rule of Section 904(f)(1) that recaptures the benefit of an overall foreign loss by recharacterizing foreign-source income earned in a subsequent tax year as U.S.-source income. The U.S. loss normally does not reduce foreign tax. Furthermore, when a U.S.-source loss is allocated to and reduces the foreign-source income in one or more limitation baskets, it will result in a reduction in the applicable Section 904 limitation(s) and may result in loss of foreign tax credits in the current year or a reduction in the amount of excess credits that could be carried back or carried forward under Section 904(c). The proper result following a U.S.-source loss would be to recharacterize subsequent U.S.-source income equal to the amount of the previously resourced U.S. loss as foreign-source income and allocate it to the baskets to which the U.S. loss had been previously allocated until the full amount of allocated U.S. losses has been "recaptured" in each basket.

For tax years starting after 2006, the 2004 JOBS Act has eliminated the previous lack of symmetry between the treatment of overall U.S. and overall foreign losses. It allows a U.S. taxpayer the foreign-source income of which has been reduced by an overall U.S.-source loss to recharacterize a portion of its U.S.-source income in each succeeding year as foreign-source. § 904(g). The amount of U.S.-source income that is recharacterized (or resourced) as foreign-source income in each of the subsequent years is the lesser of

(1) the amount of the previously unrecharacterized overall U.S.-source loss in prior tax years or

(2) 50 percent of taxpayer's U.S.-source income for the succeeding tax year.

§ 904(g)(1).

Any U.S.-source income recharacterized as foreign-source income under this rule is allocated among and increases the various foreign tax credit limitation baskets in the same proportions as those baskets were reduced by the prior overall U.S.-source loss. § 904(g)(3).

[¶ 7075]

4. RECAPTURE OF FOREIGN LOSSES ON SALE OF CONTROLLED FOREIGN CORPORATE STOCK

As discussed at ¶ 7060, if property used in a trade or business outside the United States is disposed of at a gain, 100 percent of the gain up to the amount of an overall foreign-source loss not previously resourced is recharacterized as U.S.-source income. A comparable resourcing rule was added in Section 904(f)(3)(D) by the 2004 JOBS Act for certain dispositions of the stock of a controlled foreign corporation. A disposition of such stock by a U.S. person who controls the foreign corporation through ownership of more than 50 percent (by vote or value) of its stock results in foreign-source income that is subject to being resourced as U.S.-source income. The amount resourced is equal to the lesser of (1) the excess of the fair market value of the stock over its adjusted basis or (2) the amount of prior unresourced overall foreign losses. § 904(f)(3)(D).

Although this resourcing rule is applicable whether or not gain or loss is recognized on the transaction, a number of exceptions are made for various restructurings. Excluded from the resourcing rule are:

(1) certain contributions to corporations or partnerships under Section 351 or 721 and

(2) certain acquisitions by a taxpayer or a member of its consolidated group of assets of a controlled foreign corporation in exchange

for stock of a controlled foreign corporation in a Section 332 liquidation or a reorganization under Section 368(a)(1).

§ 904(f)(3)(D)(iii), (iv).

However, any gain recognized in connection with any of these restructurings, for example, as a result of receipt of boot, triggers a recapture of overall foreign losses to the extent of such gain.

[¶ 7080]

PROBLEMS

1. Galaxy Corporation ("Galaxy"), a U.S. corporation, manufactures binoculars, telescopes and other optical equipment in its plant in San Diego, California. Galaxy conducts an extensive research and development operation in San Diego which has developed a sizeable number of inventions in the optics area that have been patented in the United States and in most industrialized countries. Galaxy granted on January 1 of year 1 a nonexclusive license covering foreign patents on one of its important inventions to an unrelated company organized under the laws of the Czech Republic that manufactures special binoculars for use at night. On January 1 of year 1, Galaxy also acquired a 30–percent interest in GP S.A., an investment corporation organized under the laws of Poland. The remaining 70 percent of the stock of GP S.A. is owned by an unrelated Polish corporation. All of GP S.A.'s income is foreign personal holding company income sourced in Eastern Europe. In addition, on January 1 of year 1, Galaxy established an export sales branch in Hungary to handle export sales of optical products Galaxy purchases from unrelated manufacturers in the United States. All income (or loss) of the branch is sourced in Hungary.

Galaxy's results for year 1 were as follows:

— Galaxy received royalties from the Czech licensee of $100,000, which were subject to a Czech withholding tax of ten percent ($10,000).

— Galaxy received from GP S.A. a dividend of $150,000 out of the affiliate's pre-Polish-tax earnings of $1,000,000, on which it paid Polish corporate income tax of $500,000. The dividend was subject to a Polish withholding tax of five percent ($7,500).

— The Hungarian sales branch had a loss of $100,000.

— Galaxy had $700,000 of taxable income from its U.S. operations all sourced in the United States.

Assume that Galaxy's effective U.S. tax rate is 35 percent. Under Section 904, how much foreign tax will Galaxy be allowed to credit for year 1?

2. How, if at all, would the results change if the foreign patents licensed by Galaxy to the Czech licensee were unrelated to Galaxy's business and had been purchased by Galaxy from an independent third party immediately before Galaxy entered into the license with the Czech licensee?

3. How, if at all, would your answer to Problem 2 change if the Hungarian sales branch had taxable income of $100,000, on which it paid

Hungarian corporate income tax of $30,000 and Galaxy had a U.S.-source operating loss of $100,000 from its U.S. operations. Under Section 904, how much foreign tax would Galaxy be allowed to credit for year 1?

4. Assume that the facts during year 1 are the same as in Problem 3 and that, in year 2, the facts are the same as in Problem 3, except that Galaxy has $700,000 of U.S.-source taxable income. Under Section 904, how much foreign tax will Galaxy be allowed to credit in year 2?

5. Assume the facts are the same as in Problem 1, except that during year 1 the Hungarian sales branch had a loss of $500,000. Under Section 904, how much foreign tax will Galaxy be allowed to credit for year 1?

6. Assume the facts remain the same as in Problem 5, except that the Hungarian sales branch has income of $600,000 in year 2, on which it paid Hungarian corporate income tax of $180,000. How much foreign tax will Galaxy be allowed to credit in year 2?

[¶ 7085]

D. LOOK-THROUGH RULES

Under the Section 904(d)(3) look-through rules, if a U.S. shareholder (as defined in Section 951(b)) includes in income actual dividends, constructive dividends under Subpart F (e.g., Subpart F inclusions), interest, rents or royalties from a controlled foreign corporation (as defined in Section 957(a)), the appropriate limitation basket for the income is determined not with reference to the character of the item of income itself (e.g., as a dividend, interest or a royalty) but with reference to the underlying income of the controlled foreign corporation. § 904(d)(3). To this extent, the controlled foreign corporation is treated, in effect, as a flow-through entity or a conduit. If none of the underlying income of the controlled foreign corporation would be included in a separate limitation basket (most importantly, the passive income basket), then none of the actual or constructive dividends, interest, rents or royalties received by the U.S. shareholder from the controlled foreign corporation would be so included; all will be included in the general limitation basket.

As discussed at ¶ 7030, the rationale for this treatment is that in the case of an international business consisting of a U.S. parent corporation and a number of foreign corporations it controls, Congress thought it appropriate to treat the group as if it were a single economic unit headquartered in the United States operating through foreign branches. Under this rationale, it becomes appropriate to allow essentially the same cross-crediting of foreign taxes within a particular foreign tax credit limitation basket as would be possible if a U.S. corporation were, in fact, operating abroad through branches. If foreign branches were involved, cross-crediting of high foreign taxes on income that is included in the passive income basket or the general limitation basket would be permitted against the U.S. tax otherwise payable on foreign-source income in that basket that had been subject to a relatively low or to no foreign tax. The Section 904(d)(3) look-through rules produce roughly the same result for foreign tax credit limitation purposes if foreign operations are conducted, not through branches, but through controlled foreign corporations. Note that Congress did not apply the branch analogy far enough in connection with controlled foreign corporations to eliminate application of the deferral principle discussed in Chapter 6.

Because in the 1986 Act, Congress concluded that the single economic unit analysis could not be applied to dividends and other payments made by noncontrolled Section 902 foreign corporations, the look-through rules were not applied to them. Dividends received from each noncontrolled foreign corporation by a U.S. corporation owning between 10 and 50 percent of the stock of the foreign corporation were included in a separate former Section 904(d)(1)(E) basket. As discussed at ¶ 7030, this restrictive regime was liberalized in the 1997 and 2004 Acts. The former Section 904(d)(1)(E) basket treatment was repealed retroactively by the 2004 JOBS Act, and a look-through rule is applied to all dividends paid to a U.S. corporation by a 10/50 foreign corporation for tax years starting after 2002. § 904(d)(4). However, no look-through rule applies to interest, rents and royalties paid by a 10/50 foreign corporation to a U.S. corporation. See ¶ 7030.

With respect to controlled foreign corporations, look-through treatment is mandated by Section 904(d)(3)(A). It provides that dividends, interest, rents and royalties received by a U.S. shareholder from a controlled foreign corporation are not to be treated as income falling within a separate limitation basket except to the extent attributable to or allocable to income of the controlled foreign corporation in that separate basket. While Section 904(d)(3)(A) contains the general look-through rule, the extent to which Subpart F inclusions, interest, rents, royalties and dividends are attributable to or allocable to underlying income of the controlled foreign corporation is determined under subsections (B), (C) and (D) of Section 904(d)(3). The attribution and allocation rules are generally those employed by the regulations in other contexts. See ¶¶ 7095 through 7120. However, in the case of interest paid by a controlled foreign corporation to a U.S. shareholder, a special direct allocation rule under Section 954(b)(5) applies. See ¶ 7100.

Section 904(d)(3)(E) contains some special rules concerning the consequences under the look-through rules if either of two relief provisions under the controlled foreign corporation provisions applies. The first links the Section 954(b)(3)(A) de minimis exception to the definition of foreign base company income to determining the foreign tax credit limitation basket into which the underlying income of the controlled foreign corporation falls. The second applies only to actual dividends paid and certain constructive dividends deemed paid by the controlled foreign corporation. It provides that if what would otherwise be passive income (other than financial services income) is excluded from foreign base company income by election under Section 954(b)(4) because it is subject to a high foreign tax burden, it is also excluded from the passive income basket and therefore is included in the general limitation basket. These rules, as far as they go, are intended to increase harmonization of the Subpart F rules and the Section 904(d)(3) look-through rules for foreign tax credit limitation purposes.

[¶ 7090]

1. DE MINIMIS EXCEPTION; 70–PERCENT FULL–INCLUSION RULE

If the gross foreign base company income (and gross insurance income) of a controlled foreign corporation is less than five percent of the corporation's total gross income and less than $1 million, none of the corporation's gross income will be treated as foreign base company income. § 954(b)(3)(A). If this de minimis rule applies, then for purposes of the Section 904(d)(3) look-through rules, all of the foreign base company income of the controlled foreign corporation (unless it is financial services income) is included in the general limitation basket. § 904(d)(3)(E).

Unlike the case of the de minimis rule, there is no linkage between the full-inclusion rule of Section 954(b)(3)(B) and the foreign tax credit limitation look-through rules. Under Section 954(b)(3)(B), if more than 70 percent of the gross income of a controlled foreign corporation is foreign base company income, all of its income is treated as such. If Section 954(b)(3)(B) applies, this treatment has no effect under the Section 904(d)(3) look-through rules on determining into what basket amounts actually paid or deemed paid by a controlled foreign corporation to a U.S. shareholder fall. Thus, if 20 percent of the gross income of a controlled foreign corporation is general limitation income, that characterization will not be altered under the look-through rules even if the rest of its gross income is passive income in the form of foreign personal holding company income.

[¶ 7095]

2. EXCEPTION FOR PASSIVE INCOME OF CONTROLLED FOREIGN CORPORATION NOT AVAILED OF TO REDUCE TAX

Under a Section 954(b)(4) election, discussed at ¶ 6165, none of what would otherwise be foreign base company income will generally be treated as foreign base company income if it is subject to an effective foreign tax rate greater than 90 percent of the top U.S. corporate income tax rate. Reg. § 1.954–1(d). If this high-foreign-tax test is met with respect to what would otherwise be passive income of a controlled foreign corporation, under Section 904(d)(3)(E), all of that income will be treated, under the Section 904(d)(3) look-through rules, as general limitation income to the extent that it is paid as an actual dividend or is deemed paid as a constructive dividend resulting from an investment in U.S. property under Section 951(a)(1)(B). This high-foreign-tax rule does not apply to a Subpart F inclusion of undistributed Subpart F income under Section 951(a)(1)(A) because if the Section 954(b)(4) election is made, there is no foreign base company income that could result in a Subpart F inclusion under Section 951(a)(1)(A). § 904(d)(3)(G).

This special rule of Section 904(d)(3)(E) applies to lower-tier as well as to first-tier controlled foreign corporations. For example, if income of a second-tier controlled foreign corporation is excluded from foreign base company income under Section 954(b)(4), an actual dividend out of that income is also excluded from the passive income basket in the hands of the first-tier controlled foreign corporation under the look-through rules. This is the case even if a dividend paid out of that income is Subpart F income to the first-tier controlled foreign corporation.

Section 904(d)(3)(E) does not apply for purposes of the Section 904(d)(3) look-through rules to interest, rents and royalties. It does not apply to those payments because they are typically deductible and therefore not taxed to the payor.

[¶ 7100]

3. DIRECT ALLOCATION OF INTEREST PAYMENTS

In applying the look-through rules to interest payments by a controlled foreign corporation to a U.S. shareholder (or to another controlled foreign corporation related to the U.S. shareholder), those interest payments are generally allocated first to the payor corporation's gross foreign personal holding company income that is passive income to the extent of such income. §§ 954(b)(5) and 904(d)(3)(C). Consequently, to the extent so allocated, the interest in the hands of the U.S. shareholder is subject to the passive income limitation. The direct interest allocation provision applies for both Subpart F and foreign tax credit limitation purposes.

The rationale for treating interest paid by a controlled foreign corporation to a U.S. shareholder as properly allocable first to gross passive foreign personal holding company income is that it would generally be as easy for the U.S. shareholder (the ultimate recipient of the passive income) to arrange to receive the passive income directly from the ultimate payor (e.g., borrower) as to arrange to receive it through a controlled foreign corporation. Note that the scope of the direct-allocation-of-interest rule goes beyond allocating interest payments by a controlled foreign corporation against its passive interest receipts. The allocation is also made against all passive foreign personal holding company income, such as passive royalty income.

For example, assume that a U.S. corporation lends funds to and receives $3,000 in interest from its controlled foreign corporation, which has $10,000 of gross income, including $2,000 of gross Subpart F foreign personal holding company income that is passive income. Of the interest paid to the U.S. corporation $2,000 will be allocated in full to the controlled foreign corporation's gross passive foreign personal holding company income and will therefore be subject to the passive income limitation in the hands of the U.S. parent corporation. This allocation reduces the passive foreign personal holding company income of the controlled foreign corporation dollar-for-dollar, but not below zero. Thus, (disregarding other deductions) $1,000 of the controlled foreign corporation's gross passive foreign personal holding company income remains after deducting the $2,000 of interest it pays to its U.S. shareholder and may be the subject of a Subpart F inclusion. See Reg. § 1.904–5(c)(2)(ii).

[¶ 7105]

4. RELATIONSHIP BETWEEN LOOK–THROUGH RULES AND RULES CALLING FOR SEPARATE BASKET CLASSIFICATION

Under Section 904(d)(3)(A) and (F), the foreign tax credit limitation baskets for dividends, interest, rents and royalties received from a controlled foreign corporation by a U.S. shareholder are determined exclusively with reference to the underlying income of the controlled foreign corporation. Thus, for example, interest received by the U.S. shareholder of a controlled foreign corporation that would otherwise meet the definition of export financing interest will be classified with reference to the underlying income of the controlled foreign corporation to which it is allocable.

There is one qualification to the general rule that the look-through rules prevail. In determining whether the "high-tax kickout" applies to interest, royalties, rents or dividends received by a U.S. shareholder from a controlled foreign corporation, the level of foreign tax borne by the U.S. shareholder (rather than the controlled foreign corporation payor) is determinative. § 904(d)(3)(F)(ii).

[¶ 7110]

5. APPLICATION OF LOOK–THROUGH RULES TO SPECIFIC ITEMS OF INCOME

Section 904(d)(3)(A) calls for separate basket treatment for dividends, Subpart F inclusions, interest, rents and royalties received by a U.S.

shareholder from a controlled foreign corporation only to the extent they are attributable or allocable to underlying income of the controlled foreign corporation in a separate category or basket. The rules for determining to what extent the inclusion by the U.S. shareholder of income from the controlled foreign corporation is attributable or allocable to separate categories of the controlled foreign corporation's income depend on the nature of the inclusion.

Note that fees paid by a controlled foreign corporation to a U.S. shareholder for services rendered by the latter abroad are not subject to the Section 904(d)(3) look-through rules. This is presumably because they would constitute general limitation income without the application of those rules.

[¶ 7115]

a. Subpart F Inclusions

For purposes of the look-through rule of Section 904(d)(3)(B), a Subpart F inclusion under Section 951(a)(1)(A) (e.g., as a result of undistributed Subpart F income) is attributable only to the specific category or categories of income that caused the inclusion and not to other categories of the controlled foreign corporation's income. Reg. § 1.904–5(c)(1)(i). This is essentially a tracing rule that looks specifically to the basket or baskets of underlying income that caused the inclusion under Section 951(a)(1)(A). This rule is unlike the look-through rule applicable to actual dividends and other constructive dividends (resulting, for example, under Section 951(a)(1)(B) from an investment in U.S. property), under which all of the income of the controlled foreign corporation is taken into account.

For example, if after allocating and apportioning deductions, 60 percent of a wholly owned controlled foreign corporation's undistributed income consists of foreign base company sales income and the remaining 40 percent is not foreign base company income, the foreign base company sales income will be a Subpart F inclusion to a U.S. shareholder. All of this inclusion will be attributable to the foreign base company sales income and will fall into the general limitation basket. If, however, the remaining 40 percent is foreign base company income in the form of interest, all of the undistributed income will be a Subpart F inclusion. In this case, 60 percent of the Subpart F inclusion is attributable to the sales income and falls into the general limitation basket and the remaining 40 percent is attributable to the interest and falls into the passive income basket. § 904(d)(3)(B). A Subpart F inclusion under Section 951(a)(1)(A) must be grossed up under Section 78 by the amount of any indirect foreign tax credit under Section 960 available to a U.S. corporate shareholder. The amount of the gross-up is treated as an additional Subpart F inclusion under Section 951(a)(1)(A) for purposes of the Section

§ 904(d)(3)(B) look-through rule, rather than as a dividend covered by Section 904(d)(3)(G).

[¶ 7120]

b. Interest

With respect to interest from a controlled foreign corporation included in the income of a U.S. shareholder, the direct-allocation-of-interest rule under Sections 904(d)(3)(C) and 954(b)(5) applies. As discussed in ¶ 7100, all interest paid by the controlled foreign corporation to a U.S. shareholder must first be allocated to foreign personal holding income of the controlled foreign corporation that is passive income to the extent thereof. Reg. § 1.904–5(c)(2)(ii)(C).

Any interest received by the U.S. shareholder that exceeds the amount allocated to passive foreign personal holding company income of the controlled foreign corporation is generally allocated to the general limitation basket.

[¶ 7125]

c. Royalties and Rents

Under Section 904(d)(3)(C), royalties and rents received by a U.S. shareholder from a controlled foreign corporation fall into a separate basket to the extent that they are "properly allocable" to income in that basket. Reg. § 1.904–5(c)(3) provides that this allocation is made pursuant to Reg. § 1.861–8 through Temp. Reg. § 1.861–14T. Any amount not allocable to income in a separate basket is allocable to income in the general limitation basket.

[¶ 7130]

d. Actual Dividends and Constructive Dividends under Sections 951(a)(1)(B) and 1248(a)

When a U.S. shareholder receives or is deemed to receive an actual dividend or a constructive dividend under Section 951(a)(1)(B) from a controlled foreign corporation, the U.S. shareholder may be required, under the look-through rules, to allocate part or all of the dividend to a separate limitation basket. The amount of this allocation is based on the ratio of the corporation's earnings and profits in that basket to the corporation's total earnings and profits. § 904(d)(3)(D); Reg. § 1.904–5(c)(4)(i). Constructive dividends deemed received by a U.S. shareholder subject to look-through treatment include those resulting from an investment of earnings in U.S. property under Section 951(a)(1)(B). As discussed at ¶ 6245, they also include gains on the sale or exchange by a U.S. shareholder of stock of a controlled foreign corporation, which are treated as dividends to the extent of the shareholder's pro rata share of post–1962 undistributed earnings under Section 1248(a).

If the U.S. corporation obtains an indirect foreign tax credit under Section 902 or Section 960 for corporate income taxes paid by the controlled foreign corporation, the actual or constructive dividend must be increased (grossed up) by the amount of the indirect credit. § 78. The Section 78 gross-up amount is treated as a dividend also subject to the dividend look-through rule of Section 904(d)(3)(D). § 904(d)(3)(G).

[¶ 7135]

6. ORDERING RULES

A particular controlled foreign corporation may, in a single tax year, pay rents, royalties, interest and dividends to a U.S. shareholder and may be deemed to distribute one or more Subpart F inclusions under Section 951(a)(1)(A) and constructive dividends under Sections 951(a)(1)(B) and Section 1248(a) to that shareholder. Therefore, it is necessary under the Section 904(d)(3) look-through rules to decide the order in which the various payments should be characterized. It would seem appropriate to characterize, first, rents, royalties and interest, which are deductible in calculating earnings and profits of the controlled foreign corporation that will be the measure of actual dividends or Subpart F inclusions. Of these deductible payments, the direct-interest-allocation rule may make it appropriate to characterize initially interest paid by the controlled foreign corporation to its U.S. shareholder. Next royalties and rents can be considered. Then Subpart F inclusions under Section 951(a)(1)(A) or constructive dividends under Sections 951(a)(1)(B) and 1248(a) should be characterized, followed by any actual dividends paid in the tax year. This is broadly the approach adopted in the ordering rules discussed at ¶ 7140 for cases in which the look-through rules must be applied to payments received (or deemed to be received) by one controlled foreign corporation or other look-through entity from another.

[¶ 7140]

7. APPLICATION OF LOOK–THROUGH RULES TO DIVIDENDS, INTEREST, RENTS AND ROYALTIES RECEIVED BY ONE LOOK–THROUGH ENTITY FROM ANOTHER

The regulations provide that the Section 904(d)(3) look-through rules also apply to dividend, interest, rent and royalty payments made and Subpart F inclusions deemed to be made by a look-through entity (such as a controlled foreign corporation or a partnership) to a related look-through entity. Reg. § 1.904–5(k)(2).[5]

Thus, if all of the stock of controlled foreign corporation S and controlled foreign corporation T is owned by U.S. corporation P, any interest, rent or royalty payment by S to T will be characterized for purposes of the Section 904 limitation rules by applying the Section 904(d)(3) look-through rules.

Reg. § 1.904–5(k) provides rules for determining the order in which payments are characterized when one look-through entity makes payments or is deemed to make payments of more than one type to a related look-through entity. Thus, one controlled foreign corporation may pay to and receive from a related controlled foreign corporation royalties, rents and interest. In addition, if the first controlled foreign corporation is a shareholder of the second, the first may receive a dividend from the second.

Reg. § 1.904–5(k)(2) states that the following types of income are to be characterized in the following order:

(i) Rents and royalties;

(ii) Interest;

(iii) Subpart F inclusions and distributive shares of partnership income; and

(iv) Dividend distributions.

If an entity both receives from and pays to a related look-through entity any of these types of income, the income received is characterized before the income paid. In addition, the amount of interest paid, directly or indirectly, by a look-through entity to a related look-through entity must be offset against and reduce any interest received, directly or indirectly, by the former entity from the latter entity before the ordering rules are applied.

[¶ 7145]

E. ALLOCATION AND APPORTIONMENT OF DEDUCTIONS IN CALCULATING LIMITATIONS

In determining the foreign-source taxable income of a U.S. person that falls within each foreign tax credit limitation basket, deductions must be allocated and apportioned against the gross income falling within that basket. These allocations and apportionments are generally effected in accordance with the rules discussed at ¶¶ 2220 et seq.

5. Two look-through entities are related for this purpose if one owns (directly or indirectly) stock possessing more than 50 percent of the voting power or value of the other. They are also related if the same U.S. shareholders own (directly or indirectly) stock possessing more than 50 percent of the total voting power (in the case of a corporation) or more than 50 percent of the total value of each look-through entity. Reg. § 1.904–5(i)(1). For a partnership, value is determined with reference to capital and profits interests. Reg. § 1.904–5(h)(4).

The special rules relating to the allocation and apportionment of interest, discussed at ¶ 2230, generally apply. However, in connection with the allocation of interest deductions against foreign-source gross income in various baskets, in certain circumstances, the regulations under Section 864(e)(7)(C) require application of a special rule, sometimes called the "CFC netting rule." Reg. § 1.861–10(e). The purpose of this rule is to discourage U.S. shareholders from borrowing funds and re-lending them to controlled foreign corporations with the objective of improving the allocation and apportionment of interest expense for foreign tax credit limitation purposes over what would result if the controlled foreign corporations directly borrowed the funds. Under the regulation, if a U.S. shareholder has both a relatively large amount of loans to controlled foreign corporations ("excess related group indebtedness") and relatively large borrowings from third parties outside the affiliated group ("excess U.S. shareholder indebtedness") in the tax year, it must allocate to its foreign-source gross income in the various foreign tax credit limitation baskets specified portions of the interest it pays to third-party lenders.

In addition, under the Section 904(d)(3) look-through rules, interest paid by a controlled foreign corporation to a U.S. shareholder or a related controlled foreign corporation may be subject to the special direct-allocation-of-interest rule discussed at ¶ 7100.

The existing rules for allocation of interest, discussed at ¶ 2230, which generally apply for purposes of determining the limitations on the foreign tax credit, are to be modified by providing a special one-time election under Section 864(f) to the common parent corporation of a U.S. affiliated group of corporations. To reduce the tax revenue lost by this election, its effective date has been delayed until tax years starting after 2020. Under the election, the foreign-source taxable income of the U.S. members of an affiliated group is determined by allocating and apportioning interest expense of the U.S. members of a worldwide affiliated group on a worldwide basis (i.e., as if all worldwide members of the group were a single corporation). If the common parent of an affiliated group makes this election, the taxable income of the U.S. members of the worldwide affiliated group from sources outside the United States is determined by allocating and apportioning the third-party interest expense of those U.S. members to foreign-source income in an amount equal to the excess (if any) of

(1) the worldwide affiliated group's worldwide third-party interest expense multiplied by the ratio which foreign assets of the worldwide affiliated group bears to the total assets of the worldwide affiliated group, over

(2) the third-party interest expense incurred by foreign members of the group to the extent such interest would be allocated to foreign sources if Section 864(f) were applied separately to the foreign members of the group.

For purposes of the elective rule, the worldwide affiliated group means all corporations in an affiliated group (as that term is defined under present law for interest allocation purposes) as well as all controlled foreign corporations that, in the aggregate, either directly or indirectly, would be members of such an affiliated group if Section 1504(b)(3) did not apply (i.e., in which at least 80–percent of the vote and value of the stock of such corporations is owned by one or more other corporations included in the affiliated group).

[¶ 7150]

F. DECONSOLIDATION TO MANIPULATE FOREIGN TAX CREDIT LIMITATIONS

Section 904(j) authorizes issuance of regulations to prevent manipulation of foreign tax credit limitations by affiliated groups. Assuming that two or more U.S. corporations would be members of the same affiliated group (i) if Section 1504(b) were applied without regard to the exceptions it contains and (ii) if the constructive ownership rules of Section 1563(e) applied for purposes of Section 1504(a), regulations may provide for resourcing of income of the corporations or changes to the consolidated return regulations as necessary to prevent the avoidance of the separate foreign tax credit limitations.

A group of U.S. affiliated corporations filing a consolidated return computes its Section 904(d)(1) foreign tax credit limitations on a group basis. Reg. § 1.1502–4(a), (c) and (d). Congress was concerned that by removing a U.S. corporation from an affiliated group, the group might increase its foreign tax credit limitations. This would be the result if foreign-source deductions could be concentrated in a U.S. affiliate that had predominantly U.S.-source income and if that corporation could be excluded from the consolidated return.

A U.S. corporation could be eliminated from the group in three ways. First, a non-includible corporation (e.g., a foreign corporation) can be inserted into a chain of U.S. corporations, with the result that all U.S. corporations below the non-includible corporation are excluded from the group. Second, a non-includible corporation may serve as the common parent of a brother-sister group. Finally, U.S. corporations that are eligible to file a consolidated return might choose not to do so.

The following example is given in the House Report of the abuse that deconsolidation could involve:

> An affiliated group filing a consolidated return (hereinafter referred to as a "consolidated group") must choose the benefits of the foreign tax credit (as opposed to taking deductions for foreign income taxes) on a group-wise basis (Treas. Reg. sec. 1.1502–4(a)). Each foreign tax credit limitation to which a consolidated group is subject

> varies directly with the ratio of the foreign source taxable income of the group subject to that limitation to the entire taxable income of the group (Treas. Reg. sec. 1.1502–4(c) and (d)).
>
> For example, assume that one member of an affiliated group that files a consolidated return is a domestic corporation with a net foreign source loss of $100 from manufacturing, and U.S. source taxable income from manufacturing of $200. Assume that the income of the other members of the group consists of $100 of foreign source [passive] income subject to $34 of foreign income tax. This group has no net foreign source taxable income, no current foreign tax credit, and, assuming that the relevant U.S. rate is 34 percent, a U.S. tax liability of $68 which is equal to, appropriately, the amount of its U.S. source taxable income ($200) times its U.S. tax rate.
>
> Now assume that the members of the affiliated group own all of the stock of a foreign corporation or all of the interests in a partnership. Assume that 21 percent of the stock of the domestic corporation with a foreign loss is owned by this foreign corporation or partnership. Under this assumption, the domestic corporation is still wholly owned by the affiliated group, albeit indirectly through a controlled entity that is not an includible corporation, but the domestic corporation with the foreign loss is *not* a member of the affiliated group for purposes of filing a consolidated return. The consolidated return filed by the remaining group of corporations would show $100 of passive foreign source income and $34 of creditable foreign income tax subject to the separate foreign tax credit limitation on passive income, resulting in no net U.S. tax. The non-affiliated domestic corporation with $200 of U.S. source income and $100 of foreign loss would pay only $34 of U.S. tax. That is, until there is a foreign loss recapture in a subsequent taxable year, the controlled group pays half the U.S. tax that would be owed in the case where 80 percent or more of stock of the domestic corporation with the foreign loss is owned directly by an includible corporation.

H.R. Rep. No. 247, 101st Cong., 1st Sess. 1292–93 (1989).

Reg. § 1.904(i)–1 was adopted to deal with this issue. It defines affiliates to prevent elimination of U.S. corporations from the consolidated return group and requires each affiliate to be treated as if it were part of the same consolidated return group for the part of the year during which the corporations involved were affiliates. Reg. § 1.904(i)–1(a) and (b). Under the regulation, in the above example, the nonaffiliated domestic corporation is treated as an affiliate that is a member of the consolidated group, and the U.S. tax on the group is $68. This forced consolidation applies only for purposes of the foreign tax credit provisions of Sections 901 through 908, 960 and 59(a).

Under the regulations, each affiliate must compute foreign-source taxable income or loss in each foreign tax credit basket and the results of all the affiliates' calculations are then combined for each basket. At this point, the rules of Section 904(f) relating to losses, discussed at ¶¶ 7055 through 7080, are applied. Reg. § 1.904(i)-l(a)(1). Finally, aggregate resulting taxable income for each basket must be allocated pro rata among the affiliates under any consistently applied reasonable method. Reg. § 1.904(i)-l(a)(2).

[¶ 7155]

PROBLEM

A U.S. corporation X, which files a consolidated tax return, owns indirectly (through entities that are not includible corporations) 80 percent or more of the stock of two U.S. subsidiary corporations, Y and Z. Assume that all income is subject to U.S. tax at a 35–percent rate. For the tax year, X has no taxable income or loss, Y has $400 of U.S.-source income and $200 of foreign-source general limitation loss and Z has $200 of pre-tax foreign-source general limitation taxable income and has paid $80 of foreign income tax. What is the aggregate U.S. tax liability of X, Y and Z?

[¶ 7160]

G. PRESERVING U.S.–SOURCE INCOME

Until the adoption of a separate basket limitation for passive income, there was a strong incentive for U.S. taxpayers to convert U.S.-source income into foreign-source income by running the income through a related foreign corporation. Even within the passive income limitation basket it might well have been advantageous to convert U.S.-source passive income into foreign-source income. Before 1984, the source rules providing that interest and dividend income derived from foreign corporations was generally foreign-source income offered an opportunity for such a conversion. If some of a taxpayer's U.S.-source income could be moved into one of the taxpayer's foreign subsidiaries, when that income was returned to the taxpayer as dividends (or interest), it would be foreign-source income under the generally applicable source rules discussed in Chapter 2. This income could be used to increase the applicable foreign tax credit limitation.

For example, if a U.S. corporation borrowed funds from its controlled foreign corporation, under appropriate circumstances, the U.S. corporation could deduct the bulk of the interest it paid to the controlled foreign corporation against its U.S.-source income. The interest thus received by the controlled foreign corporation from its U.S. parent would bear little or no foreign tax and would be Subpart F income includible in the U.S. corporation's income as a foreign-source Subpart F inclusion. This foreign-source income would increase the U.S. corporation's limitation on the foreign tax credit.

In 1984, Congress added Section 904(h), to prevent manipulation of the source of income in this manner. Section 904(h) does not change the general source rules, but rather, treats certain income from a United States-owned foreign corporation as U.S.-source income *solely* for the purposes of the Section 904 foreign tax credit limitations. A United States-owned foreign corporation ("USOFC") is any foreign corporation of which 50 percent or more of the total voting power or value of the stock is held directly or indirectly by U.S. citizens, resident aliens, corporations, partnerships and trusts or estates. § 904(h)(6). The indirect ownership rules of Section 958(a)(2) and the option constructive ownership rule of Section 318(a)(4) apply in determining stock ownership for purposes of this definition.

Three kinds of income are covered by the special sourcing rule of Section 904(h).

First, under Section 904(h)(4), dividends from U.S.-owned foreign corporations are considered U.S.-source income in accordance with the following formula:

$$\frac{\text{U.S.-source earnings and profits}}{\text{Worldwide earnings and profits}} \times \text{Dividend} = \text{U.S.-source income}$$

Second, interest paid by a USOFC to a U.S. shareholder will be treated as U.S.-source income if the interest is properly allocable to income of the foreign corporation for the tax year from U.S. sources. § 904(h)(3)(B). (The interest would not be subject to U.S. withholding tax because it is treated as U.S. source only for purposes of the foreign tax credit limitations.) Under a de minimis rule, the interest and dividend rules do not apply if less than ten percent of the foreign corporation's earnings and profits is attributable to U.S. sources. § 904(h)(5).

Finally, constructive inclusions under Section 951(a)(1)(A) and (B) with respect to controlled foreign corporations and PFIC inclusions from a qualified electing fund are treated as U.S.-source income to the extent such inclusions are attributable to income of the USOFC from U.S. sources. § 904(h)(1) and (2).

As discussed at ¶ 7042, Section 904(h)(10) contains a coordination rule providing that any income normally treated as U.S.-source under the foregoing special sourcing rule, but that is treated as foreign-source under a tax treaty, will be treated as foreign-source if the taxpayer chooses the benefit of the coordination rule. However, such income and the associated foreign creditable taxes are subject to a separate foreign tax credit limitation under Sections 902, 904, 907 and 960.

[¶ 7165]

H. TAX PLANNING UNDER SEPARATE LIMITATIONS

Requiring that eight specific categories of foreign-source income be subjected to separate limitation calculations under subparagraphs (A) through (H) of former Section 904(d)(1) dramatically increased the complexity of the foreign tax credit limitation regime and dramatically narrowed the pre–1986 Act overall limitation, the remains of which were embodied in the former Section 904(d)(1)(I) general limitation basket for tax years beginning before 2007. That change obviously reduced the planning possibilities for generating low-taxed or tax-free foreign-source taxable income that could be included in the numerator of the general limitation fraction to enable the use of what would otherwise have been excess foreign tax credits. For tax years beginning after 2006, reducing the number of limitation baskets from eight to two principal baskets reduced the complexity of the separate basket limitation regime. It also reduced the important narrowing of the general limitation basket under the prior regime. Nevertheless, even under current law with only two principal baskets, which include an expanded passive income category basket, the narrowing remains significant. Notwithstanding the current narrowing of the general limitation basket, the possibilities for achieving tax savings through the cross-crediting mechanism remain extensive. Consider in connection with the problems below what opportunities remain for the U.S. taxpayer engaged in foreign business to absorb excess foreign tax credits by generating types of low-taxed or tax-free foreign income that can be blended with high-taxed foreign income in the general limitation calculation. Before tackling the problems included below to illustrate the interaction between the controlled foreign corporation provisions and the foreign tax credit limitations, consider the following suggestions on methodology.

[¶ 7170]

I. METHODOLOGY FOR ANALYSIS

When dealing with actual payments of rents, royalties, interest or dividends or constructive dividends under Subpart F to a U.S. person from a foreign corporation, it will usually be helpful, first, to analyze the Subpart F consequences, if any, and, second, to consider into what limitation basket the item of income includible by the U.S. person should be put.

The analysis will frequently involve the following distinct steps:

1. Is the foreign corporation from which the U.S. person actually receives or is deemed to receive income a controlled foreign corporation

(as defined in Section 957(a)) and is the U.S. person a U.S. shareholder (as defined in Section 951(b)) of that corporation?

2. If the answer to either of the foregoing questions is, no, the basket into which the income received by the U.S. person must be put will not be affected by the Section 904(d)(3) look-through rules. For example, a royalty received by a U.S. corporate or individual shareholder from a noncontrolled foreign corporation will go into the Section 904(d)(1)(A) basket for passive income, unless it is or is deemed to be derived in an active business, in which case it will go into the general limitation basket. Dividends received by a U.S. corporation that owns at least ten percent of the voting stock of a 10/50 foreign corporation are subject to a special look-through rule under Section 904(d)(4). This look-through rule does not apply to interest, rent or royalty payments.

3. If the foreign payor corporation is a controlled foreign corporation and the recipient is a U.S. shareholder, the Section 904(d)(3) look-through rules will apply in determining into which baskets interest, rents, royalties, actual dividends, constructive dividends under Section 951(a)(1)(B) and Subpart F inclusions under Section 951(a)(1)(A) will fall.[6]

4. Assuming the payor is a controlled foreign corporation, the next step should be to determine whether the controlled foreign corporation has foreign base company income (which is treated as Subpart F income) or earnings invested in U.S. property (or both) that may result in Subpart F inclusions or constructive dividends to a U.S. shareholder under Sections 951(a)(1)(A) or (B). In making these determinations, payments of deductible interest, royalties and rents by the controlled foreign corporation to its U.S. shareholder will reduce the amount of the controlled foreign corporation's earnings that could be treated as a constructive dividend or Subpart F inclusion or as an actual dividend.

5. An appropriate next step would be to determine into what category or basket each type of the underlying income received by the controlled foreign corporation falls. This identification is necessary in order to be able to apply the Section 904(d)(3) look-through rules. These require that the proper limitation basket for payments of dividends, interest, royalties and rents actually made, and Subpart F inclusions deemed made, by the controlled foreign corporation to the U.S. shareholder be determined with reference to the underlying income of the controlled foreign corporation to which such payments are attributable or allocable. The same is true with respect to dividends paid by a 10/50 foreign corporation to a U.S. corporate shareholder under the Section 904(d)(4) look-through rules.

6. The final step is to determine into which basket actual payments of dividends, interest, rents, royalties, Subpart F inclusions under Section 951(a)(1)(A) and constructive dividends under Section 951(a)(1)(B) should

6. Although not involved in the problems below, a constructive dividend under Section 1248(a) when a U.S. shareholder realizes gain on sale of stock of a controlled foreign corporation is also subject to the Section 904(d)(3) look-through rules.

be placed under the Section 904(d)(3) and Section 904(d)(4) look-through rules. Because, as noted above, payments of interest, royalties and rents are deductible by the payor controlled foreign corporation in determining the amount of its earnings includible in the U.S. shareholder's income as a Subpart F inclusion under Section 951(a)(1)(A), it is logical to begin by characterizing these items under Section 904(d). Because interest may be subject to the direct-allocation-of-interest rule of Sections 954(b)(5) and 904(d)(3)(C), it seems simplest to start with this and then move to rents and royalties. Then Subpart F inclusions under Section 951(a)(1)(A) are treated under Section 904(d)(3)(B) as included in the same basket as the underlying Subpart F income that caused the inclusion. Constructive dividends under Section 951(a)(1)(B) are treated coming proportionately from the remaining underlying baskets of passive and general limitation income. Section 904(d)(3)(D).

Finally, actual dividend distributions in the tax year should be considered. To the extent that such distributions reflect amounts included in the U.S. shareholder's income as Subpart F inclusions or constructive dividends under Section 951(a)(1)(A) or (B) in the current or a previous year, the distribution is treated as previously taxed income and is tax-free. § 959(a). To the extent it is taxable, it is treated under Section 904(d)(3)(D) as included in the same basket or baskets as the earnings distributed.

[¶ 7175]

PROBLEMS

In the interest of simplification, assume in each of the following problems that any controlled foreign corporation was organized on January 1 of the tax year concerned and its tax year is the calendar year. Thus, except as otherwise indicated, post–1986 undistributed earnings and post–1986 foreign taxes will equal those for the current tax year described in the problem. All transactions occur in the current tax year except as otherwise stated. Where relevant, assume that a U.S. corporation's effective U.S. tax rate is 35 percent, and disregard deductions for expenses not specifically mentioned.

1. Cosmos Inc. ("Cosmos"), a Delaware corporation, is about to establish a wholly owned French subsidiary, Cosmos France S.A. ("Cosmos France"), which will manufacture and sell electronic equipment in France. Cosmos France is expected to have earnings before French corporate income tax (and taxable income for French tax purposes) of $200,000 per year, which will be subject to the French corporate income tax of 38 percent and, when distributed as dividends, will be subject to a French withholding tax of five percent under the terms of the United States–France Income Tax Treaty. Cosmos expects to have worldwide taxable income of $1 million. Dividends paid by Cosmos France will therefore carry with them foreign tax credits in excess of the applicable general limitation of Section 904(d)(1)(B). Consider whether the following categories of income may be useful in absorbing at least

some of these excess credits, assuming that all of the earnings and profits of Cosmos France are distributed currently:

a. Dividends and interest from a wholly owned subsidiary of Cosmos organized under Bermuda law, which owns and operates a hotel in Bermuda and all of the income of which is hotel services income earned in Bermuda. There is no corporate income tax in Bermuda, and no withholding tax will be imposed on dividends or interest paid by the Bermuda company.

b. Dividends and interest from a joint venture Irish manufacturing corporation, which manufactures electronic equipment in Ireland and sells it throughout Europe. The common stock of this corporation is 50 percent owned by Cosmos and 50 percent owned by an unrelated Dutch corporation. The earnings of the Irish corporation are exempt from Irish corporate and withholding taxes under a ten-year tax holiday. Would the result be affected if Cosmos owned, in addition to 50 percent of the common stock, all of a class of nonvoting preferred stock of the Irish corporation?

c. Interest paid by export customers of Cosmos located in various foreign countries on loans made by Cosmos to finance purchases made by these customers of Cosmos products. These products are manufactured by Cosmos in the United States with raw materials and components at least 60 percent of which are of U.S. origin and will be used outside the United States. Assume that some of this interest will be exempt from foreign withholding tax and that the rest will be subject to withholding taxes ranging from five percent to 20 percent.

d. Interest from Cosmos France on a loan from Cosmos to Cosmos France, which is deductible for purposes of the French corporate income tax and exempt from French withholding tax.

2. Alpha Corp. ("Alpha"), a Delaware corporation, owns all of the stock of Alpha Bermuda, a corporation organized under the laws of Bermuda. Alpha manufactures plastic utensils that it sells in the United States and abroad. Utensils for the export market are sold to Alpha Bermuda, which resells them at a mark-up to unrelated distributors around the world, passing title to the distributors at the port of destination. During the tax year, Alpha Bermuda had earnings from its sales operations of $1 million, which were free of tax in Bermuda. No payments of any kind were made by Alpha Bermuda to Alpha during the year. How are these transactions treated under Subpart F and the Section 904 limitations?

3. Beta Inc. ("Beta"), a Delaware corporation, owns all of the shares of Beta S.A., a Swiss corporation. Beta S.A. has $1 million of gross income for the tax year, which includes $960,000 of income from the manufacture and sale of widgets in Switzerland, $10,000 of foreign base company services income and $30,000 of foreign personal holding company income. Beta S.A. pays $100,000 of interest, $50,000 of royalties and no dividends to Beta. How are these transactions treated under Subpart F and the Section 904 limitations?

4. Gamma Inc. ("Gamma"), a Delaware corporation, owns all of the stock of Gamma Singapore & Co. ("Gamma Singapore"), a Singapore corpora-

tion. Gamma Singapore earns $1 million in the tax year, of which $750,000 is foreign personal holding company income and $250,000 is services income that is not financial services income or foreign base company services income. No dividends or other payments of any kind are paid by Gamma Singapore to Gamma. How are these transactions treated under Subpart F and the Section 904 limitations?

5. Delta Inc. ("Delta"), a Delaware corporation, owns all of the stock of Delta Korea Co. ("Delta Korea"), a South Korean corporation. Delta manufactures electrical connectors, at least 80 percent of the value of which is attributable to components and materials of U.S. origin, and sells them to unrelated purchasers in the United States and abroad. Delta Korea provides financing to unrelated foreign purchasers in connection with their purchases from Delta but is not engaged in the conduct of a banking, financing or similar business. Delta Korea also provides sales support services on behalf of Delta to foreign purchasers of Delta equipment outside South Korea. During the tax year, Delta Korea has $1.8 million of gross income, consisting of $1.2 million in fees for rendering the sales support services and $600,000 of interest paid by the foreign purchasers of Delta's inventory property. The fees and interest are exempt from withholding taxes in the source countries. During the year, Delta Korea pays to Delta $700,000 of interest for a loan of working capital and $100,000 of royalties under a license of Delta's foreign trademarks. How are these transactions treated under Subpart F and the Section 904 limitations?

6. Acme Inc. ("Acme U.S."), a Delaware corporation, owns all of the stock of Acme U.K. Sales Co. ("Acme U.K."), a United Kingdom corporation. Acme U.S. manufactures large machine tools, some of which it sells to Acme U.K. Acme U.K. then resells the tools at a mark-up to distributors in the United Kingdom. Acme U.K. has gross income of $1.7 million consisting of the following:

(i) $1.2 million is attributable to the purchase-and-resale transactions,

(ii) $200,000 is gross royalty income received under a license to an independent German licensee of a German patent unrelated to the business of Acme U.S. or Acme U.K., which was purchased from an unrelated person two years ago by Acme U.K., and

(iii) $300,000 is gross interest income received on a loan to an independent distributor in Belgium unrelated to export sales made by Acme U.S., which interest is subject to a Belgian withholding tax of ten percent.

None of the value of the equipment manufactured by Acme U.S. and sold to Acme U.K. is attributable to products imported into the United States. Acme U.S. lends funds to Acme U.K. to enable it to purchase the machine tools from Acme U.S., and Acme U.K. pays $100,000 of interest to Acme U.S. on this financing during the tax year. It also pays $150,000 to Acme U.S. on an unrelated loan. The interest payments are exempt from U.K. withholding tax under the United States–United Kingdom Income Tax Treaty. How are these transactions treated under Subpart F and the Section 904 limitations?

7. Tau Corporation ("Tau"), a Delaware corporation, is engaged in the manufacture and sale of furniture. Tau owns 100 percent of the stock of Tau N.V., a Dutch corporation which has a post–1986 pool of undistributed earnings and profits of $10 million. Of this amount, $9 million is attributable to income from the manufacture and sale of furniture in the Netherlands. The Dutch corporate tax is imposed on this income at a 36–percent rate, but foreign-source dividends and interest are exempt from tax. The remaining $1 million consists of $500,000 of dividends and $500,000 of interest received from a Swiss corporation, in which Tau N.V. owns 40 percent of the stock (the remaining 60 percent being owned by an unrelated foreign person) and which earns all of its income from the manufacture and sale of upholstery fabrics in Switzerland. The Swiss corporate income tax is imposed on the income of the Swiss corporation at a 20–percent rate. The dividends are subject to a Swiss withholding tax of five percent and the interest to a Swiss withholding tax of ten percent. Tau N.V. pays a dividend of $10 million to Tau. How are these transactions treated under Subpart F and the Section 904 limitations?

8. How will the results in Problem 7 be affected, if at all, if Tau N.V. owns 51 percent of the Swiss corporation?

9. Sigma Corporation ("Sigma"), a Delaware corporation, is engaged in the manufacture and sale of sailboards and surfboards in the United States. Sigma owns all of the stock of Sigma, K.K. ("Sigma Japan"), a Japanese corporation that owns all of the stock of Sigma Export Sales Co. ("Sigma Bermuda"), a Bermuda corporation. Sigma Japan is engaged in the manufacture and sale of sailboards in Japan. Sigma Bermuda purchases sailboards and surfboards from Sigma and Sigma Japan and sells them at a mark-up to independent distributors located in many countries other than Bermuda, the United States and Japan, passing title to customers at the port of destination. Sigma Japan pays $500,000 of interest to Sigma Bermuda on a loan of working capital. Sigma Bermuda's income consists exclusively of $3 million of income from the previously described purchase and resale of sailboards and surfboards and the $500,000 of interest from Sigma Japan. Sigma Japan receives $5 million of income from the manufacture and sale of sailboards in Japan. It also receives from Sigma Bermuda $1 million in royalties for use of trademarks in foreign countries other than Japan, which are derived in the active conduct of Sigma Japan's business and $1 million in interest from Sigma Bermuda on a loan to Sigma Bermuda to finance its purchase of sailboards from Sigma Japan. Sigma Japan pays a dividend of $2 million to Sigma. How are these transactions treated under Subpart F and the Section 904 limitations?

10. Epsilon Corp. ("Epsilon"), a Delaware corporation, is engaged in the engineering and construction business in the United States and abroad. It owns as an investment all of the stock of Epsilon S.A., a French corporation, which owns three apartment buildings in Paris. The management of the buildings is conducted by an independent French real estate management firm, which is paid a management fee by Epsilon S.A. Epsilon S.A. has only

one employee, a bookkeeper who works part-time and maintains the books and records of the corporation. Epsilon S.A.'s income consists exclusively of $200,000 of rent from the three buildings. Epsilon S.A. leases its own office premises from Epsilon and pays to Epsilon $100,000 of annual rent, which is deductible by Epsilon S.A. but is subject to a French withholding tax of $25,000. Epsilon can properly allocate and apportion $30,000 of expenses against the $100,000 of the gross rent paid to it by Epsilon S.A. Assume that the net rental income of Epsilon S.A. after deductions for business expenses (including the $100,000 of rent paid to Epsilon) is subject to French corporate income tax of 38 percent. How is the rent received by Epsilon and by Epsilon S.A. treated under Subpart F and the Section 904 limitations? Is there a Subpart F inclusion to Epsilon? If so, how is it treated for purposes of the Section 904 limitations?

[¶ 7180]

J. POLICY CONSIDERATIONS

The foregoing discussion of the rules associated with the separate basket limitation regime invites consideration of whether the objective of reducing opportunities for cross-crediting of excess foreign tax credits generated by high-taxed foreign-source income justifies the complexity of the limitation rules now in place. This subject is explored in the following Report issued by the Treasury Department, before Congress enacted the 2004 JOBS Act, which made some of the changes discussed.

[¶ 7185]

U.S. TREASURY DEPARTMENT, INTERNATIONAL TAX REFORM: AN INTERIM REPORT

19–28 (Jan. 1993).

For each separate limitation, (i) gross income items in the limitation category must be identified, (ii) expenses must be allocated to the category, (iii) creditable taxes attributable to the category must be determined, (iv) "look-through" rules may have to be applied, (v) a credit carryover mechanism must be provided and (vi) losses incurred in the category must be addressed. The obvious compliance and administrative burdens associated with these operations multiply with the addition of each new category for which a taxpayer must compute a limitation.

Yet approximately 75 percent of all foreign source income falls within the general limitation category. It is not clear that the gains derived in terms of efficiency and tax base preservation justify the potential complexity associated with subjecting only a quarter of all foreign source income to eight separate limitations. To answer this question, it will be necessary to determine the average number of separate limitations that U.S. multinational corporations must apply. If this average number is low (e.g., two or three limitations), the provision of multiple separate limitation categories may not be as great a source of complexity, in practice, as it may appear. On the other hand, U.S. multinationals faced with more than two or three separate limitations bear compliance burdens that would seem disproportionate in relation to potential gains. In connection with the ongoing study, post–1986 tax return data is being examined with this issue in mind. Pending the results of this analysis, this section describes various options for streamlining the existing separate limitation categories.

a. Expansion of passive limitation category. * * * The passive limitation category could be expanded * * * to include other low-taxed income now subject to separate limitations, e.g., shipping and financial services income. The legislative history of the Tax Reform Act of 1986 suggests that the separate limitations for shipping and financial services income were motivated both by a concern for preservation of U.S. residual tax and by a desire to mitigate inefficient incentives that might otherwise arise for combination of low-taxed shipping or financial services businesses with other high-taxed businesses. Inclusion of shipping and financial services income within the passive limitation category could address these concerns, while reducing the compliance burden for multinational corporations earning both passive income and shipping or financial services income. Although it would permit cross-crediting of high taxes (if any) paid on shipping or financial services income against low-taxed passive income, this potential erosion of the tax base may be too insignificant to justify separate limitations.

Other separate limitations that might be folded into the passive limitation are those for dividends from a DISC or former DISC, taxable income attributable to foreign trade income of a FSC, and distributions from a FSC or former FSC out of earnings attributable to foreign trade income. [The FSC rules were repealed, effective September 30, 2000, and replaced by an extraterritorial income exclusion regime, which has also been repealed, but with substantial continuing benefits available in 2005 and 2006 and in some cases beyond. See ¶ 11,230.] This income typically bears little or no foreign tax and benefits from favorable tax treatment under U.S. law. While these characteristics are reason for excluding this income from the general limitation category, it is not clear that individual limitations are justified.

b. Inclusion of active income within general limitation category. Simplification might also be achieved by including the active income now subject to separate limitations within the general limitation category. For example, rather than including shipping and financial services income within the passive limitation category, these types of income could be included in the general category. General limitation treatment would reflect a greater emphasis on competitiveness. As discussed above, however, this approach would increase cross-crediting opportunities and could result in inefficient business combinations and erosion of the U.S. tax base. In addition, it could increase administrative and compliance burdens by requiring that a distinction be drawn between the passive investment income and the active income of a financial services business.

c. High withholding tax interest. Another separate limitation often proposed for elimination is high withholding tax interest. The premise of this separate limitation is that the economic burden of a flat rate withholding tax on interest is more likely to be borne by the foreign borrower than by a U.S. lender. If so, U.S. financial institutions lending to foreign borrowers would benefit (in the absence of the separate limitation) from the imposition of a high withholding tax on interest income. The economic burden of this tax would be passed through to the foreign borrower (via a higher interest rate), but the credit granted for the withholding tax could shelter other financial services income from residual U.S. tax. A U.S. financial institution could thus have a marginal incentive to make loans to foreign borrowers rather than to U.S. borrowers.

On the other hand, cross-crediting is tolerated within other categories of business income, despite potential incentives for offshore investment. U.S. financial institutions have also argued that the separate limitation is anti-competitive, because their inability to cross-credit high foreign withholding taxes requires them to make loans on a "net-of-tax" basis, while their foreign competitors can absorb these taxes through cross-crediting against other income. Further analysis of lending practices and post–1986 income tax return data is necessary to evaluate these competing arguments. If the separate limitation is retained, however, some simplification could be achieved by restricting its application to financial institutions, which are the primary source of concern.

d. "High-tax kickout." "High-taxed income" * * * is removed from the passive category and included in the general limitation category (the "high-tax kickout"). * * * [T]he determination of effective foreign tax rates can be difficult, even though income grouping rules are provided. Thus it is worth reconsidering the need for the high-tax kickout.

The most obvious effect of the high-tax kickout is to prevent cross-crediting within the passive limitation. Passive income is highly mobile, however, and thus is rarely subject to high rates of foreign tax (unless it is earned in a high-tax country for non-tax reasons). Moreover, a concern for cross-crediting within the passive category is inconsistent with the toleration of cross-crediting within other separate limitation categories. Thus a concern for cross-crediting would not appear to justify retention of the high-tax kickout.

A second function of the high-tax kickout is to backstop the regulatory definition of "active rents and royalties," which are excluded from foreign personal holding company income under section 954(c)(2)(A) and thus, appropriately, from the passive category. The high-tax kickout ensures that rents and royalties which are, by virtue of their active nature, subject to high rates of foreign tax are excluded from the passive category—even if they would not technically qualify as active rents and royalties under the general regulatory definition. This function might be better served, however, within the regulations under section 954. For example, regulatory authority could be provided for incorporation of a tax rate test in the definition of "active rents and royalties;" while this would still require determinations of effective foreign tax rate, these determinations generally would be limited to rents and royalties (for foreign tax credit purposes).

The third function of the high-tax kickout is to prevent manipulation of the expense allocation rules to shift taxes from limitation categories with excess credits to categories with excess limitation. For example, a CFC [controlled foreign corporation] with excess credits in the general limitation category can engage in simultaneous loans, one as borrower and the other as lender, to create equal amounts of interest income and expense; the interest income may be entirely passive limitation income, but the corresponding interest expense is apportioned to reduce taxable income in all limitation categories (as well as U.S. source income). The tax effect of this transaction (which is a "wash," from an economic perspective) is that high foreign taxes actually paid on general limitation income are attributed to income in the passive limitation category and thus may offset residual U.S. tax on other, low-taxed passive income. The high-tax kickout, together with the "netting" rule of Treas. Reg. § 1.904–5(c)(2) (which allocates related person interest expense of a CFC directly against passive income of the CFC), inhibits this manipulation of the expense allocation rules.

This third function of the high-tax kickout is the most difficult to achieve by other means. It has been suggested, however, that the potential for "tax shifting" through expense allocation is sufficiently limited that it could be addressed with a general anti-abuse rule directed at "back-to-back" loans and other "wash" transactions. This approach would clearly reduce compliance burdens, although it could increase the administrative burden associated with enforcement of the foreign tax credit limitation. Alternatively, it is possible that extension of the "netting" rule of Treas. Reg. § 1.904–5(c)(2) to apply to all related and unrelated person interest income and expense of a CFC could address the potential for manipulation without requiring effective tax rate determinations.

As the foregoing discussion illustrates, there is considerable potential for simplification of the foreign tax credit limitation rules, if reduced emphasis on efficiency and tax base preservation is acceptable. The fact that the separate limitation rules are probably the most frequently cited example of complexity in the international provisions would seem to justify at least some reduction in the precision with which these objectives are sought under current law.

* * *

An additional source of complexity in the foreign tax credit rules are the rules relating to the treatment of losses * * *.

a. Treatment of losses. Under Code section 904(f)(5), a separate limitation loss (i.e., an excess of deductions allocated to foreign source income in a separate limitation category over the income in that category) is reallocated to other separate limitation categories in proportion to the income in those categories. When income is generated in the loss category in a subsequent year, that income is reallocated to the categories previously reduced by the loss in order to recapture the loss.

Similarly, an overall foreign loss reduces taxable U.S. source income in the year generated and thus the U.S. tax on U.S. source income earned in that year. Code section 904(f) recaptures the loss, however, by resourcing foreign source income earned in a later year as domestic source. Resourcing applies to an amount of foreign source income equal to the amount of the overall foreign loss, but the amount resourced in any single year is limited to 50 percent of the taxpayer's foreign source income in that year (unless the taxpayer elects a higher percentage). The effect of the resourcing is to reduce the foreign tax credit limitation in the subsequent year(s); the amount of U.S. tax may be increased by a corresponding amount, in which case the rule effectively recaptures the prior reduction in U.S. tax on U.S. source income that resulted from the foreign source loss. The rule is intended to prevent taxpayers from deriving a "double benefit," i.e., a deduction to reduce U.S. tax on U.S. source income and the ability to claim a foreign tax credit in a later income year (assuming that the foreign country where the loss was incurred does not permit loss carryovers).

These reallocation and recapture rules introduce considerable complexity to the foreign tax credit determination. In addition, it is often remarked that the lack of symmetry between the current treatment of overall foreign and domestic losses results in excessive taxation of foreign source income. Under Code section 904(f)(5)(D), domestic losses are allocated among foreign source separate limitation categories in proportion to the income in those categories. The allocation of a domestic loss to foreign source income reduces the foreign tax credit limitation in the loss year, and residual U.S. tax liability with respect to foreign source income may be increased as a result. Yet recapture of the overall domestic loss as foreign source income is not permitted when domestic source income is earned in a subsequent year; moreover, if there is positive worldwide income in the year in which the domestic loss is incurred, the domestic loss will not be carried forward to reduce U.S. source income in a subsequent year. The result can be excessive taxation over a period of years.

Recapture of overall domestic losses has been proposed on several occasions * * *. An alternative approach, that could prove simpler, would be to revise the rules for both overall *and* separate limitation losses to reallocate all losses of any category or source on a pro rata basis to all other categories with positive income. This proposal could be combined with recapture rules; alternatively, a loss in any category could be permitted to reduce income in other categories on a pro rata basis, but would also continue forward within its own category to reduce the limitation for that category in future years. The latter solution would limit recapture to the loss category—a potentially simpler rule.

A third possibility would be to require that a loss in a separate limitation category be carried forward (solely for foreign tax credit purposes) for consumption within its own limitation category, rather than reallocated to other limitation categories and subsequently recaptured. This proposal is probably simpler than the two alternatives described above. However, its effect would be to apply a separate limitation loss to reduce U.S. source income in the year incurred, without recapture. Arguably, the lack of relationship between the separate limitation loss and the U.S. source income makes this approach less logical than the pro rata alternative.

Finally, to the extent that symmetry, as well as simplification, are primary goals in this context, symmetrical treatment of overall foreign and domestic losses could also be achieved by retaining the current rules for overall domestic losses and repealing the overall foreign loss provisions of Code section 904(f)(1). This option would achieve the greatest gains in terms of simplification. However, it is arguable that the repeal of section 904(f)(1) would erode U.S. tax jurisdiction over U.S. source income by increasing incentives for taxpayers to use foreign losses against U.S. source income, while claiming foreign tax credits to limit U.S. tax on foreign source income. This could be accomplished by operating foreign, loss-generating businesses through foreign branches, while earning foreign source income through foreign subsidiaries eligible for deferral. In examining this issue, it is important to consider whether the "loss-branch-to-profitable-subsidiary" strategy is a significant concern. On the one hand, taxpayers are generally able to control the extent to which loss-generating assets are held in branch or subsidiary form; on the other hand, a safeguard exists to discourage this practice (i.e., the branch loss recapture rules of section 367(a)(3)(C)).

[¶ 7190]

NOTE

Based on its further evaluation of the policy alternatives, Congress enacted the changes contained in the 2004 JOBS Act, most of which become effective for tax years starting after 2006. Some of the changes were discussed in the foregoing Treasury Report. Has Congress gone far enough or too far in liberalizing the limitations on the foreign tax credit?

A more sweeping proposal to reduce the tax advantages derived by U.S. taxpayers from the cross-crediting opportunities available under current law was contained in the Obama Administration's proposal to determine the foreign tax credit on a pooling basis:

> Under the proposal, a U.S. taxpayer would determine its deemed paid foreign tax credit on a consolidated basis based on the aggregate foreign taxes and earnings and profits of all of the foreign subsidiaries with respect to which the U.S. taxpayer can claim a deemed paid foreign tax credit (including lower tier subsidiaries described in section 902(b)). The deemed paid foreign tax credit for a taxable year would be determined based on the amount of the consolidated earnings and profits of the foreign subsidiaries repatriated to the U.S. taxpayer in that taxable year. The Secretary would be granted authority to issue any Treasury regulations necessary to carry out the purposes of the proposal.

U.S. Treas. Dep't, General Explanations of the Administration's Fiscal Year 2011 Revenue Proposals 41 (Feb. 2010).

The proposal has not been enacted. If it were enacted, would it be an effective bar to the tax savings available through cross-crediting under current law?

CHAPTER 8

TRANSFER PRICING

■ ■ ■

[¶ 8000]

A. STATEMENT OF THE PROBLEM

The term "transfer pricing" is often used to refer to the setting of prices on all types of transactions between related parties. It would apply to fixing the price on a sale of goods from one member of a corporate family to another, the royalty rate under a patent license, the fees under a services agreement, the interest rate on a loan and the amount payable on any other intercompany transaction.

Except in situations in which consolidated returns are filed, every U.S. and foreign corporation is at least a potential taxpayer. The U.S. income tax liability for each corporation is determined by its profits and losses. Taxable income for a U.S. corporation is its net income from worldwide operations. The U.S. tax for a foreign corporation depends on whether it has income effectively connected with a U.S. trade or business and whether it is receiving other U.S.-source income. The validity of the tax results of applying the general rules is in doubt, however, when some or all of the transactions of the corporation may have been undertaken without the usual economic motivation of maximizing revenues while minimizing costs.

Transfer pricing issues have long been a source of concern to tax officials. The stakes can be demonstrated by a simple example. Suppose that two corporations, Supplier Co. and Producer Co., are owned by a single shareholder. Supplier produces parts, all of which are sold to Producer. Producer uses the parts in the manufacture of consumer goods that are sold on the open market. The economic return to the shareholder for a year is effectively measured by the difference between the revenues produced as a result of sales by Producer and the costs incurred by both corporations. The prices paid by Producer to Supplier have no economic consequence.

Those prices may, however, generate enormous tax differences. If Producer is organized in a developing country where it enjoys an income tax holiday and Supplier is a U.S. corporation taxable on worldwide income at the usual rates, there is an obvious incentive to establish a price between the two corporations that minimizes the net income of Supplier and maximizes the net income of Producer. If the shareholder is a U.S. person, the profits accruing to Producer will usually be subjected to tax in the United States at some later time (when dividends are paid, shares are sold or the corporation is liquidated), but the shareholder would have enjoyed the substantial benefits of deferral of U.S. tax during the intervening, perhaps extended, period. If the shareholder is a foreign person, potential U.S. income taxes may be permanently avoided.

The amounts at stake for the Treasury and taxpayers in transfer pricing controversies are substantial. In one well known study, the IRS estimated an annual revenue loss of $2.8 billion as a result of transfer pricing abuses. See U.S. Treas. Dep't Inspector General for Tax Administration, Final Audit Report: The Controls for Examination Processes for Industry Cases with International Transfer Pricing Issues Can Be Improved, Reference Number 2004–30–133 (Sept. 10, 2004). However, some private estimates of revenue loss are substantially higher. For example, one academic study estimated that abusive transfer pricing practices by multinational groups resulted in the loss of $53 billion in tax revenues in 2001. See 12 Tax Mgmt. Trans. Pricing Rep. (BNA) 213 (July 23, 2003). Further, the amounts at issue in transfer pricing cases are often very large. For example, it was reported that only four companies filed transfer pricing cases in 2004. These four cases, however, challenged a total of $8.4 billion in Section 482 allocations. 13 Tax Mgmt. Trans. Pricing Rep. (BNA) 903 (Jan. 19, 2005). In a widely reported settlement of a transfer pricing dispute, Glaxo SmithKline Holdings (America) paid $3.4 billion. U.S. Treas. Dep't, Report to the Congress on Earnings Stripping, Transfer Pricing and U.S. Income Tax Treaties 34 (Nov. 2007) ("2007 Treasury Report").

Problems of transfer pricing confront the tax officials of virtually all countries. The approach codified in the U.S. tax law has for many years been one of the prototypes for addressing the issue. Similar provisions can be found in the tax laws of most other countries. It should be noted, however, that questions of transfer pricing are not limited to income taxes. Minority shareholders confront similar issues in situations in which controlling interests cause a company to enter into transactions with other entities that they (but not the minority) own or control. A portion of the theoretical response to the tax question, therefore, is comparable to standards evolved under corporate law.

The difficult conceptual and administrative issues arising in connection with transfer pricing abuse and the defenses thereto have been a particularly lively item on the tax policy agenda. Sometimes it is argued that U.S. tax laws are being enforced inadequately against foreign interests participating in the U.S. economy. Sometimes it is argued that transfer pricing arrangements used by U.S. corporations move profits offshore and effectively export U.S. jobs, always a hot political issue.

As part of the Tax Reform Act of 1986, Congress directed the IRS to undertake a study of the operation of transfer pricing mechanisms, particularly with respect to the exploitation of intangible property. The result was the publication in 1988 of "A Study of Intercompany Pricing under Section 482 of the Code" (commonly referred to as the "Section 482 White Paper"). IRS Notice 88–123, 1988–2 C.B. 458. The publication of the Section 482 White Paper triggered a debate among tax administrators and professionals that resulted in the promulgation of a series of proposed regulations. After lengthy discussion and extensive amendment, new regulations were issued in final form in 1994 through 1996. Note that many of the cases and rulings in this Chapter arose for tax years prior to the adoption of the current regulations.

As the materials that follow clearly indicate, much time and thought and many resources have been directed at the issue of transfer pricing. These materials do not, however, constitute the end of the story, but only its current status. While the 2004 JOBS Act contained no substantive provisions dealing directly with issues of transfer pricing, it required the Treasury Department to:

> conduct a study regarding the effectiveness of current transfer pricing rules and compliance efforts in ensuring that cross-border transfers and other related-party transactions, particularly transactions involving intangible assets, service contracts, or leases cannot be used improperly to shift income out of the United States. The study shall include a review of the contemporaneous documentation and penalty rules under section 6662 of the * * * Code * * *, a review of the regulatory and administrative guidance implementing the principles of section 482 * * * to transactions involving intangible property and services and to cost-sharing arrangements, and an examination of whether increased disclosure of cross-border transactions should be required.

2004 JOBS Act, § 806. Further, Congress mandated that the study set forth "specific recommendations to address all abuses identified in the study." The 2007 Treasury Report fulfilled this requirement and has been the focus of extensive discussion about responses to transfer pricing abuses.

[¶ 8005]

B. STATUTORY RESPONSE: SECTION 482

1. AUTHORITY TO ADJUST

The vehicle for addressing problems of transfer pricing is set forth in a well known and widely cited provision of the Code. Section 482 states that:

> In any case of two or more organizations, trades, or businesses * * * owned or controlled directly or indirectly by the same interests, the [IRS] may distribute, apportion, or allocate gross income, deductions, credits, or allowances, between or among [them], if [it] determines that such distribution, apportionment, or allocation is necessary in order to prevent evasion of taxes or clearly to reflect the income of any [of them].

The provision applies whether or not the taxpayers are incorporated, whether they are domestic or foreign and whether or not they are "members of an affiliated group." Reg. § 1.482–1(i)(1).

The regulations explain that the purpose of the provision is to place "a controlled taxpayer [i.e., a member of a commonly controlled group] on a tax parity with an uncontrolled taxpayer by determining the *true taxable income* of the controlled taxpayer." Reg. § 1.482–1(a)(1) (emphasis added). The appropriate standard is usually characterized as fair market value or "arm's length" pricing. Reg. § 1.482–1(b)(1). In general, this standard is met if the results of a transaction are consistent with the results that would obtain if the parties were not related. As in other instances in which the value of noncash assets or of services must be determined, the difficulty of applying this standard will depend partly on the nature of the transaction being analyzed. The fair market value of a fungible security or commodity traded on established markets may be determined by reference to the financial pages of a newspaper or Internet sources. Determining the value of property not regularly traded will often be a substantially more difficult task.

Section 482 is exclusively a weapon for use by the IRS; it cannot be invoked even as a shield by the taxpayer. However, the regulations permit a taxpayer to report on a timely filed tax return results of controlled transactions "based upon prices different from those actually charged" if it is "necessary to reflect an arm's length result." Reg. § 1.482–1(a)(3). However, taxpayers may not compel the IRS to invoke Section 482. A determination by the IRS to effect an adjustment under Section 482 carries a strong presumption of correctness. A taxpayer seeking to challenge the adjustment bears the burden of proving that it is arbitrary, capricious or unreasonable. See, e.g., American Terrazzo Strip Co. v. Commissioner, 56 T.C. 961 (1971) (acq.).

The task of bearing this burden to overcome a proposed IRS adjustment under Section 482 may be formidable. Successfully demonstrating that the IRS analysis is inappropriate or inaccurate will not suffice. In one well-known decision, for example, the U.S. Court of Claims sustained the proposed IRS adjustment and offered some telling observations about the nature of the burden confronting a taxpayer:

In reviewing the Commissioner's allocation of income under Section 482, we focus on the reasonableness of the result, not the details of the examining agent's methodology.

* * *

* * * The amount of reallocation would not be easy for us to calculate if we were called upon to do it ourselves, but Section 482 gives that power to the Commissioner and we are content that his amount (totaling some $18 million) was within the zone of reasonableness. The language of the statute and the holdings of the courts recognize that the Service has broad discretion in reallocating income. * * * A "broad brush" approach to this inexact field seems necessary * * *.

E.I. DuPont De Nemours & Co. v. United States, 608 F.2d 445, 454–55 (Ct.Cl. 1979), cert. denied, 445 U.S. 962 (1980).

In Perkin–Elmer Corp. v. Commissioner, 66 T.C.M. (CCH) 634 (1993), the IRS formally abandoned its pricing adjustment theory prior to the trial. Judge Tannenwald concluded that the taxpayer had met the burden of showing the IRS allocations to be "arbitrary, capricious, or unreasonable." He noted further, however, that such a finding "does not relieve [the taxpayer] of its burden of proving that the transactions * * * meet the arm's length standard; if it fails to do so, the Court must decide the proper allocations of income * * *."

Section 482 is not restricted in its application to international transactions. Many of the applications of the authority that it provides have occurred in wholly domestic situations. This Chapter deals only with transfer pricing issues in the international context.

No additional income will normally result to the taxpayers considered as a group from an adjustment under Section 482. However, where one corporation is domestic and one foreign (as in the example of Supplier and Producer), the U.S. income tax consequences to the group may be considerable.

The adjustment of an item under Section 482 for one controlled taxpayer is accompanied by appropriate collateral adjustments, such as correlative allocations, deductions, conforming adjustments and setoffs, to one or more other members of the controlled group. Reg. § 1.482–1(g). In the case of related corporations, for example, an adjustment under Section 482 to reduce the price of items sold by one to the other will increase net income to the buyer but will reduce net income to the seller. Another example is set forth in Rev. Proc. 99–32, 1999–2 C.B. 296, where the taxable income of a U.S. subsidiary was increased in respect of transactions with its foreign parent. The IRS ruled that the foreign parent could make cash payments to reflect the Section 482 adjustments without increasing the taxable income of the U.S. subsidiary.

[¶ 8010]

2. RELEVANCE OF TAXPAYER MOTIVATION

Taxpayers may seek to avoid an adjustment by showing that prices were not established to avoid taxes. For example, the presence of minority shareholders of a corporation who have rights that can be asserted against non-arm's length transfer pricing arrangements might be offered as proof that prices were not intentionally skewed away from market values. In other situations, it might be shown that the managers of different corporations, even within a closely integrated operating group, were competing vigorously to produce high profits for the entities for which they were responsible.

Such circumstances will not themselves be a defense to an adjustment under Section 482. The authority of the IRS to make adjustments does not necessarily depend on any tax-motivated behavior by the taxpayers involved. It arises not only in the case of "evasion" but also in any circumstances in which adjustments are necessary "clearly to reflect * * * income." An appropriate adjustment cannot be avoided on the ground that the taxpayer did not consider tax consequences or that the total taxes paid by all of the related entities in all nations were higher than the tax payable in the United States. As a practical matter, of course, the discovery by IRS agents of evidence that pricing arrangements were established purposefully to avoid U.S. taxes is likely to increase the probability of an adjustment under Section 482 and of the special Section 482 adjustment penalties discussed at ¶ 8170.

[¶ 8015]

3. OWNERSHIP OR CONTROL

The definitional reach of Section 482 is broad, covering virtually any conceivable business arrangement between or among any commonly controlled individuals, businesses or types of entity. Reg. § 1.482–1(i)(1), (2). The potential reach of the provision is extended further by the broad definition of "control" that is applied. The regulations provide that control means "any kind of control, direct or indirect, whether legally enforceable, and however exercisable or exercised." The regulations assert further that the "reality," rather than the "form," of the control will be "decisive" and that "[a] presumption of control arises if income or deductions have been arbitrarily shifted." Control might also be found where two or more unrelated taxpayers act in concert or with a common goal or purpose. Reg. § 1.482–1(i)(4). The control tests can be applied on the basis of relationships extant at the time transactions are planned. For example, in DHL Corp. v. Commissioner, 285 F.3d 1210 (9th Cir. 2002), the court found that the control requirement was satisfied for purposes of Section 482 even though control did not necessarily exist at the time the transaction was actually concluded.

[¶ 8020]

4. APPLICATIONS OF SECTION 482 TO INTERNATIONAL TRANSACTIONS

a. Breadth of Application

The example of Supplier and Producer is one case in which there is an incentive for the IRS to use Section 482 to increase tax collections by allocating income to the U.S. corporation. Adjustments may occur in other circumstances as well. The application of the foreign tax credit provisions with their complex limitations (see Chapters 5 and 7) may invite the application of Section 482 to assure an accurate measure of foreign- and U.S.-source income and deductions. Attempts by taxpayers to shift income to tax haven subsidiaries in circumstances that avoid constructive dividend treatment under the special rules for controlled foreign corporations discussed in Chapter 6 may result in the application of Section 482.

[¶ 8025]

b. Potential Secondary Consequences

As the following Ruling indicates, adjustments under Section 482 may have a direct impact on U.S. tax liabilities even when they concern foreign entities engaged in foreign transactions.

[¶ 8030]

REVENUE RULING 78–83

1978–1 C.B. 79.

* * *

The taxpayer, *P*, a domestic corporation, owned all of the stock of *X*, a foreign corporation incorporated in country *M*. *X* produces and exports fiber for sale on the world market, but due to monetary restrictions, *X* has had difficulty in securing dollars needed to pay refunds to foreign customers and to pay travel expenses of its employees outside country *M*. *P*, therefore, formed *Y*, a wholly owned foreign corporation incorporated in country *T* to act on behalf of *X* to receive part of the sales price charged by *X*. Thereafter, some of these dollars accumulated by *Y* were used to pay the above-mentioned refunds and expenses, as well as certain promotion expenses in connection with the fiber sales. *P* provided incidental services for *X* in connection with these disbursements, but performed no services in connection with the fiber sales. The funds diverted from *X* to *Y* were in excess of the amounts necessary to provide *Y* with reasonable compensation for its services to *X* and to reimburse *Y* for the expenses it incurred on behalf of *X*.

Section 301(a) * * * provides * * * that a distribution of property * * * made by a corporation to a shareholder with respect to its stock shall [generally] be treated in the manner provided in subsection (c).

Section 301(c) * * * provides, in part, that in the case of a distribution to which subsection (a) applies, that portion of the distribution which is a dividend * * * shall be included in gross income.

Section 1.301–1(c) of the * * * Regulations provides that section 301 is not applicable to an amount paid by a corporation to a shareholder unless the amount is paid to the shareholder in his capacity as such. A distribution to a shareholder in his capacity as such, need not be formally declared and paid but may take the form of a constructive dividend.

Section 482 * * * provides authority to distribute, apportion or allocate gross income, deductions, and credits among related organizations, trades, or businesses if it is necessary in order to clearly reflect the income of such entities or to prevent the evasion of taxes.

Section 482 * * * applies to transactions between brother-sister corporations involving the performance of services by one for the benefit of the other that result in significant shifting of income.

Where an allocation is made under section 482 as a result of an excessive charge for services rendered between brother-sister corporations, the amount of the allocation will be treated as a distribution to the controlling shareholder with respect to the stock of the entity whose income is increased and as a capital contribution by the controlling shareholder to the other entity involved in the transaction. See Rev. Rul. 69–630, 1969–2 C.B. 112, relating to a bargain sale between brother-sister controlled corporations.

A constructive dividend is paid when a corporation diverts property, directly or indirectly, to the use of a shareholder without expectation of repayment, even though no formal dividend has been declared.

Generally, in those cases involving corporations controlled by the same persons, the courts have found a constructive dividend to have been distributed to the common shareholders where one of the corporations was used as a device for siphoning off the earnings and profits. * * *

However, a constructive dividend is a diversion of the property, not of the income. Income is a characterization which tax law attributes to certain receipts of property, whereas a constructive distribution is that of property itself. Thus, where property is transferred from one affiliate to a sister corporation without adequate consideration therefor, there is a constructive distribution to the common parent whether or not the motive for the transfer was an attempt improperly to allocate income or deductions between the corporations.

However, any amount diverted to *Y* for disbursements on behalf of *X*, or as reasonable compensation for services rendered to *X*, would not be considered as constructive dividend income to *P*.

Accordingly, the income of *X* diverted to *Y* in excess of the disbursements on behalf of *X* and reasonable compensation for services of *Y* will be treated as a distribution taxable as a dividend to *P* to the extent of the earnings and profits of *X*, and a capital contribution by *P* to *Y*.

[¶ 8035]

5. EFFECT OF FOREIGN LAW

a. Foreign Restrictions on Market Operations

While taxpayer motives will not be determinative of the application of Section 482, the "clear" reflection of income must comport with legal, as well as market, realities. In a number of cases the taxpayer has sought to avoid a proposed adjustment under Section 482 on the ground that it was restricted by legal requirements of a foreign country.

For example, in Procter & Gamble Co. v. Commissioner, 961 F.2d 1255 (6th Cir.1992), the taxpayer ("P & G") was a U.S. corporation that owned all of the stock of P & G A.G. ("AG"), a Swiss corporation. AG in turn owned all of the stock of Espana, a Spanish corporation. The IRS asserted an adjustment under Section 482 to increase royalty income paid by Espana to AG. Such royalties would have been treated as Subpart F income immediately taxable to P & G. See ¶ 6085. The adjustment was opposed by P & G on the ground that applicable Spanish law prohibited the payment of such royalties. Although acknowledging the provisions of Spanish law cited by the taxpayer, the IRS argued that the taxpayer's subsidiaries could have obtained an exception from Spanish authorities and that the Spanish requirements were temporary and were eventually relaxed. However, the Tax Court's decision accepting the taxpayer's argument was affirmed by the court of appeals.

A number of cases involved the "Aramco Advantage," which arose from the imposition of resale price restrictions by the Government of Saudi Arabia on the sale of crude oil extracted in that country. In Exxon v. Commissioner, 66 T.C.M. (CCH) 1707 (1993), the court cited the decision in the *Procter & Gamble* case in support of its holding that the IRS was precluded from allocating profits attributable to the excess of the market price of comparable crude oil over the Saudi official selling price. The decision was good news for Exxon and its shareholders. The adjustment proposed by the IRS would have increased Exxon's taxes by $2 billion.[1] In

1. It was also good news for a number of others. An Exxon official announced that the company had paid $25 million in fees to outside counsel, legal experts and witnesses. This figure did not include the salaries of in-house counsel. 246 BNA Daily Tax Rep. G–7 (Dec. 28, 1993).

an appeal consolidated with another case, the Tax Court decision was affirmed in Texaco, Inc. v. Commissioner, 98 F.3d 825 (5th Cir.1996), cert. denied, 520 U.S. 1185 (1997).

The current regulations provide that "a foreign legal restriction will be taken into account only to the extent that it is shown that the restriction affected an uncontrolled taxpayer under comparable circumstances for a comparable period of time." Reg. § 1.482–1(h)(2). The effect of such foreign legal restrictions will be considered, moreover, only if they are publicly promulgated, generally applied and not attributable to a commercial transaction between the taxpayer and the foreign government. The restrictions must explicitly prohibit the payment or receipt required by the Section 482 adjustment. The taxpayer must exhaust all available remedies for seeking a waiver and must not have engaged in arrangements to circumvent the restriction.

If there is no evidence indicating the effect of foreign legal restrictions on uncontrolled taxpayers, the regulations permit the taxpayer relief to the extent that the restricted amount may be treated as deferrable income. However, to qualify for such treatment the taxpayer must establish that payment or receipt of the arm's length amount was prohibited by a foreign legal restriction meeting all of the requirements of the above paragraph. In addition, prior to being contacted by the IRS the taxpayer must have elected to be treated under this deferred income accounting method and identified the affected transactions and applicable foreign legal restrictions. Reg. § 1.482–1(h)(2)(iii).

[¶ 8040]

b. Transfer Pricing Adjustments Resulting in Double Taxation

The thrust of Section 482 is to reallocate income or deductions between related entities but to leave the total amount of income of the group unchanged. Of course, this is one matter when all the entities are in the United States, but it is an entirely different situation when one or more of them is foreign and not subject to U.S. taxing jurisdiction. In that case, the IRS may increase the income and the taxes of a U.S. corporation, but it has no direct way to reduce commensurately the income and thus the taxes of the foreign entity. However, if the income of the foreign entity should ever become relevant for U.S. tax purposes, it will be adjusted to reflect the Section 482 decision. Such an adjustment might be made, for example, in figuring the parent's foreign tax credit on a dividend from its foreign subsidiary. See Reg. § 1.482–1(g)(2). But often with an international transaction, an IRS correlative adjustment is of no use, and there can be no assurance that tax officials in the foreign country will make an adjustment that correlates with that made by the IRS in a way that will avoid international double taxation.

Tax officials in other countries, moreover, typically have authority to adjust income tax consequences that is similar to the authority provided to the IRS by Section 482. The exercise of such authority by a foreign tax agency may result in double taxation or other adverse tax consequences. Suppose, for example, that taxing authorities in the United Kingdom conclude that prices charged by a U.S. parent for sales to a British subsidiary were too high. An adjustment is made which increases the tax liability of the British subsidiary. Note, however, that the U.S. parent has already determined its U.S. tax liability based on the transfer price that was actually charged and collected. Since the taxpayer cannot compel the IRS to effect an adjustment under Section 482, the net result may well be that both countries tax the same element of income earned by the two related companies. However, when (as in the case of the United Kingdom) a U.S. tax treaty applies, administrative relief for the taxpayer may be available under the competent authority mechanism to avoid double taxation.

The U.S. Model Treaty (Appendix A) provides an example of a form of agreement to cooperate in exercising the power to adjust transfer prices. Article 9(1) of the Model Treaty authorizes both countries to challenge transfer prices where:

> a) an enterprise of a Contracting State participates directly or indirectly in the management, control or capital of an enterprise of the other Contracting State; or
>
> b) the same persons participate directly or indirectly in the management, control, or capital of an enterprise of a Contracting State and an enterprise of the other Contracting State,
>
> and in either case conditions are made or imposed between the two enterprises in their commercial or financial relations that differ from those that would be made between independent enterprises * * * .

Article 25 provides for the "competent authorities" of the two countries to endeavor to apply their laws, including transfer pricing requirements, in such a way as to avoid taxation not in accordance with the treaty. This provision may be invoked in situations where tax officials of the two countries are asserting inconsistent adjustments based on transactions between related entities.

Suppose, for example, that a U.S. corporation sells goods to a British subsidiary for $100 per unit. The IRS, asserting its authority under Section 482, contends that the correct price should have been $120 and proposes a material assessment. The Inland Revenue in London, asserting similar authority under British tax laws, contends that the correct price should have been $80 per unit and proposes a material assessment. The related taxpayers are confronting a situation in which the same $40 of profit ($120 − $80) may be taxed in both jurisdictions. Moreover, the operation of the foreign tax credit provisions of the Code will not necessarily mitigate the double tax. Treaty provisions, such as Article 25 of the

U.S. Model Treaty, contemplate that the competent authorities of the two countries will consult to endeavor to determine a price that will apply in both countries. While the result may not be the best from the taxpayer's total tax perspective, if the competent authorities can agree, the $40 of income per unit will not be subject to tax in both countries.

[¶ 8045]

C. APPROACHES TO ARM'S LENGTH PRICING

1. THE IMPORTANCE AND EVOLUTION OF REGULATIONS

While the statutory language of Section 482 is relatively straightforward, the practical considerations that arise in the attempt to apply the arm's length standard raise many complicated conceptual issues. The arm's length standard normally requires reference to comparable transactions and relevant comparative data. As reflected by the materials that follow, the different approaches to comparability invoke quite different evidentiary requirements. As you examine the approaches reflected in the regulations, consider how they might be used by executives of a group of related corporations to establish transfer prices that would be safe from IRS challenge.

As indicated earlier, the Section 482 White Paper initiated an extended period of regulatory revision and reform. The application of the new regulations adopted in its wake to various transactional arrangements is discussed at later points in this Chapter. More detailed analysis of transfer pricing issues involving intangible property is set forth in Chapter 12. Before examining the these regulations in detail as they apply to different types of transactions, several basic elements should be noted.

The regulations provide that "[i]n determining the true taxable income of a controlled taxpayer, the standard to be applied in every case is that of a taxpayer dealing at arm's length with an uncontrolled taxpayer." The regulations also note, however, that "because identical transactions can rarely be located, whether a transaction produces an arm's length result generally will be determined by reference to the results of comparable transactions under comparable circumstances." Reg. § 1.482–1(b)(1).

In many situations, previous regulations provided a series of alternative methods of approaching the question of comparability which were specified in rank order of preference. If the most preferred approach was impossible, the next was to be used. The current regulations have modified that approach:

> The arm's length result of a controlled transaction must be determined under the method that, under the facts and circumstances,

> provides the most reliable measure of an arm's length result. Thus, there is no strict priority of methods, and no method will invariably be considered to be more reliable than others.

Reg. § 1.482–1(c)(1). Not surprisingly, the inherent ambiguity in the implementation of this so-called "best method rule" has generated substantial discussion among tax practitioners and tax administrators as to whether the purposes of Section 482 have been advanced thereby in a way that increases fairness, consistency and predictability.

The "best method rule" in general means that, if two or more methods are permissible, the arm's length result must be determined under the one that provides the most reliable measure under the facts and circumstances of the transaction. The primary factors to be considered in selecting the best method include the degree of comparability between the controlled and uncontrolled transaction and the quality of the data and assumptions used in the analysis. Reg. § 1.482–1(c)(2). Of particular importance are the completeness and accuracy of the underlying data, the reliability of the assumptions and the sensitivity of the results to possible deficiencies. Reg. § 1.482–1(c)(2)(ii).

Finally, while prior regulations contemplated adjustments to reflect various differences between the controlled transaction and the uncontrolled comparison, the current regulations identify a number of factors under the various methods of approaching comparability deserving particular attention. The comparability of controlled and uncontrolled transactions is to be evaluated by the following factors:

> **i. *Functions.*** The economic functions carried out and resources employed by the parties involved in the controlled and uncontrolled transactions must be identified and compared.
>
> **ii. *Contractual terms.*** The contractual terms of the controlled and uncontrolled transactions must be analyzed. Relevant terms include the form of consideration, volume of sales, scope and terms of warranties, rights to updates or modifications, duration of the agreement, collateral transactions or ongoing business relations and credit and payment terms.
>
> **iii. *Risks.*** The comparability of risks involved in the controlled and uncontrolled transactions must be considered. These include market risks, risks associated with the success or failure of research and development activities, financial risks, credit and collection risks, product liability risks and general business risks.
>
> **iv. *Economic conditions.*** The conditions of the controlled and uncontrolled transactions must be weighed. These include the similarity in size and composition of geographic markets, the market level, market shares, location-specific costs of the factors of production, extent of competition, economic condition of the industry and alternatives reasonably available to the parties.

v. ***Nature of property or services.*** The property or services that are the basis of both the controlled and uncontrolled transactions must be compared. The regulations emphasize that any intangible property "embedded" in tangible property must be included in such comparison.

Each factor is then discussed at some length and examples are provided of their applicability. See generally Reg. § 1.482–1(d).

The regulations also specify "special circumstances" that may affect the analysis. The enumeration derives in part from factors considered in earlier judicial opinions. They include:

i. ***Market share strategy.*** Price differentials attributable to attempts to enter a market or expand a market share may be considered.

ii. ***Differences in geographic markets.*** If it is necessary to compare transactions in another market, differences in the market that might affect the comparison should be considered.

iii. ***Location savings.*** If different geographic locations account for cost differentials, they should be weighed in the comparison.

See generally Reg. § 1.482–1(d)(4).

Transactions not made in the ordinary course of business and transactions in which a principal purpose is to establish a basis for comparison will not be considered a "reliable measure" of an arm's length result. Reg. § 1.482–1(d)(4)(iii).

Finally, the current regulations explicitly recognize that comparisons may yield different results and that the various methods will not necessarily generate results with mathematical certainty. They note that the application of a best method may produce "a number of results from which a range of reliable results may be derived." In such case, no adjustment will be made if the taxpayer's results fall within such a range, called the "arm's length range." Reg. § 1.482–1(e). The regulations describe the preferred approach to determining the arm's length range and offer examples of its application. The arm's length range is determined "ordinarily" by applying the best pricing method to two or more transactions "of similar comparability." Reg. § 1.482–2. However, if the uncontrolled comparables are not sufficiently similar or if adjustments to reflect differences cannot be effected, a statistical model using all comparables must be developed to determine an acceptable range. Reg. § 1.482–1(e)(2)(iii)(B).

[¶ 8050]

2. INTEREST ON DEBT

The determination of appropriate levels of interest or original issue discount, explicit or implicit, in debt arrangements between even unrelated taxpayers is a common part of modern tax jurisprudence. See, e.g., §§ 483, 1273 and 7872. Section 482 can also be used to require adjustments in the effective interest paid between controlled entities. Safe haven rates are provided if the lender is not regularly in the business of making loans. These rates, as with other provisions of the Code, are based on the "applicable Federal rate." Reg. § 1.482–2(a)(2). An interest rate will generally satisfy the arm's length standard if it is not less than 100 percent and not more than 130 percent of the applicable Federal interest rate on debt of comparable maturity. Reg. § 1.482–2(a)(2)(iii)(B).

[¶ 8055]

3. RENTAL OF TANGIBLE PROPERTY

The regulations provide that the application of the arm's length standard to rental arrangements requires a comparison of rental arrangements with independent parties "under similar circumstances considering the period and location of the use, the owner's investment in the property or rent paid for the property, expenses of maintaining the property, the type of property involved, its condition, and all other relevant facts." Reg. § 1.482–2(c)(2)(i). If a lessee subleases to a related party, the rent will generally include "all of the deductions claimed by the * * * lessee which are attributable to the property." Such deductions include rent, maintenance and repair, utilities and management. Reg. § 1.482–2(c)(2)(iii).

[¶ 8060]

4. PROVISION OF SERVICES

a. General Rule

The regulations provide that an arm's length standard for services is "the amount * * * charged for * * * similar services in independent transactions * * * between unrelated parties under similar circumstances considering all relevant facts." Reg. § 1.482–2(b)(3).

Any task involving a determination of fair market value or arm's length prices is heavily dependent on factual analysis. The decision of the Tax Court that follows reflects a rather thorough exploration of a complex array of relevant facts. The court of appeals determined that the decision of the Tax Court judge was "clearly erroneous." As you consider his thoughtful analysis, can you discern the clear error?

[¶ 8065]

UNITED STATES STEEL CORP. v. COMMISSIONER

United States Tax Court, 1977.
36 T.C.M. (CCH) 586 (1977), rev'd, 617 F.2d 942 (2d Cir.1980).

QUEALY, JUDGE: * * *.

* * *

As the world's largest producer of steel, petitioner required a corresponding supply of iron ore for processing at its "works." Extensive deposits of iron ore were discovered in the state of Bolivar, Venezuela. Petitioner organized a corporation under Delaware law, Orinoco Mining Company, to develop those deposits. As the development proceeded, it became necessary to provide a means of transporting the ore from the mine site to the petitioner's steel mills in the United States. After considering various alternatives, petitioner organized Navios Corporation, a Liberian shipping company, for that purpose. [Liberia has long been known as a tax haven jurisdiction, and has been used extensively as a place for incorporating ship-owning corporations.] Both the mining company and the shipping company were wholly owned subsidiaries of the petitioner.

One of the primary considerations, if not the controlling consideration, for thus separating the mining function from the transportation function was to enable the petitioner to minimize the taxes due to Venezuela by limiting its reach to the income attributable to the mining of the ore. Consistent therewith, petitioner established a price for the ore F.O.B. Puerto Ordaz, Venezuela, at which price such ore would be sold to any and all producers of steel either in the United States or in other countries.

With respect to the transportation charges, Navios enabled the petitioner to provide for the transportation of the ore from Venezuela to United States ports, as well as to foreign buyers, without subjecting the income realized therefrom to tax either in Venezuela or in the United States. In addition, Navios could obtain the savings attributable to "foreign flag" operations to the extent that Navios might ultimately decide to own or to operate the ships itself. The decision thus to divorce the shipping operations from the mining operations was a sound business decision not subject to question because the avoidance of United States income taxes was also a consideration.

It was contemplated from the outset that Navios would ultimately acquire by charter, or otherwise, a fleet of ore carriers capable of transporting up to 10,000,000 tons of iron ore per year. Once the navigational and other problems were resolved, the bulk of the fleet would be obtained under long-term time charters, many of the vessels to be built to specifications suitable for the lifting of iron ore under navigational conditions existing or anticipated in Venezuela and at the major ports of delivery. During the years before the Court, Navios completed the assembly of such fleet.

The petitioner was both a user and a supplier of iron ore in the United States. Through the Oliver Mining Company, a subsidiary or division, petitioner supplied iron ore to other steel producers. Such ore was supplied at a price established each year as of April 1, by one or more independent producers and adopted by the industry. In making its Venezuelan ore available to the United States market, petitioner was not willing to offer such ore at a price which would undercut the established price for domestic ore. At the direction of the petitioner, Navios would thus establish transportation rates for the movement of the iron ore from Venezuela to United States ports which, when added to the cost of the ore F.O.B. Puerto Ordaz, Venezuela, would result in a delivered cost compatible with the price of domestic ore. Both petitioner, and any other users of Venezuelan ore, were to be charged that same price. However, there was no obligation on the purchaser of Venezuelan ore to utilize the transportation services of Navios. In fact, a subsidiary of Bethlehem Steel Company, and the largest independent purchaser of Venezuelan ore from Orinoco, took such ore F.O.B. Puerto Ordaz and transported it to United States ports on Bethlehem controlled ships.

In reliance on section 482, respondent has allocated to petitioner a portion of the charges by Navios for the transportation of iron ore from Puerto Ordaz, Venezuela to the petitioner at designated United States ports. Respondent has determined that 25 percent of the transportation charges by Navios for delivery of iron ore to the petitioner, together with a port differential charged on account of shipments to the Fairless Works, Morrisville, Pennsylvania, should be allocated to the petitioner pursuant to that section. The resulting amounts allocated to the petitioner are, as follows:

Year	Allocation
1957	$11,072,585
1958	13,042,107
1959	13,624,330
1960	14,402,384
Total	$52,141,406

Section 482 provides that, in the case of two or more controlled corporations, respondent may allocate income among subsidiary corporations if he determines that such allocation is necessary in order to prevent the evasion of taxes or clearly to reflect the income of any of such corporations. It is clear from the record in this case that petitioner controlled both Orinoco and Navios, as a matter of law through the ownership by petitioner of all of the outstanding stock of both, and as a matter of fact because the actions taken by both Orinoco and Navios were taken at the direction of the petitioner.

Section 482 grants to the respondent broad discretionary authority to "distribute, apportion, or allocate gross income, deductions, credits, or allowances" between controlled corporations where the respondent determines that such action is necessary in order to prevent an evasion of taxes or clearly to reflect the income of any of such controlled corporations. Notwithstanding such broad authority, respondent has in his regulations provided various guidelines for the application of section 482. (Regulations § 1.482–1 et seq.) In substance, the regulations recognize that where the price at which the goods are sold, or the charge for which the services are rendered, are comparable to the amount that would have been charged in a transaction between independent parties, there is no occasion to allocate income or deductions under section 482.

* * *

* * * [P]etitioner argues that its income was not, in fact, distorted and U.S. income taxes are not evaded by its purchases of transportation services from Navios. In support of this position, petitioner relies on the fact that unrelated steel producers paid Navios the same rates as petitioner; that petitioner paid an unrelated carrier of iron ore more than it paid Navios for transportation from Chile to the United States on a comparable basis; and, that Navios' rates were comparable to the rates charged in the ore voyage charter market.

While allegations made by petitioner in support of its argument may be factually correct, respondent is able to point to other transactions which would tend to prove the opposite. For example, a subsidiary corporation of Bethlehem Steel Corporation, the largest independent purchaser of Venezuelan ore from Orinoco, did not purchase transportation services from Navios. Presumably, Bethlehem found that it could do the job for less.

With respect to the charter market for ore carrying vessels, it is clear from the record that during the years involved in this proceeding there were no published charter rates for ore carriers of any significance. Individual rates selected both by petitioner and respondent depended upon particular conditions at that time, and did not constitute a measure of what might be a reasonable charge for a continuing relationship involving the transportation of more than 10 million tons of iron ore per year. The comparability tests in the regulations cannot be relied on because the transportation of iron ore on the basis proposed by the petitioner and Navios had never been done previously. There could be no "independent transactions with unrelated parties under the same or similar circumstances" within the meaning of section 1.482–1(d)(3) of the regulations.

The petitioner cites other factors in support of the reasonableness of the rates charged by Navios, such as the risks faced by Navios, the comparable earnings of Navios with selected transportation companies, and the comparable profits of Navios and Orinoco in relationship to their respective costs of operation. The question is whether, assuming all of these considerations, the transportation charges were "arm's length." After all of these risks are factored in, there remains the question whether petitioner would have been willing to contract for such rates, on the same assumptions, with an independent transportation company. Conversely, whether an independent transportation company would have been willing to supply the transportation services for less.

Finally, the petitioner contends that there is no occasion for the reallocation of the transportation charges between Navios and petitioner because the price charged by Orinoco for the ore F.O.B. Puerto Ordaz and the transportation charges by Navios to the port of destination, when taken together, resulted in a delivered price for the Venezuelan ore which was comparable to the price of domestic ore paid and charged by the petitioner on the Great Lakes. Hence, petitioner argues that its income was not distorted, and that no taxes were evaded, regardless of the reasonableness of the shipping charges. If petitioner's position is sound, it would be immaterial what price was charged by Navios to transport the ore from Venezuela to U.S. ports. Accordingly, the Court will direct itself to this argument before considering the reasonableness of the transportation charges.

With respect to this issue the question resolves itself into whether an allocation of the shipping charges is necessary in order to prevent the evasion of taxes or clearly to reflect the income of petitioner within the meaning of section 482. Petitioner contends, and the respondent does not seriously question, that the delivered cost of the Venezuelan ore to petitioner's mills in the United States was comparable to the cost of domestic ore. It would follow that petitioner's cost of producing steel was the same regardless of the source of the ore. In fact, it might even be assumed that if Orinoco had sold the ore on a delivered basis, and supplied the shipping either directly or by contract with Navios, respondent would have been bound by his regulations. For the petitioners to adopt such a course of action would, however, be self-defeating. While there would be no additional liability for income taxes due to the United States, the resulting additional income would have been taxable by the government of Venezuela.

The petitioner would seem to take the position that if there is to be an allocation of the transportation charges, or the income resulting therefrom, such allocation should be between Orinoco and Navios. In other words, if the shipping charges were excessive, such excess is attributable to the inadequacy of the price for the ore F.O.B. Puerto Ordaz and not to the delivered cost of the ore at the U.S. ports. In effect, the petitioner would have this Court reallocate the income as between Orinoco, Navios and petitioner. That approach would ignore the requirement that the charges paid by petitioner for the transportation of the ore must be judged in the light of what might be expected if such transportation had been negotiated separately between petitioner and an unrelated carrier. * * *

* * *

The price of the Venezuelan ore was set at a lower figure F.O.B. Puerto Ordaz, coupled with an equalization factor in the transportation charges, which would be available to outside purchasers without jeopardizing the Lake Erie price. Except for Bethlehem Steel Company, most purchasers would not be in a position to contract independently for transportation of the ore to the site of their mills. As was expected, so long as the delivered price was competitive with the cost of domestic ore, most customers would avail themselves of the transportation services offered by Navios.

On the other hand, with planned shipments of up to 10 million tons per year, petitioner admittedly could have contracted with Universe Tankships, Inc.,—and possibly Hendy International—for the transportation of the ore from Puerto Ordaz to its mills for considerably less than the rates charged by Navios. With the cooperation of the parties, the Court has reconstructed hypothetical rates at which an independent carrier, such as Universe Tankships, would have been willing to provide the transportation services provided by Navios. It is clear that the rates charged by Navios substantially exceeded the rates which would have been charged for the same services in an arm's-length negotiation between the parties and a nonrelated carrier, such as Universe Tankships. Petitioner could have bought the services for less. To fail to do so, thereby enabling Navios to reap the benefit of excessive freight rates, is precisely the type of situation dealt with in section 482. * * *

Having determined that the allocation of the portion of the income or services of Navios to the petitioner is justified under section 482 in order to prevent the distortion of the income of petitioner and its controlled corporation, which results in the evasion or avoidance of U.S. income taxes, the Court is faced with the more difficult problem of arriving at the proper amount to be allocated in each year. For this purpose, the Court has considered various alternative bases.

At the outset, the management of Navios selected a return of 10 percent of costs, and later a return of 20 percent of costs, as a basis for providing a reasonable profit. While the actual return which resulted from the rates charged to unrelated shippers is considerably less than 20 percent, Navios could not charge those shippers any more than it charged petitioner. For this reason, the lesser return is not regarded as having any particular significance. Suffice to say, that both Navios and the petitioner contemplated a return of from 10 to 20 percent on cost as a basis for justifying the freight charges.

There is some dispute between the parties with respect to the appropriate costs to be considered in arriving at a rate of return. In our opinion, the cost of inland freight should not be taken into account. Such charges had no relation to the services provided by Navios. When it suited petitioner's convenience, inland freight was charged directly to the customer.

On the other hand, idle vessel expense is both appropriate and necessary in determining the cost of ocean transportation. Such expense represented the cost applicable to those ships which were taken out of service due to the fact that larger and more efficient vessels became available, as the navigational depths permitted the use of the new ore carriers. It is the savings which resulted from such carriers that gives rise, in part, to the excessive income which is being allocated from Navios to the petitioner.

Finally, any rate of return on cost should not reflect income taxes, either hypothetical or actual, which might apply to the resulting income. The amount of taxes due would depend on varying factors, peculiar to the corporate organization and activities of a particular carrier.

[The judge then applied these principles to the data that was in evidence. The IRS had used an approach that looked to profits and determined that a certain percentage of Navios' profits was in excess of what would fairly reflect income. The judge used two alternative methods of determining what Navios' revenues would have been if a market price had been charged for the services. First, he extrapolated hypothetical rates for 1957–1960 from what Universe and Hendy charged in the 1954 contracts with U.S. Steel, adding adjustments to account for increased costs, risk and profits. As a check on the accuracy of this historical approach, the judge also constructed hypothetical rates based on estimates of what Navios' costs had been in the tax years in question, adjusting these estimates to allow for risk and profit. He then chose the method which, for each tax year, would result in the lowest reallocation in favor of the IRS.]

* * *

Upon the basis of the foregoing, it is the opinion of the Court that in order to properly reflect the income of Navios and the petitioner and to prevent evasion or avoidance of taxes, within the meaning of section 482, there should be allocated to the petitioner as additional income for the taxable years involved the following amounts:

Year	Allocation
1957	$2,300,000
1958	4,500,000
1959	12,200,000
1960	8,000,000
Total	$27,000,000

* * *

[¶ 8070]

NOTES

1. Appellate courts, applying the "clearly erroneous" standard, are generally disinclined to reverse factual determinations at the trial level. In the preceding case, however, the court of appeals reversed on appeal. Its decision was based primarily on comparisons with sales of transportation services by Navios to independent shippers. 617 F.2d 942 (2d Cir.1980). The court noted that the freight paid by U.S. Steel was the same as that "actually charged for the same service in transactions with independent buyers * * *." 617 F.2d at 947. Such services offered to independent shippers were sufficiently comparable to those performed for U.S. Steel to be used as a measure under Section 482 even though U.S. Steel shipped far more tonnage each year than the independents. The court of appeals decision is discussed extensively in *Bausch & Lomb Inc. v. Commissioner*, at ¶ 8105.

2. Although reversed, the Tax Court opinion is an interesting example of analysis under Section 482. It also presents a realistic view of the complex structuring of a major foreign investment. The final plan reflects a mixture of tax and business considerations. Why might the taxpayer wish to set a low price for the ore F.O.B. Puerto Ordaz? Why might it wish to set a high price for its transport by sea?

3. GAC Produce ("GAC") was an Arizona corporation, owned by the Canelos family, which distributed fresh produce from Mexico in the United States. The family owned several other business entities in the United States and Mexico, which the court determined to constitute a controlled group under Section 482. GAC entered into a contract with an unrelated company, Sun Country Produce ("Sun Country"), for a number of years pursuant to which GAC was paid a commission for produce which it distributed for Sun Country and Sun Country agreed to provide certain marketing services in the United States to GAC and Mexican members of the controlled group. While the control group as a whole profited from the arrangement, commissions paid to GAC under the contract did not even cover its fixed costs. The court determined that the commission paid by Sun Country to GAC failed the arm's length standard and that GAC had been willing to accept losses on the contract because of benefits to Mexican members in the controlled group. The court used agreements between GAC and unrelated Mexican growers as the

basis for a Section 482 allocation. GAC Produce Co. v. Commissioner, 77 T.C.M. (CCH) 1890 (1999).

4. The IRS sometimes argues that entities used to avoid tax are shams that should be wholly disregarded for tax purposes. Such an argument was advanced in Hospital Corp. of America v. Commissioner, 81 T.C. 520 (1983) (nonacq.). The taxpayer ("HCA") was a U.S. corporation engaged in hospital management. It operated hospitals through a series of U.S. and foreign subsidiaries. When approached by the Kingdom of Saudi Arabia to manage the King Faisal Specialist Hospitals in Riyadh, HCA organized a subsidiary in the Cayman Islands, which in turn negotiated and performed the contract. HCA performed services for and provided technology to the Cayman corporation. The IRS argued that the Cayman corporation should be disregarded and that all income earned under the contract should be taxed directly to HCA. Alternatively, the IRS urged that an adjustment under Section 482 should be made of 100 percent of the revenues earned under the contract. The court rejected both positions, but approved a lesser Section 482 adjustment based on the applicable arm's length standards both for the provision of services and technology.

5. In United Parcel Service of America, Inc. ("UPS") v. Commissioner, 254 F.3d 1014 (11th Cir. 2001), the court considered an arrangement intended to shift certain income to a subsidiary established in Bermuda. The arrangement involved income generated by "excess-value charges" imposed by UPS and paid by customers who sent parcels with a declared value in excess of $100. Shares of the Bermuda subsidiary ("OPL") were distributed as a taxable dividend to UPS shareholders. UPS then purchased an insurance policy for the benefit of its customers from an independent insurance company ("National Union"), which effectively assumed the risk of damage or loss for excess-value shipments. National Union in turn concluded a reinsurance contract with OPL under which OPL assumed the risk of loss. National Union paid premiums to OPL equal to the payments it had received from UPS less commissions, fees and excise taxes.

The Tax Court accepted the corporate separateness of OPL. However, the court noted that a taxpayer cannot simply assign income to another entity to avoid tax and concluded that the somewhat complex arrangements intended to reduce U.S. income taxes by paying insurance premiums through an intermediary to its Bermuda subsidiary were "sham transactions lacking in economic substance." As a result, the court held that UPS could not deduct the payments that it had made.

On appeal, UPS attacked the Tax Court's economic-substance analysis. Its principal argument was that the plan had economic substance, and thus was not a "sham," because it involved genuine exchanges of reciprocal obligations among real, independent entities. The court of appeals noted that the "economic effects" required to entitle a transaction to respect included the creation of genuine obligations enforceable by an unrelated party and that such obligations were present in this case. The court further noted that the "business purpose" test applied by the Tax Court was too restrictive, and that it was not necessary to show that tax considerations were not a part of the rationale for the transactions under scrutiny. Finding that the arrangements in question had real economic effects and business purpose, the court of appeals reversed. However, the case was remanded to the Tax Court to consider specific challenges under Section 482 that were not reached initially because of the Tax Court's determination that the transaction was a sham.

[¶ 8075]

b. Alternative Methods

The general principles applied under Section 482 obtain in determining an acceptable pricing arrangement for the provision of services to a related entity. The regulations set forth a list of potentially acceptable methods for determining the appropriate arm's length price for the provisions of services. The method must be applied in accordance with the best method rule of Reg. § 1.482–1(c), the comparability analysis of Reg. § 1.482–1(d) and the arm's length range of § 1.482–1(e). The permissible methods are:

1. The Services Cost Method (the eligibility for which is limited, as discussed at ¶ 8077).
2. The Comparable Uncontrolled Services Price Method. ("CUSP").
3. The Gross Services Margin Method
4. The Cost of Services Plus Method.
5. The Comparable Profit Method ("CPM").
6. The Profit Split Method.
7. Unspecified Methods (that may be acceptable to the IRS).

Reg. § 1.482–9(a). These methods are analogous to those developed and authorized for use in connection with the sale of property, which are discussed in more detail at ¶ 8115. The regulations provide extensive examples of the way in which each of the methods is intended to be applied.

[¶ 8077]

c. Limited Safe Haven: Services Cost Method

The task of applying the basic principles of Section 482 to the provision of services has proved to be particularly challenging. Under prior regulations, a kind of safe haven was provided when the service was not considered to be an integral part of the business of either the renderer or the recipient. As a result, when the payment for services was equal to the direct and indirect costs of performing the services, it would generally not be challenged. Reg. § 1.482–9(b)(3). It was not necessary to include a profit calculation in such situations.

The parameters of the safe haven have been modified by the establishment of the Services Cost Method ("SCM") in the current regulations. Reg. § 1.482–9(b). Under the SCM, the arm's length standard will considered satisfied when the relevant price is at least equal to the total cost of providing the services. However, the regulations limit the circumstances when the SCM may apply.

To be eligible for treatment under the SCM, the services must be a controlled service transaction or a group of such transactions and must either be a specifically covered service or a low-margin covered service. Reg. § 1.482–9(b)(3). A list of specifically covered services is set forth in Rev. Proc. 2007–13, 2007–1 C.B. 295. Low-margin covered services are transactions in which the median comparable markup is not more than seven percent. Reg. § 1.482–9(b)(3)(i), (ii).

Certain service transactions will never be eligible for treatment under the SCM. They include the following activities:

1. Manufacturing.
2. Production.
3. Extraction, exploration, or processing of natural resources.
4. Construction.
5. Reselling, distribution, acting as a sales or purchasing agent, or acting under a commission or other similar arrangement.
6. Research, development, or experimentation.
7. Engineering or scientific.
8. Financial transactions, including guarantees.
9. Insurance or reinsurance.

Reg. § 1.482–9(b)(4). The SCM will also not be available for services that the taxpayer reasonably concludes contributes significantly to key competitive advantages, core capabilities, or fundamental risks of success of failure of the trades or business of the controlled group. Reg. § 1.482–9(b)(5).

[¶ 8080]

d. Provision of Management Services or Supervision of Investment?

Section 482 clearly applies to the provision of services to a related party, but investors can be expected to take steps to supervise their investments. In Young & Rubicam v. United States, 410 F.2d 1233 (Ct.Cl. 1969), employees of a U.S. corporate shareholder undertook certain tasks in respect of foreign subsidiaries. The IRS argued that Section 482 required the subsidiaries to compensate their parent for all such efforts. The taxpayer argued that the exercise of supervisory responsibility by a shareholder of the corporation which it owns should not be the subject of an allocation under Section 482. The court, noting that there was no evidence that the parent corporation's employees "performed specific managerial services for specific subsidiaries," concluded that the IRS allocation "was improper." 410 F.2d at 1247.

There has been concern that the result in the *Young & Rubicam* case could lead to the relatively facile avoidance of the principles of Section 482. Regulations have been promulgated to deal with so-called "stewardship expenses." Such expenses are defined to be those incurred by a corporation resulting from activities the sole effect of which is either to protect the corporation's capital investment in the related corporation or to facilitate compliance by the shareholder-corporation with reporting, legal or regulatory requirements relevant to the investment. Regular management activities would not usually qualify for such treatment. Reg. § 1.861–9(*l*)(3)(iv).

5. SALE OF TANGIBLE PERSONAL PROPERTY

[¶ 8085]

a. The Previous Regulations

The previous regulations prescribed the following techniques for applying arm's length standards in respect of sales of tangible property:

i. Comparable Uncontrolled Price Method.

ii. Resale Price Method.

iii. Cost Plus Method.

iv. Other "Appropriate" Method.

The alternative methods were prescribed in order of preference. If the most preferred method could not be applied, the next was invoked. These approaches are still countenanced by the current regulations. However, under the "best method rule" they are no longer presented in order of preference; the method providing the most reliable arm's length price must be used. The meaning of the various approaches under the current regulations is discussed at ¶ 8115.

Although the Ruling and case that follow are based upon the prior regulations, they provide good examples of the conceptual and practical problems raised in the implementation of the relatively simple idea of an arm's length standard.

[¶ 8090]

b. Aspects of Comparability

Finding comparable transactions may be a complicated task. As the regulations suggest, an appropriate standard will consider many possible factors: a comparison of product specifications, transaction terms and (as the following Ruling indicates) markets themselves.

[¶ 8095]

REVENUE RULING 87–71

1987–2 C.B. 148.

* * *

S, a wholly owned foreign mining subsidiary of domestic corporation *P*, operates an iron ore mine in a foreign country. The ore is extracted from the ground and loaded at the mine for shipment by rail to a seaport. The ore is a direct shipping grade ore suitable for blast furnace feed and needs no concentration. After nonmining transportation, the ore is unloaded from rail cars at the seaport and loaded on seagoing vessels for shipment to purchasers.

All of the ore is sold at the port to various purchasers, including *P* and unrelated purchasers in geographic market *A* and unrelated persons in geographic market *B*. The ore is processed in the geographic market of each purchaser. All sales prices include the cost of transportation to the purchasers in both geographic markets. The cost of transportation to the purchasers in both geographic markets is the same. Due to economic conditions existing in each marketplace, *S* is able to sell its ore to unrelated purchasers in geographic market *B* at a price which is substantially higher than the price at which the ore is sold to unrelated purchasers located in market *A*. The economic conditions have a definite but not reasonably ascertainable effect on the price of ore in each market.

The price charged by *S* for the sale of ore to *P* is substantially higher than the price charged for the sale of ore to unrelated purchasers located in geographic market *A*.

LAW AND ANALYSIS

Section 1.482–2(e)(1) of the * * * [former] Regulations provides that, where one member of a group of controlled entities sells or otherwise disposes of tangible property to another member of such group at other than an arm's length price, the district director may make appropriate allocations to reflect an arm's length price for such sale or disposition. An arm's length price is the price that an unrelated party would have paid for the property under the same circumstances. Section 1.482–2(e)(1)(v) of the [former] regulations provides that the selling price, for purposes of section 482 * * *, of mineral products (other than oil and gas) sold to related parties at the stage at which mining ends will be determined under the provisions of section 1.613–4. Section 1.613–4 provides rules for the determination of gross income from minerals (other than oil and gas) at the stage at which mining ends.

Under the facts of this case, the direct shipping grade ore was extracted and shipped by rail to the seaport. The only processes applied at the mine were extraction and loading for shipment to the port. Therefore, mining ended when the ore was loaded for shipment to the port. This was followed by nonmining transportation to the port prior to sale. Since a nonmining process involving transportation occurred before the sale in the case of both related and unrelated party sales, the special rule in section 1.482–2(e)(1)(v) of the [former] regulations does not apply.

The determination of an arm's length selling price under section 1.482–2(e)(2) of the [former] regulations is primarily factual. [Former] [s]ection 1.482–2(e)(2)(ii) provides that uncontrolled sales are considered comparable to controlled sales if the circumstances involved in the uncontrolled sales are so nearly identical to the controlled sales that any differences can be reflected by a reasonable number of adjustments to the price of the uncontrolled sales. Differences can be reflected by adjusting prices only where such differences have a definite and reasonably ascertainable effect on price. One difference which may affect the price of property is a difference in the geographic market in which the sale takes place.

In this case, the economic conditions present in geographic market *B* have a definite effect on the price of ore sold in that marketplace. However, the amount of the adjustment in price to reflect the difference in economic conditions cannot be reasonably ascertained. Thus, the price of ore sold to unrelated purchasers in geographic market *B* cannot be adjusted to account for differences in economic conditions in the two geographic markets and, therefore, cannot be considered to be comparable to the arm's length price charged for ore in geographic market A.

In *Paccar, Inc. and Subsidiaries v. Commissioner*, 85 T.C. 754 (1985), [the] Tax Court held that the comparable uncontrolled price method was not applicable due, in part, to the fact that the controlled sales and uncontrolled sales were made into different geographic markets and the adjustments needed to account for the differences in the geographic markets had not been established.

The uncontrolled sales by *S* to purchasers in geographic market A, in which *P* is located, are comparable to the sales *S* made to *P*. The price *S* charged *P* for ore is substantially higher than the price charged to unrelated purchasers located in the same market. Accordingly, the price *S* charged *P* for ore is not an arm's length price.

HOLDING

The provisions of section 1.482–2(e)(2) of the [former] regulations are applicable under the circumstances described, and only the uncontrolled sales made to the purchasers located in geographic market A are considered in establishing arm's length selling price for purposes of section 482 * * *.

* * *

[¶ 8100]

c. A Judicial View of Comparability

Transfer pricing cases are particularly dependent upon specific economic and financial facts. Judicial decisions are often long and necessarily complex. Because each derives from peculiar facts, they tend to be of modest precedential value. Despite these realities and the fact that future cases will increasingly apply the current regulations, it is instructive to follow the judicial reasoning in a complex case. The following case was well known and widely watched by the international tax community. Consider what evidence would have to be mustered by the taxpayer and the IRS to support their respective contentions about the appropriate price for a very profitable then new product.

The following case required the application of the former regulations in a fairly common situation. The taxpayer moves its production to another country where there are lower production costs and where the government provides substantial tax incentives. The foreign production subsidiary then sells a portion of its product to a U.S. affiliate for marketing in the United States. The portion of the case that follows involves the application of Section 482 to the price paid for the product by the U.S. marketing affiliate to the foreign production subsidiary. Another part of the decision addressed the pricing of the use of intangibles. The financial and tax objectives of the plan are fairly obvious. The judicial analysis of many complex facts and factors suggests that the application of the standards of comparability is not.

[¶ 8105]

BAUSCH & LOMB INC. v. COMMISSIONER

United States Tax Court, 1989.
92 T.C. 525, aff'd, 933 F.2d 1084 (2d Cir.1991).

[Bausch & Lomb Inc. ("B & L") is a U.S. corporation engaged in the business of manufacturing and selling scientific and ophthalmic instruments and products. B & L, which held nonexclusive rights in Europe and the United States to manufacture soft contact lenses, formed Bausch & Lomb Ireland, Ltd. ("B & L Ireland"), a wholly owned Irish subsidiary, to manufacture and sell soft contact lenses. B & L Ireland was entitled to special Irish tax incentives and subsidized financing. B & L transferred to B & L Ireland two nonexclusive licenses, terminable by either party on giving prescribed notice, to use patented and unpatented technology associated with the spin cast method of manufacturing soft contact lenses. B & L was one of several licensees of the patent on the lens, but apparently there were no patent rights in Ireland on the lenses or the manufacturing processes. Through use of the spin cast method, which B & L had developed, B & L was able by 1981 to produce soft contact lenses for approximately $1.50 per lens, while alternative production methods used by its competitors resulted in costs of at least $3.00 per lens.

Starting production using the B & L technology in 1981, B & L Ireland sold all of its output in 1981 and 1982 (although it was not required to do so) to B & L or to B & L foreign affiliates at a price of $7.50 per lens. The buyer paid freight, insurance and custom duties, which totaled about $.62 per lens. B & L Ireland also paid to B & L a royalty of five percent of its net sales of lenses for the right to use the spin cast manufacturing process.

The IRS proposed adjustments under Section 482 both with respect to the prices charged by B & L Ireland to B & L for the lenses and the royalties paid by B & L Ireland to B & L for use of the technology. This segment of a very thorough (and very long) analysis deals with the price of the lenses. The royalty analysis is omitted.]

KÖRNER, JUDGE: * * *.

* * *

We have found as fact that petitioners had sound business reasons for the establishment of B & L Ireland. Petitioners had reason to believe that manufacturing capacity at its Rochester Facility was inadequate to meet expected increases in soft contact lens demand. Petitioner determined that it was prudent to establish additional manufacturing capacity overseas in order to minimize regulatory delays, establish an alternative supply source to the Rochester Facility, and to have a facility capable of more efficiently servicing the increasingly important European markets. Ireland was determined to be the location at which these objectives could be realized most cost effectively due to the incentives offered by the Republic of Ireland to induce the location of manufacturing facilities within the Republic. Since a non-Irish company could not receive section 84 [a reference to Irish law] financing, there were sound business reasons for incorporating an Irish manufacturing facility rather than merely operating the facility as a division of B & L. Although it is possible that B & L could have established the Irish facility in a manner which resulted in a greater United States tax, it is axiomatic that a taxpayer is not obligated to arrange his affairs in a manner which maximizes his tax burden. * * * Thus respondent's determination must stand or fall based on the "clear reflection of income" prong of section 482.

As a preliminary matter, we must first address respondent's contention that it is inappropriate to analyze the transfer price and royalty rate used by B & L separately, on the theory that B & L and B & L Ireland would have constructed their relationship in a different manner had they been conducting their affairs at arm's length. Respondent argues that B & L would never have agreed to license its spin cast technology which allowed it to produce soft contact lenses for approximately $1.50 per lens and then purchase lenses from the licensee for $7.50 per lens. Respondent argues that B & L would have been unwilling to pay an independent third party much more than its costs would have been had it chosen to produce the contact lenses itself. He is indifferent as to whether the royalty is increased or the transfer price is decreased as long as the result is that B & L Ireland receives only its costs of production and a reasonable mark up. In essence, respondent argues that B & L Ireland was little more than a contract manufacturer the sale of whose total production was assured and who thus was not entitled to the return normally associated with an enterprise which bears the risk as to the volume of its product it will be able to sell and at what price.

Respondent's argument would have some merit had we found that B & L was required to purchase B & L Ireland's production of soft contact lenses. In such a case, B & L Ireland would indeed have been a contract manufacturer in substance despite the fact that ostensibly the license agreement and product purchases were not interdependent. However, we have found as fact that no such purchase requirement existed. All of the documents generated by B & L in evaluating the feasibility of the Irish lens facility indicate that it was intended to serve the foreign markets with limited possible importation of Irish lenses into the United States in the event of production problems at the Rochester Facility. That B & L would import substantial quantities of Irish lenses into the United States should worldwide demand not meet expectations was not guaranteed. Nor did B & L Ireland have a guarantee that the transfer price it received for its lenses would remain at $7.50 per lens. In actuality, the transfer price was reduced to $6.50 in 1983 due to market pressures. The most that can be said is that B & L Ireland had certain expectations as to the volume and price of lenses it could anticipate selling to B & L or its affiliates. However, such expectations are no different than those which any supplier has with regard to the business of a major customer and do not constitute a guarantee which effectively insulated B & L Ireland from market risks. In a case where the license of intangibles and sale of the product manufactured to the licensor were interdependent, then the separate royalty rate and transfer price would be unimportant as long as the net result is satisfactory. The same cannot be said in this instance where both the volume and price of sales to the licensor are subject to variation. The transfer price and the royalty rate each has independent significance and will thus be examined separately.

* * *

Petitioners contend that they have presented ample evidence of comparable, uncontrolled sales of soft contact lenses which establish that the $7.50 per lens price charged by B & L Ireland to B & L was at or below the price which would have been charged by uncontrolled manufacturers to distributors for similar lenses. Specifically, petitioners point to sales to distributors by Lombart, American Hydron, American Optical, and Hydrocurve of soft contact lenses during 1980 through 1982. No sale cited by petitioner took place for a price less than the $7.50 charged by B & L Ireland. Alternatively, petitioners argue that application of the resale-price method to the facts of this case lends further support to the arm's-length nature of the $7.50 transfer price.

Respondent contends that neither the comparable-uncontrolled price or resale-price methods are applicable herein. He argues that the sales by manufacturers to distributors cited by petitioners on the one hand, and the sales by B & L Ireland to B & L on the other, are not sufficiently similar to function as comparables. He also urges that dissimilarities between B & L and the distributors cited by petitioners render inappropriate reference to the markup percentages of these distributors in application of the resale-price method.

Specifically, respondent urges that the disparities in the volumes of lenses sold by B & L Ireland to B & L and those purchased by independent distributors from manufacturers indicate that these distributors and B & L operated at different levels of the market. He hypothesizes that any distributor who purchased lenses in the quantities purchased by B & L from B & L Ireland would have demanded and received significant volume discounts in purchase price.

The second distinction respondent finds significant is that whereas B & L was an integrated manufacturer and distributor of soft contact lenses with a worldwide sales and marketing force and a substantial research and development function, the distributors cited by petitioners performed only distribution functions. Respondent hypothesizes that at arm's length B & L would not be willing to pay as much for soft contact lenses as other distributors since, unlike non-integrated distributors, it needed the profit from soft contact lens sales to support these additional functions.

Finally, respondent urges that it is inconceivable that at arm's length B & L, which possessed the technology and present ability to manufacture contact lenses at a cost far below that achievable by any of its competitors, would go into the open market and pay $7.50 per lens for a product it could produce itself for approximately $1.50 even though other distributors without this capability would consider the $7.50 a market price.

Although he never explicitly says so, respondent contends that the cost-plus method is the only proper method for determination of the price B & L would have paid for B & L Ireland soft contact lenses at arm's length. Based on the testimony of his economic expert, Dr. David Bradford, respondent determined that an arm's-length price would be "in the neighborhood" of $2.25 to $3.00 per lens. Dr. Bradford based his conclusion on his finding that B & L produced 7.1 million lenses in 1981 at a cost of $1.50 per lens. He studied the gross profit margins of several soft contact lens manufacturers, most notably NPDC, Danlex Corporation, and the Amsco/Lombart division of the American Sterilization Company and found that these companies employed gross markups ranging from 22 to 141 percent. Applying this gross markup to B & L's production costs, Dr.

Bradford determined that an arm's-length price would be $1.82 to $3.62. He further posited that the quantities purchased by B & L and the fact that the hypothetical manufacturer would not have to support sales or research and development functions dictated a figure at the lower end of this range. He thus determined a 50–100 percent markup was most likely, resulting in a lens price of between $2.25 and $3.00.

We have found as fact that B & L functioned as a distributor with respect to lenses it purchased from B & L Ireland. We fail to see the significance of the fact that B & L engaged in other functions in addition to distribution with respect to soft contact lenses. We have also found that daily wear soft contact lenses of any manufacturer are generally considered a fungible commodity. Therefore, the third party purchase agreements identified by petitioner qualify as comparable uncontrolled sales for purposes of application of the comparable uncontrolled price method. However, these sales differ from those of B & L Ireland to B & L in that the buyers, unlike B & L, were not required to pay an additional $0.62 of duty and freight charges on their purchases. We therefore must reduce the sales prices identified by petitioner by $0.62 in order to make those transactions comparable to the sales at issue.

After giving effect to the above adjustment, we find that use of the comparable-uncontrolled-price method of determining an arm's-length price is mandatory. The third-party transactions identified by petitioner provide ample evidence that the $7.50 per-lens price charged by B & L Ireland is equal or below prices which would be charged for similar lenses in uncontrolled transactions.

Only the Lombart agreements which contain separate prices for standard and thin lenses suggest a market price below the $7.50 plus freight and duty charged by B & L Ireland. However, we place more weight on the Lombart agreements which, similar to B & L Ireland pricing, charge a single price for either standard or thin lenses. The $8.50 charged by Lombart, less the $0.62 adjustment described above exceeds the $7.50 charged by B & L.[16]

We place particular reliance on the Second Circuit's opinion in *United States Steel Corp. v. Commissioner*, 617 F.2d 942 (2d Cir.1980), revg. T.C. Memo. 1977–140. We are constrained to follow Second Circuit precedent since that circuit is where an appeal of this decision would lie. * * *

U.S. Steel Corp. involved the prices charged the taxpayer by its wholly owned subsidiary, Navios, for transporting iron ore from Venezuela to the United States. Although United States Steel was by far Navios' largest

16. Even the Lombart agreements, which charge $7.50 for standard lenses and $8.45 for thin lenses, do not support finding that a uniform price of $7.50 is other than a market price. The average of these two prices is $7.98. When reduced by the $0.62 adjustment described above this equals $7.36. Although this amount is lower than the $7.50 charged by B & L Ireland, the variance is so small (less than 2 percent) as to be insignificant and cannot support a finding that B & L Ireland's price was excessive, especially when examined in light of the other agreements identified by petitioner.

customer, Navios also transported significant amounts of ore from Venezuela to the United States for unrelated parties at the same price it charged United States Steel. This Court refused to accept these uncontrolled sales as comparables for purposes of applying the comparable-uncontrolled-price method because the unrelated parties with whom Navios did business, unlike U.S. Steel, did not have a continuing relationship with Navios for the transportation of over 10 million tons of ore per year. *U.S. Steel Corp. v. Commissioner*, T.C. Memo. 1977–140, revd. 617 F.2d 942 (2d Cir.1980). In other words, at arm's length Navios would have charged a lower price to U.S. Steel than to other customers in order to retain U.S. Steel as a high volume, long-term customer. The second circuit reversed on the ground that Navios' transactions with uncontrolled parties were sufficiently comparable to permit application of the comparable-uncontrolled-price method stating:

> We think it is clear that if a taxpayer can show that the price he paid or was charged for a service is "the amount which was charged or would have been charged for the same or similar services in independent transactions with or between unrelated parties" it has earned the right, under the Regulations, to be free from section 482 reallocation despite other evidence tending to show that its activities have resulted in a shifting of tax liability among controlled corporations. Where, as in this case, the taxpayer offers evidence that the same amount was actually charged for the same service in transactions with independent buyers, the question resolves itself into an evaluation of whether or not the circumstances of the sales to independent buyers are "similar" enough to sales to the controlling corporation under the circumstances "considering all relevant facts." * * * U.S. Steel Corp. v. Commissioner, 617 F.2d at 947.

The Second Circuit rejected this Court's position that the standard against which the rate paid by United States Steel should be measured is what a reasonable charge would be for a continuing relationship involving the transportation of more than 10 million tons of iron ore per year stating:

> To say that [the independent importer] was buying a service from Navios with one set of expectations about duration and risk, and Steel another, may be to recognize economic reality; but it is also to engraft a crippling degree of economic sophistication onto a broadly drawn statute which—if "comparable" is taken to mean "identical," as Judge Quealy would read it—would allow the taxpayer no safe harbor from the Commissioner's virtually unrestricted discretion to allocate. U.S. Steel Corp. v. Commissioner, 617 F.2d at 951.

We find that the purchases of contact lenses by B & L from B & L Ireland present an analogous situation. To posit that B & L, the world's largest marketer of soft contact lenses, would be able to secure a more favorable price from an independent manufacturer who hoped to establish a long-term relationship with a high volume customer may be to recognize economic reality, but to do so would cripple a taxpayer's ability to rely on the comparable-uncontrolled-price method in establishing transfer pricing by introducing to it a degree of economic sophistication which appears reasonable in theory, but which defies quantification in practice.

Although *U.S. Steel* dealt with the performance of services, we see no reason why its rationale should not also apply to other aspects of section 482, including the sale of tangible property. Nor do we find significant the fact that the comparables in *U.S. Steel* were transactions by the taxpayer with unrelated purchasers, whereas the comparables here do not involve petitioner. The regulations identify both situations as potentially giving rise to comparable uncontrolled prices. See sec. 1.482–2(e)(2)(ii), Income Tax Regs.

Respondent's argument that the disparities in the volumes of lenses purchased by B & L from B & L Ireland on the one hand and the purchases petitioner claims are comparable on the other, render the two incomparable is unpersuasive. Although many of the manufacturers cited by petitioners offered volume discounts to large volume purchasers, there is no evidence of any manufacturer's offering discounts for annual purchases in excess of 75,000 units. It is unrealistic to presume, as does respondent, that comparable discounts would be given for purchases above this level. Manufacturers presumably give volume discounts since high volumes allow them to spread their fixed manufacturing costs over more units and thus allow them to attain lower unit costs of production. At some point, however, the economies of scale achievable through increased production will begin to diminish and a manufacturer's unit production costs will approach an irreducible minimum.

The market price for any product will be equal to the price at which the least efficient producer whose production is necessary to satisfy demand is willing to sell. During 1981 and 1982, the lathing methods were still the predominant production technologies employed in the soft contact lens industry. American Hydron, an affiliate of NPDC and a strong competitor in the contact lens market, was able to produce 466,348 and 762,379 soft contact lenses using the lathing method in 1981 and 1982, for $6.18 and $6.46 per unit, respectively. It is questionable whether any of B & L Ireland's competitors, save B & L, could profitably have sold soft contact lenses during the period in issue for less than the $7.50 charged by B & L Ireland. The fact that B & L Ireland could, through its possession of superior production technology, undercut the market and sell at a lower price is irrelevant. Petitioners have shown that the $7.50 they paid for lenses was a "market price" and have thus "earned the right to be free from a section 482 reallocation." *U.S. Steel Corp. v. Commissioner*, supra at 947.

Finally, respondent argues that B & L *could have* produced the contact lenses purchased from B & L Ireland itself at lesser cost. However,

B & L *did not* produce the lenses itself. The mere power to determine who in a controlled group will earn income cannot justify a section 482 allocation of the income from the entity who actually earned the income. * * * B & L Ireland was the entity which actually produced the contact lenses. Respondent is limited to determining how the sales to B & L by B & L Ireland would have been priced had the parties been unrelated and negotiating at arm's length. We have determined that the $7.50 charged was a market price. We thus conclude that respondent abused his discretion and acted arbitrarily and unreasonably in reallocating income between B & L and B & L Ireland based on use of a transfer price for contact lenses other than the $7.50 per lens actually used. When conditions for use of the comparable-uncontrolled-price method are present, use of that method to determine an arm's-length price is mandated. Sec. 1.482–2(e)(1)(ii), Income Tax Regs. Therefore, we need not consider petitioner's alternative position—that application of the resale-price method supports the arm's-length nature of the $7.50 transfer price. We note, however, that application of such method lends further support to the arm's-length nature of B & L Ireland's $7.50 sales price. Uncontrolled purchases and resales by American Optical, Southern, Bailey–Smith, and Mid–South indicate gross profit percentages of between 22 and 40 percent were common among soft contact lens distributors. This is confirmed by the testimony of Thomas Sloan, president of Southern, who testified that he tried to purchase lenses from manufacturers at prices which allowed Southern to maintain a reasonable profit margin of between 25 and 40 percent. Applying a 40–percent gross margin to B & L's average realized price of $16.74 and $15.25 for domestic sales in 1981 and 1982, respectively, indicates a lens cost of $10.04 and $9.15, respectively—well above the $7.50 received by B & L Ireland for its lenses and also above the $8.12 cost to B & L when freight and duty are added.

* * *

[¶ 8110]

NOTE

The argument that arrangements are mere shams (see ¶ 8070, Notes 4 and 5) can arise in connection with sales of property. In U.S. Gypsum Co. v. United States, 452 F.2d 445 (7th Cir.1971), the taxpayer's group of companies included an export corporation that owned gypsum rock as it fell from a dockside conveyer belt until it landed in the hold of a ship. In affirming a decision reallocating income from the export corporation to the U.S. parent, the court noted the familiar observation that taxpayers may arrange their affairs to gain tax advantages. It observed further, however, that "[t]he fact that a taxpayer may properly arrange its affairs to minimize taxation does not give it license to create purposeless entities or to engage in transactions with subsidiaries which independent parties would not dream of concluding." 452

F.2d at 451. For those who prefer illustrated versions of tax-avoidance endeavors, the decision of the district court, 304 F.Supp. 627, 639 (N.D.Ill. 1969), includes the following depiction:

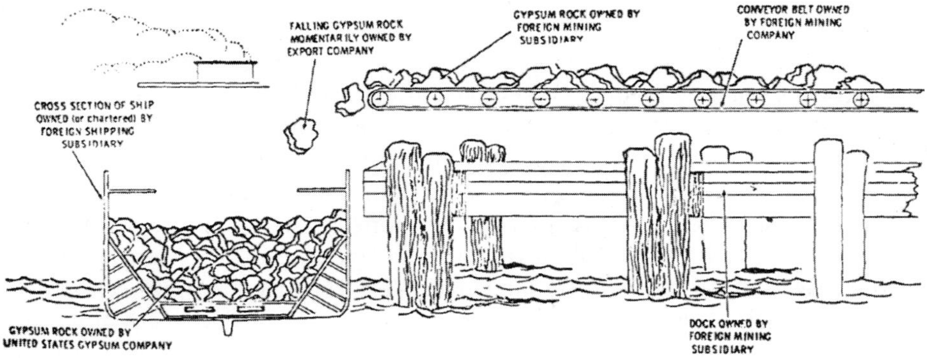

[¶ 8115]

d. The Current Regulations

The current regulations describe five methods for judging the acceptability of a transfer price for the sale of tangible personal property, along with a sixth category called "unspecified methods." They include the three methods authorized by prior regulations: the comparable uncontrolled price, resale price and cost plus methods, augmented by the comparable profits and the profit split methods. Consistent with the "best method rule," they do not prescribe an order of preference among the alternative methods. Reg. § 1.482–3(a).

The regulations are fairly explicit. In each instance, the regulations provide that adjustments must be made to reflect differences between the controlled transactions and the uncontrolled transactions to which comparison is being made. In many instances, the regulations enumerate such differences and provide examples of the way in which possible adjustments should be analyzed.

The first enumerated method is characterized as the "comparable uncontrolled price method" ("CUP method"). Reg. § 1.482–3(a)(1). The basic approach is to examine comparable sales where the parties are unrelated. These may include sales by a member of the controlled group to an unrelated party, sales by an unrelated party to a member of the controlled group and sales made in which neither party is a member of the controlled group. Reg. § 1.482–3(b).

The second is the "resale price method." Reg. § 1.482–3(a)(2). Under this approach the price for the controlled transaction is equal to the resale price to an uncontrolled buyer less an "appropriate gross profit." The appropriate gross profit is determined by multiplying the applicable resale price by the "gross profit margin" (expressed as a percentage of total revenue derived from sales) earned in comparable uncontrolled transactions. Reg. § 1.482–3(c)(2)(iii). The regulations state that a typical situation where the resale price method may be useful is one "involving the purchase and resale of tangible property in which the reseller has not added substantial value to the tangible goods by physically altering the goods" or through use of an intangible. Reg. § 1.482–3(c)(1).

The third is the "cost plus method." Reg. § 1.482–3(a)(3). Under this approach the transfer price is generally equal to the cost of production plus an amount determined by the application of a "gross profit markup" to that cost. The gross profit markup is "expressed as a percentage of cost, earned in comparable uncontrolled transactions." Reg. § 1.482–3(d)(2)(ii). The regulations state that "[t]he cost plus method is ordinarily used in cases involving the manufacture, assembly, or other production of goods that are sold to related parties." Reg. § 1.482–3(d)(1).

The fourth is the "comparable profits method" ("CPM"). Reg. § 1.482–3(a)(4). This method determines an arm's length result based on profit level indicators derived from similarly situated uncontrolled taxpayers. Reg. § 1.482–5(a). The controlled party that has the least complex, readily available and accurate financial data from which to draw a comparison will be the party to whom the test is applied and is called the "tested party." Reg. § 1.482–5(b)(2)(i). Comparability for these purposes is heavily dependent on resources employed and risks assumed, and not necessarily product similarity. Reg. § 1.482–5(c)(2)(ii) and (iii). Adjustments must be made for all material differences between the tested party and the uncontrolled taxpayers serving as the basis for comparison. Reg. § 1.482–5(c)(2)(iv).

Under the CPM, the arm's length price is calculated by applying a profit level indicator (derived from a comparable taxpayer) to the "financial data related to the tested party's most narrowly identifiable business activity" which includes the controlled transaction. Reg. § 1.482–5(b)(1). Acceptable profit level indicators (which measure the ratio of profits to either costs incurred or resources employed) include the rate of return on capital employed and financial ratios. Reg. § 1.482–5(b)(4). Other indicators are not precluded from use if they would provide an accurate estimate of profits. Reg. § 1.482–5(b)(4)(iii). The rate of return on capital employed is the ratio of operating profit to operating assets. Reg. § 1.482–5(b)(4)(i). The acceptable financial ratios include the ratio of operating profit to sales and the ratio of gross profit to operating expenses. Reg. § 1.482–5(b)(4)(ii). The appropriate profit level indicator depends upon which characteristics the tested party and the comparable party share. The safe harbor range is applicable if the same profit level indicator is used for all cases. Reg. § 1.482–5(b)(3).

The fifth is the "profit split method." Reg. § 1.482–3(a)(5). Under this method the operating profit or loss is determined from the most narrowly identifiable business activity of the controlled taxpayer which includes the controlled transaction. Reg. § 1.482–6(a). Such profit or loss is then divided between the controlled parties based upon "the relative value of each controlled taxpayer's contributions" to the success of the activity. The value of each party's contributions is to be based upon "the functions performed, risks assumed, and resources employed * * *." Reg. § 1.482–6(b).

The division can be accomplished in one of two ways: the comparable profit split or the residual profit split. Reg. § 1.482–6(c)(1). Comparability for these purposes is most dependent upon those factors important to the CPM. Reg. §§ 1.482–5(c)(2), –6(c)(2)(ii)(B)(*1*). Adjustments are allowed for minor differences, but the comparable profit split method may not be used if material differences exist between the combined operating profit (expressed as a percentage of combined assets) of the controlled and uncontrolled parties. Reg. § 1.482–6(c)(2)(ii)(B)(*1*).

The residual profit split calls for the application of a two-step process. First, the operating income is allocated to each party by reference to the market rate of return for its routine contributions to the activity. Reg. § 1.482–6(c)(3)(i)(A). Routine contributions are those made by uncontrolled taxpayers involved in similar business activities for which market returns can be identified. They include contributions of tangible property, services and intangibles which similarly situated uncontrolled parties generally own. The market rate of return is determined by reference to uncontrolled parties engaged in similar activities. If any intangibles are involved which will not be accounted for in the first step, the residual profit attributable to them will be allocated according to the relative value of the contributions of the parties. Reg. § 1.482–6(c)(3)(i)(B).

The sixth is the "unspecified method," described in Reg. § 1.482–3(e)(1). The method selected is to be applied in accordance with Reg. § 1.482–1, and should take into account the general principle that all of the "realistic alternatives" should be considered.

[¶ 8120]

e. Statutory Limitation on Imported Inventory

Section 1059A provides that property imported into the United States in a transaction that is, directly or indirectly, between related persons will have a cost or inventory basis not greater than the "customs value" of the property. The customs value is the amount used to determine customs and any other duties imposed on the import of the property. Section 1059A effectively establishes the maximum cost that the related party may use for tax purposes. Note that the taxpayer may use a tax cost that is less than the customs value if it satisfies the requirements of Section 482. Reg. § 1.1059A–1(c)(1).

[¶ 8122]

NOTE

Compaq Computer Corp. ("Compaq U.S.") purchased printed circuit boards ("PCAs") from its Asian subsidiary ("Compaq Asia") for use in Compaq computers. The IRS alleged that Compaq U.S. had paid $232 million in excess of the arm's length price for the PCAs. The IRS used several theories at various stages of the dispute, but finally based its determination on a modified cost plus method emphasizing that Compaq Asia had earned higher net profit margins than comparable companies. Although initially seeking to justify its prices under a cost plus methodology, at trial Compaq U.S. persuaded the court that a CUP method was appropriate and that there was ample evidence showing that the transactions in question were consistent with arm's length standards established by prices paid by Compaq U.S. for PCAs purchased from unrelated suppliers. The court concluded that the taxpayer had satisfied its burden of showing that the IRS allocations were "arbitrary, capricious, or unreasonable." Compaq Computer Corp. v. Commissioner, 78 T.C.M. (CCH) 20 (1999).

[¶ 8125]

PROBLEMS

1. Speakerhouse is a Delaware corporation that manufactures small CD systems. Its current model, the S24, is sold directly to retailers in the United States for $150 per system and carries a suggested retail price of $250. It is, however, commonly discounted to sell at about $200. The total costs (direct and indirect) to Speakerhouse for its manufacture and sale are $120.

Swistereo, incorporated in Switzerland, is a wholly owned subsidiary of Speakerhouse. It handles the distribution of the S24 to wholesalers throughout Europe. The wholesalers are unrelated individuals or corporations. Swistereo also handles the distribution of the RT3000 in Europe. The RT3000 is a small CD system manufactured by Sany, a Japanese corporation completely unrelated to Speakerhouse or Swistereo. The RT3000, which employs more advanced technology, is sold at retail throughout Europe at about $450 (all prices are stated in U.S. dollars for convenience). Swistereo sells them to wholesalers for $300 and pays Sany $225 each for them. Swistereo does no advertising or repackaging for the RT3000 or, indeed, anything other than performing the basic function of selling to wholesalers throughout Europe.

Swistereo performs the same functions for its parent Speakerhouse with regard to the S24, but in addition repackages the CD systems and does some advertising throughout Europe. These two extra services average out to a cost (to Swistereo) of about $10 per system. Swistereo sells the systems to wholesalers for $200 and they retail throughout Europe at between $250 and $300.

Speakerhouse has discovered through sources that it prefers not to disclose that the cost to Sany of producing a small CD system is only $80.

Speakerhouse has also learned that its major American competitor, Soundsgood, plans to market aggressively its small CD system, the S–G–2–4, in Europe where it has never before been sold. The S–G–2–4 has almost identical specifications as the S24. Soundsgood has contracted with RadioGeneva, an unrelated Swiss company, to handle the distribution of the S–G–2–4. But for the fact that Soundsgood and RadioGeneva are unrelated, their business operations, resources employed and risks assumed are remarkably similar to those of Speakerhouse and Swistereo. Speakerhouse does not know the costs of production to Soundsgood, but it has learned that the profit on the sales of S–G–2–4 is to be equally divided between Soundsgood and RadioGeneva. Speakerhouse executives believe that the arrangement was intended to increase marketing efforts in Europe so that Soundsgood can gain a substantial market share rather quickly.

For various reasons, Speakerhouse would like to make the price on the S24 to Swistereo as low as possible while avoiding an IRS adjustment. You are asked for advice. Based on the above statement of facts, give your views on how the price should be set and what it should be. Consider which of the five specifically authorized methods might be applied on the basis of the available data. What facts, if any, would have to be gathered in order to apply any of the methods? How could the taxpayer obtain such information?

2. USM, a U.S. manufacturing corporation, sells electrical gizmos to foreign distribution subsidiaries and to unrelated foreign distributors. The terms of sales are substantially the same except that the price charged to subsidiaries is a delivered price, while the price charged to unrelated distributors is f.o.b. USM's factory. Is the comparable sales method applicable in this case?

3. Would your answer in Problem 2 change if the sole difference was that USM affixes its valuable trademark to electrical gizmos sold to its subsidiaries, but not to unrelated distributors?

4. Would your answer in Problem 2 change if the sole difference was that the subsidiaries resold to European customers while the unrelated distributors sold in Asia?

5. Compco, a U.S. corporation, produces CD–ROM disk drivers in the United States. Compco uses a wholly owned subsidiary, Pacifico, which was organized in Singapore, to distribute products in Asia. Compco charges Pacifico $70 per unit delivered to Pacifico's warehouse in Singapore. The cost of shipment is $2 per unit. Compco also sells the same product to unrelated wholesalers and distributors in other parts of the world. Compco charges such customers $80 per unit under a contract providing sales are f.o.b. Compco's factory in the United States. You are the IRS agent responsible for the case. What method should be applied in determining whether to seek an adjustment under Section 482? What adjustment would you recommend?

6. How would your response to Problem 5 be affected if sales to unrelated distributors were at $60 per unit?

7. How would your response to Problem 5 be affected if Compco affixed its own valuable trademark to the CD–ROMs distributed by Pacifico in Asia, but did not do so with respect to products sold in other parts of the world?

D. EXPLOITATION OF INTANGIBLE PROPERTY

[¶ 8130]

1. INTRODUCTION

As the foregoing materials indicate, the application of arm's length standards to transactions between related taxpayers can invoke a very complex analysis of broad-ranging and sometimes elusive facts. The task is never more difficult than in transactions involving the exploitation of such intangible properties as patents, copyrights, trademarks, confidential manufacturing knowhow and trade secrets. There are several reasons for the high degree of complexity. Almost by definition, the assets involved are not susceptible to facile evaluation because they are peculiar or unique. In fact, their peculiarity or uniqueness often contributes substantially to their value. Further, the legal transfer of intangible property can be achieved relatively simply by the execution of documents of sale or license coupled with the provision of information. The ease of transferring ownership of or rights to use intangible property has led to the development of relatively simple means of effecting tax-avoidance arrangements.

The basic techniques are straightforward and well known. Suppose, for example, that a U.S corporation has developed valuable technology as a result of investment over time in research and development. If that technology can be transferred to a foreign entity organized in a tax haven jurisdiction, the technology under certain licensing and/or sale arrangements can be exploited throughout the world without subjecting the income to U.S. taxes until profits are repatriated into the United States. This was, in essence, the business plan that produced the *Bausch & Lomb* case, at ¶ 8105.

The IRS has devoted substantial resources to these problems. In part because the results in court have been mixed, coping with the problem of transfer pricing where technology or other intangibles are elements of the situation has been the object of particularly vigorous attention.

[¶ 8135]

2. PRIOR REGULATIONS

The regulations have historically reflected the attempt of the IRS to apply arm's length pricing concepts to transactions involving the exploitation of intangibles broadly defined in Section 936(h)(3)(B) and Reg. § 1.482–4(b). Comparability has been the articulated standard, but the application of this deceptively simple idea has been attended by enormous difficulty. Recognizing the particular difficulties of finding comparable transactions, the former regulations listed 12 factors that "to the extent appropriate * * * may be considered in arriving at the amount of the arm's length consideration." If these factors did not provide an acceptable answer, the regulations suggested consideration of "[a]ny other fact or circumstance which unrelated parties would have been likely to consider in determining the amount of an arm's length consideration for the property." Reg. § 1.482–2A(d)(2)(iii)(*m*).

Two of the more popular methods that were developed by the courts under the former regulations were the profit split method and the application of ratios intended to estimate an appropriate return. Under the profit split method, the net profit of the integrated activity involving the exploitation of the intangible asset was allocated to the related parties in accordance with their respective economic contributions. Ratios actually applied by the courts included comparisons of gross income to total operating costs and the rate of return on capital within the applicable industry.

The relatively long list of appropriate factors did not necessarily facilitate the work of judges called upon to resolve disputes between the IRS and taxpayers. One might empathize with the task confronting the trial judge who decided Sunstrand Corp. v. Commissioner, 96 T.C. 226 (1991).

In the *Sunstrand* case, the taxpayer was a U.S. corporation engaged in the manufacture and sale of many products, including the constant speed drive ("CSD"). The CSD was an extremely complex avionic device used to drive an airplane engine's generator at a constant speed regardless of the speed of the engine, thereby assuring constant electric current within the aircraft.

Sundstrand Pacific Ltd. ("SunPac") was a subsidiary of Sundstrand organized and operated in the Republic of Singapore. Pursuant to a license agreement concluded in 1975, Sundstrand gave SunPac the exclusive right to use technology for the manufacture of certain CSD spare parts in Singapore, the nonexclusive right to sell such parts anywhere in the world and other associated rights and powers. Sundstrand also agreed to provide SunPac with data, plans and technical assistance. In return therefor, SunPac agreed to pay Sundstrand a royalty equal to two percent of the net selling price of the spare parts. During the tax years in question, Sundstrand purchased all of SunPac's output at Sundstrand's catalog price less a 15–percent discount pursuant to a distributor agreement concluded in 1976.

The IRS sought to allocate $15.2 million of SunPac's profits to Sundstrand. The court found that the IRS adjustments could not be supported and undertook its own analysis. It held that Sundstrand should have paid a price for parts equal to 20 percent less than catalog prices (rather than the 15–percent less transfer price) and should have received royalties of ten percent (rather than the two percent actually received). The winner may be difficult to determine. The IRS collected approximately 40 percent of the dollars sought. The following segment of the court's very long opinion reflects the difficulty of the task:

> Before we begin, we must say that our attempt to determine an appropriate arm's-length price for the SunPac parts to a large extent has been stymied by the poor state of the record in this case. We found the record to be one more of obfuscation than of enlightenment. The complexity of our task was exacerbated by the contentiousness of the parties. They at times seemed to be antagonists rather than adversaries.
>
> The problems with the record began even in the examination stage when petitioner, for whatever ill-conceived reasons of its own, decided to stop cooperating with respondent's agents, and thereafter refused to furnish any additional information to the revenue agents. Petitioner, therefore, from the beginning hampered respondent's attempts to determine the true taxable income of the related parties. Considering the complex nature of cases such as this, petitioner thereby put respondent at an extreme disadvantage.
>
> After petitioner filed the petition, there followed a long and protracted period during which both sides repeatedly sought our intervention on matters which we believe the parties could have, and should have, resolved between themselves. Some of the difficulties the parties encountered during the discovery phase of the proceeding could have been avoided had respondent focused upon a viable theory of the case early on in the proceedings. (In fact, respondent waited until the briefing stage to propound his new services theory, a time which we have held was much too late * * *.) Petitioner unnecessarily complicated matters by seemingly complying with our informal discovery directions and formal discovery orders strictly on terms of what it wanted to produce and not what respondent sought.
>
> Consequently, we have labored through over 2,000 pages of testimony, hundreds of stipulations and exhibits, and nearly 2,000 proposed findings of fact (most of which were objected to by the adversary) to find the facts, many of which we believe could have been stipulated to before the trial with a little more effort by counsel. We regret to say, but feel we must, that we found the record inundated with an inordinate amount of useless information while other important information is nowhere to be found. It is obvious to us that we were too tolerant with the parties during the pretrial proceedings.
>
> However, we must determine the appropriate arm's-length consideration for the SunPac parts on the record before us. Our task was not easy but we have shouldered the yoke, and the parties now must reap what they have sowed.

96 T.C. at 374–75.

The penalty provisions and documentation requirements discussed at ¶ 8160 were designed in large measure to prevent the type of evidentiary debacle reflected in the *Sunstrand* litigation.

[¶ 8140]

3. THE CURRENT REGULATIONS

The current regulations sought to implement the Section 482 White Paper call for a fuller explanation of the arm's length standards in transactions involving intangibles. The regulations now provide for the use of four possible methods. Reg. § 1.482–4(a). Of course, the "best method rule" applies to their use.

The regulations authorize the use of the CPM and profit split methods, which also apply to sales of tangible property and which are described above at ¶¶ 8115 et seq. The regulations also authorize the "comparable uncontrolled transaction" method ("CUT method") as well as "unspecified methods."

The CUT method is applied when there are transactions involving the same or comparable intangible properties. Differences in contractual terms or economic conditions present when the transactions are effected may require adjustments. Reg. § 1.482–4(c)(1). Both comparables must be used in connection with similar products or processes within the same general industry or market and have a similar profit potential. Profit potential is based on the net present value of the profit "considering the capital investment and start-up expenses required, the risks to be assumed, and other relevant considerations." Reg. § 1.482–4(c)(2)(iii)(B)(*1*)(*ii*). Further, the regulations list particular factors to be considered in connection with the application of Section 482 to transactions involving intangibles. Reg. § 1.482–4(c)(2)(iii)(B)(*2*).

There are also requirements relating to the transfer of an intangible in conjunction with the transfer of tangible property. As long as the "embedded intangible" is not transferred with any right to its exploitation other than in the ordinary course of resale of the product produced with the technology, the transfer will be considered a transfer of tangible property subject to the appropriate rules. Reg. § 1.482–3(f). If the right to exploit the intangible beyond the ordinary course of resale exists, it is appropriate to consider separate prices for the tangible and intangible components involved in the transfer.

The application of the current regulations to transactions involving the exploitation of intangible property rights is discussed in detail in Chapter 12 in the context of other issues arising from the exploitation of intangible property rights abroad. See ¶¶ 12,200 et seq.

[¶ 8145]

4. EXTENDING THE STATUTORY REACH—"SUPER-ROYALTY" PROVISION

Concern with the possibility of avoiding taxes on the exploitation by foreign affiliates of technology developed in the United States resulted in the inclusion of the following amendment to Section 482 as part of the Tax Reform Act of 1986: "In the case of any transfer (or license) of intangible property * * *, the income with respect to such transfer or license shall be commensurate with the income attributable to the intangible." This provision, which has come to be called the "super-royalty" provision, was also added to Section 367(d), which deals with transfers of intangibles to foreign corporations. See ¶ 12,205.

The impact of this formulation may not seem self-evident. However, the current regulations provide substantial amplification of the principles. Reg. § 1.482–7.

In order to implement the super-royalty provision, the royalty or other consideration payable by the transferee of intangible property rights to its commonly controlled owner is subject to periodic review and adjustment by the IRS. The purpose is to ensure that the consideration paid over time remains commensurate with the income produced by the intangible in the hands of the transferee. Any transfer of an intangible for more than one year between commonly controlled persons is subject, in principle, to this periodic review and adjustment in part so that taxpayers cannot defeat transfer price challenges through the establishment of long-term licensing arrangements. This requirement clearly has the potential for creating excessive administrative and compliance burdens on taxpayers and the IRS alike. To avoid this result, the regulations include a series of exceptions that, under prescribed circumstances, preclude multiple adjustments of the consideration over the life of a multiyear transfer of intangible property. See ¶ 12,245.

[¶ 8150]

5. COST SHARING ARRANGEMENTS

Under Temp. Reg. § 1.482–7T, an arrangement called cost sharing is provided as a basic alternative to arm's length royalty arrangements between related parties with respect to intangibles. In general, a cost sharing arrangement is an agreement between two or more persons to share the costs and risks of research and development as they are incurred in exchange for a specified interest in any intangible property that is developed. Because each participant receives rights to any intangibles developed under the arrangement, no royalties are payable by the participants for exploiting their rights to such intangibles.

Cost sharing arrangements obviate the uncertainties of attempting to fix arm's length royalties for intangibles that are often inherently difficult, if not impossible, to value with confidence. What is the disadvantage of cost sharing? If you represented a U.S.-based multinational corporation that has excess foreign tax credits, would you advise your client to make marketing and manufacturing intangibles available to foreign affiliates under licenses calling for arm's length royalties or under a cost sharing arrangement? Note that cost sharing is an alternative to earning foreign-source royalties, which, unlike cost sharing payments, normally contain a substantial profit element. Moreover, royalties are often subject to little or no foreign tax and would often be general limitation income for purposes of the Section 904 limitations on the foreign tax credit either because they meet the active-business test or under the Section 904(d)(3) look-through rules if received from controlled foreign corporations engaged in active business. See ¶ 7085. The rules applicable to cost sharing arrangements are discussed in detail at ¶¶ 12,260 et seq.

The Conference Committee Report to the 1986 Act states that, while Congress intends to permit cost sharing arrangements, it expects them to produce results consistent with the purposes of the commensurate-with-income standards in Section 482—i.e., that the "income allocated among the parties reasonably reflect the actual economic activity undertaken by each." H.R. Conf. Rep. No. 841, 99th Cong., 2d Sess. II–638 (1986).

The temporary regulations provide that the general arm's length principles of Section 482 will apply to cost sharing arrangements. They require that cost sharing arrangements between or among controlled participants must provide for the sharing of intangible development costs ("IDC") in proportion to their respective shares of reasonably anticipated benefits ("RAB"). Temp. Reg. § 1.482–7T(a)(1). The arm's length standard will be satisfied "if, and only if, each controlled participant's IDC share equals its RAB share." Temp. Reg. § 1.482–7T(a)(4).

Certain requirements must be met if the cost sharing agreement is to be treated as "qualified." The agreement must be in writing and must reflect a sharing of the costs of developing intangibles based upon the participants' respective shares of anticipated benefits from exploiting them. It must provide for adjustments to account for changes in economic conditions, business operations and practices and the ongoing development of intangibles.

Developing an appropriate response to cost sharing arrangements under Section 482 has been a particularly challenging task. The IRS and the Treasury issued temporary regulations in 2009 that prescribe a new analytical framework and somewhat new terminology for dealing with cost sharing arrangements. The basic elements of the temporary regulations are discussed at ¶¶ 12,265–12,300.

[¶ 8155]

6. REACTION BY OTHER GOVERNMENTS

There is usually another side of the international allocation debate. The belief by U.S. tax collectors that multinational groups are not paying an appropriate tax in the United States as a result of transfer pricing policies suggests that some other entities in some other countries may be reporting too much income. Actions intended to move such "excess" income into the hands of entities subject to U.S. tax implies that there should be less income reported to the tax authorities in the other countries. It is not surprising, therefore, that tax officials in a number of other countries have expressed concern about the consequences to them of both the super-royalty provisions and the approaches to determining proper intercompany prices reflected initially in the Section 482 White Paper and then in the regulations.

E. ADMINISTRATION OF TRANSFER PRICING ISSUES

[¶ 8160]

1. REPORTING AND DOCUMENTATION REQUIREMENTS AND PENALTIES

As part of its focus on transfer pricing issues, Congress established a series of reporting requirements, documentation requirements and penalties to assist the IRS in the implementation of its Section 482 authority.

[¶ 8165]

a. Reporting and Documentation Requirements

Section 6038A provides authority to require annual reporting by U.S. corporations that are 25–percent foreign-owned. Section 6038C provides authority to require additional reporting with respect to foreign corporations engaged in a U.S. business.

The basic requirements of Sections 6038A and 6038C may be summarized as follows:

1. Any foreign corporation that conducts a trade or business in the United States and any U.S. corporation that is 25–percent owned by a foreign person is required to file an annual information return indicating the name, principal place of business, nature of business and countries in which any related party is organized or resident and reporting transactions with foreign parties that are "related" (under a broad definition including a 25–percent shareholder) to the reporting corporation.

2. Each reporting corporation is required to maintain (and perhaps to create) books and records, and these documents must be maintained either in the United States or, if outside the United States, under an agreement permitting ready access to them by the IRS. The records must reflect an overview of the business, its organizational structure, an analysis of the economic and legal factors affecting pricing, a description of alternative pricing methods considered and the reasons for not using them, a description of all controlled transactions and a description of all uncontrolled comparables considered. Moreover, the taxpayer must produce such records within 30 days of any request by the IRS. Reg. § 1.6662–6(d)(2).

3. Each foreign person related to a reporting corporation must designate that corporation to accept service of process as the related party's agent in connection with any IRS request or summons for records or testimony concerning related party transactions. Thus, IRS summonses for foreign-based documents and testimony involving a U.S. taxpayer can be served on related foreign persons through the reporting corporation.

4. Failure to comply with these rules may result in substantial monetary penalties and in some cases may permit the IRS to determine unilaterally the reporting corporation's taxable income from related party transactions.

The regulations, however, establish several exceptions to the various requirements of Section 6038A. First, they adopt a de minimis rule for a reporting corporation if the aggregate value of all payments made to and received from foreign related parties with respect to related party transactions is not more than $5 million and is less than ten percent of its U.S. gross income. Such a corporation is not required to comply with the record maintenance requirement. Also, its foreign related parties are not subject to the agency designation rules. Reg. § 1.6038A–1(i).

The regulations also adopt a "small corporation" exception to provide an exemption for small corporations that may be unable to satisfy the ten-percent-of-gross-income requirement of the de minimis rule. Under this small corporation exception, any corporation having less than $10 million in U.S. gross receipts for a tax year will be exempt from the record maintenance requirement and its foreign related parties will be exempt from the agency designation rules. Reg. § 1.6038A–1(h).

Reporting corporations entitled to the benefits of the de minimis rule or the small corporation exception are still subject to the information-reporting requirements. Moreover, neither the de minimis rule nor the small corporation exception exempts the reporting corporation from the provisions of Section 6001, which imposes a general record maintenance requirement.

Another exception is provided to certain foreign corporations that are residents of countries with which the United States has an income tax treaty. If such a corporation does not have a permanent establishment in the United States under the terms of the applicable treaty, the corporation will not be treated as a reporting corporation and thus will not be subject to any of the requirements of Section 6038C. Reg. § 1.6038A–1(c)(5)(i). Section 6114 requires, however, that the foreign corporation notify the IRS that it is entitled to the benefit of the treaty.

[¶ 8170]

b. Penalty Provisions

Other provisions are intended to enhance the ability of the IRS to use Section 482 effectively and to increase revenues in certain cases in which adjustments are made. Section 6662(e) applies the 20–percent "accuracy-related penalty" in respect of certain large adjustments under Section 482. This transactional penalty applies when the price of property or services in a transaction is adjusted to an amount that is twice as much (or half as much, depending on the direction of the adjustment) as the transfer price actually charged. Alternatively, the so-called net Section 482 adjustment penalty, also imposed at the 20–percent rate, applies when the net transfer price adjustment in any tax year exceeds the lesser of $5 million or ten percent of gross receipts. § 6662(e)(1)(B)(ii). Adjustments involving solely foreign corporations that do not affect the determination of U.S.-source income or taxable income effectively connected with a U.S. trade or business are not included in determining whether the penalty is to be imposed. § 6662(e)(3)(B)(iii). No penalty is imposed if the underpayment of tax does not exceed $10,000 for Subchapter C corporations or $5,000 for most other taxpayers. § 6662(e)(2).

For purposes of the net Section 482 adjustment penalty, an exception applies if the taxpayer has documentation establishing that it reasonably used one of the methods set forth under the Section 482 regulations (or another method designed clearly to reflect income if those specified do not do so). § 6662(e)(3)(B). The regulations also require that such method have provided the most reliable measure of an arm's length price. Reg. § 1.6662–6(d)(2)(ii).

The 20–percent penalty is doubled to 40 percent if the price is adjusted to an amount that is four times or one quarter the amount actually charged (depending on the direction of the adjustment), or if the price adjustment exceeds the lesser of $20 million or 20 percent of gross income. § 6662(h). All penalties are measured by the amount of tax underpaid.

[¶ 8175]

2. ADVANCE PRICING AGREEMENTS

As the regulations and the cases indicate, the application of the arm's length standard has historically involved an extensive analysis of a broad range of potentially relevant facts about commodities, transactions, risks, transaction terms and applicable markets. The IRS has generally been unwilling to give advance rulings with respect to questions of fact. IRS officials have, however, developed a process for granting advance pricing agreements ("APAs") on certain international pricing arrangements.

The taxpayer is given the opportunity to secure an APA on the basis of the advance provision to the IRS of a full explanation of pricing practices. The APA would apply for a specific period (for example, three years with the possibility of further extensions), during which time the taxpayer would be assured that no adjustment would be proposed under Section 482. As in the case of private letter rulings generally, the APA would not protect a taxpayer who had provided inaccurate or incomplete information or who acts in a way inconsistent with the representations that were made.

The procedural requirements for eliciting an APA are prescribed in great detail in Revenue Procedure 2006–9, 2006–1 C.B. 278. The taxpayer is required "to provide a detailed explanation and analysis of why the proposed TPM [transfer pricing method] is the best method with the meaning of [Reg.] § 1.482–1(c)." Moreover, the taxpayer request must "illustrate application of each proposed TPM by applying it, in a consistent format, to the prior three taxable years' financial and tax data of the partes to the covered transactions." If such data are not available, "the request should include an illustration based on projected or hypothetical data, as well as a description of the source of the data." Revenue Procedure 2006–9 also prescribes requirements for obtaining approval of a cost sharing agreement.

While the APA is designed to apply prospectively, it has been used by the IRS and taxpayers as a device for eliciting agreement with respect to transfer pricing disputes in past years. In effect the parties agree to resolve the existing dispute by reference to the conceptual approach reflected in the APA.

The purpose of an APA is obviously to provide a degree of predictability with respect to transfer pricing issues. The value of the added predictability of an APA in terms of U.S. income tax law is, however, somewhat diminished if the taxpayer contemplates transfer pricing challenges in other countries. Where possible, efforts have been made by the IRS and the taxing authorities in treaty partner countries to develop an APA with a taxpayer that will be accepted by both taxing jurisdictions.

[¶ 8185]

3. ALTERNATIVE APPROACHES TO ISSUES OF APPORTIONMENT

The approach prescribed by Section 482 for allocating the profits of integrated economic operations respects the separateness of even closely related corporate entities and focuses on transactional accuracy. There are other conceptual devices for addressing the proper apportionment of income among affiliated corporations operating in two or more countries. A number of states in the United States have established a formulary approach in the application of their income tax laws. One common form is to multiply the net income of an integrated group of corporations by a ratio determined by comparing certain factors (often labor costs, asset values and sales receipts) within the state to the total of the factors throughout the world. This approach has been opposed by foreign-based multinationals whose taxes have been increased by its application and by a number of foreign governments.

Is such an approach obviously less appropriate than that reflected by Section 482? It has been suggested that a formulary approach might be used to deal with transfer pricing issues at the international level, and that such an approach might even be specified in tax treaties. What practical questions of administration would be avoided? What new problems would be created?

A number of developing countries have used an interesting alternative to transactional pricing analysis in dealing with foreign investors in natural resource exploitation. At least partially in lieu of an income tax, production-sharing agreements are sometimes concluded between the host government (or an entity owned by the host government) and the foreign investor. Such an agreement typically specifies the quantity of the product of the operation that will be allocated to each party, which then markets its share of production. Counting barrels of oil turns out to be somewhat easier than finding comparable arm's length transactions.

Another approach used by some developing and some developed countries as well is to determine the taxable income of a local branch of a foreign corporation under certain circumstances based on an arbitrary formula (called in French a "forfaitaire"), usually treating the taxable income as equal to a stated percentage (e.g., 10–15 percent) of the expenses of the local branch. This approach acknowledges the difficulty of determining the "true" amount of gross income of a multinational enterprise that should be allocated to a local branch and, in the interest of simplicity and predictability, opts for making the arbitrary assumption that the net income to be taxed equals simply a specific percentage of the expenses of the branch. This percentage is fixed in advance often in a ruling by the tax administration. Since the expenses of the branch are reflected on its local books, while the gross income properly attributable to the branch often will not be, this approach eases the burden of administration and provides certainty for the taxpayer and the local tax authority alike. A similar approach has been taken in some countries with respect to locally incorporated headquarters subsidiaries that provide administrative and other services to affiliated corporations. See, e.g., Reg. § 1.901–2(b)(3)(ii), Ex. 1.

[¶ 8190]

4. THE CHALLENGE OF GLOBAL TRADING

Some may view the "profit split" approach to be a form of formulary apportionment. Consider the following explanation by the IRS of the approach that will be taken in the issuance of APAs in respect of "functionally fully integrated operations in the global trading of commodities and derivative financial products." The issues discussed here are only some of the many concerns of the IRS about the tax consequences of dealing with properties that can be effectively moved between branch offices in different countries in an instant.

[¶ 8191]

IRS NOTICE 94–40

1994–1 C.B. 351.

* * *

BACKGROUND

Historically, financial markets have been limited by the national boundaries within which they operated. However, the world's financial markets are becoming more integrated because of technological developments, financial innovation, and regulatory changes. Many financial intermediaries trade commodities and derivative financial products around the clock by maintaining traders in offices around the world ("global trading").

Four general functions are common to global trading operations; trading, sales, management, and support. A trader quotes prices, initiates buy and sell transactions, and determines whether and how to hedge transactions. A salesperson advises clients about ways to manage the price, interest rate, and currency exchange risks associated with their assets and liabilities, with a view toward selling them a derivative financial product or commodity. A manager controls or monitors the level of risk to which the institution is exposed and sets trading limits. Finally, the support function performs various wide-ranging activities that assist the first three functions; including technology and information systems development and provision, credit analysis of customers and counterparties, accounting, contract administration, and coordination of the transportation and delivery of physical commodities.

Different companies have integrated these functions in varying degrees for a variety of business reasons. However, two broad types of organization can be distinguished: operations that are functionally fully integrated and those that are not.

Global trading operations of companies that are functionally fully integrated are characterized by the centralized management of risk and personnel. The business is managed as one global position for purposes of risk management rather than several discrete businesses. Thus, a trading book is not independently maintained for each trading location. Rather, one book is maintained and the trading authority for that book is "passed" from trading location to trading location at the close of each trading day for that trading location (the "global book"). To assist in the management of the risk, a central credit department monitors the credit-related exposure of the transactions entered into by the traders. This information is used by the home office to establish credit guidelines and customer credit limits to be applied by traders throughout the company.

The book for each product, or group of products, typically has one head trader or book manager who allocates trading limits for each trading location and determines guidelines for the book. The head trader is responsible for the economic performance of that book. Accordingly, the head trader is in frequent communication with other traders employed by the company. The head trader, therefore, acts as overseer of other trading personnel.

In a functionally fully integrated operation each office may be capable of performing the same functions as any other, subject to limits, procedures, and guidelines imposed by the home office. For example, it is common for one office to locate a seller of a commodity or derivative financial product and another office to locate a buyer, while either of those offices or a third office hedges the transaction. Each office in such a transaction contributes to the overall profitability of the global business.

The APA process has proven to be a useful vehicle to allocate the income of a functionally fully integrated global trading business between taxing jurisdictions. For each of the APAs concluded with taxpayers operating these businesses, the Service used a profit split method to allocate income of related operations between taxing jurisdictions. In each case, a taxpayer and the Service entered into an APA and the competent authorities of the United States and a treaty partner entered into an agreement to allocate the income pursuant to that method. The Service, treaty partners, and taxpayers found that the use of a profit split method to allocate the income of these functionally fully integrated global trading businesses was appropriate because of the volume and nature of transactions involved in these APAs. For these taxpayers, the profit split method permits the allocation of income in a way that reflects the contribution of each trading location to the profitability of the global book.

In the case of integrated businesses operating through separately incorporated subsidiaries located in different tax jurisdictions, the APAs were entered into pursuant to the authority of section 482 of the Code and an applicable income tax treaty. For integrated businesses incorporated in one tax jurisdiction but operating through unincorporated branches in other tax jurisdictions, the APAs were entered into pursuant to the authority of income tax treaties.

APA PROCESS

Generally, APAs issued to taxpayers that have functionally fully integrated operations in the global trading area have covered transactions in commodities and derivative financial products, as well as the related hedges used to minimize price risk or interest and currency exchange rate risk. APAs in the global trading area have been issued to domestic corporations trading through a subsidiary or branch located in a country with which the U.S. maintains an income tax convention ("treaty country"). They have also been issued to corporations that are located in treaty countries and that trade in the United States through a branch. Although the Service has not yet negotiated an APA with a foreign corporation trading in the United States through a domestic subsidiary, there is no procedural obstacle to issuing such an APA.

The APA process is a flexible procedure whereby a taxpayer decides which global books it wants covered. Each of these APAs was tailored to take account of the unique facts and circumstances of the taxpayer. These APAs divided the business' worldwide trading profits or losses among the trading locations according to an agreed upon profit split method.

FACTORS USED IN GLOBAL TRADING APAS

Set forth below is a general description of the global trading APAs that the Service has concluded with functionally fully integrated taxpayers. In each of these APAs, the Service, the taxpayer, and a treaty partner agreed that the worldwide income for each global book to be covered by the APA should be allocated among the taxpayer's trading locations pursuant to a profit split method. The method was intended to measure the economic activity of each trading location and its contribution to the overall profitability of the worldwide business. Three critical factors were identified: 1) the relative value of the trading location (the "value factor"), 2) the risk associated with a trading location (the "risk factor"), and 3) the extent of the activity of each trading location (the "activity factor"). Each of the factors was weighted to reflect its relative contribution to the overall profitability of a taxpayer's worldwide business. Moreover, the APAs did not adopt a uniform measurement of these factors; rather, different measurements were adopted in each APA to reflect the taxpayer's particular facts and circumstances as closely as possible. Relevant considerations in adopting a measurement for each factor included: the taxpayer's management structure and management information system capability, the functions performed, risks assumed, and capital employed by each trading location.

The value factor is a direct measure of the contribution of a trading location to the worldwide profits of that business. Trading commodities or derivative financial products generates the profit and loss for the business. For the taxpayers covered by these APAs, traders were the most significant resource in generating trading profit or loss for the company because they typically had customer lists and knowledge of the market. Traders are responsible for negotiating prices at which trades will be made, executing the transactions, and determining the hedging strategies to be used. Their compensation often is based upon a salary and a discretionary incentive bonus that depends upon their contribution to the profitability of the book. The sum of the compensation paid to traders in a particular trading location is a direct indication of the trading location's contribution to the profitability of the worldwide book. Thus, the Service, the taxpayer, and the participating treaty partner viewed compensation of the traders at a trading location as the best measure of the value of a trading location. Accordingly, this factor was weighted more heavily than others.

The risk factor measures the potential risk to which a particular trading location exposes the worldwide capital of the organization. This factor provides an important indication of the contribution of that trading location to the production of gross profits of the business. Based on the unique characteristics of each taxpayer, the risk factor was measured in several different ways, such as the maturity weighted volume of swap transactions (determined by multiplying the notional amount of each swap transaction entered into by its maturity) or open commodity positions at the end of the year entered into in that trading location. Sometimes this factor was weighted more heavily than others.

The activity factor serves as another measure of a trading location's contribution to the production of gross profits of the business. This factor was measured by reference to the compensation of key support people at a trading location (for example, back office support) or the net present value of transactions executed at a trading location (determined by aggregating the present values of the cash flows computed at the inception of each transaction for each trading location).

APPLICATION OF THE METHOD

The first step in applying the agreed upon method is to determine the amount of trading profits or losses to which the method will apply. Typically, this includes worldwide profits and losses from trading the class of commodities or derivative financial products and related hedges that the taxpayer and the Service have agreed to include within the APA, less expenses that are directly related to the production of trading income or loss, such as compensation of certain personnel, trading computer systems, and broker commissions (the "worldwide net income or loss"). Other expenses, including office supplies, rent, and communications, were allocated to the trading locations that incurred them. However, expenses that are required to be computed under specific Code or regulatory rules, such as interest expense deductions under § 1.861–9T of the * * * Regulations or § 1.882–5 of the regulations, were allocated under the appropriate provisions.

The second step in applying the method is to calculate the ratio that results from each factor. For example, to determine the ratio for the value factor, the total U.S. trader compensation is divided by the total worldwide trader compensation. That result, possibly multiplied by a weighting factor, is the ratio for the value factor.

Once the three ratios are determined, the percentage of worldwide net income or loss attributable to the U.S. is calculated by taking the sum of the three factors and dividing them by the sum of the weights given to each factor.

Finally, to determine the amount of worldwide net income or loss attributable to the U.S., the worldwide profit or loss is multiplied by the percentage described above.

* * *

[¶ 8192]

NOTE

As recognized in the IRS Notice, the world's financial markets are becoming increasingly integrated by technological development, financial innovation and regulatory change. The IRS has proposed regulations that provide special methods in applying the arm's length standard to global dealing operations. The proposed regulations seem to be based upon IRS Notice 94–40, which dealt generally with global dealing issues in the context of APA policy.

The proposed regulations determine the allocation of income and deductions when two or more controlled taxpayers are participants in a global dealing operation. Prop. Reg. § 1.482–8(a)(1). The allocation of income and deductions deriving from such operation is to be determined by one of the following methods:

1. The comparable uncontrolled financial transaction method. Prop. Reg. § 1.482–8(b)(1).
2. The gross margin method. Prop Reg. § 1.482–8(c)(1).
3. The gross markup method. Prop Reg. § 1.482–8(d)(1).
4. The profit split method. Prop. Reg. § 1.482–8(e)(1).
5. Other unspecified methods. Prop. Reg. § 1.482–8(f).

Further, the methods must be applied in accordance with the best method rule, the comparability rule and general arm's length analysis.

The proposed regulations apply when there are two or more controlled "participants" in a "global dealing operation." A global dealing operation "consists of the execution of customer transactions, including marketing, sales, pricing and risk management activities in a particular financial product or line of financial products in multiple tax jurisdictions or through multiple participants." Prop. Reg. § 1.482–8(a)(2). However, lending activities and investment transactions are not included within the global dealing definition and are not governed by the proposed regulations.

A participant is a controlled taxpayer that is either a regular dealer in securities or a member of a group of controlled taxpayers that includes a regular dealer in securities if the member conducts one or more activities related to the activities of such a dealer. Prop. Reg. § 1.482–8(a)(2)(ii). The related activities include marketing, sales, pricing, risk management or brokering activities. They do not include credit analysis, accounting, back office services, general supervision and control over the policies of the controlled taxpayer, or the provision of guarantees.

Finally, the proposed regulations also provide that the provisions of Reg. § 1.863–3(h) will apply to determine the source of income, gain or loss from transactions involved in a global dealing operations among qualified business units. Prop. Reg. § 1.482–8(g).

[¶ 8195]

5. USE OF ARBITRATION

The extensive documentary evidence, technical detail and importance of economic and financial theory in the adjudication of transfer pricing disputes are sometimes cited by proponents of the expanded use of arbitration to resolve transfer pricing cases. Tax Court Rule 124 permits the use of arbitration and at least one voluntary binding arbitration of a transfer pricing case has been concluded. The case involved a Singapore subsidiary of Apple Computer, Inc. One commentator has observed that the Singapore subsidiary was held to be entitled to earn more than 50 percent of the amount originally claimed by Apple; that Apple's time to decision (which is nonappealable) was reduced by about four years compared with the time required for a judicial trial and appeal—a factor that enhances the taxpayer's ability to plan for the future; that Apple's professional fees were $4 to $5 million less than they would have been in litigation; and that Apple had the benefit of confidentiality, which would have been sacrificed in a trial with a public record. Although the Apple case was not settled, the commentator opined that the arbitration process is often conducive to settlement because usually each party must, as a practical matter, back off from its initial position. See Fuller, "Apple Arbitration," 7 Tax Notes Int'l 1046 (1993).

Because both governments have an interest in the resolution of conflicting positions regarding international transfer pricing controversies, it has been suggested that arbitration provides a useful avenue for resolving different viewpoints between tax authorities in different countries dealing with the same transaction. During the past several decades, a number of treaties concluded by the United States, such as the 1993 treaty with the Netherlands (Art. 29) and the 1993 treaty with Mexico (Art. 26), contain provisions authorizing, but not requiring, resort to binding arbitration if the competent authorities cannot negotiate a price acceptable to both sides. No such arbitration has, however, yet been reported.

A major change of policy has occurred in the past few years. The United States has for the first time agreed to the inclusion in income tax treaties of a provision obligating the treaty partners to submit to binding arbitration in certain instances when mutual agreement cannot be reached under the negotiating process specified in the treaty. At the time of the publication of this volume, treaties in force with Germany (Art. 25(5) and (6)), Belgium (Art. 24(7)), Canada (Art. 21(6) and (7)) and France (Art. 26(5)) include such a provision for binding arbitration.

In each of these treaties, a special form of arbitration is provided. It is often called "baseball arbitration" because it is patterned after a technique used to resolve salary disputes between professional baseball players and team owners. The unique feature of this form of arbitration is that both sides submit a final number. In most arbitration procedures, the arbitrator(s) can reach any decision supported by the evidence. However, in baseball arbitration and provisions of the tax treaties, the arbitrator must choose one of the final submissions of the two parties. The structure penalizes the party that submits an unreasonable number, thereby bringing the two sides together with a resultant increase in the probability of a negotiated settlement. Such an approach would seem peculiarly appropriate in situations when the tax administrations of the two treaty partners are challenging the same transfer price.

CHAPTER 9

FOREIGN CURRENCY

■ ■ ■

A. INTRODUCTION

[¶ 9000]

1. NATURE OF ISSUES

For U.S. income tax purposes, a taxpayer's gross income, deductions and tax liability are generally measured and determined in U.S. dollars. Foreign currencies are treated in effect as another form of noncash property, the value of which must be reflected as income, deductions or credits in U.S. dollar equivalents when calculating the taxpayer's U.S. income tax liability.

This basic principle can be illustrated with the following simple example. Suppose that a U.S. citizen is an international lawyer who has an office in New York but who works for part of a tax year with clients in the United Kingdom and in Japan. The attorney receives fees of $60,000 from U.S. clients, 100,000 U.K. pounds from British clients and 1,000,000 Japanese yen from Japanese clients. The gross income of the attorney is $60,000 plus the dollar value of the British pounds and Japanese yen. For example, if one U.K. pound could be exchanged for $1.80 and if one Japanese yen could be exchanged for $.01 (i.e., the exchange rate is 100 yen = $1), the lawyer would have gross income for the year of $250,000 ($60,000 in U.S. cash, $180,000 worth of U.K. pounds and $10,000 worth of Japanese yen). There are also other income tax consequences. Applying the normal rules for taxpayers receiving income in the form of property other than cash, the lawyer has an adjusted basis in the foreign currencies equal to the amount of gross income (their value in U.S. dollars) that had been recognized upon their receipt ($180,000 in the U.K. pounds and $10,000 in the Japanese yen).

Because foreign currencies are treated as noncash property, the tax consequences of owning and disposing of foreign currencies may involve the realization and recognition of gains and losses in respect of them. Suppose, for example, that the lawyer holds the British pounds and

Japanese yen for a period of time. When the lawyer converts the foreign currencies into U.S. dollars, their worth (measured in U.S. dollars) may have changed during the period that the lawyer held them. Differences between the U.S. dollars received by the lawyer at the time of the conversion and the lawyer's adjusted basis in the foreign currencies will constitute gain or loss determined under Section 1001 of the Code. Issues then arise concerning the character (capital gain or ordinary income) and the geographic source (U.S. or foreign) of the foreign currency exchange gain or loss.

Other transactions involving foreign currencies may be more complex. Suppose that a U.S. citizen borrows 100,000 Canadian dollars when the exchange rate is 1 U.S. dollar = 1 Canadian dollar. The debt is repaid when 1 U.S. dollar = 1.25 Canadian dollars so that the borrower is required to use only 80,000 U.S. dollars to repay the debt. It has long been held that the borrower has realized and must recognize income of 20,000 U.S. dollars. See, e.g., Church's English Shoes, Ltd. v. Commissioner, 24 T.C. 56 (1955), aff'd per curiam, 229 F.2d 957 (2d Cir.1956). If the exchange rates had moved in the opposite direction so that 1 U.S. dollar = .75 Canadian dollars, the borrower would realize a loss. Would it be deductible? As discussed later in this Chapter, in the case of an individual or partnership borrower, the answer to this question depends on whether the foreign exchange loss was incurred in connection with a business or other profit-seeking activity. If realized by a corporate borrower, the loss would normally be deductible.

The issues raised by these simple examples reflect the basic considerations inherent in many international business relationships and transactions of much more complexity. While the application of general rules of taxation may permit determination of the tax consequences of the simple transactions described above, other transactions are less susceptible to simple analysis. How should a foreign branch of a U.S. corporation deal with foreign currencies produced by 1,000 sales transactions and 2,000 separate expenditures during a tax year in which exchange rates change daily? How should the U.S. parent of a foreign subsidiary calculate an indirect foreign tax credit under Section 902 when it receives a dividend distribution out of the accumulated earnings of the foreign subsidiary that have been derived from ten years of successful operations and that have been subject to foreign income tax payments made periodically over ten years during which exchange rates have changed constantly? How should a U.S. parent of a controlled foreign corporation calculate the amount of a Subpart F inclusion under Section 951(a)(1)(A) triggered by the subsidiary's Subpart F income for a tax year during which exchange rates have changed on a daily basis throughout the year?

[¶ 9005]

2. LEGISLATIVE REFORM

As suggested in the preceding section, the potential issues attributable to the presence of foreign currency in a transaction often arise in circumstances of substantial factual complexity. These issues have been addressed in different ways during most of the time since the establishment of the U.S. income tax. Before 1986, however, there were almost no Code or regulation provisions prescribing rules for foreign currency transactions and those that existed were only of limited application. Instead, the rules governing the taxation of foreign currency transactions were largely contained in a number of court decisions and revenue rulings, which provided conflicting answers on some questions and did not even address other questions. The result was a substantial degree of uncertainty and conceptual inconsistency.

The Tax Reform Act of 1986 included a relatively comprehensive set of provisions (Sections 985–989) intended to establish at least the fundamental principles for the taxation of foreign currency transactions. In the manner that has become an increasingly common element of tax jurisprudence, these statutory provisions authorize the promulgation of extensive regulations to elaborate on the fundamental principles. Many of these regulations have already been issued. The Taxpayer Relief Act of 1997 made a number of changes to these rules, largely in an attempt to simplify the provisions and thereby reduce taxpayer compliance costs and government administrative expenses relating to the provisions.

The materials in this Chapter derive essentially from the 1986 and 1997 legislation, the legislative history accompanying the legislation and the regulations that have been issued thus far. Because the specific application of the conceptual principles often requires the application of complex accounting methodologies beyond the scope of this book, the objective of this Chapter is to provide an introduction to the conceptual principles in the context of the most common transactional forms to which they are intended to apply.

[¶ 9010]

3. FOREIGN EXCHANGE MARKETS

The tax law in the foreign currency area is formed and applied against the background of the foreign exchange markets. Prices in those markets (that is, exchange rates) move in accordance with supply and demand if the market is unregulated. Other things remaining equal, if Americans drink more Scotch whiskey, the United States will import more whiskey from the United Kingdom, the demand for pounds sterling to pay for the whiskey will go up and the price in U.S. dollars of sterling will rise. That is, the exchange rate will move from, say, \$1.80 = 1 pound to \$1.90 = 1 pound.

The process contains a built-in stabilizer. As the price of sterling rises against the dollar, imported Scotch and all other U.K. goods automatically become more expensive for Americans. Americans then buy fewer of them, thus reducing our demand for sterling. At the same time, the fall in the value of the dollar from 1 pound = $1.80 to 1 pound = $1.90 (as in the above example) will make U.S. goods less expensive for British customers. As a result, British customers will buy more U.S. goods and, therefore, need to buy more U.S. dollars. And this will tend to increase the price of the dollar.

Because of such built-in stabilizers, many argue that freely floating exchange rates comprise the best system of international exchange and will keep exchange rates hovering around the "correct" level. Others argue for government-fixed rates or, more commonly, fixed limits within which exchange rates may fluctuate, fearing that private speculators will cause distortions and wide swings of exchange rates that will interfere with international trade and capital movements. Throughout the 20th Century fixed rates predominated. Governments often used a pegging system that prevented exchange rates from freely moving in response to supply and demand except within narrow limits.

The technique of pegging rates is, in essence, simple. If the British pound were to be pegged at $1.70, the British government or its monetary authority would stand ready to buy pounds at $1.70 whenever their price fell to $1.69 and to sell pounds at $1.70 whenever the price rose to $1.71. So long as the monetary authority was able to do this, the price would be effectively pegged at $1.70. In fact, the pegging government would normally allow some leeway. So long as the pound fluctuated between $1.68 and $1.72, for example, the government would stay out of the exchange market.

A problem under this system arose when the supply of the pound at $1.68 greatly exceeded its demand. The monetary authority might be forced to use up large amounts of its gold and foreign exchange reserves to maintain the $1.68 price. If the monetary authority believed it was losing too much foreign exchange by supporting its currency, it would abruptly announce a devaluation, very likely of a substantial amount, and would thereafter support its currency only at the new lower level. Thus, this system is characterized by substantial periods of exchange rate stability, interrupted occasionally by large, abrupt changes.

In recent decades the United States and much of the world have turned to floating rates. The current system is sometimes called a "dirty float" because governments are likely to enter the exchange market at their discretion and support their currencies without announcement or at previously unannounced levels.

B. STRUCTURE OF CODE PROVISIONS

[¶ 9015]

1. BASIC PRINCIPLES

The statutory provisions added by the 1986 Act reflect several basic principles. Every taxpayer and virtually every separate business enterprise (including an unincorporated foreign branch of a U.S. corporation) will be regarded as operating in one principal currency, called the "functional currency." The special rules set forth in Sections 985–989 effectively prescribe methods of dealing with various circumstances in which currencies other than the functional currency are acquired or used in some way. In general, those rules undertake to provide methods for determining when gains and losses in respect of nonfunctional currencies will be recognized for tax purposes and for determining the character and source of any such gains and losses. Two basic methods of translation have been developed: the separate transactions method and the profit and loss method. The identification of the functional currency is crucial to the operation of these rules.

Under the separate transactions method, used if the functional currency is the U.S. dollar, transactions in any foreign currency are translated into dollars on a transaction-by-transaction basis. The disposition of foreign currency in various types of transactions results in the recognition of foreign exchange gain or loss, which is generally accounted for separately from any gain or loss attributable to the underlying transaction. By contrast, under the profit and loss method, used if the functional currency is foreign, daily business transactions are not translated into U.S. dollars. Instead, translation is deferred until necessary for some U.S. tax purpose, such as the calculation of the earnings or loss of a foreign branch for the year or determination of the U.S. tax consequences when a dividend is received by a U.S. taxpayer from a foreign corporation. Thus, for example, a U.S. taxpayer with a foreign branch the functional currency of which is a foreign currency first measures the untranslated results of the branch's foreign operations (net income or loss) for a tax year in the functional currency, and then translates the net income or loss into U.S. dollars at a prescribed exchange rate for the year.

[¶ 9020]

2. DETERMINING THE FUNCTIONAL CURRENCY

Section 985(b)(1)(A) states the general rule that the functional currency will be "the dollar." (For purposes of simplification, the term "dollar" or the "$" symbol, when used in this Chapter, will always refer to U.S. dollars unless otherwise indicated.) However, the functional currency of a "qualified business unit" ("QBU") will be "the currency of the economic environment in which a significant part of such unit's activities" is "conducted and which is used by such unit in keeping its books and records." § 985(b)(1)(B). The functional currency of the QBU will be the dollar if its activities "are primarily conducted in dollars." § 985(b)(2). A QBU will also have the dollar as its functional currency if it has the United States as its residence (as defined in Section 988(a)(3)(B), discussed below at ¶ 9035), it "does not keep books and records in the [non-U.S.] currency of any economic environment in which a significant part of its activities is conducted" or it produces income or loss that is effectively connected with the conduct of a U.S. trade or business. Reg. § 1.985–1(b)(1)(iii)-(v).

Section 989(a) defines a QBU as "any separate and clearly identified unit of a trade or business of a taxpayer which maintains separate books and records." A corporation is a QBU. A foreign branch operation of a U.S. corporation would also in most instances be a QBU. The branch must, however, be conducting activities that constitute a trade or business and maintain a separate set of books and records with respect to such activities. Reg. § 1.989(a)–1(b)(2)(ii). If the branch is an integral extension of a U.S. operation not capable of producing income independently (such as a financing vehicle), it will not be a QBU. In that event, the transactions of the foreign branch would be treated with all other transactions of the corporation of which it is a part.

Determining whether activities are a trade or business for this purpose depends upon an analysis of all the surrounding facts and circumstances. A trade or business for this purpose generally "is a specific unified group of activities that constitutes (or could constitute) an independent economic enterprise entered into for profit" if the expenses related to the activities are deductible under Section 162 or 212. To be a trade or business for this purpose, "a group of activities must ordinarily include [(1)] every operation which forms a part of, or a step in, a process by which an enterprise may earn income or profit * * * [and (2)] the collection of income and the payment of expenses." A vertical, functional or geographic division of the same trade or business may qualify as a trade or business, and, hence, a separate QBU for Section 989 purposes. By contrast, activities "merely ancillary to a trade or business" do not qualify as a trade or business for Section 989 purposes. Moreover, the regulations make clear that an individual's activities as an employee are not by themselves a trade or business for Section 989 purposes. Reg. § 1.989(a)–1(c).

An individual is generally not a QBU and must, therefore, use the dollar as the functional currency. A partnership, trust or estate is a QBU of the partners or beneficiaries. Activities of an individual, partnership, trust or estate, however, may qualify as a separate QBU if they constitute a separate trade or business for which a separate set of books and records is maintained. Reg. § 1.989(a)–1(b)(2). The regulations also provide that any activity producing income or loss that is effectively connected with a

U.S. trade or business is to be treated as a separate QBU with the dollar as the functional currency. Reg. § 1.989(a)–1(b)(3).

These principles for determining whether a QBU exists for Section 989 purposes are illustrated by the following examples drawn from Reg. § 1.989(a)–1(e).

Example 1. DC, a U.S. corporation, manufactures machinery parts in the United States for export to various countries. DC sells its machinery parts in France through a branch office in Paris, which has its own employees who solicit, accept and fill orders for the machinery parts. DC maintains a separate set of books and records for all transactions conducted by the Paris office. DC is a QBU by reason of its corporate status. The Paris branch office is a separate QBU because the sale of the machinery parts is a separate trade or business for Section 989 purposes and a complete and separate sets of books and records is maintained for the Paris branch.

Example 2. DC2, a U.S. corporation, incorporates FC, a wholly owned subsidiary in Germany. DC2 is a manufacturer of widgets that markets the widgets abroad through FC. FC has branch offices in France and Italy that are responsible for marketing DC2's widgets in those countries. The French and Italian branches each has its own employees, solicits, accepts and fills orders and maintains a separate set of books and records. DC2 and FC are separate QBUs because of their corporate status. The French and Italian branches are QBUs of FC because each constitutes a separate trade or business for Section 989 purposes (although each is a geographical division of the same trade or business) and complete and separate sets of books and records of the operations of both branches are maintained.

Example 3. DC3, a U.S. corporation, manufactures widgets in the United States for sale throughout the world. DC3 conducts all of its sale operations in the United States. DC3 employs an individual, who is a U.S. resident, to act as a courier to deliver sales documents to customers in Germany. A separate set of books and records relating to the individual's activities in Germany is maintained. The individual's activities in Germany do not constitute a separate QBU for DC3 because they are merely ancillary to DC3's manufacturing and sales business in the United States. The individual does not have a QBU because an individual's activities as an employee by themselves are not a trade or business for Section 989 purposes. By contrast, if DC3 had set up a wholly owned German subsidiary whose sole activity was the courier function, the German subsidiary would constitute a QBU for Section 989 purposes by reason of its corporate status.

Example 4. An individual, who is a U.S. resident, owns all the stock of FC2, a foreign corporation. FC2's sole activity is trading in stocks and securities. FC2 is a QBU because of its corporate status.

Example 5. An individual, who is a U.S. resident, markets and sells in the United States and Italy several products produced by other U.S. manufacturers. The individual has an office in Italy and employs a salesperson in Italy to manage its activities in Italy. The individual maintains a separate set of books and records for its Italian activities. The individual's activities in Italy are a QBU because the individual's Italian activities are a trade or business for Section 989 purposes and a complete and separate set of books and records for the Italian activities is maintained.

With respect to the "economic environment" of a QBU used to determine its functional currency, the regulations provide that "all the facts and circumstances" are to be taken into account. Relevant factors will include:

— The currency of the country in which the QBU is a resident.

— The currencies of the QBU's cash flows.

— The currencies in which the QBU generates revenues and incurs expenses.

— The currencies in which the QBU borrows and lends.

— The currencies of the QBU's sales markets.

— The currencies in which the QBU's pricing and other financial decisions are made.

— The duration of the QBU's business operations.

— The significance and/or volume of the QBU's independent activities.

Reg. § 1.985–1(c)(2). Examples of the application of these factors are set forth at Reg. § 1.985–1(f).

A QBU that would otherwise have to use a foreign functional currency may be permitted under the regulations to elect to treat the dollar as its functional currency if it keeps books and records in dollars or uses a method of accounting that "approximates a separate transactions method." § 985(b)(3). This method (sometimes called the "dollar approximate separate transactions method" or "DASTM"), which is explained more fully at Reg. § 1.985–3, basically requires conversion into dollar equivalents when discrete transactions in other currencies occur. This election to use the dollar as the functional currency has been authorized for a QBU that would otherwise have used a "hyperinflationary currency." Reg. § 1.985–2(b).

Once the functional currency of the QBU has been established, any change in the functional currency will be treated as a change in the taxpayer's method of accounting. § 985(b)(4). Thus, the functional currency must be used for the year established and all later tax years unless the IRS grants permission to change it. Reg. § 1.985–4.

[¶ 9025]

3. FIXING THE EXCHANGE RATE

To implement the foreign currency rules, it is always necessary to determine an appropriate exchange rate. This task is not easy in an era of constantly fluctuating exchange rates. It is particularly difficult when rates have changed frequently over a long period of time and the profit and loss method is applied.

In the case of transactions of a taxpayer, other than a QBU using a foreign functional currency, the translation of foreign currency into dollars generally is made using the "spot rate" on the date of the transaction. See Reg. § 1.988–2. In the case of a QBU using a foreign functional currency, Section 989(b) provides that the "appropriate exchange rate" means—

— In the case of an actual dividend distribution from a corporation, the "spot rate" on the date that the distribution is included in income. § 989(b)(1).

— In the case of a sale or exchange of stock in a foreign corporation treated as a dividend under Section 1248 (discussed at ¶ 6245), the spot rate on the date that the deemed dividend is included in income. § 989(b)(2).

— In the case of constructive dividend inclusions under the anti-deferral rules in Section 951(a)(1)(A) or 1293(a) (see Chapter 6), the average exchange rate for the tax year of the foreign corporation. § 989(b)(3).

—In the case of any other QBU of a taxpayer, the average exchange rate for the tax year of the QBU. § 989(b)(4).

For this purpose, Section 989(b) treats any amount included in a U.S. shareholder's income under Section 951(a)(1)(B) as a result of a controlled foreign corporation's investment in U.S. property as an actual distribution made on the last day of the tax year of the inclusion.

The regulations define spot rate as one "demonstrated to the satisfaction of the [IRS] to reflect a fair market rate of exchange available to the public for currency under a spot contract in a free market and involving representative amounts." In the absence of such a showing by the taxpayer, the regulations state that the IRS may make a determination in its "sole discretion." Reg. § 1.988–1(d)(1).

In some countries there is a differential between the official exchange rate and the free market rate. Transactions involving the latter may in some cases be of dubious legality. In a number of developing countries there may be two foreign exchange "windows." One window will effect exchanges at the official rate for qualified transactions that are encouraged by the government. The other window will use a floating free market rate. Under these circumstances, "the spot rate shall be the rate which most clearly reflects the taxpayer's income. Generally, this shall be the free market rate." Reg. § 1.988–1 (d)(4)(i).

Exchange rates determined over a period of time will be based on "the weighted average exchange rate" for the tax year. This rate is defined by the regulations to be "the simple average of the daily exchange rates (determined by reference to a qualified source of exchange rates * * *), excluding weekends, holidays and any other nonbusiness days for the taxable year." Reg. § 1.989(b)–1.

C. SEPARATE TRANSACTIONS METHOD

[¶ 9030]

1. FOREIGN CURRENCY GAINS AND LOSSES—DEFINITIONS

Transactions in a foreign currency of a taxpayer, other than a QBU using a foreign functional currency, must be translated into dollars on a transaction-by-transaction basis. Most of these transactions in a business context are governed by Section 988 and are labeled "section 988 transactions." Section 988 transactions include four separate categories:

(i) Acquisition of a debt instrument or becoming an obligor under a debt instrument (i.e., lending or borrowing a foreign currency). § 988(c)(1)(B)(i).

(ii) Accrual of an item of gross income or expense that is received or paid later. § 988(c)(1)(B)(ii).

(iii) Entering into or acquiring a forward currency contract, futures contract or similar financial instrument. § 988(c)(1)(B)(iii).

(iv) Disposition of a nonfunctional currency. § 988(c)(1)(C).

Section 988 covers most but not all separate foreign currency transactions. It does not, for example, encompass nonbusiness transactions. See ¶ 9065.

"Foreign currency gain" is defined for purposes of Section 988 as "gain from a section 988 transaction to the extent such gain does not exceed gain realized by reason of changes in exchange rates on or after the booking date and before the payment date." § 988(b)(1). "Foreign currency loss" is correspondingly defined in Section 988(b)(2). Thus, if the taxpayer has a loss on the overall Section 988 transaction, there is no foreign currency gain even if a favorable change in the exchange rates reduced the amount of the overall loss on the transaction. Correspondingly, if the taxpayer has a gain on the overall Section 988 transaction, there is no foreign currency loss even if an unfavorable change in the exchange rates reduced the amount of the overall gain on the transaction.

> *Example*. A U.S. corporation buys a pound sterling instrument for 100 pounds when one pound = $1.80. The cost and adjusted basis of the instrument are therefore $180.
>
> If the instrument is sold for 200 pounds when one pound = $2, the corporation's realized gain is $220 ($400 amount realized minus adjusted basis of $180). However, its foreign currency gain is measured by the difference between the exchange rates on the booking and disposition dates and therefore equals $20, calculated by multiplying the $.20 difference in the exchange rates by the original price of the instrument in pound sterling (100 pounds).
>
> If the instrument is sold for 200 pounds when one pound = $.90, i.e., at a price equal to $180, no gain or loss is realized and therefore there is no currency gain or loss.
>
> If the instrument is sold for 200 pounds when one pound = $1.00, i.e., at a price equal to $200, the corporation has a realized gain of $20 on the transaction. However, there is no foreign currency gain because the gain was not realized by reason of changes in the exchange rates but in spite of them.
>
> If the instrument is sold for 200 pounds when one pound = $.50, i.e., at a price equal to $100, there is a loss of $80 and all of it would be a foreign currency loss (because all of the loss is realized by reason of changes in the exchange rates).

Although the discussion throughout this section of the Chapter is presented in the context of situations in which the QBU's functional currency is the dollar, the principles applied here are the same for a QBU having a foreign functional currency. Where the discussion here converts foreign currencies into the dollar, a QBU having a foreign currency as its functional currency would convert other currencies (including the dollar) into its functional currency by using essentially the same rules as those discussed here.

[¶ 9035]

2. FOREIGN CURRENCY GAINS AND LOSSES—CHARACTER AND SOURCE

Key elements of the 1986 Act provisions governing the taxation of foreign exchange gains and losses are rules determining the character (ordinary or capital) and geographical source (U.S. or foreign) of such gains and losses. The following excerpt from Staff of Joint Comm. on Tax'n, 100th Cong., 1st Sess., General Explanation of the Tax Reform Act of 1986, at 1086–89 (1987), explains the Code provisions governing the character and source of exchange gains and losses:

> Prior law was unclear regarding the character, the timing of recognition, and the source of gain or loss due to fluctuations in the

exchange rate of foreign currency. Further, no rules were prescribed for determining when the results of a foreign operation could be recorded in a foreign currency, and taxpayers were permitted to use a method of translating foreign currency results into U.S. dollars that was inconsistent with general Federal income tax principles. The result of prior law was uncertainty of tax treatment for many legitimate business transactions, as well as opportunities for tax-motivated transactions. The Congress determined that a comprehensive set of rules should be provided for the U.S. tax treatment of transactions involving foreign currency.

* * *

Character of exchange gain or loss

Effect of exchange gain or loss on interest denominated in a foreign currency

Commentators observed that a loan denominated in a foreign currency may reflect a "true" U.S.-dollar interest rate plus an anticipated annual exchange gain or loss. For example, a U.S. taxpayer who borrows a currency that is viewed as strong in relation to the dollar would pay less interest (in nominal terms) than if the taxpayer had borrowed dollars (because the lender expects to be repaid with appreciated currency). Conversely, if the taxpayer borrows currency of a country experiencing high rates of inflation, so that the currency is viewed as weak in relation to the dollar, the taxpayer would pay more annual interest (in nominal terms) than if dollars had been borrowed. In such cases, at least to the extent the parties' expectations prove to be correct, or the parties hedge their positions, it is arguable that nominal interest is understated or overstated, respectively.

The relationship between the dollar price of foreign currency in the forward market and the market interest rate for such currency relative to the dollar supports the view that exchange gain or loss should be treated as interest income or expense. On the other hand, other factors (e.g., a borrower's creditworthiness) affect the stated rate of interest on a foreign currency debt, making it difficult to separate that portion of exchange gain or loss that is equivalent to interest. Even commentators who favor the interest equivalency approach for certain purposes (e.g., characterization) question the result for other Federal income tax purposes (e.g., rules that disallow interest allocable to investments such as tax-exempt bonds). Further, although expectations regarding a currency's future value are material in setting the rate of return on a financial asset or liability, exchange gain or loss could be more or less than expected.

Treatment of exchange gain or loss as ordinary income or loss

The Act does not adopt the interest equivalency approach in its entirety, but reflects the position that characterizing exchange gain or loss as ordinary income or loss for most purposes is a pragmatic solution to an issue about which tax scholars and practitioners hold disparate views. The Act authorizes the Secretary to treat exchange gain or loss as interest income or expense in appropriate circumstances (e.g., in the case of hedging transactions where a taxpayer's expectations about future exchange rates are locked in).

It was considered whether unanticipated exchange gain or loss on a financial asset or liability should be characterized as capital gain or loss. This approach was not followed because it is difficult to distinguish anticipated exchange gain or loss from unanticipated exchange gain or loss. Anticipated exchange gain or loss could be measured with reference to the premium or discount element in a forward contract had one been obtained; however, forward contracts are not available in all currencies and do not trade at all maturities. Even where anticipated exchange gain or loss is determinable (e.g., where a taxpayer enters into a forward contract), the Act treats all such gain or loss as ordinary in nature to reduce discontinuities in the law. * * * A limited exception to this treatment is provided for certain contracts that constitute capital assets in the hands of the taxpayer and are properly identified as speculative investments.

Timing of recognition

Advocates of the interest equivalency approach suggested that a taxpayer's interest income or expense should be adjusted (upwards or downwards) on a current basis, to reflect the "true" borrowing cost or interest income. The current accrual of exchange gain or loss on a borrowing is said to be necessary to properly allocate the additional "interest" to each year the borrowing is outstanding (to match income and expense).

The Congress was not persuaded that exchange gain or loss should be currently accrued in most cases. Because a right to receive (or an obligation to pay) foreign currency is not a right (or obligation) to receive (or pay) a fixed number of dollars, it would be problematical to require income inclusions (or permit deductions) due to exchange gain or loss that could be lost through subsequent exchange rate fluctuations.

The Secretary is authorized to prescribe rules for the current accrual of exchange gain or loss in certain hedging transactions. Further, although it was determined that the Secretary has adequate regulatory authority under the OID and below-market-loan rules to require the proper matching of income and expense on most foreign currency denominated loans (including any extension of credit), the Act grants additional regulatory authority to recharacterize interest and principal payments with respect to obligations denominated in hyperinflationary currencies (where use of the market rate of interest appropriate to the currency might result in a mismatching of income and expense).

Sourcing rules

Exchange gain on a financial asset or liability could be viewed as either foreign source (if ordinary in nature) or domestic source (if treated as capital gain and prior-law section 904(b)(3)(C) applied). The source of a loss on repayment was even less clear. Commentators suggested the following possibilities for allocating exchange losses: (1) exchange loss could be apportioned between domestic and foreign source income in the proportions that these amounts bear to each other in the aggregate, (2) an analogue to the "title passage" rule could apply to allocate losses to foreign source income, or (3) the loss could be allocated by reference to the source of the gain or loss from the underlying transaction.

The Congress determined that the overriding consideration should be to provide certainty regarding the source of exchange gain or loss. The Act accomplishes this result by providing definitive rules that are consistent with the treatment of foreign currency as personal property and the amendments to the sourcing rules in section [865]. In general, the Act requires the sourcing of exchange gains and the allocation of exchange losses by reference to the residence of the taxpayer or qualified business unit of the taxpayer on whose books the underlying transaction is properly reflected. For most U.S. taxpayers, this rule will result in the treatment of exchange gain or loss as domestic source or allocable thereto. This result reflects the fact that, in most cases, exchange gains realized by a U.S. taxpayer will not be subject to foreign tax. Moreover, this result will tend to neutralize the effect of exchange gain or loss on the calculation of foreign tax credits (unlike prior law, under which wide swings in exchange rates could result in unpredictable reductions in net foreign source income). Under regulations, exchange gain or loss on certain hedging transactions will be treated in a manner that is consistent with income or expense on the underlying transaction.

Under the separate transactions method, foreign currency gains are generally characterized as ordinary income, and deductible foreign currency losses are generally treated as ordinary losses. § 988(a)(1)(A). The rationale for such treatment is based partially on analogies to interest income or expense. However, foreign currency gain or loss is treated as actual interest income or expense only in limited circumstances prescribed in the regulations, such as in certain integrated hedging transactions. § 988(a)(2); Reg. § 1.988–5. Note that the foreign currency gain or loss on a Section 988 transaction is treated as ordinary in character regardless of the extent to which the foreign currency exchange rate fluctuations giving rise to the gain or loss are actually attributable to changes in interest rates rather than to some other factor such as changes in international trade flows. Is this treatment of foreign currency gain or loss as conclusively ordinary in character appropriate from a tax policy point of view?

The source of foreign currency gain or loss is generally determined by the residence of the taxpayer or the QBU on whose books the asset, liability or item of income or expense appears and not by the currency in respect of which the gain or loss has been realized. § 988(a)(3)(A). Residence, however, is specially defined for this purpose in Section 988(a)(3)(B).

An individual's residence is determined by the location of the individual's tax home as defined in Section 911(d)(3). The residence of a corporation, partnership, trust or estate is the United States if the entity qualifies as a U.S. person under Section 7701(a)(30); in other cases, the residence is outside the United States, except that the residence of a QBU is the country of its principal place of business. § 988(a)(3)(B); Reg. § 1.988–4(d)(1).

[¶ 9040]

3. RECEIPT OF INCOME IN FOREIGN CURRENCY

When income is received by a cash method taxpayer in the form of foreign currency, there is no need to apply special rules. Income under Section 61 is equal to the dollar value at the spot rate of the foreign currency at the time it is received. The character of the income item depends on the reason for its receipt. It would not usually constitute foreign currency gain.

When income is realized in a foreign currency by an accrual method taxpayer, the same principle applies at the time of the accrual. However, when the account receivable is in fact collected, the dollar value may differ from the amount accrued as income. Any difference between the amount reported as income and the dollar value of the foreign currency at the time it is collected will be treated as a foreign currency gain or loss (depending on the direction of change in the applicable exchange rates). § 988(c)(1)(B)(ii) and (c)(1)(C). In effect, the taxpayer is treated as being the obligor on a loan of the amount of the accrued income item. See ¶ 9080.

4. EXPENDITURES OF FOREIGN CURRENCY

[¶ 9045]

a. General Rules

All foreign currencies held by taxpayers for which the functional currency is the dollar will have adjusted bases determined at the time of acquisition. Suppose, for example, that Internaco, a U.S. corporation, acquires 10 million Norwegian kroner for $1 million. When exchange rates change and the dollar weakens against the krone, Internaco converts the 10 million kroner into $1.1 million. Internaco has realized a foreign currency gain of $100,000. § 988(c)(1)(C); Reg. § 1.988–2(a)(2)(i). If Internaco converts the 10 million kroner into $1.1 million worth of U.K. pounds, it will also realize a foreign currency gain of $100,000. The gain will not be treated as a like-kind exchange under Section 1031, and it will be recognized as ordinary income. Reg. § 1.988–2(a)(1)(ii).

The same result might obtain if Internaco spends its kroner for other property. Suppose that Internaco decides to acquire a building in Norway for the 10 million kroner. Because of changes in exchange rates, however, the 10 million kroner are worth $1.1 million at the time of purchase of the building. Internaco will have a foreign currency gain of $100,000. The adjusted basis of the building will be $1.1 million. If the value of the kroner at the time of the purchase of the building were only $900,000, Internaco would realize a foreign currency loss of $100,000 and the adjusted basis of the building would be $900,000. Reg. § 1.988–2(a)(2)(ii)(B).

[¶ 9050]

b. Treatment of Foreign Currency Received on Sale of Property

Consider the operation of the foreign currency rules if Internaco should subsequently dispose of the building. For purposes of simplicity, assume that Internaco never used the building and therefore took no depreciation deductions with respect to it. The basis is unchanged. Internaco sells the building for 10 million kroner, which are once again worth $1 million. If the adjusted basis were $900,000, Internaco would realize a gain of $100,000. Even though the gain is in fact attributable to variations in the foreign exchange rates (since the building is still worth 10 million kroner), it will not be characterized under the rules as foreign currency gain. The sale of the building is not a Section 988 transaction. The gain will be attributable to the investment in the building, potentially taxable as a capital gain rather than ordinary income.

If the adjusted basis of the building were $1.1 million, Internaco would realize a loss with respect to the building of $100,000. Even though the dollar value of the building had diminished solely as a result of a reduction in the value of the krone, the resulting loss would be treated as a loss on disposition of the building and not as a foreign currency loss.

The regulations provide that the IRS may recharacterize a transaction if the effect of the transaction is to avoid Section 988 or to create a Section 988 transaction where it is inappropriate. For example, a taxpayer with appreciated foreign currencies may transfer the currencies to a corporation in a nontaxable transaction under Section 351. While the sale of the currencies would have produced ordinary income, the sale of the stock might be a capital gain. The IRS could, therefore, challenge the taxpayer's characterization of the transaction. Reg. § 1.988–1(a)(11)(i), (ii), Ex.

[¶ 9055]

c. Adjusted Basis of Foreign Currency Bank Accounts

In the foregoing examples, the adjusted basis in dollars of the foreign currencies held by various taxpayers was easily ascertainable. If a taxpayer maintains a bank account in a foreign currency, the adjusted basis of a specific expenditure from the account is impossible to determine since there is no way to actually track the amounts deposited. The regulations allow the taxpayer to determine the adjusted basis "under any reasonable method that is consistently applied from year to year." Reg. § 1.988–2(a)(2)(iii)(B). Since the conceptual problem is very similar to that involved in typical inventory valuations, it is not surprising that the regulations explicitly authorize a first in-first out method, a last in-last out method or a pro-rata method.

[¶ 9060]

d. Accrual of Expenses in Foreign Currencies

When an accrual method taxpayer accrues a deductible expense, the amount of the deduction will be based on the exchange rate at the time of the accrual. If there is a modification of the exchange rate between then and the time when the expenditure is paid, foreign currency gain or loss will occur (i.e., the difference between the amount taken as a deduction and the dollar value of the foreign currency at the time it is paid). § 988(c)(1)(B)(ii). In effect, the taxpayer is treated as having borrowed the amount of the deduction item. See ¶ 9080.

[¶ 9065]

e. Foreign Currency for Personal Usage

Section 988(e) provides that the special statutory regime will not apply to individuals except in the trade or business or investment context. Reg. § 1.988–1(a)(9). When foreign exchange has been acquired for personal usage, translation is governed by case law and rulings.

Suppose that Ingrid travels to Egypt to celebrate her graduation from college. She spends $1,000 to acquire 8,000 Egyptian pounds (i.e., the exchange rate is $1 = 8 Egyptian pounds). During her trip, however, the exchange rate changes to $1 = 7 pounds. Would Ingrid realize gain every time she spends her Egyptian pounds? Conversely, if the rate should move in the other direction, say to $1 = 9 Egyptian pounds, would Ingrid realize a loss with every purchase? Happily for Ingrid and the workload of the IRS, such detailed accounts need not be maintained. Neither gain nor loss will be taken into account for federal tax purposes. See Reg. § 1.988–1(a)(9)(ii), Ex. 2. Suppose, however, that Ingrid returns to the United States with 1,000 Egyptian pounds. When she converts the pounds back into dollars, would she realize a gain or loss, depending on the direction that the exchange rate has moved? What is the amount and character of any resulting gain or loss? Is the gain taxable or the loss deductible?

As the following Revenue Ruling concludes, Ingrid would realize a foreign currency gain or loss on the conversion. However, under Section 988(e)(2), as added to the Code in 1997, an individual's exchange gain from the disposition of foreign currency in a "personal transaction" is not taxable provided that the gain on the transaction does not exceed $200. For this purpose, the statute defines the term "personal transaction" to mean any transaction other than one with respect to which properly allocable expenses are deductible as trade or business expenses under Section 162 or expenses incurred in the production or conservation of income under Section 212(1) or (2). The term "personal transaction" does, however, encompass an individual's foreign currency transactions entered into in connection with business travel deductible under Section 162(a)(2). Thus, if Ingrid has exchange gain of $200 or less on the conversion, the gain would not be taxable to her under Section 988(e)(2). By contrast, if Ingrid has an exchange gain of more than $200 on the conversion, her entire gain would be taxable in the manner provided in the Ruling below. What if Ingrid realizes a loss on the conversion transaction?

[¶ 9070]

REVENUE RULING 74–7

1974–1 C.B. 198.

* * *

The question presented is whether, after the conversion of United States dollars into foreign currency by a United States citizen traveling in the foreign country, the reconversion of the foreign currency into dollars may be treated as an exchange of property held for productive use in trade or business or for investment for property of a like kind to be held for productive use in trade or business or for investment, under section 1031 * * *. If not, the further question presented is whether the gain or loss realized on such a transaction by a taxpayer, who is not a dealer in foreign currency, constitutes capital gain or loss under section 1221 * * *.

The taxpayer, a United States citizen, while traveling in a foreign country deposited United States dollars in a bank in that country. At his request, the bank converted these dollars to that country's currency for the taxpayer's personal use. The taxpayer was not a dealer in foreign currency and was not engaged in trade or business in the foreign country. During his travels there were no transactions in the foreign bank account. At the conclusion of his stay, the taxpayer requested the bank to reconvert the foreign currency to dollars and close his account. The value of the foreign currency, measured in terms of dollars, differed at the time the account was closed from the value when the account was opened.

Section 1031(a) * * * provides, in part, that no gain or loss shall be recognized if property held for productive use in trade or business or for investment is exchanged solely for property of a like kind to be held either for productive use in trade or business or for investment.

In the instant case, the foreign currency does not constitute property held for productive use in trade or business or for investment, and therefore the reconversion is not a like kind exchange under section 1031(a) * * *.

Section 1221 * * * provides, in part, that the term "capital asset" means property held by the taxpayer, but does not include certain specified property. Section 1.1221–1(a) of the * * * Regulations provides, in part, that the term "capital assets" includes all classes of property not specifically excluded by section 1221.

In the instant case, the foreign currency is not excluded from the definition of capital assets contained in section 1221 * * *.

Accordingly, the foreign currency is a capital asset and any gain or loss realized on the reconversion by the taxpayer is a capital gain or capital loss.

* * *

[¶ 9075]

NOTES

1. As mentioned above, an individual who has exchange gain from a personal transaction in excess of the $200 limit in Section 988(e)(2) will continue to be taxed as provided in the Ruling. As a matter of tax policy, should gain from the conversion of foreign currency for personal usage be treated as taxable income?

2. The Ruling states that a loss on the foreign currency conversion would be a capital loss. But would the loss be deductible? Because such loss did not arise in a trade or business or income-producing activity, it is not deductible under Section 165 and is a nondeductible personal loss. By contrast, if the individual's foreign currency loss arises in a transaction with respect to which properly allocable expenses are deductible as trade or business expenses under Section 162 or expenses incurred in the production or conservation of income under Section 212(1) or (2), the loss would be deductible by the individual under Section 165. Note that the 1997 amendments to Section 988(e) did not change the treatment of losses arising from personal transactions involving foreign currency.

5. DEBT IN FOREIGN CURRENCY

[¶ 9080]

a. General Rules

When a taxpayer for whom the dollar is the functional currency lends or borrows in another currency, interest income or deductions (if any) will depend on the applicable exchange rate at the time of payment or accrual. However, as in the example cited at the beginning of the Chapter, there may be a gain or loss realized when the principal is repaid. The transaction is a Section 988 transaction, and the gain or loss is treated as foreign currency gain or loss. Because such gain or loss is treated as ordinary, the rule in effect either increases or reduces the effective costs paid or income received in connection with the transaction. Foreign currency gains and losses are not, however, treated as interest as such except in limited situations. Reg. § 1.988–3(c)(1). For example, under Reg. § 1.988–3(c)(2), foreign currency losses in respect of debt on which interest would be exempt under Section 103 are treated as an offset to the interest and are not, therefore, deductible.

Another issue concerns whether a debtor-taxpayer's gain from a loan in foreign currency can qualify as discharge-of-indebtedness income for Section 108 purposes. In Philip Morris Inc. v. Commissioner, 104 T.C. 61, aff'd, 71 F.3d 1040 (2d Cir.1995), cert. denied, 517 U.S. 1220 (1996), the taxpayer had obtained a loan in foreign currency and repaid it with fewer U.S. dollars. It contended that the resulting profit was income from the discharge of indebtedness entitled to the deferral benefits of Section 108. The Tax Court and the Second Circuit rejected the taxpayer's argument and held that the profit was foreign currency gain to which Section 108 did not apply. Although this case arose under pre–1986 Act law, the result should be the same under Section 988 of current law.

[¶ 9085]

b. Foreign Currency Debt for the Acquisition or Sale of Personal Use Property

Where foreign currency debt has been established in connection with the acquisition or sale of personal use property, several of the rules reflected in this Chapter may have to be applied to different elements of the transaction, as reflected in the following Revenue Ruling.

[¶ 9090]

REVENUE RULING 90–79

1990–2 C.B. 187.

ISSUE

Can an individual U.S. citizen offset the gain (or loss) realized from the sale of a personal residence with a loss (or gain) realized from the repayment of a nonfunctional currency denominated mortgage loan used to finance the purchase of the residence?

FACTS

In 1986 *A*, an individual U.S. citizen, purchased property in country *X* that *A* used exclusively as a personal residence. The purchase price was 95,000*y*. *A* financed the purchase with a loan of 85,000*y* when $1 equalled 1*y*, and 10,000*y* cash payment. In 1989 *A* sold the personal residence for 142,500*y*, and used 85,000*y* of the sale proceeds to repay the outstanding principal balance of the mortgage. At the time of the sale and repayment, $1 equaled .95*y*.

A's basis in the personal residence is $95,000 (95,000*y* at $1 equals 1*y*). The amount realized upon the sale of the residence is $150,000 (142,500*y* at $1 equals .95*y*); therefore, *A* realizes a gain of $55,000 ($150,000 − $95,000).

A's functional currency under section 985(b)(1) * * * is the United States dollar (dollar). The *y* is a nonfunctional currency with respect to *A*. None of the expenses incurred by *A* in connection with the purchase, financing, or sale of the personal residence were deductible under section 162 (relating to trade or business expenses) or section 212(1) or (2) (relating to expenses for the production of income).

LAW AND ANALYSIS

Section 985(a) * * * generally provides that all income tax determinations shall be made in a taxpayer's functional currency. An individual may have a qualified business unit (QBU) that has a non-dollar functional currency. *See* section 1.989(a)–1(b) of the * * * Regulations. However, an activity that does not generate expenses that are deductible under either section 162 or section 212(1) or (2) does not qualify as a QBU. *See* section 1.989(a)–1(c) of the regulations. Therefore, *A* must make all income tax determinations with respect to the purchase, financing, and sale of the personal residence in the dollar.

Section 988 * * * provides rules for the treatment of "section 988 transactions" including becoming an obligor under a mortgage. Section 988(c)(1)(B)(i). However, under section 988(e), the rules of section 988 apply to a transaction entered into by an individual only to the extent expenses allocable to the transaction meets the requirements of section 162 or section 212(1) or (2). Because there are no expenses properly allocable to the mortgage that meet the requirements of either section 162 or section 212(1) or (2), the rules of section 988 do not apply to *A*'s becoming an obligor under the mortgage. Therefore, the law predating section 988 governs. *See* S. Rep. No. 99–313, 99th Cong., 2d Sess. 468–69 (1986) * * *.

Under the law predating section 988, the borrowing and repayment of the mortgage loan is a separate transaction from the purchase and sale of the personal residence. * * * The repayment of the mortgage by *A* constitutes a closed, and therefore, taxable transaction. * * *

Since the *y* increased in value against the dollar between the time *A*'s liability was fixed (at the time of the borrowing) and the time *A* repaid the loan, the amount of dollars required to retire the debt exceeded the dollar value of the amount originally borrowed. Therefore, *A* realized a loss on the loan repayment. The amount of the loss is $4,474. (The dollar value of 85,000*y* borrowed: $85,000, less the dollar value of 85,000*y* used to repay the loan: $89,474.)

Section 165(a) * * * provides generally that a deduction shall be allowed for losses sustained during a taxable year and not compensated for by insurance or otherwise. Section 165(c) limits the loss deduction for individuals to losses incurred in a trade or business, losses incurred in any transaction entered into for profit, and casualty losses. Thus, an individual is not allowed to deduct all realized losses. *See Billman v. Commissioner*, 73 T.C. 139 (1979), where the Tax Court denied an individual a loss resulting from the devaluation of a foreign currency.

A's loss was not incurred in an activity or as the result of an event described in section 165(c) * * *. Therefore *A* may not deduct the $4,474 realized loss. Similarly, if *A* had realized a loss on the sale of the personal residence and a gain on the repayment of the mortgage, *A* could not deduct the loss.

HOLDING

An individual may not offset the gain (or loss) realized from the sale of a personal residence with a loss (or gain) realized on the repayment of a nonfunctional currency denominated mortgage loan used to finance the purchase of the residence.

* * *

[¶ 9095]

NOTES

1. Is the holding in the last paragraph of Revenue Ruling 90–79 consistent with the general premises of Section 988? If so, on what rationale?

2. In Quijano v. United States, 93 F.3d 26 (1st Cir.1996), cert. denied, 519 U.S. 1059 (1997), the taxpayers had purchased a U.K. personal residence in 1986, financed through a mortgage loan in pounds sterling. They made capital improvements to the residence, which they paid in pounds sterling. In 1990, they sold the residence for pounds sterling and paid off the mortgage loan. The exchange rate was one pound sterling = $1.49 at the time of purchase, but was one pound sterling = $1.82 at the time of sale. The taxpayers attempted to compute both their adjusted basis in the residence and their amount realized on the sale by using the exchange rate in effect when the house was sold, thus reducing the amount of their capital gain on the sale of the residence by the loss on the mortgage loan transaction due to the decline in the value of the dollar. The First Circuit, however, upheld the position of the IRS that the borrowing and repayment on the mortgage loan were a separate transaction from the purchase and sale of the personal residence. Moreover, since the foreign exchange loss on the mortgage loan transaction was not incurred in a trade or business or other profit-making activity, it was not deductible under Section 165.

Because the taxpayers' functional currency was the U.S. dollar, in determining their capital gain on the sale of the residence, they had to compute their adjusted cost basis for the residence by using the exchange rates in effect when they purchased it and made improvements to it and their amount realized by using the exchange rate in effect when they sold it. The court rejected the taxpayers' argument that the pound sterling was their functional currency for the personal residence, reasoning that the purchase and sale of the residence was not carried out by a "qualified business unit," within the meaning of Section 985(b)(1).

[¶ 9100]

6. FOREIGN CURRENCY CONTRACTS

Section 988(c)(1)(B)(iii) treats as a Section 988 transaction the entering into or acquiring of "any forward contract, futures contract, option, or similar financial instrument." There are, however, several circumstances in which the normal Section 988 transaction rules will not be applied to such property.

If a regulated foreign currency futures contract or nonequity option is subject to the requirements of Section 1256 (which generally require marking to market and recognition of gain or loss each year), Section 988 will not apply unless the taxpayer so elects. Absent such an election, the character of such gains and losses will depend on general tax principles and may, therefore, be treated as capital gain or loss. § 988(c)(1)(D)(i). Further, Section 988 will not apply to instruments marked to market under Section 1256 that are held by certain "qualified funds," which are partnerships established to deal in "options, futures, or forwards with respect to commodities." § 988(c)(1)(E). Such instruments will be subject to the normal rules under Section 1256.

Special rules are also provided with respect to "Section 988 hedging transactions." To the extent provided in Reg. § 1.988–5, such transactions are "integrated and treated as a single transaction" with the underlying transaction being hedged. § 988(d). Foreign currency gains or losses in such situations are, accordingly, merged with the results of the underlying transaction, the nature of which will normally determine the character and source of the overall gain or loss.

A hedging transaction is one in which the taxpayer seeks primarily to reduce the risk of currency fluctuations with respect to property held or to be held by the taxpayer or with respect to borrowing or lending made or to be made by the taxpayer. Hedging transactions must, however, be identified as such to the IRS when they are initiated. § 988(d)(2)(A). A taxpayer cannot await the result of the transaction and then decide whether it is to be treated under the hedging rules. § 988(d)(2)(B).

The following excerpt from Staff of Joint Comm. on Tax'n, 100th Cong., 1st Sess., General Explanation of the Tax Reform Act of 1986, at 1102–03 (1987), explains the hedging rules:

> The Act authorizes the issuance of regulations that address the treatment of transactions that are part of a section 988 hedging transaction. The Congress included this regulatory authority to provide certainty of tax treatment for foreign currency hedging transactions that are fast becoming commonplace (such as fully hedged foreign currency borrowings) and to insure that such a transaction is taxed in accordance with its economic substance. No inference is intended as to the proper treatment of these transactions under prior law. A section 988 hedging transaction includes certain transactions entered into primarily to reduce the risk of (1) foreign currency exchange rate fluctuations with respect to property held or to be held by the taxpayer, or (2) foreign currency fluctuations with respect to borrowings or obligations of the taxpayer. A section 988 hedging transaction is to be identified by the taxpayer or the Secretary.
>
> To the extent provided in regulations, in the case of any transaction giving rise to foreign currency gain or loss that is part of a section 988 hedging transaction (determined without regard to whether any position in the hedge would be marked to market under section 1256), all positions in the hedging transaction are integrated and treated as a single transaction, or otherwise treated consistently (e.g., for purposes of characterizing the nature of income or the sourcing rules). The Congress intends that these regulations address two different categories of hedging transactions.
>
> The first category is a narrow class of fully hedged transactions that are part of an integrated economic package through which the taxpayer (by simultaneously combining a bundle of financial rights and obligations) has assured itself of a cash flow that will not vary with movements in exchange rates. With respect to this category, the

Congress intends that such rights and obligations be integrated and treated as a single transaction with respect to that taxpayer. For example, in the case of a fully hedged foreign currency borrowing, a taxpayer with the dollar as its functional currency will borrow foreign currency and hedge its exposure by entering into a series of forward purchase contracts or a single swap agreement.

The forward contracts or swap agreement will assure the taxpayer of a stream of foreign currency flows to make interest and principal payments with respect to the foreign currency borrowing. The taxpayer, although it has borrowed foreign currency, is not at risk with respect to currency fluctuations because it has locked in the dollar cost of its future foreign currency requirements. The Congress intends that regulations treat the entire package as a dollar borrowing with dollar interest payments with respect to the borrower. This integration approach is not limited to U.S. dollar denominated transactions; thus, the rules also apply where several transactions are entered into by a U.S. dollar functional-currency taxpayer to establish a foreign currency position.

In the case of a foreign currency borrowing hedged with a series of forward purchase contracts, the rules of section 1271, *et seq.* and 163(e) shall apply in determining the appropriate interest deduction. The Congress intends that similar rules apply to synthetic dollar securities (e.g., a transaction in which a taxpayer with the dollar as its functional currency purchases a foreign currency denominated debt obligation and sells forward all interest and principal payments to assure itself a stream of fixed dollar flows). The regulations pertaining to integrated hedging transactions will be restricted to transactions that are, in substance, equivalent to a transaction denominated in the taxpayer's functional currency or a nonfunctional currency.

The second category of hedging transactions involves transactions that are not entered into as an integrated financial package but are designed to limit a taxpayer's exposure in a particular currency (e.g., the acquisition of a foreign currency denominated liability to offset exposure with regard to a foreign currency denominated asset). These regulations need not provide for complete integration (e.g., the form of a foreign currency borrowing may be respected and the interest deduction determined by reference to the spot rate on the date of payment). Where appropriate, these regulations should provide for consistent treatment with respect to character, source, and timing.

The Congress intends that both sets of regulations relating to hedging transactions provide rules to prevent taxpayers from selectively identifying only those transactions where the hedging rules are favorable to the taxpayer. * * *

[¶ 9105]

PROBLEMS

1. National Exporters is a U.S. corporation that sells throughout Europe but has no branches in any other country. National Exporters uses the accrual method of tax accounting. During year 1, the corporation began to export to Japan. It opened a bank account with a Tokyo bank into which sales proceeds in Japanese yen were deposited. During year 1, there were three major transactions with Japanese customers. In January (when $1 = 130 yen), the corporation accrued sales income of 1.3 million yen. In June (when $1 = 140 yen), the corporation accrued sales income of 1.4 million yen. In September (when $1 = 150 yen), the corporation accrued sales income of 1.5 million yen. Payment in respect of the January and June sales was received almost immediately and was deposited in the Tokyo account before any change in the exchange rate. When payment was received for the September sales, the exchange rate was $1 = 135 yen. The only expenditures from the account were 360,000 yen paid in November (when $1 = 120 yen) to cover costs of a trip to Japan by the president of the corporation to meet with prospective customers. On December 31 of year 1, $1 = 100 yen. Determine the U.S. income tax consequences for National Exporters as a result of the foregoing events.

2. In year 1 (when $1 = 200 Russian rubles), Emilio, a U.S. citizen, borrowed two million rubles. He repaid the loan in year 5, when $1 = 100 rubles. How much foreign currency gain or loss has Emilio realized?

3. Assume that Emilio used the two million rubles to purchase a house in year 1. The loan was secured by a mortgage on the house. In year 5, Emilio sold the house for four million rubles and repaid the loan when $1 = 100 rubles. He kept the remaining two million rubles in a Russian bank. Assuming that Emilio held the house as rental property, what are the U.S. income tax consequences of all of the events? How would your answer change if Emilio used the house as his principal residence? (Ignore the impact of any depreciation deductions taken in respect of the house.)

4. How would your answers in Problems 2 and 3 be affected if the exchange rate in year 5 were $1 = 400 rubles?

5. New York Imports ("Imports"), a Delaware corporation, has its office in Manhattan and imports foreign goods for resale in the United States. It keeps its books in dollars. In July of year 1, it ordered a shipment of artificial flowers from an Argentine supplier on credit for 30,000 Argentine pesos, payable January 30 of year 2. The flowers duly arrived in September and were sold to customers in October at a profit. Through November of year 1, the exchange rate of the Argentine peso was $1 = 3 Argentine pesos. On December 1, the Argentine peso was devalued to $1 = 4 Argentine pesos. On January 30 of year 2, Imports paid its debt for the flowers having that day purchased the 30,000 Argentine pesos for $7,500. How does Imports figure its cost for the flowers and consequently its income from sale of the flowers in

year 1? It paid 30,000 pesos. Is its cost $10,000 ($1 = 3 pesos)? Or $7,500 ($1 = 4 pesos)? Assuming its cost is $10,000, does Import have taxable income upon payment of the debt on January 30 of year 2?

6. Kate, a U.S. citizen and an attorney, takes a vacation in Denmark. When she arrives in Denmark, she spends $1,000 for 5,000 Danish kroner. She spends all of the kroner during her holiday except for 500 kroner that she keeps as a souvenir. As she arrives at the airport to catch her flight home, she learns that the Government of Denmark has taken action to reduce the value of the krone so that $1 = 10 kroner. Are there any U.S. income tax consequences of the foregoing events for Kate? What if she converts her remaining kroner for $50? Would either answer change if Kate were on a business trip to Denmark to consult with a ship-owning client?

7. How would your answers in Problem 6 change if Kate had paid $1,000 for 20,000 Danish kroner when she arrived in Denmark (i.e., $1 = 20 kroner), spent only 12,000 kroner during her holiday in Denmark and converted her remaining 8,000 kroner at the end of the trip for $800 (i.e., the value of the krone had increased to $1 = 10 kroner)?

8. How would your answers in Problem 6 change if Kate paid $1,000 for 20,000 Danish kroner when she arrived in Denmark, spent 18,000 kroner during her holiday in Denmark and converted her remaining 2,000 kroner at the end of the trip for $200?

9. International Factories, Inc. is a U.S. corporation that contracts to construct complete factories in developing countries. It has no foreign branches. In year 1, the corporation entered into a contract to construct a complete textile factory in Thailand for 300 million Thai baht. At that time, the exchange rate was $1 = 30 baht. Immediately upon concluding the contract, the corporation purchased, at a cost of $100,000, a currency contract entitling it to purchase $10 million in year 3 for 300 million baht. In year 3 (when the exchange rate was $1 = 40 baht), the factory was completed. The corporation received 300 million baht, which it immediately converted to $10 million under the currency contract. The factory cost $8 million to construct. What are the U.S. income tax consequences of the foregoing events?

D. PROFIT AND LOSS METHOD

[¶ 9110]

1. GENERAL DESCRIPTION

The principal alternative to the separate transactions method is the profit and loss method. The basic approach here is to apply conversion rules to the net results of operating in foreign currencies over time. The primary situations in which the profit and loss method is applied are in the measure of income from a foreign branch that is a QBU with a foreign functional currency and the determination of the tax consequences resulting from actual dividend distributions by foreign subsidiaries with foreign functional currencies to U.S. corporations (see Chapter 5) and from constructive dividends (i.e., inclusions under Section 951(a)(1)(A) or 951(a)(1)(B) of Subpart F, deemed dividends on the sale or exchange of stock of a controlled foreign corporation under Section 1248 or qualified electing fund inclusions under Section 1293 of the PFIC rules) deemed distributed by foreign corporations that use foreign functional currencies (see Chapter 6).

[¶ 9115]

2. BRANCH TRANSACTIONS

Section 987 prescribes the regime for dealing with a foreign branch that is a QBU using a foreign functional currency. The basic approach is to determine profit or loss of the foreign branch for the tax year in its functional currency and then to translate the profit or loss at the "appropriate exchange rate." § 987. The appropriate exchange rate generally is the average exchange rate for the tax year. § 989(b)(4).

The proposed regulations under Section 987 were substantially revised in 2006. See Prop. Reg. §§ 1.987–1 through–10. The 2006 version of the proposed regulations adopted the "foreign exchange exposure pool" method for calculating the taxable income of a branch. REG–208270–86, 2006–2 C.B. 698, 699–715, summarized these proposed regulations and explained the rationale for the major changes from an earlier set of proposed regulations, as follows:

> [*1. Overview and summary.*]
>
> * * * In general, the foreign exchange exposure pool method provides that the income of a QBU that is subject to section 987 ("section 987 QBU") is determined by reference to the items of income, gain, deduction and loss booked to the QBU in its functional currency, adjusted to reflect U.S. tax principles. With certain exceptions, items of income, gain, deduction and loss of a section 987 QBU are translated into the functional currency of the QBU's owner at the average exchange rate for the year. However, the basis of historic assets and deductions for depreciation, depletion, and amortization of such assets are translated at the historic exchange rate. Translating these items at the historic exchange rate differs from the approach taken in the 1991 proposed regulations, which instead uses the average exchange rate. Although using the average exchange rate for translating such items might be simpler than using the historic exchange rate, it leads to the generation of non-economic foreign currency gains or losses * * *.
>
> The foreign exchange exposure pool method uses a balance sheet approach to determine exchange gain or loss, which is then recognized upon a remittance. Use of a balance sheet approach allows taxpayers and the IRS to distinguish between those items whose value fluctuates with respect to changes in the functional currency of the owner

and those which do not. Under this method, exchange gain or loss with respect to "marked items" is identified annually but is pooled and deferred until a remittance is made. The IRS and the Treasury Department believe that section 988(c) identifies the items that should be treated as giving rise to exchange gain or loss for purposes of section 987. Accordingly, a marked item is generally defined as an asset or liability that would generate section 988 gain or loss if such asset or liability were held or entered into directly by the owner the section 987 QBU.

When a section 987 QBU makes a remittance, a portion of the pooled and deferred exchange gain or loss is recognized. In general, the amount taken into account is an amount equal to the product of the owner's portion of the section 987 QBU's net unrecognized exchange gain or loss, multiplied by the owner's remittance proportion. The owner's remittance proportion generally is equal to the quotient of the amount of the remittance, divided by the aggregate basis of the section 987 QBU's gross assets (as reflected on its year-end balance sheet), without reduction for the remittance.

The source and character of exchange gain or loss recognized under section 987 for all purposes of the Code, including sections 904(d), 907 and 954, is determined by reference to the source and character of the income derived from the section 987 QBU's assets. [Section 987 gain or loss continues to be treated as ordinary income or loss. See Prop. Reg. § 1.987–6(a).]

The IRS and the Treasury Department believe that the foreign exchange exposure pool method is consistent with section 987 and legislative intent for several reasons. First, the foreign exchange exposure pool method uses a profit and loss statement to determine the items of income, gain, deduction and loss of a section 987 QBU in its functional currency. This allows proper characterization of items of income, gain, deduction and loss. Second, exchange gain or loss must be taken into account only with respect to items of branch capital and earnings whose value fluctuates with changes in exchange rates by reference to the owner's functional currency. This comports both with Congressional intent that taxpayers recognize exchange gain or loss (but only economic exchange gain or loss) inherent in branch capital and branch earnings and with authority granted under section 987(3) to identify appropriate translation rates. Third, exchange gain or loss is recognized under section 987 only upon a remittance. Finally, the foreign exchange exposure pool method is an appropriate interpretation of the "blended" approach of section 987—that is, it incorporates certain aspects of the profit and loss method and the net worth method.

2. *Taxpayers subject to section 987 and related definitions.*

The IRS and the Treasury Department believe that section 987 should only apply where an individual or corporation (whether foreign or domestic) has activities that constitute a trade or business under § 1.989(a)–1(c) and the trade or business has a functional currency different from the individual or corporation. In such cases, the individual or corporation will be subject to the rules of the proposed regulations if the individual or corporation is the owner of a section 987 QBU. A section 987 QBU is defined in § 1.987–1(b)(2) as an eligible QBU that has a functional currency different from its owner.

An eligible QBU is defined in § 1.987–1(b)(3) of the proposed regulations. Generally, an eligible QBU is an activity of an individual, corporation, partnership or DE [disregarded entity under the check-the-box regulations] that is a trade or business as defined in § 1.989(a)–1(c); maintains separate books and records as defined in § 1.989(a)–1(d) and assets and liabilities used in conducting such activities are reflected on such books and records; and the activities are not subject to the dollar approximate separate transaction (DASTM) rules of § 1.985–3. A corporation is not an eligible QBU. An individual is not a QBU under § 1.989(a)–1(b)(2)(i) and therefore cannot be an eligible QBU. In addition, and as discussed in this preamble, neither a partnership nor a DE is an eligible QBU.

In the case of ownership other than through a partnership (that is, direct ownership), the individual or corporation is treated as the owner of an eligible QBU if the individual or corporation is the tax owner of the assets and liabilities of the eligible QBU. For purposes of determining direct ownership, an individual or corporation will be treated as a direct owner of the assets and liabilities of an eligible QBU if it owns a DE that holds an eligible QBU. In such case, because the DE is not recognized as a separate entity, it cannot be a QBU under section 989 and, therefore, is not treated as an eligible QBU under the proposed regulations. However, the activities of the DE, which are treated for purposes of the Code as carried on directly by its owner, can qualify as an eligible QBU of the DE's owner.

* * *

* * * [T]he proposed regulations provide that for purposes of applying the foreign exchange exposure pool method each individual or corporation that is a partner in a partnership will be considered to own indirectly an eligible QBU consisting of a portion of the assets and liabilities of the partnership allocated to it under § 1.987–7. If such eligible QBU has a different functional currency from the partner and therefore is a section 987 QBU, the foreign exchange exposure pool method is applied with respect to those assets and liabilities. In addition, the proposed regulations provide rules for converting the items of section 987 taxable income or loss of a section 987 QBU into the functional currency of the partner (when neces-

sary), and rules coordinating this aggregate approach with other provisions of subchapter K.

* * *

3. De minimis rule for certain indirectly owned section 987 QBUs.

The IRS and the Treasury Department recognize that it may be administratively burdensome for taxpayers to apply certain aspects of the proposed regulations to section 987 QBUs indirectly owned through relatively small interests in partnerships. As a result, the proposed regulations provide a de minimis election for certain indirectly owned section 987 QBUs. Under this rule, an individual or corporation that owns a section 987 QBU indirectly through a partnership may elect not to take into account the section 987 gain or loss of such section 987 QBU, provided such individual or corporation owns, directly or indirectly, less than five percent of the section 987 partnership. Constructive ownership rules apply for purposes of determining whether the less than five percent ownership threshold is satisfied.

This de minimis exception only applies to recognition of section 987 gain or loss with respect to a section 987 QBU. Thus, owners of section 987 QBUs that qualify under the de minimis exception must comply with all other aspects of the proposed regulations, including the requirement to take into account the section 987 taxable income or loss with respect to such section 987 QBUs.

* * *

4. Exchange rates.

Section 1.987–1(c)(1)(i) defines the spot rate as the rate determined under the principles of § 1.988–1(d)(1), (2) and (4) on the relevant day. Section 1.987–1(c)(1)(ii) allows taxpayers to elect to use spot rate conventions that reasonably approximate the spot rate on a particular day. It is anticipated that taxpayers will be able to conform the spot rate convention for section 987 to the spot rate conventions used under FAS 52 for financial accounting purposes. This is intended to simplify the calculations required under section 987.

In a similar attempt to simplify calculations, § 1.987–1(c)(2) defines the yearly average exchange rate as an average exchange rate for the taxable year computed under any reasonable method that is consistently applied.

Finally, § 1.987–1(c)(3) defines the historic exchange rate by reference to the spot rate on the day that assets are transferred to (or acquired by) the section 987 QBU, or on the day that liabilities are assumed (or entered into) by the section 987 QBU. The reference to the spot rate as defined in § 1.987–1(c)(1)(i) and (ii) allows taxpayers to elect to use spot rate conventions for these purposes.

5. Definitions of a section 987 marked item and a section 987 historic item.

The definitions of a section 987 marked item and a section 987 historic item are central to the foreign exchange exposure pool method. When taken into account in the context of the calculation of net unrecognized section 987 gain or loss under § 1.987–4, the definitions distinguish those items that generate section 987 gain or loss from those that do not. The IRS and the Treasury Department believe that section 988 identifies those items properly treated as giving rise to exchange gain or loss for purposes of section 987. Thus, a marked item as defined in § 1.987–1(d) is an asset or liability reflected on the books and records of the section 987 QBU that both (1) would generate section 988 gain or loss if held or entered into directly by the owner of the section 987 QBU and (2) is not a section 988 transaction to the section 987 QBU. It is important to exclude section 988 transactions of a section 987 QBU because section 988 already requires the section 987 QBU to recognize gain or loss from such transactions. Thus, treating such transactions as marked items for purposes of section 987 would result in double counting. Marked items give rise to exchange gain or loss under section 987. Historic items, which are defined in § 1.987–1(e) as items other than marked items, do not give rise to exchange gain or loss under section 987.

* * *

B. Section 1.987–2 Attribution of Items to an Eligible QBU; the Definition of a Transfer, and Related Rules.

1. Attribution of items to an eligible QBU.

i. Overview.

A section 987 QBU is not itself a taxpayer and does not have its own taxable income. Items of income, gain, deduction and loss must nonetheless be attributed to such section 987 QBU for purposes of determining the owner's taxable income. The items of income, gain, deduction and loss attributed to a section 987 QBU are generally determined in the functional currency of the section 987 QBU and then translated into the functional currency of the owner. The aggregate translated amount is the section 987 taxable income or loss of the section 987 QBU. Thus, attribution rules are necessary to determine which items of income, gain, deduction and loss are attributed to the section 987 QBU.

Under section 987(3), assets and liabilities must be attributed to a section 987 QBU in order to determine the amount of section 987 gain or loss of such QBU. In some cases, a section 987 QBU of a taxpayer will not be held through an entity separate from the taxpayer that can legally own assets and incur liabilities. In addition, not all the assets and liabilities of an entity that is separate from the taxpayer may be attributable to a section 987 QBU for purposes of section 987. Moreover, assets and liabilities may constitute a section 987 QBU of a taxpayer even when such assets and liabilities are owned or incurred by separate legal entities. As a result, assets and liabilities of the taxpayer (or of entities owned by the taxpayer that are not themselves taxpayers) must be attributed to the section 987 QBU.

Neither section 987 nor the underlying legislative history provides explicit rules for attributing a taxpayer's items of income, gain, deduction, or loss to a section 987 QBU to determine the QBU's section 987 taxable income or loss. Similarly, no explicit rules are provided in the statute or legislative history for attributing a taxpayer's assets or liabilities to a section 987 QBU to determine the section 987 gain or loss of such QBU.

* * *

ii. Books and records method—general rule.

* * *

* * * [T]he proposed regulations adopt a books and records method for allocating items to an eligible QBU. The proposed regulations provide that, subject to certain exceptions, items are attributable to an eligible QBU to the extent they are reflected on the separate set of books and records of such eligible QBU, as defined in § 1.989(a)–1(d). The proposed regulations make clear that these rules apply solely for purposes of section 987. Thus, for example, the attribution rules contained in the proposed regulations do not apply for purposes of allocating and apportioning interest expense under section 864(e).

iii. Exception for non-portfolio stock, interests in partnerships and certain acquisition indebtedness.

As discussed above, the IRS and the Treasury Department believe that the assets and liabilities reflected on the books and records of an eligible QBU are a reasonable approximation of the assets and liabilities that are used in the trade or business of the eligible QBU and, therefore, should be taken into account for purposes of section 987. However, the IRS and the Treasury Department believe that certain assets and liabilities should not be attributed to an eligible QBU, even if such assets and liabilities are reflected on the books and records of such QBU. The IRS and the Treasury Department believe that non-portfolio stock and interests in partnerships (and liabilities to acquire such assets), even if reflected on the books and records of the eligible QBU, should not be attributed to such QBU for purposes of section 987. This is consistent with the principle stated above that a section 987 QBU cannot be an owner of another section 987 QBU. Excluding non-portfolio stock is also consistent with the principle that non-portfolio stock cannot be used in, or held for the use in, the conduct of a trade or business in the United States. See § 1.864–4(c)(2)(iii).

As a result, the proposed regulations provide that stock of a corporation (whether domestic or foreign) and an interest in a partnership (whether domestic or foreign) are not considered to be on the books and records of an eligible QBU. The proposed regulations provide an exception, however, for portfolio stock where the owner of the eligible QBU owns (directly or constructively) less than ten percent of the total voting power or value of the stock of such corporation. The proposed regulations also provide that indebtedness incurred to acquire stock or a partnership interest that is not treated as being reflected on the books and records of an eligible QBU should similarly be excluded from the books and records. Finally, the proposed regulations provide that items of income, gain, deduction and loss arising from ownership of stock, a partnership interest, or related acquisition indebtedness that is excluded from the general books and records rule, shall similarly not be treated as being on the books and records of the eligible QBU.

* * *

3. Definition of a transfer.

* * *

The definition of a transfer under the proposed regulations includes transactions that are regarded for both legal and tax purposes, and transactions that are regarded for legal purposes, but disregarded as transactions for tax purposes (''disregarded transactions''). For this purpose, the term disregarded transaction is treated as including the recording of an asset or liability on one set of books and records, if the recording is the result of such asset or liability being removed from another set of books and records of the same person or entity (including a DE or partnership).

The proposed regulations provide that an asset or liability is treated as transferred to or from a section 987 QBU if, as a result of a disregarded transaction, such asset or liability is reflected, or is not reflected, respectively, on the books and records of the section 987 QBU. For example, if an owner of a section 987 DE loans cash to the section 987 QBU held by the section 987 DE, the loan is disregarded for Federal income tax purposes. However, as a result of such disregarded transaction, the loaned cash is reflected on the books and records of the section 987 QBU and, therefore, is treated as transferred to such section 987 QBU.

* * *

v. Change in form of ownership.

* * *

The IRS and the Treasury Department believe that changes in form of ownership should result in a transfer only to the extent such change affects the assets and liabilities attributable to the section 987 QBU of the owner. As a result, the proposed regulations provide that a mere change in form of ownership of a section 987 QBU does not result in a transfer to or from the section 987 QBU. Instead, the proposed regulations provide that the determination of whether a transfer has occurred in such cases should be made under the general transfer rules, discussed above. * * *

vi. General tax law principles.

The proposed regulations clarify that general tax law principles, including the circular cash flow, step-transaction, and substance-over-form doctrines apply for purposes of determining whether there is a transfer of an asset or liability to or from a QBU. For example, if a shareholder of a corporation that directly owns a section 987 QBU transfers property to the corporation and the property is recorded on the books and records of the corporation's section 987 QBU, the shareholder is first treated as transferring the property to the corporation, and then the corporation is treated as transferring the property to the section 987 QBU in a disregarded transaction.

* * *

5. Translation of items transferred to a section 987 QBU.

The proposed regulations provide translation rules for the transfer of assets and liabilities to a section 987 QBU. Under the proposed regulations, if an asset or a liability is transferred to a section 987 QBU, such items are translated into the QBU's functional currency at the spot rate on the day of transfer. No translation is required for assets or liabilities denominated in the functional currency of the section 987 QBU.

The proposed regulations provide special rules for items transferred to a section 987 QBU where such items are denominated in (or determined by reference to) the owner's functional currency. Such items are not translated and instead are carried on the balance sheet in the owner's functional currency since no foreign currency exposure with respect to the owner is created by such items.

* * *

C. Section 1.987–3 Determination of the items of section 987 taxable income or loss of an owner of a section 987 QBU.

In general, the term "section 987 taxable income" refers to the items of income, gain, deduction or loss attributed to the section 987

QBU under § 1.987–2(b), translated into the functional currency of the owner. The allocation of expenses such as interest under other provisions are not taken into account for this purpose. Section 987 taxable income is calculated by determining each item of income, gain, deduction or loss in the section 987 QBU's functional currency under § 1.987–3(a), and then translating those items into the owner's functional currency using the exchange rates provided in § 1.987–3(b). Items of income, gain, deduction or loss of a section 987 QBU that are denominated in (or determined by reference to) the functional currency of the owner are not translated and are not treated as section 988 transactions to the section 987 QBU. Transactions denominated in (or determined by reference to) a currency that is neither the functional currency of the owner nor of the section 987 QBU are subject to the generally applicable rules under section 988 determined with respect to the functional currency of the section 987 QBU.

When basis recovery is required with respect to an historic asset, either in computing gain or loss on the sale or exchange of such asset, or in determining cost recovery deductions (such as depreciation or depletion), the proposed regulations require the use of the historical exchange rate associated with the particular asset. Thus, for example, where a section 987 QBU sells an historic asset, the amount realized will be translated into the owner's functional currency using the yearly average exchange rate (or, if properly elected, the spot rate), but the adjusted basis will be translated using the historic exchange rate associated with that asset. The use of different exchange rates for amount realized and adjusted basis is designed to more closely reflect the economic gain or loss to the owner of the section 987 QBU than the 1991 proposed regulations. The same is true for depreciation or other cost recovery deductions that are claimed with respect to historic assets of a section 987 QBU.

Special translation rules are provided with respect to the disposition of marked assets (other than functional currency cash of the section 987 QBU). Generally, the amount realized and basis are translated at the same exchange rates. The purpose of these special rules is to assure that foreign currency gain or loss (as opposed to gain or loss not related to movements in exchange rates) is reflected through the balance sheet calculations of § 1.987–4 and not through the profit and loss calculations of § 1.987–3. Cash is not included in these special rules because the disposition of cash cannot generate profit or loss to the section 987 QBU for purposes of § 1.987–3.

D. Section 1.987–4 Determination of net unrecognized section 987 gain or loss of a section 987 QBU.

Section 1.987–4 provides the mechanics for determining "net unrecognized section 987 gain or loss" and, when combined with § 1.987–5, form the mathematical core of the foreign exchange exposure pool method. In summary, § 1.987–4 uses a balance sheet to distinguish the items of a section 987 QBU that give rise to section 987 gain or loss (section 987 marked items) from those that do not (section 987 historic items). This approach avoids the distortions caused by the 1991 proposed regulations that impute section 987 gain or loss to all assets of a section 987 QBU, even those assets the value of which does not fluctuate with currency movements. Generally, annual comparison of the change in the value of section 987 marked items on the opening and closing balance sheets due to changes in exchange rates gives rise to unrecognized section 987 gain or loss. This unrecognized section 987 gain or loss is aggregated with similar amounts determined for prior years (to the extent not previously taken into account) and is taken into account by the owner under the rules of § 1.987–5 upon a remittance by the section 987 QBU.

Under § 1.987–4(a) and (b), net unrecognized section 987 gain or loss is computed annually and is equal to the sum of the "unrecognized section 987 gain or loss for the current taxable year" and the "net accumulated unrecognized section 987 gain or loss for all prior taxable years." A section 987 QBU's net accumulated unrecognized section 987 gain or loss for all prior taxable years is the aggregate of the unrecognized section 987 gain or loss determined under § 1.987–4(d) for all prior taxable years (to which these regulations apply) reduced by the amounts taken into account under § 1.987–5 upon a remittance for all such taxable years. For section 987 QBUs in existence prior to the effective date of these regulations, a section 987 QBU's net accumulated unrecognized section 987 gain or loss includes amounts taken into account under the transition rules of § 1.987–10.

Unrecognized section 987 gain or loss is determined under a seven step calculation. Under the first step in § 1.987–4(d)(1), the "owner functional currency net value" of the section 987 QBU is determined under § 1.987–1(e) at the close of the taxable year in the functional currency of the owner. This is a balance sheet calculation under which the basis (or amount, in the case of a liability) of each section 987 marked item is translated into the owner's functional currency at the spot rate on the last day of the taxable year. Section 987 historic items are translated into the owner's functional currency at the historic exchange rate and, therefore, do not give rise to exchange gain or loss. The amount of liabilities determined in the owner's functional currency is subtracted from the value of the assets determined in the owner's functional currency to result in the owner functional currency net value of the section 987 QBU at the close of the taxable year. The owner functional currency net value of the section 987 QBU at the close of the preceding taxable year is subtracted from the owner functional currency net value of the section 987 QBU at the close of the current taxable year to yield the change in owner functional currency net value of the section 987 QBU for the taxable year expressed in the owner's functional currency.

Generally, three components are reflected in the change in owner functional currency net value of the section 987 QBU for a taxable year. First, taxable income or loss of the section 987 QBU will result in increases or decreases in net assets, and will therefore affect net value. Second, transfers of assets or liabilities to or from the section 987 QBU will affect net value. Finally, any remaining change in net value (as measured in the owner's functional currency) results from changes in the value of the section 987 QBU's marked assets and liabilities. In order to isolate the change in value due to foreign currency movements with respect to section 987 marked assets and liabilities, the other changes must be reversed out. That is the function of steps 2 through 7 of § 1.987–4(d).

The unrecognized section 987 gain or loss when aggregated with similar amounts for prior years (that were not previously taken into account) yields a pool of "net unrecognized section 987 gain or loss" all or part of which is to be triggered upon a remittance or termination.

E. Section 1.987–5 Recognition of Section 987 Gain or Loss.

Section 1.987–5 of the proposed regulations provides the method for determining the amount of section 987 gain or loss a taxpayer must recognize in a taxable year. Generally, the amount of section 987 gain or loss recognized in a taxable year equals the net unrecognized section 987 gain or loss of the section 987 QBU determined under § 1.987–4 on the last day of such taxable year, multiplied by the owner's remittance proportion. The pool of net unrecognized section 987 gain or loss includes both unrecognized section 987 gain or loss on marked items for the current year and unrecognized section 987 gain or loss on marked items for prior years (that has not yet been taken into account). A portion of the § 1.987–4 pool of unrecognized section 987 gain or loss is triggered by a net transfer or "remittance" to the owner by a section 987 QBU during the owner's taxable year. Generally, the owner's remittance proportion is equal to the quotient of the amount of the remittance divided by the aggregate adjusted basis of the section 987 QBU's gross assets (as reflected on its year end balance sheet), without reduction for the remittance.

* * *

Section 1.987–5(c) of the proposed regulations defines a remittance as the excess of total transfers from the section 987 QBU to the owner determined in the owner's functional currency on an annual basis over total transfers from the owner to the section 987 QBU determined on an annual basis. Solely for purposes of determining the amount of a remittance under § 1.987–5(c), the amount of liabilities transferred from the owner to the section 987 QBU is treated as a transfer of assets from the section 987 QBU to the owner. Similarly, the amount of liabilities transferred from the section 987 QBU to the owner is treated as a transfer of assets from the owner to the section 987 QBU. The IRS and the Treasury Department recognize that section 987 QBUs actively engaged in business may have a significant number of transactions that are treated as transfers to and from the owner pursuant to § 1.987–2(c). It is anticipated that the annual netting rule will help to reduce complexity and administrative burden for taxpayers and the IRS by treating the net amount of transfers as a single annual remittance. For purposes of determining the annual remittance, only assets and liabilities considered transferred pursuant to § 1.987–2(c) will be taken into account.

The remittance is divided by the total adjusted basis of section 987 gross assets, expressed in the functional currency of the owner, reflected on the section 987 QBU balance sheet pursuant to § 1.987–2 (increased by the amount of the remittance) to determine the remittance proportion. The IRS and the Treasury Department considered a number of different measures for determining the amount of section 987 gain or loss triggered upon a remittance. The adjusted basis of gross section 987 QBU assets was selected as the measure because it avoids administrative concerns raised by alternative methods and limits the potential volatility associated with the recognition of section 987 gain or loss. * * *

* * *

H. Section 1.987–8 Termination of a Section 987 QBU.

1. General termination rules.

The proposed regulations set forth circumstances in which a section 987 QBU will terminate. For purposes of § 1.987–5, a termination of a section 987 QBU is treated as a remittance of all the gross assets of the section 987 QBU to its owner. The termination rules recognize that an owner carries on a trade or business through its section 987 QBU and when the owner stops conducting that trade or business through its section 987 QBU, any section 987 gain or loss should be recognized in full. Thus, a termination generally occurs when: (1) the activities of the section 987 QBU cease; (2) substantially all of the assets (as defined in section 368(a)(1)(C)) of the section 987 QBU are transferred to its owner; or (3) the owner of the section 987 QBU ceases to exist.

In addition, a termination occurs when a foreign corporation that is a controlled foreign corporation (CFC) that is the owner of a section 987 QBU ceases to be a CFC because at that point any section 987 gain or loss cannot be subpart F income and may be deferred indefinitely.

2. *Exceptions for certain section 381 transactions.*

Section 987 gain or loss generally arises during the period that an owner has a section 987 QBU. The section 987 gain or loss is analogous in some respects to a tax attribute under section 381. As a result, the proposed regulations provide that a termination does not generally occur when other tax attributes under section 381 are carried over in a liquidation under section 332 or an asset reorganization under section 368(a). However, inbound and outbound liquidations and reorganizations terminate a section 987 QBU because these transactions materially change the circumstances in which section 987 gain or loss is taken into account.

* * *

4. *Section 351 exchanges and transactions within a consolidated group.*

The proposed regulations provide that a termination occurs when the owner of a section 987 QBU transfers the QBU to another corporation in exchange for stock in a transaction qualifying under section 351. The termination occurs because the owner no longer has a section 987 QBU.

* * *

The amount of foreign income taxes on the income of the branch will be determined for purposes of the direct foreign tax credit under the rules set forth in Section 986, as substantially revised in 1997. Under revised Section 986, a taxpayer that uses the accrual method to account for foreign taxes for purposes of the foreign tax credit generally translates foreign income taxes accrued into U.S. dollars at the average exchange rate for the tax year to which the taxes relate (rather than at the exchange rate for the date of payment). § 986(a)(1)(A). This rule does not apply to (1) any foreign income taxes paid more than two years after the close of the tax year to which the taxes relate; (2) any foreign income taxes paid before the start of the tax year to which the taxes relate; or (3) any foreign income taxes the liability for which is denominated in any inflationary currency. § 986(a)(1)(B), (C). This rule obviously also does not apply to a taxpayer that uses the cash method to account for foreign taxes. All foreign taxes that do not qualify for translation at the average exchange rate for the year must be translated at the exchange rate in effect for the date of payment of the taxes to the foreign country. § 986(a)(2)(A). However, Section 986(a)(3) provides regulatory authority for the Treasury Department to allow the use of specified average exchange rates for the period during which the taxes are paid instead of actual daily exchange rates on the date of payment.

The 2004 JOBS Act added Section 986(a)(1)(D) to the Code, which provides an election for a taxpayer that otherwise is required under

Section 986(a)(1)(A) to translate foreign taxes into U.S. dollars using the average exchange rate for the tax year. This election applies to "any foreign income taxes the liability for which is denominated in any currency other than in the taxpayer's functional currency." Under this provision, such a taxpayer may elect to use the exchange rate at the time that the foreign taxes are paid instead of the average exchange rate for the tax year. Once made, the election applies to the tax year for which it was made and all later tax years unless revoked with the IRS's consent. The statute authorizes the Treasury and the IRS to issue regulations applying this election to foreign income taxes attributable to a qualified business unit.

If the foreign income tax paid differs from the amount of foreign tax accrued or if the foreign income tax is fully or partially refunded, the taxpayer must notify the IRS, which will redetermine the taxpayer's U.S. tax liability. See § 905(c)(1)(A), (C); Temp. Reg. § 1.905–4T. Under the revisions to Sections 905(c) and 986 made by the 1997 Act, a redetermination will also take place for any portion of accrued foreign income taxes that remain unpaid more than two years after the close of the tax year to which the taxes relate. §§ 905(c)(1)(B); 986(a)(1)(B)(i), (a)(2)(A). In effect, the previous accrual of any foreign tax that is unpaid as of that date is disallowed. See H.R. Conf. Rep. No. 220, 105th Cong., 1st Sess. 614 (1997). However, if the foreign income tax is paid within the two-year period, no redetermination will be made under current law even though the actual U.S. dollar value of the foreign tax paid may differ from the accrued amount due to foreign currency fluctuations. See §§ 905(c)(1)(B) and 986(a)(1); H.R. Conf. Rep. No. 220, 105th Cong., 1st Sess. 614–15 (1997).

Redetermined foreign taxes paid are generally translated into U.S. dollars using the exchange rate applicable on the date the foreign tax adjustment is paid to the foreign country. § 986(a)(2)(B)(i). If foreign taxes are refunded or credited to the taxpayer by a foreign country, the redetermined amount of taxes paid is translated into U.S. dollars using the exchange rate as of the date of the original payment of the taxes. § 986(a)(2)(B)(ii). In the case of a direct foreign tax credit, accrued foreign income taxes paid more than two years after the close of the tax year to which the taxes relate are taken into account for the tax year to which the taxes relate, but are translated using the exchange rates in effect as of the time of payment of the taxes. See § 986(a)(2)(A); H.R. Conf. Rep. No. 220, 105th Cong., 1st Sess. 614–15 (1997).

Example. DC, a domestic corporation that uses the accrual method for foreign tax credit purposes, accrues in year 1 100 units of foreign tax owing to Country Y. Country Y's currency is not inflationary. The year 1 Country Y foreign tax is unpaid at the end of year 1. DC does not make an election under Section 986(a)(1)(D). Under Section 986(a)(1), DC translates the 100 units of Country Y foreign tax into U.S. dollars using the average exchange rate for year 1. If DC pays the 100 units of Country Y foreign tax in year 2 or year 3, DC is not required to redetermine its foreign tax for year 1 even if the dollar value of the foreign tax paid differs from the accrued amount due to foreign currency fluctuations. If, however, any portion of the accrued Country Y tax for year 1 remains unpaid as of the end of year 3, DC must redetermine its accrued foreign tax under Section 905(c) for year 1 to eliminate the accrued but unpaid Country Y tax and reduce its foreign tax credit. If DC pays the disallowed tax in year 4, DC must again redetermine its Country Y foreign tax and foreign tax credit for year 1, but the year 1 tax paid by DC in year 4 is translated into U.S. dollars using the exchange rate in effect for the date of payment in year 4. See H.R. Conf. Rep. No. 220, 105th Cong., 1st Sess. 614–15 (1997).

[¶ 9120]

3. FOREIGN SUBSIDIARIES

Section 986 prescribes the methods applicable to translating earnings and taxes of foreign affiliates of U.S. corporations that have a foreign functional currency. Note that a foreign currency translation may not be necessary until the affiliate distributes or is deemed to distribute dividends (e.g., as a Subpart F inclusion) to a U.S. taxpayer. At that time, if the shareholder is a U.S. corporation owning at least ten percent of the foreign affiliate's voting stock, it must report dividend income but is also entitled to an indirect foreign tax credit under Section 902 or 960. To determine the amount includible in income and the indirect foreign tax credit, it is normally necessary to translate into dollars the amount of the includible dividend, the amount of earnings and profits from which the dividend is paid and the amount of foreign tax associated with the distribution.

As discussed at ¶ 9115, under revised Section 986, accrued foreign taxes paid within two years after the close of the tax year to which the taxes relate are translated into U.S. dollars using the average exchange rate for the tax year to which the taxes relate. Accrued foreign taxes paid more than two years after the tax year to which the taxes relate, before the start of the tax year to which the taxes relate or in an inflationary currency are translated into U.S. dollars at the spot rate on the date of payment. Any refund or credit of foreign tax is translated at the spot rate on the date of the original payment of the foreign taxes, and any increase in foreign taxes resulting from an adjustment is translated at the spot rate in effect on the date the adjustment is paid. An adjustment under Section 905(c) is triggered by refunds or adjustments of foreign taxes or by the foreign corporation's failure to pay accrued foreign taxes within two years after the tax year to which they relate. However, Section 905(c)(1) gives the Treasury regulatory authority to allow adjustments to the payor foreign corporation's pools of post–1986 foreign income taxes and post–

1986 undistributed earnings in lieu of redetermining foreign taxes for purposes of the indirect credit.

Beyond this, the applicable rules vary depending on whether the distribution takes the form of an actual dividend distribution, gain on disposition of stock of a controlled foreign corporation that is treated as a constructive dividend under Section 1248 or a deemed distribution under Section 951(a)(1)(A) or 951(a)(1)(B) of Subpart F or Section 1293 of the PFIC provisions.

If an actual dividend is involved, the amount of the dividend and the amount of earnings and profits out of which it is paid in the foreign corporation's foreign functional currency are translated into dollars at the spot rate on the date the distribution is included in the shareholder's income. §§ 986(b); 989(b)(1). The same rules apply in the case of gain on a disposition of stock of a controlled foreign corporation that is treated as a constructive dividend under Section 1248. §§ 986(b); 989(b)(2). Thus, for actual distributions and constructive dividends under Section 1248, no exchange gain or loss is separately recognized as the result of exchange rate fluctuations between the time earnings and profits arise and the time of distribution.

In the case of a deemed distribution of Subpart F income under Section 951(a)(1)(A), the amount of the deemed distribution and the earnings and profits out of which the deemed distribution is made are translated at the average exchange rate for the tax year. §§ 986(b); 989(b)(3). When Subpart F income taxed under Section 951(a)(1)(A) is subsequently distributed, foreign currency gain or loss is recognized to the extent of changes in exchange rates between the original inclusion of the deemed distribution and the time of the actual distribution of previously taxed income.

The average exchange rate for the tax year is also used to translate inclusions with respect to a PFIC under Section 1293(a). §§ 986(b); 989(b)(3). The rules for recognizing exchange gain or loss with respect to the distribution of previously taxed income also apply to previously taxed PFIC income. By contrast, any amount included in income under Section 951(a)(1)(B), concerning earnings invested in U.S. property under Section 956, is treated as an actual distribution made on the last day of the tax year in which the amount is included. § 989(b) (last sentence). Accordingly, under Section 989(b)(1), the appropriate exchange rate is the spot rate on the last day of the tax year of inclusion.

As discussed at ¶ 9115, the 2004 JOBS Act added a new election in Section 986(a)(1)(D) for a taxpayer that otherwise is required under Section 986(a)(1)(A) to translate foreign taxes into U.S. dollars using the average exchange rate for the tax year. This provision allows such a taxpayer to elect to use the exchange rate at the time that the foreign taxes are paid instead of the average exchange rate for the tax year. Once elected, this provision applies to the tax year for which it was made and all later tax years unless revoked with the IRS's consent. Note, however, that this election applies only to the translation of foreign taxes and foreign tax adjustments; it does not apply to the translation of a foreign corporation's earnings and profits or to the translation of dividends or constructive inclusions under either the Subpart F or PFIC rules.

[¶ 9125]

PROBLEMS

1. Global Car Parts, Ltd. is a U.S. corporation that established a Jamaican subsidiary to manufacture certain automobile parts. During its first year, the subsidiary earned 500,000 Jamaican dollars and paid taxes of 100,000 Jamaican dollars when the exchange rate was US $1 = .80 Jamaican dollar. The average exchange rate for year 1 was US $1 = 1 Jamaican dollar. No dividends were paid in year 1. During year 2, the Jamaican subsidiary broke even but paid a dividend of 200,000 Jamaican dollars. The spot exchange rate on the date the dividend was distributed and included in the parent corporation's income was US $1 = 1.20 Jamaican dollars. After recalling the mechanics of the indirect foreign tax credit, determine the gross income that must be reported by the parent corporation and the maximum indirect foreign tax credit that might be available in respect thereof. Assume that Subpart F did not require a constructive dividend of any of the Jamaican subsidiary's year 1 income to Global Car Parts, Ltd.

2. American Paper Co. is a U.S. corporation with several foreign subsidiaries. During year 1, its Cayman subsidiary (for which the U.K. pound was the functional currency) had Subpart F income of 100,000 U.K. pounds that was taxed immediately to American Paper Co. The average exchange rate during year 1 was $2 = 1 U.K. pound. During year 2, the Cayman subsidiary made a distribution of 50,000 U.K. pounds, which was appropriately treated as previously taxed income under Subpart F. At the time of the distribution, the exchange rate was $1.75 = 1 U.K. pound. What are the U.S. income tax consequences for American Paper Co. in year 2?

3. On May 1, 2010, DC Corporation, a U.S. corporation that has the U.S. dollar as its functional currency, established a Japanese branch that has the yen as its functional currency. On May 1, 2010 (when the spot exchange rate was $1 = 100 Japanese yen), DC Corporation transferred the following assets to the Japanese branch: $1,000 (which the Japanese branch immediately converted into 100,000 Japanese yen) and raw land with an adjusted basis of $500. On May 1, 2010, the Japanese branch also borrowed 10,000 Japanese yen from a local bank. During the period from May 1, 2010, through December 31, 2010, the Japanese branch earned a total of 13,000 yen of income items and incurred a total of 2,000 yen of currently deductible expenses. All of the items of income earned and all of the expenses incurred in 2010 by the Japanese branch were received and paid in Japanese yen. The spot exchange rate on December 31, 2010, was $1 = 120 Japanese yen, and

the average exchange rate for 2010 was $1 = 110 yen. Determine the amount of the Japanese branch's net unrecognized Section 987 gain or loss for 2010.

4. Assume the facts are the same as in Problem 3, except that in the following year, 2011, the Japanese branch earned a total of 19,000 yen of income items and incurred a total of 4,000 yen of currently deductible expenses. All of the Japanese branch's income items earned and expenses incurred in 2011 were received and paid in Japanese yen. On April 1, 2011 (when the spot exchange rate was $1 = 130 Japanese yen), the Japanese branch sold the raw land for its then fair market value of 15,600 yen. On December 31, 2011 (when the spot exchange rate was $1 = 115 Japanese yen), the Japanese branch transferred 34,500 Japanese yen to DC Corporation. The average exchange rate for 2011 was $1 = 125 Japanese yen. Determine the amount of the Japanese branch's net unrecognized Section 987 gain or loss for 2011 and determine DC Corporation's Section 987 gain or loss recognized with respect to the Japanese branch for 2011.

CHAPTER 10

INTERNATIONAL TAX-FREE EXCHANGES

■ ■ ■

[¶ 10,000]

A. INTRODUCTION

Whenever a U.S. person decides to establish a business abroad that will be conducted by a foreign corporation, it will be necessary to capitalize the foreign corporation with a transfer of cash and other property in exchange for its stock. When appreciated property, such as equipment or intangible property rights (e.g., foreign patents, knowhow and trademarks), is transferred to a foreign corporation, gain will often be realized by the U.S. person. This gain will be recognized and subject to U.S. tax unless one of the tax-free-exchange (or nonrecognition) provisions of the Code applies. The imposition of U.S. tax on a transfer of appreciated property to a foreign corporation will be a substantial deterrent to the transfer of property. Accordingly, the tax planner will seek to ensure that the transaction is structured in a way to minimize or eliminate the initial U.S. tax burden.

If a U.S. corporation is liquidated and its assets are distributed to foreign shareholders, U.S. tax will be imposed on the gain realized by the distributing corporation except to the extent that a tax-free-exchange provision provides otherwise.

If the stock or assets of a U.S. corporation are acquired by a foreign corporation in exchange for stock of the foreign corporation, or if, conversely, a foreign corporation is acquired for stock of a U.S. corporation, gain realized by U.S. shareholders and the U.S. corporation will also be subject to tax, except to the extent that the gain is sheltered by a tax-free-exchange provision. Even an acquisition of one foreign corporation by another foreign corporation involving U.S. shareholders who exchange their stock in the acquired corporation for stock in the acquiring corporation may be subject to U.S. tax unless the transaction qualifies as a tax-free exchange. Similarly, if a foreign corporation engages in a recapitalization or a reincorporation, U.S. shareholders who exchange their original stock or securities of the foreign corporation for new stock or securities will be taxed on any gain realized, except to the extent that a nonrecognition provision applies.

Under the Code, gain or loss realized in exchanges of property in connection with a variety of transactions involving only U.S. corporations will go unrecognized if the requirements of the applicable tax-free-exchange provision are met. Such transactions include transfers of property to a controlled corporation, liquidation of a controlled subsidiary into its corporate parent and certain corporate reorganizations. When the transaction involves one or more corporations organized in a foreign country, however, nonrecognition of gain is limited and frequently a transfer of appreciated assets or stock of a U.S. corporation to a foreign corporation is subject to a significant U.S. tax burden.

The basic problem is the need to protect the right of the country of residence of the transferor corporation or shareholder to tax gains realized by its taxpayer in the transaction. The concern of that country is that, if not taxed immediately, the gain will escape its tax net permanently. Since 1932, Section 367 and its predecessor provisions have provided the mechanism for protecting the U.S. taxing jurisdiction in transactions involving transfers by U.S. taxpayers of appreciated property in exchange for stock when one or more foreign corporations are involved.

Section 367 was originally aimed at preventing tax-free transfers by U.S. taxpayers of appreciated property to foreign corporations that could then sell the property free of U.S. tax. H.R. Rep. No. 708, 72d Cong., 1st Sess. 20 (1932); S. Rep. No. 665, 72d Cong., 1st Sess. 26–27 (1932). The reach of this provision has been broadened over the years to apply to a broad spectrum of transactions involving transfers both into and out of the United States and, as a result of the enactment of Subpart F, to a variety of transactions involving only foreign corporations.

Section 367 has two basic purposes today. First, it stands sentinel to ensure that (with certain exceptions) a U.S. tax liability (sometimes called a "toll charge") is imposed when property with untaxed appreciation is transferred beyond U.S. taxing jurisdiction. It generally accomplishes this objective by treating the foreign transferee corporation as not qualifying as a "corporation" for purposes of certain tax-free-exchange provisions. Because such provisions apply only to "corporations," the U.S. transferor will recognize taxable gain on the transfer.

> *Example.* DC, a U.S. corporation, owns inventory property with an adjusted basis of $50,000 and a current fair market value of $100,000. During the current year, DC transfers the inventory to FC, a newly formed foreign corporation, in exchange for all of FC's stock. Ignoring Section 367(a) for the moment, DC would not recognize any gain on the transfer by reason of the nonrecognition provisions in Section 351 of the Code. FC would obtain a carryover basis of $50,000 in the inventory under Section 362(a). If FC later sells the inventory for $100,000, passing title to the customer abroad, its gain on the sale

of the property would not be subject to U.S. tax because FC is a foreign taxpayer and is not taxable on such gain under Section 881 or 882. (FC's gain on the sale of the inventory would be foreign-source income under Sections 865(b) and 862(a)(6) and the United States generally does not tax the foreign-source income of foreign persons.) Thus, the $50,000 of taxable gain inherent in the inventory at the time of the transfer to FC could permanently escape U.S. taxation even though the gain accrued while the property was owned by a U.S. person (DC) unless FC distributes its earnings to DC or DC has a constructive dividend under one of the anti-deferral regimes.

Section 367(a) prevents this result by treating FC as not a corporation for Section 351 purposes. Thus, DC's transfer to FC would not qualify for nonrecognition treatment under Section 351 and DC's realized gain of $50,000 on the transfer would be recognized and subject to U.S. income tax at the time of transfer.

Second, Section 367 ensures that the earnings of a controlled foreign corporation (to the extent they are not currently taxed to U.S. shareholders) do not avoid U.S. tax because they are shifted to an entity that is not a controlled foreign corporation as a result of some corporate reorganization or other transaction. In this latter respect, Section 367 is the mechanism that ensures the enforcement of the rules of Section 1248, which require dividend treatment when a U.S. shareholder sells or exchanges stock in a controlled foreign corporation or the corporation is liquidated. The principal purpose of Section 1248 is to prevent a U.S. shareholder of a controlled foreign corporation from realizing gain on its undistributed earnings at the cost only of the tax on long-term capital gains by selling its stock or liquidating the corporation. See ¶ 6245.

B. NONRECOGNITION-OF-GAIN TRANSACTIONS

[¶ 10,005]

1. CORPORATE FORMATIONS: TRANSFERS OF APPRECIATED PROPERTY TO FOREIGN CORPORATION

When property is transferred to a corporation in exchange for stock, recognition of gain or loss is governed by Section 351 and, if gain on a transfer to a foreign corporate transferee is involved, by Section 367 as well. Under Section 351, no gain or loss is recognized (1) if property is transferred to a U.S. corporation by one or more persons solely in exchange for stock in the corporation and (2) if immediately after the exchange such person or persons are in control[1] of the corporation.

1. "Control" for this purpose means ownership of at least 80 percent of the total combined voting power of all classes of stock entitled to vote and at least 80 percent of the total number of shares of each other class of stock. § 368(c).

Section 351 thus may come into play whenever property with a value greater or less than its tax basis is transferred to a newly formed corporation by the initial subscribers to its stock. It may also operate to prevent recognition of gain or loss when such property is transferred to an existing corporation. As discussed in the example above, however, where a transfer of property to a *foreign* corporation in exchange for its stock is involved, the nonrecognition of *gain* under Section 351 will apply only to the extent provided in Section 367. If *loss* is realized on the exchange, and the transaction meets the requirements of Section 351, the loss will not be recognized; Section 367 does not apply.

The kinds of property most often raising the question of possible qualification under Sections 351 and 367 are inventory, equipment depreciated below fair market value, manufacturing intangibles (e.g., patents and knowhow) and marketing intangibles (e.g., trademarks and trade names). These intangibles often have a zero or very low basis because research and experimental costs and advertising costs have been deducted currently. Assets such as these are frequently transferred to a foreign corporation when a foreign business is established or expanded. Sometimes the existence of a transfer of appreciated property is not immediately obvious. For example, if a going sales business previously conducted by a division of a U.S. corporation is taken over by a foreign subsidiary corporation, a transfer of valuable goodwill (possibly having a zero basis) may be involved.

Contributions to the capital of a corporation by its shareholders normally are treated as nontaxable to both the corporation and the contributing shareholder. However, when property is contributed to the capital of a foreign corporation by one or more transferors who in the aggregate own at least 80 percent of the total combined voting power of the foreign corporation's stock, the contribution is treated for purposes of Section 367 as a constructive transfer in exchange for the corporation's stock equal in value to the fair market value of the contributed property. § 367(c)(2). Thus, a U.S. transferor may be taxable on any gain (i.e., fair market value of the contributed property in excess of the adjusted basis of the property) realized on the constructive exchange because Section 367(a) prevents the transfer from qualifying for nonrecognition-of-gain treatment under Section 351. Moreover, to the extent provided in regulations, Section 367(f) requires that a U.S. person's transfer of appreciated property to a foreign corporation as paid-in surplus or a contribution to capital be treated as a fair market sale and that the gain on such sale be recognized. Unlike Section 367(c)(2), the latter provision applies without regard to whether the transferor (or a group of such transferors) owns 80 percent or more of the voting stock of the transferee corporation.

[¶ 10,010]

2. CORPORATE LIQUIDATIONS

Amounts distributed to shareholders in complete liquidation generally are treated for U.S. tax purposes as distributions in exchange for the stock relinquished. § 331(a). Accordingly, under this general rule, a complete liquidation is the occasion for the recognition of the gain or loss represented by the difference between the value of the liquidation distribution and the shareholder's tax basis in the stock surrendered. Generally, the character of the gain or loss concerned will be capital and, if the holding period requirement has been met, any such gain or loss will be treated as long-term capital gain or loss. Under Section 1248, however, if a controlled foreign corporation is liquidated, the gain realized by a ten-percent-or-more U.S. shareholder may be taxed as a dividend to the extent that it reflects that shareholder's share of post–1962 earnings and profits of the corporation. See ¶ 6245. Note that, without regard to Section 367, the liquidating corporation normally recognizes gain or loss on the distribution of property to shareholders in complete liquidation of its stock (except that loss on certain distributions to related persons is not recognized). § 336.

In the case of the liquidation of a U.S. subsidiary corporation into a U.S. parent corporation, if certain requirements are met, the parent corporation's gain or loss on the receipt of the liquidating distributions is not recognized under Section 332 and the subsidiary corporation's gain or loss on the liquidating distributions of property to its parent corporation is not recognized under Section 337(a). Those requirements, set forth in Section 332(b), are:

> (1) the parent corporation must own, on the date the plan of liquidation is adopted and continuously thereafter until receipt of the liquidating distribution, stock possessing at least 80 percent of the total combined voting power of all classes of the subsidiary's stock entitled to vote and at least 80 percent of the total value of all other classes of stock (except certain nonvoting, nonconvertible preferred stock); *and either*
>
> (2) the distribution by the subsidiary must occur within the tax year of the plan's adoption and be in complete cancellation or redemption of all its stock; *or*
>
> (3) the plan of liquidation must call for transfer of all the subsidiary's property concerned within three years from the end of the tax year in which the first distribution is made and the transfer must actually be completed within this period.

Under Section 367(e)(2), when a U.S. subsidiary of a foreign corporation is liquidated, nonrecognition of gain under Sections 332 and 337 will apply only as provided in Reg. § 1.367(e)–2. See ¶ 10,100.

[¶ 10,015]

3. SECTION 368(a)(1) REORGANIZATIONS

The Code provides for nonrecognition of gain or loss realized in connection with a considerable number of corporate organizational changes. These include acquisitive and other reorganizations defined in Section 368(a)(1) and divisive reorganizations under Section 355. They are permitted on a tax-free basis on the rationale that they involve merely changes in the organizational forms for the conduct of business and that there should be no tax penalty imposed on formal organizational adjustments that are dictated by business considerations.

Reorganizations, as defined in Section 368(a)(1), include statutory mergers and consolidations, acquisitions by one corporation of the stock or assets of another corporation, recapitalizations, changes in form or place of organization and certain corporate transfers in a Title 11 or similar bankruptcy case. If the transaction qualifies as a reorganization, neither gain nor loss will be recognized by the corporation or corporations involved or by their shareholders who may exchange their stock for other stock or by certain security holders who may exchange their securities for other securities of a party to the reorganization (with certain exceptions and qualifications). See §§ 354, 356, 361 and 1032. Also, in the case of a qualifying reorganization, the tax attributes (e.g., tax basis of assets, net operating losses and earnings and profits) of a corporation whose assets are acquired carry over to the acquiring corporation. See § 381. This carryover of tax attributes is subject to certain limits. See §§ 382 through 384.

The purpose of the reorganization provisions is to permit on a tax-free basis "such readjustments of corporate structures made in one of the particular ways specified in the Code, as are required by business exigencies and which effect only a readjustment of continuing interest[s] in property under modified corporate forms." Reg. § 1.368–1(b). Implicit in this statement of purpose are three general requirements for qualification of a transaction as a tax-free reorganization: (1) the transaction must have a business purpose, Gregory v. Helvering, 293 U.S. 465 (1935), Reg. § 1.368–1(b); (2) the original owners must retain a continued proprietary interest in the reorganized corporation (the "continuity of interest" requirement), Reg. § 1.368–1(e); and (3) in an acquisitive reorganization, the acquiring corporation must either continue the acquired corporation's historic business or use a significant portion of the acquired corporation's historic business assets in a business (the "continuity of business enterprise" requirement), Reg. § 1.368–1(d).

The basic types of reorganizations are:

(1) ***Type A reorganization*** (statutory merger). For many years, an adjustment involving a foreign corporation could not qualify as a

statutory merger or consolidation (Type A reorganization) if the surviving corporation was not a U.S. corporation because the prior regulations required that a qualifying merger or consolidation had to be effected pursuant to the corporation laws of the United States, one of the states or the District of Columbia. However, the regulations were amended in 2006 to provide that "a statutory merger or consolidation is a transaction effected pursuant to the statute or statutes necessary to effect the merger or consolidation, in which transaction, as a result of the operation of such statute or statutes" (1) all of the assets (other than those distributed in the transaction) and all of the liabilities of each combining entity of the transferor unit become the assets and liabilities of one or more of the combining entities of the transferee unit; and (2) each combining entity of the transferor unit ceases its separate legal existence for all purposes. Reg. § 1.368–2(b)(1)(ii). Thus, under the current regulations, a merger or consolidation effected under the laws of a foreign jurisdiction or a U.S. possession can qualify as a Type A reorganization, regardless of whether the surviving transferee corporation is a U.S. or foreign corporation. See, e.g., Reg. § 1.368–2(b)(1)(iii), Exs. 13, 14.

In the context of international corporate acquisitions, tax-free statutory mergers often take the form of forward triangular mergers, in which the acquired corporation is merged into a subsidiary of the acquiring corporation; these mergers must meet the requirements of Section 368(a)(2)(D). International tax-free statutory mergers may also take the form of reverse triangular mergers, in which a subsidiary of the acquiring corporation is merged into the acquired corporation; these mergers must meet the requirements of Section 368(a)(2)(E).

(2) ***Type B reorganization*** (acquisition by one corporation, in exchange solely for all or part of its voting stock or voting stock of its parent corporation, of the stock of another corporation, if the acquiring corporation has "control" (see footnote 1 supra) of the acquired corporation immediately after the acquisition).

(3) ***Type C reorganization*** (acquisition of substantially all of the assets of a corporation by another corporation, in exchange for part or all of the latter's voting stock, or the voting stock of its parent corporation, followed by liquidation of the acquired corporation).

(4) ***Type D reorganization*** (a transfer by a corporation of part or all of its assets to another corporation if immediately after the transfer the transferor and/or its shareholders are in control of the transferee corporation and if the stock or securities of the transferee corporation are distributed in a transaction qualifying under Section 354, 355 or 356).

(5) ***Type E reorganization*** (recapitalization of a corporation).

(6) ***Type F reorganization*** (change in identity, form or place of incorporation of a corporation).

(7) ***Type G reorganization*** (a transfer by a corporation of part or all of its assets to another corporation in a Title 11 or similar bankruptcy case if the stock or securities of the transferee of the assets are distributed in a transaction qualifying under Section 354, 355 or 356).

Section 368(a)(1) plays a definitional role only; the provisions providing for nonrecognition of gain or loss are Sections 354, 356 and 361[2] and it is these sections, not Section 368(a)(1), that are referred to in Section 367(a)(1). Reorganizations defined in Section 368(a)(1) involving one or more foreign corporations will be accorded nonrecognition-of-gain treatment only to the extent permitted under Section 367 and the regulations issued thereunder. The rules differ depending on whether the transaction is deemed to involve an outbound transfer under Section 367(a), which involves a transfer of assets or stock from a U.S. person to a foreign person, or a nonoutbound transfer under Section 367(b), which involves a transfer of assets or stock from a foreign person to a U.S. person or from one foreign person to another foreign person.

[¶ 10,020]

4. CORPORATE DIVISIONS

Corporate divisions under Section 355 include:

The ***spin-off*** (distribution by one corporation to its shareholders of the stock of a controlled subsidiary corporation),

The ***split-off*** (similar to the spin-off, except that the shareholders of the parent corporation give up a portion of their stock in the parent in exchange for the controlled subsidiary's stock), and

The ***split-up*** (parent corporation distributes its stock in two or more controlled subsidiaries in complete liquidation).

Under Section 355, the parent (distributing) corporation is permitted to distribute stock or securities in a controlled subsidiary without recognition of gain or loss if the following conditions are met:

(1) The distributing corporation must control[3] the subsidiary (or subsidiaries) the stock or securities of which are distributed;

(2) Immediately after the distribution, both the distributing corporation and the controlled subsidiary (or subsidiaries) must be

2. The treatment of "boot" and liabilities in connection with corporate reorganizations is dealt with in Sections 356 and 357. The acquiring corporation's carryover tax basis in the assets or stock acquired in the transaction is covered in Section 362(b) and the shareholder's substituted basis in the stock and securities received in the transaction is covered in Section 358. The transfer of tax attributes (e.g., earnings and profits and net operating losses) is covered in Section 381, subject to certain limits in Sections 382 through 384.

3. "Control" is defined in Section 368(c). See note 1 supra.

engaged in the active conduct of a trade or business (or, if the assets of the distributing corporation consist solely of stock and securities in two or more controlled subsidiaries, each of the latter must be so engaged);[4]

(3) Certain tests must be met with respect to the amount of stock and securities of the controlled subsidiary (or subsidiaries) that is distributed (Section 355(a)(1)(D));

(4) The transaction must not be used principally as a device for the distribution of the earnings and profits of any corporation involved; and

(5) The distribution must not constitute a disqualified distribution (as defined in Section 355(d)) or a distribution to which Section 355(e), (f) or (g) applies.

[¶ 10,023]

5. ANTI-IMPORTATION OF LOSS RULES

Congress became concerned with the fact that various corporate transactions were structured to take advantage of the carryover basis rules of Section 362. In the case of built-in loss property (i.e., property with a basis in excess of the fair market value of the property at the time it was acquired by the corporation in a carryover basis transaction), Congress was concerned that taxpayers were using incorporation and reorganization transactions to create duplicate corporate losses from a single economic loss. Congress also was concerned with taxpayers importing economic, built-in losses into the U.S. tax system that arose before the property was subject to U.S. taxing jurisdiction. See S. Rep. No. 192, 108th Cong., 1st Sess. 125 (2003). The 2004 JOBS Act added Section 362(e), which limits a corporation's Section 362 basis in the case of certain transactions involving built-in loss property.

The first of these limitation rules applies if (1) gain or loss with respect to the property is not subject to U.S. tax in the hands of the transferor immediately before the transfer; (2) gain or loss with respect to the property is subject to U.S. tax in the hands of the transferee immediately after the transfer; and (3) the transfer involves the importation of a net built-in loss, i.e., the transferee's total adjusted bases of the properties that are transferred in the transaction would (but for this limitation provision) exceed the fair market value of the properties immediately after the transaction. If these conditions are met, Section 362(e)(1) limits the transferee corporation's basis in each property acquired in the transaction to its fair market value immediately after the transaction.

4. This requirement is met only if the trade or business concerned (1) was actively conducted during the five years before the distribution; (2) was not acquired during that period in a taxable transaction; and (3) was not conducted by another corporation the control of which was acquired during that period in a taxable transaction. § 355(b)(2).

The second of these limitation rules applies only to a corporation's basis in property in a Section 351 exchange that is governed by the basis rule in Section 362(a), but that does not fall within the limitation rule in Section 362(e)(1) described above. § 362(e)(2)(A)(i). In addition, for this second limitation rule to apply, the corporate transferee's total adjusted bases of the properties transferred must (but for this limitation rule) exceed the fair value of such properties immediately after the transaction. § 362(e)(2)(A)(ii). If these conditions are met, the transferee's aggregate adjusted bases of the properties transferred will be limited to the fair market value of the properties immediately after the transaction. The aggregate reduction in adjusted basis required by this limitation rule must be allocated among the properties transferred in proportion to each property's respective built-in loss immediately before the transaction. § 362(e)(2)(B). (Note that unlike the limitation rule in Section 362(e)(1), described above, Section 362(e)(2) does *not* limit the corporation's basis in each property to its fair market value immediately after the transaction.) Although the statutory language is not clear on the point, proposed regulations issued in 2006 would clarify that if more than one transferor transfers property to a corporation in a transaction described in Section 362(a), the rules in Section 362(e)(2) (including the determination of whether the property transferred to the corporation has a net built-in loss) are separately applied to each transferor. See Prop. Reg. § 1.362–4(b)(2); REG–110405–05, 2006–2 C.B. 1004, 1005. The statute also allows the transferor and transferee to elect jointly to avoid application of the corporate transferee basis limitation rule in Section 362(e)(2) by the transferor agreeing to limit its Section 358 basis in the stock received from the corporation in the exchange to the fair market value of the stock immediately after the transfer. § 362(e)(2)(C).

[¶ 10,025]

C. LEGISLATIVE AND ADMINISTRATIVE BACKGROUND

To understand the current rules in Section 367 and the complex regulations issued under that provision, it is helpful to consider briefly the legislative and administrative background in which those rules evolved. Before the Tax Reform Act of 1976, if a U.S. taxpayer wanted to avoid recognition of gain in an incorporation, liquidation, reorganization or other transaction involving a foreign corporation, Section 367 required the taxpayer to obtain a ruling from the IRS before the transaction to the effect that the transaction was not in pursuance of a plan having as one of its principal purposes the avoidance of U.S. income tax. Although the standard used in the statute was subjective, the IRS normally issued a favorable ruling only if the transaction met certain objective standards set forth in Rev. Proc. 68–23, 1968–1 C.B. 821 (sometimes called the "367

Guidelines") and the taxpayer agreed to pay U.S. tax on the gain realized on the transfer of certain so-called "tainted assets" (e.g., inventory or liquid or passive investment assets) as to which the IRS was persuaded that there was inherently significant tax-avoidance potential.

The Tax Reform Act of 1976 revised Section 367 to draw a distinction between (1) so-called "outbound" transactions covered by Section 367(a), which involved transfers of property (other than certain stock or securities of a foreign corporation) by a U.S. person to a foreign corporation in an exchange described in Section 332, 351, 354, 355, 356 or 361, and (2) all other so-called "nonoutbound" transactions covered by Section 367(b). Under the revised statute, a taxpayer still had to obtain a ruling for outbound transactions, unless the regulations provided otherwise, but the ruling could be obtained within 183 days after the start of the transfer. Moreover, the 1976 Act created a declaratory judgment procedure under which a taxpayer could obtain judicial review in the Tax Court of adverse rulings, failures to rule and unfavorable conditions attached to favorable rulings. No ruling was required for nonoutbound transactions, which were governed by temporary regulations.

Congress, however, became concerned with the difficulties encountered by the IRS in administering the revised statute. The Tax Court had interpreted the "principal purpose" test in Section 367(a) as allowing the tax-free transfer of property to a foreign corporation unless avoidance of U.S. income taxes was a purpose that was first in importance. See Dittler Bros., Inc. v. Commissioner, 72 T.C. 896 (1979). Congress concluded that this decision was preventing the IRS "from restricting tax avoidance transfers that the provisions of [Section 367(a)] were intended to combat." Staff of Joint Comm. on Tax'n, 98th Cong., 2d Sess., General Explanation of the Revenue Provisions of the Deficit Reduction Act of 1984, at 427 (1984).

Congress also was concerned with the treatment of foreign marketing and manufacturing intangibles, such as trademarks, trade names, patents and knowhow, under the IRS ruling process. A U.S. taxpayer could develop the intangible in the United States, deduct the costs of such development against U.S.-source income, and then under the 367 Guidelines often obtain a favorable ruling from the IRS allowing a tax-free transfer of the foreign rights in the intangibles to a foreign corporation. The foreign corporation would thereafter earn the income from the intangible in a foreign business, which income would escape any U.S. income tax unless and until the foreign corporation's earnings were distributed to its U.S. shareholders.

To deal with these concerns, the Tax Reform Act of 1984 substantially restructured and revised the provisions of Section 367 and former Sections 1491–1494 (which imposed an excise tax on certain outbound transfers). The 1984 Act eliminated the declaratory judgment procedure for reviewing IRS rulings under Section 367 and replaced the required-ruling process itself with a new general rule under Section 367(a) governing outbound transfers by a U.S. person to a foreign corporation described in Section 332, 351, 354, 356 or 361. Under the new general rule, the foreign corporation is treated as *not* a "corporation" for purposes of the enumerated Code provisions, which means that the U.S. transferors will not qualify for nonrecognition treatment.

This general rule of taxability under Section 367(a) is subject to a number of exceptions, which largely codify many aspects of the treatment of outbound transfers under the pre–1984 IRS ruling process but also make some significant changes. The principal exception to the general rule of taxability applies to transfers of property to be used in the active conduct of a foreign trade or business. See ¶¶ 10,040 et seq. Such transfers are generally tax-free, subject to some important exceptions. Under one of those exceptions, a U.S. person must recognize gain on the transfer of certain "tainted assets" to the foreign corporation that do not qualify for the active trade or business exception. See ¶ 10,045. In addition, a U.S. person must recognize gain on the incorporation of certain foreign branches that have generated losses and provided the U.S. person with deductions that offset its other income. See ¶ 10,095. Furthermore, gain on transfers of the stock or securities of a U.S. or foreign corporation will be taxed under Section 367(a) unless one of the special exceptions for such transfers is available. See ¶¶ 10,075 et seq. Finally, manufacturing and marketing intangibles are subject to special rules in Section 367(d) (as further revised by the Tax Reform Act of 1986), which treat the transferor as receiving constructive ordinary income royalties over the life of each intangible transferred. See ¶ 10,090.

The 1986 Act amended Section 367(d) to require that payments with respect to an intangible that a U.S. person transfers to a foreign corporation in a Section 351 or 361 exchange "be commensurate with the income attributable to the intangible." Congress made this change "to fulfill the objective that the division of income between related parties reasonably reflect the relative economic activity undertaken by each." Staff of Joint Comm. on Tax'n, 100th Cong., 1st Sess., General Explanation of the Tax Reform Act of 1986, at 1015 (1987).

Congress came to view former Sections 1491 through 1494, which imposed an excise tax on certain outbound property transfers, as a trap for the unwary. Accordingly, the Taxpayer Relief Act of 1997 repealed the excise tax provisions of Sections 1491–1494. To replace these provisions, the 1997 Act added new reporting requirements and several other new provisions to the Code, including one applicable to transfers of property by a U.S. person to a foreign estate or trust. See ¶ 10,125. The 1997 Act also amended Section 367(d) to provide that constructive royalty payments under Section 367(d) would be treated as foreign-source income to the same extent that an actual royalty payment would be treated as foreign-source income (i.e., under the normal royalty income source rules, royalties from the use of a foreign intangible generally are foreign-source income). See ¶ 10,090.

In 2004, Congress became concerned with so-called "corporate inversion" transactions in which a former publicly owned U.S. parent corporation would become a subsidiary of a foreign corporation. As a result of the inversion transaction, the new foreign parent corporation would be publicly owned and would not be a controlled foreign corporation, thus escaping the reach of Subpart F. Congress believed that the rules in Section 367 did not prevent corporations from undertaking these transactions which were motivated in part by the fact that the tax benefits at the corporate level exceeded the U.S. tax that would have to be paid by the corporation's shareholders under the Section 367 rules. Accordingly, as discussed at ¶ 10,088, in the 2004 JOBS Act, Congress enacted new provisions to deal with this problem. Under one of these provisions, new Section 7874, a foreign corporation may be treated as a U.S. corporation for federal income tax purposes, if certain conditions are met, thus denying the corporate taxpayer the intended tax benefits to be obtained from the inversion transaction. Finally, as discussed at ¶¶ 10,090 and 12,130, the JOBS Act also made clear that constructive royalty payments under Section 367(d) are treated as royalties for purposes of applying the foreign tax credit limitations in Section 904.

D. SECTION 367(a) REQUIREMENTS FOR OUTBOUND TRANSFERS

[¶ 10,030]

1. INTRODUCTION AND OVERVIEW

All outbound transfers by U.S. persons of appreciated property to foreign corporations and to certain other foreign persons will give rise to recognized gain to the extent required in subsections (a) and (c) through (e) of Section 367 and the regulations implementing them. A variety of transactions are involved. The common factor is that each transaction involves an outbound transfer of property.

Gain recognized on an item-by-item basis under Section 367(a) will in no event exceed the gain that would have been recognized on a taxable sale of the item. Temp. Reg. § 1.367(a)–1T(b)(3)(i). The character (ordinary income or capital gain) and source (U.S. or foreign) of gain recognized under Section 367(a) is generally determined as if the U.S. transferor had disposed of the transferred property in a taxable exchange with the transferee foreign corporation. Temp. Reg. § 1.367(a)–1T(b)(4)(i)(A). Generally no losses are recognized by reason of the operation of Section 367(a). Temp. Reg. § 1.367(a)–1T(b)(1) and (b)(3)(ii).

Notwithstanding that Section 367(a)(1) may deny nonrecognition treatment to a transfer, appropriate adjustments to earnings and profits, basis and other affected items must be made according to the otherwise applicable rules as if the nonrecognition provision had applied to the transfer, but taking into account the gain recognized by the transferor under Section 367(a)(1). Any increase in the adjusted basis of property received by the foreign corporation resulting from the application of Sections 367(a)(1) and 362 must be allocated to the transferred property with respect to which gain is recognized under Section 367(a)(1) in proportion to the "amount realized" by the U.S. transferor on each item of property transferred to the foreign corporation. Temp. Reg. § 1.367(a)–1T(b)(4)(i)(B).

> *Example.* DC, a U.S. corporation, transfers inventory with a fair market value of $100,000 and an adjusted basis of $70,000 to FC, a foreign corporation, in exchange for all of FC's stock. Title to the inventory passes to FC in the United States. Notwithstanding the normal nonrecognition rule in Section 351, Section 367(a) requires DC to recognize gain of $30,000 on the transfer. Under Section 1221(a)(1), DC's gain on the sale of this inventory is ordinary income. Under Sections 865(b) and 861(a)(6) and Reg. § 1.861–7(c), the gain is U.S.-source income because title to the inventory passes in the United States.
>
> Appropriate adjustments to various items must be made as if Section 351 had applied to the transfer. For example, DC's basis in the FC stock will be determined under Section 358 and will be $100,000, i.e., a substituted basis of $70,000 (DC's basis in the inventory), increased by the $30,000 gain recognized on the transfer under Section 367(a)(1). FC's basis in the inventory will be determined under Section 362(a) and will be $100,000, i.e., a carryover of DC's basis of $70,000 in the inventory, increased by the $30,000 gain recognized by DC under Section 367(a)(1).

[¶ 10,035]

2. TRANSFERS SUBJECT TO SECTION 367(a)

Section 367(a) provides a general rule of taxability with respect to outbound transfers of property in exchange for other property in transactions described in Section 332, 351, 354, 356 or 361 by stating that a foreign corporation will not be considered a corporation that could qualify for nonrecognition of gain under one of the enumerated Code sections. The exchange will be tax-free only to the extent specifically provided in the Code and regulations.

The drafting of these Code sections is somewhat convoluted. The point is that the enumerated tax-free-exchange provisions apply only when U.S. corporations are involved in the exchange; if a foreign corporation is not treated as a corporation, the gain is recognized and taxed.

The transaction subject to Section 367(a) that is most commonly encountered is probably a transfer of property to a foreign corporation in exchange for its stock under Section 351. A liquidation of an 80–percent-owned U.S. subsidiary into its foreign parent corporation is also encompassed by the terms of Section 367(a) but is specifically dealt with in Section 367(e)(2).

Other transactions that less obviously involve outbound transfers of property are also subject to Section 367(a). Acquisition of the stock or assets of a U.S. corporation in exchange for stock of a foreign corporation in a reorganization described in Section 368(a) is normally within the scope of Section 367(a). Triangular Type A mergers, whether in the form of a forward triangular merger described in Section 368(a)(2)(D) or a reverse triangular merger described in Section 368(a)(2)(E), in which the shareholders of the acquired U.S. corporation exchange their stock in the U.S. corporation for stock in a foreign corporation, are treated as an indirect transfer of stock by the U.S. shareholders to the foreign corporation. Reg. § 1.367(a)–3(d)(1)(i), (ii) and (d)(3), Exs. 1, 2. The same analysis applies to a triangular Type B reorganization in which a U.S. person transfers stock in the acquired U.S. corporation to a U.S. subsidiary of the foreign corporation in exchange for stock of the foreign corporation. Reg. § 1.367(a)–3(d)(1)(iii) and (d)(3), Ex. 5. A U.S. shareholder is also deemed to make a transfer of stock of a U.S. corporation if substantially all of its assets are acquired by a U.S. subsidiary of a foreign corporation in exchange for stock of the foreign corporation in a triangular Type C reorganization and the U.S. acquired corporation is then liquidated. Reg. § 1.367(a)–3(d)(1)(iv) and (d)(3), Ex. 6.

Example 1. A French corporation acquires a U.S. corporation through the merger of the French corporation's wholly owned U.S. subsidiary into the U.S. acquired corporation in a reverse triangular merger described in Section 368(a)(2)(E). The shareholders of the U.S. acquired corporation exchange the stock they formerly held in that corporation for voting stock issued by the French corporation. The U.S. acquired corporation is the surviving U.S. entity. Under Section 367(a)(1), the U.S. shareholders of the U.S. acquired corporation are treated as having transferred their shares in the U.S. corporation to the French corporation in exchange for its shares. This is an outbound transaction and, unless an exception to Section 367(a)'s general rule of taxability applies, Section 354(a)'s nonrecognition provisions will not be available to shield the U.S. shareholders from tax on the gain realized on the disposition of their U.S. corporation stock.

Example 2. The result would be the same if the U.S. acquired corporation were merged into a U.S. subsidiary that is wholly owned by the French corporation, in what is called a forward triangular merger under Section 368(a)(2)(D). In this case, the surviving corporation is the French corporation's wholly owned U.S. subsidiary, but the U.S. shareholders of the U.S. acquired corporation are again deemed to have exchanged their shares in the acquired corporation for shares in the French corporation, resulting in an outbound transfer subject to Section 367(a).

Example 3. The same analysis applies if substantially all of the assets of the U.S. acquired corporation are acquired by the wholly owned U.S. subsidiary of the French corporation in a triangular Type C reorganization under Section 368(a)(1)(C) in exchange for voting stock of the French corporation. In this case, the U.S. acquired corporation distributes the voting stock of the French corporation to its shareholders in liquidation in exchange for the shares they previously held in the U.S. acquired corporation.

Distributions described in Section 355 (or so much of Section 356 as relates to it) by a U.S. corporation to a foreign person were excluded from the coverage of Section 367(a) by the Tax Reform Act of 1986 and covered instead by Section 367(e)(1). This change was thought to be necessary as a technical matter because nonrecognition of gain in a Section 355 distribution does not depend on whether the distributee is a corporation. Gain on such distributions involving outbound transactions is to be recognized under principles similar to those embodied in Section 367(a) to the extent provided in regulations. Section 355 transactions not involving an outbound transfer are covered by Section 367(b). See ¶ 10,160.

Section 367(a)(4) provides that a transfer by a U.S. person of an interest in a partnership (whether U.S. or foreign) to a foreign corporation is to be treated as a transfer of the person's pro rata share of the assets of the partnership. There is a narrow exception for the transfer of a limited partnership interest regularly traded on an established securities market, which is treated as a transfer of stock or securities. Temp. Reg. § 1.367(a)–1T(c)(3)(ii)(C). If, moreover, a U.S. or foreign partnership transfers property to a foreign corporation, a U.S. partner is treated as having transferred a proportionate share of the property for purposes of Section 367(a). Temp. Reg. § 1.367(a)–1T(c)(3)(i)(A).

Example. DP, a partnership, has four equal partners, one of whom, C, is a U.S. citizen. DP transfers appreciated property to FC, a foreign corporation, in an exchange governed by Section 367(a)(1). Each of the partners of DP is treated as having indirectly transferred 25 percent of each partnership asset to FC. The indirect transfer of property by C, the partner who is a U.S. person, i.e., 25 percent of each asset transferred to FC, is treated as a transfer governed by Section 367(a)(1). The gain recognized on the transfer of 25 percent of each asset to FC is taxable to C, unless an exception to or special rule in Section 367(a)(1) applies.

If a foreign business organization is classified for U.S. tax purposes as an entity other than a corporation (e.g., it is classified as a partnership) (see ¶¶ 13,035 et seq.) and thereafter changes its classification to an association taxable as a corporation, the change is deemed to be a transfer by the former entity of its assets to a foreign corporation under Section 351. Temp. Reg. § 1.367(a)–1T(c)(6).

Section 367(a) provides that, if a U.S. person transfers property to a foreign corporation in an exchange described in Section 332, 351, 354, 356 or 361, the corporate status of the transferee is disregarded and any gain is taxable unless one of the exceptions or special rules applies. Thus, the focus is on the exceptions and special rules.

It should be emphasized that qualifying for nonrecognition of gain under any of the exceptions in Section 367(a) or (d) is conditioned on meeting the notice requirements of Section 6038B. Failure to comply with these requirements will result in immediate gain recognition and a penalty. See ¶ 10,115.

3. EXCEPTION FOR PROPERTY TRANSFERRED FOR USE IN ACTIVE CONDUCT OF FOREIGN TRADE OR BUSINESS

[¶ 10,040]

a. Generally

The touchstone of nontaxability under Section 367(a) is whether the property is transferred for use in the active conduct of a foreign trade or business. Under Section 367(a)(3)(A), except as provided in regulations and in Section 367(a)(3)(B), gain is not recognized with respect to any property transferred for use by a foreign corporation in the active conduct of a trade or business outside the United States. The theory underlying this provision is that the business purpose for the transfer overrides the concern of Congress that the property may be transferred outside the U.S. taxing jurisdiction. In effect, if the transfer meets the requirements of the active foreign trade or business exception, the transfer is presumed not to be for tax-avoidance purposes.

The temporary regulations deal in some detail with what constitutes the active conduct of a trade or business outside the United States. To determine whether property qualifies for the active conduct of a trade or business exception, four questions must be answered:

(1) What is the transferee's trade or business?

(2) Do the transferee's activities constitute the active conduct of that trade or business?

(3) Is the trade or business conducted outside of the United States?

(4) Is the transferred property used or held for use in the trade or business?

Temp. Reg. § 1.367(a)–2T(b)(1). Making each of these determinations requires a consideration of all the facts and circumstances.

A trade or business is "a specific unified group of activities that constitute (or could constitute) an independent economic enterprise carried on for profit." To meet the definition of a trade or business for this purpose, a group of activities "must ordinarily include every operation which forms a part of, or a step in, a process by which an enterprise may earn income or profit," and must normally include both the collection of income and the payment of expenses. Any activity generating expenses that would be deductible only under Section 212 if an individual were conducting the activity is not a trade or business for this purpose. Moreover, the holding of investments in stock, securities, land or other property for one's own account and the casual sales of such investments are not a trade or business for this purpose. If the activities of the transferee foreign corporation do not constitute a trade or business, then the active trade or business exception does not apply to any transfer of property to such corporation, regardless of the level of activities that the corporation carries on. Temp. Reg. § 1.367(a)–2T(b)(2).

Example. FC, a foreign corporation, is a wholly owned marketing subsidiary of DC. FC engages in marketing activities in various foreign countries on behalf of DC. FC's marketing activities are such that they could be independently carried on for profit and they include both the collection of income and the payment of expenses. FC's marketing activities meet the definition of a trade or business even though FC acts exclusively for DC and has operations that are fully integrated with DC. The key is that FC's activities include every operation that is part of a process by which an independent enterprise could earn income or profit.

A foreign corporation actively conducts a trade or business only if its officers and employees "carry out substantial managerial and operational activities." This requirement may be met even though independent contractors carry out "incidental activities" of the trade or business on behalf of the foreign corporation. However, only the activities of the foreign corporation's officers and employees are taken into account in determining whether the corporation's officers and employees perform substantial managerial and operational activities. For this purpose, the foreign corporation's officers and employees are treated as including "the officers and employees of related entities who are made available to and supervised on a day-to-day basis by, and whose salaries are paid by (or reimbursed to the lending related entity by), the transferee foreign corporation." Temp. Reg. § 1.367(a)–2T(b)(3). If, however, the foreign corporation merely contracts out its activities to the related entity for an arm's length fee, it will not be treated as actively conducting a trade or business. Temp. Reg. § 1.367(a)–2T(b)(3), Ex.

Example. FC conducts the trade or business of manufacturing widgets. However, FC contracts with Y, a foreign corporation that is unrelated to FC, to perform a substantial amount of the manufacturing activity for an arm's length fee. (The activities performed by Y are not merely incidental activities.) Y performs its work for FC as an independent contractor. FC does not actively conduct the trade or business of manufacturing. If, however, FC owned 60 percent of the stock of Y, supervised the employees of Y on a day-to-day basis in doing the manufacturing work and paid the salaries of Y's employees, FC would be treated as actively conducting the trade or business of manufacturing.

To meet the requirement that the trade or business be actively conducted outside the United States, "the primary managerial and operational activities of the trade or business must be conducted outside the United States and immediately after the transfer the transferred assets must be located outside the United States." The regulations further explain this as a requirement that substantially all the transferred assets be located outside the United States, not that every item of transferred property be used outside of the United States. Accordingly, incidental items of transferred property located in the United States may qualify for the exception, provided that "substantially all" of the transferred assets are located outside the United States. Temp. Reg. § 1.367(a)–2T(b)(4).

Property is treated as used or held for use in a foreign corporation's trade or business if it is—

(1) Held for the principal purpose of promoting the present conduct of the trade or business;

(2) Acquired and held in the ordinary course of the trade or business; or

(3) Held in a direct relationship to the trade or business.

The regulations treat property as held in a direct relationship to a trade or business if it is held to meet the present needs of the trade or business and not its future needs. Accordingly, property is not treated as held in a direct relationship to a trade or business if it is held for the purpose of future diversification into a new trade or business, future expansion of the trade or business, future plant replacement or future business contingencies. Temp. Reg. § 1.367(a)–2T(b)(5).

Under a special rule, the determination of whether a trade or business that produces rents or royalties is actively conducted is to be made under the principles of Section 954(c)(2)(A) and the accompanying regulations (but without regard to whether the rents or royalties are received from an unrelated party). Temp. Reg. § 1.367(a)–2T(e)(1). (Section 954(c)(2)(A) is discussed at ¶ 6085.)

With certain exceptions, the active trade or business exception does not apply if a foreign corporation receives property in an exchange described in Section 367(a)(1) and as part of the same transaction transfers the property to another person. For this purpose, the regulations treat a subsequent transfer within six months of the initial transfer as part of the same transaction. Moreover, a subsequent transfer more than six months after the initial transfer may be treated as part of the same transaction under step-transaction principles. Temp. Reg. § 1.367(a)–2T(c)(1).

[¶ 10,045]

b. Assets Automatically Tainted Under Section 367(a)

Section 367(a) imposes a toll charge tax on the income realized on transfers of certain tainted assets even though they will be used in the active conduct of a foreign trade or business. Categories of tainted assets under Section 367(a) include (1) property described in Section 1221(a)(1) or 1221(a)(3)—relating to inventory and certain narrowly defined intellectual property (e.g., a copyright held by the creator of the work); (2) installment obligations, accounts receivable or similar property to the extent that the taxpayer has not previously included the principal amount in income; (3) property with respect to which the transferor is a lessor at the time of the transfer, unless the transferee was the lessee, the transferee will lease the property to third persons and meet the conditions in Temp. Reg. § 1.367(a)–4T(c)(1) and (c)(2) or, with respect to vessels or aircraft, the lessee will lease the property to third persons and meet the conditions in Temp. Reg. § 1.367(a)–4T (Temp. Reg. § 1.367(a)–4T is discussed at ¶ 10,050); (4) foreign currency and other property denominated in foreign currency (e.g., installment obligations, accounts receivable and other obligations calling for payment in foreign currency);[5] and (5) depreciable property to the extent that gain reflects depreciation deductions that have been taken against U.S.-source income. Temp. Reg. §§ 1.367(a)–4T(b) and –5T; Staff of Joint Comm. on Tax'n, 98th Cong., 2d Sess., General Explanation of the Revenue Provisions of the Deficit Reduction Act of 1984, at 432–35 (1984). Gain is also recognized with respect to a transfer to a foreign corporation of assets of a foreign branch with cumulative previously deducted losses under Section 367(a)(3)(C). See ¶ 10,095. Most intangible assets (except those covered by Section 1221(a)(3)) are treated as tainted in every case and are subject to special toll-charge rules under Section 367(d) and its regulations. See ¶ 10,090.

Recapture gain is required to be recognized as ordinary income on the transfer of depreciable property used in the United States (whether or not it is thereafter used in an active business abroad) to the extent that depreciation deductions previously claimed by the taxpayer with respect to the transferred property would be recaptured if the property were sold.

5. There is an exception for property denominated in a foreign currency of the country of the transferee foreign corporation that was acquired in the ordinary course of the transferor's business which will be carried on by the transferee. Temp. Reg. § 1.367(a)–5T(d)(2). In addition, under a special gain limitation rule, the gain recognized on a transfer of foreign currency or other property denominated in foreign currency is limited to the gain realized on the transfer of such property minus any loss realized as part of the same transaction on the transfer of such property. Temp. Reg. § 1.367(a)–5T(d)(3).

Temp. Reg. § 1.367(a)–4T(b). The amount to be recaptured as ordinary income is the full recapture amount multiplied by the proportion of U.S. use to total use of the property concerned. Temp. Reg. § 1.367(a)–4T(b)(3).

Stock and securities are not treated as assets that are tainted per se. Transfers of stock and securities to a foreign corporation will be exempt from tax under Section 367(a)(1) if they fall within one of the exceptions discussed at ¶¶ 10,075 et seq.

[¶ 10,050]

c. Property to Be Leased by Transferee

Temp. Reg. § 1.367(a)–4T(c)(1) treats tangible property transferred to a foreign corporation that the corporation will lease to others as transferred for use in the active conduct of a trade or business outside of the United States only if three requirements are met. The requirements are:

> "(i) The transferee's leasing of the property constitutes the active conduct of a leasing business;
>
> (ii) The lessee of the property is not expected to, and does not, use the property in the United States; and
>
> (iii) The transferee has need for substantial investment in assets of the type transferred."

For the transferee's leasing to constitute the active conduct of a leasing business, the foreign corporation's employees must perform substantial marketing, customer service, repair and maintenance and other substantial operational activities with respect to the transferred property outside the United States.

Note that a transfer of real property located outside the United States may qualify under this rule. However, this rule does not apply to a transfer of inventory or other property held primarily for sale to customers in the ordinary course of the transferor's business.

Even though the transfer of tangible property to be leased by the transferee foreign corporation does not meet the above requirements, it will be treated as transferred for use in the active conduct of a trade or business under a de minimis leasing rule if one of two alternative tests is met. Under the first test, the transfer of the tangible property will be treated as transferred for use in the active conduct of a trade or business if the transferee foreign corporation uses the property in the active conduct of a trade or business but leases the property "during occasional brief periods when the property would otherwise be idle, such as an airplane leased during periods of excess capacity." Under the second test, which applies only to real property located outside the United States, the transfer of the property will be treated as transferred for use in the active conduct of a trade or business if the transferred real property will be used primarily in the active conduct of a trade or business of the foreign corporation and no more than ten percent of the square footage will be leased to others. Temp. Reg. § 1.367(a)–4T(c)(2).

A special rule applies to aircraft or vessels transferred to a foreign corporation that leases such aircraft or vessels to others for use predominantly outside the United States. The transfer of the property is treated as transferred for use in the active conduct of a trade or business if the foreign corporation's employees "perform substantial managerial and operational activities of leasing aircraft or vessels outside the United States." Temp. Reg. § 1.367(a)–4T(c)(3).

[¶ 10,055]

d. Property to Be Sold

Property is not treated as transferred for use in the active conduct of a trade or business if, at the time of the transfer, it is reasonable to believe that, in the foreseeable future, the transferee will sell or otherwise dispose of any material portion of the transferred property other than in the ordinary course of business. Temp. Reg. § 1.367(a)–4T(d).

[¶ 10,060]

e. Oil and Gas Working Interests

A working interest in oil and gas properties is treated as transferred for use in the active conduct of a trade or business if certain requirements set forth in the regulations are met and, at the time of the transfer, the transferee has no intention to farm out or otherwise transfer any part of the working interest. Temp. Reg. § 1.367(a)–4T(e).

[¶ 10,065]

f. Compulsory Transfers

Under an exception that applies to certain so-called compulsory transfers, the regulations presume property to be transferred for use in the active conduct of a trade or business outside the United States if two requirements are met. First, the property must have been previously in use in the foreign country in which the transferee foreign corporation was organized. Second, the transfer must be either legally required by the foreign government of that country as a condition of doing business in the country or "[c]ompelled by a genuine threat of immediate expropriation by the foreign government." Temp. Reg. § 1.367(a)–4T(f).

[¶ 10,070]

g. Exception Not Applicable to Certain Reorganization Transfers Involving U.S. Corporate Transferors

Under Section 367(a)(5), the active trade or business exception will not apply to a reorganization exchange governed by Section 361 if the transferor corporation is controlled by individuals or by more than five U.S. corporations. For example, if a U.S. corporation owned entirely by individuals transfers substantially all of its assets to a foreign corporation in exchange for stock in the foreign corporation in a C reorganization, the active trade or business exception will not apply to the reorganization exchange between the U.S. transferor corporation and the transferee foreign corporation. Thus, Section 367(a)(1) will override Section 361, and the U.S. corporation will have to recognize gain on the asset transfer, unless one of the other exceptions in Section 367(a) applies.

[¶ 10,075]

4. SPECIAL RULES FOR STOCK OR SECURITIES OF CORPORATIONS

The general rule of taxability applies to transfers of stock or securities by a U.S. person to a foreign corporation unless an exception is available. See Reg. § 1.367(a)–3(a). Some exceptions require the execution of a closing agreement between the IRS and the U.S. transferor under which the transferor must agree to recognize taxable gain on the transferee corporation's later disposition of the transferred stock or securities (a "gain-recognition agreement"). The gain-recognition agreement requires the U.S. transferor to recognize any realized gain in the transferred stock or securities not recognized at the time of transfer if the transferee foreign corporation disposes of the transferred stock or securities during the five-year gain-recognition period. Gain recognition to the U.S. transferor is also triggered if the corporation the stock or securities of which were transferred to the foreign corporation (the "transferred corporation") disposes of substantially all of its assets. (There are various other gain-triggering events described in the regulations.) If the transferee foreign corporation disposes of the transferred stock or securities (or the transferred corporation disposes of substantially all of its assets) during the five-year period in which the gain-recognition agreement is in effect, the U.S. transferor must recognize any previously unrecognized gain plus pay an interest charge to compensate for the benefit of deferral of the U.S. tax on the unrecognized gain. If gain is triggered under the gain-recognition agreement, the U.S. transferor files an amended return for the original year of transfer, reporting the recognized gain and the interest charge. Alternatively, the U.S. transferor may elect to report the gain, plus the interest charge, on the return for the year in which the triggering event occurs. Reg. § 1.367(a)–8.

[¶ 10,080]

a. Exception for Transfers of Stock or Securities of a Foreign Corporation

The regulations provide an exception to Section 367(a)(1) for transfers of the stock or securities of a foreign corporation by a U.S. person to a foreign corporation. The U.S. transferor will obtain nonrecognition-of-gain treatment on the transfer under the normal rules of Section 351, 354, 356 or 361 if the exception applies. The requirements for the exception vary for U.S. transferors owning less than five percent of the voting power and value of the stock of the transferee foreign corporation and those owning five percent or more of the voting power or value of the transferee corporation's stock. For purposes of determining the ownership of the transferee corporation, the constructive ownership rules of Section 318, as modified by Section 958(b) of the controlled foreign corporation provisions, apply. See Reg. § 1.367(a)–3(b).

If the U.S. transferor owns less than five percent of the total voting power and total value of the stock of the transferee foreign corporation, the U.S. transferor will obtain nonrecognition-of-gain treatment on the transfer of the stock or securities of a foreign corporation without having to file a gain-recognition agreement. A U.S. transferor owning five percent or more of either the total voting power or total value of the transferee corporation's stock will obtain nonrecognition-of-gain treatment on the transfer only by entering into a five-year, gain-recognition agreement with the IRS. Reg. § 1.367(a)–3(b)(1). The gain-recognition agreement must meet the detailed requirements of Reg. § 1.367(a)–8.

Example. DC1, a U.S. corporation, owns 36 percent of the stock of FS, a foreign corporation, and DC2, another U.S. corporation that is not related to DC1, owns four percent of the stock of FS. The other 60 percent of the FS stock is owned by foreign persons unrelated to DC1 or DC2. As part of a plan of reorganization, DC1 exchanges its 36–percent stock interest in FS and DC2 exchanges its four-percent stock interest in FS for stock of FC, another foreign corporation unrelated to DC1 or DC2. After the reorganization exchange, DC1 owns nine percent of FC and DC2 owns one percent of FC. This reorganization transaction qualifies as a B reorganization. Section 367(a)(1) will not apply to override nonrecognition treatment for DC1 and DC2 if the requirements of Reg. § 1.367(a)–3(b) are met. Thus, Section 367(a)(1) will not trigger gain recognition and DC1 will obtain nonrecognition treatment under Section 354 if it enters into a five-year, gain-recognition agreement with the IRS. Because DC2 owns less than five percent of both the total voting power and value of the stock of FC after the exchange, DC2 will obtain nonrecognition treatment under Section 354 without having to file a gain-recognition agreement.

If a U.S. transferor transfers stock in a controlled foreign corporation in which it is a U.S. shareholder but does not receive back stock in a controlled foreign corporation in which it is a U.S. shareholder, the transaction is not automatically taxable under Section 367(a)(1). Instead, both Section 367(a) and (b) apply to the exchange. If the U.S. transferor is required to file a gain-recognition agreement to obtain nonrecognition-of-gain treatment and fails to do so, Section 367(a)(1) applies and the U.S. transferor's gain will be fully taxable. Moreover, all or some portion of that gain may be treated as a dividend under Section 1248. If the U.S. transferor is required to file a gain-recognition agreement to obtain nonrecognition-of-gain treatment and does so, Section 367(b) requires the U.S. transferor to include in income the Section 1248 amount attributable to the stock exchange. See ¶¶ 10,130–10,150. The amount of gain covered by the gain-recognition agreement equals the amount of gain realized on the transfer minus the inclusion under Section 367(b). See Reg. § 1.367(a)–3(b)(2); T.D. 8770, 1998–2 C.B. 3, 5. The concurrent application of Section 367(a) and (b) to certain transactions is further discussed at ¶ 10,130.

[¶ 10,085]

b. Exception for Transfers of Stock or Securities of a U.S. Corporation

Transfers by a U.S. person of stock and securities of a U.S. corporation to a foreign corporation are generally taxable under Section 367(a)(1), unless the exception for U.S. transferors with no more than 50–percent ownership of the transferee, described below, applies. Reg. § 1.367(a)–3(a).

Under Reg. § 1.367(a)–3(c)(1), a transfer of stock or securities of a U.S. corporation by a U.S. person to a foreign corporation is not taxable under Section 367(a)(1) if all of the following five conditions are met:

(1) The U.S. corporation the stock or securities of which are transferred (the "U.S. target company") complies with certain reporting requirements in Reg. § 1.367(a)–3(c)(6);

(2) No more than 50 percent of each of the total voting power and the total value of the transferee foreign corporation's stock is received in the transaction, in the aggregate, by U.S. transferors;

(3) No more than 50 percent of each of the total voting power and the total value of the transferee foreign corporation's stock is owned, in the aggregate, immediately after the transfer by U.S. persons who are either officers, directors or five-percent-or-more shareholders (by value) of the U.S. target company immediately before the transfer;

(4) The transferee foreign corporation or an affiliate of the transferee foreign corporation has been engaged in the active conduct of a

trade or business that is substantial in comparison to the U.S. target company's trade or business, for the entire 36–month period before the date of the transfer and, at the time of transfer, neither the transferors nor the transferee foreign corporation have an intention to substantially dispose of or discontinue that trade or business. A foreign corporation is treated as meeting this substantiality requirement, if, at the time of transfer, the fair market value of the transferee foreign corporation is equal to or greater than the fair market value of the U.S. target company. See Reg. § 1.367(a)–3(c)(3); and

(5) Either (i) the U.S. transferor owns less than five percent of both the total voting power and the total value of the transferee foreign corporation's stock immediately after the transfer (in which event no gain-recognition agreement is necessary to qualify for the exception); or (ii) a five-percent-or-more U.S. transferor enters into a five-year, gain-recognition agreement with the IRS under Reg. § 1.367(a)–8 and complies with the reporting requirements of Section 6038B.

For purposes of determining the ownership of stock, securities or other property in applying these requirements, the constructive ownership rules of Section 318, as modified by Section 958(b), apply. Reg. § 1.367(a)–3(c)(4)(iv). The regulations presume that persons who transfer stock or securities of the U.S. target company or other property to the transferee foreign corporation are U.S. persons. Reg. § 1.367(a)–3(c)(2). This presumption can be rebutted if the U.S. target company (1) obtains ownership statements as specified in Reg. § 1.367(a)–3(c)(5)(i) from a sufficient number of persons that transfer U.S. target company stock or securities (or other property) in the transaction that are not U.S. persons to show that the 50–percent-U.S.-transferors threshold has not been exceeded and (2) the U.S. target company attaches to its timely filed U.S. tax return for the tax year in which the transfer occurs a statement containing certain information specified in the regulations. Reg. § 1.367(a)–3(c)(7).

Example. DC, a U.S. corporation, owns all of the stock of DS, a U.S. corporation. FC is a foreign corporation unrelated to DC. Pursuant to a plan of reorganization, DC transfers all of the DS stock to FC in exchange for FC stock. This exchange qualifies as a B reorganization. If, immediately after the exchange, DC owns more than 50 percent of the stock of FC, the exception in Reg. § 1.367(a)–3(c) will not apply. Accordingly, Section 367(a)(1) will override Section 354 and require DC to recognize its gain on the transfer of the DS stock to FC. If, immediately after the exchange, DC owns 50 percent or less of the total voting power and value of the FC stock, the fair market value of FC is equal to or greater than the fair market value of DS at the time of transfer and FC otherwise meets the active conduct of a trade or business requirements and the other requirements discussed above, the exception in Reg. 1.367(a)–3(c) will apply provided that DC enters into a five-year, gain-recognition agreement. If so, DC will be able to obtain nonrecognition treatment under Section 354 on the exchange. If DC owns less than five percent of both the total voting power and value of FC immediately after the exchange, the exception in Reg. § 1.367(a)–3(c) will apply and DC will not recognize its gain on the transfer of the DS stock to FC without having to enter into a five-year, gain-recognition agreement.

[¶ 10,086]

c. Corporate Inversion or Expatriation Transactions

The regulations regarding transfers of the stock or securities of a U.S. corporation to a foreign corporation, discussed above, reflect, in part, concerns of the Treasury Department and the IRS regarding so-called "corporate inversion" or "corporate expatriation" transactions—transactions in which a publicly held U.S. corporation having one or more foreign subsidiaries becomes a U.S. subsidiary of one of those foreign subsidiaries or a newly organized foreign corporation through a stock or asset exchange intended to come within the reorganization provisions of the Code. The Treasury and the IRS are justifiably concerned that these restructurings are being undertaken for tax-avoidance purposes. See IRS Notice 94–46, 1994–1 C.B. 356. After the transaction, the former shareholders of the U.S. parent corporation own stock of a foreign corporation that is *not* a controlled foreign corporation (within the meaning of Section 957) because it is publicly held and, therefore, is *not* subject to the Subpart F anti-deferral rules, discussed in Chapter 6. Thus, the restructured group's foreign operations will not generally be subject to current U.S. tax. Moreover, U.S. tax on the restructured group's U.S. operations may be reduced through deductible payments made by the now U.S. subsidiary corporation to the foreign parent corporation (which is often incorporated in a low-tax or no-tax country that may have a favorable treaty with the United States). The Treasury Department further explains its concerns in the following excerpt from a 2002 report.

[¶ 10,087]

U.S. TREASURY DEPARTMENT, CORPORATE INVERSION TRANSACTIONS: TAX POLICY IMPLICATIONS

17–20 (May 2002).

* * *

A. Introduction

Inversion transactions are not new. However, until recently they were a relatively isolated phenomenon. Recently there has been a marked increase in the frequency of inversion transactions and the size of the companies involved. At the same time, the range of industries in which these transactions are occurring is broadening. These increases reflect an evolution in the perception of these transactions. As more inversion transactions are consummated, more companies find it acceptable from a public relations standpoint to contemplate such a transaction. Indeed, in those industries in which there have been several inversion transactions, other companies within the industry may feel competitive pressure to consider an inversion.

Stock market conditions likely have been a factor in the recent increase in inversion activity. Most inversion transactions have been structured as [s]tock [t]ransactions, which are taxable to the company's shareholders. However, as a result of several factors, the resulting shareholder-level tax may be less significant today. In general, stock prices have fallen considerably in the past two years. The three most widely-quoted indices of U.S. corporate share prices, the Dow Jones Industrial Average, the Standard & Poor's 500, and the Nasdaq Composite, have fallen roughly 20 percent, 30 percent, and 70 percent, respectively, from the all-time highs reached in 2000. This is particularly significant in light of the trend in shareholder turnover, which indicates that shareholders are holding stock for a shorter period of time, thereby reducing the potential for built-in gain. For example, the annual percentage turnover rates (i.e., the number of shares traded over the total number of shares outstanding) for the New York Stock Exchange have increased from 36 percent in 1980, to 46 percent in 1990, and to 88 percent in 2000.

There also has been a significant increase in shareholdings by persons and entities that are not likely to be sensitive to U.S. capital gains tax, such as tax-exempt investors and certain institutional shareholders. Between 1981 and 2001, foreign persons increased their U.S. stock holdings from 5.4 percent to 12.4 percent. The holdings by mutual funds increased even more significantly, from 2.7 percent in 1981 to 18.7 percent in 2001. Mutual funds have some tax-exempt holders such as IRAs. Moreover, mutual fund managers appear to be less sensitive to tax considerations.

Although these market conditions have facilitated the recent inversion activity, they are not what motivates the transactions. U.S.-based multinational companies and their shareholders are making the decision to undertake an inversion transaction in large part because of overall tax savings. Through an inversion transaction, a U.S.-based multinational group can substantially reduce or eliminate the U.S. corporate-level tax on income from its foreign operations [through the inverted corporate structure's avoidance of the Subpart F rules]. In addition, the inversion transaction may be used to achieve a reduction in the U.S. corporate-level tax on income from U.S. operations [through "base-stripping," deductible payments of interest or royalties from the now U.S. subsidiary to the foreign parent corporation, often organized in a low-tax or no-tax country that may have a tax treaty with the United States]. An inversion is complicated as a transactional matter but may be virtually transparent as an operational matter. The fact that our tax law operates so that substantial reductions in U.S. taxes are available through a transaction that is more form than substance is troubling to policy makers and the public alike.

Nevertheless, in considering the appropriate response to the recent inversion activity, it is important not to lose sight of the fact that in many cases the same types of tax reduction may be achieved through other means. A start-up venture that contemplates both U.S. and foreign operations must choose a location for its corporate parent. While the natural choice for a U.S.-based venture may be a U.S. parent corporation, that often will not be the most tax-efficient choice. By forming initially through a foreign parent corporation, the venture can enjoy the same tax savings as would be available through a subsequent inversion transaction.

The U.S. tax reduction achieved through an inversion transaction also is available to a foreign acquiror of a U.S.-based multinational group. Following the acquisition, the group may be restructured to achieve substantial reductions in U.S. tax on the income of both foreign and U.S. operations of the former U.S. group. Short of an acquisition of the entire U.S.-based group, a foreign company may acquire the foreign operations of the U.S. group. The movement of those foreign operations out of the U.S. group to the foreign acquiror also results in a substantial reduction or elimination of U.S. tax on the income from such operations.

In the last few years, foreign acquisitions of U.S. companies have grown substantially. Foreign acquisitions of U.S. businesses were $90.9 billion in 1997, $234 billion in 1998, $266.5 billion in 1999, and $340 billion in 2000. There are many economic factors and business reasons that underlie foreign acquisitions of U.S. companies. Even so, the disparity in tax treatment between multinational companies based in the United States and those based in our major trading partners must be recognized and considered as foreign-based multinationals increase their investment in the United States.

B. Cost Differences and Their Effects

Inversion transactions implicate fundamental issues of tax policy. The U.S. tax system can operate to provide a cost advantage to foreign-based multinational companies over U.S.-based multinational companies. Inversions demonstrate this cost advantage in its purest form. By reorganizing to create an offshore parent corporation in a no-tax jurisdiction, a U.S.-based group can reduce its tax liability significantly without any real changes in its business operations and without negatively affecting its access to capital markets. However, this cost advantage is not limited to corporations that invert. Foresighted planners can obtain this same cost advantage by incorporating offshore from the outset. Moreover, a foreign corporation can gain a cost advantage with respect to the operations of an existing U.S. group through a takeover of that group, which may be either friendly or hostile.

The cost advantage accorded by the U.S. tax system to foreign-based multinational companies relative to U.S.-based multinational companies can have significant effects on the way business activity is conducted. Foreign-based multinationals may achieve increased market share by passing the tax savings on to customers in the form of reduced prices. This increased market share translates into reduced business opportunities for U.S.-based multinationals. The differential in U.S. tax treatment also may affect acquisitions of U.S.-based multinational groups, with a foreign-based acquiror able to pay more for the acquisition because of the post-acquisition tax savings unavailable to a U.S. acquiror. Therefore, the likelihood is increased that a foreign acquiror will prevail over a U.S. competitor in an acquisition bidding war.

These changes in business activity can have effects on the U.S. tax system. A shift from U.S.-based multinational structures to foreign-based multinational structures, however accomplished, can erode the U.S. corporate income tax base. More business activity will be conducted in the form that allows enjoyment of a relative reduction in U.S. tax liability. The income from the purely foreign operations of a foreign-based company can escape U.S. corporate-level tax altogether. Moreover, there are techniques available under current law that can result in a reduction in the U.S. corporate-level tax on income from the U.S. operations of a foreign-based company.

In addition, changes in business form can affect the location of business activity. A foreign-headquartered company may make locational decisions that are very different from those a U.S.-headquartered company would make. A foreign-based company that has grown through increases in market share due to cost advantages or through acquisitions may make different supply and investment choices than the U.S.-based company it replaced or acquired. Locational decisions that shift business activity away from the United States have an adverse effect on U.S. jobs, U.S. business, and the U.S. economy overall. Of course, any such shift also affects the U.S. corporate income tax base.

The policy response to corporate inversion transactions should be broad enough to address the underlying differences in the U.S. tax treatment of U.S.-based companies and foreign-based companies, without regard to how foreign-based status is achieved. An approach that addresses only inversion transactions runs the serious risk of simply encouraging the other forms of transaction that can be used to accomplish the same tax results, whether it is original foreign incorporation or foreign acquisition of a U.S. multinational group. The increased inversion activity seen recently is a symptom, and the concerns implicated can be addressed most effectively and most fully by addressing the underlying causes.

An appropriate immediate response should address the U.S. tax advantages that are available to foreign-based companies because of the ability to reduce the U.S. corporate-level tax on income from U.S. operations. It also is necessary to address the U.S. tax disadvantages that are caused for U.S.-based companies because of the U.S. tax treatment of income from their foreign operations. * * * In addition, consideration should be given to the overall U.S. corporate income tax burden. Our tax system should be reviewed and evaluated relative to the tax systems of our major trading partners; fundamental structural issues include the relative share of the tax burden on the corporate sector and the persistent difficulties in properly measuring income and appropriately allocating the tax burden on that basis.

* * *

[¶ 10,088]

d. 2004 JOBS Act Provisions and Tax Treaty Provisions Aimed at Corporate Inversion Transactions

In 2004, corporate inversion transactions became a prime focus of Congress as a result of several well-publicized inversion transactions during the prior decade (e.g., the inversion transactions involving Tyco Corporation and Cooper Industries) as well as one that was not completed largely because of the legislative and administrative focus on these transactions (i.e., a proposed inversion transaction involving The Stanley Works). The corporate inversion issue generated a vigorous political debate, in part because of concern by some members of Congress that the tax savings arising from these transactions were causing U.S. multinational corporate groups to shift business operations, manufacturing plants and jobs abroad, with a resulting adverse effect on U.S. job opportunities and the overall U.S. economy (as mentioned in the Treasury Report, excerpted at ¶ 10,087). The House Ways and Means Committee Report accompanying the enactment of the 2004 JOBS Act describes the corporate inversion problem, as follows:

> Under present law, a U.S. corporation may reincorporate in a foreign jurisdiction and thereby replace the U.S. parent corporation of a multinational corporate group with a foreign parent corporation. These transactions are commonly referred to as inversion transactions. Inversion transactions may take many different forms, including stock inversions, asset inversions, and various combinations of and variations on the two. Most of the known transactions to date have been stock inversions. In one example of a stock inversion, a U.S. corporation forms a foreign corporation, which in turn forms a domestic merger subsidiary. The domestic merger subsidiary then merges into the U.S. corporation, with the U.S. corporation surviving, now as a subsidiary of the new foreign corporation. The U.S. corpora-

tion's shareholders receive shares of the foreign corporation and are treated as having exchanged their U.S. corporation shares for the foreign corporation shares. An asset inversion reaches a similar result, but through a direct merger of the top-tier U.S. corporation into a new foreign corporation, among other possible forms. An inversion transaction may be accompanied or followed by further restructuring of the corporate group. For example, in the case of a stock inversion, in order to remove income from foreign operations from the U.S. taxing jurisdiction, the U.S. corporation may transfer some or all of its foreign subsidiaries directly to the new foreign parent corporation or other related foreign corporations.

In addition to removing foreign operations from the U.S. taxing jurisdiction, the corporate group may derive further advantage from the inverted structure by reducing U.S. tax on U.S.-source income through various earnings stripping or other transactions. This may include earnings stripping through payment by a U.S. corporation of deductible amounts such as interest, royalties, rents, or management service fees to the new foreign parent or other foreign affiliates. In this respect, the post-inversion structure enables the group to employ the same tax-reduction strategies that are available to other multinational corporate groups with foreign parents and U.S. subsidiaries, subject to the same limitations (e.g., secs. 163(j) and 482).

Inversion transactions may give rise to immediate U.S. tax consequences at the shareholder and/or the corporate level, depending on the type of inversion. In stock inversions, the U.S. shareholders generally recognize gain (but not loss) under section 367(a), based on the difference between the fair market value of the foreign corporation shares received and the adjusted basis of the domestic corporation stock exchanged. To the extent that a corporation's share value has declined, and/or it has many foreign or tax-exempt shareholders, the impact of this section 367(a) "toll charge" is reduced. The transfer of foreign subsidiaries or other assets to the foreign parent corporation also may give rise to U.S. tax consequences at the corporate level (e.g., gain recognition and earnings and profits inclusions under secs. 1001, 311(b), 304, 367, 1248 or other provisions). The tax on any income recognized as a result of these restructurings may be reduced or eliminated through the use of net operating losses, foreign tax credits, and other tax attributes.

In asset inversions, the U.S. corporation generally recognizes gain (but not loss) under section 367(a) as though it had sold all of its assets, but the shareholders generally do not recognize gain or loss, assuming the transaction meets the requirements of a reorganization under section 368.

H.R. Rep. No. 548, pt. 1, 108th Cong., 2d Sess. 243–44 (2004).

To remove the incentive to engage in corporate inversion transactions, Congress included several provisions in the 2004 JOBS Act aimed at this problem.

First, the JOBS Act added Section 7874 to the Code, which defines two different types of corporate inversion transactions and provides a different set of tax consequences to reach each type of inversion transaction.[6] This provision had a retroactive effective date and applied to tax years ending after March 4, 2003 (but it did not affect the highly publicized inversion transactions that generated the congressional concern). It has a broad-ranging scope and critics have argued that it goes well beyond what was necessary to deal with the tax policy issues raised by tax-motivated inversion transactions. The House Conference Committee Report explained Section 7874, as follows:

> ***Transactions involving at least 80 percent identity of stock ownership***
>
> The first type of inversion is a transaction in which, pursuant to a plan or a series of related transactions: (1) a U.S. corporation becomes a subsidiary of a foreign-incorporated entity or otherwise transfers substantially all of its properties to such an entity in a transaction completed after March 4, 2003; (2) the former shareholders of the U.S. corporation hold (by reason of holding stock in the U.S. corporation) 80 percent or more (by vote or value) of the stock of the foreign-incorporated entity after the transaction; and (3) the foreign-incorporated entity, considered together with all companies connected to it by a chain of greater than 50 percent ownership (i.e., the "expanded affiliated group"), does not have substantial business activities in the entity's country of incorporation, compared to the total worldwide business activities of the expanded affiliated group. The provision denies the intended tax benefits of this type of inversion by deeming the top-tier foreign corporation to be a domestic corporation for all purposes of the Code.
>
> In determining whether a transaction meets the definition of an inversion under the proposal, stock held by members of the expanded affiliated group that includes the foreign incorporated entity is disregarded. For example, if the former top-tier U.S. corporation receives

6. As mentioned in Chapters 1 and 6, in a tax reform report issued in 2005, the Staff of the Joint Committee on Taxation proposed new rules for determining the residence of publicly traded foreign entities. This proposal would determine a publicly traded foreign incorporated entity's residence based on the location of its primary management and control. For this purpose, a corporation's place of primary management and control is "where the executive officers and senior management of the corporation exercise day-to-day responsibility for the strategic, financial and operational policy decision making for the company (including direct and indirect subsidiaries)." See Staff of Joint Comm. on Tax'n, 109th Cong., 1st Sess., Options to Improve Tax Compliance and Reform Tax Expenditures, at 179–80 (2005). This proposal would constitute a more comprehensive solution to the tax policy issues raised by corporate inversion transactions. As discussed at ¶ 6060, however, this proposal, if enacted into law, would create uncertainty concerning the residency of publicly traded foreign corporations for U.S. tax purposes and thereby increase compliance costs for taxpayers and administration costs for the IRS.

stock of the foreign incorporated entity (e.g., so-called "hook" stock), the stock would not be considered in determining whether the transaction meets the definition. Similarly, if a U.S. parent corporation converts an existing wholly owned U.S. subsidiary into a new wholly owned controlled foreign corporation, the stock of the new foreign corporation would be disregarded. Stock sold in a public offering related to the transaction also is disregarded for these purposes.

Transfers of properties or liabilities as part of a plan a principal purpose of which is to avoid the purposes of the proposal are disregarded. In addition, the Treasury Secretary is granted authority to prevent the avoidance of the purposes of the proposal, including avoidance through the use of related persons, pass-through or other noncorporate entities, or other intermediaries, and through transactions designed to qualify or disqualify a person as a related person or a member of an expanded affiliated group. Similarly, the Treasury Secretary is granted authority to treat certain non-stock instruments as stock, and certain stock as not stock, where necessary to carry out the purposes of the proposal.

Transactions involving at least 60 percent but less than 80 percent identity of stock ownership

The second type of inversion is a transaction that would meet the definition of an inversion transaction described above, except that the 80–percent ownership threshold is not met. In such a case, if at least a 60–percent ownership threshold is met, then a second set of rules applies to the inversion. Under these rules, the inversion transaction is respected (i.e., the foreign corporation is treated as foreign), but any applicable corporate-level "toll charges" for establishing the inverted structure are not offset by tax attributes such as net operating losses or foreign tax credits. Specifically, any applicable corporate-level income or gain required to be recognized under sections 304, 311(b), 367, 1001, 1248, or any other provision with respect to the transfer of controlled foreign corporation stock or the transfer or license of other assets by a U.S. corporation as part of the inversion transaction or after such transaction to a related foreign person is taxable, without offset by any tax attributes (e.g., net operating losses or foreign tax credits). This rule does not apply to certain transfers of inventory and similar property. These measures generally apply for a 10–year period following the inversion transaction.

Under the proposal, inversion transactions include certain partnership transactions. Specifically, the proposal applies to transactions in which a foreign-incorporated entity acquires substantially all of the properties constituting a trade or business of a domestic partnership, if after the acquisition at least 60 percent of the stock of the entity is held by former partners of the partnership (by reason of holding their partnership interests), provided that the other terms of the basic

> definition are met. For purposes of applying this test, all partnerships that are under common control within the meaning of section 482 are treated as one partnership, except as provided otherwise in regulations. In addition, the modified "toll charge" proposals apply at the partner level.

H.R. Conf. Rep. No. 755, 108th Cong., 2d Sess. 560–62 (2004) (footnotes omitted).

Second, the JOBS Act added Section 4985 to the Code, which imposes an excise tax on certain individuals who hold stock options and other stock-based compensation in a corporation in the case of certain inversion transactions involving the corporation. The excise tax applies to the value of specified stock compensation held, directly or indirectly, by or for the benefit of a disqualified individual, or a member of the individual's family (as defined in Section 267), at any time during the 12–month period starting six months before the corporation's expatriation date. § 4985(a)(2); see H.R. Conf. Rep. No. 755, 108th Cong., 2d Sess. 563 (2004). The rate of the excise tax is equal to the preferential rate of tax on long-term capital gains in Section 1(h)(1)(C). § 4985(a)(1). A disqualified individual is any individual who is, with respect to a corporation, at any time during the 12–month period starting six months before the corporation's expatriation date, subject to the requirements of Section 16(a) of the Securities and Exchange Act of 1934 with respect to the corporation or any member of the corporation's expanded affiliated group, or who would be subject to those requirements if the corporation were an issuer of securities referred to in that provision of the securities laws. § 4985(e)(1). This group generally includes certain top-level officers, directors and ten–percent-or-greater shareholders of a corporation. See H.R. Conf. Rep. No. 755, 108th Cong., 2d Sess. 563 (2004). The excise tax is generally imposed only if gain is recognized in whole or in part by any shareholder on account of certain corporate inversion transactions. § 4985(c).

Third, the JOBS Act added Section 6043A to the Code, which requires the acquiring corporation in any taxable acquisition to file an information return with the IRS in accordance with forms or regulations issued by the Treasury and the IRS.

Fourth, Section 424 of the JOBS Act required the Treasury Department to conduct a study of the effectiveness of the earnings stripping provisions in the Code, which was to include the following issues:

> (1) the effectiveness of Section 163(j) in preventing the shifting of income out of the United States;
>
> (2) whether any deficiencies in these earnings stripping provisions place U.S. businesses at a competitive disadvantage relative to foreign businesses;
>
> (3) the effect of earnings striping activities on the U.S. tax base;

(4) whether laws of other countries facilitate the stripping of earnings out of the United States; and

(5) whether changes in the earnings stripping provisions would affect U.S. jobs.

The Treasury Department issued that report in 2007. See U.S. Treas. Dep't, Report to the Congress on Earnings Stripping, Transfer Pricing and U.S. Income Tax Treaties (Nov. 2007) ("2007 Treasury Report").

Finally, Section 806 of the JOBS Act required the Treasury to conduct studies of various issues relating to the corporate expatriation problem and report back to the Congress. The three studies to be prepared by the Treasury were:

(1) A study regarding "the effectiveness of current transfer pricing rules and compliance efforts in ensuring that cross-border transfers and other related-party transactions, particularly transactions involving intangible assets, service contracts, or leases cannot be used improperly to shift income out of the United States";

(2) A study of U.S. income tax treaties "to identify any inappropriate reductions in United States withholding tax that provide opportunities for shifting income out of the United States, and to evaluate whether existing anti-abuse mechanisms are operating properly"; and

(3) A study of the effectiveness of the tax provisions relating to corporate expatriation.

These items also were the subject of the 2007 Treasury Report cited above.

In addition to these legislative changes, the United States in 2004 also negotiated protocols to tax treaties with several countries that had served as the residence country for the foreign parent corporation in some of these inversion transactions. Under the amended limitation-on-benefits provisions in these protocols, a resident corporation of the treaty country is entitled to claim benefits under the treaty only if it can establish a substantial presence in the treaty country through either the public trading of its stock on a specified exchange or meeting stock ownership and base erosion tests. See United States–Barbados Tax Treaty, Art. 22; United States–Netherlands Tax Treaty, Art. 26. Thus, the tightening of the limitation-of-benefits provisions in tax treaties is yet another avenue for the United States to pursue in trying to prevent abusive corporate inversion transactions.

[¶ 10,090]

5. SPECIAL RULES FOR INTANGIBLES

Introduction. As discussed above, Congress recognized that transfers of manufacturing and marketing intangibles to a foreign corporation presented special problems. Before 1984, a U.S. taxpayer would develop such intangibles and often deduct the costs of such development against its U.S.-source income. The U.S. taxpayer would then transfer the intangible to a foreign corporation for use in an active trade or business abroad, often obtaining a favorable ruling from the IRS allowing the transfer to be tax-free. The income from exploitation of the intangible would thereafter be earned by the foreign corporation, largely free of any current U.S. income tax. Even if a toll charge were imposed on the U.S. taxpayer at the time of transfer, it would not necessarily remedy the tax-avoidance potential inherent in these transfers. The value of the intangible at time of transfer was often uncertain and speculative, resulting in an amount of gain recognition at the time of transfer that would not reflect the ultimate value of the intangible. To deal with these problems, special rules for intangibles were adopted by tax legislation in 1984 and 1986 and are set forth in Sections 367(d) and 482.

Constructive royalty payments under Section 367(d). Under Section 367(d), marketing and manufacturing intangibles, as broadly defined in Section 936(h)(3)(B),[7] are treated as a special class of tainted asset. In every case involving the transfer of such assets in a transaction falling within Section 351 or 361, the transferor is treated as having sold the property in exchange for payments that are contingent on the productivity, use or disposition of such property. These imputed or constructive royalty payments must reasonably reflect the amounts that would have been received annually in the form of such payments over the useful life of such property. § 367(d)(2)(A)(ii)(I). Under the regulations, the transferor must continue to recognize the constructive royalties over the useful life of the intangible, but not in excess of 20 years. Temp. Reg. § 1.367(d)–1T(c)(3). These deemed royalty payments are treated as ordinary income to the U.S. transferor. § 367(d)(2)(C); Temp. Reg. § 1.367(d)–1T(c)(1).

As a result of tax legislation enacted in 1986, Section 367(d) now provides that, in the case of any transfer of intangible property in a Section 351 or 361 exchange, the royalty income with respect to such transfer is to be commensurate with the income attributable to the intangible. This means that the constructive royalty is calculated in an amount that represents an arm's length charge for the use of the property (as determined under the Section 482 regulations). Temp. Reg. § 1.367(d)–1T(c)(1). This "super-royalty" provision authorizes review and possible adjustment of the royalty on a periodic basis, subject to exceptions spelled out in the regulations. See ¶ 12,130.

7. Intangible property is defined in Section 936(h)(3)(B) as any (1) patent, invention, formula, process, design, pattern or knowhow, (2) copyright, literary, musical or artistic composition, (3) trademark, trade name or brand name, (4) franchise, license or contract, (5) method, program, system, procedure, campaign, survey, study, forecast, estimate, customer list or technical data or (6) any similar item, which property has substantial value independent of the services of any individual. For a similar definition of intangible property, see Reg. § 1.482–4(b).

Source of Section 367(d) payments and treatment for foreign tax credit limitation purposes. Under a change to the statute made in 1997, the source of constructive royalty payments under Section 367(d) is determined under the normal source rules for royalties in Sections 865(d)(1)(B), 861(a)(4) and 862(a)(4). Thus, the constructive royalty payments will be foreign-source income to the extent that the intangible is used outside the United States. Since such constructive royalty income is not likely to be subject to any foreign tax, the effect of this source rule is to provide the U.S. transferor with low- or zero-taxed foreign-source income for purposes of the foreign tax credit limitations. Such income can absorb excess foreign tax credits on other high-taxed foreign-source income falling within the same foreign tax credit limitation category.

As discussed in more detail at ¶ 12,130, the 2004 JOBS Act amended Section 367(d)(2)(C) to provide that deemed payments under Section 367(d) are treated as royalties for purposes of applying the foreign tax credit limitations in Section 904. This change is effective retroactively to amounts treated as received under Section 367(d)(2) on or after August 5, 1997. The result is that the Section 904(d)(3) look-through rules will apply if the constructive Section 367(d) payments are treated as received from a controlled foreign corporation. If, instead, the Section 367(d) constructive payments are treated as received from a noncontrolled foreign corporation or from another related or unrelated party, these payments will fall into the general category income limitation basket if derived in the active conduct of the transferor's trade or business, or, if not so derived, generally will fall into the passive category income limitation basket.

Earnings and profits adjustment and treatment of Section 367(d) payments for Subpart F purposes. Section 367(d)(2)(B) calls for an appropriate reduction in the earnings and profits of the foreign corporation to reflect the royalty-like payments deemed paid by the foreign corporation. See Temp. Reg. § 1.367(d)–1T(c)(2)(i). For purposes of Subpart F, the transferee foreign corporation may treat such constructive royalty payments as properly allocated and apportioned to gross income subject to Subpart F. Temp. Reg. § 1.367(d)–1T(c)(2)(ii).

> *Example.* DC, a U.S. corporation, owns all of the stock of FS, a foreign corporation. (FS is a controlled foreign corporation (within the meaning of Section 957(a).) DC incurs and deducts under Sections 162 and 174 various expenses relating to the development of a patented invention. After completing development of the patented invention, DC transfers the patent to FS in a transaction that, in the absence of Section 367(d), would qualify for nonrecognition treatment under Section 351. FS uses the patent in its manufacturing business. Section 367(d) will treat DC as having sold the property to FS in exchange for payments that are contingent on the productivity, use or disposition of such property. These constructive royalty payments will be calculated in an amount that reflects an arm's length charge for use of the

patent. DC will recognize the constructive royalties over the useful life of the patent (but not in excess of 20 years).

These constructive royalty payments are treated as ordinary income to DC. Moreover, since they represent payment for the use of the patent outside the United States (i.e., for the foreign rights to the patent), the constructive royalties are treated as foreign-source income under Section 862(a)(4). Because these constructive royalty payments are treated as received by DC from a controlled foreign corporation, FS, the look-through rules in Section 904(d)(3) will apply to determine which category the payments fall into for foreign tax credit limitation purposes.

For Subpart F purposes, FS may treat these constructive royalty payments as allocated and apportioned to its Subpart F income. FS will reduce its earnings and profits to reflect these constructive royalty payments.

Exclusion of transfers of foreign goodwill or going concern value from Section 367(d) treatment. Transfers of foreign goodwill or going concern value are excluded from the operation of Section 367(d). Temp. Reg. § 1.367(d)–1T(b). They are defined as the residual value of a business operation conducted outside the United States after all other tangible and intangible assets have been identified and valued. The value of the right to use a corporate name in a foreign country is treated as foreign goodwill or going concern value. Temp. Reg. § 1.367(a)–1T(d)(5)(iii).

Identity of transferor of the intangible for Section 367(d) purposes. In T.D. 8770, 1998–2 C.B. 3, 8, the Treasury and the IRS issued a revised temporary regulation which clarifies that certain rules under Section 367(a) also will apply for purposes of determining the identity of the transferor treated as making an outbound transfer of an intangible subject to the constructive royalty rules under Section 367(d). See Temp. Reg. § 1.367(d)–1T(a). In T.D. 8770, 1998–2 C.B. 3, 8, the Treasury and the IRS indicated their belief that the identity of the transferor of the intangible has been and must continue to be consistent under both Sections 367(a) and 367(d). Thus, for example, if a partnership transfers an intangible to a foreign corporation in a transaction that qualifies as a Section 351 exchange, each U.S. partner is treated as transferring the partner's share of the intangible in a transfer that is subject to the constructive royalty rules in Section 367(d). Consequently, this rule prevents a U.S. person from using a partnership as an intermediary for transferring an intangible to a foreign corporation to avoid Section 367(d).

Actual royalties under license agreement as alternative to constructive royalty treatment under Section 367(d). As an alternative to constructive royalties under Section 367(d), a U.S. transferor may prefer to enter into a license agreement with the transferee foreign corporation providing for actual royalties to the U.S. transferor for use of the intangible. Actual royalties will be subject to Section 482, which generally authorizes the IRS to reallocate income, deductions, credits and allowances between related parties to reflect what the arrangements would have been if those parties had been dealing as independent parties at arm's length. See ¶ 12,200. Like Section 367(d), Section 482, as amended in the 1986 tax reform legislation, provides that, in the case of any transfer or license of marketing and manufacturing intangible property, the income with respect to such transfer or license shall be commensurate with the income attributable to the intangible. Thus, using an actual license does not eliminate the possibility of periodic adjustments by the IRS to the amount of the royalty.

Although the U.S. tax treatment of actual and constructive royalties may be the same, the foreign tax consequences may differ. An actual royalty may incur a foreign withholding tax, while a constructive royalty may not, a factor favoring the constructive royalty approach. However, an actual royalty may be deductible by the foreign transferee for foreign tax purposes, while a constructive royalty may not be, a factor favoring the actual license approach. Moreover, the actual royalty results in a cash receipt to the transferor, while a constructive royalty does not.

Dispositions of transferred intangible accelerating U.S. transferor's gain recognition under Section 367(d). A disposition of the transferred intangible either directly by the transferee foreign corporation's sale of the intangible or indirectly by the U.S. transferor's sale of the stock of the transferee foreign corporation may accelerate gain recognition by the U.S. transferor under Section 367(d). § 367(d)(2)(A)(ii)(II). Thus, if, during the useful life of the intangible, the transferee foreign corporation disposes of the intangible to an unrelated person, the U.S. transferor is required to include in gross income the difference between the amount realized on the disposition of the intangible and the adjusted basis of the intangible at the time of original transfer. Temp. Reg. § 1.367(d)–1T(f). Similar treatment applies to a disposition by the U.S. transferor of the transferee foreign corporation's stock to an unrelated person (i.e., the U.S. transferor includes in gross income the difference between the fair market value of the intangible on date of sale of the stock and the transferor's original basis in the transferred intangible). Any amount of gain taxed on this deemed sale of the intangible reduces the amount of gain taxable to the U.S. transferor on the sale of the stock. Temp. Reg. § 1.367(d)–1T(d). If the transferee foreign corporation transfers the intangible to a related person, the U.S. transferor will continue to report the constructive royalty payments on the transferred intangible under the usual rules in Section 367(d). Temp. Reg. § 1.367(d)–1T(f)(3). If the U.S. transferor transfers the stock of the transferee foreign corporation to a related U.S. person, the related U.S. person must report the constructive royalty payments on the transferred intangible under the usual rules in Section 367(d). Temp. Reg. § 1.367(d)–1T(e)(1). If the U.S. transferor transfers the stock of the transferee foreign corporation to a related foreign person, the stock transfer is not treated as a disposition of the intangible and the U.S. transferor must continue to report the constructive royalty payments under the usual rules in Section 367(d). Temp. Reg. § 1.367(d)–1T(e)(3).

Election to treat transfer of the intangible as a deemed sale at fair market value. Under certain circumstances, a U.S. transferor may prefer having the transfer of the intangibles to the foreign corporation taxed entirely at the time of transfer as a taxable sale of the intangible for its fair market value at a fixed price, rather than taxed as royalties over the life of the intangible (which may increase over time under the "commensurate with income" standard). The regulations permit the taxpayer to elect to treat the transfer of the intangible as a sale at its fair market value if certain requirements are met. If this election is made, the taxpayer includes as ordinary gross income in the year of transfer the difference between the fair market value of the intangible on the date of transfer and its adjusted basis. Temp. Reg. § 1.367(d)–1T(g)(2). This income should normally be U.S.-source income under Section 865(d)(1)(A) and 865(a) and Temp. Reg. § 1.367(d)–1T(g)(2), which makes this election disadvantageous for the U.S. transferor for purposes of the foreign tax credit limitations.

The regulations permit a taxpayer to make this deemed sale election in three situations. First, the taxpayer may so elect if the intangible is an operating intangible. Temp. Reg. § 1.367(d)–1T(g)(2)(i). An operating intangible is an intangible of a type not normally licensed or transferred in transactions between unrelated parties for consideration contingent on use of the intangible. Examples include surveys, long-term purchase or supply contracts, customer lists and studies. Temp. Reg. § 1.367(a)–1T(d)(5)(ii).

Second, the taxpayer may elect deemed sale treatment if the transfer is legally required by the government in the country of incorporation of the transferee corporation or is compelled by a genuine threat of immediate expropriation by such government. Temp. Reg. § 1.367(d)–1T(g)(2)(ii).

Third, the taxpayer may elect deemed sale treatment if—

(1) The taxpayer transferred the intangible to the foreign corporation within three months of the organization of that corporation as part of the original plan of capitalization of the corporation;

(2) Immediately after the transfer of the intangible, the taxpayer owns at least 40 percent but not more than 60 percent of the total voting power and total value of the transferee foreign corporation's stock;

(3) Immediately after the transfer of the intangible, foreign persons unrelated to the U.S. transferor own at least 40 percent of the total voting power and total value of the transferee corporation's stock;

(4) Intangibles constitute at least 50 percent of the fair market value of property transferred by the taxpayer to the foreign corporation; and

(5) The transferred intangible will be used in the active conduct of a trade or business outside the United States and will not be used for the manufacture or sale of products in or for use or consumption in the United States.

Temp. Reg. § 1.367(d)–1T(g)(2)(iii).

Regulatory authority to apply Section 367(d) treatment to transfers of intangibles to partnerships. In 1997, Congress added Sections 367(c)(3) and 721(d) to the Code. These provisions give the Treasury regulatory authority to apply the constructive royalty treatment under Section 367(d) to transfers of intangible property by a U.S. person to a partnership in circumstances consistent with the purposes of Section 367(d). No regulations have yet been issued under this provision.

[¶ 10,095]

6. BRANCH LOSS RECAPTURE RULES

Introduction. Special concerns are presented when a U.S. taxpayer operated the active foreign business as a branch before transferring the business to a foreign corporation and that branch incurred losses (i.e., deductions in excess of income). The foreign branch losses reduced the amount of the U.S. taxpayer's worldwide income subject to U.S. income tax, and, yet, as a result of the incorporation of the branch, the later income generated by the foreign business generally will escape current U.S. income tax as it is realized by the foreign corporation (i.e., it is foreign-source income realized by a foreign corporation and, thus, not taxable under Sections 881 and 882). To deal with these concerns, Congress enacted the branch loss recapture rules of Section 367(a)(3)(C).

Basic operation of the branch loss recapture rules. Under the branch loss recapture rules, a U.S. person that transfers part or all of the assets of a foreign branch to a foreign corporation in a Section 367(a)(1) exchange must recognize as recapture gain certain of the previously deducted cumulative losses of the branch. A foreign branch is defined for this purpose as an integral business operation carried on by a U.S. person outside the United States. Temp. Reg. § 1.367(a)–6T(g)(1).

The amount of gain to be recognized is the sum of the previously deducted ordinary losses and the sum of the previously deducted capital losses (both amounts to be adjusted by certain items, as explained below). Temp. Reg. § 1.367(a)–6T(b)(1). The recapture rules apply without regard to whether the assets of the foreign branch are transferred for use in the active conduct of a trade or business outside the United States. Temp. Reg. § 1.367–6T(b)(2).

Previously deducted ordinary losses are recaptured as ordinary income and previously deducted capital losses are recaptured as capital gain. Gain recognized under these rules is treated as foreign-source income. Temp. Reg. § 1.367(a)–6T(c)(1).

These branch loss recapture rules must be separately applied to each foreign branch that a taxpayer transfers to a foreign corporation. Thus, the previously deducted losses of one branch may not be offset by the income of another branch for purposes of determining the amount of gain that must be recognized under these rules. Temp. Reg. § 1.367(a)–6T(g)(2).

Because various provisions requiring recognition of gain overlap, gain that is taxable under the branch loss recapture rule of Section 367(a)(3)(C) could also be taxable under Section 367(a)(3)(A) and (B) (gain on assets not used in active business abroad and gain on tainted assets) or be subject to Section 904(f)(3) recapture under the overall foreign loss rules subject to the general limit or "cap" that the total gain to be recognized under Section 367(a) cannot exceed the gain that would have been recognized if the assets had been sold individually without offsetting individual losses against individual gains. Temp. Reg. § 1.367(a)–1T(b)(3). An effort has been made to adjust for these overlapping provisions, as explained below.

The basic approach of Section 367(a)(3)(C) is to require recognition of gain realized on the incorporation of the branch to the extent that the previously deducted losses of the branch exceed:

(1) Any taxable income of the branch realized after the last loss year through the end of the year in which the incorporation occurred; and

(2) Any amount of gain recognized under Section 904(f)(3) on the disposition of foreign property.

Therefore, the first step is to add the taxable income of the branch recognized through the close of the tax year of the incorporation (including gain recognized on the transfers involved in the incorporation itself under Section 367(a)) and the Section 904(f)(3) gain. This total is the amount by which the previously deducted losses must be reduced. Temp. Reg. § 1.367(a)–6T(e) elaborates on this step by requiring that the following amounts be totaled and then applied to reduce previously deducted losses:

(1) Any taxable income of the branch recognized (other than under Section 367(a)) through the close of the year in which the incorporation occurs;

(2) The amount recaptured under Section 904(f)(3) as a result of the transfers of appreciated assets of the branch (i.e., recognized gain on the transfer of branch assets not exceeding a prior overall foreign loss);

(3) Gain recognized under Section 367(a) (other than gain recognized under the branch loss recapture rules themselves). Such gain will include gain on property transferred to the foreign corporation not for use in the active conduct of business outside of the United States (Section 367(a)(3)(A)), gain on tainted assets (Section 367(a)(3)(B)) and gain recognized on certain transfers of stock or securities;

(4) Amounts recognized under Section 904(f)(3) on previous transfers of branch assets attributable to losses of a foreign branch; and

(5) Amounts previously recognized under the branch loss recapture rules of Section 367(a)(3)(C) on a previous transfer of branch assets.

Amounts listed above representing ordinary income first reduce the sum of previously deducted branch ordinary losses and then (if any such income is remaining) reduce the sum of previously deducted branch capital losses. Similarly, amounts listed above representing capital gains first reduce the sum of previously deducted branch capital losses and then (if any such gains are remaining) reduce the sum of previously deducted ordinary losses. Temp. Reg. § 1.367(a)–6T(e)(1).

Previously deducted branch losses for each branch loss year are also reduced by adjustments for expired net ordinary and capital losses and for unused expired foreign tax credits and investment tax credits. See Temp. Reg. § 1.367(a)–6T(d).

Any previously deducted branch losses that remain after being reduced by the total of the amounts set forth above will be "recaptured" (i.e., recognized) as foreign-source income to the extent of gain realized on assets not included in the above list, subject to the general limit or cap on recognized gain referred to above. Such assets would include, for example, gain realized on the transfer of marketing and manufacturing intangibles and gain realized on assets used in the active conduct of a trade or business. Excluded from such gain would be gain from the transfer of intangibles recognized under Section 904(f)(3), which would already have been included in the total amount by which previously deducted losses are reduced.

Example. In year 1, DC, a domestic corporation, established a branch in Ireland. In year 7, DC organized FC, a corporation organized under the laws of Ireland, and transferred all of the assets of the Irish branch to FC, including intangibles. At the time of transfer, the assets of the branch had a total fair market value of $2,500,000 and a total adjusted basis of $500,000 (with each asset having a fair market value in excess of its adjusted basis). Thus, DC has realized gain of $2,000,000 on the transfer of the branch assets to FC.

DC's Irish branch had income and losses in the following amounts for years 1 through 7:

Year	*Ordinary income (loss)*	*Capital gain (loss)*
Year 1	(200,000)	0
Year 2	(300,000)	(100,000)
Year 3	(400,000)	0
Year 4	300,000	0
Year 5	(200,000)	0
Year 6	75,000	20,000
Year 7	100,000	0

DC had no unused net operating losses, net capital losses, investment tax credits or foreign tax credits. DC did not have any recognized gain under Section 904(f)(3) by reason of the year 7 transfer or any prior transfer. DC also had no recognized gain on the transfer under Section 367(a), other than by reason of the branch loss recapture rules.

Initially, the branch has previously deducted ordinary losses of $1,100,000 and previously deducted capital losses of $100,000. These amounts are reduced by the taxable income of the branch earned before the transfer, consisting of $475,000 of ordinary income and $20,000 of long-term capital gains. The ordinary income of $475,000 first reduces the previously deducted ordinary losses of $1,100,000 to $625,000, and the long-term capital gains of $20,000 first reduce the previously deducted capital losses of $100,000 to $80,000. (The capital losses were deductible by DC in year 2 under Section 1211 because DC had capital gains from other activities in year 2.) Thus, the previously deducted losses of DC's Irish branch are $625,000 of ordinary losses and $80,000 of capital losses.

Under the branch loss recapture rules, in year 7, DC must recognize $625,000 of ordinary income and $80,000 of long-term capital gain. This income is treated as foreign-source income.

Overlap between branch loss recapture rules, Section 904(f)(3) and Section 367(d). When the transfer of branch assets can result in recognition of gain under both the branch loss recapture rules and Section 904(f)(3), the above rules, in effect, give priority to Section 904(f)(3) by requiring that branch losses subject to recapture must first be reduced by gain recognized under Section 904(f)(3). One result of giving priority to Section 904(f)(3) is to treat that part of the gain as U.S.-source income under Section 904(f). Temp. Reg. § 1.367(a)–6T(e)(5).

The overall cap on the amount of branch loss recapture discussed above includes gain that is recognized on the transfer of intangibles. Accordingly, intangibles are potentially taxable under Section 904(f)(3), the branch loss recapture rules and Section 367(d). To deal with the overlap, the regulations provide that income recognized on the transfer of intangibles under Section 904(f)(3) or the branch loss recapture rules will be credited against the annual royalty payments that the transferor would otherwise be required to recognize with respect to the intangibles under Section 367(d). Temp. Reg. § 1.367(d)–1T(g)(3). The amount of gain recognized with respect to intangibles under Section 904(f)(3) or the branch loss recapture rules for purposes of this credit is determined by the following formula:[8]

$$\text{Loss recapture income} \times \frac{\text{Gain from intangibles under Section 904(f)(3) or Temp. Reg. § 1.367(a)–6T}^{8}}{\text{Gain from all branch assets on which a gain is realized}}$$

Anti-abuse rule. Because of the possibility that the branch loss recapture rules might be avoided by transferring the branch to a U.S. corporation which would then transfer the assets to a foreign corporation under the active trade or business exception, an anti-abuse rule has been added to the temporary regulations. If the transfer of assets to a U.S. corporation is made for the principal purpose of avoiding the branch loss recapture rules, the transfer will be treated as if made directly to the foreign corporation. Temp. Reg. § 1.367(a)–6T(h).

[¶ 10,100]

7. LIQUIDATION OF U.S. CORPORATION INTO FOREIGN PARENT CORPORATION

Section 367(e)(2) denies nonrecognition-of-gain treatment to a U.S. corporation making a liquidating distribution to a foreign corporation that owns 80 percent or more of its stock by providing that subsections (a) and (b)(1) of Section 337 do not apply, except as otherwise provided in regulations. Thus, under the general rule, the U.S. corporation will recognize gain or loss on the distribution of the property to the foreign parent corporation. Reg. § 1.367(e)–2(b)(1)(i). However, the regulations contain an overall loss limitation rule, which limits the loss recognized on assets distributed to the amount of gain recognized on other assets. Reg. § 1.367(e)–2(b)(1)(ii)(B).

The Conference Committee Report on the 1986 Act, H.R. Conf. Rep. No. 841, 99th Cong., 2d Sess. II–202 (1986), indicated that "regulations may permit nonrecognition if the appreciation on the distributed property is not being removed from the U.S. taxing jurisdiction." In accordance with this suggestion, the regulations provide an exception to the general rule of taxability when the property distributed in liquidation is used by

8. Gain from intangibles does not include gain on transfers of foreign goodwill or going concern value and certain copyrights, literary, musical or artistic compositions or a transfer of intangibles that the taxpayer elects to have treated as a sale. Temp. Reg. § 1.367(d)–1T(g)(3).

the foreign corporate distributee in a U.S. trade or business for ten years after the date of the distribution. Reg. § 1.367(e)–2(b)(2)(i). The rationale for the exception is that, unlike the case in which the assets distributed in liquidation are transferred outside of the U.S. taxing jurisdiction, when the assets continue to be used in a U.S. business, the income they generate and the unrealized appreciation inherent in them (because the distributee takes a carryover basis under Section 334(b)(1)) continue to be subject to U.S. tax. There may also be a branch profits tax on a withdrawal by the foreign distributee of those assets from use in the U.S. business. To take advantage of this exception, a statement containing extensive information must be filed with the IRS by the distributing corporation.

Under the exception for assets used in a U.S. business, if distributed property is disposed of by the foreign distributee during the ten-year period after the liquidating distribution and any gain is reported by it on a timely filed U.S. income tax return, the distributing U.S. corporation is not required to recognize gain retroactively as a result of the distribution. Reg. § 1.367(e)–2(b)(2)(i)(E)(*1*). If the foreign distributee does not report the gain, however, the U.S. distributing corporation must do so. If the foreign distributee withdraws the property from the U.S. business but does not dispose of it, the U.S. distributing corporation must recognize the gain realized but not recognized on the original distribution. The foreign distributee corporation must file an amended return for the year of the liquidating distribution on behalf of the domestic liquidating corporation, reporting the gain realized on the distribution, plus accrued interest on the additional tax calculated from the due date of the domestic liquidating corporation's U.S. income tax return for the year of the distribution to the date on which the additional tax for that year is paid. Reg. § 1.367(e)–2(b)(2)(i)(E)(*2*).

A U.S. distributing corporation normally does not recognize gain or loss on the distribution in liquidation to a foreign parent corporation of a U.S. real property interest. Gain is recognized, however, if the U.S. corporation distributes stock in a former U.S. real property holding corporation that is treated as a U.S. real property interest for five years under Section 897(c)(1)(A)(ii). Reg. § 1.367(e)–2(b)(2)(ii).

In addition, a U.S. distributing corporation normally does not recognize gain or loss on the distribution of the stock of an 80 percent U.S. subsidiary corporation to a foreign parent corporation. To qualify for this exception, the distributing corporation must attach to its federal income tax return for the year of the distribution a statement containing the information specified in the regulations. If the U.S. distributing corporation is a U.S. real property holding corporation at the time of the liquidation (or is a former U.S. real property holding corporation the stock of which is treated as U.S. real property interest for five years under Section 897(c)(1)(A)), the exception will apply only to the distribution of the stock of an 80 percent U.S. subsidiary corporation that is a U.S. real property holding corporation at the time of liquidation and immediately thereafter. Moreover, under an anti-abuse rule in the regulations, the exception will not apply if a principal purpose of the distribution of the 80 percent U.S. subsidiary's stock is the avoidance of U.S. tax that would have been imposed on the U.S. distributing corporation's disposition of the stock to an unrelated party. Reg. § 1.367(e)–2(b)(2)(iii).

The foreign distributee corporation's basis in property subject to these rules is the same as the U.S. distributing corporation's basis in the property immediately before the liquidation, increased by the gain and reduced by the loss recognized by the U.S. distributing corporation on the distribution of the property. Reg. § 1.367(e)–2(b)(3)(i).

If the U.S. corporation distributes a partnership interest in liquidation, the U.S. distributing corporation is treated as if it had distributed a proportionate share of the property of the partnership. The foreign distributee corporation's basis in the distributed partnership interest is the same as the U.S. distributing corporation's basis in the partnership interest immediately before the distribution, increased by the gain and reduced by the loss recognized by the distributing corporation on the distribution of the interest. However, a distribution of a publicly traded partnership interest is treated as a distribution of stock (not the distribution of a partnership interest). Reg. § 1.367(e)–2(b)(1)(iii).

As mentioned in Chapter 4, the 2004 JOBS Act added new Section 332(d) to the Code. This provision treats a distribution to a foreign corporation in complete liquidation of an "applicable holding company" (i.e., domestic holding company that has been in existence for less than five years) as a Section 301 distribution. Thus, neither Section 331 nor Section 332 applies to such a distribution and the distribution will be treated as a dividend to the foreign corporate distributee to the extent of the domestic holding company's earnings and profits. The purpose of this provision is to prevent withholding tax abuse by foreign corporations that "establish a U.S. holding company to receive tax-free dividends from U.S. operating companies, liquidate the U.S. holding company to distribute the U.S. earnings free of U.S. withholding taxes, and then reestablish another U.S. holding company, with the intention of escaping U.S. withholding taxes." S. Rep. No. 192, 108th Cong., 1st Sess. 125 (2003). More precisely, an "applicable holding company" is a U.S. corporation (1) that is a common parent of an affiliated group (as defined in Section 1504(a), but without regard to Section 1504(b)(2) and (4)), (2) the stock of which is directly owned by the distributee foreign corporation, (3) substantially all of the assets of which are stock in other members of the affiliated group, and (4) that has not been in existence at all times during the five years immediately before the date of the liquidation. § 332(d)(2). However, if the foreign corporate distributee of the distribution is a controlled foreign corporation, the distribution will be treated as a Section 331 distribution.

§ 332(d)(3). The statute authorizes the Treasury and the IRS to issue regulations to prevent the abuse of this provision. § 332(d)(4).

[¶ 10,105]

8. LIQUIDATION OF FOREIGN CORPORATION INTO FOREIGN PARENT CORPORATION

The general rule established by the temporary regulations is that a foreign corporation does not recognize gain with respect to property it distributes in complete liquidation to a foreign parent corporation meeting the stock ownership tests of Section 332(b). Reg. § 1.367(e)–2(c)(1). Gain is recognized, however, on the distribution of any property (other than U.S. real property interests) used by the distributing foreign corporation in the conduct of a U.S. trade or business at the time of the liquidation. Reg. § 1.367(e)–2(c)(2)(i)(A). An exception to this recognition-of-gain rule applies if the distributee foreign corporation continues for a ten-year period to use the property in the conduct of a trade or business within the United States and the distributing and distributee corporations file an appropriate statement with the IRS. Reg. § 1.367(e)–2(c)(2)(i)(B).

It is unclear why, in the case of a liquidation of a foreign corporation into another foreign corporation, U.S. tax should be imposed if the distributee ceases to use the distributed assets in a U.S. business. Any foreign corporation is free to withdraw appreciated assets from a U.S. business and use them to produce income that is exempt from U.S. tax, subject to possible imposition of branch profits tax on previously reinvested earnings. The foreign corporate distributee takes a carryover basis in the distributed assets in a Section 332 liquidation and unrealized appreciation in assets withdrawn from a U.S. business remain subject to U.S. tax if the assets are disposed of within ten years under Section 864(c)(7).

[¶ 10,110]

9. OUTBOUND SECTION 355 DISTRIBUTIONS

Section 367(e)(1) provides that, in the case of a distribution described in Section 355 (or so much of Section 356 as relates to Section 355) by a U.S. corporation to a foreign person, gain is to be recognized under principles similar to those of Section 367. Since the foreign distributee in a Section 355 distribution may be an individual, partnership, trust or estate, as well as a foreign corporation, recognition of gain to the distributing corporation may not be achieved, as it is in the other exchanges enumerated in Section 367(a)(1), in a Section 355 distribution by simply not treating a foreign corporation as a corporation for purposes of Section 355. Accordingly, Section 355 distributions are dealt with specifically in the regulations.

The regulations establish, as a general rule, that if a U.S. corporation distributes stock or securities of a corporation in a transaction that otherwise qualifies under Section 355(a) to a person who is not a "qualified U.S. person," the distributing corporation recognizes gain (but not loss) under Section 367(e)(1). Reg. § 1.367(e)–1(b)(1). A "qualified U.S. person" for this purpose is a U.S. citizen, resident alien or corporation. If the distributed corporation is a controlled foreign corporation of which the distributing corporation is a U.S. shareholder, part or all of the taxable gain may be treated as a dividend under Section 1248(a). However, under the current regulations, this gain-recognition rule will apply only to a U.S. distributing corporation's distribution of the stock or securities of a *foreign* corporation. Thus, the regulations now specifically provide that a U.S. distributing corporation does not recognize gain under this rule on the distribution of the stock or securities of a *U.S.* corporation. Reg. § 1.367(e)–1(c).

If the U.S. distributing corporation does trigger this gain-recognition rule by distributing the stock or securities of a foreign corporation to distributees who are not qualified U.S. persons in a Section 355 transaction, the gain recognized by the distributing corporation is the excess of the fair market value of the stock or securities distributed to such distributees (determined as of the time of the distribution) over the corporation's adjusted basis in such stock or securities. Reg. § 1.367(e)–1(b)(3). The regulations presume all distributions subject to this gain-recognition rule to be to persons who are not qualified U.S. persons, Reg. § 1.367(e)–1(d)(1), unless the U.S. distributing corporation rebuts the presumption in the manner provided in the regulations:

> ***Non-publicly traded distributing corporation.*** If the class of stock or securities of the U.S. distributing corporation (in respect of which stock or securities of the controlled corporation are distributed) is not regularly traded on a qualified exchange or market, the distributing corporation may rebut the presumption only by identifying the qualified U.S. persons to which controlled corporation stock or securities were distributed and by certifying the amount of stock or securities distributed to such qualified U.S. persons. Reg. § 1.367(e)–1(d)(2).
>
> ***Five-percent-or-more shareholders of publicly traded distributing corporation.*** If the class of stock or securities of the U.S. distributing corporation (in respect of which stock or securities of the controlled corporation are distributed) is regularly traded on a qualified exchange or market, and the distributee owns at least five percent of that class of stock or securities of the corporation, the corporation may rebut the presumption only by identifying the qualified U.S. persons to which controlled corporation stock or securities were distributed and by certifying the amount of stock or securities distributed to such qualified U.S. persons. Reg. § 1.367(e)–1(d)(3)(i).
>
> ***Other distributees of publicly traded U.S. distributing corporation.*** If the class of stock or securities of the U.S. distributing corporation (in respect of which stock or securities of the controlled

corporation are distributed) is regularly traded on a qualified exchange or market, and the distributee is *not* a five-percent-or-more shareholder of that class of stock or securities of the corporation, the corporation may rebut the presumption "by relying on and providing a reasonable analysis of shareholder records and other relevant information that demonstrates a number of distributees that are qualified U.S. persons." The regulations permit the taxpayer to rely on this analysis, unless it is later determined that there are actually fewer distributees who are qualified U.S. persons than were shown in the analysis. Reg. § 1.367(e)–1(d)(3)(ii).

Whether or not the U.S. distributing corporation must recognize gain under Section 367(e)(1) and the regulations, the foreign distributee is not required to recognize gain if the requirements of Section 355 are met. In other words, the distribution is treated as a nonrecognition transaction to the foreign distributee. Reg. § 1.367(e)–1(b)(4).

[¶ 10,115]

10. REPORTING REQUIREMENT

So that the IRS will be informed of outbound transfers covered by Section 367(a) and (e)(1), as well as transfers of property by a U.S. person to a foreign partnership, Section 6038B requires the U.S. persons involved to notify the IRS of the existence of these transactions. A U.S. person who fails to notify the IRS and cannot show reasonable cause for such failure will pay a penalty equal to ten percent of the fair market value of the property at the time of the exchange. There is a $100,000 limit on the amount of the penalty with respect to any exchange, unless the failure was due to intentional disregard. § 6038B(c). The statute of limitations for assessment with respect to recognized gain under Section 367(a) or (e)(1) is extended until three years after notice is given to the IRS. § 6501(c)(8).

[¶ 10,120]

PROBLEMS

1. Analytical Equipment Company ("AEC") is a U.S. corporation engaged in the manufacture and sale of office automation systems. If AEC transfers the following assets to a wholly owned subsidiary organized under the laws of the Cayman Islands ("AEC (Cayman)"), in exchange for all of the subsidiary's stock, which of the assets will be automatically tainted under Section 367(a)?

a. 500,000 Cayman Islands dollars;

b. Accounts receivable from Cayman customers expressed in Cayman dollars;

c. 10,000 desktop systems (for immediate sale);

d. 1,000 copiers (to be leased to European customers);

e. All of AEC's interest in "Datamaitre," a word processing program designed for European users; or

f. AEC's just-purchased warehouse in the Cayman Islands.

2. Assume that Datamaitre generates revenue of $5 million per year in the hands of the new Cayman subsidiary and $500,000 per year is an amount that reasonably reflects the amount AEC would have received as an arm's length fair market royalty had AEC licensed Datamaitre to AEC (Cayman) rather than transferred it outright. How much must AEC include in income to reflect the transfer of Datamaitre to AEC (Cayman)? What if, after three years, AEC (Cayman) sells Datamaitre to an unrelated Jamaican corporation? Alternatively, what if, after three years, AEC sells all of its stock in AEC (Cayman) to an unrelated Jamaican corporation? What is the source of the income to AEC in each case?

3. Suppose that AEC had operated in the Cayman Islands as a branch for three years before the incorporation of AEC (Cayman) with the following results:

Year	*Branch Net Income*
Year 1	($1,000)
Year 2	($2,000)
Year 3	$ 500

On December 31 of year 3, AEC's Cayman branch transferred to the new Cayman subsidiary assets used in the active conduct of a trade or business and not otherwise tainted under Section 367(a)(3), the fair market value of which exceeded their basis by $2,000, and assets used in the active conduct of a trade or business but tainted under Section 367(a)(3)(B), the fair market value of which exceeded their basis by $500. Assuming that AEC previously deducted the branch losses in years 1 and 2, what amount must AEC include in gross income under the branch loss recapture rules?

4. If the facts are the same as in Problem 3, except that the realized gain on the transfer of untainted assets is only $1,000, what amount must AEC include in its gross income?

5. Assume that the facts are the same as in Problem 3, except that AEC establishes its branch in the Cayman Islands on December 31 of year 4, and that the branch breaks even that year. If AEC derives $1,000 of income from foreign sources other than through the Cayman branch and earns $2,000 in U.S.-source income in year 4, how much of the branch loss is subject to recapture?

6. Assume that AEC's branch in the Cayman Islands has $2,000 in cumulative previously deducted losses at the time of its incorporation as a subsidiary. The branch transfers to the new subsidiary assets with a fair market value in excess of their basis of $2,000. These assets include Datamaitre, the word processing program, which has a fair market value in excess of

basis of $1,000 and which would give rise to constructive royalty payments under Section 367(d) of $500 per year. How much branch loss recapture gain will be recognized? How much income must AEC recognize under Section 367(d) during the first two years of the newly incorporated subsidiary's operations?

7. DC, a U.S. corporation, owns 40 percent of the stock of FC1, a corporation organized in the Netherlands. C1, a U.S. citizen who resides in New York, owns five percent of the stock of FC1. C1 does not own any stock of DC and is not otherwise a "related person" of DC. FC2, a corporation organized in Germany and unrelated to DC or C1, owns the remaining 55 percent of the outstanding stock of FC1. FC3, a publicly traded corporation organized in Spain, will acquire all of the FC1 stock from DC, C and FC2 under a reorganization plan pursuant to Section 368(a)(1)(B). In accordance with that plan, DC, C1 and FC2 transfer their FC1 stock to FC3 in return solely for FC3 voting stock. Before the reorganization exchange, neither DC nor C1 owned any shares of FC3 stock. After the reorganization exchange, DC owns 16 percent of FC3 and C owns 2 percent of FC3. What are the U.S. income tax consequences to DC and C1 as a result of this reorganization exchange?

8. Domestic Parent, a U.S. corporation, owns 95 percent of the outstanding stock of Domestic Subsidiary, also a U.S. corporation. C2, a U.S. citizen who resides in California, owns five percent of the outstanding Domestic Subsidiary stock. C2 does not own any stock of Domestic Parent and is not otherwise a "related person" of Domestic Parent. Domestic Parent and C2 transfer to Foreign Parent, a corporation organized in Italy, all of their Domestic Subsidiary stock solely for voting stock of Foreign Parent. This reorganization exchange will take place pursuant to Section 368(a)(1)(B). Assume that neither Domestic Parent nor C2 owned any Foreign Parent stock before the reorganization exchange.

a. What are the U.S. income tax consequences to Domestic Parent and C2 if, immediately after the stock-for-stock exchange, Domestic Parent and C2 each owns less than five percent of both the total voting power and value of the Foreign Parent stock?

b. How would your answer change if the facts are the same as in Problem 8.a., except that, immediately after the stock-for-stock exchange, Domestic Parent owns more than five percent, but less than 45 percent, of both the total voting power and value of the Foreign Parent stock and C2 owns less than five percent of both the total voting power and value of the Foreign Parent stock?

c. How would your answer change if the facts are the same as in Problem 8.a., except that, immediately after the stock-for-stock exchange, Domestic Parent owns more than 50 percent of both the total voting power and value of the Foreign Parent stock and C2 owns less than five percent of both the total voting power and value of the Foreign Parent stock?

[¶ 10,125]

E. TRANSFERS OF APPRECIATED PROPERTY TO A PARTNERSHIP OR TRUST

Under former Sections 1491–1494, an excise tax generally applied to transfers of property, whether otherwise tax-free or taxable, by U.S. persons (including U.S. corporations, partnerships and estates and trusts) to foreign corporations, foreign partnerships and foreign estates and trusts. However, in the case of transfers of property to foreign corporations, the tax applied only to property treated as paid-in surplus or as a contribution to capital. The amount of the excise tax was equal to 35 percent of the transferor's gain that was not recognized at the time of the transfer. Because these provisions were viewed as traps for the unwary and added unnecessary complexity to the taxation of international transactions, Congress repealed Sections 1491–1497 in tax legislation enacted in 1997.

Congress replaced these excise tax provisions with a new Code section that requires gain recognition on the transfer of appreciated property by a U.S. person to a foreign trust or estate (except to the extent that regulations provide otherwise). See § 684. Congress also gave the Treasury and the IRS expanded regulatory authority to treat transfers of property to foreign corporations by U.S. persons as paid-in surplus or contributions to capital as fair market sales and require gain recognition on such sales. See § 367(f). The 1997 legislation also added Section 721(c), which provides regulatory authority to require gain recognition on a transfer by a U.S. person of appreciated property to a partnership in the situation where the gain when recognized by the partnership would be allocable to a foreign partner. Finally, the 1997 legislation added extensive information reporting requirements for controlled foreign partnerships and transfers to such partnerships comparable to those for controlled foreign corporations. See §§ 6038 and 6038B.

F. APPLICATION OF SECTION 367(b) TO NONOUTBOUND TRANSFERS

[¶ 10,130]

1. BACKGROUND

Section 367(b) and the regulations issued under it cover exchanges that do not involve an outbound transfer covered by Section 367(a). Specifically, in the case of any exchange described in Section 332, 351, 354, 355, 356 or 361 in connection with which there is no outbound transfer subject to Section 367(a)(1), a foreign corporation will be considered to be a corporation. As a result, the general rule with respect to nonoutbound transfers is nonrecognition of gain, subject to the exceptions set forth in the regulations issued under Section 367(b).

Section 367(b)(2) calls for regulations dealing with the sale or exchange of stock or securities in a foreign corporation by a U.S. person, including regulations providing for recognition of gain or inclusion of amounts in gross income as a dividend, or both, or deferral of gain or other amounts for taxation at a later date. In addition, the regulations are to provide for adjustments in earnings and profits and basis of stock, securities and assets.

T.D. 8862, 2000–1 C.B. 466, 466–67, described the policy of Section 367(b), as follows:

> The principal purpose of section 367(b) is to prevent the avoidance of U.S. tax that can arise when the Subchapter C provisions apply to transactions involving foreign corporations. The potential for tax avoidance arises because of differences between the manner in which the United States taxes foreign corporations and their shareholders and the manner in which the United States taxes domestic corporations and their U.S. shareholders.
>
> The Subchapter C [corporate tax] provisions generally have been drafted to apply to domestic corporations and U.S. shareholders, and thus do not fully take into account the cross-border aspects of U.S. taxation (such as deferral, foreign tax credits, and section 1248). Section 367(b) was enacted to help ensure that international tax considerations in the Code are adequately addressed when the Subchapter C provisions apply to an exchange involving a foreign corporation. Because determining the proper interaction of the Code's international and Subchapter C provisions is "necessarily highly technical," Congress granted the [Treasury and IRS] broad regulatory authority to provide the "necessary or appropriate" rules, rather than enacting a complex statutory regime. * * *

Although the regulations that have been issued under Section 367(b) are highly complex, their basic thrust is to implement taxation under Section 1248 in transactions that would otherwise be exempt from tax under a tax-free-exchange provision. The purpose of Section 1248 is to prevent a U.S. shareholder from realizing upon the accumulated earnings of a controlled foreign corporation by selling its stock or liquidating it at the cost only of any preferential rate of tax on long-term capital gains. See ¶ 6245. Thus, the Section 367(b) regulations require current taxation as an ordinary income deemed dividend of amounts of earnings of a controlled foreign corporation that might otherwise escape U.S. taxation and permit deferral of U.S. tax on amounts of income or gain associated with a controlled foreign corporation that remain within the taxing jurisdiction of the United States. The Section 367(b) regulations generally only impose tax when a controlled foreign corporation is involved in a transaction that would otherwise qualify as a tax-free exchange. If an exchange described in Section 332, 351, 354, 355, 356 or 361 involves only foreign corporations that are not controlled foreign corporations, no gain would be recognized.

In general, if a U.S. shareholder of a controlled foreign corporation exchanges, in a nonoutbound transaction, shares of that corporation for shares of another controlled foreign corporation as to which the shareholder is also a U.S. shareholder, as defined in Section 1248(a)(2), no gain is recognized. See Reg. § 1.367(b)–4(b). Recognition of gain and Section 1248 dividend income can be postponed until the U.S. shareholder disposes of stock of the controlled foreign corporation received in the exchange. Recognition of dividend income under Section 1248 is deferred through the mechanism of attributing appropriate amounts of the earnings and profits of the controlled foreign corporation, the shares of which are transferred, to the stock the shareholder receives in the transferee controlled foreign corporation. See Reg. §§ 1.367(b)–7 and 8. The amounts so attributed include the "1248 amount" and the "all earnings and profits amount," which are discussed at ¶ 10,135. Reg. § 1.367(b)–2(c) and (d). As a result of this attribution, the appropriate attributed amounts become characteristics of the stock of the controlled foreign corporation that the U.S. shareholder receives in the exchange, and, when this stock is disposed of, dividend consequences under Section 1248 may be imposed. In addition, the controlled foreign corporation the stock of which is received by the U.S. shareholder inherits the earnings and profits of the controlled foreign corporation the stock of which is exchanged and of any of its lower-tier corporations (while the earnings and profits of the latter controlled foreign corporation and its lower-tier corporations are reduced by the same amount).

If the exchanging shareholder was a U.S. shareholder of the controlled foreign corporation, the stock of which was exchanged, but is not a U.S. shareholder of the transferee corporation (e.g., because the exchanging shareholder receives stock of a U.S. corporation or stock of a foreign corporation that is not a controlled foreign corporation or as to which it is not a U.S. shareholder), it must pay its Section 1248 tax liability. This means that the exchanging shareholder must include in gross income, as a deemed dividend, the "Section 1248 amount" attributable to the stock exchanged to the extent that the fair market value of the stock exchanged exceeds its adjusted basis. Any additional gain will be treated as gain from the sale or exchange of the stock. Reg. § 1.367(b)–4(b).

In the event of a liquidation of a foreign corporation controlled (within the meaning of Section 1504(a)(2)) by a U.S. corporation or the acquisition by a U.S. corporation of all of a foreign corporation's assets in an asset acquisition described in Section 368(a)(1), the U.S. corporation must include in income as a deemed dividend the "all earnings and profits amount" attributable to its stock in the foreign subsidiary. Reg. § 1.367(b)–3(b)(3).

Reg. § 1.367(b)–1(c) requires a U.S. person to file a notice setting forth the details of the exchange as an attachment to the taxpayer's timely filed federal income tax return for the year in which the gain is realized in the Section 367(b) exchange.

Concurrent application of Section 367(a) and (b). Reg. § 1.367(a)–3(b)(2) provides rules governing the concurrent application of Section 367(a) and (b) to transfers of stock of a foreign corporation. As the IRS and the Treasury explain in REG–125628–01, 2005–1 C.B. 536, 540:

> This [concurrent application] may occur, for example, when a U.S. shareholder exchanges stock of a foreign corporation (foreign acquired corporation) for stock of another foreign corporation (foreign acquiring corporation). See § 1.367(a)–3(b)(1). It may also occur when an acquiring corporation (foreign or domestic) acquires the assets of a foreign acquired corporation, and the U.S. shareholder exchanges stock of the foreign acquired corporation for stock of the foreign parent of the acquiring corporation in a triangular reorganization.
>
> The U.S. person's exchange of stock of the foreign acquired corporation for stock of either the foreign acquiring corporation or the foreign parent is subject to section 367(a). See § 1.367(a)–3(b) and (d). If the exchanging U.S. shareholder owns 5 percent or more (by vote or value) of the stock of the foreign acquiring corporation or the foreign parent immediately after the exchange, the shareholder recognizes gain, if any, under section 367(a), unless the shareholder enters into a gain recognition agreement as provided in § 1.367(a)–8. If the exchanging shareholder is not a 5–percent shareholder, then the exchanging shareholder does not recognize gain, if any, on the exchange.
>
> The U.S. shareholder's exchange described above also may be subject to section 367(b). If the exchanging U.S. shareholder is a section 1248 shareholder of the foreign acquired corporation, and the stock of the foreign acquiring corporation (or its foreign parent corporation) is not stock in a corporation that is a CFC as to which the U.S. shareholder is a section 1248 shareholder immediately after the exchange, then the exchanging shareholder must include in income the section 1248 amount with respect to the stock exchanged. See § 1.367(b)–4. If, instead, a domestic acquiring corporation acquires the assets of a foreign acquired corporation, and the U.S. shareholder exchanges stock of the foreign acquired corporation for stock of the foreign parent of the acquiring corporation in a triangular reorganization, then the exchanging shareholder must include in income the all earnings and profits amount with respect to the stock of the acquired corporation. See § 1.367(b)–3. Unlike the section 1248 amount, the all earnings and profits amount is not limited by the shareholder's gain inherent in the stock of the foreign acquired corporation.

In cases where section 367(a) and (b) apply concurrently to a transaction, existing § 1.367(a)–3(b)(2) provides that section 367(b) will not apply if the transfer is taxable under section 367(a). If the transfer is taxable under section 367(a), the exchanging U.S. shareholder will recognize gain inherent in the exchanged stock (subject to recharacterization as dividend income under section 1248). If the transfer is not taxable under section 367(a), because the exchanging U.S. shareholder either is not a 5–percent shareholder or enters into a gain recognition agreement, then section 367(b) applies and the exchange is subject to either § 1.367(b)–3 or 1.367(b)–4 at the shareholder level.

Questions with respect to the concurrent application of section 367(a) and (b) have arisen in situations that otherwise would require inclusion of the all earnings and profits amount under §§ 1.367(b)–3. If the all earnings and profits amount is greater than the section 367(a) gain with respect to the stock of the foreign acquired corporation, under current law the exchanging shareholder effectively may elect to be taxed on the lesser amount of gain under section 367(a) simply by failing to file a gain recognition agreement. In that case, section 367(b) would not apply and the shareholder would avoid inclusion in income of the greater all earnings and profits amount.

The ability to elect to recognize the lesser gain inherent in the stock exchanged in such cases is inconsistent with the policies of section 367(b) that apply to inbound transactions, including preventing conversion of tax deferral into tax forgiveness and ensuring that the domestic acquiring corporation's section 381 carryover basis reflects an after-tax amount. Accordingly, the IRS and Treasury believe that the all earnings and profits amount provisions under §§ 1.367(b)–3 should not operate electively in these cases. * * *

Regulations proposed in 2005 and issued in final form in 2006 modify the concurrent application of Section 367(a) and (b) to transactions that require the inclusion in income of the "all earnings and profits amount" under Section 367(b). Under Reg. § 1.367(a)–3(b)(2)(i), for exchanges subject to Reg. § 1.367(b)–3 and Section 367(a), Section 367(b) applies before Section 367(a) and the shareholder has to include in income the "all earnings and profits amount." In such a case, the "all earnings and profits amount" inclusion increases the exchanging shareholder's adjusted basis for purposes of determining the amount of the shareholder's gain under Section 367(a). See Reg. § 1.367(a)–3(d)(3), Ex. 15. Consequently, if the "all earnings and profits amount" exceeds the shareholder's inherent gain in the stock, no gain will be recognized under Section 367(a) in this situation. If the transaction in question does not involve an inclusion of the "all earnings and profits amount" (e.g., a "Section 367(b) exchange" governed by Reg. § 1.367(b)–4, discussed at ¶ 10,150), the ordering rules under the then existing regulations did not change. REG–125628–01, 2005–1 C.B. 536, 540.

[¶ 10,135]

2. AMOUNTS OF ATTRIBUTED EARNINGS UNDER SECTION 1248 AND TREATMENT OF DEEMED DIVIDENDS

There are two distinct amounts of attributed earnings and profits that play a central role in the mechanisms adopted in the regulations under Section 367(b). These mechanisms ensure that ordinary income, deemed dividend treatment will be imposed when a U.S. shareholder disposes of stock in a controlled foreign corporation in a manner other than a tax-free exchange for stock of another controlled foreign corporation of which the shareholder is a U.S. shareholder. The two amounts are defined as follows:

1. ***"Section 1248 amount"*** means the net positive earnings and profits, if any, that would have been attributable to the stock of the foreign corporation exchanged and includible in income as a deemed dividend under Section 1248 if the stock had been sold by the shareholder. Stated differently, the Section 1248 amount is the previously untaxed post–1962 earnings that would be taxed as a dividend under Section 1248(a) if the stock had been sold. Reg. § 1.367(b)–2(c)(1).

2. ***"All earnings and profits amount"*** means the net positive earnings and profits, if any, for all tax years which are attributable to the stock of the foreign corporation exchanged under Section 1248 and the regulations under that provision. However, in determining the "all earnings and profits amount" under the principles of Section 1248 and its regulations, the requirements of Section 1248 that are not relevant to determining a shareholder's pro rata portion of earnings and profits are ignored. Thus, the "all earnings and profits amount" is determined without regard to whether the exchanging shareholder owned a ten-percent-or-greater interest in the foreign corporation's stock or whether the foreign corporation was a controlled foreign corporation at any time during the five prior years. The "all earnings and profits" amount also is determined without regard to whether the earnings and profits of the foreign corporation were accumulated while the corporation was a controlled foreign corporation or in pre- or post–1962 years. Reg. § 1.367(b)–2(d).

In some circumstances, the Section 367(b) regulations require an exchanging shareholder to include deemed dividends in income in order to implement the policies of Section 1248. The regulations treat such deemed dividends as actual dividends for purposes of the Internal Revenue Code.[9]

---

9. Moreover, amounts treated as dividends under Reg. § 1.367(b)–2(e)(2) may constitute "qualified dividend income" for purposes of the preferential tax rates in Section 1(h)(11) if the

This means that they are treated as paid out of the earnings and profits of a foreign corporation and reduce the earnings and profits of the corporation. In addition, the regulations treat a deemed dividend as having been paid through intermediate owners (when appropriate). See Reg. § 1.367(b)–2(e)(2).

These deemed dividends under the Section 367(b) regulations are distinguishable from deemed dividends under Section 1248 itself. A deemed dividend under Section 1248 is not treated as a dividend at the corporate level and does not reduce the corporation's earnings and profits. Instead, to prevent double taxation of the same amounts, Section 959 treats the shareholder-level inclusion under Section 1248 as previously taxed earnings and profits and, thus, not taxable on later distribution.

3. RULES FOR NONOUTBOUND LIQUIDATIONS AND REORGANIZATIONS

[¶ 10,140]

a. Complete Liquidation of Foreign Subsidiary into U.S. Parent under Section 332 or U.S. Corporation's Acquisition of the Assets of a Foreign Corporation in a Section 368(a)(1) Transaction

Under the current regulations, the U.S. corporation has to include in income as a deemed dividend the "all earnings and profits amount." Reg. § 1.367(b)–3(b)(3).

Under Section 334(b)(1), as amended by the 2004 JOBS Act, a domestic corporation's basis in property distributed in a Section 332 liquidation of a foreign subsidiary corporation is limited to the fair market value of the property distributed at the time of liquidation if the aggregate adjusted bases of such property distributed in liquidation would (but for this limitation) exceed the fair market value of the property immediately after the liquidation. Congress enacted this provision because of its concern that foreign-generated built-in losses (i.e., losses that were generated while the property was outside of U.S. taxing jurisdiction) were being imported in various corporate transactions and used to shelter U.S. income from taxation. See S. Rep. No. 192, 108th Cong., 1st Sess. 125 (2003).

controlled foreign corporation is a "qualified foreign corporation" and the other requirements of Section 1(h)(11) are met. See IRS Notice 2004–70, § 4, 2004–2 C.B. 724, 726. Amounts treated as dividends under Reg. § 1.367(b)–2(e)(2) with respect to a foreign corporation that is not a controlled foreign corporation may constitute "qualified dividend income" if the corporation otherwise meets the definition of a "qualified foreign corporation" and the other requirements of Section 1(h)(11) are met. 2004–2 C.B. at 726 n.5. Section 1(h)(11) will expire for tax years starting after 2010 unless it is extended or made permanent by Congress in new legislation.

[¶ 10,145]

b. Complete Liquidation of Foreign Subsidiary into Foreign Parent

The distributee foreign corporation will be treated as a corporation for purposes of Sections 332, 334(b)(1) and 381(a)(1). Thus, gain is not recognized. Reg. § 1.367(b)–1(b)(1). See ¶ 10,105 for the foreign subsidiary's consequences.

[¶ 10,150]

c. Acquisitive Reorganizations and Section 351 Exchanges

T.D. 8862, 2000–1 C.B. 466, 467, explained the policy underlying the Section 367(b) regulations in this area, as follows:

> The principal policy considerations of section 367(b) with respect to inbound nonrecognition transactions is the appropriate carryover of attributes from foreign to domestic corporations. This consideration has interrelated shareholder-level and corporate-level components. At the shareholder level, the section 367(b) regulations are concerned with the proper taxation of previously deferred earnings and profits. At the corporate level, the section 367(b) regulations are concerned with both the extent and manner in which the tax attributes carry over in light of the variations between the Code's taxation of foreign and domestic corporations.

Reg. § 1.367(b)–4 applies to the acquisition by a foreign corporation of the stock or assets of another foreign corporation in a reorganization described in Section 368(a)(1)(A), (B), (C), (D), (E), (F) or (G) or a Section 351 exchange transaction. In general, exchanging shareholders in such a transaction have to include in income as a deemed dividend the Section 1248 amount attributable to their stock if the transaction meets one of three tests. Reg. § 1.367(b)–4(b).

The first test is met if a U.S. person is a Section 1248 shareholder of the foreign acquired corporation immediately before the exchange, and does not receive stock in a controlled foreign corporation as to which the U.S. person is a Section 1248 shareholder immediately after the exchange. Reg. § 1.367(b)–4(b)(1). A "Section 1248 shareholder" is a U.S. person who meets the ownership requirements of Section 1248(a)(2) or 1248(c)(2) with respect to a foreign corporation. Reg. § 1.367(b)–2(b)(1).

The second, alternative test is met if (1) the exchanging shareholder receives preferred stock in exchange for common stock; (2) immediately after the exchange a U.S. corporation owns a sufficient amount of the voting stock of the foreign acquiring corporation to qualify for the indirect foreign tax credit with respect to a distribution from such corporation; and

(3) immediately before the exchange the foreign acquired corporation and the foreign acquiring corporation were not members of the same affiliated group under Section 1504(a) (without regard to Section 1504(b)) based on more than 50 percent, rather than at least 80 percent, ownership. Reg. § 1.367(b)–4(b)(2).

The third, alternative test applies to an exchange pursuant to a recapitalization under Section 368(a)(1)(E). The test is met (1) if during the 24–month period immediately before or after the date of recapitalization, the corporation that undergoes the recapitalization (or a predecessor or successor corporation) also engages in a transaction that would meet the second test above, but for the requirement that preferred stock be received, either as the foreign acquiring or acquired corporation; and (2) the recapitalization exchange is described in Reg. § 1.367(b)–4(b)(2)(i)(C). Reg. § 1.367(b)–4(b)(3).

Suppose that income is not required to be recognized under these rules. In such cases, for purposes of applying Section 1248 or 367(b) to later exchanges, earnings and profits to which the foreign acquiring corporation succeeds under Section 381 are deemed to have been accumulated by the acquiring corporation in the same years in which they were accumulated by the acquired corporation, and the exchanging shareholder is deemed to have owned stock in the acquiring corporation for the period during which it owned stock in the acquired corporation. Reg. § 1.367(b)–4(d).

[¶ 10,155]

PROBLEMS

1. American Holdings Inc., a U.S. corporation, owns all of the outstanding stock of Pasta SpA, an Italian corporation. Pasta SpA has post–1986 undistributed earnings and profits of $1,000, has paid cumulative foreign taxes of $500 and has a basis of $200 in its assets. Pasta SpA's shares have unrealized appreciation (i.e., fair market value in excess of basis) of $2,000 in American Holdings Inc.'s hands. If American Holdings Inc. liquidates Pasta SpA into itself, what amount(s) must American Holdings Inc. include in its gross income? What amount(s) would American Holdings Inc. include if Pasta SpA's shares have unrealized appreciation of $200 in American Holdings Inc.'s hands?

2. If the facts are the same as in Problem 1 except that American Holdings Inc. held its Pasta SpA shares indirectly, through Overseas S.A., a first-tier wholly owned Swiss controlled foreign corporation, and if Pasta SpA were liquidated into Overseas S.A., how much gain would Overseas S.A. recognize on the liquidation?

3. American Holdings Inc. exchanges its shares of Pasta SpA, a first-tier controlled foreign corporation, for five percent of the outstanding stock of Ciel S.A., a French corporation that is not a controlled foreign corporation after

the exchange. At the time of the exchange, Pasta SpA has earnings and profits of $2,000 and has paid cumulative foreign taxes of $500. The Pasta SpA shares have unrealized appreciation of $1,000 in American Holdings Inc.'s hands. What amount must American Holdings Inc. include in its gross income? What amount is American Holdings Inc. entitled to take as an indirect foreign tax credit?

4. American Holdings Inc. owns all of the outstanding stock of Pasta SpA, which in turn owns all of the stock of Milan Enterprises SpA, an Italian corporation. Pasta SpA exchanges its shares of Milan Enterprises SpA for shares of Ciel S.A., a French corporation, in which American Holdings Inc. has a five-percent interest. The exchange results in Pasta SpA having a ten-percent interest in Ciel S.A., which is not a controlled foreign corporation after the exchange. Milan Enterprises SpA has earnings and profits of $200 at the time of the exchange and has paid cumulative foreign taxes of $50. What are the federal income tax consequences of the foregoing exchange?

5. Domestic Manufacturing, Inc., a U.S. corporation, owns all of the stock of Foreign Subsidiary, Inc., a controlled foreign corporation. Domestic Manufacturing, Inc. has an adjusted basis of $100 in its stock in Foreign Subsidiary, Inc., the value of which is $200. The Section 1248 amount with respect to the stock is $60. Foreign Acquiring Corporation, a foreign corporation, is owned entirely by nonresident alien individuals unrelated to either Domestic Manufacturing, Inc. or Foreign Subsidiary, Inc. Foreign Acquiring Corporation acquires all of the stock of Foreign Subsidiary, Inc. from Domestic Manufacturing, Inc. in exchange for ten percent of the stock of Foreign Acquiring Corporation in a reorganization meeting the requirements of Section 368(a)(1)(B). What are the federal income tax consequences of the foregoing exchange?

4. NONOUTBOUND CORPORATE DIVISIONS (SECTION 355)

[¶ 10,160]

a. General Description

Section 355 describes a number of corporate division transactions in which a corporation distributes at least 80 percent of the stock of a corporation that it controls, within the meaning of Section 368(c), and which do not involve an outbound transfer covered by Section 367(e)(1). The distribution may take the form of a spin-off, split-off or split-up (¶ 10,020) and, if an asset transfer to the controlled corporation is involved, it may also constitute a Type D reorganization (¶ 10,015).

The Section 367(b) regulations establish different rules for nonoutbound corporate divisions involving (1) a distributing corporation that is a U.S. corporation and a controlled corporation that is a foreign corporation; (2) a distributing corporation that is a controlled foreign corporation and the stock of the controlled corporation is distributed pro rata to each of the distributing corporation's shareholders; and (3) a distributing corporation that is a controlled foreign corporation and the stock of the controlled corporation is not distributed pro rata to each of the distributing corporation's shareholders. Reg. § 1.367(b)–5(b), (c) and (d). The regulations treat all distributees in any of these three types of transactions as "exchanging shareholders" that realize income in a Section 367(b) exchange. Reg. § 1.367(b)–5(a)(2).

In general, only corporate divisions in which assets begin and end in foreign corporations or begin in foreign corporations and end in U.S. corporations are subject to the Section 367(b) regulations. As discussed at ¶ 10,110, under the final Section 367(e)(1) regulations, any outbound Section 355 distribution by a U.S. corporation to a non-U.S. person of the stock or securities of a controlled corporation that is a foreign corporation gives rise to the recognition of gain to the distributing corporation as an outbound transaction. Reg. § 1.367(e)–1. By contrast, if the U.S. corporation distributes the stock or securities of a controlled corporation that is a U.S. corporation, gain recognition is not triggered under the final Section 367(e)(1) regulations.

[¶ 10,165]

b. Distribution by U.S. Corporation

Under the final Section 367(b) regulations, when a U.S. corporation distributes stock of a controlled corporation that is a foreign corporation, whether the U.S. corporation must recognize gain depends on whether the distributee is an individual or corporation. If the distributee is an individual, the controlled corporation is not considered to be a corporation and, consequently, the distributing corporation is required to recognize any gain (but not loss) realized on the distribution. Reg. § 1.367(b)–5(b)(1)(ii).

If, however, the distributee is a corporation, the controlled corporation is considered to be a corporation and, consequently, the U.S. distributing corporation does not recognize gain on the distribution. Reg. § 1.367(b)–5(b)(1)(i). The distributing corporation must treat the distributee as an individual unless it can identify that the distributee is a corporation in accordance with the shareholder identification requirements in the regulations. Reg. § 1.367(b)–5(b)(3).

These rules do not apply to a foreign distributee to the extent that gain is recognized under Section 367(e)(1) and the regulations issued under that provision. Reg. § 1.367(b)–5(b)(2). In addition, special rules apply if the distributee is a partnership, trust or estate. See Reg. § 1.367(b)–2(k).

[¶ 10,170]

c. Distribution by Foreign Corporation

If a distribution is made by a foreign corporation that is not a controlled foreign corporation to a U.S. shareholder, Reg. § 1.367(b)–5 does not apply. In such a case, the normal rules applying to a Section 355 distribution are applicable, and no gain is recognized to the distributing corporation or the exchanging shareholder.

If the distribution is made by a controlled foreign corporation, then the distributee's Section 1248 amount must be taken into account to the extent that the distributee shareholder's Section 1248 amount (determined on a hypothetical exchange of its stock in the distributing or controlled corporation) decreases after the distribution with respect to either the distributing or controlled corporation. Reg. § 1.367(b)–5(c), (d).

In the case of a *pro rata distribution* to the distributing corporation's shareholders, the reduction in the Section 1248 amount with respect to stock in the distributing or controlled corporation reduces the basis of the distributee in that stock, and any excess over basis is included in the distributee's income as a deemed dividend. Reg. § 1.367(b)–5(c)(2). Under a basis redistribution rule, the distributee's basis in the stock of the distributing or controlled corporation (whichever is applicable) is increased by the amount of the required decrease in basis in the other stock. However, the distributee's basis in such stock cannot be increased above the fair market value of the stock and cannot be increased to the extent that the decrease reduces the distributee's postdistribution Section 1248 amount with respect to the stock. Reg. § 1.367(b)–5(c)(4).

If the *distribution is non-pro rata* to the distributing corporation's shareholders, each distributee must include in income as a deemed dividend the amount of any reduction in the Section 1248 amount with respect to either the distributing or controlled corporation. This rule applies even to a shareholder of the distributing corporation who receives no stock but whose Section 1248 amount decreases after the distribution. Reg. § 1.367(b)–5(d).

If the exchanging shareholder is a controlled foreign corporation, the deemed dividend inclusion is excluded from the controlled foreign corporation's foreign personal holding company income under Section 954(c). Reg. § 1.367(b)–5(f).

[¶ 10,175]

5. ALLOCATION AND CARRYOVER OF TAX ATTRIBUTES; BASIS AND HOLDING PERIOD RULES

In 2000, detailed proposed regulations were issued concerning the carryover of tax attributes, such as earnings and profits and foreign income tax accounts, when two corporations combine in a Section 367(b) transaction. The proposed regulations also dealt with the allocation of certain tax attributes when a corporation distributes the stock of another corporation in a Section 367(b) transaction. Some, but not all, of these proposed regulations have been issued in final form.

Reg. § 1.367(b)–3 provides rules that govern the carryover of certain foreign taxes, net operating loss and capital loss carryovers and earnings and profits from a foreign acquired corporation to a U.S. acquiring corporation. Under those rules, excess foreign taxes under Section 904(c) allowable to a foreign acquired corporation under Section 906 carry over to a U.S. acquiring corporation, but no other foreign taxes paid or accrued by the foreign acquired corporation carry over to the U.S. acquiring corporation. Reg. § 1.367(b)–3(d)(1). Net operating loss and capital loss carryovers and earnings and profits (or deficits in earnings and profits) of a foreign acquired corporation carry over to a U.S. acquiring corporation only to the extent that such amounts are effectively connected with the conduct of a U.S. trade or business or, in the context of an applicable U.S. income tax treaty, are attributable to a U.S. permanent establishment. Reg. § 1.367(b)–3(e) and (f).

Reg. § 1.367(b)–7 provides rules for determining how a foreign surviving corporation succeeds to and takes into account the earnings and profits and foreign income taxes of a foreign acquiring corporation and a foreign acquired corporation. REG–116050–99, 2000–2 C.B. 520, 525, summarizes these provisions when they were issued in proposed form, as follows:

> The proposed regulation attempts to preserve the character of earnings and profits and foreign income taxes to the extent possible in light of the applicable statutory limitations, as well as the relevant policy and administrative concerns. * * * Accordingly, the proposed rules provide that, to the extent possible, pooled earnings and profits (and foreign income taxes) remain pooled [and subject to the post–1986 Act pooling system for determining the indirect credit under Section 902], earnings and profits (and foreign income taxes) in annual layers remain in annual layers [and subject to the pre–1986 Act, year-by-year tracing system for determining the indirect credit under Section 902], foreign income taxes trapped before the transaction remain trapped after the transaction, and earnings and profits

(and foreign income taxes) remain in the same basket [for foreign tax credit limitation purposes] before and after the transaction.

Prop. Reg. § 1.367(b)–8, issued in 2006, contains rules that would apply in divisive reorganizations and would provide that the rules of Reg. § 1.312–10 apply generally to allocate earnings and profits between a distributing and controlled corporation. However, these rules are modified to reflect international tax policy concerns. Finally, Reg. § 1.367(b)–9 provides rules that apply to foreign F reorganizations and foreign-to-foreign Section 381 transactions in which either the foreign acquired corporation or foreign acquiring corporation is newly created.

Reg. § 1.367(b)–13 provides basis and holding period rules for certain Section 367(b) transactions involving a foreign corporation with Section 1248 shareholders. The purpose of these rules is to preserve relevant Section 1248 amounts. See REG–125628–01, 2005–1 C.B. 536, 537.

[¶ 10,180]

PROBLEMS

1. Southern Cross, Inc. is a U.S. corporation that owns all of the stock of Southern Cross Holdings, another U.S. corporation. Southern Cross Holdings, in turn, owns all of the stock of Bahia S.A., a Brazilian corporation. The shares of Bahia S.A. held by Southern Cross Holdings have a fair market value of $5,100 and a basis of $100. Bahia S.A. has earnings and profits of $3,000, $1,000 of which is attributable to Subpart F income for the current tax year. Bahia S.A. has paid cumulative foreign taxes of $600, $200 of which is attributable to Subpart F income included by Southern Cross Holdings in its gross income. Southern Cross Holdings distributes all of its Bahia S.A. stock to Southern Cross, Inc., in exchange for 20 percent of Southern Cross, Inc.'s stock in Southern Cross Holdings in a transaction that meets the requirements of Section 355. To what extent must Southern Cross Holdings recognize gain on the disposition of its Bahia S.A. stock? Will gain be recognized by Southern Cross, Inc. on the exchange?

2. North American Co. ("North American"), a U.S. corporation, owns all the outstanding stock of Australian Overseas, Ltd. ("Australian Overseas"), an Australian corporation. Australian Overseas, in turn, owns all of the outstanding stock of Pacific Co., a U.S. corporation. North American's shares in Australian Overseas have a fair market value of $9,000 and a basis in North American's hands of $1,500; Australian Overseas' shares in Pacific Co. have a fair market value of $1,000. Australian Overseas has earnings and profits of $9,000. In the current year, North American exchanges ten percent of its Australian Overseas shares for all of Australian Overseas' shares in Pacific Co. in a transaction that meets the requirements of Section 355. What are the U.S. tax consequences to North American?

CHAPTER 11

INTERNATIONAL SALE OF GOODS

■ ■ ■

[¶ 11,000]

A. OVERVIEW

The focus of this Chapter is on the tax aspects of planning export sales into one or more foreign countries of products that are manufactured, either in the United States by a U.S. corporation or in a foreign country by a U.S. corporation or one of its foreign subsidiaries. While business considerations in most cases should and will be paramount, there are some legal and tax factors that should be taken into account. The basic business planning problem is to determine what organizational and contractual arrangements should be adopted to implement such a marketing program. This problem involves two levels.

First, it is necessary to select appropriate arrangements for handling export sales into the particular foreign country concerned. The choice here may be rendered difficult by the number of alternatives and the complex set of legal and business factors that come into play. For example, sales might be handled by a foreign subsidiary organized under the laws of the country in which the customers are located. This subsidiary may be owned entirely by the U.S. corporation or owned jointly by the U.S. corporation and one or more other (perhaps local) investors. Alternatively, sales might be handled by selling directly to an independent local distributor or through a dependent or an independent local agent.[1] Other possibilities would be to establish a local sales facility or to rely entirely on periodic visits by sales employees of the U.S. exporter. In recent years, a growing volume of export sales have involved the Internet. U.S. sellers may sell exported products through computer software on web sites maintained on

1. There is wide diversity in the terminology used to describe representatives abroad who are involved in selling imported goods. The terms "dealer," "distributor," "sales representative," "agent," "commission agent" and "broker" are commonly used, often with no effort to discriminate with care among various distinguishable legal relationships. In the discussion that follows, the term "distributor" will be used to denote an enterprise that buys and resells imported goods for its own account. The term "agent" will denote an enterprise that performs various sales services for the account of its foreign principal but that does not purchase or sell for its own account.

servers located in the United States, in the customer's country or in a third country. Under each of these broad alternatives, there are many ancillary problems to be solved. For example, to what extent will the sales operations (including the determination of prices and other terms of sale to the customer) be controlled by the U.S. exporter? To what extent should a dependent agent, an independent agent or a software agent maintained on a web site hosted by an independent service provider be given power to negotiate the terms of and to conclude sales agreements on behalf of the U.S. exporter? Should warehouse and servicing facilities be maintained abroad, and, if so, what organizational and operational arrangements should be adopted for them? Commercial, tax and antitrust laws in the United States and abroad may have an important bearing on the handling of these and related problems.

The second level of the organizational problem is selecting an appropriate organization for handling the overall export sales program. Should worldwide or regional marketing efforts be handled by a division of the U.S. corporation or by a U.S. subsidiary, possibly one that qualifies as a Domestic International Sales Corporation ("DISC")? Or would using a foreign corporation be more advantageous? Formerly, as discussed at ¶¶ 11,155 et seq., a foreign corporation could qualify as a Foreign Sales Corporation ("FSC"), which resulted in a reduction of U.S. tax on a portion of its export income. Following the decision by the World Trade Organization ("WTO") Dispute Settlement Body ("DSB") holding that the FSC provisions involved an export subsidy prohibited by WTO agreements, the FSC regime was repealed in 2000. As a result, no foreign corporation could qualify as a FSC after September 30, 2000. The FSC regime was replaced by the extraterritorial income ("ETI") exclusion regime, under which a portion of a U.S. taxpayer's extraterritorial income, which typically included (but was not limited to) income from exports, was exempt from U.S. tax. However, in a proceeding initiated by what is now the European Union ("EU"), the WTO DSB ruled that the ETI regime was, like the FSC, an illegal export subsidy under the WTO agreements. The WTO authorized the imposition by the EU of sanctions in the form of retaliatory customs duties on goods imported from the United States to encourage the United States to end the export subsidy. As discussed at ¶ 11,230, the 2004 JOBS Act repealed the ETI exclusion but with generous transitional rules that permitted substantial ETI benefits to be available in 2005 and 2006 and even beyond on export transactions effected pursuant to a binding contract in effect on September 17, 2003. Subsequently, these transitional rules were also held by the WTO DSB to violate WTO agreements.

In practice, the two levels of the organizational issues presented in planning U.S. export transactions often have a close interrelationship that must be considered in drafting an overall organizational and operational blueprint for implementation of an export program.

B. ARRANGEMENTS FOR HANDLING EXPORT SALES INTO A PARTICULAR FOREIGN COUNTRY

[¶ 11,005]

1. FOREIGN INCOME TAXES

The starting point for an assessment of the risk of incurring foreign income tax in connection with export operations is an examination, usually in collaboration with local experts, of the tax law of the countries into which export sales will be made. A U.S. enterprise that makes export sales directly to independent parties abroad and has no representative or office abroad will not, under the tax laws of most countries, be subject to liability for income taxes in the country in which the importer is located. If the U.S. firm sells in the importer's country through a locally organized subsidiary, the income of the latter will, of course, be subject to the usual local corporate income taxes. Whether the U.S. firm will also be subject to foreign income tax will depend on the nature of the subsidiary's business activity and its relationship to the U.S. parent. If, in lieu of a local subsidiary, the U.S. enterprise enters into a contractual relationship with a sales agent or sets up some kind of office or other facility in the foreign country, there may be substantial exposure on the part of the U.S. firm to foreign income tax liability. The nature of the U.S. firm's relationship with the foreign agent or the foreign office or other facility and the latter's method of carrying on its activities will, in most cases, have an important bearing on the impact of foreign income taxes.

If the export income of the U.S. exporting enterprise would be subject to tax under the law of an importer's country, it is necessary to consider the possible application of any income tax treaty in effect between the United States and the foreign country concerned. To the extent that treaty provisions are not dispositive, the normally applicable rules of the foreign income tax system will control.

In most cases, foreign income taxes imposed in connection with export operations will be creditable against the U.S. income tax of the U.S. exporter. Not infrequently, however, the Section 904 limitations on the foreign tax credit, discussed in Chapters 5 and 7, will limit the amount of foreign tax that can be credited. As discussed in these chapters, there are two baskets of income under Section 901(d)(1) to which the foreign tax credit limitation of Section 904(a) is separately applied. The two baskets are the passive category income basket, Section 904(d)(1)(A), and the general category income basket, Section 904(d)(1)(B). When the limitations come into play, they may limit opportunities for cross-crediting and underscore the importance of minimizing foreign income taxes imposed on export income.

The potential impact of the foreign tax credit limitations on the planning of exports from the United States may be illustrated by an example. When a U.S. corporation receives a dividend from a wholly owned foreign manufacturing subsidiary, the dividend will often be included in the foreign tax credit general limitation basket under the Section 904(d)(3) look-through rules. If the combined foreign corporate income tax and withholding tax relating to this dividend are higher than the effective U.S. corporate tax, the foreign income taxes with respect to the dividend distribution will exceed the Section 904(d)(1)(B) general limitation on the foreign tax credit (computed solely with reference to this dividend). If this excess is to be creditable, it will be necessary for the U.S. corporation to have other foreign-source general limitation income taxed at a rate lower than the U.S. corporate tax. One method of absorbing some or all of this excess foreign tax credit would be for the exporter to arrange its export sales so that (1) they generate some foreign-source income and (2) such income is exempt from foreign tax.

Loss of foreign tax credit could also result in a case involving export income alone. If a U.S. exporter sells through a foreign sales branch products it manufactures in the United States and passes title to the customer outside the United States, a portion of the export income will be deemed to be from U.S. sources. §§ 865(b) and 863(b). This portion will, therefore, not be included in the numerator of the foreign tax credit general limitation fraction. If, however, the foreign tax authorities under their source-of-income rules and any applicable tax treaty take the position that the entire export income is attributable to the foreign sales branch and is therefore subject to the applicable foreign corporate taxes, the limitation may, depending on the foreign tax rate, prevent taking a full foreign tax credit for the foreign tax on the export income.

A more dramatic case arises if the U.S. exporter passes title to exported products at the U.S. port of shipment, and the foreign tax authorities hold that all of the export income is attributable to the foreign sales branch and is subject to foreign income tax. Assume that the U.S. exporter has no other foreign-source income in the general limitation basket that is subject to a low foreign tax or no foreign tax. Because all of the export income will be treated as U.S.-source under U.S. tax law, no foreign tax credit will be available for the foreign tax on the export income.

[¶ 11,010]

2. INCOME TAX TREATIES: THE PERMANENT ESTABLISHMENT CONCEPT

The device incorporated in each of the U.S. income tax treaties for the purpose of allocating jurisdiction to tax income generated by international sales of goods is the concept of the "permanent establishment." See

¶ 3165. The basic provision applicable to export profits found in the applicable treaties is phrased as follows in paragraph 1 of Article VII of the U.S. treaty with Canada:

Article VII

BUSINESS PROFITS

> 1. The business profits of a resident of a Contracting State shall be taxable only in that State unless the resident carries on business in the other Contracting State through a permanent establishment situated therein. If the resident carries on, or has carried on, business as aforesaid, the business profits of the resident may be taxed in the other State but only so much of them as is attributable to that permanent establishment.

Convention Between the United States of America and Canada with Respect to Taxes on Income and on Capital, U.S.-Can., Sept. 26, 1980, T.I.A.S. No. 11,087.

Many foreign countries also apply the permanent establishment concept as the basic criterion for fixing the scope of taxing jurisdiction over foreign persons engaged in domestic business even in the absence of an applicable income tax treaty.

The income tax treaties negotiated by the United States during the last 45 years or so tend to be patterned after the OECD Model Tax Convention, and the 2006 U.S. Treasury Model Treaty (Appendix A) follows the OECD Model quite closely. But, there are important differences between older U.S. treaties and more recent ones and even between treaties that generally follow the OECD Model. The OECD Model Tax Convention on Income and Capital and accompanying commentary have been revised frequently in recent years. As part of an ongoing process, updates and amendments are made periodically without complete revisions of the Model. See OECD Committee on Fiscal Affairs, Model Tax Convention on Income and Capital (2 vols. updated as of July 22, 2010) ("OECD Model Tax Convention").

[¶ 11,015]

3. EXTENT OF EXPOSURE TO FOREIGN INCOME TAXATION

If an income tax treaty applies and if the U.S. enterprise is present in the foreign country through a permanent establishment, the U.S. enterprise exposes itself to income tax liability in that country, and the amount of income subject to foreign tax liability may be affected by the terms of the applicable treaty. For example, the United States–Greece income tax treaty, which is an older treaty, provides that if a permanent establishment of a U.S. enterprise is found to exist in Greece, the U.S. enterprise may be subject to Greek tax on its entire industrial and commercial profits from all sources within Greece. This provision would permit attributing maximum "force of attraction" to the permanent establishment. Thus, if a U.S. corporation has several offices and agents in Greece, only one of which constitutes a permanent establishment, the U.S. corporation might, if Greek tax law so provides, be held liable for Greek income tax on the total amount of its Greek-source income, even though much of that income is not attributable to a permanent establishment.

It is clear that a more limited approach is taken in the U.S. treaties with Belgium and South Korea and most other U.S. tax treaties (as well as the U.S. Model Treaty). Under these treaties, only so much of the U.S. enterprise's profits as are actually attributable to the permanent establishment may be taxed by the host country.

Unfortunately, the treaties do not ensure that income attributable to the permanent establishment and therefore subject to foreign tax will be considered to be income from foreign sources for purposes of the general income limitation on the U.S. foreign tax credit under Section 904(d)(1)(B). Therefore, the possibility of double taxation remains. This defect could be cured by permitting only income having its source in the foreign country concerned to be attributed to the foreign permanent establishment and by negotiating uniform source-of-income rules for application by the United States and the treaty partner.

All of the treaties explicitly provide, in effect, that in determining commercial profits subject to tax under the permanent establishment provision, the tax authorities will not be bound by the profits allocated by the foreign enterprise to the local establishment; rather the taxable income of the permanent establishment will be deemed to be the income that it might be expected to earn if it were dealing as an unrelated party on an arm's length basis with the foreign enterprise of which it is a part. The treaties generally provide that all expenses allocable to the permanent establishment are to be allowed in computing taxable income, and they make clear that such allowable deductions include executive and general administrative expenses. The treaties also generally provide that expenses allocable to the permanent establishment are deductible wherever incurred. Accordingly, deductions are permitted for an appropriate portion of the U.S. head office expense and, in some cases, for research and experimental expenses. The treaties do not provide specific rules for allocating expenses or losses to a permanent establishment, but defer to the rules of the treaty partner concerned. See ¶¶ 3185 and 3187.

When a permanent establishment has been created in a foreign country to which income can be attributed, the establishment will usually be subject to the income taxes normally imposed by that country on the branch of a foreign corporation. The effective tax burden on a branch may be significantly higher or lower than that imposed on a subsidiary organized under local law. It is likely to be lower if there is no foreign tax equivalent of the U.S. branch profits tax on the unreinvested profits of the permanent establishment.

It is important to keep in mind, moreover, that even though a U.S. enterprise creates a permanent establishment in a foreign country to which income is attributable under the treaty, the country may choose not to exercise the full extent of the taxing jurisdiction permitted by the treaty. In a number of foreign countries, for example, Belgium and the Netherlands, it has been possible to establish a so-called "headquarters" or "coordination" branch office that will either be exempted from taxation or be taxed on a highly favorable basis. See ¶ 13,005. Such arrangements can be worked out notwithstanding the facts that a permanent establishment has been created and that, consequently, under the treaty, the usual income tax of the country in which the headquarters or coordination office is established could be imposed on the income attributable to that establishment.

[¶ 11,020]

4. DEFINITION OF PERMANENT ESTABLISHMENT

The various treaties to which the United States is a party sometimes differ in the way in which they define permanent establishment. These differences can play an important role in planning the procedures and organizational and contractual arrangements for exporting into a country with which the United States has an income tax treaty. The relatively recent income tax treaties to which the United States is a party tend to follow the pattern of Article 5 of the 2006 U.S. Model Treaty, but even among the newer treaties there are important differences. The definition of permanent establishment in some of the older treaties differs in basic respects from that of the newer treaties.

To provide a focus for examining the significance of some of those differences, the permanent establishment definitions contained in the U.S. treaties with Belgium and South Korea, which are examples of newer treaties, and in the U.S. treaty with Greece, which is an older treaty, are set forth below. These definitions are followed by a series of questions on the foreign income tax consequences of implementing export sales into those countries in various ways.

[¶ 11,025]

a. United States–Greece Tax Treaty (entered into force December 30, 1953)

Article II–General Definitions

* * *

[(1)](i) The term "permanent establishment", when used with respect to an enterprise of one of the Contracting States, means a branch, factory or other fixed place of business, but does not include an agency unless that agent has, and habitually exercises, a general authority to negotiate and conclude contracts on behalf of such enterprise or has a stock of merchandise from which he regularly fills orders on behalf of such enterprise. An enterprise of one of the Contracting States shall not be deemed to have a permanent establishment in the other Contracting State merely because it carries on business dealings in such other Contracting State through a bona fide commission agent, broker or custodian acting in the ordinary course of his business as such. The fact that an enterprise of one of the Contracting States maintains in the other Contracting State a fixed place of business exclusively for the purchase of goods or merchandise shall not of itself constitute such fixed place of business a permanent establishment of such enterprise. When a corporation of one Contracting State has a subsidiary corporation which is a corporation of the other Contracting State or which is engaged in trade or business in such other Contracting State, such subsidiary corporation shall not, merely because of that fact, be deemed to be a permanent establishment of its parent corporation.

* * *

Article III

(1) An enterprise of one of the Contracting States shall not be subject to taxation by the other Contracting State in respect of its industrial or commercial profits unless it is engaged in trade or business in the other Contracting State through a permanent establishment situated therein. If it is so engaged the other Contracting State may impose the tax only upon the income of such enterprise from sources within such other State.

(2) Where an enterprise of one of the Contracting States is engaged in trade or business in the other Contracting State through a permanent establishment situated therein, there shall be attributed to such permanent establishment the industrial or commercial profits which it might be expected to derive if it were an independent enterprise engaged in the same or similar activities under the same or similar conditions and dealing at arm's length with the enterprise of which it is a permanent establishment, and the profits so attributed shall, subject to the law of such other Contracting State, be deemed to be income from sources within such other Contracting State.

(3) In determining the industrial or commercial profits from sources within one of the Contracting States of an enterprise of the other Contracting State, no profits shall be deemed to arise from the mere purchase of goods or merchandise within the former Contracting State by such enterprise.

* * *

Convention between The United States of America and the Kingdom of Greece for the Avoidance of Double Taxation and the Prevention of Fiscal Evasion with Respect to Taxes on Income, U.S.-Greece, Feb. 20, 1950, 5 U.S.T. 47.

[¶ 11,030]

b. United States–South Korea Tax Treaty (entered into force October 20, 1979)

Article 8

BUSINESS PROFITS

(1) Industrial or commercial profits of a resident of one of the Contracting States shall be exempt from tax by the other Contracting State unless such resident is engaged in industrial or commercial activity in that other Contracting State through a permanent establishment situated therein. If such resident is so engaged, tax may be imposed by that other Contracting State on the industrial or commercial profits of such resident but only on so much of such profits as are attributable to the permanent establishment.

(2) Where a resident of one of the Contracting States is engaged in industrial or commercial activity in the other Contracting State through a permanent establishment situated therein, there shall in each Contracting State be attributed to the permanent establishment the industrial or commercial profits which would be attributable to such permanent establishment if such permanent establishment were an independent entity engaged in the same or similar activities under the same or similar conditions and dealing wholly independently with the resident of which it is a permanent establishment.

(3) In the determination of the industrial or commercial profits of a permanent establishment, there shall be allowed as deductions expenses which are reasonably connected with such profits, including executive and general administrative expenses, whether incurred in the Contracting State in which the permanent establishment is situated or elsewhere.

(4) No profits shall be attributed to a permanent establishment of a resident of one of the Contracting States in the other Contracting State merely by reason of the purchase of goods or merchandise by that permanent establishment, or by the resident of which it is a permanent establishment, for the account of that resident.

* * *

Article 9

PERMANENT ESTABLISHMENT

(1) For purposes of this Convention, the term "permanent establishment" means a fixed place of business through which a resident of one of the Contracting States engages in industrial or commercial activity.

(2) The term "fixed place of business" includes but is not limited to:

(a) A branch;

(b) An office;

(c) A factory;

(d) A workshop;

(e) A warehouse;

(f) A store or other sales outlet;

(g) A mine, quarry, or other place of extraction of natural resources; and

(h) A building site or construction or installation project which exists for more than 6 months.

(3) Notwithstanding paragraphs (1) and (2), a permanent establishment shall not include a fixed place of business used only for one or more of the following:

(a) The use of facilities for the purpose of storage, display, or delivery of goods or merchandise belonging to the resident;

(b) The maintenance of a stock of goods or merchandise belonging to the resident for the purpose of storage, display, or delivery;

(c) The maintenance of a stock of goods or merchandise belonging to the resident for the purpose of processing by another person;

(d) The maintenance of a fixed place of business for the purpose of purchasing goods or merchandise, or for collecting information, for the resident;

(e) The maintenance of a fixed place of business for the purpose of advertising, for the supply of information, for scientific research, or for similar activities which have a preparatory or auxiliary character, for the resident; or

(f) The maintenance of a building site or construction or installation project which does not exist for more than 6 months.

(4) Even if a resident of one of the Contracting States does not have a permanent establishment in the other Contracting State under paragraphs (1) through (3) of this Article, nevertheless he shall be deemed to have a permanent establishment in that other Contracting State if he engages in trade or business in that other Contracting State through an agent who—

(a) Has an authority to conclude contracts in the name of that resident and regularly exercises that authority in that other Contracting State, unless the exercise of the authority is limited to the purchase of goods or merchandise for the account of the resident; or

(b) Maintains in that other Contracting State a stock of goods or merchandise belonging to that resident from which he regularly fills orders or makes deliveries.

(5) Notwithstanding subparagraphs (a), (c) and (d) of paragraph (3), if a resident of one of the Contracting States has a fixed place of business in the other Contracting State and goods or merchandise are either:

(a) Subjected to processing in that other Contracting State by another person (whether or not purchased in that other Contracting State); or

(b) Purchased in that other Contracting State (and such goods or merchandise are not subjected to processing outside that other Contracting State)

such resident shall be considered to have a permanent establishment in that other Contracting State, if all or part of such goods or merchandise is sold by or on behalf of such resident for use, consumption, or disposition in that other Contracting State.

(6) Notwithstanding the provisions of paragraphs (4) and (5), a resident of one of the Contracting States shall not be deemed to have a permanent establishment in the other Contracting State merely because such resident engages in industrial or commercial activity in that other Contracting State through a broker, general commission agent or any other agent of an independent status, where such broker or agent is acting in the ordinary course of his business.

(7) The fact that a resident of one of the Contracting States is a related person (as defined under Article 11 (Related Persons)) with respect to a resident of the other Contracting State or with respect to a person who engages in industrial or commercial activity in that other Contracting State (whether through a permanent establishment or otherwise) shall not be taken into account in determining whether that resident of the first-mentioned Contracting State has a permanent establishment in that other Contracting State.

Convention Between the United States of America and the Republic of Korea for the Avoidance of Double Taxation and the Prevention of Fiscal Evasion with Respect to Taxes on Income and the Encouragement of International Trade and Investment, U.S.-S. Korea, June 4, 1976, 30 U.S.T. 5253.

[¶ 11,035]

c. United States–Belgium Tax Treaty (entered into force December 28, 2007)

Article 5

PERMANENT ESTABLISHMENT

1. For the purposes of this Convention, the term "permanent establishment" means a fixed place of business through which the business of an enterprise is wholly or partly carried on.

2. The term "permanent establishment" includes especially:

a) a place of management;

b) a branch;

c) an office;

d) a factory;

e) a workshop; and

f) a mine, an oil or gas well, a quarry, or any other place of extraction of natural resources.

3. a) A building site or construction or installation project constitutes a permanent establishment only if it lasts for more than twelve months.

b) An installation used for the exploration for natural resources constitutes a permanent establishment in a Contracting State only if it lasts or the activity continues in that State for more than twelve months.

4. Notwithstanding the preceding provisions of this Article, the term "permanent establishment" shall be deemed not to include:

a) the use of facilities solely for the purpose of storage, display or delivery of goods or merchandise belonging to the enterprise;

b) the maintenance of a stock of goods or merchandise belonging to the enterprise solely for the purpose of storage, display or delivery;

c) the maintenance of a stock of goods or merchandise belonging to the enterprise solely for the purpose of processing by another enterprise;

d) the maintenance of a fixed place of business solely for the purpose of purchasing goods or merchandise, or of collecting information, for the enterprise;

e) the maintenance of a fixed place of business solely for the purpose of carrying on, for the enterprise, any other activity of a preparatory or auxiliary character;

f) the maintenance of a fixed place of business solely for any combination of the activities mentioned in subparagraphs a) through e), provided that the overall activity of the fixed place of business resulting from this combination is of a preparatory or auxiliary character.

5. Notwithstanding the provisions of paragraphs 1 and 2, where a person—other than an agent of an independent status to whom paragraph 6 applies—is acting on behalf of an enterprise and has and habitually exercises in a Contracting State an authority to conclude contracts that are binding on the enterprise, that enterprise shall be deemed to have a permanent establishment in that State in respect of any activities that the person undertakes for the enterprise, unless the activities of such person are limited to those mentioned in paragraph 4 that, if exercised through a fixed place of business, would not make this fixed place of business a permanent establishment under the provisions of that paragraph.

6. An enterprise shall not be deemed to have a permanent establishment in a Contracting State merely because it carries on business in that State through a broker, general commission agent, or any other agent of an independent status, provided that such persons are acting in the ordinary course of their business as independent agents.

7. The fact that a company that is a resident of a Contracting State controls or is controlled by a company that is a resident of the other Contracting State, or that carries on business in that other State (whether through a permanent establishment or otherwise), shall not be taken into account in determining whether either company has a permanent establishment in that other State.

* * *

Article 7

BUSINESS PROFITS

1. The profits of an enterprise of a Contracting State shall be taxable only in that State unless the enterprise carries on business in the other Contracting State through a permanent establishment situated therein. If the enterprise carries on business as aforesaid, the profits of the enterprise may be taxed in the other State but only so much of them as are attributable to that permanent establishment.

2. Subject to the provisions of paragraph 3, where an enterprise of a Contracting State carries on business in the other Contracting State through a permanent establishment situated therein, there shall in each Contracting State be attributed to that permanent establishment the profits that it might be expected to make if it were a distinct and independent enterprise engaged in the same or similar activities under the same or similar conditions.

3. In determining the profits of a permanent establishment, there shall be allowed as deductions expenses that are incurred for the purposes of the permanent establishment, including executive and general administra-

tive expenses so incurred, whether in the State in which the permanent establishment is situated or elsewhere.

4. No profits shall be attributed to a permanent establishment by reason of the mere purchase by that permanent establishment of goods or merchandise for the enterprise.

Convention Between the Government of The United States Of America and the Government of The Kingdom Of Belgium for the Avoidance Of Double Taxation and the Prevention of Fiscal Evasion with Respect to Taxes on Income, U.S.-Belg., Nov. 27, 2006, S. TREATY DOC. No. 110–3 (2007).

[¶ 11,040]

d. Permanent Establishment and the Taxation of Export Income

Definitions of permanent establishment in the more recent tax treaties to which the United States is a party, such as the treaties with Belgium and South Korea excerpted above, typically draw an important distinction between an independent agent acting in the ordinary course of its business and all other agents. Little is done, however, to define the criteria on which the distinction is to be based. Paragraphs 4, 5 and 6 of the Article 5 definition of permanent establishment contained in the OECD Model Tax Convention on Income and on Capital (as revised on July 22, 2010)("OECD Model Tax Convention"), vol. I, at M–13 and M–14, provide as follows:

> 4. Notwithstanding the preceding provisions of this Article, the term "permanent establishment" shall be deemed not to include:
>
> a) the use of facilities solely for the purpose of storage, display or delivery of goods or merchandise belonging to the enterprise;
>
> b) the maintenance of a stock of goods or merchandise belonging to the enterprise solely for the purpose of storage, display or delivery;
>
> c) the maintenance of a stock of goods or merchandise belonging to the enterprise solely for the purpose of processing by another enterprise;
>
> d) the maintenance of a fixed place of business solely for the purpose of purchasing goods or merchandise or of collecting information, for the enterprise;
>
> e) the maintenance of a fixed place of business solely for the purpose of carrying on, for the enterprise, any other activity of a preparatory or auxiliary character;
>
> f) the maintenance of a fixed place of business solely for any combination of activities mentioned in sub-paragraphs a) to e), provid-

ed that the overall activity of the fixed place of business resulting from this combination is of a preparatory or auxiliary character.

5. * * * [W]here a person—other than an agent of an independent status to whom paragraph 6 applies—is acting on behalf of an enterprise and has, and habitually exercises, in a Contracting State an authority to conclude contracts in the name of the enterprise, that enterprise shall be deemed to have a permanent establishment in that State in respect of any activities which that person undertakes for the enterprise, unless the activities of such person are limited to those mentioned in paragraph 4 which, if exercised through a fixed place of business, would not make this fixed place of business a permanent establishment under the provisions of that paragraph.

6. An enterprise shall not be deemed to have a permanent establishment in a Contracting State merely because it carries on business in that State through a broker, general commission agent or any other agent of an independent status, provided that such persons are acting in the ordinary course of their business.

The accompanying commentary to the OECD Model Tax Convention Paragraphs 5 and 6 (OECD Model Tax Convention, vol. I, at C(5)–18 through C(5)–24) ("OEDC Commentary") contains some helpful elaboration.

For example, with respect to paragraph 5, the Commentary notes that an agent in the customer's country (other than an independent agent acting in the ordinary course of its business) who has authority to conclude contracts in the name of the foreign enterprise is not restricted to an agent who enters into contracts literally in the name of the enterprise. It also includes an agent who concludes contracts that are binding on the enterprise even if these contracts are not actually in the name of the enterprise. OECD Commentary ¶ 32.1. This would appear to include a contract binding on an undisclosed principal. The Commentary also highlights that an agent can be a permanent establishment if he solicits and negotiates (but does not formally accept orders) which are forwarded to the foreign enterprise where the transaction is routinely approved. OECD Commentary ¶ 33.

With respect to paragraph 6, the Commentary indicates that a person will be treated as an independent agent acting in the ordinary course of business only if he is independent of the foreign enterprise both legally and economically. Id. at ¶ 37. In determining whether an agent is not legally independent, an important criterion is whether the agent is subject to detailed instructions or to comprehensive control by the foreign principal. Id. at ¶ 38. A related criterion is whether the agent is subject to significant control with respect to the manner in which he carries out his work. Id. at ¶ 38.3. Reliance by the principal on the special skill and knowledge of the agent tends to support the existence of legal independence. Id. at ¶ 38.3. Legal independence is less likely to be present if the functions of the agent are performed entirely or almost entirely on behalf of one enterprise over a long period of time although this factor is not by itself determinative. It must be weighed in the light of all the facts and circumstances. Id. at ¶ 38.6.

The Commentary also indicates that whether entrepreneurial risk is borne by the agent or the foreign enterprise is an important criterion. Id. at ¶ 38. Although not specifically so stated, this criterion is presumably related to whether the agent is economically independent of the enterprise.

Another paragraph of the Commentary deals with a subsidiary which is organized in the customer's country and owned by the foreign enterprise. If the subsidiary functions as a sales agent of its parent enterprise, it will be treated as a permanent establishment of the enterprise only under the same conditions prescribed in paragraph 5 of Article 5 for any unrelated agent. Thus, if the subsidiary has the authority to conclude contracts in the name of its parent, which it habitually exercises, it will be a permanent establishment unless it qualifies as an independent agent acting in the ordinary course of its business. Id. at ¶ 41.

The OECD Commentary, while limited in scope, is particularly significant in view of the relative dearth of interpretative material available in the United States concerning the meaning of tax treaty concepts.

In Taisei Fire & Marine Insurance Co. v. Commissioner, 104 T.C. 535 (1995)(acq.), at ¶ 3175, the Tax Court examined whether an unrelated U.S. corporation that conducted a reinsurance business as agent on behalf of four Japanese insurance companies constituted an independent agent acting in the ordinary course of its business under the United States–Japan Income Tax Treaty. In the absence of U.S. administrative guidance the court relied on the pertinent OECD commentary concerning the definition of an independent agent and found that such an agent must be legally *and* economically independent of its foreign principal. The government conceded that the U.S. agent was acting in the ordinary course of its business. The court found that the U.S. corporate agent was legally independent of its Japanese principals because they did not exercise comprehensive control over, or give detailed instructions to, their agent. In addition, the U.S. agent was held to be economically independent because it bore entrepreneurial risk. It had to earn enough commissions based on a percentage of gross premiums paid to its principals to cover its expenses and there was no assurance that it would be able to do so.

The U.S. Treasury Department's Technical Explanation to the 2006 U.S. Model Treaty (Appendix B) contains the current articulation of the U.S. Treasury's views concerning the criteria to be applied in determining whether an agent is legally and economically independent for purposes of the Model. It states, at p. 18:

Whether the agent and the enterprise are independent is a factual determination. Among the questions to be considered are the extent to which the agent operates on the basis of instructions from the enterprise. An agent that is subject to detailed instructions regarding the conduct of its operations or comprehensive control by the enterprise is not legally independent.

In determining whether the agent is economically independent, a relevant factor is the extent to which the agent bears business risk. Business risk refers primarily to risk of loss. An independent agent typically bears risk of loss from its own activities. In the absence of other factors that would establish dependence, an agent that shares business risk with the enterprise, or has its own business risk, is economically independent because its business activities are not integrated with those of the principal. Conversely, an agent that bears little or no risk from activities it performs is not economically independent * * *.

Another relevant factor in determining whether an agent is economically independent is whether the agent acts exclusively or nearly exclusively for the principal. Such a relationship may indicate that the principal has economic control over the agent. A number of principals acting in concert also may have economic control over an agent. The limited scope of the agent's activities and the agent's dependence on a single source of income may indicate that the agent lacks economic independence. It should be borne in mind, however, that exclusivity is not in itself a conclusive test: an agent may be economically independent notwithstanding an exclusive relationship with the principal if it has the capacity to diversify and acquire other clients without substantial modifications to its current business and without substantial harm to its business profits. Thus, exclusivity should be viewed merely as a pointer to further investigation of the relationship between the principal and the agent. Each case must be addressed on the basis of its own facts and circumstances.

Consider in connection with the following problems how much authority and discretion can be given to an agent (including an employee) without giving rise to a permanent establishment. There is a wide range of functions and powers that can be vested in an agent in connection with export sales. For example, an agent could simply solicit sales on the seller's standard terms and conditions of sale, with all orders being subject to acceptance by the seller's export division in the United States. At the other end of the scale, an agent can be given authority to carry out all aspects of the export sales, including negotiation of prices and other terms of sale, acceptance of orders, effecting deliveries from inventory maintained in a warehouse and invoicing and collection. Under what circumstances does the distinction between an independent agent acting in the ordinary course of its business and another agent become important?

What factors are relevant in identifying an independent agent acting in the ordinary course of its business as distinguished from any other agent? From a tax policy perspective, are the distinctions drawn in the definition of permanent establishment justifiable?

[¶ 11,045]

PROBLEMS

1. Assume that Cosmos Corporation ("Cosmos"), a U.S. corporation, makes export sales of products it manufactures to an independent distributor in South Korea that buys from Cosmos and resells for its own account. Cosmos has no sales office or other facility in South Korea. Its only contacts with South Korea consist of (1) visits to the distributor by its export division sales employees headquartered in the United States who are authorized to solicit orders (on the standard conditions of sale imposed by Cosmos) from the distributor but have no authority to negotiate prices or terms of the export sales or to accept orders (orders are subject to acceptance by Cosmos in the United States) and (2) communications, including order confirmations, shipping documents and invoices sent from the United States to the distributor relating to export sales. Could the income realized by Cosmos on these sales be subject to South Korean income tax?

2. If the Cosmos employees referred to in Problem 1 had and regularly exercised the authority not only to solicit orders on the standard terms and conditions of sale required by the Cosmos export division but also to accept such orders while visiting the distributor in South Korea, would the result be different?

3. If the facts were as stated in Problem 1 except that the distributor was located in Greece and the Cosmos export division employees had no authority to negotiate the price or other terms of the sale, but only to solicit and accept orders on the standard terms and conditions of sale required by the Cosmos export division, could income realized by Cosmos from the export sales be subject to Greek income tax?

4. Assume that Cosmos sells directly to customers in Belgium and South Korea through agents in Belgium and in South Korea, who solicit sales and have authority to conclude sales contracts binding on Cosmos which they regularly exercise and receive commissions for their sales efforts. The commissions are fixed at ten percent of the sale prices of Cosmos products they sell. All sales must be made on Cosmos' standard conditions of sale, but terms of payment, including prices within parameters set by Cosmos, may be determined by the agents. The agents are manufacturers' representatives who sell products manufactured by a variety of suppliers. Could income realized by Cosmos on these sales be taxed in Belgium or South Korea?

5. Cosmos establishes offices in Seoul, South Korea, and Athens, Greece, that engage only in (1) handling South Korean and Greek market research and advertising (all sales being made directly by the Cosmos export division in the United States to independent distributors) and (2) purchasing South

Korean-made and Greek-made components that are shipped (without further processing) to Cosmos in the United States for incorporation in Cosmos' manufactured products. Would the offices constitute permanent establishments?

6. Would the result in Problem 5 be different if some of the South Korean- or Greek-made components were resold by the Cosmos offices to South Korean or Greek manufacturers?

7. Cosmos establishes offices in Seoul and Athens at which it locates staffs of engineers who provide advice to potential customers in South Korea and Greece concerning how Cosmos products can be adapted to meet customers' technical requirements and who provide after-sales services for Cosmos products as required under Cosmos warranties to customers in those countries. Has a permanent establishment been created in either country?

8. Assume that the facts are the same as in Problem 1, except that Cosmos maintains warehouses in Brussels, Seoul and Athens in which its products are displayed and from which deliveries are regularly made to distributors from inventories maintained in these warehouses. Is there a permanent establishment under any of the applicable treaties?

9. Assume that, in addition to the facts set forth in Problem 8, products maintained in the warehouses are sent to independent local painting firms to be painted and polished before being displayed and delivered to local distributors who purchase them pursuant to export sales orders accepted by the Cosmos export division in the United States. Has a permanent establishment been created under any of the applicable treaties?

10. If the products referred to in Problem 9 were shipped, after processing, only to distributors located outside Belgium, South Korea and Greece, would the result be altered?

11. If Cosmos establishes wholly owned subsidiaries in Belgium, South Korea and Greece that buy from Cosmos and resell at a markup and fill the role played by the independent distributors in Problem 1 and if the facts are otherwise as stated in Problem 1, could the subsidiaries be regarded as permanent establishments of Cosmos so that Cosmos could be subjected to foreign income tax on income generated by its export sales to its subsidiary-distributors?

12. Suppose that the sales subsidiaries functioned as agents of Cosmos, that their employees regularly negotiated export sale contracts and entered into such contracts binding on Cosmos in return for commissions paid by Cosmos, but that deliveries were made directly from Cosmos to the local customers. Could Cosmos be subject to Belgian, South Korea or Greek income tax as a result of the activities of the sales agent subsidiaries?

13. Assume that Cosmos has three divisions, one engaged in manufacturing and selling radios, the second engaged in manufacturing and selling refrigerators and the third engaged in manufacturing and selling children's toys. The toy division has large sales offices in Brussels, Seoul and Athens, which are engaged in soliciting, negotiating and accepting sales contracts for exports from the United States for toys. The other two divisions handle their

export sales in the manner described in Problem 1 with no office in the foreign country. Can Belgium, South Korea and Greece subject the income realized by Cosmos on export sales of radios and refrigerators to income tax under the applicable treaties?

14. To what extent do the treaties control the issues of how much gross income must be included and what expenses (including those incurred outside the country concerned) may be deducted in determining the taxable income of the permanent establishment?

15. A U.S. architectural firm has designed in its U.S. offices motels to be built in Belgium, South Korea and Greece. To supervise the building of the motels by local construction concerns, the firm establishes temporary offices at the building sites, which are staffed with employees of the U.S. firm responsible for the supervision of construction. The supervision is completed and the offices closed less than one year after they were opened. Can the U.S. architectural firm be subjected to income tax by Belgium, Greece and South Korea?

[¶ 11,050]

5. PERMANENT ESTABLISHMENT IN THE CONTEXT OF INTERNATIONAL ELECTRONIC COMMERCE

Perhaps the most significant development in international business over the last 20 years has been the growth in international electronic commerce ("e-commerce") involving the supply of tangible and intangible property and services over the Internet. The permanent establishment concept was largely developed in the context of sales of personal property in traditional commerce, and it attached central importance to the existence of a fixed place of business. However, as stated in a U.S. Treasury Report on policy implications of global electronic commerce:

> Electronic commerce, on the other hand, may be conducted without regard to national boundaries and may dissolve the link between an income-producing activity and a specific location. From a certain perspective, electronic commerce does not seem to occur in any physical location but instead takes place in the nebulous world of cyberspace. Persons engaged in electronic commerce could be located anywhere in the world and their customers will be ignorant of, or indifferent to, their location.

U.S. Treas. Dep't, Selected Tax Policy Implications Of Global Electronic Commerce 20 (Nov. 1996).

Pursuant to the Internet Tax Freedom Act of 1998 47 U.S.C.A § 151, the Advisory Commission on Electronic Commerce released a report in May, 2000, in which it asserted that taxation of e-commerce must be globally consistent. Toward this end, the Commission concluded that the goal of neutral, fair and nondiscriminatory taxation of e-commerce must be achieved in cooperation with the OECD. Multiple amendments have extended the Act, currently through 2010, without modification of the policy of deference to OECD standards on international e-commerce. Internet Tax Freedom Act Amendments Act of 2007, Pub. L. 110–108, §§ 2–6 (2007).

International electronic commerce has been an important focus for study by the OECD Committee on Fiscal Affairs ("CFA"). The CFA issued on October 8, 1998, a report entitled, "A Borderless World: Realising the Potential of Electronic Commerce" ("CFA E–Commerce Report"), the proposals contained in which have been endorsed by the OECD Ministers. Among its main conclusions the touchstone is stated as follows:

> 4. The taxation principles which guide governments in relation to conventional commerce should also guide them in relation to electronic commerce. The CFA believes that at this stage of development in the technological and commercial environment, existing taxation rules can implement these principles.

The CFA E–Commerce Report then sets forth, at p. 4, the broad tax principles that should apply to electronic commerce. These principles, each of which is described in a sentence or two, are so abstract as to provide little meaningful guidance, include neutrality, efficiency, certainty and simplicity, effectiveness and fairness and flexibility.

The CFA E–Commerce Report also makes the following comment on international tax arrangements, at p. 5:

> *International tax arrangements and co-operation*
>
> (ix) While the OECD believes that the principles which underlie the international norms that it has developed in the area of tax treaties and transfer pricing (through the Model Tax Convention and the Transfer Pricing Guidelines) are capable of being applied to electronic commerce, there should be a clarification of how the Model Tax Convention applies with respect to some aspects of electronic commerce.

There will, of course, be cases in which U.S. suppliers of goods on the Internet will find that business considerations make it necessary to have a fixed place of business in the foreign country treaty partner in which customers are located. At such a facility goods offered for sale on the Internet can be demonstrated, sold, returned or serviced. In this case, the U.S. person will clearly have a fixed place of business in that country that may be a permanent establishment under a treaty patterned on the OECD Model Tax Convention. But in some cases there may be no obvious fixed place of business but merely computer data and software associated with sales through a web site maintained on a server located in the customer's country that will raise the question whether the web site and the server constitute a permanent establishment. For example, a U.S. person may solicit and accept orders for goods from foreign customers through a web site on a computer server maintained by an independent Internet Service Provider ("ISP") in the foreign treaty country in which the customer is located. Even if the ISP's server were regarded as a fixed place of business, it could not be imputed to the foreign seller if the ISP merely hosts the seller's web site and the web sites of others and is not an agent of the seller. Even if the ISP were the U.S. seller's agent, it would frequently be an independent agent acting in the ordinary course of its business and therefore not a permanent establishment under paragraph 6 of Article 5 of the OECD Model. Moreover, it could be argued that because a server can be located anywhere outside the foreign country in which the customers are located without detriment to the customers, who are typically indifferent to its location, the existence of a server located in the foreign treaty partner through which goods are sold to customers in that country should not constitute a permanent establishment even if it is maintained by the U.S. seller. Consider whether the OECD has accepted that view in the Commentary changes, some of which are summarized below.

The OECD has determined that human intervention with respect to computer equipment in a fixed location is not a requirement for the existence of a permanent establishment. Whether the computer equipment in a fixed location constitutes a permanent establishment will depend on whether the functions performed through that equipment exceed the scope of the preparatory or auxiliary activities referred to in paragraph 4 of Article 5 of the OECD Model. See OECD Clarification on the Application of the Permanent Establishment Definition in E–Commerce: Changes to the Commentary on Article 5, ¶¶ 9 and 14 (2000).

In response to the rise of global electronic commerce, the OECD Directorate on Financial Fiscal and Enterprise Affairs has agreed on a number of changes (prepared by the CFA) to the Commentary on Article 5 of the OECD Model Tax Convention, vol. I, at C(5)–24 through C(5)–28 ("OECD Commentary") which speak to some of the new issues raised.

The Commentary draws a distinction between computer equipment, such as a server, which can under certain circumstances be a permanent establishment, and an Internet web site, which consists of the data and software used by, or stored on, that equipment. An Internet web site is not tangible property and has by itself no location that can be a "place of business." However, a server on which the web site is stored and through which it is accessible is tangible property which will have a physical location and may constitute a fixed place of business and a permanent establishment. Id. at ¶ 42.2.

Frequently, a web site through which a foreign enterprise carries on its business is hosted on the server of an ISP. In that case, the enterprise has no physical presence at the server's location. However, if the enterprise owns or leases the server on which its web site is hosted, the server, if physically located in the customer's country, could be a permanent establishment there. Id. at ¶ 42.6. That could be the result even if no employees of the enterprise are located at the server. The analogy is drawn of equipment that operates automatically with no need for human intervention, such as, automatic pumping equipment used in the exploitation of natural resources. Id. at ¶ 42.6.

Another point discussed in the Commentary is that computer equipment, such as a server, will not constitute a permanent establishment if the operations carried on through the equipment are limited to activities that are "preparatory or auxiliary." Under paragraph 4 of Article 5, a fixed place in the customer's country will not be a permanent establishment if it carries on some or all of the activities that are identified in that paragraph as preparatory or auxiliary to the business of selling products on the Internet. The following example is given:

> [If the] location is used to operate a server that hosts a web site which, as is often the case, is used exclusively for advertising, displaying a catalogue of products or providing information to potential customers, paragraph 4 will apply and the location [of the server] will not constitute a permanent establishment. If, however, the typical functions related to a sale are performed at the location (for example, the conclusion of the contract with the customer, the processing of the payment and the delivery of the products are performed automatically through the equipment located there), these activities cannot be considered to be merely preparatory or auxiliary.

Id. at ¶ 42.9.

Another issue discussed deals with whether, under paragraph 5, an ISP's server on which the enterprise's web site is hosted may be deemed to be a permanent establishment. The Commentary states that this will generally not occur because the ISP will not be an agent of the enterprise to which the web site belongs because it (the ISP) will not have authority to conclude contracts in the name of the enterprise or, in any event, if it were an agent of the enterprise, it would be an independent agent acting in the ordinary course of its business if it hosts web sites of multiple enterprises. Moreover, the web site is not included in the definition of a "person" under Article 3 of the OECD Model Convention and, therefore, the Commentary concludes, paragraph 5 of Article 5 cannot apply. Id. at ¶ 42.10.

Perhaps the more important question, discussed in Note 1 at ¶ 11,055, is whether a web site software agent hosted on a server located outside the customer's country that is given the authority, which it habitually exercises, to conclude contracts binding on the enterprise should treated under paragraph 5 as the functional equivalent of a human agent and as a permanent establishment.

[¶ 11,055]

PROBLEMS

Assume that Cosmos Corporation ("Cosmos"), a U.S. corporation, is selling products it manufactures in the United States to customers located in Brazil and assume that Brazil is party to an income tax treaty with the United States (although in fact it currently is not). The treaty contains an Article 5 identical to Article 5 of the OECD Model Tax Convention. Consider whether, taking into account the OECD Commentary on Article 5 discussed above, Cosmos will be regarded as having a permanent establishment in Brazil under each of the following sets of circumstances:

1. Cosmos maintains a web site on a server owned by an unrelated Internet Service Provider ("ISP") in Brazil. The web site contains a catalogue of products for sale and prices. Orders for the products may be transmitted by customers in Brazil to the web site, which will further transmit them to the Cosmos Export Division in New York. The Export Division will accept the orders and arrange for shipment to and billing of customers in Brazil. Assume that the ISP hosts a large number of web sites for clients selling to customers in Brazil in addition to Cosmos and is paid by these clients on the same basis as it is paid by Cosmos.

2. The facts are the same as in Problem 1, but the web site also accepts orders and the customer has to tender payment to the web site by supplying relevant credit card information. The web site electronically issues delivery instructions to the warehouse maintained by Cosmos in the United States.

3. The facts are the same as in Problem 2, but Cosmos itself owns, maintains and operates the server located in Brazil.

4. The facts are the same as in Problem 2, but Cosmos owns, maintains and operates the server located in Bermuda, a country in which there is no income tax.

5. Does the OECD Commentary attach too much importance to a server owned (or leased) in Brazil by Cosmos on which the Cosmos web site is hosted when the server can readily be located outside Brazil, and the purchaser in Brazil is indifferent to its location? Does the OECD Commentary attach too little significance to the existence of a web site serving Brazilian customers hosted on a server maintained outside Brazil?

[¶ 11,060]

NOTES

1. A U.S. seller of property using the Internet may operate a web site that can function as a kind of software agent. Such an agent can carry out a variety of activities including the conclusion of contracts related to commercial transactions on behalf of and binding on the U.S. principal (Cosmos). Like a human agent, a web site software agent may assist the foreign customer to find the product desired, answer customer questions, solicit an order, negoti-

ate contract terms within prescribed limits, conclude the sales contract, arrange for shipping and handle credit arrangements and payment. If Cosmos effected export sales to Brazilian customers through such a Cosmos web site software agent operated from a server owned by it and located outside Brazil, under the OECD Commentary, it would apparently not open the door to taxation by Brazil of the income generated by the transaction because there would be no permanent establishment in Brazil. There would be no fixed place of business in Brazil and no physical "person" (as defined in Article 3 of the OECD Model Tax Convention) in Brazil with power to enter into contracts binding on the foreign principal.

2. The more fundamental policy question, of course, is whether the definition of permanent establishment in the OECD Model Tax Convention and in U.S. tax treaties should be changed to accommodate more appropriately international electronic commerce. The OECD Committee on Fiscal Affairs has established a Technical Advisory Group (on Monitoring the Application of Existing Treaty Norms for the Taxation of Business Profits in the Context of Electronic Commerce) to examine how the current treaty rules for the taxation of business profits apply in the context of electronic commerce and examine proposals for alternative rules. The Technical Advisory Group concluded that technological change in e-commerce does not justify changing the rules for taxation of business profits. OECD, Are the Current Treaty Rules for Taxing Business Profits Appropriate for E–Commerce? Final Report (Dec. 19, 2005). Consequently, the Group also declined to pursue several proposals which would have required changes to the Model Convention definition of permanent establishment specifically for e-commerce. A later report issued by the Committee on Fiscal Affairs and endorsed by the OECD Council indicates no change in policy on attribution of profits in e-commerce is called for. OECD, Report on the Attribution of Profits to Permanent Establishments (July 18, 2008).

[¶ 11,065]

C. INTRODUCTION TO USE OF FOREIGN OR U.S. CORPORATION TO HANDLE EXPORT SALES

Two leading organizational alternatives for handling a U.S. corporation's overall export program are (1) use of a U.S. corporation and (2) use of a foreign corporation. Prior to September 30, 2000, certain foreign corporations engaged in export operations could qualify as FSCs (foreign sales corporations) and receive special tax benefits. Although FSC benefits could continue for a limited period under special transition rules, no foreign corporation could qualify as a FSC after that date. The FSC regime was repealed because it was held by the World Trade Organization ("WTO") Dispute Settlement Body ("DSB") to violate WTO agreements prohibiting export subsidies. See ¶ 11,185.

The FSC regime, which required use of a foreign corporation, was replaced by the extraterritorial income ("ETI") exclusion, under which a U.S. taxpayer, often a U.S. corporation, could elect to exclude from its gross income a portion of income from sale or leasing of property for use outside the United States and from the rendering of various services outside the United States. The exclusion produced tax benefits comparable to the FSC benefits it was replacing, but the benefits were more extensive because, unlike the FSC, which required that property sold be manufactured in the United States, the ETI exclusion applied even if the products were manufactured by the U.S. taxpayer outside the United States. In response to a proceeding brought by the European Union, the WTO DSB held that the ETI exclusion regime also conferred on U.S. taxpayers export subsidies prohibited under WTO agreements. The European Union was authorized by the WTO to impose retaliatory customs duties of some four billion dollars on U.S. exports. To end the imposition of these sanctions, the U.S. Congress repealed the ETI exclusion regime. Congress replaced the ETI regime with a tax benefit for U.S. corporations that will not be subject to characterization as an export subsidy because it benefits U.S. production generating U.S. as well as foreign sales. This benefit takes the form of a deduction of a percentage of the taxpayer's income from U.S. production activities. The percentage was three percent for 2005, increasing to nine percent for 2010 and thereafter. See § 199, discussed at ¶ 11,230.

U.S. manufacturing corporations may handle exports to foreign countries through an export division of the U.S. manufacturing corporation itself. Alternatively, they may set up one or more wholly owned U.S. subsidiaries to carry on this activity. In either case, the U.S. corporation may operate through one or more foreign branch offices. U.S. manufacturing corporations have traditionally taken steps to ensure that title will pass on its exported products outside the United States. If they do so, under the source rules of sections 865(b) and 863(b)(2) and the regulations, usually 50 percent of the export income will be foreign-source. See ¶ 2160. If that income bears no foreign tax under foreign law or under a tax treaty (e.g., because no permanent establishment has been established in the customers' countries), the income will often be helpful in absorbing excess foreign tax credits.

In the case of a U.S. corporation that has a relatively small quantity of export sales, a significant deferral of U.S. tax may be realized (at the cost of an interest charge on the deferred tax) by handling exports of U.S.-made products through a U.S. corporation that qualifies as a Domestic International Sales Corporation ("DISC"). See ¶ 11,150.

[¶ 11,070]

D. USE OF A FOREIGN EXPORT CORPORATION

While some business and operational advantages may be gained through the use of a foreign corporation as the vehicle for a foreign export program, a significant consideration in pursuing this route is likely to be the promise of tax savings.

An export sales corporation may be established in a foreign country in which the taxes on income from international trading activities are well below both the 35–percent maximum U.S. corporate tax rate and the corporate income tax rates applicable in the countries in which the foreign customers are located. If so, the after-tax accumulation of export income may be greater than would be the case if sales were handled through a U.S. corporation or a corporation organized under the laws of the customer's country. However, as discussed at ¶ 11,085, the Code provisions relating to controlled foreign corporations sharply limit the situations in which tax savings can be achieved in this way.

The possibility of accumulating export profits in a foreign export corporation free of U.S. tax results from three basic rules of U.S. tax law. The first of these rules provides that, with the limited exceptions contained in Section 864(c)(4), a foreign corporation is subject to U.S. tax only on its U.S.-source income. §§ 881(a), 864(c)(2) and (3) and 882(a) and (b). The second and third relate to the determination of source of income for U.S. tax purposes. These rules provide (i) that the source of income resulting from the performance of services is determined by the place where the services are performed, Sections 861(a)(3) and 862(a)(3), and (ii) that the source of income resulting from the purchase and resale of inventory property is determined by the place where the sale is consummated, i.e., generally where the "rights, title, and interest of the seller in the property are transferred to the buyer." §§ 865(b), 861(a)(6) and 862(a)(6), and Reg. § 1.861–7(c).

There are two basic ways in which a foreign export corporation can be operated to ensure that none of its export-related income will be considered to be from U.S. sources. First, the export corporation may be paid commissions by the U.S. producer for sales activities carried on by the export corporation outside the United States with the sales of goods being made directly by the U.S. producer to the foreign purchaser. Second, the export corporation may actually purchase the exported goods from the U.S. producer and resell them at a higher price to the foreign purchaser passing title to the goods outside the United States.

[¶ 11,075]

1. COMMISSION APPROACH

A foreign export corporation can be used to accumulate export profits in the form of arm's length commissions paid by its U.S. parent corporation for sales services rendered by the export corporation. The basic requirement for this type of operation is the carrying out of substantial sales activities outside the United States. Such foreign activities are necessary to justify the payment of substantial commissions to the export corporation and to establish that the source of the commission income is outside the United States.

If all the sales activities of the export corporation's sales personnel are to be deemed to occur outside the United States, it is normally necessary to establish a foreign headquarters for the export corporation from which such foreign sales personnel can operate. If the sales personnel operated out of an office located in the United States, the IRS would properly take the position that some of the sales services were performed in the United States, thus giving rise to income effectively connected with a U.S. business that is subject to U.S. tax.

If the export corporation is a controlled foreign corporation, export sales commissions may constitute foreign base company sales or services income to the foreign corporation which may be taxed to the U.S. parent corporation as a Subpart F inclusion.

[¶ 11,080]

2. PURCHASE AND RESALE APPROACH

The second basic method of operating a foreign export corporation involves having the corporation purchase the exported products from its U.S. parent corporation (or one of its affiliates) at an arm's length price and resell them abroad at a reasonable markup to foreign customers. As suggested above, the foundation for this type of operation is the Section 862(a)(6) source rule, which provides that income from the purchase of inventory property within and its sale without the United States is income from sources without the United States. This rule has been construed by the judicial decisions dealing with the issue to mean that the source of income resulting from the sale of personal property is generally the place where the title passes to the buyer. This principle is reflected in the regulations issued under Section 861. Reg. § 1.861–7(c). Thus, if a foreign export corporation purchases from its U.S. parent in the United States and resells at a higher price to a foreign purchaser with title passing from the export corporation to the foreign purchaser outside the United States, the profit realized on the resale is treated as foreign-source income.

The passage-of-title test affords the taxpayer a simple mechanism for manipulating the source of income from the purchase and resale of inventory property. See the materials beginning at ¶ 2115, and particularly the *A.P. Green Export* case, at ¶ 2120. The most important formality is ensuring that there is evidence that the seller and buyer agree that title is to pass on the export sale of U.S.-made products at the port of destination or other location abroad. If the appropriate formalities are observed, all of the trading income is treated as foreign-source income. This is so even if the foreign export corporation operates from an office in the United States, provided that an office or other fixed place of business of that corporation in a foreign country materially participates in the export sales. § 865(e)(2). Such foreign-source income is not itself subject to U.S. tax. See § 864(c)(4)(B)(iii). However, if the export corporation is a controlled foreign corporation, the trading income will often constitute foreign base company sales income to the foreign export corporation which may be taxed as a Subpart F inclusion to the U.S. parent corporation. See ¶ 11,085.

An example of an exporter's conditions of sale adopted to provide a foundation for contending that buyer and seller have agreed that title passes outside the United States is set forth below:

> 1. Unless otherwise indicated, the purchase price shall consist of the basic price plus all costs of delivering the products to Buyer at the port or point of entry, including without limitation ocean, air or other freight, marine, air or other insurance, consular fees and U.S. port and forwarding fees.
>
> 2. All property rights in products shipped by Seller to Buyer, including title to, beneficial ownership of, control over, and the risk of loss or damage to such products, shall remain with Seller until such products arrive at the port or point of entry. The products shall be deemed to arrive at the port or point of entry, in the case of ocean or air shipments, at the time and place at which they are unloaded by the international carrier in Buyer's country and, in the case of land shipments, at the time and place in Buyer's country at which the products enter such country. No sale shall be deemed to have taken place unless and until the products arrive at the port or point of entry. References such as C. & F., C.I.F., F.A.S., F.O.B., C.O.D. or similar terms shall be used solely to calculate prices. Such terms, the time, method or place of payment or of endorsement or delivery of shipping documents, the method of shipment, the manner of consignment, the contents of Buyer's purchase order or Seller's invoice or other documents or papers relating to the sales transaction shall not be deemed to limit or alter the foregoing rights of Seller in the products.
>
> 3. Buyer agrees that it will, upon request by Seller, take any actions and provide any certificates, undertakings or other papers required of Buyer to enable Seller to effect the exportation of the products from the United States, and that it will, when the products

arrive at the port or point of entry, accept title, ownership, control over, and the risk of loss or damage to such products, accept delivery thereof and take all actions and pay all duties, taxes, fees, charges or other costs of whatever nature necessary to effect the importation.

4. Seller will insure for its own benefit products shipped to Buyer until such products arrive at the port or point of entry. Where laws or regulations of Buyer's country require Buyer to take out insurance, the policy shall be for the benefit of Seller, whether or not Seller is named as an insured in such policy, until the products arrive at the port or point of entry in Buyer's country. Where possible under the laws and regulations of Buyer's country, the policy shall provide that it is for the benefit of Seller and/or Buyer "as their interests may appear." Where Buyer insures, Buyer will be allowed an appropriate credit against the purchase price for the insurance premiums paid by Buyer, and the purchase price shall not include any insurance premiums paid by Seller. The taking out of insurance by Buyer shall not affect Seller's property rights in the products as provided in paragraph 2.

5. Where the laws or regulations of Buyer's country require Buyer to pay the portion of the purchase price attributable to ocean, air or other freight costs, a credit in the amount of such costs paid by Buyer shall be allowed against the purchase price.

6. All orders accepted by Seller shall be subject to the terms and conditions set forth herein, and Seller's acceptance incorporating the terms and conditions specified herein and the agreement represented thereby may be changed only by further written agreement between Seller and Buyer. In case of conflict between any of the terms and conditions herein prescribed and any provision of Buyer's order or other communications relating to the sales transaction, the terms and conditions herein prescribed shall prevail.

[¶ 11,085]

3. IMPACT OF THE CONTROLLED FOREIGN CORPORATION PROVISIONS ON USE OF A FOREIGN EXPORT CORPORATION

One of the major targets of the controlled foreign corporation provisions of Subpart F was the tax savings that could be realized under prior law by handling international trading activities through a foreign corporation incorporated in a tax haven country. These provisions dealt effectively with the great majority of situations in which use of a controlled foreign corporation to conduct trading operations produced important tax savings. The typical foreign export corporation is organized in a tax haven country as a wholly owned subsidiary of a U.S. corporation and, accordingly, it falls within the "controlled foreign corporation" definition of Section 957(a). If its earnings either (i) result from purchase of goods manufactured by its U.S. parent corporation or a related person in the United States and their resale to purchasers outside the country of incorporation of the foreign export corporation or (ii) take the form of commissions or other fees for services rendered in connection with such transactions, these earnings will usually constitute "foreign base company sales income," and, in the case of sales services, they may also constitute "foreign base company services income." Under most circumstances, this income will be included in Subpart F income taxed to the U.S. parent corporation as a Subpart F inclusion. § 954(d). Nonetheless, in special circumstances there remain potential tax savings to be realized through the use of foreign export corporations. Consider some of the possibilities in connection with the materials that follow.

[¶ 11,090]

a. Definition of Foreign Base Company Sales Income

If a controlled foreign corporation manufactures goods in its country of incorporation, the income it generates by their sale cannot be foreign base company sales income. As illustrated in the following case, issues may arise as to whether the activities of the foreign corporation may be considered to constitute the manufacture of the products it sells under the standards set forth in Reg. § 1.954–3(a)(2) and (4), in which case its income will not be foreign base company sales income.

[¶ 11,095]

DAVE FISCHBEIN MFG. CO. v. COMMISSIONER

United States Tax Court, 1972.
59 T.C. 338 (acq.).

IRWIN, JUDGE: * * *.

* * *

The issues remaining for our decision [include:] * * * whether Dave Fischbein Company must include in its income for 1964 through 1967 under section 951(a)(1)(A)(i) * * *, certain income earned in the years 1963 through 1966 by its Belgian subsidiary, Compagnie Fischbein, S.A., from the sale of bag-closing machines on the basis that such income constituted "subpart F" income of the variety defined in section 954(d)(1) as "foreign base company sales income." * * *

FINDINGS OF FACT

* * *

[Dave Fischbein Manufacturing Company, a U.S. corporation, (hereafter "DFMC")] is engaged in the manufacture of bag-closing equipment, including sewing machines and related items. DFMC sells this equipment * * * to [Dave Fischbein Company, also a U.S. corporation (hereafter "DFC")] * * *.

* * *

A bag-closing machine is a type of sewing machine used to close the mouth of an open bag. These machines are used in the animal feed, seed, fertilizer, food-processing, and other industries.

* * *

On March 1, 1956, DFC organized a wholly-owned subsidiary, Compagnie Fischbein, S.A. (hereafter CFSA), under the laws of Belgium to sell Fischbein bag closers throughout the world. * * *

At the time CFSA was organized it was decided that CFSA would purchase the component parts for bag-closing machines from DFMC and from unrelated suppliers in Belgium rather than purchase finished machines from DFMC. This decision was based upon two primary reasons. First, it was important that the machines sold by CFSA be of Belgian origin so that they would qualify for Belgian certificates of origin. This was important from the standpoint of tariffs, quantity restrictions and similar measures in the Common Market. Second, it was cheaper for CFSA to complete its own finished machines in Belgium because of the lower labor and overhead costs in Belgium.

* * * In 1963 through 1966 CFSA had the following number of employees:

Year	Office	Mechanics	Total
1963	2	7	9
1964	2	8	10
1965	2	9	11
1966	2	8	10

* * *

Approximately 95 percent of CFSA's sales of bag-closing machines were to exclusive distributors in the various countries of Europe, Africa and elsewhere. * * *

* * *

The bag-closing machines sold by CFSA generally were serviced by the local distributors through whom they were sold to the end users. These distributors employed mechanics who were trained by CFSA's personnel either at CFSA's plant in Brussels or at the distributors' places of business. Moreover, CFSA provided its distributors with special repair kits for use in making repairs.

* * *

By 1967 DFMC was the largest exclusive bag-closing manufacturer in the United States and throughout the world.

CFSA purchased most of the components of the bag-closing machines directly from DFMC. In 1956, CFSA began immediately to sell Fischbein bag-closing machines. CFSA also purchased from DFMC components for the accessories to the bag-closing machines * * *.

Rather than purchase standard component parts such as screws, nuts, motors, belts, cord sets, needles and switches from DFMC, which DFMC had to purchase from unrelated suppliers, CFSA purchased these parts from unrelated suppliers in Belgium. There were four main reasons for the purchase of certain component parts locally in Belgium. First, the Belgian government encouraged CFSA to use locally-made products to the extent possible. In fact, CFSA also tried to use Belgian air and shipping lines for parts and machines sent to or from Belgium. Second, many of the parts could be bought by CFSA at lower prices in Belgium than it could obtain them from DFMC. Third, * * * the local purchase of these parts avoided certain customs difficulties. Fourth, since CFSA sold its bag-closing machines primarily in Europe, several components of CFSA's machines had to comply with European standards that could not be satisfied by American-made products. * * *

In the years in question CFSA had in Brussels a fully equipped factory with all the tools and equipment necessary for it to turn the machines into finished products.

* * *

Except for the larger items of equipment such as the drill press, the various tools were located at the work stations of the individual mechanics. A work station consisted of a bench with compartments for the component parts of the bag-closing machines and a stool for the mechanic. Each work station had vises, an electric motor controlled by a rheostat, a spotlight and all the other tools necessary to enable the mechanic to complete the segment of the assembly of completed machines assigned to him. A special work station was provided for electrical work (i.e., wiring of machines), and this work station was equipped with the electrical equipment required for that work.

The parts illustration of the sewing head and electric drive handle of the Model D bag-closing machine shows that the completed machine consists of 198 different types of component parts. Because certain of these parts are used more than once during CFSA's assembly of the bag-closing machine, a total of 283 parts comprise the final product.

Most of these parts were received by CFSA from DFMC in fabricated form according to DFMC's blueprints for such parts. The mechanics at the CFSA plant in Brussels, in operations consisting of 58 different steps and averaging approximately six hours of combined working time, tailored these parts to each other in order to complete the assembly of a finished bag-closing machine. The tailoring process was required because many of the more sophisticated parts were not ready for use in finished machines without additional mechanical work such as reaming, lapping, and mating. The six-hour operation of completing the bag-closing machines included electrical testing of the machine and "time runs" in which each machine is tested at various speeds of operation.

Some of the components of the bag-closing machine, for example, the housing and handle of the machine, remain recognizable in the finished bag-closing machine which CFSA sells.

During the years 1963–1967, inclusive, CFSA's operations did not account for 20 percent or more of the total cost of the bag-closing machines it sold.

OPINION

* * *

The term "subpart F income," insofar as it is relevant in this case, is defined to include the controlled foreign corporation's "foreign base company income." In turn, the Code defines "foreign base company income" to include the controlled foreign corporation's "foreign base company sales income."

* * * [S]ales by a controlled foreign corporation produce foreign base company sales income * * * [under Section 954(d)(1)] only if they relate to goods which are produced, manufactured, grown or extracted outside the country in which the controlled foreign corporation is organized and are sold for use, consumption or disposition outside that country.

On the other hand, if the sales outside the foreign country relate to goods which are produced, manufactured, constructed, grown or extracted *within* the country in which the controlled foreign corporation is organized, then such sales do not produce "foreign base company sales income."

* * *

Petitioner DFC argues herein that, under the scheme of the Code, the regulations, and the legislative history of subpart F, the operations of CFSA amount to production, manufacture, or construction of bag-closing machines and, hence, the income derived by CFSA from the sales of these machines is not foreign base company sales income. At the very least petitioner contends the operations constituted major assembly.

In order to determine the merit of DFC's contention on this point, we must first examine respondent's regulations interpreting the definition of foreign base company sales income found in section 954(d)(1) * * *.

* * *

* * * [R]egulation [§ 1.954–3(a)(2) and (4)] espouses both a substantive and objective test for satisfaction. The objective test offers a safe harbor of compliance if the foreign corporation's operations account for 20 percent or more of the total cost of goods sold. Failure to obtain this safe harbor, however, does not prevent compliance through satisfaction of the substantive test.

Although the term "minor assembling" is found in the regulations and the Senate and House Committee reports on the 1962 Revenue Act, its counterpart, "major assembling" is only referred to specifically in the Senate Report. The relevant language is found in S. Rept. No. 1881, 87th Cong., 2d Sess., p. 84 (1962) * * *:

> The "foreign base company sales income" referred to here means income from the purchase and sale of property, without any appreciable value being added to the product by the selling corporation. This does not, for example, include cases where any significant amount of manufacturing, *major assembling,* or construction activity is carried on with respect to the product by the selling corporation. On the other hand, activity such as minor assembling, packaging, repackaging or labeling will not be sufficient to exclude the profits from this definition. [Emphasis supplied.]

We are of the opinion, based on the facts presented here, that under the scheme of the Code, the regulations, and the pertinent legislative history of subpart F, the income generated by CFSA from its sales of bag-closing machines is *not* "foreign base company sales income" includable in the income of its "United States shareholder," DFC.

It seems clear that the operations of CFSA are not akin to the examples of "substantial transformation" given in section 1.954–3(a)(4)(ii), Income Tax Regs., i.e., transforming wood pulp into paper; steel rods into screws or bolts; and tuna fish into canned fish.

However, the operations of CFSA in connection with the components it purchased *do* amount to the manufacture of a product (sec. 1.954–3(a)(4)(iii) of the regulations) since they are substantial and, at the least, must be considered either the "major assembly" or manufacture, in part, of portable bag-closing machines.

We agree, as per examples (1) (industrial engines) and (2) (automobiles) found in section 1.954–3(a)(4)(iii), Income Tax Regs., the product sold herein, a portable bag-closing machine, is not sufficiently distinguishable from some of its components to constitute a substantial transformation of the purchased parts since the housing and handle remain recognizable as such in the finished machine.

Although the automobile operation in example (2) resulted in a final product not sufficiently distinguishable from some of its components, the substantive test of this regulation was still satisfied because the operations of the foreign corporation were substantial in nature and generally considered to constitute manufacture of a product.

We consider CFSA's operations are similarly substantial and, therefore, CFSA also satisfies the substantive test of the regulation. CFSA (a) tailors and finishes some of its purchased components in order to place these parts in usable condition; (b) puts these tailored components and others together in a 6–hour, 58–step process to form salable quality bag-closing machines; and (c) possesses in its plant all of the tools and equipment necessary for these activities. As a result of CFSA's operations, the purchaser of one of these devices is guaranteed a carefully put together, well tested and operable machine.

These operations are not similar to "packaging, repackaging, labeling, or minor assembly" which cannot, in any event, be considered the equivalent of manufacture, production, or construction for purposes of section 954(d)(1). Sec. 1.954–3(a)(4)(iii), Income Tax Regs. CFSA's operations are certainly more significant than the packaging of "knock-down" radio kits given as example (3) in section 1.954–3(a)(4)(iii). There is nothing minor, insignificant, or insubstantial about the utilization of proper equipment, by trained personnel, in a time consuming process which has, as its final result, a high calibre portable bag-closing machine.

We, therefore, disagree with respondent's contention that the components purchased by CFSA were so perfect that they only had to be simply put together in short periods of time, by not too highly skilled mechanics, whose tasks in this operation were nothing more than ministerial functions. Contrariwise, the record is abundant that the purchased parts were not perfect, that many of them had to be individually tailored and tested in order to have a completed, functioning sewing machine, that the mechanics were trained and experienced and used skill and judgment in performing their tasks, and that they were not performing purely ministerial functions. It was the calibre of CFSA's mechanics which resulted in a smooth running operation rather than a lack of complexity of the operations.

The operations of CFSA herein are found to be significant major assembly of portable bag-closing machines, substantial in nature, and to constitute the manufacture of a product. Consequently, the income in question is not "foreign base company sales income," includable in the income of CFSA's "United States shareholder," DFC.

[¶ 11,100]

b. Basic Rules Relating to Sales and Manufacturing Branches

As illustrated in the *Fischbein* case above, if the controlled foreign corporation itself manufactures the goods it sells, its income is generally excluded from the definition of foreign base sales company income. This rule suggests the question: what is the result if the controlled foreign corporation itself manufactures products in Country A but sells them through a branch established in Country B where the sales income will be taxed at a significantly lower rate than would apply if the income were taxed in Country A? The assumption made here is that Country A makes use of the territorial system of international taxation under which Country A does not tax income attributable to a branch in Country B. Because the Country B branch is part of the Country A corporation, it would seem that the controlled foreign corporation would be considered to manufacture the product it sells and therefore the resulting income would not be foreign base company income under Section 954(d)(1). This favorable result, however, is precluded in many situations by the special branch rule of Section 954(d)(2). Under this rule, for purposes of the foreign base company sales income definition, a sales branch is treated as a separate subsidiary when it has substantially the same effect as if it were a wholly owned subsidiary of the controlled foreign corporation. The regulations make this determination by applying a tax-rate-disparity test. A sales branch in Country B is treated as having substantially the same effect as a subsidiary if it is subject to an effective rate of Country B tax that is less than 90 percent of, and at least five percentage points less than, the rate that would apply if the sales income were taxed by Country A. Reg. § 1.954–3(b)(1)(i)*(b)*. The regulations apply a similar approach if the controlled foreign corporation organized in Country A manufactures the products it sells through a manufacturing branch in Country B, but the tax-rate-disparity test is reversed. See Reg. § 1.954–3(b)(1)(ii)(*b*). The manufacturing branch arrangement is discussed in Rev. Rul. 75–7 and the *Ashland Oil* case below.

[¶ 11,105]

REVENUE RULING 75–7

1975–1 C.B. 244, revoked by Rev. Rul. 97–48, 1997–2 C.B. 89.

Advice has been requested whether a controlled foreign corporation realizes foreign base company income, within the meaning of section 954(a) * * *, under the circumstances described below.

X, a controlled foreign corporation within the meaning of section 957(a) * * * was incorporated in country *M*. *X* purchased specific metal ore concentrate in the United States and Canada from related persons, within the meaning of section 954(d)(3).

Conversion of the ore concentrate into a ferroalloy was accomplished by *X*, pursuant to an arm's length contract, through *Y*, an unrelated foreign corporation incorporated in country *O*. The conversion of the ore concentrate required intricate chemical and metallurgical processing involving highly skilled labor working in accordance with scientific controls. *Y*'s plant in country *O* was one of the few plants in the world equipped to accomplish the conversion.

Y had no present, nor was it contemplated that it would have any future affiliation, directly or indirectly, with *X*, other than contractual obligations arising under arm's length contracts. *Y* had no present, nor was it contemplated that it would have any future, financial participation in the nature of a joint venture or other risk or profit sharing arrangement in the manufacture of the ferroalloy.

Under the terms of the contract *X* paid *Y* a conversion fee. The ore concentrate, before and during processing, and the finished product remained the sole property of *X* at all times. *X* alone purchased all raw material and other ingredients necessary in the processing operation and bore the risk of loss at all times in connection with the operation. Complete control of the time and quantity of production was vested in *X*. Complete control of the quality of the product was also vested in *X*, and *Y* was at all times required to use such processes as were directed by *X*. *X*, could, when the occasion warranted it, send engineers or technicians to *Y*'s plant to inspect, correct, or advise with regard to the processing of the ore concentrate into the finished product.

The negotiation and consummation of the sale of the finished product were solely the responsibility of *X*. Profits or losses resulting from the sale of the finished product were solely *X*'s, *Y*'s only financial interest in the entire transaction was the fee paid by *X* for the conversion of the ore. The finished product was sold by *X* to unrelated parties in foreign countries, other than *M*, for use, consumption, or disposition in such other foreign countries. The effective tax rate in country *M* was 46 percent while the effective tax rate in country *O* was 38.5 percent.

Section 954(a) * * * provides, in general, that the term "foreign base company income" means the sum of the foreign personal holding company income, the foreign base company sales income, and the foreign base company services income, for the taxable year.

Section 954(d)(1) * * * provides, in part, that the term "foreign base company sales income" means income derived in connection with the purchase of personal property from a related person and its sale to any person, the sale of personal property to any person on behalf of a related person, or the purchase of personal property from any person on behalf of a related person when the property which is purchased is extracted outside the country under the laws of which the controlled foreign corporation is created or organized, and the property is sold for use or disposition outside such foreign country.

Section 1.954–3(a)(4)(i) of the * * * Regulations provides, in part, that foreign base company sales income does not include income of a controlled foreign corporation derived in connection with the sale of personal property manufactured, produced, or constructed by such corporation in whole or in part from personal property which it has purchased. A foreign corporation will be considered, for purposes of section 1.954–3(a)(4)(i), to have manufactured, produced, or constructed personal property which it sells, if the property sold is in effect not the property which it purchased. In the case of the manufacture, production, or construction of personal property, the property sold will be considered, for purposes of section 1.954–3(a)(4)(i), as not being the property which is purchased, if the provisions of section 1.954–3(a)(4)(ii) are satisfied.

Section 1.954–3(a)(4)(ii) of the regulations provides, in part, that if purchased personal property is substantially transformed prior to sale, the property sold will be treated as having been manufactured, produced, or constructed by the selling corporation.

Section 1.954–3(b)(1)(ii) of the regulations provides, in relevant part, that if a controlled foreign corporation carries on manufacturing, producing, constructing, growing, or extracting activities by or through a branch or similar establishment located outside the country under the laws of which such corporation is created or organized and the use of the branch or similar establishment for such activities with respect to personal property purchased or sold by or through the remainder of the controlled foreign corporation has substantially the same tax effect as if the branch or similar establishment were a wholly owned subsidiary corporation of such controlled foreign corporation, the branch or similar establishment and the remainder of the controlled foreign corporation will be treated as separate corporations for purposes of determining foreign base company sales income of such corporation. See section 954(d)(2) * * *.

The use of the branch or similar establishment will be considered to have substantially the same tax effect as if it were a wholly-owned subsidiary corporation of the controlled foreign corporation if income allocated to the remainder of the controlled foreign corporation is, by statute, treaty obligation, or otherwise, taxed in the year when earned at an effective rate of tax that is less than 90 percent of, and at least 5 percentage points less than, the effective rate of tax that would apply to such income under the laws of the country in which the branch or similar establishment is located.

Under the contractual arrangement between *X* and *Y*, the performance by *Y* of the operations whereby the ore concentrate is processed into a ferroalloy is considered to be a performance by *X*. Therefore, *X* will be treated as having "substantially transformed personal property" within the meaning of section 1.954–3(a)(4) of the regulations.

Furthermore, since *X* is conducting a manufacturing activity outside country *M*, it will be considered to do so through a branch or similar establishment within the meaning of section 1.954–3(b)(1)(ii) of the regulations. However, since the effective rate of tax in country *M* is higher than the rate of tax in country *O*, the manufacturing activity of *X* conducted in country *O* will not be considered to have substantially the same tax effect as a wholly-owned subsidiary corporation of *X* within the meaning of section 1.954–3(b)(1)(ii).

Accordingly, the income derived by *X* upon the sale of the ferroalloy will not constitute "foreign base company income" within the meaning of section 954(a) * * *.

[¶ 11,110]

ASHLAND OIL, INC. v. COMMISSIONER

United States Tax Court, 1990.
95 T.C. 348.

NIMS, CHIEF JUDGE: * * *

Petitioner Ashland Oil, Inc., a domestic corporation with its principal office in Ashland, Kentucky, is the parent company of petitioner Ashland Technology, Inc., a domestic corporation * * *. Respondent determined deficiencies in the Federal income taxes of the subsidiary, Ashland Technology, Inc. * * *. Respondent determined the identical deficiencies for the parent, Ashland Oil, Inc., as transferee for the primary liability of Ashland Technology, Inc.

During the years at issue, and prior to its 1981 acquisition by Ashland Oil, Inc., the name of Ashland Technology, Inc., was United States Filter Corporation (U.S. Filter). * * *

The statutory provision here involved is section 954(d)(2), which by its terms applies to a controlled foreign corporation (hereinafter sometimes referred to as a CFC) carrying on activities through a "branch or similar establishment." The substantive issues before us are: (1) whether section 954(d)(2) applies to a contractual manufacturing arrangement between a CFC and another corporation, which corporation is unrelated to the CFC apart from the contractual arrangement; and, if so, (2) whether section 1.954–3(b)(1)(ii), Income Tax Regs., which treats manufacturing branches as within the scope of section 954(d)(2), is invalid.

BACKGROUND

* * *

U.S. Filter was a domestic corporation. Drew Chemical Corporation (Drew Chemical) was a wholly-owned domestic subsidiary of U.S. Filter. Drew Ameroid International (Drew Ameroid), a wholly-owned foreign subsidiary of Drew Chemical, was organized in 1973 under the laws of Liberia, in large part to save income taxes. Drew Ameroid, with its principal office in Athens, Greece, was a "controlled foreign corporation" of Drew Chemical within the meaning of section 957(a), and Drew Chemical was a "United States shareholder" of Drew Ameroid within the meaning of section 951(b).

Drew Chemical was engaged in the manufacture and sale of industrial and marine chemical products. Drew Ameroid purchased and sold marine chemicals and other personal property, and did not itself manufacture any of the products it sold. The products sold by Drew Ameroid were manufactured or produced outside Liberia, and were also sold for use, consumption, and disposition outside Liberia.

Much of the record concerns the business relationship between Drew Ameroid and Societe Des Produits Tensio–Actifs et Derives, Tensia, S.A. (Tensia).

Tensia was organized in 1950 as a corporation under the laws of Belgium, which was also the location of its principal place of business. Tensia manufactured household and industrial detergents, soaps, and other cleaning products, including marine chemicals. No Tensia stock or other interest was owned, directly or indirectly within the meaning of section 958, by U.S. Filter, Drew Chemical, Drew Ameroid, or any of their affiliates. Similarly, neither Tensia nor any of its affiliates owned, directly or indirectly within the meaning of section 958, any stock or other interest in U.S. Filter, Drew Chemical, Drew Ameroid, or any of their affiliates. Tensia was not a related person with respect to Drew Ameroid within the meaning of section 954(d)(3).

Drew Ameroid and Tensia entered into a manufacturing, license and supply agreement (the agreement) as of September 15, 1973. * * *

Under the agreement, Drew Ameroid transferred to Tensia proprietary technical information, trade secrets, specifications, know-how, and other information (including designs, drawings, formulas, methods, techniques, and processes), to be used by Tensia in manufacturing, processing, and/or compounding approximately 25 products for Drew Ameroid. Tensia, for its part, agreed to adhere strictly to production and quality control specifications. The selling price for a product sold by Tensia to Drew Ameroid was the cost of the raw materials and packaging to Tensia plus a "conversion fee," which included labor, overhead, financing, and remuneration (profit) to Tensia. Assuming that Tensia satisfactorily performed its contractual obligations under the agreement, Tensia was guaranteed a profit.

Tensia purchased raw materials, for use in meeting its obligations under the agreement, from several sources. Tensia purchased most of these raw materials, however, from vendors suggested by Drew Ameroid or from Drew Ameroid affiliates functioning as sourcing intermediaries. Tensia, rather than Drew Ameroid, owned the raw materials while they were in that state.

The agreement required Tensia to deliver products within 30 days of the receipt of an order from Drew Ameroid. Tensia delivered the products directly to Drew Ameroid or to whomever Drew Ameroid designated, using labeling and packaging instructions provided by Drew Ameroid. As labeled by Tensia, a given product bore trademarks and tradenames of Drew Ameroid, an affiliate of Drew Ameroid, or a customer of Drew Ameroid.

The negotiation and consummation of the finished product resales were solely the responsibility of Drew Ameroid. As with the raw materials, Tensia owned the finished products until purchased by Drew Ameroid or its affiliates.

The agreement provided that during its term, and for two years after its termination, Tensia could not manufacture or sell products similar to those covered by the agreement for distribution to the same customers.

At least one employee of Drew Chemical or Drew Ameroid visited Tensia's manufacturing facilities monthly.

Tensia's gross sales under the agreement never exceeded eight percent of its total gross sales * * *. In contrast, at least 80 percent of Drew Ameroid's income was attributable to the resale of products manufactured by Tensia. Drew Ameroid had overall profits * * *.

* * *

In his notices of deficiency, respondent determined that the manufacture of products by Tensia for Drew Ameroid, and the subsequent sales by Drew Ameroid to unrelated third parties, resulted in foreign base company sales income under the "branch or similar establishment" rule of section 954(d)(2).

DISCUSSION

A United States shareholder (Drew Chemical in this case) of a controlled foreign corporation (Drew Ameroid) generally must include in gross income a pro rata share of the CFC's subpart F income for the taxable year. Sec. 951(a)(1). Subpart F income includes, among other things, foreign base company income. Sec. 952(a)(2). Foreign base company income includes, among other things, foreign base company sales income. Sec. 954(a)(2).

* * *

Generally, in order for income to be considered foreign base company sales income, the property purchased must be manufactured or produced outside the country in which the CFC is organized and must also be sold for use outside that country. Sec. 954(d)(1)(A) and (B). Although the CFC here, Drew Ameroid, was organized in Liberia, the subject property was manufactured in Belgium and sold for use outside Liberia.

Because Drew Ameroid and Tensia were not related persons and respondent does not contend that Drew Ameroid's pertinent sales were made to related persons, the general principles of section 954(d) do not attribute foreign base company sales income to Drew Ameroid. Nonetheless, respondent maintains that foreign base company sales income results from the so-called "branch rule" of section 954(d)(2) * * *.

The specific disputed issue is whether Tensia is a "branch or similar establishment" under section 954(d)(2). Petitioners argue that Tensia is not a branch within the ordinary meaning of the term and that "similar establishment" cannot be justifiably construed to include Tensia. Respondent appears to use three principal arguments, in various overlapping combinations, in asserting that Tensia is indeed a "branch or similar establishment." The factors most emphasized by respondent are congressional intent, the tax rate disparity between Belgium and Liberia, and the business relationship between Drew Ameroid and Tensia.

Respondent's most general contention is that Congress, in enacting the branch rule of section 954(d)(2), intended it to be a broad "loophole closing" provision. The applicable loophole here, according to respondent, is any arrangement that separates the manufacturing and sales functions so as to avoid or limit tax on the sales. Because the statute does not define "branch or similar establishment," respondent's position necessitates a venture into the legislative history to trace the evolution of the branch rule.

Prior to the Revenue Act of 1962, * * * a foreign corporation controlled by U.S. shareholders was ordinarily not subject to U.S. tax on foreign source income. The income became subject to U.S. tax only when it took the form of dividends distributed to the United States shareholders. President Kennedy, in 1961, characterized this tax deferral as undesirable and advocated its elimination in developed countries and in situations involving low-tax jurisdictions known as "tax havens." * * *

The House Ways and Means Committee conceded that its bill did not go as far as the President's recommendations. H. Rept. No. 1447, 87th Cong., 2d Sess. (1962) * * *. The House bill included no provision comparable to the branch rule, but targeted purchase and sale transactions between related persons, defined vaguely in terms of ownership or control, as generating foreign base company sales income. * * *

The Secretary of the Treasury, Douglas Dillon, submitted a statutory draft, relating in part to foreign base company sales income, during hearings before the Senate Finance Committee. * * * This draft, which included a proposed section 954(d), reworded the House bill's "ownership or control" related-person standard to a "control" standard defined in terms of stock ownership, and listed individuals, partnerships, trusts, estates, and corporations as persons qualified to be related persons with respect to a CFC. The proposed section 954(d) also included a version of the branch rule, which, like the rest of the proposed section 954(d), does not vary significantly from section 954(d) as eventually enacted. Secretary Dillon described the controlled foreign corporation portion of the draft as consistent with "the more limited tax-haven approach" of the House bill. * * *

The Senate Finance Committee included the branch rule in its bill, in the form that was later enacted, and retained Secretary Dillon's related-person standard. * * * In comparing its amendments to the House provisions, the committee reported that "In the area of * * * income from sales subsidiary operations, your committee's provision is much the same as the House bill." * * * Although there is a discussion highlighting the "more significant changes" and amendments that "differ considerably" from House provisions, there is no mention of the branch rule in this discussion. * * * The branch rule is instead described later, without any apparent emphasis, in a "general explanation" section:

> Also included in foreign base company sales income are operations handled through a branch (rather than a corporate subsidiary) operating outside of the country in which the controlled foreign corporation is incorporated, if the combined effect of the tax treatment accorded the branch, by the country of incorporation of the controlled foreign corporation and the country of operation of the branch, is to treat the branch substantially the same as if it were a subsidiary corporation organized in the country in which it carries on its trade or business. * * *

The House–Senate Conference Committee report discusses the branch rule only briefly:

> The Senate amendment provides that foreign branches of a controlled foreign corporation shall, under certain circumstances, be treated as wholly owned subsidiary corporations for purposes of determining the foreign base company sales income of the controlled foreign corporation * * *. * * *

* * *

In the absence of a specified technical definition, a statutory term should be given its normal and customary meaning. * * * Our review of the legislative history, highlighted above, leads us to conclude that Congress did not intend the word "branch" in section 954(d)(2) to take on a meaning other than its ordinary meaning in a business and accounting sense.

Resort to dictionaries is an acceptable means of discerning ordinary usage. * * * Petitioners suggest, as a foundation, a definition from Black's Law Dictionary, p. 170 (5th ed. 1979): "Division, office, or other unit of business located at a different location from main office or headquarters." A specialized business dictionary cited by petitioners similarly stresses an "office" in a different location than the "parent company."

Respondent rejects petitioners' proposed definition as too narrow, yet offers no alternative that purports to represent normal and customary usage. We find nothing in the legislative history that is inconsistent with petitioners' definition. We recognize, however, that petitioners' proposal, without clarification of the nature of divisions and units, seems to shift the definitional problem rather than resolve it. Nonetheless, respondent admits that petitioners' definition does not cover Tensia. Regardless of the precise ordinary meaning of "branch," we are confident that such meaning does not encompass Tensia, an unrelated corporation operating under an arm's-length contractual arrangement with Drew Ameroid.

Respondent maintains that the "or similar establishment" language of section 954(d)(2) should be broadly construed to cover Tensia. We read "similar establishment," however, to mean an establishment that bears the typical characteristics of an ordinary-usage branch, yet goes by another name for accounting, financial reporting, local law, or other purposes. Respondent's expansive reading of the term, to include Tensia, is not supported by the legislative history. The Senate Finance Committee and the House–Senate Conference Committee do not even mention the term "similar establishment" in generally describing the branch rule in their respective reports. * * *

Respondent's position on congressional intent would be more persuasive if Congress had granted specific regulatory authority to the Secretary of the Treasury to define "branch or similar establishment." Section 954(d)(2) does grant specific regulatory authority, but, as is apparent from the sentence structure of that section, the authority becomes operative only if a branch or similar establishment is a given. In other words, the Secretary has a specific grant of authority to address certain consequences flowing from the existence of a branch or similar establishment, but does not have such authority to determine what a branch or similar establishment is. The legislative history confirms our reading of the statute:

> Paragraph (2) of section 954(d) provides that in situations in which the carrying on of activities by a controlled foreign corporation through a branch or similar establishment * * * has substantially the same effect as if such branch or similar establishment were a wholly owned subsidiary corporation deriving such income, *then, under regulations prescribed by the Secretary of the Treasury or his delegate*, the income attributable to the carrying on of such activities of such branch or similar establishment shall be treated as income derived by a wholly owned subsidiary * * *. * * *

In sum, we reject respondent's contention that Congress intended the branch rule to apply to "any arrangement" with a specified tax effect.

Respondent's second principal argument also relates to demonstrable tax avoidance, but primarily in the joint context of the statute and regulations. As already noted, the statute and legislative history do not define "branch or similar establishment." The regulations also do not directly define the phrase. Sec. 1.954–3(b)(1), (2), and (3), Income Tax Regs. The illustrations in section 1.954–3(b)(4), Income Tax Regs., invariably assume away the definitional issue by presupposing the existence of branches denoted as "branch B" and "branch C."

Respondent argues, however, that the statute and regulations indirectly define "branch or similar establishment" in that they invoke principles of tax rate disparity between the foreign countries involved.

* * * Petitioners do not challenge respondent's assertion that Belgium had an effective tax rate substantially exceeding that of Liberia during the years at issue.

Respondent's argument draws upon the statutory requirement that the branch have "substantially the same effect as if such branch * * * were a wholly owned subsidiary corporation deriving such income." Sec. 954(d)(2). Because the regulations seemingly implement this provision through a tax rate disparity test, such a disparity between manufacturing and sales locations arguably serves to define a branch or similar establishment.

We find respondent's emphasis on tax rate disparities misplaced for several reasons. Most notably, again with reference to the wording of the statute, the provision respondent draws from the statute merely describes restrictively *which* branches and similar establishments are subject to the operative provisions of section 954(d)(2). Section 954(d)(2) says, in effect: "Begin with the entire class of the CFC's branches and similar establishments located in other countries. From this group, select those that have 'substantially the same effect' and apply the provisions hereafter." If an establishment is not in the nature of a branch in the first instance, it cannot become so through the application of a restrictive modifying provision.

Furthermore, the legislative history, rather than focusing on tax rate disparities, presents the "substantially the same effect" statutory provision as relating to a different and more straightforward concept: similar foreign tax treatment of branches and corporate subsidiaries. Branch operations are included in foreign base company sales income if—

> the combined effect of the tax treatment accorded the branch, by the country of incorporation of the controlled foreign corporation and the country of operation of the branch, is to treat the branch substantially the same as if it were a subsidiary corporation organized in the country in which it carries on its trade or business. * * *

See Staff of the Comm. on Ways and Means, Comparative Analysis of Differences in House and Senate Versions of H.R. 10650 "The Revenue Act of 1962" 22–23 (Sept. 14, 1962) (Senate bill applies to branches "if such branches are, for tax purposes, treated as subsidiaries under foreign law"); Staff of the Comm. on Ways and Means, "The Revenue Act of 1962" Comparative Analysis of Prior Law and Provisions of Public Law 87–834 (H.R. 10650) 11 (Oct. 19, 1962) (for purposes of foreign base company sales income, "a branch may be treated as a subsidiary if so treated under foreign law") * * *.

* * *

Respondent's third recurring theme is that the nature of the business relationship between Drew Ameroid and Tensia makes the latter a branch or similar establishment. Respondent likens Tensia to an agent of Drew

Ameroid, based on factors that include Drew Ameroid's control over Tensia's manufacturing operations under the agreement, the allocation of risk between the two, and the anticipated lengthy term of the relationship.

We have already indirectly considered this issue in our analysis of respondent's broad "loophole closing" argument. In that context, we determined that Congress intended the term "branch" to have its customary business meaning and the term "similar establishment" to serve a fine-tuning purpose rather than an expansionary one. A separately incorporated manufacturing entity operating pursuant to an arm's-length agreement, with the CFC having no direct or indirect stock interest in that entity (and vice versa), does not fall within any customary meaning of "branch" of which we are aware. In these circumstances, the degree of control exercised by Drew Ameroid over a part of Tensia's manufacturing operations, any disproportionate risk borne by Drew Ameroid relative to Tensia, and the anticipated length of the relationship are irrelevant considerations.

This conclusion does not seem to us to be unjustifiably permissive to taxpayers, primarily because neither Drew Ameroid nor its U.S. shareholder, Drew Chemical, had a claim to any of Tensia's manufacturing income derived under the arm's-length agreement or otherwise.

The significance of Tensia's manufacturing income is apparent when viewed in the context of the tax policy considerations that underlie the subpart F provisions. The two undesirable concepts emphasized throughout the legislative history are tax deferral and tax havens. Tax deferral refers to a foreign corporation's retention of foreign source earnings, resulting in the deferral of U.S. tax until the foreign corporation distributes dividends to its U.S. shareholders. Tax havens are favorable, low-tax jurisdictions.

A typical situation targeted by section 954(d)(1) is a sales subsidiary in a relatively low-tax jurisdiction, all of the voting stock of which is owned by a manufacturing CFC in a relatively high-tax jurisdiction. In a greatly simplified sense, the U.S. shareholders of this CFC realize income roughly equal to the subsidiary's ultimate sales revenue less the CFC's cost to manufacture the property. Some form of intercorporate pricing, however, splits the income in two, and the sales end is taxed at a lower rate than the manufacturing end. The statute deems this situation unacceptable, presumably because of the tax deferral and tax haven implications, and attributes foreign base company sales income to the CFC, which becomes gross income to the U.S. shareholders.

Tensia's Belgian manufacturing activity for Drew Ameroid bears neither the tax haven nor the tax deferral stigma. Belgium is not the purported tax haven here, Liberia is. Indeed, it is this relative tax rate disparity that provides respondent with the foothold from which to invoke the operative regulations applicable to manufacturing branches. See sec. 1.954–3(b)(1)(ii), Income Tax Regs. Tensia's activities also did not directly give rise to tax deferral, at least as contemplated and described by the President and Congress. Drew Ameroid had no claim to Tensia's manufacturing income and thus had no corresponding distributable amount that it was retaining in lieu of distributing dividends to Drew Chemical in the United States.

These tax policy considerations, we believe, explain why Tensia can be classified differently than a subsidiary or an unincorporated establishment of Drew Ameroid, even though Drew Ameroid had a large measure of control here over the manufacture of the products it sold.

One possible response to this tax policy analysis is that Drew Ameroid's sales operation had both tax deferral and tax haven implications, and Drew Ameroid's activities alone should be enough to support implementation of the branch rule. This position, however, is not consistent with the limits respondent places on the branch rule in his opposition brief:

It must be emphasized that respondent has not applied the manufacturing branch rule to an ordinary purchase of finished goods from a third-party supplier. Respondent agrees that the purchase from an unrelated supplier and resale of goods in the ordinary course by a CFC does not result in foreign base company sales income. * * *

We take this to mean that respondent would not apply the branch rule to a CFC's spontaneous (rather than contracted for) purchase of fungible (rather than custom-made) finished goods. In both respondent's conceded example and the situation before us in this case, there are no substantial tax deferral or tax haven implications attributable to the finished goods supplier. In our view, the applicability of the branch rule should be the same in both situations.

* * *

We hold that Tensia is not a "branch or similar establishment" of Drew Ameroid within the meaning of section 954(d)(2). In light of this holding, we need not consider petitioners' alternative position that the regulations relating to manufacturing branches are invalid. * * *

[¶ 11,115]

NOTE

The *Ashland Oil* decision was followed in Vetco, Inc. v. Commissioner, 95 T.C. 579 (1990). The *Vetco* case involved a wholly owned Swiss subsidiary ("VIAG") of Vetco, Inc., a California corporation. VIAG sold pipe and pipe connectors to independent parties for use in offshore oil drilling. A wholly owned U.K. subsidiary ("VOL") of VIAG provided a variety of services to VIAG (principally welding of connectors to pipe), which were billed to VIAG at cost plus five percent. Because VIAG did not *actually* purchase from VOL the products VIAG sold, the IRS apparently concluded that the sales income realized by VIAG could not be classified as foreign base company sales income under Section 954(d)(1) by itself without benefit of the manufacturing branch rule. The income could not be treated as foreign base company sales income unless VOL could be treated as a manufacturing branch for purposes of Section 954(d)(2). The IRS argued that VOL should be treated as a manufacturing branch from which VIAG purchased the products it sold and that the income realized by VIAG should be treated as foreign base company sales income. The court rejected the IRS's argument that a wholly owned subsidiary could be treated as a manufacturing branch for purposes of the manufacturing branch rule.

[¶ 11,120]
REVENUE RULING 97–48

1997–2 C.B. 89.

* * *

In Rev. Rul. 75–7, 1975–1 C.B. 244, a controlled foreign corporation entered into an arm's length contract with an unrelated contract manufacturer located outside of its country of incorporation. Under the contract, the unrelated contract manufacturer agreed to perform manufacturing services for the controlled foreign corporation. Under the facts described in Rev. Rul. 75–7, the processing activities of the unrelated contract manufacturer were considered to be performed by the controlled foreign corporation outside its country of incorporation through a branch or similar establishment for purposes of section 954(d)(1) and (2) * * *.

In Ashland Oil, Inc. v. Commissioner, 95 T.C. 348 (1990), the Tax Court held that a manufacturing corporation unrelated to a controlled foreign corporation cannot be a branch or similar establishment of the controlled foreign corporation. See also, Vetco, Inc. v. Commissioner, 95 T.C. 579 (1990) (wholly-owned subsidiary of a controlled foreign corporation cannot be a branch or similar establishment of the controlled foreign corporation).

The Service will follow the *Ashland* and *Vetco* opinions. The activities of a contract manufacturer cannot be attributed to a controlled foreign corporation for purposes of either section 954(d)(1) or section 954(d)(2) * * * to determine whether the income of a controlled foreign corporation is foreign base company sales income. * * *

Pursuant to the authority of section 7805(b), for taxable years of a controlled foreign corporation starting before December 8, 1997, the principles of Rev. Rul. 75–7 may be relied upon to attribute the activities of a contract manufacturer to the controlled foreign corporation. A taxpayer that relies on Rev. Rul. 75–7 to attribute the activities of a contract manufacturer to a controlled foreign corporation for purposes of section 954(d)(1), however, must treat the contract manufacturing activities as being performed through a branch or similar establishment of the controlled foreign corporation for purposes of section 954(d)(2). The Service has never been of the view that Rev. Rul. 75–7 allows the activities of a contract manufacturer performed outside the controlled foreign corporation's country of incorporation to be attributed to the controlled foreign corporation without treating those activities as performed through a branch or similar establishment of the controlled foreign corporation.

With the revocation of Rev. Rul. 75–7, the Service's position on the treatment of contract manufacturing for purposes of section 954(d) is harmonized with its position on the treatment of contract manufacturing for purposes of section 863(b) (see § 1.863–3(c) of the * * * Regulations (production activity limited to activity conducted directly by taxpayer)).

* * *

[¶ 11,125]

c. Controlled Foreign Corporation Manufacturing Under the Substantial Contribution Test

Section 954(d)(1) and Reg. § 1.954–3(a)(4)(i) exclude from foreign base company sales income a controlled foreign corporation's income derived from the sale of goods that it manufactures. A controlled foreign corporation is treated as a manufacturer if either a substantial transformation of the property sold is effected by the controlled foreign corporation or, if purchased components are part of the property sold, the activities of the controlled foreign corporation in connection with the property sold are substantial in nature and are generally considered to constitute manufacturing. See ¶ 11,095. In Revenue Ruling 97–48, the IRS held that this exclusion could not apply when an unrelated contract manufacturer performs activities that would satisfy § 954(d)(1) if the activities had been performed by the controlled foreign corporation itself.

During the years following Revenue Ruling 97–48, the proliferation of the use of international contract manufacturing arrangements by controlled foreign corporations gave rise to a need for new regulatory guidance to realistically reflect modern cross-border manufacturing of goods by unrelated contract manufacturers. In 2008, the Treasury released proposed regulations intended to address this issue. The preamble to the proposed regulations affirmed the position of the Treasury and the IRS as follows:

> In Rev. Rul. 97–48 the IRS revoked Rev. Rul. 75–7. Rev. Rul. 97–48 states that the IRS will follow *Ashland Oil, Inc.* v. *Commissioner* and *Vetco, Inc.* v. *Commissioner*, and therefore confirms that the IRS will not treat a separate contract manufacturer as a branch for purposes of section 954(d)(2). In addition, Rev. Rul. 97–48 rules that the activities of a contract manufacturer cannot be attributed to a CFC for purposes of either section 954(d)(1) or section 954(d)(2) to determine whether the income of a CFC is FBCSI. However, the ruling

> does not address the circumstances under which the activities of the CFC itself may qualify as manufacturing when a contract manufacturing or similar arrangement is in place.

REG–124590–07, 2008–1 C.B. 801, 803.

The same preamble articulated the policy motivations behind the regulation that would become Reg. § 1.954–3(a)(4)(iv):

> Final regulations addressing FBCSI were first published in 1964 * * *. Since then, global economic expansion and globalization have led to significant changes in manufacturing. Many multinational groups have extensive manufacturing networks * * *. These cross-border manufacturing networks are created primarily to leverage expertise and cost efficiencies. In addition, the use of contract manufacturing arrangements has become a common way of manufacturing products because of the flexibility and efficiencies it affords. Accordingly, updated rules in this area are important to the continued competitiveness of U.S. businesses operating abroad.

Id.

The "substantial contribution" test was designed to bridge the gap between the existing tests for substantial transformation and component manufacturing activity performed by the controlled foreign corporation itself and the prohibited attribution of the manufacturing activities of an unrelated contract manufacturer to the controlled foreign corporation for which those activities are performed. As the name suggests, the test deems a controlled foreign corporation to have manufactured a product when it makes a "substantial contribution" through the activities of its employees to the manufacture of the product by the contract manufacturer. Because Revenue Ruling 97–48 maintained the position that a contract manufacturer's activities cannot be attributed to the controlled foreign corporation for the purposes of determining whether the controlled foreign corporation has manufactured the product, the substantial contribution test is a significant compromise that essentially takes the form of an exception to the general rule of non-attribution. The non-attribution of an unrelated contract manufacturer's manufacturing activities to the controlled foreign corporation is preserved by treating the controlled foreign corporation as the manufacturer of the product based on activities *it* performs through its *own employees*. Under the new test, the contract manufacturer's manufacturing activities are effectively imputed to the controlled foreign corporation only if the controlled foreign corporation's employees make a substantial contribution to their performance. In this case the controlled foreign corporation is deemed to satisfy the Reg. § 1.954–3(a)(4)(i) manufacturing exception. Reg. § 1.954–3(a)(4)(iv) is therefore clearly focused on whether the activities of the controlled foreign corporation's employees related to the contract manufacturer's manufacturing operations rise to a level of substance that makes it appropriate to treat the manufacturing as having been performed by the controlled foreign corporation.

Reg. § 1.954–3(a)(4)(iv) provides in relevant part as follows:

(iv) Substantial contribution to manufacturing of personal property—(a) In general. If an item of personal property would be considered manufactured, produced, or constructed (under the principles of paragraph (a)(4)(ii) or (a)(4)(iii) of this section) prior to sale by the controlled foreign corporation had all of the manufacturing, producing, and constructing activities undertaken with respect to that property prior to sale been undertaken by the controlled foreign corporation through the activities of its employees, then this paragraph (a)(4)(iv) applies. If this paragraph (a)(4)(iv) applies and if the facts and circumstances evince that the controlled foreign corporation makes a substantial contribution through the activities of its employees to the manufacture, production, or construction of the personal property sold, then the personal property sold by the controlled foreign corporation is manufactured, produced, or constructed by such controlled foreign corporation.

(b) Activities. The determination of whether a controlled foreign corporation makes a substantial contribution through the activities of its employees to the manufacture, production, or construction of the personal property sold involves, but will not necessarily be limited to, consideration of the following activities:

(1) Oversight and direction of the activities or process pursuant to which the property is manufactured, produced, or constructed (under the principles of paragraph (a)(4)(ii) or (a)(4)(iii) of this section).

(2) Activities that are considered in, but that are insufficient to satisfy, the tests provided in paragraphs (a)(4)(ii) and (a)(4)(iii) of this section.

(3) Material selection, vendor selection, or control of the raw materials, work-in-process or finished goods.

(4) Management of manufacturing costs or capacities (for example, managing the risk of loss, cost reduction or efficiency initiatives associated with the manufacturing process, demand planning, production scheduling, or hedging raw material costs).

(5) Control of manufacturing related logistics.

(6) Quality control (for example, sample testing or establishment of quality control standards).

(7) Developing, or directing the use or development of, product design and design specifications, as well as trade secrets, technology, or other intellectual property for the purpose of manufacturing, producing, or constructing the personal property.

(c) Application of substantial contribution test.—When considering whether a controlled foreign corporation makes a substantial

contribution to the manufacture, production, or construction of the personal property, the performance of any activity in paragraph (1)(4)(iv)*(b)* of this section will be taken into account. The performance or lack of performance of any particular activity in paragraph (a)(4)(iv)*(b)* of this section, or of a particular number of activities in (a)(4)(iv)*(b)* of this section, is not determinative. The weight accorded to the performance of any quantum of any activity (whether or not specified in paragraph (a)(4)(iv)*(b)* of this section) will vary with the facts and circumstances of the particular business. * * *

The substantial contribution test represents a taxpayer-favorable policy shift in a direction away from the position that was taken by the IRS and rejected by the court in the *Ashland Oil* case If the IRS's position had been upheld in *Ashland Oil*, the result would have been that in many cases the income realized by a controlled foreign corporation on sale of products manufactured by an unrelated contract manufacturer would have constituted foreign base company sales income under the manufacturing branch rule. The IRS sought to retain much of the broadened definition of foreign base company sales income it failed to achieve in *Ashland Oil* by reaffirming, in Revenue Ruling 97–48, ¶ 11,120, its rejection of any attribution of manufacturing activities of an unrelated contract manufacturer to the controlled foreign corporation. However, as part of the updated rules in Reg. § 1.954–3(a)(4)(iv), described in the preamble above, as "important to the continued competitiveness of U.S. businesses operating abroad," the substantial contribution test has significantly narrowed the scope of foreign base company sales income. Does this change represent sound tax policy?

[¶ 11,130]

PROBLEMS

1. Suppose that a U.S. corporation has a wholly owned manufacturing subsidiary in the Netherlands and it establishes a branch office in Switzerland. The Swiss branch handles all sales of the products manufactured in the Netherlands to non-Dutch customers. Leaving aside U.S. tax considerations, such an organizational structure could be particularly advantageous because the combined Swiss–Dutch tax burden on the income from non-Dutch sales will be markedly less than if the non-Dutch sales were handled directly by the Dutch manufacturing subsidiary.[2] Assume that the effective Dutch and Swiss corporate income tax rates on manufacturing and sales income are 35 percent and 18 percent, respectively. Under such an organizational structure, does the trading income escape classification as foreign base company sales income because the products have not been purchased from a related person but have been manufactured by the controlled foreign corporation?

2. The benefit derives from the fact that the sales income of the branch would be taxed in Switzerland at rates well below the Dutch corporate rates and would be free of tax in the Netherlands, which uses a territorial system of international taxation in this context.

2. Consider the classification of sales income in a case in which a controlled foreign corporation incorporated in Switzerland handles non-Swiss sales in Europe through a Swiss office (the sales profit of which is subject to Swiss income tax at the rate of 18 percent). The products sold by the Swiss office are manufactured by a manufacturing branch of the Swiss corporation established in the Netherlands where manufacturing income is taxed at a 35–percent rate. Can the position taken in Reg. § 1.954–3(b)(1)(ii) that a manufacturing branch may, under the prescribed circumstances, be treated as a separate corporation for purposes of applying the definition of foreign base company sales income be justified on the basis of the literal terms of Section 954(d)(2) or the legislative history discussed in the *Ashland Oil* case? Note that the court's analysis in *Ashland Oil* made it unnecessary for it to decide this issue.

3. Precision Marine Corp. ("PM U.S."), a U.S. corporation, is engaged in the manufacture and sale of power boats inside and outside the United States. PM U.S. owns 100 percent of the stock of PM Bermuda ("PM Bermuda"), a corporation organized under Bermuda law. PM Bermuda is engaged in the production of marine electronic navigational and communications equipment ("marine equipment") that it sells at a profit to PM U.S., passing title in Bermuda. PM U.S. installs appropriate items of marine equipment it buys from PM Bermuda in power boats PM U.S. sells to its unrelated distributors outside Bermuda. All of the marine equipment is manufactured for PM Bermuda by an unrelated contract manufacturer ("CM"), located in Monterrey, Mexico. CM buys for the account of PM Bermuda components from unrelated suppliers outside Bermuda and engages in substantial manufacturing activities to produce the marine equipment. Under its contract with CM, PM Bermuda owns throughout CM's manufacturing process the components, work-in-progress and finished products, and PM Bermuda has the rights (i) to control the acquisition by CM of components used by CM in its manufacturing of the marine equipment, (ii) to exercise oversight and control over CM's operations involved in its manufacture of the marine equipment and (iii) to supervise and control the use of intangibles that are licensed by PM Bermuda to CM for use in the manufacture by CM of the marine equipment. Because CM has established a record of outstanding efficiency and quality control, PM Bermuda's employees limit the exercise of their rights of supervision and control to random checks each week of the quality of the finished products manufactured by CM. PM Bermuda pays CM an arm's length conversion fee for CM's manufacturing activities based on the type and number of items produced by CM. Is the income realized by PM Bermuda on its sales of marine equipment to PM U.S. foreign base company sales income?

4. Juicer Inc. ("Juicer U.S.") is a U.S. corporation that owns all of the outstanding stock of Juicer Singapore PLC ("Juicer Singapore"), a corporation organized under the laws of Singapore, which is subject to an effective foreign income tax rate of 10 percent. Juicer Singapore sells juicer machines that convert fruits and vegetables to juices to Juicer U.S., which resells them to unrelated distributors in the Western Hemisphere. The machines are manufactured under contract with Juicer Singapore by unrelated contract

manufacturers CM–C, CM–J and CM–V, which are incorporated in China, Japan and Vietnam, respectively. Under each of the following sets of circumstances, would Juicer Singapore generate foreign base company sales income upon sale of the juicer machines to Juicer U.S.?

a. The contract with CM–C specifies that Juicer Singapore provides and owns throughout the manufacturing process the raw materials and components used to manufacture the juicer machines. Juicer Singapore also owns and licenses to CM–C the manufacturing patents needed by CM–C in the manufacture of the juicer machines. Pursuant to the contract, a Juicer Singapore employee visits CM–C quarterly to evaluate the quality of the work process, the effective use of the manufacturing patents and the final products ready for shipment to Juicer U.S. The employee is empowered to require CM–C to remediate promptly any deficiencies in the manufacturing process. Juicer Singapore pays a conversion fee to CM–C related to the quantity of machines produced. Juicer Singapore has the right, which it exercises, to have its employees train CM–C employees at Juicer Singapore's expense before the involvement of those CM–C employees in the manufacture of juicer machines.

b. The contract with CM–J specifies that Juicer Singapore is not obligated to provide any raw materials or components, which are selected and purchased by CM–J. The contract gives Juicer Singapore the right to supervise the manufacturing process and to conduct quality control checks on finished juicers. The CM–J factory is operated entirely by robots that were designed, built, installed and serviced by Juicer U.S. The robots are programmed with tolerance-measuring systems and if juicers are not in accordance with quality standards set forth in the contract, employees of Juicer U.S. are authorized to stop production and adjust the robot or robots involved. Because the robots have consistently demonstrated a high level of accuracy and reliability, the Juicer Singapore employee responsible for supervising the CM–J production only visits the factory once a month to check the robots. While onsite, the Juicer Singapore employee consults with the Juicer U.S. employee who monitors the robots remotely and verifies that the production is within specification. The Juicer Singapore employee also performs a random sampling of the manufacturing process and finished products for quality control purposes at CM–J's factory every other month.

c. The contract with CM–V specifies that Juicer Singapore provides the raw materials and components used in the manufacture of the juicers by CM–V, and Juicer Singapore is responsible for monitoring quality control on the final products but does not supervise the production process itself. The Juicer Singapore employee responsible for the quality control oversight has chosen to hire an unrelated project manager to monitor quality control. However, the manner in which the project manager carries out its responsibilities is not controlled by Juicer Singapore. The project manager cannot instruct CM–V to make changes to its process based on his findings. Instead, he is obligated to notify the Juicer Singapore employee of quality deficiencies, and the latter is authorized to direct CM–V to make changes to conform to quality standards prescribed in the contract.

d. Assume the same facts as in Problem 4.c., except the project manager makes monthly reports of quality deficiencies to the Juicer Singapore employee. In this case, the Juicer Singapore employee is obligated to exercise his authority to stop production immediately until the deficiencies are eliminated.

[¶ 11,132]

d. Rules Relating to Multiple Sales and Manufacturing Branches

Temporary regulations, which became effective in 2009, provide guidance on identifying foreign base company sales income in situations involving more than one sales or manufacturing branch in various combinations. If a controlled foreign corporation carries on purchasing or selling activities through more than one branch (or similar establishment) located outside the country under the laws of which that corporation is organized, then the sales (or purchase) branch allocation-of-income rule and tax-rate-disparity test of Reg. § 1.954–3(b)(1)(i)(*b*) are applied separately to the income derived by each such branch by treating that branch as if it were the only branch of the controlled foreign corporation and as if any such other branches were separate corporations. This treatment is applied in determining whether the use of branch in question has substantially the same tax effect as if that branch were a wholly owned subsidiary corporation of the controlled foreign corporation. Temp. Reg. § 1.954–3T(b)(1)(i)(*c*).

If a manufacturing branch located outside the country of the controlled foreign corporation, the remainder of which corporation is involved in purchasing or selling the products manufactured by the branch, has substantially the same effect as a wholly owned subsidiary of the controlled foreign corporation, the branch and the remainder of the corporation are treated as separate corporations for purposes of determining the foreign base company sales income of the corporation. Temp. Reg. § 1.954–3T(b)(1)(ii)(*a*).

If a controlled foreign corporation carries on the manufacturing of different tools through more than one manufacturing branch outside the country of the controlled foreign corporation, the manufacturing branch income-allocation rule and tax-rate-disparity test of Reg. § 1.954–3(b)(1)(ii)(*b*) are applied separately to each branch as if each branch were the only manufacturing branch and as if the other branches were separate corporations for purposes of determining whether each such branch has the same tax effect as if it were a wholly owned subsidiary of the controlled foreign corporation. Temp. Reg. § 1.954–3T(b)(1)(ii)(*c*)(2).

> *Example.* Controlled foreign corporation X is a Country M corporation, which is subject to the M income tax of 10 percent. X has a manufacturing branch, Branch A, in Country A that manufactures machine tools and is subject to an A income tax of 20 percent. X also

has a manufacturing branch, Branch B, in Country B that manufactures hand tools and is subject to a B income tax of 12 percent. Both types of the manufactured tools are sold by X to a related person in Country D. Employees of X engage only in sales activities in Country M related to tools manufactured by Branch A and Branch B. The manufacturing branch allocation-of-income rule and tax-rate-disparity test of § 1.954–3(b)(1)(ii)(*b*) are applied separately to Branch A and Branch B with respect to the sales income of controlled foreign corporation X. Branch A would have substantially the same tax effect as a wholly owned subsidiary of X because X's tax rate (10 percent) is less than 90 percent of, and at least five percentage points less than, Branch A's tax rate (20 percent). However, Branch B would not have substantially the same effect as a wholly owned subsidiary of X because its income tax (12 percent) would be too close to X's (10 percent) to meet the tax-rate-disparity test. Temp. Reg. § 1.954–3T(b)(1)(ii)(*c*)(2), Ex. Therefore, the sales income derived by X from sales of machine tools manufactured by Branch A, but not the sales income derived by X from sales of hand tools manufactured by Branch B, would be foreign base company sales income.

If a controlled foreign corporation has a manufacturing branch and two selling branches that sell the products manufactured by the manufacturing branch, the manufacturing branch allocation-of-income rule and the tax-rate-disparity test of Reg. § 1.954–3(b)(1)(ii)(*b*) are applied separately to the income of each selling branch by treating each as though it alone were the remainder of the controlled foreign corporation for purposes of determining whether the manufacturing branch has substantially the same tax effect as if it were a wholly owned subsidiary of the controlled foreign corporation. Temp. Reg. § 1.954–3T(b)(1)(ii)(*c*)(1).

Example. Controlled foreign corporation X is a Country M corporation, which is subject to an M income tax of 10 percent. X has a Branch A in Country A that manufactures widgets in Country A and is subject to an A income tax of 40 percent. X has a sales Branch B in Country B that sells widgets manufactured by Branch A and is subject to a B income tax of 10 percent. X also has a sales Branch C in Country C that sells widgets manufactured by Branch A and is subject a to C income tax of 38 percent. The customers who buy the widgets are located in countries other than M, A, B and C. X is not engaged in any activities beyond those engaged in by Branches A, B and C. The manufacturing branch allocation-of-income and tax-rate-disparity test of Reg. § 1.954–3(b)(1)(ii)(*b*) are applied to the sales income of Branch B as though it alone were the remainder of the corporation. Branch B would have substantially the same effect as a wholly owned subsidiary of X because its tax rate (10 percent) is less than 90 percent of, and at least five percentage points less than, the tax rate imposed on the manufacturing income of Branch A (40 percent). Branch C would not have substantially the same effect as a wholly owned subsidiary of X because its tax rate (38 percent) is too close to Branch A's (40 percent) to meet the tax-rate-disparity test. Temp. Reg. § 1.954–3T(b)(1)(ii)(*c*)(1), Ex. Therefore, Branch B would, but Branch C would not, be treated as a wholly owned subsidiary of X for purposes of applying the definition of foreign base company sales income, and the income of Branch B, but not of Branch C, would be foreign base company sales income.

The temporary regulations go on to deal with further aspects related to varied combinations of sales and manufacturing branches. See Temp. Reg. § 1.954–3T(b)(1)(ii)(*c*)(3)–(b)(4).

[¶ 11,135]

e. Other Tax Savings Through Use of Foreign Export Corporation

There are some other situations in which the use of a foreign corporation to handle export sales of U.S.-made goods to foreign countries may produce significant tax savings notwithstanding the controlled foreign corporation provisions.

One obvious possibility is to organize the foreign export corporation on a joint venture basis with the U.S. corporation holding no more than 50 percent of the voting power and of the value of the outstanding stock (the remaining 50 percent being held by an unrelated foreign person) so that the export corporation avoids classification as a controlled foreign corporation. The utility of this arrangement will normally be restricted to the situation in which the U.S. corporation has entered into a joint manufacturing venture with a foreign corporation, and it is decided for tax or other reasons to have a separate corporation handle export sales of products manufactured by the jointly owned manufacturing corporation. For foreign tax credit limitation purposes, dividends from the trading corporation would be subject to the Section 904(d)(4) look-through rule. This treatment applies to dividends paid by a foreign corporation of which a U.S. corporation owns between ten and 50 percent of the stock. In this case, the dividends will normally fall into the foreign tax credit general income limitation basket and will be useful in absorbing excess foreign tax credits associated with active business income. See ¶ 7030.

Then, too, if "non-base company" activities, such as manufacturing, that produce non-foreign base company income can be carried out by a controlled foreign corporation in the country of its incorporation, it may be possible to prevent its export income from being classified as foreign base company income by relying on the de minimis rule of Section 954(b)(3). Under that rule, if the gross foreign base company income of the controlled foreign corporation is less than the smaller of (1) five percent of its total gross income or (2) $1 million, none of the gross income will be treated as foreign base company income. Consider the potential for sheltering what would otherwise be foreign base company income by combining the export business with another business (e.g., hotel operations) that generates a large amount of gross income in relation to net income because operating expenses are relatively high.

Many U.S. corporations engaged in international business are paying foreign income taxes that exceed the applicable Section 904(d)(1) limitations on the amount of foreign taxes they may credit against their U.S. income tax. The effective U.S. corporate income tax burden is lower than that imposed in many industrialized countries, and the Section 904(d)(1) separate basket limitations on the foreign tax credit, although liberalized in the 2004 JOBS Act, may prevent a taxpayer from combining certain types of low-taxed foreign-source income with other types of high-taxed foreign income to increase the amount of the applicable foreign tax credit limitation.

Because many U.S. corporations have excess foreign tax credits, they will seek types of foreign-source income that are subject to little or no tax abroad and that can be used in the numerator of the general income limitation basket fraction to increase the amount of that limitation. A possibility would be to pass title abroad on products manufactured in the United States and exported. Under the Section 863(b)(2) source-of-income rule (see ¶ 2160), a substantial portion of the income (often 50 percent under the allocation method permitted by Reg. § 1.863–3(b)(1)), would be foreign-source income. If this income were free of foreign tax, it would absorb excess foreign tax credits with respect to other income falling within the general income limitation basket. See ¶ 11,005. Approximately the same result could be achieved (albeit at greater administrative cost) by having a wholly owned foreign export company in a tax-free jurisdiction, such as Bermuda, that would buy products manufactured by the U.S. parent corporation in the United States and resell those products at a markup to foreign customers, passing title to them outside the United States. The export income would be totally free of foreign tax, assuming no tax is imposed by the country in which the customer is located. The income earned would be foreign base company sales income, which would be taxed as a constructive Subpart F inclusion dividend to the U.S. parent corporation under Subpart F. However, under the foreign tax credit look-through rules of Section 904(d)(3), the dividend would be regarded as active general limitation income, which would fall into the numerator of the general income limitation foreign tax credit calculation. See ¶ 7085.

Also of interest to a U.S. corporation in an excess foreign tax credit position would be the possibility of using a wholly owned tax haven base company to handle export sales for a wholly owned manufacturing company in a relatively high-tax *foreign* country. This could result in moving the export sales income from the manufacturing corporation in the country in which it would be subject to a high tax to a tax haven, where that income would be tax-free. The income would be foreign base company sales income, which would be taxed as a constructive Subpart F inclusion dividend to the U.S. parent corporation under Section 951. But the income would be free of foreign tax (again, assuming no tax would be imposed by the country in which the customer is located) and would, under the Section 904(d)(3) look-through rules, fall into the numerator of the general limitation calculation, thereby increasing the amount of the general income limitation. The result would probably be to alleviate the excess foreign tax credit problem. In this situation, a wholly owned tax haven foreign export corporation would be used to reduce the foreign tax burden on income from the export of products manufactured abroad and thereby improve the U.S. parent corporation's overall U.S. and foreign tax situation. It would do this by permitting the U.S. parent to cross-credit the excess foreign tax credit generated by the high-taxed general limitation manufacturing income against U.S. tax otherwise imposed on the Subpart F inclusion deemed received from the foreign export corporation which would be exempt from foreign tax.

[¶ 11,140]

f. Export Trade Corporations

In enacting the controlled foreign corporation provisions of Subpart F in 1962, Congress took away with one hand most of the tax advantages formerly obtainable through the use of a tax haven foreign export corporation. Yet, in the same tax act, it somewhat paradoxically gave back with the other hand some of these benefits by enacting Sections 970 and 971, which relate to "export trade corporations." The latter step was apparently motivated primarily by balance of payments considerations and a desire not to have the controlled foreign corporation provisions eliminate all tax incentives to exports of products manufactured in the United States.

Section 970 provides that, in the case of a controlled foreign corporation that is an export trade corporation, Subpart F income taxable as a constructive dividend to its U.S. shareholders is reduced within specified limits by as much of its foreign base company income as consists of export trade income, as defined in Section 971(b). Thus, the U.S. shareholders of a controlled foreign corporation will not be taxed on its undistributed foreign base company income if the controlled foreign corporation is an export trade corporation to the extent that it earns "export trade income." However, under Section 970(a), the exclusion for foreign base company income constituting export trade income may not exceed the lesser of:

(1) ten percent of export-related gross receipts of the export trade corporation, or

(2) 150 percent of its "export promotion expenses."

The export trade income on which U.S. tax is to be deferred is also limited to the portion of this income that is invested by the export trade corporation in "export trade assets." § 970(a)(2). Any amount of export trade income on which taxation has been deferred because of such investments will subsequently be taxed to the extent that there is a decrease in export trade assets.

An export trade corporation is defined as a controlled foreign corporation that derives 90 percent of its gross income (for the prior three-year period) from sources outside the United States and that derives 75 percent or more of its gross income (for the same three-year period) from export trade income. § 971(a)(1).

Legislation relating to the Domestic International Sales Corporation, enacted in 1971, which is discussed in the following section, provided that no corporation that did not then qualify as an export trade corporation could thereafter so qualify. However, a corporation that qualified as an export trade corporation then can continue to do so unless it fails to qualify for three consecutive years. § 971(a)(3).

E. U.S. TAX SUBSIDIES TO ENCOURAGE U.S. EXPORTS

[¶ 11,145]

1. A BRIEF SUMMARY

There have been many twists and turns in the U.S. taxation of income from exports of goods and services. Before enactment of the controlled foreign corporation provisions of Subpart F, many U.S. corporations handled exports of U.S.-made products through foreign export corporations organized in tax havens, which would purchase goods manufactured by related U.S. corporations and resell them at a markup to foreign customers or would serve as a sales agent for export sales in return for commissions. In either case, the objective was to defer any U.S. income tax liability indefinitely by accumulating and reinvesting in the export business or other foreign businesses the income realized by the foreign export corporation. The controlled foreign corporation provisions enacted in 1962 altered the picture significantly by including the export income earned by such foreign export corporations in the definition of "foreign base company sales income" of Section 954(d), which would usually be taxed as a constructive Subpart F inclusion dividend to its U.S. parent corporation, thus ending any deferral of U.S. tax. See ¶ 6140.

As discussed at ¶ 11,140, deferral within limits was retained for controlled foreign corporations that qualified as "export trade corporations." The export trade corporation provisions, however, were not regarded as an adequate tax incentive to increasing the volume of U.S. exports, in part because use of a foreign corporation was relatively complicated and expensive for small exporters. In an effort to introduce a more effective incentive regime, the provisions concerning the Domestic International Sales Corporation ("DISC") were enacted in 1971 as the principal tax incentive to exports. The DISC was permitted to defer the U.S. corporate tax indefinitely on a portion of its export income, without having to pay interest to the U.S. Treasury on the deferred tax.

Eventually, for the reasons discussed below, the DISC was replaced as the principal export tax incentive by the Foreign Sales Corporation ("FSC"). A portion of the income of a FSC from U.S. exports was exempt from U.S. corporate tax and could be distributed to U.S. shareholders free of U.S. tax at the shareholder level. Thus, unlike the export trade corporation and the DISC which accorded a deferral of U.S. tax on some export income, the FSC provided an exemption from U.S. tax for a significant portion of export income. Moreover, although the FSC provisions contained incentives to convert export trade corporations and DISCs into FSCs, there was no compulsion to do so. Thus, the export trade corporation (which at least theoretically could continue to be used by some exporters) and the DISC (which may continue to be used by some small exporters) continue to subsist. As discussed at ¶ 11,185, the FSC provisions were held to be export subsidies in violation of World Trade Organization ("WTO") agreements and were repealed on November 15, 2000. However, then existing FSCs were permitted to continue to enjoy FSC benefits through December 31, 2000, and in some cases for a limited period thereafter.

The FSC provisions were replaced in the 2000 legislation by the extraterritorial income ("ETI") exclusion regime. This regime effectively exempted from U.S. tax a portion of the extraterritorial income of U.S. taxpayers, which included predominantly income from U.S. exports. The ETI exclusion was also held to violate the prohibition of WTO agreements against export subsidies. The ETI exclusion regime was repealed on October 22, 2004, by the JOBS Act. However, repeal was subject to generous transitional rules that permitted a continuation of the exclusion benefits for two years and sometimes longer. These rules have also been held to violate WTO agreements. See ¶ 11,230. In the JOBS Act, Congress abandoned efforts to fashion tax benefits that were contingent on exports and instead provided a special deduction from all gross income (whether or not export-related) from U.S. production activities broadly defined. See § 199, discussed at ¶ 11,230.

[¶ 11,150]

2. TREATMENT OF DOMESTIC INTERNATIONAL SALES CORPORATIONS

Under the DISC provisions, which were enacted in 1971 as Sections 991 through 997 of the Code, U.S. corporate tax is deferred on a portion of a DISC's export-related income. Thus, the deferral regime, preserved by the export trade corporation provisions, continued to survive in modified form in the DISC provisions. Under the DISC regime, the profits of a

DISC are not taxed to the DISC, but are taxed to the shareholders of the DISC when distributed or deemed distributed to them. § 995(a) and (b). Each year, a DISC is deemed to have distributed a portion of its income, thereby subjecting that income to current taxation in the hands of its shareholders. § 995(b). Tax can generally be deferred on the remaining portion of the DISC's taxable income until (i) the income is actually distributed to the DISC shareholders, (ii) a shareholder disposes of the DISC stock, (iii) the DISC is liquidated, (iv) the stock of the DISC is distributed, exchanged or sold, (v) the corporation ceases to qualify as a DISC or (vi) the DISC election is terminated or revoked. § 995(b)(2)(A), (c)(1). In the typical case, a DISC is a wholly owned U.S. subsidiary of a U.S. corporation, with the result that actual distributions and deemed distributions from DISCs are subject to U.S. corporate tax.

In connection with enactment in 1984 of provisions with respect to the FSC, the DISC provisions were amended to restrict benefits of deferral to relatively small DISCs by permitting deferral of tax only with respect to 16/17ths of the taxable income attributable to a maximum of $10 million of qualified export receipts. § 995(b)(1)(E) and (F). Because qualification for DISC deferral comes at the cost of an interest charge on the amount of tax deferred, corporations qualifying for deferral under current law are often called interest-charge DISCs. They are further discussed at ¶¶ 11,195 et seq.

[¶ 11,155]

3. ENACTMENT OF THE FSC PROVISIONS

Following its introduction, the DISC became the subject of a dispute between the United States and certain other parties to the General Agreement on Tariffs and Trade ("GATT"), the multinational trade agreement that preceded the WTO agreements. The other parties contended that the DISC amounted to an illegal export subsidy in violation of the GATT. In 1976, a GATT panel determined that the DISC had some characteristics of an illegal export subsidy. In the case of the DISC, the Panel Report pointed to the failure to charge interest on deferred taxes as the offending export subsidy. Although the United States had not conceded that the DISC violated the GATT, it did agree in December 1981 to the adoption by the GATT Council of the GATT Panel Reports on the DISC and the export tax practices of Belgium, France and the Netherlands, (the "1981 Decision").

The 1981 Decision provided that GATT signatories were not required to tax export income attributable to economic processes located outside their territorial limits. Furthermore, the 1981 Decision also stated that arm's length pricing principles should be observed in transactions between exporting enterprises and foreign buyers under common control. Finally, the 1981 Decision stated that the GATT did not prohibit the adoption of measures to avoid the double taxation of foreign-source income.

A debate in the GATT Council, the then ruling body of the GATT, ensued in early 1982 on the interpretation of the 1981 Decision as it applied to the DISC. This debate delayed progress on other issues of critical interest to the United States.

The European Economic Communities ("EEC") argued that the DISC was an illegal export subsidy because it allowed indefinite deferral of direct taxes on income from exports earned through business activity conducted in the United States with no charge for interest on the taxes deferred. The United States defended the DISC on the ground that its effect on trade as an incentive for exports approximated the effect of the territorial system of taxation used by Belgium, France and the Netherlands and found to be consistent with the GATT in the 1981 Decision. The majority of the GATT Council members urged the United States to bring the DISC clearly into conformity with the GATT. The EEC went one step further and requested authorization from the GATT Council to take retaliatory action against the United States. The EEC alleged that the DISC had provided more than $2 billion in subsidies for U.S. exports to EEC member countries over the previous 10 years.

The DISC debate in the GATT Council highlighted the potential danger of a breakdown in the GATT dispute settlement process and the isolation of the United States over the DISC issue. To remove the DISC as a contentious issue and to avoid further disputes over retaliation, in March 1983, the Administration approved the general outlines of a proposal to replace the DISC with a new system of taxation of export income earned by a FSC. The FSC was designed in a manner intended to comply with the GATT prohibition against export subsidies. The FSC provisions were enacted in 1984.

The portion of the 1981 Decision holding that a country was not required to tax income from economic processes occurring outside its territory was adopted to accommodate territorial systems of international taxation used by a number of European countries, under which export income attributable to a foreign permanent establishment is exempt from taxation in the exporter's home country. Consequently, it was concluded by Congress that certain export income attributable to economic activities occurring outside the United States could be exempted from U.S. tax to afford U.S. exporters treatment comparable to that customarily obtained by exporters under territorial systems of taxation.

[¶ 11,160]

F. TAX TREATMENT OF THE FOREIGN SALES CORPORATION

The special tax regime for FSCs, enacted in 1984 and contained in former Sections 921 through 927 and 291(a)(4) of the Code, largely supplanted the prior DISC regime. However, while the DISC (like the export trade corporation) enjoyed only a deferral of U.S. tax on a portion of its export-related income (albeit often an indefinite deferral), the FSC enjoyed a permanent exemption of a portion of its export income from U.S. tax. Moreover, the amount of the tax benefit for most U.S. exporters was enlarged by the FSC regime.

In general, a FSC is a foreign corporation engaged in selling U.S. goods (or in providing certain services) abroad. Typically, the FSC operates as a wholly owned subsidiary of a U.S. producer and sells products supplied by its U.S. parent.[3] As with the DISC provisions, the idea behind the FSC provisions was to create a tax incentive for exports of goods produced in the United States. If a corporation qualified for and elected FSC status, the tax benefit accorded the FSC was an exemption from the U.S. corporate income tax for a significant part of its export-related income. Former § 921(a). This part, moreover, could be distributed as a dividend tax-free to the U.S. parent corporation of the FSC because the distribution, unlike distributions from most foreign corporations, qualified for a 100–percent dividends-received deduction. Former § 245(c)(1)(A).

The FSC provisions contained a number of requirements and qualifications designed, broadly speaking, to ensure that a FSC had a genuine presence outside the United States and that its income exempted from U.S. tax was attributable to substantial commercial activity conducted outside the United States. These requirements were intended (i) to comply with the 1981 GATT Decision that an exemption from tax was permitted only if the economic processes that give rise to the income take place outside the United States and (ii) to accord treatment comparable to exemptions from home country tax accorded to export earnings under a territorial system of international taxation.

[¶ 11,165]

1. FORMAL REQUIREMENTS FOR FSC QUALIFICATION

Under former Section 922(a), to qualify as a FSC, a corporation had to meet a number of formal requirements of which the most notable were the following:

3. In many cases, a FSC was a controlled foreign corporation. However, if a controlled foreign corporation elected to be taxed as a FSC, its exempt foreign trade income was not subject to constructive dividend treatment under Subpart F under a prior version of Section 952(b).

(1) A FSC had to be a foreign corporation created or organized under the laws of a qualified foreign country or certain U.S. possessions. For a foreign country to qualify, there had to be in effect between that country and the United States an appropriate bilateral or multilateral exchange-of-information agreement meeting the standards of the Caribbean Basin legislation, Section 274(h)(6)(C), or an income tax treaty with respect to which the Treasury certified that the exchange-of-information program was adequate to prevent tax avoidance. Former § 927(e)(3).

(2) The corporation had to meet certain organizational requirements and to elect to be treated as a FSC. Former § 922(a)(2).

(3) The board of directors of a FSC had to include at least one individual who was not a U.S. resident but who could be a U.S. citizen. Former § 922(a)(1)(E); former Reg. § 1.922–1(j).

(4) The corporation had to maintain an office in a foreign country or possession that could qualify as a jurisdiction in which a FSC could be organized, at which it maintained a set of permanent records and books of account. Former § 922(a)(1)(D)(i)-(ii); former Reg. § 1.922–1(i). A FSC also had to maintain certain tax records at a location within the United States. Former § 922(a)(1)(D)(iii).

[¶ 11,170]

2. FOREIGN TRADING GROSS RECEIPTS

If a corporation was eligible and elected to be a FSC, a portion of the FSC's "foreign trade income" was exempt from U.S. tax. Income qualified as "foreign trade income" only if it was gross income attributable to "foreign trading gross receipts." Former § 923(b). A FSC was treated as having "foreign trading gross receipts" only if (1) the management of the FSC was carried on outside the United States and (2) the economic processes from which the income was earned took place outside the United States. Former § 924(b)(1).

To be treated as having foreign trading gross receipts, the management of the FSC had to take place outside the United States. Former § 924(b)(1)(A). This requirement was met if: (1) all meetings of its board of directors and shareholders were held outside the United States; (2) its principal bank account was maintained in a U.S. possession or a foreign country meeting the exchange-of-information requirements of former Section 927(e)(3); and (3) all dividends, legal and accounting fees and compensation of officers and directors were paid out of foreign bank accounts. Former § 924(c).

In addition to the foreign management requirement, the FSC was treated as having foreign trading gross receipts only if the economic processes that generated the income were located outside the United States. Former § 924(b)(1)(B). This requirement was met only if the FSC

(1) participated outside the United States in the solicitation (other than advertising), the negotiation or the making of a contract relating to the transaction and

(2) incurred outside the United States direct costs attributable to the transaction equal to

(a) at least 50 percent of the total direct costs attributable to the transaction with respect to five categories of sales-related activities: (i) advertising and sales promotion, (ii) processing of customer orders and the arranging for delivery, (iii) transportation to the customer, (iv) preparation and sending of the invoice and receipt of payment and (v) assumption of credit risk, or, alternatively,

(b) at least 85 percent of the direct costs attributable to any two of the five categories of sales-related activities.

Former § 924(d) and (e).

In addition, the income of the FSC was required to be determined on the basis of actual arm's length prices or on the basis of special administrative pricing formulas. Former § 925(a). This rule was intended to respond to the GATT's 1981 Decision that called for the application generally of an arm's length standard in setting transfer prices between a foreign export corporation and the related parties supplying the products exported from the United States.

[¶ 11,175]

3. DETERMINATION OF AMOUNT OF FOREIGN TRADE INCOME

Once the FSC was able to demonstrate that it had foreign trading gross receipts, it had to calculate the amount of its "foreign trade income" before it could calculate the portion that was exempt from U.S. tax. The FSC's foreign trade income was calculated by reducing the amount of "foreign trading gross receipts" by the "transfer price" paid by the FSC. Former Temp. Reg. § 1.923–1T(a).

The FSC could adopt one of two alternatives for determining the transfer price paid by the FSC: (1) arm's length pricing or (2) if certain requirements were met, either of two special administrative pricing rules. Former § 925(a).

After determining the amount of foreign trade income of the FSC, the next step was to calculate the amount of foreign trade income that was exempt from U.S. tax. The exempt portion varied depending on whether it was calculated by using arm's length pricing or one of the two administrative pricing rules.

(i) Arm's length pricing. If arm's length pricing was used, 30 percent of the FSC's gross foreign trade income (exclusive of income attributable to intangibles identified in former Section 927(a)(2)(B)) was exempt foreign trade income if, as in the usual case, the shareholder of the FSC was a U.S. corporation; 32 percent was exempt in other cases. Former §§ 923(a)(2) and 291(a)(4)(A).

(ii) Administrative pricing rules. If the administrative pricing rules were used, 15/23 of the foreign trade income derived from the transaction was treated as exempt foreign trade income and qualified for the exemption from U.S. income tax, assuming that the shareholder of the FSC was a U.S. corporation; 16/23 qualified if the shareholder was not a U.S. corporation. Former §§ 923(a)(3) and 291(a)(4)(B).

To achieve exemption from U.S. tax for a portion of the foreign trade income, the Code treated exempt foreign trade income of the FSC as foreign-source income that was not effectively connected with the conduct of a trade or business within the United States. Former § 921(a).

[¶ 11,180]

4. FSC TAXATION

A U.S. corporation was generally entitled to a 100–percent dividends-received deduction for distributions from a FSC out of earnings and profits attributable to foreign trade income, other than certain non-exempt income. Former § 245(c)(1)(A). Thus, exempt foreign trade income was not taxed at the level of the FSC or at the level of its U.S. corporate shareholder(s).

A FSC generally was not allowed a foreign tax credit for foreign income taxes paid or accrued with respect to exempt foreign trade income. Former § 906(b)(5). In addition, a shareholder of a FSC was generally not eligible for a foreign tax credit with respect to a foreign withholding tax imposed on a dividend attributable to foreign trade income. Consequently, to enjoy the maximum benefit from the U.S. tax exemption, the FSC had to be organized in a foreign country or U.S. possession in which, as a matter of domestic tax law, there was little or no corporate tax on the foreign trade income of the FSC exempt from U.S. tax and little or no withholding tax on dividend distributions out of such income.

Under pre-2007 law, two categories of FSC-related income were subject to separate basket foreign tax credit limitations (like DISC dividends). The first category was taxable income attributable to foreign trade income (at the FSC level). Former § 904(d)(1)(G). The second category of income was distributions received by a shareholder from a FSC or former FSC out of earnings and profits attributable to foreign trade income or certain interest or carrying charges related to such income. Former § 904(d)(1)(H). Because no foreign tax credit was to be available for the foreign taxes that a FSC incurred on exempt foreign trade income, the function of the separate limitation treatment was to prevent foreign trade income from increasing the limitation applicable to any other basket of income under Section 904(d)(1). Such an increase might effectively permit a credit for foreign taxes on that income that would otherwise not be available. Under current law, the second category of FSC-related income identified above (like DISC dividends) is placed in the passive category income basket as "specified passive category income." § 904(d)(2)(B)(v)(II).

[¶ 11,185]

G. DEMISE OF THE FSC AND ENACTMENT AND DEMISE OF ITS SUCCESSOR, THE EXTRATERRITORIAL INCOME EXCLUSION REGIME

Notwithstanding the effort of Congress to fashion the FSC provisions to approximate the exemptions available under the territorial systems of international taxation used by a number of European countries, the European Communities ("EC"), filed a complaint with the WTO alleging that the tax reductions accorded to FSCs under the Code were illegal export subsidies. A WTO Dispute Settlement Body ("DSB") panel ruled on October 8, 1999, that the FSC tax benefits violated the GATT Agreement on Subsidies and Countervailing Measures ("SCM Agreement") and the Agreement on Agriculture, which prohibit subsidies contingent on export performance. The panel report gave the United States until October 1, 2000, to comply with these agreements; this decision was affirmed by a WTO DSB appeals panel on February 24, 2000 and was adopted by the DSB on March 20, 2000. United States—Tax Treatment for "Foreign Sales Corporations", WTO WT/DS 108/26 April 25, 2003. The deadline for U.S. compliance was extended by the WTO to November 1. Id.

On November 15, 2000, the FSC Repeal and Extraterritorial Income Exclusion Act of 2000 ("2000 Act") was enacted. The 2000 Act repealed the pre-existing FSC rules and replaced them with an exclusion from the gross income of a U.S. taxpayer for extraterritorial income ("ETI") in the form of certain "qualifying foreign trade income."

No corporation could elect to be a FSC after September 30, 2000. 2000 Act, § 5(b)(1). However, under the transition rules, FSC benefits were continued for FSCs in existence on that date for transactions made in the ordinary course of business before 2002 and for transactions pursuant to a binding contract in effect on September 30, 2000, between a FSC and an unrelated person. Moreover, a FSC could elect to have the ETI exclusion regime apply to these transactions in lieu of the FSC rules.

In an apparent effort to sidestep the WTO DSB ruling that the FSC benefits were unlawful export subsidies, in part, because they were contingent on exports, the ETI exclusion was not limited to income from U.S. exports, did not require the use of a foreign corporation and permitted the manufacturing to be done outside the United States. In general, the exclusion regime appeared to be an attempt to align the Code more closely than the FSC provisions with the territorial systems used by some of the European countries. The ironic result was that the change once again increased the tax benefit to most U.S. exporters and added an estimated $1.5 billion to the projected $25 billion five-year cost of the FSC benefits. Bus. Week, Sept. 4, 2000, at p. 103.

Not surprisingly, the EC objected to the U.S. ETI exclusion regime, and on November 17, 2000, asked the WTO to approve retaliatory sanctions against U.S. products to compensate the EC for damages allegedly suffered as a result of the FSC tax benefits accorded to U.S. exporters. The EC also requested that a WTO DSB panel rule on whether the FSC replacement legislation was in compliance with the WTO agreements that prohibit export subsidies. The EC took the position that the extraterritorial income exclusion continued to provide a significant illegal export subsidy to more than half of total U.S. exports to the direct detriment of European companies. The EC also contended that the ETI legislation made the tax benefits contingent on use of at least 50 percent domestic rather than imported materials, which the EC argued was also illegal under the SCM Agreement.

In January 2002, the WTO DSB adopted the WTO Panel and Appellate Body reports agreeing with the European Union ("EU"), (which replaced the EC), and held the extraterritorial income exclusion regime also contained export subsidies in violation of the WTO Agreements. 2002 WL 44907 (W.T.O.). A previously initiated arbitration procedure was then reactivated by the WTO at the request of the EU to determine the sanctions that could be imposed in the form of tariff duties on U.S. exports to compensate the EU companies for the damages suffered as a result of the export subsidies accorded to U.S. exporters. On August 30, 2002, the arbitration granted the EU authority to impose duties on U.S. imports (more technically, suspend concessions previously granted under WTO trade agreements) in an amount up to $4.043 billion. The tariffs were authorized at a rate of 100 percent ad valorem above existing bound custom duties on the list of products prepared by the EU. Imposition of the sanctions was delayed to March 1, 2003, in the expectation that the U.S. Congress would promptly repeal the ETI exclusion regime.

In order to end the retaliatory tariff duties imposed by the EU on specified goods imported from the United States, Congress enacted section 101 of the 2004 JOBS Act, which was signed into law on October 22, 2004, and which repealed the ETI exclusion regime of former Section 114, but adopted transitional rules (also held to violate WTO agreements) that allowed substantial ETI benefits to continue for 2005 and 2006 and in some cases beyond. See ¶ 11, 230.

[¶ 11,190]

H. SPECIAL RULES FOR SMALL BUSINESSES: INTEREST–CHARGE DISC

To provide relief for small businesses that might find the foreign-management and economic-activity requirements of the FSC provisions burdensome, two alternatives were provided to the FSC: the interest-charge DISC and the small FSC. The provisions relating to the small FSC were repealed along with FSC provisions generally in the 2000 Act. The interest-charge DISC remains available for relatively small-scale U.S. exporters.

[¶ 11,195]

1. INTEREST–CHARGE DISC

A DISC may defer the U.S. tax on its taxable income attributable to $10 million or less of qualified export receipts for each tax year. This treatment is subject to the requirement that certain amounts must be deemed to be distributed and therefore lose the benefit of deferral. For example, 50 percent of the income attributable to military property is treated as distributed. Of the excess of the DISC's taxable income over certain specifically identified deemed distributions, 1/17th is deemed distributed. § 995(b)(1)(F). (This cutback in DISC deferral is comparable to the former corporate preference cutback of the exempt income of a FSC under former Section 291(a)(4).) Thus, except for the 1/17th cutback and other deemed distributions, substantially all of the typical DISC's taxable income attributable to $10 million or less of qualified export receipts may be accumulated and the tax thereon deferred. However, an interest charge will be imposed on the shareholders of the DISC. The amount of the interest is based on the tax that would have been due on the undistributed income if the income had been distributed. § 995(f)(1).

The tax that would otherwise have been due on the undistributed income, termed the shareholder's DISC-related deferred tax liability, is the excess of (i) the shareholder's tax liability for the shareholder's tax year computed as if the deferred DISC income had been included in the shareholder's income over (ii) the shareholder's actual tax liability for the year which reflects the deferral. § 995(f)(2).

Deferred DISC income generally means the excess of accumulated DISC income at the end of the prior tax year over the amount by which actual distributions out of accumulated DISC income exceed the current tax year's DISC income. § 995(f)(3). The rate of interest imposed on the shareholder's DISC-related deferred tax liability is determined by reference to a base period Treasury bill rate. This rate is the annual rate of interest that is equivalent to the average investment yield of U.S. Treasury bills with maturities of 52 weeks which were auctioned during the one-year period ending on September 30 of the calendar year ending with the close of the tax year of the shareholder. § 995(f)(4).

Taxable income of the DISC attributable to qualified export receipts that exceed $10 million is deemed distributed. § 995(b)(1)(E). Thus, if export receipts exceed $10 million, the DISC would not be disqualified; there would merely be no deferral of tax on taxable income attributable to the excess receipts. DISCs that are members of the same controlled group of corporations under Section 993(a)(3) would be treated as a single corporation for purposes of the $10 million rule, and the $10 million is deemed to be allocated among the members of the group. § 995(b)(4).

To qualify as a DISC, the corporation must (1) be incorporated under the laws of any of the States or the District of Columbia, (2) have only one class of stock, (3) have outstanding capital stock with a par or stated value of at least $2,500, (4) elect to be treated as a DISC and (5) meet an export gross-receipts test and an export-assets test. § 992(a)(1).

The export gross-receipts test requires that at least 95 percent of the corporation's gross receipts consist of qualified export receipts. § 992(a)(1)(A). In general, qualified export receipts are receipts, including commission receipts, derived from the sale or lease for use outside the United States of export property or from the furnishing of services related to the sale or lease of export property. Certain receipts for managerial services performed by a DISC for an unrelated DISC are qualified export receipts. Interest on any obligation which is a qualified export asset is also a qualified export receipt. § 993(a). Export property must be manufactured, produced, grown or extracted in the United States and held primarily for sale, lease, rent, consumption or disposition outside the United States. § 993(c).

The export-assets test requires that at least 95 percent of the corporation's assets constitute qualified export assets. § 992(a)(1)(B). Qualified export assets include principally inventories of export property, necessary operational equipment and supplies, trade receivables from export sales, producer's loans, working capital, obligations of domestic corporations organized solely to finance export sales under guaranty agreements with the Export–Import Bank and obligations issued, guaranteed or insured by the Export–Import Bank or the Foreign Credit Insurance Association. § 993(b).

The DISC provisions include special elective intercompany pricing rules, which may be used in lieu of the general intercompany pricing rules of Section 482 to determine the profits which a DISC may earn on products that it purchases from a related company and then resells for export or that it sells on a commission basis. In general, a DISC may earn up to four percent of gross export receipts from a transaction or 50 percent of the combined taxable income of the DISC and its related party from an export transaction; in either case, the DISC is also deemed to earn ten percent of export promotion expenses. Alternatively, the DISC and its related party may use pricing determined under the usual arm's length rules of Section 482. § 994(a).

[¶ 11,200]

a. Producer's Loans

One of the major innovations of the DISC system of tax deferral lay in the ability of the DISC to make its undistributed export profits available to its U.S. parent manufacturing company (or any other U.S. manufacturer of export property) through "producer's loans" without losing the benefit of the tax deferral. Because a producer's loan is not taxed as a dividend, it affords the U.S. parent company a means of withdrawing the tax-deferred export profit of the DISC at no tax cost, except the interest on the shareholder's deferred tax. All producer's loans must bear interest at an arm's length rate in accordance with the standards set by Section 482.

A "producer's loan" must meet certain requirements prescribed in Section 993(d) at the time it is made, but once qualified, such a loan is not disqualified by subsequent events. The loan must be designated a "producer's loan"; it must be evidenced by a note with a term of not more than five years; it can be made only to a person engaged in the United States in the production of export property; and, when added to the unpaid balances of all other producer's loans, it must not exceed the accumulated DISC income. § 993(d)(1). Moreover, to insure that outstanding loans to a particular borrower will qualify as producer's loans only to the extent of that borrower's export-related assets, the cumulative amount of loans to a given borrower is limited to an amount determined by multiplying the sum of:

(1) the amount of the borrower's adjusted basis in plant, machinery, equipment and supporting production facilities in the United States (at the beginning of the tax year);

(2) the amount of the borrower's property held for sale, lease or rental to customers in the ordinary course of business (at the beginning of the tax year); and

(3) the aggregate amount of the borrower's research and experimental expenditures in the United States during all prior tax years

by the percentage ratio of (a) the borrower's receipts for the three tax years preceding the current tax year from sales or leases outside the United States of property that would be export property if held by a DISC to (b) the borrower's gross receipts over the same period from the sale or lease of inventory property generally. § 993(d)(2). In addition, to ensure that producer's loans will be reflected in appropriate increased investment, the qualifying amount of producer's loans for the tax year may not exceed the sum of (i) the excess of the borrower's adjusted basis in the assets referred to in (1) and (2), above, at the end of the tax year over its basis in such assets at the beginning of the year and (ii) the borrower's research and experimental expenditures in the United States for such year. § 993(d)(3). Notwithstanding these limitations, there need be no tracing of the proceeds of producer's loans; the producer is not required to show that specific export-related manufacturing facilities or equipment have been financed with the proceeds of producer's loans.

To prevent the use of producer's loans to increase investment in foreign facilities, the amount of a DISC's tax-deferred income is reduced by the amount of any foreign investment attributable to such loans.

To prevent a disqualification of the DISC through unintentional failure to meet the 95–percent-export-gross-receipts or 95–percent-export-assets tests in a particular year, under certain conditions a DISC may make after-year-end deficiency distributions with regard to disqualifying items. § 992(c). If the DISC had at least 70 percent of its gross receipts in the form of qualified export receipts during the tax year, and at least 70 percent of its assets in the form of qualified export assets, a distribution of the income derived from non-qualified gross receipts (if the DISC fails to meet the export gross-receipts test) and the value of the non-qualified export assets held at the end of the year (if it fails to meet the export-assets test) can be made at any time within eight and one-half months after the close of the DISC's tax year. § 992(c)(3).

[¶ 11,205]

b. Tax Treatment of DISC Income

The DISC itself is not taxed on any of its income. § 991. Rather, it is the shareholder of the DISC that may be subject to taxation on a portion of the DISC's earnings and profits. § 995(a). In general, the portion of the DISC's income that does not qualify for deferral is taxed to its shareholders as a dividend currently, whether or not it is actually distributed, while the remainder is taxed to them when it is actually distributed as a dividend, when it is "deemed distributed," when the shareholder sells or otherwise disposes of stock in the DISC or when the corporation ceases to qualify as a DISC. § 995(b) and (c).

Under Section 995(b)(1), a shareholder is *deemed* to have received a distribution taxable as a dividend in an amount equal to the shareholder's pro rata share of the sum (or, if smaller, the earnings and profits of the DISC for the taxable year) of:

(1) the gross interest from producer's loans;

(2) the gain recognized by the DISC on the sale or exchange of property (other than qualified export assets) that was transferred to

the DISC in a transaction in which no gain was recognized, but only to the extent of the gain not recognized on the earlier transfer;

(3) the gain recognized by the DISC on the sale or exchange of property (except inventory), even if a qualified export asset, previously transferred to it in a tax-free transaction, but only to the extent that the transferor's gain was not recognized and would have been treated as ordinary income if the property had been sold;

(4) 50 percent of the taxable income of the DISC for the tax year attributable to military property;

(5) the taxable income of the DISC for the tax year attributable to qualified export receipts that exceed $10 million;

(6) the sum of

(a) 1/17th of the excess of the taxable income of the DISC for the tax year, before reduction for any distributions during the year, over the sum of the amounts deemed distributed for the tax year under subparagraphs (1), (2), (3), (4) and (5) above;

(b) an amount equal to 16/17ths of the amount determined under clause (a) multiplied by the international boycott factor determined under Section 999 with respect to operations involving participation in or cooperation with an international boycott; and

(c) any illegal bribe, kickback or other payment (within the meaning of Section 162(c)) paid by or on behalf of the DISC directly or indirectly to an official, employee or agent of a government; and

(7) the amount of foreign investment attributable to producer's loans (as defined in Section 995(d)) of a DISC for the tax year.

Item (7) is aimed at preventing the flow of tax-deferred profits of the DISC into the financing of foreign plants, equipment and other foreign assets. The effect of this foreign investment limitation is that the tax-deferred portion of the DISC's profits will be deemed to be distributed and taxed as a dividend to the shareholder to the extent of the "amount of foreign investment attributable to producer's loans" for the tax year. This amount is defined as the smallest of (i) the "net increase in foreign assets" by members of the controlled group of companies to which the DISC belongs; (ii) the "actual foreign investment" by domestic members of the group after 1971; or (iii) the amount of the DISC's outstanding producer's loans to members of the group. § 995(d)(1).

Actual dividend distributions to shareholders come first out of any income previously taxed (that is, income "deemed distributed") and then out of any untaxed income accumulated by the DISC. § 996(a)(1).

[¶ 11,210]

c. Sale or Other Disposition of DISC Stock

Gain from certain dispositions of DISC stock is included in the shareholder's gross income as a dividend to the extent of the accumulated tax-deferred DISC income attributable to the shareholder's stock. This treatment is applicable whenever stock in a DISC (or former DISC) is disposed of either in a transaction (such as a sale) in which gain is recognized or in a transaction (such as a reorganization) in which gain would not otherwise be recognized and in which the DISC ceases to exist as a separate corporate entity. § 995(c).

[¶ 11,215]

d. Termination of DISC Status

Upon termination of the DISC election or disqualification of the DISC, the earnings and profits of the DISC on which U.S. taxes have been deferred during the years in which the corporation qualified as a DISC are deemed distributed to the shareholders. § 995(b)(2)(A). The shareholders are taxed on their pro rata share of the deferred income in equal installments over the ten years after termination or disqualification or over such shorter period as does not exceed twice the number of immediately preceding consecutive tax years during which the corporation qualified as a DISC. § 995(b)(2)(B).

[¶ 11,220]

e. Profits Attributable to DISC: Intercompany Pricing Rules

In the case of export property sold to a DISC by a related party, the Section 482 arm's length standards are augmented, pursuant to Section 994(a), by two safe harbor pricing rules. No reallocations are required under Section 482 if the intercompany pricing is such that the DISC will not derive more taxable income than the greater of:

(1) four percent of the qualified export receipts on sales by the DISC, plus ten percent of the export promotion expenses of the DISC attributable to those receipts; or

(2) 50 percent of the combined taxable income of the DISC and the related person attributable to the qualified export receipts on the sale of export property, plus ten percent of the export promotion expenses attributable to those receipts.

Export promotion expenses include those expenses incurred to advance the distribution or sale of export property for use, consumption or distribution outside the United States, exclusive of income taxes. § 994(c). Although both of the pricing rules generally are to be applied on a product-by-product basis, the rules may be applied on the basis of product lines. Reg. § 1.994–1(c)(7)(i).

Where a DISC is attempting to establish a market abroad or seeking to maintain a market abroad for exports, Reg. § 1.994–2 sets forth special marginal costing rules governing the allocation of expenses incurred on the sale of the export property for purposes of determining the combined taxable income of the related person and the DISC. For the purpose of applying the second pricing rule, the regulation allows the combined taxable income on the sale of export property to reflect a profit equal to that which the DISC and a related party would earn if they took into account only the marginal costs of producing the property.

Neither the four-percent method nor the 50–50–profit-split method can be applied to cause a loss to the related supplier while the DISC is earning a net profit. Reg. § 1.994–1(e)(1)(i); see Archer–Daniels–Midland Co. v. United States, 37 F.3d 321 (7th Cir. 1994).

[¶ 11,225]

f. Availability of Foreign Tax Credit

Actual and constructive dividends from a DISC (or former DISC) are treated as dividends from foreign sources (i.e., assimilated to dividends from a foreign corporation) to the extent they are attributable to qualified export receipts (other than U.S.-source interest) of the DISC. § 861(a)(2)(D). Thus, a DISC shareholder is entitled to a Section 902 indirect foreign tax credit with respect to any foreign income taxes paid by the DISC. However, a DISC shareholder for purposes of the Section 904(d)(1) limitations on the foreign tax credit cannot use its excess foreign tax credits with respect to income in the general category income basket to offset its U.S. tax liability on dividends received by the shareholder from the DISC. These dividends are placed in the passive category income basket as specified passive category income. § 904(d)(2)(B)(v)(I). Thus, cross-crediting within the passive category income basket will be permitted.

[¶ 11,230]

I. THE EXTRATERRITORIAL INCOME EXCLUSION REGIME

The principal provisions embodying the exclusion for extraterritorial income were former Section 114 and former Sections 941 through 943, enacted by the 2000 Act. The Act repealed the FSC rules contained in former Sections 921 through 927 of the Code, subject to the transition rules discussed at ¶ 11,185, and it substituted an extraterritorial income ("ETI") exclusion. Under this regime gross income for U.S. tax purposes did not include the portion of extraterritorial income that met the definition of "qualifying foreign trade income." Former § 114(a) and (b). "Extraterritorial income" was gross income attributable to foreign trading gross receipts as defined in former Section 942. Former § 114(e). Because the exclusion of such extraterritorial income precluded international double taxation, no foreign tax credit was allowed for foreign income taxes paid with respect to such excluded income. Former § 114(d). Moreover, under U.S. income tax principles that generally deny deductions for expenses related to exempt income, otherwise deductible expenses that were allocated and apportioned to excluded qualifying foreign trade income were generally disallowed. Former § 114(c)(1). Deductions properly allocated and apportioned to extraterritorial income from any transaction are to be allocated proportionately between excluded and nonexcludable extraterritorial income. Former § 114(c)(2).

The ETI regime applied in the same manner with respect to both individuals and corporations who were U.S. taxpayers. In addition, the exclusion from gross income applied for individual and corporate alternative minimum tax purposes. The following summary of the exclusion regime draws extensively on H.R. Conf. Rep. No. 106–1004, 106th Cong., 2d Sess. 207 (2000).

Qualifying foreign trade income was defined as "the amount of gross income which, if excluded, would result in a reduction of the taxable income of the taxpayer equal to the greatest of

> (A) 30 percent of the foreign sale and leasing income derived by the taxpayer from the transaction;
>
> (B) 1.2 percent of the foreign trading gross receipts derived by the taxpayer from the transaction; or
>
> (C) 15 percent of the foreign trade income derived by the taxpayer from the transaction."

Former § 941(a)(1). If the method based on 1.2 percent of the foreign trading gross receipts was used, the amount of qualifying foreign trade income was limited to twice the qualifying foreign trade income that would have resulted using 15 percent of the foreign trade income. Id. The three methods were applied to reduce *taxable* income, and qualifying foreign trade income was an exclusion from *gross* income. Therefore, after determining the reduction of taxable income under the method selected by the taxpayer, that amount had to be "grossed up" for related expenses in order to determine the amount of gross income excluded.

The amount of qualifying foreign trade income could be determined either on a transaction-by-transaction basis or on an aggregate basis for groups of transactions, provided that the groups were based on product lines or recognized industry or trade usage. Former § 943(b)(1)(B). Qualifying foreign trade income had to be reduced by illegal bribes, kickbacks and similar payments, former Section 941(a)(5)(B), and the amount that resulted by multiplying such income by the international boycott factor used under Section 999(c)(1) in connection with operations involving participation in or cooperation with an international boycott. Former § 941(a)(5)(A). See ¶ 14,070.

As noted above, qualifying foreign trade income was determined with reference to "foreign trading gross receipts," "foreign trade income" or "foreign sale and leasing income." Former § 941(a)(1). "Foreign trading gross receipts" were gross receipts derived through "economic processes" carried on outside the United States that were receipts (1) from the sale, exchange or other disposition of qualifying foreign trade property; (2) from the lease or license of qualifying foreign trade property; (3) for services which were related and subsidiary to the sale, exchange, disposition, lease or rental of qualifying foreign trade property; (4) for engineering or architectural services for construction projects located outside the United States and (5) for the performance of certain managerial services for unrelated persons in furtherance of the producing of foreign trade receipts if at least 50 percent of the foreign trading gross receipts (excluding those for managerial services) fell into categories (1), (2) or (3). Former § 942(a)(1). The FSC regulations dealing with the definition of foreign trading gross receipts were to apply.

A taxpayer could elect to treat gross receipts from a transaction as not constituting foreign trading gross receipts. Former § 942(a)(3). As a consequence of such an election, the taxpayer could utilize any related foreign tax credits in lieu of the exclusion as a means of avoiding double taxation.

"Foreign trade income" meant the taxable income of the taxpayer attributable to its foreign trading gross receipts. Former § 941(b)(1). "Foreign sale and leasing income" included foreign trade income derived by the taxpayer in connection with the leasing or licensing of qualifying foreign trade property for use by the lessee or licensee outside the United States. Former § 941(c)(1)(B).

As under the FSC regime, gross receipts from each transaction were foreign trading gross receipts only if generated through certain economic processes that took place outside the United States. Former § 942(b)(1). An exception from the foreign economic processes requirement was provided for taxpayers with foreign trading gross receipts for the year of $5 million or less. Former § 942(c)(1). For this purpose, the receipts of related persons were aggregated and, in the case of pass-through entities, the determination of whether the foreign trading gross receipts exceeded $5 million was made both at the entity and at the partner/shareholder level. Former § 942(c)(2) and (3).

As noted above, gross receipts were treated as foreign trading gross receipts only if the gross receipts were derived from a transaction involving sale, lease or license for use outside the United States of "qualifying foreign trade property" or certain related services or engineering or architectural services. Qualifying foreign trade property was property manufactured, produced, grown or extracted ("manufactured") that was held primarily for sale, lease or rental, in the ordinary course of a trade or business, for direct use, consumption or disposition outside the United States (including Puerto Rico). Former § 943(a)(1)(A) and (B). Importantly, not more than 50 percent of the fair market value (based on its appraised value for customs purposes) of qualifying foreign trade property could be attributable to (1) the fair market value of articles manufactured outside the United States plus (2) the direct costs of labor performed outside the United States. Former § 943(a)(1)(C).

In a radical departure from the FSC rules, under the ETI exclusion regime, property could be treated as qualifying foreign trade property whether manufactured inside or outside the United States. Former § 943(a)(1)(A). However, as under the FSC regime, property constituted qualifying foreign trade property only if it was held primarily for lease, sale or rental, in the ordinary course of business, for direct use, consumption or disposition outside the United States. Former § 943(a)(1)(A) and (B).

As in the case of the FSC, certain property was excluded from the definition of qualifying foreign trade property. The exclusions included: (1) property leased or rented by the taxpayer for use by a related person, (2) certain intangibles, (3) oil and gas (or any primary product thereof), (4) products subject to export restrictions, (5) unprocessed softwood timber and (6) property designated by Executive Order as in short supply. Former § 943(a)(3) and (4).

With respect to property that was manufactured outside the United States, rules were provided to ensure consistent U.S. tax treatment with respect to manufacturers. To be treated as qualifying foreign trade property, such property had to be manufactured by (1) a U.S. corporation, (2) an individual who was a U.S. citizen or resident, (3) a foreign corporation that elected to be subject to U.S. taxation in the same manner as a U.S. corporation, or (4) a partnership or other pass-through entity all of the partners or owners of which were described in (1), (2), or (3) above. Former § 943(a)(2). Thus, property manufactured by a foreign branch of a U.S. corporation qualified.

Under former Section 943(e)(1), certain foreign corporations could elect, on an original return, to be treated as U.S. corporations. Such election was available for a foreign corporation (1) that manufactured property in the ordinary course of the corporation's trade or business or (2) if substantially all of its gross receipts were foreign trading gross receipts. Former § 943(e)(2). In order to make this election, the foreign corporation had to waive all benefits granted to such corporation by the United States pursuant to any income tax treaty. Absent such a waiver, it would have been unclear, for example, whether the permanent establishment article of a relevant tax treaty would override the electing corporation's treatment as a U.S. corporation under this provision.

Section 101 of the 2004 JOBS Act repealed the ETI exclusion of former Section 114 in an effort to comply with the determination by the

WTO that the exclusion constituted an illegal export subsidy. As discussed at ¶ 11,185, repeal was necessitated by retaliatory sanctions imposed by the EU under authorization of the WTO in the form of tariffs at increasingly punitive rates on certain goods that were imported from the United States. The repeal of the ETI exclusion, however, was not outright.

There are two sets of transitional rules contained in Section 101(d)-(f) of the JOBS Act. The first provides that the ETI exclusion remains in effect for any transaction between the taxpayer and a person who was not a related person (as defined in former Section 943(b)(3)) which occurs pursuant to a binding contract in effect on September 17, 2003. A binding contract includes a purchase option, renewal option or replacement option, which is included in the contract and is enforceable against the seller or lessor.

The second transitional rule applies to all transactions that would have qualified for the ETI exclusion before repeal. Under this rule, taxpayers were entitled to 80 percent of the ETI benefits for transactions during 2005 and 60 percent for transactions during 2006. Foreign corporations that elected to be treated as U.S. corporations in order to claim ETI benefits could revoke such elections within one year of enactment of the JOBS Act without recognition of gain or loss, subject to anti-abuse rules as prescribed in regulations.

Although the EU terminated the retaliatory customs duties on U.S. exports after repeal of the ETI regime in the JOBS Act, the EU attacked the liberal transitional rules. The EU requested that the WTO Dispute Settlement Body establish a panel to determine whether these rules themselves constituted an export subsidy in violation of WTO agreements. On September 30, 2005, the WTO announced the decision of the panel upholding the EU position that the ETI regime transitional rules violated WTO agreements. Panel Report, United States—Tax Treatment for "Foreign Sales Corporations", WT/DS 108/RW2, Sept. 30, 2005.

To ease the economic pain caused by elimination of ETI benefits, the JOBS Act provided a new deduction in Section 199 for corporations, pass-through entities and individuals of increasing percentages of income from "qualified production activities" in the United States. For tax years starting in 2010, the deduction percentage reached nine percent. § 199(a)(1). The deduction is limited to 50 percent of the wages paid by the taxpayer during the calendar year that ends in the tax year for which the deduction is allowable. § 199(b).

The deduction is also allowed in calculating the alternative minimum tax. § 199(d)(6). Certain affiliated corporate groups (defined to include 50 percent-owned U.S. and foreign corporations) are treated as a single taxpayer and the deduction is allocated among the members in proportion to each member's respective amount (if any) of qualified production activities income. § 199(d)(4). The effect of the deduction is to reduce in stages (corresponding to the increasing levels of the deduction) the maximum U.S. tax on qualifying income in 2010 and thereafter to 32 percent. The effect of the phase-in may be summarized as follows:

Taxable Year	2005–2006	2007–2009	2010 and later
Manufacturing Deduction Percentage	3%	6%	9%
Equivalent Manufacturing Tax-rate Reduction	1%	2%	3%
Resulting Effective Tax Rate	34%	33%	32%

This deduction is available whether or not the U.S. taxpayer ever claimed ETI benefits.

[¶ 11,235]

J. FINANCING OF EXPORTS

If a U.S. person lends funds to a foreign purchaser of goods manufactured in the United States with predominately U.S.-origin materials and components, the interest received will be excluded from the separate basket for passive income because it will qualify as export financing interest. § 904(d)(2)(B)(iii)(I) and (d)(2)(G). As export financing interest, it will be included in the Section 904(d)(1)(B)) general income limitation basket. The interest will normally be deductible by the borrower, and in many cases the interest will be exempt from withholding tax in the borrower's country. Occasionally, the exemption from withholding tax will be granted under the tax law of the borrower's country. More often, it will be provided by an applicable tax treaty, provided that the interest is not attributable to a permanent establishment maintained by the lender in the borrower's country. If the interest is exempt from tax in the source country and falls in the general limitation basket, it will be helpful in absorbing excess foreign tax credits otherwise generated by other general limitation income.

Notwithstanding the generally applicable exclusion from passive income for export financing interest, such interest may be considered passive income if it constitutes related person factoring income under Section 864(d)(1) or (6). As discussed at ¶ 6090, Section 864(d)(1) treats income from a trade or service receivable acquired from a related person as "interest" and Section 864(d)(6) does the same for interest received by a controlled foreign corporation on a loan to any person to finance the purchase of inventory or services from a related person. As discussed at ¶ 7010, income treated as interest under either of these rules falls into the passive income basket. Temp. Reg. § 1.904–4T(h)(3).

Under the related person factoring rules, if a U.S. corporation wants to provide export financing for exported goods manufactured in the United States by a related person, the form adopted may make an important difference. If the U.S. corporation buys receivables from the related person, the corporation's resulting income is treated as income that falls in the passive income basket, but if the U.S. corporation lends funds directly to the person buying the goods from the related person, the interest will be export financing interest that falls in the general limitation basket. See Temp. Reg. § 1.904–4T(h)(3)(ii); Reg. § 1.904–4(h)(2), (4), Exs. 2, 3.

If a controlled foreign corporation buys trade or service receivables from a related person or lends funds to a purchaser (whether related or unrelated) of goods manufactured by the U.S. parent corporation of the controlled foreign corporation, the income is treated as interest which is generally excluded from export financing interest and falls into the passive income basket. § 864(d)(5)(A)(i) and (6); Temp. Reg. § 1.904–4T(h)(3)(i).

However, in the case in which a controlled foreign corporation buys receivables from a related person, Section 864(d)(7) provides that income that would otherwise be treated as interest under Section 864(d)(1) will not be so treated if the person acquiring the receivables and the related person are organized in the same foreign country and certain other requirements are met. Temp. Reg. § 1.864–8T(d). If this same-country exception applies, this related person factoring income will fall into the general limitation basket.

[¶ 11,240]

K. EXPORT INCENTIVE POLICY ISSUES

As discussed above, over the years Congress followed a fairly consistent pattern of providing tax incentives to encourage exports. The most obvious examples have been the Western Hemisphere trade corporation (discussed in the *A.P. Green Export Co.* case at ¶ 2120), the export trade corporation, the DISC, the FSC and, most recently, the extraterritorial income exclusion, which was repealed, subject to liberal transitional rules, by the 2004 JOBS Act. Before 1962, a controlled foreign corporation in a tax haven could earn income from U.S. exports free of foreign tax and free of U.S. tax until the income was distributed to U.S. shareholders. All of these incentives lowered the effective total U.S. tax burden on export income and therefore enabled the U.S. exporter to charge lower prices without reducing net profit. This was done either by reducing the U.S. tax rate on export income (Western Hemisphere trade corporation), by exempting a portion of the export income from tax (FSC and extraterritorial income exclusion) or by permitting deferral of U.S. tax on some or all of the export income (pre–1962 controlled foreign corporation, export trade corporation and DISC). All of these tax benefits for exports, except the interest-charge DISC, have been repealed.

Another important export tax benefit that has been preserved is the benefit accorded export income under Sections 865(b) and 863(b) that permit a U.S. manufacturer to create foreign-source export income by passing title on exports outside the United States. This income is general limitation income and when, as is often the case, it bears no foreign tax, it permits use of excess foreign tax credits generated by other high-taxed general limitation income.

In addition, other less dramatic tax incentives for exports, which have been retained in the Code, are the various respects in which favorable treatment is accorded to export financing interest under the Section 904 limitations on the foreign tax credit.

These tax incentives to export income violate the principle of capital-export neutrality to the extent that they create a tax disincentive to investment in manufacturing facilities abroad. The following excerpt from Joint Comm. on Tax'n, 102d Cong., 1st Sess., Factors Affecting the International Competitiveness of the United States, at 256–57 (1991), suggests that these export incentives or, more bluntly, export subsidies, reduce the overall economic welfare of the United States:

> A fundamental decision facing any U.S. business is whether to locate some portion of production overseas. In the case of business that sells products overseas, the investment location decision to invest abroad or domestically can be influenced by the availability of tax incentives for exports. Export subsidies, like tariffs that penalize imports, reduce global economic welfare. Furthermore, although they undoubtedly improve the lot of the favored export sector, they generally can be expected to reduce the overall economic welfare of the nation providing the subsidy. Nevertheless, tax and other export incentives may reduce the incentive of U.S. businesses to locate production abroad. There are two major U.S. tax incentives providing favorable treatment to the taxation of income from exports. The first of these is the so-called "title passage rule" and the second are the [since repealed] provisions available to exporters who make use of foreign sales corporations ("FSCs").
>
> ***Title Passage Rule***
>
> As a general rule of U.S. taxation, the residence of the seller determines the source of income from the sale of personal property. However, a major exception is provided in that sales of inventory are sourced in the location where the goods are sold—generally where title passes. In the case where goods are manufactured in the United States and sold overseas, regulations provide an allocation formula which may result in as little as one-half of this income being sourced domestically, even though most of the value is added in the United

States and the income from these sales might not be subject to any foreign income tax. The title passage rule provides additional foreign tax credits to multinational enterprises with high foreign taxes by increasing foreign source income and, thus, the foreign tax credit limitation. The title passage rule, therefore, potentially provides a strong incentive for a U.S. firm that pays high foreign taxes on other income not to locate some portion of its additional production overseas. On the other hand, in order to take advantage of the rule, some portion of activity generally must take place overseas in order to generate the high foreign taxes that shelter income sourced foreign under the rule. Therefore, the title passage rule has much less incentive effect, for either domestic or outbound investment, or for exports, on a company with no foreign investment or tax liability. The rule may, however, make such a company an attractive takeover target to a high foreign-taxpaying company that can benefit from the former company's ability to generate untaxed foreign source income. The tax expenditure budget indicates that the title passage rule will provide an $18 billion subsidy to exporters over the 1992–1996 period.

As a result of the prohibition of WTO agreements against tax subsidies for exports, Congress has been compelled to repeal all direct export subsidies, except the modest export incentive embodied in the interest-charge DISC provisions. The most significant remaining tax benefit for exports from the United States is the title passage rule. Presumably because it is not a direct subsidy to exports, this rule has not been alleged by U.S. trade competitors to violate the WTO prohibitions against tax subsidies contingent on exports.

The assumption on which all of the tax benefits accorded by Congress in the last several decades to encourage exports are based is that exports increase U.S. jobs and improve the current trade portion of the U.S. international balance of payments. While it is clear that the tax benefits intended to encourage exports have significantly reduced the tax burden on major U.S. exporters, it is not clear whether a commensurate increase in exports has resulted. Thus, there remains the fundamental policy question of whether tax incentives to exports, or more broadly to extraterritorial income, can be justified when viewed in the context of the overall economic welfare of the United States.

Chapter 12

Exploitation of Intangible Property Rights Abroad

■ ■ ■

[¶ 12,000]

A. INTRODUCTION

In considering the U.S. and foreign tax aspects of exploiting abroad intangible property rights, such as rights to foreign patents, confidential knowhow, trade secrets, copyrights, trademarks and franchises, it is convenient to analyze separately five different situations:

(1) the licensing of intangible property rights to an independent or affiliated licensee in consideration for continuing royalties;

(2) the transfer of intangible property rights to an independent or affiliated transferee in exchange for royalty-like or fixed payments that are treated as capital gain;

(3) the transfer of intangible property rights to a foreign corporation in exchange for its stock (e.g., in a Section 351 exchange or a Section 361 reorganization exchange) or as a contribution to capital;

(4) the sharing of intangible property rights pursuant to a cost sharing arrangement under which related parties agree to share the cost and risks of developing intangible property in return for an interest in any intangible property created and

(5) the handling of international licensing of foreign intangible property rights through a foreign base company organized in a country having favorable legal and tax regimes.

Transfers of intangible property between commonly controlled persons involved in any of the foregoing situations are subject to the basic requirement that the pricing arrangements meet the arm's length standards imposed by Section 482, discussed in Chapter 8 and ¶¶ 12,200 et seq. The IRS is, in effect, empowered to shift income, deductions and credits between commonly controlled persons in order to produce the tax results that would have been obtained if the commonly controlled persons had been dealing as independent parties at arm's length.

"Intangible" for purposes of the Section 482 regulations is given the following definition, which closely tracks the definition in Section 936(h)(3)(B) for purposes of the former Puerto Rico and possessions tax credit:

> * * * [A]n asset that comprises any of the following items and has substantial value independent of the services of any individual—
>
> (1) Patents, inventions, formulae, processes, designs, patterns, or know-how;
>
> (2) Copyrights and literary, musical, or artistic compositions;
>
> (3) Trademarks, trade names, or brand names;
>
> (4) Franchises, licenses, or contracts;
>
> (5) Methods, programs, systems, procedures, campaigns, surveys, studies, forecasts, estimates, customer lists, or technical data; and
>
> (6) Other similar items. For purposes of section 482, an item is considered similar to those listed in paragraph (b)(1) through (5) of this section if it derives its value not from its physical attributes but from its intellectual content or other intangible properties.

Reg. § 1.482–4(b).

A new element was introduced by the Tax Reform Act of 1986, which added the following sentence to Section 482:

> In the case of any transfer (or license) of intangible property (within the meaning of Section 936(h)(3)(B)), the income with respect to such transfer or license shall be commensurate with the income attributable to the intangible.

A similar provision was added to Section 367(d) (see ¶ 12,130). The uncertainties created by this provision, which has come to be called the "super-royalty" provision, are discussed in ¶ 12,205.

Eventually, detailed regulations were issued clarifying how the arm's length standard is to be applied to the various categories of transfers of intangibles between commonly controlled taxpayers. These regulations, which also clarify the requirement that the income of the transferor be commensurate with the income attributable to the intangible, are discussed in ¶¶ 12,215 through 12,250.

In a number of contexts, it is important to distinguish among various types of intangible property. For example, differing tax consequences may turn on whether the subject matter of a particular transfer agreement is foreign trademarks, franchise rights, patents or unpatented confidential knowhow.

B. LICENSING INTANGIBLE PROPERTY RIGHTS TO AN INDEPENDENT OR AFFILIATED LICENSEE IN CONSIDERATION FOR CONTINUING ROYALTIES

[¶ 12,005]

1. TAX INCENTIVES TO LICENSING

U.S. tax considerations generally do not represent a major incentive to the licensing of intangible property rights by a U.S. licensor to unaffiliated parties abroad or to affiliates not controlled by the licensor. Such licensing is usually adopted as a technique for exploiting intangible property for business reasons quite independently of tax factors. For example, the licensing of foreign patents and knowhow is a classic method of obtaining a return from foreign markets on research and development expenditures without making a major investment abroad. However, in some cases, a U.S. corporation that is in an excess foreign tax credit position will be able to use excess foreign tax credits against the U.S. tax on royalties from unaffiliated or affiliated but noncontrolled licensees abroad under licenses of foreign patents and knowhow. Because royalties are often subject to little or no tax in the foreign country in which the licensee is located, if they fall in the general category income limitation basket, they can be particularly helpful in absorbing excess foreign tax credits generated by other high-taxed general limitation income. The royalties will be general limitation income only when they qualify as royalties that are derived in the active conduct of a trade or business whether received from unrelated or related persons. Temp. Reg. § 1.904–4T(b)(2)(iii). If they so qualify, they are excluded from passive income under Sections 904(d)(2)(A)(i) and 954(c)(2)(A) and therefore are treated as general limitation income subject to the Section 904(d)(1)(B) limitation on the U.S. foreign tax credit.

Moreover, tax factors may influence the *form* in which transfers of intangible rights to noncontrolled foreign transferees are cast. Before the elimination of the preferential tax rate on long-term capital gains realized by corporations, transfers of intangible property rights were often structured with the objective of having the payments qualify for long-term capital gains treatment. Under current law, while an individual enjoys a preference in the rate of tax on long-term capital gains, the sole tax advantage of capital gain treatment for a corporation is that capital losses can be deducted only against its capital gains. Thus, a corporation that has a capital loss carryforward or anticipates capital losses in the current year or in future years will have an incentive to qualify intangible property right transfers as sales of capital or Section 1231 assets.

Tax considerations often create major incentives for the licensing of intangible property rights to foreign affiliates controlled by the licensor. Under the Section 904(d)(1)(B) general income limitation on the foreign tax credit, a U.S. corporation may have an incentive to set up foreign licensing arrangements when a substantial portion of the U.S. corporation's foreign-source income is in the form of dividends from operating controlled foreign corporations located in high-tax countries. If the foreign taxes on profits distributed as dividends are in excess of the U.S. effective corporate tax rate, the dividend income will generate excess foreign tax credit. This excess credit could be used against the U.S. taxes on foreign-source income received from controlled foreign corporations in the form of royalties that are tax-exempt or taxed at a lower foreign tax rate than the effective U.S. corporate rate as a result of foreign law or an applicable income tax treaty. This conclusion assumes that the controlled foreign corporation is engaged in the manufacture and sale of products or other active business operations and that the dividends and royalties it pays to its U.S. parent corporation will both fall within the Section 904(d)(1)(B) general income foreign tax credit limitation basket under the Section 904(d)(3) look-through rules. Unless the U.S. corporation has some foreign-source income, such as royalty income, which has been subjected to foreign income taxes at rates lower than the effective U.S. corporate tax rate and which is included in the general limitation basket, the excess credit for foreign taxes imposed at rates in excess of the U.S. rate may not be usable in the current year but may be eligible to be carried back or forward under Section 904(c).

[¶ 12,010]

2. TAX TREATMENT OF ROYALTIES IN THE SOURCE COUNTRY

Under the tax laws of most foreign countries, royalty payments under an exclusive or nonexclusive license are deductible by the licensee as business expenses. If the licensor and licensee are related entities, however, the amount of the royalties will often be closely scrutinized by the foreign tax authorities, and the deduction will be denied to the extent that the royalties are excessive when judged against the standard of a royalty rate that might reasonably have been adopted by independent parties dealing at arm's length. A similar arm's length standard is contained in the U.S. income tax treaties. See, e.g., U.S. Model Treaty (Appendix A), Art.12(4). The portion of a royalty deduction denied as excessive is usually treated for tax purposes as a dividend.

The U.S. income tax treaties also provide that royalties under exclusive or nonexclusive licenses are exempt from income tax or are subject to reduced tax in the source country so long as the licensor does not have a permanent establishment in that country to which the royalties are attributable. If such treaty exemption does not apply, royalties are subject to the normally applicable (or reduced treaty) rate of tax that must be withheld by the licensee in the source country on royalties paid to foreign licensors. Occasionally, such royalties are exempt from withholding tax under the law of the source country.

When an agreement transferring foreign patents to a foreign transferee is cast in the form of an outright assignment or sale in consideration for fixed payments or royalty-like contingent payments spread over the life of the patents or a specified number of years, the law of the source country may not permit the payments to be deducted as expenses. Rather, the payments may have to be capitalized as the cost of the patents and amortized by the transferee over the shorter of the remaining life of the patents or term of the agreement. Furthermore, when intangible property rights, such as trademarks or knowhow, have no determinable life or the license under which rights thereto are granted does not have a fixed term, it may be impossible under local law for the transferee to amortize the cost thereof. Amortization rates may be subject to negotiation with the local tax authorities, and it may be possible, even if the payments are contingent on the transferee's sales, to obtain approval for an amortization deduction schedule that corresponds with the annual payments called for under the agreement. This is the position in the United States when there has been a sale of a patent in return for payments geared to the transferee's production or sales.[1] Under many U.S. income tax treaties, fixed or contingent payments under an assignment or sale of intangible property rights are exempt from income taxation in the source country, provided the recipient has no permanent establishment there to which the rights are attributable. They may also be exempt under the law of the source country.

[¶ 12,015]

3. TAX TREATMENT OF ROYALTIES IN THE UNITED STATES; THE ACTIVE–BUSINESS TEST

Royalties received by a U.S. licensor from a foreign licensee under a patent, knowhow or trademark license are treated for U.S. tax purposes as ordinary income unless, under the principles to be examined in the following section, the license is treated as a sale of a capital or a Section 1231 asset, the income from which is characterized as capital gain. Any foreign income taxes withheld at the source are creditable for purposes of the direct foreign tax credit under Section 901 or Section 903 within the limits set by Section 904. Other taxes, including turnover taxes, imposed upon royalties by the source country are generally not creditable, but are

1. See Associated Patentees, Inc. v. Commissioner, 4 T.C. 979 (1945) (acq.).

deductible, for U.S. tax purposes. Expenses of the licensor properly allocated and apportioned to the royalties are deductible in computing taxable income for U.S. tax purposes. Those expenses will include amortization deductions taken over the useful life of the intangibles (e.g., the life of the foreign patent) or, in the case of purchased amortizable Section 197 intangibles, over the 15–year period beginning with the month of their purchase.

As suggested at ¶ 12,005, it will be important to determine whether royalties received directly by a U.S. person from foreign licensees are derived in the active conduct of a trade or business. If they are, such royalties received from a licensee that is not a related person to the recipient under Section 954(d)(3) will fall in the Section 904(d)(1)(B) general income limitation basket for foreign tax credit limitation purposes. Under Temp. Reg. § 1.904–4T(b)(2)(iii), this treatment has been also extended to royalties received from related persons. (Such royalties from related persons will still be treated as foreign personal holding company income under Subpart F.) Royalties received by a U.S. shareholder from a controlled foreign corporation are subject to the Section 904(d)(3) look-through rules. Because royalties are often subject to a low rate of foreign tax or to no foreign tax in the licensee's country, if they qualify as general limitation income, they will usually be very helpful in absorbing excess tax credits that are generated by other general limitation income. If the royalties from unrelated or related licensees (other than controlled foreign corporations) are not derived in the active conduct of business, they will fall in the Section 904(d)(1)(A) passive income basket and will be of benefit only in absorbing excess foreign tax credits with respect to passive income.

Under the original Subpart F rules, the active-business test for royalties received from unrelated persons applied only to *controlled foreign corporations* under Section 954(c)(2)(A). If this test was met, royalties were excluded from the definition of foreign personal holding company income that could be taxed as a Subpart F inclusion to U.S. shareholders although not actually distributed to them. Under the separate basket regime for calculating foreign tax credits introduced in the 1986 Act, however, the active-business test became applicable to *U.S. persons* because passive income of a U.S. person is defined as income that would constitute foreign personal holding company income if received by a controlled foreign corporation. Consequently, if a U.S. person receives royalties from persons who are not related persons as defined in Section 954(d)(3) and the royalties are derived in the active conduct of a trade or business, the royalties are excluded from the passive income basket and fall in the general limitation basket. §§ 904(d)(2)(A)(i) and 954(c)(2)(A). Under Temp. Reg. § 1.904–4T(b)(2)(iii), the same is true even if the royalties are received (after September 20, 2004) from related persons.

Reg. § 1.954–2(d)(1) expands the active-business concept by providing that the test will be met (by a controlled foreign corporation or a U.S. person) if royalties are received from licensing intangible property covered by either of the following two descriptions:

> (i) Property that the licensor has developed, created or produced, or has acquired and added substantial value to, but only so long as the licensor is regularly engaged in the development, creation or production of, or in the acquisition of and addition of substantial value to, property of such kind; or
>
> (ii) Property that is licensed as a result of the performance of marketing functions by such licensor if the licensor, through its own officers or staff of employees located in a foreign country, maintains and operates an organization in such country that is regularly engaged in the business of marketing, or of marketing and servicing, the licensed property and that is substantial in relation to the amount of royalties derived from the licensing of the property.

Under the former description, U.S. corporations that exploit inventions generated through their own research and development efforts by licensing them for royalties will meet the active-business test. The regulations go on to spell out a safe harbor test for determining whether a foreign organization that is involved exclusively in marketing and servicing foreign patent rights obtained from others will be considered to be substantial in relation to the royalties received. An organization will be considered substantial if "active licensing expenses" equal at least 25 percent of "adjusted licensing profit." Reg. § 1.954–2(d)(2)(ii).

[¶ 12,020]

PROBLEM

Comet Corporation ("Comet"), a U.S. corporation, is in the regular business of buying U.S. and foreign pharmaceutical patents from small laboratories. Comet has a staff of employees in the United States who include scientists, technicians and administrative, financial and marketing personnel. Comet's employees are responsible for designing production equipment, testing the patented processes, shepherding the drugs through clinical trials and the procedures required for Food and Drug Administration approvals and eventually commercializing them, by licensing the inventions to unrelated large drug companies in the United States and abroad in return for royalties equal to a specified percentage of the net sales by the licensees.

What is the source of royalties received by Comet? In what foreign tax credit limitation basket do they fall?

[¶ 12,025]

C. CAPITAL GAINS LICENSING

If an assignment or license of foreign patents, trademarks or knowhow constitutes a transfer of all substantial rights to the intangible property concerned, the assignment or license will, under certain circumstances, be deemed a sale of a capital asset[2] or a "Section 1231 asset"[3] for tax purposes. E.g., E.I. Du Pont de Nemours & Co. v. United States, 432 F.2d 1052 (3d Cir.1970). In this case, royalties received by the transferor are treated as the purchase price for the intangible property rights concerned and may be treated as long-term capital gain, assuming that the applicable holding period requirement is met and that the intangible property rights concerned do not constitute inventory property and are not held by the U.S. transferor primarily for sale to customers in the ordinary course of business.[4]

Most of the tax law bearing on capital gains licensing has developed in the patent and trademark areas and, in these areas, the basic principles are generally well established. In the area of knowhow licensing, however, there is less certainty concerning the applicable principles, although Rev. Rul. 64–56, at ¶ 12,145, and a number of cases have shed considerable light on the views of the IRS and the courts.

[¶ 12,030]

1. PATENTS, KNOWHOW, COPYRIGHTS AND TRADEMARKS AS CAPITAL OR SECTION 1231 ASSETS

A transfer of patents, knowhow, trade secrets, trademarks, trade names or copyrights can result in a long-term capital gain to the transferor only if the property rights concerned constitute capital or Section 1231 assets. Each of these intangibles involves a monopoly or quasi-monopoly enjoyed by the owner and therefore constitutes property. As such, each intangible may qualify as a capital or Section 1231 asset if not held as inventory or primarily for sale to customers.

---

2. Section 1235 provides that a transfer for value of all substantial rights in a patent by certain "holders" is deemed to constitute a sale or exchange of a capital asset held more than one year. Because a corporation cannot qualify as a "holder," Section 1235 is not considered in detail in this discussion.

3. Section 1231 assets consist of real property or depreciable or amortizable personal property used in trade or business and held for more than one year, with exceptions spelled out in Section 1231(b). Patents normally constitute Section 1231 assets. See ¶ 12,030.

4. Property properly includible in inventory and property held primarily for sale to customers in the ordinary course of a trade or business are excluded from the definition of capital assets under Section 1221(a)(1) and from the definition of Section 1231 assets under Section 1231(b)(1)(A) and (B).

[¶ 12,035]

a. Patents, Patent Applications and Trademarks

A patent is an exclusive right granted to an inventor to use, manufacture and sell the patented invention and to exclude others from doing so. It is essentially a monopoly issued to the patentee in exchange for publication of the invention disclosed in the application. In the United States and in many, but not all, foreign countries the patent is valid for 21 years from the date of application. A trademark protects the holder's exclusive right to use a registered mark on specified goods in commerce. It may be renewed without limit.

It is beyond dispute that patents and patent applications may constitute capital assets. See, e.g., Commissioner v. Celanese Corp. of America, 140 F.2d 339 (D.C.Cir.1944). Further, if patents are used in trade or business, as they normally are when held by a corporation, they constitute amortizable property and as such will be deemed to qualify as Section 1231 assets, (e.g., Merck & Co. v. Smith, 261 F.2d 162 (3d Cir.1958)), provided that the applicable holding period requirement is met. It is also clear that trademarks and trade names and their associated goodwill are usually capital assets, Reid v. Commissioner, 26 T.C. 622 (1956) (acq.), unless they constitute amortizable Section 197 intangibles, in which case they will be Section 1231 assets.

[¶ 12,040]

b. Knowhow

Proprietary knowhow is essentially secret or confidential information not known to the public that may not lawfully be disclosed to third parties without the authorization of its discoverer or its owner. The right to prevent unauthorized disclosure effectively prevents use of the information by others, and it thereby invests the discoverer or owner with a kind of practical exclusivity in the information that is analogous to (although by no means equivalent to) the exclusivity of the patentee. The patent confers a statutory monopoly; confidential knowhow confers a monopoly in fact.

It is more difficult to draw the boundaries of the capital asset classification when proprietary knowhow, rather than a patent is involved, principally because proprietary knowhow is often closely linked to services that cannot be assimilated to property. A considerable number of cases deal with the circumstances under which knowhow will constitute a capital asset for purposes of capital gains licensing. See, e.g., Taylor–Winfield Corp. v. Commissioner, 57 T.C. 205 (1971), aff'd, 467 F.2d 483 (6th Cir.1972). Unless they constitute purchased amortizable Section 197 intangibles, most forms of knowhow are not depreciable or amortizable.

Therefore, they can constitute capital, but not Section 1231, assets. The relevant criteria for determining whether knowhow is "property" for capital gains purposes appear to overlap to a considerable extent those criteria discussed at ¶ 12,145, which apply in determining what knowhow is treated as "property" for purposes of Section 351. Unpatented inventions, Taylor v. Commissioner, 16 T.C. 376 (1951) (nonacq.), and secret processes, Commercial Solvents Corp. v. Commissioner, 42 T.C. 455 (1964) (acq.), constitute capital assets that may be licensed on a capital gains basis. Rev. Rul. 64–56, at ¶ 12,145, indicates that the IRS accepts the view that for capital gains purposes the kinds of knowhow that are treated as property and therefore generally as capital assets include:

(1) anything qualifying as "secret processes and formulas" within the meanings of Sections 861(a)(4) and 862(a)(4) and

(2) any other secret information as to a device or process, in the general nature of a patentable invention, without regard to whether a patent has been applied for and without regard to whether it is patentable in the patent law sense.

Beyond this, the IRS proceeds on a case-by-case basis along the broad lines suggested in Rev. Rul. 64–56, at ¶ 12,145. Thus, for example, the fact that the information is recorded on paper or some other material will not, in itself, be viewed by the IRS as an indication that the information is property.

There is judicial support for the view that any trade secret with respect to which the owner has a right to prevent unauthorized disclosure constitutes property that will qualify as a capital asset. E.I. Du Pont de Nemours & Co. v. United States, 288 F.2d 904 (Ct.Cl.1961). Also, Rev. Rul. 64–56, at ¶ 12,145, indicates that a prerequisite to classifying transferred knowhow as property, rather than as services, is that the country in which the transferee is to operate must afford substantial legal protection against the unauthorized disclosure and use of the process, formula or other secret information. The Ruling also indicates that the performance of certain services in conjunction with the transfer of "property" will not prevent the consideration from being treated as capital gain in its entirety. These include:

(1) services performed in conjunction with the production of the knowhow, except perhaps where such knowhow has been developed especially for the transferee, and

(2) services performed in connection with the actual transfer of the property where such services are merely ancillary and subsidiary to the property transfer, such as demonstrating and explaining the use of the property, assisting in the effective "starting-up" of the property and performing under a guarantee relating to such starting-up.[5]

5. Rev. Rul. 64–56, at ¶ 12,145. "Ancillary and subsidiary services," however, would not include training the transferee's employees in skills of any grade through expertness (for

[¶ 12,045]

c. Copyrights

Under the Copyright Act, the copyright owner is granted exclusive rights to do and authorize any of the following:

> (1) to reproduce the copyrighted work in copies or phonorecords;
>
> (2) to prepare derivative works based upon the copyrighted work;
>
> (3) to distribute copies or phonorecords of the copyrighted work to the public by sale or other transfer of ownership, or by rental, lease or lending;
>
> (4) in the case of literary, musical, dramatic, and choreographic works, pantomimes, and motion pictures and other audiovisual works, to perform the copyrighted work publicly;
>
> (5) in the case of literary, musical, dramatic, and choreographic works, pantomimes, and pictorial, graphic, or sculptural works, including the individual images of a motion picture or other audiovisual work, to display the copyrighted work publicly; and
>
> (6) in the case of sound recordings, to perform the copyrighted work publicly by means of a digital audio transmission.

17 U.S.C.A. § 106. Each of these rights is a monopoly that constitutes a separate item of property.

Under the Copyright Term Extension Act of 1998, copyrights created on or after January 1, 1978, endure for the life of the creator and 70 additional years. For works created by multiple authors, the term extends through the life of the last surviving author plus an additional 70 years. Finally, for works that are anonymous, pseudonymous or made for hire, the copyright term extends either for 95 years from first publication or 120 years from its creation, whichever term expires first. If the anonymous or pseudonymous author is revealed the term reverts to life of the creator plus 70 years. 17 U.S.C.A. § 302.

None of the property rights inherent in a copyright can qualify as a capital or Section 1231 asset if it is held by the taxpayer whose personal efforts created the copyrighted work. §§ 1221(a)(3)(A) and 1231(b)(1)(C). (An exception is contained in Section 1221(b)(3), under which, if the taxpayer so elects, copyrights in self-created musical works can qualify as capital assets.) Creator is defined by the regulations to include a taxpayer who personally "performs creative or productive work which affirmatively contributes to the creation of the property." Reg. §§ 1.1221–1(c)(3) and

---

example, in any recognized profession, craft or trade), continuing technical assistance after the starting-up phase or, generally, assistance in the construction of a plant building to house machinery transferred or to house machinery to be used in applying a patented or other process or formula.

1.1231–1(c)(1)(ii). This encompasses joint or collective work. Creator also includes a taxpayer who "directs and guides others in the performance of such work." Id. This definition would preclude capital asset or Section 1231 asset treatment for an employer with respect to a copyrighted work created by an employee. Moreover, even copyrighted work purchased from an independent contractor who created it could be denied capital asset treatment if the taxpayer is found to have directed or guided the creation of the work. The regulations do not elaborate on, or provide safe harbors with respect to, what is meant by direction or guidance. Presumably, it would include providing detailed specifications for the created work. Generally, the only taxpayers in whose hands copyrights could qualify as capital or Section 1231 assets would be purchasers of copyrights who were not involved in directing or guiding their creation (except for creators of musical works under Section 1221(b)(3), noted above).

[¶ 12,050]

2. THE "SALE" REQUIREMENT

a. Sales of Patents

To give rise to the realization of a capital gain, there must be a "sale or exchange" of a capital or a Section 1231 asset. If the gain is to qualify for treatment as a long-term capital gain, the asset must be held for more than a year when it is sold. §§ 1222(3), 1231(a)(3)(A)(ii)(II) and 1231(b)(1). For purposes of the present discussion, this requirement necessitates an examination of what constitutes a "sale" of intangible property rights under the applicable tax law principles.

There are two basic methods by which a transfer of rights to a patent can be effected to qualify as a "sale" for tax purposes. First, the patent may be assigned. Second, the transferee may be granted an exclusive license to use, manufacture and sell the patented invention (and products embodying it) within a defined geographical area for the remaining life of the patent. In this second case, the transferor retains legal title to the patent, but because the transferee obtains all the rights the patent monopoly confers, the exclusive license is deemed to constitute a transfer of all substantial rights to the patent and is treated for tax purposes as a sale.

One factor that tends to create a preference for the exclusive license, as compared with an outright assignment, is that it usually avoids the expense and taxes, including patent registration fees and possibly excise or turnover taxes, that may be involved when a patent is assigned. In addition, a right reserved by the transferor to recapture the patent rights in the event of such occurrences as inadequate production and sales by the transferee or bankruptcy or expropriation of the transferee can normally be better protected under an exclusive license than under an assignment. An exclusive license also enables the licensor to retain the right to use the patented invention in certain functional applications or in a geographical area within the country that has issued the patent, while granting exclusive rights to the licensee with respect to the remaining applications or geographical area.

Whether the transfer is in the form of an assignment or a qualifying exclusive license, the consideration under the agreement will be treated as giving rise to a long-term capital gain (or loss) whether it is expressed in terms of (i) a single fixed payment, (ii) fixed payments for a specified number of years or (iii) contingent royalty-like payments for a period of years (possibly the life of the patent) based on the production, sales or income of the transferee. See, e.g., United States v. Carruthers, 219 F.2d 21 (9th Cir.1955); Rev. Rul. 58–353, 1958–2 C.B. 408. The agreement may provide for the furnishing of certain technical services by the transferor which are ancillary and subsidiary to the patent rights transferred without sacrificing capital gain treatment of the entire consideration. See, e.g., Rev. Rul. 64–56, at ¶ 12,145.

When a transfer of patent rights to an independent foreign person is involved, the transferor will typically want to retain various controls over the transferred patent rights. The transferor may want to retain the right to terminate the agreement and recapture the patent rights on the occurrence of specified events, such as the royalties under the agreement falling below certain levels, the transferee being expropriated or the imposition of exchange controls preventing royalty payments in convertible currency. Also, the transferor will often wish to place restrictions on the right of the transferee to sublicense or assign, to retain the right to bring or defend or to participate in the bringing, or defense of, infringement actions. If certain rights such as these are retained by the transferor, they may have the individual or cumulative effect of persuading the IRS or a court to conclude that the transferor has not relinquished all substantial rights to the patent as is required if the transfer is to constitute a sale for tax purposes.

In general, the transaction will be characterized as a sale even if the transferor retains the right to terminate the agreement and recapture the patent rights upon the occurrence of an event not within the transferor's control. For example, it has been held that in a sale transaction the transferor may retain the right to terminate if the transferee's production falls below a specified minimum, Watson v. United States, 222 F.2d 689 (10th Cir.1955), or if the transferee goes into bankruptcy or receivership, Commissioner v. Celanese Corp. of America, 140 F.2d 339 (D.C.Cir.1944). However, if the triggering event were wholly within the licensor's control or if the licensor held the right to terminate the license at will, the transfer would not be treated as a sale. Young v. Commissioner, 269 F.2d 89 (2d Cir.1959).

If the event that triggers the licensor's right to terminate is not readily ascertainable, or depends to some extent on the licensor's judgment, it becomes less clear whether the transfer can qualify as a sale. It has been held that a transfer will qualify as a sale even if the transferor retains the right to terminate if the transferee (1) fails to maintain high standards of quality and sanitation, V.H. Moberg v. Commissioner, 305 F.2d 800 (5th Cir.1962) and Estate of Gowdey v. Commissioner, 307 F.2d 816 (4th Cir.1962), which are franchise and trademark cases relying on precedents in the patent field, (2) violates the agreement in any way, Allen v. Werner, 190 F.2d 840 (5th Cir.1951), or (3) endangers its ability to carry on the business or perform its obligations as determined solely by the transferor, Rouverol v. Commissioner, 42 T.C. 186 (1964) (nonacq.). Other courts, however, have denied the existence of a sale when the transferor retained the right to terminate in the event of (1) the failure of the transferee to maintain high standards of quality and sanitation, T.E. Moberg v. Commissioner, 310 F.2d 782 (9th Cir.1962) (a franchise and trademark case relying on precedents in the patent field), or (2) the failure of the transferee to develop its territory fully or to use reputable distributors and high quality products in accomplishing that full development, Wernentin v. United States, 218 F.Supp. 465 (S.D.Iowa 1963), aff'd in part, rev'd in part, 354 F.2d 757 (8th Cir.1965). These courts have stated that the right to terminate the license agreement must, for tax purposes, be limited by a fixed and definite standard and not merely depend on the transferor's judgment.

Retention by the transferor either of a veto right over sublicensing or further assignment by the transferee or of a right to bring or defend infringement actions will generally not be sufficient to preclude the finding of a sale. See, e.g., Watson v. United States, 222 F.2d 689 (10th Cir.1955). However, the retention of these rights in conjunction with other rights, such as a right to compel the licensee to sublicense to parties selected by the licensor, may have the cumulative effect of vitiating treatment as a sale. Watkins v. United States, 149 F.Supp. 718 (D.Conn. 1957), aff'd, 252 F.2d 722 (2d Cir.), cert. denied, 357 U.S. 936 (1958).

A license will generally not meet the exclusivity requirement if the transferor retains the right to sublicense others within the transferee's territory. Redler Conveyor Co. v. Commissioner, 303 F.2d 567 (1st Cir. 1962). If the license is made subject to a prior nonexclusive license to another in the same area, the weight of authority supports the view that the transfer can nonetheless qualify as a sale. E.g., MacDonald v. Commissioner, 55 T.C. 840 (1971) (acq.). The licensor-seller may manufacture the patented article for the licensee-buyer of the patent if the licensee-buyer retains the right, under the license, to select other manufacturers for its production needs. Puschelberg v. United States, 330 F.2d 56 (6th Cir. 1964).

An important issue that remains to be finally resolved by the courts is whether it is inconsistent with a sale characterization for the licensor to retain the right to use the invention in one or more functional applications while all other rights are transferred to the licensee. A number of cases have been decided involving individuals who qualified as "holders" for purposes of Section 1235 and who sought long-term capital gain treatment under the provisions of that section. The regulations issued under Section 1235 specifically state that a license will not constitute a transfer of all substantial rights that will qualify for capital gain treatment under Section 1235 if the licensor retains rights to exploit the invention in one or more applications. Reg. § 1.1235–2(b). The courts have sustained the validity of this regulation. E.g., Mros v. Commissioner, 493 F.2d 813 (9th Cir.1974). In addition, the Section 1235 regulations provide that transferring patent rights in a geographical area smaller than the country covered by the patent precludes qualification of the transfer as a sale. Reg. § 1.1235–2(b). This position has also received judicial support. E.g., Kueneman v. Commissioner, 68 T.C. 609 (1977), aff'd, 628 F.2d 1196 (9th Cir.1980).

Although the requirement that all substantial rights in patents or knowhow be transferred is common to Sections 1222 and 1231, on the one hand, and Section 1235, on the other, the courts have generally applied less stringent standards under Sections 1222 and 1231 than under Section 1235, particularly with respect to whether geographical or functional subdivision of the patent or knowhow precludes qualification of the transfer as a sale. The following case involves exclusive licenses that effect a functional subdivision of foreign patent rights.

[¶ 12,055]

E.I. DU PONT DE NEMOURS & CO. v. UNITED STATES

United States Court of Appeals, Third Circuit, 1970.
432 F.2d 1052.

FULLAM, DISTRICT JUDGE:

[The first of the two unrelated issues raised is] whether funds received by the taxpayer in exchange for the assignment of certain Brazilian patents were taxable as ordinary income or as capital gain * * *.
* * *

I.

THE BRAZILIAN PATENTS ISSUE

The taxpayer was the owner of eight Brazilian patents relating to the manufacture of nylon fibers. All were process patents, but four also covered apparatus used in the manufacture of the fibers and four included claims having applicability to dacron as well.

In January 1954, the taxpayer entered into two related agreements with a French chemical corporation, Societa Rhodiaceta (hereinafter Rhodiaceta) and its Brazilian affiliate, Companhia Brasileira Rhodiaceta (hereinafter CBR), the effect of which was to transfer rights in all of these eight

Brazilian patents to CBR, for a consideration of $5,500,000, so that CBR could engage in the manufacture of nylon in Brazil. Of the agreed payment, $4,094,000 was paid during 1954, and in its tax return for that year, the taxpayer included this amount as ordinary income. Thereafter, a timely claim for refund was filed, on the theory that this payment should have been treated as a capital gain. When the refund was refused, the taxpayer brought suit in the court below and recovered judgment in its favor.

The record discloses the following background to this transaction: In 1946, the taxpayer had assigned to Rhodiaceta its nylon patents in France, Belgium, Spain and Switzerland, and had made available to Rhodiaceta its current nylon technology; and in exchange Rhodiaceta had agreed to pay the taxpayer a continuing royalty. In 1948, Rhodiaceta had licensed the taxpayer under its cellulose acetate yarn patents in the United States and Canada, in exchange for which the taxpayer had agreed to pay Rhodiaceta a continuing royalty. In 1950, Rhodiaceta sought to obtain from the taxpayer nylon rights for CBR under the taxpayer's Brazilian nylon patents. On March 20, 1952, after extended negotiations, these rights were granted to CBR by a non-exclusive license, under which CBR immediately paid a security deposit of $250,000 and agreed to pay a continuing royalty through 1974. On the same date, the taxpayer executed a separate agreement with Rhodiaceta under which the taxpayer agreed, *inter alia*, to make available to Rhodiaceta the taxpayer's entire nylon technology up to September 30, 1952, and authorized its use by Rhodiaceta and its licensees, including CBR; and Rhodiaceta agreed to cancel the taxpayer's continuing royalty obligation under the 1948 cellulose acetate yarn agreement.

Insofar as Rhodiaceta was concerned, the agreement was carried out, but the provisions of the 1952 license agreement with CBR could not be carried [out] because the Brazilian Government refused to approve the agreement and to make available the necessary foreign exchange. It further appeared that the Brazilian government opposed in principle any non-exclusive licensing arrangement, particularly one which would be likely to produce a recurring drain on its dollar reserves.

Thereafter, negotiations continued with a view toward obviating these difficulties. It was the position of Rhodiaceta and CBR that they were interested only in exclusive nylon rights in Brazil, and that, for foreign exchange reasons, it would be helpful to channel the transfer through Rhodiaceta. The taxpayer was willing to grant exclusive nylon rights, on a fixed-price basis, payable over a very short period. Moreover, the taxpayer felt constrained by the terms of a recent antitrust decree to reserve the right to import into Brazil nylon lawfully manufactured in the United States.

The ultimate outcome of these negotiations was the transaction now under scrutiny. The taxpayer entered into the two agreements referred to above, one with Rhodiaceta dated January 4, 1954, and the other with CBR dated January 19, 1954, the net effect of which was to transfer to Rhodiaceta and CBR the exclusive right to make, use and sell nylon in Brazil, and to license others to do so, for the full life of the patents, subject to the taxpayer's reserved right to import, for a total consideration of $5,500,000, part of which was to be paid by CBR and part by Rhodiaceta.

It is undisputed that the taxpayer had held the patent rights in question for more than six months [the then applicable holding period] prior to the transfer, and had not held them for sale to customers. Accordingly, the only question is whether the transfer constituted a sale of such rights within the meaning of sections 1222 and 1231 * * *. Neither the Code itself, nor treasury regulations define what constitutes a sale for capital gains purposes.

Patent rights are intangible property rights, the transfer of which may qualify as a sale for capital gain purposes. The precise form and terminology of the transfer are not controlling, so long as it transfers exclusive rights for the full life of the patent. * * * As stated by this Court in Merck & Co., Inc. v. Smith, [261 F.2d 162 (3d Cir.1958)] at page 164:

> "* * * a transfer of all of the substantial rights in a patent is deemed an assignment and qualifies the transferor for capital gains treatment. A transfer of anything less is called a license with a resultant assessment of the tax at ordinary income rates."

To determine whether the taxpayer did transfer all of the substantial rights in the patents in question, the key question is whether the transferor retained any rights which, in the aggregate, have substantial value. * * *

In the present case, the government contends that the taxpayer retained the following valuable rights in connection with the transfer:

1. The right to import into Brazil nylon lawfully manufactured elsewhere;

2. The right to control any subsequent licensing or assignment of the rights granted Rhodiaceta and CBR with respect to the use of the patented process and apparatus in making nylon;

3. The right to make any use it saw fit (including manufacturing under its own auspices, licensing, sale, etc.) of the patent rights in connection with dacron; and

4. The right to manufacture for sale the apparatus covered by the patent or to license others to manufacture the apparatus for use, in connection with the manufacture of fibers other than nylon (especially dacron).

The District Court carefully analyzed all of the rights retained by the taxpayer, and specifically found that they were of no substantial value. On appeal, the Government contends that each of these findings was erroneous, and that, in any event, the District Court erred in treating each right individually and in failing to make a finding that, in the aggregate, the retained rights had substantial value.

In our view, this latter argument represents a too narrow reading of the District Court opinion. After analyzing each of the rights individually, and finding it valueless, the District Court concluded that the taxpayer had not retained substantial rights in the patents, and that the transfer qualified for capital gains treatment. Indeed, at the conclusion of this discussion of the various retained rights, Chief Judge Wright expressly stated:

> "No substantial rights in the eight patents transferred having been retained, the 1954 transactions constituted a sale of those patents, the proceeds of which are entitled to capital gains treatment." 296 F.Supp. 823, 833.

Accordingly, the only issue before this Court is whether the District Court findings are clearly erroneous. We have concluded that the record adequately supports the findings of the District Court.

1. *Right to import.* There was ample evidence in the record to justify the conclusion that the reservation by the taxpayer of the right to import nylon into Brazil, and to license others to do so, preserved nothing of value to the taxpayer. The parties contemplated that the government of Brazil would adhere to its policy of excluding such imports, once a Brazilian company entered the market. Subsequent events have borne out the accuracy of this assumption.

In this connection, we note, but need not pass upon, taxpayer's further argument that this reservation was included in the agreement because it was believed to be required by the provisions of an antitrust decree; hence, the argument goes, the taxpayer lacked the legal capacity to transfer a right to preclude imports, so that this right should be deemed non-existent rather than retained.

Moreover, it is by no means clear that the (theoretical) right to import into Brazil nylon lawfully manufactured in the United States (presumably, under taxpayer's American patents) derogates from the completeness of the transfer of the Brazilian patents. Rather, such rights would seem to be more directly related to the independent American patent rights.

2. *Right to sell and sublicense equipment.* As noted above, four of the eight patents transferred covered apparatus as well as process. The two 1954 agreements (Article V of the Rhodiaceta agreement and Article III of the CBR agreement) can be read to mean that, while both grantees received the right to make and use, in their own plants, the apparatus and equipment covered by the patents, neither grantee had the right to sell such equipment. The agreements can also be read to mean that while CBR had the right to sublicense others to make, use and sell nylon, it did not have the right to sublicense others to make and use the required equip-

ment. The District Court found that the only limitation, insofar as Rhodiaceta is concerned, was the inability to sell equipment; and that, "* * * the manufacture of equipment for sale to other fiber producers is a function separate and distinct from manufacture of equipment for use in one's own fiber production. Accordingly, the apparatus patents in issue here are divisible along that line." * * *

Insofar as CBR is concerned, the District Court found that, under the foregoing interpretation of the agreements, the taxpayer in effect reserved to itself a veto power over CBR's ability to sublicense production use and sale of nylon. The District Court concluded that this veto power was of no substantial value.

* * *

In our view, the District Court was correct in concluding that, assuming the taxpayer retained a veto power over sublicensing, that fact would not mean that the taxpayer failed to transfer substantially all rights in the patents. In Rollman v. Commissioner of Internal Revenue, 244 F.2d 634 (4th Cir.1957), the transfer documents expressly provided that the grantee could not grant sublicenses under the patents except with the written consent of the transferor. The court held:

> "Such limitation does not interfere with the full use of the patent by the assignee * * * Moreover, the assignor retains no use of the patent for himself by reason of the limitation since he has granted the exclusive rights to the assignee and cannot grant a sublicense without the purchaser's consent." (At page 640)

* * *

3. *The dacron rights*. Four of the eight patents in question are at least theoretically applicable to dacron as well as nylon, but only the nylon rights were transferred. The District Court found that the retained dacron rights were not of substantial value, and that, in any event, they were severable. The government here challenges both of these findings.

It is apparent that the District Court was persuaded by the testimony presented on behalf of the taxpayer, to the effect that the patents were of extremely minor importance in the manufacture of dacron; that dacron could be manufactured without resort to the processes and equipment covered by these patents; and that use of these patents for dacron in Brazil was foreclosed by the basic Whitfield and Dixon patent, owned by Imperial Chemical Industries, Ltd. In view of this evidence, we certainly cannot say that the District Court's finding of no substantial value was clearly erroneous.

Moreover, we agree with the District Court's conclusion that, for capital gains purposes, the nylon rights, considered independently, were proper subjects for a sale. For such purposes, patent rights are divisible between different industries and different industrial products. * * *

For the foregoing reasons, we have concluded that the District Court was correct in deciding that the reservation of dacron rights * * * did not amount to a reservation of anything having substantial value, derogating from the completeness of the transfer of the nylon rights.

* * *

For the foregoing reasons, the Judgment of the District Court, insofar as it concerns the Brazilian patents issue, will be affirmed.

[¶ 12,060]

NOTE

The preceding decision in *Du Pont* and Bell Intercontinental Corp. v. United States, 381 F.2d 1004 (Ct.Cl.1967), which predate the functional and geographical subdivision cases decided under Section 1235, support the conclusion that a taxpayer may retain rights to exploit an invention in one or more functional applications without vitiating a "sale" of the rights to the invention in one or more other applications.

There is also authority (again predating the Section 1235 cases) supporting the position that retention of rights in an area encompassing a portion of the United States is not inconsistent with a sale. E.g., Reid v. Commissioner, 26 T.C. 622 (1956) (acq.) (trademarks and patents). The unresolved question is whether the courts in dealing with Section 1222 and 1231 transactions will now follow the decisions holding that either a geographical or a functional subdivision of patents will preclude finding a transfer of all substantial rights for purposes of Section 1235. One significant difference between the issues in the two contexts is that regulations under Section 1235 specifically take the positions that have been sustained by the courts of appeals. No Section 1222 or 1231 regulations apply, and differing standards seem implied by Rev. Rul. 69–482, 1969–2 C.B. 164, which states that "holders" who cannot qualify their transfers under Section 1235 for capital gains treatment may do so under Sections 1222 and 1231.

[¶ 12,065]

PROBLEMS

1. Cyber Corporation ("Cyber"), a U.S. corporation, intends to grant an exclusive license under Mexican patents to an independent licensee in Mexico. Assume that the license would otherwise qualify as a sale. Consider whether, if the agreement provides for retention by Cyber of the right to terminate the license and recapture the rights to the Mexican patents under the following alternative circumstances, the transfer would fail to qualify as a sale for U.S. tax purposes:

   a. After the license has been in effect for ten years;

b. Mexico imposes exchange controls that prevent the licensee from paying royalties in U.S. dollars as required under the license;

c. Upon the bankruptcy of the licensee;

d. The licensee fails to reach specified and reasonably attainable levels of production and sales within three years of the inception of the license;

e. The licensee fails to use best efforts to develop the market within Mexico;

f. The licensee fails to maintain the quality standards specified in an annex to the license;

g. The licensee fails to supply the reasonable needs of customers in Mexico or

h. The licensor retains a right to veto any sublicensing by the licensee.

2. Would your analysis change if Cyber did not have the right to terminate the agreement and recapture the licensed patent rights, but, instead, upon the happening of any of the above-specified events, the exclusive license would become nonexclusive? If the license became nonexclusive, Cyber would be enabled to sell the patented products into Mexico or grant a nonexclusive license to another licensee in Mexico.

[¶ 12,070]

b. Sales of Confidential Knowhow and Other Trade Secrets

When a transfer of confidential knowhow or another trade secret is involved, some guidance as to what constitutes a sale for tax purposes can be obtained from the principles which have been elaborated in the patent and trademark fields. Since, however, the property rights inhering in knowhow, unlike those inhering in a patent or trademark, do not depend upon a monopoly granted within a fixed area by governmental authority, some caution must be exercised in applying the patent and trademark analogies.

[¶ 12,075]

E.I. DU PONT DE NEMOURS & CO. v. UNITED STATES

United States Court of Claims, 1961.
288 F.2d 904.

JONES, CHIEF JUDGE:

* * *

The second part of this case deals with plaintiff's disclosure of a secret process and the treatment of income received in exchange. The plaintiff developed an electrolytic process for producing the metal sodium. The process was at first thought not to be patentable and was kept secret. However, the process was put into commercial use by the plaintiff. In 1948, Associated Ethyl Corporation, Ltd., a British corporation (hereafter referred to as Associated) sought to obtain plaintiff's secret process. On May 15, 1950, a written contract was made whereby plaintiff agreed to transfer the complete blueprints and operational characteristics of the process to Associated in consideration of the sum of $225,000. In addition, the plaintiff promised "not to assert against [Associated] any patent covering the construction or use of sodium cells, the licensing rights of which were possessed by du Pont." Associated agreed to keep the process secret for 5 years. No restrictions were placed on plaintiff's right to disclose the process. The contract placed no restrictions on Associated's use of the process anywhere in the world.

On December 18, 1950, plaintiff agreed to grant similar rights to the electrolytic cell to the Ethyl Corporation, a Delaware corporation, in exchange for $400,000.

In 1952, patents did issue both in the United States and in Great Britain covering certain functional features of the electrolytic cells.

For the purposes of this case the Government concedes that the secret process was "property" within the meaning of section 117(a) [now Section 1222] of the Internal Revenue Code; that plaintiff was not in the business of selling secret processes; and that this particular secret process was not held primarily for sale to customers in the ordinary course of trade or business.

In dispute is the question whether the disclosure of the secret process in exchange for $225,000 constituted a "sale" of the process within the meaning of section 117 [Section 1222]. Only if there was a sale is plaintiff entitled to preferential capital treatment of the gain realized on the transaction. Plaintiff maintains that merely having disclosed its secret process to another, it is somehow poorer; something has been irretrievably given away; that since money was received in exchange for this something given away, a sale of property must have occurred.

The propriety of classifying confidential disclosures of ideas as dealings in property has been under discussion in this country since the time of Jefferson, who stated:

> "If nature has made any one thing less susceptible than others of exclusive property, it is the action of the thinking power called an idea * * *. Its peculiar character, too, is that no one possesses the less because every other possesses the whole of it. He who receives an idea from me receives instruction himself without lessening mine; as he who lights his taper at mine, receives light without darkening me." [Writings of Thomas Jefferson, Vol. 6, pp. 180–181, H. A. Washington ed. (1854).]

Justice Holmes, in an injunction proceeding to prevent a former employee of plaintiff from disclosing secret processes which he had learned while in plaintiff's employ, in E. I. Du Pont De Nemours Powder Co. v. Masland, 1917, 244 U.S. 100, 102 * * *, made the following statement:

> "Whether the plaintiffs have any valuable secret or not the defendant knows the facts, whatever they are, through a special confidence that he accepted. The property may be denied but the confidence cannot be. Therefore the starting point for the present matter is not property or due process of law, but that the defendant stood in confidential relations with the plaintiffs, or one of them."

We quote from Judge Learned Hand, in Cheney Bros. v. Doris Silk Corporation, (2d Cir.1929) 35 F.2d 279, 280, the following:

> "* * * a man's property [in an idea] is limited to the chattels which embody his invention." * * *

Were we to accept plaintiff's position without qualification, it would be similar to concluding that a lawyer makes a sale of property when he discloses an estate plan to a client, and a doctor makes a sale when he discloses the diagnosis of his patient's ills. * * *

In another light, however, the transfer of a trade secret may be a transaction equivalent to a sale, in the same manner that a patent assignment is considered a sale. In each case the transferee or assignee gets more than mere information. Of greater importance, he obtains what he believes to be a competitive advantage, a means for commercial exploitation and reward.

Without question, there are important differences between patents and trade secrets. Under the Constitution a patent secures to the inventor the exclusive rights to his discovery. A form of monopoly is given in exchange for the full disclosure and public dedication of a new and useful invention. * * * Information contained in a patent is public, widely distributed, and generally known by those interested in a particular art. Inevitably the patented idea becomes common knowledge, yet the patentee retains the right to prevent the manufacture, use and sale of the invention during the life of the patent. 35 U.S.C. § 154. The patent owner may affirmatively act to prevent anyone else from using the patented invention; even to prevent such use by a second inventor who discovers the same idea entirely on his own. It follows that no disposition of a patent is complete without some transfer of this right to prevent infringement.

A trade secret is any information not generally known in a trade. It may be an unpatented invention, a formula, pattern, machine, process, customer list, customer credit list, or even news. The information is frequently in the public domain. Anyone is at liberty to discover a particular trade secret by any fair means, as by experimentation or by examination and analysis of a particular product. Moreover, upon discovery the idea may be used with impunity. A plurality of individual discoverers may have protectible wholly separate rights in the same trade secret. However, the owner of a trade secret has no protectible rights in the *idea* itself any more than a lawyer has in his estate plan or a doctor in his diagnosis. Unlike an estate plan or a diagnosis, a trade secret, as a tool for commercial competition, derives much of its value from the fact of its secrecy. It is truly valuable only so long as it is a secret, for only so long does it provide an advantage over competitors. It follows that the essential element of a trade secret which permits of ownership and which distinguishes it from other forms of ideas is the right in the discoverer to prevent unauthorized disclosure of the secret. No disposition of a trade secret is complete without some transfer of this right to prevent unauthorized disclosure.

However different these concepts of trade secrets and patents may appear to be, there is an important similarity; they are both means to competitive advantage. The value in both lies in the rights they give to their owners for monopolistic exploitation. The owner of a patent can make something which no one else can make because no one else is permitted. But circumstances are frequently such that the owner of a trade secret can make something which no one else can make because no one else knows how. The patent owner has a monopoly created by law; the trade secret owner has a monopoly in fact. In both cases there exists the possibility of either limited or complete transfers of the right to the exclusive use of an idea.

A person may pay the owner of a patent for the privilege of operating under the patent without liability for infringement. This is the simple license situation * * * and is not considered a "sale" under the tax law. * * * Again, a person may pay the owner of a patent for the privilege of operating under the patent without liability for infringement, and in addition may pay for the residual right possessed by the patent owner, that being the right to prevent all others from operating under the patent. This is an assignment * * * and is treated as a "sale" under the tax law. In both cases there has been a sacrifice of an exclusive market and the establishment of a potential competitor where formerly the law guaranteed there would be none. Yet unquestionably the money received from the license is ordinary income to the owner of the patent, while the money received from the assignment may be treated as capital gain.

Compare the situation which obtains with trade secrets. A person may pay the discoverer of a trade secret for its disclosure, but in fact the disclosure which is purchased carries with it the right to use the trade secret without liability to the owner. This is the instant case. Again, a person may pay the discoverer of a trade secret for disclosure (i.e., the privilege of using the trade secret) and in addition pay for the residual right possessed by the discoverer—the right to prevent unauthorized disclosure. And this right to prevent unauthorized disclosure is effectively, as stated above, the right to prevent anyone else from using the secret process. * * *

Just as the grant of the naked right to operate under a patent in exchange for money results in ordinary income to the owner of the patent, so the simple disclosure and grant of the privilege of using a trade secret in exchange for money must also result in ordinary income to the discoverer of the trade secret. In both instances there has been no disposition of interest sufficient to meet the "sale" requirement of the Code. * * * When a patent owner gives not only the right to operate under the patent but in addition conveys all or a part of his remaining rights in the patent (particularly the right to exclude others from using the idea) in exchange for money, the disposition is complete. The transaction satisfies the "sale" requirement of the Code, and any gain on the transaction may be entitled to capital treatment. Similarly, when the owner of a trade secret gives the right to use the secret and in addition conveys his most important remaining right, the right to prevent unauthorized disclosure (and effectively the right to prevent further use of the trade secret by others) there is a complete disposition of the trade secret. This transaction meets the "sale" requirement of the Code and any gain would be entitled to preferential capital treatment.

In the case before us the plaintiff did not transfer to Associated the right to prevent further disclosure of the secret process. In fact, Associated could do nothing to prevent the subsequent disclosure of the secret by plaintiff to Ethyl of Delaware. Because of this, we find that the disposition of the trade secret did not meet the requirements of a "sale." Accordingly, the gain realized on the transaction must be taxed as ordinary income. Any other rule would encourage tax avoidance by providing a broad avenue for the conversion of ordinary royalty income into capital gain.

[¶ 12,080]

NOTE

If knowhow transferred cannot be shown to have a limited period of utility, applying the trademark analogy would seem to require a license to be in perpetuity in order to qualify as a sale. Rev. Rul. 64–56, at ¶ 12,145. The IRS has ruled, however, that an unqualified transfer of the exclusive right to use a trade secret until it becomes public knowledge and is no longer protectible under the applicable law of the country where the transferee is to operate will constitute a "transfer" for purposes of Section 351. Rev. Rul. 71–564, 1971–2 C.B. 179. Because the IRS appears to apply similar standards in the two contexts, such a transfer presumably would also qualify as a sale for purposes of capital gains treatment.

As illustrated in the *Du Pont* case at ¶ 12,075, the courts, in articulating the requirements that must be met if a license of secret processes is to constitute a "sale," have relied on the patent analogy. Specifically, they have held that the transferee must obtain the right to prevent future unauthorized disclosures by the transferor, thus preserving the exclusivity of the transferred rights. See also Hooker Chemicals & Plastics Corp. v. United States, 591 F.2d 652 (Ct.Cl.1979). It seems clear that a grant to the transferee of exclusive rights to utilize the knowhow within a defined area is, in and of itself, a sufficient grant of the "right to prevent unauthorized disclosure," if, under the applicable local law, the exclusive licensee of knowhow has the right to prevent unauthorized disclosures by the licensor and by others (including the licensee's employees) if a breach of contract or confidence is involved. R. Ellis, Trade Secrets § 385 (1953).

In Rev. Rul. 64–56, at ¶ 12,145, the IRS set down guidelines pertaining to the transfer of knowhow to a controlled corporation under Section 351. In general, applying the patent analogy, the IRS will require the transfer of all substantial rights in the "property" involved, in order to qualify as a "transfer" of "property" under Section 351. Regarding secret information in particular, the IRS indicated that a qualifying transfer will generally require an unqualified grant, until the information is no longer protectible under applicable law, of the exclusive right, within a given country, to:

(1) use a secret process or other similar secret information,

(2) use a secret formula, and use and sell the products derived from it, where both are elements of the transferor's property right or

(3) make, use and sell an unpatented but secret product.

However, see *E.I. Du Pont de Nemours & Co. v. United States*, at ¶ 12,160, in which the Court of Claims held that a nonexclusive license of foreign patents will qualify as a "transfer" under Section 351(a) even though it would not qualify as a sale.

Note that the IRS appears to require that exclusive rights within a particular country be granted if all substantial rights to knowhow are to be deemed transferred. This contrasts with the cases in the patent field, which hold that exclusive rights to a patent in a geographical area comprising only part of a country may constitute a sale. See Marco v. Commissioner, 25 T.C. 544 (1955) (acq.). *But see* e.g., Kueneman v. Commissioner, 68 T.C. 609 (1977), aff'd, 628 F.2d 1196 (9th Cir.1980). The IRS view, thus, may be unjustifiably narrow. See ¶ 12,050.

The IRS's use of the word "unqualified" indicates that the problems in the patent area relating to retention of rights by the transferor (see ¶ 12,050) are likely to have their analogues when dealing with knowhow transfers. One question of particular interest centers on the right of the transferor to restrict further disclosures of the trade secret by the transferee. Once the notion of limiting the exclusive right in the knowhow to a particular country is accepted, it would seem clear that the transferor should retain the right to restrict the transferee from disclosing the secret information for use outside that particular country. Indeed, if this were not the case, it is likely that the transferor would have no way of protecting its special rights to the secret information in other countries.

Less clear is the case in which the transferor seeks to restrict disclosures by the transferee for use within the transferee's own country. Perhaps the transferor would want to restrict disclosure only to those employees of the transferee who would be willing to execute agreements stipulating that they would keep the secret information confidential. Certain protection against further disclosure within the geographical area in which exclusive rights are granted may be essential to prevent trade secrets from becoming generally known and thereby losing their value. Such protection would also be necessary to ensure that the transferee will receive and maintain a competitive advantage within its exclusive area so that the transferor who receives royalties geared to the transferee's sales will be adequately compensated for the knowhow sold. While such a restriction would not abridge the "exclusive" nature of the transferee's rights, it would permit the transferor to prevent use by others of the information within the country concerned. Here the holdings in the patent area permitting the transferor to retain a veto power over sublicensing would appear to be relevant. See, e.g., Watson v. United States, 222 F.2d 689 (10th Cir.1955).

In Hooker Chemicals & Plastics Corp. v. United States, 591 F.2d 652, 662 (Ct.Cl.1979), the Court of Claims considered a provision in parallel exclusive knowhow licenses that provided:

> [The transferee] agrees to hold in confidence and safeguard the secrecy of all of the know-how received by it under this Agreement so long as such know-how is not generally known to the public, *provided, however, that it may disclose such know-how to the extent necessary in connection with the manufacture, use, sale or licensing of* the [chemicals or chemical techniques] to which it pertains. (Emphasis supplied.)

In rejecting the government's contention that this clause indicated that the transferor intended to preserve its property rights in the territories covered by the licenses, which would be inconsistent with a sale characterization, the court stated:

> * * * The transferees had an obligation of confidentiality but could disclose the know-how, where necessary, in the manufacture, use, sale, and licensing of it. The obligation therefore did not circumscribe the transferee's total use of the know-how.
>
> What it did do is recognize an obvious fact that once a secret is out of the bag, it becomes much less valuable. That value remained important for the transferees in the * * * territories [covered by the licenses in issue] and for the plaintiff in North America and elsewhere worldwide. As such, it represents a reasonable method used to prevent the unauthorized disclosure of the know-how beyond the * * * territories and was therefore not a substantial right of value retained in the transferred know-how.

Finally, the IRS may also require a showing that the country in which the transferee is to operate affords to the transferee substantial legal protection against the unauthorized disclosure and use of the confidential knowhow or other trade secret by the transferor and possibly by others if the disclosure constitutes a breach of agreement or confidence. See Rev. Rul. 64–56, at ¶ 12,145.

[¶ 12,085]

c. Sales of Franchises, Trademarks and Trade Names

An exclusive and perpetual license of a franchise, trademark or trade name constitutes a sale even if the license is limited to an area geographically smaller than the country granting the trademark or trade name protection. See e.g., Rainier Brewing Co. v. Commissioner, 7 T.C. 162 (1946), aff'd per curiam, 165 F.2d 217 (9th Cir.1948). However, if the transferor retains one or more significant rights described in Section 1253(b)(2), the transfer will not be treated as a sale.

[¶ 12,090]

d. Sales of Copyrights; Gains Treated as Ordinary Income

With respect to a copyright, there is no doubt that distinct functional aspects of a copyright can be "sold" for U.S. tax purposes. The Court of Claims held in Herwig v. United States, 105 F.Supp. 384, 389 (Ct.Cl.1952), that an "exclusive and perpetual grant of any one of the 'bundle of rights' which make up a copyright [constitutes] a 'sale' of personal property rather than a mere 'license.' "The court also commented as follows:

> While it has been suggested that the splitting up of the right on a geographical basis appears less feasible with respect to a copyright than with respect to patents or trademarks, even in the copyright field an agreement of this kind would be possible; e.g., a grant of the rights to dramatize productions limited to certain cities. * * *

Id. at 388.

The IRS has ruled that consideration received by a proprietor of a copyright for a grant transferring the exclusive right to exploit the copyrighted work in a medium of publication throughout the life of the copyright will be treated as the proceeds from a sale of property whether the purchase price is fixed or cast in the form of royalty-like payments. Rev. Rul. 54–409, 1954–2 C.B. 174, modified by Rev. Rul. 60–226, 1960–1 C.B. 26.

In fact, the IRS's emphasis on medium of publication seems misplaced. The Copyright Act provides that the copyright owner is granted the exclusive rights to exploit any and all of the separate rights set forth in Section 106. See ¶ 12,045. Each of these rights may be transferred, subdivided, owned and enforced independently of the others. 17 U.S.C.A. § 201(d). Accordingly, any exclusive transfer of any of the separate rights conferred by the Copyright Act for the life of the copyright concerned will probably qualify as a sale for tax purposes even if limited to a specific geographical area.

Regulations have been issued on the tax treatment of international transfers of computer programs for purposes of specified provisions of the Code relating to international transactions. Reg. § 1.861–18. The regulations characterize transfers of computer programs as sales, exchanges, leases or licenses, depending upon the circumstances. Reg. § 1.861–18(a)(2). A computer program is defined as "a set of statements or instructions to be used directly or indirectly in a computer in order to bring about a certain result" and it includes any media, user manuals, documentation, database or similar item incidental to operation of the computer program. Reg. § 1.861–18(a)(3).

For purposes of these regulations, Reg. § 1.861–18(c)(2) identifies four copyright "rights":

(1) the right to make copies of the computer program for distribution to the public;

(2) the right to prepare derivative computer programs based on the copyrighted computer program;

(3) the right to make a public performance of the computer program; and

(4) the right to publicly display the computer program.

The transfer of any of these rights is treated as the transfer of a copyright right. A copyrighted "article" is defined in the regulations as "a copy of a computer program from which the words can be perceived, reproduced, or otherwise communicated, either directly or with the aid of a machine or device." Reg. § 1.861–18(c)(3).

A transfer of a computer program is treated as one of the following:

(1) a transfer of a copyright right in the computer program;

(2) a transfer of a copy of the computer program (a copyrighted article);

(3) the provision of services for the development or modification of the program; or

(4) the provision of knowhow relating to computer programming techniques.

Any transaction including more than one of the foregoing transactions will generally be treated as a number of separate transactions each of which will be treated as one of the foregoing. Reg. § 1.861–18(b)(2).

In classifying a transfer of a copyright as a sale (or exchange) or license, the regulations provide that if "all substantial rights" in the copyright right are transferred, the transfer will be treated as a sale (or exchange); if not, it will be treated as a license. The term over which payments are to be made is irrelevant to the determination of whether the transfer is a sale (or exchange) or a license. Reg. § 1.861–18(f). A nonsale transfer of a copy of a computer program is treated as a lease (not a license). Reg. § 1.861–18(f)(2).

The regulations provide the following source rules:

(1) income from sales or exchanges of copyrighted articles is sourced under Section 861(a)(6), 862(a)(6), 863, 865(a), 865(b), 865(c) or 865(e), as appropriate. If held as inventory, the usual inventory source rules apply. Reg. § 1.861–18(f)(2). See ¶¶ 2115 and 2160.

(2) Income from the leasing of a computer program or the licensing of copyright rights in a computer program is sourced under Section 861(a)(4) or 862(a)(4), as appropriate. Reg. § 1.861–18(f)(2).

(3) Income from the sale or exchange of a copyright right is sourced under Section 865(a), 865(c), 865(d), 865(e) or 865(h), as appropriate.

The OECD released on February 1, 2001, the final report of its Technical Advisory Group on tax treaty characterization issues arising from e-commerce. The report analyzes 28 separate categories of e-commerce transactions and characterizes the income produced by them for purposes of the OECD Model Tax Convention. Of the 28 transactions, the income from 26 will normally be taxed as business profits under Article 7 of the OECD Model Convention and only two as royalties under Article 12. For example, in the case of transactions that allow customers to download software or other digital products for the customer's own use, as opposed to commercial purposes, the income will be treated as business profits. However, if the download involves the granting of the right to use the copyright in a digital product, the transaction will give rise to royalties. Treaty Characterization Issues Arising from E–Commerce: Final Report to Working Party No. 1 of the OECD Committee on Fiscal Affairs 5–6 (OECD Feb. 1, 2001).

It is important to note that, under certain circumstances, the foreign rights to use computer software may be patentable either as a process or a method implemented by a computer as a means for accomplishing some function, or as part of a machine, apparatus or system which utilizes the software to perform some function. If the software is patented or patentable, the tax rules applicable to transfers of foreign patents and patentable inventions will presumably apply.

[¶ 12,095]

3. SALES OF PATENT AND KNOWHOW RIGHTS TO A FOREIGN CONTROLLED CORPORATION

The opportunities available to a U.S. person for realizing tax savings through capital gains licensing of controlled foreign corporations were markedly narrowed by Section 1249, which provides that any gain realized on a sale or exchange of a patent, an invention, model or design (whether or not patented), a copyright, a secret formula or process or "any other similar property right" to a foreign corporation "controlled" by the transferor will be treated as ordinary income rather than capital gain. For this purpose, control means the ownership, directly or indirectly and constructively (under the rules of Section 958), of stock of the foreign corporation possessing more than 50 percent of the total combined voting power of all classes of stock entitled to vote. § 1249(b). Thus, patent or knowhow transfers can generate long-term capital gains only if the transfers are made to a foreign corporation, 50 percent or less of the voting power of which is owned by the U.S. transferor.

The enactment of Section 1249 put an end to a tax-saving arrangement sometimes referred to as the patent and knowhow "bailout." A U.S. corporation with valuable foreign patents and knowhow rights was often unwilling for business reasons to grant a sufficiently unqualified exclusive license to independent licensees to enable the royalties to be treated as generating long-term capital gain. Such a corporation typically transferred to a wholly owned foreign licensing base company an unqualified exclusive license for a royalty expressed as a percentage of the income to be realized by the base company from exploitation by the latter of the foreign intangible property rights. The foreign base company could then license independent licensees, retaining any restrictions and controls desired from a business point of view, under licenses that could not constitute "sales" for U.S. tax purposes if made by the U.S. corporation itself. The royalties received by the U.S. corporation from the foreign base company, however, did qualify for long-term capital gain treatment and, therefore, through this device it was possible to convert a portion of what would otherwise have been ordinary income royalties from independent licensees into long-term capital gain royalties from the wholly owned licensing base company.

Section 1249 was rendered largely superfluous by the elimination in 1986 of the distinction between the tax rate applicable to long-term capital gain and that applicable to ordinary income. It regained some importance when the distinction was subsequently restored in the case of individuals. In the case of corporations, currently, the only substantive difference between capital gains and ordinary income is that capital losses of a corporation can be offset only against capital gains (long-term or short-term).

[¶ 12,100]

4. TRANSFERS OF TRADEMARKS, TRADE NAMES, FRANCHISES AND RELATED INTANGIBLES WITH RETAINED RIGHTS

Section 1249 does not apply to trademarks, trade names or franchises, but a transfer of rights of this kind is subject to a different set of restrictions on capital gain treatment. Under Section 1253, gain on a transfer of a trademark, trade name or franchise will be treated as ordinary income rather than capital gain if the transferor retains any significant power, right or continuing interest with respect to the transferred property. Section 1253(b)(2) defines "significant power, right, or continuing interest" as including, but not limited to, the following:

(1) a right to disapprove any assignment of such interest, or any part thereof,

(2) a right to terminate at will,

(3) a right to prescribe the standards of quality of products used or sold, or of services furnished, and of the equipment and facilities used to promote such products or services,

(4) a right to require that the transferee sell or advertise only products or services of the transferor,

(5) a right to require that the transferee purchase substantially all of its supplies and equipment from the transferor and

(6) a right to payments contingent on the productivity, use or disposition of the subject matter of the interest transferred, if such payments constitute a substantial element under the transfer agreement.

Note that, unlike the approach of Section 1249 with respect to patents, inventions, copyrights and similar rights, the extent of the stock ownership of the transferor in the transferee is immaterial under Section 1253.

International transfers of franchises are an important and growing category of international transactions. Burger King, KFC, McDonald's and Pizza Hut are only a few of the well known names encountered in countries around the world. Transfers of such franchises encompass a very large range of functional activities, including, for example, providing services of various types, selling or leasing property and selling or licensing computer software. It is not uncommon to find that transfers of intangible property such as patents, confidential knowhow, trademark rights, copyrights and computer software accompany or are an integral part of a franchise transfer. Even though the income realized from the transfer of the franchise itself may be ordinary income under Section 1253, it is possible that gain on a transfer of related patents, knowhow, copyrights or software might qualify for long-term capital gain treatment if the transfer qualifies as a discrete sale separable from the franchise transfer.

Accordingly, an issue that sometimes arises under Section 1253 is the scope of a franchise that involves related intangibles. In the following case, the taxpayers argued that computer software licenses to foreign licensees were not covered by Section 1253. If covered by Section 1253, the payments received would have been taxed as ordinary income rather than as capital gain. In the alternative, the taxpayers argued that, in any event, licenses of related intangibles, identified as the "Sort Program," "trade secrets" and "licensed technology," should be treated as transfers separate from the franchise transfer. If so treated, these licenses, the taxpayers argued, qualified as sales on which the gains should have been taxed as long-term capital gains.

[¶ 12,105]

SYNCSORT INC. v. UNITED STATES

United States Court of Federal Claims, 1994.
31 Fed.Cl. 545.

ANDEWELT, JUDGE:

In these consolidated tax refund actions, plaintiffs, Syncsort Incorporated (Syncsort) and Assadour O. Tavitian (individually and as "Tax Matters Person" of Syncsort), seek to recover income taxes paid for tax years 1979 through 1985 on payments Syncsort received pursuant to licensing agreements it entered with four foreign computer consulting firms. Plaintiffs contend that the Internal Revenue Service (IRS) improperly required plaintiffs to treat these payments as ordinary income for federal income tax purposes instead of permitting the more beneficial tax treatment [then] available for capital gains. These actions are presently before the court on cross-motions for summary judgment. For the reasons set forth below, defendant's motion for summary judgment is granted and plaintiffs' cross-motion is denied.

I.

The material facts are not in dispute. During tax years 1979 through 1985, Syncsort principally was engaged in the business of marketing and leasing or licensing a computer program referred to as "SyncSort" (the Sort Program). The basic function of the Sort Program was to sort unorganized individual data records in a specified sequence, e.g., in alphabetical or chronological order. In the domestic market, Syncsort offered its customers a computer tape of the Sort Program plus support services. The support services included installing the Sort Program, training a customer's systems programmers to use the Sort Program, fine-tuning the parameters of the Sort Program to the boundaries of the customer's computer environment, and maintaining the Sort Program by correcting any defects or "bugs" or by referring the customer to the pertinent portions of the operation manuals and/or user guides. In addition, separate from fine-tuning the parameters of the Sort Program, Syncsort apparently also engaged in certain "customized actions" which involved the customer's individual computer system. Using confidential information about the Sort Program, Syncsort modified the customer's systems software so as to enable the customer to secure greater efficiencies in the sorting process carried out by the Sort Program. * * *

Four foreign computer consulting firms contacted Syncsort and expressed an interest in Syncsort's business. After determining not to exploit the relevant foreign markets on its own, Syncsort entered licensing agreements with these four firms, Pandata NV (Pandata), The Shell Company of Australia Limited (Shell), Computing Benefits (Proprietary) Limited (Computing Benefits), and Software Engineering Co., Ltd. (Software Engineering). In the respective agreements, Syncsort granted each of the four licensees, inter alia, an exclusive license in a specified geographic area to promote, advertise, duplicate, use, sublicense, and sublease the Sort Program, and to use the associated Syncsort trademarks.[1] The licensing agreements also provided for the transfer to the licensees of "Trade Secrets" and "Licensed Technology," which apparently correspond to the confidential information Syncsort used in providing the Sort Program and related services to its domestic customers.[2] The "Licensed Technology" consisted of technological information and marketing data including charts and diagrams relating to the Sort Program's "object code," a master tape of the "object code," sales promotion information, advertising material, contracts, and brochures. The "Trade Secrets" consisted of confidential information about the Sort Program necessary to enable the licensees to "customize" their customers' systems software so as to permit the Sort Program to operate most efficiently.

In the respective licensing agreements, plaintiffs granted exclusive marketing rights to Pandata in the Soviet Union, the Middle East, North Africa, Southwest Asia, and various European countries; to Shell in Australia and New Zealand; to Computing Benefits in South Africa; and to Software Engineering in Japan and Korea. Each of the licensees agreed to use its best efforts to market the Sort Program within its exclusive territory. As consideration for the license, rights, and disclosures made by Syncsort under the licensing agreements, each licensee agreed to pay Syncsort a fixed royalty ranging from 25 to 50 percent of the gross revenues the licensee earned from "marketing" the Sort Program, including revenues received for maintaining the Sort Program. In the Pandata agreement, Pandata also agreed to pay Syncsort $200,000 in addition to the fixed royalty.

1. The Computing Benefits licensing agreement is unique in that it also permitted Computing Benefits to sell the Sort Program.

2. "Trade Secrets" and "Licensed Technology" are defined in a generally consistent manner in the licensing agreements with Pandata, Computing Benefits, and Shell. For example, the Pandata agreement defines the terms, in pertinent part, as follows:

> (b) The term "Licensed Technology" shall mean (i) technical information, charts and diagrams relating to, and a master tape of the "object code" of, each version of the [Sort Program] in sufficient detail to enable [the licensee] (x) to make duplicate copies of [the Sort Program], (y) to install [the Sort Program] for, and deliver the same to, its customers, and (z) to service the same, and (ii) marketing data, such as sales promotion and advertising material, contracts and brochures used by [Syncsort] in marketing the [Sort Program].
>
> (c) The term "Trade Secret" shall mean the compilation or partial compilation of information relating to the Licensed Technology which will be disclosed to the licensee. . . .

For each of the tax years in issue, Syncsort recorded the payments it received from these licensees on its Schedule D tax form under Part II, entitled "Long–Term Capital Gains and Losses—Assets Held More Than One Year." From 1979 through 1984, Syncsort described the income source under Part II as "Sale of Franchises." For 1985, Syncsort changed the description to "Sale of Know How." The IRS first disputed plaintiffs' classification of the income received under the licenses for tax years 1979 through 1983. The IRS alleged that plaintiffs should have treated the payments as ordinary income instead of capital gains. Syncsort paid the additional funds sought by the IRS for these tax years and then filed a refund claim. After the IRS denied Syncsort's refund request, Syncsort filed two separate suits in this court seeking a refund for tax years 1979 through 1982, and 1983, respectively. Thereafter, for tax years 1984 and 1985, the IRS, on the same grounds as for tax years 1979 through 1983, assessed additional taxes against plaintiff Assadour O. Tavitian, both as "Tax Matters Person" of Syncsort and in his individual capacity. After Syncsort's shareholders paid these additional assessments, Syncsort and Tavitian filed a third suit seeking a refund for tax years 1984 and 1985. This court consolidated the three actions.

In its motion for summary judgment, defendant contends that each of the four licenses in issue constitutes a transfer of a franchise and that pursuant to [Section] 1253, all money received from such transfers must be treated as ordinary income for federal income tax purposes. In their cross-motion, plaintiffs respond with two alternative arguments. First, plaintiffs contend that the licensing agreements do not involve the transfer of a franchise within the scope of Section 1253. Second, plaintiffs argue that even assuming the licensing agreements included in part a transfer of a franchise within the scope of Section 1253, the agreements also transferred other intangible assets to the licensees—the Sort Program, "Licensed Technology," and "Trade Secrets"—which are not covered by Section 1253. Plaintiffs argue that at a minimum, the revenues attributable to the transfer of these intangible assets should receive capital gains treatment.

* * *

II.

* * * Section 1253, * * * entitled "Transfers of franchises, trademarks, and trade names," was enacted in response to a series of conflicting court decisions dealing with the extent to which franchisees' payments to franchisors qualify for capital gains treatment. * * * Section 1253(a) provides that "[a] transfer of a franchise, trademark, or trade name shall not be treated as a sale or exchange of a capital asset if the transferor retains any significant power, right, or continuing interest with respect to the subject matter of the franchise, trademark, or trade name." Thus, when applying Section 1253(a) to the instant facts, the court must make

two pertinent determinations. First, the court must determine whether a transfer of a franchise is involved and, second, if such a transfer is involved, the court must determine whether Syncsort maintained the requisite "power, right, or continuing interest with respect to the subject matter of the franchise."

Turning to the first determination, Section 1253(b)(1) defines "franchise" as "includ[ing] an agreement which gives one of the parties to the agreement the right to distribute, sell, or provide goods, services, or facilities within a specified area." Herein, each of the four licensing agreements fits within that definition. As described above, in each agreement, Syncsort granted the licensee the exclusive right within a designated area to distribute and provide a specific product, i.e., the Sort Program. Each agreement also provided the licensee with the right to use technological information and trade secrets to provide related services.

Turning to the second determination of whether Syncsort maintained a "significant power, right, or continuing interest with respect to the subject matter of the franchise," * * * in each of the four agreements, Syncsort maintained significant rights over the subject matter of the franchise, i.e., the Sort Program and the support services related to the Sort Program. In its agreements with Pandata, Shell, and Computing Benefits, Syncsort maintained the right to disapprove any assignment of the licensees' interest (Section 1253(b)(2)(A)) and to prescribe standards of quality for the copies of the Sort Program that were sublicensed or subleased to end-users (Section 1253(b)(2)(C)). In its agreements with Computing Benefits and Software Engineering, Syncsort required the licensees to refrain from marketing any competitive computer programs (Section 1253(b)(2)(D)). In all four agreements, Syncsort received payments contingent on the use or disposition of the Sort Program and such payments constituted a substantial element under each transfer agreement (Section 1253(b)(2)(F)).[6] Thus, the four licensing agreements fall within the literal scope of Section 1253(a). Each agreement constitutes a transfer of a franchise and in each agreement, Syncsort retained significant rights with respect to the subject matter of that franchise.

III.

Plaintiffs do not dispute that the literal reach of Section 1253 applies to the instant agreements. Plaintiffs do, however, dispute that Section

6. In addition to the rights specifically listed in Section 1253(b)(2), Syncsort maintained other rights, powers, and interests that can at least be argued to be "significant." In all four agreements, Syncsort, inter alia, retained control over the terms and/or conditions of sublicenses, maintained confidentiality with respect to information concerning the basic design of the Sort Program, and maintained standards over the display of Syncsort trademarks. The agreements with Pandata, Shell, and Computing Benefits also obliged the licensees to disclose to Syncsort all modifications to or improvements of the Sort Program that the licensees invented, developed, or adopted during the terms of the licensing agreements. The agreements with Pandata, Shell, and Software Engineering also provided Syncsort with either some control over the price at which the licensees could sublicense or sublease the Sort Program or access to information concerning this price.

1253 should be applied literally herein. Plaintiffs contend that Congress intended Section 1253 to reach only those situations where the franchisor participates much more actively in the franchisee's business than did Syncsort.

Where, as here, the statutory language, in pertinent part, is unambiguous, a court must interpret the statute consistent with its unambiguous language unless the legislative history demonstrates "a clearly expressed legislative intention to the contrary." * * * Plaintiffs herein rely primarily upon the following portion of the legislative history of Section 1253, which appears in substantially the same form in both of the pertinent Senate and House Committee Reports. The House Report provides, in relevant part:

> It would appear that the retention of significant rights, powers, or continuing interests by the franchisor in the subject matter of the franchise is equivalent to active operational control and is inconsistent with a sale of property.
>
> Moreover, it has been pointed out that some franchisors participate substantially in the day-to-day management of the franchisee's business activities and operations or, in other words, carry on what amounts to active commercial participation in the business by the transferor of the franchise. In other words, it would appear that the franchisor had reserved what may be regarded as an operational interest in the subfranchise if he participates in its management by conducting activities such as sales promotion (including advertising), sales and management training, employee training programs, holding of national meetings for franchisees, providing the franchisee with blue prints or formulas, and other forms of continuing assistance.

H.R. Rep. No. 413, 91st Cong., 1st Sess., Pt. 1, 162 (1969). * * *

But this statement hardly constitutes a "clearly expressed legislative intention" that Congress intended Section 1253 to reach only those situations where the franchisor is involved in the management of the franchisee's business on a day-to-day basis. The observation that "*some* franchisors participate substantially in the day-to-day management of the franchisee's business activities" (emphasis added) necessarily recognizes that other franchisors do not, but nothing in the quoted portion indicates that Congress intended Section 1253 to reach only the first group of franchisors. Moreover, the ultimate conclusion expressed in this portion of the legislative history is that the "retention of significant rights, powers, or continuing interests by the franchisor in the subject matter of the franchise is equivalent to active operational control and is inconsistent with the sale of property." In Section 1253(b)(2), Congress proceeded specifically to define those rights that it considered to be "significant" and hence "inconsistent with the sale of property." Thus, once the court determines that a transfer of a franchise is involved and that the franchisor retained significant rights as defined in Section 1253(b)(2), the court's inquiry, in pertinent part, is complete and Section 1253 necessarily applies. The legislative history of Section 1253 does not anticipate that in situations where the franchisor retains rights specifically listed in Section 1253(b)(2), the court will perform its own analysis to measure the significance of those rights to determine whether retention amounted to "operational control."

Herein, the right of each licensee to distribute and provide the Sort Program and related services constitutes a franchise within the meaning of Section 1253(b)(1), and with respect to that franchise, Syncsort maintained significant rights listed in Section 1253(b)(2). Therefore, under the mandate of Section 1253, plaintiffs are not entitled to claim long-term capital gains on payments allocable to these franchise transfers.

IV.

In the alternative, plaintiffs argue that even assuming each of the four licensing agreements included the transfer of a franchise within the scope of Section 1253, all royalty payments Syncsort received under the four licensing agreements should not necessarily be denied capital gains treatment. Plaintiffs argue that the phrase "transfer of a franchise" in Section 1253(a) must be narrowly construed to encompass only the transfer of the naked intangible "right to distribute, sell, or provide goods, services, or facilities within a specified area." Plaintiffs contend that all other assets, tangible or intangible, that may be transferred in connection with the franchise fall outside of Section 1253(a), and hence must be evaluated for capital gains treatment under the other provisions * * * of the Internal Revenue Code.

Plaintiffs contend that in addition to granting the licensees the right to distribute the Sort Program, the license agreements also transferred the Sort Program, "Licensed Technology" and "Trade Secrets." Plaintiffs argue that the amount of payments made by the licensees attributable to the transfer of these other intangible assets falls outside of Section 1253(a) and qualifies for capital gains treatment. Because the license agreements provided for fixed royalty payments based on total revenues and did not allocate the payments among the transferred assets, plaintiffs argue that this court must allocate the royalty payments between payments attributable to the transfer of the naked "right to distribute ... " and payments attributable to the transfer of the Sort Program, "Licensed Technology," and "Trade Secrets."

V.

The wording of Section 1253 and the pertinent legislative history do not support plaintiffs' proposed narrow interpretation of the phrase "transfer of a franchise." As noted above, Section 1253(b)(1) defines "franchise" as follows: "The term 'franchise' *includes* an agreement which gives one of the parties to the agreement the right to distribute, sell, or provide goods, services, or facilities, within a specified area" (emphasis added). By using the term "includes," the statutory definition is open ended. To say that the term franchise "includes" an agreement which contains a certain specified provision is to acknowledge that the term may also include other, unspecified arrangements. *See* [Section] 7701(c)("The terms 'includes' and 'including' when used in a definition contained in this title shall not be deemed to exclude other things otherwise within the meaning of the term defined."). * * * Plaintiffs err by interpreting Section 1253(b)(1) as though it states that a franchise "*is* an agreement which gives ... the right to distribute ... "rather than "*includes* an agreement which gives ... the right to distribute.... "

A related indication in the statutory definition of "franchise" that plaintiffs' proposed interpretation is too narrow is that the statutory definition does not focus exclusively on the grant of the "right to distribute ... " but rather refers to the agreement which contains such a grant (" 'franchise' includes an agreement which gives ... the right to distribute ... "). The statutory focus on the "agreement" indicates that a "franchise" may include assets transferred in the same agreement other than the "right to distribute.... "

The legislative history similarly does not favor plaintiffs' proposed interpretation of Section 1253. * * *

VI.

A franchise is a business. Congress enacted Section 1253 in response to a franchise boom in which franchisors licensed various assets to franchisees and thereby helped establish the franchisees in the business of distributing, selling, or providing the goods, services, or facilities within specified areas. * * * To conduct the franchised business, a franchisee typically needs not only the naked right to distribute, sell, or provide, the goods, services, or facilities, but also other unique intangible assets that are integral to the providing of such goods, services, or facilities. Plaintiffs' effort herein to interpret "transfer of a franchise" as limited to the transfer of the naked right to distribute, sell, or provide, and to exclude these other unique and integral intangible assets ignores the essential nature of the franchise as a business.

In the instant action, Syncsort, in effect, franchised aspects of its domestic business. Syncsort chose not to conduct its business in certain foreign markets on its own and instead to exploit its assets in foreign markets by licensing its business to existing foreign firms. The licenses granted the firms access to the Sort Program, "Licensed Technology," and "Trade Secrets," which Syncsort utilized in its United States business. Syncsort thereby, in effect, permitted the foreign firms to emulate Syncsort's domestic business in foreign markets.

The three assets at issue—the Sort Program, "Licensed Technology," and "Trade Secrets"—are unique intangible assets that are an integral part of each of the franchised businesses created in the agreements. There is no contention that these assets have use other than in connection with the franchised business, *i.e.,* other than in the provision of the Sort Program and related services. The Sort Program is the essence of the franchise arrangements. Without access to the Sort Program, the franchisees would have no product to distribute. The "Licensed Technology" and "Trade Secrets" similarly are integral to the franchisees' ability to market and provide services relating to the Sort Program in the specified areas. The "Licensed Technology" allowed the franchisees to duplicate the Sort Program for sale to customers, and facilitated the franchisees' servicing and marketing of the Sort Program. The "Trade Secrets," which the franchisees specifically targeted in their pre-licensing communications with Syncsort, permitted the franchisees to offer increased efficiencies in the Sort Program's sorting process. * * * Hence, without the transfer of the Sort Program, "Licensed Technology," and "Trade Secrets," the licensees could not have distributed and provided the Sort Program and related services.

Viewing a "transfer of a franchise" as encompassing only the transfer of the intangible right to distribute products and provide services and not also as including the transfer of other unique intangible assets integral to the provision of such products and related services produces a fundamentally inaccurate picture of the business relationship created by a franchise transfer. This court will not promote such a distorted picture unless the statutory language or the legislative history requires such a result. As described above, the language and legislative history of Section 1253 point in the opposite direction and indicate that a "transfer of a franchise" includes more than merely the transfer of the naked right that plaintiffs propose here.

In summary, the court concludes that the three unique intangible assets plaintiffs transferred to the franchisees—the Sort Program, "Licensed Technology," and "Trade Secrets"—fall within the reach of "transfer of a franchise" under Section 1253. Hence, income received in connection with the transfer of the franchise that is attributable to the transfer of these three assets must be treated as ordinary income for federal income tax purposes.

[¶ 12,110]

5. IMPUTED ORIGINAL ISSUE DISCOUNT

If patent, trademark or knowhow rights are sold by a corporation for a stated dollar amount payable in installments, some or all of which are due more than six months after the date of sale, and no interest or an inadequate interest rate on the unpaid installments is provided for,

Section 1274 requires that a portion of each installment due more than six months after the date of sale be treated as original issue discount (OID). Section 1274 comes into play whenever the stated redemption price at maturity of the installment obligation exceeds the imputed principal amount. § 1274(c)(1)(A). The imputed principal amount is equal to the sum of the present values of all payments due under the obligation, discounted at 100 percent of the applicable federal rate (short-term, mid-term or long-term, depending on the term of the installment obligation) determined under Section 1274(d). The discount rate cannot exceed nine percent, compounded semiannually, if the principal amount of the debt obligation does not exceed $2.8 million (to be adjusted for inflation). The seller must include in ordinary income the sum of the daily portion of OID for each day of the tax year the obligation is held, whether the seller is on a cash or an accrual method of tax accounting, and the buyer may deduct corresponding amounts. However, if the seller is on an accrual basis and is not a dealer, buyer and seller may jointly elect to use the cash method with respect to a debt instrument, the principal amount of which does not exceed $2 million (to be adjusted for inflation).

If the intangibles are sold on an installment basis for a total price of $250,000 or less and inadequate interest is stated, Section 1274 does not apply, but additional interest is imputed under Section 483 for each installment due more than six months after the sale. The portion of the installment payments that is treated as imputed additional interest is equal to the excess of the sum of the payments due under the contract over the sum of (1) the present values of such payments (determined by using a discount rate equal to the applicable federal rate under Section 1274(d), compounded semiannually) and (2) any stated interest due under the contract. The end result is similar, whether OID is imputed under Section 1274 or unstated interest is imputed under Section 483, except that under Section 483 the seller (lender) and buyer (borrower) may report the imputed interest in accordance with their usual tax accounting method (e.g., cash or accrual method).

Sales or exchanges by individual holders of patent rights described in Section 1235(a) are not subject to the Section 1274 imputation-of-OID rules or the Section 483 imputation-of-unstated-interest rules if the consideration is contingent on the productivity, use or disposition of the property transferred. §§ 483(d)(4) and 1274(c)(3)(E).

[¶ 12,115]

6. SOURCE OF INCOME

Income from the sale or exchange of intangible property is deemed to have its source in the country of the seller's residence to the extent that the income is not contingent on the productivity, use or disposition of the intangible property right. § 865(a) and (d)(1)(A). Intangible property for this purpose includes "any patent, copyright, secret process or formula, goodwill, trademark, trade name, franchise or other like property." § 865(d)(2). Thus, sale of foreign rights to intangible property by a U.S. corporation to a foreign corporation for a fixed price will give rise to U.S.-source income.

If, however, the price for the foreign rights to the intangible is contingent on the productivity, use or disposition of the intangible, the royalty source rule of Section 862(a)(4) applies. § 865(d)(1)(B). Under this rule, the source is the country in which the intangible is used. For example, if rights to knowhow in France are sold by the U.S. corporation to a foreign corporation for a price expressed as a royalty contingent on (e.g., expressed as a percentage of) the net sales of the products embodying the knowhow, the sales income will be foreign-source income. This would be the case whether or not the transfer constitutes a sale for U.S. tax purposes.

The foregoing source rules are subject to a special "depreciation override" rule which is applicable to any sale of depreciable or amortizable intangible property, such as a patent, the adjusted basis (or cost) of which may be recovered through depreciation or amortization deductions over the remaining life of the patent or over a 15–year period in the case of a patent that constitutes an amortizable Section 197 intangible. § 865(d)(4). Gain on the sale of a patent up to the amount of depreciation or amortization deductions previously taken is sourced under the rules for sales of depreciable property in Section 865(c), except that gain in excess of prior depreciation or amortization deductions (called "depreciation adjustments" in Section 865(c)) is sourced under the intangible property rules of Section 865(d) rather than under the inventory property rules. § 865(d)(4)(B). Under the depreciable property rules, gain realized on a sale up to the amount of prior depreciation or amortization deductions is U.S.-source gain to the extent that the prior depreciation or amortization deductions offset U.S-source income or is foreign-source gain to the extent that the depreciation or amortization deductions offset foreign-source income. Thus, if a French patent for which prior depreciation or amortization deductions had offset foreign-source income were sold by a U.S. corporation for a fixed price, the part of the gain realized equal to the prior depreciation or amortization deductions would be foreign-source gain. The remainder of the gain would be U.S.-source gain under Section 865(a). The depreciation override rule does not apply to foreign rights to unpatented knowhow or foreign trademarks or trade names to the extent they are not amortizable or depreciable. The depreciation override applies if they are amortizable Section 197 intangibles.

A special source rule applies to goodwill. If goodwill is sold for a fixed price, the income will be deemed to have its source in the country in which the goodwill was generated (e.g., by incurring advertising expenses). § 865(d)(3). Goodwill is often closely associated, if not inextricably bound up, with a trademark or trade name. It is unclear how, in such a case, the goodwill is to be separated from the trademark or trade name when a fixed purchase price is involved. If goodwill is sold or licensed (with or without a related trademark or trade name) for a royalty, the royalty source rules of Sections 861(a)(4) and 862(a)(4) apply. § 865(d)(1)(B).

International Multifoods Corp. v. Commissioner, 108 T.C. 25 (1997), involved a sale by International Multifoods of its Asian and Pacific Mister Donut Operations for $2,050,000. The court held that goodwill was not sold separately from franchise rights and trademarks, and, accordingly, the gain realized by the U.S. corporation was U.S.-source income under Section 865(a)(1) and (d)(1)(A). The court noted that intangible assets such as trademarks and franchises were "inextricably related" to goodwill, and concluded that the special source rule for goodwill

> is applicable only where goodwill is separate from the other intangible assets that are specifically listed in section 865(d)(2). If the sourcing provision contained in section 865(d)(3) also extended to the goodwill element embodied in the other intangible assets enumerated in section 865(d)(2), the exemption would swallow the rule. Such an interpretation would nullify the general rule that income from the sale of an intangible asset by a U.S. resident is to be sourced in the United States.

108 T.C. at 37–38. Of the sale price, $300,000 was attributable to the covenant of International Multifoods not to compete in the buyer's territory. This portion of the price was held to be foreign-source ordinary income. See ¶ 2080.

[¶ 12,120]

PROBLEM

Review Problem 7 at ¶ 2215.

[¶ 12,125]

7. APPLICABLE FOREIGN TAX CREDIT LIMITATION

If the sale by a U.S. person of an intangible produces foreign-source income under the source rules just reviewed, the seller must determine into which of the Section 904(d) foreign tax credit limitation baskets the income falls.

Dealing with this issue requires that a distinction be drawn between sales to controlled foreign corporations and sales to others. If the foreign buyer is not a controlled foreign corporation as defined in Section 957(a), the gain will fall in the Section 904(d)(1)(A) passive income basket if it would be foreign personal holding company had it been received by a controlled foreign corporation. § 904(d)(2)(A)(i). Section 954(c)(1)(B)(i) includes in foreign personal holding company income, gain from the sale (or exchange) of property that gives rise to foreign personal holding company income after applying the active-business-unrelated-person exception of Section 954(c)(2)(A). Reg. § 1.954–2(e)(1). Thus, if the intangible had previously generated royalties that were paid to the U.S. seller by persons who were not related under Section 954(d)(3) and that were derived in the active conduct of a trade or business, gain on its sale would be excluded from foreign personal holding company income and the passive income basket and would fall into the general income limitation basket. Reg. § 1.954–2(e)(2)(i) and (3)(i). Temp. Reg. § 1.904–4T(b)(2)(iii) also includes in the general income limitation basket royalties derived in the active conduct of a trade or business and received from *related* persons. See ¶ 12,015. It would seem to follow that the same treatment would be given to gain on the sale of intangibles producing such royalties as to gain on the sale of intangibles producing income from unrelated persons.[6]

What is the result if the intangible sold has not previously been licensed? If it is used (or held for use) in the business of the seller, it is apparently not regarded as not giving rise to income under Section 954(c)(1)(B)(iii). Reg. § 1.954–2(e)(3)(iv). As a result, gain on its sale would seem to be included in the Section 904(d)(1)(B) general income limitation basket. However, if foreign intangible property is not regarded as used (or held for use) in the seller's foreign business, gain on its sale may be included in the Section 904(d)(1)(A) passive income basket.

If a manufacturing intangible is sold by a U.S. corporation to a foreign corporation that is controlled under Sections 957(a) and 1249 for a contingent, royalty-like price, Section 1249 requires that the purchase price be treated as ordinary income, rather than as capital gain.[7] This being so, it is unclear whether the Section 904(d)(3) look-through rules would apply to the purchase price royalties. The fact that purchase price royalties are assimilated to ordinary income royalties for purposes of determining their source under Sections 865(d)(1)(B), 861(a)(4) and 862(a)(4) and under Article 12(2)(b) of the 2006 Treasury Model Tax Treaty (Appendix A) suggests that the same treatment would be appropriate here. If the look-through rules apply, the applicable basket for the purchase price royalties would depend on the underlying income of the controlled foreign corporation. If all of that underlying income were Section 904(d)(1)(B) general limitation income, all of the purchase price

6. The same-country-related-person exception for royalties under Section 954(c)(3)(A)(ii) is not applicable to royalties received by a U.S. person. § 954(c)(1)(B)(i). Therefore, gain on sale of intangibles producing royalties covered by this exception would fall in the seller's passive income basket. Reg. § 1.954–2(e)(i). If, however, such royalties were derived in the active conduct of the seller's trade or business, gain on the sale of the intangible would appear to fall into the general income limitation basket. Temp. Reg. § 1.904–4T(b)(2)(iii).

7. If the price were fixed, the gain would be U.S.-source, and no foreign tax credit limitation issue would arise. § 865(d)(1)(A).

royalties would be similarly treated. See ¶ 7110. If the look-through rules do not apply to the purchase price royalties, the analysis in the preceding paragraph would seem to apply.

Because the definitions of controlled foreign corporation under Sections 957(a) and 1249(b) differ (the latter encompassing only more than 50 percent of the corporation's total combined voting power), gain on the sale of manufacturing intangibles for a royalty-like purchase price to a foreign corporation that is controlled under Section 957(a), but not under Section 1249, could qualify as capital gain under Section 1222, 1231 or 1235. In this case, the Section 904(d)(3) look-through rules would not apply, and the proper limitation basket would be determined under the analysis discussed above that applies when a sale of manufacturing intangibles is made to an unrelated person.

Under Section 1253, gains from sales or exchanges of foreign marketing intangibles, such as trademarks, trade names and franchises, are usually treated as gains from the sale of non-capital assets rather than as capital gain. See ¶ 12,100. In Tomerlin v. Commissioner, 87 T.C. 876, 888–892 (1986), the Tax Court held that ordinary income from the sale of a trademark was not a royalty for personal holding company purposes. Therefore, the Section 903(d)(3) look-through rules would probably not apply to gain treated as ordinary income under Section 1253, and the analysis above relating to sales of manufacturing intangibles to unrelated persons would seem to be applicable.

D. TRANSFER OF INTANGIBLE PROPERTY RIGHTS TO A FOREIGN CORPORATION IN EXCHANGE FOR STOCK OR AS CONTRIBUTION TO CAPITAL

[¶ 12,130]

1. TRANSFER IN EXCHANGE FOR STOCK

When a U.S. corporation making a direct investment in a foreign corporation contributes intangible property rights to the enterprise, it may consider the possibility of transferring these rights in exchange for stock. The corporation supplying the intangible rights may make such a transfer whether it emerges as the owner of 100 percent or some lesser percentage of the stock of the transferee foreign corporation.

In most cases, intangible property rights transferred to a foreign corporation will have a value in excess of their tax cost or basis. In the case of patents and knowhow, this will often result from the fact that research and development costs have been previously expensed by the transferor (i.e., deducted currently pursuant to Section 174, rather than capitalized), and, in the case of trademarks, from the fact that advertising and promotion costs, which are incurred to enhance the value of the trademark, have similarly been deducted currently. Thus, when intangible property rights are exchanged for stock having an equal value, gain will typically be realized by the transferor.

On such a transfer any gain realized will be recognized and taxed unless Section 351 (or, in the case of a tax-free reorganization, Section 361) operates to prevent its recognition. Whether recognized gain will be treated as ordinary income or long-term capital gain turns on the nature of the intangible property, the period for which the transferor has held the property, the nature of the transfer and the relationship between the transferor and transferee. See ¶¶ 12,025 et seq.

Before enactment of the Tax Reform Act of 1984, a U.S. corporation or other taxpayer that transferred intangible property to a foreign corporation could avoid any tax on the gain realized on the transaction by qualifying the transaction for nonrecognition of gain under Section 351. This result could be achieved only if the substantive requirements of this provision were met and if a ruling under Section 367 were obtained from the IRS to the effect that the exchange was not in pursuance of a plan having as one of its principal purposes the avoidance of federal income taxes. To meet the requirements of Section 351 for nonrecognition of gain, there had to be a "transfer" of "property" solely in exchange for stock and immediately after the transfer, the transferor or transferors of property had to own 80 percent of the voting power and 80 percent of the number of shares of each class of nonvoting stock of the transferee. For purposes of this 80–percent requirement, all persons who transfer cash or other property in exchange for stock as part of the same transaction are aggregated.

The impetus for the basic changes enacted in 1984 to the taxation of intangible property rights under Sections 351 and 367(a) derived principally from the fact that the taxpayer could under pre-existing law develop intangible property, such as patents, knowhow, trademarks and other manufacturing and marketing intangibles in the United States, deduct the costs thereof against U.S.-source income and then transfer the foreign rights to these intangibles tax-free to a foreign corporation for use in connection with its foreign manufacturing and marketing operations. The tension was particularly acute in the case of manufacturing intangibles. The U.S. taxpayer benefited from important U.S. tax incentives given for conducting research and development in the United States. Research or experimental expenditures could be currently deducted under Section 174 rather than capitalized, thus reducing income subject to U.S. income tax. A tax credit equal to 20 percent of certain incremental research expenses was available. Half of all expenditures for U.S. research and experimental activities reduced U.S.-source but not foreign-source income for purposes of the Section 904(a) limitation on foreign tax credits. This enabled many U.S. businesses to credit a larger portion of their foreign tax burdens than would be possible under the normal rules reflected in Reg. § 1.861–8, which would have required more than one half of those expenditures to be allocated against foreign-source income.

If the research expenditures resulted in valuable patents or technological knowhow, the U.S. taxpayer could transfer the foreign rights to a wholly owned manufacturing and marketing corporation abroad. Then, if the intangibles were to be used in connection with a foreign manufacturing business, the products of which would be sold abroad, under prior law, a favorable ruling would be issued by the IRS without imposition of tax on any of the gain realized. If the foreign corporation were set up in a low-tax or a tax-holiday jurisdiction, there would be little or no foreign tax on the income generated by the intangibles, and U.S. tax would be deferred unless and until the earnings were distributed as dividends to the U.S. corporation.

As a result of the enactment in 1984 of Section 367(d), a transfer of any intangible property, as broadly defined in Section 936(h)(3)(B), including but not limited to marketing and manufacturing intangibles (such as trademarks, trade names, patents and technical knowhow) to a foreign corporation can no longer be effected free of tax. Section 367(d) provides that, except as may otherwise be provided in regulations, in the case of a transfer of any intangible property to a foreign corporation in exchange for stock that meets the requirements of Section 351 (or of a tax-free reorganization), the U.S. transferor is not subject to tax on the full amount of the gain realized on the exchange. The transferor will be deemed, however, to have sold the intangible property in exchange for constructive periodic payments. These are deemed to be payments that are contingent on the productivity, use or disposition of such property and that reasonably reflect the amounts that would have been received (1) annually over the useful life of such property or (2) in a disposition following such transfer (whether direct or indirect) at the time of the disposition.

These constructive royalty-like payments are treated under Section 367(d)(2)(C) as ordinary income. Section 367(d)(2)(B) calls for an appropriate reduction in the earnings and profits of the foreign corporation to reflect the payments deemed paid by the foreign corporation. The reference to direct or indirect disposition is intended to cover a disposition of either the transferred intangible by the transferee corporation or a disposition of the transferor's stock interest in the transferee corporation. The amount of income taxed upon such a disposition will depend on the value of the intangible at the time of the disposition. Although under the 1984 Act, the constructive payments were treated as U.S.-source income, the 1997 Act repealed this special source rule and made the general royalty source rules (in this case the foreign-source rule of Section 862(a)(4)) applicable. No change was made in the rule treating the constructive royalties as ordinary income even if there is a transfer of all substantial rights to a foreign corporation that is not controlled by the U.S. transferor under Section 1249. But for the special rule of Section 367(d)(2)(C), the consideration for such a taxable exchange would often generate a capital gain rather than ordinary income. See ¶¶ 12,025 et. seq.

Thus, as a result of the 1984 and 1997 changes, a Section 351 exchange of intangible property for a foreign corporation's stock will be treated as if the transferor had sold the property for constructive (or deemed) royalty-like payments, which will be taxed as they are deemed to be received over the life of the intangibles concerned (even though no such payments are in fact made by the transferee). Temp. Reg. § 1.367(d)–1T. Moreover, the amount of constructive royalty included by the transferor in gross income annually over the life of the property must represent an appropriate arm's length charge determined under Section 482 and Reg. § 1.482–4.

Intangible property is defined as any (1) patent, invention, formula, process, design, pattern or knowhow, (2) copyright, literary, musical or artistic composition, (3) trademark, trade name or brand name, (4) franchise, license or contract, (5) method, program, system, procedure, campaign, survey, study, forecast, estimate, customer list or technical data, or (6) any similar item, if the property has substantial value independent of the services of any individual. Temp. Reg. § 1.367(a)–1T(d)(5)(i). Note the breadth of this definition, particularly items (5) and (6). The only exceptions are set forth in Temp. Reg. § 1.367(d)–1T(b), which excludes from Section 367(d) transfers of "foreign goodwill or going concern value" (Temp. Reg. § 1.367(a)–1T(d)(5)(iii)) and of copyrights and certain comparable intangibles (Temp. Reg. § 1.367(a)–5T(b)(2)). Foreign goodwill and going concern value are defined as the residual value of a business operation conducted outside of the United States after all other tangible and intangible assets have been identified and valued. Temp. Reg. § 1.367(a)–1T(c)(5)(iii).

The temporary regulations contain rules for cases in which there is a later direct or indirect disposition of the intangible property transferred or of stock of the transferee corporation. In general, deemed annual license payments will continue if the disposition is made to a related person, as defined in Temp. Reg. § 1.367(d)–1T(h), while gain must be recognized immediately by the transferor if the disposition is to an unrelated person. Temp. Reg. § 1.367(d)–1T(d) through (f).

The valuation problems inherent in the requirement that a constructive arm's length royalty be established for all intangibles transferred to a foreign corporation in a Section 351 or 361 exchange are formidable, and they were compounded by enactment of Section 367(d)(2)(A). This provision, which is similar to the super-royalty provision added to Section 482 by the Tax Reform Act of 1986, states that the constructive royalty payments shall "be commensurate with the income attributable to the intangible." See ¶ 12,205. In order to ensure compliance, the constructive royalties are subject to periodic review and adjustment by the IRS. This requirement in the context of Section 482 is discussed in the Treasury's Section 482 White Paper. See ¶ 12,210. With respect to its application under Section 367(d), the White Paper states, in part, as follows (1988–2 C.B. at 473):

> 2. *Interaction with Section 367(d).* Section 367(d), enacted as part of the 1984 Tax Reform Act, provides that when intangible property is transferred by a U.S. person to a foreign corporation in a transaction described in section 351 or 361, the transferor shall be treated as receiving annual payments, over the useful life of the property, contingent on productivity or use of the property, regardless of whether such payments are actually made. These payments are treated as U.S. source income. [This rule was repealed by the 1997 Act, making the foreign-source rule of Section 862(a)(4) applicable.] A subsequent disposition to an unrelated party of either the intangible property or the stock in the transferee triggers immediate gain recognition. The 1986 Act made the commensurate with income standard applicable in computing payments attributable to the transferor under section 367(d). * * * [S]ection 367(d) may also suggest that certain exceptions from the periodic payment approach may be appropriate—e.g., transfers to corporations in which an unrelated corporation has a substantial enough interest that an objective valuation of the transferred intangible can be considered to be arm's length.
>
> Sales and licenses of intangibles are generally not subject to section 367(d), since they are not transactions described in section 351 or 361. The temporary regulations state that, when an actual license or sale has occurred, an adjustment to the consideration received by the transferor shall be made solely under section 482, without reference to section 367(d). However, if the purported sale or license to the related person is for no consideration or if the terms of the purported sale or license differ so greatly from the substance of an arm's length transfer that the transfer should be considered a sham, the transfer will be treated as falling within section 367(d).

Also, the problem of determining useful lives of assets, such as knowhow, a customer list or a brand name—a sampling of a very wide range of intangibles, can be challenging. Section 367(d) may require a long-term royalty in the case of assets with indeterminate lives. The temporary regulations state only that the useful life of intangible property is the entire period over which it has value but in no event will exceed 20 years. If intangible property derives its value from secrecy or protections afforded by law, the useful life terminates when the property is no longer secret or is no longer legally protected. Temp. Reg. § 1.367(d)–1T(c)(3).

The stated purpose for the 1997 Act change making Section 367(d) constructive royalties subject to the royalty source rule of Section

862(a)(4) applicable to royalties for the use of foreign intangibles was to facilitate the acquisition by U.S. persons of interests in foreign joint ventures that are licensees of U.S. technology and other intangibles. But it leaves in place some significant uncertainties concerning the treatment of the constructive royalties called for by Section 367(d). One uncertainty results principally from the fact that constructive royalties remain subject to the commensurate-with-the-income test and the periodic review and adjustment that the application of that test may imply. Moreover, the Section 367(d) "constructive" royalties result in no cash to the transferor with which to pay the tax on those royalties, and if no actual payment is made, the constructive royalties may not be deductible by the transferee under the tax law of the foreign-source country.

The transferor accruing the constructive (but unpaid) royalty sets up the payment as an account receivable, actual payment of which results in no includible income. No interest is accrued and no bad debt deduction can be taken with respect to such a receivable. Temp. Reg. § 1.367(d)–1T(g)(1)(i).

In rare cases, the transferor may prefer to have the gain realized on a transfer of intangibles in exchange for stock of a foreign corporation recognized in its entirety and taxed at the time of transfer. For example, the transferor might have an operating loss to offset the gain or might want to avoid the uncertainties of possible periodic review and adjustment of a Section 367(d) deemed royalty. The regulations permit the transferor to elect to have the transfer treated as a sale at its fair market value if specified, quite restrictive conditions are met. The income would be treated as U.S.-source ordinary income. Temp. Reg. § 1.367(d)–1T(g)(2). See ¶ 10,090.

An odd aspect of Section 367(d)(2)(C), noted above, is that, if the transfer of intangibles to a foreign corporation that is not controlled by the transferor constitutes a transfer of all substantial rights to the property, the transaction, if held to be taxable, should be characterized as a sale. In this case, the gain would qualify for long-term capital gain treatment, assuming that the property qualifies as a capital or Section 1231 asset that has been held for the requisite holding period of more than one year. However, while Section 367(d)(2)(C) treats the transaction as a sale, the constructive payments are necessarily treated as ordinary income even if all substantial rights have been transferred.

Finally, because Section 367(d) characterizes the transfer of foreign intangible rights for stock as a sale, but treats the proceeds as ordinary income, some uncertainty arose as to the application of the 904(d) foreign tax credit limitation regime. If the transferee foreign corporation is a controlled foreign corporation under Section 957(a), constructive royalty-like payments might be assimilated to actual royalties. If so, the Section

904(d)(3) look-through rules would apply under which the applicable foreign tax credit limitation basket would depend upon the underlying income of the transferee corporation to which the royalties are properly allocable. § 904(d)(3)(C). If the transferee corporation is not a controlled foreign corporation, the constructive payments could be treated as gain from the sale of foreign intangibles. Such gain would fall into the limitation basket called for under the regulations applicable generally to gain from the sale of foreign intangibles discussed at ¶ 12,125. This analysis could have resulted in treating the payments as falling within the passive income basket. The 2004 JOBS Act resolved this uncertainty retroactively by providing that constructive payments under Section 367(d) received on or after August 5, 1997 are treated as royalties for purposes of applying the foreign tax credit limitations. § 367(d)(2)(C).

Thus, if constructive Section 367(d) payments are received from a controlled foreign corporation, the Section 904(d)(3) look-through rules will apply. If received from a noncontrolled foreign corporation or from another related or unrelated party, they will fall into the general income limitation basket if derived in the active conduct of the transferor's trade or business. See ¶ 12,015. If not so derived, they will generally fall into the passive income basket.

[¶ 12,131]

2. REPEAL OF THE EXCISE TAX

Another major change made by the 1997 Act was to repeal the 35 percent excise tax imposed under former Sections 1491 through 1494 and the information-reporting rules that applied to transfers of appreciated property by a U.S. person to various foreign entities, such as foreign trusts, estates, partnerships and, in some cases, corporations.

Instead of the excise tax that applied under prior law to a transfer by a U.S. person to a foreign corporation as paid-in surplus or as a contribution to capital in a transaction not otherwise described in Section 367 (e.g., a capital contribution by a non-shareholder), regulatory authority is granted under Section 367(f) to treat such transfer as a fair market value sale and to require recognition of the gain realized. Instead of the excise tax that applied under prior law to transfers to foreign partnerships, regulatory authority is also granted by the 1997 Act to apply the constructive royalty treatment of Section 367(d) to transfers of intangibles to foreign partnerships and to source the royalties under the normal royalty source rule of Section 862(a)(4). Similarly, regulatory authority is granted to provide for gain recognition on a transfer of appreciated property to any partnership in cases in which such gain would be includible in the gross income of a foreign partner. §§ 367(d)(3), 721(c) and (d).

[¶ 12,135]

PROBLEMS

1. The IRS position for years has been that a transfer of intangibles to a foreign corporation will not qualify as a "transfer" of "property" for purposes of Section 351 unless it constitutes a transfer of all substantial rights, i.e., would qualify as a sale if the transaction were taxable. This position was rejected in E.I. du Pont de Nemours & Co. v. United States, at ¶ 12,160, but has never been abandoned by the IRS. In view of the provisions of Section 367(d), what tax consequences turn on whether the transaction qualifies under Section 351?

2. In the light of Section 367(d), why would taxpayers elect to transfer intangible properties to foreign corporations in Section 351 exchanges? Could advantages be gained by transferring intangible property rights to a foreign corporation under actual license agreements in return for actual royalties rather than through Section 351 transfers in exchange for stock in the transferee? Both are subject to periodic review and adjustment by the IRS under the test requiring that actual or constructive royalties be commensurate with the income of the transferee attributable to the transferred intangible. An actual royalty may qualify for treatment as long-term capital gain; a constructive royalty under Section 367(d) could not. Moreover, an actual royalty results in cash to the transferor while the Section 367(d) deemed royalty does not. An actual royalty will normally be deductible by the transferee, a section 367(b) royalty may not be. Part of the "bite" of Section 367(d) results from the fact that a U.S. corporation participating in a foreign joint venture corporation may be compelled by the requirements of its foreign partner or of the foreign government to take stock in exchange for its intangible property contribution rather than burden the joint venture corporation and the foreign country's current balance of payments with the payment of actual royalties.

[¶ 12,140]

3. "PROPERTY" REQUIREMENT

It is clear that patents, patent applications, trademarks, trade names and associated goodwill constitute "property" for purposes of Section 351. Although Section 936(h)(3)(B)(i) includes "knowhow" as a form of intangible property, as Rev. Rul. 64–56, presented below, suggests, the status of "knowhow" as property is not always clear. In part, this is attributable to the fact that the term "knowhow," as generally used, encompasses a wide range of elements. Often included under this extensive umbrella are inventions, secret processes or secret formulas that are unpatented or unpatentable; technical information that may be embodied in tangible specifications, designs, blueprints and the like and technical information and skills that are not or cannot be reduced to tangible form and that must be communicated through the rendering of technical assistance by the personnel who have accumulated the information and skills involved.

[¶ 12,145]

REVENUE RULING 64–56

1964–1 C.B. (Part 1) 133.

The Internal Revenue Service has received inquiries whether technical "know-how" constitutes property which can be transferred, without recognition of gain or loss, in exchange for stock * * * under Section 351 * * *.

The issue has been drawn to the attention of the Service, particularly in cases in which a manufacturer agrees to assist a newly organized foreign corporation to enter upon a business abroad of making and selling the same kind of product as it makes. The transferor typically grants to the transferee rights to use manufacturing processes in which the transferor has exclusive rights by virtue of process patents or the protection otherwise extended by law to the owner of a process. The transferor also often agrees to furnish technical assistance in the construction and operation of the plant and to provide on a continuing basis technical information as to new developments in the field.

Some of this consideration is commonly called "know-how." In exchange, the transferee typically issues to the transferor all or part of its stock.

* * *

Since the term "know-how" does not appear in section 351 * * *, its meaning is immaterial in applying this section, and the Service will look behind the term in each case to determine to what extent, if any, the items so called constitute "property * * * transferred to a corporation * * * in exchange for stock."

The term "property" for purposes of section 351 * * * will be held to include anything qualifying as "secret processes and formulas" within the meaning of sections 861(a)(4) and 862(a)(4) * * * and any other secret information as to a device, process, etc., in the general nature of a patentable invention without regard to whether a patent has been applied for * * * and without regard to whether it is patentable in the patent law sense * * *. Other information which is secret will be given consideration as "property" on a case-by-case basis.

The fact that information is recorded on paper or some other physical material is not itself an indication that the information is property. * * *

It is assumed for the purpose of this Revenue Ruling that the country in which the transferee is to operate affords to the transferor substantial legal protection against the unauthorized disclosure and use of the process, formula, or other secret information involved.

Once it is established that "property" has been transferred, the transfer will be tax-free under section 351 [before enactment of Section

367(d)] even though services were used to produce the property. Such is generally the case where the transferor developed the property primarily for use in its own manufacturing business. However, where the information transferred has been developed specially for the transferee, the stock received in exchange for it may be treated as payment for services rendered. See [Regenstein v. Commissioner, 35 T.C. 183 (1960)], where the taxpayer developed a plan for selling insurance which he ultimately sold to certain insurance companies. The court held that the consideration received was payment for services.

Where the transferor agrees to perform services in connection with a transfer of property, tax-free treatment will be accorded if the services are merely ancillary and subsidiary to the property transfer. Whether or not services are merely ancillary and subsidiary to a property transfer is a question of fact. Ancillary and subsidiary services could be performed, for example, in promoting the transaction by demonstrating and explaining the use of the property, or by assisting in the effective "starting-up" of the property transferred, or by performing under a guarantee relating to such effective starting-up. * * * Where both property and services are furnished as consideration, and the services are not merely ancillary and subsidiary to the property transfer, a reasonable allocation is to be made.

Training the transferee's employees in skills of any grade through expertness, for example, in a recognized profession, craft, or trade is to be distinguished as essentially educational and, like any other teaching services, is taxable when compensated in stock or otherwise, without being affected by section 351 * * *. However, where the transferee's employees concerned already have the particular skills in question, it will ordinarily follow as a matter of fact that other consideration alone and not training in those skills is being furnished for the transferee's stock.

Continuing technical assistance after the starting-up phase will not be regarded as performance under a guarantee, and the consideration therefor will ordinarily be treated as compensation for professional services, taxable without regard to section 351 * * *. * * *

Assistance in the construction of a plant building to house machinery transferred, or to house machinery to be used in applying a patented or other process or formula which qualifies as property transferred, will ordinarily be considered to be in the nature of an architect's or construction engineer's services rendered to the transferee and not merely rendered on behalf of the transferor in producing, or promoting the sale or exchange of, the things transferred. Similarly, advice as to the lay-out of plant machinery and equipment may be so unrelated to the particular property transferred as to constitute no more than a rendering of advisory services to the transferee.

The transfer of all substantial rights in property of the kind hereinbefore specified will be treated as a transfer of property for purposes of section 351 * * *. The transfer will also qualify under section 351 * * * if the transferred rights extend to all of the territory of one or more countries and consist of all substantial rights therein, the transfer being clearly limited to such territory, notwithstanding that rights are retained as to some other country's territory. * * *

The property right in a formula may consist of the method of making a composition and the composition itself, namely the proportions of its ingredients, or it may consist of only the method of making the composition. Where the property right in the secret formula consists of both the composition and the method of making it, the unqualified transfer in perpetuity of the exclusive right to use the formula, including the right to use and sell the products made from and representing the formula, within all the territory of the country will be treated as the transfer of all substantial rights in the property in that country.

The unqualified transfer in perpetuity of the exclusive right to use a secret process or other similar secret information qualifying as property within all the territory of a country, or the unqualified transfer in perpetuity of the exclusive right to make, use and sell an unpatented but secret product within all the territory of a country, will be treated as the transfer of all substantial rights in the property in that country.

[¶ 12,150]

NOTE

In Rev. Rul. 71–564, 1971–2 C.B. 179, the IRS liberalized the requirement that the transfer be in perpetuity by recognizing that what is required is a transfer of a trade secret for its full life. The Ruling stated that an unqualified transfer of the exclusive right to use a trade secret until it becomes public knowledge and no longer protectible under the applicable law of the country where the transferee is to operate constitutes a transfer of property for purposes of Rev. Rul. 64–56.

The central problem is to distinguish property from services. Note that the IRS in Rev. Rul. 64–56 was unwilling to commit itself in advance to recognize as property any knowhow that did not fall within the description of "secret information as to a device, process, formula etc., in the general nature of a patentable invention;" the status of other information will be determined on a case-by-case basis. There is room for considerable skepticism about the distinction the IRS appears to draw between secret information relating to a device or process in the general nature of a patentable invention and other secret information, especially when the problem is viewed in the light of cases indicating that confidentiality and the legal protection of the holder against unauthorized disclosure are the most significant indicia of "property" in this context. E.g., Commercial Solvents Corp. v. Commissioner, 42 T.C. 455 (1964) (acq.); E.I. du Pont de Nemours & Co. v. United States, at ¶ 12,075. There is also authority for the view that secret information concerning customers constitutes property, e.g., Commissioner v. Killian, 314 F.2d 852 (5th Cir. 1963), and that trade secrets generally fall within the tax law concept of property. See Ruppert & Pansius, "Transfers of Knowhow under Section 351," 55 Denv. U. L. Rev. 223 (1978). Included in the definition of intangible property are any method, program, system, procedure, campaign, survey, study, forecast, estimate, customer list, technical data and any similar item. § 936(h)(3)(B). However, in Rev. Rul. 64–56 the IRS rejects the relevance of the fact that the "knowhow" is reduced to the printed page. See also Rev. Proc. 69–19, 1969–2 C.B. 301.

Rev. Rul. 64–56 implies that knowhow will be considered property only if the law of the country in which it is to be used affords substantial protection against unauthorized disclosure. Presumably this means at the least that, under the foreign law of unfair competition or its counterpart, any unauthorized disclosure of the knowhow to a third party by an employee or agent of the owner without the consent of the owner is an actionable tort.

Before the 1984 Act, the Code required that a ruling be obtained from the IRS if a transfer of property in exchange for stock of a transferee foreign corporation were to qualify for nonrecognition of gain under Sections 351 and 367. As a condition to obtaining such a ruling with respect to transfers of knowhow in exchange for stock, the IRS required in Rev. Proc. 69–19, 1969–2 C.B. 301, 302 that the following representations be made by the taxpayer:

* * *

SEC. 3 STATEMENTS TO BE INCLUDED IN RULING REQUESTS.

> .01 * * * "It is represented that the 'information' being transferred in exchange for stock under section 351 is 'property' within the meaning of Revenue Ruling 64–56, C.B. 1964–1 (Part I), 133, and as such is afforded substantial legal protection against unauthorized disclosure and use under the laws of the country from which it is being transferred. It is further represented that any services to be performed in connection with the transfer of the property are merely ancillary and subsidiary to the property transfer within the meaning of Revenue Ruling 64–56 or the transferor will be compensated by a fee negotiated at arm's length (in consideration other than stock or securities of the transferee unless such stock or securities are identified) for any other services to be performed on behalf of the transferee."
>
> .02 In making such representations the taxpayer should in his request for ruling describe the "information" involved and state that:
>
> (a) the "information" is secret in that it is known only by the owner and those confidential employees who require the "information" for use in the conduct of the activities to which it is related and adequate safeguards have been taken to guard the secret against unauthorized disclosure, and
>
> (b) the "information" represents a discovery and, while not necessarily patentable, the "information" is original, unique, and novel.

.03 The statements and representations described in .01 and .02 above must be based upon the following criteria and facts and the request for a ruling should affirmatively state the presence or absence of such criteria or facts by reference to this subsection of this Revenue Procedure:

(a) The "information" is not revealed by a patent, is not the subject of a patent application, nor is it disclosed by the product on which it is used or to which it is related.

(b) The "information" does not represent mere knowledge, or efficiency resulting from experience, or mere skill in manipulation or total accumulated experience and skill of the transferor.

(c) The "information" involved is not merely the rights to tangible evidence of information such as blueprints, drawings or other physical material on which it is recorded.

(d) The "information" has not been developed especially for the transferee.

(e) The "information" is not in the form of assistance in the construction of a plant building or advice as to the layout of machinery and equipment.

(f) The "information" is not training of the transferee's employees that is essentially educational in nature.

(g) Technical information of a related or similar nature such as new developments in the field will not be furnished on a continuing basis without adequate compensation therefor in the manner prescribed for services in the statement in subsection .01 above.

SEC. 4. CONCLUSION.

If the above representations are made by the transferor the Service will consider for purposes of the requested ruling that the country in which the transferee is to operate affords to the transferor substantial legal protection against the unauthorized disclosure and use of the information.

[¶ 12,155]

4. "TRANSFER" REQUIREMENT

Rev. Rul. 64–56, at ¶ 12,145, takes the position that to qualify under Section 351 the transfer must be of "all substantial rights" to the property concerned. Rev. Rul. 69–156, 1969–1 C.B. 101, indicates that this is the same test that is applied in determining whether a transfer constitutes a "sale" for tax purposes. But see the *Du Pont* case, at ¶ 12,160. Thus, an outright and unconditional assignment would clearly qualify. In this case, legal title to the property is transferred and, if a patent, trademark or copyright is involved, steps must be taken to have the transferee registered as the owner in the appropriate register.

Typically, however, the transferor prefers to effect the transfer by exclusive license rather than by assignment. This is so because the license technique facilitates the retention by the transferor of certain controls over the use of the property rights by the transferee and the recovery of those rights in certain events, such as the bankruptcy or expropriation of the transferee. Usually retention of certain controls and rights of recapture are especially important, as a business matter, to the U.S. transferor in the joint venture context when that transferor holds only a minority or a 50–percent noncontrolling equity participation in the transferee. For example, if the transferee fails to utilize the intangible property rights effectively, the transferor may wish to have the right to terminate the license and regain the intangible property rights concerned. In addition, the transferor may wish to retain the right to veto any sublicensing by the transferee. The use of an exclusive license also may make it possible for the transferor to transfer exclusive rights to less than all of the geographical area (i.e., the country) covered by a patent or to fewer than all of the functional applications to which an invention may be suited. See ¶ 12,060.

The retention of strings by the transferor in an exclusive license that is exchanged for stock in a foreign corporation presents problems analogous to those in connection with licensing on a capital-gains basis, discussed at ¶¶ 12,025 et seq. The IRS may take the position that the retention of strings by the transferor will prevent the license from qualifying as a Section 351 "transfer."

Finally, it should be noted that the transfer requirement is closely intertwined with the "property" requirement, and if certain rights, such as the rights to use an invention in certain applications, are retained by the transferor, the IRS may take the position that the bundle of licensed rights do not constitute "property" for purposes of Section 351.

[¶ 12,160]

E.I. DU PONT DE NEMOURS & CO. v. UNITED STATES

United States Court of Claims, 1973.
471 F.2d 1211.

DAVIS, JUDGE:

We are narrowly concerned with only one issue * * *—the application of section 351 * * *.

In 1959, Du Pont was engaged in the domestic sale and exportation (to France, among other places) of urea herbicides. Although doing the manufacturing in this country, the company owned French patents for the product. French law provided that French-patented items must be manufactured in France within three years of the issuance of the patent. If this were not done, the owner had to grant, upon request, a license to a French producer. In order to forestall that result, with its potential loss of income,

Du Pont organized (in October 1959) a wholly-owned French subsidiary, Du Pont de Nemours (France) S.A., to manufacture the herbicide in France.[2] By agreement in December 1959 plaintiff granted to the subsidiary a royalty-free, non-exclusive license to make, use and sell urea herbicides under the French patents. Du Pont thereby gave up its right to assert patent infringement against the subsidiary's products for the duration of the license, which was for the remaining life of the patents. The subsidiary had the right to sublicense manufacturing for its own needs, but any other sublicensing could only be done with the parent's consent. In exchange for this grant, and in lieu of royalties, Du Pont received stock in the subsidiary valued at $411,500. After the award of the license, the subsidiary proceeded to arrange for manufacture of the herbicides for its own account by an unrelated French firm.

Before undertaking this arrangement, taxpayer requested rulings from the Commissioner of Internal Revenue as to whether the proposed transaction would comply with the requirements of sections 351 and 367 * * *. Section 351(a), as enacted in the 1954 Code and in effect in 1959, provided that:

> (a) General Rule.—No gain or loss shall be ... recognized if property is transferred to a corporation by one or more persons solely in exchange for stock or securities in such corporation and immediately after the exchange such person or persons are in control (as defined in section 368(c)) of the corporation. For purposes of this section, stock or securities issued for services shall not be considered as issued in return for property.

Section 367 declared that, if the transaction involved transfer of property to a foreign corporation in exchange for its stock, nonrecognition would only be granted if it were established to the Commissioner's satisfaction that the exchange were not part of a plan for the avoidance of federal income tax. The Internal Revenue Service ruled in November 1959 that the demands of section 367 were met, but not those of section 351. It was said that "[s]ince all substantial rights of the patents will not be transferred * * * to the new French company, such patents will not be considered property within the meaning of section 351 * * *." Despite this holding, Du Pont proceeded with the incorporation of the subsidiary, and the grant of the non-exclusive license, but the worth of the affiliate's stock was not included as income in taxpayer's 1959 return. Since the shares received by Du Pont were valued at $411,500, and it claimed no basis in the patents, the size of the present claim by defendant for setoff is $411,500.

---

2. If forced to grant a license to a French manufacturer, Du Pont feared that the French market would be cut off for all non-French producers of the herbicide. In that situation, the license royalties Du Pont would receive would approximate, it thought, only one third of the income it could expect through its own French manufacturer.

There is no question, of course, that plaintiff meets the condition of section 351 that it must be in control of the subsidiary after the transaction. The controversy implicates the other prime elements of the provision: "property", "transfer", "exchange." The Government has vacillated somewhat in tying the articulation of its position to one or another of those statutory terms. The 1959 ruling given to taxpayer deemed the patent rights transferred to the subsidiary not to be "property". Conceding that this "did not adequately express the basis for the Government's action," the defendant now stresses the reasoning of Rev. Rul. 69–156, 1969–1 Cum. Bull. 101:

> The grant of patent rights to a corporation will constitute a transfer of property within the meaning of section 351 of the Code only if the grant of these rights in a transaction which would ordinarily be taxable, would constitute a sale or exchange of property rather than a license for purposes of determining gain or loss. In order for such a grant of patent rights to * * * constitute a sale or exchange, the grant must consist of all substantial rights to the patent.

The present emphasis is thus on the "exchange" requirement, with that factor being equated with the concept of "sale or exchange" under the capital gains provisions of the Code. If a transaction does not qualify as a "sale or exchange" for those purposes, it cannot (according to the defendant) be a "transfer" of "property" "in exchange" under section 351. On that view, the Government would be entitled to its offset since it is settled that the proceeds of a grant of a simple non-exclusive patent license are not eligible for capital gains treatment. To attain that status there must normally be a transfer of an interest in all substantial rights to the patent, or of exclusive rights in a defined area. * * *

I.

The first and principal problem, then, is whether section 351 embodies the same notions as the capital gains provisions * * *. In searching out the answer, we look to the language of the sections being compared, their individual purposes, their history and context, as well as their treatment by the courts.

Congress, it is plain, did not use identical wording. First, section 351 speaks of "property", not of "capital assets", and the Government concedes that section 351 can apply to property which is not a capital asset. * * * Second, the capital gains part of the Code uses "sale or exchange" of an asset * * * [see § 1222], while section 351 is phrased in terms of property "transferred * * * in exchange." This latter difference is obviously not controlling, but the fact that the drafters made the distinction in language cautions against a wholesale and automatic adoption by section 351 of the concepts of the capital gains provisions. The bare words of the statutes do not compel, or even favor, their parallel application, as might have been the case if they were worded identically. With some indulgence to defendant, we can count the language as basically neutral in itself.

However, we do view the contrasting purposes of the two parts of the Code as undermining, affirmatively and seriously, the Government's position. In order to qualify for the tax relief of lower rates under the capital gains provisions, there must be complete divestiture of the taxpayer's interest in property of a particular nature, capital assets. In such cases, there is no doubt about the actual flow of gain to the taxpayer from an outside source. Section 351, on the other hand, is not concerned with situations involving true severance of control and true flow of gain, but, rather, with instances which Congress considered as revealing illusory or artificial relinquishment of control and illusory or artificial gain. The transferor in section 351 cases is required to remain in control, albeit indirectly, after the transfer. There is, in short, a transfer in form only, a technical transfer not one of substance. The section is designed to give present tax relief for internal rearrangements of the taxpayer's own assets, accompanied by no sacrifice of control and no real generation of income for the owner—and to defer taxation until a true outside disposition is made.

* * *

This direct opposition in the aims of the two sets of provisions—the capital gains sections stressing the completeness of disposition by the taxpayer while section 351 is grounded in the taxpayer's continuance in control—supplies a compelling reason for putting aside, in applying the latter, capital gains formulations. Where the goals of two pieces of legislation are contradictory, it is appropriate, if the words permit, to treat them independently and to let the application of each be governed by its own separate purpose.

* * *

This emphasis on the taxpayer's continuous interest and continuous control, as the essence of section 351, is convincing to us, and persuades strongly against defendant's point that the requirement of full disposition as a precondition to a "sale or exchange" for capital gains purposes should be imported into [section] 351. In view of the congressional aim in the latter provision to disregard dispositions which are merely formal and do not have economic or commercial reality, it is proper to accept, as a "transfer * * * in exchange," those dispositions which are less than substantially complete. If the transactions that most look like complete dispositions, but in reality are not dispositions at all, are free of tax because they are not deemed true dispositions, then transactions that have less appearance of complete dispositions should also be free, so long as control is maintained over what is transferred through the receipt of the transferee's stock. It would be odd to hold that a transfer had to look most like a complete disposition in order to avoid being treated for tax purposes as a complete disposition.

If Du Pont had made a full assignment of the patents to its subsidiary, the Government would agree that section 351 was entirely satisfied—and yet the taxpayer would have made no more of a true disposition to an outsider than in the present situation; in reality there would be no greater severance of control. In terms of the ends of section 351, there is no more reason for that transaction to be covered than the one we have here. In other words, in this respect the capital gains concept of a "sale and exchange" is simply irrelevant to section 351, which has a quite different purpose and an independent postulate. To insist, nevertheless, on applying that alien notion is to bring about disparate results not rationally connected to the fundamental principle behind section 351—the paradigmatic example of "mechanical jurisprudence."

Defendant's best counter-argument is that the predecessors of section 351 and the capital-gain-and-loss provisions had their joint birth in the Revenue Act of 1921 where they were placed in very close proximity, and that this juxtaposition continued for many years. Until 1954, the recognition provision for "sales or exchanges" and the exceptions to the recognition provision (including the forerunners of section 351) were positioned next to each other. * * * The Government draws the conclusion that, at least where a nonrecognition section uses the word "exchange," Congress intended the very same meaning to be given to that term as in the "sale or exchange" recognition provisions; those nonrecognition sections should simply be read, defendant says, as subordinate exceptions to the general provision providing for recognition of gain from a "sale or exchange."

There is obviously some force to this textual contention, but an "inference drawn from the juxtaposition and cross referencing" of related sections will be overborne by other more powerful factors. * * * We think that is true here. The elements of cognate origin and statutory juxtaposition are outbalanced by the great variance between the purposes of [section] 351 and of the capital gains sections, and by the clear irrelevance of the concepts from the latter, which defendant invokes, to the goals and theory of the former. And, as we have already said, the bare terminology of [section] 351 is not so identical to that of the capital gains sections that a court might feel driven by the parallelism of language to treat them as twins, despite the clear difference in purpose.

II.

Having rejected defendant's chief point that "transfer * * * in exchange" under section 351 is tied to and has the same scope as "sale or exchange" under the capital gains sections, we still have to determine whether [section] 351, as an autonomous provision, covers plaintiff's transaction. * * *

Once the capital gains concepts are seen as irrelevant, it is not difficult to find that the non-exclusive license handed over to the subsidiary was "property". Both patents themselves and the exclusive licensing of patents have long been considered "property" under [section] 351. It is not a far step to include a non-exclusive license of substantial value—commonly thought of in the commercial world as a positive business asset. Unless there is some special reason intrinsic to the particular provision (as there is with respect to capital assets), the general word "property" has a broad reach in tax law. * * * For section 351, in particular, courts have advocated a generous definition of "property", * * * and it has been suggested in one capital gains case that non-exclusive licenses can be viewed as property though not as capital assets. * * *

We see no adequate reason for refusing to follow these leads. Defendant now concedes that the license was "property" in the hands of the transferee, but does not agree that Du Pont gave up any "property." But, as taxpayer says, although the rights granted were "not all the rights under the patents, they were perpetual, irrevocable, and quite substantial in value." Taxpayer surrendered its right to assert infringement against the subsidiary even though it retained the right to prevent others from operating under the patent. The subsidiary could proceed without fear of an infringement suit. One chunk of rights was permanently severed from the main property—the patent. In common understanding, this segment can easily be considered "property" transferred, although it was not a full cross section of the patent. Nothing in the legislative purpose of section 351 counsels a narrower reading. Congress, as we have said, wished to free taxpayers from immediate tax where they remained in control of valuable items, even though the taxpayer made some intra-business rearrangements, and to postpone the tax until complete disposition to an outsider. That objective fits this case exactly; Du Pont remains in control, and there has not as yet been a disposition to an outsider. Under the theory of the section, there is no reason for tax at this time.

Similarly with the other statutory elements of "transfer" and "exchange." Freed of the capital gains gloss, those terms plainly apply to this transaction. Du Pont handed over something of value and received stock in return; in normal understanding there was a mutual exchange. * * * And, again, the aim of section 351 is advanced and fulfilled by applying it to taxpayer's transaction.

To all of this the defendant's answer—aside from its primary contention rejected in Part I, *supra*—is that, if nonexclusive licenses are covered by [section] 351, it will be extremely difficult to determine what portion of the transferor's basis for his patent should be carried over to a non-exclusive license, when the licensor retains the right to issue an indeterminate number of additional licenses. Generally, by section 362(a), the transferee's basis for the transferred property would be the "same as it would be in the hands of the transferor,'' increased by the amount of gain recognized by the transferor through the transfer. * * *

In this particular case there is no problem of basis allocation since Du Pont claims no basis in the French patents. But we need not rest on that happenstance. Other cases have presented similar problems of proper allocation between retained and transferred value, and the courts have been able to reach satisfactory solutions. * * *

* * *

For these reasons, we hold that section 351 applies to taxpayer's transaction, and defendant is not entitled to the offset it claims. Plaintiff's motion for partial summary judgment is granted, the defendant's cross-motion is denied, and the defendant's claimed offset with respect to this transaction is disallowed.

[¶ 12,165]

5. TRANSFER AS CONTRIBUTION TO CAPITAL

If foreign rights to intangible property are transferred as a contribution to capital of a foreign corporation, there will generally be no gain or loss for U.S. tax purposes because there is considered to be no sale or exchange. There is, however, an important exception to this general rule. Section 367(c)(2) provides that a contribution to capital will be treated as a constructive exchange for stock when one or more transferors own directly (or by attribution of ownership under Section 318(a)) at least 80 percent of the total combined voting power of all classes of stock of the transferee corporation immediately after the transfer. In this case the exchange will be subject to the tax treatment prescribed by Section 367(d). See ¶ 12,130. Under this provision, the transferee is deemed to make constructive royalty payments to the transferor that are subject to tax as ordinary income from foreign sources and that may be subject to periodic adjustment under the super-royalty provision discussed at ¶ 12,205.

In cases not covered by Section 367(c)(2), a contribution of foreign rights to intangible property to a foreign corporation not in exchange for stock (or to a foreign partnership or trust) is to the extent provided in regulations (not yet issued) to be treated as a sale for an amount equal to the fair market value of the property. § 367(f).

[¶ 12,170]

6. FOREIGN TAXES IN CONNECTION WITH TRANSFER OF INTANGIBLE PROPERTY RIGHTS IN EXCHANGE FOR STOCK OR AS CONTRIBUTION TO CAPITAL

Income tax is often not imposed in foreign countries in connection with a transfer of intangible property rights by a U.S. corporation in exchange for stock of a transferee foreign corporation or as a contribution to capital. Even if the transferee corporation issued debt obligations in consideration for the transfer of intangible property and the transaction were treated as a sale, the transferor would usually not be subject to income tax on any gain realized, provided that it has no permanent establishment in the transferee's country to which the gain is attributable. This will normally be the result if a tax treaty is applicable and may also be the result under foreign law in the absence of an applicable treaty.

In cases in which the transfer is effected in exchange for stock or as a contribution to capital, any registration and stamp taxes normally associated with an issuance of stock or increase in capital would be payable.

E. BASE COMPANY LICENSING

[¶ 12,175]

1. INCENTIVES TO BASE COMPANY LICENSING

A U.S. corporation planning an extensive program for the exploitation of intangible property rights abroad may conclude that the program can best be conducted by an organization established outside the United States. A well located foreign licensing headquarters, which is able to follow closely foreign industrial and marketing developments, will often be in a better position to seek out effective licensees and opportunities to obtain equity participations in foreign enterprises through the contribution of intangible property rights than a licensing organization headquartered in the United States.

Although the opportunities for tax savings are narrowly circumscribed as a result of the controlled foreign corporation provisions of the Code, discussed in Chapter 6, there may still be tax incentives to base company licensing. In some cases, a significant impetus to using a base company for foreign licensing derives from the fact that a considerably larger after-tax profit can be achieved by accumulating royalties in a base company than by having such royalties paid directly to a U.S. licensor corporation. Thus, to take an example, royalties paid by a Belgian licensee to a Swiss base company are exempt from income tax in Belgium; they are free of the Belgian corporate tax because they are deductible by the payor and they are exempt from the Belgian withholding tax under the Belgium–Switzerland Income Tax Treaty. The royalties are subject to tax in Switzerland in certain cantons at rates not in excess of 20 percent. Hence, if we ignore the expenses that would be incidental to the earning of this royalty income and the Belgian value added tax which would be applicable to royalties paid to a Swiss or a U.S. licensor, out of $100 of royalty paid by the Belgian licensee, there would be a profit after taxes in Switzerland of approximately $80. By contrast, if that royalty were paid directly to the U.S. corporation and taxed as ordinary income, the after-tax profit would be only $65 after imposition of a 35 percent U.S. corporate tax.

This saving is dependent on the base company's royalty income not being foreign personal holding company income, which would be treated as a Subpart F inclusion to the U.S. parent corporation. It therefore requires that the base company's licensing income be excluded from foreign base company income, most commonly under the active-business-unrelated-person exception of Section 954(c)(2)(A) but also possibly under the same-country-related-person exception of Section 954(c)(3)(A) or under the de minimis exception of Section 954(b)(3). The amount of the saving will also be influenced by the rate of tax on royalty income imposed by the country in which the base company is established and the rate of withholding tax imposed by the licensee's country on royalties received by the base company; the lower the tax in the base company country and the withholding tax at the source, the greater the tax saving from accumulating the royalty income in the base company will be.

Another factor that may make accumulating royalty income in a licensing base company attractive is that it is often possible to achieve a much larger after-tax accumulation by drawing off a given amount from an operating foreign subsidiary in the form of a royalty paid to a base company than in the form of dividend paid to a U.S. parent corporation or to the base company. This benefit is also contingent on the royalties being excluded from foreign personal holding company income.

In some cases, an important tax incentive to licensing through a foreign base company will be the possibility of using the base company's royalty income, which is often subject to low or to no withholding tax in the source country as the result of an applicable income tax treaty or foreign law, to absorb excess foreign tax credits generated by other foreign-source income, such as dividends, that is subject to relatively high foreign taxes. This benefit turns on the base company's royalties being treated as general limitation income rather than as passive income for purposes of the Section 904 limitations on the foreign tax credit. It can be achieved in two principal situations discussed at ¶ 12,190. First, if the royalties received by the base company are excluded from the definition of foreign personal holding company income under one of the applicable exceptions, most probably the active-business-unrelated-person exception, they will constitute general limitation income. Moreover, under Temp. Reg. § 1.904–4T(b)(2)(iii), the same treatment would be accorded to royalties from related persons for purposes of the limitations on the foreign tax credit (but not for purposes of Subpart F).

Second, under the Section 904(d)(3) look-through rules, even if royalty income received by the controlled foreign corporation from unrelated persons (or related persons under Temp. Reg. § 1.904–4T(b)(2)(iii)(A)) is foreign personal holding company income to the base company, it may still be placed in the general limitation basket under a special affiliated corporation rule. Temp. Reg. § 1.904–4T(b)(2)(iii)(B). See ¶ 12,190. Under this rule, if the U.S. parent corporation meets the active-business test, the base company is deemed to do so also for purposes of the Section 904 limitations. The result is that the royalty income of the base company falls into the general limitation basket.

Under the Section 904(d)(3) look-through rules, the general limitation royalty income of the base company can be used to absorb excess credits of the U.S. parent corporation associated with other general limitation income. This is true whether that royalty income is treated as a Subpart F inclusion or is distributed as a dividend, or the base company pays interest, rents or royalties to its U.S. parent corporation properly allocable to such royalty income of the base company.

[¶ 12,180]

2. SELECTION OF BASE COUNTRY FOR LICENSING OPERATIONS

The first important attribute for a country in which a licensing base company could advantageously be established is a tax system under which foreign-source royalties are exempt from taxation or are subject to taxes imposed at relatively low rates.

A second important attribute for a licensing base company country from a tax point of view is the existence of a network of income tax treaties between the base company country and the countries in which the foreign licensees will be located. Such treaties are important because they normally reduce or eliminate the income taxes on royalties which would otherwise be withheld at the source, provided that the base company licensor has no permanent establishment in the source country to which the royalties are attributable. The existence of income tax treaties is, of course, significant only where the countries in which prospective licensees are located are party to such treaties with countries that otherwise qualify as base company countries for foreign licensing activities. When the licensee is located in a country having no such tax treaties, the relative tax burden in the base company country on foreign-source royalties will be the primary tax factor favoring one base company country over another.

A country frequently selected as a base for licensing operations is Switzerland because it combines a relatively low rate of tax on foreign-source royalties with a broad tax treaty network. Although in Switzerland significant taxes are imposed on foreign-source royalties, these taxes are considerably lower than the income taxes normally imposed on royalties in the source countries which are eliminated by the Swiss income tax treaties. Accordingly, when a licensee is located in a country having a tax treaty with Switzerland, greater tax savings can be realized if the licensor base company is located in Switzerland than if the licensor were a Bermuda company. If the licensor were a Bermuda company, no tax would be imposed in Bermuda, but the full withholding tax on the royalties would be imposed in the source country because Bermuda is not a party to a significant tax treaty network. If, however, a licensee is located in a country that is party to no income tax treaties with potential base company countries, greater tax savings will be realized by using a Bermuda than by using a Swiss licensing company.

[¶ 12,185]

3. EFFECT OF SUBPART F ON LICENSING THROUGH A CONTROLLED FOREIGN CORPORATION

Certain provisions of Subpart F have an important impact on the licensing of intangible property rights abroad by a foreign corporation falling within the definition of a controlled foreign corporation. Royalty income meeting the definition of "foreign personal holding company income" in Section 954(c) will, in many cases, be treated as foreign base company income and, in turn, as Subpart F income that will be taxed to ten-percent U.S. shareholders as a constructive dividend even though not distributed to them.

If the foreign licensing company avoids the controlled foreign corporation definition, for example, because 50 percent of the voting power and value of its stock is owned by foreign interests, Subpart F has no impact on the tax advantages of base company licensing. As noted above, even if the licensing company is a controlled foreign corporation, base company licensing will also produce savings if the royalty income can escape the "foreign personal holding company income" definition.

A narrow exception to this definition that may be helpful is set forth in Section 954(c)(3)(A). That exception provides that foreign personal holding company income does not include royalties and similar payments received from a "related person" (as defined in Section 954(d)(3)) for the use of, or the privilege of using, property within the country under the laws of which the controlled foreign corporation is created or organized. Thus, royalties received by a Swiss licensing company from a related person under a license of Swiss patents would avoid classification as foreign personal holding company income.

A much more important exception is embodied in Section 954(c)(2)(A), which excludes from foreign personal holding company income royalties that are "derived in the active conduct of a trade or business" and that are received from a person other than a "related person" (as defined in Section 954(d)(3)). Here the key problem is how much activity by the controlled foreign corporation associated with licensing will be required to meet the "derived in the active conduct of a trade or business" test. Reg. § 1.954–2(d) provides a detailed definition of this concept. See ¶ 12,015.

Even if the licensing company is a controlled foreign corporation and its royalty income is foreign personal holding company income, this income may be sheltered from U.S. tax by one of the relief provisions of Subpart F, such as the de minimis exception of Section 954(b)(3)(A). The high-foreign-tax exception of Section 954(b)(4) will not apply if, as is usually the case, the licensing company is organized in a low-tax country.

[¶ 12,190]

4. EFFECT OF FOREIGN TAX CREDIT LIMITATIONS ON LICENSING THROUGH CONTROLLED FOREIGN CORPORATION

When the U.S. parent corporation is in or near an excess foreign tax credit position, licensing through a controlled foreign licensing corporation may be of assistance in absorbing excess foreign tax credits. Such licensing may result in a lower foreign tax burden on foreign-source royalties than if the royalties were earned by the U.S. parent corporation. These low-taxed royalties will be helpful in absorbing excess foreign tax credits if they are included in the foreign tax credit general limitation basket of Section 904(d)(1)(B). If the royalty income of the base company, which is a controlled foreign corporation, is excluded from the Section 954(c) definition of foreign personal holding company income because, for example, under Section 954(c)(2)(A), it is derived in the active conduct of a trade or business and is received from an unrelated person, it will not be treated as passive income in the Section 904(d)(1)(A) basket. Instead, such royalty income will be subject to the Section 904(d)(1)(B) general limitation. Temp. Reg. § 1.904–4T(b)(2)(iii)(A) accords the same treatment to such royalties received from a related person. In this situation, under the Section 904(d)(3) look-through rules, any actual dividends received by the U.S. parent corporation out of the base company's royalty income will be general limitation income that can be mixed with other general limitation income of the parent that bears relatively high foreign taxes. The same will be true of any interest, rents or royalties paid by the controlled foreign corporation to its U.S. parent corporation that are properly allocable to the latter's general limitation royalty income. Thus, the high foreign taxes can be cross-credited against the U.S. taxes that would otherwise be imposed on the licensing corporation's royalty income subject to low foreign taxes. In this way, foreign tax credits that would otherwise exceed the general limitation can be used.

Even if royalty income is included in the licensing corporation's foreign personal holding company income, it may be treated as Section 904(d)(1)(B) general limitation income because it is deemed to be derived in an active business under the special affiliated corporation rule of Temp. Reg. § 1.904–4T(b)(2)(iii)(B). For purposes of the foreign tax credit limitations, a foreign licensing corporation at least 80–percent owned by a U.S.

parent corporation will be deemed to meet the derived-in-the-active-business test of Section 954(c)(2)(A) if the U.S. parent corporation meets this test.[8] Accordingly, if the U.S. parent met the active-business test because its research facilities developed the invention or knowhow concerned, its 80–percent-owned licensing base company would also be deemed to do so. This rule does not apply for purposes of the controlled foreign corporation provisions. Thus, if the foreign licensing corporation itself does not meet the active-business test, its royalty income will be foreign personal holding company income that may be taxed as a Subpart F inclusion to its U.S. parent. However, under this special affiliated corporation rule, the Subpart F inclusion will be general limitation income and under the Section 904(d)(3) look-through rules will be general limitation income in the hands of its parent corporation that can be used to absorb excess foreign tax credits generated by other general limitation income. See Temp. Reg. § 1.904–4T(b)(2)(iv), Ex. 2. The same result will obtain if the foreign licensing corporation pays dividends, interest, rents or royalties to its U.S. parent that are allocable to the former's general limitation royalty income.

Foreign tax credit considerations alone, however, will rarely be an incentive to conducting international licensing through a controlled foreign licensing corporation. This is so because if licensing income of such a corporation qualifies as general limitation income, as it normally must if it is to be helpful in absorbing excess foreign tax credits, it would also constitute general limitation income if received directly by the U.S. parent. Thus, interposition of a controlled foreign licensing corporation does not improve the foreign tax credit limitation picture unless royalties received directly by the U.S. parent are subject to withholding taxes in the licensee's country that are higher than the combination of the withholding tax in the licensee's country and the corporate income tax in the country in which the licensing corporation is incorporated. The rates of withholding taxes will often be determined by applicable income tax treaties between the licensee's country, on the one hand, and the United States or the licensing corporation's country, on the other.

[¶ 12,195]

5. TRANSFER OF INTANGIBLE PROPERTY RIGHTS TO A BASE COMPANY

If foreign intangible property rights are transferred to a foreign base company in exchange for stock in a transaction otherwise qualifying for nonrecognition of gain under Section 351, Section 367(d) provides, as discussed at ¶ 12,130, that, except as may be provided in regulations, the

8. Temp. Reg. § 1.904–4T(b)(2)(iii)(B) changes the definition of affiliated group to include only U.S. members and controlled foreign corporations in which U.S. members own, directly or indirectly, at least 80 percent of the value and voting power of the stock. See ¶ 7010.

transferor is not subject to tax on the full amount of the gain realized on the transfer. Instead, the transferor is treated as having sold the property in exchange for royalty-like payments contingent upon the productivity, use or disposition of such property, which will be taxed to the transferor as ordinary income from foreign sources and will be subject to periodic adjustment under the super-royalty provision of Section 367(d)(2)(A)(ii).

As noted at ¶ 12,165, a transfer of intangible property rights as a contribution to the capital of a base company of which at least 80 percent of the voting stock is owned by the transferor will be deemed to be an exchange for stock subject to tax under Section 367(d) even if no stock, as a formal matter, is issued to the transferor in exchange for those property rights. § 367(c)(2). A transfer by contribution to capital not treated as an exchange for stock could, under regulations yet to be issued, be treated as a taxable sale for the fair market value of the intangible. § 367(f). See ¶ 12,165.

The U.S. transferor may not find acceptable the tax treatment dictated by Section 367(d), under which constructive royalty payments are invariably treated as ordinary income even though no actual payments (which, unlike constructive payments, would be deductible in the source country) are received. Instead, the U.S. transferor will frequently prefer to transfer the intangible property rights to a foreign base company under a license agreement that calls for the payment of actual royalties. This would result in receipt of cash royalty payments, by the U.S. transferor, which would be deductible by the licensee-payor. See ¶ 12,130.

If the U.S. transferor owns more than 50 percent of the voting power of the base company, Section 1249 precludes capital gains treatment of royalties that would otherwise qualify for such treatment. However, capital gains treatment would apparently be available if the U.S. transferor owned only 50 percent of the *voting power* of the foreign licensing company transferee even if the latter were a controlled foreign corporation because the transferor owned more than 50 percent of the *value* of the transferee's stock. Capital gains treatment may also be feasible if the base company is jointly owned by the U.S. transferor and an independent foreign party, and the former owns 50 percent or less of the voting power and value of the stock. Because only individuals enjoy a preferential rate of U.S. taxation on long-term capital gains under current law, a U.S. corporation will normally seek capital gains only if it has (or anticipates having in the future) capital losses which may be offset against those gains. Even if capital gains treatment is not sought or cannot be achieved, actual ordinary income royalties under a license agreement transferring foreign rights to intangibles will be treated under Section 862(a)(4) as having a source outside the United States, which, as noted at ¶ 12,190 above, may be beneficial in increasing the applicable Section 904(d) limitation on the foreign tax credit. The same would be true of constructive foreign-source royalties if foreign rights to intangibles are transferred to the foreign base company in exchange for stock.

Ordinary income royalties contingent on productivity or use of the intangible property rights abroad by the licensee will be taxed only when received or accrued under normal tax accounting principles. If the purchase price for a sale of foreign intangible property rights to a foreign base company is cast in the form of fixed or contingent payments payable for a specified number of years, such installments will be taxed to the U.S. transferor only when received under the Section 453 installment sale method, provided that the transfer meets the requirements of that method. In either case, an immediate tax on the entire amount of appreciation inherent in the intangible property rights is avoided. As discussed at ¶ 12,110, if no interest or inadequate interest is charged with respect to future payments of purchase price, original issue discount may be imputed under Section 1274 or interest may be imputed under Section 483.

[¶ 12,197]

PROBLEMS

Seaborne Inc. ("Seaborne"), a U.S. corporation, is engaged in the manufacture of power boats for sale inside and outside the United States. Seaborne is considering a program that will tap more effectively into the European market for power boats. Seaborne has a considerable number of important patents registered in the United States, Canada and the European Union ("EU") countries, all of which relate to power boat manufacturing inventions. All of these inventions were developed by Seaborne's own research and development facility in the United States. Seaborne has not yet used, licensed or otherwise earned income on its EU country patents, and no depreciation or amortization deductions have been allowable or taken by Seaborne on these patents. The patents have a value of $20 million and a U.S. tax basis of $1 million.

Seaborne has decided to establish its own wholly owned manufacturing corporation (*société anonyme*) organized under French law, ("Seaborne France"), in Toulon, France. Seaborne France would manufacture power boats in France and sell them to unrelated distributors in the EU. It will be at least three years before Seaborne France will be ready to begin manufacturing operations. Seaborne is considering the following alternatives:

a. Assume that Seaborne would grant Seaborne France a nonexclusive license to use, manufacture and sell the patented inventions and boats incorporating them under the EU patents owned by Seaborne. The license would run throughout the EU for the life of the patents. Under the first alternative, Seaborne would require Seaborne France to pay royalties in U.S. dollars of 5 percent of the annual net sales by Seaborne France of the licensed boats it manufactures and sells. Under the second alternative, the nonexclusive license would be exchanged not for royalties but for shares of the stock of Seaborne France worth $20 million. What are the tax consequences of these alternatives and which would produce the more desirable U.S. and French tax consequences for Seaborne?

b. Seaborne is also considering not granting a license to Seaborne France directly but granting a license similar to the license described in the first alternative of the preceding paragraph a. to a wholly owned licensing subsidiary of Seaborne, called Seaborne Licensing ("SL"), to be organized as a corporation (*Aktiengesellschaft*) under the laws of Switzerland. The only difference in the license granted by Seaborne would be that the royalty to be paid by SL to Seaborne would be 30 percent of the gross royalty income realized by SL under licenses it granted to others. At the outset, SL would grant licenses similar to the license described in the first alternative of the preceding paragraph a. to Seaborne France and to unrelated EU companies that would manufacture outside Switzerland components needed by Seaborne France and unrelated companies that manufacture power boats. The unrelated licensees of SL would be selected by Seaborne, and Seaborne would be responsible for any license negotiations. SL's employees would include an administrator charged with monitoring the manufacturing operations by the licensees under the licenses granted by SL and an accountant charged with auditing the royalties SL receives. For the first three years, SL's only income would be the royalties from these unrelated EU manufacturers. Would the royalty income that would be received by SL under this proposal from licenses it granted to the unrelated EU manufacturing companies be foreign personal holding company income under the controlled foreign corporation rules of Subpart F?

c. In what foreign tax credit limitation basket would the royalty income that would be received by Seaborne from SL under the proposal described in the preceding paragraph b. be placed?

F. THE REQUIREMENT FOR ARM'S LENGTH PRICING BETWEEN RELATED PERSONS

[¶ 12,200]

1. SECTION 482

As discussed in Chapter 8, under Section 482, the IRS is empowered to reallocate income, deductions, credits and allowances among business enterprises controlled directly or indirectly by the same interests as may be necessary clearly to reflect the income of each such enterprise. In effect, the IRS is empowered to shift income, deductions and credits in order to produce the tax results that would have been obtained if the related parties had been dealing as independent parties at arm's length.

The Section 482 arm's length standard applies to all transfers between related parties of intangible property, as defined in Reg. § 1.482–4(b). Thus, the arm's length standard applies whether the transfer is in the form of (1) a license, (2) a sale or (3) a Section 351 (or Section 361) transfer to a corporation in exchange for stock, for which a constructive royalty is required under Section 367(d). It also applies to transfers of existing intangibles effected under qualifying cost sharing arrangements. See ¶ 12,260. The regulations under Section 482 contain detailed rules for determining the arm's length consideration for transfers of intangible property between commonly controlled parties. Reg. §§ 1.482–4 through –7T. The general standard is that of "a taxpayer dealing at arm's length with an uncontrolled taxpayer." Reg. § 1.482–1(b)(1).

[¶ 12,205]

2. THE "SUPER-ROYALTY" PROVISION

In 1986, the super-royalty provision was added to Section 482 and to Section 367(d) (see ¶ 12,130). The new provision, which required the consideration for a transfer of intangible property between related parties to be "commensurate with the income attributable to the intangible," created substantial uncertainties, which had to await the issuance of regulations in 1994 for clarification. What is meant by "commensurate with the income attributable to the intangible?" Does "income" refer to gross income, net sales income, net profit or something else? Evidently, periodic (in some cases, an annual) review and adjustment by the IRS of royalty or other compensation rates with the benefit of hindsight seemed to be contemplated.

Some light on the intent of Congress could be gleaned from the House Committee Report which provided:

> The committee does not intend * * * that the inquiry as to the appropriate compensation for the intangible be limited to the question of whether it was appropriate considering only the facts in existence at the time of the transfer. The committee intends that consideration also be given the actual profit experience realized as a consequence of the transfer. Thus, the committee intends to require that the payments made for the intangible be adjusted over time to reflect changes in the income attributable to the intangible. The bill is not intended to require annual adjustments when there are only minor variations in revenues. However, it will not be sufficient to consider only the evidence of value at the time of the transfer. Adjustments will be required when there are major variations in the annual amounts of revenue attributable to the intangible.
>
> * * * As under present law, all the facts and circumstances are to be considered in determining what pricing methods are appropriate in cases involving intangible property, including the extent to which the transferee bears real risks with respect to its ability to make a profit from the intangible * * *. However, the profit or income stream generated by or associated with intangible property is to be given primary weight.

H.R. Rep. No. 426, 99th Cong., 1st Sess. 403, 425–26 (1985).

Among the issues raised by the super-royalty provision is the possible adverse reaction of the foreign taxing jurisdiction if the IRS seeks to increase the royalty paid by a foreign subsidiary to its U.S. parent corporation. The reaction may be particularly pronounced if the increase proposed by the IRS occurs some years after the original license was executed (and an initial arm's length royalty was fixed) because the foreign subsidiary has been able to generate an unexpectedly high profit through use of the intangible licensed to it by the U.S. parent. What will be the effect of the provisions of U.S. tax treaties that call for arm's length royalties between related parties but say nothing of a requirement that the royalty be commensurate with the income attributable to the intangible or of periodic reexamination and possible adjustment of royalty rates by the IRS?

[¶ 12,210]

3. SECTION 482 WHITE PAPER

In response to a request from the Congress, the Treasury Department issued on October 18, 1988, A Study of Intercompany Pricing under Section 482 of the Code, IRS Notice 88–123, 1988–2 C.B. 458 ("Section 482 White Paper"). This study examined the theory and administration of Section 482 with particular attention to transfers of intangible property and presented findings and recommendations of the Treasury and the IRS. The study was intended to elicit comments from interested parties as a prelude to the issuance of revised regulations under Section 482.

[¶ 12,215]

4. FINAL REGULATIONS

As discussed in Chapter 8, implementing the innovations discussed in the Section 482 White Paper proved challenging. A series of proposed and temporary regulations preceded the issuance of final regulations on the pricing of intangibles in 1994. Reg. §§ 1.482–4 through –6. A series of final, proposed and temporary regulations concerning cost sharing arrangements were issued in 1995 and 2003. The process culminated with the issuance in 2009 of Temp. Reg. § 1.482–7T. See ¶ 12,260.

[¶ 12,220]

a. Basic Concepts

The starting point under the regulations is identifying the owner of the intangible. The basic concepts are that the intangible's owner is the party that should be taxed on the income generated when rights to it are made available to a related person under any type of arrangement and that the income realized by the owner should at least equal the amount that an independent party would have paid for the intangible under the same circumstances. Normally, the legal owner of the right to exploit an intangible will be treated as the owner for purposes of Section 482. Reg. § 1.482–4(f)(3)(ii)(A). The owner of intangible property that is not legally protected will generally be the person that bore the greatest part of the development costs. Reg. § 1.482–4(f)(3)(ii)(B). Because, by hypothesis, the owner and the related person enjoying rights to the intangible are commonly controlled (e.g., one by the other or both by a common owner), the regulations refer to the owner as the controlled owner and the party using rights to the intangible as the controlled person.

The general rule is that when a controlled person pays inadequate consideration for the right to exploit an intangible, and the transferor retains a substantial interest in the intangible, the arm's length consideration should be in the form of a royalty, unless under the particular circumstances a different form of payment is more appropriate. Reg. § 1.482–4(f)(1). In any event, the consideration must be commensurate with the income attributable to the intangible. § 482. In order to meet this standard, Reg. § 1.482–4(f)(2) provides that, if an intangible is transferred for a period exceeding one year, the consideration charged is generally subject to annual review and adjustment by the IRS to ensure that it is commensurate over time with the income generated by the intangible in the hands of the transferee.

If a lump-sum payment is called for under a license or other transfer agreement, it is potentially subject to periodic adjustments to the same extent as agreements providing for periodic royalty payments. Reg. § 1.482–4(f)(5). For purposes of determining whether the lump-sum payment satisfies the arm's length standard and whether periodic adjustments are required, the lump sum must be treated as an advance payment of a stream of royalty payments ("equivalent royalty amounts") over the life of the agreement. The "equivalent royalty amount" attributable to each year serves as the basis for determining if the consideration is arm's length. In addition, if a periodic adjustment is called for by Reg. § 1.482–4(f)(2), the royalty that was deemed to have been prepaid for the tax year in question will be set off against the arm's length royalty determined for such year, and the difference will be treated as an additional payment in the year of the adjustment that is of the same character as the initial lump-sum payment.

Annual review and adjustment of the consideration for every intangible transfer would obviously impose a heavy administrative burden on taxpayers and the IRS. A series of important exceptions discussed at ¶ 12,245 eliminate this requirement under specified circumstances.

[¶ 12,225]

b. Methods for Determining Arm's Length Pricing

Reg. § 1.482–4(a) authorizes the use of the following methods for determining arm's length pricing for transfers of intangible property between related parties: (i) the comparable uncontrolled transaction ("CUT") method, (ii) the comparable profit method ("CPM"), (iii) profit split methods ("PSM"), and (iv) further unspecified methods. The method to be used in a particular case must be selected under the best method rule, which requires use of the method that, under the facts and circumstances, provides the "most reliable measure" of an arm's length result. Reg. § 1.482–1(c).

The arm's length consideration for the transfer of an intangible is not governed either by prevailing industry average royalty rates or the consideration paid in uncontrolled transactions that are not comparable to the controlled transaction. Reg. § 1.482–4(f)(5).

[¶ 12,230]

c. Comparable Uncontrolled Transaction ("CUT") Method

The CUT method generally provides the most direct and reliable measure of an arm's length royalty. It may be used if the same intangible is transferred in both the controlled and uncontrolled transactions and only minor differences exist between the uncontrolled and the controlled transactions, provided that these differences have a definite and reasonably ascertainable effect on pricing and that appropriate adjustments are made for them. Reg. § 1.482–4(c)(2)(ii).

Although all the general factors for determining comparability of the controlled and uncontrolled transactions described in Reg. § 1.482–1(d)(3) must be considered, Reg. § 1.482–4(c)(2)(iii) emphasizes that the CUT method is particularly dependent on the intangibles involved being the same or comparable and on similarity in the terms of contractual arrangements and economic conditions. To be considered comparable both intangibles must be used in connection with similar products or processes within the same general industry or market and must have similar profit potential. Reg. § 1.482–4(c)(2)(iii)(B). Basically, controlled and uncontrolled transfers of intangibles used for the same product type in the same industry (such as patents on a pharmaceutical product) will be comparable if they are anticipated to generate substantially the same pre-tax benefits for the transferees.

To conclude that the profit potential of two intangibles is similar, it is necessary to have an acceptably reliable measure of the profit potential of the two intangibles. The profit potential of an intangible involves calculating the net present value of the benefits to be derived from use of the intangible by the transferee. Profit potential is most reliably measured by direct calculations, based on reliable projections, of the net present value of the benefits to be realized through use of the intangible. While this information frequently will be available with respect to the controlled transaction, it normally will not be available with respect to an uncontrolled transaction unless one of the controlled persons was a party to it. In recognition of this difficulty, the regulations provide that, in certain cases, it may be acceptable to refer to evidence other than projections to compare profit potentials. For example, such evidence may include the terms of the transfers, the uniqueness of the intangibles and their stage of development. Reg. § 1.482–4(c)(2)(iii)(B)(*1*)(*ii*) and –4(c)(2)(iii)(B)(*2*)(*ii*). Such indirect comparisons of profit potentials will be most useful in cases in which it is not possible to calculate directly the profit potential of the intangibles in either the controlled or uncontrolled transaction. An example would be a transfer of an intangible that relates to a component of a manufactured product consisting of many components (such as an automobile). In such a case, it would obviously be difficult to calculate with reliability the net present value of the profit attributable to the intangible that was transferred in the controlled transaction.

[¶ 12,235]

d. The Comparable Profits Method ("CPM")

The CPM, as described in Reg. § 1.482–5, may be used to determine the arm's length consideration for intangible property where the CUT method cannot be employed because a comparable uncontrolled transaction has not been identified. The CPM relies on the general principle that similarly situated taxpayers will tend to earn similar returns over a reasonable period of time. In essence, it involves imputing to the related transferee a level of operating profit that would be earned by an unrelated similarly situated transferee. The CPM determines the arm's length consideration for a controlled transaction by referring to objective measures of operating profit (profit level indicators) derived from uncontrolled persons that engage in similar activities with other uncontrolled persons under similar circumstances. Thus, to use a simplified example, if one comparable unrelated transferee earns an operating profit of $400,000 a year from use of an intangible, applying that profit level to the controlled transferee using a comparable intangible under comparable circumstances makes it possible to calculate what arm's length royalty the controlled transferee should have paid to the owner for the intangible. A difficulty with this method is that if, as would commonly be the case, the controlled person has use of multiple intangibles, it will often not be possible to identify an uncontrolled comparable person that has the use of similarly valuable intangibles. If a comparable uncontrolled person is identified, the operating profit of that person is compared with the operating profit of the controlled person using appropriate profit level indicators. If the CUT method is inapplicable and if, in the rather unlikely event that such an uncontrolled person can be identified and the relevant data on operating profit can be obtained, the CPM may prove to be the most reliable.

The profit level indicators that are used to evaluate operating profit include two types of measures: the rate of return on capital and financial ratios. Reg. § 1.482–5(b)(4). Other profit level indicators not specifically described in the regulations may be employed, provided that they provide the most reliable measure of an arm's length result under the best method rule. Reg. § 1.482–5(b)(4)(iii). Any measure of profit based on objective measures of profitability derived from uncontrolled taxpayers that engage in similar business activities under similar circumstances could be employed.

In determining an arm's length royalty under the CPM, the taxpayer's average reported operating profit for the year under review and the preceding two tax years ordinarily will be compared to the average profit of the uncontrolled comparable persons for the same period. Reg. § 1.482–5(b)(4). Comparison of multiple year profit averages is thought to provide a more accurate reflection of a taxpayer's transfer pricing practices than an analysis based on a single year and thus reduces the effect of short-term variations in operating profit that may be unrelated to transfer pricing.

If the taxpayer's average reported operating profit for this period falls outside the arm's length range determined under Reg. § 1.482–1(e)(2), the IRS may make an adjustment. This arm's length range will ordinarily be from the 25th to the 75th percentile of the results derived from uncontrolled comparables. Reg. § 1.482–1(e)(2)(iii)(C). In most cases, any adjustment required will be made to the median of the operating profits of the comparable uncontrolled persons for the tax year. See Reg. § 1.482–5(e), Ex. 2.

The comparability factors that must be taken into account under the CPM are set forth in Reg. § 1.482–5(c)(2). In particular, Reg. § 1.482–5(c)(2)(ii) provides that, while all the comparability factors described in Reg. § 1.482–1(d)(3) must be considered, comparability under the CPM is particularly dependent on resources employed and risks assumed. Further, since resources and risks are directly related to functions performed, functional comparability is also an important consideration under the CPM. Moreover, comparability under the CPM may be adversely affected by other factors that have little effect on comparability under the CUT method, such as management efficiency.

Adjustments must be made for all material differences to the extent that such adjustments improve the reliability of the analysis. Reg. § 1.482–5(c)(2)(iv). All items that have a material effect on the profit level indicators must be accounted for consistently and, if necessary to obtain this consistency, adjustments must be made. Reg. § 1.482–5(c)(3)(ii). An additional factor that may affect reliability under the CPM is the ability to allocate costs and other items between the relevant business activity and the other activities of the controlled taxpayer or the uncontrolled taxpayers.

Only infrequently is the CPM likely to prove to be the best method to measure the arm's length character of a royalty rate for a particular intangible transfer. The CPM looks to the operating profit of the entire enterprise, rather than operating profit attributable to a particular intangible. It focuses on the total operating profit based on all functions performed, capital invested and risks assumed. The CPM also looks to profitability of uncontrolled taxpayers that engage in similar business activities under similar circumstances. This seems somewhat odd because one of the purposes of the commensurate-with-income standard was to "make it clear that industry norms * * * do not provide a safe-harbor minimum payment for related party intangibles transfers." H.R. Rep. No. 426, 99th Cong., 1st Sess. 425 (1985).

[¶ 12,240]

e. Profit Split Methods ("PSM")

If members of a controlled group are engaged in a functionally integrated business and each member uses valuable intangibles, it will normally be difficult to identify comparable uncontrolled transactions and comparable uncontrolled transferees of comparable intangibles that can be used to determine arm's length pricing for particular intangible transfers. Without comparable transactions or comparable uncontrolled holders of similar intangible rights, neither the CUT method nor the CPM can be used. In this situation, a profit split method may be applied.

Reg. § 1.482–6 describes profit split methods. The basic approach of a profit split method is to estimate an arm's length return by (1) comparing the relative economic contributions that the parties make to the success of a business venture and (2) dividing the returns from that venture between them on the basis of the relative value of such contributions. The relative value of each controlled taxpayer's contribution to the success of the relevant business activity must be determined in a manner that reflects the functions performed, risks assumed and resources employed by each participant in the relevant business activity, consistent with the comparability provisions of Reg. § 1.482–1(d)(3). Such an allocation is intended to correspond to the division of profit or loss that would result from an arrangement between uncontrolled taxpayers, each performing functions similar to those of the various controlled taxpayers engaged in the relevant business activity.

Two profit split methods are provided: the comparable profit split and the residual profit split. A comparable profit split is derived from the combined operating profit of uncontrolled taxpayers, the transactions and activities of which are similar to those of the controlled taxpayers in the relevant business activity. Each uncontrolled taxpayer's percentage of the combined operating profit or loss is used to allocate the combined operating profit or loss of each controlled taxpayer involved in the relevant business activity. Reg. § 1.482–6(c)(2).

The residual profit split method determines an arm's length consideration in a two-step process. Reg. § 1.482–6(c)(3). First, using other methods such as the CPM, market returns for routine functions are estimated and allocated to the parties that performed them. The remaining, residual amount is then allocated between the parties on the assumption that this residual is attributable to intangible property contributed to the activity by the controlled taxpayers. Using this assumption, the residual is divided based on the estimate of the relative value of the parties' contributions of such property. Since the fair market value of the intangible property usually will not be readily ascertainable, other measures of the relative values of intangible property may be used, including capitalized intangible development expenses.

Under the best method rule, methods that determine an arm's length result based on the results of transactions between uncontrolled taxpayers are generally considered to be more reliable than methods (such as the residual profit split) that only rely on such transactions in part. Therefore, the results of the methods based solely on results of transactions between uncontrolled taxpayers will be selected under the best method rule unless the data necessary to apply them is relatively incomplete or unreliable. Under the best method rule, the residual profit split generally would be considered a method of last resort.

Reg. § 1.482–6(c)(3)(ii)(C) identifies several other factors that may affect the reliability of the residual profit split method. In addition to allocation of costs, income and assets and accounting consistency, another factor to take into account under the residual profit split, is the reliability of the estimate of the value of intangible property. The reliability of this method may be adversely affected if capitalized costs of development are used to estimate the value of intangible property because such costs may bear no relation to the market value of the intangible.

[¶ 12,245]

f. Special Rules Precluding Periodic Adjustments

As noted above, the consideration for a transfer of the use of an intangible for more than one year is generally subject to an annual adjustment to ensure that it is commensurate with the income attributable to the intangible in the hands of the controlled transferee. An adjustment may be made for the current year, although no adjustments were made for prior years. Reg. § 1.482–4(f)(2)(i). If, in every case, annual review of, and possible adjustment of, the consideration received by the owner of an intangible from a related transferee were required, the regulations would involve very heavy administrative and compliance burdens for taxpayers and the IRS. To avoid this result, the regulations include a series of important exceptions that, under prescribed circumstances, preclude multiple adjustments throughout the life of the intangible transfer. Reg. § 1.482–4(f)(2)(ii). These exceptions include the following:

(A) ***Transactions involving the same intangible.*** No periodic adjustments will be made if the consideration paid for the intangible is determined to be an arm's length amount under the CUT method for the first year based on a transfer of the same intangible to an uncontrolled taxpayer under substantially the same circumstances. Reg. § 1.482–4(f)(2)(ii)(A). Thus, for example, the consideration for the transfer of an intangible to a controlled taxpayer in one country could be determined to be arm's length based on the transfer of the same intangible under similar circumstances to an uncontrolled taxpayer in another country in which the relevant economic conditions are substantially similar to those in the first country.

(B) ***Transactions involving a comparable intangible.*** If the arm's length result is derived from the application of the CUT method based on the transfer of a comparable intangible under comparable circumstances to those of the controlled transaction, no adjustment for a subsequent year will be made if each of the following facts is established:

(1) The controlled taxpayers entered into a written agreement (controlled agreement) that provided for an amount of consideration with respect to each tax year subject to such agreement, such consideration was an arm's length amount for the first tax year in which substantial periodic consideration was required to be paid under the agreement and such agreement remained in effect for the tax year under review;

(2) There is a written agreement setting forth the terms of the comparable uncontrolled transaction relied upon to establish the arm's length consideration (uncontrolled agreement), which contains no provisions that would permit any change to the amount of consideration, a renegotiation or a termination of the agreement in circumstances comparable to those of the controlled transaction in the tax year under review;

(3) The controlled agreement is substantially similar to the uncontrolled agreement;

(4) The controlled agreement limits use of the intangible to a specified field or purpose in a manner that is consistent with industry practice and any such limitation in the uncontrolled agreement;

(5) There were no substantial changes in the functions performed by the controlled transferee after the controlled agreement was exe-

cuted, except changes required by events that were not foreseeable; and

(6) The total profits actually earned or the total cost savings actually realized by the controlled taxpayer from the exploitation of the intangible in the year under examination, and all past years, are not less than 80 percent nor more than 120 percent of the prospective profits or cost savings that were foreseeable when the comparability of the uncontrolled agreement was established.

Reg. § 1.482–4(f)(2)(ii)(B).

(C) ***Methods other than the CUT method.*** Under methods other than the CUT method, no subsequent adjustment will be made if each of the following is established:

(1) The controlled taxpayers entered into a written agreement (controlled agreement) that provided for an amount of consideration with respect to each tax year subject to such agreement, and such agreement remained in effect for the tax year under review;

(2) The consideration called for in the controlled agreement was an arm's length amount for the first tax year in which substantial periodic consideration was required to be paid, and relevant supporting documentation was prepared contemporaneously with the execution of the controlled agreement;

(3) There have been no substantial changes in the functions performed by the transferee since the controlled agreement was executed, except changes required by events that were not foreseeable; and

(4) The total profits actually earned or the total cost savings realized by the controlled transferee from the exploitation of the intangible in the year under examination, and all past years, are not less than 80 percent nor more than 120 percent of the prospective profits or cost savings that were foreseeable when the controlled agreement was entered into.

Reg. § 1.482–4(f)(2)(ii)(C).

(D) ***Extraordinary events.*** No periodic adjustments will be made if the aggregate actual profits fall outside the permissible 80 to 120 percent band of projected profits or cost savings and if this variation from the projected results was due to extraordinary events. These are events that could not reasonably have been anticipated (including natural or man-made disasters, but not more routine events such as the failure of a market to develop as anticipated) and all the other requirements of either (B) or (C) above are satisfied. Reg. § 1.482–4(f)(2)(ii)(D).

(E) ***Five-year test.*** Reg. § 1.482–4(f)(2)(ii)(E) provides that, if the requirements of either paragraph (B) or (C) above are met for the five-year period starting with the year in which substantial periodic consideration is first paid, no periodic adjustments will thereafter be made.

[¶ 12,250]

g. Allocations for Assistance

Allocations may be made with respect to assistance provided to the owner by other parties that assisted in the development of the intangible. Reg. § 1.482–4(f)(4)(i). Assistance does not include expenditures of a routine nature that an unrelated party dealing at arm's length would be expected to incur under similar circumstances. For instance, even in the absence of a license agreement transferring the right to exploit a trademark to an unrelated distributor, a distributor may be expected to incur a certain amount of advertising and other marketing expenses that could increase the value of the trademark. If an uncontrolled distributor would incur such expenses without reimbursement by the owner of the intangible, then no allocation with respect to similar levels of expenses would be made under Section 482 in the case of a distributor that is a member of the controlled group to which the legal owner of the trademark belongs. On the other hand, an allocation could be made if the expenses were greater than those an unrelated party would have incurred without some form of compensation.

[¶ 12,255]

PROBLEM

Pharma Corporation ("Pharma") is a U.S. corporation engaged in the development, manufacture and sale of pharmaceuticals in the United States and foreign countries. As a result of its research and development efforts in the United States, Pharma discovered drug A, a safe and effective drug for use in the treatment of disease T, a serious infectious disease. Drug A is a significant improvement over other available treatments for disease T, and Pharma has obtained patents covering drug A in the United States and in various foreign countries. Pharma has not completed the necessary clinical trials for drug A, and has not yet obtained necessary government authorization to market drug A in the United States or any foreign country.

In addition to its own research and development activities, Pharma actively seeks to expand its product line by obtaining licenses from unrelated parties covering promising pharmaceutical agents in the treatment of human diseases. As part of these efforts, Pharma obtained a license to make, use and sell in the United States drug B, a safe and effective drug for use in the treatment of disease V, another serious infectious disease. This license was obtained from Worlddrug, S.A., an unrelated foreign pharmaceutical company that developed drug B and that holds patents on drug B in the United States and in various foreign countries. Drug B represents a significant improvement over other treatments currently available for disease V, and, under the "use restrictions'' contained in the license agreement between Pharma and Worlddrug, S.A., Pharma may use or sell drug B only for use in the treatment of disease V. Clinical trials on drug B have not been completed, and sale of the drug has not yet been approved by the United States or foreign governments. Pharma estimates that, within the first two years of its introduction in the United States, drug B will achieve annual sales of at least $300 million, with potentially higher sales thereafter. Pharma further estimates that drug B will achieve an average annual profit from sales in the United States of at least $100 million over the life of the drug. Based on this estimate of the profit potential for drug B, and in the face of competing license offers to Worlddrug, S.A. from other independent U.S. pharmaceutical companies unrelated to Pharma or Worlddrug, S.A., Pharma agreed to pay Worlddrug, S.A. a royalty of 12 percent of sales.

During this same period, Pharma granted its wholly owned foreign subsidiary, Pharma International (''International''), a license in perpetuity to make, use and sell drug A in foreign countries but only for use in the treatment of disease T. Pharma estimates that within the first two years of its introduction into the foreign market, drug A will achieve annual sales of at least $300 million, with potentially higher sales thereafter, and should achieve an average annual profit of at least $100 million from sales in the foreign market over the life of the drug. The license agreement provides for a royalty rate of 12 percent of sales, based on the rate paid by Pharma to Worlddrug, S.A. for the license related to drug B.

At the same time, Pharma also granted International a license in perpetuity to make, use and sell drug C in foreign countries, but only for use in the treatment of disease W. Pharma is the discoverer and patent holder of drug C. Drug C is comparable to drugs A and B in that all three drugs are protected by patents, treat serious health problems, represent significant improvements over other treatments available for the relevant diseases, are expected to achieve sales of at least $300 million in the first two years, with potentially higher sales thereafter, and are expected to achieve average annual profits from sales in their respective geographic markets of at least $100 million over their economic lives. However, at the time drug C was licensed to International, all clinical trials had been completed, and Pharma had obtained all necessary governmental authorizations to market drug C for treatment of disease W. To reflect the fact that drug C was licensed at a later stage of development than were drugs A and B, and to compensate Pharma for the increased costs incurred to obtain government authorizations, the royalty rate on drug C was set at 14 percent of sales.

Consider whether the royalties payable by International to Pharma can be justified as arm's length under the Section 482 regulations.

[¶ 12,260]

5. COST SHARING ARRANGEMENTS

The Section 482 regulations contain an important exception to the general rule that an arm's length royalty or other consideration must be paid by a related enterprise when intangibles are transferred to it by an enterprise controlled by the same interests. Intangibles may be shared between two or more related enterprises under an arrangement that provides for the sharing of the costs and risks of developing intangible property in return for an interest in the intangible property that may be produced. Under a qualifying cost sharing arrangement, the related person receiving an interest in intangible property is not required to pay an arm's length royalty for its use; it need only bear or pay an appropriate share of the cost of the research and development concerned.

When Section 482 was amended to require that consideration for intangible property transferred between commonly controlled enterprises be commensurate with the income of the transferee attributable to the intangible, the Conference Committee Report indicated that Congress did not intend to preclude the use of bona fide research and development cost sharing arrangements as an appropriate method of allocating between commonly controlled persons income and expense attributable to intangibles. The Report stated, however, that for cost sharing arrangements to produce results consistent with the commensurate-with-the-income standard, the following requirements must be met:

> (1) a cost sharer should be expected to bear its portion of all research and development costs, on unsuccessful as well as successful products, within an appropriate product area * * *,
>
> (2) the allocation of costs generally should be proportionate to profit as determined before deductions for research and development expenses, and
>
> (3) to the extent that one related party contributes funds toward research and development at a significantly earlier point in time than another, or is otherwise putting its funds at risk to a greater extent than the other, that party should receive an appropriate return on its investment.

H.R. Conf. Rep. No. 841, 99th Cong., 2d Sess. II–638 (1986).

The Section 482 White Paper suggested that, in general, a bona fide cost sharing arrangement ("CSA") should have certain prescribed provisions. For example, participants should be assigned exclusive rights in a specific geographic area in intangibles developed under it (and should predict benefits and divide costs accordingly) and that only intangibles involved in manufacturing should generally be developed under a CSA. IRS Notice 88–123, 1988–2 C.B. 458, 496. The White Paper also discussed as follows the requirement that a qualifying CSA contain appropriate buy-in and buy-out provisions:

> [A] party to a cost sharing arrangement that has contributed funds or incurred risks for development of intangibles at an earlier stage must be appropriately compensated by the other participants—hence the requirement for a buy-in payment. One of the primary reasons for

> adopting most sharing provisions is to avoid the necessity of valuing intangibles. Yet, if there are intangibles that are not fully developed that relate to the research to be conducted under the cost-sharing arrangement, it is necessary to value them in order to determine an appropriate buy-in payment.
>
> There are three basic types of intangibles subject to the buy-in requirement. A participant may own preexisting intangibles at various stages of development that will become subject to the arrangement. A company may also have conducted basic research not associated with any product. Finally, there may be a going concern value associated with a participant's research facilities and capabilities that will be utilized. [The transfer of such intangibles is now referred to in the temporary regulations as a "platform contribution."]
>
> Fully developed intangibles command a royalty to the extent used by other participants and are generally not appropriately incorporated into a cost sharing arrangement. Thus, royalties for preexisting developed intangibles may not be included in the buy-in payment * * *.
>
> The buy-in payment should reflect the full fair market value of all intangibles utilized in the arrangement and not merely costs incurred to date * * *.
>
> A "buy-out" occurs when a participant withdraws from a cost sharing arrangement. Having funded a portion of research and development prior to withdrawal, that person owns a share of whatever the agreement has borne to date and must be compensated by the other participants for the value of what the arrangement has produced to date and not merely reimbursed for costs incurred to date.
>
> A "secondary buy-in" is required when new members are admitted after a cost sharing arrangement is in place. If a new member is acquiring a portion of the geographic rights of one of the original participants, any buy-in amount should be paid to the affiliate whose geographic rights are being reduced. * * *

IRS Notice 88–123, 1988–2 C.B. at 497.

The IRS issued proposed cost sharing regulations in 1992, which generally allowed more flexibility than anticipated by the White Paper, relying on anti-abuse tests rather than requiring standard cost sharing provisions. Final regulations taking a generally similar approach were issued in 1995 and liberalized in 1996. These regulations (referred to in the 2009 temporary regulations as "former § 1.482–7" and herein as the "QCSA Regulations" or "Reg. § 1.482–7A") spelled out in rather general terms the requirements that had to be met by a "qualified cost sharing arrangement" ("QCSA"), but did not deal in detail with determining appropriate buy-in or buy-out payments.

In 2003 the pendulum that had been moving in the direction of encouraging the use of cost sharing arrangements began to swing in the other direction. That year the regulations were amended to require for the first time that stock-based compensation (such as the cost of stock options) be treated as an intangible development cost to be shared in the case of employees whose basic compensation was so classified.

A major objective of proposed regulations issued in August 2005, Prop. Reg. § 1.482–7, REG–144615–02, 2005–2 C.B. 625, was to tighten the rules relating to the buy-in payment requirement under the QCSA regulations. The principal impetus for change was a growing awareness that some U.S. multinational corporations were using CSAs to shift large amounts of profit generated by foreign intangibles by transferring them to controlled foreign corporations in low- or no-tax countries.

On February 7, 2006, at a hearing of the Senate Finance Committee, the following is a portion of the colloquy that is reported to have occurred:

> The Chairman: * * *
>
> For example, the Wall Street Journal reported that a four-year-old Irish subsidiary of Microsoft called Round Island One, Limited, "has a thin roster of employees, but controls more than $16 billion in Microsoft assets. Virtually unknown in Ireland, on paper it has quickly become one of the countries [sic] biggest companies, with a gross product of nearly $9 billion in 2004."
>
> According to the article, much of this profit is from licensing software code that originated in the United States. Reporting this profit in Ireland helps Microsoft save half a billion dollars in annual tax revenue.
>
> The press reports indicate that it is through cost sharing arrangements that companies like Microsoft are able to accomplish such dramatic tax savings.
>
> These companies enter into cost sharing arrangements with their foreign subsidiaries, giving those subsidiaries the right to a share of whatever income or loss is generated by the intellectual property developed under the arrangements. Instead of receiving royalties from their foreign subsidiaries, the U.S. parent receives buy-in payments up front.
>
> Now, the Treasury Department has recently proposed an overhaul of cost sharing regulations and, based upon these press reports, Treasury review of this area is very timely.
>
> So, Mr. Secretary, would you please comment on the priority given to finalizing these regulations?
>
> Secretary [of the Treasury John W.] Snow: Mr. Chairman, it is a clear priority for us. We share your concern, the concern you have just articulated. There is a clear danger here that there has been migration of intellectual and other intangible property offshore. This type of migration can be accomplished through the cost sharing sort of

> arrangements that you described. We feel that the existing rules have not been effective in getting at this problem.
>
> * * *

Unofficial Transcript of Finance Committee Hearing on Fiscal 2007 Budget, available at 2006 TNT 31–15 (Feb. 15, 2006).

The August 2005 proposed regulations called for a new analytical framework for CSAs (subsequently implemented in the 2009 temporary regulations). The proposed regulations included guidance on evaluating the arm's length buy-in payments that must be paid to a contributing participant and paid by a benefitting participant with respect to external contributions of non-fully developed intangibles made by participants in a CSA. The preamble to the proposed regulations summarized the new framework as follows:

> For purposes of determining the results that would have been realized under an arm's length cost sharing arrangement, the proposed regulations adopt as a fundamental concept an investor model for addressing the relationships and contributions of controlled participants in a cost sharing arrangement. Under this model, each controlled participant may be viewed as making an aggregate investment, attributable to both cost contributions (ongoing share of intangible development costs) and external contributions (the preexisting advantages which the parties bring into the arrangement), for purposes of achieving an anticipated return appropriate to the risks of the cost sharing arrangement over the term of the development and exploitation of the intangibles resulting from the arrangement.
>
> * * *
>
> There are special implications that are derived from determining the arm's length compensation for external contributions in line with the investor model. In evaluating that arm's length compensation, it is appropriate, consistent with the investor model, to determine (1) what an investor would pay at the outset of a cost sharing arrangement for an opportunity to invest in that arrangement, and (2) what a participant with external contributions would require as compensation at the outset of a cost sharing arrangement to allow an investor to join in the investment. The appropriate "price" of undertaking a risky investment is typically determined at the time the investment is undertaken, based on the ex ante expectations of the investors.

REG–144615–02, 2005–2 C.B. 625, 626–627.

The proposed regulations did more than provide enhanced guidance on determining the arm's length buy-in amounts to be paid by and to participants in a CSA consistent with the investor model. They also permitted the IRS to make periodic adjustments necessary to produce arm's length payments by and to controlled participants that appropriately reflect the profit potential of intangibles transferred to the arrangement. Moreover, the proposed regulations contained a kind of safe harbor. If specified documentation requirements had been met, the IRS would generally have been precluded from making a periodic adjustment with respect to a controlled participant if the ratio of (i) the present value of the participant's share of profits from cost shared intangibles to (ii) the present value of its contributions to the arrangement fell into a range between two and one-half ("band of comfort").

On January 5, 2009, the currently applicable temporary regulations, Temp. Reg. § 1.482–7T, became effective, but with some complex transitional rules that call for different applicable rules for two categories of CSA:

(1) A CSA in force on or after January 5, 2009, which is governed by the temporary regulations.

(2) A CSA in force prior to January 5, 2009, which qualified as a QCSA under the QCSA regulations and which remains subject, in part, to the QCSA regulations and, in part, to the temporary regulations with adjustments called for in the Coordinated Issue Paper on Section 482 CSA Buy–In Adjustments ("CSA–CIP"), LMSB–04–0907–62 (September 27, 2007). The CSA–CIP indicates that the transfer pricing methods contained in the temporary regulations will generally correspond to the best methods under the QCSA regulations. A QCSA is thus effectively subject to the buy-in payment rules of the temporary regulations. A QCSA continues to be subject to the applicability of the QCSA regulations only if the written QCSA agreement is amended, if necessary, to conform with the temporary regulations, is not materially expanded, and if, subject to specified exceptions, the activities of the controlled participants comply with the temporary regulations. The specified exceptions to the applicability of the temporary regulations to QCSAs include (i) the exclusive divisional interest requirement; (ii) the new cost sharing transaction ("CST") and platform contribution transaction ("PCT") rules; (iii) the September 2, 2009 deadline for filing the CSA Statement; (iv) the annual return requirement and (v) the periodic adjustment rules of the temporary regulations. With respect to these issues, QCSAs remain generally subject to the QCSA regulations. Temp. Reg. § 1.482–7T(m). (Both categories of CSAs are collectively referred to herein as "qualifying CSAs.")

The temporary regulations contain periodic adjustment rules, discussed below, that impose more specific parameters on the calculation of the buy-in payments required for CSAs under the investor model than those called for in the QCSA regulations and the 2005 proposed regulations.

[¶ 12,265]

a. Requirements for a Qualifying Cost Sharing Arrangement

QCSA Reg. § 1.482–7A(a)(1) defines a QCSA as an agreement for sharing costs of development of one or more intangibles in proportion to the participants' shares of reasonably anticipated benefits ("RABs") from their exploitation of interests in any intangibles that are developed.

If a QCSA exists, no Section 482 allocation of arm's length royalties or equivalent payments can be made by the IRS. The IRS can only adjust the cost sharing payments to make each controlled participant's share of the relevant intangible development costs equal to its share of RABs from use of the intangibles developed. Reg. § 1.482–7A(a)(2). To be treated as a QCSA and thus be insulated from risk of royalty allocations, the arrangement must meet four formal requirements enumerated in QCSA Reg. § 1.482–7A(b). Specifically, the arrangement must:

(1) Include two or more participants;

(2) Provide a method to calculate each controlled participant's share of intangible development costs, based on factors that can reasonably be expected to reflect the participant's share of anticipated benefits;

(3) Provide for adjustment to the controlled participant's shares of intangible development costs to account for changes in economic conditions, the business operations and practices of the participants and the ongoing development of intangibles under the arrangement and

(4) Be recorded in a document that is contemporaneous with the formation (and any revision) of the CSA that includes:

(i) A list of the arrangement's participants, and any other member of the controlled group that will benefit from the use of intangibles developed under the CSA;

(ii) The information described in paragraphs (2) and (3) above;

(iii) A description of the scope of the research and development to be undertaken, including the intangible or class of intangibles intended to be developed;

(iv) A description of each participant's interest in any covered intangibles;

(v) The duration of the arrangement and

(vi) The conditions under which the arrangement may be modified or terminated and the consequences of such modification or termination, such as the interest that each participant will receive in any covered intangibles.

Accounting, documentation and reporting requirements are also included. QCSA Reg. § 1.482–7A(i), (j).

Under the temporary regulations, a qualifying CSA must be a written agreement by controlled participants to share the costs of developing cost shared intangibles in proportion to their RAB shares, and controlled participants must comply with specified substantive and administrative rules. The substantive rules include the following:

(i) The controlled participants must commit to, and in fact engage in, cost sharing transactions ("CSTs"). This means that the controlled participants make payments to each other ("CST Payments") as necessary to ensure that in each taxable year, each controlled participant's share of intangible development costs ("IDCs") is in proportion to its respective RAB share.

(ii) The controlled participants must commit to, and in fact engage in, platform contribution transactions ("PCTs") to the extent there are platform contributions. In a PCT, each controlled participant ("PCT Payor") is obligated to make arm's length payments ("PCT Payment") to each other controlled participant ("PCT Payee") that provides a platform contribution.

(iii) Each controlled participant must receive a non-overlapping divisional interest in the cost shared intangibles without any further obligation to compensate another controlled participant for such interest.

Temp. Reg. § 1.482–7T(b)(1).

Under the administrative rules, each controlled participant must comply substantially with the CSA contractual, documentation, accounting and reporting requirements. Temp. Reg. § 1.482–7T(k).

A qualifying CSA must have a defined "intangible development activity" (or under the QCSA regulations "intangible development area") (both hereinafter "IDA"). The CSA constitutive contract must describe the IDA, including the intangible or class of intangibles reasonably anticipated to be developed. Temp. Reg. § 1.482–7T(k)(1)(ii)(B).

A CSA produces results that are consistent with an arm's length result within the meaning of Reg. § 1.482–1(b)(1) only if "each controlled participant's IDC share * * * equals its RAB share, each controlled participant compensates its RAB share of the value of all platform contributions by other controlled participants, and all other requirements of Temp. Reg. § 1.482–7T are met." Temp. Reg. § 1.482–7T(a)(4).

[¶ 12,270]

b. Cost Shared Intangibles and Participants

The intangibles developed under a CSA are referred to as "cost shared intangibles" (or under the QCSA regulations, "covered intangibles"). A cost shared intangible is defined broadly as "any intangible (within the meaning of Reg. § 1.482–4b) that is developed by the IDA." Temp. Reg. § 1.482–7T(j)(1)(i). This includes any intangible whether or not its development was foreseen at the inception of the CSA.

Thus, the regulations do not adopt the view of the Section 482 White Paper that CSAs should generally encompass only intangibles used in manufacturing. Examples are given of CSAs covering the development of training materials for entry-level employees and of computer software, which imply wide flexibility in what may be brought within the concept of "cost shared intangible." Temp. Reg. § 1.482–7T(e)(2)(ii)(E), Exs. 8, 9. "Intangible" is defined broadly for purposes of Section 482 to include any item (including the obvious examples of patents, knowhow, copyrights, trademarks and franchises) "if it derives its value not from its physical attributes but from its intellectual content or other intangible properties." Reg. § 1.482–4(b). The unstated assumption of the regulations appears to be that CSAs may cover any intangible as so defined.

Unrelated persons—"uncontrolled participants"—may participate in a qualifying CSA. Commonly controlled taxpayers—"controlled participants"—may be participants if they meet certain conditions. Temp. Reg. § 1.482–7T(a)(1). All members of a group of controlled entities created or organized within a single country and subjected to an income tax by such country on their combined income are treated as a single participant. Temp. Reg. § 1.482–7T(j)(2)(i). To qualify as a controlled participant, a controlled taxpayer, as defined under Reg. § 1.482–1(i)(5), must be a party to the CSA agreement and must reasonably anticipate that it will derive benefits from exploiting one or more cost shared intangibles. Temp. Reg. § 1.482–7T(j)(1)(i).

A controlled person that does not qualify as a controlled participant may furnish assistance (e.g., as a contract researcher) to the controlled participants in connection with a CSA. In this case, the appropriate compensation for such assistance in the research and development undertaken is governed by the rules in Reg. § 1.482–4(f)(4) relating to allocations with respect to assistance provided to the owner. Temp. Reg. § 1.482–7T(a)(3)(i). Each controlled participant would be deemed to incur as part of its IDCs a share of such compensation equal to its RAB share. In the case of a controlled research entity that furnishes services under an arrangement that is not a CSA, the appropriate arm's length compensation would generally be determined under the principles prescribed in Temp. Reg. § 1.482–1T(b)(2)(iii) relating to performance of services by one controlled person for another. Temp. Reg. § 1.482–7T(a)(3)(iv).

[¶ 12,275]

c. Development Costs and Reasonably Anticipated Benefits

Temp. Reg. § 1.482–7T(d)(1) defines intangible development costs ("IDCs") of a controlled participant as all of its costs in cash or in kind (including stock-based compensation) that are directly identified with, or are reasonably allocated to, the IDA. Included are costs incurred in attempting to develop reasonably anticipated cost shared intangibles (regardless of whether such costs ultimately lead to development of those intangibles) and other intangibles developed unexpectedly. Also included are the arm's length rental charges for the use of any land or depreciable tangible property directly identified with or reasonably allocable to the IDA. Excluded are acquisition costs for such land and property after formation of a CSA. Temp. Reg. § 1.482–7T(d)(1)(iii).

In recent years an issue has surfaced concerning whether IDCs include stock-based compensation provided by a controlled participant, often in the form of stock options. In 2003, QCSA Reg. § 1.482–7A(d)(2) was issued, taking the position (previously articulated in a 2002 proposed regulation) that operating expenses include any stock-based compensation, such as restricted stock, stock options and stock appreciation rights, provided to an employee or independent contractor related to a CSA. Under Temp. Reg. § 1.482–7T(d)(3)(ii), the determination of whether stock-based compensation is directly identified with or reasonably allocable to the IDA is to be made as of the date the stock-based compensation is granted. The regulation deals in detail with permissible methods for measuring the cost associated with stock-based compensation. In general, the operating expense attributable to stock-based compensation is the amount allowable as a deduction. Temp. Reg. § 1.482–7T(d)(3)(iii)(A). However, with respect to options on publicly traded stock, the controlled participants in a qualifying CSA may elect to treat as operating expense the relevant amount reflected as a charge against earnings in audited financial statements (or in footnotes) prepared in accordance with U.S. generally accepted accounting principles. Temp. Reg. § 1.482–7T(d)(3)(iii)(B).

In Xilinx, Inc. v. Commissioner, 125 T.C. 37 (2005), which involved pre–2002 tax years, the Tax Court held that in the absence of evidence that unrelated parties dealing at arm's length would require a sharing of the expense of employee stock-based compensation under a CSA, the IRS was barred from allocating such costs to a controlled foreign participant by Reg. § 1.482–1(b)(1). This regulation states: "In determining the true taxable income of a controlled taxpayer, the standard to be applied in every case is that of a taxpayer dealing at arm's length with an uncontrolled taxpayer." In Xilinx, Inc. v. Commissioner, 567 F.3d 482 (9th Cir. 2009), the Ninth Circuit reversed the Tax Court in a two-to-one majority decision, holding that under the canon of statutory construction that a specific statute (or regulation) trumps a general statute (or regulation), the specific requirement of Reg. § 1.482–7(d)(1) (applicable to pre–2003 CSAs) that "all costs" be allocated under a CSA must trump the general arm's length standard of Reg. § 1.482–1(b)(1). Xilinx filed a petition for rehearing, soon accompanied by multiple amicus briefs filed on behalf of concerned corporations. The government filed a response in opposition in which it endorsed the Ninth Circuit outcome but not the analysis the court had adopted, instead arguing that the commensurate-with-the-income requirement for transfer of intangibles under section 367(d)(2)(A)(ii) does not require parity with uncontrolled transactions. Without rehearing the case, the original panel withdrew its prior opinion and issued a two-to-one decision that upheld the Tax Court decision by reasoning that the purpose of Section 482 is to establish parity between transactions of related persons and unrelated persons. Xilinx, Inc. v. Commissioner, 598 F.3d 1191, 1196 (9th Cir. 2010). Revised regulations applicable to post–2002 tax years, as well as the temporary regulations, which expressly include stock based compensation as a cost that must be shared under a CSA, have not yet been considered by the courts.

[¶ 12,277]

d. Controlled Participant's Share of IDCs

Each controlled participant in a CSA must bear a share of the IDCs incurred in developing cost shared intangibles (or under the QCSA regulations, "covered intangibles") that is equal to the participant's share of the reasonably anticipated benefits ("RABs") to be derived from the use of the developed intangibles. These benefits under a particular CSA are the sum of additional revenue generated, plus cost savings, minus any cost increases, from exploiting cost shared intangibles. Temp. Reg. § 1.482–7T(j)(1)(i). A particular controlled participant's RAB share is equal to its reasonably anticipated benefits divided by the sum of the RAB shares of all controlled participants. Temp. Reg. § 1.482–7T(e)(1)(i). A controlled participant's RAB share must be determined on the most reliable basis. This rule echoes the best method rule used for determining the most reliable measure of an arm's length result under Reg. § 1.482–1(c). The measure used for estimating a controlled participant's RAB share must be consistent for all such participants, and the participant's share may be measured directly or indirectly, whichever produces the most reliable estimate, and it may be necessary to make adjustments to account for material differences between the activities that controlled participants perform in connection with exploitation of covered intangibles, such as manufacturing and wholesale or retail distribution. Temp. Reg. § 1.482–7T(e)(2)(i). A direct measure would be based on additional revenue to be generated or costs to be saved. Indirect measures, which may in some cases be more reliable, would include units used, produced or sold, sales and operating profit. Temp. Reg. § 1.482–7T(e)(2)(ii). Required documentation must provide projections used to estimate benefits and update RAB shares and must explain the measure used and why it is the most reliable available. Temp. Reg. § 1.482–7T(e)(1).

The total pool of RABs and each controlled participant's RAB share are subject to adjustment by the IRS. Temp. Reg. § 1.482–7T(e)(1)(I) states: "For purposes of determining RAB shares at any given time, reasonably anticipated benefits must be estimated over the entire period, past and future, of exploitation of the cost shared intangibles, and must reflect appropriate updates to take into account the most current reliable data regarding past and projected future results available at such time."

Projections used to estimate benefits generally include a determination of the time period between the inception of the research and development and the receipt of benefits, a projection of the time over which benefits will be received and a projection of the benefits anticipated for each year in which it is anticipated that the intangible will generate benefits. However, if benefit shares are not expected to change significantly over time, current annual benefit shares may be used in lieu of projections. Temp. Reg. § 1.482–7T(e)(2)(iii).

A significant divergence between projected and actual benefit shares may indicate that the projections were not reliable, in which case the IRS can adjust RAB shares. Temp. Reg. § 1.482–7T(i)(2)(ii)(A). A significant divergence is defined as a divergence in excess of 20 percent between projected and actual benefit shares. If there is a significant divergence, which is not due to an extraordinary unforeseeable event, the IRS may use actual benefits as the most reliable basis for measuring benefits. Temp. Reg. § 1.482–7T(i)(2)(ii)(A). Conversely, no allocation will be made based on a divergence that is not considered significant as long as the projection is made using the most reliable basis for measuring benefits.

For purposes of the 20–percent test, all non-U.S. controlled participants are treated as a single controlled participant. The purpose of this rule is to ensure that a divergence by a foreign controlled participant with a very small share of the total costs will not necessarily trigger an adjustment of cost shares. Temp. Reg. § 1.482–7T(i)(2)(ii)(D), Ex. 4.

[¶ 12,280]

PROBLEM

Astra Corporation ("Astra") is a U.S. corporation with two wholly owned foreign subsidiaries, FS1 and FS2. All three corporations enter into a qualifying CSA. The participants project that shares of anticipated benefits will be as follows: Astra 45 percent, FS1 35 percent and FS2 20 percent. Actual benefits for years 1 and 2 prove to be as follows: Astra 50 percent, FS1 20 percent and FS2 30 percent. Can the IRS adjust the cost shares under these circumstances?

[¶ 12,285]

e. Buy–In and Buy–Out Rules

Typically when a CSA is established, one or more of the controlled participants contribute existing intangible property to the CSA that benefits one or more other controlled participants. As noted above, when this occurs each benefitted participant must make an arm's length buy-in payment to the contributing member or members. Thus, for example, if a U.S.-based multinational corporation enters into a CSA with a wholly owned subsidiary established in a low- or no-tax foreign country and transfers to the subsidiary existing intangible property, the subsidiary is required to make an arm's length buy-in payment equal to the value of the contributed intangible property. This payment could take the form of lump-sum, installment payments or a royalty. In the case of a QCSA, the amounts of buy-in payments required to be paid are determined under standards prescribed in the CSA–CIP, which are generally similar to those contained in the temporary regulations. In addition to the buy-in payment, under the CSA the subsidiary need only pay a share of the IDCs proportionate to the RAB the subsidiary is expected to derive from its use of the cost shared intangibles. It is not uncommon, especially in areas such as technology hardware and software, pharmaceuticals and medical devices, for the profit generated by the subsidiary from the cost shared intangibles under the CSA to exceed markedly amounts the subsidiary has paid to its parent corporation as buy-in payment and its share of the IDCs. Outsized amounts of income earned under CSAs by tax haven foreign subsidiaries owned by U.S.-based multinationals have resulted in increasingly aggressive focus by the Treasury, IRS and the Congress on the determination of appropriate buy-in payments. As a result of tightened rules and enforcement with respect to buy-in payment valuation, IRS audits have resulted in billions of dollars of buy-in payment adjustments, many of which are have not yet been resolved. In 2006, for example, reported CSA-related adjustments by the IRS totaled $26 billion, of which $23 billion related to buy-in payments. 14 Tax Mgmt. Trans. Pricing Rep. (BNA) 720 (Jan. 18, 2006).

The temporary regulations contain detailed provisions relating to the determination of buy-in and buy-out provisions aimed at narrowing the flexibility previously enjoyed by controlled participants. In the temporary regulations, contributions to a CSA of existing intangibles by a controlled participant are labelled "platform contributions." A platform contribution is defined as "any resource, capability, or right that a controlled participant has developed, maintained or acquired externally to the IDA (whether prior to or during the course of the CSA) that is reasonably anticipated to contribute to developing cost shared intangibles." Temp. Reg. § 1.482–7T(c)(1). If a controlled participant makes a platform contribution to a CSA in what is labelled a PCT, each other controlled participant, PCT Payor, must make an arm's length PCT Payment to each PCT Payee that makes a platform contribution. Under Temp. Reg. § 1.482–7T(a)(2), the arm's length amount must be determined under other sections of the section 482 regulations, supplemented by Temp. Reg. § 1.482–7T(g).

The regulations provide five methods for valuing buy-in payments: (1) the comparable uncontrolled transaction method, which looks to a comparable cost sharing arrangement with an uncontrolled party; (2) the income method, which examines the present value of the projected income from the contributing participant's best realistic alternative (e.g., a hypothetical license royalty); (3) the acquisition price method, which looks to the acquisition price of a part or all of an organization's stock or assets that were recently acquired in an arm's length transaction, multiplied by the PCT Payor's RAB share; (4) the market capitalization method, which is based on the average market capitalization of a publicly traded PCT Payee, multiplied by the PCT Payor's RAB share and (5) the residual profit split method, which evaluates whether the allocation of combined operating profit or loss attributable to one or more PCTs is arm's length by reference to each participant's contribution to that combined profit or loss. In addition, unspecified methods may be used under some circumstances. Temp. Reg. § 1.482–7T(g)(3)–(8). See ¶¶ 12,220–12,240. The rules of the temporary regulations did not come as a surprise as a result of the CSA–CIP issued on September 27, 2007. The CSA–CIP indicated that transfer pricing methods similar to those now contained in the temporary regulations would generally be deemed the best methods under the QCSA regulations.

The framework for determining the best method that must be used for determining the arm's length value of a PCT is the investor model. Temp. Reg. § 1.482–7T(g)(2)(ii) states, in part, as follows:

> In particular, the relative reliability of an application of any method depends on the degree of consistency of the analysis with the applicable contractual terms and allocation of risk under the CSA and this section among the controlled participants as of the date of the PCT, unless a change in such terms or allocation has been made in return for arm's length consideration. In this regard, a CSA involves an upfront division of the risks as to both reasonably anticipated obligations and reasonably anticipated benefits over the reasonably anticipated term of the CSA Activity. Accordingly, the relative reliability of an application of a method also depends on the degree of consistency of the analysis with the assumption that, as of the date of the PCT, each controlled participant's aggregate net investment in the CSA Activity (attributable to platform contributions, operating contributions * * *, operating cost contributions * * * and cost contributions) is reasonably anticipated to earn a rate of return equal to the appropriate discount rate for the controlled participant's CSA Activity over the entire period of such CSA Activity.

The regulations generally permit the IRS to make periodic adjustments to buy-in payments for any open tax year and all subsequent tax years if the IRS determines with respect to a particular PCT (called the "Trigger PCT") that a controlled participant has realized an "Actually Experienced Return Ratio" ("AERR") that is outside a specified "Periodic Return Ratio Range" ("PRRR"). Temp. Reg. § 1.482–7T(i)(6)(i). The

AERR is the present value of total benefits ("PVTB") divided by the present value of investment ("PVI"). In computing PVTB and PVI, present values are computed using the Applicable Discount Rate ("ADR") determined under Temp. Reg. § 1.482–7T(g)(2)(v). PRRR will generally consist of return ratios that are not less than .667 nor more than 1.5. But if the controlled participant has not substantially complied with appropriate CSA documentation requirements, the PRRR return ratios are not less than .8 nor more than 1.25. Temp. Reg. § 1.482–7T(i)(6)(ii). The regulations provide a number of exceptions, however, under which no adjustment can be made. For example, if failure to fall within the PRRR range is due to extraordinary events beyond the participants' control that could not be reasonably anticipated at the time of the buy-in, or if the AERR would fall within the PRRR if the AERR were recomputed with certain specified adjustments (such as adjustments to reflect delayed exploitation of the intangible), no adjustment can be made. In addition, no adjustment can be made when the same platform contribution is made to an uncontrolled party on substantially similar terms as the controlled transaction, and the requirements of the CUT method are satisfied. Temp. Reg. § 1.482–7T(i)(6)(vi)(A).

If, after any IDC allocations made by the IRS to make each participant's share of IDCs equal its share of RABs authorized by § 1.482–7T(i), the economic substance of the arrangement is nevertheless inconsistent with the terms of the arrangement over a period of years (for example, through a consistent pattern of one controlled participant bearing an inappropriately high or low share of the IDCs), the IRS may impute an agreement consistent with the participants' actual course of conduct. In that case, one or more of the participants that bore a disproportionately greater share of costs would be deemed to own a greater interest in cost shared intangibles than provided under the arrangement and must receive arm's length buy-in payments from the other participants. Temp. Reg. § 1.482–7T(i)(5).

If a new controlled participant joins a qualifying cost sharing agreement and thereby acquires an interest in cost shared intangibles, it must make an arm's length payment to each controlled participant from whom such interest was acquired. Temp. Reg. § 1.482–7T(a)(3)(iii). Conversely, if a controlled participant relinquishes an interest under the arrangement, it must receive an arm's length buy-out payment from the remaining controlled participants whose interests are thereby increased. Temp. Reg. § 1.482–7T(f)(2). Buy-in payments owed are netted against payments owing, and only the net amount need be paid. Temp. Reg. § 1.482–7T(g)(2)(iv). When there is a transfer of an interest in a cost shared intangible, the intangible valuation rules of Reg. §§ 1.482–1 and 1.482–4 through 1.482–6 apply (supplemented by Temp. Reg. § 1.482–7T(f)(4) when a change in participation in the CSA is involved). Temp. Reg. § 1.482–7T(a)(3)(ii).

[¶ 12,290]

f. Divisional Interests

Unlike the position set forth in the White Paper that each controlled participant be assigned exclusive rights in a specific geographic area to intangibles developed under a CSA, the QCSA regulations require in the case of QCSAs only that each participant be assigned an "interest" in covered intangibles that is documented in the QCSA. The temporary regulations require for CSAs, other than QCSAs, that each controlled participant be assigned one of three types of non-overlapping "divisional interest" in cost shared intangibles with no obligation to compensate another controlled participant. The non-overlapping interest under each divisional basis must be exclusive and perpetual and encompass all profits attributable to that interest. The alternative divisional interests include the following:

1. A territorial-based division that involves dividing the world into two or more non-overlapping geographic territories. Each participant must be given the right to exploit the intangible in its territory. Temp. Reg. § 1.482–7T (b)(4)(ii).

2. A field-of-use-based division that involves dividing all interests in cost shared intangibles on the basis of all anticipated uses to which they can be put. Each controlled participant must be assigned at least one anticipated use, and one controlled participant must be assigned the right to exploit the cost shared intangibles in any unanticipated uses. Temp. Reg. § 1.482–7T(b)(4)(iii).

3. Other divisional bases can be used only if they meet the following special requirements:

   (i) The basis clearly and unambiguously divides all interests in the intangibles among all controlled participants;

   (ii) The consistent use of the basis can be dependably verified from the records kept by the controlled participants;

   (iii) The rights of participants to exploit cost shared intangibles are non-overlapping, exclusive and perpetual and

   (iv) The resulting benefits enjoyed by each controlled participant are predictable with reasonable reliability.

An example given that would qualify in this category involves two facilities manufacturing the same product in different locations each owned by one of two controlled participants in a CSA. Each facility is functioning at or near capacity so that production can not feasibly be shifted. Temp. Reg. § 1.482–7T(b)(4)(iv), Ex. 2.

g. Other Rules

Two rules are of special importance to a foreign participant. First, a qualifying CSA will not be treated for U.S. tax purposes as a partnership.

QCSA Reg. § 1.482–7A(a)(1); Temp. Reg. § 1.482–7T(j)(2)(iii). Second, a foreign participant will not be treated as engaged in a U.S. trade or business solely by virtue of its participation in a CSA involving U.S. research and development activities. QCSA Reg. § 1.482–7A(a)(1); Temp. Reg. § 1.482–7T(j)(2)(ii).

CST payments made by a controlled participant in a qualifying CSA are generally treated as deductible amounts of research and development expense. These amounts are reduced by any CST payments received from other participants. A net approach is applied in the interest of simplicity and generally to preserve the character of costs actually incurred by a participant to the extent not reimbursed. Because CST payments involve no income, they are exempt from withholding tax in the United States and in foreign countries that recognize CSAs. Finally, any payment that in substance constitutes a CST payment will be treated as such, regardless of its characterization under foreign law. This rule is intended to enable foreign entities to participate in CSAs with U.S. controlled participants even if foreign law does not recognize cost sharing.

[¶ 12,295]

h. Evaluation of Cost Sharing Arrangements

Some U.S.-based multinational corporations have eschewed cost sharing in favor of arm's length royalties. Frequently, the principal tax factor is that participation by the U.S. parent corporation (or U.S. group) with foreign affiliates in a qualifying CSA produces no foreign-source income to the U.S. parent (or group). Accordingly, participation in a CSA cannot improve the foreign tax credit position of a U.S. corporation that is, as many are, in an excess foreign tax credit position. On the other hand, if royalties are received from affiliated or controlled foreign corporations, these royalties normally contain a profit element, and the profit will be foreign-source income that is frequently subject to little or no foreign tax. As a result, royalties will often increase the applicable foreign tax credit limitation for U.S.-based multinational corporations and will be helpful in ameliorating a current or anticipated excess foreign tax credit position.

Under the Section 904(d)(3) look-through rules for determining the limitations on the foreign tax credit, royalties from operating controlled foreign corporations will typically fall into the general income limitation basket. If royalties are exempt from foreign withholding tax, as is often the result under an applicable tax treaty between the United States and a source country, or are subject to a low or no withholding tax under the law of the source country, such royalties are helpful in absorbing excess foreign tax credits generated by other foreign-source general limitation income. Because cost sharing payments contain no income element, they cannot produce a comparable benefit. Accordingly, a U.S. taxpayer that is in an excess foreign tax credit position or is concerned that it may be in such a position in the future may elect to avoid cost sharing in favor of having controlled foreign affiliates pay royalties.

There are, however, other considerations that may persuade a foreign-based multinational group and, in many cases, a U.S.-based multinational group, to adopt cost sharing rather than royalty arrangements. Having international affiliates share the cost of research and development and thereby obtain the right to use developed intangibles in their operations will frequently reflect the natural business logic underlying a multinational's international business operations more accurately than royalty arrangements. Efficiency is promoted by permitting the location of research facilities in countries where they can function most effectively. Relative simplicity is another attraction of cost sharing. The complexities and administrative burdens inherent in having to fix arm's length royalties that will pass muster under the Section 482 regulations and their counterparts under foreign tax systems in the context of differing tax rates are avoided. Moreover, some U.S.-based multinational corporations have used CSAs as the vehicle for shifting income generated by cost shared intangibles to one or more controlled foreign corporations established in low- or no-tax foreign countries at the cost of buy-in payments that are in some cases dwarfed by the income derived by the controlled foreign corporation through exploitation of the intangibles. This benefit is now being counterbalanced to a growing extent by the increased audit vigor being brought to bear by the IRS, abetted by the more demanding requirements of the CSA–CIP and the temporary regulations.

Because fixing appropriate cost shares of a group of commonly controlled corporations is more straightforward and more readily verifiable than fixing arm's length royalties, a CSA offers the prospect of reduced potential for controversy with the IRS and with foreign tax authorities. Under the Section 482 regulations, the determinations of which affiliate is the owner of an intangible and what amount of royalty or other consideration must be paid to the owner by other members of the group for licenses or other transfers of the intangible require the application of complex methodologies and numerous judgments. These judgments not infrequently give rise to difficult three-party disputes among the taxpayer, the IRS and foreign tax authorities.

By contrast, under a qualifying CSA, the areas for potential controversy are more limited. They focus on the relatively narrow issues of identifying the pool of costs relevant to the IDA, the pool of reasonably anticipated benefits and the proper division of the costs among participants. The most difficult valuation issues often relate to setting the appropriate buy-in payments required when a CSA is initiated, the buy-out payment for a participant withdrawing from the arrangement or payments required when participants bear shares of IDCs that are disproportionate to their RAB shares. Of these, clearly the determination of the buy-in payments for controlled participants when a CSA is newly established has in itself become a central and growingly complex issue that has produced an inordinate level of controversy—a level that is very likely to increase as the IRS audits taxpayer implementation of the requirements of the CSA–CIP and of the temporary regulations.

[¶ 12,300]

6. PROPOSALS FOR REFORM

In the Staff of the Joint Committee on Taxation's Description of Revenue Provisions Contained in the President's Fiscal Year 2010 Budget Proposal, the following observations were made:

> Empirical evidence
>
> Empirical evidence indicating that U.S. multinationals continue to shift income to low-tax foreign jurisdictions has led many to question the effectiveness of the current transfer pricing rules. Most recently, the General Accountability Office ("GAO") reported in 2008 that the average tax rates on the foreign operations of U.S. multinationals vary considerably by country, and that most of the countries studied with relatively low average tax rates have income shares significantly larger than their shares of the business measures least likely to be affected by inappropriate income shifting practices: physical assets, compensation and employment. The GAO found that the opposite relationship holds for most of the high tax countries that it studied.
>
> In 2007, a Treasury Department study of the effectiveness of the transfer pricing rules examined the relationship between CFC profitability (measured by the ratio of operating profits to sales) and the statutory tax rate of the CFC's jurisdiction. * * * Using information from tax filings for the years 1996, 2000 and 2002, the study found an inverse relationship between pre-tax profitability and tax rates. In other words, the data generally showed that pre-tax operating margins are higher in low-tax countries and lower in high-tax countries. Based on this analysis, the Treasury study concluded that there is some potential for income shifting under the current regulations, and that this potential is perhaps most acute with respect to cost sharing arrangements involving intangibles. The Treasury study acknowledges, however, that many factors affect profitability, and that while the results are consistent with income shifting, a more refined empirical analysis is necessary to isolate income shifting through non-arm's length pricing.
>
> The Treasury study's findings are consistent, however, with those of empirical studies conducted by economists, beginning in the early 1990s and continuing through today, which include controls for various non-tax factors. * * *

> In 2003, another study examined the sources of income shifting, focusing on the role of intangible assets. The study used firm-level data from 1996 corporate tax filings (supplemented by data from public filings), and controlled for U.S. parent and CFC non-tax characteristics. Like previous studies, this study found an inverse relationship between local statutory rates and reported earnings. More specifically, however, this study found that "about half of the observed difference in profitability between high and low tax countries seems to be accounted for by the shifting of income derived from industrial intangibles."
>
> The conclusions reached by the Treasury and in other studies regarding the role of intangibles in income shifting are not surprising. Transfer pricing issues involving high-value intangibles are particularly difficult to resolve, due to the unique nature of those assets. Transactions involving these assets generally are not readily comparable to other third party transactions. In fact, some analysts concluded that the transfer of valuable intangible assets to low tax subsidiaries without adequate compensation (such as through appropriately priced royalties) is probably one of the most important income-shifting methods.
>
> The difficult problem presented by intangibles is further illustrated by data involving Ireland, which currently taxes active business income at a 12.5 percent rate. Another analysis reports that information from Treasury 2002 tax files for certain CFCs in manufacturing indicates that the ratios of pre-tax profits to sales are almost three times higher in Ireland on average than the mean ratio of pre-tax profits to sales for all such CFCs. According to the authors, "these 'excess' profits presumably reflect the fact that very valuable intellectual property is located in Ireland and the royalties paid back to the United States, while significant, do not fully reflect" the contribution of the U.S. parent.

Staff of Joint Comm. on Tax'n, Description of Revenue Provisions Contained in the President's Fiscal Year 2010 Budget Proposal, Part Three: Provisions Related to the Taxation of Cross–Border Income and Investment, at 26–29 (Sept. 2009) (footnotes omitted).

The proposal made by the Obama Administration in its budgets for 2010 and 2011 with respect to intangible transfers would clarify that the definition of intangible property for purposes of Sections 367(d) and 482 includes workforce in place, goodwill and going concern value. And that in a transfer of multiple intangible properties, such properties may be valued on an aggregate basis where doing so achieves a more reliable result. The proposal would also clarify that intangible property must be valued at its highest and best use, as such property would change hands between a willing buyer and a willing seller, neither being under any compulsion to buy or to sell and both having reasonable knowledge of relevant facts.

The Staff of the Joint Committee's analysis of the proposal is, in part, as follows:

> The proposal does not modify the basic approach of the existing transfer pricing rules with regard to income from intangible property. Instead, its scope is limited to clarification of certain definitional and methodological issues that have arisen in IRS examinations of the value attributed to intangible property at the time it is transferred offshore. * * *
>
> Clarification of the definition of intangible property
>
> In recent years, two areas in particular have been the focus of increased transfer pricing audits and proposed adjustments with respect to transfers of intangible property. The first is the adequacy of the buy-in payment for existing intangible property made available to controlled affiliates pursuant to cost sharing arrangements; these cases are typically evaluated by the IRS under section 482. The second is the adequacy of compensation paid by a CFC for intangible property transferred in connection with the recent wave of outbound restructurings of U.S. manufacturing operations * * *; these cases are typically evaluated by the IRS under sections 367(d) and 482.
>
> IRS audits of these transactions frequently involve disputes regarding whether goodwill, going concern value and workforce in place are intangible property for which compensation must be provided. Both sections 367(d) and 482 reference the definition of intangible property provided in section 936(h)(3)(B), but those items (among others) are not expressly included in that definition. Taxpayers, therefore, have taken the position that transfers of such property are not compensable.
>
> The IRS view, however, is that any workforce in place, goodwill and going concern value that may exist (the existence of these items itself often disputed by the IRS) are intangible property under section 936(h)(3)(B), because they constitute "similar items" under section 936(h)(3)(B)(vi). In particular, the IRS position is that goodwill, going concern value and workforce in place must be "similar items" because they are like the listed items; moreover, Congress arguably envisioned goodwill and going concern value as "similar items" because the legislative history of section 367(d) contemplates an exclusion of foreign goodwill or going concern value that would otherwise have been unnecessary. Alternatively, for transactions to which section 482 applies, even if these items were not treated as intangibles within the meaning of section 936(h)(3)(B), the IRS could be expected to argue that their transfer must nonetheless be fully compensated under the general rules of section 482 (which is not limited to compensation of intangible property). In addition, where intangible property is made available in conjunction with the provision of services, the IRS argues that it must be fully compensated under section 482, even though

> there is no separate transfer. The distance between the two positions is great—whereas the IRS sees the issue as a question of determining the arm's length pricing of such transactions, taxpayers deny that any price is required in the first place.
>
> With regard to goodwill and going concern value, audit disputes concern both the threshold treatment of these items as intangibles and, to the extent that such treatment is required, the scope of the exception under section 367(d) for foreign goodwill or going concern value. * * *

Id. at 37–39.

In an effort to add another arrow to the IRS quiver in dealing with inappropriate shifting of income generated by foreign intangibles to a controlled foreign corporation established in a low- or no-tax foreign country, the Obama Administration's tax proposals for fiscal year 2011 included the following:

> Under the proposal, if a U.S. person transfers an intangible from the United States to a related controlled foreign corporation that is subject to a low foreign effective tax rate in circumstances that evidence excessive income shifting, then an amount equal to the excessive return would be treated as subpart F income in a separate foreign tax credit limitation basket.

U.S. Treas. Dep't, General Explanations of the Administration's Fiscal Year 2011 Revenue Proposals 43 (Feb. 2010). Legislation implementing either of the foregoing proposals has not been enacted.

[¶ 12,305]

7. USE OF ADVANCE PRICING AGREEMENTS

Under the Section 482 regulations covering transfer pricing for intangibles there are obviously many areas for potential disagreement between commonly controlled taxpayers, on the one hand, and the IRS and foreign tax authorities, on the other.

One technique for eliminating most, if not all, the areas of potential dispute with respect to determining appropriate arm's length consideration for intangible transfers, including cost sharing arrangements, would be for the taxpayer to request and negotiate an advance pricing agreement ("APA") with the IRS. As discussed in Chapter 8, through an APA, it may be possible for a taxpayer and the IRS to establish taxpayer-specific resolutions of the various factual issues that arise in connection with a particular intangible transfer.

Moreover, the competent authority mechanism under applicable income tax treaties between the United States and foreign countries in which eligible participants are located may be made an integral part of the APA process. See ¶ 8175. Thus, using the APA process offers an opportunity to confront and resolve differences with the tax authorities of treaty partners and with the IRS on the full range of issues under a particular intangible transfer before the transfer is implemented and under a CSA before the constitutive agreement is signed.

CHAPTER 13

DIRECT INVESTMENT ABROAD

■ ■ ■

[¶ 13,000]

A. DIRECT INVESTMENT ABROAD THROUGH FOREIGN BRANCH OR FOREIGN COMPANY

A direct investment by a U.S. corporation in a foreign country may take the form of the establishment of a branch of that corporation in the foreign country or the acquisition of an equity interest in one of the forms of business organization recognized under the laws of that country. In this context, a *direct* investment, as typically distinguished from a *portfolio* investment, involves a sufficiently large interest in the foreign enterprise's voting equity to carry with it a significant participation in and influence over management of the enterprise.

[¶ 13,005]

1. OPERATION THROUGH A FOREIGN BRANCH

There are a number of nontax factors that may make setting up a wholly owned direct investment in a foreign country in the form of a branch attractive. Although establishing a branch necessitates qualifying the U.S. corporation (or one of its subsidiaries) to do business under the laws of the foreign country concerned, operation through a branch will usually obviate compliance with certain legal requirements relating to the organization and operation of business entities set up under local law. Thus, branch operation will eliminate complications that might result from corporate law requirements as to the minimum number of shareholders required in a corporate enterprise, the nationality of directors and the location of directors' and shareholders' meetings.

Occasionally foreign, and more often U.S., tax considerations will encourage branch operation. If, for example, the foreign enterprise is engaged in the exploration, development and exploitation of solid mineral resources abroad, operating through a branch will enable the U.S. corporation to use percentage depletion with respect to qualifying foreign solid mineral production.

In many cases, however, operating through a branch will entail burdens and risks that would not be involved if a wholly owned corporation were organized under local law. One factor that tends to make branch operation unattractive is that a U.S. corporation operating through a foreign branch normally cannot limit its liability to the assets owned by that branch. Moreover, the operation of a branch in another country will generally subject the U.S. corporation to the exercise of in personam jurisdiction in that country. Also, the organization and operation of a branch may involve some rather burdensome requirements for the filing of documents and reports. Normally the corporate charter and bylaws of the U.S. or other corporation of which the branch is an extension must be translated, registered and published as a part of the qualification procedure. Regular publication of information concerning the worldwide operations of the corporation may be required. Moreover, the local tax regime may be relatively inhospitable to branch operation either because branch profits are subjected to higher taxes (including perhaps a branch profits tax) than distributed earnings of a corporation organized under the laws of the foreign country concerned or because there is greater uncertainty as to how the taxable profit will be computed than would be the case if the operation were conducted by a local corporation.

As discussed previously, U.S. taxes will be imposed currently on the profits of a foreign branch of a U.S. corporation, subject to a direct credit against U.S. income taxes for foreign income taxes paid or accrued. This may create a strong incentive to organize a foreign subsidiary corporation, which will enjoy the advantage of deferral of U.S. tax so long as profits are accumulated. This will be true whenever the foreign operations are to be conducted in a country in which the corporate income tax burden is substantially lower than the effective income tax burden in the United States. The deferral is advantageous because the profits from a branch would be immediately taxed in the United States and the benefit of the lower foreign tax burden would be lost.

When the foreign tax rates are lower than the U.S. rates, however, it may be possible in some cases to use a branch approach and still gain the advantage of deferring U.S. taxes until ultimate distribution of profits to the U.S. corporation by having the operation conducted through a branch of a wholly owned foreign base company of the U.S. corporation. This advantage is based on the assumption that the base company, although typically a controlled foreign corporation, will not receive types of income that will be treated as a constructive dividend to its U.S. parent corporation under Subpart F.

The desirability of operating through a branch may depend, to a considerable extent, on the functions to be carried out by the foreign enterprise. As already noted, when solid mineral exploration and exploitation are involved, certain U.S. tax factors may make branch operations attractive. Branch operation is also often used in connection with (i) sale of U.S. exports into the foreign country concerned or (ii) purchase of materials and components in the foreign country and their importation into the United States. International export or import trading through a foreign branch will be free of foreign tax if an income tax treaty applies and if, under the terms of that treaty, the branch does not constitute a permanent establishment to which the trading income is attributable. See ¶¶ 11,010–11,015. The result may be the same under a foreign country's tax law in the absence of an applicable tax treaty. If the trading is carried out by a local corporation, the resulting income will almost certainly be subject to foreign tax unless the corporation is established in a tax haven.

U.S. corporations that have or that plan extensive foreign operations have also used branch operations in connection with foreign "headquarters" facilities, the function of which is supervising and coordinating some or all of the corporation's foreign activities. A number of Western European countries tax the branches of foreign corporations falling within the "headquarters" classification on a highly favorable basis. To qualify as a "headquarters" operation, it must generally be shown that the branch will not be engaged in commercial activities but will be limited to supervising and coordinating specified foreign operations. These may include international procurement, manufacturing and sales activities. In some cases the "headquarters" branch will be taxed on a formulary basis, which will produce a very modest tax burden. For example, in some instances, it has been possible to obtain rulings that a headquarters branch of a foreign corporation will be subject to the normal foreign corporate income taxes on an assumed net income equal to ten percent of the branch's expenses or an assumed gross income equal to 110 percent of its expenses (which produces the same result). In other cases, moreover, it has been possible for a branch of a U.S. corporation to obtain a complete exemption from local income taxes if its activities are limited to "supervision, research and coordination."

Although use of the branch approach is not uncommon if the functions of the foreign facility include foreign mining operations, trading activities or supervisory headquarters-type functions, when manufacturing or service operations are involved, the disadvantages of branch operation usually outweigh the advantages. Moreover, branch operation may be precluded by practical necessities when the venture is to involve joint equity ownership by the U.S. corporation and by one or more other parties, who will often be located in the country in which the business is to be established.

If the foreign business is expected to result in losses at least for an initial period, it may be desirable for a U.S. corporation to operate as a branch even when manufacturing or service operations are involved. If the business is conducted through a branch of a U.S. corporation, rather than a foreign subsidiary, the losses may be deducted currently against other income of the U.S. corporation and thereby reduce the current U.S. corporate income tax burden. If realized by a foreign corporation, the losses would produce no current U.S. or foreign tax benefit. In assessing the desirability of operating through a foreign branch to permit current use of initial losses, it is essential to evaluate the effects of the current loss on the calculation of the Section 904 foreign tax credit limitations. Foreign-source loss will reduce the numerator of the applicable Section 904(d) limitation fraction by the same amount as the denominator, and it is possible that an overall foreign loss may be produced that will be subject to "recapture" under Section 904(f)(1). See the discussion at ¶ 7060. If the foreign business becomes profitable and incorporation of the branch is contemplated, it will be important to consider the branch loss recapture rules of Section 367(a)(3)(C). See ¶ 10,095.

[¶ 13,010]

2. OPERATION THROUGH A FOREIGN BUSINESS ORGANIZATION

When the choice is open between conducting active business operations in a foreign country through a branch and through a wholly owned corporation, a variety of factors, some of which have already been noted, should be considered. In addition to the advantage of limited liability, the use of a locally organized corporation may be simpler and less expensive than qualification of a branch. It may also have the advantage of identifying the enterprise more closely with the local scene. When the corporate income tax burden in the country in which the operations are to be conducted is significantly lower than the burden in the United States, the use of a foreign corporation will often be advantageous. This is true because it will permit accumulation and reinvestment of profits free of U.S. tax as long as profits are not distributed to the U.S. shareholder. (This assumes that the taxpayer will be able to avoid the anti-deferral rules of Subpart F.) This factor is particularly important when the foreign country grants incentives in the form of tax reductions or tax holidays to approved investments.

Suppose that the business is to involve one or more unrelated foreign investors in addition to the U.S. investor. In such cases, it will normally be appropriate, if not essential, to have the business conducted by a form of business organization created under the laws of the country in which the business operations will be conducted.

After deciding to use a form of business organization established under foreign law, the U.S. investor must decide what form of business organization to adopt. In civil law countries, the available forms of business organization typically include at least the corporation, the limited liability company, the limited partnership, the limited partnership with shares, the general partnership and the contractual joint venture. See ¶ 13,025. Of particular interest is the civil law limited liability company, which at one time had no close counterpart in U.S. law. Over the course of the last four decades, however, all states of the United States and the District of Columbia have enacted legislation recognizing the limited liability company patterned on the civil law form, in which all equity owners enjoy limited liability. The limited liability company found in the civil law systems has certain features of the corporation (for example, limited liability and, in most cases, continuity of existence) and others of a partnership (for example, absence of freely transferable equity shares and typically no requirement for centralized management through a board of directors).

In some situations, U.S. tax factors exercise a strong influence over the choice of the particular form of local business organization to be employed. To receive the benefit of the U.S. tax advantages already mentioned in the solid mineral exploitation field, it would be essential for a U.S. corporation, not conducting operations through a branch, to adopt a form of business organization in the foreign country concerned that would not be treated as a foreign corporation for U.S. tax purposes. This is so because, as previously noted, the tax advantages concerned are accorded only to U.S. taxpayers. The same is true if the U.S. corporation seeks to use anticipated initial losses to offset income from other investments. In these cases, a foreign business organization must be selected that will not be characterized as an "association" taxable as a corporation for U.S. tax purposes. To gain these U.S. tax advantages the choice could be made from among the limited liability company, general partnership, limited partnership, contractual joint venture or other form of business organization that can qualify to be treated for U.S. tax purposes as a partnership or as a branch (if wholly owned by the U.S. corporation). The advantages would be forfeited if a foreign law corporation were used.

Barring these special considerations that make partnership treatment desirable, however, an enterprise with multiple owners will usually be cast in the form of a business organization that will be classified as a corporation for U.S. tax purposes. Formerly, whether a limited liability company would be treated as a corporation or as a partnership for U.S. tax purposes would depend upon its attributes, and it was usually possible to tailor those attributes to ensure either partnership or corporation classification, whichever were desired. See ¶ 13,030. Entity classification regulations (or, as they are commonly called, the "check-the-box" regulations) have been issued, however, that permit the U.S. taxpayer to elect whether an entity organized under foreign law other than as a corporation will be treated as a partnership or a corporation for U.S. tax purposes. Such elective classification treatment most commonly applies to a foreign limited liability company. See ¶ 13,035.

In a case in which the foreign enterprise is 100–percent-owned by a U.S. corporation, it is usually a simple matter for the business to be organized under the applicable foreign law in a manner that will produce the desired classification for U.S. tax purposes. Under the check-the-box regulations, use of a form of business organization under foreign law that corresponds to a U.S. corporation will assure classification as a corporation, and if a foreign limited liability company is used, it may elect to be treated either as a corporation or as a branch (a "disregarded entity") for U.S. tax purposes. If a foreign business entity is treated as a corporation for foreign tax purposes but as a branch for U.S. tax purposes, it is often referred to as a "hybrid entity" or, more specifically, a "hybrid branch." The choice of entity issue may be more challenging when the foreign business is a joint venture in which one or more foreign investors own part of the equity because these investors may have objectives relating to the classification of the business organization that conflict with those of the U.S. investor. This classification issue is discussed in the context of international joint ventures at ¶ 13,115.

[¶ 13,015]

PROBLEMS

Western Metals ("Western") is a U.S. corporation engaged in mining in the United States. At present, it is planning its first foreign venture, a copper ore mine in Country Z. The initial capital required is $300 million, all of which, according to the agreement made between Western and the Country Z government ("the Agreement"), must be in equity (not debt). Western intends to provide the full $300 million out of its accumulated earnings.

The ore will be mined from the sands of the Kanga, Country Z's largest river, by a new dredging process patented and now owned by Process, Inc., a wholly owned U.S. subsidiary corporation of Western. Process, Inc. has previously deducted all of its costs of developing the process. All dredging will take place on one large bend in the Kanga. From there the ore will be transported 20 miles by rail to Mtweya, a deep water port, where it will be sorted and then sold F.O.B. ("Free On Board") Mtweya.

The Agreement provides for (1) a royalty to the Country Z government of $4 per ton, which is a fair market royalty; (2) a Country Z income tax of 30 percent on net profits; (3) net profits to be computed in essentially the same manner as under the Internal Revenue Code, except that percentage depletion is not allowed (since Western has no "cost" for the ore body, no depletion of any kind will be allowed under Country Z law for removal of the ore); (4) no Country Z withholding tax on dividends or royalties; and (5) a deduction for a "fair" royalty payable to Process, Inc., for use of its process patent. Based on its economic analysis Western has concluded that a royalty of anywhere from $5 million to $10 million per year would be acceptable to the Country Z Ministry of Mines, to the Country Z Inland Revenue Service and, under Section 482, to the IRS.

Gross income from sale of the ore F.O.B. Mtweya (five million tons) is estimated to be $200 million per annum. Expenses, including the Country Z royalty, but not including the royalty to Process, Inc., or depletion, are estimated to be $150 million per annum.

Western intends to withdraw from the Country Z project $20 million annually (before U.S. taxes) for use in the United States in its business and the business of Process, Inc. The $20 million includes whatever royalty is set on the Process, Inc. patent. For the foreseeable future all other cash flow will be reinvested in the project in Country Z.

Assume that the U.S. corporate income tax rate is 35 percent, that Western's U.S.-source income is $200 million and that the percentage depletion available for copper mined abroad is 14 percent of the gross income from the copper mine property (less royalties and rents paid with respect to the property) but not to exceed 50 percent of the taxpayer's taxable income from the property. The start-up period is very short and can be disregarded; assume full investment, production and income from the beginning of year 1. See § 901(e).

1. Consider whether, from a tax standpoint, the Country Z operation should be run as a branch of Western or as a corporation organized under Country Z law of which Western would own 100 percent of the stock. Assume further that the Country Z corporation would be treated as a corporation for U.S. tax purposes.

2. Consider whether the royalty to Process, Inc., should be set on the low end ($5 million), the high end ($10 million) or somewhere in the middle of the acceptable range.

3. Assume the facts are as stated in Problem 1, except: (1) the Country Z income tax rate is 55 percent on net profits; (2) Western has various other foreign branch mining ventures producing large amounts of income bearing an average foreign tax rate of 25 percent; (3) the royalty to Process, Inc. is set at $10 million a year; and (4) the Country Z project is organized as a branch. How much annual excess tax credit will be available from the Country Z project to offset U.S. tax otherwise due on the foreign-source general limitation income from Western's other foreign mining branches? See § 901(e).

4. Assume the facts are as stated in Problem 1, except that Western is involved in other foreign mining ventures and it expects to have annual excess foreign tax credits with respect to foreign-source general limitation income from these ventures of $5 million. Would this fact alter the analysis?

3. CHARACTERIZATION OF THE FOREIGN BUSINESS ORGANIZATION FOR U.S. TAX PURPOSES

[¶ 13,020]

a. Introduction

If it is decided to organize a business in a civil law country in one of the forms of business organization available under the laws of the country concerned, one complicating feature that will frequently be encountered is a requirement that a civil law company have at least two (and sometimes more than two) equity owners. This rule is premised on the conceptual basis for creation of a company under civil law, which is generally that of contract. A company is created by a contract between two or more equity owners which must be registered in the commercial registry. This may often be accomplished by the creation of two U.S. special purpose subsidiaries which then become the equity owners of the civil law company.

In connection with establishing a direct investment abroad, a threshold decision is whether the venture will be organized in the form of an incorporated entity that would correspond to the corporation of U.S. law or in the form of some other entity, such as a limited liability company, a limited or general partnership or a contractual joint venture.

There are some basic differences between the usual corporation and the usual unincorporated forms of business organizations. The corporate form offers limited liability to all investors and, at least in the case of the corporation under U.S. law and its civil law counterpart, a well-developed body of substantive law governing the rights of the shareholders. When two (or more) shareholders are involved, effective and enforceable control arrangements can usually be worked out in appropriate cases to ensure both representation of each participant on the board of directors (or other body responsible for supervising management) and veto rights in either or both participants over certain corporate decisions. In addition, unless special classes of stock or debt obligations are used, each venturer's share of profits and its share of the tax burden borne by the joint enterprise is governed by its share of the jointly owned corporate entity's capital stock.

In the case of a contractual joint venture, partnership or other unincorporated form of business organization, limited liability may not be available unless the participant concerned interposes a subsidiary corporation to hold its interest in the joint enterprise. Control arrangements involve the problem that either participant may be able to bind the partnership or a joint venture vis-à-vis third parties in contravention of the agreement between the co-venturers. They also involve the problem that agreements concerning how the venture will be managed may not be specifically enforceable under many civil law systems. Certain unincorporated forms may, however, offer some flexibility in allocating book income, tax deductions and credits and cash distributions between the partners in proportions differing from their equity contributions.

One consideration that may influence the choice will be the foreign tax burden on the undistributed or distributed earnings of the various business forms that may be otherwise suitable for use under the particular circumstances. It is impossible to generalize about this question. The important thing is to examine the treatment of each alternative under the tax laws of the country in which the joint enterprise will be established.

If the foreign income tax can be fully credited against U.S. tax, reducing the foreign tax burden on distributed earnings may be of no significance. However, when the foreign tax burden on distributed earnings exceeds the U.S. corporate tax burden or the U.S. corporation is otherwise in or near an excess foreign tax credit position, an important objective is likely to be reducing as much as feasible the foreign tax burden on distributed earnings of any joint venture abroad. A foreign tax burden in excess of the Section 904 limitations may thus induce the U.S. participant to press for selection of an unincorporated form of business organization if it will involve a reduced foreign tax burden. The same consideration has prompted the use of foreign tax haven holding companies to reduce the foreign tax burden on distributed earnings from a foreign corporation. See ¶ 13,155.

[¶ 13,025]

b. Civil Law Forms of Business Organization

As suggested above, the civil law systems, which have been adopted in a significant number of major industrial countries, such as Belgium, France, Germany, Italy, Japan, Spain, the Netherlands and the countries of Latin America, offer a greater number of business forms than countries that have adopted the Anglo–American model. The latter include, in addition to the United States and the United Kingdom, many former British colonies, some of which are now members of the British Commonwealth, such as Australia, Canada, New Zealand and many countries in the Caribbean. The traditional business forms available in Anglo–American systems have been the corporation (usually called "company" in the British practice), the limited partnership and the general partnership. A relatively new business form has rapidly emerged in the Anglo–American world called the limited liability company ("LLC"), which is patterned after its counterpart in the civil law systems.

The civil law systems provide for a business form that is closely analogous to the corporation of U.S. law, namely the *société anonyme* ("*S.A.*"), the *sociedad anónima* ("*S.A.*") and the *Aktiengesellschaft* ("*A.G.*"). This civil law form is translated as "corporation" in the United States.

Another business form that is widely used in many civil law countries is the *société à responsabilité limitée* ("*SARL*"), *sociedad de responsabilidad limitada* ("*SRL*") and the *Gesellschaft mit beschränkter Haftung* ("GmbH"). This entity is called a "limited liability company" in the United States, and a business form very similar to it has been adopted in all states of the United States, the District of Columbia and a number of foreign countries with an Anglo–American legal tradition. Its principal attraction in the United States is that it affords limited liability to all its equity owners and yet it can elect to be treated as a partnership for U.S. tax purposes under the check-the-box regulations, discussed at ¶ 13,035.

The civil law counterpart to the limited partnership of Anglo–American law is the *société en commandite simple*, *sociedad en commandita simple* and *Kommanditgesellschaft* (*"K.G."*). The usual English translation is "limited partnership." Under a variation generally not available under Anglo–American law, this civil law form may be created with transferable shares, in which case it is labelled a *société en commandite par actions*, *sociedad en commandita por acciones* or *Kommanditgesellschaft auf aktien*. Finally, the civil law systems offer the counterpart of the general partnership of Anglo–American law in the form of the *société en nom collectif*, *sociedad colectiva* and *Offene Handelsgesellschaft* (*"OHG"*).

If the direct investment is to be a joint venture involving two or more equity owners, it may be possible to organize it as a contractual joint venture. Here the rights and obligations of the parties will be largely spelled out in the constitutive contract; there will usually not be a relevant body of governing substantive law except the law relating to business contracts generally. The civil law forms of general and limited partnership and contractual joint venture will usually be treated as a partnership for U.S. and foreign tax law purposes, subject to the right to elect to have the entity taxed as a corporation for U.S. tax purposes under the check-the-box regulations.

[¶ 13,030]

c. Former Section 7701 Regulations

The characterization of a business organization organized under U.S. or foreign law as a corporation or a partnership for U.S. tax purposes was for many years governed by the entity classification regulations issued under Section 7701(a)(2) and (3) of the Code (hereinafter "former Section 7701 regulations"). Former Reg. §§ 301.7701–1 through 301.7701–4. The picture has, however, been substantially altered under the check-the-box regulations, which often permit the organization to elect to be treated for U.S. tax purposes either as a corporation or as a conduit, flow-through or fiscally transparent entity (i.e., in effect, as a partnership or if it has only one member, as a disregarded entity or branch). The election is available to any business entity organized under foreign law except the foreign law counterpart of a U.S. corporation, which is required, even under the check-the-box regulations, to be treated as a corporation for U.S. tax purposes.

In characterizing a business entity as a corporation or partnership, the former Section 7701 regulations invoked the six corporate characteristics identified by the Supreme Court in Morrissey v. Commissioner, 296 U.S. 344 (1935): (1) associates, (2) objective to carry on business and divide the profits, (3) continuity of life, (4) centralized management, (5) free transferability of ownership interests and (6) limited liability. Because the existence of (1) and (2) are common to both the corporation and the partnership, in differentiating between these business forms, only the remaining four corporate characteristics were considered. A highly mechanical test was adopted: "An unincorporated organization shall not be classified as an association [taxable under the Code as a corporation] unless such organization has more corporate characteristics than non-corporate characteristics." Former Reg. § 301.7701–2(a)(3). Thus, if an unincorporated business organization had no more than two of the four corporate characteristics (3) through (6), it was characterized as a partnership for U.S. tax purposes.

An organization had the corporate characteristic of continuity of life if the death, insanity, bankruptcy, retirement, resignation or expulsion of any member would not cause a dissolution of the organization. Former Reg. § 301.7701–2(b)(1). An organization had centralized management if any person (or group of persons that does not include all of the equity owners) had continuing exclusive authority to make the management decisions necessary to the conduct of the organization's business. Former Reg. § 301.7701–2(c)(1). An organization had the corporate characteristic of free transferability of interests if persons owning substantially all of the equity interests in the organization had the power, without the consent of other members, to substitute for themselves in the organization persons who were not previously equity owners. Former Reg. § 301.7701–2(e)(1). An organization had limited liability if under local law there was no equity owner who was personally liable for the debts of or claims against the organization. Former Reg. § 301.7701–2(d).

When a business organization created under foreign law was involved, foreign law determined the legal relationships of the members of the organization with one another and with the public and their interests in the organization's assets. Rev. Rul. 88–8, 1988–1 C.B. 403. But the characterization for U.S. tax purposes turned on the application to those relationships of the tests set forth in the former Section 7701 regulations. These tests were based on the corporate characteristics referred to above.

The form of foreign business organization that was most often characterized as a corporation for foreign tax purposes, but as a partnership for U.S. tax purposes, was the civil law limited liability company. If all of the equity owners were directly involved in management, if the equity shares were not transferable by one owner without the consent of the others and if death, insanity, expulsion, resignation, retirement or bankruptcy of an equity owner would terminate the existence of the company, under the former Section 7701 regulations, the organization was normally regarded as lacking the three corporate characteristics of centralized management, free transferability of interests and continuity of life. Accordingly, such an organization was characterized as a partnership. Indeed, it was enough to ensure that it lacked only two of these three corporate characteristics to achieve partnership characterization, and it was frequently possible to achieve this result. Thus, it was the limited liability company organized under foreign law that was most often selected by investors who wanted both limited liability for all investors and partnership classification for U.S. tax purposes.

[¶ 13,035]

d. Replacement of the Former Entity–Classification Regulations With an Elective Check-the-Box System

In IRS Notice 95–14, 1995–1 C.B. 297, the IRS and the Treasury announced that they were considering simplifying the classification regulations to allow taxpayers to treat domestic unincorporated business organizations and certain foreign business organizations as partnerships or as associations taxable as corporations on an elective basis. The rationale underlying the proposed change was described in the Notice as follows:

> The existing classification regulations are based on the historical differences under local law between partnerships and corporations. However, many states recently have revised their statutes to provide that partnerships and other unincorporated organizations may possess characteristics that have traditionally been associated with corporations, thereby narrowing considerably the traditional distinctions between corporations and partnerships. For example, some partnership statutes have been modified to provide that no partner is unconditionally liable for all of the debts of the partnership. Similarly, almost all states have enacted statutes allowing the formation of limited liability companies. These entities are designed to provide liability protection to all members and to otherwise resemble corporations, while generally qualifying as partnerships for federal tax purposes. *See, e.g.,* Rev. Rul. 88–76, 1988–2 C.B. 360.
>
> One consequence of the narrowing of the differences under local law between corporations and partnerships is that taxpayers can achieve partnership tax classification for a non-publicly traded organization that, in all meaningful respects, is virtually indistinguishable from a corporation. Taxpayers and the Service, however, continue to expend considerable resources in determining the proper classification of domestic unincorporated business organizations. * * * In addition, small unincorporated organizations may not have sufficient resources and expertise to apply the current classification regulations to achieve the tax classification they desire.

With respect to foreign entities, the principal impetus for applying an elective approach was the ease with which the civil law limited liability company's characteristics could be manipulated in order to ensure partnership classification for U.S. tax purposes even though all the equity owners enjoyed limited liability. The IRS and Treasury recognized in IRS Notice 95–14 (1995–1 C.B. at 298) that the following special considerations came into play with respect to foreign business entities:

> The first is that presently there is no foreign analogue to a state-law corporation and, therefore, no foreign organization that is automatically treated as a corporation for federal tax purposes. Thus, an elective system that follows exactly the approach * * * for domestic unincorporated organizations would apply to all foreign organizations, without exception. The Service and Treasury are considering the appropriateness and feasibility of identifying particular forms of foreign organizations that, like state-law corporations, would automatically be treated as corporations.
>
> A second consideration in the foreign area is the possibility of inconsistent, or hybrid, entity classification; that is, classification as a taxable entity in one country but as a flow-through entity (e.g., a partnership) under the tax laws of another country. An elective approach could expand the potential that exists under the current classification regulations for hybrid structures. The Service and Treasury are considering whether it is appropriate to address inconsistent classification in any rules to be proposed and also are considering how the tax benefits or detriments that may result from inconsistent classification can be addressed through the tax treaty process.
>
> A third consideration in the foreign area is that a purely elective approach could have a substantive effect on entity classification by increasing taxpayers' flexibility to achieve their desired classification of certain foreign organizations. Under the present rules, taxpayers holding interests in foreign organizations are not always as able as those holding interests in domestic organizations to achieve their desired result. Because any change in the existing classification regulations is intended generally to simplify the rules without resulting in a substantial change in the classification of unincorporated organizations, the Service and Treasury must consider whether an elective approach should be modified with respect to foreign organizations.

In May 1996, proposed regulations were issued under which elective treatment would be made available to unincorporated business organizations under U.S. and foreign law to replace former Regs. §§ 301.7701–1 through –3. An introduction to the new regime in the IRS Notice of Proposed Rule–Making and Hearing, 61 Fed. Reg. 21,989 (May 13, 1996) stated:

> Treasury and the IRS believe that it is appropriate to replace the increasingly formalistic rules under the current regulations with a much simpler approach that generally is elective. To further simplify this area, the proposed regulations provide similar rules for organizations that have a single owner.

> With respect to foreign organizations, Notice 95–14 (1995–1 C.B. 297) observed that, while the distinctions are similarly formalistic, the classification process under the current regulations involves even more complexities and requires greater resources than does the classification process for domestic organizations. For example, the classification of a foreign organization involves not only a review of organizational documents, but also a thorough understanding of the controlling foreign law. Accordingly, the simplified system provided under the proposed regulations extends to foreign organizations as well, with certain modifications * * *.
>
> In light of the increased flexibility under an elective regime for the creation of organizations classified as partnerships, the Treasury Department and the IRS will continue to monitor carefully the uses of partnerships in the international context and will issue appropriate substantive guidance when partnerships are used to achieve results that are inconsistent with the policies and rules of particular Code provisions or of U.S. tax treaties.
>
> * * *
>
> Proposed Section 301.7701–2 specifies those business entities that automatically are classified as corporations for federal tax purposes. Any other business entity that is recognized for federal tax purposes may choose its classification under the rules of proposed Section 301.7701–3. Those rules provide that a business entity with at least two members can be classified as either a partnership or an association [taxable as a corporation] and that a business entity with a single member can be classified as an association or can be disregarded as an entity separate from its owner.

The final check-the-box regulations, Reg. §§ 301.7701–1 through –3, became effective on January 1, 1997. They generally adopt the approach of the proposed regulations. It had long been possible under the laws of many foreign countries, particularly civil law countries, to create a limited liability company (e.g., a *GmbH* or a *limitada*), in which all members would enjoy limited liability and that would be treated as a corporation under the foreign tax system, but treated as a partnership for U.S. tax purposes under the former Section 7701 regulations. Such an entity would be exempt from U.S. tax at the entity level and would qualify for flow-through treatment of income, deductions and other tax attributes. If it had only one shareholder, the foreign entity would be disregarded and thus treated as an extension of its owner for U.S. tax purposes. Under the check-the-box regulations, there is no need to manipulate the characteristics of the civil law limited liability company to achieve flow-through treatment for U.S. tax purposes.

The elective approach (to business entity classification) thus recognizes and accepts the reality that, in most cases, the characteristics of a limited liability company could under prior law be manipulated to achieve classification either as a corporation or as a partnership (or if it had a single owner, as a disregarded entity) and that often the classification was essentially elective in practical terms. The elective regime has the virtue of avoiding the large amount of taxpayer and IRS time and effort previously required to process ruling requests regarding the classification of particular entities.

An entity organized under U.S. law as a state law corporation is always treated as an association taxable as a corporation for federal tax purposes. The final check-the-box regulations adopt an analogous scheme for foreign entities. The regulations set forth a list of business entities organized under the law of identified foreign countries that will always be treated as associations taxable as corporations for U.S. tax purposes. These include, for example, the *Aktiengesellschaft* of German and Swiss law, the *sociedad anónima* of Spanish and Mexican law and the *société anonyme* of French law. Reg. § 301.7701–2(b)(8). This list of foreign entities that are automatically classified as corporations for U.S. tax purposes (often referred to as "per se corporations") has been expanded periodically since the original issuance of the check-the-box regulations. The expansion has usually taken the form of adding countries and their form of business organization that is treated as a per se corporation for U.S. purposes. A relatively recent addition to the per se corporation list that is not organized in a single country is the European public limited liability company *Societas Europaea* ("SE"). Reg. § 301.7701–2(b)(8)(i). The European Union Council Regulation 2157/2001, 2001 O.J. (L294), that created the SE on October 8, 2004, has legal effect in all of the Member States of the European Economic Area (which includes the European Union plus Norway, Iceland and Liechtenstein). An SE must have a registered office in one of the Member States and in addition may have registered offices in others. T.D. 9197, 2005–1 C.B. 985.

Any entity organized under foreign law that is not required to be classified as a corporation under the check-the-box regulations is an "eligible entity" and as such is eligible to elect to be classified either as a corporation or a flow-through entity for federal tax purposes. Reg. § 301.7701–3(a). If the entity has at least two equity owners (members) and makes the latter election, it is classified as a partnership for U.S. tax purposes, even if taxed as a corporation for foreign law purposes. If it has only one equity owner (member) and makes the election, the entity is disregarded as an entity separate from its owner and is treated as a branch of a corporate owner or an extension of the sole proprietorship of an individual owner. Reg. § 301.7701–2(c)(2).

Default rules provide for classification of foreign entities that decide not to, or fail to, make an election. Reg. § 301.7701–3(b). These rules are intended to match taxpayers' probable expectations in the absence of an election (and thus to reduce the number of elections that will be needed).

If at least one equity owner of a foreign entity that has at least two owners has unlimited liability, the entity will be classified as a partnership in default of an election. If it has only one owner, the entity will be classified as a branch of a corporate owner or an extension of an individual proprietorship (i.e., it is disregarded as an entity separate from its owner). Reg. § 301.7701–3(b)(2)(A) and (C). If all of the owners of the entity enjoy limited liability, in default of an election, the entity will be classified as a corporation for U.S. tax purposes. Reg. § 301.7701–3(b)(2)(B). Grandfathering rules are applicable to entities in existence on May 8, 1996, when the regulations were initially proposed, that generally permit such entities to retain the status they had on that date. Reg. § 301.7701–2(d).

If the classification of a foreign entity has not previously been relevant for U.S. tax purposes, its classification will be determined under the foregoing rules when it first becomes relevant. A foreign entity's classification becomes relevant when it affects the liability of any persons for federal income tax or information reporting purposes. Reg. § 301.7701–3(d).

A change in an entity's classification will often have tax consequences in addition to determining whether the entity is treated as a flow-through entity or a taxable entity for U.S. tax purposes. For example, if an eligible entity previously classified as a partnership elects to be classified as a corporation, the following transactions are deemed to occur: The partnership contributes all of its assets and liabilities to the corporation in exchange for stock in the corporation, and immediately thereafter, the partnership liquidates by distributing the corporation's stock to its partners. Conversely, if an eligible entity previously classified as a corporation elects to be classified as a partnership, the following transactions are considered to be involved: The corporation distributes all of its assets and liabilities to its shareholders in complete liquidation, and immediately thereafter, the shareholders contribute all of the distributed assets and liabilities to a newly formed partnership. Reg. § 301.7701–3(g)(1). The tax treatment of the transactions deemed to occur as a result of an election to change an entity's classification is determined under the provisions of the Code that generally apply to such transactions and general principles of tax law, such as the step-transaction doctrine. Reg. § 301.7701–3(g)(2)(i).

Regulations have been issued to clarify the classification of a business entity that is chartered, created or organized in more than one country. Reg. § 301.7701–2(b)(9). Classifying such an entity for U.S. tax purposes requires two steps. The first is to determine whether, under the check-the-box regulations, the entity is treated as a corporation or a non-corporate entity (a partnership or disregarded entity). The second is to determine whether the entity is foreign or domestic. A business entity (including a disregarded entity) is domestic if it is created or organized as any type of entity (e.g., corporation, general or limited partnership or limited liability company) in the United States. If it is not domestic, it is treated as foreign.[1] Reg. § 301.7701–5.

Thus, if the entity is classified as a corporation because it is incorporated in the United States, it is treated as a domestic corporation for U.S. tax purposes even though its form of organization in a foreign country (e.g., as a limited liability company) would not have required it to be treated as a corporation for U.S. tax purposes. If, on the other hand, an entity is classified as a corporation because of its form of organization in a foreign country, it is also treated as a domestic corporation for U.S. tax purposes if it is organized as any form of entity in the United States (e.g., corporation, limited liability company or partnership).

Example. BE is an entity with a single equity owner organized as a corporation under the laws of Country X. It is treated for U.S. tax purposes as a per se corporation under Reg. § 301.7701–2(b)(8)(i). Some years after its formation BE files a certificate of domestication in State Y, one of the states of the United States, as a limited liability company with the result that it is treated as a limited liability company under the laws of that state. For U.S. tax purposes (absent a contrary election) the limited liability company would ordinarily be treated as a disregarded entity. Neither Country X nor State Y requires BE to terminate its charter in Country X as a result of the domestication. Therefore, BE is a dually chartered entity and is treated as a domestic corporation for U.S. tax purposes. See Reg. § 301.7701–2(b)(9)(ii), Ex.1.

[¶ 13,040]

e. The "Hybrid Entity" Problem

One obvious consequence of the check-the-box regulations has been to facilitate the creation of entities, such as civil law limited liability companies, that are treated as separately taxable corporations under foreign law but as flow-through entities (either as partnerships or wholly owned entities that are disregarded) for U.S. tax purposes. Such dual character entities are often referred to as "hybrid entities" or, if wholly owned by a single equity owner, as "hybrid branches."

The ready availability of controlled or wholly owned hybrid entities and branches quickly led to their use by U.S. corporations and foreign corporations controlled by U.S. corporations to reduce the foreign tax burden by having the foreign hybrid entity or branch (treated as a taxable

1. Rev. Rul. 2004–76, 2004–2 C.B. 111, deals with the issue of which U.S. tax treaty applies to payments made by a U.S. resident payor to a foreign corporation that is a dual resident of two foreign countries (because it is incorporated in one and has its management in the other). The United States is party to a tax treaty with each of these countries. Both foreign countries are themselves parties to a tax treaty under which the foreign corporation is treated as a resident of one of them (because its management is there). The Ruling concludes that U.S. treaty with that country is controlling.

corporation under foreign law) pay deductible royalties, interest, rents and other payments to its parent entity, whether a U.S. corporation or its controlled foreign corporation. Because these payments would be deductible for foreign tax purposes, they would reduce the amount of foreign tax imposed on the hybrid entity or branch. If the parent of a wholly owned foreign hybrid entity were a U.S. corporation, this reduction would be particularly helpful when the hybrid entity was operating in a high tax country by reducing or eliminating excess foreign tax credits that would otherwise be generated by the foreign corporate income tax and dividend withholding tax when the entity distributed its earnings. Payments deductible by the foreign hybrid entity would be treated as intra-entity payments that were tax-free to the U.S. corporation.

When the parent entity of a wholly owned foreign hybrid was a controlled foreign corporation of a U.S. corporation, there was the added benefit that royalties, interest and rents from the hybrid entity were simply intra-entity remittances. Consequently, they usually would not be treated as items of Subpart F income in the hands of the controlled foreign corporation.

The use of hybrid branches of controlled foreign corporations to avoid having intra-entity payments classified as foreign personal holding company income prompted the IRS to issue IRS Notice 98–11, 1998–1 C.B. 433, as a prelude to issuance of proposed and temporary regulations. Broadly speaking, this Notice treated a hybrid branch as an entity separate and distinct from the rest of the controlled foreign corporation that owned it. However, under pressure from U.S.-based multinational corporations and Congress, the IRS subsequently withdrew IRS Notice 98–11 and the regulations. See IRS Notice 98–35, 1998–2 C.B. 34. Under the temporary and proposed regulations certain intra-entity remittances of interest, rents and royalties by the hybrid branch to its controlled foreign corporation parent could have been classified as foreign personal holding company income for purposes of Subpart F. This treatment would have applied to such intra-entity remittances received from a hybrid branch by a controlled foreign corporation either directly or through a partnership as if they were payments from a separate entity.

The Conference Committee report concerning the Internal Revenue Service Restructuring and Reform Act of 1998 stated as follows:

> The conferees expect that the Congress will consider the international tax policy issues relating to the treatment of hybrid transactions under the subpart F provisions of the Code, and will consider taking legislative action as deemed appropriate. In this regard, the conferees expect that the Congress will consider the impact of any legislation or administrative guidance in this area on affected taxpayers and industries. The conferees strongly recommend that the Department of the Treasury also take into account the impact of any administrative guidance in this area on affected taxpayers and indus-

tries. No [implication] is intended regarding the authority of the Department of the Treasury or the Internal Revenue Service to issue the Notice [IRS Notice 98–11] or the regulations, or to issue any other notice or regulation which reaches the same or similar results with respect to the treatment of hybrid transactions under subpart F.

H.R. Conf. Rep. No. 599, 105th Cong., 2d Sess. 314 (1998).

In July 1999, proposed regulations dealing with hybrid branches were issued. Prop. Reg. § 1.954–9, REG–113909–98, 1999–2 C.B. 125. Under these proposed regulations, payments received by a controlled foreign corporation from a hybrid branch would be recharacterized as Subpart F income if three conditions are met:

(i) A hybrid branch payment must be made between specified entities;

(ii) The hybrid branch payment must reduce foreign tax; and

(iii) The hybrid branch payment must fall within the definition of one of the categories of foreign personal holding company income.

Prop. Reg. § 1.954–9(a)(1).

Specified entities would include the following:

(i) A controlled foreign corporation and its hybrid branch;

(ii) Hybrid branches of a controlled foreign corporation;

(iii) A partnership in which a controlled foreign corporation is a partner (either directly or through one or more branches or other partnerships) and a hybrid branch of the partnership; or

(iv) Hybrid branches of a partnership in which a controlled foreign corporation is a partner (either directly or through one or more branches or other partnerships).

Prop. Reg. § 1.954–9(a)(2).

For purposes of the proposed regulations, a number of other definitions are introduced. A hybrid branch would mean an entity that

(i) is disregarded as an entity separate from its owner for federal tax purposes and is owned (including ownership through branches) by either a controlled foreign corporation or a partnership in which a controlled foreign corporation is a partner (either directly or indirectly through one or more branches or partnerships);

(ii) is treated as fiscally transparent by the United States; and

(iii) is treated as non-fiscally transparent by the country in which the payor entity, any owner of a fiscally-transparent payor entity, the controlled foreign corporation or any intermediary partnership is created, organized or has substantial assets.

Prop. Reg. § 1.954–9(a)(6)(iii). A hybrid branch payment is defined as the gross amount of any payment (or accrual) which, under the tax laws of any foreign jurisdiction to which the payor is subject, is regarded as a payment between two separate entities but which, under U.S. income tax principles, is not income to the recipient because it was between two parts of a single entity. Prop. Reg. § 1.954–9(a)(6)(iv).

The hybrid branch payment would be recharacterized as Subpart F income only if the hybrid branch payment meets the tax disparity test. It would do so if it is taxed to the payee in the year when earned at an effective rate of tax that is less than 90 percent of, and at least five percentage points less than, the hypothetical effective rate of tax imposed on the hybrid branch payment if taxed to the payor. Prop. Reg. § 1.954–9(a)(5)(iv)(A). The hypothetical effective rate of tax imposed on the hybrid payment would be:

> (i) For the tax year of the payor in which the hybrid branch payment is made, the amount of income taxes that would have been paid or accrued by the payor if the hybrid branch payment had not been made, less the amount of income taxes paid or accrued by the payor, divided by
>
> (ii) The amount of the hybrid branch payment.

Prop. Reg. § 1.954–9(a)(5)(iv)(B).

[¶ 13,045]

NOTE

The hybrid branch proposed regulations, if and when finalized, would generally not be effective to classify as Subpart F income any hybrid branch payment until the first year of the U.S. shareholder of the controlled foreign corporation starting on or after the expiration of five calendar years from the date of finalization of the regulations. IRS Notice 98–35, 1998–2 C.B. 34. The long delay by the IRS and Treasury in taking further action on the proposed regulations and the long-postponed effective date envisioned in them suggest that they are not likely ever to become effective.

[¶ 13,050]

f. Check-the-Box Regulations and International Tax Arbitrage

As suggested at ¶ 1133, international or cross-border tax arbitrage is the name frequently given to arrangements designed to produce tax savings through exploitation of differences between the U.S. and foreign tax rules on such matters as determining the source of income and deductions, classification of entities and determining the residence of entities for tax purposes. In the context of direct investment abroad there are many opportunities for such arbitrage. Some of the more significant of these lie in the use of hybrid entities (and particularly hybrid branches), which is facilitated by the check-the-box regulations.

A simple illustration would be afforded by a U.S. corporation that owns a smaller-than-ten-percent interest in the voting equity of a foreign joint venture set up in a form of business organization under foreign law that must be treated as a corporation for U.S. tax purposes under the check-the-box regulations. Because the U.S. corporation owns less than ten percent of the voting stock of the foreign corporation, the U.S. corporation would not be entitled to an indirect (or direct) foreign tax credit for foreign corporate taxes imposed on the joint venture corporation's income. If, however, the joint venture is organized as a limited liability company or other entity under foreign law that qualifies as an "eligible entity" under the check-the-box regulations, an election can be made to have the joint venture entity characterized as a partnership for U.S. tax purposes. Under this election, the foreign taxes would be creditable by the U.S. corporation as a direct credit under Section 901. This is so because a partner is deemed to pay its share of income tax paid by the hybrid entity, which is treated as a partnership for U.S. tax purposes even though it is treated as a corporation for foreign tax purposes.

Using a foreign hybrid entity as the vehicle for a direct investment that is wholly or majority owned by a U.S. corporation can also produce tax benefits. These benefits may be particularly significant if the investment is made in a high-tax foreign country.

> *Example*. USC, a U.S. corporation, owns 100 percent of the equity shares of FC, a limited liability company organized under the laws of Country A. The company is treated as a taxable entity for Country A tax purposes, and its income is taxed at the rate of 40 percent. If USC makes a loan of working capital to FC, FC will typically be entitled to deduct for Country A tax purposes the interest that it pays to USC. But if an election is made under the check-the-box regulations to have FC treated for U.S. tax purposes as a disregarded entity (i.e., a hybrid branch of USC), the interest will not be taxed in the United States because it is simply regarded as an intra-entity transfer within USC. The effect is a reduction in the foreign tax of FC, but without a correlative income inclusion to USC. A similar benefit can be achieved if the hybrid branch makes other payments to USC that are deductible for Country A tax purposes, such as royalties, rents and payments for services.

Significant benefits may also be available if the U.S. corporation operates abroad through a wholly owned tax haven foreign base company, which is a controlled foreign corporation and is the parent of an operating company organized in a second foreign country.

> *Example*. USC, a U.S. corporation, owns all of the stock of FC1, a foreign base company incorporated under the laws of Country A, a tax haven. FC1 is a controlled foreign corporation. FC1, in turn, owns all of the stock of FC2, a company organized as a limited liability company under the tax laws of Country B. FC2 is engaged in the

manufacture and sale of widgets in Country B. This manufacturing company is taxed as a corporation in Country B. If an election is made under the check-the-box regulations to have FC2 treated as a disregarded entity (i.e., a hybrid branch) for U.S. tax purposes, payments such as interest and royalties paid by FC2 to FC1 will normally be deductible for Country B tax purposes and will result in a reduction in the Country B corporate income tax payable by FC2. However, these payments would not be treated as Subpart F income to FC1 because the payments are regarded simply as intra-entity payments within FC1.

In both examples, a deduction reduces the foreign income tax payable without a correlative income inclusion that can be taxed. In both, the inconsistent treatment of the payments concerned is the result of an election under the check-the-box regulations to have the payor treated as a disregarded entity for U.S. tax purposes although it is treated as a taxable entity for foreign tax purposes. The election gives rise to inconsistent characterizations of FC2 in Country A and Country B that create the tax arbitrage opportunity. The combination of a deduction in the foreign country of the payor and no correlative income inclusion to the payee is sometimes described as a "double dip" transaction.

In the second example, the Subpart F regime is being subverted by the election to have FC2, the Country B limited liability company (which is a taxable entity in Country B), treated as a transparent or disregarded entity for U.S. tax purposes with the result that it is treated as a hybrid branch of FC1, the controlled foreign corporation. (The sales and manufacturing branch rules under Section 954(d)(2) do not come into play because both activities occur in Country B.)

Yet another example of potential tax savings through international arbitrage involves a sale by a controlled foreign corporation of its wholly owned foreign operating company. The operating company is organized as a limited liability company, which elects to be treated as a hybrid branch.

Example. USC, a U.S. corporation, owns all of the stock of FC1, a corporation organized under the laws of Country A, a tax haven. FC1 is treated as a taxable corporation for U.S. and Country A purposes. FC1, a controlled foreign corporation, owns all of the equity shares of FC2, a limited liability company organized under the laws of Country B. FC2 is treated for Country B purposes as a taxable corporation. If FC2 were treated as a corporation for U.S. tax purposes, gain on the sale of its equity shares by FC1 would be foreign personal holding company income and could result in a Subpart F inclusion to USC. FC2, however, is an eligible entity and elects to be treated as a disregarded entity (i.e., a hybrid branch) for U.S. tax purposes. As a result, the sale of the equity shares of FC2 by FC1 is treated for U.S. tax purposes as a sale by FC1 of the operating assets of FC2. Gain on the sale of operating assets realized by FC1 will usually not be foreign personal holding company income and will not result in a Subpart F inclusion to USC.

Again, in this "check and sell transaction" the election under the check-the-box regulations subverts the policy underlying Subpart F. As discussed at ¶ 6105, the basic issue presented in the preceding example was considered by the Tax Court in Dover Corp. v. Commissioner, 122 T.C. 324 (2004). The *Dover* case involved a more complex set of facts but in essence held that the "check and sell" transaction would be respected and be treated for U.S. tax purposes as a sale by a controlled foreign corporation of the operating assets of a foreign entity rather than as a sale of its stock. Therefore, the gain realized was not treated as foreign personal holding company income.

In July 1999, the IRS and Treasury issued Prop. Reg. § 1.954–9, REG–113909–98, 1999–2 C.B. 125, excerpted at ¶ 13,040, which targeted various abusive international tax arbitrage transactions involving controlled foreign corporations and their hybrid branches. The regulations encompass the treatment under Subpart F of various payments to controlled foreign corporations by their hybrid branches. These proposed regulations provide that hybrid branch payments that would otherwise not be foreign personal holding company income of a controlled foreign corporation would be recharacterized as Subpart F income under the following circumstances:

(1) A "hybrid branch payment" (e.g., a royalty, rent or interest payment) is made between a controlled foreign corporation and its hybrid branch;

(2) The hybrid branch payment reduces the foreign tax of the payor;

(3) The hybrid branch payment would be foreign personal holding company income if made between controlled foreign corporations; and

(4) There is a specified tax rate disparity between the tax rate on the payment in the hands of the payee and the hypothetical tax rate that would have applied if the payment had been taxed to the payor. The hybrid branch payment would meet this test if the tax to the payee were less than 90 percent of, and at least five percentage points less than, the hypothetical tax to the payor if it retained the payment.

The proposed regulation was generally to become effective only for payments made in tax years starting five years after the regulation became final. Prop. Reg. § 1.954–0(c).

In view of the long period of inaction, it seems unlikely that these proposed regulations will ever become effective. However, if the regulations did become final regulations, would they cover any or all of the three examples of the use of hybrid branches set forth above?

Prop. Reg. § 1.954–9 was not the only regulatory action contemplated by the IRS and the Treasury to deal with abuses of the check-the-box regulations in the international arena. In November 1999, the IRS and the Treasury issued former Prop. Reg. § 301.7701–3(h), REG–110385–99, 1999–2 C.B. 670, concerning cases in which "an extraordinary transaction" occurred in close proximity to an election by a foreign entity to change its classification to disregarded entity status under the check-the-box regulations. In the event that such an extraordinary transaction occurred, the entity would not be treated as a disregarded entity but as a corporation for U.S. tax purposes. An "extraordinary transaction" was defined to include a sale, exchange, transfer or other disposition of a ten percent or greater interest in a foreign eligible entity during a period starting one day before an election to be converted to a disregarded entity and ending 12 months thereafter. Former Prop. Reg. § 301.7701–3(h)(1)(i)(A)-(B) (1999).

These proposed regulations were criticized as overly broad and as undermining the increased certainty promoted by the check-the-box regulations. The upshot was the decision by the IRS and Treasury to withdraw Prop. Reg. § 301.7701–3(h). This withdrawal was accompanied by the following comment:

> The IRS and Treasury remain concerned about cases in which a taxpayer, seeking to dispose of an entity, makes an election to disregard it merely to alter the tax consequences of the disposition. The IRS will continue to pursue the application of other principles of existing law (such as the substance over form doctrine) to determine the proper tax consequences in such cases. As the Supreme Court has noted: "To permit the true nature of a transaction to be disguised by mere formalisms, which exist solely to alter tax liabilities, would seriously impair the effective administration of the tax policies of Congress." *Commissioner v. Court Holding Co.*, 324 U.S. 331, 334 (1945).
>
> In addition, the IRS and Treasury are continuing to examine the potential use of the entity classification regulations to achieve results inconsistent with the policies and rules of particular Code provisions or of U.S. tax treaties. In contrast to the approach of the extraordinary transaction rule, which would operate to change the classification of an entity if certain conditions are met, this examination will focus on ensuring that the substantive rules of particular Code provisions and U.S. tax treaties reach appropriate results notwithstanding changes in entity classification.

IRS Notice 2003–46, 2003–2 C.B. 53.

As may be apparent from the foregoing, no effective defense has as yet been mounted against abuses of the check-the-box regulations with respect to the election of disregarded entity status by foreign "eligible entities." Consider the extent to which the following proposal of the Staff of the Joint Committee on Taxation in 2005 would curtail the use of hybrid branches to avoid the impact of Subpart F.

[¶ 13,055]

STAFF OF JOINT COMMITTEE ON TAXATION, OPTIONS TO IMPROVE TAX COMPLIANCE AND REFORM TAX EXPENDITURES

109th Cong., 1st Sess.
183–85 (Comm. Print 2005).

Under the proposal, an organization must be treated as a corporation for Federal tax purposes if the organization: (1) is a separate business entity organized under foreign law; and (2) has only a single member. This proposal overrides any contrary result that may have been obtained under the current entity classification regulations. In all other respects, those regulations remain in force.

If a branch, local office, or other organization does not rise to the level of a separate business entity (e.g., if it is not established as a separate legal entity under the relevant local law), then the branch, office, or organization is not subject to this proposal, and thus is not treated as a corporation for Federal tax purposes.

Domestic business entities and non-single-member foreign business entities are generally not subject to the proposal and thus remain eligible for elective entity classification to the extent so eligible under the current regulations. However, the Treasury Secretary may issue regulations extending the application of this provision to: (1) a non-single-member foreign business entity, in cases in which a membership interest is issued to a person related to another member, with a principal purpose of preventing the entity from being classified as a corporation under the provision;[411] or (2) a domestic business entity that has a CFC [controlled foreign corporation] as its sole member.

Effective Date

The provision applies to taxable years beginning one year or more after the date of enactment.

Discussion

As noted above, although the "check the box" regulations have produced some simplification benefits with respect to both domestic and foreign entities, the regulations also have created some unintended tax-avoidance opportunities as applied to foreign entities. In particular, it appears that the availability of single-member disregarded entities has

411. Persons are considered related for this purpose if they meet a greater-than–50–percent common-control standard under rules similar to those of section 954(d)(3).

facilitated the avoidance of current taxation under subpart F in situations in which subpart F normally would apply.

For example, payments of interest, dividends, rent, and royalties between CFCs often generate subpart F income, but similar payments between a disregarded entity and a CFC do not, even if the disregarded entity is treated as a separate corporation under applicable foreign tax law, and thus may be deducting the payment for foreign tax purposes. In these cases, commonly referred to as "hybrid branch arrangements," the ability to avoid subpart F may combine with favorable results under foreign tax law to distort investment decisions, arguably making it more attractive in some cases to locate investments abroad than in the United States. Ensuring that these transactions are taxed under subpart F could both correct the misallocation of capital away from the United States and raise additional revenue. On the other hand, some would argue that this sort of inconsistent treatment of a transaction by the countries concerned is an inevitable result of cross-border activity in a world with diverse tax systems, that the appropriate U.S. tax treatment of a transaction should not depend on the results that a taxpayer might be able to achieve under foreign tax law, and that capital import neutrality is promoted by allowing these transactions to avoid taxation under subpart F.[412] Regardless of whether these particular tax results are viewed with approval or disapproval, hybrid branch arrangements illustrate well how a "check the box" election may be used to secure tax results that would have appeared difficult or impossible to achieve under the current statutory subpart F rules.

While hybrid branch arrangements are perhaps the first and best-known example of how a "check the box" election can be used to circumvent subpart F, other similar uses for the election have been found. For example, the sale of stock of an operating company by a CFC generally would give rise to subpart F income, but if an election to disregard the company is in effect, then the transaction may be treated as a sale of operating assets, thus avoiding the creation of subpart F income.[413] As in the case of hybrid branch arrangements, a mere election, with no non-tax economic effect, may transform what would have been subpart F income into an item exempt from subpart F.[414]

412. In 1998 the IRS proposed, and then withdrew, regulations that sought to prevent this particular use of the "check the box" regulations. See Notice 98–11, 1998–1 C.B. 433; former Temp. Treas. Reg. sec. 1.954–9T, adopted in T.D. 8767, 1998–1 C.B. 875; Notice 98–35, 1998–2 C.B. 34. More recently, both the House-and Senate-passed versions of AJCA [American Jobs Creation Act of 2004] included a provision that would have allowed taxpayers to achieve tax results similar to those achieved via hybrid branch arrangements in connection with payments between two CFCs, thus obviating the need to establish a hybrid branch, but this provision was not adopted in the final version of AJCA.

413. See, e.g., Dover Corp. v. Commissioner, 122 T.C. 324 (2004).

414. Under section 412 of AJCA, certain sales of partnership interests by controlled foreign corporations no longer give rise to subpart F income. AJCA did not extend a similar approach to the sale of stock by a controlled foreign corporation, which still gives rise to subpart F income.

While a certain degree of electivity already prevailed as a practical matter under the pre–1997 entity classification rules, and tax results similar to those described above may have been attainable under some circumstances before 1997, the expressly elective approach of the current regulations has removed some frictions that may have acted as a brake on some of the tax planning involving the classification of entities. In particular, the ability to disregard single-member foreign business entities may have impaired the intended functioning of subpart F in some respects.

The proposal strikes a balance between the goal of simplification and the policies reflected in the substantive provisions of the Code by generally retaining the elective approach of the current entity classification regulations, but providing that single-member business entities organized under foreign law must be treated as corporations for Federal tax purposes. This approach will not prevent every arrangement that might be thought to be abusive, as not all abuses require the use of a separate disregarded entity, but the approach will render it considerably more difficult in many cases for taxpayers to use the entity classification rules to frustrate the intent of the international tax provisions of the Code. A wide range of potentially abusive transactions that are currently disregarded for purposes of the substantive rules of the Code would be "regarded" under the proposal, thereby providing a greater opportunity to apply and adjust those rules in an appropriate manner, whether that be to allow or to disallow a particular tax result.

While the overall structuring flexibility available to taxpayers under this approach is considerably less than what prevails under the current entity classification regulations, it is generally still greater than the flexibility that prevailed before 1997. Because this approach would have the effect of upsetting taxpayer expectations that have developed over the last several years of experience with the current regulations, the proposal includes a delayed effective date, in order to enable taxpayers to restructure arrangements that were established in reliance on the current regulations.

[¶ 13,060]

NOTE

Is the proposal of the Staff of the Joint Committee an adequate response to the abuses involving circumvention of the controlled foreign corporation regime? Should consideration be given to a more drastic change such as denying the check-the-box election altogether to entities organized under foreign law or ending deferral of U.S. tax on all types of income earned by a controlled foreign corporation?

[¶ 13,062]

The Obama Administration's budget proposal for fiscal year 2010 included a modified version of the 2005 proposal of the Staff of the Joint Committee with exceptions for (i) a wholly owned foreign eligible entity organized under the law of the same country as that in which the single owner is organized and (ii) a first-tier foreign entity wholly owned by a U.S. person. The proposal, which would have been effective for tax years beginning after 2010, read as follows:

> The proposal provides that a foreign eligible entity may be treated as a disregarded entity only if the single owner of the eligible entity is created or organized in, or under the law of, the foreign country in, or under the law of, which the foreign eligible entity is created or organized. Therefore, a foreign eligible entity with a single owner that is created or organized in a country other than that of its single owner would be treated as a corporation for Federal tax purposes. Except in cases of U.S. tax avoidance, the proposal would generally not apply to a first-tier foreign eligible entity wholly owned by a U.S. person. The tax treatment of the conversion to a corporation of a foreign eligible entity treated as a disregarded entity would be consistent with current Treasury regulations and relevant tax principles.

Staff of Joint Comm. on Tax'n, 111th Cong., 1st Sess., Description of Revenue Provisions Contained in the President's Fiscal Year 2010 Budget Proposal, Part Three: Provisions Related to the Taxation of Cross–Border Income and Investment, at 110 (Sept. 2009).

The Joint Committee Staff's analysis included the following comments:

> Under present law, the hybrid branch arrangements described in Notice 98–11 and the 1999 proposed regulations permit taxpayers to achieve results similar to those permitted by section 954(c)(6). Payments of interest, dividends, rent, and royalties between a disregarded entity and a CFC do not generate subpart F income, even if the disregarded entity is treated as a separate corporation under applicable foreign tax law and thus the CFC may be deducting the payment for foreign tax purposes. Prior to the enactment of section 954(c)(6), similar payments made between two CFCs located in different countries would generate subpart F income; under the look-through rule, however, they often do not, again even in cases in which the payments are deductible by the payor for foreign tax purposes. Both sets of rules permit taxpayers to move foreign earnings from one CFC to another CFC located in a different country, potentially reducing foreign tax liability without incurring U.S. tax—indeed, that is the stated purpose of the look-though rule.

Section 954(c)(6) expires for taxable years beginning after December 31, 2009. The Administration has proposed extending section 954(c)(6) for one additional year (through 2010), but its subsequent expiration would then dovetail with this proposal's 2011 effective date. That is, under the Administration's proposals (and assuming no further extension of section 954(c)(6)), cross-border payments of the types contemplated by hybrid branch structures or by section 954(c)(6) could not be made in taxable years beginning after December 31, 2010, with the same favorable tax results that are achieved today.

By facilitating the reduction of foreign tax liability, both hybrid branch structures and the look-through rule can encourage indefinite deferral of U.S. tax on foreign income through continued foreign reinvestment of foreign earnings. Both may also affect the timing and utilization of foreign tax credits under some circumstances (or in conjunction with other techniques), by facilitating the separation of relatively high-taxed and low-taxed foreign-source income and permitting a taxpayer to more effectively isolate and time the distribution of high-taxed income to maximize the taxpayer's ability to use the foreign tax credits under the section 904 limitation (while also minimizing the amount of low-taxed income that is repatriated to the United States). These techniques arguably may make the tax treatment of the foreign earnings of U.S. multinationals more comparable to that of an exemption system—the tax system applicable to many of their competitors—which some may view as beneficial. However, these techniques arguably may also make foreign reinvestment of foreign earnings significantly more attractive than repatriation and reinvestment of those earnings in the United States, thus exacerbating the investment distortion already inherent in the deferral regime that some may view as detrimental.

Hybrid branch arrangements are perhaps the first and best-known example of how a check-the-box election can be used to circumvent subpart F, but other similar uses for the election have been found. For example, the sale of stock of an operating company by a CFC generally would give rise to subpart F income, but if an election to disregard the company is in effect, then the transaction may be treated as a sale of operating assets, thus avoiding the creation of subpart F income. As in the case of hybrid branch arrangements, a mere election, with no nontax economic effect, may transform what would have been subpart F income into an item exempt from subpart F.

The proposal would address these techniques, while retaining the basic elective regime of the entity classification rules, by providing that single-member business entities organized under foreign law generally must be treated as corporations for Federal tax purposes. As

> a consequence, a wide range of transactions that are currently disregarded for Federal tax purposes would be "regarded," and the proposal (in conjunction with the expiration of section 954(c)(6)) would reduce opportunities for avoidance of subpart F and manipulation of the foreign tax credit limitation.
>
> The proposal includes, however, certain exceptions. First, the proposal would not apply in cases in which the single-member entity is organized in the same country as its owner. Consequently, it would appear to permit taxpayers to continue to use hybrid branches to achieve results similar to those of the "same-country" exception of section 954(c)(3), but in circumstances in which that exception might not otherwise apply. This exception appears to be intended to allow U.S. multinational enterprises to maintain foreign holding companies to receive dividends from foreign subsidiaries free of foreign withholding tax, principally within the European Union. Second, the proposal would not generally apply to a first-tier foreign eligible entity wholly owned by a U.S. person, except in cases of U.S. tax avoidance. Third, the proposal would not apply to domestic eligible entities or multi-member foreign eligible entities.

Id. at 110–112 (footnotes omitted).

This proposal was not included in the Obama Administration's budget proposals for fiscal year 2011, and Congress has not enacted legislation limiting the applicability of the check-the-box regulations to any foreign entities. Thus, the opportunities for international tax arbitrage through the use by controlled foreign corporations established in low-tax or no-tax countries of hybrid branches created under the check-the-box regulations remains unimpaired, except to extent that abuses can be successfully attacked by the IRS using current law anti-abuse doctrines.

[¶ 13,065]

g. Dual Resident Corporations and Dual Consolidated Losses

Opportunities for tax savings through international tax arbitrage can also arise when there are inconsistencies between the rules in two relevant countries for determining the residence of corporations. For example, a corporation organized in the United States is treated as a U.S. resident, subject to U.S. tax on its worldwide net income with losses wherever incurred being deductible. Under Section 1501 of the Code and regulations issued pursuant to Section 1502, a U.S. corporation is permitted to file a consolidated tax return with other U.S. corporations in an affiliated group. An affiliated group consists, broadly speaking, of one or more chains of U.S. corporations connected by stock ownership (excluding certain preferred stock) of at least 80 percent of the vote and value with a common U.S. parent. § 1504. If two or more U.S. corporations are members of an affiliated group that files a consolidated return, the losses of any one of the group generally may offset or eliminate tax on the income of one or more other members of the group. § 1504(a).

Inconsistencies arise because some other countries use criteria other than place of incorporation to determine whether a corporation is a domestic resident for their tax purposes. For example, countries, such as the United Kingdom and Australia, treat a corporation as a domestic resident if it is managed or controlled there, regardless of where the corporation is incorporated. If a corporation is a resident under this test, it will typically be taxed by the country of residence on its worldwide net income with losses wherever incurred being deductible. If certain conditions are met, these countries allow losses of a resident corporation to reduce or eliminate tax on income of other commonly controlled domestic corporations. See generally Staff of Joint Comm. on Tax'n, 100th Cong., 1st Sess., General Explanation of the Tax Reform Act of 1986, at 1063 (1987) (hereinafter "General Explanation of the 1986 Act").

Because of the application of differing criteria for determining corporate residence it is possible for a U.S. corporation to incorporate a foreign subsidiary under the laws of a foreign country that determines the residence of a corporation not on the basis that it is incorporated there but on the basis of where the corporation's management or control is located. If the foreign corporation's top management is located in the United States but the corporation is not engaged in business operations in the United States, the corporation might be exempt from income tax in the United States and in the country in which it is incorporated.

In a sense, the converse is the case in which the management of a U.S. corporation is located in a country, such as the United Kingdom or Australia, that treats it as a domestic corporation because its management is located there. Under these circumstances the corporation has dual residence (i.e., is a dual resident corporation) and will often be subject to the corporate income tax imposed by both the United States and the foreign country concerned. (Double taxation in the United States is, of course, usually mitigated or eliminated by the U.S. foreign tax credit and, in many cases, by applicable income tax treaties.)

A dual resident corporation is frequently the U.S. parent corporation of one affiliated group of corporations in the United States (as described above) and another affiliated group in the foreign country that also treats the group as a taxable resident. Such a dual resident corporation might find opportunities to engage in "double-dipping" with respect to losses and expense items that may be deducted under the tax laws of both United States and the foreign country concerned.

Absent a legislative fix by Congress, if a corporation was a resident of both the United States and a foreign country and the foreign country allowed the loss of the dual resident corporation to offset the income of another foreign corporation (frequently a member of a foreign affiliated group filing a consolidated return), then the dual resident corporation could use any loss it generated twice. The loss could offset income that was subject to U.S. tax but not foreign tax and also offset income subject to foreign tax but not to U.S. tax. It could arise from an operating loss or from interest on loans used to finance other members of the groups. Basically, the U.S. corporation could use the same deduction for U.S. and foreign purposes. This was the "double-dip."

The Staff of the Joint Committee explained the need for legislation to deal with double-dipping abuses as follows:

> Losses (however derived) that a corporation uses to offset foreign tax on income that the United States does not subject to current tax should not also be used to reduce any other corporation's U.S. tax. Disallowing such losses allows foreign and U.S. investors to compete in the U.S. economy under tax rules that put them in the same competitive position. By allowing "double-dipping" (use of a deduction by two different groups), the prior treatment of dual resident companies gave an undue tax advantage to certain foreign investors that made U.S. investments.
>
> For example, under prior law, a profitable U.K. company would acquire a profitable U.S. target by establishing a dual resident holding company to own the shares of the U.S. target. The dual resident company borrowed funds with which to buy the target. The interest expense of the dual resident company appeared on both the U.K. and the U.S. returns. It was conceivable that an affiliated group could have worldwide profits from operating in just two countries, the United Kingdom and the United States, yet, by using the dual resident company device, pay no current taxes to either country.
>
> As an example, assume that a U.K. corporation earned $100 of income before purchasing a U.S. target. The target produced $100 of income. To finance the purchase of the target, the U.K. corporation established a dual resident company that incurred interest expense of $100. The dual resident company effectively shared its loss with its U.K. parent, so the group's U.K. taxable income shrank from $100 to 0. In the United States, the dual resident company consolidated with its subsidiary, the U.S. target, so U.S. taxable income was zero. Despite worldwide profits of $100, earned solely in the United States and the United Kingdom, the group owed no current tax to any country.
>
> In the example above, the U.K. corporation reduced its U.K. tax on U.K. income (and its worldwide tax on worldwide income) by making the investment in the United States through the dual resident company device. That is, the marginal tax rate on that investment was negative. That result occurred even though the target's income exactly offset the expenses of financing the acquisition. By contrast, if a similar U.S. corporation bought the same U.S. target corporation

through the use of the same amount of debt, it would not reduce its tax. For example, assume that a U.S. corporation earned $100 of income before purchasing a U.S. target. The target produced $100 of income. To finance the purchase of the target, the U.S. corporation established a holding company that incurred interest expense of $100. The holding company effectively shared its loss with the other members of the U.S. group but the group's taxable income remained at $100. There was no reduction of the group's total tax liability, as there was when a U.K. corporation bought a U.S. corporation through the use of the dual resident corporation device. Congress believed that the dual resident company device created an undue incentive for U.K. corporations (and Australian corporations) to acquire U.S. corporations and otherwise to gain an advantage in competing in the U.S. economy against U.S. corporations. Similarly, the dual resident company device created an undue incentive for U.S. corporations to acquire foreign rather than domestic assets.

General Explanation of the 1986 Act, at 1064–65.

To deal with the double-dip international tax arbitrage opportunities for dual resident corporations, Congress enacted Section 1503(d) as part of the 1986 Act. Section 1503(d)(1) provides that the dual consolidated loss of a dual resident corporation for any tax year cannot reduce the taxable income of any other U.S. member of the affiliated group for that or any other tax year. A dual consolidated loss is defined essentially as a net operating loss of a U.S. corporation that is taxed by a foreign country on its worldwide income or on a residence basis. § 1503(d)(2)(A). The Staff of the Joint Committee describes the thrust of Section 1503(d) as follows:

The Act provides that if a U.S. corporation is subject to a foreign country's tax on worldwide income, or on a residence basis as opposed to a source basis, any net operating loss it incurs cannot reduce the taxable income of any other member of a U.S. affiliated group for that or any other taxable year. (A net operating loss of such a corporation is referred to as a "dual consolidated loss.") A company may be subject to foreign tax on a residence basis because its place of effective management is in a foreign country or for other reasons. Where a U.S. corporation is subject to foreign tax on a residence basis, then, under the Act, for U.S. purposes, its loss will be available to offset income of that corporation in other years, but not income of another U.S. corporation. Regulatory authority is provided to exempt a U.S. corporation from this rule to the extent that its losses do not offset the income of foreign corporations for foreign tax purposes.

* * *

Congress did not perceive any relevant distinction between a deduction that arises on account of interest expense and one that arises on account of some other expense, or between a deduction for a

> payment to a related party and one for a payment to an unrelated party. Therefore, the provision applies to any dual consolidated loss regardless of the type of deductions that caused it.
>
> The Act's provision applies to losses of dual resident companies whether or not any of the income of any foreign corporation that the dual resident corporation's loss may reduce in the foreign country is or will be subject to U.S. tax. Congress applied this provision to all foreign corporations that could benefit from a dual resident corporation's net operating loss, whether or not the foreign corporation's earnings are or will be subject to U.S. tax, for two reasons.
>
> First, Congress believed that this application is fair; Congress was not aware of a case where the use of one company's deduction by two other companies each of which is resident in only one jurisdiction makes sense as a matter of tax policy. Second, Congress was aware of arguments that denying loss-sharing only when the income protected from foreign tax was not or would not be subject to U.S. tax discriminated against foreign-owned U.S. corporations. The Act's provision will apply to losses shared with foreign corporations whose earnings will be subject to U.S. tax (which are typically U.S.-controlled) as well as to losses shared with foreign corporations whose earnings are never subject to U.S. tax (which are typically foreign-controlled). Congress was aware that some have attempted to argue that the provision discriminates against foreign-controlled U.S. entities by somehow imposing on those entities some requirement for loss-sharing not imposed on U.S.-controlled U.S. entities. Congress found no merit in this argument. If this provision somehow is found to conflict with any treaty, the provision is to be effective notwithstanding the treaty.

General Explanation of the 1986 Act, at 1065.

Since the enactment of Section 1503(d), the IRS and Treasury have issued temporary, proposed and final regulations, which have been updated and amended over the years. The regulations state the general principle that a dual consolidated loss cannot offset the taxable income of any U.S. affiliate for the tax year of the loss or any other tax year. And this is generally so, regardless of whether the loss offsets income of another person under foreign tax law and whether the income that the loss may offset is, has been or will be subject to U.S. tax. The same limitation on loss use applies to a separate unit of a U.S. corporation as if the separate unit were the corporation's wholly owned subsidiary. Reg. § 1.1503–2(b)(1). "Separate unit" for purpose of Section 1503(d) includes a foreign branch (as defined in Temp. Reg. § 1.367(a)–6T(g)(1)), a partnership interest, a trust interest and an interest in a hybrid entity treated as a corporation under foreign law. Reg. § 1.1503–2(c)(3)(i). In determining whether a separate unit has a dual consolidated loss for the tax year, the separate unit computes its taxable income (or loss) as if it were a separate U.S. corporation. Reg. § 1.1503–2(d)(1)(ii). Two foreign branches owned by a single U.S. corporation in the same foreign country are treated as one if they are consolidated under foreign tax law. Reg. § 1.1503–2(c)(3)(ii).

A dual consolidated loss may not be used to offset the taxable income of another corporation that succeeds to the tax attributes of a dual resident corporation under Section 381 as a result of a nonrecognition transaction (e.g., a Section 332 liquidation or a tax-free reorganization). Also, a dual consolidated loss of a separate unit of a U.S. corporation cannot be used to offset the income of a U.S. corporation after the termination, liquidation, sale or other disposition of the separate unit. However, if a dual resident corporation transfers its assets to another corporation in a transaction subject to section 381, and the acquiring corporation is a (i) dual resident corporation of the same foreign country of which the transferor dual resident corporation is a resident or (ii) a U.S. corporation that carries on the business activities of the transferor dual resident corporation as a separate unit, then income generated by the transferee dual resident corporation, or separate unit, may be offset by the carryover losses of the transferor dual resident corporation. In addition, if a U.S. corporation transfers a separate unit to another U.S. corporation in a transaction subject to section 381, the income generated by the separate unit following the transfer may be offset by the carryover losses of the separate unit. Reg. § 1.1503–2(b)(2). The Section 1503(d) limitation is illustrated in the regulations by the following examples:

> *Example 1.* P, a domestic corporation, owns all of the outstanding stock of DRC, a domestic corporation. P and DRC file a consolidated U.S. income tax return. DRC is managed and controlled in Country W, a country that determines the tax residence of corporations according to their place of management and control. Therefore, DRC is a dual resident corporation and any net operating loss it incurs is a dual consolidated loss. In Years 1 through 3, DRC incurs dual consolidated losses. Under this paragraph (b), the dual consolidated losses may not be used to offset P's income on the group's consolidated U.S. income tax return. At the end of Year 3, DRC sells all of its assets and discontinues its business operations. DRC is then liquidated into P, pursuant to the provisions of section 332. Normally, under section 381, P would succeed to, and be permitted to utilize, DRC's net operating loss carryovers. However, this paragraph (b) prohibits the dual consolidated losses of DRC from reducing P's income for U.S. tax purposes. Therefore, DRC's net operating loss carryovers will not be available to offset P's income.
>
> *Example 2.* The facts are the same as in *Example 1,* except that DRC does not sell its assets and, following the liquidation of DRC, P continues to operate DRC's business as a separate unit (e.g., a branch). DRC's loss carryovers are available to offset P's income generated by the assets previously owned by DRC and now held by the separate unit.

Reg. § 1.1503–2(b)(4), Exs. 1, 2.

Section 1503(d)(2)(B) provides that, to the extent permitted by regulation, the disallowance of dual consolidated losses does not apply to a net operating loss that does not offset the income of any foreign corporation under foreign law. The regulations implement this rule by exempting from dual consolidated loss treatment losses incurred in a foreign country that does not permit the dual resident corporation to use its losses to offset income of any other person recognized in the same tax year or in any other tax year. Reg. § 1.1503–2(c)(5)(ii)(A).

Moreover, under prescribed circumstances, a U.S. consolidated group, an unaffiliated dual resident corporation or an unaffiliated U.S. owner of a separate unit can be exempted by election from the prohibition against using a dual consolidated loss to offset income of a U.S. affiliate. Specifically, an election (a "(g)(2)(i) election") can be made not to use the loss to offset income of a foreign corporation. If this election is made, the loss can be used to offset income of another U.S. member of the U.S. affiliated group. Reg. § 1.1503–2(g)(2). The electing party (e.g., the U.S. consolidated group) must file with its tax return an agreement that includes an undertaking to comply with the regulations and a certification that no portion of the dual consolidated loss has been or will be used to offset the income of any other person under the tax laws of a foreign country. Reg. § 1.1503–2(g)(2)(i)(C), (E). If such an agreement is filed and a subsequent "triggering event" occurs (e.g., there is a foreign use of the loss or the dual resident corporation is sold or otherwise leaves the consolidated group), the dual consolidated loss generally must be recaptured and included in gross income in the tax year of the event (plus an interest charge). Furthermore, unless covered by questions included in a corporate tax return (Form 1120) or accompanying schedules, the electing party must file with its tax return a certification for each of the 15 tax years after the dual consolidated loss arose that the losses, expenses or deductions making up the dual consolidated loss have not been used to offset the income of another person under foreign tax law. Reg. § 1.1503–2(g)(2)(vi)(B).

The regulations also provide that the dual consolidated loss rules will not be applied if the dual resident corporation or U.S. owner of a separate unit elects to deduct the loss in the United States pursuant to an agreement entered into between the United States and a foreign country that puts into place an elective procedure through which losses offset income of only one country. Reg. § 1.1503–2(g)(1).

Reg. § 1.1503–2(c)(15)(iv) contains "a mirror legislation" rule to deal with situations in which a foreign country enacts a tax law that operates in a manner similar to the U.S. dual consolidated loss rule. The backdrop to this regulation is described as follows by the Staff of the Joint Committee:

> Congress was concerned that a foreign country, in response to this U.S. legislation, might deny loss-sharing to its corporate residents that are incorporated in the United States. In fact, in response to this U.S. legislation, the United Kingdom has indicated that it will seek to prevent the use of interest-deduction-related losses generated by U.S. corporations that are U.K. residents against the taxable income of other U.K. residents. Congress, foreseeing adoption of such a rule by (for example) the United Kingdom, did not intend that such a rule of foreign law cause all the revenue gain from termination of the dual resident company device to inure to the benefit of the foreign revenue authority. (If the U.S. rule had applied only to companies whose losses actually reduced the income of a foreign corporation, then after application of, for example, a U.K. rule that denies loss-sharing to U.S. corporations that are U.K. residents, the Act's new rule would have had no possible impact on a U.S. corporation resident in the United Kingdom).
>
> Instead, Congress intended that the U.S. Treasury Department pursue with the appropriate authorities of any foreign country adopting the approach that the United Kingdom has adopted a bilateral agreement allowing losses of a dual resident company to offset income of affiliates in only one country. When such an agreement is effective, or when the circumstances otherwise insure that the United States obtains an appropriate share of revenue from Congress' action in ending use of this dual resident company device, then Congress intended that regulations exempt from "dual consolidated loss" treatment losses that do not offset the income of any foreign corporation. * * *

General Explanation of the 1986 Act, at 1065–66.

Thus, the basic purpose of the mirror legislation rule is to prevent the revenue gain resulting from the disallowance of the double-dip benefit of a dual consolidated loss from inuring entirely to the foreign country. The rule was held to be valid in British Car Auctions, Inc. v. United States, 35 Fed. Cl. 123 (1996), aff'd without opinion, 116 F.3d 1497 (Fed. Cir. 1997).

More specifically, the rule provides that if the law of a foreign country denies the use of a loss of a dual resident corporation (or separate unit) to offset the income of another person because the dual resident corporation (or separate unit) is also taxed by a different country (e.g., the United States) on its worldwide income or on a residence basis, the loss is deemed to be used to offset income of another person in the foreign country. In this case no (g)(2) election can be made, because it would permit use of the loss in the United States. The intent of the rule is to prevent the foreign country from enacting a law that would give a taxpayer the sole option of using the dual consolidated loss to offset U.S. income.

On October 6, 2006, the United States concluded a competent authority agreement with the United Kingdom. See Announcement 2006–86,

2006–2 C.B. 842. The agreement applies to dual consolidated losses attributable to certain United Kingdom permanent establishments that are otherwise subject to both Section 1503(d) and mirror legislation enacted by the United Kingdom. In general, under the agreement taxpayers can elect to use the loss in either the United Kingdom or the United States, but not both.

[¶ 13,070]

4. PLANNING PROBLEMS POSED BY SECTION 904 LIMITATIONS

In planning a direct investment abroad, an important problem resulting from the Section 904(d)(1) separate limitations on the foreign tax credit, discussed in Chapters 5 and 7, is the possible loss of potential foreign tax credits in cases in which income from the investment is subject to foreign income taxes in excess of the effective rate of the U.S. corporate income tax. The challenge is to structure transactions and investments in a way that will make use of what would otherwise be potential foreign tax credits that would exceed the applicable Section 904 limitations. The foreign tax credit separate basket regime under Section 904(d) significantly complicates the challenge.

Suppose, for example, that a U.S. corporation plans to establish a wholly owned subsidiary in Country A that will engage in the manufacture and sale of computer chips. Assume that the U.S. corporation has no other income from foreign sources and that $200,000 of before-tax profits will be distributed as dividends by the Country A subsidiary, which will bear a 38 percent Country A corporate tax, amounting to $76,000. Thus, the cash dividend net of the Country A corporate tax will be $124,000, which will bear a dividend withholding tax (reduced to five percent under the United States–Country A tax treaty) of $6,200. The full $76,000 will qualify for the Section 902 indirect credit ($124,000 dividend/$124,000 post–1986 earnings × $76,000 corporate tax) and the $6,200 withholding tax will qualify for the Section 901 direct credit. The U.S. corporation must include in income $200,000, which represents the actual dividend of $124,000, grossed up under Section 78 by the indirect credit of $76,000. Under the Section 904(d)(3) look-through rules, the dividend will be included in the general income foreign tax credit limitation basket because the underlying income of the Country A subsidiary is active business income from manufacture and sales. The maximum amount of credit that may be taken under this limitation is computed as follows (assuming that the worldwide taxable income of the U.S. corporation is $1 million and that the effective U.S. corporate tax rate is 35 percent):

Foreign-source general limitation taxable income $200,000 / Worldwide taxable income $1,000,000	×	Total U.S. tax $350,000	=	General Limitation $70,000

Thus, $12,200 of potential foreign tax credit (total Country A taxes of $82,200 less the $70,000 limitation) is being generated, but it cannot be used because of the foreign tax credit limitation. If the U.S. corporation's sole source of foreign-source income continues to be the Country A subsidiary dividend, the carryback and carryover of excess foreign tax credits under Section 904(c) will not provide relief from international double taxation.

Since this excess foreign tax credit is potentially available as a direct dollar-for-dollar offset against U.S. tax, its use becomes a prime objective for the tax advisor. One need only glance at the limitation formula to realize that one way to permit use of at least some of the unused credit is to introduce into the numerator of the fraction foreign-source income of a type that falls within the Section 904(d)(1)(B) general limitation basket and that is subject to a foreign income tax burden of less than the effective U.S. corporate tax of 35 percent.

What suggestions would you as a tax planner make? Would it be helpful to have the U.S. corporation lend substantial sums to its Country A subsidiary in order to generate foreign-source interest payments? Such payments would be deductible in computing the subsidiary's net income subject to Country A corporate income tax and would, under the United States–Country A tax treaty, be subject to a Country A withholding tax of ten percent, assuming the U.S. corporation has no permanent establishment in Country A to which the interest would be attributable. What would be the effect, if any, on this plan of the separate basket limitation for passive income and the look-through rules for controlled foreign corporations in Section 904(d)(3)? Alternatively, would it be helpful for the U.S. corporation to deposit funds in an interest-bearing account in a Country A bank on which the interest is exempt from Country A tax?

Assuming that the U.S. corporation has a significant amount of export business, would it help to pass title to the foreign buyer, not when the goods are turned over to the international carrier in the United States, but rather when the goods arrive at the foreign port? See §§ 865(b) and 863(b)(2), and Reg. § 1.863–3(b)(1).

Another possibility might be for the Country A subsidiary to pay a royalty to the U.S. parent corporation for patent or knowhow rights in Country A under a nonexclusive license agreement. This royalty would be deductible in computing the subsidiary's net income subject to Country A corporate income tax. It would be exempt from Country A withholding tax by virtue of the United States–Country A tax treaty, provided, again, that the U.S. corporation has no permanent establishment in Country A to which the royalties would be attributable. Assume that, instead of distributing a dividend out of $200,000 of earnings before the 38–percent Country A corporate tax, the Country A subsidiary distributes a dividend out of before-tax earnings of $150,000 and pays a royalty of $50,000. Will this permit use of part or all of the $12,200 of excess foreign tax credit that would be generated if a dividend out of $200,000 of before-tax earnings were distributed?

Still another possibility would be for the U.S. corporation to provide managerial and technical services in Country A to its Country A subsidiary in consideration for the payment by the latter of arm's length fees. Assume that these fees would be deductible by the Country A subsidiary and would be exempt from withholding tax in Country A. Would this arrangement help absorb excess foreign tax credits generated by dividends received by the U.S. corporation from the Country A subsidiary?

[¶ 13,075]

5. CAPITALIZATION OF THE FOREIGN CORPORATION

In planning the capitalization of a foreign corporation, consideration will normally be given to whether debt or special classes of stock should be used in addition to voting common stock. The use of a substantial amount of debt may be advantageous for U.S. and foreign tax reasons. Interest on debt is generally deductible for foreign corporate income tax purposes. In addition, under the law of some countries, interest is exempt from withholding tax. Moreover, under many U.S. income tax treaties, interest is exempt from, or subject to a reduced rate of, withholding tax, provided that the interest is not attributable to a permanent establishment maintained by the U.S. creditor in the country in which the corporate debtor is located. As discussed at ¶ 13,070, interest can be particularly important to a U.S. corporation that is in or near an excess foreign tax credit position. Foreign-source interest subject to a low- or no-foreign tax received by a U.S. corporation from a controlled foreign corporation is subject to the Section 904(d)(3) look-through rules and can often be included in the numerator of the general income foreign tax credit limitation fraction, thereby permitting a foreign tax credit for foreign taxes that might otherwise not be creditable.

The use of debt in the capital structure of a foreign corporation may be advantageous for another reason. Through repayment of the principal amount of the debt a substantial amount of the investor's initial cash investment can be recovered free of foreign and U.S. tax. By contrast, in the case of a U.S. corporation that owns only common or preferred stock and no debt obligations of a foreign corporation, the recovery of part of the investment tax free is normally not possible because redemption of stock of a wholly or majority owned subsidiary usually results in dividend treatment. § 302. It is important to note, however, that dividend treatment of a ten-percent U.S. corporate shareholder of a foreign corporation may be more advantageous than tax-free repayment of debt. A dividend carries with it indirect foreign tax credit under Section 902 for a portion of the foreign corporate income tax on distributed earnings, whereas no indirect credit accompanies the repayment of debt.

The tax advantages to be gained by having a shareholder lend some funds to its controlled foreign corporation rather than contribute them as equity have resulted in the recurrent problem of determining under what circumstances the putative loan from a shareholder to its controlled corporation will be treated as equity for U.S. or foreign tax purposes. Under U.S. law, this issue has traditionally been left to the vagaries of litigation with each case turning on its own facts and having little precedential value. Moreover, attempts to provide guidance through regulations issued pursuant to Section 385 have failed.

In the case of a foreign joint venture company in which the equity is divided between the U.S. corporation and a foreign company, two classes of common stock may be used to implement arrangements for ensuring representation of both participants on the board of directors. These classes of common stock are usually identical except that one class may elect, or make binding nominations for, a specified number of directors, and the other class may do so for the remainder of the directors. See ¶ 13,095. In the unusual case in which one participant is to receive an assured dividend return on a priority basis, preferred stock may be used. This creates no special tax problems except that any use of preferred stock, convertible preferred stock and convertible debentures requires that a wary eye be maintained on Section 305. The result of that provision can be taxable dividend consequences to a shareholder when, although the shareholder receives no actual cash dividend, the shareholder's proportionate interest in the corporation's earnings or assets is increased at the same time cash or property is distributed to one or more other shareholders.

Another issue to be considered in connection with planning the capital structure of the foreign company is whether various types of property, including intangible property (e.g., patents, knowhow, trademarks or copyrights), tangible personal property and real property, should be transferred to the foreign company in exchange for an equity interest or made available in some other way, such as through a sale, lease or license. A number of questions may be implicated in the decision as to how to make such property available. For a detailed discussion with respect to intangible property, see Chapter 12.

The mode of transfer may control the source of income recognized, which may have important consequences under the Section 904 limitations on the foreign tax credit. Also at stake may be the amount and character of the recognized income: Will income realized be recognized? Will the income be treated as capital gain or ordinary income? Will the income be characterized for foreign tax credit limitation purposes as general limitation income or income assigned to the passive income limitation basket? Can the transferor and transferee definitively determine the amount of consideration to be paid by the transferee without risk of subsequent adjustment by the IRS?

The character of the income and whether the transferor and transferee can definitively fix the amount paid by the transferee may be affected by whether the transferee is a controlled foreign corporation of which the transferor is a U.S. shareholder and whether the transferor and transferee are commonly controlled parties for purposes of Section 482.

To illustrate the range of issues that may be involved, consider the following four alternative methods of transferring intangible manufacturing property, such as foreign patents, to a foreign corporation in which the transferor has an equity investment:

1. The foreign patents could be transferred in exchange for stock in a transaction qualifying generally for nonrecognition of gain under Section 351. See ¶¶ 12,130–12,160. However, Section 367(d) requires that the transferor be deemed to have sold the patents for constructive annual royalty-like payments over the life of the patents. § 367(d)(2). The income, moreover, is treated as foreign-source ordinary income (rather than capital gain) and the amount of the income is uncertain because the payments must be commensurate with the income attributable to the intangible in the hands of the transferee corporation. This implies periodic review and possible adjustment by the IRS. Bear in mind that the constructive royalty-like payments result in no cash to the transferor and are not likely to be deductible by the transferee.

2. The patents might be sold for a purchase price expressed as a royalty. In this case, the gain to the extent of previously deducted amounts of amortization will be treated as U.S.- or foreign-source gain, depending on whether the deductions had offset U.S.- or foreign-source income. § 865(c). Gain in excess of the amortization deductions would have a foreign source under the royalty rule. §§ 865(d)(1)(B) and 862(a)(4). Under Section 1249, the character of the income is ordinary income if the transferee is a foreign corporation controlled by the transferor (under the Section 1249 definition of "control", which refers exclusively to more than 50 percent of the total combined voting power). For foreign tax credit limitation purposes, the income would be passive royalty income subject to the separate Section 904(d)(1)(A) limitation if the patents had been previously licensed and had generated passive income. Alternatively, if the

patents had been previously licensed and produced general limitation income in the form, for example, of royalties received from unrelated persons (or related persons under Temp. Reg. § 1.904–4T(b)(2)(iii)) and derived in the active conduct of business, the sale proceeds would be subject to the general income limitation. If the patents previously produced no royalty income, the gain would apparently fall into the general income limitation basket only if the patents qualify as property used in the transferor's business. Reg. § 1.954–2(e)(3)(iv). If the patents had not been used in business abroad, they may not meet this test, in which case, gain on their sale would be passive income. If the transferor and transferee are commonly controlled under Section 482, the amount of the consideration is subject to the commensurate-with-the-income standard and to periodic adjustment by the IRS.

3. The patents may be sold to the foreign corporation for a fixed price. In this case, like the preceding alternative, gain to the extent of amounts of previously deducted amortization is sourced under Section 865(c). However, gain in excess of prior amortization deductions is given a U.S. source under the residence-of-the-seller rule. §§ 865(d)(1)(A) and 865(a). To the extent that the sale produces foreign-source income under Section 865(c), the analysis concerning the applicable foreign tax credit limitation and Section 482 is the same as under the second alternative.

4. The patent rights may be transferred in exchange for royalties under a license that does not qualify as a sale. In this case the royalties will be foreign-source ordinary income under Section 862(a)(4). For foreign tax credit limitation purposes, if the transferee is a controlled foreign corporation, the royalties will be characterized under the Section 904(d)(3) look-through rules, often as general limitation income. If the transferee is not a controlled foreign corporation, the royalties will be classified as passive income, subject to the Section 904(d)(1)(A) limitation, unless, as will often be true, they are derived by the transferor in the active conduct of a trade or business under Section 954(c)(2)(A). If they are so derived, they will constitute general limitation income. If the transferor and transferee are commonly controlled entities for purposes of Section 482, however, the royalties will be subject to periodic readjustment by the IRS under the commensurate-with-the-income standard, but any adjustment upward will be treated as foreign-source income.

The foregoing analysis suggests that a U.S. transferor of patents to a foreign corporation in which it owns all or part of the equity will often choose the fourth alternative if the transferor is concerned about the need to absorb excess foreign tax credits that may be generated with respect to other foreign-source income.

A similar analysis should be undertaken with respect to other intangibles that may be transferred to the foreign company. Confidential know-how, copyrights, franchises, trademarks, trade names, goodwill and other intangibles encompassed by the expansive Section 936(h)(3)(B) definition of intangible property are all susceptible to such analysis. However, some important differences with regard to source and character of the income and the capacity of the transferor and transferee to fix definitively the amount of consideration may be involved. For example, confidential know-how, trademarks and trade names are normally not amortizable, and consequently gain on their sale will not be subject to the Section 865(c) source rules for depreciable (or amortizable) property unless they constitute amortizable Section 197 intangibles. Trademarks, trade names and franchises are subject to the special rules of Section 1253, which will often require that gain on their sale be treated as ordinary income.

Transfers of tangible personal property, such as equipment, and real property to a foreign corporation raise comparable issues. In each case, it is important to analyze the tax consequences of the various alternative modes of making the property available to the foreign corporation. Depreciable equipment and real property can be transferred to a foreign corporation in exchange for stock, and the only gain recognized will be recapture of previously deducted depreciation. No constructive rental payments may be imputed, as may be done under Section 367(d) with respect to intangibles. If the property is sold, gain on a sale of foreign real property will be foreign-source under Section 862(a)(5), while gain on a sale of depreciable personal property will be sourced under Section 865(c). The gain will be Section 1231 gain except for ordinary income depreciation recapture under Sections 1245 and 1250. For foreign tax credit limitation purposes, the gain will usually be treated as general limitation income under Sections 904(d)(2)(A) and 954(c)(1)(B). See Reg. § 1.954–2(e)(3). If the property is leased to a foreign corporation, the rentals will be passive income, unless the rentals are derived in the active conduct of a business whether received from unrelated (or, under Temp. Reg. § 1.904–4T(b)(2)(iii), related) persons, in which event they will be general limitation income. In addition, if the transferee is a controlled foreign corporation of which the transferor is a U.S. shareholder, the Section 904(d)(3) look-through rules will apply and the rentals will be classified as general limitation income to the extent they are allocable to general limitation income of the foreign corporation. If the transferor and transferee are commonly controlled entities, any payments made by the transferee are subject to adjustment by the IRS at the outset to comply with the arm's length standard under Section 482. However, the commensurate-with-the-income standard does not apply and therefore periodic readjustment by the IRS would not be a risk.

[¶ 13,080]

B. SOME TAX ASPECTS OF INTERNATIONAL JOINT VENTURES

In many cases, investments by U.S. corporations in foreign countries will be carried out on a joint venture basis. In international business, the term "joint venture" is often used in a broad, nontechnical sense to denote any kind of international business undertaking that involves participation by two or more equity owners. In the context of direct investment, a foreign joint venture normally involves the setting up of a corporation, limited liability company or some other form of business organization under the laws of the foreign country, in which the U.S. corporation and a local enterprise will have equity participations.

There are many reasons for the creation of a joint venture. For example, participation of local interests may be required by law or by governmental policy of the foreign country concerned or the U.S. participant may lack sufficient available capital to finance the venture alone. Many U.S. corporations find that profitable operations in some foreign markets can generally be reached more quickly when the enterprise is established in conjunction with an existing local enterprise experienced in local production, marketing and administrative matters. Local participation may also contribute to facilitating contacts with local businesses and governmental agencies.

Setting up a joint venture abroad involves some special problems. When the U.S. corporation has a majority of the equity, the most critical item is often to ensure that the local minority shareholders cannot paralyze the enterprise in the event of a falling out between the parties. Here, careful drafting of the joint venture agreement and the articles of incorporation and by-laws (in civil law systems, typically combined in one document) of the joint venture company is of paramount importance. Also, various rights granted under local law to minority shareholders in the corporation and the limited liability company, respectively, may significantly influence which is chosen. When the U.S. corporation is in a minority position, it will attempt to choose the business form and draft the corporate articles and by-laws with an eye to ensuring protection of its rights as a minority shareholder and, when feasible, to buttressing its influence over management of the enterprise. The U.S. investor may be able to accept a minority of the voting equity and at the same time retain some measure of managerial control through a variety of devices, such as a management contract or a right in the U.S. corporation to terminate, within a limited number of years, a patent license without which the joint enterprise could not function. Control arrangements adopted for an international joint venture organized as a foreign corporation may have important potential U.S. tax implications, particularly those associated with whether the control arrangements will result in the joint venture entity's being classified as a controlled foreign corporation. See ¶¶ 13,105–13,120.

The following discussion will focus on the most common type of joint venture for the U.S. corporation abroad—the direct investment in a form of business organization in which the equity is divided between the U.S. corporation and a local business or investor in the foreign country concerned.

[¶ 13,085]

1. LEGAL INSTRUMENTS

In setting up a joint venture, the first step in negotiations will often be the preparation of a brief outline of the basic terms of the proposed venture. This document will typically cover in broad outline such matters as:

(1) The scope of the venture and arrangements for expansion (e.g., what products are to be manufactured or services to be offered and marketed initially and how the list may be revised);

(2) The form of foreign business organization to be selected as the joint venture vehicle;

(3) The division of voting equity;

(4) The amount of capital required for the first few years of the venture and how it is to be supplied;

(5) The nature of the contributions to the capital of the joint venture entity;

(6) The identity or method of selection of key managerial personnel of the joint venture and their successors;

(7) The size and constitution of the board of directors or its counterpart (if appropriate for the particular form of business organization);

(8) Any special arrangements for supplying patent rights and knowhow to the joint venture company by either or both of the participants;

(9) Provisions relating to use of franchises, trademarks and trade names where appropriate;

(10) Marketing arrangements; and

(11) A right of first refusal exercisable by each participant if the other should seek to sell its interest to a third party.

This outline (often embodied in a "Memorandum or Letter of Intent" or a "Heads of Agreement") is usually not intended as a binding document; rather, it is an expression of mutual intent with respect to the basic features of the deal from a business point of view. On the basis of this outline, the detailed negotiations and drafting of the formal implementing instruments will be carried out. Needless to say, however, this outline is a highly important document. It will be difficult, as a practical matter, for either party to depart materially in later negotiations from positions it agreed to initially and included in the outline.

The specific arrangements concerning the establishment and operation of the joint venture are normally set forth in a joint venture agreement between the equity holders. This document will cover in detail all aspects of the venture. As a rule, various additional documents are attached to and incorporated by reference in this agreement. These documents will include the charter and by-laws or other constitutive instruments of the proposed joint venture and any collateral agreements that may be involved, such as patent, knowhow or trademark license agreements, technical assistance agreements, management contracts and employment contracts for key personnel. If either or both participants are providing debt capital, the loan agreement or agreements would be attached. Also, it may be appropriate to attach distributorship or agency agreements relating to projected sales by or for the joint venture.

[¶ 13,090]

2. CONTROL ARRANGEMENTS FOR A JOINT VENTURE COMPANY

In negotiating the joint venture arrangement, many of the important legal problems cluster around the question of control. The U.S. legal adviser's objective is, broadly speaking, to maximize the U.S. participant's control over the management of the joint venture.

If the joint venture is organized as a corporation or limited liability company organized under the laws of a civil law country, it will normally be essential to incorporate the arrangements concerning control, shareholders' rights and related matters in the corporate constitutive instrument. This instrument combines the functions of the charter (or certificate of incorporation or articles of incorporation) and bylaws of an Anglo–American corporation. In countries with legal systems following the Anglo–American approach, control arrangements are often embodied principally in an agreement between the two shareholders of the joint venture company.

The problems of control will vary, of course, depending upon the percentage of the voting equity of the joint venture company that is to be held by the U.S. participant.

[¶ 13,095]

a. U.S. Participant With a Minority of the Voting Equity and Effective Control in Hands of Foreign Participant

When the U.S. participant is to hold a minority of the equity and the foreign participant is to exercise effective day-to-day control over the running of the business, the major objective is to maximize the U.S. participant's influence over management of the enterprise and to ensure that the U.S. participant will have enough information about the enterprise to exercise this influence effectively.

Here another word should be said about the form of business organization. In connection with a joint venture in a civil law country, it will often be preferable from the minority participant's point of view to have the enterprise conducted through a corporation rather than a limited liability company. This preference is based on the fact that the rights of a minority shareholder under local corporate law are generally more fully developed and articulated in the case of the corporation than in the case of the limited liability company. However, U.S. tax considerations, discussed at ¶ 13,035, may argue for use of a limited liability company.

Minority rights under foreign corporate laws differ widely but, generally speaking, a minority shareholder that depends solely on the rights accorded under local law is left in a quite vulnerable position. It is normally essential to supplement these rights by including special protections in the corporate constitutive instrument.

As a minimum, the U.S. minority participant should insist on representation on the board of directors (or other managerial board) of the joint venture company. Also, the U.S. minority participant should insist that its representatives have reasonable rights to inspect the corporate books and records. If these rights are not provided without qualification under the applicable corporate law, they should be covered in the constitutive instrument of the joint venture company.

In a civil law country, the problem of ensuring representation of the minority participant on the board of directors or managerial board is usually more complex than would be the case with an Anglo–American corporation. Cumulative voting and voting trusts are normally not recognized in civil law countries and a shareholders' agreement limiting the shareholders' freedom to vote may be void or unenforceable. If valid at all, the shareholders' agreement is usually enforceable in a civil law country only by an action for damages and not by an action for specific performance. As a result of the difficulties inherent in proving the existence and quantum of damages, the damage action will usually prove to be an inadequate sanction to ensure compliance with the terms of the agreement. The device most commonly adopted when a civil law corporation is involved is to provide for two classes of voting stock and to provide that the class of stock held by the minority participant has the right to elect or, in effect, to require the election of, a specified number of directors (typically proportional to its equity participation).

To achieve this result, it is often necessary to adopt a device that will not run afoul of the rule sometimes encountered in civil law countries that all shares must have the right to vote for all directors. Where this rule is in effect, it may be necessary to adopt the technique of permitting the class of stock held by the minority shareholder to make binding nominations of two or more persons to fill each of a specified number of positions on the board of directors.[2] In this way, all of the shareholders must vote for one of the persons nominated by the minority participant for each directorship allocated to the minority. In a number of civil law countries each director must own at least one share. Accordingly, minority representation may be assured simply by providing that a specified number of directors must be owners of the separate class of stock held by the minority shareholder.

Another protection that should be sought for the U.S. minority participant is a veto right over acts by the joint venture company that would be adverse to the interests of the minority participant. The most effective method for achieving this result is to include in the corporate constitutive instrument quorum and voting majority requirements for director and shareholder action that will permit the U.S. minority participant to block significant corporate acts to which it objects. These will vary with the circumstances, but, as a minimum, the veto right should cover such matters as amendment of the corporation's constitutive instrument, new investments, material change in the business, contracts with affiliated companies or shareholders, sale of a substantial portion of the joint venture company's assets, acquisitions, mergers, issuance of additional capital stock and borrowing by the corporation other than in the ordinary course of business. In addition, preemptive rights, if not guaranteed under local corporate law, should be expressly reserved in the constitutive instrument. The U.S. minority participant should also insist that the joint venture company be required to have its books audited annually by an independent accounting firm designated by or acceptable to the minority participant.

The U.S. minority participant may want some assurance that dividends will be distributed regularly by the joint venture company out of its earnings. If desired, this should be covered explicitly in the constitutive instrument. Thus, the constitutive instrument may provide that a certain minimum percentage of the par value of the shares or of the year's net income is to be paid as dividends annually.

Sometimes the position of the minority participant can be buttressed effectively by creating leverage that operates independently of any direct

2. At least two nominations for each directorship are frequently required to preserve the fiction that the arrangement does not deprive shareholders of freedom of choice.

control over corporate acts. For example, if the U.S. minority participant is to supply patent rights or technical assistance to the joint venture company without which it could not operate effectively, giving the U.S. participant the right to terminate the license or technical service agreement after a prescribed initial period would give it considerable leverage in matters relating to management of the joint venture company.

Any number of variations on this theme are possible. For example, the U.S. participant might retain the sole right to manufacture certain key components required in the joint venture company's operations. The U.S. participant might also retain control over trademarks under which the joint venture company's products will be marketed, perhaps by controlling a separate company that will handle marketing. If the U.S. participant is to supply debt financing, it might take a security interest in a portion of the foreign participant's voting stock under an arrangement that would enable the U.S. participant to vote this portion of the stock on some or all questions of business policy in the event of a default or possibly while the indebtedness remains unpaid. In some cases, a combination of such devices can be used concurrently or in series with a cumulative effect that permits the U.S. minority participant to exercise a high degree of influence, if not effective control, over management of the joint venture company.

[¶ 13,100]

b. U.S. Participant With a Less Than Controlling Interest in the Voting Equity but With Effective Control

In some cases, for a variety of reasons, the joint venturers may agree that the U.S. participant is to hold less than a controlling interest in the stock of a joint venture corporation but is to be placed in effective control.

In some civil law countries, there are serious legal roadblocks to vesting managerial control in a participant owning 50 percent or less of the capital stock of a jointly owned corporation. The unavailability of the voting trust and the obstacles to the enforceability of a shareholders' agreement have already been noted. In a civil law country the absence of specific enforcement of shareholders' agreements may, in some cases, be partially remedied by providing penalties in the form of liquidated damages. But even this measure often leaves the noncontrolling shareholder in a less than satisfactory position.

In some civil law countries devices involving two classes of stock with different voting rights are precluded by the general rule that each share of stock must have at least one vote and must have a vote proportional to the percentage of capital that it represents. In such countries, it seems doubtful whether a holder of a minority of the equity capital could be given, in effect, the right to elect a majority of the directors through one of the devices already discussed that involve creation of two classes of stock with each share having one vote but with a majority of the board of directors necessarily elected from persons nominated by the minority shareholder.

In civil law countries in which a holder of 50 percent or less of the equity cannot be given power directly or indirectly to name the majority of the board of directors of a corporation (the *société anonyme* or its equivalent), it may be desirable to consider the possibility of using the limited liability company (*SARL* or its equivalent) as the vehicle for the venture. In the case of the limited liability company, there is generally no need for a board of directors or managers. The enterprise can be managed by a single manager who can be appointed in the original corporate constitutive instrument to serve for an indefinite period. Under the laws of some civil law countries, unless the constitutive instrument otherwise provides, the sole manager of a limited liability company may be dismissed only for cause. When this is the case, the U.S. participant holding 50 percent or less of the equity can enjoy a broad measure of control over the management of the enterprise on a long-term basis by designating the sole manager initially in the limited liability company constitutive instrument. This could be buttressed by providing in the constitutive instrument that certain important corporate acts, including amendment of the constitutive instrument, can be taken only by a qualified majority, which is set high enough to give the U.S. participant a veto.

Another possible alternative for vesting certain elements of managerial control in a U.S. minority participant would be the use of a management contract. "Management contract" is a broad term used to describe a whole range of contractual arrangements under which specified aspects of management of an enterprise are undertaken by another party. Before reliance is placed on a management contract as the means for vesting effective control over management in a minority shareholder, however, it is necessary to consider carefully the extent to which managerial functions may properly be delegated by the directors of the joint venture company and the extent to which the agreement can be effectively enforced in the event of a clash between the person exercising managerial powers under the contract and the directors of the joint venture company.

[¶ 13,105]

c. U.S. Participant With a Majority of the Voting Equity and Effective Control

When the joint venturers decide that the U.S. participant will hold a controlling interest in the voting equity and will exercise managerial control, the problem of selecting effective control devices is often a relatively simple one.

The strongest position for the U.S. participant would be achieved by retaining the right through its majority control of the voting equity to elect a majority of the board of directors or other managerial body. Also, the U.S. participant should provide in the constitutive instrument, whenever permitted by local corporate law, for shareholder voting majorities that will make it impossible for the minority shareholder to block important corporate actions desired by the U.S. participant.

When, as will commonly be the case, the minority participant is to be represented on the board of directors or other managerial body, this representation will have to be provided for by adopting one of the devices previously discussed. Here, however, it will be desirable from the U.S. participant's point of view to ensure that quorum and voting majority requirements for director and shareholder action are set so that the minority participant's representatives will not be able to block corporate action thought to be important by the U.S. participant.

[¶ 13,110]

d. Special Problems of a 50–50 Joint Venture

When the equity of the joint venture is to be owned equally by the two participants, the control problems vary depending upon the basic agreement between the parties. If they decide that the U.S. participant is to have control over day-to-day management, the problem is the one previously discussed of selecting organizational arrangements that will effectively vest day-to-day control in a party holding less than a majority interest in the equity.

If the foreign partner is to enjoy effective day-to-day control, the U.S. participant will want at the least to exercise a veto over certain corporate acts and to ensure that it is fully informed as to company operations. This can be accomplished most directly by ensuring that the U.S. participant will be able to elect at least half of the board of directors or comparable body and by requiring that specified corporate acts be approved by an absolute majority of the board or, when appropriate, the shareholders. If possible under the local corporate law, the position of the U.S. participant can be made even stronger by vesting in it the right to designate the chief executive officer or to elect a majority of the board of directors who retain control over major policy decisions, while the foreign partner is empowered to handle day-to-day management under a management contract.

One possibility for implementing equality in managerial control between joint venturers would be to divide responsibility for day-to-day management concurrently between the two participants. This could be effected by providing in the constitutive instrument that two co-chief executives, one representing each participant, must act together to bind the corporation. Another possibility is to divide responsibility functionally, for example, by placing one participant's representative in charge of administration and sales and the other participant's representative in charge of production and technical matters. For practical reasons, however, this arrangement is generally a much less satisfactory one than having one person direct the day-to-day operations of the enterprise. If desired, the chief executive officer could be independent of, but acceptable to, both participants or this position could be filled during specified periods alternately by a nominee of each participant.

In the true 50–50 joint venture, neither party can dictate major policy decisions without the concurrence of the other. And this, of course, opens the door to the possibility of deadlock. What, if anything, should be done in organizing a 50–50 joint venture to cope with the possibility of deadlock? The resolution of this issue may have important potential U.S. tax implications.

It is sometimes felt that the best way to deal with potential deadlock is not to attempt to make provision for it at all. The theory is that there will usually be very strong pressure on the participants to reach an accommodation in order to preserve their respective investments. This will be especially true in a country, in which, if there is a continuing deadlock, the courts have the power to order liquidation of the company under the supervision of a court-appointed receiver—normally the last thing that either party wants.

Another possibility is to provide, as a last-ditch measure, a device whereby one party may either buy out, or be bought out by, the other party. A number of variations on this approach are possible. Under one arrangement either party may initiate the buy-out by offering to purchase the other's stock at a price set by the initiating party. The responding party then has the option of selling its 50–percent interest at that price or buying the initiating party's stock at that price. This mechanical buy-out device has the advantage that one party is left holding all the stock and no liquidation is required. However, once the initiating party sets the buy-out mechanism in motion, the automatic result is that one party's stock interest will be purchased by the other and yet the initiating party loses virtually all control over the outcome. This absence of control is intended to ensure that the initiating party will set a fair price. Thus, this type of deadlock-resolution mechanism is sometimes referred to as "joint venture roulette." A number of variations can be used.

For example, the initiating party may offer to buy the 50–percent interest of the other at a price set by an appraisal by an independent party. The responding party then has the option to sell or buy the initiating party's interest at that price. Under another approach, each party may be permitted to initiate the buy-out procedure by either (1) offering to *sell* all of its shares to the other party or (2) offering to *buy* all the shares owned by the other party for an amount fixed by independent appraisal. The responding party may then be given the option of accepting the initiating party's offer or directing liquidation of the joint venture corporation.

Another possibility is to provide for an auction-type arrangement. Either party may initiate the buy-out by offering a specified price for the other's stock; the responding party then has the choice of accepting the offer or making a counter-offer to purchase the initiating party's stock at a higher price. The initiating party may then either accept the counter-offer or make another higher offer. The procedure continues until an offer is accepted.

Another approach to the deadlock problem is to provide for arbitration of issues on which the parties are deadlocked. The major drawback here is that many questions involving business judgment do not lend themselves very satisfactorily to resolution by an arbitrator who is less familiar with the business than the joint venture participants.

In short, the problem of how to deal with the possibility of deadlock is one that must be resolved ad hoc in the case of each 50–50 joint venture in the light of the particular circumstances.

3. U.S. TAX CONSIDERATIONS IN ORGANIZING A JOINT VENTURE ABROAD

[¶ 13,115]

a. Selecting a Form of Business Organization

Selecting the optimal form of business organization for the joint venture will usually involve choosing between a corporation, a limited liability company or some form of general or limited partnership organized under foreign law. Occasionally, the venture may simply be organized pursuant to a joint venture contract, such as a joint operating agreement, that does not purport to be a partnership under foreign or U.S. law. Often business considerations will play a dominant role in making the selection, but U.S. and foreign tax considerations may be highly significant. The most important of these is usually whether the foreign law entity will be a corporation treated as such for U.S. purposes or some other entity that will be free under the check-the-box regulations to elect to be treated either as a partnership or a corporation for U.S. tax purposes under the rules discussed in ¶¶ 13,020 et seq.

In many cases business considerations will suggest the choice of a corporation or a limited liability company because business in the foreign country concerned is usually conducted in one of these forms. However, in some cases business factors may suggest the choice of a foreign partnership organized under foreign law.

An example of considerations that might lead to choice of a general partnership form is afforded by a joint venture in a civil law country organized as a civil law general partnership (*société en nom collectif* or its equivalent). This entity may offer greater flexibility in the control arrangements than are feasible in a corporation or limited liability company.

For example, under French law, in the case of a *société anonyme* ("*S.A.*"), a 40–percent equity owner could not be given a right to elect one half of the board of directors, while in a *société en nom collectif*, such minority owner could be given a role in management equal to that of the 60–percent owner. A U.S. corporation may be designated the manager of a *société en nom collectif*, but not of a limited liability company ("*SARL*"). In addition, there is more flexibility in handling the usual joint venture restrictions on the right of transfer and the right of first refusal with respect to each participant's equity interest in a *société en nom collectif* than in the case of an *S.A.* or an *SARL*. Furthermore, a partner in a *société en nom collectif* can contribute in exchange for an equity interest its own obligation to provide property or services in the future, such as an agreement to supply patents and knowhow to be acquired in the future or an agreement to supply raw materials over a period of years. Such a contribution cannot generally be exchanged for equity in an *S.A.* or an *SARL*.

Of the available business forms for a foreign joint venture only the foreign law corporation, as identified in Reg. § 301.7701–2(b)(8), will automatically be treated as a corporation (sometimes referred to as a "per se corporation") for U.S. tax purposes. Under the check-the-box regulations, any other business form can elect to be taxed either as a partnership or a corporation. Thus, a general partnership, a limited partnership and a limited liability company, whether organized under the laws of a civil country or a country utilizing an Anglo–American legal regime, will be eligible to elect to be treated as a partnership for U.S. tax purposes.

If the business organization selected for the joint venture is classified as a corporation for U.S. tax purposes, a number of important U.S. tax consequences will turn on whether the foreign corporation will be treated as a controlled foreign corporation.

[¶ 13,120]

b. Classification of a Jointly Owned Foreign Corporation as a Controlled Foreign Corporation

The U.S. tax consequences that turn on whether a foreign corporation, the voting stock of which is owned in part by a U.S. person and in part by a foreign person, is classified as a controlled foreign corporation are discussed in Chapter 6 and will only be summarized here. A controlled foreign corporation is defined as a foreign corporation of which more than 50 percent of (1) the combined voting power of all classes of stock entitled to vote or (2) the total value of the stock is owned, directly, indirectly or constructively, by U.S. shareholders, i.e., U.S. persons, each of whom, directly, indirectly or constructively, owns at least ten percent of the total combined voting power of the corporation's voting stock.

Thus, if the U.S. participant owns more than 50 percent of the voting stock of a jointly owned foreign corporation, the corporation will normally be classified as a controlled foreign corporation. In some situations, even if the U.S. participant owns 50 percent or less of the voting stock, but nonetheless exercises effective control over some aspects of management, it may be possible that the jointly owned foreign corporation will be classified as a controlled foreign corporation. See ¶¶ 13,125–13,135.

Under current law, in the typical case, one of the most important U.S. tax consequences that flows from classification of the foreign joint venture corporation as a controlled foreign corporation relates to the determination of the Section 904 limitations on the U.S. foreign tax credit. If the joint venture is a controlled foreign corporation, the Section 904(d)(3) look-through rules for determining the applicable foreign tax credit limitations of Section 904 apply to actual dividends, Subpart F inclusions, interest, royalties and rents actually received or deemed to be received by a ten-percent U.S. corporate shareholder. In cases in which a controlled foreign corporation earns exclusively general limitation income, foreign taxes attributable to interest, rents, royalties, Subpart F inclusions and actual dividends derived from that corporation by its U.S. shareholder will be subject to the Section 904(d)(1)(B) general income limitation. This situation will normally maximize the likelihood that any excess foreign tax credits, whether generated by dividends from the joint venture corporation or other general limitation income, will be usable.

If the foreign corporation is not a controlled foreign corporation, dividends paid to ten-percent U.S. corporate shareholders are subject to the look-through rule of Section 904(d)(4). Thus, if the underlying earnings of the noncontrolled foreign corporation are all general limitation income, a dividend to such U.S. corporate shareholders will be included in the general limitation basket. The Section 904(d)(4) look-through rule does not, however, apply to interest, rents and royalties paid by a noncontrolled foreign corporation to a ten-percent U.S. corporate shareholder. Therefore, such income items are often subject to the passive income limitation with the result that they are not likely to be helpful in absorbing excess foreign tax credits generated by general limitation income, including dividends from the foreign corporation.

Important in this context are the differing foreign tax credit limitation rules (particularly the look-through rules) applicable to controlled and noncontrolled foreign corporations, if the foreign corporation will earn general limitation income (which includes foreign base company sales income and foreign base company services income). As a result of these rules, having the corporation qualify as a controlled foreign corporation will often have foreign tax credit advantages that will outweigh the disadvantages of that status. See ¶ 7085.

The disadvantages of classification of a foreign corporation as a controlled foreign corporation have been discussed in Chapter 6 and need only to be briefly recapitulated here. If the jointly owned corporation is a controlled foreign corporation, certain types of income (the most common of which are collectively referred to as "foreign base company income") may be classified as Subpart F income. Under Subpart F of the Code, this income may be taxed directly as a Subpart F inclusion to a U.S. person owning at least ten percent of the corporation's combined voting power, even though not actually distributed. This constructive dividend treatment results in any tax year in which these types of gross income, in the aggregate, equal or exceed, under the de minimis rule, the lesser of five percent of the total gross income of the corporation or $1 million. See ¶ 6160. The same treatment may be accorded to certain income of a controlled foreign corporation that participates in, or cooperates with, an international boycott as described in Section 999 or that makes illegal bribes, kickbacks or other payments directly or indirectly to an official, employee or agent of a government. § 952(a)(3)(B) and (a)(4) and Chapter 14.

If the jointly owned corporation is a controlled foreign corporation, investments of earnings of the corporation in a variety of types of U.S. property may be treated as constructive dividends to any ten-percent U.S. shareholder under Sections 951(a)(1)(B) and 956. Investment in U.S. property for this purpose has a broader scope than one might expect. For example, it may include any debt or equity investment in a U.S. corporation affiliated with the controlled foreign corporation, any investment in tangible property in the United States, an acquisition of a right to use patents and knowhow in the United States and any guarantee or pledge by the controlled foreign corporation of the obligation of a U.S. person. See ¶¶ 6200–6220.

In addition, under Section 1248, a ten-percent U.S. shareholder of a controlled foreign corporation will, under certain circumstances, be taxed upon gain realized from sale or exchange of the stock of such corporation (including gain realized on liquidation) as if such gain were a dividend rather than capital gain. This dividend treatment applies to the extent that the gain reflects the U.S. shareholder's pro rata share of the post–1962 earnings and profits of the foreign corporation while it was a controlled foreign corporation. Dividend treatment may, in fact, be more advantageous to a U.S. corporate (as opposed to an individual) shareholder than capital gain treatment because a corporation is not entitled to a preferential tax rate on long-term capital gains and a dividend carries with it an indirect foreign tax credit for foreign corporate taxes under Section 960, whereas a capital gain would not. See ¶ 6245.

Under Section 1249, patents, secret processes and similar intangible property rights can be transferred by the U.S. participant to the joint venture corporation on a basis that will permit the payments received to qualify as long-term capital gains only if the transferee jointly owned corporation is not controlled by the transferor. Under Section 1249, control is defined in terms of ownership of more than 50 percent of the voting power of the foreign corporation's stock. In contrast to the Section

957(a) definition of controlled foreign corporation, under Section 1249 the value of the stock owned is irrelevant. See ¶ 12,095.

Finally, if the jointly owned corporation is a controlled foreign corporation, the U.S. participant will have to file with the IRS extensive annual information reports concerning the income and operations of the foreign corporation pursuant to Sections 6038 and 6046. It will also have to keep records prescribed by Section 964(c) and the regulations thereunder.

As noted above, the statutory test of control in the definition of controlled foreign corporation is stated in terms of ownership of more than 50 percent of (1) the total combined voting power of the foreign corporation or (2) the value of the stock of the foreign corporation. The regulations state that, in determining whether the U.S. participant will be deemed to own more than 50 percent of the total combined voting power of a jointly owned foreign corporation, all the surrounding facts and circumstances will be considered, and any arrangement to shift formal voting power away from the U.S. shareholder will not be given effect if in reality voting power is retained. Reg. § 1.957–1(b)(2). With respect to arrangements involving more than one class of stock, the regulations provide that if a U.S. shareholder owns shares of a foreign corporation which has another class of stock outstanding, the voting power ostensibly provided such other class of stock will be deemed owned by any person on whose behalf it is exercised. If not exercised, that voting power will be disregarded if (1) the percentage of voting power of such other class of stock is substantially greater than its proportionate share of the corporate earnings, (2) the facts indicate that the shareholders of such other class do not exercise their voting rights independently or fail to exercise such voting rights and (3) a principal purpose of the arrangement is to avoid the classification of the corporation as a controlled foreign corporation. Reg. § 1.957–1(b)(2).

Another feature of the regulations that is of particular relevance in the context of international joint ventures is the rule that a U.S. shareholder will be deemed to own more than 50 percent of the total combined voting power if it has the power to elect, appoint or replace the person or body of persons exercising, with respect to a foreign corporation, the powers ordinarily exercised by the board of directors of a U.S. corporation. Reg. § 1.957–1(b)(1). This test is interesting in that it involves an attempt to apply standards of U.S. corporate law to non-U.S. corporate entities to which—especially in the case of the civil law countries—they fit only imperfectly.

Uncertainty as to whether a jointly owned foreign corporation will be classified as a controlled foreign corporation is particularly prone to arise in the case of the 50–50 foreign joint venture corporation, as a result of control and deadlock-resolution arrangements or other circumstances that have the effect of vesting a large measure of voting, managerial or operating control in the U.S. shareholder. Obviously, if the U.S. participant holds 50 percent of the equity and has the right to elect one half of the members of the board of directors or other governing body, the joint venture company will be a controlled foreign corporation if any persons elected or designated by the U.S. participant have the right to cast the deciding vote in the event of a tie vote in such body or to exercise for the duration of any deadlock the powers ordinarily exercised by such governing body. What, however, is the result if the U.S. participant has a deciding vote on some but not all of the matters normally decided by the board of directors of a U.S. corporation or has the right to name a manager who has some but not all of those powers? One complicating factor is that the board of directors of the civil law counterpart of the corporation and the manager or managers of the civil law limited liability company usually do not exercise all of the powers normally exercised by the board of directors of a U.S. corporation. For example, the shareholders, not the directors or managers, of a civil law corporation or limited liability company usually must decide whether a dividend is to be distributed.

The following case was decided when the definition of controlled foreign corporation turned exclusively on whether the U.S. person owned more than 50 percent of the total combined voting power of the foreign corporation. It illustrates that a foreign corporation only 50 percent of the stock of which is owned by a U.S. person may be classified as a controlled foreign corporation as a result of factors not involving directly the voting power of the stock owned.

[¶ 13,125]

ESTATE OF WEISKOPF v. COMMISSIONER

United States Tax Court, 1975.
64 T.C. 78, aff'd per curiam, 538 F.2d 317 (2d Cir.1976).

[One of the two issues considered by the Tax Court was whether, for purposes of applying Section 1248, a foreign corporation was a "controlled foreign corporation" as defined in Section 957(a).

Technicon Instruments Corp. ("Technicon"), a U.S. corporation wholly owned by Whitehead and Weiskopf, was primarily engaged in the manufacture and sale of scientific instruments, the most important of which was the "AutoAnalyzer."

Technicon Instruments Co., Ltd. (Limited), a wholly owned subsidiary of Technicon, was organized in the United Kingdom in the late 1950s to assemble AutoAnalyzers from parts made in the United States by Technicon for sale in the United Kingdom. Subsequently, it started its own manufacturing and selling operations in the United Kingdom. In or about 1963, Technicon expanded the manufacturing capacity of Limited so as to enable it to supply AutoAnalyzers to the world market outside the United States.

To gain exemption from income and profits tax on all trading income from outside the United Kingdom, the board of directors of Limited (Weiskopf, Whitehead, Carr and Evans) implemented a plan to establish an Overseas Trade Corporation ("OTC"). Because a company wholly owned by Whitehead and Weiskopf would have been subject to a "surtax direction," a tax similar to accumulated earnings tax under the U.S. tax law, which would have partially negated the tax benefits of an OTC, the board discussed several different alternatives for decontrolling the proposed OTC. Whitehead and Weiskopf finally agreed to an arrangement in which 50 percent "of the votes" would go to a public British company.

Carr proposed to Franklin, a representative of Romney, an independent U.K. finance company, that Romney invest in the proposed OTC. The dividend to be paid on Romney's investment (12½ percent) was substantially higher than the then-prevailing bank interest rates. Franklin agreed to this arrangement.

On November 22, 1963, Intapco, Inc., was incorporated under the laws of the State of New York. Intapco was formed to hold stock in Ininco, Ltd., the proposed OTC. Intapco had two classes of stock authorized consisting of 100 shares of common and 500 shares of preferred stock. Upon incorporation, Whitehead subscribed to 70 shares of common stock, for which he paid $7,000. Weiskopf subscribed to 490 shares of preferred stock, for which he paid $49,000. Par value of both preferred and common stock was $100 per share. On November 24, 1963, Intapco and Weiskopf entered into an agreement that granted Weiskopf the option to convert up to 70 shares of his preferred stock into common stock share for share.

On November 28, 1963, Ininco was incorporated under the laws of the United Kingdom. It qualified as an OTC under U.K. law and as such was exempt from U.K. income and profit tax on its trading income from outside the United Kingdom.

The share capital of Ininco was divided into three classes of stock as follows: (1) 250 preferred ordinary shares; (2) 250 deferred ordinary shares; and (3) 175 second preferred ordinary shares. From the inception of Ininco and through February 24, 1966, Romney owned all of the 250 preferred ordinary shares of Ininco, for which it paid 25,000 pounds. Intapco owned all of the 250 deferred ordinary shares and all of the 175 second preferred ordinary shares, for which it paid 2,500 pounds and 17,500 pounds, respectively.

The preferred ordinary shares and the deferred ordinary shares of Ininco were entitled to one vote per share and the majority of each class of stock was entitled to appoint not more than two directors of Ininco. The second preferred ordinary shares had no voting rights. The preferred ordinary shares were to receive a cumulative dividend of 12½ percent per annum. The articles also provided that both Romney and Intapco were subject to the requirement that their interest in Ininco be offered first to the remaining shareholders before being sold to another person.

On November 29, 1963, Intapco, Romney and Ininco entered into a "Shareholders Agreement." Upon the sale of stock, the price to be paid to the selling shareholder for the offered shares was the amount which the shares would receive on liquidation of the corporation. Under the articles of association of Ininco, upon liquidation of that corporation, the owners of the preferred ordinary shares and the second preferred ordinary shares were entitled to receive the par value of those shares plus unpaid dividends, if any. The balance, if any, was distributable to the deferred ordinary shares.

Upon dissolution of or sale of stock in Ininco, the agreement provided that the shareholders had no rights with respect to continued handling of its product lines. The agreement also provided that in view of the even division of control of Ininco between the holders of the preferred ordinary and the deferred ordinary shares, the parties would endeavor to prevent a deadlock that would impede the normal conduct of the business of the company.

Ininco became engaged in the business of selling AutoAnalyzers, manufactured by Limited, to the world market outside of the United States and the United Kingdom. Limited continued to sell AutoAnalyzers it manufactured in the U.K. market. Ininco would purchase AutoAnalyzers from Limited and pay for the products. It in turn would sell the AutoAnalyzers to agents and distributors overseas, some of which were affiliated in some manner with Technicon. It went through an evolutionary period at this time from the use of independent agents and distributors to establishing offices in foreign countries. One of the purposes of establishing Ininco was to take advantage of the U.K. tax benefits and thereby build up capital to finance a rapidly expanding export business of Technicon. Ininco would provide credit terms for offices, which were overseas and affiliated with Technicon. There was no written agreement between Ininco and Limited relating to the sale of AutoAnalyzers for any extended period of time beyond the fulfillment of each order.

There was no provision in the articles of association of Ininco to break any deadlock vote which might arise. Franklin and Goldwater were appointed to the board of directors of Ininco by Romney. Weiskopf and Whitehead were appointed to the board of directors of Ininco by Intapco.

Evans, the managing director of Limited, was also the managing director who ran Ininco to all intents and purposes. (The managing director in a U.K. corporation is the equivalent of a president of a U.S. corporation.)

The special treatment accorded by the United Kingdom to an OTC was abolished by legislation effective as of April 6, 1966. Since Ininco would no longer be exempt from U.K. income and profit tax on its current income, it no longer served the purpose for which it was originally intended, and Weiskopf and Whitehead decided to terminate its existence. It was determined that liquidation of Ininco by Intapco and Romney would result in the imposition of a 40–percent British tax on the liquidation distributions. U.K. law, however, permitted a nonresident to receive dividends in gross that would not be subject to such tax. Carr approached Intapco with the suggestion that, because of favored tax provisions, Intapco stock be sold to a Hong Kong company. Carr worked out arrangements for sale of Intapco stock (owned by Whitehead and Weiskopf) and Ininco stock (owned by Romney) to Hong Kong Holdings, Ltd.

On December 6, 1965, Whitehead, Weiskopf and Intapco entered into an agreement whereby Weiskopf exercised his option to convert 50 of his shares of preferred stock in Intapco into 50 shares of common stock upon execution of the sale agreement to Hong Kong Holdings.

On December 21, 1965, Carr approached Franklin to ask whether Romney was prepared to dispose of or deal its holdings in Ininco, because Intapco and Technicon "weren't going to use Ininco again." Franklin testified that at first he objected to sale of Romney's interest in Ininco, as the investment had been viewed as being of long-term duration. Franklin suggested that some premium element be added for Romney in order to obtain its approval of the prospective sale of its stock in Ininco to Hong Kong Holdings.

On February 21, 1966, Hong Kong Holdings entered into an agreement with Whitehead and Weiskopf to buy their stock in Intapco. Whitehead and Weiskopf then considered establishing manufacturing and selling operations outside of the United Kingdom. In 1966, AutoAnalyzers were manufactured and sold by Technicon (Ireland) Ltd., an Irish corporation wholly owned by Weiskopf and Technicon. Technicon (Ireland) took over the markets previously serviced by Ininco. Limited continued to manufacture and sell for the U.K. market, on a much smaller scale than when it supplied products to Ininco. After the transfer of the stock of Ininco to Hong Kong Holdings, Ininco did not solicit any new orders of AutoAnalyzers.

The total amount received by Whitehead for his stock in Intapco was $1,100,654.16. The total amount received by Weiskopf for his stock in Intapco was $1,155,220.17.]

WILES, JUDGE:

* * *

The main issue for determination is whether any part of the gain realized by Whitehead and Weiskopf upon the transfer of their interest in Intapco must be treated as a dividend under the provisions of section 1248.

Section 1248 provides generally that, if a United States person sells stock in a foreign corporation and such person owns ten percent or more of the total combined voting power of classes of stock entitled to vote when the corporation is a "controlled foreign corporation," the gain recognized should be included in gross income as a dividend to the extent of the earnings and profits of the foreign corporation. Section 1248(e) provides that if a domestic corporation was formed or availed of principally for the holding of stock of a foreign corporation, the sale of the stock of the domestic corporation should be treated as a sale of the stock of the foreign corporation.

Section 957(a) defines the term "controlled foreign corporation" as any foreign corporation of which more than 50 percent of the total combined voting power of all classes of stock entitled to vote is owned by United States shareholders on any day during the taxable year of such foreign corporation. [An alternative definition based on more than 50 percent of the value of the foreign corporation's stock has since been added to Section 957(a).]

Since Intapco was formed principally for the holding of stock in Ininco, and since Whitehead and Weiskopf were United States persons who owned ten percent or more of the total combined voting power of Ininco, the application of section 1248 in this case turns on whether Ininco was a controlled foreign corporation as defined in section 957(a).

Petitioners contend that since 50 percent of the voting rights were held by Romney, a foreign corporation, Ininco is not a controlled foreign corporation within the definition of section 957(a). Respondent contends that Whitehead and Weiskopf, in effect, retained voting control of Ininco by virtue of the overall arrangement under which Romney purchased and retained its stock interest in Ininco.

It is clear that Romney owned, at least on the books, 50 percent of the voting rights in Ininco; therefore, it does not come within the literal definition of controlled foreign corporation. A mere technical compliance with section 957(a), however, is not sufficient to exclude petitioners from its application. * * * The 50–percent test of section 957(a) was intended to exclude from the definition of controlled foreign corporations only those foreign corporations which are not subject to the dominion and control of the United States shareholders. * * * We must determine whether the substance of the transaction in this case was that which the statute intended, specifically a real and meaningful ownership of at least 50 percent of the voting power in Ininco by non-United States shareholders.

While we recognize the rights of taxpayers to arrange their transactions in a manner intended to minimize tax liabilities, we also note that such transactions must have substance in order to achieve the intended result. * * * After analysis of the evidence in this case, we hold that Whitehead and Weiskopf retained dominion and control of Ininco in spite of Romney's 50–percent voting interest. Ininco was therefore a controlled foreign corporation as defined in section 957(a) and section 1248 is applicable to the transfer of the Intapco stock to Hong Kong Holdings in 1966.

We rely heavily on the opinions of *Kraus v. Commissioner*, 490 F.2d 898 (2d Cir.1974), and *Garlock, Inc. v. Commissioner*, 489 F.2d 197 (2d Cir.1973), cert. denied 417 U.S. 911 (1974), in determining the relevant factors to be considered in deciding this issue.

Section 1.957–1(b)(2), Income Tax Regs., provides in part that "any arrangement to shift formal voting power away from United States shareholders of a foreign corporation will not be given effect if in reality voting power is retained." * * *

The Second Circuit, in the *Garlock* case, stated that "It is significant also that the terms of the arrangement worked out were such that the preferred shareholders would have no interest in disturbing the taxpayer's continued control." That factor applies to the present situation. Romney was given an investment interest which was made attractive by paying a dividend rate in excess of the market for money advanced. Also, by virtue of the articles of association of Ininco and the shareholders' agreement dated November 29, 1963, Romney had a quite limited stake in the business. The articles of association provided that, upon liquidation, Romney was entitled only to a return of the par value of the stock (i.e., Romney's investment in the corporation). The shareholders' agreement entered into by Romney and Intapco provided that, upon sale of its stock, Romney had to offer its stock interest in Ininco to Intapco at a price measured by the amount to be received upon liquidation. Thus, as a practical matter, Romney could expect to receive only a return of its investment whether it attempted to sell its interest or forced a liquidation of Ininco.

Petitioners argue that both Romney and Intapco were subject to the requirement that their interest in Ininco be offered first to the remaining shareholders and therefore these provisions could not have been utilized by Whitehead and Weiskopf to retain control over Ininco. As a practical matter, provisions of the articles of association and the shareholders' agreement dated November 29, 1963, did serve the purpose of ensuring that Romney had no real interest in disturbing control of Ininco, as it could only obtain a return of its investment no matter which method it followed. If Intapco offered its interest in Ininco to Romney, the latter would have been required to pay Intapco whatever profits had been accumulated in Ininco. Even if Romney wished to pay Intapco this amount, any incentive to do so was negated by the fact that the business of Ininco was dependent upon a continued supply of AutoAnalyzers from Limited. Since the owners of Intapco also controlled Limited and thereby could, and eventually did, cut off sale of AutoAnalyzers to Ininco, the rights possessed by Romney lacked any real substance. It is thus clear that Romney had little, if any, interest in disturbing the effective control of Ininco by Whitehead and Weiskopf through Intapco and Limited.

A second factor which indicates that Whitehead and Weiskopf retained control and dominion over Ininco despite Romney's 50–percent voting rights was retention of complete and unfettered control by Limited over Ininco's only product line, the AutoAnalyzer. Since Ininco had no contract with Limited assuring it of any supply beyond current orders, the use of Ininco as an exporting business could have been halted at any time by a firm over which Whitehead and Weiskopf had control. Whitehead testified that he was aware that he could stop supplying the AutoAnalyzers to Ininco and thereby "essentially" terminate its business.

The shareholders' agreement dated November 29, 1963, further strengthened the control which Whitehead and Weiskopf had over Ininco by providing that, after dissolution of or sale of stock in Ininco, the shareholders had no rights with respect to continued handling of its product lines. Since Whitehead and Weiskopf were the sole shareholders of Technicon, whose wholly owned subsidiary was Limited, and thus had control over the manufacture of the AutoAnalyzer, the agreement realistically served only to prevent Romney from any future rights to the use of the AutoAnalyzer should Limited decide to cut off the supply of the products to Ininco. These circumstances further lessened the possibility that Romney would have any interest in disturbing or challenging the control of Whitehead and Weiskopf. Although we find it difficult to believe that a party with 50 percent of the voting power of a corporation would enter into an arrangement in which its only product line could be withdrawn at any time by action of the remaining 50–percent shareholders, we do not foreclose the possibility that such an arrangement might be entered into at arm's length. When, however, these circumstances are present in conjunction with other factors indicating that dominion and control are possessed by United States shareholders, the control which Whitehead and Weiskopf maintained over the continued supply of the AutoAnalyzer becomes a significant factor.

Petitioners have made much of the fact that Ininco was set up as a "deadlock" company with neither Intapco nor Romney holding the power to control the votes of the board of directors. They also cite the November 29 shareholders' agreement wherein the parties "in view of the even division of control" agreed to endeavor to avoid a deadlock situation and the rights to arbitration in case of differing interpretations of that agreement. This Court and the Second Circuit in the *Garlock* case viewed the presence of an arbitration provision to be an unrealistic business solution. In any event, any deadlock which occurred in running Ininco could have been solved by Whitehead and Weiskopf by merely terminating Ininco as a seller of the AutoAnalyzers, as it in fact did, when the OTC provisions were repealed.

Furthermore, Romney got 50 percent of the voting shares in Ininco for which it paid 25,000 pounds. In return it got an assured 12½ percent dividend and, by virtue of the articles of association of Ininco and the November 29, 1963, shareholders' agreement, only the right to a return of its investment upon sale or liquidation. It defies credulity that Romney would have advanced more money than Intapco and received only 12½ percent of the dividends to be paid by a company that was to be exempt from United Kingdom taxes on its profits if it truly obtained 50 percent of the voting power of that company.

Any remaining doubt as to the control and domination which Whitehead and Weiskopf retained over Ininco is resolved upon examination of the manner in which Ininco was terminated and the holdings of Romney were eliminated. After it was learned that the OTC provisions were to be repealed, Whitehead and Weiskopf, in discussions with Carr, decided that Ininco would no longer serve any useful purpose and that it should be terminated. Carr, after conference with others, concluded that a sale of stock to a Hong Kong corporation provided the best means taxwise of "getting rid of" Ininco. Carr then approached Hong Kong Holdings to arrange for sale of the stock and eventual liquidation by it of Ininco. In anticipation of this sale, Weiskopf, Whitehead, and Intapco entered into an agreement whereby Weiskopf was to exercise his option. This agreement was dated December 6, 1965. On December 22, 1965, Franklin wrote Carr a letter concerning their conversation "yesterday" regarding the possible sale of Romney's interest in Ininco. Thus, Carr approached Franklin after the transfer of Intapco's interest in Ininco had been arranged. Even Romney's limited rights under the shareholders' agreement were ignored by petitioner. Moreover, Carr testified that he went to Franklin to ask "whether he was prepared to dispose of or deal with his holding of Romney because Intapco of New York weren't going to use or Technicon Instruments weren't going to use Ininco again." Romney had no viable alternative but to sell its interest in Ininco to the buyer which Carr had located. If it refused to do so, the most that it could have done was force a liquidation or offer its stock interest to Intapco and receive a return of its investment. Since Intapco, by unilateral decision, had decided to cut off the supply of Ininco's only product line, it would be unrealistic to argue that Romney had any choice but to assent to sale of its interest in Ininco. Thus, even though Romney possessed 50 percent of the voting rights of Ininco, it lacked any real or meaningful power to influence decisions affecting the future of Ininco or its business.

Petitioners contend that Romney agreed to sell its interest in Ininco only after being promised and receiving a premium over and above the normal dividend rate. This contention apparently is offered to show that Romney acted independently of Intapco and asserted its power as a 50–percent owner of the voting rights in Ininco. We cannot accept petitioners' contention. First, the facts are unclear whether such a premium was paid. Second, the payment of a premium of 900 pounds from a corporation whose net worth had increased from 45,000 pounds upon incorporation to over 800,000 pounds in less than 3 years does not appear to be sufficient incentive to induce a party to give up its ostensible 50–percent ownership of that corporation. To the contrary, the 900 pounds premium, if paid, appears to be a "nuisance value" payment intended to prevent Romney from forcing liquidation, which could have resulted in the imposition of a 40–percent United Kingdom tax on the earnings to be distributed to Intapco.

A final factor in determining that Whitehead and Weiskopf retained dominion and control over Ininco is an examination of the overall transaction. The primary corporation throughout this period was Technicon. The entire transaction was arranged so that this business, through affiliates, would keep control of the sale of the AutoAnalyzer and expand its worldwide business. Thus, Ininco was utilized to service and expand a worldwide market previously supplied by Technicon. At the same time, funds accumulated in Ininco because of its exempt tax status were utilized to provide credit for the establishment of foreign offices (Technicon affiliates) which would sell AutoAnalyzers in foreign countries. After repeal of the OTC provisions rendered Ininco of little use to Technicon, Whitehead and Weiskopf terminated its business by cutting off its supply of AutoAnalyzers and transferring its worldwide manufacturing and selling operation to Ireland.

Romney was powerless to alter the course of these events in any meaningful way even though it had 50 percent of the voting rights of Ininco. It was, by virtue of the articles of association and the shareholders' agreement dated November 29, 1963, in a position only to force liquidation of Ininco. Furthermore, the operation of Ininco was run as if it were merely a Technicon or Limited affiliate. Evans acted as virtual managing director of Ininco, as well as director of Limited. Also, the business of Ininco was operated from the offices of Limited. The overall effect of these facts leaves no doubt that Whitehead and Weiskopf retained complete dominion and control over Ininco during its entire period of incorporation.

[¶ 13,130]

REVENUE RULING 70–426

1970–2 C.B. 157.

Advice has been requested whether, under the circumstances described below, a foreign corporation is a controlled foreign corporation within the meaning of section 957 * * *.

Y, a foreign corporation, has two classes of capital stock outstanding, as follows: 100 shares of no par value class A stock and 100 shares of $1.00 par value class B stock. Each class of outstanding stock has the same voting rights. The class B stock has a preference as to assets on dissolution of the corporation to the extent of its par value and a preference to annual dividends equal to the greater of a small fixed amount or a minor percentage of *Y*'s annual income. *X*, a domestic corporation, owns all shares of class A stock. All the shares of class B stock are owned equally by two individuals who are citizens and residents of the foreign country in which *Y* is incorporated. The corporate charter of *Y* is for one year with an annual renewal requiring the approval of the shareholders owning 75 percent of the combined voting power of all classes of stock entitled to vote.

Section 957(a) * * * provides, in general, that the term "controlled foreign corporation" means any foreign corporation of which more than 50 percent of the total combined voting power of all classes of stock entitled to vote [or, under current law, of the total value of all classes of stock] is owned by United States shareholders on any day during the taxable year of such corporation.

Section 1.957–1(b)(1) of the * * * Regulations provides that in determining whether United States shareholders own the requisite percentage of total combined voting power of all classes of stock entitled to vote, consideration will be given to all the facts and circumstances of each case. In all cases, however, United States shareholders of a foreign corporation will be deemed to own the requisite percentage of total combined voting power with respect to such corporation—

> (i) if they have the power to elect, appoint, or replace a majority of that body of persons exercising the powers ordinarily exercised by the board of directors of a domestic corporation;
>
> (ii) if any persons elected or designated by such shareholders have the power, where such shareholders have the power to elect exactly one-half of the members of such governing body of such foreign corporation, either to cast a vote deciding an evenly divided vote of such body or, for the duration of any deadlock which may arise, to exercise the powers ordinarily exercised by such governing body; or
>
> (iii) if the powers which would ordinarily be exercised by the board of directors of a domestic corporation are exercised with respect to such foreign corporation by a person whom such shareholders have the power to elect, appoint, or replace.

Section 1.957–1(b)(2) of the regulations provides that any arrangement to shift formal voting power away from United States shareholders of a foreign corporation will not be given effect if in reality voting power is retained. The mere ownership of stock entitled to vote does not by itself mean that the shareholder owning such stock has the voting power of such stock for purposes of section 957 * * *. This section of the regulations further provides that if there is any agreement, whether express or implied, that any shareholder will not vote his stock or will vote it only in a special manner, or that shareholders owning stock having not more than 50 percent of the total combined voting power will exercise voting power normally possessed by a majority of stockholders, then the nominal ownership of the voting power will be disregarded in determining which shareholders actually hold such voting power, and this determination will be made on the basis of such agreement.

Section 1.957–1(b)(2) of the regulations also provides that where United States shareholders own shares of one or more classes of stock of a foreign corporation which has another class of stock outstanding, the voting power ostensibly provided such other class of stock will be deemed owned by any person on whose behalf it is exercised or, if not exercised, will be disregarded if the percentage of voting power of such other class of stock is substantially greater than its proportionate share of the corporate earnings, if the facts indicate that the shareholders of such other class of stock do not exercise their voting rights independently or fail to exercise such voting rights, and if a principal purpose of the arrangement is to avoid the classification of such foreign corporation as a controlled foreign corporation under section 957 * * *.

Y's charter has a one year life and the annual renewal of the charter requires the approval of 75 percent of the combined voting power of all classes of stock entitled to vote. Thus *X*, owning 50 percent of the total combined voting power of *Y*, has the power to readily force *Y* into liquidation. *X* is therefore, deemed to own the requisite percentage of the total combined voting power with respect to *Y* under section 1.957–1(b)(1) of the regulations.

Accordingly, under the circumstances noted above, *X* is deemed to own the voting power ostensibly attached to the class B stock owned by the foreign stockholders, and *Y* is a controlled foreign corporation under section 957 * * *.

[¶ 13,135]

PROBLEMS

1. Your objective is to ensure that a 50–50 owned joint venture organized as a corporation under the laws of Country A will be classified for U.S. tax purposes as a controlled foreign corporation. Evaluate the likelihood that each of the following would achieve that objective:

a. The chief executive of the foreign joint venture corporation, who represents the U.S. participant, is named in the original constitutive instrument. Under Country A law, such an executive could be named to serve for the life of the corporation or until removed by a majority vote of the shareholders. Thus, the U.S. participant could block the executive's removal.

b. The U.S. participant or its representative is given certain managerial powers over the jointly owned foreign corporation under a management contract. The contract vests in the U.S. participant some, but less than all, of the powers normally exercised by the board of directors of a U.S. corporation.

c. In the event of deadlock, the U.S. participant is given the right to terminate a license agreement under which it has licensed to the jointly owned foreign corporation patents and knowhow essential to the latter's manufacturing operations. Compare Rev. Rul. 70–426, at ¶ 13,130.

2. Would use of any of the deadlock-resolution mechanisms discussed at ¶ 13,110 (such as one of the joint venture roulette devices) result in classification of the 50–50 owned joint venture corporation as a controlled foreign corporation?

3. Particularly difficult situations to evaluate are 50–50 jointly owned foreign corporations with respect to which, either by contract or otherwise, the U.S. participant enjoys certain leverage apart from its 50 percent interest in the corporation's voting stock. For example, suppose that the U.S. participant is given the power to cut off supplies of materials without which the jointly owned corporation could not function effectively, to accelerate the maturity on essential loans it has made to the jointly owned corporation or to terminate trademark rights or distribution arrangements important to profitable marketing of the products of the jointly owned corporation. Consider in this connection the emphasis given by the Tax Court in the *Estate of Weiskopf* case, at ¶ 13,125, to the fact that the U.S. corporation, which (through Limited, its U.K. manufacturing subsidiary) supplied products sold by the foreign sales corporation. Although the U.S. shareholders owned only 50 percent of the voting stock of the 50–50 company, they could decide to terminate the supply of such products at any time. Should such leverage in the hands of the U.S. participant be enough to require the conclusion that it owns more than 50 percent of the total combined *voting power* of the foreign corporation?

In considering these questions, review, in addition to the materials above, *CCA, Inc. v. Commissioner*, at ¶ 6045, and, especially, *Koehring Co. v. United States*, at ¶ 6050.

A question that pervades this area is whether the taxpayer who seeks to have the 50–50 foreign joint venture corporation qualify as a controlled foreign corporation can rely on decisions in such cases as *Koehring* or *Estate of Weiskopf*, in which the IRS successfully sought controlled foreign corporation classification.

Of interest on a cautionary note in this context is Framatome Connectors USA, Inc. v. Commissioner, 118 T.C. 32 (2002), aff'd without opinion, 2004–2 U.S.T.C. ¶ 50,364 (2d Cir. 2004). This case involved a Japanese joint venture corporation in which Burndy–US, a U.S. corporation (a predecessor of Framatome Connectors USA), owned 50 percent of the voting stock and two independent Japanese companies each owned 25 percent. One of the issues was whether, as petitioners argued, the joint venture corporation was a controlled foreign corporation for the tax year 1992 because it was effectively controlled by Burndy–US. If the joint venture was a controlled foreign corporation, the Section 904(d)(3) look through rules would have been applicable, and dividends received by Burndy–US from the joint venture corporation would have been included in the general limitation basket. The position of the

IRS was that the joint venture corporation was not a controlled foreign corporation and therefore the dividends had to be included in the since-repealed separate basket under former Section 904(d)(1)(E) for dividends from each noncontrolled Section 902 corporation. Under this treatment, urged by the IRS, excess foreign tax credits generated by Burndy–US's general limitation income could not be cross-credited against the U.S. tax on the joint venture dividends and were accordingly disallowed.

The petitioners' primary argument was that a 50–percent shareholder has more than 50 percent of the voting power of a corporation foreign joint venture if that shareholder actually controls the joint venture. Petitioners relied on a number of cases so holding, including *Koehring Co. v. United States*, at ¶ 6050, and *Estate of Weiskopf*, at ¶ 13,125. The court in *Framatome*, however, found these cases to be distinguishable and held that the joint venture corporation was not a controlled foreign corporation. The court stated that the government had prevailed in those cases by relying on Reg. § 1.957–1(b)(2) and by invoking the doctrine of substance over form. The court went on to state that a taxpayer may invoke the doctrine of substance over form to disavow a transactional form of its own choosing "if the motive of the taxpayer is not primarily tax avoidance." 118 T.C. at 48. Here, the petitioners in years prior to 1987 (when the 1986 Act first made controlled foreign corporation status advantageous) had taken the position that the Japanese joint venture was not a controlled foreign corporation. They changed their position only for 1987 through 1992 when there was a U.S. tax advantage in doing so. The court therefore held that petitioners could not invoke the doctrine because their change in position was motivated by tax avoidance.

But, in any event, the court went on to find that the U.S. corporation did not in fact control the joint venture. The articles of association required a supermajority vote of more than 80 percent to make a series of eight important decisions, such as amending the articles, electing directors and auditors, changing the capital, selling an essential part of the business and making or altering license agreements. Moreover, under the joint venture agreement, each of the joint venture shareholders had a veto right over six important categories of corporate decisions, including payment of dividends, changes in capital, changes in license agreements, acquisition or disposition of shares of other companies, transfer of a major part of the business and entrusting management to a third party. The court also found that, under the articles and the joint venture agreement, the U.S. corporation did not have the unilateral right to designate a majority of the board of directors or the president or to resolve deadlocks; nor could it force a dissolution of the corporation. The court concluded that the supermajority voting requirement, the veto rights in each shareholder, the rules relating to directors and other circumstances precluded a finding that the U.S. corporation had more than 50 percent of the voting power. The court also found that the 50–percent interest of the U.S. corporation did not, principally as a result of the factors mentioned above, have a value in excess of 50 percent of the value of all of the joint venture corporation's outstanding stock. Thus, Burndy–US did not hold more than 50 percent of the voting power or value of the Japanese joint venture corporation, and it, accordingly, could not be treated as a controlled foreign corporation.

[¶ 13,140]

4. LOOK–THROUGH TREATMENT THROUGH USE OF A PARTNERSHIP

Suppose that the U.S. participant in a 50–50 foreign manufacturing joint venture is not in a position to ensure that if the joint venture is organized under foreign law as a corporation treated as a per se corporation for U.S. tax purposes under Reg. § 301.7701–2(b)(8), it will qualify as a controlled foreign corporation. The objective is to insure that interest, royalties and rents paid by the joint venture corporation will qualify for look-through treatment under Section 904(d)(3). If they do so qualify, these payments will usually fall into the Section 904(d)(1)(B) general limitation basket. How can the U.S. participant achieve this objective?

One possibility for achieving look-through treatment for interest, royalties and rents would be to interpose a U.S. partnership owned 50–50 by the two participants to hold 100 percent of the foreign manufacturing corporation. Another would be to use an entity under foreign law as the vehicle for the venture that can elect to be classified as a partnership for U.S. tax purposes under the check-the-box regulations. If an entity classified as a partnership for U.S. tax purposes is used, interest, royalties and rents received by the U.S. participant will normally flow through as general limitation income. If the U.S. or foreign partner insists on limited liability, it will often be possible to use a limited liability company that will elect to be classified as a partnership under the check-the-box regulations.

[¶ 13,145]

a. Interposing a U.S. Partnership

Assume that foreign law considerations or the needs of the foreign partner make it mandatory to use a foreign law entity that will be classified as a corporation for U.S. tax purposes and that the U.S. participant's objective is flow-through treatment of the entity's general limitation income for foreign tax credit limitation purposes. Assume further that the U.S. participant will own 50 percent or less of the equity so that look-through treatment under Section 904(d)(3) will not be available with respect to interest, royalties and rents paid to the U.S. participant. What are the possibilities?

One possibility would be to interpose a partnership organized under U.S. law in which the U.S. participant would own 50 percent (or less) of the equity while the foreign partner would own the remaining 50 percent (or more). This partnership would own 100 percent of the foreign corporation that would actually conduct the business of the joint venture abroad. As a result of the U.S. partnership's owning all of the stock of the foreign corporation, the corporation will be treated as a controlled foreign corporation, and the U.S. participant's share of the interest, royalties and rents received by the partnership from the controlled foreign corporation will fall into the general limitation basket of Section 904(d)(1)(B). Or will it? Is there risk that the IRS might disregard the partnership and treat the U.S. corporation as owning directly only 50 percent of the stock of the foreign corporation conducting the joint venture? Important in this context are the partnership anti-abuse rules in Reg. § 1.701–2.

The anti-abuse regulations give the IRS the authority to treat a partnership as an aggregate of its partners in whole or in part, rather than as an entity, as may be appropriate to carry out the purpose of any provision of the Code or regulations. If, in the above hypothetical, the partnership were treated as an aggregate, the U.S. corporation would be treated as owning only 50 percent of the foreign corporation actually conducting the venture, which would therefore not be a controlled foreign corporation. Reg. § 1.701–2(f), Ex. 3, however, appears to insulate use of the partnership from aggregate treatment in this case. That regulation treats the foreign corporation as a controlled foreign corporation because all of its stock is owned by the U.S. partnership, which is accorded entity treatment.

Another possibility would be to substitute for the U.S. partnership in the above arrangement, a U.S. limited liability company that elects to be treated as a partnership for U.S. tax purposes. This should also result in flow-through treatment to the U.S. participant for interest, royalties and rents received from the foreign corporation, but there is no authority directly on point.

[¶ 13,150]

b. Selecting a Jointly Owned Foreign Business Organization That Will Be Classified as a Partnership

If the jointly owned foreign legal entity is characterized as a partnership, rather than as a corporation for U.S. income tax purposes, the partnership is treated as a conduit and flow-through treatment applies. Thus, gross income of the joint venture is includible directly in the income of the U.S. partner; expenses and losses of the entity can be taken currently as deductions by the U.S. participant for U.S. tax purposes and foreign taxes imposed on the income of the joint venture entity are considered to be imposed directly on the partners.

As suggested above, partnership classification may be significant when a U.S. corporate participant holds a 50 percent or smaller interest in the equity of the joint venture. In such a case, if the joint venture entity is classified as a corporation, the Section 904(d)(3) look-through rules will not apply to interest, royalties and rents received by the U.S. corporation from the foreign joint venture corporation. In any event, a look-through rule will be applied to dividends paid by a foreign corporation in which the U.S. corporate participant owns between ten and 50 percent of the stock (a 10/50 foreign corporation). § 904(d)(4). If, however, the joint venture entity is classified as a partnership for U.S. tax purposes, a look-through rule applies because the partnership is treated as a conduit or flow-through entity. The basket into which interest, royalties and rents received by each partner and each partner's distributive share of partnership income falls is determined by the limitation basket or baskets into which underlying income of the partnership falls. If all of the partnership's income is general limitation income, the interest, royalties and rents and the distributive share of any U.S. partners will also be general limitation income.

If the venture is conducted by a limited liability company organized under foreign law and the equity owners elect to have the company treated as a partnership for U.S. tax purposes, the entity may be a hybrid. See ¶ 13,040. That is, it may be treated as a corporation for foreign tax purposes but a partnership under U.S. tax rules. If so, not only will interest, royalties and rents paid by the limited liability company to U.S. equity owners be treated as general limitation income, but they may well be deductible for foreign tax purposes and thus be exempt from the foreign corporate income tax, thereby reducing the foreign tax burden imposed on the limited liability company. If a tax treaty is applicable they may also be subject to a reduced, or to no, foreign withholding tax.

Partnership classification will also be important if the equity owners are U.S. citizens, resident aliens or corporations that will own less than a ten-percent interest in the voting equity of a foreign joint venture company. If the joint venture vehicle is classified as a corporation for U.S. tax purposes, these shareholders would not be entitled to an indirect foreign tax credit under Section 902 for foreign taxes imposed on the foreign corporation's income. If, however, the joint venture entity is classified as a partnership for U.S. tax purposes, the foreign taxes imposed on the partnership's income are considered to be imposed on the partners. The result is that these taxes qualify for the direct foreign tax credit under Section 901. Because foreign corporate income taxes are often a significant burden, this result is often important.

Partnership classification may also be important when losses are expected during an initial start-up period. This factor, indeed, may make it desirable to inaugurate the joint venture in an unincorporated business form and to convert to a business form characterized as a corporation for U.S. tax purposes after the period of initial losses is over and profitable operations commence. The conversion is likely, however, to give rise to a significant tax liability under rules calling for recapture of previously deducted losses when a branch or partnership is incorporated. See ¶ 10,-

095. Foreign losses may also give rise to adverse consequences under Section 904(f) with respect to calculation of U.S. foreign tax credit limitations. See ¶¶ 7060 and 7065.

In addition, if the foreign entity is treated as a partnership for U.S. tax purposes, the U.S. participant will enjoy the U.S. tax benefits, such as percentage depletion, accorded to U.S. taxpayers in connection with solid mineral operations.[3] If the foreign business entity is treated as a corporation for U.S. tax purposes, it will be considered to be a foreign corporation that is not entitled to these benefits.

Partnership characterization also implies, however, immediate U.S. income tax on the U.S. participant's share of the income of the foreign enterprise, whether or not the income is remitted to the U.S. participant. The undistributed earnings of a foreign corporation will not be subject to U.S. corporate tax unless the foreign corporation is a controlled foreign corporation or a passive foreign investment company, and certain conditions are fulfilled. This deferral of U.S. tax is particularly important if the joint venture is subject to a lower foreign corporate tax than the effective U.S. corporate tax rate or is exempt from tax in a tax haven or under a tax holiday in the foreign country intended to encourage foreign investment. There are, in addition, a number of special rules applicable to controlled foreign corporations discussed at ¶ 13,120 and more extensively in Chapter 6 that can come into play only if the foreign entity is classified for U.S. tax purposes as a corporation.

[¶ 13,155]

C. POSSIBLE TAX SAVINGS THROUGH INTERPOSITION OF A FOREIGN HOLDING COMPANY

In connection with planning a direct investment abroad, it may prove to be advantageous from a tax point of view to interpose a wholly owned foreign corporation ("holding company") organized under the laws of a third country between the U.S. corporation and the foreign operating corporation. Assuming that the holding company is classified as a per se corporation for U.S. tax purposes, it will, of course, be a controlled foreign corporation. The foreign operating corporation, some of the stock of which is owned by the holding company, may itself be a controlled foreign corporation. If so, the Section 904(d)(3) look-through rules will be applied to any interest, rents, royalties and dividends paid by it to the interposed holding company. These items of income will usually be foreign base company income to the holding company. See ¶ 6025. If the operating

3. Similar advantages will result if the foreign enterprise is characterized as a simple co-ownership or a joint operating agreement (which under certain circumstances can elect not to be taxed as a partnership for U.S. income tax purposes under Section 761).

corporation earns only general limitation income, these payments in the hands of the holding company will be characterized as general limitation income under the look-through rules.

If the foreign operating corporation is not a controlled foreign corporation, any payments of interest, rents and royalties it makes to the holding company may be foreign personal holding company income, which is passive basket income. By contrast, dividends paid by such a corporation will be subject to look-through treatment under Section 904(d)(4). In either case, the dividend, interest, rent and royalty income of the holding company would be taxed as a Subpart F inclusion to the U.S. corporation, and there would normally be no advantage to be gained by accumulating such income from the operating corporation in the holding company. Nevertheless, the use of the holding company can be advantageous in occasional situations even when much or all of the U.S. corporation's share of the earnings of the foreign operating corporation will be distributed currently as actual dividends or taxed as constructive Subpart F inclusions through the holding company to the U.S. parent corporation. This may be the case when the latter's aggregate foreign income tax burden exceeds the foreign tax credit general income limitation. If the use of an interposed holding company can reduce the foreign tax burden on distributed earnings of a foreign operating corporation below the level that would obtain if the earnings were distributed directly by the foreign operating corporation to the U.S. parent, the reduction will be an absolute saving because it represents tax that would not be creditable against the U.S. tax.

When holding companies are used in this context, the availability of income tax treaties to reduce withholding tax on dividends at the source may be particularly important. The U.S. investor engages in outbound treaty shopping to select a country that has a favorable tax treaty with the country in which the investment is to be made. The holding company will be incorporated in the treaty country. Consequently, holding companies are often organized in jurisdictions, such as Austria, the Netherlands or Switzerland, which offer the combined advantage of little or no tax on foreign-source dividend income and a broad tax treaty network reducing withholding taxes otherwise imposed on such dividend income by the source country. An Austrian or a Dutch holding company, which is itself wholly owned by the U.S. parent corporation, may be interposed to hold the shares of operating corporations in certain countries that are party to a tax treaty with Austria or the Netherlands. Such treaties can reduce the total foreign tax burden on distributed earnings of the operating corporation substantially below the burden that would apply if the U.S. corporation owned its interest in the operating corporation directly.

For example, if a 50–percent stock interest in an Italian joint venture corporation is owned directly by a U.S. corporation, the Italian dividend withholding tax rate is ten percent. However, if the stock is owned by an

Austrian holding company, the dividend is exempt from both the Italian withholding tax (under the Austria–Italy Income Tax Treaty) and from the Austrian corporate tax.

Withholding tax savings under the Austria–Italy treaty more than outweigh the five-percent Austrian withholding tax under the U.S.–Austria treaty on dividends paid by the holding company to its U.S. parent corporation. Moreover, although the dividend income of the holding company will be taxed as a constructive Subpart F inclusion to the U.S. parent, the Austrian withholding tax can be avoided by accumulating rather than distributing the holding company's dividend income.

As discussed at ¶ 4090, many U.S. income tax treaties now contain "limitation of benefits" provisions that are designed to restrict treaty shopping of this kind to reduce U.S. taxes. As yet, anti-treaty-shopping provisions are relatively uncommon in treaties between countries other than the United States. For example, the Austria–Italy Income Tax Treaty does not contain one.

Until a statutory change in 2010, it was also possible that additional international tax arbitrage benefits could be achieved by interposing a foreign holding company organized as a limited liability company. An example is afforded by Guardian Industries Corp. v. United States, 477 F.3d 1368 (Fed. Cir. 2007). The Federal Circuit affirmed a decision by the Court of Federal Claims and held that an election under the check-the-box regulations by a Luxembourg limited liability holding company to be treated as a disregarded entity enabled the U.S. parent corporation to obtain a direct foreign tax credit for Luxembourg corporate taxes on undistributed earnings of the holding company's Luxembourg operating subsidiaries. Because the Luxembourg holding company filed a combined return with its Luxembourg operating subsidiaries, under Luxembourg law the holding company was solely liable for the Luxembourg taxes on the entire Luxembourg combined group. Hence, the election to have the holding company disregarded permitted the U.S. parent to be treated as the payor of the Luxembourg taxes on the undistributed earnings of the Luxembourg operating companies. As a result, the U.S. parent was entitled to claim an immediate direct foreign tax credit under Section 901 for Luxembourg taxes on earnings of the Luxembourg operating subsidiaries on which U.S. tax was deferred until (if ever) those earnings were distributed. The deferral resulted from the treatment of the operating subsidiaries (as distinguished from the holding company) as separate corporations (presumably per se corporations under the check-the-box regulations) for U.S. tax purposes. The result in the *Guardian Industries* case would be changed under new Section 909, enacted in 2010. Broadly, Section 909 provides that when there is a foreign tax credit splitting event involving a foreign income tax paid or accrued by a taxpayer, the foreign tax is not taken into account for U.S. income tax purposes and, consequently is not creditable, until the tax year in which the related income on which the tax is imposed is taken into account. See ¶ 5,010.

CHAPTER 14

INTERNATIONAL BOYCOTT AND FOREIGN BRIBERY PROVISIONS

■ ■ ■

[¶ 14,000]

A. USING TAX LAW TO ADVANCE FOREIGN POLICY OBJECTIVES

Throughout this book attention has been devoted to considerations of appropriate international income tax policy in the context of international economic objectives, administrative considerations and fairness to taxpayers. Sometimes tax rules are created on the basis of other considerations. There are many instances in which purely domestic income tax rules have been tailored to advance political and social objectives. It is not surprising, therefore, to discover that in various circumstances the rules for taxing international transactions have also been adopted with a view to advancing international political objectives.

An example of the impact of international political considerations on the development of tax policy is the denial of foreign tax credits in respect of income taxes paid to certain ostracized countries discussed at ¶ 5125. This Chapter deals with two additional examples. The first arises from the establishment by many Arab states of economic sanctions against Israel, which included a widespread boycott of persons doing business with Israel. As part of its longstanding support of Israel, Congress adopted a so-called anti-boycott program intended to deter U.S. individuals and corporations from cooperating with the Arab boycott. This program is implemented under the Export Administration Act of 1979, 50 App. U.S.C.A. §§ 2402(5) and 2407 (West 2010), and the Internal Revenue Code, and is administered by both the Commerce Department and the IRS.

The issue of bribery abroad by U.S. individuals and corporations has also occupied the attention of Congress. Despite the contention that the extraterritorial application of strictures on the bribery of foreign officials would not affect behavior in other places and would simply lead to the loss of economic opportunities to competitors in other countries, Congress eventually adopted the Foreign Corrupt Practices Act of 1977, 15 U.S.C.A. §§ 78dd–1, 78dd–2, 78ff(a) (West 2010). The Act applies sanctions against certain U.S. individuals and corporations that engage in foreign bribery. The sanctions are reflected in the Foreign Corrupt Practices Act and the Internal Revenue Code. In this case, the sanctions are administered by both the Department of Justice and the IRS.

This Chapter focuses on the elements of the anti-boycott and the foreign bribery provisions that are reflected in the Code and administered by the IRS.

B. INTERNATIONAL BOYCOTT PROVISIONS

[¶ 14,005]

1. INTRODUCTION

Section 999 imposes various tax penalties on taxpayers that "participate in or cooperate with" an international boycott. The purpose of the provision is to deter participation in or cooperation with international secondary or tertiary boycotts to which the United States is opposed.

A primary boycott is one imposed by a country on individuals, entities, property and transactions within the boycotting country. For example, the U.S. prohibition on most exports by U.S. persons to Cuba is a primary boycott. A secondary boycott extends the restrictions imposed by the boycotting country[1] beyond the country directly boycotted to "blacklisted" persons, i.e., those doing business with the boycotted country's government, or one of its companies or nationals. A tertiary boycott extends the boycott restrictions to others doing business with persons affected by the secondary boycott.

Although the anti-boycott provisions are generalized to encompass all international boycotts, they were enacted principally in response to the Arab boycott of Israel. If there is participation in or cooperation with an international boycott[2] in connection with a specific business operation, the current tax sanctions are these:

(1) foreign income taxes attributable to the operation may not be credited against U.S. income taxes, § 908(a) and

(2) undistributed income from the operation that is earned by a controlled foreign corporation or a Domestic International Sales Cor-

---

1. Section 999(a)(1) defines a boycotting country as either: (A) a country which is on the list published pursuant to Section 999(a)(3) (the following countries were on the latest version of the list: Kuwait, Lebanon, Libya, Qatar, Saudi Arabia, Syria, United Arab Emirates and Republic of Yemen. List of countries requiring cooperation with an International Boycott, 75 Fed. Reg. 44,842 (July 29, 2010) or (B) any other country if the reporting person knows or has reason to know that boycott cooperation is required as a condition of doing business within such country). The status of Iraq remains under review by the Department of the Treasury. Id.

2. Both "participation in" and "cooperation with" a boycott may trigger the applicable penalties under Section 999(c). For the sake of brevity, "boycott cooperation" is generally used in the text to cover both.

poration (DISC) is deemed distributed to the corporation's shareholders. §§ 952(a)(3) and 995(b)(1)(F)(iii)

If the taxpayer cannot clearly show the amounts of foreign taxes and income attributable to specific boycott-related operations, the tax penalties are determined by reference to the "international boycott factor." This factor is generally defined as the ratio of boycott-related operations to worldwide operations outside of the United States.

The international boycott provisions also require certain persons to report to the Treasury the existence of operations in countries implementing an international boycott. Acts of boycott cooperation, and requests therefor, must also be disclosed.

Except for temporary regulations regarding the calculation of the international boycott factor, no proposed or final regulations have been issued. However, the Treasury has released Guidelines, consisting of a series of Questions and Answers (hereinafter "Questions"), interpreting the international boycott provisions of Section 999. 43 Fed. Reg. 3454 (1978).

2. GENERAL SCOPE OF INTERNATIONAL BOYCOTT PROVISIONS

[¶ 14,010]

a. Persons Subject to International Boycott Provisions

Taxpayers otherwise entitled to a direct or indirect foreign tax credit or the benefits of deferral of U.S. tax on earnings of controlled foreign corporations or DISCs may be denied all or part of those tax benefits if any of the following cooperates with an international boycott:

(1) the taxpayer;

(2) any member of a controlled group of corporations (determined on the basis of *more than 50 percent* ownership) of which the taxpayer is a member (§ 999(a)(1), (b)(1), (c)(1));

(3) any corporation controlled (determined on the basis of *50 percent or greater* ownership) by the taxpayer (§ 999(e)(1));

(4) any person controlling the corporation (determined on the basis of *50 percent or greater* ownership) (§ 999(e)(2));

(5) a foreign corporation that is not a controlled foreign corporation but that is at least ten percent owned by the taxpayer and that generates an indirect foreign tax credit (Question A–19) or

(6) a foreign corporation that is a controlled foreign corporation, that is at least ten percent owned by the taxpayer and that generates an indirect foreign tax credit or earnings entitled to deferral of U.S. tax.

The taxpayer may be a U.S. or foreign corporation, an individual, a partnership or a trust.

The jurisdictional reach of the tax element of the anti-boycott program is substantial. In contrast to the boycott provisions of the Export Administration Act, the international boycott provisions of the Internal Revenue Code apply whether or not U.S. interstate or foreign commerce is involved. Thus, for example, actions constituting boycott cooperation taken by foreign nationals employed by a 50 percent owned foreign subsidiary of a U.S. taxpayer in an entirely foreign transaction may have significant U.S. income tax consequences under the international boycott provisions.

The reporting requirements imposed under Section 999 apply to all U.S. persons who have operations in, or related to, or who are related to other persons having operations in, or related to, a boycotting country (Question A–1) or with such country's government, nationals or companies.

[¶ 14,015]

b. Activities Subject to International Boycott Provisions

Section 999(b)(3) provides that a person participates in or cooperates with an international boycott if that person *agrees*:

(A) as a condition of doing business directly or indirectly within a country or with the government, a company or a national of a country—

(1) to refrain from doing business with or in a country which is the object of the boycott or with the government, companies or nationals of that country (which would be an example of a secondary boycott);

(2) to refrain from doing business with any U.S. person engaged in trade in a country which is the object of the boycott or with the government, companies or nationals of that country (which would be an example of a tertiary boycott);

(3) to refrain from doing business with any company the ownership or management of which is made up, in whole or in part, of individuals of a particular nationality, race or religion, or to remove (or refrain from selecting) corporate directors who are individuals of a particular nationality, race or religion; or

(4) to refrain from employing individuals of a particular nationality, race or religion; or

(B) as a condition of the sale of a product to the government, a company or a national of a country, to refrain from shipping or insuring that product on a carrier owned, leased or operated by a person who does not participate in or cooperate with an international boycott (within the meaning of subparagraph (A)).

Under Section 999(b)(4), penalties do not, however, attach to any agreement by a person:

> (A) to meet requirements imposed by a foreign country with respect to an international boycott if U.S. law or regulations, or an Executive Order, sanctions participation in, or cooperation with, that international boycott;
>
> (B) to comply with a prohibition on the importation of goods produced in whole or in part in any country that is the object of an international boycott; or
>
> (C) to comply with a prohibition imposed by a country on the exportation of products obtained in such country to any country that is the object of an international boycott.

Thus, a primary boycott may be respected by an individual or entity investing or doing business in the boycotting country. The specific categories of penalized and exempt activities are discussed in detail below.

Section 999(a)(1) requires that a taxpayer report on IRS Form 5713 all operations in, or related to, boycotting countries (or with the government, a company or a national of a boycotting country). Taxpayers must also specifically report both requests to cooperate with a boycott and actual cooperation. § 999(a)(2).

[¶ 14,020]

3. THE CONCEPT OF AGREEMENT

Boycott cooperation exists only if, as a condition of doing business or as a condition of the sale of a product, a person *agrees* to certain boycott-related conduct. § 999(b)(3). The concept of agreement is therefore critical to an understanding of the international boycott provisions.

The Internal Revenue Code and the Guidelines provide guidance, but no clear standards, as to when the requisite agreement will be found to exist. The agreement may be written or oral. Questions H–1A and H–2. The agreement may be inferred from a course of conduct. The circumstances under which an agreement may be inferred from a given course of conduct, however, are difficult to describe in the abstract. The Introductory Statement to the Guidelines indicates that "whether an agreement can be inferred from a given course of conduct is an evidentiary question which turns on the probative value of particular facts and circumstances." The Guidelines contain numerous questions and answers which state that, while the activities described therein do not in and of themselves constitute a boycott agreement, such activities will be evidence that, together with "other factors," may support an inference that such a boycott agreement exists. See, e.g., Questions H–3, H–5, H–7, H–9, H–13, H–15, H–17, H–23, H–24, H–25, H–32 and M–9. Thus, for example, while neither entering into an agreement containing a clause stating that the laws of a boycotting country will "apply" to the performance of the agreement (Question H–3) nor furnishing information in response to clearly boycott-related inquiries (Question H–17) itself constitutes boycott cooperation, a boycott agreement "could be inferred from an overall course of conduct that includes [such activities] in addition to other factors." Question H–17. Examples of "other factors" include the termination or lessening of preexisting business relationships with blacklisted[3] firms or with the boycotted country that cannot be justified by nonboycott considerations and the refusal to enter into such business relationships where there are opportunities and compelling business reasons for engaging in such relationships. Questions H–3 and H–17.

Actions consistent with boycott requirements that are not justified by valid business reasons will be suspect. Question H–9, for example, describes a situation in which a company excludes individuals of a particular religion from consideration for employment on a project in a boycotting country. The answer indicates that "it is highly unlikely here that there are valid business reasons" for the company's action. Although an exporter to a boycotting country that does not purchase goods of blacklisted companies because such goods would be denied entry into the boycotting country has not thereby agreed to cooperate, that course of conduct is one factor that may support the inference of cooperation. Question H–5. See Questions H–23 and M–8 for a similar rule respecting selection of shippers and insurers in the light of applicable boycotting country laws. When there is no boycott clause in a contract, but the local law requires as a prerequisite to obtaining an import license a certificate indicating that the goods were not manufactured by a blacklisted person and were not shipped on a blacklisted ship, merely providing (even repeatedly) the certificate at the time of import does not appear to be boycott cooperation. However, an *agreement* to provide such a certificate would be. Question H–32; see also Questions H–33, H–1A and H–1B. Providing a similar certificate pursuant to a letter of credit constitutes boycott cooperation since the terms of the letter of credit itself will be deemed to be part of the agreement. Question H–8.

A company's response to an invitation to tender that requires the successful tenderer to enter into an agreement to refrain from doing business with blacklisted suppliers will not be cooperation if the company does not win the contract, withdraws the tender, or wins the contract but deletes the boycott clause from the eventual agreement. In the event that the company's tender is rejected or withdrawn, an agreement to cooperate may nevertheless be inferred in other direct or indirect business transac-

3. As employed in the Guidelines, the term "blacklist" is generally used to refer to lists maintained by boycotting countries of persons who engage in activities that are inconsistent with the boycott. Question H–1A.

tions from the company's stated willingness to accept the boycott clause, if such willingness is coupled with other factors. If the company deletes the boycott clause in bad faith or in an attempt to mask an unstated understanding to cooperate with an international boycott, the deletion will be disregarded, and an agreement will be deemed to have been made. Questions H–24, H–25 and H–26.

An agreement to "comply" with the laws of a boycotting country is boycott cooperation, while, as noted above, an agreement that such laws will "apply" to the performance of the contract is only one factor that, along with others, could support an inference of boycott cooperation. Compare Question H–3 with Question H–4. Similarly, acknowledgment that a branch or subsidiary is "subject to" the laws, regulations, requirements and administrative practices of a boycotting country in connection with the incorporation of the subsidiary or the registration of the branch is one factor that, in addition to others, could support an inference of boycott cooperation. Question H–7. An agreement that disputes under a contract will be resolved in accordance with the laws of a boycotting country does not constitute boycott cooperation, nor does it give rise to an inference thereof. Question H–16.

If an agreement to cooperate with the boycott is found to exist, it is immaterial whether a person intends to abide by, or actually abides by, such agreement. Question H–18; see also Question I–4. The mere fact of having entered into an agreement triggers the tax penalties, even where the person would have taken the action agreed to for nonboycott reasons. Question K–3.

Even if the taxpayer does not personally enter into an agreement to cooperate with the boycott, certain actions of third parties may be attributed to the taxpayer. Thus, the Guidelines provide that, if the taxpayer establishes a relationship with another party in order to facilitate cooperation with the boycott, acts of boycott cooperation by such other party may be attributed to the taxpayer. See Questions A–11 and H–22. But see Question M–3.

4. SPECIFIC TYPES OF PENALIZED CONDUCT

[¶ 14,025]

a. Discriminatory Refusals to Do Business

A taxpayer will face the disallowance of tax benefits by agreeing, as a condition of doing business directly or indirectly within a country or with the government, a company or a national of a country, to refrain from doing business (1) with or in the boycotted country or with the government, companies or nationals of the boycotted country, (2) with a U.S. person engaged in trade in a boycotted country or with the government, companies or nationals of a boycotted country or (3) with any company whose ownership or management is made up, in whole or in part, of individuals of a particular nationality, race or religion.

With respect to refusals to do business with or in a boycotted country, its companies or nationals, the Guidelines state that a provision in a licensing agreement with a company of a boycotting country under which a person agrees not to enter into any agreement with any national of the boycotted country with respect to the use in such country of patents and trademarks will constitute boycott cooperation. Question I–3. An agreement to refrain from doing some types of business in a boycotted country but not in others is boycott cooperation (Question H–21), as is an agreement by a person not to supply a boycotting country with goods produced or manufactured with capital originating in a boycotted country. Question I–6. An agreement not to assign a contract with a boycotting country to a company incorporated under the laws of the boycotted country without the prior approval of the boycotting country will support an inference of boycott cooperation unless valid business reasons can be shown for this provision apart from the boycott. Question I–7.

Finally, a bank does not cooperate with the boycott by confirming and making payment on a letter of credit requiring the payee that is *not* organized under the laws of a boycotted country to provide a certificate to that effect, because the bank is not thereby refusing to do business with a company organized in the boycotted country. Question I–8. Presumably, the bank would be cooperating with the boycott if the payee were organized under the laws of the boycotted country. Question I–8; see also Question H–29A. The bank would also be cooperating if it agreed with a boycotting country to certify that it will not confirm letters of credit relating to the export of goods to the boycotted country. Question H–30.

The Guidelines contain a number of rules regarding refusals to do business with any U.S. person engaged in trade in a boycotted country or with a boycotted country's government, companies or nationals. Because Section 999(b)(3)(A)(ii) covers only refusals to do business with U.S. persons, a refusal to do business with a foreign person *solely* because it engages in trade in a boycotted country will not be penalized. Questions J–2B and J–11.[4] An agreement not to deal with any blacklisted company will, however, constitute boycott cooperation even if no U.S. company is presently blacklisted, because a U.S. company could be added to the blacklist in the future. Questions J–4 and H–1A. Any agreement not to enter into subcontracts with or purchase goods from a U.S. person named on a blacklist will generally constitute boycott cooperation, even if that person is not engaged in trade with the boycotted country. Question J–2A; see also Questions H–1A and M–7. In each instance, the presumption of boycott cooperation can be rebutted by evidence that the blacklist is

4. The term "U.S. person" includes a U.S. citizen or resident alien, a U.S. partnership, a U.S. corporation and a U.S. estate or trust. § 7701(a)(30). The term does not appear to include a foreign corporation engaged in a trade or business in the United States. Question A–1.

maintained for reasons other than furtherance of the boycott. Questions J–2A and H–1A.

An agreement to subcontract only with named subcontractors would also give rise to an inference of cooperation if the list on its face indicates a pattern of excluding blacklisted companies, unless it can be shown that the exclusion is not boycott-based. Question H–14. An agreement not to subcontract with a number of named subcontractors whose past performance has been unsatisfactory for other than boycott reasons, thus, does not constitute cooperation. Question J–1. An agreement to subcontract only with a specific subcontractor who in fact is not on the blacklist and who was named by a boycotting country would not be boycott cooperation, although it is not totally clear that this result would obtain if the contractor knew that the designation of the subcontractor was boycott-based. See Question J–10. However, an agreement by a U.S. person to obtain goods from a specific U.S. supplier named by a boycotting country purchaser, when coupled with a requirement that the U.S. person pass on to the purchaser a certificate from the specific U.S. supplier that it is not blacklisted, will constitute boycott cooperation. Question H–1B. See Question H–34, in which an agreement by a manufacturer to certify that its products contain no components produced by blacklisted companies is cooperation. From these and other provisions of the Guidelines (Questions H–13 and H–15), it is clear that a person must use caution in agreeing to give another party discretion to dictate with whom it may deal (e.g., by specific right of designation or approval).

A bank engages in boycott cooperation if it confirms a letter of credit requiring the beneficiary to certify that it is not blacklisted, unless two conditions are met. First, the beneficiary is neither a boycotted country person nor a U.S. person. Second, the bank does not have reason to know that the beneficiary will not be able to obtain the required certificate because of the nationality, race or religion of the beneficiary's ownership, management or directors. Question H–29A. A similar result follows if the letter of credit requires a certificate that the manufacturer of the goods is not blacklisted. Question H–29B. A bank also cooperates if a boycotting country deposits money with a branch of the bank on the condition that the branch will make loans only to companies that can supply certificates that they are not blacklisted. Question H–33.

A bid requirement that a supplier furnish goods or equipment on a delivered in boycotting country basis or that a supplier reimburse the purchaser for the purchase price and freight, plus interest, in the event that the supplier's goods are denied entry into the boycotting country does not constitute a refusal to do business. The Guidelines reason that blacklisted companies are unable to meet these requirements, not because of any agreement between the purchaser and the boycotting country, but rather because of the laws of the boycotting country. Questions J–7 and J–8.

The Guidelines are relatively brief regarding what constitutes a refusal to do business with a company whose ownership or management is made up, in whole or in part, of individuals of a particular nationality, race or religion. One example in the Guidelines finds boycott cooperation where a leader of an underwriting syndicate, pursuant to the request of a boycotting country, excludes a company from the syndicate because of the religion of its directors. Question K–3. The result is the same if the company's participation in the syndicate is conditioned upon its removal of directors who are boycotted country nationals. Question K–4. A requirement that an exporter obtain goods from a supplier designated by a boycotting country along with a certificate that the supplier is not blacklisted is boycott cooperation (even where the supplier is not organized in the United States or in the boycotted country) if the exporter has reason to know that it cannot obtain the certificate because of the race, religion or nationality of the supplier's ownership, management or directors. Question H–1B; see also Questions H–29A and H–29B. The confirmation of or payment on a letter of credit requiring a certificate that the board of directors of the payee does not contain any nationals of the boycotted country also constitutes boycott cooperation. Question K–5. However, an agreement by an exporter of goods to the boycotting country that the goods will not bear any mark symbolizing a particular religion of a boycotted country is not boycott cooperation. Question K–1.

[¶ 14,030]

b. Discriminatory Employment Practices

Agreement to a provision precluding employment (whether within a boycotting country or abroad) of individuals who are members of a particular religion or who are nationals of the boycotted country clearly constitutes boycott cooperation. Questions L–1 and L–5. An agreement to employ only nationals of the United States or of the contracting country is not. Question L–2. The provision is said to be an even-handed exclusion of nationals of both friendly and unfriendly countries. An agreement to employ a specified percentage or an increased number of nationals of the contracting country also is not cooperation. Question L–3. Finally, the employment of an individual for a position in a boycotting country may be conditioned upon the individual's obtaining a visa from the boycotting country without constituting boycott cooperation. Questions H–10, H–11 and H–12.

[¶ 14,035]

c. Discriminatory Shipping and Insurance Arrangements

The Guidelines indicate that an agreement to refrain from using a blacklisted shipper or insurer will constitute boycott cooperation. Questions M–1 and M–7. Compliance with the terms of a letter of credit that require a certificate as to the identity of the shipper or insurer will not, in and of itself, constitute cooperation, but together with other factors may evidence a course of conduct from which cooperation may be inferred. Question M–9. Sales made on F.A.S. (Free Alongside Ship) terms pursuant to which the purchaser is responsible for arranging shipping and insurance do not result in boycott cooperation by a U.S. seller. This is the case even if the seller has reason to know that the purchaser will arrange shipping and insurance with carriers and insurers who participate in the boycott and the terms of shipment were changed from C.I.F. (Cost, Insurance and Freight) to F.A.S. so that the seller could avoid selecting the shipper and insurer on a boycott basis. Questions M–2 and M–3. The purchaser's agent may, however, be deemed to have cooperated with the boycott if instructions of the purchaser to abide by a blacklist are followed. Question M–4.

The Guidelines permit, as a precaution against confiscation or damage, the seller to agree not to ship goods to or from the boycotting country on a vessel registered in a boycotted country or owned or operated by companies or nationals of such country or on a vessel that during the voyage calls at a boycotted country while the goods are on board. Question M–5. The Guidelines further do not penalize agreements with a boycotting country to ship exclusively on ships registered under the laws of such country. Question M–6.

[¶ 14,040]

5. EXCEPTIONS TO THE INTERNATIONAL BOYCOTT PROVISIONS

Section 999(b)(4) establishes limited exceptions to the international boycott provisions. As noted above, tax benefits will not be disallowed as a result of an agreement by a person to cooperate in an international boycott sanctioned by the United States. An example of such a boycott was the one previously applied against South Africa as a result of its long since terminated *apartheid* practices. See Question P, 52 Fed. Reg. 25,118 (July 2, 1987).

The most important set of exceptions to the international boycott provisions permits compliance with a primary boycott imposed by a foreign country with respect to imports from or exports to a boycotted country. This exception for primary boycotts reflects recognition by Congress of the sovereign right of all countries to control their own imports and exports. Thus, the Guidelines permit a person to agree not to import into a boycotting country goods produced in whole or in part in a boycotted country, or containing any parts, raw materials or labor from such country. Question I–1. Similarly a bank may, without penalty, confirm and make payment on a letter of credit requiring a certificate that the goods comply with such a condition. Question H–31. Capital, however, is treated differently from parts and labor: an agreement not to use any capital originating in a boycotted country in the production or manufacture of goods will constitute boycott cooperation because it represents a discriminatory refusal to do business. Question I–6.

In further implementation of the primary boycott exception, the Guidelines provide that an agreement not to export to a boycotted country goods produced in a boycotting country will not constitute penalized boycott cooperation. Question I–5. See Question M–5, which indicates that it may be agreed that exports to or from a boycotting country will be shipped on a vessel that is not owned, controlled, operated or chartered by the boycotted country or companies or nationals of such country, or that calls at a boycotted country while the exports are aboard. Subsequent purchasers may also be required to undertake not to send such goods to the boycotted country, provided that the goods are "substantially unaltered" at the time of resale. Question J–9.

The primary boycott import and export exceptions are available only for compliance with "prohibitions." Compliance with presumed policies of a boycotting country would not appear to be covered by the exceptions, unless the policies are embodied in the laws, regulations, administrative requirements or practices of the boycotting country. See Questions I–1 and I–5.

[¶ 14,045]

6. PRESUMPTIONS EXTENDING BOYCOTT COOPERATION TAINT

Once it has been established under Section 999(b)(3) that a person has cooperated with an international boycott, certain other operations of the same person and of certain related persons are presumed to involve such cooperation. The governing rules are found in Section 999(b)(1) and (e).

[¶ 14,050]

a. Definition of Operations in Boycotting Country

A special presumption arises if a person, or a member of a controlled group[5] that includes the person, cooperates with an international boycott. As a result of such cooperation, all operations of such person or group *in* any country that requires cooperation with that boycott as a condition of doing business within that country (or with the government, companies or nationals thereof) are presumed to be operations in connection with which such cooperation occurs. This presumption is not applied if the person can clearly demonstrate that a particular operation is a clearly separate and identifiable operation involving no boycott cooperation. § 991(b)(1).

5. See ¶ 14,055 for discussion of what constitutes a "controlled group."

"Operations" have been interpreted to encompass all forms of business or commercial activities and transactions, whether or not productive of income. These activities include, but are not limited to, selling, purchasing, leasing, licensing, banking, financing and similar activities, extracting, processing, manufacturing, producing, constructing, transporting and activities ancillary to the foregoing. "Operations" also include rendering of services of any kind. Question B–1. The performance of services by an employee in a boycotting country are not operations of the employee and therefore do not require reporting by such employee. Question B–3.

The geographical scope of the presumption under Section 999(b)(1) depends on which countries are included in a list published by the Treasury Department of countries which require or may require participation in or cooperation with an international boycott (within the meaning of subsection (b)(3)). The presence of a country on this list is not conclusive as to whether that country requires such cooperation and the absence of a country does not mean that it will not be considered to require such cooperation.

For purposes of the Section 999(b)(1) presumption (as well as for reporting purposes (see ¶ 14,080)), it is important to distinguish among operations "*in* a boycotting country," operations "*with* the government, a company or a national of a boycotting country" and operations "*related to* a boycotting country." An operation "in" is defined in the Guidelines as any operation carried on in whole or in part in such a country. An operation "with" is any operation carried on outside a boycotting country either for or with the government, a company or a national of such country. An operation "related to" is any operation carried on outside a boycotting country for the government, a company or a national of a nonboycotting country if the person engaged in the operation knows or has reason to know that the specific goods, services or funds produced by the operation are intended for use in a boycotting country, for use by or for the benefit of the government, a company or a national of a boycotting country or for use in forwarding or transporting to a boycotting country. Question B–1.

Since the Section 999(b)(1) presumption is phrased in terms of operations "in" a boycotting country, it extends only to operations actually carried on in whole or in part in such countries. If a person has cooperated with a boycott imposed by one country, all operations of the person *in* that and all other countries requiring cooperation in the same boycott will be presumed to involve boycott cooperation, but operations of that person wholly outside the boycotting countries even if "with" governments, companies or nationals of, or "related to," other boycotting countries will not be swept in by the presumption. Question D–1. The Guidelines state, however, that operations outside the boycotting countries "will be considered to be operations in connection with which there was participation in or cooperation with an international boycott if so warranted by the facts." Question D–1.

[¶ 14,055]

b. Controlled Groups and Related Persons

Section 999(b)(1) also contains a presumption that if any member of a controlled group cooperates with a boycott, all operations *in* boycotting countries—not just the operations of that member, but of the entire group—will be presumed to involve boycott cooperation. For this purpose, Section 993(a)(3) defines a controlled group with reference to Section 1563(a), except that "more than 50 percent" is substituted for "at least 80 percent" wherever the latter phrase appears in Section 1563(a).

Generally, controlled groups include parent-subsidiary groups, brother-sister groups and combined groups in which the members are related by stock ownership of more than 50 percent. A parent-subsidiary group is any group of one or more chains of corporations connected through stock ownership with a common parent if (1) the parent owns more than 50 percent of the stock of at least one subsidiary (excluding for this purpose stock owned directly by other subsidiaries) and (2) more than 50 percent of the stock of each subsidiary is owned by other subsidiaries or the parent. §§ 993(a)(3) and 1563(a)(1). Two or more corporations are a brother-sister group if five or fewer persons who are individuals, trusts or estates own more than 50 percent of the stock of each corporation, taking into account the stock ownership of each such person only to the extent such stock ownership is identical with respect to each corporation. §§ 993(a)(3) and 1563(a)(2). Finally, three or more corporations constitute a combined group if each is a member of either a parent-subsidiary group or a brother-sister group, and the parent of the former is a member of the latter. §§ 993(a)(3) and 1563(a)(3). The percentage of stock ownership tests may be met either in terms of value or voting power. § 1563(a). Certain attribution rules may apply to determine stock ownership. § 1563(d) and (e).

Further presumptions affecting related persons are contained in Section 999(e). Under this Section, if a person controls a corporation, cooperation with an international boycott by either the person or the controlled corporation is presumed to be such cooperation by both. Control is defined by reference to Section 304(c) as the ownership of *50 percent or more* of the stock of a corporation (in contrast to the presumption regarding controlled groups in which stock ownership of *more than 50 percent* is required). For purposes of this test, the stock attribution rules of Section 318(a) apply without regard to the 50–percent limitations in Section 318(a)(2)(C) and (3)(C). Thus, stock owned by the shareholders of a corporation is treated as owned by the corporation, and stock owned by the corporation (other than stock owned by shareholders that is treated as owned by the corporation) is treated as owned by each shareholder in the proportion that the value of the shareholder's stock bears to the value of all the stock in the corporation. In addition, a person controlling a corporation is deemed to control any other corporation which that corporation itself controls. § 304(c)(1). It is unclear from the statute whether this presumed cooperation would trigger the presumption under Section 999(b)(1), although the Joint Committee Staff's General Explanation of the Tax Reform Act of 1976 (hereinafter "General Explanation of the 1976 Act") indicated that it would.[6] Unfortunately, the Guidelines do not discuss the application of Section 999(e). It is also unclear whether the cooperation of one 50–percent shareholder of a corporation is attributed to the corporation and then, by again applying the presumption, to the other 50–percent shareholder. For example, in the case of a 50–50 corporate joint venture between a corporation of a boycotting country and a U.S. person, is the boycott cooperation of the former first imputed to the joint venture company and then from the joint venture company to the U.S. person? Neither the Guidelines nor the General Explanation of the 1976 Act discusses this question.

[¶ 14,060]

c. Rebutting the Presumptions; "Clearly Separate and Identifiable Operations"

Taxpayers may rebut the presumptions discussed at ¶¶ 14,050 and 14,055. This may be done by showing that all or certain of their operations in or related to boycotting countries are clearly separate and identifiable from the operation in connection with which there was actual boycott cooperation and that no boycott cooperation occurred in respect of such separate and identifiable operations. § 999(b)(2). The Guidelines list five factors that may be considered in determining whether an operation is clearly separate and identifiable from an operation with respect to which boycott cooperation occurred (Question D–3):

(1) Were the two operations conducted by different corporations, partnerships or other business entities?

(2) Were the operations, whether conducted by separate entities or not, supervised by different management personnel?

(3) Did the operations involve distinctly different products or services?

(4) Were the operations undertaken pursuant to separate and distinct contracts?

(5) If business operations in the countries conducting the international boycott in question were not continuous over time, was each transaction separately negotiated and performed?

6. See Staff of Joint Comm. on Tax'n, 94th Cong., 2d Sess., General Explanation of the Tax Reform Act of 1976, at 285 (1976).

This list of factors is not intended to be exhaustive and the relative weight to be assigned to each factor depends on the facts and circumstances of the particular case. The Guidelines warn that even a positive answer to all five of the above questions will not result in a determination that an operation is separate and identifiable if a contrary conclusion is warranted by the facts. Question D–3.

Applying the above factors, the Guidelines state that the activities of separately managed divisions of a company, marketing different products through different offices, constitute separate and identifiable operations. Question D–3, Ex. (c). On the other hand, the production and marketing of different goods by two wholly owned subsidiaries of a common parent corporation, using the same manufacturing and office facilities and the same management personnel, are a single operation. Question D–3, Ex. (e).

[¶ 14,065]

7. COMPUTATION OF TAX PENALTIES

The international boycott provisions provide two alternative methods for computing the loss of tax benefits: the international boycott factor method and the specifically attributable taxes and income method. Taxpayers must elect yearly which method to use. § 999(c).

In the case of a controlled group, each member may separately choose which of the two alternative methods of computation it wishes to use. However, all members of the controlled group filing a consolidated return must use the same method. Question F–5.

[¶ 14,070]

a. The International Boycott Factor

The first method for computing the tax penalties imposed as a result of boycott cooperation makes use of the "international boycott factor." This factor is defined in Section 999(c)(1) as a fraction. The numerator of the fraction reflects the foreign operations of a person (or, in the case of a controlled group, foreign operations of the group that includes that person) that are operations in or related to a group of countries associated in carrying out an international boycott with which that person or a member of that controlled group cooperated during the tax year. The denominator of the fraction reflects the entire *foreign* operations of that person or group, as the case may be.

The boycott factor is determined in accordance with regulations by reference to purchases, sales and payroll. According to Temp. Reg. § 7.999–1(c)(2)(i), the numerator of the fraction is the sum of:

(1) Purchases made from all boycotting countries associated in carrying out a particular international boycott,

(2) Sales made to or from all boycotting countries associated in carrying out a particular international boycott and

(3) Payroll paid or accrued for services performed in all boycotting countries associated in carrying out a particular international boycott.

The above rules (1) and (2) in effect ignore the distinctions among operations "in," "with" or "related to." Thus, when the international boycott factor is used, the taxpayer is allowed to exclude from the numerator the amount of purchases, sales and payroll that is demonstrated to be attributable to clearly separate and identifiable operations in connection with which there was no boycott cooperation. The denominator of the boycott factor is defined to include purchases, sales and payroll connected with any country other than the United States.

Once the international boycott factor has been determined, it is used in computing the tax penalties under Sections 908, 952(a)(3) and 995(b)(1)(F)(ii). Under Section 908, the amount of the foreign tax credits otherwise allowable (including both direct and indirect foreign tax credits under Sections 901, 902 and 960 after the application of the limitations of Sections 904 and 907) are reduced by the product of that amount and the relevant international boycott factor. Question N–1A. Foreign taxes otherwise creditable as a direct foreign tax credit under Section 901 that are not creditable because of Section 908 are deductible. §§ 908(b) and 275(a)(4); Questions N–4 and N–5. Indirect foreign tax credits under Sections 902 and 960 that are denied creditability by reason of boycott cooperation are not deductible. Questions N–4 and N–5. The Guidelines contain rules for the treatment of foreign tax credit carryforwards and carrybacks. In general, when tax credits are carried from a year in which the international boycott factor is applied to any other year, the international boycott factor for the year from which such taxes are carried determines the amount of such taxes not creditable in the other year. Questions N–1A to N–5.

As discussed in Chapter 6, a controlled foreign corporation's Subpart F income may be treated as a constructive dividend (technically, a Subpart F inclusion) to the corporation's U.S. shareholders. Section 952(a)(3) adds to the Subpart F income of a controlled foreign corporation, an amount equal to the product of the international boycott factor and the income of the controlled foreign corporation that would not otherwise be deemed to be constructively distributed to U.S. shareholders. Finally, the Code permits the deferral of tax on a portion of the taxable income of a DISC. Section 995(b)(1)(F), however, reduces the amount of taxable income on which tax is otherwise deferrable by the product of that amount and the international boycott factor.

It should be apparent from the above discussion that the international boycott factor method, under certain circumstances, could result in a substantial loss of tax benefits even though few of those tax benefits are attributable to operations involving boycott cooperation. This result can occur because the loss of tax benefits under this method is measured by the product of the international boycott factor multiplied by the *world-wide* foreign tax credits and income benefitting from deferral of or exemption from U.S. tax.

[¶ 14,075]

b. Specifically Attributable Taxes and Income

The use of the international boycott factor can be avoided if the taxpayer (including individual members of a controlled group[7]) clearly shows that the foreign taxes paid and income earned for the tax year are attributable to certain specific operations that are not in or related to boycotting countries. § 999(b)(2)(A). The principles of Reg. § 1.861–8 are applicable in determining income and taxes attributable to specific operations. Question F–6. Under the specifically attributable taxes and income method, a taxpayer loses those tax benefits attributable (1) to specific operations *in or related to* boycotting countries in connection with which there was boycott cooperation and (2) to operations *in* boycotting countries, all of which are subject to the Section 999(b)(1) presumption. See ¶ 14,050. This result will not obtain, however, if the operations have been shown to be separate and identifiable operations in connection with which there has been no boycott cooperation. Question N–1B; see also Question F–8. The distinctions among operations "in," "with" or "related to," and the discussion of such terms in connection with the Section 999(b)(1) presumptions, discussed at ¶ 14,050, is critical in computing the loss of benefits under the specifically attributable taxes and income method. By contrast, these distinctions are ignored under the international boycott factor method. The Section 904 limitations on the foreign tax credit, discussed in Chapters 5 and 7, are applied after otherwise creditable foreign taxes have been reduced to reflect boycott cooperation under the specifically attributable taxes and income method. Question N–1B.

[¶ 14,080]

8. REPORTING REQUIREMENTS

To assist in the enforcement of the substantive measures described above and to provide a basis for the annual reports that the Treasury is required to submit to Congress, certain persons must report to the Treasury on IRS Form 5713 the following information under Section 999(a):

7. Any group member may avoid application of the factor altogether by attributing foreign taxes and income to its own operations. Questions F–3 and F–5. A corporation may not, however, apply the international boycott factor to some (but not all) of its operations and attribute income and foreign taxes to the rest. Question F–4. All members of a group filing a consolidated return must compute the loss of tax benefits using the same method. Question F–5.

(A) operations in or related to a country (or with the government, a company or a national of a country) that implements an international boycott (Question A–1);[8]

(B) cooperation with an international boycott;

(C) requests to cooperate with an international boycott and

(D) the nature of operations in connection with which cooperation or requests to cooperate with an international boycott occur.

The reporting requirements imposed by the international boycott provisions apply not only to U.S. taxpayers who may lose tax benefits as a result of boycott cooperation, but to all U.S. persons who have operations in or who are related to other persons having operations in, or related to, a boycotting country (Question A–1) or with such country's government, nationals or companies. Specifically, the reporting requirement covers any U.S. person who

(A) has operations in, or related to, a boycotting country (or with the government, a company or a national of a boycotting country);

(B) is a member of a controlled group, another member of which has such operations;

(C) is a U.S. shareholder (within the meaning of Section 951(b)), and who actually owns stock, (within the meaning of Section 958(a)) of a foreign corporation that has such operations;

(D) is a partner in a partnership that has such operations or

(E) is the owner of a trust that has such operations.

Question A–1.

A taxpayer who willfully fails to report may be subject to up to one year in prison, a $25,000 fine or both. § 999(f).

[¶ 14,085]

9. LOSS OF FOREIGN TAX CREDITS

Direct credits under Section 901 (e.g., for foreign withholding taxes on dividends paid by a foreign corporation) will be lost only if the person claiming them cooperates with an international boycott in connection with its investment in a foreign corporation or branch and if its investment is a clearly separate and identifiable operation. For this purpose, it is not relevant whether the foreign corporation itself cooperates with an international boycott. Question N–3.

---

8. Note that *operations* in or related to these countries must be reported even if they fall within the scope of Section 999(b)(4)(B) or 999(b)(4)(C) (relating to compliance with primary boycott import and export exceptions), but not if they are covered by Section 999(b)(4)(A) (boycotts sanctioned by U.S. law). Questions A–9 and A–10. Acts (and requests therefor) within the exceptions for compliance with import and export prohibitions are not, however, reportable as requests to cooperate or cooperation.

The loss of indirect credits under Section 902, on the other hand, may in some circumstances depend on whether the foreign corporation involved cooperates with an international boycott. If the U.S. shareholder chooses to apply the international boycott factor, that factor is applied to all its foreign tax credits, both direct and indirect, and thus whether the foreign corporation cooperates does not affect the computation of lost tax credit benefits. Questions A–19 and F–5. By contrast, if the U.S. shareholder cooperates with a boycott and computes lost credits under the specifically attributable taxes and income method of Section 999(c)(2), it will lose its indirect credit to the extent that it is unable to show that the taxes paid by the foreign corporation are attributable to operations of the foreign corporation (1) that are not in or related to a boycotting country, (2) that, although related to a boycotting country, involved no cooperation with the boycott or (3) that are in a boycotting country but are clearly separate and identifiable from operations in connection with which there was boycott cooperation. Question A–19. Even if such shareholder does not itself cooperate with the boycott, it appears that indirect foreign tax credits may be denied the shareholder if the foreign corporation cooperates with the boycott. See General Explanation of the 1976 Act, at 283. The Guidelines do not deal with this situation, instead limiting themselves to a discussion of situations in which the U.S. shareholder is required to compute the loss of benefits as a result of its own operations by applying either the international boycott factor or the specifically attributable taxes and income method.

[¶ 14,090]

PROBLEMS

1. In planning an operation with respect to which boycott cooperation may be required, what is the significance of the availability of the method of specifically attributing taxes to specified operations as an alternative to the use of the international boycott factor? Would it normally be prudent to try to plan such an operation in a manner that enables the U.S. person to demonstrate that the operation is clearly separate and identifiable from all other operations of the person in boycotting countries, as well as to identify the taxes and income attributable to this operation?

2. Assume that the Government of Country X, an oil-producing state on the Persian Gulf, was requiring that purchasers of crude oil agree to the following stipulations in their crude oil purchase agreements:

(A) Buyer undertakes that crude oil covered by this Contract or any blend of it shall not be sold to or transported through Israel, and that Buyer shall at all times comply with all the laws, regulations and rules of Country X relating to the destination of crude oil purchased hereunder in force from time to time.

(B) Buyer undertakes that all vessels employed by it to transport the crude oil covered by this Contract shall not be from those listed in the blacklist issued by the Israel Boycott Bureau of the League of Arab States or be unacceptable to the authorities at the port of loading concerned.

(C) Buyer undertakes, whenever required, to submit to Seller or its representative within a reasonable time, the discharge certificate of each shipment duly endorsed by the Country X representative (or any other acceptable representative) in the country of destination.

If a U.S. company agreed to these provisions, would it constitute boycott cooperation?

3. After months of negotiation, certain U.S. oil companies agreed to the following revised terms in their agreements to purchase Country X crude oil:

(A) Buyer undertakes that crude oil covered by this Contract or any blend of it shall not be sold to or transported through Israel, and that the Buyer shall at all times comply with all the laws, regulations and rules of Country X relating to the destination of crude oil purchased hereunder in force from time to time.

(B) Buyer undertakes that all rules and regulations of the loading port authority shall apply to vessels employed by it to transport crude oil covered by this Contract. Such rules and regulations include, among other things, the unacceptability of vessels listed in the blacklist issued by the Israel Boycott Bureau of the League of Arab States.

(C) Buyer undertakes, whenever required, to submit to Seller or its representative within a reasonable time the discharge certificate of each shipment duly endorsed by the Country X representative (or any other acceptable representative) in the country of destination.

Is the distinction between an agreement to "comply" with the laws of a boycotting country, which by itself is boycott cooperation, and an agreement that such laws will "apply" to the performance of the contract, which by itself is not, a proper one? What policy considerations justify it? If an agreement provides, as does, in effect, paragraph (B) of the revised version of the Country X crude oil agreement, that the laws of the boycotting country, including the anti-Israel boycott rules, "shall apply" to the performance of the contract, will entering into the agreement constitute boycott cooperation? Suppose the contract provides that "the laws of the boycotting country will apply to the performance of the contract and the U.S. company will agree to indemnify the boycotting country against any loss it realizes as a result of violation by the U.S. company of the laws of the boycotting country." Would agreeing to this provision constitute boycott cooperation?

4. United States Oil Company ("USOC") agreed to refrain from doing business with Israel as a condition for establishing a petrochemical plant as a branch in Country X. If USOC were otherwise eligible under Sections 901 and 904 for total foreign tax credits of $500,000, of which $35,000 are attributable to the Country X tax on the taxable income from Country X, what effect would the penalty imposed under Section 999 have on these credits? Assume that USOC's foreign operations generated the following for the current tax year:

	Operations in Country X	*Total Foreign Operations*
Total		
Purchases	$ 500,000	$1,500,000
Sales	$1,250,000	$5,000,000
Payroll	$ 250,000	$1,500,000
Taxable Income	$ 100,000	$1,000,000

Would USOC benefit from electing to identify the specific taxes and income attributable to its operations in Country X? § 999(c)(2).

5. Galaxy, Ltd. ("Galaxy"), is a U.K. corporation that exports various products to different parts of the world. At one time it was very successful in several Arab countries in the Middle East. However, when all of the stock of Galaxy was acquired several years ago by Amfirst Inc., a U.S. corporation on the Arab blacklist because of its investments in Israel, Galaxy was blacklisted. Since that time Galaxy has done no business in those Arab states. It has never done any business in Israel.

All of the shares of Galaxy, which remains on the Arab blacklist, were acquired last year by Starstripe Co. ("Starstripe"), a U.S. corporation that has never been involved in business in any country in the Middle East and is not on the Arab blacklist. The executives of Galaxy, none of whom is a U.S. citizen or resident, would like to regain its business position in the Arab countries. They wish to take steps to have Galaxy removed from the blacklist and reestablish its prior profitable business. Executives of Starstripe are, however, very concerned about the potential impact of the international boycott provisions.

What advice would you give to Starstripe, Galaxy and their executives?

[¶ 14,095]

C. TREATMENT OF BRIBES, KICKBACKS OR SIMILAR PAYMENTS TO FOREIGN GOVERNMENT OFFICIALS OR AGENTS

The Code also contains three provisions dealing with certain bribes, kickbacks or similar payments made abroad. First, the definition of Subpart F income includes the sum of the amounts of any illegal bribes, kickbacks or other payments (within the meaning of Section 162(c)) paid by or on behalf of a controlled foreign corporation during the tax year directly or indirectly to an official, employee or agent in fact of a government. § 952(a)(4). Second, in determining the earnings and profits of a controlled foreign corporation under the Section 964 rules, the amount of any illegal bribe, kickback or other payment within the meaning of Section 162(c) may not decrease earnings and profits (or increase a deficit in earnings and profits). § 964(a). These provisions cover only payments that would be unlawful under the Foreign Corrupt Practices Act of 1977 if the payor were a U.S. person. §§ 952(a) and 964(a).[9] Third, illegal bribes, kickbacks or other payments made by or on behalf of a DISC are deemed distributions and subject to U.S. tax in the hands of the shareholders, thereby losing the benefit of deferral. § 995(b)(1)(F)(iii).

The Foreign Corrupt Practices Act distinguishes between true bribes and facilitating or expediting payments (sometimes referred to as "grease" payments) to secure the performance of "routine governmental action." Such payments, well known and widely practiced in some parts of the world, are not treated as bribes because the foreign officials take actions that should, in any event, be taken under applicable local law.

The United States has played a leading role in encouraging other major industrialized countries to criminalize, and deny tax deductions for, bribes, kickbacks and other similar payments to foreign officials. In response to strong U.S. pressure, the members of the Council of the Organization for Economic Cooperation and Development recommended on April 11, 1996, that OECD member states change their tax laws to deny tax deductions for bribes, kickbacks and like payments to foreign officials. A further significant step has been the Convention on Combating Bribery of Foreign Public Officials in International Business Transactions, negotiated under the auspices of the OECD, which went into effect on February 15, 1999. The Convention, which as of March, 2009 had been ratified by 38 countries, obligates parties to adopt legislation making it a crime to offer, promise or give a bribe to a foreign public official and providing for mutual legal assistance in combating such bribery. 37 I.L.M. 1 (1998).

On January 1, 1999, a Criminal Convention on Corruption was signed by member States of the Council of Europe and a number of other states, requiring parties to criminalize bribery of domestic and foreign public officials and money laundering of proceeds from corruption offenses. 38 I.L.M. 505 (1999). Previously, the Organization of American States had adopted an Inter–American Convention Against Corruption. 35 I.L.M. 724 (1996).

[¶ 14,100]

D. SOME POLICY CONSIDERATIONS

Both the income tax penalties with respect to participation in or cooperation with an international boycott and with respect to bribes, kickbacks or similar payments are rather stark examples of using the Code to achieve nontax objectives. Are tax penalties such as these an

9. Interestingly, the provisions of the Foreign Corrupt Practices Act may apply to payments to a foreign official for the purpose of tax evasion in a foreign country. See United States v. Kay, 359 F.3d 738 (5th Cir. 2004), which sets forth a detailed analysis of the legislative history of the Act in a case involving alleged bribes paid to Haitian officials to evade customs taxes.

effective means of discouraging the proscribed conduct? In these cases, the tax penalties are supplemental to the rules that directly prohibit and punish the conduct concerned. In the case of boycott cooperation the prohibitions are contained in regulations under the Export Administration Act of 1979 administered by the Commerce Department. 50 App. U.S.C.A. §§ 2402(5) and 2407 (1991). In the case of the Foreign Corrupt Practices Act of 1977, 15 U.S.C.A. §§ 78dd–1, 78dd–2 and 78ff(a) (West 2010), the criminal penalties for the prohibited conduct are enforced by the Justice Department.

There are several important differences between the elements of the two programs administered by the IRS and those administered by other agencies. One is that the jurisdictional reach of the tax provisions is greater. Situations that may invoke tax penalties may not violate the Export Administration Act and the Foreign Corrupt Practices Act because they involve non-U.S. persons.

Another difference is that enforcement action by the Commerce and Justice Departments is likely to be made public. By contrast, if a taxpayer chooses to do business in ways penalized only under either of the two tax regimes, the public is unlikely to become aware of it because of the confidentiality that attaches to tax returns and information furnished to the IRS in connection with tax audits and tax controversies settled administratively.

APPENDIX A

UNITED STATES MODEL INCOME TAX CONVENTION OF NOVEMBER 15, 2006

■ ■ ■

CONVENTION BETWEEN THE GOVERNMENT OF THE UNITED STATES OF AMERICA AND THE GOVERNMENT OF ______ FOR THE AVOIDANCE OF DOUBLE TAXATION AND THE PREVENTION OF FISCAL EVASION WITH RESPECT TO TAXES ON INCOME

The Government of the United States of America and the Government of ___, desiring to conclude a Convention for the avoidance of double taxation and the prevention of fiscal evasion with respect to taxes on income, have agreed as follows:

Article 1
GENERAL SCOPE

1. This Convention shall apply only to persons who are residents of one or both of the Contracting States, except as otherwise provided in the Convention.

2. This Convention shall not restrict in any manner any benefit now or hereafter accorded:

a) by the laws of either Contracting State; or

b) by any other agreement to which the Contracting States are parties.

3. a) Notwithstanding the provisions of subparagraph b) of paragraph 2 of this Article:

i) for purposes of paragraph 3 of Article XXII (Consultation) of the General Agreement on Trade in Services, the Contracting States agree that any question arising as to the interpretation or application of this Convention and, in particular, whether a taxation measure is within the scope of this Convention, shall be determined exclusively in accordance with the provisions of Article 25 (Mutual Agreement Procedure) of this Convention; and

ii) the provisions of Article XVII of the General Agreement on Trade in Services shall not apply to a taxation measure unless the competent authorities agree that the measure is not within the scope of Article 24 (Non–Discrimination) of this Convention.

b) For the purposes of this paragraph, a "measure" is a law, regulation, rule, procedure, decision, administrative action, or any similar provision or action.

4. Except to the extent provided in paragraph 5, this Convention shall not affect the taxation by a Contracting State of its residents (as determined under Article 4 (Resident)) and its citizens. Notwithstanding the other provisions of this Convention, a former citizen or former long-term resident of a Contracting State may, for the period of ten years following the loss of such status, be taxed in accordance with the laws of that Contracting State.

5. The provisions of paragraph 4 shall not affect:

a) the benefits conferred by a Contracting State under paragraph 2 of Article 9 (Associated Enterprises), paragraphs 1 b) , 2 , and 5 of Article 17 (Pensions, Social Security, Annuities, Alimony, and Child Support), paragraphs 1 and 4 of Article 18 (Pension Funds), and Articles 23 (Relief From Double Taxation), 24 (Non–Discrimination), and 25 (Mutual Agreement Procedure); and

b) the benefits conferred by a Contracting State under paragraph 2 of Article 18 (Pension Funds), Articles 19 (Government Service), 20 (Students and Trainees), and 27 (Members of Diplomatic Missions and Consular Posts), upon individuals who are neither citizens of, nor have been admitted for permanent residence in, that State.

6. An item of income, profit or gain derived through an entity that is fiscally transparent under the laws of either Contracting State shall be considered to be derived by a resident of a State to the extent that the item is treated for purposes of the taxation law of such Contracting State as the income, profit or gain of a resident.

Article 2

TAXES COVERED

1. This Convention shall apply to taxes on income imposed on behalf of a Contracting State irrespective of the manner in which they are levied.

2. There shall be regarded as taxes on income all taxes imposed on total income, or on elements of income, including taxes on gains from the alienation of property.

3. The existing taxes to which this Convention shall apply are:

a) in the case of ___:

b) in the case of the United States: the Federal income taxes imposed by the Internal Revenue Code (but excluding social security and unemployment taxes), and the Federal excise taxes imposed with respect to private foundations.

4. This Convention shall apply also to any identical or substantially similar taxes that are imposed after the date of signature of the Convention in addition to, or in place of, the existing taxes. The competent authorities of the Contracting States shall notify each other of any changes that have been made in their respective taxation or other laws that significantly affect their obligations under this Convention.

Article 3

GENERAL DEFINITIONS

1. a) For the purposes of this Convention, unless the context otherwise requires: a) the term "person" includes an individual, an estate, a trust, a partnership, a company, and any other body of persons;

b) the term "company" means any body corporate or any entity that is treated as a body corporate for tax purposes according to the laws of the state in which it is organized;

c) the terms "enterprise of a Contracting State" and "enterprise of the other Contracting State" mean respectively an enterprise carried on by a resident of a Contracting State, and an enterprise carried on by a resident of the other Contracting State; the terms also include an enterprise carried on by a resident of a Contracting State through an entity that is treated as fiscally transparent in that Contracting State;

d) the term "enterprise" applies to the carrying on of any business;

e) the term "business" includes the performance of professional services and of other activities of an independent character;

f) the term "international traffic" means any transport by a ship or aircraft, except when such transport is solely between places in a Contracting State;

g) the term "competent authority" means:

i) in ___, ___; and

ii) in the United States: the Secretary of the Treasury or his delegate;

h) the term "___" means ;

i) the term "United States" means the United States of America, and includes the states thereof and the District of Columbia; such term also includes the territorial sea thereof and the sea bed and subsoil of the submarine areas adjacent to that territorial sea, over which the United States exercises sovereign rights in accordance with international law; the term, however, does not include Puerto Rico, the Virgin Islands, Guam or any other United States possession or territory;

j) the term "national" of a Contracting State means:

i) any individual possessing the nationality or citizenship of that State; and

ii) any legal person, partnership or association deriving its status as such from the laws in force in that State;

k) the term "pension fund" means any person established in a Contracting State that is:

i) generally exempt from income taxation in that State; and

ii) operated principally either:

A) to administer or provide pension or retirement benefits; or

B) to earn income for the benefit of one or more persons described in clause A).

2. As regards the application of the Convention at any time by a Contracting State any term not defined therein shall, unless the context otherwise requires, or the competent authorities agree to a common meaning pursuant to the provisions of Article 25 (Mutual Agreement Procedure), have the meaning which it has at that time under the law of that State for the purposes of the taxes to which the Convention applies, any meaning under the applicable tax laws of that State prevailing over a meaning given to the term under other laws of that State.

Article 4

RESIDENT

1. For the purposes of this Convention, the term "resident of a Contracting State" means any person who, under the laws of that State, is liable to tax therein by reason of his domicile, residence, citizenship, place of management, place of incorporation, or any other criterion of a similar nature, and also includes that State and any political subdivision or local authority thereof. This term, however, does not include any person who is liable to tax in that State in respect only of income from sources in that State or of profits attributable to a permanent establishment in that State.

2. The term "resident of a Contracting State" includes:

a) a pension fund established in that State; and

b) an organization that is established and maintained in that State exclusively for religious, charitable, scientific, artistic, cultural, or educational purposes, notwithstanding that all or part of its income or gains may be exempt from tax under the domestic law of that State.

3. Where, by reason of the provisions of paragraph 1, an individual is a resident of both Contracting States, then his status shall be determined as follows:

a) he shall be deemed to be a resident only of the State in which he has a permanent home available to him; if he has a permanent home available to him in both States, he shall be deemed to be a resident only of the State with which his personal and economic relations are closer (center of vital interests);

b) if the State in which he has his center of vital interests cannot be determined, or if he does not have a permanent home available to him in either State, he shall be deemed to be a resident only of the State in which he has an habitual abode;

c) if he has an habitual abode in both States or in neither of them, he shall be deemed to be a resident only of the State of which he is a national;

d) if he is a national of both States or of neither of them, the competent authorities of the Contracting States shall endeavor to settle the question by mutual agreement.

4. Where by reason of the provisions of paragraph 1 a company is a resident of both Contracting States, then if it is created or organized under the laws of one of the Contracting States or a political subdivision thereof, but not under the laws of the other Contracting State or a political subdivision thereof, such company shall be deemed to be a resident of the first-mentioned Contracting State. In all other cases involving dual resident companies, the competent authorities of the Contracting States shall endeavor to determine the mode of application of the Convention to such company. If the competent authorities do not reach such an agreement, that company will not be treated as a resident of either Contracting State for purposes of its claiming any benefits provided by the Convention.

5. Where by reason of the provisions of paragraphs 1 and 2 of this Article a person other than an individual or a company is a resident of both Contracting States, the competent authorities of the Contracting States shall by mutual agreement endeavor to determine the mode of application of this Convention to that person.

Article 5

PERMANENT ESTABLISHMENT

1. For the purposes of this Convention, the term "permanent establishment" means a fixed place of business through which the business of an enterprise is wholly or partly carried on.

2. The term "permanent establishment" includes especially:

a) a place of management;

b) a branch;

c) an office;

d) a factory;

e) a workshop; and

f) a mine, an oil or gas well, a quarry, or any other place of extraction of natural resources.

3. A building site or construction or installation project, or an installation or drilling rig or ship used for the exploration of natural resources, constitutes a permanent establishment only if it lasts, or the exploration activity continues for more than twelve months.

4. Notwithstanding the preceding provisions of this Article, the term "permanent establishment" shall be deemed not to include:

a) the use of facilities solely for the purpose of storage, display or delivery of goods or merchandise belonging to the enterprise;

b) the maintenance of a stock of goods or merchandise belonging to the enterprise solely for the purpose of storage, display or delivery;

c) the maintenance of a stock of goods or merchandise belonging to the enterprise solely for the purpose of processing by another enterprise;

d) the maintenance of a fixed place of business solely for the purpose of purchasing goods or merchandise, or of collecting information, for the enterprise;

e) the maintenance of a fixed place of business solely for the purpose of carrying on, for the enterprise, any other activity of a preparatory or auxiliary character;

f) the maintenance of a fixed place of business solely for any combination of the activities mentioned in subparagraphs a) through e), provided that the overall activity of the fixed place of business resulting from this combination is of a preparatory or auxiliary character.

5. Notwithstanding the provisions of paragraphs 1 and 2, where a person—other than an agent of an independent status to whom paragraph 6 applies—is acting on behalf of an enterprise and has and habitually exercises in a Contracting State an authority to conclude contracts that are binding on the enterprise, that enterprise shall be deemed to have a permanent establishment in that State in respect of any activities that the person undertakes for the enterprise, unless the activities of such person are limited to those mentioned in paragraph 4 that, if exercised through a fixed place of business, would not make this fixed place of business a permanent establishment under the provisions of that paragraph.

6. An enterprise shall not be deemed to have a permanent establishment in a Contracting State merely because it carries on business in that State through a broker, general commission agent, or any other agent of

an independent status, provided that such persons are acting in the ordinary course of their business as independent agents.

7. The fact that a company that is a resident of a Contracting State controls or is controlled by a company that is a resident of the other Contracting State, or that carries on business in that other State (whether through a permanent establishment or otherwise), shall not be taken into account in determining whether either company has a permanent establishment in that other State.

Article 6

INCOME FROM REAL PROPERTY

1. Income derived by a resident of a Contracting State from real property, including income from agriculture or forestry, situated in the other Contracting State may be taxed in that other State.

2. The term "real property" shall have the meaning which it has under the law of the Contracting State in which the property in question is situated. The term shall in any case include property accessory to real property (including livestock and equipment used in agriculture and forestry), rights to which the provisions of general law respecting landed property apply, usufruct of real property and rights to variable or fixed payments as consideration for the working of, or the right to work, mineral deposits, sources and other natural resources. Ships and aircraft shall not be regarded as real property.

3. The provisions of paragraph 1 shall apply to income derived from the direct use, letting, or use in any other form of real property.

4. The provisions of paragraphs 1 and 3 shall also apply to the income from real property of an enterprise.

5. A resident of a Contracting State who is liable to tax in the other Contracting State on income from real property situated in the other Contracting State may elect for any taxable year to compute the tax on such income on a net basis as if such income were business profits attributable to a permanent establishment in such other State. Any such election shall be binding for the taxable year of the election and all subsequent taxable years unless the competent authority of the Contracting State in which the property is situated agrees to terminate the election.

Article 7

BUSINESS PROFITS

1. The profits of an enterprise of a Contracting State shall be taxable only in that State unless the enterprise carries on business in the other Contracting State through a permanent establishment situated therein. If the enterprise carries on business as aforesaid, the profits of the enter-

prise may be taxed in the other State but only so much of them as are attributable to that permanent establishment.

2. Subject to the provisions of paragraph 3, where an enterprise of a Contracting State carries on business in the other Contracting State through a permanent establishment situated therein, there shall in each Contracting State be attributed to that permanent establishment the profits that it might be expected to make if it were a distinct and independent enterprise engaged in the same or similar activities under the same or similar conditions. For this purpose, the profits to be attributed to the permanent establishment shall include only the profits derived from the assets used, risks assumed and activities performed by the permanent establishment.

3. In determining the profits of a permanent establishment, there shall be allowed as deductions expenses that are incurred for the purposes of the permanent establishment, including executive and general administrative expenses so incurred, whether in the State in which the permanent establishment is situated or elsewhere.*

4. No profits shall be attributed to a permanent establishment by reason of the mere purchase by that permanent establishment of goods or merchandise for the enterprise.

---

* Protocol or Notes should include the following language: It is understood that the business profits to be attributed to a permanent establishment shall include only the profits derived from the assets used, risks assumed and activities performed by the permanent establishment. The principles of the OECD Transfer Pricing Guidelines will apply for purposes of determining the profits attributable to a permanent establishment, taking into account the different economic and legal circumstances of a single entity. Accordingly, any of the methods described therein as acceptable methods for determining an arm's length result may be used to determine the income of a permanent establishment so long as those methods are applied in accordance with the Guidelines. In particular, in determining the amount of attributable profits, the permanent establishment shall be treated as having the same amount of capital that it would need to support its activities if it were a distinct and separate enterprise engaged in the same or similar activities. With respect to financial institutions other than insurance companies, a Contracting State may determine the amount of capital to be attributed to a permanent establishment by allocating the institution's total equity between its various offices on the basis of the proportion of the financial institution's risk-weighted assets attributable to each of them. In the case of an insurance company, there shall be attributed to a permanent establishment not only premiums earned through the permanent establishment, but that portion of the insurance company's overall investment income from reserves and surplus that supports the risks assumed by the permanent establishment.

5. For the purposes of the preceding paragraphs, the profits to be attributed to the permanent establishment shall be determined by the same method year by year unless there is good and sufficient reason to the contrary.

6. Where profits include items of income that are dealt with separately in other Articles of the Convention, then the provisions of those Articles shall not be affected by the provisions of this Article.

7. In applying this Article, paragraph 6 of Article 10 (Dividends), paragraph 4 of Article 11 (Interest), paragraph 3 of Article 12 (Royalties), paragraph 3 of Article 13 (Gains) and paragraph 2 of Article 21 (Other Income), any income or gain attributable to a permanent establishment during its existence is taxable in the Contracting State where such permanent establishment is situated even if the payments are deferred until such permanent establishment has ceased to exist.

Article 8

SHIPPING AND AIR TRANSPORT

1. Profits of an enterprise of a Contracting State from the operation of ships or aircraft in international traffic shall be taxable only in that State.

2. For purposes of this Article, profits from the operation of ships or aircraft include, but are not limited to:

a) profits from the rental of ships or aircraft on a full (time or voyage) basis;

b) profits from the rental on a bareboat basis of ships or aircraft if the rental income is incidental to profits from the operation of ships or aircraft in international traffic; and

c) profits from the rental on a bareboat basis of ships or aircraft if such ships or aircraft are operated in international traffic by the lessee.

Profits derived by an enterprise from the inland transport of property or passengers within either Contracting State shall be treated as profits from the operation of ships or aircraft in international traffic if such transport is undertaken as part of international traffic.

3. Profits of an enterprise of a Contracting State from the use, maintenance, or rental of containers (including trailers, barges, and related equipment for the transport of containers) shall be taxable only in that Contracting State, except to the extent that those containers are used for transport solely between places within the other Contracting State.

4. The provisions of paragraphs 1 and 3 shall also apply to profits from participation in a pool, a joint business, or an international operating agency.

Article 9

ASSOCIATED ENTERPRISES

1. Where:

a) an enterprise of a Contracting State participates directly or indirectly in the management, control or capital of an enterprise of the other Contracting State; or

b) the same persons participate directly or indirectly in the management, control, or capital of an enterprise of a Contracting State and an enterprise of the other Contracting State, and in either case conditions are made or imposed between the two enterprises in their commercial or financial relations that differ from those that would be made between independent enterprises, then any profits that, but for those conditions, would have accrued to one of the enterprises, but by reason of those conditions have not so accrued, may be included in the profits of that enterprise and taxed accordingly.

2. Where a Contracting State includes in the profits of an enterprise of that State, and taxes accordingly, profits on which an enterprise of the other Contracting State has been charged to tax in that other State, and the other Contracting State agrees that the profits so included are profits that would have accrued to the enterprise of the first-mentioned State if the conditions made between the two enterprises had been those that would have been made between independent enterprises, then that other State shall make an appropriate adjustment to the amount of the tax charged therein on those profits. In determining such adjustment, due regard shall be had to the other provisions of this Convention and the competent authorities of the Contracting States shall if necessary consult each other.

Article 10

DIVIDENDS

1. Dividends paid by a company that is a resident of a Contracting State to a resident of the other Contracting State may be taxed in that other State.

2. However, such dividends may also be taxed in the Contracting State of which the company paying the dividends is a resident and according to the laws of that State, but if the dividends are beneficially owned by a resident of the other Contracting State, except as otherwise provided, the tax so charged shall not exceed:

a) 5 percent of the gross amount of the dividends if the beneficial owner is a company that owns directly at least 10 percent of the voting stock of the company paying the dividends;

b) 15 percent of the gross amount of the dividends in all other cases.

This paragraph shall not affect the taxation of the company in respect of the profits out of which the dividends are paid.

3. Notwithstanding paragraph 2, dividends shall not be taxed in the Contracting State of which the company paying the dividends is a resident if:

a) the beneficial owner of the dividends is a pension fund that is a resident of the other Contracting State; and

b) such dividends are not derived from the carrying on of a trade or business by the pension fund or through an associated enterprise.

4. a) Subparagraph a) of paragraph 2 shall not apply in the case of dividends paid by a U.S. Regulated Investment Company (RIC) or a U.S. Real Estate Investment Trust (REIT). In the case of dividends paid by a RIC, subparagraph b) of paragraph 2 and paragraph 3 shall apply. In the case of dividends paid by a REIT, subparagraph b) of paragraph 2 and paragraph 3 shall apply only if:

i) the beneficial owner of the dividends is an individual or pension fund, in either case holding an interest of not more than 10 percent in the REIT;

ii) the dividends are paid with respect to a class of stock that is publicly traded and the beneficial owner of the dividends is a person holding an interest of not more than 5 percent of any class of the REIT's stock; or

iii) the beneficial owner of the dividends is a person holding an interest of not more than 10 percent in the REIT and the REIT is diversified.

b) For purposes of this paragraph, a REIT shall be "diversified" if the value of no single interest in real property exceeds 10 percent of its total interests in real property. For the purposes of this rule, foreclosure property shall not be considered an interest in real property. Where a REIT holds an interest in a partnership, it shall be treated as owning directly a proportion of the partnership's interests in real property corresponding to its interest in the partnership.

5. For purposes of this Article, the term "dividends" means income from shares or other rights, not being debt-claims, participating in profits, as well as income that is subjected to the same taxation treatment as income from shares under the laws of the State of which the payer is a resident.

6. The provisions of paragraphs 2 through 4 shall not apply if the beneficial owner of the dividends, being a resident of a Contracting State, carries on business in the other Contracting State, of which the payer is a resident, through a permanent establishment situated therein, and the holding in respect of which the dividends are paid is effectively connected

with such permanent establishment. In such case the provisions of Article 7 (Business Profits) shall apply.

7. A Contracting State may not impose any tax on dividends paid by a resident of the other State, except insofar as the dividends are paid to a resident of the first-mentioned State or the dividends are attributable to a permanent establishment, nor may it impose tax on a corporation's undistributed profits, except as provided in paragraph 8 , even if the dividends paid or the undistributed profits consist wholly or partly of profits or income arising in that State.

8. a) A company that is a resident of one of the States and that has a permanent establishment in the other State or that is subject to tax in the other State on a net basis on its income that may be taxed in the other State under Article 6 (Income from Real Property) or under paragraph 1 of Article 13 (Gains) may be subject in that other State to a tax in addition to the tax allowable under the other provisions of this Convention.

b) Such tax, however, may be imposed:

i) on only the portion of the business profits of the company attributable to the permanent establishment and the portion of the income referred to in subparagraph a) that is subject to tax under Article 6 or under paragraph 1 of Article 13 that, in the case of the United States, represents the dividend equivalent amount of such profits or income and, in the case of ___, is an amount that is analogous to the dividend equivalent amount; and

ii) at a rate not in excess of the rate specified in paragraph 2 a) .

Article 11

INTEREST

1. Interest arising in a Contracting State and beneficially owned by a resident of the other Contracting State may be taxed only in that other State.

2. Notwithstanding the provisions of paragraph 1:

a) interest arising in ___ that is determined with reference to receipts, sales, income, profits or other cash flow of the debtor or a related person, to any change in the value of any property of the debtor or a related person or to any dividend, partnership distribution or similar payment made by the debtor or a related person may be taxed in the Contracting State in which it arises, and according to the laws of that State, but if the beneficial owner is a resident of the other Contracting State, the interest may be taxed at a rate not exceeding 15 percent of the gross amount of the interest;

b) interest arising in the United States that is contingent interest of a type that does not qualify as portfolio interest under United States law may be taxed by the United States but, if the beneficial owner of the interest is a resident of ___, the interest may be taxed at a rate not exceeding 15 percent of the gross amount of the interest; and

c) interest that is an excess inclusion with respect to a residual interest in a real estate mortgage investment conduit may be taxed by each State in accordance with its domestic law.

3. The term "interest" as used in this Article means income from debt-claims of every kind, whether or not secured by mortgage, and whether or not carrying a right to participate in the debtor's profits, and in particular, income from government securities and income from bonds or debentures, including premiums or prizes attaching to such securities, bonds or debentures, and all other income that is subjected to the same taxation treatment as income from money lent by the taxation law of the Contracting State in which the income arises. Income dealt with in Article 10 (Dividends) and penalty charges for late payment shall not be regarded as interest for the purposes of this Convention.

4. The provisions of paragraphs 1 and 2 shall not apply if the beneficial owner of the interest, being a resident of a Contracting State, carries on business in the other Contracting State, in which the interest arises, through a permanent establishment situated therein, and the debt-claim in respect of which the interest is paid is effectively connected with such permanent establishment. In such case the provisions of Article 7 (Business Profits) shall apply.

5. Where, by reason of a special relationship between the payer and the beneficial owner or between both of them and some other person, the amount of the interest, having regard to the debt-claim for which it is paid, exceeds the amount which would have been agreed upon by the payer and the beneficial owner in the absence of such relationship, the provisions of this Article shall apply only to the last-mentioned amount. In such case the excess part of the payments shall remain taxable according to the laws of each State, due regard being had to the other provisions of this Convention.

Article 12

ROYALTIES

1. Royalties arising in a Contracting State and beneficially owned by a resident of the other Contracting State may be taxed only in that other State.

2. The term "royalties" as used in this Article means:

a) payments of any kind received as a consideration for the use of, or the right to use, any copyright of literary, artistic, scientific or other work (including cinematographic films), any patent, trademark, design or model, plan, secret formula or process, or for information concerning industrial, commercial or scientific experience; and

b) gain derived from the alienation of any property described in subparagraph a), to the extent that such gain is contingent on the productivity, use, or disposition of the property.

3. The provisions of paragraph 1 shall not apply if the beneficial owner of the royalties, being a resident of a Contracting State, carries on business in the other Contracting State through a permanent establishment situated therein and the right or property in respect of which the royalties are paid is effectively connected with such permanent establishment. In such case the provisions of Article 7 (Business Profits) shall apply.

4. Where, by reason of a special relationship between the payer and the beneficial owner or between both of them and some other person, the amount of the royalties, having regard to the use, right, or information for which they are paid, exceeds the amount which would have been agreed upon by the payer and the beneficial owner in the absence of such relationship, the provisions of this Article shall apply only to the last-mentioned amount. In such case the excess part of the payments shall remain taxable according to the laws of each Contracting State, due regard being had to the other provisions of the Convention.

Article 13

GAINS

1. Gains derived by a resident of a Contracting State that are attributable to the alienation of real property situated in the other Contracting State may be taxed in that other State.

2. For the purposes of this Article the term "real property situated in the other Contracting State" shall include:

a) real property referred to in Article 6 (Income from Real Property);

b) where that other State is the United States, a United States real property interest; and

c) where that other State is ___,

i) shares, including rights to acquire shares, other than shares in which there is regular trading on a stock exchange, deriving their value or the greater part of their value directly or indirectly from real property referred to in subparagraph a) of this paragraph situated in ___; and

ii) an interest in a partnership or trust to the extent that the assets of the partnership or trust consist of real property situated in ___, or of shares referred to in clause i) of this sub-paragraph.

3. Gains from the alienation of movable property forming part of the business property of a permanent establishment that an enterprise of a Contracting State has in the other Contracting State, including such gains

from the alienation of such a permanent establishment (alone or with the whole enterprise), may be taxed in that other State.

4. Gains derived by an enterprise of a Contracting State from the alienation of ships or aircraft operated or used in international traffic or personal property pertaining to the operation or use of such ships or aircraft shall be taxable only in that State.

5. Gains derived by an enterprise of a Contracting State from the alienation of containers (including trailers, barges and related equipment for the transport of containers) used for the transport of goods or merchandise shall be taxable only in that State, unless those containers are used for transport solely between places within the other Contracting State.

6. Gains from the alienation of any property other than property referred to in paragraphs 1 through 5 shall be taxable only in the Contracting State of which the alienator is a resident.

Article 14

INCOME FROM EMPLOYMENT

1. Subject to the provisions of Articles 15 (Directors' Fees), 17 (Pensions, Social Security, Annuities, Alimony, and Child Support) and 19 (Government Service), salaries, wages, and other similar remuneration derived by a resident of a Contracting State in respect of an employment shall be taxable only in that State unless the employment is exercised in the other Contracting State. If the employment is so exercised, such remuneration as is derived therefrom may be taxed in that other State.

2. Notwithstanding the provisions of paragraph 1, remuneration derived by a resident of a Contracting State in respect of an employment exercised in the other Contracting State shall be taxable only in the first-mentioned State if:

a) the recipient is present in the other State for a period or periods not exceeding in the aggregate 183 days in any twelve month period commencing or ending in the taxable year concerned;

b) the remuneration is paid by, or on behalf of, an employer who is not a resident of the other State; and

c) the remuneration is not borne by a permanent establishment which the employer has in the other State.

3. Notwithstanding the preceding provisions of this Article, remuneration described in paragraph 1 that is derived by a resident of a Contracting State in respect of an employment as a member of the regular complement of a ship or aircraft operated in international traffic shall be taxable only in that State.

Article 15

DIRECTORS' FEES

Directors' fees and other compensation derived by a resident of a Contracting State for services rendered in the other Contracting State in his capacity as a member of the board of directors of a company that is a resident of the other Contracting State may be taxed in that other Contracting State.

Article 16

ENTERTAINERS AND SPORTSMEN

1. Income derived by a resident of a Contracting State as an entertainer, such as a theater, motion picture, radio, or television artiste, or a musician, or as a sportsman, from his personal activities as such exercised in the other Contracting State, which income would be exempt from tax in that other Contracting State under the provisions of Articles 7 (Business Profits) and 14 (Income from Employment) may be taxed in that other State, except where the amount of the gross receipts derived by such entertainer or sportsman, including expenses reimbursed to him or borne on his behalf, from such activities does not exceed twenty thousand United States dollars ($20,000) or its equivalent in ___ for the taxable year of the payment.

2. Where income in respect of activities exercised by an entertainer or a sportsman in his capacity as such accrues not to the entertainer or sportsman himself but to another person, that income, notwithstanding the provisions of Article 7 (Business Profits) or 14 (Income from Employment), may be taxed in the Contracting State in which the activities of the entertainer or sportsman are exercised unless the contract pursuant to which the personal activities are performed allows that other person to designate the individual who is to perform the personal activities.

Article 17

PENSIONS, SOCIAL SECURITY, ANNUITIES, ALIMONY, AND CHILD SUPPORT

1. a) Pensions and other similar remuneration beneficially owned by a resident of a Contracting State shall be taxable only in that State.

b) Notwithstanding subparagraph a), the amount of any such pension or remuneration arising in a Contracting State that, when received, would be exempt from taxation in that State if the beneficial owner were a resident thereof shall be exempt from taxation in the Contracting State of which the beneficial owner is a resident.

2. Notwithstanding the provisions of paragraph 1, payments made by a Contracting State under provisions of the social security or similar legislation of that State to a resident of the other Contracting State or to a

citizen of the United States shall be taxable only in the first-mentioned State.

3. Annuities derived and beneficially owned by an individual resident of a Contracting State shall be taxable only in that State. The term "annuities" as used in this paragraph means a stated sum paid periodically at stated times during a specified number of years, or for life, under an obligation to make the payments in return for adequate and full consideration (other than services rendered).

4. Alimony paid by a resident of a Contracting State to a resident of the other Contracting State shall be taxable only in that other State. The term "alimony" as used in this paragraph means periodic payments made pursuant to a written separation agreement or a decree of divorce, separate maintenance, or compulsory support, which payments are taxable to the recipient under the laws of the State of which he is a resident.

5. Periodic payments, not dealt with in paragraph 4, for the support of a child made pursuant to a written separation agreement or a decree of divorce, separate maintenance, or compulsory support, paid by a resident of a Contracting State to a resident of the other Contracting State, shall be exempt from tax in both Contracting States.

Article 18

PENSION FUNDS

1. Where an individual who is a resident of one of the States is a member or beneficiary of, or participant in, a pension fund that is a resident of the other State, income earned by the pension fund may be taxed as income of that individual only when, and, subject to the provisions of paragraph 1 of Article 17 (Pensions, Social Security, Annuities, Alimony and Child Support), to the extent that, it is paid to, or for the benefit of, that individual from the pension fund (and not transferred to another pension fund in that other State).

2. Where an individual who is a member or beneficiary of, or participant in, a pension fund that is a resident of one of the States exercises an employment or self-employment in the other State:

a) contributions paid by or on behalf of that individual to the pension fund during the period that he exercises an employment or self-employment in the other State shall be deductible (or excludible) in computing his taxable income in that other State; and

b) any benefits accrued under the pension fund, or contributions made to the pension fund by or on behalf of the individual's employer, during that period shall not be treated as part of the employee's taxable income and any such contributions shall be allowed as a deduction in computing the taxable income of his employer in that other State.

The relief available under this paragraph shall not exceed the relief that would be allowed by the other State to residents of that State for contributions to, or benefits accrued under, a pension plan established in that State.

3. The provisions of paragraph 2 of this Article shall not apply unless:

a) contributions by or on behalf of the individual, or by or on behalf of the individual's employer, to the pension fund (or to another similar pension fund for which the first-mentioned pension fund was substituted) were made before the individual began to exercise an employment or self-employment in the other State; and

b) the competent authority of the other State has agreed that the pension fund generally corresponds to a pension fund established in that other State.

4. a) Where a citizen of the United States who is a resident of ___ exercises an employment in ___ the income from which is taxable in ___, the contribution is borne by an employer who is a resident of ___ or by a permanent establishment situated in ___, and the individual is a member or beneficiary of, or participant in, a pension plan established in ___,

i) contributions paid by or on behalf of that individual to the pension fund during the period that he exercises the employment in ___, and that are attributable to the employment, shall be deductible (or excludible) in computing his taxable income in the United States; and

ii) any benefits accrued under the pension fund, or contributions made to the pension fund by or on behalf of the individual's employer, during that period, and that are attributable to the employment, shall not be treated as part of the employee's taxable income in computing his taxable income in the United States.

b) The relief available under this paragraph shall not exceed the lesser of:

i) the relief that would be allowed by the United States to its residents for contributions to, or benefits accrued under, a generally corresponding pension plan established in the United States; and

ii) the amount of contributions or benefits that qualify for tax relief in. ___

c) For purposes of determining an individual's eligibility to participate in and receive tax benefits with respect to a pension plan established in the United States, contributions made to, or benefits accrued under, a pension plan established in ___ shall be treated as contributions or benefits under a generally corresponding pension plan established in the United States to the extent relief is available to the individual under this paragraph.

d) This paragraph shall not apply unless the competent authority of the United States has agreed that the pension plan generally corresponds to a pension plan established in the United States.

Article 19

GOVERNMENT SERVICE

1. Notwithstanding the provisions of Articles 14 (Income from Employment), 15 (Directors' Fees), 16 (Entertainers and Sportsmen) and 20 (Students and Trainees):

a) Salaries, wages and other remuneration, other than a pension, paid to an individual in respect of services rendered to a Contracting State or a political subdivision or local authority thereof shall, subject to the provisions of subparagraph b), be taxable only in that State;

b) such remuneration, however, shall be taxable only in the other Contracting State if the services are rendered in that State and the individual is a resident of that State who:

i) is a national of that State; or

ii) did not become a resident of that State solely for the purpose of rendering the services.

2. Notwithstanding the provisions of paragraph 1 of Article 17 (Pensions, Social Security, Annuities, Alimony, and Child Support):

a) any pension and other similar remuneration paid by, or out of funds created by, a Contracting State or a political subdivision or a local authority thereof to an individual in respect of services rendered to that State or subdivision or authority (other than a payment to which paragraph 2 of Article 17 applies) shall, subject to the provisions of subparagraph b) , be taxable only in that State;

b) such pension, however, shall be taxable only in the other Contracting State if the individual is a resident of, and a national of, that State.

3. The provisions of Articles 14 (Income from Employment), 15 (Directors' Fees), 16 (Entertainers and Sportsmen) and 17 (Pensions, Social Security, Annuities, Alimony, and Child Support) shall apply to salaries, wages and other remuneration, and to pensions, in respect of services rendered in connection with a business carried on by a Contracting State or a political subdivision or a local authority thereof.

Article 20

STUDENTS AND TRAINEES

1. Payments, other than compensation for personal services, received by a student or business trainee who is, or was immediately before visiting a Contracting State, a resident of the other Contracting State, and who is present in the first-mentioned State for the purpose of his full-time education or for his full-time training, shall not be taxed in that State,

provided that such payments arise outside that State, and are for the purpose of his maintenance, education or training. The exemption from tax provided by this paragraph shall apply to a business trainee only for a period of time not exceeding one year from the date the business trainee first arrives in the first-mentioned Contracting State for the purpose of training.

2. A student or business trainee within the meaning of paragraph 1 shall be exempt from tax by the Contracting State in which the individual is temporarily present with respect to income from personal services in an aggregate amount equal to $9,000 or its equivalent in [other currency] annually. The competent authorities shall, every five years, adjust the amount provided in this subparagraph to the extent necessary to take into account changes in the U.S. personal exemption and the standard deduction.

3. For purposes of this Article, a business trainee is an individual:

a) who is temporarily in a Contracting State for the purpose of securing training required to qualify the individual to practice a profession or professional specialty; or

b) who is temporarily in a Contracting State as an employee of, or under contract with, a resident of the other Contracting State, for the primary purpose of acquiring technical, professional, or business experience from a person other than that resident of the other Contracting State (or a person related to such resident of the other Contracting State).

Article 21

OTHER INCOME

1. Items of income beneficially owned by a resident of a Contracting State, wherever arising, not dealt with in the foregoing Articles of this Convention shall be taxable only in that State.

2. The provisions of paragraph 1 shall not apply to income, other than income from real property as defined in paragraph 2 of Article 6 (Income from Real Property), if the beneficial owner of the income, being a resident of a Contracting State, carries on business in the other Contracting State through a permanent establishment situated therein and the income is attributable to such permanent establishment. In such case the provisions of Article 7 (Business Profits) shall apply.

Article 22

LIMITATION ON BENEFITS

1. Except as otherwise provided in this Article, a resident of a Contracting State shall not be entitled to the benefits of this Convention otherwise accorded to residents of a Contracting State unless such resident is a "qualified person" as defined in paragraph 2.

2. A resident of a Contracting State shall be a qualified person for a taxable year if the resident is:

a) an individual;

b) a Contracting State, or a political subdivision or local authority thereof;

c) a company, if:

i) the principal class of its shares (and any disproportionate class of shares) is regularly traded on one or more recognized stock exchanges, and either:

A) its principal class of shares is primarily traded on one or more recognized stock exchanges located in the Contracting State of which the company is a resident; or

B) the company's primary place of management and control is in the Contracting State of which it is a resident; or

ii) at least 50 percent of the aggregate vote and value of the shares (and at least 50 percent of any disproportionate class of shares) in the company is owned directly or indirectly by five or fewer companies entitled to benefits under clause i) of this subparagraph, provided that, in the case of indirect ownership, each intermediate owner is a resident of either Contracting State;

d) a person described in paragraph 2 of Article 4 of this Convention, provided that, in the case of a person described in subparagraph a) of that paragraph, more than 50 percent of the person's beneficiaries, members or participants are individuals resident in either Contracting State; or

e) a person other than an individual, if:

i) on at least half the days of the taxable year, persons who are residents of that Contracting State and that are entitled to the benefits of this Convention under subparagraph a), subparagraph b), clause i) of subparagraph c), or subparagraph d) of this paragraph own, directly or indirectly, shares or other beneficial interests representing at least 50 percent of the aggregate voting power and value (and at least 50 percent of any disproportionate class of shares) of the person, provided that, in the case of indirect ownership, each intermediate owner is a resident of that Contracting State, and

ii) less than 50 percent of the person's gross income for the taxable year, as determined in the person's State of residence, is paid or accrued, directly or indirectly, to persons who are not residents of either Contracting State entitled to the benefits of this Convention under subparagraph a), subparagraph b), clause i) of subparagraph c), or subparagraph d) of this paragraph in the form of payments that are deductible for purposes of the taxes covered by this Convention in the person's State of residence (but not including arm's length payments in the ordinary course of business for services or tangible property).

3. a) A resident of a Contracting State will be entitled to benefits of the Convention with respect to an item of income derived from the other State, regardless of whether the resident is a qualified person, if the resident is engaged in the active conduct of a trade or business in the first-mentioned State (other than the business of making or managing investments for the resident's own account, unless these activities are banking, insurance or securities activities carried on by a bank, insurance company or registered securities dealer), and the income derived from the other Contracting State is derived in connection with, or is incidental to, that trade or business.

b) If a resident of a Contracting State derives an item of income from a trade or business activity conducted by that resident in the other Contracting State, or derives an item of income arising in the other Contracting State from a related person, the conditions described in subparagraph a) shall be considered to be satisfied with respect to such item only if the trade or business activity carried on by the resident in the first-mentioned Contracting State is substantial in relation to the trade or business activity carried on by the resident or such person in the other Contracting State. Whether a trade or business activity is substantial for the purposes of this paragraph will be determined based on all the facts and circumstances.

c) For purposes of applying this paragraph, activities conducted by persons connected to a person shall be deemed to be conducted by such person. A person shall be connected to another if one possesses at least 50 percent of the beneficial interest in the other (or, in the case of a company, at least 50 percent of the aggregate vote and value of the company's shares or of the beneficial equity interest in the company) or another person possesses at least 50 percent of the beneficial interest (or, in the case of a company, at least 50 percent of the aggregate vote and value of the company's shares or of the beneficial equity interest in the company) in each person. In any case, a person shall be considered to be connected to another if, based on all the relevant facts and circumstances, one has control of the other or both are under the control of the same person or persons.

4. If a resident of a Contracting State is neither a qualified person pursuant to the provisions of paragraph 2 nor entitled to benefits with respect to an item of income under paragraph 3 of this Article the competent authority of the other Contracting State may, nevertheless, grant the benefits of this Convention, or benefits with respect to a specific item of income, if it determines that the establishment, acquisition or maintenance of such person and the conduct of its operations did not have as one of its principal purposes the obtaining of benefits under this Convention.

5. For purposes of this Article:

a) the term "recognized stock exchange" means:

i) the NASDAQ System owned by the National Association of Securities Dealers, Inc. and any stock exchange registered with the U.S. Securities and Exchange Commission as a national securities exchange under the U.S. Securities Exchange Act of 1934;

ii) stock exchanges of ___; and

iii) any other stock exchange agreed upon by the competent authorities;

b) the term "principal class of shares" means the ordinary or common shares of the company, provided that such class of shares represents the majority of the voting power and value of the company. If no single class of ordinary or common shares represents the majority of the aggregate voting power and value of the company, the "principal class of shares" are those classes that in the aggregate represent a majority of the aggregate voting power and value of the company

c) the term "disproportionate class of shares" means any class of shares of a company resident in one of the Contracting States that entitles the shareholder to disproportionately higher participation, through dividends, redemption payments or otherwise, in the earnings generated in the other State by particular assets or activities of the company; and

d) a company's "primary place of management and control" will be in the Contracting State of which it is a resident only if executive officers and senior management employees exercise day-to-day responsibility for more of the strategic, financial and operational policy decision making for the company (including its direct and indirect subsidiaries) in that State than in any other state and the staff of such persons conduct more of the day-to-day activities necessary for preparing and making those decisions in that State than in any other state.

Article 23

RELIEF FROM DOUBLE TAXATION

1. In the case of ___, double taxation will be relieved as follows:

2. In accordance with the provisions and subject to the limitations of the law of the United States (as it may be amended from time to time without changing the general principle hereof), the United States shall allow to a resident or citizen of the United States as a credit against the United States tax on income applicable to residents and citizens:

a) the income tax paid or accrued to ___ by or on behalf of such resident or citizen; and

b) in the case of a United States company owning at least 10 percent of the voting stock of a company that is a resident of ___ and from which the United States company receives dividends, the income tax paid or accrued to ___ by or on behalf of the payer with respect to the profits out of which the dividends are paid.

For the purposes of this paragraph, the taxes referred to in paragraphs 3 a) and 4 of Article 2 (Taxes Covered) shall be considered income taxes.

3. For the purposes of applying paragraph 2 of this Article, an item of gross income, as determined under the laws of the United States, derived by a resident of the United States that, under this Convention, may be taxed in ___ shall be deemed to be income from sources in. ___

4. Where a United States citizen is a resident of ___:

a) with respect to items of income that under the provisions of this Convention are exempt from United States tax or that are subject to a reduced rate of United States tax when derived by a resident of ___ who is not a United States citizen, ___ shall allow as a credit against ___ tax, only the tax paid, if any, that the United States may impose under the provisions of this Convention, other than taxes that may be imposed solely by reason of citizenship under the saving clause of paragraph 4 of Article 1 (General Scope);

b) for purposes of applying paragraph 2 to compute United States tax on those items of income referred to in subparagraph a), the United States shall allow as a credit against United States tax the income tax paid to ___ after the credit referred to in subparagraph a); the credit so allowed shall not reduce the portion of the United States tax that is creditable against the ___ tax in accordance with subparagraph a); and

c) for the exclusive purpose of relieving double taxation in the United States under subparagraph b), items of income referred to in subparagraph a) shall be deemed to arise in ___ to the extent necessary to avoid double taxation of such income under subparagraph b).

Article 24

NON-DISCRIMINATION

1. Nationals of a Contracting State shall not be subjected in the other Contracting State to any taxation or any requirement connected therewith that is more burdensome than the taxation and connected requirements to which nationals of that other State in the same circumstances, in particular with respect to residence, are or may be subjected. This provision shall also apply to persons who are not residents of one or both of the Contracting States. However, for the purposes of United States taxation, United States nationals who are subject to tax on a worldwide basis are not in the same circumstances as nationals of ___ who are not residents of the United States.

2. The taxation on a permanent establishment that an enterprise of a Contracting State has in the other Contracting State shall not be less favorably levied in that other State than the taxation levied on enterprises of that other State carrying on the same activities.

3. The provisions of paragraphs 1 and 2 shall not be construed as obliging a Contracting State to grant to residents of the other Contracting State any personal allowances, reliefs, and reductions for taxation purposes on account of civil status or family responsibilities that it grants to its own residents.

4. Except where the provisions of paragraph 1 of Article 9 (Associated Enterprises), paragraph 5 of Article 11 (Interest), or paragraph 4 of Article 12 (Royalties) apply, interest, royalties, and other disbursements paid by a resident of a Contracting State to a resident of the other Contracting State shall, for the purpose of determining the taxable profits of the first-mentioned resident, be deductible under the same conditions as if they had been paid to a resident of the first-mentioned State. Similarly, any debts of a resident of a Contracting State to a resident of the other Contracting State shall, for the purpose of determining the taxable capital of the first-mentioned resident, be deductible under the same conditions as if they had been contracted to a resident of the first-mentioned State.

5. Enterprises of a Contracting State, the capital of which is wholly or partly owned or controlled, directly or indirectly, by one or more residents of the other Contracting State, shall not be subjected in the first-mentioned State to any taxation or any requirement connected therewith that is more burdensome than the taxation and connected requirements to which other similar enterprises of the first-mentioned State are or may be subjected.

6. Nothing in this Article shall be construed as preventing either Contracting State from imposing a tax as described in paragraph 8 of Article 10 (Dividends).

7. The provisions of this Article shall, notwithstanding the provisions of Article 2 (Taxes Covered), apply to taxes of every kind and description imposed by a Contracting State or a political subdivision or local authority thereof.

Article 25

MUTUAL AGREEMENT PROCEDURE

1. Where a person considers that the actions of one or both of the Contracting States result or will result for such person in taxation not in accordance with the provisions of this Convention, it may, irrespective of the remedies provided by the domestic law of those States, and the time limits prescribed in such laws for presenting claims for refund, present its case to the competent authority of either Contracting State.

2. The competent authority shall endeavor, if the objection appears to it to be justified and if it is not itself able to arrive at a satisfactory solution, to resolve the case by mutual agreement with the competent authority of the other Contracting State, with a view to the avoidance of

taxation which is not in accordance with the Convention. Any agreement reached shall be implemented notwithstanding any time limits or other procedural limitations in the domestic law of the Contracting States. Assessment and collection procedures shall be suspended during the period that any mutual agreement proceeding is pending.

3. The competent authorities of the Contracting States shall endeavor to resolve by mutual agreement any difficulties or doubts arising as to the interpretation or application of the Convention. They also may consult together for the elimination of double taxation in cases not provided for in the Convention. In particular the competent authorities of the Contracting States may agree:

a) to the same attribution of income, deductions, credits, or allowances of an enterprise of a Contracting State to its permanent establishment situated in the other Contracting State;

b) to the same allocation of income, deductions, credits, or allowances between persons;

c) to the settlement of conflicting application of the Convention, including conflicts regarding:

i) the characterization of particular items of income;

ii) the characterization of persons;

iii) the application of source rules with respect to particular items of income;

iv) the meaning of any term used in the Convention;

v) the timing of particular items of income;

d) to advance pricing arrangements; and

e) to the application of the provisions of domestic law regarding penalties, fines, and interest in a manner consistent with the purposes of the Convention.

4. The competent authorities also may agree to increases in any specific dollar amounts referred to in the Convention to reflect economic or monetary developments.

5. The competent authorities of the Contracting States may communicate with each other directly, including through a joint commission, for the purpose of reaching an agreement in the sense of the preceding paragraphs.

Article 26

EXCHANGE OF INFORMATION AND ADMINISTRATIVE ASSISTANCE

1. The competent authorities of the Contracting States shall exchange such information as may be relevant for carrying out the provisions of this Convention or of the domestic laws of the Contracting States

concerning taxes of every kind imposed by a Contracting State to the extent that the taxation thereunder is not contrary to the Convention, including information relating to the assessment or collection of, the enforcement or prosecution in respect of, or the determination of appeals in relation to, such taxes. The exchange of information is not restricted by paragraph 1 of Article 1 (General Scope) or Article 2 (Taxes Covered).

2. Any information received under this Article by a Contracting State shall be treated as secret in the same manner as information obtained under the domestic laws of that State and shall be disclosed only to persons or authorities (including courts and administrative bodies) involved in the assessment, collection, or administration of, the enforcement or prosecution in respect of, or the determination of appeals in relation to, the taxes referred to above, or the oversight of such functions. Such persons or authorities shall use the information only for such purposes. They may disclose the information in public court proceedings or in judicial decisions.

3. In no case shall the provisions of the preceding paragraphs be construed so as to impose on a Contracting State the obligation:

a) to carry out administrative measures at variance with the laws and administrative practice of that or of the other Contracting State;

b) to supply information that is not obtainable under the laws or in the normal course of the administration of that or of the other Contracting State;

c) to supply information that would disclose any trade, business, industrial, commercial, or professional secret or trade process, or information the disclosure of which would be contrary to public policy (ordre public).

4. If information is requested by a Contracting State in accordance with this Article, the other Contracting State shall use its information gathering measures to obtain the requested information, even though that other State may not need such information for its own purposes. The obligation contained in the preceding sentence is subject to the limitations of paragraph 3 but in no case shall such limitation be construed to permit a Contracting State to decline to supply information because it has no domestic interest in such information.

5. In no case shall the provisions of paragraph 3 be construed to permit a Contracting State to decline to supply information requested by the other Contracting State because the information is held by a bank, other financial institution, nominee or person acting in an agency or a fiduciary capacity or because it relates to ownership interests in a person.

6. If specifically requested by the competent authority of a Contracting State, the competent authority of the other Contracting State shall provide information under this Article in the form of depositions of

witnesses and authenticated copies of unedited original documents (including books, papers, statements, records, accounts, and writings).

7. Each of the Contracting States shall endeavor to collect on behalf of the other Contracting State such amounts as may be necessary to ensure that relief granted by the Convention from taxation imposed by that other State does not inure to the benefit of persons not entitled thereto. This paragraph shall not impose upon either of the Contracting States the obligation to carry out administrative measures that would be contrary to its sovereignty, security, or public policy.

8. The requested State shall allow representatives of the requesting State to enter the requested State to interview individuals and examine books and records with the consent of the persons subject to examination.

[9.] The competent authorities of the Contracting States may develop an agreement upon the mode of application of this Article, including agreement to ensure comparable levels of assistance to each of the Contracting States, but in no case will the lack of such agreement relieve a Contracting State of its obligations under this Article.

Article 27

MEMBERS OF DIPLOMATIC MISSIONS AND CONSULAR POSTS

Nothing in this Convention shall affect the fiscal privileges of members of diplomatic missions or consular posts under the general rules of international law or under the provisions of special agreements.

Article 28

ENTRY INTO FORCE

1. This Convention shall be subject to ratification in accordance with the applicable procedures of each Contracting State, and instruments of ratification will be exchanged as soon thereafter as possible.

2. This Convention shall enter into force on the date of the exchange of instruments of ratification, and its provisions shall have effect:

a) in respect of taxes withheld at source, for amounts paid or credited on or after the first day of the second month next following the date on which the Convention enters into force;

b) in respect of other taxes, for taxable periods beginning on or after the first day of January next following the date on which the Convention enters into force.

3. Notwithstanding paragraph 2, the provisions of Article 26 (Exchange of Information and Administrative Assistance) shall have effect from the date of entry into force of this Convention, without regard to the taxable period to which the matter relates.

Article 29

TERMINATION

This Convention shall remain in force until terminated by a Contracting State. Either Contracting State may terminate the Convention by giving notice of termination to the other Contracting State through diplomatic channels. In such event, the Convention shall cease to have effect:

a) in respect of taxes withheld at source, for amounts paid or credited after the expiration of the 6 month period beginning on the date on which notice of termination was given; and

b) in respect of other taxes, for taxable periods beginning on or after the expiration of the 6 month period beginning on the date on which notice of termination was given.

IN WITNESS WHEREOF, the undersigned, being duly authorized thereto by their respective Governments, have signed this Convention.

DONE at ______ in duplicate, in the English and ______ languages, both texts being equally authentic, this ___ day of ____, 20___.

FOR THE GOVERNMENT OF THE UNITED STATES OF AMERICA:	FOR THE GOVERNMENT OF ______________________:

Appendix B

2006 United States Model Income Tax Treaty— U.S. Treasury Department's Technical Explanation

■ ■ ■

This is a technical explanation of the Convention between the United States and [the other Contracting State][1] for the avoidance of double taxation and the prevention of fiscal evasion with respect to taxes on income, signed on [date] (the "Convention").

Negotiations took into account the U.S. Department of the Treasury's current tax treaty policy, and the United States Model Income Tax Convention of November 15, 2006. Negotiations also took into account the Model Tax Convention on Income and on Capital, published by the Organisation for Economic Cooperation and Development (the "OECD Model"), and recent tax treaties concluded by both countries.

The Technical Explanation is an official guide to the Convention. It reflects the policies behind particular Convention provisions, as well as understandings reached with respect to the application and interpretation of the Convention. References in the Technical Explanation to "he" or "his" should be read to mean "he or she" or "his and her."

ARTICLE 1 (GENERAL SCOPE)

Paragraph 1

Paragraph 1 of Article 1 provides that the Convention applies only to residents of the United States or the other Contracting State except where the terms of the Convention provide otherwise. Under Article 4 (Resident) a person is generally treated as a resident of a Contracting State if that person is, under the laws of that State, liable to tax therein by reason of

---

1. To enhance readability, this Model Technical Explanation uses the term "the other Contracting State"; the actual name of the other Contracting State should be used throughout the text of the Technical Explanation to an actual treaty.

his domicile, citizenship, residence, or other similar criteria. However, if a person is considered a resident of both Contracting States, Article 4 provides rules for determining a State of residence (or no State of residence). This determination governs for all purposes of the Convention.

Certain provisions are applicable to persons who may not be residents of either Contracting State. For example, paragraph 1 of Article 24 (Non–Discrimination) applies to nationals of the Contracting States. Under Article 26 (Exchange of Information and Administrative Assistance), information may be exchanged with respect to residents of third states.

Paragraph 2

Paragraph 2 states the generally accepted relationship both between the Convention and domestic law and between the Convention and other agreements between the Contracting States. That is, no provision in the Convention may restrict any exclusion, exemption, deduction, credit or other benefit accorded by the tax laws of the Contracting States, or by any other agreement between the Contracting States. The relationship between the non-discrimination provisions of the Convention and other agreements is addressed not in paragraph 2 but in paragraph 3.

Under paragraph 2, for example, if a deduction would be allowed under the U.S. Internal Revenue Code (the "Code") in computing the U.S. taxable income of a resident of the other Contracting State, the deduction also is allowed to that person in computing taxable income under the Convention. Paragraph 2 also means that the Convention may not increase the tax burden on a resident of a Contracting States beyond the burden determined under domestic law. Thus, a right to tax given by the Convention cannot be exercised unless that right also exists under internal law.

It follows that, under the principle of paragraph 2, a taxpayer's U.S. tax liability need not be determined under the Convention if the Code would produce a more favorable result. A taxpayer may not, however, choose among the provisions of the Code and the Convention in an inconsistent manner in order to minimize tax. For example, assume that a resident of the other Contracting State has three separate businesses in the United States. One is a profitable permanent establishment and the other two are trades or businesses that would earn taxable income under the Code but that do not meet the permanent establishment threshold tests of the Convention. One is profitable and the other incurs a loss. Under the Convention, the income of the permanent establishment is taxable in the United States, and both the profit and loss of the other two businesses are ignored. Under the Code, all three would be subject to tax, but the loss would offset the profits of the two profitable ventures. The taxpayer may not invoke the Convention to exclude the profits of the profitable trade or business and invoke the Code to claim the loss of the loss trade or business against the profit of the permanent establishment. (See Rev. Rul. 84–17, 1984–1 C.B. 308.) If, however, the taxpayer invokes the Code for the taxation of all three ventures, he would not be precluded from invoking the Convention with respect, for example, to any dividend income he may receive from the United States that is not effectively connected with any of his business activities in the United States.

Similarly, nothing in the Convention can be used to deny any benefit granted by any other agreement between the United States and the other Contracting State. For example, if certain benefits are provided for military personnel or military contractors under a Status of Forces Agreement between the United States and the other Contracting State, those benefits or protections will be available to residents of the Contracting States regardless of any provisions to the contrary (or silence) in the Convention.

Paragraph 3

Paragraph 3 specifically relates to non-discrimination obligations of the Contracting States under the General Agreement on Trade in Services (the "GATS"). The provisions of paragraph 3 are an exception to the rule provided in paragraph 2 of this Article under which the Convention shall not restrict in any manner any benefit now or hereafter accorded by any other agreement between the Contracting States.

Subparagraph (a) of paragraph 3 provides that, unless the competent authorities determine that a taxation measure is not within the scope of the Convention, the national treatment obligations of the GATS shall not apply with respect to that measure. Further, any question arising as to the interpretation of the Convention, including in particular whether a measure is within the scope of the Convention shall be considered only by the competent authorities of the Contracting States, and the procedures under the Convention exclusively shall apply to the dispute. Thus, paragraph 3 of Article XXII (Consultation) of the GATS may not be used to bring a dispute before the World Trade Organization unless the competent authorities of both Contracting States have determined that the relevant taxation measure is not within the scope of Article 24 (Non–Discrimination) of the Convention.

The term "measure" for these purposes is defined broadly in subparagraph (b) of paragraph 3. It would include, for example, a law, regulation, rule, procedure, decision, administrative action or guidance, or any other form of measure.

Paragraph 4

Paragraph 4 contains the traditional saving clause found in all U.S. treaties. The Contracting States reserve their rights, except as provided in paragraph 5, to tax their residents and citizens as provided in their internal laws, notwithstanding any provisions of the Convention to the contrary. For example, if a resident of the other Contracting State performs professional services in the United States and the income from the services is not attributable to a permanent establishment in the United States, Article 7 (Business Profits) would by its terms prevent the

United States from taxing the income. If, however, the resident of the other Contracting State is also a citizen of the United States, the saving clause permits the United States to include the remuneration in the worldwide income of the citizen and subject it to tax under the normal Code rules (i.e., without regard to Code section 894(a)). However, subparagraph 5(a) of Article 1 preserves the benefits of special foreign tax credit rules applicable to the U.S. taxation of certain U.S. income of its citizens resident in the other Contracting State. See paragraph 4 of Article 23 (Relief from Double Taxation).

For purposes of the saving clause, "residence" is determined under Article 4 (Resident). Thus, an individual who is a resident of the United States under the Code (but not a U.S. citizen) but who is determined to be a resident of the other Contracting State under the tie-breaker rules of Article 4 would be subject to U.S. tax only to the extent permitted by the Convention. The United States would not be permitted to apply its statutory rules to that person to the extent the rules are inconsistent with the treaty.

However, the person would be treated as a U.S. resident for U.S. tax purposes other than determining the individual's U.S. tax liability. For example, in determining under Code section 957 whether a foreign corporation is a controlled foreign corporation, shares in that corporation held by the individual would be considered to be held by a U.S. resident. As a result, other U.S. citizens or residents might be deemed to be United States shareholders of a controlled foreign corporation subject to current inclusion of Subpart F income recognized by the corporation. See, Treas. Reg. section 301.7701(b)–7(a)(3).

Under paragraph 4, each Contracting State also reserves its right to tax former citizens and former long-term residents for a period of ten years following the loss of such status. Thus, paragraph 4 allows the United States to tax former U.S. citizens and former U.S. long-term residents in accordance with Section 877 of the Code. Section 877 generally applies to a former citizen or long-term resident of the United States who relinquishes citizenship or terminates long-term residency if either of the following criteria exceed established thresholds: (a) the average annual net income tax of such individual for the period of 5 taxable years ending before the date of the loss of status, or (b) the net worth of such individual as of the date of the loss of status. The thresholds are adjusted annually for inflation. The United States defines "long-term resident" as an individual (other than a U.S. citizen) who is a lawful permanent resident of the United States in at least 8 of the prior 15 taxable years. An individual is not treated as a lawful permanent resident for any taxable year if such individual is treated as a resident of a foreign country under the provisions of a tax treaty between the United States and the foreign country and the individual does not waive the benefits of such treaty applicable to residents of the foreign country.

Paragraph 5

Paragraph 5 sets forth certain exceptions to the saving clause. The referenced provisions are intended to provide benefits to citizens and residents even if such benefits do not exist under internal law. Paragraph 5 thus preserves these benefits for citizens and residents of the Contracting States.

Subparagraph (a) lists certain provisions of the Convention that are applicable to all citizens and residents of a Contracting State, despite the general saving clause rule of paragraph 4:

(1) Paragraph 2 of Article 9 (Associated Enterprises) grants the right to a correlative adjustment with respect to income tax due on profits reallocated under Article 9.

(2) Paragraphs 1 b), 2, and 5 of Article 17 (Pensions, Social Security, Annuities, Alimony and Child Support) provide exemptions from source or residence State taxation for certain pension distributions, social security payments and child support.

(3) Paragraph 1 of Article 18 (Pension Fund) provides an exemption for certain investment income of pension funds located in the other Contracting State, while paragraph 4 provides benefits for certain contributions by or on behalf of a U.S. citizen to certain pension funds established in the other Contracting State.

(4) Article 23 (Relief from Double Taxation) confirms to citizens and residents of one Contracting State the benefit of a credit for income taxes paid to the other or an exemption for income earned in the other State.

(5) Article 24 (Non–Discrimination) protects residents and nationals of one Contracting State against the adoption of certain discriminatory practices in the other Contracting State.

(6) Article 25 (Mutual Agreement Procedure) confers certain benefits on citizens and residents of the Contracting States in order to reach and implement solutions to disputes between the two Contracting States. For example, the competent authorities are permitted to use a definition of a term that differs from an internal law definition. The statute of limitations may be waived for refunds, so that the benefits of an agreement may be implemented.

Subparagraph (b) of paragraph 5 provides a different set of exceptions to the saving clause. The benefits referred to are all intended to be granted to temporary residents of a Contracting State (for example, in the case of the United States, holders of non-immigrant visas), but not to citizens or to persons who have acquired permanent residence in that State. If beneficiaries of these provisions travel from one of the Contracting States to the other, and remain in the other long enough to become residents under its internal law, but do not acquire permanent residence status (i.e., in the U.S. context, they do not become "green card" holders) and are not citizens of that State, the host State will continue to grant these benefits even if they conflict with the statutory rules. The benefits preserved by this paragraph are: (1) the host country exemptions for government service salaries and pensions under Article 19 (Government Service), certain income of visiting students and trainees under Article 20 (Students and Trainees), and the income of diplomatic agents and consular officers under Article 27 (Members of Diplomatic Missions and Consular Posts); and (2) the beneficial tax treatment of pension fund contributions under paragraph 2 of Article 18 (Pension Funds).

Paragraph 6

Paragraph 6 addresses special issues presented by fiscally transparent entities such as partnerships and certain estates and trusts. Because different countries frequently take different views as to when an entity is fiscally transparent, the risk of both double taxation and double non-taxation are relatively high. The intention of paragraph 6 is to eliminate a number of technical problems that arguably would have prevented investors using such entities from claiming treaty benefits, even though such investors would be subject to tax on the income derived through such entities. The provision also prevents the use of such entities to claim treaty benefits in circumstances where the person investing through such an entity is not subject to tax on the income in its State of residence. The provision, and the corresponding requirements of the substantive rules of Articles 6 through 21, should be read with those two goals in mind.

In general, paragraph 6 relates to entities that are not subject to tax at the entity level, as distinct from entities that are subject to tax, but with respect to which tax may be relieved under an integrated system. This paragraph applies to any resident of a Contracting State who is entitled to income derived through an entity that is treated as fiscally transparent under the laws of either Contracting State. Entities falling under this description in the United States include partnerships, common investment trusts under section 584 and grantor trusts. This paragraph also applies to U.S. limited liability companies ("LLCs") that are treated as partnerships or as disregarded entities for U.S. tax purposes.

Under paragraph 6, an item of income, profit or gain derived by such a fiscally transparent entity will be considered to be derived by a resident of a Contracting State if a resident is treated under the taxation laws of that State as deriving the item of income. For example, if a company that is a resident of the other Contracting State pays interest to an entity that is treated as fiscally transparent for U.S. tax purposes, the interest will be considered derived by a resident of the U.S. only to the extent that the taxation laws of the United States treats one or more U.S. residents (whose status as U.S. residents is determined, for this purpose, under U.S. tax law) as deriving the interest for U.S. tax purposes. In the case of a partnership, the persons who are, under U.S. tax laws, treated as partners of the entity would normally be the persons whom the U.S. tax laws would treat as deriving the interest income through the partnership. Also, it follows that persons whom the United States treats as partners but who are not U.S. residents for U.S. tax purposes may not claim a benefit for the interest paid to the entity under the Convention, because they are not residents of the United States for purposes of claiming this treaty benefit. (If, however, the country in which they are treated as resident for tax purposes, as determined under the laws of that country, has an income tax convention with the other Contracting State, they may be entitled to claim a benefit under that convention.) In contrast, if, for example, an entity is organized under U.S. laws and is classified as a corporation for U.S. tax purposes, interest paid by a company that is a resident of the other Contracting State to the U.S. entity will be considered derived by a resident of the United States since the U.S. corporation is treated under U.S. taxation laws as a resident of the United States and as deriving the income.

The same result obtains even if the entity were viewed differently under the tax laws of the other Contracting State (e.g., as not fiscally transparent in the first example above where the entity is treated as a partnership for U.S. tax purposes). Similarly, the characterization of the entity in a third country is also irrelevant, even if the entity is organized in that third country. The results follow regardless of whether the entity is disregarded as a separate entity under the laws of one jurisdiction but not the other, such as a single owner entity that is viewed as a branch for U.S. tax purposes and as a corporation for tax purposes under the laws of the other Contracting State. These results also obtain regardless of where the entity is organized (i.e., in the United States, in the other Contracting State or, as noted above, in a third country).

For example, income from U.S. sources received by an entity organized under the laws of the United States, which is treated for tax purposes under the laws of the other Contracting State as a corporation and is owned by a shareholder who is a resident of the other Contracting State for its tax purposes, is not considered derived by the shareholder of that corporation even if, under the tax laws of the United States, the entity is treated as fiscally transparent. Rather, for purposes of the treaty, the income is treated as derived by the U.S. entity. These principles also apply to trusts to the extent that they are fiscally transparent in either Contracting State. For example, if X, a resident of the other Contracting State, creates a revocable trust in the United States and names persons resident in a third country as the beneficiaries of the trust, the trust's income would be regarded as being derived by a resident of the other Contracting State only to the extent that the laws of the other Contracting State treat X as deriving the income for its tax purposes, perhaps through application of rules similar to the U.S. "grantor trust" rules.

Paragraph 6 is not an exception to the saving clause of paragraph 4. Accordingly, paragraph 6 does not prevent a Contracting State from taxing an entity that is treated as a resident of that State under its tax law. For example, if a U.S. LLC with members who are residents of the other Contracting State elects to be taxed as a corporation for U.S. tax purposes, the United States will tax that LLC on its worldwide income on a net basis, without regard to whether the other Contracting State views the LLC as fiscally transparent.

ARTICLE 2 (TAXES COVERED)

This Article specifies the U.S. taxes and the taxes of the other Contracting State to which the Convention applies. With two exceptions, the taxes specified in Article 2 are the covered taxes for all purposes of the Convention. A broader coverage applies, however, for purposes of Articles 24 (Non–Discrimination) and 26 (Exchange of Information and Administrative Assistance). Article 24 (Non–Discrimination) applies with respect to all taxes, including those imposed by state and local governments. Article 26 (Exchange of Information and Administrative Assistance) applies with respect to all taxes imposed at the national level.

Paragraph 1

Paragraph 1 identifies the category of taxes to which the Convention applies. Paragraph 1 is based on the OECD Model and defines the scope of application of the Convention. The convention applies to taxes on income, including gains, imposed on behalf of a Contracting State, irrespective of the manner in which they are levied. Except with respect to Article 24 (Non–Discrimination), state and local taxes are not covered by the Convention.

Paragraph 2

Paragraph 2 also is based on the OECD Model and provides a definition of taxes on income and on capital gains. The Convention covers taxes on total income or any part of income and includes tax on gains derived from the alienation of property. The Convention does not apply, however, to social security charges, or any other charges where there is a direct connection between the levy and individual benefits. Nor does it apply to property taxes, except with respect to Article 24 (Non–Discrimination).

Paragraph 3

Paragraph 3 lists the taxes in force at the time of signature of the Convention to which the Convention applies. The existing covered taxes of the other Contracting State are identified in subparagraph (a) of paragraph 3. Subparagraph 3(b) provides that the existing U.S. taxes subject to the rules of the Convention are the Federal income taxes imposed by the Code, together with the excise taxes imposed with respect to private foundations (Code sections 4940 through 4948). Social security and unemployment taxes (Code sections 1401, 3101 , 3111 and 3301) are specifically excluded from coverage.

Paragraph 4

Under paragraph 4, the Convention will apply to any taxes that are identical, or substantially similar, to those enumerated in paragraph 3, and which are imposed in addition to, or in place of, the existing taxes after [ ], the date of signature of the Convention. The paragraph also provides that the competent authorities of the Contracting States will notify each other of any changes that have been made in their laws, whether tax laws or non-tax laws, that affect significantly their obligations under the Convention. Non-tax laws that may affect a Contracting State's obligations under the Convention may include, for example, laws affecting bank secrecy.

ARTICLE 3 (GENERAL DEFINITIONS)

Article 3 provides general definitions and rules of interpretation applicable throughout the Convention. Certain other terms are defined in other articles of the Convention. For example, the term "resident of a Contracting State" is defined in Article 4 (Resident). The term "permanent establishment" is defined in Article 5 (Permanent Establishment). These definitions are used consistently throughout the Convention. Other terms, such as "dividends," "interest" and "royalties" are defined in specific articles for purposes only of those articles.

Paragraph 1

Paragraph 1 defines a number of basic terms used in the Convention. The introduction to paragraph 1 makes clear that these definitions apply for all purposes of the Convention, unless the context requires otherwise. This latter condition allows flexibility in the interpretation of the treaty in order to avoid results not intended by the treaty's negotiators.

Subparagraph 1(a) defines the term "person" to include an individual, a trust, a partnership, a company and any other body of persons. The definition is significant for a variety of reasons. For example, under Article 4, only a "person" can be a "resident" and therefore eligible for most benefits under the treaty. Also, all "persons" are eligible to claim relief under Article 25 (Mutual Agreement Procedure).

The term "company" is defined in subparagraph 1(b) as a body corporate or an entity treated as a body corporate for tax purposes in the state where it is organized. The definition refers to the law of the state in which an entity is organized in order to ensure that an entity that is treated as fiscally transparent in its country of residence will not get inappropriate benefits, such as the reduced withholding rate provided by subparagraph 2(b) of Article 10 (Dividends). It also ensures that the Limitation on Benefits provisions of Article 22 will be applied at the appropriate level.

The terms "enterprise of a Contracting State" and "enterprise of the other Contracting State" are defined in subparagraph 1(c) as an enterprise carried on by a resident of a Contracting State and an enterprise carried on by a resident of the other Contracting State. An enterprise of a Contracting State need not be carried on in that State. It may be carried on in the other Contracting State or a third state (e.g., a U.S. corporation doing all of its business in the other Contracting State would still be a U.S. enterprise).

Subparagraph 1(c) further provides that these terms also encompass an enterprise conducted through an entity (such as a partnership) that is treated as fiscally transparent in the Contracting State where the entity's owner is resident. The definition makes this point explicitly to ensure that the purpose of the Convention is not thwarted by an overly technical application of the term "enterprise of a Contracting State" to activities carried on through partnerships and similar entities. In accordance with Article 4 (Resident), entities that are fiscally transparent in the country in which their owners are resident are not considered to be residents of a Contracting State (although income derived by such entities may be taxed as the income of a resident, if taxed in the hands of resident partners or other owners). It could be argued that an enterprise conducted by such an entity is not conducted by a resident of a Contracting State, and therefore would not benefit from provisions applicable to enterprises of a Contracting State. The definition is intended to make clear that an enterprise conducted by such an entity will be treated as carried on by a resident of a Contracting State to the extent its partners or other owners are residents. This approach is consistent with the Code, which under section 875 attributes a trade or business conducted by a partnership to its partners and a trade or business conducted by an estate or trust to its beneficiaries.

Subparagraph (d) defines the term "enterprise" as any activity or set of activities that constitutes the carrying on of a business. The term "business" is not defined, but subparagraph (e) provides that it includes the performance of professional services and other activities of an independent character. Both subparagraphs are identical to definitions recently added to the OECD Model in connection with the deletion of Article 14 (Independent Personal Services) from the OECD Model. The inclusion of the two definitions is intended to clarify that income from the performance of professional services or other activities of an independent character is dealt with under Article 7 (Business Profits) and not Article 21 (Other Income).

Subparagraph 1(f) defines the term "international traffic." The term means any transport by a ship or aircraft except when such transport is solely between places within a Contracting State. This definition is applicable principally in the context of Article 8 (Shipping and Air Transport). The definition combines with paragraphs 2 and 3 of Article 8 to exempt from tax by the source State income from the rental of ships or aircraft that is earned both by lessors that are operators of ships and aircraft and by those lessors that are not (e.g., a bank or a container leasing company).

The exclusion from international traffic of transport solely between places within a Contracting State means, for example, that carriage of goods or passengers solely between New York and Chicago would not be treated as international traffic, whether carried by a U.S. or a foreign carrier. The substantive taxing rules of the Convention relating to the taxation of income from transport, principally Article 8 (Shipping and Air Transport), therefore, would not apply to income from such carriage. Thus, if the carrier engaged in internal U.S. traffic were a resident of the other Contracting State (assuming that were possible under U.S. law), the United States would not be required to exempt the income from that transport under Article 8. The income would, however, be treated as business profits under Article 7 (Business Profits), and therefore would be taxable in the United States only if attributable to a U.S. permanent establishment of the foreign carrier, and then only on a net basis. The gross basis U.S. tax imposed by section 887 would never apply under the circumstances described. If, however, goods or passengers are carried by a carrier resident in the other Contracting State from a non-U.S. port to, for example, New York, and some of the goods or passengers continue on to Chicago, the entire transport would be international traffic. This would be true if the international carrier transferred the goods at the U.S. port of entry from a ship to a land vehicle, from a ship to a lighter, or even if the overland portion of the trip in the United States was handled by an independent carrier under contract with the original international carrier, so long as both parts of the trip were reflected in original bills of lading. For this reason, the U.S. Model refers, in the definition of "international traffic," to "such transport" being solely between places in the other Contracting State, while the OECD Model refers to the ship or aircraft being operated solely between such places. The U.S. Model language is intended to make clear that, as in the above example, even if the goods are carried on a different aircraft for the internal portion of the international voyage than is used for the overseas portion of the trip, the definition applies to that internal portion as well as the external portion.

Finally, a "cruise to nowhere," i.e., a cruise beginning and ending in a port in the same Contracting State with no stops in a foreign port, would not constitute international traffic.

Subparagraph 1(g) designates the "competent authorities" for the other Contracting State and the United States. The U.S. competent authority is the Secretary of the Treasury or his delegate. The Secretary of the Treasury has delegated the competent authority function to the Commissioner of Internal Revenue, who in turn has delegated the authority to the Deputy Commissioner (International) LMSB. With respect to interpretative issues, the Deputy Commissioner (International) LMSB acts with the concurrence of the Associate Chief Counsel (International) of the Internal Revenue Service.

The geographical scope of the Convention with respect to the other Contracting State is set out in subparagraph 1(h).

The geographical scope of the Convention with respect to the United States is set out in subparagraph 1(i). It encompasses the United States of America, including the states, the District of Columbia and the territorial sea of the United States. The term does not include Puerto Rico, the Virgin Islands, Guam or any other U.S. possession or territory. For certain purposes, the term "United States" includes the sea bed and subsoil of undersea areas adjacent to the territorial sea of the United States. This extension applies to the extent that the United States exercises sovereignty in accordance with international law for the purpose of natural resource exploration and exploitation of such areas. This extension of the definition applies, however, only if the person, property or activity to which the Convention is being applied is connected with such natural resource exploration or exploitation. Thus, it would not include any activity involving the sea floor of an area over which the United States exercised sovereignty for natural resource purposes if that activity was unrelated to the exploration and exploitation of natural resources. This result is consistent with the result that would be obtained under Section 638, which treats the continental shelf as part of the United States for purposes of natural resource exploration and exploitation.

The term "national," as it relates to the United States and to the other Contracting State, is defined in subparagraphs 1(j). This term is relevant for purposes of Articles 19 (Government Service) and 24 (Non–Discrimination). A national of one of the Contracting States is (1) an individual who is a citizen or national of that State, and (2) any legal person, partnership or association deriving its status, as such, from the law in force in the State where it is established.

Subparagraph (k) defines the term "pension fund" to include any person established in a Contracting State that is generally exempt from income taxation in that State and that is operated principally to provide pension or retirement benefits or to earn income for the benefit of one or more such arrangements. In the case of the United States, the term "pension fund" includes the following: a trust providing pension or retirement benefits under a Code section 401(a) qualified pension plan, profit sharing or stock bonus plan, a trust providing pension or retirement benefits under a Code section 403(b) plan, a trust that is an individual retirement account under Code section 408, a Roth individual retirement account under Code section 408A , or a simple retirement account under Code section 408(p), a trust providing pension or retirement benefits under a simplified employee pension plan under Code section 408(k) , a trust described in section 457(g) providing pension or retirement benefits under a Code section 457(b) plan, and the Thrift Savings Fund (section

7701(j)). Section 401(k) plans and group trusts described in Revenue Ruling 81–100 and meeting the conditions of Revenue Ruling 2004–67 qualify as pension funds because they are covered by Code section 401(a).

Paragraph 2

Terms that are not defined in the Convention are dealt with in paragraph 2.

Paragraph 2 provides that in the application of the Convention, any term used but not defined in the Convention will have the meaning that it has under the law of the Contracting State whose tax is being applied, unless the context requires otherwise, or the competent authorities have agreed on a different meaning pursuant to Article 25 (Mutual Agreement Procedure). If the term is defined under both the tax and non-tax laws of a Contracting State, the definition in the tax law will take precedence over the definition in the non-tax laws. Finally, there also may be cases where the tax laws of a State contain multiple definitions of the same term. In such a case, the definition used for purposes of the particular provision at issue, if any, should be used.

If the meaning of a term cannot be readily determined under the law of a Contracting State, or if there is a conflict in meaning under the laws of the two States that creates difficulties in the application of the Convention, the competent authorities, as indicated in paragraph 3(c)(iv) of Article 25 (Mutual Agreement Procedure), may establish a common meaning in order to prevent double taxation or to further any other purpose of the Convention. This common meaning need not conform to the meaning of the term under the laws of either Contracting State.

The reference in paragraph 2 to the internal law of a Contracting State means the law in effect at the time the treaty is being applied, not the law as in effect at the time the treaty was signed. The use of "ambulatory" definitions, however, may lead to results that are at variance with the intentions of the negotiators and of the Contracting States when the treaty was negotiated and ratified. The reference in both paragraphs 1 and 2 to the "context otherwise requir[ing]" a definition different from the treaty definition, in paragraph 1, or from the internal law definition of the Contracting State whose tax is being imposed, under paragraph 2, refers to a circumstance where the result intended by the Contracting States is different from the result that would obtain under either the paragraph 1 definition or the statutory definition. Thus, flexibility in defining terms is necessary and permitted.

ARTICLE 4 (RESIDENT)

This Article sets forth rules for determining whether a person is a resident of a Contracting State for purposes of the Convention. As a general matter only residents of the Contracting States may claim the benefits of the Convention. The treaty definition of residence is to be used only for purposes of the Convention. The fact that a person is determined to be a resident of a Contracting State under Article 4 does not necessarily entitle that person to the benefits of the Convention. In addition to being a resident, a person also must qualify for benefits under Article 22 (Limitation on Benefits) in order to receive benefits conferred on residents of a Contracting State.

The determination of residence for treaty purposes looks first to a person's liability to tax as a resident under the respective taxation laws of the Contracting States. As a general matter, a person who, under those laws, is a resident of one Contracting State and not of the other need look no further. For purposes of the Convention, that person is a resident of the State in which he is resident under internal law. If, however, a person is resident in both Contracting States under their respective taxation laws, the Article proceeds, where possible, to use tie-breaker rules to assign a single State of residence to such a person for purposes of the Convention.

Paragraph 1

The term "resident of a Contracting State" is defined in paragraph 1. In general, this definition incorporates the definitions of residence in U.S. law and that of the other Contracting State by referring to a resident as a person who, under the laws of a Contracting State, is subject to tax there by reason of his domicile, residence, citizenship, place of management, place of incorporation or any other similar criterion. Thus, residents of the United States include aliens who are considered U.S. residents under Code section 7701(b) . Paragraph 1 also specifically includes the two Contracting States, and political subdivisions and local authorities of the two States, as residents for purposes of the Convention.

Certain entities that are nominally subject to tax but that in practice are rarely required to pay tax also would generally be treated as residents and therefore accorded treaty benefits. For example, a U.S. Regulated Investment Company (RIC) and a U.S. Real Estate Investment Trust (REIT) are residents of the United States for purposes of the treaty. Although the income earned by these entities normally is not subject to U.S. tax in the hands of the entity, they are taxable to the extent that they do not currently distribute their profits, and therefore may be regarded as "liable to tax." They also must satisfy a number of requirements under the Code in order to be entitled to special tax treatment.

A person who is liable to tax in a Contracting State only in respect of income from sources within that State or capital situated therein or of profits attributable to a permanent establishment in that State will not be treated as a resident of that Contracting State for purposes of the Convention. Thus, a consular official of the other Contracting State who is posted in the United States, who may be subject to U.S. tax on U.S. source investment income, but is not taxable in the United States on non-U.S. source income (see Code section 7701(b)(5)(B)), would not be considered a resident of the United States for purposes of the Convention. Similarly, an enterprise of the other Contracting State with a permanent establishment in the United States is not, by virtue of that permanent establishment, a resident of the United States. The enterprise generally is subject to U.S. tax only with respect to its income that is attributable to the U.S. permanent establishment, not with respect to its worldwide income, as it would be if it were a U.S. resident.

Paragraph 2

Paragraph 2 provides that certain tax-exempt entities such as pension funds and charitable organizations will be regarded as residents of a Contracting State regardless of whether they are generally liable to income tax in the State where they are established. The paragraph applies to legal persons organized under the laws of a Contracting State and established and maintained in that State to provide pensions or other similar benefits pursuant to a plan, or exclusively for religious, charitable, scientific, artistic, cultural, or educational purposes. Thus, a section 501(c) organization organized in the United States (such as a U.S. charity) that is generally exempt from tax under U.S. law is a resident of the United States for all purposes of the Convention.

Paragraph 3

If, under the laws of the two Contracting States, and, thus, under paragraph 1, an individual is deemed to be a resident of both Contracting States, a series of tie-breaker rules are provided in paragraph 3 to determine a single State of residence for that individual. These tests are to be applied in the order in which they are stated. The first test is based on where the individual has a permanent home. If that test is inconclusive because the individual has a permanent home available to him in both States, he will be considered to be a resident of the Contracting State where his personal and economic relations are closest (i.e., the location of his "centre of vital interests"). If that test is also inconclusive, or if he does not have a permanent home available to him in either State, he will be treated as a resident of the Contracting State where he maintains an habitual abode. If he has an habitual abode in both States or in neither of them, he will be treated as a resident of the Contracting State of which he is a national. If he is a national of both States or of neither, the matter will be considered by the competent authorities, who will assign a single State of residence.

Paragraph 4

Paragraph 4 seeks to settle dual-residence issues for companies. A company is treated as resident in the United States if it is created or organized under the laws of the United States or a political subdivision. If, as is frequently the case, a company is treated as a resident of the other Contracting State if it is either incorporated or managed and controlled there, dual residence can arise in the case of a U.S. company that is managed and controlled in the other Contracting State. In other cases, a company may be a dual resident because it was originally incorporated in one Contracting State but has "continued" into the other Contracting State. Paragraph 4 thus attempts to deal with each of these situations.

Under paragraph 4, the residence of a dual resident company will be in the Contracting State under the laws of which it is created or organized if it is created or organized under the laws of only one of the other Contracting States. Thus, if a company is a resident of the United States because it is incorporated under the laws of one of the states and is a resident of the other Contracting State because its place of effective management is in that State, then it will be a resident only of the United States. However, if the incorporation test does not resolve the question because, for example, the company was incorporated in one Contracting State and continued into the other Contracting State, but the first-mentioned Contracting State does not recognize the migration and continues to treat the company as a resident, then the competent authorities will try to determine a single State of residence for the company.

If the competent authorities do not reach an agreement on a single State of residence, that company may not claim any benefit accorded to residents of a Contracting State by the Convention. The company may, however, claim any benefits that are not limited to residents, such as those provided by paragraph 1 of Article 24 (Non–Discrimination). Thus, for example, a State cannot discriminate against a dual resident company.

Dual resident companies also may be treated as a resident of a Contracting State for purposes other than that of obtaining benefits under the Convention. For example, if a dual resident company pays a dividend to a resident of the other Contracting State, the U.S. paying agent would withhold on that dividend at the appropriate treaty rate because reduced withholding is a benefit enjoyed by the resident of the other Contracting State, not by the dual resident company. The dual resident company that paid the dividend would, for this purpose, be treated as a resident of the United States under the Convention. In addition, information relating to dual resident companies can be exchanged under the Convention because, by its terms, Article 26 (Exchange of Information and Administrative Assistance) is not limited to residents of the Contracting States.

Paragraph 5

Dual residents other than individuals or companies (such as trusts or estates) are addressed by paragraph 5. If such a person is, under the rules of paragraph 1, resident in both Contracting States, the competent authorities shall seek to determine a single State of residence for that person for purposes of the Convention.

ARTICLE 5 (PERMANENT ESTABLISHMENT)

This Article defines the term "permanent establishment," a term that is significant for several articles of the Convention. The existence of a permanent establishment in a Contracting State is necessary under Article 7 (Business Profits) for the taxation by that State of the business profits of a resident of the other Contracting State. Articles 10, 11 and 12 (dealing with dividends, interest, and royalties, respectively) provide for reduced rates of tax at source on payments of these items of income to a resident of the other State only when the income is not attributable to a permanent establishment that the recipient has in the source State. The concept is also relevant in determining which Contracting State may tax certain gains under Article 13 (Gains) and certain "other income" under Article 21 (Other Income).

Paragraph 1

The basic definition of the term "permanent establishment" is contained in paragraph 1. As used in the Convention, the term means a fixed place of business through which the business of an enterprise is wholly or partly carried on. As indicated in the OECD Commentary to Article 5 (see paragraphs 4 through 8), a general principle to be observed in determining whether a permanent establishment exists is that the place of business must be "fixed" in the sense that a particular building or physical location is used by the enterprise for the conduct of its business, and that it must be foreseeable that the enterprise's use of this building or other physical location will be more than temporary.

Paragraph 2

Paragraph 2 lists a number of types of fixed places of business that constitute a permanent establishment. This list is illustrative and non-exclusive. According to paragraph 2, the term permanent establishment includes a place of management, a branch, an office, a factory, a workshop, and a mine, oil or gas well, quarry or other place of extraction of natural resources.

Paragraph 3

This paragraph provides rules to determine whether a building site or a construction, assembly or installation project, or an installation or drilling rig or ship used for the exploration of natural resources constitutes a permanent establishment for the contractor, driller, etc. Such a site or activity does not create a permanent establishment unless the site, project, etc. lasts, or the exploration activity continues, for more than twelve months. It is only necessary to refer to "exploration" and not "exploitation" in this context because exploitation activities are defined to constitute a permanent establishment under subparagraph (f) of paragraph 2. Thus, a drilling rig does not constitute a permanent establishment if a well is drilled in only six months, but if production begins in the following month the well becomes a permanent establishment as of that date.

The twelve-month test applies separately to each site or project. The twelve-month period begins when work (including preparatory work carried on by the enterprise) physically begins in a Contracting State. A series of contracts or projects by a contractor that are interdependent both commercially and geographically are to be treated as a single project for purposes of applying the twelve-month threshold test. For example, the construction of a housing development would be considered as a single project even if each house were constructed for a different purchaser.

In applying this paragraph, time spent by a sub-contractor on a building site is counted as time spent by the general contractor at the site for purposes of determining whether the general contractor has a permanent establishment. However, for the sub-contractor itself to be treated as having a permanent establishment, the sub-contractor's activities at the site must last for more than 12 months. If a sub-contractor is on a site intermittently, then, for purposes of applying the 12–month rule, time is measured from the first day the sub-contractor is on the site until the last day (i.e., intervening days that the sub-contractor is not on the site are counted).

These interpretations of the Article are based on the Commentary to paragraph 3 of Article 5 of the OECD Model, which contains language that is substantially the same as that in the Convention. These interpretations are consistent with the generally accepted international interpretation of the relevant language in paragraph 3 of Article 5 of the Convention.

If the twelve-month threshold is exceeded, the site or project constitutes a permanent establishment from the first day of activity.

Paragraph 4

This paragraph contains exceptions to the general rule of paragraph 1, listing a number of activities that may be carried on through a fixed place of business but which nevertheless do not create a permanent establishment. The use of facilities solely to store, display or deliver merchandise belonging to an enterprise does not constitute a permanent establishment of that enterprise. The maintenance of a stock of goods belonging to an enterprise solely for the purpose of storage, display or delivery, or solely for the purpose of processing by another enterprise does not give rise to a permanent establishment of the first-mentioned enterprise. The maintenance of a fixed place of business solely for the purpose of purchasing goods or merchandise, or for collecting information, for the enterprise, or for other activities that have a preparatory or auxiliary character for the enterprise, such as advertising, or the supply of information, do not constitute a permanent establishment of the enterprise. Moreover, subparagraph 4(f) provides that a combination of the activities described in the other subparagraphs of paragraph 4 will not give rise to a permanent establishment if the combination results in an overall activity that is of a preparatory or auxiliary character.

Paragraph 5

Paragraphs 5 and 6 specify when activities carried on by an agent or other person acting on behalf of an enterprise create a permanent establishment of that enterprise. Under paragraph 5, a person is deemed to create a permanent establishment of the enterprise if that person has and habitually exercises an authority to conclude contracts that are binding on the enterprise. If, however, for example, his activities are limited to those activities specified in paragraph 4 which would not constitute a permanent establishment if carried on by the enterprise through a fixed place of business, the person does not create a permanent establishment of the enterprise. The OECD Model uses the term "in the name of that enterprise" rather than "binding on the enterprise." This difference is intended to be a clarification rather than a substantive difference. As indicated in paragraph 32 to the OECD Commentaries on Article 5, paragraph 5 of the Article is intended to encompass persons who have "sufficient authority to bind the enterprise's participation in the business activity in the State concerned."

The contracts referred to in paragraph 5 are those relating to the essential business operations of the enterprise, rather than ancillary activities. For example, if the person has no authority to conclude contracts in the name of the enterprise with its customers for, say, the sale of the goods produced by the enterprise, but it can enter into service contracts in the name of the enterprise for the enterprise's business equipment, this contracting authority would not fall within the scope of the paragraph, even if exercised regularly.

Paragraph 6

Under paragraph 6, an enterprise is not deemed to have a permanent establishment in a Contracting State merely because it carries on business in that State through an independent agent, including a broker or general commission agent, if the agent is acting in the ordinary course of his business as an independent agent. Thus, there are two conditions that must be satisfied: the agent must be both legally and economically independent of the enterprise, and the agent must be acting in the ordinary course of its business in carrying out activities on behalf of the enterprise.

Whether the agent and the enterprise are independent is a factual determination. Among the questions to be considered are the extent to which the agent operates on the basis of instructions from the enterprise. An agent that is subject to detailed instructions regarding the conduct of its operations or comprehensive control by the enterprise is not legally independent.

In determining whether the agent is economically independent, a relevant factor is the extent to which the agent bears business risk. Business risk refers primarily to risk of loss. An independent agent typically bears risk of loss from its own activities. In the absence of other factors that would establish dependence, an agent that shares business risk with the enterprise, or has its own business risk, is economically independent because its business activities are not integrated with those of the principal. Conversely, an agent that bears little or no risk from the activities it performs is not economically independent and therefore is not described in paragraph 6.

Another relevant factor in determining whether an agent is economically independent is whether the agent acts exclusively or nearly exclusively for the principal. Such a relationship may indicate that the principal has economic control over the agent. A number of principals acting in concert also may have economic control over an agent. The limited scope of the agent's activities and the agent's dependence on a single source of income may indicate that the agent lacks economic independence. It should be borne in mind, however, that exclusivity is not in itself a conclusive test; an agent may be economically independent notwithstanding an exclusive relationship with the principal if it has the capacity to diversify and acquire other clients without substantial modifications to its current business and without substantial harm to its business profits. Thus, exclusivity should be viewed merely as a pointer to further investigation of the relationship between the principal and the agent. Each case must be addressed on the basis of its own facts and circumstances.

Paragraph 7

This paragraph clarifies that a company that is a resident of a Contracting State is not deemed to have a permanent establishment in the other Contracting State merely because it controls, or is controlled by, a company that is a resident of that other Contracting State, or that carries on business in that other Contracting State. The determination whether a permanent establishment exists is made solely on the basis of the factors described in paragraphs 1 through 6 of the Article. Whether a company is a permanent establishment of a related company, therefore, is based solely on those factors and not on the ownership or control relationship between the companies.

ARTICLE 6 (INCOME FROM REAL PROPERTY)

Paragraph 1

The first paragraph of Article 6 states the general rule that income of a resident of a Contracting State derived from real property situated in the other Contracting State may be taxed in the Contracting State in which the property is situated. The paragraph specifies that income from real property includes income from agriculture and forestry. Given the availability of the net election in paragraph 5, taxpayers generally should be able to obtain the same tax treatment in the situs country regardless of whether the income is treated as business profits or real property income.

This Article does not grant an exclusive taxing right to the situs State; the situs State is merely given the primary right to tax. The Article does not impose any limitation in terms of rate or form of tax on the situs State, except that, as provided in paragraph 5, the situs State must allow the taxpayer an election to be taxed on a net basis.

Paragraph 2

The term "real property" is defined in paragraph 2 by reference to the internal law definition in the situs State. In the case of the United States, the term has the meaning given to it by Reg. § 1.897–1(b). In addition to the statutory definitions in the two Contracting States, the paragraph specifies certain additional classes of property that, regardless of internal law definitions, are within the scope of the term for purposes of the Convention. This expanded definition conforms to that in the OECD Model. The definition of "real property" for purposes of Article 6 is more limited than the expansive definition of "real property" in paragraph 1 of Article 13 (Capital Gains). The Article 13 term includes not only real property as defined in Article 6 but certain other interests in real property.

Paragraph 3

Paragraph 3 makes clear that all forms of income derived from the exploitation of real property are taxable in the Contracting State in which the property is situated. This includes income from any use of real property, including, but not limited to, income from direct use by the owner (in which case income may be imputed to the owner for tax purposes) and rental income from the letting of real property. In the case of a net lease of real property, if a net election has not been made, the gross rental payment (before deductible expenses incurred by the lessee) is treated as income from the property.

Other income closely associated with real property is covered by other Articles of the Convention, however, and not Article 6. For example, income from the disposition of an interest in real property is not considered "derived" from real property; taxation of that income is addressed in Article 13 (Gains). Interest paid on a mortgage on real property would be covered by Article 11 (Interest). Distributions by a U.S. Real Estate Investment Trust or certain regulated investment companies would fall under Article 13 (Gains) in the case of distributions of U.S. real property gain or Article 10 (Dividends) in the case of distributions treated as dividends. Finally, distributions from a United States Real Property Holding Corporation are not considered to be income from the exploitation of real property; such payments would fall under Article 10 or 13.

Paragraph 4

This paragraph specifies that the basic rule of paragraph 1 (as elaborated in paragraph 3) applies to income from real property of an enterprise. This clarifies that the situs country may tax the real property income (including rental income) of a resident of the other Contracting State in the absence of attribution to a permanent establishment in the situs State. This provision represents an exception to the general rule under Articles 7 (Business Profits) that income must be attributable to a permanent establishment in order to be taxable in the situs state.

Paragraph 5

The paragraph provides that a resident of one Contracting State that derives real property income from the other may elect, for any taxable year, to be subject to tax in that other State on a net basis, as though the income were attributable to a permanent establishment in that other State. The election may be terminated with the consent of the competent authority of the situs State. In the United States, revocation will be granted in accordance with the provisions of Treas. Reg. section 1.871–10(d)(2).

ARTICLE 7 (BUSINESS PROFITS)

This Article provides rules for the taxation by a Contracting State of the business profits of an enterprise of the other Contracting State.

Paragraph 1

Paragraph 1 states the general rule that business profits of an enterprise of one Contracting State may not be taxed by the other Contracting State unless the enterprise carries on business in that other Contracting State through a permanent establishment (as defined in Article 5 (Permanent Establishment)) situated there. When that condition is met, the State in which the permanent establishment is situated may tax the enterprise on the income that is attributable to the permanent establishment.

Although the Convention does not include a definition of "business profits," the term is intended to cover income derived from any trade or business. In accordance with this broad definition, the term "business profits" includes income attributable to notional principal contracts and other financial instruments to the extent that the income is attributable to a trade or business of dealing in such instruments or is otherwise related to a trade or business (as in the case of a notional principal contract entered into for the purpose of hedging currency risk arising from an active trade or business). Any other income derived from such instruments is, unless specifically covered in another article, dealt with under Article 21 (Other Income).

The term "business profits" also includes income derived by an enterprise from the rental of tangible personal property (unless such tangible personal property consists of aircraft, ships or containers, income from which is addressed by Article 8 (Shipping and Air Transport)). The inclusion of income derived by an enterprise from the rental of tangible personal property in business profits means that such income earned by a resident of a Contracting State can be taxed by the other Contracting State only if the income is attributable to a permanent establishment maintained by the resident in that other State, and, if the income is taxable, it can be taxed only on a net basis. Income from the rental of tangible personal property that is not derived in connection with a trade or business is dealt with in Article 21 (Other Income).

In addition, as a result of the definitions of "enterprise" and "business" in Article 3 (General Definitions), the term includes income derived from the furnishing of personal services. Thus, a consulting firm resident in one State whose employees or partners perform services in the other State through a permanent establishment may be taxed in that other State on a net basis under Article 7, and not under Article 14 (Income from Employment), which applies only to income of employees. With respect to the enterprise's employees themselves, however, their salary remains subject to Article 14.

Because this article applies to income earned by an enterprise from the furnishing of personal services, the article also applies to income derived by a partner resident in a Contracting State that is attributable to personal services performed in the other Contracting State through a partnership with a permanent establishment in that other State. Income which may be taxed under this article includes all income attributable to the permanent establishment in respect of the performance of the personal services carried on by the partnership (whether by the partner himself, other partners in the partnership, or by employees assisting the partners) and any income from activities ancillary to the performance of those services (e.g., charges for facsimile services).

The application of Article 7 to a service partnership may be illustrated by the following example: a partnership formed in the other Contracting State has five partners (who agree to split profits equally), four of whom are resident and perform personal services only in the other Contracting State at Office A, and one of whom performs personal services at Office B, a permanent establishment in the United States. In this case, the four partners of the partnership resident in the other Contracting State may be taxed in the United States in respect of their share of the income attributable to the permanent establishment, Office B. The services giving rise to income which may be attributed to the permanent establishment would include not only the services performed by the one resident partner, but also, for example, if one of the four other partners came to the United States and worked on an Office B matter there, the income in respect of those services. Income from the services performed by the visiting partner would be subject to tax in the United States regardless of whether the visiting partner actually visited or used Office B while performing services in the United States.

Paragraph 2

Paragraph 2 provides rules for the attribution of business profits to a permanent establishment. The Contracting States will attribute to a permanent establishment the profits that it would have earned had it been a distinct and separate enterprise engaged in the same or similar activities under the same or similar conditions and dealing wholly independently with the enterprise of which it is a permanent establishment.

The "attributable to" concept of paragraph 2 provides an alternative to the analogous but somewhat different "effectively connected" concept in Code section 864(c). In effect, paragraph 2 allows the United States to tax the lesser of two amounts of income: the amount determined by applying U.S. rules regarding the calculation of effectively connected income and the amount determined under Article 7 of the Convention. That is, a taxpayer may choose the set of rules that results in the lowest amount of taxable income, but may not mix and match.

In some cases, the amount of income "attributable to" a permanent establishment under Article 7 may be greater than the amount of income that would be treated as "effectively connected" to a U.S. trade or business under section 864. For example, a taxpayer that has a significant amount of foreign source royalty income attributable to a U.S. branch may find that it will pay less tax in the United States by applying section 864(c) of the Code, rather than the rules of Article 7, if the foreign source royalties are not derived in the active conduct of a trade or business and thus would not be effectively connected income. But, as described in the Technical Explanation to Article 1(2), if it does so, it may not then use Article 7 principles to exempt other income that would be effectively connected to the U.S. trade or business. Conversely, if it uses Article 7 principles to exempt other effectively connected income that is not attributable to its U.S. permanent establishment, then it must include the foreign source royalties in its net taxable income even though such royalties would not constitute effectively connected income.

In the case of financial institutions, the use of internal dealings to allocate income within an enterprise may produce results under Article 7 that are significantly different than the results under the effectively connected income rules. For example, income from interbranch notional principal contracts may be taken into account under Article 7, notwithstanding that such transactions may be ignored for purposes of U.S. domestic law. Under the consistency rule described above, a financial institution that conducts different lines of business through its U.S. permanent establishment may not choose to apply the rules of the Code with respect to some lines of business and Article 7 of the Convention with respect to others. If it chooses to use the rules of Article 7 to allocate its income from its trading book, it may not then use U.S. domestic rules to allocate income from its loan portfolio.

The profits attributable to a permanent establishment may be from sources within or without a Contracting State. However, as stated in paragraph 2, the business profits attributable to a permanent establishment include only those profits derived from the assets used, risks assumed, and activities performed by, the permanent establishment.

The language of paragraph 2, when combined with paragraph 3 dealing with the allowance of deductions for expenses incurred for the purposes of earning the profits, incorporates the arm's-length standard for purposes of determining the profits attributable to a permanent establishment. As noted below with respect to Article 9, the United States generally interprets the arm's length standard in a manner consistent with the OECD Transfer Pricing Guidelines.

The notes confirm that the arm's length method of paragraphs 2 and 3 consists of applying the OECD Transfer Pricing Guidelines, but taking into account the different economic and legal circumstances of a single legal entity (as opposed to separate but associated enterprises). Thus, any of the methods used in the Transfer Pricing Guidelines, including profits methods, may be used as appropriate and in accordance with the Transfer Pricing Guidelines. However, the use of the Transfer Pricing Guidelines applies only for purposes of attributing profits within the legal entity. It does not create legal obligations or other tax consequences that would result from transactions having independent legal significance.

For example, an entity that operates through branches rather than separate subsidiaries will have lower capital requirements because all of the assets of the entity are available to support all of the entity's liabilities (with some exceptions attributable to local regulatory restrictions). This is the reason that most commercial banks and some insurance companies operate through branches rather than subsidiaries. The benefit that comes from such lower capital costs must be allocated among the branches in an appropriate manner. This issue does not arise in the case of an enterprise that operates through separate entities, since each entity will have to be separately capitalized or will have to compensate another entity for providing capital (usually through a guarantee).

Under U.S. domestic regulations, internal "transactions" generally are not recognized because they do not have legal significance. In contrast, the rule provided by the notes is that such internal dealings may be used to allocate income in cases where the dealings accurately reflect the allocation of risk within the enterprise. One example is that of global trading in securities. In many cases, banks use internal swap transactions to transfer risk from one branch to a central location where traders have the expertise to manage that particular type of risk. Under the Convention, such a bank may also use such swap transactions as a means of allocating income between the branches, if use of that method is the "best method" within the meaning of regulation section 1.482–1(c). The books of a branch will not be respected, however, when the results are inconsistent with a functional analysis. So, for example, income from a transaction that is booked in a particular branch (or home office) will not be treated as attributable to that location if the sales and risk management functions that generate the income are performed in another location.

Because the use of profits methods is permissible under paragraph 2, it is not necessary for the Convention to include a provision corresponding to paragraph 4 of Article 7 of the OECD Model.

Paragraph 3

This paragraph is the same as paragraph 3 of Article 7 of the OECD Model. Paragraph 3 provides that in determining the business profits of a permanent establishment, deductions shall be allowed for the expenses incurred for the purposes of the permanent establishment, ensuring that business profits will be taxed on a net basis. This rule is not limited to expenses incurred exclusively for the purposes of the permanent establishment, but includes expenses incurred for the purposes of the enterprise as a whole, or that part of the enterprise that includes the permanent establishment. Deductions are to be allowed regardless of which accounting unit of the enterprise books the expenses, so long as they are incurred for the purposes of the permanent establishment. For example, a portion of the interest expense recorded on the books of the home office in one State may be deducted by a permanent establishment in the other if properly allocable thereto. The amount of expense that must be allowed as a deduction is determined by applying the arm's length principle.

As noted above, the notes provide that the OECD Transfer Pricing Guidelines apply, by analogy, in determining the profits attributable to a permanent establishment. Accordingly, a permanent establishment may deduct payments made to its head office or another branch in compensation for services performed for the benefit of the branch. The method to be used in calculating that amount will depend on the terms of the arrangements between the branches and head office. For example, the enterprise could have a policy, expressed in writing, under which each business unit could use the services of lawyers employed by the head office. At the end of each year, the costs of employing the lawyers would be allocated to each business unit according to the amount of services used by that business unit during the year. Since this appears to be a kind of cost-sharing arrangement and the allocation of costs is based on the benefits received by each business unit, it would be an acceptable means of determining a permanent establishment's deduction for legal expenses. Alternatively, the head office could agree to employ lawyers at its own risk, and to charge an arm's length price for legal services performed for a particular business unit. If the lawyers were under-utilized, and the "fees" received from the business units were less than the cost of employing the lawyers, then the head office would bear the excess cost. If the "fees" exceeded the cost of employing the lawyers, then the head office would keep the excess to compensate it for assuming the risk of employing the lawyers. If the enterprise acted in accordance with this agreement, this method would be an acceptable alternative method for calculating a permanent establishment's deduction for legal expenses.

The notes also specify that a permanent establishment cannot be funded entirely with debt, but must have sufficient capital to carry on its activities as if it were a distinct and separate enterprise. To the extent that the permanent establishment does not have such capital, a Contracting State may attribute such capital to the permanent establishment and deny an interest deduction to the extent necessary to reflect that capital attribution. The method prescribed by U.S. domestic law for making this attribution is found in Treas. Reg. Section 1.882–5. Both Section 1.882–5 and the method prescribed in the notes start from the premise that all of the capital of the enterprise supports all of the assets and risks of the enterprise, and therefore the entire capital of the enterprise must be allocated to its various businesses and offices.

However, section 1.882–5 does not take into account the fact that some assets create more risk for the enterprise than do other assets. An independent enterprise would need less capital to support a perfectly-hedged U.S. Treasury security than it would need to support an equity security or other asset with significant market and/or credit risk. Accordingly, in some cases section 1.882–5 would require a taxpayer to allocate more capital to the United States, and therefore would reduce the taxpayer's interest deduction more, than is appropriate. To address these cases, the notes allow a taxpayer to apply a more flexible approach that takes into account the relative risk of its assets in the various jurisdictions in which it does business. In particular, in the case of financial institutions other than insurance companies, the amount of capital attributable to a permanent establishment is determined by allocating the institution's total equity between its various offices on the basis of the proportion of the financial institution's risk-weighted assets attributable to each of them. This recognizes the fact that financial institutions are in many cases required to risk-weight their assets for regulatory purposes and, in other cases, will do so for business reasons even if not required to do so by regulators. However, risk-weighting is more complicated than the method prescribed by Section 1.882–5. Accordingly, to ease this administrative burden, taxpayers may choose to apply the principles of Treas. Reg. Section 1.882–5(c) to determine the amount of capital allocable to its U.S. permanent establishment, in lieu of determining its allocable capital under the risk-weighed capital allocation method provided by the notes, even if it has otherwise chosen to apply the principles of Article 7 rather than the effectively connected income rules of U.S. domestic law.

Paragraph 4

Paragraph 4 provides that no business profits can be attributed to a permanent establishment merely because it purchases goods or merchandise for the enterprise of which it is a part. This paragraph is essentially identical to paragraph 5 of Article 7 of the OECD Model. This rule applies only to an office that performs functions for the enterprise in addition to purchasing. The income attribution issue does not arise if the sole activity of the office is the purchase of goods or merchandise because such activity does not give rise to a permanent establishment under Article 5 (Permanent Establishment). A common situation in which paragraph 4 is relevant is one in which a permanent establishment purchases raw materials for the enterprise's manufacturing operation conducted outside the United States and sells the manufactured product. While business profits may be attributable to the permanent establishment with respect to its sales activities, no profits are attributable to it with respect to its purchasing activities.

Paragraph 5

Paragraph 5 provides that profits shall be determined by the same method each year, unless there is good reason to change the method used. This rule assures consistent tax treatment over time for permanent establishments. It limits the ability of both the Contracting State and the enterprise to change accounting methods to be applied to the permanent establishment. It does not, however, restrict a Contracting State from imposing additional requirements, such as the rules under Code section 481, to prevent amounts from being duplicated or omitted following a change in accounting method. Such adjustments may be necessary, for example, if the taxpayer switches from using the domestic rules under section 864 in one year to using the rules of Article 7 in the next. Also, if the taxpayer switches from Convention-based rules to U.S. domestic rules, it may need to meet certain deadlines for making elections that are not necessary when applying the rules of the Convention.

Paragraph 6

Paragraph 6 coordinates the provisions of Article 7 and other provisions of the Convention. Under this paragraph, when business profits include items of income that are dealt with separately under other articles of the Convention, the provisions of those articles will, except when they specifically provide to the contrary, take precedence over the provisions of Article 7. For example, the taxation of dividends will be determined by the rules of Article 10 (Dividends), and not by Article 7, except where, as provided in paragraph 6 of Article 10, the dividend is attributable to a permanent establishment. In the latter case the provisions of Article 7 apply. Thus, an enterprise of one State deriving dividends from the other State may not rely on Article 7 to exempt those dividends from tax at source if they are not attributable to a permanent establishment of the enterprise in the other State. By the same token, if the dividends are attributable to a permanent establishment in the other State, the dividends may be taxed on a net income basis at the source State full corporate tax rate, rather than on a gross basis under Article 10 (Dividends).

As provided in Article 8 (Shipping and Air Transport), income derived from shipping and air transport activities in international traffic described in that Article is taxable only in the country of residence of the enterprise regardless of whether it is attributable to a permanent establishment situated in the source State.

Paragraph 7

Paragraph 7 incorporates into the Convention the rule of Code section 864(c)(6) . Like the Code section on which it is based, paragraph 7 provides that any income or gain attributable to a permanent establishment during its existence is taxable in the Contracting State where the permanent establishment is situated, even if the payment of that income or gain is deferred until after the permanent establishment ceases to exist. This rule applies with respect to paragraphs 1 and 2 of Article 7 (Business Profits), paragraph 6 of Article 10 (Dividends), paragraph 4 of Article 11 (Interest), paragraph 3 of Articles 12 (Royalties) and 13 (Gains) and paragraph 2 of Article 21 (Other Income).

The effect of this rule can be illustrated by the following example. Assume a company that is a resident of the other Contracting State and that maintains a permanent establishment in the United States winds up the permanent establishment's business and sells the permanent establishment's inventory and assets to a U.S. buyer at the end of year 1 in exchange for an interest-bearing installment obligation payable in full at the end of year 3. Despite the fact that Article 13's threshold requirement for U.S. taxation is not met in year 3 because the company has no permanent establishment in the United States, the United States may tax the deferred income payment recognized by the company in year 3.

Relationship to Other Articles

This Article is subject to the saving clause of paragraph 4 of Article 1 (General Scope) of the Model. Thus, if a citizen of the United States who is a resident of the other Contracting State under the treaty derives business profits from the United States that are not attributable to a permanent establishment in the United States, the United States may, subject to the special foreign tax credit rules of paragraph 4 of Article 23 (Relief from Double Taxation), tax those profits, notwithstanding the provision of paragraph 1 of this Article which would exempt the income from U.S. tax.

The benefits of this Article are also subject to Article 22 (Limitation on Benefits). Thus, an enterprise of the other Contracting State and that derives income effectively connected with a U.S. trade or business may not claim the benefits of Article 7 unless the resident carrying on the enterprise qualifies for such benefits under Article 22.

ARTICLE 8 (SHIPPING AND AIR TRANSPORT)

This Article governs the taxation of profits from the operation of ships and aircraft in international traffic. The term "international traffic" is defined in subparagraph 1(f) of Article 3 (General Definitions).

Paragraph 1

Paragraph 1 provides that profits derived by an enterprise of a Contracting State from the operation in international traffic of ships or aircraft are taxable only in that Contracting State. Because paragraph 6 of Article 7 (Business Profits) defers to Article 8 with respect to shipping income, such income derived by a resident of one of the Contracting States may not be taxed in the other State even if the enterprise has a permanent establishment in that other State. Thus, if a U.S. airline has a ticket office in the other State, that State may not tax the airline's profits attributable to that office under Article 7. Since entities engaged in international transportation activities normally will have many permanent establishments in a number of countries, the rule avoids difficulties that would be encountered in attributing income to multiple permanent establishments if the income were covered by Article 7 (Business Profits).

Paragraph 2

The income from the operation of ships or aircraft in international traffic that is exempt from tax under paragraph 1 is defined in paragraph 2.

In addition to income derived directly from the operation of ships and aircraft in international traffic, this definition also includes certain items of rental income. First, income of an enterprise of a Contracting State from the rental of ships or aircraft on a full basis (i.e., with crew) is income of the lessor from the operation of ships and aircraft in international traffic and, therefore, is exempt from tax in the other Contracting State under paragraph 1. Also, paragraph 2 encompasses income from the lease of ships or aircraft on a bareboat basis (i.e., without crew), either when the income is incidental to other income of the lessor from the operation of ships or aircraft in international traffic, or when the ships or aircraft are operated in international traffic by the lessee. If neither of those two conditions apply, income from the bareboat rentals would constitute business profits. The coverage of Article 8 is therefore broader than that of Article 8 of the OECD Model, which covers bareboat leasing only when it is incidental to other income of the lessor from the operation of ships of aircraft in international traffic.

Paragraph 2 also clarifies, consistent with the Commentary to Article 8 of the OECD Model, that income earned by an enterprise from the inland transport of property or passengers within either Contracting State falls within Article 8 if the transport is undertaken as part of the international transport of property or passengers by the enterprise. Thus, if a U.S. shipping company contracts to carry property from the other Contracting State to a U.S. city and, as part of that contract, it transports the property by truck from its point of origin to an airport in the other Contracting State (or it contracts with a trucking company to carry the property to the airport) the income earned by the U.S. shipping company from the overland leg of the journey would be taxable only in the United States. Similarly, Article 8 also would apply to all of the income derived from a contract for the international transport of goods, even if the goods were transported to the port by a lighter, not by the vessel that carried the goods in international waters.

Finally, certain non-transport activities that are an integral part of the services performed by a transport company, or are ancillary to the enterprise's operation of ships or aircraft in international traffic, are understood to be covered in paragraph 1, though they are not specified in paragraph 2. These include, for example, the provision of goods and services by engineers, ground and equipment maintenance and staff, cargo handlers, catering staff and customer services personnel. Where the enterprise provides such goods to, or performs services for, other enterprises and such activities are directly connected with or ancillary to the enterprise's operation of ships or aircraft in international traffic, the profits from the provision of such goods and services to other enterprises will fall under this paragraph.

For example, enterprises engaged in the operation of ships or aircraft in international traffic may enter into pooling arrangements for the purposes of reducing the costs of maintaining facilities needed for the operation of their ships or aircraft in other countries. For instance, where an airline enterprise agrees (for example, under an International Airlines Technical Pool agreement) to provide spare parts or maintenance services to other airlines landing at a particular location (which allows it to benefit from these services at other locations), activities carried on pursuant to that agreement will be ancillary to the operation of aircraft in international traffic by the enterprise. Also, advertising that the enterprise may do for other enterprises in magazines offered aboard ships or aircraft that it operates in international traffic or at its business locations, such as ticket offices, is ancillary to its operation of these ships or aircraft. Profits generated by such advertising fall within this paragraph. Income earned by concessionaires, however, is not covered by Article 8. These interpretations of paragraph 1 also are consistent with the Commentary to Article 8 of the OECD Model.

Paragraph 3

Under this paragraph, profits of an enterprise of a Contracting State from the use, maintenance or rental of containers (including equipment for their transport) are exempt from tax in the other Contracting State, unless those containers are used for transport solely in the other Contracting State. This result obtains under paragraph 3 regardless of whether the recipient of the income is engaged in the operation of ships or aircraft in international traffic, and regardless of whether the enterprise has a permanent establishment in the other Contracting State. Only income from the use, maintenance or rental of containers that is incidental to other income from international traffic is covered by Article 8 of the OECD Model.

Paragraph 4

This paragraph clarifies that the provisions of paragraphs 1 and 3 also apply to profits derived by an enterprise of a Contracting State from participation in a pool, joint business or international operating agency. This refers to various arrangements for international cooperation by carriers in shipping and air transport. For example, airlines from two countries may agree to share the transport of passengers between the two countries. They each will fly the same number of flights per week and share the revenues from that route equally, regardless of the number of passengers that each airline actually transports. Paragraph 4 makes clear that with respect to each carrier the income dealt with in the Article is that carrier's share of the total transport, not the income derived from the passengers actually carried by the airline. This paragraph corresponds to paragraph 4 of Article 8 of the OECD Model.

Relationship to Other Articles

The taxation of gains from the alienation of ships, aircraft or containers is not dealt with in this Article but in paragraph 4 of Article 13 (Gains).

As with other benefits of the Convention, the benefit of exclusive residence country taxation under Article 8 is available to an enterprise only if it is entitled to benefits under Article 22 (Limitation on Benefits). This Article also is subject to the saving clause of paragraph 4 of Article 1 (General Scope) of the Model. Thus, if a citizen of the United States who is a resident of the other Contracting State derives profits from the operation of ships or aircraft in international traffic, notwithstanding the exclusive residence country taxation in paragraph 1 of Article 8, the United States may, subject to the special foreign tax credit rules of paragraph 4 of Article 23 (Relief from Double Taxation), tax those profits as part of the worldwide income of the citizen. (This is an unlikely situation, however, because non-tax considerations (e.g., insurance) generally result in shipping activities being carried on in corporate form.)

ARTICLE 9 (ASSOCIATED ENTERPRISES)

This Article incorporates in the Convention the arm's-length principle reflected in the U.S. domestic transfer pricing provisions, particularly Code section 482. It provides that when related enterprises engage in a transaction on terms that are not arm's-length, the Contracting States may make appropriate adjustments to the taxable income and tax liability of such related enterprises to reflect what the income and tax of these enterprises with respect to the transaction would have been had there been an arm's-length relationship between them.

Paragraph 1

This paragraph is essentially the same as its counterpart in the OECD Model. It addresses the situation where an enterprise of a Contracting State is related to an enterprise of the other Contracting State, and there are arrangements or conditions imposed between the enterprises in their commercial or financial relations that are different from those that would have existed in the absence of the relationship. Under these circumstances, the Contracting States may adjust the income (or loss) of the enterprise to reflect what it would have been in the absence of such a relationship.

The paragraph identifies the relationships between enterprises that serve as a prerequisite to application of the Article. As the Commentary to the OECD Model makes clear, the necessary element in these relationships is effective control, which is also the standard for purposes of section 482. Thus, the Article applies if an enterprise of one State participates directly or indirectly in the management, control, or capital of the enterprise of the other State. Also, the Article applies if any third person or persons participate directly or indirectly in the management, control, or capital of enterprises of different States. For this purpose, all types of control are included, i.e., whether or not legally enforceable and however exercised or exercisable.

The fact that a transaction is entered into between such related enterprises does not, in and of itself, mean that a Contracting State may adjust the income (or loss) of one or both of the enterprises under the provisions of this Article. If the conditions of the transaction are consistent with those that would be made between independent persons, the income arising from that transaction should not be subject to adjustment under this Article.

Similarly, the fact that associated enterprises may have concluded arrangements, such as cost sharing arrangements or general services agreements, is not in itself an indication that the two enterprises have entered into a non-arm's-length transaction that should give rise to an adjustment under paragraph 1. Both related and unrelated parties enter into such arrangements (e.g., joint venturers may share some development costs). As with any other kind of transaction, when related parties enter into an arrangement, the specific arrangement must be examined to see whether or not it meets the arm's-length standard. In the event that it does not, an appropriate adjustment may be made, which may include modifying the terms of the agreement or re-characterizing the transaction to reflect its substance.

It is understood that the "commensurate with income" standard for determining appropriate transfer prices for intangibles, added to Code section 482 by the Tax Reform Act of 1986, was designed to operate consistently with the arm's-length standard. The implementation of this standard in the section 482 regulations is in accordance with the general principles of paragraph 1 of Article 9 of the Convention, as interpreted by the OECD Transfer Pricing Guidelines.

This Article also permits tax authorities to deal with thin capitalization issues. They may, in the context of Article 9, scrutinize more than the rate of interest charged on a loan between related persons. They also may examine the capital structure of an enterprise, whether a payment in respect of that loan should be treated as interest, and, if it is treated as interest, under what circumstances interest deductions should be allowed to the payor. Paragraph 2 of the Commentary to Article 9 of the OECD Model, together with the U.S. observation set forth in paragraph 15, sets forth a similar understanding of the scope of Article 9 in the context of thin capitalization.

Paragraph 2

When a Contracting State has made an adjustment that is consistent with the provisions of paragraph 1, and the other Contracting State agrees that the adjustment was appropriate to reflect arm's-length conditions, that other Contracting State is obligated to make a correlative adjustment (sometimes referred to as a "corresponding adjustment") to the tax liability of the related person in that other Contracting State. Although the OECD Model does not specify that the other Contracting State must agree with the initial adjustment before it is obligated to make the correlative adjustment, the Commentary makes clear that the paragraph is to be read that way.

As explained in the Commentary to Article 9 of the OECD Model, Article 9 leaves the treatment of "secondary adjustments" to the laws of the Contracting States. When an adjustment under Article 9 has been made, one of the parties will have in its possession funds that it would not have had at arm's length. The question arises as to how to treat these funds. In the United States the general practice is to treat such funds as a dividend or contribution to capital, depending on the relationship between the parties. Under certain circumstances, the parties may be permitted to restore the funds to the party that would have the funds had the transactions been entered into on arm's length terms, and to establish an account payable pending restoration of the funds. See Rev. Proc. 99–32, 1999–2 C.B. 296.

The Contracting State making a secondary adjustment will take the other provisions of the Convention, where relevant, into account. For example, if the effect of a secondary adjustment is to treat a U.S. corporation as having made a distribution of profits to its parent corporation in the other Contracting State, the provisions of Article 10 (Dividends) will apply, and the United States may impose a 5 percent withholding tax on the dividend. Also, if under Article 23 the other State generally gives a credit for taxes paid with respect to such dividends, it would also be required to do so in this case.

The competent authorities are authorized by paragraph 3 of Article 25 (Mutual Agreement Procedure) to consult, if necessary, to resolve any differences in the application of these provisions. For example, there may be a disagreement over whether an adjustment made by a Contracting State under paragraph 1 was appropriate.

If a correlative adjustment is made under paragraph 2, it is to be implemented, pursuant to paragraph 2 of Article 25 (Mutual Agreement Procedure), notwithstanding any time limits or other procedural limitations in the law of the Contracting State making the adjustment. If a taxpayer has entered a closing agreement (or other written settlement) with the United States prior to bringing a case to the competent authorities, the U.S. competent authority will endeavor only to obtain a correlative adjustment from the other Contracting State. See, Rev. Proc. 2002–52, 2002–31 I.R.B. 242, Section 7.04.

Relationship to Other Articles

The saving clause of paragraph 4 of Article 1 (General Scope) does not apply to paragraph 2 of Article 9 by virtue of an exception to the saving clause in paragraph 5(a) of Article 1. Thus, even if the statute of limitations has run, a refund of tax can be made in order to implement a correlative adjustment. Statutory or procedural limitations, however, cannot be overridden to impose additional tax, because paragraph 2 of Article 1 provides that the Convention cannot restrict any statutory benefit.

ARTICLE 10 (DIVIDENDS)

Article 10 provides rules for the taxation of dividends paid by a company that is a resident of one Contracting State to a beneficial owner that is a resident of the other Contracting State. The article provides for full residence country taxation of such dividends and a limited source-State right to tax. Article 10 also provides rules for the imposition of a tax on branch profits by the State of source. Finally, the article prohibits a State from imposing taxes on a company resident in the other Contracting State, other than a branch profits tax, on undistributed earnings.

Paragraph 1

The right of a shareholder's country of residence to tax dividends arising in the source country is preserved by paragraph 1, which permits a Contracting State to tax its residents on dividends paid to them by a company that is a resident of the other Contracting State. For dividends from any other source paid to a resident, Article 21 (Other Income) grants the residence country exclusive taxing jurisdiction (other than for dividends attributable to a permanent establishment in the other State).

Paragraph 2

The State of source also may tax dividends beneficially owned by a resident of the other State, subject to the limitations of paragraphs 2 and 3. Paragraph 2 generally limits the rate of withholding tax in the State of source on dividends paid by a company resident in that State to 15 percent of the gross amount of the dividend. If, however, the beneficial owner of the dividend is a company resident in the other State and owns directly shares representing at least 10 percent of the voting power of the company paying the dividend, then the rate of withholding tax in the State of source is limited to 5 percent of the gross amount of the dividend. Shares are considered voting shares if they provide the power to elect, appoint or replace any person vested with the powers ordinarily exercised by the board of directors of a U.S. corporation.

The benefits of paragraph 2 may be granted at the time of payment by means of reduced rate of withholding tax at source. It also is consistent with the paragraph for tax to be withheld at the time of payment at full statutory rates, and the treaty benefit to be granted by means of a subsequent refund so long as such procedures are applied in a reasonable manner.

The determination of whether the ownership threshold for subparagraph (a) of paragraph 2 is met for purposes of the 5 percent maximum rate of withholding tax is made on the date on which entitlement to the dividend is determined. Thus, in the case of a dividend from a U.S. company, the determination of whether the ownership threshold is met generally would be made on the dividend record date.

Paragraph 2 does not affect the taxation of the profits out of which the dividends are paid. The taxation by a Contracting State of the income of its resident companies is governed by the internal law of the Contracting State, subject to the provisions of paragraph 4 of Article 24 (Non–Discrimination).

The term "beneficial owner" is not defined in the Convention, and is, therefore, defined as under the internal law of the country imposing tax (i.e., the source country). The beneficial owner of the dividend for purposes of Article 10 is the person to which the income is attributable under the laws of the source State. Thus, if a dividend paid by a corporation that is a resident of one of the States (as determined under Article 4 (Residence)) is received by a nominee or agent that is a resident of the other State on behalf of a person that is not a resident of that other State, the dividend is not entitled to the benefits of this Article. However, a dividend received by a nominee on behalf of a resident of that other State would be entitled to benefits. These limitations are confirmed by paragraph 12 of the Commentary to Article 10 of the OECD Model. See also paragraph 24 of the Commentary to Article 1 of the OECD Model.

Special rules, however, apply to shares that are held through fiscally transparent entities. In that case, the rules of Article 1(6) will apply to determine whether the dividends should be treated as having been derived by a resident of a Contracting State. If so, then the source country rules will apply to determine whether that person, or another resident of the other Contracting State, is the beneficial owner of the income, as required by paragraph 2, and satisfies any other requirements for the specified benefits, such as the ownership threshold of subparagraph 2(a).

For example, assume that PCo, a company that is a resident of the other Contracting State, owns all of the outstanding shares in ThirdDE, an entity that is disregarded for U.S. tax purposes that is resident in a third country. ThirdDE owns 100% of the stock of USCo. The other Contracting State views ThirdDE as fiscally transparent under its domestic law, and taxes PCo currently on the income derived by ThirdDE. In this case, PCo is treated as deriving the dividends paid by USCo under

Article 1(6). PCo is also the beneficial owner of the dividends under U.S. law, because an entity with a single owner that has made an election under Treas. Reg. Section 301.7701–3(a) is disregarded as an entity separate from its owner.[2] Moreover, PCo is treated as owning the shares of USCo directly. The Convention does not address what constitutes direct ownership for purposes of Article 10. As a result, whether ownership is direct is determined under the internal law of the country imposing tax (i.e., the source country) unless the context otherwise requires. Accordingly, a company that holds stock through such an entity will generally be considered to directly own such stock for purposes of Article 10.

This result may change, however, if ThirdDE is regarded as non-fiscally transparent under the laws of the other Contracting State. Assuming that ThirdDE is treated as non-fiscally transparent by the other Contracting State, the income will not be treated as derived by a resident of the other Contracting State for purposes of the Convention. However, ThirdDE may still be entitled to the benefits of the U.S. tax treaty, if any, with its country of residence. In the case of hybrid entities (that is, an entity that is treated as fiscally transparent under the laws of one State and non-fiscally transparent under the laws of the other, or of a third State), it may be that the person who "derives" the income under Article 1(6) is not the same person as the "beneficial owner" under Article 10. This will not prevent a claim for treaty benefits, so long as each of the requirements is met by one or more residents of the other Contracting State. For example, assume the same facts, except that the intermediate entity is SubDE, an entity organized in the other Contracting State, but treated as a disregarded entity for U.S. tax purposes. Paragraph 2(a) provides that the reduced withholding rate is available to a company that is the beneficial owner of the dividend and, which owns, directly, at least 10 percent of the shares of USCo. Under the laws of the other Contracting State, SubDE is taxable as a corporation. Accordingly, the dividend is treated as derived by a resident of the other Contracting State, SubDE, under the rules of Article 1(6). From the U.S. perspective, SubDE does not exist as a separate entity. Accordingly, the combined entity that is SubDE and PCo satisfy the requirements that the beneficial owner be a resident of the other Contracting State and that the shares of USCo be held directly. In addition, the analysis and result are unchanged if all of the outstanding shares in SubDE are owned by an individual who is a resident of the other Contracting State.

If PCo were not a resident of the other Contracting State, the analysis would be slightly different. From the U.S. perspective, the combined entity that is PCo and SubDE meets the 10 percent ownership requirement, and it owns the shares directly. From the perspective of the other Contracting State, SubDE is a resident of the other Contracting State. Accordingly, all

2. It is assumed in each of these examples that none of the parties has entered into an arrangement that would shift the benefits and burdens of ownership to a third party.

of the requirements of Articles 1(6) and 10(2)(a) are met, and the 5% withholding rate applies to the dividends paid by USCo. Alternatively, PCo might be able to claim an exemption from the withholding tax altogether under another tax treaty to which the United States is a party. That would be the case if PCo were established in, and a resident of, a country with which the United States has entered into a tax treaty eliminating the withholding tax on dividends, and that other country viewed SubDE as fiscally transparent.

The same principles would apply in determining whether companies holding shares through fiscally transparent entities such as partnerships, trusts, and estates would qualify for benefits. As a result, companies holding shares through such entities may be able to claim the benefits of subparagraph (a) under certain circumstances. The lower rate applies when the company's proportionate share of the shares held by the intermediate entity meets the 10 percent threshold, and the company meets the requirements of Article 1(6) (i.e., the company's country of residence treats the intermediate entity as fiscally transparent) with respect to the dividend. Whether this ownership threshold is satisfied may be difficult to determine and often will require an analysis of the partnership or trust agreement.

Paragraph 3

Paragraph 3 provides that dividends received by a pension fund may not be taxed in the Contracting State of which the company paying the tax is a resident, unless such dividends are derived from the carrying on of a business, directly or indirectly, by the pension fund or through an associated enterprise. For these purposes, the term "pension fund" is defined in subparagraph 1(k) of Article 3 (General Definitions).

The rule is necessary because pension funds normally do not pay tax (either through a general exemption or because reserves for future pension liabilities effectively offset all of the fund's income), and therefore cannot benefit from a foreign tax credit. Moreover, distributions from a pension fund generally do not maintain the character of the underlying income, so the beneficiaries of the pension are not in a position to claim a foreign tax credit when they finally receive the pension, in many cases years after the withholding tax has been paid. Accordingly, in the absence of this rule, the dividends would almost certainly be subject to unrelieved double taxation.

Paragraph 4

Paragraph 4 imposes limitations on the rate reductions provided by paragraphs 2 and 3 in the case of dividends paid by [a] RIC or a REIT.

The first sentence of subparagraph 4(a) provides that dividends paid by a RIC or REIT are not eligible for the 5 percent rate of withholding tax of subparagraph 2(a).

The second sentence of subparagraph 4(a) provides that the 15 percent maximum rate of withholding tax of subparagraph 2(b) applies to dividends paid by RICs and that the elimination of source-country withholding tax of paragraph 3 applies to dividends paid by RICs and beneficially owned by a pension fund.

The third sentence of subparagraph 4(a) provides that the 15 percent rate of withholding tax also applies to dividends paid by a REIT and that the elimination of source-country withholding tax of paragraph 3 applies to dividends paid by REITs and beneficially owned by a pension fund, provided that one of the three following conditions is met. First, the beneficial owner of the dividend is an individual or a pension fund, in either case holding an interest of not more than 10 percent in the REIT. Second, the dividend is paid with respect to a class of stock that is publicly traded and the beneficial owner of the dividend is a person holding an interest of not more than 5 percent of any class of the REIT's shares. Third, the beneficial owner of the dividend holds an interest in the REIT of not more than 10 percent and the REIT is "diversified."

Subparagraph (b) provides a definition of the term "diversified", which is necessary because the term is not defined in the Code. A REIT is diversified if the gross value of no single interest in real property held by the REIT exceeds 10 percent of the gross value of the REIT's total interest in real property. Foreclosure property is not considered an interest in real property, and a REIT holding a partnership interest is treated as owning its proportionate share of any interest in real property held by the partnership.

The restrictions set out above are intended to prevent the use of these entities to gain inappropriate U.S. tax benefits. For example, a company resident in the other Contracting State that wishes to hold a diversified portfolio of U.S. corporate shares could hold the portfolio directly and would bear a U.S. withholding tax of 15 percent on all of the dividends that it receives. Alternatively, it could hold the same diversified portfolio by purchasing 10 percent or more of the interests in a RIC. If the RIC is a pure conduit, there may be no U.S. tax cost to interposing the RIC in the chain of ownership. Absent the special rule in paragraph 4, such use of the RIC could transform portfolio dividends, taxable in the United States under the Convention at a 15 percent maximum rate of withholding tax, into direct investment dividends taxable at a 5 percent maximum rate of withholding tax or eligible for the elimination of source-country withholding tax on dividends paid to pension funds.

Similarly, a resident of the other Contracting State directly holding U.S. real property would pay U.S. tax upon the sale of the property either at a 30 percent rate of withholding tax on the gross income or at graduated rates on the net income. As in the preceding example, by placing the real property in a REIT, the investor could, absent a special rule, transform income from the sale of real estate into dividend income from the REIT, taxable at the rates provided in Article 10, significantly reducing the U.S. tax that otherwise would be imposed. Paragraph 4 prevents this result and thereby avoids a disparity between the taxation of direct real estate investments and real estate investments made through REIT conduits. In the cases in which paragraph 4 allows a dividend from a REIT to be eligible for the 15 percent rate of withholding tax, the holding in the REIT is not considered the equivalent of a direct holding in the underlying real property.

Paragraph 5

Paragraph 5 defines the term dividends broadly and flexibly. The definition is intended to cover all arrangements that yield a return on an equity investment in a corporation as determined under the tax law of the state of source, as well as arrangements that might be developed in the future.

The term includes income from shares, or other corporate rights that are not treated as debt under the law of the source State, that participate in the profits of the company. The term also includes income that is subjected to the same tax treatment as income from shares by the law of the State of source. Thus, a constructive dividend that results from a non-arm's length transaction between a corporation and a related party is a dividend. In the case of the United States the term dividend includes amounts treated as a dividend under U.S. law upon the sale or redemption of shares or upon a transfer of shares in a reorganization. See, e.g., Rev. Rul. 92–85, 1992–2 C.B. 69 (sale of foreign subsidiary's stock to U.S. sister company is a deemed dividend to extent of the subsidiary's and sister company's earnings and profits). Further, a distribution from a U.S. publicly traded limited partnership, which is taxed as a corporation under U.S. law, is a dividend for purposes of Article 10. However, a distribution by a limited liability company is not taxable by the United States under Article 10, provided the limited liability company is not characterized as an association taxable as a corporation under U.S. law.

Finally, a payment denominated as interest that is made by a thinly capitalized corporation may be treated as a dividend to the extent that the debt is recharacterized as equity under the laws of the source State.

Paragraph 6

Paragraph 6 excludes from the general source country limitations under paragraphs 2 through 4 dividends paid with respect to holdings that form part of the business property of a permanent establishment. In such case, the rules of Article 7 (Business Profits) shall apply. Accordingly, the dividends will be taxed on a net basis using the rates and rules of taxation generally applicable to residents of the State in which the permanent establishment is located, as such rules may be modified by the Convention. An example of dividends paid with respect to the business property of a permanent establishment would be dividends derived by a dealer in stock or securities from stock or securities that the dealer held for sale to customers.

Paragraph 7

The right of a Contracting State to tax dividends paid by a company that is a resident of the other Contracting State is restricted by paragraph 7 to cases in which the dividends are paid to a resident of that Contracting State or are attributable to a permanent establishment or fixed base in that Contracting State. Thus, a Contracting State may not impose a "secondary" withholding tax on dividends paid by a nonresident company out of earnings and profits from that Contracting State. In the case of the United States, the secondary withholding tax was eliminated for payments made after December 31, 2004 in the American Jobs Creation Act of 2004.

The paragraph also restricts the right of a Contracting State to impose corporate level taxes on undistributed profits, other than a branch profits tax. The paragraph does not restrict a State's right to tax its resident shareholders on undistributed earnings of a corporation resident in the other State. Thus, the authority of the United States to impose taxes on subpart F income and on earnings deemed invested in U.S. property, and its tax on income of a passive foreign investment company that is a qualified electing fund is in no way restricted by this provision.

Paragraph 8

Paragraph 8 permits a Contracting State to impose a branch profits tax on a company resident in the other Contracting State. The tax is in addition to other taxes permitted by the Convention. The term "company" is defined in subparagraph 1(b) of Article 3 (General Definitions).

A Contracting State may impose a branch profits tax on a company if the company has income attributable to a permanent establishment in that Contracting State, derives income from real property in that Contracting State that is taxed on a net basis under Article 6 (Income from Real Property), or realizes gains taxable in that State under paragraph 1 of Article 13 (Gains). In the case of the United States, the imposition of such tax is limited, however, to the portion of the aforementioned items of income that represents the amount of such income that is the "dividend equivalent amount." This is consistent with the relevant rules under the U.S. branch profits tax, and the term dividend equivalent amount is defined under U.S. law. Section 884 defines the dividend equivalent amount as an amount for a particular year that is equivalent to the income described above that is included in the corporation's effectively connected earnings and profits for that year, after payment of the corporate tax under Articles 6 (Income from Real Property), 7 (Business Profits) or 13 (Gains), reduced for any increase in the branch's U.S. net equity during the year or increased for any reduction in its U.S. net equity during the year. U.S. net equity is U.S. assets less U.S. liabilities. See Treas. Reg. section 1.884–1.

The dividend equivalent amount for any year approximates the dividend that a U.S. branch office would have paid during the year if the branch had been operated as a separate U.S. subsidiary company. In the case that the other Contracting State also imposes a branch profits tax, the base of its tax must be limited to an amount that is analogous to the dividend equivalent amount.

As discussed in the Technical Explanations to Articles 1(2) and 7(2), consistency principles require that a taxpayer may not mix and match the rules of the Code and the Convention in an inconsistent manner. In the context of the branch profits tax, the consistency requirement means that an enterprise that uses the principles of Article 7 to determine its net taxable income also must use the principles in determining the dividend equivalent amount. Similarly, an enterprise that uses U.S. domestic law to determine its net taxable income must also use U.S. domestic law in complying with the branch profits tax. As in the case of Article 7, if an enterprise switches between domestic law and treaty principles from year to year, it will need to make appropriate adjustments or recapture amounts that otherwise might go untaxed.

Subparagraph b) provides that the branch profits tax shall not be imposed at a rate exceeding the direct investment dividend withholding rate of five percent.

Relationship to Other Articles

Notwithstanding the foregoing limitations on source country taxation of dividends, the saving clause of paragraph 4 of Article 1 permits the United States to tax dividends received by its residents and citizens, subject to the special foreign tax credit rules of paragraph 4 of Article 23 (Relief from Double Taxation), as if the Convention had not come into effect.

The benefits of this Article are also subject to the provisions of Article 22 (Limitation on Benefits). Thus, if a resident of the other Contracting State is the beneficial owner of dividends paid by a U.S. corporation, the shareholder must qualify for treaty benefits under at least one of the tests of Article 22 in order to receive the benefits of this Article.

ARTICLE 11 (INTEREST)

Article 11 specifies the taxing jurisdictions over interest income of the States of source and residence and defines the terms necessary to apply the article.

Paragraph 1

Paragraph 1 generally grants to the State of residence the exclusive right to tax interest beneficially owned by its residents and arising in the other Contracting State.

The term "beneficial owner" is not defined in the Convention, and is, therefore, defined under the internal law of the State of source. The beneficial owner of the interest for purposes of Article 11 is the person to which the income is attributable under the laws of the source State. Thus, if interest arising in a Contracting State is received by a nominee or agent that is a resident of the other State on behalf of a person that is not a resident of that other State, the interest is not entitled to the benefits of Article 11. However, interest received by a nominee on behalf of a resident of that other State would be entitled to benefits. These limitations are confirmed by paragraph 8 of the OECD Commentary to Article 11. See also paragraph 24 of the OECD Commentary to Article 1.

Paragraph 2

Paragraph 2 provides anti-abuse exceptions to the source-country exemption in paragraph 1 for two classes of interest payments.

The first class of interest, dealt with in subparagraphs (a) and (b) is so-called "contingent interest." With respect to the other Contracting State, such interest is defined in subparagraph (a) as any interest arising in that State that is determined by reference to the receipts, sales, income, profits or other cash flow of the debtor or a related person, to any change in the value of any property of the debtor or a related person or to any dividend, partnership distribution or similar payment made by the debtor or a related person. Any such interest may be taxed in that Contracting State according to the laws of that State. If the beneficial owner is a resident of the other Contracting State, however, the gross amount of the interest may be taxed at a rate not exceeding 15 percent. With respect to interest arising in the United States, subparagraph (b) refers to contingent interest of a type that does not qualify as portfolio interest under U.S. domestic law. The cross-reference to the U.S. definition of contingent interest, which is found in section 871(h)(4) of the Code, is intended to ensure that the exceptions of section 871(h)(4)(c) will be applicable.

The second class of interest is dealt with in subparagraph c) of paragraph 2. This exception is consistent with the policy of Code sections 860E(e) and 860G(b) that excess inclusions with respect to a real estate mortgage investment conduit (REMIC) should bear full U.S. tax in all cases. Without a full tax at source foreign purchasers of residual interests would have a competitive advantage over U.S. purchasers at the time these interests are initially offered. Also, absent this rule, the U.S. fisc would suffer a revenue loss with respect to mortgages held in a REMIC because of opportunities for tax avoidance created by differences in the timing of taxable and economic income produced by these interests.

Paragraph 3

The term "interest" as used in Article 11 is defined in paragraph 2 to include, inter alia, income from debt claims of every kind, whether or not secured by a mortgage. Penalty charges for late payment are excluded from the definition of interest. Interest that is paid or accrued subject to a contingency is within the ambit of Article 11. This includes income from a debt obligation carrying the right to participate in profits. The term does not, however, include amounts that are treated as dividends under Article 10 (Dividends).

The term interest also includes amounts subject to the same tax treatment as income from money lent under the law of the State in which the income arises. Thus, for purposes of the Convention, amounts that the United States will treat as interest include (i) the difference between the issue price and the stated redemption price at maturity of a debt instrument (i.e., original issue discount ("OID")), which may be wholly or partially realized on the disposition of a debt instrument (section 1273), (ii) amounts that are imputed interest on a deferred sales contract (section 483), (iii) amounts treated as interest or OID under the stripped bond rules (section 1286), (iv) amounts treated as original issue discount under the below-market interest rate rules (section 7872), (v) a partner's distributive share of a partnership's interest income (section 702), (vi) the interest portion of periodic payments made under a "finance lease" or similar contractual arrangement that in substance is a borrowing by the nominal lessee to finance the acquisition of property, (vii) amounts included in the income of a holder of a residual interest in a REMIC (section 860E), because these amounts generally are subject to the same taxation treatment as interest under U.S. tax law, and (viii) interest with respect to notional principal contracts that are re-characterized as loans because of a "substantial non-periodic payment."

Paragraph 4

Paragraph 4 provides an exception to the exclusive residence taxation rule of paragraph 1 and the source-country gross taxation rule of paragraph 2 in cases where the beneficial owner of the interest carries on business through a permanent establishment in the State of source situated in that State and the interest is attributable to that permanent establishment. In such cases the provisions of Article 7 (Business Profits) will apply and the State of source will retain the right to impose tax on such interest income.

In the case of a permanent establishment that once existed in the State but that no longer exists, the provisions of paragraph 4 also apply, by virtue of paragraph 7 of Article 7 (Business Profits), to interest that would be attributable to such a permanent establishment or fixed base if it did exist in the year of payment or accrual. See the Technical Explanation of paragraph 7 of Article 7.

Paragraph 5

Paragraph 5 provides that in cases involving special relationships between the payor and the beneficial owner of interest income, Article 11 applies only to that portion of the total interest payments that would have been made absent such special relationships (i.e., an arm's-length interest payment). Any excess amount of interest paid remains taxable according to the laws of the United States and the other Contracting State, respectively, with due regard to the other provisions of the Convention. Thus, if the excess amount would be treated under the source country's law as a distribution of profits by a corporation, such amount could be taxed as a dividend rather than as interest, but the tax would be subject, if appropriate, to the rate limitations of paragraph 2 of Article 10 (Dividends). The term "special relationship" is not defined in the Convention. In applying this paragraph the United States considers the term to include the relationships described in Article 9, which in turn corresponds to the definition of "control" for purposes of section 482 of the Code.

This paragraph does not address cases where, owing to a special relationship between the payer and the beneficial owner or between both of them and some other person, the amount of the interest is less than an arm's-length amount. In those cases a transaction may be characterized to reflect its substance and interest may be imputed consistent with the definition of interest in paragraph 3. The United States would apply section 482 or 7872 of the Code to determine the amount of imputed interest in those cases.

Relationship to Other Articles

Notwithstanding the foregoing limitations on source country taxation of interest, the saving clause of paragraph 4 of Article 1 permits the United States to tax its residents and citizens, subject to the special foreign tax credit rules of paragraph 4 of Article 23 (Relief from Double Taxation), as if the Convention had not come into force.

As with other benefits of the Convention, the benefits of exclusive residence State taxation of interest under paragraph 1 of Article 11, or limited source taxation under subparagraphs 2(a) and (b), are available to a resident of the other State only if that resident is entitled to those benefits under the provisions of Article 22 (Limitation on Benefits).

ARTICLE 12 (ROYALTIES)

Article 12 provides rules for the taxation of royalties arising in one Contracting State and paid to a beneficial owner that is a resident of the other Contracting State.

Paragraph 1

Paragraph 1 generally grants to the State of residence the exclusive right to tax royalties beneficially owned by its residents and arising in the other Contracting State.

The term "beneficial owner" is not defined in the Convention, and is, therefore, defined under the internal law of the State of source. The beneficial owner of the royalty for purposes of Article 12 is the person to which the income is attributable under the laws of the source State. Thus, if a royalty arising in a Contracting State is received by a nominee or agent that is a resident of the other State on behalf of a person that is not a resident of that other State, the royalty is not entitled to the benefits of Article 12. However, a royalty received by a nominee on behalf of a resident of that other State would be entitled to benefits. These limitations are confirmed by paragraph 4 of the OECD Commentary to Article 12. See also paragraph 24 of the OECD Commentary to Article 1.

Paragraph 2

Paragraph 2 defines the term "royalties," as used in Article 12, to include any consideration for the use of, or the right to use, any copyright of literary, artistic, scientific or other work (such as cinematographic films), any patent, trademark, design or model, plan, secret formula or process, or for information concerning industrial, commercial, or scientific experience. The term "royalties" also includes gain derived from the alienation of any right or property that would give rise to royalties, to the extent the gain is contingent on the productivity, use, or further alienation thereof. Gains that are not so contingent are dealt with under Article 13 (Gains). The term "royalties," however, does not include income from leasing personal property.

The term royalties is defined in the Convention and therefore is generally independent of domestic law. Certain terms used in the definition are not defined in the Convention, but these may be defined under domestic tax law. For example, the term "secret process or formulas" is found in the Code, and its meaning has been elaborated in the context of sections 351 and 367. See Rev. Rul. 55–17, 1955–1 C.B. 388; Rev. Rul. 64–56, 1964–1 C.B. 133; Rev. Proc. 69–19, 1969–2 C.B. 301.

Consideration for the use or right to use cinematographic films, or works on film, tape, or other means of reproduction in radio or television broadcasting is specifically included in the definition of royalties. It is intended that, with respect to any subsequent technological advances in the field of radio or television broadcasting, consideration received for the use of such technology will also be included in the definition of royalties.

If an artist who is resident in one Contracting State records a performance in the other Contracting State, retains a copyrighted interest in a recording, and receives payments for the right to use the recording based on the sale or public playing of the recording, then the right of such other Contracting State to tax those payments is governed by Article 12. See Boulez v. Commissioner, 83 T.C. 584 (1984), aff'd, 810 F.2d 209 (D.C. Cir. 1986). By contrast, if the artist earns in the other Contracting State income covered by Article 16 (Entertainers and Sportsmen), for example, endorsement income from the artist's attendance at a film screening, and if such income also is attributable to one of the rights described in Article 12 (e.g., the use of the artist's photograph in promoting the screening), Article 16 and not Article 12 is applicable to such income.

Computer software generally is protected by copyright laws around the world. Under the Convention, consideration received for the use, or the right to use, computer software is treated either as royalties or as business profits, depending on the facts and circumstances of the transaction giving rise to the payment. The primary factor in determining whether consideration received for the use, or the right to use, computer software is treated as royalties or as business profits is the nature of the rights transferred. See Treas. Reg. section 1.861–18. The fact that the transaction is characterized as a license for copyright law purposes is not dispositive. For example, a typical retail sale of "shrink wrap" software generally will not be considered to give rise to royalty income, even though for copyright law purposes it may be characterized as a license.

The means by which the computer software is transferred are not relevant for purposes of the analysis. Consequently, if software is electronically transferred but the rights obtained by the transferee are substantially equivalent to rights in a program copy, the payment will be considered business profits. The term "industrial, commercial, or scientific experience" (sometimes referred to as "know-how") has the meaning ascribed to it in paragraph 11 et seq. of the Commentary to Article 12 of the OECD Model. Consistent with that meaning, the term may include information that is ancillary to a right otherwise giving rise to royalties, such as a patent or secret process.

Know-how also may include, in limited cases, technical information that is conveyed through technical or consultancy services. It does not include general educational training of the user's employees, nor does it include information developed especially for the user, such as a technical plan or design developed according to the user's specifications. Thus, as provided in paragraph 11.3 of the Commentary to Article 12 of the OECD Model, the term "royalties" does not include payments received as consideration for after-sales service, for services rendered by a seller to a purchaser under a warranty, or for pure technical assistance.

The term "royalties" also does not include payments for professional services (such as architectural, engineering, legal, managerial, medical, software development services). For example, income from the design of a refinery by an engineer (even if the engineer employed know-how in the process of rendering the design) or the production of a legal brief by a lawyer is not income from the transfer of know-how taxable under Article 12, but is income from services taxable under either Article 7 (Business Profits) or Article 14 (Income from Employment). Professional services may be embodied in property that gives rise to royalties, however. Thus, if a professional contracts to develop patentable property and retains rights in the resulting property under the development contract, subsequent license payments made for those rights would be royalties.

Paragraph 3

This paragraph provides an exception to the rule of paragraph 1 that gives the state of residence exclusive taxing jurisdiction in cases where the beneficial owner of the royalties carries on business through a permanent establishment in the state of source and the royalties are attributable to that permanent establishment. In such cases the provisions of Article 7 (Business Profits) will apply.

The provisions of paragraph 7 of Article 7 (Business Profits) apply to this paragraph. For example, royalty income that is attributable to a permanent establishment and that accrues during the existence of the permanent establishment, but is received after the permanent establishment no longer exists, remains taxable under the provisions of Article 7 (Business Profits), and not under this Article.

Paragraph 4

Paragraph 4 provides that in cases involving special relationships between the payor and beneficial owner of royalties, Article 12 applies only to the extent the royalties would have been paid absent such special relationships (i.e., an arm's-length royalty). Any excess amount of royalties paid remains taxable according to the laws of the two Contracting States, with due regard to the other provisions of the Convention. If, for example, the excess amount is treated as a distribution of corporate profits under domestic law, such excess amount will be taxed as a dividend rather than as royalties, but the tax imposed on the dividend payment will be subject to the rate limitations of paragraph 2 of Article 10 (Dividends).

Relationship to Other Articles

Notwithstanding the foregoing limitations on source country taxation of royalties, the saving clause of paragraph 4 of Article 1 (General Scope) permits the United States to tax its residents and citizens, subject to the special foreign tax credit rules of paragraph 4 of Article 23 (Relief from Double Taxation), as if the Convention had not come into force.

As with other benefits of the Convention, the benefits of exclusive residence State taxation of royalties under paragraph 1 of Article 12 are available to a resident of the other State only if that resident is entitled to those benefits under Article 22 (Limitation on Benefits).

ARTICLE 13 (GAINS)

Article 13 assigns either primary or exclusive taxing jurisdiction over gains from the alienation of property to the State of residence or the State of source.

Paragraph 1

Paragraph 1 of Article 13 preserves the non-exclusive right of the State of source to tax gains attributable to the alienation of real property situated in that State. The paragraph therefore permits the United States to apply section 897 of the Code to tax gains derived by a resident of the other Contracting State that are attributable to the alienation of real property situated in the United States (as defined in paragraph 2). Gains attributable to the alienation of real property include gains from any other property that is treated as a real property interest within the meaning of paragraph 2.

Paragraph 1 refers to gains "attributable to the alienation of real property" rather than the OECD Model phrase "gains from the alienation" to clarify that the United States will look through distributions made by a REIT and certain RICs. Accordingly, distributions made by a REIT or certain RICs are taxable under paragraph 1 of Article 13 (not under Article 10 (Dividends)) when they are attributable to gains derived from the alienation of real property.

Paragraph 2

This paragraph defines the term "real property situated in the other Contracting State." The term includes real property referred to in Article 6 (i.e., an interest in the real property itself), a "United States real property interest" (when the United States is the other Contracting State under paragraph 1), and an equivalent interest in real property situated in the other Contracting State.

Under section 897(c) of the Code the term "United States real property interest" includes shares in a U.S. corporation that owns sufficient U.S. real property interests to satisfy an asset-ratio test on certain testing dates. The term also includes certain foreign corporations that have elected to be treated as U.S. corporations for this purpose. Section 897(i).

Paragraph 3

Paragraph 3 of Article 13 deals with the taxation of certain gains from the alienation of movable property forming part of the business property of a permanent establishment that an enterprise of a Contracting State has in the other Contracting State. This also includes gains from the alienation of such a permanent establishment (alone or with the whole enterprise). Such gains may be taxed in the State in which the permanent establishment is located. A resident of the other Contracting State that is a partner in a partnership doing business in the United States generally will have a permanent establishment in the United States as a result of the activities of the partnership, assuming that the activities of the partnership rise to the level of a permanent establishment. Rev. Rul. 91–32, 1991–1 C.B. 107. Further, under paragraph 3, the United States generally may tax a partner's distributive share of income realized by a partnership on the disposition of movable property forming part of the business property of the partnership in the United States.

The gains subject to paragraph 3 may be taxed in the State in which the permanent establishment is located, regardless of whether the permanent establishment exists at the time of the alienation. This rule incorporates the rule of section 864(c)(6) of the Code . Accordingly, income that is attributable to a permanent establishment, but that is deferred and received after the permanent establishment no longer exists, may nevertheless be taxed by the State in which the permanent establishment was located.

Paragraph 4

This paragraph limits the taxing jurisdiction of the State of source with respect to gains from the alienation of ships or aircraft operated in international traffic by the enterprise alienating the ship or aircraft and from property (other than real property) pertaining to the operation or use of such ships, aircraft, or containers. Under paragraph 4, such income is taxable only in the Contracting State in which the alienator is resident. Notwithstanding paragraph 3, the rules of this paragraph apply even if the income is attributable to a permanent establishment maintained by the enterprise in the other Contracting State. This result is consistent with the allocation of taxing rights under Article 8 (Shipping and Air Transport).

Paragraph 5

Paragraph 5 provides a rule similar to paragraph 4 with respect to gains from the alienation of containers and related personal property. Such gains derived by a enterprise of a Contracting State shall be taxable only in that Contracting State unless the containers were used for the transport of goods or merchandise solely within the other Contracting State. The other Contracting State may not tax even if the gain is attributable to a permanent establishment maintained by the enterprise in that other Contracting State.

Paragraph 6

Paragraph 6 grants to the State of residence of the alienator the exclusive right to tax gains from the alienation of property other than property referred to in paragraphs 1 through 5. For example, gain derived from shares, other than shares described in paragraphs 2 or 3, debt instruments and various financial instruments, may be taxed only in the State of residence, to the extent such income is not otherwise characterized as income taxable under another article (e.g., Article 10 (Dividends) or Article 11 (Interest)). Similarly gain derived from the alienation of tangible personal property, other than tangible personal property described in paragraph 3, may be taxed only in the State of residence of the alienator.

Gain derived from the alienation of any property, such as a patent or copyright, that produces income covered by Article 12 (Royalties) is governed by the rules of Article 12 and not by this article, provided that such gain is of the type described in paragraph 2(b) of Article 12 (i.e., it is contingent on the productivity, use, or disposition of the property). Thus, under either article, such gain is taxable only in the State of residence of the alienator. Gains derived by a resident of a Contracting State from real property located in a third state are not taxable in the other Contracting

State, even if the sale is attributable to a permanent establishment located in the other Contracting State.

Relationship to Other Articles

Notwithstanding the foregoing limitations on taxation of certain gains by the State of source, the saving clause of paragraph 4 of Article 1 (General Scope) permits the United States to tax its citizens and residents as if the Convention had not come into effect. Thus, any limitation in this Article on the right of the United States to tax gains does not apply to gains of a U.S. citizen or resident. The benefits of this Article are also subject to the provisions of Article 22 (Limitation on Benefits). Thus, only a resident of a Contracting State that satisfies one of the conditions in Article 22 is entitled to the benefits of this Article.

ARTICLE 14 (INCOME FROM EMPLOYMENT)

Article 14 apportions taxing jurisdiction over remuneration derived by a resident of a Contracting State as an employee between the States of source and residence.

Paragraph 1

The general rule of Article 14 is contained in paragraph 1. Remuneration derived by a resident of a Contracting State as an employee may be taxed by the State of residence, and the remuneration also may be taxed by the other Contracting State to the extent derived from employment exercised (i.e., services performed) in that other Contracting State. Paragraph 1 also provides that the more specific rules of Articles 15 (Directors' Fees), 17 (Pensions, Social Security, Annuities, Alimony and Child Support), and 19 (Government Service) apply in the case of employment income described in one of those articles. Thus, even though the State of source has a right to tax employment income under Article 14, it may not have the right to tax that income under the Convention if the income is described, for example, in Article 17 (Pensions, Social Security, Annuities, Alimony and Child Support) and is not taxable in the State of source under the provisions of that article.

Article 14 applies to any form of compensation for employment, including payments in kind. Paragraph 1.1 of the Commentary to Article 16 of the OECD Model now confirms that interpretation.

Consistent with section 864(c)(6) of the Code , Article 14 also applies regardless of the timing of actual payment for services. Consequently, a person who receives the right to a future payment in consideration for services rendered in a Contracting State would be taxable in that State even if the payment is received at a time when the recipient is a resident of the other Contracting State. Thus, a bonus paid to a resident of a Contracting State with respect to services performed in the other Contracting State with respect to a particular taxable year would be subject to Article 14 for that year even if it was paid after the close of the year. An annuity received for services performed in a taxable year could be subject to Article 14 despite the fact that it was paid in subsequent years. In that case, it would be necessary to determine whether the payment constitutes deferred compensation, taxable under Article 14, or a qualified pension subject to the rules of Article 17 (Pensions, Social Security, Annuities, Alimony, and Child Support). Article 14 also applies to income derived from the exercise of stock options granted with respect to services performed in the host State, even if those stock options are exercised after the employee has left the source country. If Article 14 is found to apply, whether such payments were taxable in the State where the employment was exercised would depend on whether the tests of paragraph 2 were satisfied in the year in which the services to which the payment relates were performed.

Paragraph 2

Paragraph 2 sets forth an exception to the general rule that employment income may be taxed in the State where it is exercised. Under paragraph 2, the State where the employment is exercised may not tax the income from the employment if three conditions are satisfied: (a) the individual is present in the other Contracting State for a period or periods not exceeding 183 days in any 12–month period that begins or ends during the relevant taxable year (i.e., in the United States, the calendar year in which the services are performed); (b) the remuneration is paid by, or on behalf of, an employer who is not a resident of that other Contracting State; and (c) the remuneration is not borne as a deductible expense by a permanent establishment that the employer has in that other State. In order for the remuneration to be exempt from tax in the source State, all three conditions must be satisfied. This exception is identical to that set forth in the OECD Model.

The 183–day period in condition (a) is to be measured using the "days of physical presence" method. Under this method, the days that are counted include any day in which a part of the day is spent in the host country. (Rev. Rul. 56–24, 1956–1 C.B. 851.) Thus, days that are counted include the days of arrival and departure; weekends and holidays on which the employee does not work but is present within the country; vacation days spent in the country before, during or after the employment period, unless the individual's presence before or after the employment can be shown to be independent of his presence there for employment purposes; and time during periods of sickness, training periods, strikes, etc., when the individual is present but not working. If illness prevented the individual from leaving the country in sufficient time to qualify for the benefit, those days will not count. Also, any part of a day spent in the host country while in transit between two points outside the host country is not counted. If the individual is a resident of the host country for part of the taxable year concerned and a non-resident for the remainder of the year, the individual's days of presence as a resident do not count for purposes of determining whether the 183–day period is exceeded.

Conditions (b) and (c) are intended to ensure that a Contracting State will not be required to allow a deduction to the payor for compensation paid and at the same time to exempt the employee on the amount received. Accordingly, if a foreign person pays the salary of an employee who is employed in the host State, but a host State corporation or permanent establishment reimburses the payor with a payment that can be identified as a reimbursement, neither condition (b) nor (c), as the case may be, will be considered to have been fulfilled.

The reference to remuneration "borne by" a permanent establishment is understood to encompass all expenses that economically are incurred and not merely expenses that are currently deductible for tax purposes. Accordingly, the expenses referred to include expenses that are capitalizable as well as those that are currently deductible. Further, salaries paid by residents that are exempt from income taxation may be considered to be borne by a permanent establishment notwithstanding the fact that the expenses will be neither deductible nor capitalizable since the payor is exempt from tax.

Paragraph 3

Paragraph 3 contains a special rule applicable to remuneration for services performed by a resident of a Contracting State as an employee aboard a ship or aircraft operated in international traffic. Such remuneration may be taxed only in the State of residence of the employee if the services are performed as a member of the regular complement of the ship or aircraft. The "regular complement" includes the crew. In the case of a cruise ship, for example, it may also include others, such as entertainers, lecturers, etc., employed by the shipping company to serve on the ship throughout its voyage. The use of the term "regular complement" is intended to clarify that a person who exercises his employment as, for example, an insurance salesman while aboard a ship or aircraft is not covered by this paragraph.

If a U.S. citizen who is resident in the other Contracting State performs services as an employee in the United States and meets the conditions of paragraph 2 for source country exemption, he nevertheless is taxable in the United States by virtue of the saving clause of paragraph 4 of Article 1 (General Scope), subject to the special foreign tax credit rule of paragraph 4 of Article 23 (Relief from Double Taxation).

ARTICLE 15 (DIRECTORS' FEES)

This Article provides that a Contracting State may tax the fees and other compensation paid by a company that is a resident of that State for services performed in that State by a resident of the other Contracting State in his capacity as a director of the company. This rule is an exception to the more general rules of Articles 7 (Business Profits) and 14

(Income from Employment). Thus, for example, in determining whether a director's fee paid to a non-employee director is subject to tax in the country of residence of the corporation, it is not relevant to establish whether the fee is attributable to a permanent establishment in that State.

The analogous OECD provision reaches different results in certain cases. Under the OECD Model provision, a resident of one Contracting State who is a director of a corporation that is resident in the other Contracting State is subject to tax in that other State in respect of his directors' fees regardless of where the services are performed. Under the provision in the Convention, the State of residence of the corporation may tax nonresident directors with no time or dollar threshold, but only with respect to remuneration for services performed in that State. The United States has entered a reservation with respect to the OECD provision.

This Article is subject to the saving clause of paragraph 4 of Article 1 (General Scope). Thus, if a U.S. citizen who is a resident of the other Contracting State is a director of a U.S. corporation, the United States may tax his full remuneration regardless of where he performs his services.

ARTICLE 16 (ENTERTAINERS AND SPORTSMEN)

This Article deals with the taxation in a Contracting State of entertainers and sportsmen resident in the other Contracting State from the performance of their services as such. The Article applies both to the income of an entertainer or sportsman who performs services on his own behalf and one who performs services on behalf of another person, either as an employee of that person, or pursuant to any other arrangement. The rules of this Article take precedence, in some circumstances, over those of Articles 7 (Business Profits) and 14 (Income from Employment).

This Article applies only with respect to the income of entertainers and sportsmen. Others involved in a performance or athletic event, such as producers, directors, technicians, managers, coaches, etc., remain subject to the provisions of Articles 7 and 14. In addition, except as provided in paragraph 2, income earned by juridical persons is not covered by Article 16.

Paragraph 1

Paragraph 1 describes the circumstances in which a Contracting State may tax the performance income of an entertainer or sportsman who is a resident of the other Contracting State. Under the paragraph, income derived by an individual resident of a Contracting State from activities as an entertainer or sportsman exercised in the other Contracting State may be taxed in that other State if the amount of the gross receipts derived by the performer exceeds $20,000 (or its equivalent in [the currency of the other Contracting State]) for the taxable year. The $20,000 includes expenses reimbursed to the individual or borne on his behalf. If the gross receipts exceed $20,000, the full amount, not just the excess, may be taxed in the State of performance.

The OECD Model provides for taxation by the country of performance of the remuneration of entertainers or sportsmen with no dollar or time threshold. This Convention introduces the monetary threshold to distinguish between two groups of entertainers and athletes—those who are paid relatively large sums of money for very short periods of service, and who would, therefore, normally be exempt from host country tax under the standard personal services income rules, and those who earn relatively modest amounts and are, therefore, not easily distinguishable from those who earn other types of personal service income. The United States has entered a reservation to the OECD Model on this point.

Tax may be imposed under paragraph 1 even if the performer would have been exempt from tax under Article 7 (Business Profits) or 14 (Income from Employment). On the other hand. if the performer would be exempt from host-country tax under Article 16, but would be taxable under either Article 7 or 14, tax may be imposed under either of those Articles. Thus, for example, if a performer derives remuneration from his activities in an independent capacity, and the performer does not have a permanent establishment in the host State, he may be taxed by the host State in accordance with Article 16 if his remuneration exceeds $20,000 annually, despite the fact that he generally would be exempt from host State taxation under Article 7. However, a performer who receives less than the $20,000 threshold amount and therefore is not taxable under Article 16 nevertheless may be subject to tax in the host country under Article 7 or 14 if the tests for host-country taxability under the relevant Article are met. For example, if an entertainer who is an independent contractor earns $14,000 of income in a State for the calendar year, but the income is attributable to his permanent establishment in the State of performance, that State may tax his income under Article 7.

Since it frequently is not possible to know until year-end whether the income an entertainer or sportsman derived from performances in a Contracting State will exceed $20,000, nothing in the Convention precludes that Contracting State from withholding tax during the year and refunding it after the close of the year if the taxability threshold has not been met.

As explained in paragraph 9 of the Commentary to Article 17 of the OECD Model, Article 16 of the Convention applies to all income connected with a performance by the entertainer, such as appearance fees, award or prize money, and a share of the gate receipts. Income derived from a Contracting State by a performer who is a resident of the other Contracting State from other than actual performance, such as royalties from record sales and payments for product endorsements, is not covered by this Article, but by other articles of the Convention, such as Article 12 (Royalties) or Article 7 (Business Profits). For example, if an entertainer receives royalty income from the sale of live recordings, the royalty income would be exempt from source state tax under Article 12, even if the performance was conducted in the source country, although the entertainer could be taxed in the source country with respect to income from the performance itself under Article 16 if the dollar threshold is exceeded.

In determining whether income falls under Article 16 or another article, the controlling factor will be whether the income in question is predominantly attributable to the performance itself or to other activities or property rights. For instance, a fee paid to a performer for endorsement of a performance in which the performer will participate would be considered to be so closely associated with the performance itself that it normally would fall within Article 16. Similarly, a sponsorship fee paid by a business in return for the right to attach its name to the performance would be so closely associated with the performance that it would fall under Article 16 as well. As indicated in paragraph 9 of the Commentary to Article 17 of the OECD Model, however, a cancellation fee would not be considered to fall within Article 16 but would be dealt with under Article 7 (Business Profits) or 14 (Income from Employment).

As indicated in paragraph 4 of the Commentary to Article 17 of the OECD Model, where an individual fulfills a dual role as performer and non-performer (such as a player-coach or an actor-director), but his role in one of the two capacities is negligible, the predominant character of the individual's activities should control the characterization of those activities. In other cases there should be an apportionment between the performance-related compensation and other compensation.

Consistent with Article 14 (Income from Employment), Article 16 also applies regardless of the timing of actual payment for services. Thus, a bonus paid to a resident of a Contracting State with respect to a performance in the other Contracting State during a particular taxable year would be subject to Article 16 for that year even if it was paid after the close of the year. The determination as to whether the $20,000 threshold has been exceeded is determined separately with respect to each year of payment. Accordingly, if an actor who is a resident of one Contracting State receives residual payments over time with respect to a movie that was filmed in the other Contracting State, the payments do not have to be aggregated from one year to another to determine whether the total payments have finally exceeded $20,000. Otherwise, residual payments received many years later could retroactively subject all earlier payments to tax by the other Contracting State.

Paragraph 2

Paragraph 2 is intended to address the potential for circumvention of the rule in paragraph 1 when a performer's income does not accrue directly to the performer himself, but to another person. Foreign performers frequently perform in the United States as employees of, or under contract with, a company or other person.

The relationship may truly be one of employee and employer, with no circumvention of paragraph 1 either intended or realized. On the other hand, the "employer" may, for example, be a company established and owned by the performer, which is merely acting as the nominal income recipient in respect of the remuneration for the performance (a "star company"). The performer may act as an "employee," receive a modest salary, and arrange to receive the remainder of the income from his performance from the company in another form or at a later time. In such case, absent the provisions of paragraph 2, the income arguably could escape host-country tax because the company earns business profits but has no permanent establishment in that country. The performer may largely or entirely escape host-country tax by receiving only a small salary, perhaps small enough to place him below the dollar threshold in paragraph 1. The performer might arrange to receive further payments in a later year, when he is not subject to host-country tax, perhaps as dividends or liquidating distributions.

Paragraph 2 seeks to prevent this type of abuse while at the same time protecting the taxpayers' rights to the benefits of the Convention when there is a legitimate employee-employer relationship between the performer and the person providing his services. Under paragraph 2, when the income accrues to a person other than the performer, the income may be taxed in the Contracting State where the performer's services are exercised, without regard to the provisions of the Convention concerning business profits (Article 7) or income from employment (Article 14), unless the contract pursuant to which the personal activities are performed allows the person other than the performer to designate the individual who is to perform the personal activities. This rule is based on the U.S. domestic law provision characterizing income from certain personal service contracts as foreign personal holding company income in the context of the foreign personal holding company provisions. See Code section 954(c)(1)(I) . The premise of this rule is that, in a case where a performer is using another person in an attempt to circumvent the provisions of paragraph 1, the recipient of the services of the performer would contract with a person other than that performer (i.e., a company employing the performer) only if the recipient of the services were certain that the performer himself would perform the services. If instead the person is allowed to designate the individual who is to perform the services, then likely the person is a service company not formed to circumvent the provisions of paragraph 1. The following example illustrates the operation of this rule.

Example. Company O, a resident of the other Contracting State, is engaged in the business of operating an orchestra. Company O enters into a contract with Company A pursuant to which Company O agrees to carry out two performances in the United States in consideration of which Company A will pay Company O $200,000. The contract designates two individuals, a conductor and a flutist, that must perform as part of the orchestra, and allows Company O to designate the other members of the orchestra. Because the contract does not give Company O any discretion to determine whether the conductor or the flutist perform personal services under the contract, the portion of the $200,000 which is attributable to the personal services of the conductor and the flutist may be taxed by the United States pursuant to paragraph 2. The remaining portion of the $200,000, which is attributable to the personal services of performers that Company O may designate, is not subject to tax by the United States pursuant to paragraph 2. In cases where paragraph 2 is applicable, the income of the "employer" may be subject to tax in the host Contracting State even if it has no permanent establishment in the host country. Taxation under paragraph 2 is on the person providing the services of the performer. This paragraph does not affect the rules of paragraph 1, which apply to the performer himself. The income taxable by virtue of paragraph 2 is reduced to the extent of salary payments to the performer, which fall under paragraph 1.

For purposes of paragraph 2, income is deemed to accrue to another person (i.e., the person providing the services of the performer) if that other person has control over, or the right to receive, gross income in respect of the services of the performer.

Since pursuant to Article 1 (General Scope) the Convention only applies to persons who are residents of one of the Contracting States, income of the star company would not be eligible for benefits of the Convention if the company is not a resident of one of the Contracting States.

Relationship to other Articles

This Article is subject to the provisions of the saving clause of paragraph 4 of Article 1 (General Scope). Thus, if an entertainer or a sportsman who is resident in the other Contracting State is a citizen of the United States, the United States may tax all of his income from performances in the United States without regard to the provisions of this Article, subject, however, to the special foreign tax credit provisions of paragraph 4 of Article 23 (Relief from Double Taxation). In addition, benefits of this Article are subject to the provisions of Article 22 (Limitation on Benefits).

ARTICLE 17 (PENSIONS, SOCIAL SECURITY, ANNUITIES, ALIMONY, AND CHILD SUPPORT)

This Article deals with the taxation of private (i.e., non-government service) pensions and annuities, social security benefits, alimony and child support payments.

Paragraph 1

Paragraph 1 provides that distributions from pensions and other similar remuneration beneficially owned by a resident of a Contracting

State in consideration of past employment are taxable only in the State of residence of the beneficiary. The term "pensions and other similar remuneration" includes both periodic and single sum payments. The phrase "pensions and other similar remuneration" is intended to encompass payments made by qualified private retirement plans. In the United States, the plans encompassed by Paragraph 1 include: qualified plans under section 401(a), individual retirement plans (including individual retirement plans that are part of a simplified employee pension plan that satisfies section 408(k), individual retirement accounts and section 408(p) accounts), section 403(a) qualified annuity plans, and section 403(b) plans. Distributions from section 457 plans may also fall under Paragraph 1 if they are not paid with respect to government services covered by Article 19.

In the other Contracting State, the term pension applies to: [ ]. The competent authorities may agree that distributions from other plans that generally meet similar criteria to those applicable to the listed plans also qualify for the benefits of Paragraph 1.

Pensions in respect of government services covered by Article 19 are not covered by this paragraph. They are covered either by paragraph 2 of this Article, if they are in the form of social security benefits, or by paragraph 2 of Article 19 (Government Service). Thus, Article 19 generally covers section 457, 401(a), 403(b) plans established for government employees, and the Thrift Savings Plan (section 7701(j)).

However, the State of residence, under subparagraph (b), must exempt from tax any amount of such pensions or other similar remuneration that would be exempt from tax in the Contracting State in which the pension fund is established if the recipient were a resident of that State. Thus, for example, a distribution from a U.S. "Roth IRA" to a resident of the other Contracting State would be exempt from tax in the other Contracting State to the same extent the distribution would be exempt from tax in the United States if it were distributed to a U.S. resident. The same is true with respect to distributions from a traditional IRA to the extent that the distribution represents a return of non-deductible contributions. Similarly, if the distribution were not subject to tax when it was "rolled over" into another U.S. IRA (but not, for example, to a pension fund in the other Contracting State), then the distribution would be exempt from tax in the other Contracting State.

Paragraph 2

The treatment of social security benefits is dealt with in paragraph 2. This paragraph provides that, notwithstanding the provision of paragraph 1 under which private pensions are taxable exclusively in the State of residence of the beneficial owner, payments made by one of the Contracting States under the provisions of its social security or similar legislation to a resident of the other Contracting State or to a citizen of the United States will be taxable only in the Contracting State making the payment.

The reference to U.S. citizens is necessary to ensure that a social security payment by the other Contracting State to a U.S. citizen who is not resident in the United States will not be taxable by the United States.

This paragraph applies to social security beneficiaries whether they have contributed to the system as private sector or Government employees. The phrase "similar legislation" is intended to refer to United States tier 1 Railroad Retirement benefits.

Paragraph 3

Under paragraph 3, annuities that are derived and beneficially owned by a resident of a Contracting State are taxable only in that State. An annuity, as the term is used in this paragraph, means a stated sum paid periodically at stated times during a specified number of years, under an obligation to make the payment in return for adequate and full consideration (other than for services rendered). An annuity received in consideration for services rendered would be treated as either deferred compensation that is taxable in accordance with Article 14 (Income from Employment) or a pension that is subject to the rules of Article 17 (Pensions, Social Security, Annuities, Alimony, and Child Support).

Paragraphs 4 and 5

Paragraphs 4 and 5 deal with alimony and child support payments. Both alimony, under paragraph 4, and child support payments, under paragraph 5, are defined as periodic payments made pursuant to a written separation agreement or a decree of divorce, separate maintenance, or compulsory support. Paragraph 4, however, deals only with payments of that type that are taxable to the payee. Under that paragraph, alimony paid by a resident of a Contracting State to a resident of the other Contracting State is taxable under the Convention only in the State of residence of the recipient. Paragraph 5 deals with those periodic payments that are for the support of a child and that are not covered by paragraph 4. These types of payments by a resident of a Contracting State to a resident of the other Contracting State are taxable in neither Contracting State.

Relationship to other Articles

Paragraphs 1 (a), 3 and 4 of Article 17 are subject to the saving clause of paragraph 4 of Article 1 (General Scope). Thus, a U.S. citizen who is resident in the other Contracting State, and receives either a pension, annuity or alimony payment from the United States, may be subject to U.S. tax on the payment, notwithstanding the rules in those three paragraphs that give the State of residence of the recipient the exclusive taxing right. Paragraphs 1(b), 2 and 5 are excepted from the saving clause by virtue of subparagraph 5(a) of Article 1. Thus, the United States will not tax U.S. citizens and residents on the income described in those paragraphs even if such amounts otherwise would be subject to tax under U.S. law.

ARTICLE 18 (PENSION FUNDS)

Article 18 deals with cross-border pension contributions. It is intended to remove barriers to the flow of personal services between the Contracting States that could otherwise result from discontinuities in the laws of the Contracting States regarding the deductibility of pension contributions. Such discontinuities may arise where countries allow deductions or exclusions to their residents for contributions, made by them or on their behalf, to resident pension plans, but do not allow deductions or exclusions for payments made to plans resident in another country, even if the structure and legal requirements of such plans in the two countries are similar.

Paragraph 1

Paragraph 1 provides that, if a resident of a Contracting State participates in a pension fund established in the other Contracting State, the State of residence will not tax the income of the pension fund with respect to that resident until a distribution is made from the pension fund. Thus, for example, if a U.S. citizen contributes to a U.S. qualified plan while working in the United States and then establishes residence in the other Contracting State, paragraph 1 prevents the other Contracting State from taxing currently the plan's earnings and accretions with respect to that individual. When the resident receives a distribution from the pension fund, that distribution may be subject to tax in the State of residence, subject to paragraph 1 of Article 17 (Pensions, Social Security, Annuities, Alimony, and Child Support).

Paragraph 2

Paragraph 2 provides certain benefits with respect to cross-border contributions to a pension fund, subject to the limitations of paragraphs 3 and 4 of the Article. It is irrelevant for purposes of paragraph 2 whether the participant establishes residence in the State where the individual renders services (the "host State").

Subparagraph (a) of paragraph 2 allows an individual who exercises employment or self-employment in a Contracting State to deduct or exclude from income in that Contracting State contributions made by or on behalf of the individual during the period of employment or self-employment to a pension fund established in the other Contracting State. Thus, for example, if a participant in a U.S. qualified plan goes to work in the other Contracting State, the participant may deduct or exclude from income in the other Contracting State contributions to the U.S. qualified plan made while the participant works in the other Contracting State. Subparagraph (a), however, applies only to the extent of the relief allowed by the host State (e.g., the other Contracting State in the example) for contributions to a pension fund established in that State.

Subparagraph (b) of paragraph 2 provides that, in the case of employment, accrued benefits and contributions by or on behalf of the individual's employer, during the period of employment in the host State, will not be treated as taxable income to the employee in that State. Subparagraph (b) also allows the employer a deduction in computing its taxable income in the host State for contributions to the plan. For example, if a participant in a U.S. qualified plan goes to work in the other Contracting State, the participant's employer may deduct from its taxable income in the other Contracting State contributions to the U.S. qualified plan for the benefit of the employee while the employee renders services in the other Contracting State.

As in the case of subparagraph (a), subparagraph (b) applies only to the extent of the relief allowed by the host State for contributions to pension funds established in that State. Therefore, where the United States is the host State, the exclusion of employee contributions from the employee's income under this paragraph is limited to contributions not in excess of the amount specified in section 402(g) for elective contributions. Deduction of employer contributions is subject to the limitations of sections 415 and 404. The section 404 limitation on deductions is calculated as if the individual were the only employee covered by the plan.

Paragraph 3

Paragraph 3 limits the availability of benefits under paragraph 2. Under subparagraph (a) of paragraph 3, paragraph 2 does not apply to contributions to a pension fund unless the participant already was contributing to the fund, or his employer already was contributing to the fund with respect to that individual, before the individual began exercising employment in the host State. This condition would be met if either the employee or the employer was contributing to a fund that was replaced by the fund to which he is contributing. The rule regarding successor funds would apply if, for example, the employer has been taken over by a company that replaces the existing fund with its own fund, rolling membership in the old fund over into the new fund.

In addition, under subparagraph (b) of paragraph 3, the competent authority of the host State must determine that the recognized plan to which a contribution is made in the other Contracting State generally corresponds to the plan in the host State. For this purpose the U.S. pension funds eligible for the benefits of paragraph 2 include qualified plans under section 401(a), individual retirement plans (including individual retirement plans that are part of a simplified employee pension plan that satisfies section 408(k)), individual retirement accounts, individual retirement annuities, section 408(p) accounts and Roth IRAs under section 408A), section 403(a) qualified annuity plans, section 403(b) plans, section 457(b) plans and the Thrift Savings Plan (section 7701(j)).

Paragraph 4

Paragraph 4 generally provides U.S. tax treatment for certain contributions by or on behalf of U.S. citizens resident in the other Contracting

State to pension funds established in the other Contracting State that is comparable to the treatment that would be provided for contributions to U.S. funds. Under subparagraph (a), a U.S. citizen resident in the other Contracting State may exclude or deduct for U.S. tax purposes certain contributions to a pension fund established in the other Contracting State. Qualifying contributions generally include contributions made during the period the U.S. citizen exercises an employment in the other Contracting State if expenses of the employment are borne by an employer or permanent establishment in that other Contracting State. Similarly, with respect to the U.S. citizen's participation in the pension fund in the other Contracting State, accrued benefits and contributions during that period generally are not treated as taxable income in the United States.

The U.S. tax benefit allowed by paragraph 4, however, is limited under subparagraph (b) to the lesser of the amount of relief allowed for contributions and benefits under a pension fund established in the other Contracting State and the amount of relief that would be allowed for contributions and benefits under a generally corresponding pension fund established in the United States.

Subparagraph (c) provides that the benefits an individual obtains under paragraph 4 are counted when determining that individual's eligibility for benefits under a pension fund established in the United States. Thus, for example, contributions to a pension fund in the other Contracting State may be counted in determining whether the individual has exceeded the annual limitation on contributions to an individual retirement account.

Under subparagraph (d), paragraph 4 does not apply to pension contributions and benefits unless the competent authority of the United States has agreed that the pension fund established in the other Contracting State generally corresponds to a pension fund established in the United States. The notes provide that certain pension funds have been determined to "generally correspond" to funds in the other country. Since paragraph 4 applies only with respect to employees, however, the relevant plans are those that correspond to employer plans in the United States.

Relationship to other Articles

Paragraphs 1 and 4 of Article 18 are excepted from the saving clause of paragraph 4 of Article 1 by virtue of paragraph 5(a) of Article 1. Thus, the United States will allow U.S. citizens and residents the benefits of paragraphs 1 and 4. Paragraph 2 is excepted from the saving clause by subparagraph 5(b) of Article 1 with respect only to persons who are not admitted for permanent residence or citizens. Accordingly, a person who becomes a U.S. permanent resident or citizen will no longer receive a deduction for contributions to a pension fund established in the other Contracting State.

ARTICLE 19 (GOVERNMENT SERVICE)

Paragraph 1

Subparagraphs (a) and (b) of paragraph 1 deal with the taxation of government compensation (other than a pension addressed in paragraph 2). Subparagraph (a) provides that remuneration paid to any individual who is rendering services to that State, political subdivision or local authority is exempt from tax by the other State. Under subparagraph (b), such payments are, however, taxable exclusively in the other State (i.e., the host State) if the services are rendered in that other State and the individual is a resident of that State who is either a national of that State or a person who did not become resident of that State solely for purposes of rendering the services. The paragraph applies to anyone performing services for a government, whether as a government employee, an independent contractor, or an employee of an independent contractor.

Paragraph 2

Paragraph 2 deals with the taxation of pensions paid by, or out of funds created by, one of the States, or a political subdivision or a local authority thereof, to an individual in respect of services rendered to that State or subdivision or authority. Subparagraph (a) provides that such pensions are taxable only in that State. Subparagraph (b) provides an exception under which such pensions are taxable only in the other State if the individual is a resident of, and a national of, that other State.

Pensions paid to retired civilian and military employees of a Government of either State are intended to be covered under paragraph 2. When benefits paid by a State in respect of services rendered to that State or a subdivision or authority are in the form of social security benefits, however, those payments are covered by paragraph 2 of Article 17 (Pensions, Social Security, Annuities, Alimony, and Child Support). As a general matter, the result will be the same whether Article 17 or 19 applies, since social security benefits are taxable exclusively by the source country and so are government pensions. The result will differ only when the payment is made to a citizen and resident of the other Contracting State, who is not also a citizen of the paying State. In such a case, social security benefits continue to be taxable at source while government pensions become taxable only in the residence country.

Paragraph 3

Paragraph 3 provides that the remuneration described in paragraph 1 will be subject to the rules of Articles 14 (Income from Employment), 15 (Directors' Fees), 16 (Entertainers and Sportsmen) or 17 (Pensions, Social Security, Annuities, Alimony, and Child Support) if the recipient of the income is employed by a business conducted by a government.

Relationship to other Articles

Under paragraph 5(b) of Article 1 (General Scope), the saving clause (paragraph 4 of Article 1) does not apply to the benefits conferred by one of the States under Article 19 if the recipient of the benefits is neither a citizen of that State, nor a person who has been admitted for permanent residence there (i.e., in the United States, a "green card" holder). Thus, a resident of a Contracting State who in the course of performing functions of a governmental nature becomes a resident of the other State (but not a permanent resident), would be entitled to the benefits of this Article. However, an individual who receives a pension paid by the Government of the other Contracting State in respect of services rendered to that Government shall be taxable on this pension only in the other Contracting State unless the individual is a U.S. citizen or acquires a U.S. green card.

ARTICLE 20 (STUDENTS AND TRAINEES)

This Article provides rules for host-country taxation of visiting students and business trainees. Persons who meet the tests of the Article will be exempt from tax in the State that they are visiting with respect to designated classes of income. Several conditions must be satisfied in order for an individual to be entitled to the benefits of this Article.

First, the visitor must have been, either at the time of his arrival in the host State or immediately before, a resident of the other Contracting State.

Second, the purpose of the visit must be the full-time education or training of the visitor. Thus, if the visitor comes principally to work in the host State but also is a part-time student, he would not be entitled to the benefits of this Article, even with respect to any payments he may receive from abroad for his maintenance or education, and regardless of whether or not he is in a degree program. Whether a student is to be considered full-time will be determined by the rules of the educational institution at which he is studying.

The host-country exemption in the Article applies to payments received by the student or business trainee for the purpose of his maintenance, education or training that arise outside the host State. A payment will be considered to arise outside the host State if the payer is located outside the host State. Thus, if an employer from one of the Contracting States sends an employee to the other Contracting State for training, the payments the trainee receives from abroad from his employer for his maintenance or training while he is present in the host State will be exempt from tax in the host State. Where appropriate, substance prevails over form in determining the identity of the payer. Thus, for example, payments made directly or indirectly by a U.S. person with whom the visitor is training, but which have been routed through a source outside the United States (e.g., a foreign subsidiary), are not treated as arising outside the United States for this purpose.

The Article also provides a limited exemption for remuneration from personal services rendered in the host State with a view to supplementing the resources available to him for such purposes to the extent of $9,000 United States dollars (or its equivalent in the currency of the other Contracting State) per taxable year. The specified amount is intended to equalize the position of a U.S. resident who is entitled to the standard deduction and the personal exemption with that of a student who files as a non-resident alien and therefore does not. Accordingly, the competent authorities are instructed to adjust this amount every five years, if necessary, to take into account changes in the amount of the U.S. standard deduction and personal exemption.

In the case of a business trainee, the benefits of the Article will extend only for a period of one year from the time that the visitor first arrives in the host country. If, however, a trainee remains in the host country for a second year, thus losing the benefits of the Article, he would not retroactively lose the benefits of the Article for the first year. The term "business trainee" is defined as a person who is in the country temporarily for the purpose of securing training that is necessary to qualify to pursue a profession or professional specialty. Moreover, the person must be employed or under contract with a resident of the other Contracting State and must be receiving the training from someone who is not related to its employer. Thus, a business trainee might include a lawyer employed by a law firm in one Contracting State who works for one year as a stagiare in an unrelated law firm in the other Contracting State. However, the term would not include a manager who normally is employed by a parent company in one Contracting State who is sent to the other Contracting State to run a factory owned by a subsidiary of the parent company.

Relationship to other Articles

The saving clause of paragraph 4 of Article 1 (General Scope) does not apply to this Article with respect to an individual who is neither a citizen of the host State nor has been admitted for permanent residence there. The saving clause, however, does apply with respect to citizens and permanent residents of the host State. Thus, a U.S. citizen who is a resident of the other Contracting State and who visits the United States as a full-time student at an accredited university will not be exempt from U.S. tax on remittances from abroad that otherwise constitute U.S. taxable income. A person, however, who is not a U.S. citizen, and who visits the United States as a student and remains long enough to become a resident under U.S. law, but does not become a permanent resident (i.e., does not acquire a green card), will be entitled to the full benefits of the Article.

ARTICLE 21 (OTHER INCOME)

Article 21 generally assigns taxing jurisdiction over income not dealt with in the other articles (Articles 6 through 20) of the Convention to the

State of residence of the beneficial owner of the income. In order for an item of income to be "dealt with" in another article it must be the type of income described in the article and, in most cases, it must have its source in a Contracting State. For example, all royalty income that arises in a Contracting State and that is beneficially owned by a resident of the other Contracting State is "dealt with" in Article 12 (Royalties). However, profits derived in the conduct of a business are "dealt with" in Article 7 (Business Profits) whether or not they have their source in one of the Contracting States.

Examples of items of income covered by Article 21 include income from gambling, punitive (but not compensatory) damages and covenants not to compete. The article would also apply to income from a variety of financial transactions, where such income does not arise in the course of the conduct of a trade or business. For example, income from notional principal contracts and other derivatives would fall within Article 21 if derived by persons not engaged in the trade or business of dealing in such instruments, unless such instruments were being used to hedge risks arising in a trade or business. It would also apply to securities lending fees derived by an institutional investor. Further, in most cases guarantee fees paid within an intercompany group would be covered by Article 21, unless the guarantor were engaged in the business of providing such guarantees to unrelated parties.

Article 21 also applies to items of income that are not dealt with in the other articles because of their source or some other characteristic. For example, Article 11 (Interest) addresses only the taxation of interest arising in a Contracting State. Interest arising in a third State that is not attributable to a permanent establishment, therefore, is subject to Article 21.

Distributions from partnerships are not generally dealt with under Article 21 because partnership distributions generally do not constitute income. Under the Code, partners include in income their distributive share of partnership income annually, and partnership distributions themselves generally do not give rise to income. This would also be the case under U.S. law with respect to distributions from trusts. Trust income and distributions that, under the Code, have the character of the associated distributable net income would generally be covered by another article of the Convention. See Code section 641 et seq.

Paragraph 1

The general rule of Article 21 is contained in paragraph 1. Items of income not dealt with in other articles and beneficially owned by a resident of a Contracting State will be taxable only in the State of residence. This exclusive right of taxation applies whether or not the residence State exercises its right to tax the income covered by the Article.

The reference in this paragraph to "items of income beneficially owned by a resident of a Contracting State" rather than simply "items of income of a resident of a Contracting State," as in the OECD Model, is intended merely to make explicit the implicit understanding in other treaties that the exclusive residence taxation provided by paragraph 1 applies only when a resident of a Contracting State is the beneficial owner of the income. Thus, source taxation of income not dealt with in other articles of the Convention is not limited by paragraph 1 if it is nominally paid to a resident of the other Contracting State, but is beneficially owned by a resident of a third State. However, income received by a nominee on behalf of a resident of that other State would be entitled to benefits.

The term "beneficially owned" is not defined in the Convention, and is, therefore, defined as under the internal law of the country imposing tax (i.e., the source country). The person who beneficially owns the income for purposes of Article 21 is the person to which the income is attributable for tax purposes under the laws of the source State.

Paragraph 2

This paragraph provides an exception to the general rule of paragraph 1 for income that is attributable to a permanent establishment maintained in a Contracting State by a resident of the other Contracting State. The taxation of such income is governed by the provisions of Article 7 (Business Profits). Therefore, income arising outside the United States that is attributable to a permanent establishment maintained in the United States by a resident of the other Contracting State generally would be taxable by the United States under the provisions of Article 7. This would be true even if the income is sourced in a third State.

Relationship to Other Articles

This Article is subject to the saving clause of paragraph 4 of Article 1 (General Scope). Thus, the United States may tax the income of a resident of the other Contracting State that is not dealt with elsewhere in the Convention, if that resident is a citizen of the United States. The Article is also subject to the provisions of Article 22 (Limitation on Benefits). Thus, if a resident of the other Contracting State earns income that falls within the scope of paragraph 1 of Article 21, but that is taxable by the United States under U.S. law, the income would be exempt from U.S. tax under the provisions of Article 21 only if the resident satisfies one of the tests of Article 22 for entitlement to benefits.

ARTICLE 22 (LIMITATION ON BENEFITS)

Article 22 contains anti-treaty-shopping provisions that are intended to prevent residents of third countries from benefiting from what is intended to be a reciprocal agreement between two countries. In general, the provision does not rely on a determination of purpose or intention but instead sets forth a series of objective tests. A resident of a Contracting

State that satisfies one of the tests will receive benefits regardless of its motivations in choosing its particular business structure.

The structure of the Article is as follows: Paragraph 1 states the general rule that residents are entitled to benefits otherwise accorded to residents only to the extent provided in the Article. Paragraph 2 lists a series of attributes of a resident of a Contracting State, the presence of any one of which will entitle that person to all the benefits of the Convention. Paragraph 3 provides that, regardless of whether a person qualifies for benefits under paragraph 2, benefits may be granted to that person with regard to certain income earned in the conduct of an active trade or business. Paragraph 4 provides that benefits also may be granted if the competent authority of the State from which benefits are claimed determines that it is appropriate to provide benefits in that case. Paragraph 5 defines certain terms used in the Article.

Paragraph 1

Paragraph 1 provides that a resident of a Contracting State will be entitled to the benefits otherwise accorded to residents of a Contracting State under the Convention only to the extent provided in the Article. The benefits otherwise accorded to residents under the Convention include all limitations on source-based taxation under Articles 6 through 21, the treaty-based relief from double taxation provided by Article 23, and the protection afforded to residents of a Contracting State under Article 24. Some provisions do not require that a person be a resident in order to enjoy the benefits of those provisions. Article 25 is not limited to residents of the Contracting States, and Article 27 applies to diplomatic agents or consular officials regardless of residence. Article 22 accordingly does not limit the availability of treaty benefits under these provisions.

Article 22 and the anti-abuse provisions of domestic law complement each other, as Article 22 effectively determines whether an entity has a sufficient nexus to the Contracting State to be treated as a resident for treaty purposes, while domestic anti-abuse provisions (e.g., business purpose, substance-over-form, step transaction or conduit principles) determine whether a particular transaction should be recast in accordance with its substance. Thus, internal law principles of the source Contracting State may be applied to identify the beneficial owner of an item of income, and Article 22 then will be applied to the beneficial owner to determine if that person is entitled to the benefits of the Convention with respect to such income.

Paragraph 2

Paragraph 2 has six subparagraphs, each of which describes a category of residents that are entitled to all benefits of the Convention.

It is intended that the provisions of paragraph 2 will be self executing. Unlike the provisions of paragraph 4, discussed below, claiming benefits under paragraph 2 does not require advance competent authority ruling or approval. The tax authorities may, of course, on review, determine that the taxpayer has improperly interpreted the paragraph and is not entitled to the benefits claimed.

Individuals—Subparagraph 2(a)

Subparagraph (a) provides that individual residents of a Contracting State will be entitled to all treaty benefits. If such an individual receives income as a nominee on behalf of a third country resident, benefits may be denied under the respective articles of the Convention by the requirement that the beneficial owner of the income be a resident of a Contracting State.

Governments—Subparagraph 2(b)

Subparagraph (b) provides that the Contracting States and any political subdivision or local authority thereof will be entitled to all benefits of the Convention.

Publicly-Traded Corporations—Subparagraph 2(c)(i)

Subparagraph (c) applies to two categories of companies: publicly traded companies and subsidiaries of publicly traded companies. A company resident in a Contracting State is entitled to all the benefits of the Convention under clause (i) of subparagraph (c) if the principal class of its shares, and any disproportionate class of shares, is regularly traded on one or more recognized stock exchanges and the company satisfies at least one of the following additional requirements: first, the company's principal class of shares is primarily traded on one or more recognized stock exchanges located in the Contracting State of which the company is a resident; or, second, the company's primary place of management and control is in its State of residence.

The term "recognized stock exchange" is defined in subparagraph (a) of paragraph 5. It includes (i) the NASDAQ System and any stock exchange registered with the Securities and Exchange Commission as a national securities exchange for purposes of the Securities Exchange Act of 1934; (ii) [certain exchanges located in the other Contracting State]; and (iii) any other stock exchange agreed upon by the competent authorities of the Contracting States.

If a company has only one class of shares, it is only necessary to consider whether the shares of that class meet the relevant trading requirements. If the company has more than one class of shares, it is necessary as an initial matter to determine which class or classes constitute the "principal class of shares". The term "principal class of shares" is defined in subparagraph (b) of paragraph 5 to mean the ordinary or common shares of the company representing the majority of the aggregate voting power and value of the company. If the company does not have a class of ordinary or common shares representing the majority of the aggregate voting power and value of the company, then the "principal class of shares" is that class or any combination of classes of shares that represents, in the aggregate, a majority of the voting power and value of the company. Although in a particular case involving a company with several classes of shares it is conceivable that more than one group of classes could be identified that account for more than 50% of the shares, it is only necessary for one such group to satisfy the requirements of this subparagraph in order for the company to be entitled to benefits. Benefits would not be denied to the company even if a second, non-qualifying, group of shares with more than half of the company's voting power and value could be identified.

A company whose principal class of shares is regularly traded on a recognized stock exchange will nevertheless not qualify for benefits under subparagraph (c) of paragraph 2 if it has a disproportionate class of shares that is not regularly traded on a recognized stock exchange. The term "disproportionate class of shares" is defined in subparagraph (c) of paragraph 5. A company has a disproportionate class of shares if it has outstanding a class of shares which is subject to terms or other arrangements that entitle the holder to a larger portion of the company's income, profit, or gain in the other Contracting State than that to which the holder would be entitled in the absence of such terms or arrangements. Thus, for example, a company resident in the other Contracting State meets the test of subparagraph (c) of paragraph 5 if it has outstanding a class of "tracking stock" that pays dividends based upon a formula that approximates the company's return on its assets employed in the United States.

The following example illustrates this result.

Example. OCo is a corporation resident in the other Contracting State. OCo has two classes of shares: Common and Preferred. The Common shares are listed and regularly traded on the principal stock exchange of the other Contracting State. The Preferred shares have no voting rights and are entitled to receive dividends equal in amount to interest payments that OCo receives from unrelated borrowers in the United States. The Preferred shares are owned entirely by a single investor that is a resident of a country with which the United States does not have a tax treaty. The Common shares account for more than 50 percent of the value of OCo and for 100 percent of the voting power. Because the owner of the Preferred shares is entitled to receive payments corresponding to the U.S. source interest income earned by OCo, the Preferred shares are a disproportionate class of shares. Because the Preferred shares are not regularly traded on a recognized stock exchange, OCo will not qualify for benefits under subparagraph (c) of paragraph 2.

The term "regularly traded" is not defined in the Convention. In accordance with paragraph 2 of Article 3 (General Definitions), this term will be defined by reference to the domestic tax laws of the State from which treaty benefits are sought, generally the source State. In the case of the United States, this term is understood to have the meaning it has under Treas. Reg. section 1.884–5(d)(4)(i)(B), relating to the branch tax provisions of the Code. Under these regulations, a class of shares is considered to be "regularly traded" if two requirements are met: trades in the class of shares are made in more than de minimis quantities on at least 60 days during the taxable year, and the aggregate number of shares in the class traded during the year is at least 10 percent of the average number of shares outstanding during the year. Sections 1.884–5(d)(4)(i)(A), (ii) and (iii) will not be taken into account for purposes of defining the term "regularly traded" under the Convention.

The regular trading requirement can be met by trading on any recognized exchange or exchanges located in either State. Trading on one or more recognized stock exchanges may be aggregated for purposes of this requirement. Thus, a U.S. company could satisfy the regularly traded requirement through trading, in whole or in part, on a recognized stock exchange located in the other Contracting State. Authorized but unissued shares are not considered for purposes of this test.

The term "primarily traded" is not defined in the Convention. In accordance with paragraph 2 of Article 3 (General Definitions), this term will have the meaning it has under the laws of the State concerning the taxes to which the Convention applies, generally the source State. In the case of the United States, this term is understood to have the meaning it has under Treas. Reg. section 1.884–5(d)(3), relating to the branch tax provisions of the Code. Accordingly, stock of a corporation is "primarily traded" if the number of shares in the company's principal class of shares that are traded during the taxable year on all recognized stock exchanges in the Contracting State of which the company is a resident exceeds the number of shares in the company's principal class of shares that are traded during that year on established securities markets in any other single foreign country.

A company whose principal class of shares is regularly traded on a recognized exchange but cannot meet the primarily traded test may claim treaty benefits if its primary place of management and control is in its country of residence. This test should be distinguished from the "place of effective management" test which is used in the OECD Model and by many other countries to establish residence. In some cases, the place of effective management test has been interpreted to mean the place where the board of directors meets. By contrast, the primary place of management and control test looks to where day-to-day responsibility for the management of the company (and its subsidiaries) is exercised. The company's primary place of management and control will be located in the State in which the company is a resident only if the executive officers and senior management employees exercise day-to-day responsibility for more of the strategic, financial and operational policy decision making for the company (including direct and indirect subsidiaries) in that State than in the other State or any third state, and the staff that support the management in making those decisions are also based in that State. Thus, the test looks to the overall activities of the relevant persons to see where those activities are conducted. In most cases, it will be a necessary, but not a sufficient, condition that the headquarters of the company (that is, the place at which the CEO and other top executives normally are based) be located in the Contracting State of which the company is a resident.

To apply the test, it will be necessary to determine which persons are to be considered "executive officers and senior management employees". In most cases, it will not be necessary to look beyond the executives who are members of the Board of Directors (the "inside directors") in the case of a U.S. company or the members of the [ ] in the case of the other Contracting State. That will not always be the case, however; in fact, the relevant persons may be employees of subsidiaries if those persons make the strategic, financial and operational policy decisions. Moreover, it would be necessary to take into account any special voting arrangements that result in certain board members making certain decisions without the participation of other board members.

Subsidiaries of Publicly–Traded Corporations—Subparagraph 2(c)(ii)

A company resident in a Contracting State is entitled to all the benefits of the Convention under clause (ii) of subparagraph (c) of paragraph 2 if five or fewer publicly traded companies described in clause (i) are the direct or indirect owners of at least 50 percent of the aggregate vote and value of the company's shares (and at least 50 percent of any disproportionate class of shares). If the publicly-traded companies are indirect owners, however, each of the intermediate companies must be a resident of one of the Contracting States.

Thus, for example, a company that is a resident of the other Contracting State, all the shares of which are owned by another company that is a resident of that State, would qualify for benefits under the Convention if the principal class of shares (and any disproportionate classes of shares) of the parent company are regularly and primarily traded on a recognized stock exchange in that Contracting State. However, such a subsidiary would not qualify for benefits under clause (ii) if the publicly traded parent company were a resident of a third state, for example, and not a resident of the United States or the other Contracting State. Furthermore, if a parent company in the other Contracting State indirectly owned the bottom-tier company through a chain of subsidiaries, each such subsidiary in the chain, as an intermediate owner, must be a resident of the United States or the other Contracting State in order for the subsidiary to meet the test in clause (ii).

Tax Exempt Organizations—Subparagraph 2(d)

Subparagraph 2(d) provides rules by which the tax exempt organizations described in paragraph 2 of Article 4 (Resident) will be entitled to all the benefits of the Convention. A pension fund will qualify for benefits if more than fifty percent of the beneficiaries, members or participants of the organization are individuals resident in either Contracting State. For purposes of this provision, the term "beneficiaries" should be understood to refer to the persons receiving benefits from the organization. On the other hand, a tax-exempt organization other than a pension fund automatically qualifies for benefits, without regard to the residence of its beneficiaries or members. Entities qualifying under this rule generally are those that are exempt from tax in their State of residence and that are organized and operated exclusively to fulfill religious, charitable, scientific, artistic, cultural, or educational purposes.

Ownership/Base Erosion—Subparagraph 2(e)

Subparagraph 2(e) provides an additional method to qualify for treaty benefits that applies to any form of legal entity that is a resident of a Contracting State. The test provided in subparagraph (e), the so-called ownership and base erosion test, is a two-part test. Both prongs of the test must be satisfied for the resident to be entitled to treaty benefits under subparagraph 2(e).

The ownership prong of the test, under clause (i), requires that 50 percent or more of each class of shares or other beneficial interests in the person is owned, directly or indirectly, on at least half the days of the person's taxable year by persons who are residents of the Contracting State of which that person is a resident and that are themselves entitled to treaty benefits under subparagraphs (a), (b), (d) or clause (i) of subparagraph (c) of paragraph 2. In the case of indirect owners, however, each of the intermediate owners must be a resident of that Contracting State.

Trusts may be entitled to benefits under this provision if they are treated as residents under Article 4 (Residence) and they otherwise satisfy the requirements of this subparagraph. For purposes of this subparagraph, the beneficial interests in a trust will be considered to be owned by its beneficiaries in proportion to each beneficiary's actuarial interest in the trust. The interest of a remainder beneficiary will be equal to 100 percent less the aggregate percentages held by income beneficiaries. A beneficiary's interest in a trust will not be considered to be owned by a person entitled to benefits under the other provisions of paragraph 2 if it is not possible to determine the beneficiary's actuarial interest. Consequently, if it is not possible to determine the actuarial interest of the beneficiaries in a trust, the ownership test under clause i) cannot be satisfied, unless all possible beneficiaries are persons entitled to benefits under the other subparagraphs of paragraph 2.

The base erosion prong of clause (ii) of subparagraph (e) is satisfied with respect to a person if less than 50 percent of the person's gross income for the taxable year, as determined under the tax law in the person's State of residence, is paid or accrued to persons who are not residents of either Contracting State entitled to benefits under subparagraphs (a), (b), (d) or clause (i) of subparagraph (c) of paragraph 2, in the form of payments deductible for tax purposes in the payer's State of residence. These amounts do not include arm's-length payments in the ordinary course of business for services or tangible property. To the extent they are deductible from the taxable base, trust distributions are deductible payments. However, depreciation and amortization deductions, which do not represent payments or accruals to other persons, are disregarded for this purpose.

Paragraph 3

Paragraph 3 sets forth an alternative test under which a resident of a Contracting State may receive treaty benefits with respect to certain items of income that are connected to an active trade or business conducted in its State of residence. A resident of a Contracting State may qualify for benefits under paragraph 3 whether or not it also qualifies under paragraph 2.

Subparagraph (a) sets forth the general rule that a resident of a Contracting State engaged in the active conduct of a trade or business in that State may obtain the benefits of the Convention with respect to an item of income derived in the other Contracting State. The item of income, however, must be derived in connection with or incidental to that trade or business.

The term "trade or business" is not defined in the Convention. Pursuant to paragraph 2 of Article 3 (General Definitions), when determining whether a resident of the other Contracting State is entitled to the benefits of the Convention under paragraph 3 of this Article with respect to an item of income derived from sources within the United States, the United States will ascribe to this term the meaning that it has under the law of the United States. Accordingly, the U.S. competent authority will refer to the regulations issued under section 367(a) for the definition of the term "trade or business." In general, therefore, a trade or business will be considered to be a specific unified group of activities that constitute or could constitute an independent economic enterprise carried on for profit. Furthermore, a corporation generally will be considered to carry on a trade or business only if the officers and employees of the corporation conduct substantial managerial and operational activities.

The business of making or managing investments for the resident's own account will be considered to be a trade or business only when part of banking, insurance or securities activities conducted by a bank, an insurance company, or a registered securities dealer. Such activities conducted by a person other than a bank, insurance company or registered securities dealer will not be considered to be the conduct of an active trade or business, nor would they be considered to be the conduct of an active trade or business if conducted by a bank, insurance company or registered securities dealer but not as part of the company's banking, insurance or dealer business. Because a headquarters operation is in the business of managing investments, a company that functions solely as a headquarters company will not be considered to be engaged in an active trade or business for purposes of paragraph 3.

An item of income is derived in connection with a trade or business if the income-producing activity in the State of source is a line of business that "forms a part of" or is "complementary" to the trade or business conducted in the State of residence by the income recipient.

A business activity generally will be considered to form part of a business activity conducted in the State of source if the two activities involve the design, manufacture or sale of the same products or type of products, or the provision of similar services. The line of business in the State of residence may be upstream, downstream, or parallel to the activity conducted in the State of source. Thus, the line of business may provide inputs for a manufacturing process that occurs in the State of source, may sell the output of that manufacturing process, or simply may sell the same sorts of products that are being sold by the trade or business carried on in the State of source.

Example 1. USCo is a corporation resident in the United States. USCo is engaged in an active manufacturing business in the United States. USCo owns 100 percent of the shares of FCo, a corporation resident in the other Contracting State. FCo distributes USCo products in the other Contracting State. Since the business activities conducted by the two corporations involve the same products, FCo's distribution business is considered to form a part of USCo's manufacturing business.

Example 2. The facts are the same as in Example 1, except that USCo does not manufacture. Rather, USCo operates a large research and development facility in the United States that licenses intellectual property to affiliates worldwide, including FCo. FCo and other USCo affiliates then manufacture and market the USCo-designed products in their respective markets. Since the activities conducted by FCo and USCo involve the same product lines, these activities are considered to form a part of the same trade or business.

For two activities to be considered to be "complementary," the activities need not relate to the same types of products or services, but they should be part of the same overall industry and be related in the sense that the success or failure of one activity will tend to result in success or failure for the other. Where more than one trade or business is conducted in the State of source and only one of the trades or businesses forms a part of or is complementary to a trade or business conducted in the State of residence, it is necessary to identify the trade or business to which an item of income is attributable. Royalties generally will be considered to be derived in connection with the trade or business to which the underlying intangible property is attributable. Dividends will be deemed to be derived first out of earnings and profits of the treaty-benefited trade or business, and then out of other earnings and profits.

Interest income may be allocated under any reasonable method consistently applied. A method that conforms to U.S. principles for expense allocation will be considered a reasonable method.

Example 3. Americair is a corporation resident in the United States that operates an international airline. FSub is a wholly-owned subsidiary of Americair resident in the other Contracting State. FSub operates a chain of hotels in the other Contracting State that are located near airports served by Americair flights. Americair frequently sells tour packages that include air travel to the other Contracting State and lodging at FSub hotels. Although both companies are engaged in the active conduct of a trade or business, the businesses of operating a chain of hotels and operating an airline are distinct trades or businesses. Therefore FSub's business does not form a part of Americair's business. However, FSub's business is considered to be complementary to Americair's business because they are part of the same overall industry (travel) and the links between their operations tend to make them interdependent.

Example 4. The facts are the same as in Example 3, except that FSub owns an office building in the other Contracting State instead of a hotel chain. No part of Americair's business is conducted through the office building. FSub's business is not considered to form a part of or to be complementary to Americair's business. They are engaged in distinct trades or businesses in separate industries, and there is no economic dependence between the two operations.

Example 5. USFlower is a corporation resident in the United States. USFlower produces and sells flowers in the United States and other countries. USFlower owns all the shares of ForHolding, a corporation resident in the other Contracting State. ForHolding is a holding company that is not engaged in a trade or business. ForHolding owns all the shares of three corporations that are resident in the other Contracting State: ForFlower, ForLawn, and ForFish. ForFlower distributes USFlower flowers under the USFlower trademark in the other State. ForLawn markets a line of lawn care products in the other State under the USFlower trademark. In addition to being sold under the same trademark, ForLawn and ForFlower products are sold in the same stores and sales of each company's products tend to generate increased sales of the other's products. ForFish imports fish from the United States and distributes it to fish wholesalers in the other State. For purposes of paragraph 3, the business of ForFlower forms a part of the business of USFlower, the business of ForLawn is complementary to the business of USFlower, and the business of ForFish is neither part of nor complementary to that of USFlower.

An item of income derived from the State of source is "incidental to" the trade or business carried on in the State of residence if production of the item facilitates the conduct of the trade or business in the State of residence. An example of incidental income is the temporary investment of working capital of a person in the State of residence in securities issued by persons in the State of source.

Subparagraph (b) of paragraph 3 states a further condition to the general rule in subparagraph (a) in cases where the trade or business generating the item of income in question is carried on either by the person deriving the income or by any associated enterprises. Subparagraph (b) states that the trade or business carried on in the State of residence, under these circumstances, must be substantial in relation to the activity in the State of source. The substantiality requirement is intended to prevent a narrow case of treaty-shopping abuses in which a company attempts to qualify for benefits by engaging in de minimis connected business activities in the treaty country in which it is resident (i.e., activities that have little economic cost or effect with respect to the company business as a whole).

The determination of substantiality is made based upon all the facts and circumstances and takes into account the comparative sizes of the trades or businesses in each Contracting State the nature of the activities performed in each Contracting State, and the relative contributions made to that trade or business in each Contracting State. In any case, in making each determination or comparison, due regard will be given to the relative sizes of the economies in the two Contracting States.

The determination in subparagraph (b) also is made separately for each item of income derived from the State of source. It therefore is possible that a person would be entitled to the benefits of the Convention with respect to one item of income but not with respect to another. If a resident of a Contracting State is entitled to treaty benefits with respect to a particular item of income under paragraph 3, the resident is entitled to all benefits of the Convention insofar as they affect the taxation of that item of income in the State of source.

The application of the substantiality requirement only to income from related parties focuses only on potential abuse cases, and does not hamper certain other kinds of non-abusive activities, even though the income recipient resident in a Contracting State may be very small in relation to the entity generating income in the other Contracting State. For example, if a small U.S. research firm develops a process that it licenses to a very large, unrelated, pharmaceutical manufacturer in the other Contracting State, the size of the U.S. research firm would not have to be tested against the size of the manufacturer. Similarly, a small U.S. bank that makes a loan to a very large unrelated company operating a business in the other Contracting State would not have to pass a substantiality test to receive treaty benefits under Paragraph 3.

Subparagraph (c) of paragraph 3 provides special attribution rules for purposes of applying the substantive rules of subparagraphs (a) and (b). Thus, these rules apply for purposes of determining whether a person meets the requirement in subparagraph (a) that it be engaged in the active conduct of a trade or business and that the item of income is derived in connection with that active trade or business, and for making the comparison required by the "substantiality" requirement in subparagraph (b). Subparagraph (c) attributes to a person activities conducted by persons "connected" to such person. A person ("X") is connected to another person ("Y") if X possesses 50 percent or more of the beneficial interest in Y (or if Y possesses 50 percent or more of the beneficial interest in X). For this purpose, X is connected to a company if X owns shares representing fifty percent or more of the aggregate voting power and value of the company or fifty percent or more of the beneficial equity interest in the company. X also is connected to Y if a third person possesses fifty percent or more of the beneficial interest in both X and Y. For this purpose, if X or Y is a company, the threshold relationship with respect to such company or companies is fifty percent or more of the aggregate voting power and value or fifty percent or more of the beneficial equity interest. Finally, X is connected to Y if, based upon all the facts and circumstances, X controls Y, Y controls X, or X and Y are controlled by the same person or persons.

Paragraph 4

Paragraph 4 provides that a resident of one of the States that is not entitled to the benefits of the Convention as a result of paragraphs 1 through 3 still may be granted benefits under the Convention at the discretion of the competent authority of the State from which benefits are claimed. In making determinations under paragraph 4, that competent authority will take into account as its guideline whether the establishment, acquisition, or maintenance of the person seeking benefits under the Convention, or the conduct of such person's operations, has or had as one of its principal purposes the obtaining of benefits under the Convention. Benefits will not be granted, however, solely because a company was established prior to the effective date of a treaty or protocol. In that case a company would still be required to establish to the satisfaction of the Competent Authority clear non-tax business reasons for its formation in a Contracting State, or that the allowance of benefits would not otherwise be contrary to the purposes of the treaty. Thus, persons that establish operations in one of the States with a principal purpose of obtaining the benefits of the Convention ordinarily will not be granted relief under paragraph 4.

The competent authority's discretion is quite broad. It may grant all of the benefits of the Convention to the taxpayer making the request, or it may grant only certain benefits. For instance, it may grant benefits only with respect to a particular item of income in a manner similar to paragraph 3. Further, the competent authority may establish conditions, such as setting time limits on the duration of any relief granted.

For purposes of implementing paragraph 4, a taxpayer will be permitted to present his case to the relevant competent authority for an advance determination based on the facts. In these circumstances, it is also expected that, if the competent authority determines that benefits are to be allowed, they will be allowed retroactively to the time of entry into force of the relevant treaty provision or the establishment of the structure in question, whichever is later.

Finally, there may be cases in which a resident of a Contracting State may apply for discretionary relief to the competent authority of his State of residence. This would arise, for example, if the benefit it is claiming is provided by the residence country, and not by the source country. So, for example, if a company that is a resident of the United States would like to claim the benefit of the re-sourcing rule of paragraph 3 of Article 23, but it does not meet any of the objective tests of paragraphs 2 and 3, it may apply to the U.S. competent authority for discretionary relief.

Paragraph 5

Paragraph 5 defines several key terms for purposes of Article 22. Each of the defined terms is discussed above in the context in which it is used.

ARTICLE 23 (RELIEF FROM DOUBLE TAXATION)

This Article describes the manner in which each Contracting State undertakes to relieve double taxation. The United States uses the foreign tax credit method under its internal law, and by treaty.

Paragraph 1

Paragraph 1 provides that the other Contracting State will provide relief from double taxation through [the credit method/the exemption method/a mixture of the credit and exemption methods.]

Paragraph 2

The United States agrees, in paragraph 2, to allow to its citizens and residents a credit against U.S. tax for income taxes paid or accrued to the other Contracting State. Paragraph 2 also provides that the other Contracting State's covered taxes are income taxes for U.S. purposes. This provision is based on the Department of the Treasury's review of the other Contracting State's laws.

Subparagraph (b) provides for a deemed-paid credit, consistent with section 902 of the Code , to a U.S. corporation in respect of dividends received from a corporation resident in the other Contracting State of which the U.S. corporation owns at least 10 percent of the voting stock. This credit is for the tax paid by the corporation to the other Contracting State on the profits out of which the dividends are considered paid.

The credits allowed under paragraph 2 are allowed in accordance with the provisions and subject to the limitations of U.S. law, as that law may be amended over time, so long as the general principle of the Article, that is, the allowance of a credit, is retained. Thus, although the Convention provides for a foreign tax credit, the terms of the credit are determined by the provisions, at the time a credit is given, of the U.S. statutory credit.

Therefore, the U.S. credit under the Convention is subject to the various limitations of U.S. law (see, e.g., Code sections 901–908). For example, the credit against U.S. tax generally is limited to the amount of U.S. tax due with respect to net foreign source income within the relevant foreign tax credit limitation category (see Code section 904(a)), and the dollar amount of the credit is determined in accordance with U.S. currency translation rules (see, e.g., Code section 986). Similarly, U.S. law applies to determine carryover periods for excess credits and other inter-year adjustments.

Paragraph 3

Paragraph 3 provides a re-sourcing rule for gross income covered by paragraph 2. Paragraph 3 is intended to ensure that a U.S. resident can obtain an appropriate amount of U.S. foreign tax credit for income taxes paid to the other Contracting State when the Convention assigns to the other Contracting State primary taxing rights over an item of gross income.

Accordingly, if the Convention allows the other Contracting State to tax an item of gross income (as defined under U.S. law) derived by a resident of the United States, the United States will treat that item of gross income as gross income from sources within the other Contracting State for U.S. foreign tax credit purposes. In the case of a U.S.-owned foreign corporation, however, section 904(g)(10) may apply for purposes of determining the U.S. foreign tax credit with respect to income subject to this re-sourcing rule. Section 904(g)(10) generally applies the foreign tax credit limitation separately to re-sourced income. Furthermore, the paragraph 2 re-sourcing rule applies to gross income, not net income. Accordingly, U.S. expense allocation and apportionment rules, see, e.g., Treas. Reg. section 1.861–9, continue to apply to income resourced under paragraph 2.

Paragraph 4

Paragraph 4 provides special rules for the tax treatment in both States of certain types of income derived from U.S. sources by U.S. citizens who are residents of the other Contracting State. Since U.S. citizens, regardless of residence, are subject to United States tax at ordinary progressive rates on their worldwide income, the U.S. tax on the U.S. source income of a U.S. citizen resident in the other Contracting State may exceed the U.S. tax that may be imposed under the Convention on an item of U.S. source income derived by a resident of the other Contracting State who is not a U.S. citizen. The provisions of paragraph 4 ensure that the other Contracting State does not bear the cost of U.S. taxation of its citizens who are residents of the other Contracting State.

Subparagraph (a) provides, with respect to items of income from sources within the United States, special credit rules for the other Contracting State. These rules apply to items of U.S.-source income that would be either exempt from U.S. tax or subject to reduced rates of U.S. tax under the provisions of the Convention if they had been received by a resident of the other Contracting State who is not a U.S. citizen. The tax credit allowed under paragraph 4 with respect to such items need not exceed the U.S. tax that may be imposed under the Convention, other than tax imposed solely by reason of the U.S. citizenship of the taxpayer under the provisions of the saving clause of paragraph 4 of Article 1 (General Scope).

For example, if a U.S. citizen resident in the other Contracting State receives portfolio dividends from sources within the United States, the foreign tax credit granted by the other Contracting State would be limited to 15 percent of the dividend—the U.S. tax that may be imposed under subparagraph (b) of paragraph 2 of Article 10 (Dividends)—even if the shareholder is subject to U.S. net income tax because of his U.S. citizenship. With respect to royalty or interest income, the other Contracting State would allow no foreign tax credit, because its residents are exempt from U.S. tax on these classes of income under the provisions of Articles 11 (Interest) and 12 (Royalties).

Paragraph 4(b) eliminates the potential for double taxation that can arise because subparagraph 4(a) provides that the other Contracting State need not provide full relief for the U.S. tax imposed on its citizens resident in the other Contracting State. The subparagraph provides that the United States will credit the income tax paid or accrued to the other Contracting State, after the application of subparagraph 4(a). It further provides that in allowing the credit, the United States will not reduce its tax below the amount that is taken into account in the other Contracting State in applying subparagraph 4(a).

Since the income described in paragraph 4(a) generally will be U.S. source income, special rules are required to re-source some of the income to the other Contracting State in order for the United States to be able to credit the tax paid to the other Contracting State. This re-sourcing is provided for in subparagraph 4(c), which deems the items of income referred to in subparagraph 4(a) to be from foreign sources to the extent necessary to avoid double taxation under paragraph 4(b). Subparagraph 3(c)(iii) of Article 25 (Mutual Agreement Procedure) provides a mechanism by which the competent authorities can resolve any disputes regarding whether income is from sources within the United States.

The following two examples illustrate the application of paragraph 4 in the case of a U.S.-source portfolio dividend received by a U.S. citizen resident in the other Contracting State. In both examples, the U.S. rate of tax on residents of the other Contracting State, under subparagraph (b) of paragraph 2 of Article 10 (Dividends) of the Convention, is 15 percent. In both examples, the U.S. income tax rate on the U.S. citizen is 35 percent. In example 1, the rate of income tax imposed in the other Contracting State on its resident (the U.S. citizen) is 25 percent (below the U.S. rate), and in example 2, the rate imposed on its resident is 40 percent (above the U.S. rate).

	Example 1	Example 2
Subparagraph (a)		
U.S. dividend declared	$100.00	$100.00
Notional U.S. withholding tax (Article 10(2)(b))	15.00	15.00
Taxable income in other Contracting State	100.00	100.00
Other Contracting State tax before credit	25.00	40.00
Less: tax credit for notional U.S. withholding tax	15.00	15.00
Net post-credit tax paid to other Contracting State	10.00	25.00
Subparagraphs (b) and (c)		
U.S. pre-tax income	$100.00	$100.00
U.S. pre-credit citizenship tax	35.00	35.00
Notional U.S. withholding tax	15.00	15.00
U.S. tax eligible to be offset by credit	20.00	20.00
Tax paid to other Contracting State	10.00	25.00
Income re-sourced from U.S. to foreign source (see below)	28.57	57.14
U.S. pre-credit tax on re-sourced income	10.00	20.00
U.S. credit for tax paid to the other Contracting State	10.00	20.00
Net post-credit U.S. tax	10.00	0.00
Total U.S. tax	25.00	15.00

In both examples, in the application of subparagraph (a), the other Contracting State credits a 15 percent U.S. tax against its residence tax on the U.S. citizen. In the first example, the net tax paid to the other Contracting State after the foreign tax credit is $10.00; in the second example, it is $25.00. In the application of subparagraphs (b) and (c), from the U.S. tax due before credit of $35.00, the United States subtracts the amount of the U.S. source tax of $15.00, against which no U.S. foreign tax credit is allowed. This subtraction ensures that the United States collects the tax that it is due under the Convention as the State of source.

In both examples, given the 35 percent U.S. tax rate, the maximum amount of U.S. tax against which credit for the tax paid to the other Contracting State may be claimed is $20 ($35 U.S. tax minus $15 U.S. withholding tax). Initially, all of the income in both examples was from sources within the United States. For a U.S. foreign tax credit to be allowed for the full amount of the tax paid to the other Contracting State, an appropriate amount of the income must be re-sourced to the other Contracting State under subparagraph (c).

The amount that must be re-sourced depends on the amount of tax for which the U.S. citizen is claiming a U.S. foreign tax credit. In example 1, the tax paid to the other Contracting State was $10. For this amount to be creditable against U.S. tax, $28.57 ($10 tax divided by 35 percent U.S. tax rate) must be resourced to the other Contracting State. When the tax is credited against the $10 of U.S. tax on this resourced income, there is a net U.S. tax of $10 due after credit ($20 U.S. tax eligible to be offset by credit, minus $10 tax paid to the other Contracting State). Thus, in example 1, there is a total of $25 in U.S. tax ($15 U.S. withholding tax plus $10 residual U.S. tax).

In example 2, the tax paid to the other Contracting State was $25, but, because the United States subtracts the U.S. withholding tax of $15 from the total U.S. tax of $35, only $20 of U.S. taxes may be offset by taxes paid to the other Contracting State. Accordingly, the amount that must be resourced to the other Contracting State is limited to the amount necessary to ensure a U.S. foreign tax credit for $20 of tax paid to the other Contracting State, or $57.14 ($20 tax paid to the other Contracting State divided by 35 percent U.S. tax rate). When the tax paid to the other Contracting State is credited against the U.S. tax on this re-sourced income, there is no residual U.S. tax ($20 U.S. tax minus $25 tax paid to the other Contracting State, subject to the U.S. limit of $20). Thus, in example 2, there is a total of $15 in U.S. tax ($15 U.S. withholding tax plus $0 residual U.S. tax). Because the tax paid to the other Contracting State was $25 and the U.S. tax eligible to be offset by credit was $20, there is $5 of excess foreign tax credit available for carryover.

Relationship to other Articles

By virtue of subparagraph (a) of paragraph 5 of Article 1 (General Scope), Article 23 is not subject to the saving clause of paragraph 4 of Article 1. Thus, the United States will allow a credit to its citizens and residents in accordance with the Article, even if such credit were to provide a benefit not available under the Code (such as the re-sourcing provided by paragraph 3 and subparagraph 4(c)).

ARTICLE 24 (NON–DISCRIMINATION)

This Article ensures that nationals of a Contracting State, in the case of paragraph 1, and residents of a Contracting State, in the case of paragraphs 2 through 5, will not be subject, directly or indirectly, to discriminatory taxation in the other Contracting State. Not all differences in tax treatment, either as between nationals of the two States, or between residents of the two States, are violations of the prohibition against discrimination. Rather, the non-discrimination obligations of this

Article apply only if the nationals or residents of the two States are comparably situated.

Each of the relevant paragraphs of the Article provides that two persons that are comparably situated must be treated similarly. Although the actual words differ from paragraph to paragraph (e.g., paragraph 1 refers to two nationals "in the same circumstances," paragraph 2 refers to two enterprises "carrying on the same activities" and paragraph 4 refers to two enterprises that are "similar"), the common underlying premise is that if the difference in treatment is directly related to a tax-relevant difference in the situations of the domestic and foreign persons being compared, that difference is not to be treated as discriminatory (i.e., if one person is taxable in a Contracting State on worldwide income and the other is not, or tax may be collectible from one person at a later stage, but not from the other, distinctions in treatment would be justified under paragraph 1). Other examples of such factors that can lead to nondiscriminatory differences in treatment are noted in the discussions of each paragraph.

The operative paragraphs of the Article also use different language to identify the kinds of differences in taxation treatment that will be considered discriminatory. For example, paragraphs 1 and 4 speak of "any taxation or any requirement connected therewith that is more burdensome," while paragraph 2 specifies that a tax "shall not be less favorably levied." Regardless of these differences in language, only differences in tax treatment that materially disadvantage the foreign person relative to the domestic person are properly the subject of the Article.

Paragraph 1

Paragraph 1 provides that a national of one Contracting State may not be subject to taxation or connected requirements in the other Contracting State that are more burdensome than the taxes and connected requirements imposed upon a national of that other State in the same circumstances. The OECD Model prohibits taxation that is "other than or more burdensome" than that imposed on U.S. persons. This Convention omits the reference to taxation that is "other than" that imposed on U.S. persons because the only relevant question under this provision should be whether the requirement imposed on a national of the other Contracting State is more burdensome. A requirement may be different from the requirements imposed on U.S. nationals without being more burdensome.

The term "national" in relation to a Contracting State is defined in subparagraph 1(j) of Article 3 (General Definitions). The term includes both individuals and juridical persons. A national of a Contracting State is afforded protection under this paragraph even if the national is not a resident of either Contracting State. Thus, a U.S. citizen who is resident in a third country is entitled, under this paragraph, to the same treatment in the other Contracting State as a national of the other Contracting State who is in similar circumstances (i.e., presumably one who is resident in a third State).

As noted above, whether or not the two persons are both taxable on worldwide income is a significant circumstance for this purpose. For this reason, paragraph 1 specifically states that the United States is not obligated to apply the same taxing regime to a national of the other Contracting State who is not resident in the United States as it applies to a U.S. national who is not resident in the United States. United States citizens who are not residents of the United States but who are, nevertheless, subject to United States tax on their worldwide income are not in the same circumstances with respect to United States taxation as citizens of the other Contracting State who are not United States residents. Thus, for example, Article 24 would not entitle a national of the other Contracting State resident in a third country to taxation at graduated rates on U.S. source dividends or other investment income that applies to a U.S. citizen resident in the same third country.

Paragraph 2

Paragraph 2 of the Article, provides that a Contracting State may not tax a permanent establishment of an enterprise of the other Contracting State less favorably than an enterprise of that first-mentioned State that is carrying on the same activities.

The fact that a U.S. permanent establishment of an enterprise of the other Contracting State is subject to U.S. tax only on income that is attributable to the permanent establishment, while a U.S. corporation engaged in the same activities is taxable on its worldwide income is not, in itself, a sufficient difference to provide different treatment for the permanent establishment. There are cases, however, where the two enterprises would not be similarly situated and differences in treatment may be warranted. For instance, it would not be a violation of the non-discrimination protection of paragraph 2 to require the foreign enterprise to provide information in a reasonable manner that may be different from the information requirements imposed on a resident enterprise, because information may not be as readily available to the Internal Revenue Service from a foreign as from a domestic enterprise. Similarly, it would not be a violation of paragraph 2 to impose penalties on persons who fail to comply with such a requirement (see, e.g., sections 874(a) and 882(c)(2)). Further, a determination that income and expenses have been attributed or allocated to a permanent establishment in conformity with the principles of Article 7 (Business Profits) implies that the attribution or allocation was not discriminatory.

Section 1446 of the Code imposes on any partnership with income that is effectively connected with a U.S. trade or business the obligation to withhold tax on amounts allocable to a foreign partner. In the context of the Convention, this obligation applies with respect to a share of the partnership income of a partner resident in the other Contracting State, and attributable to a U.S. permanent establishment. There is no similar obligation with respect to the distributive shares of U.S. resident partners. It is understood, however, that this distinction is not a form of discrimination within the meaning of paragraph 2 of the Article. No distinction is made between U.S. and non-U.S. partnerships, since the law requires that partnerships of both U.S. and non-U.S. domicile withhold tax in respect of the partnership shares of non-U.S. partners. Furthermore, in distinguishing between U.S. and non-U.S. partners, the requirement to withhold on the non-U.S. but not the U.S. partner's share is not discriminatory taxation, but, like other withholding on nonresident aliens, is merely a reasonable method for the collection of tax from persons who are not continually present in the United States, and as to whom it otherwise may be difficult for the United States to enforce its tax jurisdiction. If tax has been over-withheld, the partner can, as in other cases of over-withholding, file for a refund.

Paragraph 3

Paragraph 3 makes clear that the provisions of paragraphs 1 and 2 do not obligate a Contracting State to grant to a resident of the other Contracting State any tax allowances, reliefs, etc., that it grants to its own residents on account of their civil status or family responsibilities. Thus, if a sole proprietor who is a resident of the other Contracting State has a permanent establishment in the United States, in assessing income tax on the profits attributable to the permanent establishment, the United States is not obligated to allow to the resident of the other Contracting State the personal allowances for himself and his family that he would be permitted to take if the permanent establishment were a sole proprietorship owned and operated by a U.S. resident, despite the fact that the individual income tax rates would apply.

Paragraph 4

Paragraph [4] prohibits discrimination in the allowance of deductions. When a resident or an enterprise of a Contracting State pays interest, royalties or other disbursements to a resident of the other Contracting State, the first-mentioned Contracting State must allow a deduction for those payments in computing the taxable profits of the resident or enterprise as if the payment had been made under the same conditions to a resident of the first-mentioned Contracting State. Paragraph [4], however, does not require a Contracting State to give non-residents more favorable treatment than it gives to its own residents. Consequently, a Contracting State does not have to allow non-residents a deduction for items that are not deductible under its domestic law (for example, expenses of a capital nature).

The term "other disbursements" is understood to include a reasonable allocation of executive and general administrative expenses, research and development expenses and other expenses incurred for the benefit of a group of related persons that includes the person incurring the expense.

An exception to the rule of paragraph 4 is provided for cases where the provisions of paragraph 1 of Article 9 (Associated Enterprises), paragraph 5 of Article 11 (Interest) or paragraph 4 of Article 12 (Royalties) apply. All of these provisions permit the denial of deductions in certain circumstances in respect of transactions between related persons. Neither State is forced to apply the non-discrimination principle in such cases. The exception with respect to paragraph 4 of Article 11 would include the denial or deferral of certain interest deductions under Code section 163(j).

Paragraph 4 also provides that any debts of an enterprise of a Contracting State to a resident of the other Contracting State are deductible in the first-mentioned Contracting State for purposes of computing the capital tax of the enterprise under the same conditions as if the debt had been contracted to a resident of the first-mentioned Contracting State. Even though, for general purposes, the Convention covers only income taxes, under paragraph 7 of this Article, the nondiscrimination provisions apply to all taxes levied in both Contracting States, at all levels of government. Thus, this provision may be relevant for both States. The other Contracting State may have capital taxes and in the United States such taxes frequently are imposed by local governments.

Paragraph 5

Paragraph 5 requires that a Contracting State not impose more burdensome taxation or connected requirements on an enterprise of that State that is wholly or partly owned or controlled, directly or indirectly, by one or more residents of the other Contracting State than the taxation or connected requirements that it imposes on other similar enterprises of that first-mentioned Contracting State. For this purpose it is understood that "similar" refers to similar activities or ownership of the enterprise.

This rule, like all non-discrimination provisions, does not prohibit differing treatment of entities that are in differing circumstances. Rather, a protected enterprise is only required to be treated in the same manner as other enterprises that, from the point of view of the application of the tax law, are in substantially similar circumstances both in law and in fact. The taxation of a distributing corporation under section 367(e) on an applicable distribution to foreign shareholders does not violate paragraph 5 of the Article because a foreign-owned corporation is not similar to a domestically-owned corporation that is accorded non-recognition treatment under sections 337 and 355.

For the reasons given above in connection with the discussion of paragraph 2 of the Article, it is also understood that the provision in section 1446 of the Code for withholding of tax on non-U.S. partners does not violate paragraph 5 of the Article.

It is further understood that the ineligibility of a U.S. corporation with nonresident alien shareholders to make an election to be an "S" corporation does not violate paragraph 5 of the Article. If a corporation elects to be an S corporation, it is generally not subject to income tax and the shareholders take into account their pro rata shares of the corporation's items of income, loss, deduction or credit. (The purpose of the provision is to allow an individual or small group of individuals the protections of conducting business in corporate form while paying taxes at individual rates as if the business were conducted directly.) A nonresident alien does not pay U.S. tax on a net basis, and, thus, does not generally take into account items of loss, deduction or credit. Thus, the S corporation provisions do not exclude corporations with nonresident alien shareholders because such shareholders are foreign, but only because they are not net-basis taxpayers. Similarly, the provisions exclude corporations with other types of shareholders where the purpose of the provisions cannot be fulfilled or their mechanics implemented. For example, corporations with corporate shareholders are excluded because the purpose of the provision to permit individuals to conduct a business in corporate form at individual tax rates would not be furthered by their inclusion.

Finally, it is understood that paragraph 5 does not require a Contracting State to allow foreign corporations to join in filing a consolidated return with a domestic corporation or to allow similar benefits between domestic and foreign enterprises.

Paragraph 6

Paragraph 6 of the Article confirms that no provision of the Article will prevent either Contracting State from imposing the branch profits tax described in paragraph 8 of Article 10 (Dividends).

Paragraph 7

As noted above, notwithstanding the specification of taxes covered by the Convention in Article 2 (Taxes Covered) for general purposes, for purposes of providing nondiscrimination protection this Article applies to taxes of every kind and description imposed by a Contracting State or a political subdivision or local authority thereof. Customs duties are not considered to be taxes for this purpose.

Relationship to Other Articles

The saving clause of paragraph 4 of Article 1 (General Scope) does not apply to this Article by virtue of the exceptions in paragraph 5(a) of Article 1. Thus, for example, a U.S. citizen who is a resident of the other Contracting State may claim benefits in the United States under this Article.

Nationals of a Contracting State may claim the benefits of paragraph 1 regardless of whether they are entitled to benefits under Article 22 (Limitation on Benefits), because that paragraph applies to nationals and not residents. They may not claim the benefits of the other paragraphs of this Article with respect to an item of income unless they are generally entitled to treaty benefits with respect to that income under a provision of Article 22.

ARTICLE 25 (MUTUAL AGREEMENT PROCEDURE)

This Article provides the mechanism for taxpayers to bring to the attention of competent authorities issues and problems that may arise under the Convention. It also provides the authority for cooperation between the competent authorities of the Contracting States to resolve disputes and clarify issues that may arise under the Convention and to resolve cases of double taxation not provided for in the Convention. The competent authorities of the two Contracting States are identified in paragraph 1(g) of Article 3 (General Definitions).

Paragraph 1

This paragraph provides that where a resident of a Contracting State considers that the actions of one or both Contracting States will result in taxation that is not in accordance with the Convention he may present his case to the competent authority of either Contracting State. This rule is more generous than in most treaties, which generally allow taxpayers to bring competent authority cases only to the competent authority of their country of residence, or citizenship/nationality. Under this more generous rule, a U.S. permanent establishment of a corporation resident in the treaty partner that faces inconsistent treatment in the two countries would be able to bring its complaint to the U.S. competent authority. If the U.S. competent authority can resolve the issue on its own, then the taxpayer need never involve the other competent authority. Thus, the rule provides flexibility that might result in greater efficiency.

Although the typical cases brought under this paragraph will involve economic double taxation arising from transfer pricing adjustments, the scope of this paragraph is not limited to such cases. For example, a taxpayer could request assistance from the competent authority if one Contracting State determines that the taxpayer has received deferred compensation taxable at source under Article 14 (Income from Employment), while the taxpayer believes that such income should be treated as a pension that is taxable only in his country of residence pursuant to Article 17 (Pensions, Social Security, Annuities, Alimony, and Child Support).

It is not necessary for a person bringing a complaint first to have exhausted the remedies provided under the national laws of the Contracting States before presenting a case to the competent authorities, nor does the fact that the statute of limitations may have passed for seeking a refund preclude bringing a case to the competent authority. Unlike the OECD Model, no time limit is provided within which a case must be brought.

Paragraph 2

Paragraph 2 sets out the framework within which the competent authorities will deal with cases brought by taxpayers under paragraph 1. It provides that, if the competent authority of the Contracting State to which the case is presented judges the case to have merit, and cannot reach a unilateral solution, it shall seek an agreement with the competent authority of the other Contracting State pursuant to which taxation not in accordance with the Convention will be avoided.

Any agreement is to be implemented even if such implementation otherwise would be barred by the statute of limitations or by some other procedural limitation, such as a closing agreement. Paragraph 2, however, does not prevent the application of domestic-law procedural limitations that give effect to the agreement (e.g., a domestic-law requirement that the taxpayer file a return reflecting the agreement within one year of the date of the agreement). Where the taxpayer has entered a closing agreement (or other written settlement) with the United States before bringing a case to the competent authorities, the U.S. competent authority will endeavor only to obtain a correlative adjustment from the other Contracting State. See Rev. Proc. 2002–52, 2002–31 I.R.B. 242, § 7.04. Because, as specified in paragraph 2 of Article 1 (General Scope), the Convention cannot operate to increase a taxpayer's liability, temporal or other procedural limitations can be overridden only for the purpose of making refunds and not to impose additional tax.

Paragraph 3

Paragraph 3 authorizes the competent authorities to resolve difficulties or doubts that may arise as to the application or interpretation of the Convention. The paragraph includes a non-exhaustive list of examples of the kinds of matters about which the competent authorities may reach agreement. This list is purely illustrative; it does not grant any authority that is not implicitly present as a result of the introductory sentence of paragraph 3. The competent authorities may, for example, agree to the same allocation of income, deductions, credits or allowances between an enterprise in one Contracting State and its permanent establishment in the other or between related persons. These allocations are to be made in accordance with the arm's length principle underlying Article 7 (Business Profits) and Article 9 (Associated Enterprises). Agreements reached under these subparagraphs may include agreement on a methodology for determining an appropriate transfer price, common treatment of a taxpayer's cost sharing arrangement, or upon an acceptable range of results under that methodology.

As indicated in subparagraph (c), the competent authorities also may agree to settle a variety of conflicting applications of the Convention. They may agree to settle conflicts regarding the characterization of particular items of income, the characterization of persons, the application of source rules to particular items of income, the meaning of a term, or the timing of an item of income.

They also may agree as to advance pricing arrangements. They also may agree as to the application of the provisions of domestic law regarding penalties, fines, and interest in a manner consistent with the purposes of the Convention.

Since the list under paragraph 3 is not exhaustive, the competent authorities may reach agreement on issues not enumerated in paragraph 3 if necessary to avoid double taxation. For example, the competent authorities may seek agreement on a uniform set of standards for the use of exchange rates. Agreements reached by the competent authorities under paragraph 3 need not conform to the internal law provisions of either Contracting State.

Finally, paragraph 3 authorizes the competent authorities to consult for the purpose of eliminating double taxation in cases not provided for in the Convention and to resolve any difficulties or doubts arising as to the interpretation or application of the Convention. This provision is intended to permit the competent authorities to implement the treaty in particular cases in a manner that is consistent with its expressed general purposes. It permits the competent authorities to deal with cases that are within the spirit of the provisions but that are not specifically covered. An example of such a case might be double taxation arising from a transfer pricing adjustment between two permanent establishments of a third-country resident, one in the United States and one in the other Contracting State. Since no resident of a Contracting State is involved in the case, the Convention does not apply, but the competent authorities nevertheless may use the authority of this Article to prevent the double taxation of income.

Paragraph 4

Paragraph 4 authorizes the competent authorities to increase any dollar amounts referred to in the Convention to reflect economic and monetary developments. Under the Model, this refers only to Article 17 (Entertainers and Sportsmen); Article 19 (Students, Trainees, Teachers and Researchers) separately instructs the competent authorities to adjust the exemption amount for students and trainees in accordance with specified guidelines. The rule under paragraph 4 is intended to operate as follows: if, for example, after the Convention has been in force for some time, inflation rates have been such as to make the $20,000 exemption threshold for entertainers unrealistically low in terms of the original objectives intended in setting the threshold, the competent authorities may agree to a higher threshold without the need for formal amendment to the treaty and ratification by the Contracting States. This authority can be exercised, however, only to the extent necessary to restore those original objectives. This provision can be applied only to the benefit of taxpayers (i.e., only to increase thresholds, not to reduce them).

Paragraph 5

Paragraph 5 provides that the competent authorities may communicate with each other for the purpose of reaching an agreement. This makes clear that the competent authorities of the two Contracting States may communicate without going through diplomatic channels. Such communication may be in various forms, including, where appropriate, through face-to-face meetings of representatives of the competent authorities.

Treaty termination in relation to competent authority dispute resolution

A case may be raised by a taxpayer under a treaty with respect to a year for which a treaty was in force after the treaty has been terminated. In such a case the ability of the competent authorities to act is limited. They may not exchange confidential information, nor may they reach a solution that varies from that specified in its law.

Triangular competent authority solutions

International tax cases may involve more than two taxing jurisdictions (e.g., transactions among a parent corporation resident in country A and its subsidiaries resident in countries B and C). As long as there is a complete network of treaties among the three countries, it should be possible, under the full combination of bilateral authorities, for the competent authorities of the three States to work together on a three-sided solution. Although country A may not be able to give information received under Article 26 (Exchange of Information) from country B to the authorities of country C, if the competent authorities of the three countries are working together, it should not be a problem for them to arrange for the authorities of country B to give the necessary information directly to the tax authorities of country C, as well as to those of country A. Each bilateral part of the trilateral solution must, of course, not exceed the scope of the authority of the competent authorities under the relevant bilateral treaty.

Relationship to Other Articles

This Article is not subject to the saving clause of paragraph 4 of Article 1 (General Scope) by virtue of the exceptions in paragraph 5(a) of that Article. Thus, rules, definitions, procedures, etc. that are agreed upon by the competent authorities under this Article may be applied by the United States with respect to its citizens and residents even if they differ from the comparable Code provisions. Similarly, as indicated above, U.S. law may be overridden to provide refunds of tax to a U.S. citizen or resident under this Article. A person may seek relief under Article 25 regardless of whether he is generally entitled to benefits under Article 22 (Limitation on Benefits). As in all other cases, the competent authority is vested with the discretion to decide whether the claim for relief is justified.

ARTICLE 26 (EXCHANGE OF INFORMATION AND ADMINISTRATIVE ASSISTANCE)

This Article provides for the exchange of information and administrative assistance between the competent authorities of the Contracting States.

Paragraph 1

The obligation to obtain and provide information to the other Contracting State is set out in Paragraph 1. The information to be exchanged is that which may be relevant for carrying out the provisions of the Convention or the domestic laws of the United States or of the other Contracting State concerning taxes of every kind applied at the national level. This language incorporates the standard in 26 U.S.C. Section 7602 which authorizes the IRS to examine "any books, papers, records, or other data which may be relevant or material." (Emphasis added.) In United States v. Arthur Young & Co., 465 U.S. 805, 814 (1984), the Supreme Court stated that the language "may be" reflects Congress's express intention to allow the IRS to obtain "items of even potential relevance to an ongoing investigation, without reference to its admissibility." (Emphasis in original.) However, the language "may be" would not support a request in which a Contracting State simply asked for information regarding all bank accounts maintained by residents of that Contracting State in the other Contracting State, or even all accounts maintained by its residents with respect to a particular bank.

Exchange of information with respect to each State's domestic law is authorized to the extent that taxation under domestic law is not contrary to the Convention. Thus, for example, information may be exchanged with respect to a covered tax, even if the transaction to which the information relates is a purely domestic transaction in the requesting State and, therefore, the exchange is not made to carry out the Convention. An example of such a case is provided in the OECD Commentary: a company resident in the United States and a company resident in the other Contracting State transact business between themselves through a third-country resident company. Neither Contracting State has a treaty with the third State. To enforce their internal laws with respect to transactions of their residents with the third-country company (since there is no relevant treaty in force), the Contracting States may exchange information regarding the prices that their residents paid in their transactions with the third-country resident.

Paragraph 1 clarifies that information may be exchanged that relates to the assessment or collection of, the enforcement or prosecution in respect of, or the determination of appeals in relation to, the taxes covered by the Convention. Thus, the competent authorities may request and provide information for cases under examination or criminal investigation, in collection, on appeals, or under prosecution.

The taxes covered by the Convention for purposes of this Article constitute a broader category of taxes than those referred to in Article 2 (Taxes Covered). Exchange of information is authorized with respect to taxes of every kind imposed by a Contracting State at the national level. Accordingly, information may be exchanged with respect to U.S. estate and gift taxes, excise taxes or, with respect to the other Contracting State, value added taxes.

Information exchange is not restricted by paragraph 1 of Article 1 (General Scope). Accordingly, information may be requested and provided under this article with respect to persons who are not residents of either Contracting State. For example, if a third-country resident has a permanent establishment in the other Contracting State, and that permanent establishment engages in transactions with a U.S. enterprise, the United States could request information with respect to that permanent establishment, even though the third-country resident is not a resident of either Contracting State. Similarly, if a third-country resident maintains a bank account in the other Contracting State, and the Internal Revenue Service has reason to believe that funds in that account should have been reported for U.S. tax purposes but have not been so reported, information can be requested from the other Contracting State with respect to that person's account, even though that person is not the taxpayer under examination.

Although the term "United States" does not encompass U.S. possessions for most purposes of the Convention, Section 7651 of the Code authorizes the Internal Revenue Service to utilize the provisions of the Internal Revenue Code to obtain information from the U.S. possessions pursuant to a proper request made under Article 26. If necessary to obtain requested information, the Internal Revenue Service could issue and enforce an administrative summons to the taxpayer, a tax authority (or a government agency in a U.S. possession), or a third party located in a U.S. possession.

Paragraph 2

Paragraph 2 also provides assurances that any information exchanged will be treated as secret, subject to the same disclosure constraints as information obtained under the laws of the requesting State. Information received may be disclosed only to persons, including courts and administrative bodies, involved in the assessment, collection, or administration of, the enforcement or prosecution in respect of, or the determination of the of appeals in relation to, the taxes covered by the Convention. The information must be used by these persons in connection with the specified functions. Information may also be disclosed to legislative bodies, such as the tax-writing committees of Congress and the Government Accountability Office, engaged in the oversight of the preceding activities. Information received by these bodies must be for use in the performance of their role in overseeing the administration of U.S. tax laws. Information received may be disclosed in public court proceedings or in judicial decisions.

Paragraph 3

Paragraph 3 provides that the obligations undertaken in paragraphs 1 and 2 to exchange information do not require a Contracting State to carry out administrative measures that are at variance with the laws or administrative practice of either State. Nor is a Contracting State required to supply information not obtainable under the laws or administrative practice of either State, or to disclose trade secrets or other information, the disclosure of which would be contrary to public policy.

Thus, a requesting State may be denied information from the other State if the information would be obtained pursuant to procedures or measures that are broader than those available in the requesting State. However, the statute of limitations of the Contracting State making the request for information should govern a request for information. Thus, the Contracting State of which the request is made should attempt to obtain the information even if its own statute of limitations has passed. In many cases, relevant information will still exist in the business records of the taxpayer or a third party, even though it is no longer required to be kept for domestic tax purposes. While paragraph 3 states conditions under which a Contracting State is not obligated to comply with a request from the other Contracting State for information, the requested State is not precluded from providing such information, and may, at its discretion, do so subject to the limitations of its internal law.

Paragraph 4

Paragraph 4 provides that when information is requested by a Contracting State in accordance with this Article, the other Contracting State is obligated to obtain the requested information as if the tax in question were the tax of the requested State, even if that State has no direct tax interest in the case to which the request relates. In the absence of such a paragraph, some taxpayers have argued that paragraph 3(a) prevents a Contracting State from requesting information from a bank or fiduciary that the Contracting State does not need for its own tax purposes. This paragraph clarifies that paragraph 3 does not impose such a restriction and that a Contracting State is not limited to providing only the information that it already has in its own files.

Paragraph 5

Paragraph 5 provides that a Contracting State may not decline to provide information because that information is held by financial institutions, nominees or persons acting in an agency or fiduciary capacity. Thus, paragraph 5 would effectively prevent a Contracting State from relying on paragraph 3 to argue that its domestic bank secrecy laws (or similar legislation relating to disclosure of financial information by financial institutions or intermediaries) override its obligation to provide information under paragraph 1. This paragraph also requires the disclosure of information regarding the beneficial owner of an interest in a person, such as the identity of a beneficial owner of bearer shares.

Paragraph 6

Paragraph 6 provides that the requesting State may specify the form in which information is to be provided (e.g., depositions of witnesses and authenticated copies of original documents). The intention is to ensure that the information may be introduced as evidence in the judicial proceedings of the requesting State. The requested State should, if possible, provide the information in the form requested to the same extent that it can obtain information in that form under its own laws and administrative practices with respect to its own taxes.

Paragraph 7

Paragraph 7 provides for assistance in collection of taxes to the extent necessary to ensure that treaty benefits are enjoyed only by persons entitled to those benefits under the terms of the Convention. Under paragraph 7, a Contracting State will endeavor to collect on behalf of the other State only those amounts necessary to ensure that any exemption or reduced rate of tax at source granted under the Convention by that other State is not enjoyed by persons not entitled to those benefits. For example, if the payer of a U.S.-source portfolio dividend receives a Form W–8BEN or other appropriate documentation from the payee, the withholding agent is permitted to withhold at the portfolio dividend rate of 15 percent. If, however, the addressee is merely acting as a nominee on behalf of a third-country resident, paragraph 7 would obligate the other Contracting State to withhold and remit to the United States the additional tax that should have been collected by the U.S. withholding agent.

This paragraph also makes clear that the Contracting State asked to collect the tax is not obligated, in the process of providing collection assistance, to carry out administrative measures that are different from those used in the collection of its own taxes, or that would be contrary to its sovereignty, security or public policy.

Paragraph 8

Paragraph 8 provides that the requested State shall allow representatives of the applicant State to enter the requested State to interview individuals and examine books and records with the consent of the persons subject to examination.

Paragraph 9

Paragraph 9 states that the competent authorities of the Contracting States may develop an agreement upon the mode of application of the Article. The article authorizes the competent authorities to exchange information on a routine basis, on request in relation to a specific case, or spontaneously. It is contemplated that the Contracting States will utilize this authority to engage in all of these forms of information exchange, as appropriate.

The competent authorities may also agree on specific procedures and timetables for the exchange of information. In particular, the competent authorities may agree on minimum thresholds regarding tax at stake or take other measures aimed at ensuring some measure of reciprocity with respect to the overall exchange of information between the Contracting States.

Treaty effective dates and termination in relation to exchange of information

Once the Convention is in force, the competent authority may seek information under the Convention with respect to a year prior to the entry into force of the Convention. Even if an earlier Convention with more restrictive provisions, or even no Convention, was in effect during the years in which the transaction at issue occurred, the exchange of information provisions of the Convention apply. In that case, the competent authorities have available to them the full range of information exchange provisions afforded under this Article. Paragraph 3 of Article 28 (Entry into Force) confirms this understanding with respect to the effective date of the Article.

A tax administration may also seek information with respect to a year for which a treaty was in force after the treaty has been terminated. In such a case the ability of the other tax administration to act is limited. The treaty no longer provides authority for the tax administrations to exchange confidential information. They may only exchange information pursuant to domestic law or other international agreement or arrangement.

ARTICLE 27 (MEMBERS OF DIPLOMATIC MISSIONS AND CONSULAR POSTS)

This Article confirms that any fiscal privileges to which diplomatic or consular officials are entitled under general provisions of international law or under special agreements will apply notwithstanding any provisions to the contrary in the Convention. The agreements referred to include any bilateral agreements, such as consular conventions, that affect the taxation of diplomats and consular officials and any multilateral agreements dealing with these issues, such as the Vienna Convention on Diplomatic Relations and the Vienna Convention on Consular Relations. The U.S. generally adheres to the latter because its terms are consistent with customary international law.

The Article does not independently provide any benefits to diplomatic agents and consular officers. Article 19 (Government Service) does so, as do Code section 893 a number of bilateral and multilateral agreements. In the event that there is a conflict between the Convention and international law or such other treaties, under which the diplomatic agent or consular official is entitled to greater benefits under the latter, the latter laws or agreements shall have precedence. Conversely, if the Convention confers a greater benefit than another agreement, the affected person could claim the benefit of the tax treaty.

Pursuant to subparagraph 5(b) of Article 1, the saving clause of paragraph 4 of Article 1 (General Scope) does not apply to override any benefits of this Article available to an individual who is neither a citizen of the United States nor has immigrant status in the United States.

ARTICLE 28 (ENTRY INTO FORCE)

This Article contains the rules for bringing the Convention into force and giving effect to its provisions.

Paragraph 1

Paragraph 1 provides for the ratification of the Convention by both Contracting States according to their constitutional and statutory requirements. Instruments of ratification shall be exchanged as soon as possible. In the United States, the process leading to ratification and entry into force is as follows: Once a treaty has been signed by authorized representatives of the two Contracting States, the Department of State sends the treaty to the President who formally transmits it to the Senate for its advice and consent to ratification, which requires approval by two-thirds of the Senators present and voting. Prior to this vote, however, it generally has been the practice for the Senate Committee on Foreign Relations to hold hearings on the treaty and make a recommendation regarding its approval to the full Senate. Both Government and private sector witnesses may testify at these hearings. After the Senate gives its advice and consent to ratification of the protocol or treaty, an instrument of ratification is drafted for the President's signature. The President's signature completes the process in the United States.

Paragraph 2

Paragraph 2 provides that the Convention will enter into force upon the exchange of instruments of ratification. The date on which a treaty enters into force is not necessarily the date on which its provisions take effect. Paragraph 2, therefore, also contains rules that determine when the provisions of the treaty will have effect.

Under paragraph 2(a), the Convention will have effect with respect to taxes withheld at source (principally dividends, interest and royalties) for amounts paid or credited on or after the first day of the second month following the date on which the Convention enters into force. For example, if instruments of ratification are exchanged on April 25 of a given year, the withholding rates specified in paragraph 2 of Article 10 (Dividends) would be applicable to any dividends paid or credited on or after June 1 of that year. This rule allows the benefits of the withholding reductions to be put into effect as soon as possible, without waiting until the following year. The delay of one to two months is required to allow sufficient time for withholding agents to be informed about the change in withholding rates. If for some reason a withholding agent withholds at a higher rate than that provided by the Convention (perhaps because it was not able to re-program its computers before the payment is made), a beneficial owner of the income that is a resident of the other Contracting State may make a claim for refund pursuant to section 1464 of the Code.

For all other taxes, paragraph 2(b) specifies that the Convention will have effect for any taxable period beginning on or after January 1 of the year following entry into force.

As discussed under Articles 25 (Mutual Agreement Procedure) and 26 (Exchange of Information), the powers afforded the competent authority under these articles apply retroactively to taxable periods preceding entry into force.

ARTICLE 29 (TERMINATION)

The Convention is to remain in effect indefinitely, unless terminated by one of the Contracting States in accordance with the provisions of Article 29. The Convention may be terminated at any time after the year in which the Convention enters into force. If notice of termination is given, the provisions of the Convention with respect to withholding at source will cease to have effect after the expiration of a period of 6 months beginning with the delivery of notice of termination. For other taxes, the Convention will cease to have effect as of taxable periods beginning after the expiration of this 6 month period.

Article 29 relates only to unilateral termination of the Convention by a Contracting State. Nothing in that Article should be construed as preventing the Contracting States from concluding a new bilateral agreement, subject to ratification, that supersedes, amends or terminates provisions of the Convention without the six-month notification period.

Customary international law observed by the United States and other countries, as reflected in the Vienna Convention on Treaties, allows termination by one Contracting State at any time in the event of a "material breach" of the agreement by the other Contracting State.

INDEX

References are to Paragraph Numbers

References are to Paragraph Numbers

References are to Paragraph Numbers

References are to Paragraph Numbers

References are to Paragraph Numbers

†